Lecture Notes in Computer Science   12623

More information about this subseries at http://www.springer.com/series/7412

Hiroshi Ishikawa · Cheng-Lin Liu ·
Tomas Pajdla · Jianbo Shi (Eds.)

Computer Vision – ACCV 2020

15th Asian Conference on Computer Vision
Kyoto, Japan, November 30 – December 4, 2020
Revised Selected Papers, Part II

 Springer

Editors
Hiroshi Ishikawa
Waseda University
Tokyo, Japan

Cheng-Lin Liu
Institute of Automation of Chinese Academy
of Sciences
Beijing, China

Tomas Pajdla
Czech Technical University in Prague
Prague, Czech Republic

Jianbo Shi
University of Pennsylvania
Philadelphia, PA, USA

ISSN 0302-9743   ISSN 1611-3349 (electronic)
Lecture Notes in Computer Science
ISBN 978-3-030-69531-6   ISBN 978-3-030-69532-3   (eBook)
https://doi.org/10.1007/978-3-030-69532-3

LNCS Sublibrary: SL6 – Image Processing, Computer Vision, Pattern Recognition, and Graphics

This Springer imprint is published by the registered company Springer Nature Switzerland AG
The registered company address is: Gewerbestrasse 11, 6330 Cham, Switzerland

Preface

The Asian Conference on Computer Vision (ACCV) 2020, originally planned to take place in Kyoto, Japan, was held online during November 30 – December 4, 2020. The conference featured novel research contributions from almost all sub-areas of computer vision.

We received 836 main-conference submissions. After removing the desk rejects, 768 valid, complete manuscripts were submitted for review. A pool of 48 area chairs and 738 reviewers was recruited to conduct paper reviews. As in previous editions of ACCV, we adopted a double-blind review process to determine which of these papers to accept. Identities of authors were not visible to reviewers and area chairs; nor were the identities of the assigned reviewers and area chairs known to authors. The program chairs did not submit papers to the conference.

Each paper was reviewed by at least three reviewers. Authors were permitted to respond to the initial reviews during a rebuttal period. After this, the area chairs led discussions among reviewers. Finally, an interactive area chair meeting was held, during which panels of three area chairs deliberated to decide on acceptance decisions for each paper, and then four larger panels were convened to make final decisions. At the end of this process, 254 papers were accepted for publication in the ACCV 2020 conference proceedings.

In addition to the main conference, ACCV 2020 featured four workshops and two tutorials. This is also the first ACCV for which the proceedings are open access at the Computer Vision Foundation website, by courtesy of Springer.

We would like to thank all the organizers, sponsors, area chairs, reviewers, and authors. We acknowledge the support of Microsoft's Conference Management Toolkit (CMT) team for providing the software used to manage the review process.

We greatly appreciate the efforts of all those who contributed to making the conference a success, despite the difficult and fluid situation.

December 2020

Hiroshi Ishikawa
Cheng-Lin Liu
Tomas Pajdla
Jianbo Shi

Organization

General Chairs

Ko Nishino   Kyoto University, Japan
Akihiro Sugimoto   National Institute of Informatics, Japan
Hiromi Tanaka   Ritsumeikan University, Japan

Program Chairs

Hiroshi Ishikawa   Waseda University, Japan
Cheng-Lin Liu   Institute of Automation of Chinese Academy
     of Sciences, China
Tomas Pajdla   Czech Technical University, Czech Republic
Jianbo Shi   University of Pennsylvania, USA

Publication Chairs

Ichiro Ide   Nagoya University, Japan
Wei-Ta Chu   National Chung Cheng University, Taiwan
Marc A. Kastner   National Institute of Informatics, Japan

Local Arrangements Chairs

Shohei Nobuhara   Kyoto University, Japan
Yasushi Makihara   Osaka University, Japan

Web Chairs

Ikuhisa Mitsugami   Hiroshima City University, Japan
Chika Inoshita   Canon Inc., Japan

AC Meeting Chair

Yusuke Sugano   University of Tokyo, Japan

Area Chairs

Mathieu Aubry   École des Ponts ParisTech, France
Xiang Bai   Huazhong University of Science and Technology,
     China
Alex Berg   Facebook, USA
Michael S. Brown   York University, Canada

Tat-Jun Chin	University of Adelaide, Australia
Yung-Yu Chuang	National Taiwan University, Taiwan
Yuchao Dai	Northwestern Polytechnical University, China
Yasutaka Furukawa	Simon Fraser University, Canada
Junwei Han	Northwestern Polytechnical University, China
Tatsuya Harada	University of Tokyo/RIKEN, Japan
Gang Hua	Wormpex AI Research, China
C. V. Jawahar	IIIT Hyderabad, India
Frédéric Jurie	Université de Caen Normandie, France
Angjoo Kanazawa	UC Berkeley, USA
Rei Kawakami	Tokyo Institute of Technology, Japan
Tae-Kyun Kim	Imperial College London, UK
Zuzana Kukelova	Czech Technical University in Prague, Czech Republic
Shang-Hong Lai	Microsoft AI R&D Center, Taiwan
Ivan Laptev	Inria Paris, France
Laura Leal-Taixe	TU Munich, Germany
Yong Jae Lee	UC Davis, USA
Vincent Lepetit	Université de Bordeaux, France
Hongdong Li	Australian National University, Australia
Guangcan Liu	NUIST, China
Li Liu	National University of Defense Technology, China
Risheng Liu	Dalian University of Technology, China
Si Liu	Beihang University, China
Yasuyuki Matsushita	Osaka University, Japan
Hajime Nagahara	Osaka University, Japan
Takayuki Okatani	Tohoku University/RIKEN, Japan
Carl Olsson	Lund University, Sweden
Hyun Soo Park	University of Minnesota, USA
Shmuel Peleg	Hebrew University of Jerusalem, Israel
Shin'ichi Satoh	National Institute of Informatics, Japan
Torsten Sattler	Chalmers University of Technology, Sweden
Palaiahnakote Shivakumara	University of Malaya, Malaysia
Hao Su	UC San Diego, USA
Siyu Tang	ETH Zurich, Switzerland
Radu Timofte	ETH Zurich, Switzerland
Yoshitaka Ushiku	OMRON SINIC X, Japan
Gul Varol	University of Oxford, UK
Kota Yamaguchi	Cyberagent, Inc., Japan
Ming-Hsuan Yang	UC Merced, USA
Stella X. Yu	UC Berkeley/ICSI, USA
Zhaoxiang Zhang	Chinese Academy of Sciences, China
Wei-Shi Zheng	Sun Yat-sen University, China
Yinqiang Zheng	National Institute of Informatics, Japan
Xiaowei Zhou	Zhejiang University, China

Additional Reviewers

Sathyanarayanan
  N. Aakur
Mahmoud Afifi
Amit Aides
Noam Aigerman
Kenan Emir Ak
Mohammad
  Sadegh Aliakbarian
Keivan Alizadeh-Vahid
Dario Allegra
Alexander Andreopoulos
Nikita Araslanov
Anil Armagan
Alexey Artemov
Aditya Arun
Yuki M. Asano
Hossein Azizpour
Seung-Hwan Baek
Seungryul Baek
Max Bain
Abhishek Bajpayee
Sandipan Banerjee
Wenbo Bao
Daniel Barath
Chaim Baskin
Anil S. Baslamisli
Ardhendu Behera
Jens Behley
Florian Bernard
Bharat Lal Bhatnagar
Uttaran Bhattacharya
Binod Bhattarai
Ayan Kumar Bhunia
Jia-Wang Bian
Simion-Vlad Bogolin
Amine Bourki
Biagio Brattoli
Anders G. Buch
Evgeny Burnaev
Benjamin Busam
Holger Caesar
Jianrui Cai
Jinzheng Cai

Fanta Camara
Necati Cihan Camgöz
Shaun Canavan
Jiajiong Cao
Jiale Cao
Hakan Çevikalp
Ayan Chakrabarti
Tat-Jen Cham
Lyndon Chan
Hyung Jin Chang
Xiaobin Chang
Rama Chellappa
Chang Chen
Chen Chen
Ding-Jie Chen
Jianhui Chen
Jun-Cheng Chen
Long Chen
Songcan Chen
Tianshui Chen
Weifeng Chen
Weikai Chen
Xiaohan Chen
Xinlei Chen
Yanbei Chen
Yingcong Chen
Yiran Chen
Yi-Ting Chen
Yun Chen
Yun-Chun Chen
Yunlu Chen
Zhixiang Chen
Ziliang Chen
Guangliang Cheng
Li Cheng
Qiang Cheng
Zhongwei Cheng
Anoop Cherian
Ngai-Man Cheung
Wei-Chen Chiu
Shin-Fang Ch'ng
Nam Ik Cho
Junsuk Choe

Chiho Choi
Jaehoon Choi
Jinsoo Choi
Yukyung Choi
Anustup Choudhury
Hang Chu
Peng Chu
Wei-Ta Chu
Sanghyuk Chun
Ronald Clark
Maxwell D. Collins
Ciprian Corneanu
Luca Cosmo
Ioana Croitoru
Steve Cruz
Naresh Cuntoor
Zachary A. Daniels
Mohamed Daoudi
François Darmon
Adrian K. Davison
Rodrigo de Bem
Shalini De Mello
Lucas Deecke
Bailin Deng
Jiankang Deng
Zhongying Deng
Somdip Dey
Ferran Diego
Mingyu Ding
Dzung Anh Doan
Xingping Dong
Xuanyi Dong
Hazel Doughty
Dawei Du
Chi Nhan Duong
Aritra Dutta
Marc C. Eder
Ismail Elezi
Mohamed Elgharib
Sergio Escalera
Deng-Ping Fan
Shaojing Fan
Sean Fanello

Moshiur R. Farazi
Azade Farshad
István Fehérvári
Junyi Feng
Wei Feng
Yang Feng
Zeyu Feng
Robert B. Fisher
Alexander Fix
Corneliu O. Florea
Wolfgang Förstner
Jun Fu
Xueyang Fu
Yanwei Fu
Hiroshi Fukui
Antonino Furnari
Ryo Furukawa
Raghudeep Gadde
Vandit J. Gajjar
Chuang Gan
Bin-Bin Gao
Boyan Gao
Chen Gao
Junbin Gao
Junyu Gao
Lin Gao
Mingfei Gao
Peng Gao
Ruohan Gao
Nuno C. Garcia
Georgios Georgakis
Ke Gong
Jiayuan Gu
Jie Gui
Manuel Günther
Kaiwen Guo
Minghao Guo
Ping Guo
Sheng Guo
Yulan Guo
Saurabh Gupta
Jung-Woo Ha
Emanuela Haller
Cusuh Ham
Kai Han
Liang Han

Tengda Han
Ronny Hänsch
Josh Harguess
Atsushi Hashimoto
Monica Haurilet
Jamie Hayes
Fengxiang He
Pan He
Xiangyu He
Xinwei He
Yang He
Paul Henderson
Chih-Hui Ho
Tuan N.A. Hoang
Sascha A. Hornauer
Yedid Hoshen
Kuang-Jui Hsu
Di Hu
Ping Hu
Ronghang Hu
Tao Hu
Yang Hua
Bingyao Huang
Haibin Huang
Huaibo Huang
Rui Huang
Sheng Huang
Xiaohua Huang
Yifei Huang
Zeng Huang
Zilong Huang
Jing Huo
Junhwa Hur
Wonjun Hwang
José Pedro Iglesias
Atul N. Ingle
Yani A. Ioannou
Go Irie
Daisuke Iwai
Krishna Murthy
   Jatavallabhula
Seong-Gyun Jeong
Koteswar Rao Jerripothula
Jingwei Ji
Haiyang Jiang
Huajie Jiang

Wei Jiang
Xiaoyi Jiang
Jianbo Jiao
Licheng Jiao
Kyong Hwan Jin
Xin Jin
Shantanu Joshi
Frédéric Jurie
Abhishek Kadian
Olaf Kaehler
Meina Kan
Dimosthenis Karatzas
Isay Katsman
Muhammad Haris Khan
Vijeta Khare
Rawal Khirodkar
Hadi Kiapour
Changick Kim
Dong-Jin Kim
Gunhee Kim
Heewon Kim
Hyunwoo J. Kim
Junsik Kim
Junyeong Kim
Yonghyun Kim
Akisato Kimura
A. Sophia Koepke
Dimitrios Kollias
Nikos Kolotouros
Yoshinori Konishi
Adam Kortylewski
Dmitry Kravchenko
Sven Kreiss
Gurunandan Krishnan
Andrey Kuehlkamp
Jason Kuen
Arjan Kuijper
Shiro Kumano
Avinash Kumar
B. V. K. Vijaya Kumar
Ratnesh Kumar
Vijay Kumar
Yusuke Kurose
Alina Kuznetsova
Junseok Kwon
Loic Landrieu

Dong Lao
Viktor Larsson
Yasir Latif
Hei Law
Hieu Le
Hoang-An Le
Huu Minh Le
Gim Hee Lee
Hyungtae Lee
Jae-Han Lee
Jangho Lee
Jungbeom Lee
Kibok Lee
Kuan-Hui Lee
Seokju Lee
Sungho Lee
Sungmin Lee
Bin Li
Jie Li
Ruilong Li
Ruoteng Li
Site Li
Xianzhi Li
Xiaomeng Li
Xiaoming Li
Xin Li
Xiu Li
Xueting Li
Yawei Li
Yijun Li
Yimeng Li
Yin Li
Yong Li
Yu-Jhe Li
Zekun Li
Dongze Lian
Zhouhui Lian
Haoyi Liang
Yue Liao
Jun Hao Liew
Chia-Wen Lin
Guangfeng Lin
Kevin Lin
Xudong Lin
Xue Lin
Chang Liu

Feng Liu
Hao Liu
Hong Liu
Jing Liu
Jingtuo Liu
Jun Liu
Miaomiao Liu
Ming Liu
Ping Liu
Siqi Liu
Wentao Liu
Wu Liu
Xing Liu
Xingyu Liu
Yongcheng Liu
Yu Liu
Yu-Lun Liu
Yun Liu
Zhihua Liu
Zichuan Liu
Chengjiang Long
Manuel López Antequera
Hao Lu
Hongtao Lu
Le Lu
Shijian Lu
Weixin Lu
Yao Lu
Yongxi Lu
Chenxu Luo
Weixin Luo
Wenhan Luo
Diogo C. Luvizon
Jiancheng Lyu
Chao Ma
Long Ma
Shugao Ma
Xiaojian Ma
Yongrui Ma
Ludovic Magerand
Behrooz Mahasseni
Mohammed Mahmoud
Utkarsh Mall
Massimiliano Mancini
Xudong Mao
Alina E. Marcu

Niki Martinel
Jonathan Masci
Tetsu Matsukawa
Bruce A. Maxwell
Amir Mazaheri
Prakhar Mehrotra
Heydi Méndez-Vázquez
Zibo Meng
Kourosh Meshgi
Shun Miao
Zhongqi Miao
Micael Carvalho
Pedro Miraldo
Ashish Mishra
Ikuhisa Mitsugami
Daisuke Miyazaki
Kaichun Mo
Liliane Momeni
Gyeongsik Moon
Alexandre Morgand
Yasuhiro Mukaigawa
Anirban Mukhopadhyay
Erickson R. Nascimento
Lakshmanan Nataraj
K. L. Navaneet
Lukáš Neumann
Shohei Nobuhara
Nicoletta Noceti
Mehdi Noroozi
Michael Oechsle
Ferda Ofli
Seoung Wug Oh
Takeshi Oishi
Takahiro Okabe
Fumio Okura
Kyle B. Olszewski
José Oramas
Tribhuvanesh Orekondy
Martin R. Oswald
Mayu Otani
Umapada Pal
Yingwei Pan
Rameswar Panda
Rohit Pandey
Jiangmiao Pang
João P. Papa

Nanne van Noord
Subeesh Vasu
Javier Vazquez-Corral
Andreas Velten
Constantin Vertan
Rosaura G. VidalMata
Valentin Vielzeuf
Sirion Vittayakorn
Konstantinos Vougioukas
Fang Wan
Guowei Wan
Renjie Wan
Bo Wang
Chien-Yi Wang
Di Wang
Dong Wang
Guangrun Wang
Hao Wang
Hongxing Wang
Hua Wang
Jialiang Wang
Jiayun Wang
Jingbo Wang
Jinjun Wang
Lizhi Wang
Pichao Wang
Qian Wang
Qiaosong Wang
Qilong Wang
Qingzhong Wang
Shangfei Wang
Shengjin Wang
Tiancai Wang
Wenguan Wang
Wenhai Wang
Xiang Wang
Xiao Wang
Xiaoyang Wang
Xinchao Wang
Xinggang Wang
Yang Wang
Yaxing Wang
Yisen Wang
Yu-Chiang Frank Wang
Zheng Wang
Scott Wehrwein

Wei Wei
Xing Wei
Xiu-Shen Wei
Yi Wei
Martin Weinmann
Michael Weinmann
Jun Wen
Xinshuo Weng
Thomas Whelan
Kimberly Wilber
Williem Williem
Kwan-Yee K. Wong
Yongkang Wong
Sanghyun Woo
Michael Wray
Chenyun Wu
Chongruo Wu
Jialian Wu
Xiaohe Wu
Xiaoping Wu
Yihong Wu
Zhenyao Wu
Changqun Xia
Xide Xia
Yin Xia
Lei Xiang
Di Xie
Guo-Sen Xie
Jin Xie
Yifan Xing
Yuwen Xiong
Jingwei Xu
Jun Xu
Ke Xu
Mingze Xu
Yanyu Xu
Yi Xu
Yichao Xu
Yongchao Xu
Yuanlu Xu
Jia Xue
Nan Xue
Yasushi Yagi
Toshihiko Yamasaki
Zhaoyi Yan
Zike Yan

Keiji Yanai
Dong Yang
Fan Yang
Hao Yang
Jiancheng Yang
Linlin Yang
Mingkun Yang
Ren Yang
Sibei Yang
Wenhan Yang
Ze Yang
Zhaohui Yang
Zhengyuan Yang
Anbang Yao
Angela Yao
Rajeev Yasarla
Jinwei Ye
Qi Ye
Xinchen Ye
Zili Yi
Ming Yin
Zhichao Yin
Ryo Yonetani
Ju Hong Yoon
Haichao Yu
Jiahui Yu
Lequan Yu
Lu Yu
Qian Yu
Ruichi Yu
Li Yuan
Sangdoo Yun
Sergey Zakharov
Huayi Zeng
Jiabei Zeng
Yu Zeng
Fangneng Zhan
Kun Zhan
Bowen Zhang
Hongguang Zhang
Jason Y. Zhang
Jiawei Zhang
Jie Zhang
Jing Zhang
Kaihao Zhang
Kaipeng Zhang

Lei Zhang
Mingda Zhang
Pingping Zhang
Qian Zhang
Qilin Zhang
Qing Zhang
Runze Zhang
Shanshan Zhang
Shu Zhang
Wayne Zhang
Xiaolin Zhang
Xiaoyun Zhang
Xucong Zhang
Yan Zhang
Zhao Zhang
Zhishuai Zhang
Feng Zhao
Jian Zhao
Liang Zhao
Qian Zhao
Qibin Zhao

Ruiqi Zhao
Sicheng Zhao
Tianyi Zhao
Xiangyun Zhao
Xin Zhao
Yifan Zhao
Yinan Zhao
Shuai Zheng
Yalin Zheng
Bineng Zhong
Fangwei Zhong
Guangyu Zhong
Yaoyao Zhong
Yiran Zhong
Jun Zhou
Mo Zhou
Pan Zhou
Ruofan Zhou
S. Kevin Zhou
Yao Zhou
Yipin Zhou

Yu Zhou
Yuqian Zhou
Yuyin Zhou
Guangming Zhu
Ligeng Zhu
Linchao Zhu
Rui Zhu
Xinge Zhu
Yizhe Zhu
Zhe Zhu
Zhen Zhu
Zheng Zhu
Bingbing Zhuang
Jiacheng Zhuo
Mohammadreza
    Zolfaghari
Chuhang Zou
Yuliang Zou
Zhengxia Zou

Contents – Part II

Low-Level Vision, Image Processing

Image Inpainting with Onion Convolutions

Shant Navasardyan$^{(\boxtimes)}$ⓘ and Marianna Ohanyanⓘ

Picsart Inc., Yerevan, Armenia
{shant.navasardyan,marianna.ohanyan}@picsart.com

Abstract. Recently deep learning methods have achieved a great success in image inpainting problem. However, reconstructing continuities of complex structures with non-stationary textures remains a challenging task for computer vision. In this paper, a novel approach to image inpainting problem is presented, which adapts exemplar-based methods for deep convolutional neural networks. The concept of *onion convolution* is introduced with the purpose of preserving feature continuities and semantic coherence. Similar to recent approaches, our onion convolution is able to capture *long-range spatial correlations*. In general, the implementation of modules with such ability in low-level features leads to impractically high latency and complexity. To address this limitations, the onion convolution suggests an efficient implementation. As qualitative and quantitative comparisons show, our method with onion convolutions outperforms state-of-the-art methods by producing more realistic, visually plausible and semantically coherent results.

Keywords: Inpainting · Onion convolution · Patch-match

1 Introduction

Image inpainting is the problem of completing missing or damaged regions in images resulting in a realistic, visually plausible, and semantically meaningful output. It can be utilized in many applications such as recovering spots or other damaged parts in images, removing unwanted objects or parts of them.

The main challenge of obtaining a high-quality image inpainting algorithm is getting both semantically consistent and visually realistic results, especially if the image contains complex scenes and structures.

Some traditional approaches [1–8] are based on texture synthesis techniques and achieve great success in producing realistic-looking texture details. However, these methods rarely give structurally or semantically reasonable outputs.

Electronic supplementary material The online version of this chapter (https://doi.org/10.1007/978-3-030-69532-3_1) contains supplementary material, which is available to authorized users.

Fig. 1. Image inpainting results of our method. Each triplet of images is composed of the original image, the image with the missing region, and our result. The method allows users to remove unwanted objects or fill missing parts in images. Please see in color. (Color figure online)

Later, some methods [9–11] were proposed to address the structural inconsistencies resulting in perfect image completions in some cases. Yet, generating coherent semantics remains beyond the abilities of traditional methods. Hence, deep learning techniques come to fill the missing region in a semantically plausible way [12–16]. Early methods [12,13,17,18] use vanilla convolutions and manage to gain fine results for small missing regions. However, for complex structures, these methods introduce blur, edge artifacts, and color inconsistencies. The reason is that vanilla convolutions treat all pixels equally, so outputs depend on the initialization of the missing pixels.

Some methods [14,15,19,20] introduce special convolutional layers which are designed to operate with only valid pixels in the input. This approach allows to gain a drastic improvement over using only vanilla convolutions. Though, these mechanisms introduce some patterns or distorted structures near the boundary of the missing region due to ineffectiveness of convolutions in modeling long-range pixel correlations.

To address this problem, two main approaches were introduced. The first approach [21–24] adopts patch-based traditional image inpainting techniques in the learning process, while the second one [15,16,25] utilizes the self-attention mechanism [26]. Both approaches perform state-of-the-art results by completing complex structures and semantics. However, in all these methods, the modules responsible for capturing long-range dependencies are designed to process tensors in which the initial missing region is roughly filled. So the output of these methods highly depends on the *coarse estimation* of the missing pixels. In some cases, networks fail to make a continuity-preserving coarse estimations, resulting in outputs with structure discontinuities (see Fig. 4).

To address this problem we introduce the onion convolution layer, which is able to preserve feature continuities and does not depend on a coarse estimation of the missing region. To make the layer keep feature continuities, we supply it with an iterative filling of the missing region starting from its boundary to the center, similar to the process of peeling an onion, so we call it *onion convolution*. Some results can be found in Fig. 1.

In general, modules capturing long-range pixel dependencies come with a high computational cost, since their implementations often require (all-to-all) pixel-wise dot-product computations. This makes the usage of such modules impractical in high resolution features. On the other hand, in the case of image inpainting, some of the computations mentioned above can be avoided. Such adaptation of these modules to the image inpainting problem was introduced in [25] for *rectangular-formed* missing regions. However it still does unnecessary computations when the missing region has an *irregular* form. To eliminate the redundant computational cost we make our own implementation with a common deep learning framework *TensorFlow* [27].

To summarize, our main contributions are the following:

- We introduce the *onion convolution* mechanism, which enables us to continuously propagate feature activations from valid pixels to the missing ones.
- To the best of our knowledge, this is the first work on using exemplar-based image inpainting techniques in deep features without coarsely estimating the pixels in the missing region.
- Onion convolution mechanism, which can capture long-range pixel dependencies, is implemented in a low computational and memory-efficient way.

The structure of the further part of this work is the following: in Sect. 2 some existing approaches to the image inpainting problem are reviewed. Then in Sect. 3 our approach is introduced in detail. In Sect. 4 our experiments, quantitative and qualitative comparisons with state-of-the-art methods, and the ablation study are presented. In Sect. 5 we make a conclusion.

2   Related Work

The existing approaches to the problem of image inpainting can be roughly divided into two groups. First group uses traditional diffusion-based or exemplar-based techniques, while the second one utilizes learning processes. In this section, a brief introduction of the mentioned groups will be held.

2.1   Traditional Non-learning Methods

Historically, image inpainting was a problem of image restoration, with the aim of removing scratches, torn parts, or text in images. Several algorithms [28,29] were suggested for this purpose, and rely on the idea of propagating image structures from the known region to the unknown by diffusion processes. Diffusion based approaches are able to produce high quality results when restoring small damaged parts in images. However, they sometimes over-smooth outputs, especially in cases when the missing region is large. To address this problem, exemplar-based methods [1-8,30-32] replicate the texture by copying patches from the known region. In [1], authors apply a patch-based technique to sample from the conditional distribution of each pixel, conditioned on its neighborhood. Later some methods [3–5] were proposed to optimize the algorithm introduced in [1]. Also, the *randomized search*, introduced in [2], can be adopted for this purpose. However, the method described in [1] completes a *single pixel at a time*, which can lead some textures to "occasionally 'slip' into a wrong part of the search space and start growing garbage" (as mentioned in limitations in [1]). To address the problem of "growing garbage", some *texture synthesis* algorithms suggest copying regions with more than one pixel at a time [6,30–32].

Though these methods perform excellent results in providing detailed textures, they fail in reconstructing complex structures or semantics.

2.2   Learning-Based Methods

After computer vision adopted deep learning techniques, researchers started experimenting with convolutional neural networks in the image inpainting problem. Deep learning allows modeling of high-level semantics, which is used to generate missing parts of objects based on the semantic information of images. Early works on image inpainting with neural networks [17,19,33] concentrate on completing locally corrupted images when missing regions are small. Later, for obtaining more structure-preserving results, some learning-based methods [34–36] have adopted structure-guidance techniques inside networks. However, some of the methods mentioned above poorly generate texture details.

Through *generative adversarial networks, GANs* [37], researchers have reached new heights in solving computer vision tasks. The ability of GANs to generate visually plausible results helps to coherently hallucinate the missing region [12,13,15,18,24]. Nevertheless, in some cases boundary artifacts and inconsistencies occur. This is caused mostly by treating all pixels equally when processing an incomplete image trough stacked vanilla convolutions. Hence, the methods with *partial convolutions* [14] and *gated convolutions* [15] are introduced. The partial convolution [14] convolves with only known pixels at each sliding window and normalize the output by the number of these known pixels. Moreover, it narrows the missing region in a rule-based manner. In contrast, the gated convolution [15] lets the network to learn how to update the missing region for each layer. Both works perform excellent results on many complicated examples.

Despite the high quality of the algorithms mentioned above, some of them fail to complete complex structures continuously. The main reason is the inability to capture long-range spatial dependencies. To eliminate this cause, some methods either adopt exemplar-based techniques [21–24] or benefit from self-attention mechanisms [15,16,25]. In [23] the authors use the technique described in [38], which replace the patches in the unknown region with their closest (in terms of similarity defined by cross-correlation) patches from the known region. Similarly, [22] uses a special case of this technique, by considering patches of size 1×1 (i.e. pixels) and combining features from both encoder and decoder for computing similarities. [15,25] introduce the *contextual attention* layer for completing the missing region based on the soft self-attention mechanism [26,39]. These works obtain great results, outperforming previous state-of-the-art methods. Though, their *long-range spatial dependency capturing* modules need to be fed with a tensor in which the missing region is coarsely initialized. This may cause structure discontinuities due to unreasonable coarse estimations. In this work the onion convolution layer is introduced to continuously propagate the information without any coarse estimation of the missing region.

3   Approach

In this section, all components of our approach are described in detail. First, we introduce our *onion convolution* mechanism and discuss some implementations. Then the inpainting network architecture and loss functions are presented.

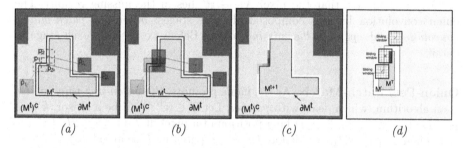

Fig. 2. Onion convolution. First we perform onion-peel patch-match in the following way: for each iteration $t = 1, \ldots, T$ the pixels in the boundary ∂M^t of the missing region M^t are considered. (a) $k_m \times k_m$ patches, centered in the boundary pixels (e.g. p_1, p_2, p_3), are matched to their corresponding patches from the source region $(M^t)^c$ (corresponding source patches are centered in $\hat{p}_1, \hat{p}_2, \hat{p}_3$). (b) $k_f \times k_f$ patches centered in the pixels $p_1, p_2, p_3, \ldots$ are replaced with their corresponding $k_f \times k_f$ patches centered in $\hat{p}_1, \hat{p}_2, \hat{p}_3, \ldots$. (c) Then the overlapping parts are aggregated by averaging, and the next missing region M^{t+1} is computed. After the onion-peel patch-match, a convolution followed by an updating of the initial missing region $M^1 = M$ is applied. (d) Some $k_c \times k_c$ convolution sliding windows, centered in the filled region $(1 - M^T)$, may overlap with the missing region M^T, hence their centers are also treated as non-valid pixels, resulting in the updating of the initial missing region $M \mapsto M'$ by the Eq. 8.

3.1   Onion Convolution

During our research, it has been validated that for getting semantically meaningful and visually realistic results, our network needs to contain a block which satisfies the following conditions:

- (*C*1) Valid/known pixels has higher impact on the output of the block than missing ones.

- (C2) The block continuously propagates the information (e.g. texture, structure, semantics) of the know region to the unknown.

All deep-learning-based methods that use only vanilla convolutions do not satisfy the condition (C1), since they treat all pixels as valid ones.

Though the *partial* [14] and *gated* [15] convolutions are designed to satisfy the condition (C1), they are unable to model long-range pixel correlations, which is necessary for satisfying the condition (C2). As we have already mentioned, some methods [15,22,23] capture long-range pixel dependencies, but do not pay a special attention on *continuously propagation of the information*, so they also do not satisfy (C2).

To make both (C1) and (C2) hold, we propose the *onion convolution layer*, illustrated in Fig. 2. It takes two arguments as input: a tensor $X \in \mathbb{R}^{H \times W \times c}$ and a binary mask $M \in \{0,1\}^{H \times W}$ indicating the missing region in the tensor X ($M_{ij} = 1$ means, that the pixel $X_{ij} \in \mathbb{R}^c$ lies in the missing region). The onion convolution layer is composed of three stages: *onion-peel patch-match*, *convolution* and *updating the missing region*. Below we describe each stage in detail.

Onion-Peel Patch-Match. As the name prompts, the *onion-peel patch-match* is an algorithm, which deals with *patches*. Let $T \in \mathbb{R}^{H \times W \times c}$ be a tensor, k be a positive integer and $p = (i, j)$ be a position of a pixel in T ($1 \le i \le H$, $1 \le j \le W$). Then by $patch_T^k(p)$ we denote the $k \times k$ patch in T centered at p.

With a usage of concepts introduced in [1], our onion-peel patch-match aims to preserve feature continuities when filling the missing region. Illustration of the approach is shown in Fig. 2(a), (b), (c).

The missing region in X is filled iteratively, initially taking $X^1 = X, M^1 = M$. For each iteration $t = 1, \ldots, T$, the boundary of the missing region M^t is filled, resulting in a tensor X^{t+1} with a missing region, indicated by M^{t+1}. So at first we need to identify the boundary of the missing region. Since the missing region is indicated by M^t, the boundary can be obtained by the morphological erosion operation on M^t with a window of size 3×3:

$$\partial M^t = M^t - erode(M^t, 3) . \tag{1}$$

Then for each point p in the boundary ∂M^t of the missing region we fill the unknown pixel X_p^t by sampling from its conditional distribution $P(X_p^t \mid X_{n(p)}^t)$ given its known neighborhood $X_{n(p)}^t$.

In order to estimate $P(X_p^t \mid X_{n(p)}^t)$, similar with [1], we consider the histogram of pixels from a set $\Omega^\varepsilon(p)$. The set $\Omega^\varepsilon(p)$ is composed of pixels, neighborhoods of which are close to the neighborhood of p. More precisely, we consider $patch_{X^t}^{k_m}(\hat{p})$ as a neighborhood of a pixel $X_{\hat{p}}^t$, and fix a function $d(\cdot, \cdot)$ (which will be detailed later) for measuring distances between patches. Then we compute the distances

$$d_{p\hat{p}} = d(patch_{X^t}^{k_m}(p) , patch_{X^t}^{k_m}(\hat{p})) \tag{2}$$

for points $\hat{p}$, which are in the known region, but are also in a neighborhood of the missing region. This neighborhood, indicated by a binary mask $(M^t)^c$ can be obtained by the morphological dilation operation:

$$(M^t)^c = dilate(M^t, dil) - M^t , \tag{3}$$

where dil is a hyper-parameter determining the region of valid pixels which are used for filling the missing ones.

After computing the distances $d_{p\hat{p}}$, the minimum distance d^* is found (the corresponding matching patches are illustrated in Fig. 2(a)). Then the set $\Omega^\varepsilon(p)$ is defined as follows:

$$\Omega^\varepsilon(p) = \{X_{\hat{p}}^t \mid (M^t)_{\hat{p}}^c = 1, \ d(patch_{X^t}^{k_m}(p), patch_{X^t}^{k_m}(\hat{p})) \leq (1+\varepsilon)d^*\} , \tag{4}$$

where ε is a hyper-parameter.

After the $\Omega^\varepsilon(p)$ is determined, one can sample from it's histogram. For simplicity we sample a pixel $X_{\hat{p}}^t$ uniformly from the set $\Omega^\varepsilon(p)$.

When $X_{\hat{p}}^t$ is chosen, $patch_{X^t}^{k_f}(p)$ is replaced with $patch_{X^t}^{k_f}(\hat{p})$ in the tensor X^t (see Fig. 2(b)). Notice that if $k_f > 1$, and we replace the corresponding patches simultaneously for all points p (in the boundary of the missing region), we will end up with multiple candidates for missing pixels X_p^t. In our algorithm these candidates are averaged to fill the pixel X_p^t for each point p in the boundary of the missing region (see Fig. 2(c)).

After replacing patches centered in all boundary points, we result in a tensor $\hat{X}^t$, and take

$$X^{t+1} = (1 - \partial M^t) \odot X^t + \partial M^t \odot \hat{X}^t . \tag{5}$$

As the boundary pixels in X^{t+1} are filled, we also update the missing region by taking

$$M^{t+1} = M^t - \partial M^t . \tag{6}$$

Now it only remains to define the distance $d(\cdot, \cdot)$. As it is crucial to satisfy the condition $(C1)$, for measuring the distance between $patch_X^{k_m}(p)$ and $patch_X^{k_m}(\hat{p})$, we use only valid pixels in $patch_X^{k_m}(p)$. More precisely, d is defined as a normalized sum of squared distances between valid pixels in $patch_X^{k_m}(p)$ and corresponding pixels in $patch_X^{k_m}(\hat{p})$:

$$d_{p\hat{p}} = \frac{1}{sum(patch_M^{k_m}(p))} ||(patch_X^{k_m}(p) - patch_X^{k_m}(\hat{p})) \odot patch_M^{k_m}(p)||_2^2 . \tag{7}$$

The result of onion-peel patch-match is denoted by O.

Convolution and Updating the Missing Region. After the onion-peel patch-match is performed, we apply a convolution with a kernel size $k_c \times k_c$ to the tensor O, resulting in a tensor we denote by C. On the other hand, some pixels in the tensor O may remain unknown (the new missing region is indicated by M^T). So during the convolution some $k_c \times k_c$ sliding windows will contain missing pixels. Hence, in the tensor C we eliminate the results of convolving in such sliding windows. To obtain the centers of such sliding windows, one can use the morphological erosion operation with the kernel size $T - [k_c/2]$:

$$M' = erode(M, T - [k_c/2]) . \tag{8}$$

We refer to M' as the *updated missing region after the onion convolution* (see Fig. 2(d)).

So, the result of the onion convolution, with parameters $k_m, k_f, k_c, dil, \varepsilon$ is the tuple $(C \odot M', M')$.

Note that the onion convolution layer satisfies conditions $(C1)$ and $(C2)$. Indeed, by designing the $M \mapsto M'$ mask updating procedure, we keep from the tensor C only the signals, which are results of convolution in sliding windows with only valid pixels. So the condition $(C1)$ holds. On the other hand, our onion-peel patch-match is a generalization of the non-parametric sampling technique [1] designed to have no visual discontinuities between the boundary of the known and generated regions. As the onion-peel patch-match is applied to deep features, it has the property of preserving feature continuities, so the condition $(C2)$ also holds.

3.2   Discussion on Implementation

Note, that the onion convolution mechanism requires pairwise distance computations between patches centered in the regions indicated by ∂M^t and $(M^t)^c$ (for each iteration $t = 1, \ldots, T$). Moreover, the L2-norm component in the Eq. 7 can be computed by using dot product due to the formula

$$||u - v||_2^2 = ||u||_2^2 - 2\langle u, v \rangle + ||v||_2^2 \tag{9}$$

for any vectors (patches) u, v. Therefore, similar to other long-range pixel dependency capturing mechanisms, we also need to calculate patch-wise dot products. In general, it is done by extracting patches

$$\mathcal{P}_{X^t}^{k_m}((M^t)^c) = \{patch_{X^t}^{k_m}(p) \mid (M^t)_p^c = 1\} \tag{10}$$

then convolving the tensor X with filters from $\mathcal{P}_{X^t}^{k_m}((M^t)^c)$.[1] This procedure contains dot product calculations also for pairs of patches, each of which is centered in the region $(M^t)^c$. To avoid these redundant computations, we merely extract patches $\mathcal{P}_{X^t}^{k_m}(\partial M^t)$ and compute distances for each pair

$$(patch_{X^t}^{k_m}(p), patch_{X^t}^{k_m}(\hat{p})) \in \mathcal{P}_{X^t}^{k_m}(\partial M^t) \times \mathcal{P}_{X^t}^{k_m}((M^t)^c) . \tag{11}$$

Our implementation is done purely with *TensorFlow* [27], resulting in an end-to-end pipeline for training and inference.

---

[1] Moreover, replacing patches followed by averaging of overlapping regions, also can be done by using *transposed convolution* operation and $\mathcal{P}_{X^t}^{k_f}((M^t)^c)$ (see [38] for details).

3.3   The Network Architecture

In our method, a generative adversarial network is used, the generator of which is the main inpainting network. As a discriminator, our approach uses the *SN-PatchGAN* introduced in [15] and based on the concept of *SN-GAN* [40].

The generator network consists of two parts: *coarse* and *refinement networks*.

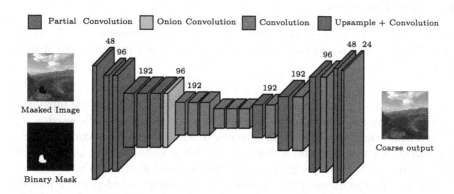

Fig. 3. The architecture of our coarse network. After each convolution the corresponding activation is used. The onion convolution layer is used with parameters $k_m = 4, k_f = 2, dil = 8, \varepsilon = 0.1, k_c = 3, T = \infty$, where $T = \infty$ means that we iteratively complete the missing region until it is filled completely.

Coarse Network. Let I be an image normalized to the range $[-1, 1]$, and M be a binary mask indicating the missing region in the image. The network is fed by two inputs: $I \odot (1 - M)$ and M. The overall architecture of our coarse model is presented in Fig. 3. Six partial convolution layers with *ELU* [41] activation are used at the beginning of the network to reduce the tensor sizes. Let's denote the output of sixth partial convolution by X. The binary mask M is resized to the size of X and is referred as the missing region indicator in the tensor X. Then the onion convolution layer (see Fig. 3). We have experimented with the hyper-parameters and the onion convolution layer position and find this is the optimal usage of it in our case. After the onion convolution layer the *ELU* activation is used. The rest of our coarse network is composed of convolutional layers and Nearest Neighbor Upsamplings, followed by convolutions. All convolutions, except the last one, are followed by activation functions *ELU*. In the end, tanh activation is used to obtain output in the range $[-1, 1]$. For details see the supplementary material.

Refinement Network. After passing the image and the missing region through the coarse network, we obtain a rough estimation of pixels in the missing region. Let us denote the output of the coarse network by I_c. For getting more detailed output, the image $I_{comp} = I_c \odot M + I \odot (1 - M)$ is formulated and passed through another network, which we call *refinement network*. The architecture of the refinement network is very similar to the refinement network used in [15]. The only difference is using vanilla convolutions instead of gated convolutions (this difference is discussed in our ablation study, see Sect. 4.3).

3.4   Loss Functions

Our loss function consists of three terms: *pixel-wise reconstruction loss* $\mathcal{L}_1$, *adversarial loss* $\mathcal{L}_{ad}$ and perceptual loss $\mathcal{L}_p$. The total loss is a weighted sum of these losses:

$$\mathcal{L} = \lambda_1 \mathcal{L}_1 + \lambda_2 \mathcal{L}_{ad} + \lambda_3 \mathcal{L}_p , \qquad (12)$$

where $\lambda_1, \lambda_2, \lambda_3$ are training hyperparameters. For optimizing the inpainting network G, the loss function $\mathcal{L}$ is minimized w.r.t. the generator's weights ω_G. At the same time, as there is an adversarial loss, $\mathcal{L}_{ad}$, it is maximized w.r.t. *SN-PatchGAN discriminator's* weights ω_D. We update ω_G and ω_D one after another at each step resulting in an equilibrium point for the GAN.

Let I_{orig} be the image, which is needed to be reconstructed given an image I with a missing region indicated by a binary mask M. Let I_c and I_r be the coarse and refinement networks' outputs, respectively. Each of our losses is discussed below in detail.

Pixel-Wise Reconstruction Loss. We penalize each of our inpainting networks in all spatial locations by minimizing the *mean absolute error* between the original image I_{orig} and reconstructions I_c and I_r (similarly as in [15]):

$$\mathcal{L}_1 = ||I_c - I_{orig}||_1 + ||I_r - I_{orig}||_1 . \qquad (13)$$

Adversarial Loss. Our discriminator gets the original images I_{orig} as real examples and composition images $I_{compos} = I_{orig} \odot (1 - M) + I_r \odot M$ as fake examples. Since the discriminator belongs to the family of *PatchGANs*, it outputs $3D$ tensors D_{real} and D_{fake}. As in [15], the *hinge loss* between the outputs of our discriminator is computed:

$$\mathcal{L}_{ad} = -\mathbb{E}[ReLU(1 - D_{real}) + ReLU(1 + D_{fake})] . \qquad (14)$$

Perceptual Loss. We also use the *perceptual (content) loss* introduced in [42], which minimizes the distance between the features of the original and the completed images obtained by the VGG-16 [43] network. Similar to [14], we compute distances between the vgg-features of three images: the original image I_{orig}, the output of the refinement network I_r and the composition image I_{compos}. More precisely, let $MP_i(X)$ be the output of the $MaxPool$ layer in the ith block, when feeding the VGG network with an image X. Then our perceptual loss is defined as follows:

$$\mathcal{L}_p = \sum_{i=1}^{3} \left[||MP_i(I_r) - MP_i(I_{orig})||_1 + ||MP_i(I_{compos}) - MP_i(I_{orig})||_1 \right] . \quad (15)$$

Thus, the total loss $\mathcal{L}$ is a weighted sum of above-mentioned three losses. In our experiments $\lambda_1 = 1, \lambda_2 = 1, \lambda_3 = 0.05$ are taken.

4 Experiments

We have experimented with the dataset Places2 [44]. Our model is trained by the ADAM optimizer [45] with learning rate 10^{-4} and parameters $\beta_1 = 0.5$, $\beta_2 = 0.999$. For all experiments, a single *NVIDIA V100 GPU* (with 16 GB RAM) is used with batch size equal to 28. Images and binary masks are resized to the size 256×256 before feeding the network; no augmentations are used. The training lasted 14 days.

To evaluate our model, we have randomly chosen a test-set from 500 images from the test set of the *Mapillary* [46] dataset. We have created random free-form masks as it was done in [15]. The masks are in different sizes equiprobable from area ranges covering $10 - 20, 20 - 30, 30 - 40$ or $40 - 50$ percents of the image area. All masks and images are resized to the size of 256×256.

Due to our efficient implementation of the onion convolution layer and the fact that our network is fully convolutional, we can also process images with resolution 512×512 (see Fig. 1).

We compare our method with state-of-the-art methods[2]: Gated Convolutions (GC) [15] and Partial Convolutions (PC) [14].

4.1 Qualitative Comparison

As shown in Fig. 4, PC [14] reconstructs semantics, but introduce some blur (e.g. rows 5 and 7 in Fig. 4), pattern (e.g. rows 1, 6 in Fig. 4) or sometimes does not preserve continuous lines (e.g. rows 1, 2, 3 in Fig. 4). GC [15] shows plausible results, but sometimes does not keep the image structure (rows 3, 4 in Fig. 4), introduce some "dirt" (row 1 in Fig. 4) or generates some strange artifacts (e.g. rows 2, 6, 7 in Fig. 4).

In comparison with these methods, our method can reconstruct detailed textures and coherently generate structures due to its property of feature continuity. Also, our method does not generate artifacts not related to the context of the image.

---

[2] For comparison we take the pretrained GC [15] model from the official repository. As there is no official implementation of the method [14] PC, we make our own, which benefits a lot from https://github.com/MathiasGruber/PConv-Keras.

Masked   PC   GC   our

Fig. 4. Comparisons of our method with PC [14] and GC [15]. For more images please see the supplementary material.

Table 1. Comparison of our method with PC [14] and GC [15].

	PSNR	SSIM	MAE
Partial Convolutions (PC)	**22.14**	0.794	0.036
Gated Convolutions (GC)	21.97	0.83	**0.029**
Onion Convolutions (our)	22	**0.835**	0.029

4.2 Quantitative Comparison

To compare our method with PC [14] and GC [15], we consider 500 images from *Mapillary* dataset [46], generate irregular missing regions and evaluate methods by calculating standard evaluation metrics *PSNR, SSIM* [47] and *Mean Absolute Error (MAE)*. The evaluation results are presented in Table 1 and show that our method outperforms the others.

As shown in the Table 1 in terms of SSIM, our method outperforms the other two. In terms of MAE, our method performs similarly with GC and better than PC. In terms of PSNR, PC is better, but it mostly comes from the fact that PC sometimes gives more smooth and blurry results, which is not looking realistic.

4.3 Ablation Study

The main idea of our approach is hooded under the mechanism of onion convolution: filling the missing region iteratively by only using valid pixels without any pre-estimating a coarse output in that region. So we start to analyze the effect of our *onion convolution layer*. Also, we analyze the impact of replacing the onion convolution with consecutive onion convolutions. Then we study the effects of the perceptual loss, the replacing gated convolutions with vanilla convolutions in the refinement network.

Effect of Onion Convolution Layer. As shown in Fig. 5, our model with onion convolution Fig. 5(b) helps the model coherently fill the missing region. Especially in the case of large missing regions, the model without onion convolutions Fig. 5(c) cannot propagate sufficient information from the known region to the unknown.

Effect of a Single Onion Convolution Instead of Consecutive Onion Convolutions. We also perform experiments with replacing the II-VI partial convolution layers with 6 onion convolution layers in our coarse model. The results are shown in Fig. 5(d). It can be noticed that sometimes this architecture leads to more structure-preserving results (e.g. column 4 in Fig. 5(d)), but in some cases it can introduce black (white) artifacts or blur.

Effect of Perceptual Loss. We also train our model without perceptual loss we have mentioned in Sect. 3. The results, presented in Fig. 5(e), show that using the perceptual loss in our case helps to avoid some patterns and inconsistencies.

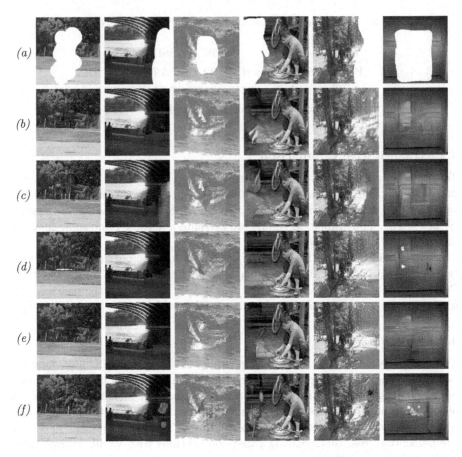

Fig. 5. *(a)* Masked image, *(b)* our model, *(c)* model without onion convolutions, *(d)* model with using a sequence of onion convolutions, *(e)* model without perceptual loss, *(f)* model with gated convolutions.

Effect of Vanilla Convolutions Instead of Gated Convolutions. We have also experimented with gated convolutions [15] in the refinement network and find out that, in our case, gated convolutions introduce artifacts as shown in Fig. 5(f). We suppose this is due to the property of "vanishing" some regions when using gated convolution (sometimes the gate of a gated convolution does not allow some information to pass through the layer).

5   Conclusion

We present a novel patch-based onion convolution mechanism for image inpainting problem. By using the ability to capture long-range pixel dependencies, the onion convolution is designed to propagate the information from known regions to missing ones. We show that our method quantitatively and qualitatively outperforms existing state-of-the-art approaches of image inpainting. It is worth noting that our onion convolution can be adopted with various architectures and learning techniques. In the future, we plan to extend this method to face completion and image super-resolution tasks.

References

1. Efros, A., Leung, T.: Texture synthesis by non-parametric sampling. In: International Conference on Computer Vision, pp. 1033–1038 (1999)
2. Barnes, C., Shechtman, E., Finkelstein, A., Goldman, D.B.: PatchMatch: a randomized correspondence algorithm for structural image editing. ACM Trans. Graph. (Proc. SIGGRAPH) **28**, 24 (2009)
3. Ashikhmin, M.: Synthesizing natural textures. In: Proceedings of the 2001 Symposium on Interactive 3D Graphics, I3D 2001, pp. 217–226. Association for Computing Machinery, New York (2001)
4. Wei, L.Y., Levoy, M.: Fast texture synthesis using tree-structured vector quantization. In: Proceedings of the 27th Annual Conference on Computer Graphics and Interactive Techniques, SIGGRAPH 2000, USA, pp. 479–488. ACM Press/Addison-Wesley Publishing Co. (2000)
5. Harrison, P.: A non-hierarchical procedure for re-synthesis of complex textures (2000)
6. Efros, A.A., Freeman, W.T.: Image quilting for texture synthesis and transfer. In: Proceedings of the 28th Annual Conference on Computer Graphics and Interactive Techniques, SIGGRAPH 2001. Association for Computing Machinery, New York, pp. 341–346 (2001)
7. Criminisi, A., Pérez, P., Toyama, K.: Object removal by exemplar-based inpainting, vol. 2, pp. 721–728 (2003)
8. Criminisi, A., Perez, P., Toyama, K.: Region filling and object removal by exemplar-based image inpainting. Trans. Img. Proc. **13**, 1200–1212 (2004)
9. Sun, J., Yuan, L., Jia, J., Shum, H.Y.: Image completion with structure propagation. ACM Trans. Graph. **24**, 861–868 (2005)
10. Hung, J., Chun-Hong, H., Yi-Chun, L., Tang, N., Ta-Jen, C.: Exemplar-based image inpainting base on structure construction. J. Softw. **3**, 57–64 (2008)
11. Huang, J.B., Kang, S.B., Ahuja, N., Kopf, J.: Image completion using planar structure guidance. ACM Trans. Graph. **33**, 1–10 (2014)
12. Pathak, D., Krähenbühl, P., Donahue, J., Darrell, T., Efros, A.A.: Context encoders: feature learning by inpainting. In: 2016 IEEE Conference on Computer Vision and Pattern Recognition (CVPR), pp. 2536–2544 (2016)
13. Iizuka, S., Simo-Serra, E., Ishikawa, H.: Globally and locally consistent image completion. ACM Trans. Graph. **36**, 1–14 (2017)
14. Liu, G., Reda, F.A., Shih, K.J., Wang, T.-C., Tao, A., Catanzaro, B.: Image inpainting for irregular holes using partial convolutions. In: Ferrari, V., Hebert, M., Sminchisescu, C., Weiss, Y. (eds.) ECCV 2018. LNCS, vol. 11215, pp. 89–105. Springer, Cham (2018). https://doi.org/10.1007/978-3-030-01252-6_6
15. Yu, J., Lin, Z., Yang, J., Shen, X., Lu, X., Huang, T.: Free-form image inpainting with gated convolution. In: 2019 IEEE/CVF International Conference on Computer Vision (ICCV), pp. 4470–4479 (2019)

16. Zheng, C., Cham, T.J., Cai, J.: Pluralistic image completion. In: 2019 IEEE/CVF Conference on Computer Vision and Pattern Recognition (CVPR), pp. 1438–1447 (2019)

17. Xie, J., Xu, L., Chen, E.: Image denoising and inpainting with deep neural networks. In: Proceedings of the 25th International Conference on Neural Information Processing Systems - Volume 1, NIPS 2012, pp. 341–349. Curran Associates Inc., Red Hook (2012)

18. Yeh, R.A., Chen, C., Lim, T.Y., Schwing, A.G., Hasegawa-Johnson, M., Do, M.N.: Semantic image inpainting with deep generative models. In: 2017 IEEE Conference on Computer Vision and Pattern Recognition (CVPR), pp. 6882–6890 (2017)

19. Ren, J.S.J., Xu, L., Yan, Q., Sun, W.: Shepard convolutional neural networks. In: NIPS (2015)

20. Xie, C., Liu, S., Li, C., Cheng, M., Zuo, W., Liu, X., Wen, S., Ding, E.: Image inpainting with learnable bidirectional attention maps. In: 2019 IEEE/CVF International Conference on Computer Vision (ICCV), pp. 8857–8866 (2019)

21. Yang, C., Lu, X., Lin, Z., Shechtman, E., Wang, O., Li, H.: High-resolution image inpainting using multi-scale neural patch synthesis (2016)

22. Yan, Z., Li, X., Li, M., Zuo, W., Shan, S.: Shift-Net: image inpainting via deep feature rearrangement. In: Ferrari, V., Hebert, M., Sminchisescu, C., Weiss, Y. (eds.) Computer Vision – ECCV 2018. LNCS, vol. 11218, pp. 3–19. Springer, Cham (2018). https://doi.org/10.1007/978-3-030-01264-9_1

23. Song, Y., et al.: Contextual-based image inpainting: infer, match, and translate. In: Ferrari, V., Hebert, M., Sminchisescu, C., Weiss, Y. (eds.) ECCV 2018. LNCS, vol. 11206, pp. 3–18. Springer, Cham (2018). https://doi.org/10.1007/978-3-030-01216-8_1

24. Liu, H., Jiang, B., Xiao, Y., Yang, C.: Coherent semantic attention for image inpainting. In: 2019 IEEE/CVF International Conference on Computer Vision (ICCV), pp. 4169–4178 (2019)

25. Yu, J., Lin, Z., Yang, J., Shen, X., Lu, X., Huang, T.S.: Generative image inpainting with contextual attention. In: 2018 IEEE/CVF Conference on Computer Vision and Pattern Recognition, pp. 5505–5514 (2018)

26. Zhang, H., Goodfellow, I., Metaxas, D., Odena, A.: Self-attention generative adversarial networks. In: Proceedings of the 36th International Conference on Machine Learning. Volume 97 of Proceedings of Machine Learning Research, Long Beach, California, USA, pp. 7354–7363. PMLR (2019)

27. Abadi, M., et al.: TensorFlow: large-scale machine learning on heterogeneous systems (2015). Software available from tensorflow.org

28. Bertalmío, M., Sapiro, G., Caselles, V., Ballester, C.: Image inpainting. In: SIGGRAPH 2000 (2000)

29. Bertalmio, M., Vese, L., Sapiro, G., Osher, S.: Simultaneous structure and texture image inpainting. IEEE Trans. Image Process. **12**, 882–889 (2003)

30. Liang, L., Liu, C., Xu, Y.Q., Guo, B., Shum, H.Y.: Real-time texture synthesis by patch-based sampling. ACM Trans. Graph. **20**, 127–150 (2001)

31. Kwatra, V., Schödl, A., Essa, I., Turk, G., Bobick, A.: Graphcut textures: image and video synthesis using graph cuts. ACM Trans. Graph. **22**, 277–286 (2003)

32. Boykov, Y., Veksler, O., Zabih, R.: Fast approximate energy minimization via graph cuts. IEEE Trans. Pattern Anal. Mach. Intell. **23**, 1222–1239 (2001)

33. Köhler, R., Schuler, C., Schölkopf, B., Harmeling, S.: Mask-specific inpainting with deep neural networks. In: Jiang, X., Hornegger, J., Koch, R. (eds.) GCPR 2014. LNCS, vol. 8753, pp. 523–534. Springer, Cham (2014). https://doi.org/10.1007/978-3-319-11752-2_43

34. Nazeri, K., Ng, E., Joseph, T., Qureshi, F.Z., Ebrahimi, M.: EdgeConnect: generative image inpainting with adversarial edge learning. ArXiv abs/1901.00212 (2019)
35. Xiong, W., et al.: Foreground-aware image inpainting. In: The IEEE Conference on Computer Vision and Pattern Recognition (CVPR) (2019)
36. Song, Y., Yang, C., Shen, Y., Wang, P., Huang, Q., Kuo, C.J.: SPG-Net: segmentation prediction and guidance network for image inpainting. CoRR abs/1805.03356 (2018)
37. Goodfellow, I.J., et al.: Generative adversarial nets. In: Proceedings of the 27th International Conference on Neural Information Processing Systems - Volume 2, NIPS 2014, pp. 2672–2680. MIT Press, Cambridge (2014)
38. Chen, T.Q., Schmidt, M.: Fast patch-based style transfer of arbitrary style. arXiv preprint arXiv:1612.04337 (2016)
39. Vaswani, A., et al.: Attention is all you need. In: Advances in Neural Information Processing Systems 30, pp. 5998–6008. Curran Associates, Inc. (2017)
40. Miyato, T., Kataoka, T., Koyama, M., Yoshida, Y.: Spectral normalization for generative adversarial networks. ArXiv abs/1802.05957 (2018)
41. Clevert, D.A., Unterthiner, T., Hochreiter, S.: Fast and accurate deep network learning by exponential linear units (ELUs). CoRR abs/1511.07289 (2015)
42. Gatys, L.A., Ecker, A.S., Bethge, M.: Image style transfer using convolutional neural networks. In: Proceedings of the IEEE Conference on Computer Vision and Pattern Recognition, pp. 2414–2423 (2016)
43. Simonyan, K., Zisserman, A.: Very deep convolutional networks for large-scale image recognition. arXiv preprint arXiv:1409.1556 (2014)
44. Zhou, B., Lapedriza, A., Khosla, A., Oliva, A., Torralba, A.: Places: a 10 million image database for scene recognition. IEEE Trans. Pattern Anal. Mach. Intell. **40**, 1452–1464 (2017)
45. Kingma, D.P., Ba, J.: Adam: a method for stochastic optimization. CoRR abs/1412.6980 (2015)
46. Neuhold, G., Ollmann, T., Rota Bulò, S., Kontschieder, P.: The mapillary vistas dataset for semantic understanding of street scenes. In: International Conference on Computer Vision (ICCV) (2017)
47. Wang, Z., Bovik, A.C., Sheikh, H.R., Simoncelli, E.P.: Image quality assessment: from error visibility to structural similarity. IEEE Trans. Image Process. **13**, 600–612 (2004)

Accurate and Efficient Single Image Super-Resolution with Matrix Channel Attention Network

Hailong Ma[✉][iD], Xiangxiang Chu[iD], and Bo Zhang[iD]

Xiaomi AI Lab, Beijing, China
{mahailong,chuxiangxiang,zhangbo11}@xiaomi.com

Abstract. In recent years, deep learning methods have achieved impressive results with higher peak signal-to-noise ratio in Single Image Super-Resolution (SISR) tasks. However, these methods are usually computationally expensive, which constrains their application in mobile scenarios. In addition, most of the existing methods rarely take full advantage of the intermediate features which are helpful for restoration. To address these issues, we propose a moderate-size SISR network named matrix channel attention network (MCAN) by constructing a matrix ensemble of multi-connected channel attention blocks (MCAB). Several models of different sizes are released to meet various practical requirements. Extensive benchmark experiments show that the proposed models achieve better performance with much fewer multiply-adds and parameters (Source code is at https://github.com/macn3388/MCAN).

1 Introduction

Single image super-resolution (SISR) attempts to reconstruct a high-resolution (HR) image from its low-resolution (LR) counterpart, which is essentially an ill-posed inverse problem since there are infinitely many HR images that can be downsampled to the same LR image.

Most of the deep learning methods discussing SISR have been devoted to achieving higher *peak signal noise ratios* (PSNR) with deeper and deeper layers, making it difficult to fit in mobile devices [3–5,8]. A lightweight framework CARN stands out for being one of the first SR methods that are applicable on mobile devices, however it comes at a cost of reduction on PSNR [7]. An information distillation network (IDN) also achieves good performance with a moderate model size [9]. Another effort that tackles SISR with neural architecture search has also been proposed [10], with their network FALSR surpassing CARN at the same level of FLOPs. Readers can find a thorough summary of state-of-the-art methods and results in [11] (Fig. 1).

© Springer Nature Switzerland AG 2021
H. Ishikawa et al. (Eds.): ACCV 2020, LNCS 12623, pp. 20–35, 2021.
https://doi.org/10.1007/978-3-030-69532-3_2

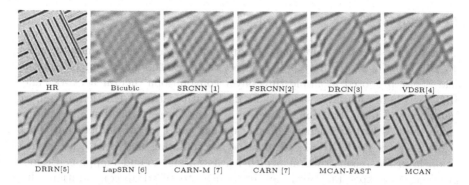

Fig. 1. Visual results with bicubic degradation (×4) on "img_092" from Urban100.

Nevertheless, it is worth pointing out that higher PSNR does not necessarily give better visual effects, for which a new measure called *perceptual index* (PI) is formulated [12]. Noteworthy works engaging perceptual performance are SRGAN [13] and ESRGAN [14], whose PSNR is not the highest, but both render more high-frequency details. However, these GAN-based methods inevitably bring about bad cases that are intolerable in practice. Our work still focuses on improving PSNR, which is a well-established distortion measure. Furthermore, our proposed model can also serve as the generator of GAN-based methods.

To seek a better trade-off between image quality and model sizes, we design an architecture called Matrix Channel Attention Network. We name its basic building block *multi-connected channel attention block* (MCAB), which is an adaptation of *residual channel attention block* (RCAB) from RCAN [8]. MCAB differs from RCAB by allowing hierarchical connections after each activation. In such a way, multiple levels of information can be passed both in depth and in breadth.

In summary, our main contributions are as follows:

- We propose a matrix channel attention network named MCAN for SISR. Our matrix-in-matrix (MIM) structure, which is composed of multi-connected channel attention blocks (MCAB), can effectively utilize the hierarchical features. We also devise a hierarchical feature fusion (HFF) block, which can be used in combination with the MIM structure. HFF can better profit the hierarchical features of MIM from the LR space.
- We build three additional efficient SR models of different sizes, namely MCAN-M, MCAN-S, MCAN-T, which correspond to the model sizes of mobile, small, and tiny, respectively. We also introduce MCAN-FAST by replacing the *sigmoid* with the *fast sigmoid* [15] to overcome the inefficiency of the sigmoid function on mobile devices, and MCAN-FAST has only a small loss of precision compared to MCAN.
- We show through extensive experiments that our MCAN family achieves higher PSNR and better perceptual results, with much fewer mult-adds and number of parameters than the state-of-the-art methods.

2   Related Work

In recent years, deep learning has been applied to many areas of computer vision [16–20]. Dong et al. [1] first applied deep learning to the image super-resolution field. They proposed a simple three-layer convolutional neural network called SRCNN, where each layer sequentially deals with feature extraction, non-linear mapping, and reconstruction. However, it needs an extra bicubic interpolation which reduces high-frequency information and adds extra computation. Their follow-up work FSRCNN [2] requires no interpolation and inserts a deconvolution layer for reconstruction, which learns an end-to-end mapping. Besides, shrinking and expanding layers are introduced to speed up computation, altogether rendering FSRCNN real-time on a generic CPU.

Meantime, VDSR presented by [3] proposes global residual learning to ease training for their very deep network. DRCN handles deep network recursively to share parameters [3]. DRRN builds two residual blocks in a recursive manner [5]. Unfortunately, these very deep architectures undoubtedly require heavy computation.

The application of DenseNet in SR domain goes to SRDenseNet [21], in which they argue that dense skip connections could mitigate the vanishing gradient problem and can boost feature propagation. It achieves better performance as well as faster speed. However, results from [10] showed that it is not efficient to connect all modules intensively because it brings extra computation, and their less dense network FALSR is also competitive.

A cascading residual network CARN is devised for a lightweight scenario [7]. The basic block of their architecture is called *cascading residual block*, whose outputs of intermediary layers are dispatched to each of the consequent convolutional layers. These cascading blocks, when stacked, are again organized in the same fashion.

Another remarkable work RCAN [8] observed that low-frequency information is hard to capture by convolutional layers which only exploit local regions. By adding multiple long and short skip connections for residual dense blocks, low-frequency features can bypass the network and thus the main architecture focuses on high-frequency information. RCAN also invented a *channel attention* mechanism via global average pooling to deal with interdependencies among channels.

3   Matrix Channel Attention Network

3.1   Network Structure

MCAN consists of four components: feature extraction (FE), a matrix-in-matrix (MIM) mapping, hierarchical feature fusion (HFF) and reconstruction, as illustrated in Fig. 2.

Specifically, we utilize two successive 3×3 convolutions to extract features from the input image in the FE stage. Let I_{LR} represent the low-resolution

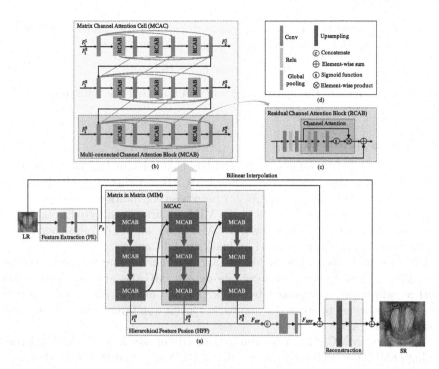

Fig. 2. (a) The overall structure of our matrix convolutional neural network (MCAN), in which MIM is set to $D = 3, K = 3, M = 3$. The blue thick arrows indicate multiple connections between two blocks. (b) Matrix channel attention cell (MCAC) composed by multi-connected channel attention block (MCAB). (c) Residual channel attention block proposed by RCAN [8].

input image and I_{HR} be the high-resolution output, this procedure can then be formulated as

$$F_0 = H_{FE}(I_{LR}) \tag{1}$$

where $H_{FE}(\cdot)$ is the feature extraction function and F_0 denotes the output features.

The nonlinear mapping is constructed by what we call a matrix-in-matrix module (MIM). Similarly,

$$F_{HF} = H_{MIM}(F_0) \tag{2}$$

where $H_{MIM}(\cdot)$ is the mapping function, to be discussed in detail in Sect. 3.2. F_{HF} stands for the hierarchical features, so named for they come from different depths of the our MIM structure. Further feature fusion can be put formally as

$$F_{HFF} = H_{HFF}(F_{HF}). \tag{3}$$

HFF will be elaborated in Sect. 3.4.

We then upscale the combination of fused feature F_{HFF} and F_0, and add it to the interpolated I_{LR} to generate the high-resolution target,

$$I_{SR} = H_{UP}(F_{HFF} + F_0) + B(I_{LR}), \qquad (4)$$

where $H_{UP}(\cdot)$ denotes the upsampling function and $B(\cdot)$ the bilinear interpolation.

3.2   Matrix in Matrix

In general, an MIM is composed of D matrix channel attention cells (MCAC). Each MCAC contains K MCABs, and each MCAB contains M residual channel attention blocks (RCAB) [8] and $M + 1$ pointwise convolution layers.

As shown in Fig. 2(a), MCACs in the MIM are firstly connected from end to end, marked by black curved arrows. MCABs inside an MCAC also contributes for connections, which are evinced by black straight arrows.

Likewise, MCABs within an MCAC are also multi-connected, indicated by blue thick arrows. Figure 2(b) shows its details: MCABs are joined one after another, which are represented by black polyline arrows. Meanwhile, orange arrows add a bridge between the pointwise convolution layers and its equivalent in the next MCAB.

Therefore, an MCAC can be seen as a matrix of size $K \times M$. An MIM containing D MCACs can be thus regarded as a $D \times K \times M$ matrix, for which reason we nicknamed the structure "matrix-in-matrix". Figure 2 gives an example of an MIM of $3 \times 3 \times 3$ matrix, containing 3 MCACs, and each MCAC has 3 MCABs. We will elaborate MCABs in Sect. 3.3.

3.3   Matrix Channel Attention Cell

In super-resolution, skip connections are popular since it reuses intermediate features while relieving the training for deep networks [3,21,22]. Nevertheless, these skip connections between modules are point-to-point, where only the output features of a module can be reused, losing many intermediate features. This can be alleviated by adding skip connections within the module, but as more intermediate features are concatenated, channels become very thick before fusion [23], which narrows transmission of information and gradients.

If we densely connect all intermediate features and modules like SRDenseNet [21], it inevitably brings in redundant connections for less important features, while the important ones become indistinguishable, which increases the training difficulty.

To address these problems, we propose a matrix channel attention cell, which is composed of several multi-connected channel attention blocks. We recursively define F_d as the outputs of an MCAC,

$$
\begin{aligned}
F_d &= H_{MCAC}^d(F_{d-1}) \\
&= H_{MCAC}^d((F_{d-1}^1, F_{d-1}^2, \ldots, F_{d-1}^K)) \\
&= (F_d^1, F_d^2, \ldots, F_d^K).
\end{aligned}
\qquad (5)
$$

Thence the output of $H_{MIM}(\cdot)$ can be composed by the combination of K-th outputs of all MCACs,

$$F_{EF} = (F_1^K, F_2^K, \ldots, F_D^K). \tag{6}$$

Multi-connected Channel Attention Block. Previous works seldom discriminate feature channels and treat them equally. Till recently a channel attention mechanism using global pooling is proposed in RCAN to concentrate on more useful channels [8]. We adopt the same channel attention block RCAB as in RCAN, also depicted in Fig. 2(c), and the difference between the two only lies in the style of connections.

Channel Attention Mechanism. We let $X = [x_1, \cdots, x_c, \cdots, x_C]$ denote an input that contains C feature maps, and the shape of each feature map be $H \times W$. Then the statistic z_c of the c-th feature map x_c is defined as

$$z_c = H_{GP}(x_c) = \frac{\sum_{i=1}^H \sum_{j=1}^W x_c(i,j)}{H \times W}, \tag{7}$$

where $x_c(i,j)$ denotes the value at index (i,j) of feature map x_c, and $H_{GP}(\cdot)$ represents the global average pooling function. The channel attention of the feature map x_c can thus be denoted as

$$s_c = f(W_U \delta(W_D z_c)), \tag{8}$$

where $f(\cdot)$ and $\delta(\cdot)$ represent the sigmoid function and the ReLU [24] function respectively, W_D is the weight set of a 1×1 convolution for channel downscaling. This convolution reduces the number of channels by a factor r. Later after being activated by a ReLU function, it enters a 1×1 convolution for channel upscaling with the weights W_U, which expands the channel again by the factor r. The computed statistic s_c is used to rescale the input features x_c,

$$\hat{x}_c = s_c \cdot x_c, \tag{9}$$

Description of RCAB. The RCAB is organized using the aforementioned channel attention mechanism. Formally it is a function $H_{RCAB}(\cdot)$ on the input features I,

$$\begin{aligned} F_{RCAB} &= H_{RCAB}(I) \\ &= s_{X_I} \cdot X_I + I \\ &= \hat{X}_I + I, \end{aligned} \tag{10}$$

where s_{X_I} is the output of channel attention on X_I, which are the features generated from the two stacked convolution layers,

$$X_I = W_2 \delta(W_1 I). \tag{11}$$

The cascading mechanism from CARN [7] makes use of intermediate features in a dense way. In order to relax the redundancy of dense skip connections, our channel attention blocks are built in a multi-connected fashion, so-called as MCAB. As shown in Fig. 2(b), each MCAB contains M residual channel attention blocks (RCAB) and $M + 1$ pointwise convolution operations for feature fusion (H_F), which are interleaved by turns. In addition to the cascading mechanism marked by green arrows, we added multi-connections between MCABs, which are marked by orange arrows.

MCAC Structure. As we mentioned before, each MCAC contains K MCABs and each MCAB is composed of M RCABs. In the d-th MCAC, we let the input and output of k-th MCAB be IM_d^k and OM_d^k, and the k-th output of the last MCAC be F_{d-1}^k, we formulate IM_d^k as follows,

$$\begin{cases} [F_0] & d = k = 0 \\ [OM_d^{k-1}] & d = 0, k \in (0, K] \\ [F_{d-1}^k] & d \in (0, D], k = 0 \\ [OM_d^{k-1}, F_{d-1}^k] & d \in (0, D], k \in (0, K] \end{cases} \tag{12}$$

In the case of $d \in (0, D], k \in (0, K], m \in (0, M]$, the m-th feature fusion convolution H_F takes multiple inputs and fuses them into $F_d^{k,m}$. Let the input of m-th RCAB be $IR_d^{k,m}$ and the output $OR_d^{k,m}$, we can write the input of m-th feature fusion convolution $IF_d^{k,m}$ as

$$\begin{cases} [F_{d-1}^k, F_d^{k-1,m+1}, F_d^{k-1,M+1}] & m = 0 \\ [OR_d^{k,m-1}, F_d^{k-1,m+1}, F_d^{k,1}, \\ \quad \ldots, F_d^{k,m-1}] & m \in (0, M] \\ [OR_d^{k,m-1}, F_d^{k,1}, \ldots, F_d^{k,M}] & m = M + 1 \end{cases} \tag{13}$$

Now we give the complete definition of the output of d-th MCAC,

$$\begin{aligned} F_d &= (F_d^1, F_d^2, \ldots, F_d^K) \\ &= H_{MCAC,d}(F_{d-1}) \\ &= H_{MCAC,d}((F_{d-1}^1, F_{d-1}^2, \ldots, F_{d-1}^K)) \\ &= (F_d^{1,M+1}, F_d^{2,M+1}, \ldots, F_d^{K,M+1}). \end{aligned} \tag{14}$$

As we have seen, the nonlinear mapping module of our proposed model is a matrix of $D \times K$. Thus its overall number of sigmoid functions can be calculated as

$$num_{f(\cdot)} = D \times K \times M \times N_{ca}, \tag{15}$$

where $f(\cdot)$ means the sigmoid function and N_{ca} indicates the number of filters in the channel attention mechanism (Fig. 3).

Table 1. Quantitative comparison with the state-of-the-art methods based on ×2, ×3, ×4 (sequentially splitted in three sets of rows in the table) SR with a bicubic degradation mode. Red/blue text: best/second-best.

Method	Scale	Train data	Mult-Adds	Params	Set5 PSNR/SSIM	Set14 PSNR/SSIM	B100 PSNR/SSIM	Urban100 PSNR/SSIM
SRCNN [1]	×2	G100+Yang91	52.7G	57K	36.66/0.9542	32.42/0.9063	31.36/0.8879	29.50/0.8946
FSRCNN [2]	×2	G100+Yang91	6.0G	12K	37.00/0.9558	32.63/0.9088	31.53/0.8920	29.88/0.9020
VDSR [4]	×2	G100+Yang91	612.6G	665K	37.53/0.9587	33.03/0.9124	31.90/0.8960	30.76/0.9140
DRCN [3]	×2	Yang91	17,974.3G	1,774K	37.63/0.9588	33.04/0.9118	31.85/0.8942	30.75/0.9133
LapSRN [6]	×2	G200+Yang91	29.9G	813K	37.52/0.9590	33.08/0.9130	31.80/0.8950	30.41/0.9100
DRRN [5]	×2	G200+Yang91	6,796.9G	297K	37.74/0.9591	33.23/0.9136	32.05/0.8973	31.23/0.9188
BTSRN [25]	×2	DIV2K	207.7G	410K	37.75/-	33.20/-	32.05/-	31.63/-
MemNet [26]	×2	G200+Yang91	2,662.4G	677K	37.78/0.9597	33.28/0.9142	32.08/0.8978	31.31/0.9195
SelNet [27]	×2	ImageNet subset	225.7G	974K	37.89/0.9598	33.61/0.9160	32.08/0.8984	-
CARN [7]	×2	DIV2K	222.8G	1,592K	37.76/0.9590	33.52/0.9166	32.09/0.8978	31.92/0.9256
CARN-M [7]	×2	DIV2K	91.2G	412K	37.53/0.9583	33.26/0.9141	31.92/0.8960	31.23/0.9194
MoreMNAS-A [28]	×2	DIV2K	238.6G	1,039K	37.63/0.9584	33.23/0.9138	31.95/0.8961	31.24/0.9187
FALSR-A [10]	×2	DIV2K	234.7G	1,021K	37.82/0.9595	33.55/0.9168	32.12/0.8987	31.93/0.9256
MCAN	×2	DIV2K	191.3G	1,233K	37.91/0.9597	33.69/0.9183	32.18/0.8994	32.46/0.9303
MCAN+	×2	DIV2K	191.3G	1,233K	38.10/0.9601	33.83/0.9197	32.27/0.9001	32.68/0.9319
MCAN-FAST	×2	DIV2K	191.3G	1,233K	37.84/0.9594	33.67/0.9188	32.16/0.8993	32.36/0.9300
MCAN-FAST+	×2	DIV2K	191.3G	1,233K	38.05/0.9600	33.78/0.9196	32.26/0.8999	32.62/0.9317
MCAN-M	×2	DIV2K	105.50G	594K	37.78/0.9592	33.53/0.9174	32.10/0.8984	32.14/0.9271
MCAN-M+	×2	DIV2K	105.50G	594K	37.98/0.9597	33.68/0.9186	32.200.8992	32.35/0.9290
MCAN-S	×2	DIV2K	46.09G	243K	37.62/0.9586	33.35/0.9156	32.02/0.8976	31.83/0.9244
MCAN-S+	×2	DIV2K	46.09G	243K	37.82/0.9592	33.49/0.9168	32.12/0.8983	32.03/0.9262
MCAN-T	×2	DIV2K	6.27G	35K	37.24/0.9571	32.97/0.9112	31.74/0.8939	30.62/0.9120
MCAN-T+	×2	DIV2K	6.27G	35K	37.45/0.9578	33.07/0.9121	31.85/0.8950	30.79/0.9137
SRCNN [1]	×3	G100+Yang91	52.7G	57K	32.75/0.9090	29.28/0.8209	28.41/0.7863	26.24/0.7989
FSRCNN [2]	×3	G100+Yang91	5.0G	12K	33.16/0.9140	29.43/0.8242	28.53/0.7910	26.43/0.8080
VDSR [4]	×3	G100+Yang91	612.6G	665K	33.66/0.9213	29.77/0.8314	28.82/0.7976	27.14/0.8279
DRCN [3]	×3	Yang91	17,974.3G	1,774K	33.82/0.9226	29.76/0.8311	28.80/0.7963	27.15/0.8276
DRRN [5]	×3	G200+Yang91	6,796.9G	297K	34.03/0.9244	29.96/0.8349	28.95/0.8004	27.53/0.8378
BTSRN [25]	×3	DIV2K	207.7G	410K	37.75/-	33.20/-	32.05/-	31.63/-
MemNet [26]	×3	G200+Yang91	2,662.4G	677K	34.09/0.9248	30.00/0.8350	28.96/0.8001	27.56/0.8376
SelNet [27]	×3	ImageNet subset	120.0G	1,159K	34.27/0.9257	30.30/0.8399	28.97/0.8025	-
CARN [7]	×3	DIV2K	118.8G	1,592K	34.29/0.9255	30.29/0.8407	29.06/0.8034	28.06/0.8493
CARN-M [7]	×3	DIV2K	46.1G	412K	33.99/0.9236	30.08/0.8367	28.91/0.8000	27.55/0.8385
MCAN	×3	DIV2K	95.4G	1,233K	34.45/0.9271	30.43/0.8433	29.14/0.8060	28.47/0.8580
MCAN+	×3	DIV2K	95.4G	1,233K	34.62/0.9280	30.50/0.8442	29.21/0.8070	28.65/0.8605
MCAN-FAST	×3	DIV2K	95.4G	1,233K	34.41/0.9268	30.40/0.8431	29.12/0.8055	28.41/0.8568
MCAN-FAST+	×3	DIV2K	95.4G	1,233K	34.54/0.9276	30.48/0.8440	29.20/0.8067	28.60/0.8595
MCAN-M	×3	DIV2K	50.91G	594K	34.35/0.9261	30.33/0.8417	29.06/0.8041	28.22/0.8525
MCAN-M+	×3	DIV2K	50.91G	594K	34.50/0.9271	30.44/0.8432	29.14/0.8053	28.39/0.8552
MCAN-S	×3	DIV2K	21.91G	243K	34.12/0.9249	30.22/0.8391	28.99/0.8021	27.94/0.8465
MCAN-S+	×3	DIV2K	21.91G	243K	34.28/0.9255	30.31/0.8403	29.07/0.8034	28.09/0.8493
MCAN-T	×3	DIV2K	3.10G	35K	33.54/0.9191	29.76/0.8301	28.73/0.7949	26.97/0.8243
MCAN-T+	×3	DIV2K	3.10G	35K	33.68/0.9207	29.8/0.8320	28.80/0.7964	27.10/0.8271
SRCNN [1]	×4	G100+Yang91	52.7G	57K	30.48/0.8628	27.49/0.7503	26.90/0.7101	24.52/0.7221
FSRCNN [2]	×4	G100+Yang91	4.6G	12K	30.71/0.8657	27.59/0.7535	26.98/0.7150	24.62/0.7280
VDSR [4]	×4	G100+Yang91	612.6G	665K	31.35/0.8838	28.01/0.7674	27.29/0.7251	25.18/0.7524
DRCN [3]	×4	Yang91	17,974.3G	1,774K	31.53/0.8854	28.02/0.7670	27.23/0.7233	25.14/0.7510
LapSRN [6]	×4	G200+Yang91	149.4G	813K	31.54/0.8850	28.19/0.7720	27.32/0.7280	25.21/0.7560
DRRN [5]	×4	G200+Yang91	6,796.9G	297K	31.68/0.8888	28.21/0.7720	27.38/0.7284	25.44/0.7638
BTSRN [25]	×4	DIV2K	207.7G	410K	37.75/-	33.20/-	32.05/-	31.63/-
MemNet [26]	×4	G200+Yang91	2,662.4G	677K	31.74/0.8893	28.26/0.7723	27.40/0.7281	25.50/0.7630
SelNet [27]	×4	ImageNet subset	83.1G	1,417K	32.00/0.8931	28.49/0.7783	27.44/0.7325	-
SRDenseNet [21]	×4	ImageNet subset	389.9G	2,015K	32.02/0.8934	28.50/0.7782	27.53/0.7337	26.05/0.7819
CARN [7]	×4	DIV2K	90.9G	1,592K	32.13/0.8937	28.60/0.7806	27.58/0.7349	26.07/0.7837

(continued)

Table 1. (*continued*)

Method	Scale	Train data	Mult-Adds	Params	Set5 PSNR/SSIM	Set14 PSNR/SSIM	B100 PSNR/SSIM	Urban100 PSNR/SSIM
CARN-M [7]	×4	DIV2K	32.5G	412K	31.92/0.8903	28.42/0.7762	27.44/0.7304	25.62/0.7694
CARN1 [29]	×4	DIV2K	11.3G	86.24K	31.13/0.88	27.93/0.76	27.20/0.72	25.05/0.74
OISR [30]	×4	-	114.2G	1.52M	32.14/0.8947	28.63/0.7819	27.60/0.7369	26.17/0.7888
IMDN [31]	×4	-	71.99G	715K	32.21/0.8948	28.58/0.7811	27.56/0.7353	26.04/0.7838
MCAN	×4	DIV2K	83.1G	1,233K	32.33/0.8959	28.72/0.7835	27.63/0.7378	26.43/0.7953
MCAN+	×4	DIV2K	83.1G	1,233K	32.48/0.8974	28.80/0.7848	27.69/0.7389	26.58/0.7981
MCAN-FAST	×4	DIV2K	83.1G	1,233K	32.30/0.8955	28.69/0.7829	27.60/0.7372	26.37/0.7938
MCAN-FAST+	×4	DIV2K	83.1G	1,233K	32.43/0.8970	28.78/0.7843	27.68/0.7385	26.53/0.7970
MCAN-M	×4	DIV2K	35.53G	594K	32.21/0.8946	28.63/0.7813	27.57/0.7357	26.19/0.7877
MCAN-M+	×4	DIV2K	35.53G	594K	32.34/0.8959	28.72/ 0.7827	27.63/0.7370	26.34/0.7909
MCAN-S	×4	DIV2K	13.98G	243K	31.97/0.8914	28.48/0.7775	27.48/0.7324	25.93/0.7789
MCAN-S+	×4	DIV2K	13.98G	243K	32.11/0.8932	28.57/0.7791	27.55/0.7338	26.06/0.7822
MCAN-T	×4	DIV2K	2.00G	35K	31.33/0.8812	28.04/0.7669	27.22/0.7228	25.12/0.7515
MCAN-T+	×4	DIV2K	2.00G	35K	31.50/0.8843	28.14/0.7689	27.29/0.7244	25.23/0.7548

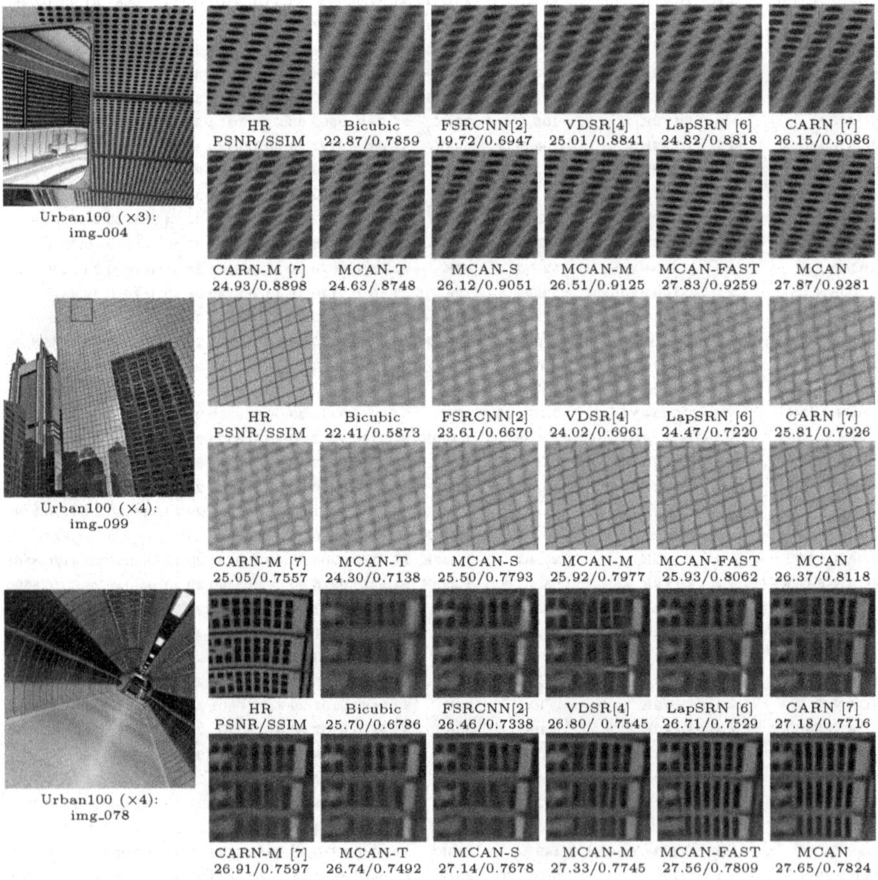

Fig. 3. Visual comparison with bicubic degradation model. Red/blue text: best/second-best. (Color figure online)

3.4   Hierarchical Feature Fusion

Since we generate multiple features through MIM during different stages, we put forward a hierarchical feature fusion (HFF) module to integrate these features hierarchically.

Particularly, we unite the outputs of the last MCAB in each MCAC as the hierarchical features of MIM, which are marked by red arrows in Fig. 2(a). In further detail, HFF takes a 3 × 3 convolution for fusion and another 3 × 3 convolution to reduce channel numbers:

$$F_{HFF} = W_F W_R [F_d^{1,M+1}, \ldots, F_d^{K,M+1}],   \tag{16}$$

where W_F and W_R are the weights of fusion convolution and the channel reduction layer.

3.5   Comparison with Recent Models

Comparison with SRDenseNet. SRDenseNet uses dense blocks proposed by DenseNet to construct a nonlinear mapping module [21]. This dense connection mechanism may lead to redundancy, in fact, not all features should be equally treated. In our work, MIM and HFF can reduce dense connections and highlight the hierarchical information. Additionally, SRDenseNet connects two blocks from point to point, which refrains transmission and utilization of intermediate features. Our proposed multi-connected channel attention block (MCAB) mitigates this problem by injecting multiple connections between blocks.

Comparison with CARN. CARN uses a cascading mechanism [7], which is also pictured in our MIM. Despite this, MIM features multiple connections between MCACs, and the outputs of different stages are relayed between MCABs. Such an arrangement makes better use of intermediate information. Another important difference is that MCAN combines the hierarchical features before upsampling via hierarchical feature fusion. This mechanism helps significantly for reconstruction.

4   Experimental Results

4.1   Datasets and Evaluation Metrics

We train our model based on DIV2K [32], which contains 800 2K high-resolution images for the training set and another 100 pictures for both the validation and test set. Besides, we make comparisons across three scaling tasks (×2, ×3, ×4) on four datasets: Set5 [33], Set14 [34], B100 [35], and Urban100 [36]. The evaluation metrics we used are PSNR [37] and SSIM [38] on the Y channel in the YCbCr space.

4.2 Implementation Details

As shown in Fig. 2, the inputs and outputs of our model are RGB images. We crop the LR patches by 64×64 for various scale tasks and adopt the standard data augmentation.

For training, we use Adam ($\beta_1 = 0.9$, $\beta_2 = 0.999$, and $\epsilon = 10^{-8}$) [39] to minimize L_1 loss within 1.2×10^6 steps with a batch-size of 64. The initial learning rate is set to 2×10^{-4}, halved every 4×10^5 steps. Like CARN [7], we also initialize the network parameters by $\theta \sim U(-k, k)$, where $k = 1/\sqrt{c_{in}}$ and c_{in} is the number of input feature maps. Inspired by EDSR [40], we apply a multi-scale training. Our sub-pixel convolution is the same as in ESPCN [41].

We choose network hyperparameters to build an accurate and efficient model. The first two layers in the FE stage contain $n_{FE} = \{64, 32\}$ filters accordingly. As for MIM, we set $D = K = M = 3$, its number of filters $n_{MIM} = 32$. Two HFF convolutions have $n_{HFF} = \{D \times 32, 32\}$ filters. The last convolution before the upsampling procedure has $n_l = 256$ filters. The reduction factor r in the channel attention mechanism is set to 8.

Table 2. Hyperparameters of our networks.

Models	n_{FE}	n_{MIM}	n_{HFF}	n_l	r
MCAN	{64,32}	32	{96,32}	256	8
MCAN-FAST	{64,32}	32	{96,32}	256	8
MCAN-M	{64,24}	24	{72,24}	128	8
MCAN-S	{32,16}	16	{48,16}	64	8
MCAN-T	{16,8}	8	{24,8}	24	4

Since the *sigmoid* function is inefficient on some mobile devices, especially for some fixed point units such as DSPs. Therefore we propose MCAN-FAST by replacing the *sigmoid* with the *fast sigmoid* [15], which can be written as,

$$f_{fast}(x) = \frac{x}{1 + |x|}. \tag{17}$$

Experiments show that MCAN-FAST has only a small loss on precision, and it achieves almost the same level of metrics as MCAN.

For more lightweight applications, we reduce the number of filters as shown in Table 2. Note in MCAN-T we also set the group as 4 in the group convolution of RCAB for further compression.

4.3 Comparisons with State-of-the-Art Algorithms

We use Mult-Adds and the number of parameters to measure the model size. We emphasize on Mult-Adds as it indicates the number of multiply-accumulate

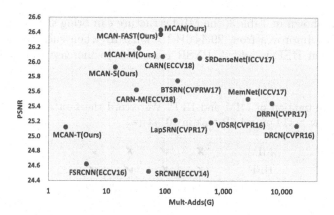

Fig. 4. MCAN models (red) compared with others (blue) on ×4 task of Urban 100. The mult-adds are calculated when the target HR image has a size of 1280×720. (Color figure online)

operations. By convention, it is normalized on 1280×720 high-resolution images. Further evaluation based on geometric self-ensemble strategy [40] are marked with '+' (Fig. 4).

Quantitative comparisons with the state-of-the-art methods are listed in Table 1. For fair comparison, we concentrate on models with comparative mult-adds and parameters.

Notably, MCAN outperforms CARN [7] with fewer mult-adds and parameters. The medium-size model MCAN-M [7] achieves better performance than the CARN-M, additionally, it is still on par with CARN with about half of its mult-adds. For short, it surpasses all other listed methods, including MoreMNAS-A [28] and FALSR-A [10] from NAS methods.

The smaller model MCAN-S emulates LapSRN [6] with much fewer parameters. Particularly, it has an average advantage of 0.5 dB on PSNR over the LapSRN on the ×2 task, and on average, MCAN-S still has an advantage of 0.4 dB. MCAN-S also behaves better than CARN-M on all tasks with half of its model size. It is worth to note that heavily compressed MCAN-S still exceeds or matches larger models such as VDSR, DRCN, DRRN, and MemNet.

The tiny model MCAN-T is meant to be applied under requirements of extreme fast speed. It overtakes FSRCNN [2] on all tasks with the same level of mult-adds.

4.4 Ablation Study

In this section, we demonstrate the effectiveness of the MIM structure and HFF through ablation study.

Matrix in Matrix. We remove the connections between MCACs and also the connections between MCABs. Hence the model comes without intermediate connections. As shown in Table 3, the MIM structure can bring significant improvements, PSNR improves from 29.44 dB to 30.25 dB when such connections are enabled. When HFF is added, PNSR continues to increase from 30.23 dB to 30.28 dB.

Table 3. Investigation of MIM and HFF. We record the best average PSNR (dB) values of Set5 & Set14 on ×4 SR task in 10^5 steps.

MIM	✗	✔	✗	✔
HFF	✗	✗	✔	✔
Avg. PSNR	29.44	30.25	30.23	30.28

Hierarchical Feature Fusion. We simply eliminate the fusion convolutions connected to MIM and consider the output of the last MCAB as the output of MIM. In this case, the intermediate features acquired by the MIM structure are not directly involved in the reconstruction. In Table 3, we observe that the HFF structure enhances PNSR from 29.44 dB to 30.23 dB. With MIM enabled, PSNR is further promoted from 30.25 dB to 30.28 dB.

5   Conclusion

In this paper, we proposed an accurate and efficient network with matrix channel attention for the SISR task. Our main idea is to exploit the intermediate features hierarchically through multi-connected channel attention blocks. MCABs then act as a basic unit that builds up the matrix-in-matrix module. We release three additional efficient models of varied sizes, MCAN-M, MCAN-S, and MCAN-T. Extensive experiments reveal that our MCAN family excel the state-of-the-art models of accordingly similar or even bigger sizes.

To deal with the inefficiency of the sigmoid function on some mobile devices, we benefit from the fast sigmoid to construct MCAN-FAST. The result confirms that MCAN-FAST has only a small loss of precision when compared to MCAN, and it can still achieve better performance with fewer mult-adds and parameters than the state-of-the-art methods.

References

1. Dong, C., Loy, C.C., He, K., Tang, X.: Learning a deep convolutional network for image super-resolution. In: Fleet, D., Pajdla, T., Schiele, B., Tuytelaars, T. (eds.) ECCV 2014, Part IV. LNCS, vol. 8692, pp. 184–199. Springer, Cham (2014). https://doi.org/10.1007/978-3-319-10593-2_13
2. Dong, C., Loy, C.C., Tang, X.: Accelerating the super-resolution convolutional neural network. In: Leibe, B., Matas, J., Sebe, N., Welling, M. (eds.) ECCV 2016, Part II. LNCS, vol. 9906, pp. 391–407. Springer, Cham (2016). https://doi.org/10.1007/978-3-319-46475-6_25

3. Kim, J., Lee, J.K., Lee, K.M.: Deeply-recursive convolutional network for image super-resolution. In: 2016 IEEE Conference on Computer Vision and Pattern Recognition, CVPR 2016, Las Vegas, NV, USA, 27–30 June 2016, pp. 1637–1645 (2016)
4. Kim, J., Lee, J.K., Lee, K.M.: Accurate image super-resolution using very deep convolutional networks. In: 2016 IEEE Conference on Computer Vision and Pattern Recognition, CVPR 2016, Las Vegas, NV, USA, 27–30 June 2016, pp. 1646–1654 (2016)
5. Tai, Y., Yang, J., Liu, X.: Image super-resolution via deep recursive residual network. In: 2017 IEEE Conference on Computer Vision and Pattern Recognition, CVPR 2017, Honolulu, HI, USA, 21–26 July 2017, pp. 2790–2798 (2017)
6. Lai, W., Huang, J., Ahuja, N., Yang, M.: Deep Laplacian pyramid networks for fast and accurate super-resolution. In: 2017 IEEE Conference on Computer Vision and Pattern Recognition, CVPR 2017, Honolulu, HI, USA, 21–26 July 2017, pp. 5835–5843 (2017)
7. Ahn, N., Kang, B., Sohn, K.-A.: Fast, accurate, and lightweight super-resolution with cascading residual network. In: Ferrari, V., Hebert, M., Sminchisescu, C., Weiss, Y. (eds.) ECCV 2018, Part X. LNCS, vol. 11214, pp. 256–272. Springer, Cham (2018). https://doi.org/10.1007/978-3-030-01249-6_16
8. Zhang, Y., Li, K., Li, K., Wang, L., Zhong, B., Fu, Y.: Image super-resolution using very deep residual channel attention networks. In: Ferrari, V., Hebert, M., Sminchisescu, C., Weiss, Y. (eds.) ECCV 2018, Part VII. LNCS, vol. 11211, pp. 294–310. Springer, Cham (2018). https://doi.org/10.1007/978-3-030-01234-2_18
9. Hui, Z., Wang, X., Gao, X.: Fast and accurate single image super-resolution via information distillation network. In: 2018 IEEE Conference on Computer Vision and Pattern Recognition, CVPR 2018, Salt Lake City, UT, USA, 18–22 June 2018, pp. 723–731 (2018)
10. Chu, X., Zhang, B., Ma, H., Xu, R., Li, J., Li, Q.: Fast, accurate and lightweight super-resolution with neural architecture search. CoRR abs/1901.07261 (2019)
11. Zhang, K., et al.: AIM 2019 challenge on constrained super-resolution: methods and results. In: 2019 IEEE/CVF International Conference on Computer Vision Workshop (ICCVW), pp. 3565–3574. IEEE (2019)
12. Blau, Y., Mechrez, R., Timofte, R., Michaeli, T., Zelnik-Manor, L.: The 2018 PIRM challenge on perceptual image super-resolution. In: Leal-Taixé, L., Roth, S. (eds.) ECCV 2018. LNCS, vol. 11133, pp. 334–355. Springer, Cham (2019). https://doi.org/10.1007/978-3-030-11021-5_21
13. Ledig, C., et al.: Photo-realistic single image super-resolution using a generative adversarial network. In: 2017 IEEE Conference on Computer Vision and Pattern Recognition, CVPR 2017, Honolulu, HI, USA, 21–26 July 2017, pp. 105–114 (2017)
14. Wang, X., et al.: ESRGAN: enhanced super-resolution generative adversarial networks. In: Leal-Taixé, L., Roth, S. (eds.) ECCV 2018. LNCS, vol. 11133, pp. 63–79. Springer, Cham (2019). https://doi.org/10.1007/978-3-030-11021-5_5
15. Georgiou, G.: Parallel distributed processing in the complex domain. Ph.D. thesis, Tulane (1992)
16. Girshick, R.B.: Fast R-CNN. In: 2015 IEEE International Conference on Computer Vision, ICCV 2015, Santiago, Chile, 7–13 December 2015, pp. 1440–1448 (2015)
17. He, K., Gkioxari, G., Dollár, P., Girshick, R.B.: Mask R-CNN. In: IEEE International Conference on Computer Vision, ICCV 2017, Venice, Italy, 22–29 October 2017, pp. 2980–2988 (2017)

18. Liu, W., et al.: SSD: single shot multibox detector. In: Leibe, B., Matas, J., Sebe, N., Welling, M. (eds.) ECCV 2016. LNCS, vol. 9905, pp. 21–37. Springer, Cham (2016). https://doi.org/10.1007/978-3-319-46448-0_2

19. Noh, H., Hong, S., Han, B.: Learning deconvolution network for semantic segmentation. In: 2015 IEEE International Conference on Computer Vision, ICCV 2015, Santiago, Chile, 7–13 December 2015, pp. 1520–1528 (2015)

20. Zhang, R., Isola, P., Efros, A.A.: Colorful image colorization. In: Leibe, B., Matas, J., Sebe, N., Welling, M. (eds.) ECCV 2016, Part III. LNCS, vol. 9907, pp. 649–666. Springer, Cham (2016). https://doi.org/10.1007/978-3-319-46487-9_40

21. Tong, T., Li, G., Liu, X., Gao, Q.: Image super-resolution using dense skip connections. In: IEEE International Conference on Computer Vision, ICCV 2017, Venice, Italy, 22–29 October 2017, pp. 4809–4817 (2017)

22. Mao, X., Shen, C., Yang, Y.: Image restoration using very deep convolutional encoder-decoder networks with symmetric skip connections. In: Advances in Neural Information Processing Systems 29: Annual Conference on Neural Information Processing Systems 2016, Barcelona, Spain, 5–10 December 2016, pp. 2802–2810 (2016)

23. Zhang, Y., Tian, Y., Kong, Y., Zhong, B., Fu, Y.: Residual dense network for image super-resolution. In: 2018 IEEE Conference on Computer Vision and Pattern Recognition, CVPR 2018, Salt Lake City, UT, USA, 18–22 June 2018, pp. 2472–2481 (2018)

24. Nair, V., Hinton, G.E.: Rectified linear units improve restricted Boltzmann machines. In: Proceedings of the 27th International Conference on Machine Learning (ICML 2010), Haifa, Israel, 21–24 June 2010, pp. 807–814 (2010)

25. Fan, Y., et al.: Balanced two-stage residual networks for image super-resolution. In: 2017 IEEE Conference on Computer Vision and Pattern Recognition Workshops, CVPR Workshops 2017, Honolulu, HI, USA, 21–26 July 2017, pp. 1157–1164 (2017)

26. Tai, Y., Yang, J., Liu, X., Xu, C.: MEMNet: a persistent memory network for image restoration. In: IEEE International Conference on Computer Vision, ICCV 2017, Venice, Italy, 22–29 October 2017, pp. 4549–4557 (2017)

27. Choi, J., Kim, M.: A deep convolutional neural network with selection units for super-resolution. In: 2017 IEEE Conference on Computer Vision and Pattern Recognition Workshops, CVPR Workshops 2017, Honolulu, HI, USA, 21–26 July 2017, pp. 1150–1156 (2017)

28. Chu, X., Zhang, B., Xu, R., Ma, H.: Multi-objective reinforced evolution in mobile neural architecture search. CoRR abs/1901.01074 (2019)

29. Li, Y., Agustsson, E., Gu, S., Timofte, R., Van Gool, L.: CARN: convolutional anchored regression network for fast and accurate single image super-resolution. In: Leal-Taixé, L., Roth, S. (eds.) ECCV 2018. LNCS, vol. 11133, pp. 166–181. Springer, Cham (2019). https://doi.org/10.1007/978-3-030-11021-5_11

30. He, X., Mo, Z., Wang, P., Liu, Y., Yang, M., Cheng, J.: ODE-inspired network design for single image super-resolution. In: Proceedings of the IEEE Conference on Computer Vision and Pattern Recognition, pp. 1732–1741 (2019)

31. Hui, Z., Gao, X., Yang, Y., Wang, X.: Lightweight image super-resolution with information multi-distillation network. In: Proceedings of the 27th ACM International Conference on Multimedia (ACM MM), pp. 2024–2032 (2019)

32. Agustsson, E., Timofte, R.: NTIRE 2017 challenge on single image super-resolution: dataset and study. In: 2017 IEEE Conference on Computer Vision and Pattern Recognition Workshops, CVPR Workshops 2017, Honolulu, HI, USA, 21–26 July 2017, pp. 1122–1131 (2017)

33. Bevilacqua, M., Roumy, A., Guillemot, C., Alberi-Morel, M.: Low-complexity single-image super-resolution based on nonnegative neighbor embedding. In: British Machine Vision Conference, BMVC 2012, Surrey, UK, 3–7 September 2012, pp. 1–10 (2012)

34. Yang, J., Wright, J., Huang, T.S., Ma, Y.: Image super-resolution via sparse representation. IEEE Trans. Image Processing **19**, 2861–2873 (2010)

35. Martin, D.R., Fowlkes, C.C., Tal, D., Malik, J.: A database of human segmented natural images and its application to evaluating segmentation algorithms and measuring ecological statistics. In: ICCV, pp. 416–425 (2001)

36. Huang, J., Singh, A., Ahuja, N.: Single image super-resolution from transformed self-exemplars. In: IEEE Conference on Computer Vision and Pattern Recognition, CVPR 2015, Boston, MA, USA, 7–12 June 2015, pp. 5197–5206 (2015)

37. Horé, A., Ziou, D.: Image quality metrics: PSNR vs. SSIM. In: 20th International Conference on Pattern Recognition, ICPR 2010, Istanbul, Turkey, 23–26 August 2010, pp. 2366–2369 (2010)

38. Wang, Z., Bovik, A.C., Sheikh, H.R., Simoncelli, E.P.: Image quality assessment: from error visibility to structural similarity. IEEE Trans. Image Processing **13**, 600–612 (2004)

39. Kingma, D.P., Ba, J.: Adam: a method for stochastic optimization. CoRR abs/1412.6980 (2014)

40. Lim, B., Son, S., Kim, H., Nah, S., Lee, K.M.: Enhanced deep residual networks for single image super-resolution. In: 2017 IEEE Conference on Computer Vision and Pattern Recognition Workshops, CVPR Workshops 2017, Honolulu, HI, USA, 21–26 July 2017, pp. 1132–1140 (2017)

41. Shi, W., et al.: Real-time single image and video super-resolution using an efficient sub-pixel convolutional neural network. In: 2016 IEEE Conference on Computer Vision and Pattern Recognition, CVPR 2016, Las Vegas, NV, USA, 27–30 June 2016, pp. 1874–1883 (2016)

Second-Order Camera-Aware Color Transformation for Cross-Domain Person Re-identification

Wangmeng Xiang[1], Hongwei Yong[1], Jianqiang Huang[2],
Xian-Sheng Hua[2], and Lei Zhang[1,2]([⊠])

[1] Department of Computing, The Hong Kong Polytechnic University,
Hung Hom, Hong Kong
{cswxiang,cshyong,cslzhang}@comp.polyu.edu.hk
[2] Artificial Intelligence Center, Alibaba DAMO Academy, Hangzhou, China
{jianqiang.hjq,xiansheng.hxs}@alibaba-inc.com

Abstract. In recent years, supervised person re-identification (person ReID) has achieved great performance on public datasets, however, cross-domain person ReID remains a challenging task. The performance of ReID model trained on the labeled dataset (source) is often inferior on the new unlabeled dataset (target), due to large variation in color, resolution, scenes of different datasets. Therefore, unsupervised person ReID has gained a lot of attention due to its potential to solve the domain adaptation problem. Many methods focus on minimizing the distribution discrepancy in the feature domain but neglecting the differences among input distributions. This motivates us to handle the variation between input distributions of source and target datasets directly. We propose a Second-order Camera-aware Color Transformation (SCCT) that can operate on image level and align the second-order statistics of all the views of both source and target domain data with original ImageNet data statistics. This new input normalization method, as shown in our experiments, is much more efficient than simply using ImageNet statistics. We test our method on Market1501, DukeMTMC, and MSMT17 and achieve leading performance in unsupervised person ReID.

1 Introduction

Person re-identification (person ReID) is an important computer vision task, which aims to identify the same person from a set of images captured under different cameras [1]. The task of person ReID is very challenging due to the large variation in camera viewpoint, lighting, resolution, and human pose etc. In recent years, supervised person ReID has achieved great performance under the single domain dataset [2–4,4–17]. State-of-the-art methods have achieved over 95% top1 accuracy and nearly 90% in mAP. Existing researches in supervised single domain person ReID methods can be roughly grouped into three categories: 1) transferring and improving powerful CNN architectures to person ReID [2–7], where off-the-shelf feature extractors are used as parts of the

© Springer Nature Switzerland AG 2021
H. Ishikawa et al. (Eds.): ACCV 2020, LNCS 12623, pp. 36–53, 2021.
https://doi.org/10.1007/978-3-030-69532-3_3

network architecture; 2) designing more effective metrics [10–15]; 3) combining priori into network architecture for fine-grained feature learning [4,8,9,16,17].

Despite supervised single domain person ReID has achieved great accuracy, the performance of the model would drop dramatically when the model is applied to an unseen new dataset. In other words, the performance of ReID model trained on the labeled source dataset (source) is often inferior on the new unlabeled target dataset, which is due to the data-bias between these two datasets (or two domains). As it is expensive to label the target datasets, many researchers treat this task as an unsupervised domain adaptation (UDA) problem. Unfortunately, many existing UDA solutions can not be simply applied to unsupervised person ReID due to the differences in problem settings. Generally, UDA setting requires the categories of source and target domain to be the same, or at least to have overlap. However, in person ReID, the identities in source and target datasets are totally different. In recent years, approaches that aim specifically to improve the performance of unsupervised domain adaptation of person ReID have been proposed [18–21]. We categorize these methods into two different settings: direct transfer and progressive learning. In the direct transfer setting, most of methods [19,20] minimize the discrepancy of two domains by applying carefully designed loss functions. While in progressive learning [21], pseudo labels are generated for training, and the model is trained in an iterative manner.

Although many methods focus on decreasing the domain discrepancy in the feature level, there are very few methods working on the image level. Several existing methods use generative adversarial networks [22] (GAN) to generate new data that are similar to the target domain for training. For example, PTGAN [18] transfers the appearance of the labeled source dataset to the unlabeled target dataset using generative adversarial networks (GAN). ECN [19] makes fine-grained camera style transfer by utilizing the camera id information in the target dataset. Camera sensor variation is pointed out in [23], and they use GAN to generate domain-specific images for every view of the camera. Our proposed method also works on image level, unlike previous works that use additional GAN for data generation, we aim to minimize the discrepancy of datasets by matching the camera-wise input distributions to the second-order ImageNet [24] data statistics. We found that there are actually two "domain shift" steps in the typical unsupervised person ReID. 1) ImageNet to the source: most methods in person ReID would use a backbone network pre-trained on ImageNet, the input distribution of ImageNet is usually different from the source dataset, which means the first domain shift is from ImageNet to source dataset. 2) source to target: the second step is domain shift from source dataset to target dataset. To solve the domain shift problem mentioned above, we apply the camera-aware color transformation, which matches every camera view individually to the ImageNet statistics. This fine-grained color transformation boosts the performance of ReID model in the cross-domain setting by a large margin. In addition, we also apply a color equalization data augmentation to increase the adaptive ability of our trained model. As far as we know, it is the first time second-order color transformation and color equalization data augmentation are applied for unsupervised person ReID. We summarize the contributions as follows:

- We propose to use the color transformation as a pre-processing step to compensate for the color changes in unsupervised person ReID in both source domain and target domain, which is a fine-grained camera-aware color transformation that can handle camera color shift and statistics changes of different cameras. It is easy to implement, fast and simple, and there is no need for tedious parameter tuning.
- We propose to use color equalization augmentation in cross-domain person ReID. This augmentation could ease the differences in the input distribution of different datasets.
- We conduct extensive experiments and ablation studies on several popular person ReID benchmarks including Market1501 [25], DukeMTMC-ReID [26], MSMT17 [18] to demonstrate the effectiveness of proposed color transformation and data augmentation solution and achieve leading performance in these datasets.

2   Related Works

2.1   Supervised Person ReID

In recent years, state-of-the-art supervised person ReID methods have achieved over 95% top1 accuracy in large-scale public datasets. Researchers have been working on novel network structures [2–4,7], combining other human body prior in the training process [8,9,27,28], more efficient loss functions [2,6,10,11,29–33] etc. For example, Sun et al. [3] used CaffeNet and ResNet as backbone networks. Chen et al. [27] developed a multi-scale network architecture with a saliency-based feature fusion. Zhou et al. [28] built a part-based CNN to extract discriminative and stable features for body appearance. Shi et al. [11] trained their network using triplet loss with hard positive pairs mining. Although these methods perform well on the single domain dataset, when directly test the model trained from the source dataset on the new unlabeled target dataset, the performance of the model would drop dramatically. This performance gap has led many researchers to cross-domain person ReID or unsupervised person ReID.

2.2   Unsupervised Domain Adaptation

Unsupervised domain adaptation (UDA) [34–36] aims to transfer knowledge from a labeled source dataset to an unlabeled target dataset. Many UDA methods focus on the feature domain and try to decrease the discrepancy of source and target feature distributions. For example, Gretton et al. [34] minimize the difference between the means of features from two domains. Sun et al. [35] learn a linear transformation that aligns the mean and covariance of feature distribution between source and target domain. Ganin et al. [36] propose a gradient reversal layer and integrate it into a deep neural network for minimizing the classification loss while maximizing domain confusion loss. Chen *et al.* [37] propose a high-order moment matching between two domains in feature space. Some existing works try to generate pseudo-labels on the target set and utilize this information for training. For example, Sener *et al.* [38] infer the labels of unsupervised target data points in a k-NN graph and jointly train a unified deep learning framework in an end-to-end fashion. Saito *et al.* [39] propose to assign pseudo-labels to unlabeled target samples based on the predictions from two classifiers trained on source samples and one network is trained by the samples to obtain target discriminative representations. However, these methods assume the class labels are the same across domains, which is not true in person ReID. In addition, they were not designed to address the camera shifts in ReID problem. Therefore they can not achieve good performance in unsupervised person ReID and some of them can not be applied to this problem.

2.3 Unsupervised Person ReID

Recently, works specifically focus on unsupervised person ReID have been proposed to tackle the scalability problem. Several methods utilize GAN to generate new data that looks similar to target domain for training. For example, Wei *et al.* [18] transfer the appearance of labeled source dataset to the unlabeled target dataset using cycle GAN [40]. Zhong *et al.* [19] make fine-grained camera style transfer by utilizing the camera id information in the target dataset. Some works use additional attribute information for cross-domain knowledge transfer. For instance, Wang *et al.* [41] propose to learn an attribute-semantic and identity discriminative feature representation space for the target domain. They utilize attribute information of person to bridge the source and target domain. Cross-camera scenes variation in person ReID is significant in many ways including image resolution, color, and viewpoints changes. These variants lead to a huge discrepancy in image statistics of images captured by different cameras. Existing methods handle cross-camera scene variation by camera-to-camera alignment at image level [19,20] or feature level [42]. Zhong *et al.* [20] try to use GAN to generate different camera style images of the target dataset. Wu *et al.* [43] consider the domain shift among different cameras and propose to keep cross camera-aware similarity consistency and intra-camera similarity preservation by minimizing two consistency loss. UPR [44] adjusts images' hue, saturation, lightness, and contrast to enhance the adaptation ability of models by data augmentation. Different from previous works, we propose a second-order color transform method that focuses on the distribution of input images. Besides, color equalization augmentation is used to make model less sensitive to the data distribution changes.

3 Proposed Method

As we mentioned in Sect. 1, we noticed that the DNNs' backbone model used for person ReID are usually pre-trained on ImageNet to obtain better performance. However, the input statistics of source and target ReID datasets (e.g.

Market1501, DukeMTMC) are different from ImageNet. Therefore, matching the color statistics of the source and target ReID dataset with ImageNet would reduce the domain discrepancy. Another observation is that the image distribution of camera views are inconsistent due to the camera sensor variation. As we can see from Fig. 1, the color of the clothes of the same person looks different under different camera views. The color mean statistic of six cameras in Market1501 in Fig. 2 shows that there are clear differences in input color distribution of different cameras. This observation motivates us to make color statistics of all the cameras be the same. More specifically, we use a linear transformation to match the first-order statistics (mean) and second-order statistics (covariance) of input images with ImageNet statistics.

Fig. 1. Samples of color changes of different camera views of Market1501. The column 1–6 and 7–12 are sampled from camera view 1 to 6 respectively. As we can see the camera view 6 (column 6,12) is very different from other camera views. (Color figure online)

3.1   Color Statistics Calculation

For color matching of different camera views, we need to obtain the statistics of datasets. Due to the limitation of computation resources, we cannot load the whole dataset into memory to make the full computation, especially for the large scale dataset (e.g. ImageNet). Therefore, we adopt an incremental computation method. Suppose $\mathbf{X}_k \in \mathbb{R}^{m \times n \times 3}$ the k-th input image of training dataset, $m \times n$ is the size of input images and 3 is the number of channels (i.e. R, G and B), and $\mathbf{x}_{ijk} \in \mathbb{R}^3$ denotes the color vector of a pixel in image $\mathbf{X}_k$. We use the following incremental rules to obtain the color mean and covariance of input images:

$$S^k[\mathbf{x}] = S^{k-1}[\mathbf{x}] + \sum_{i,j} \mathbf{x}_{ijk},$$
$$S^k[\mathbf{x}\mathbf{x}^T] = S^{k-1}[\mathbf{x}\mathbf{x}^T] + \sum_{i,j} \mathbf{x}_{ijk}\mathbf{x}_{ijk}^T, \tag{1}$$
$$N^k = N^{k-1} + mn$$

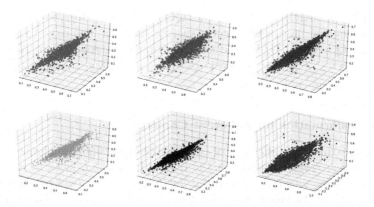

Fig. 2. Color mean statistic of different camera views on Market1501. It is clear that the scale and shape of color mean statistic distribution are different among various camera views. (Color figure online)

where $S^k[\mathbf{x}]$ and $S^k[\mathbf{x}\mathbf{x}^T]$ is the incremental statistics of the first k images, respectively, N^k is the number of pixels of the first k images, and $S^0[\mathbf{x}]$ and $S^0[\mathbf{x}\mathbf{x}^T]$ is a zero vector and matrix, respectively, and $N^0 = 0$. After we obtain the final statistics $S[\mathbf{x}]$ and $S[\mathbf{x}\mathbf{x}^T]$ of all input images, the mean and covariance matrix are:

$$\boldsymbol{\mu} = \frac{1}{N}S[\mathbf{x}], \quad \boldsymbol{\Sigma} = \frac{1}{N}S[\mathbf{x}\mathbf{x}^T] - \boldsymbol{\mu}\boldsymbol{\mu}^T \tag{2}$$

We can use these incremental rules to get mean and covariance of input images without occupying too much memory. Because we only need to save $S^k[\mathbf{x}]$, $S^k[\mathbf{x}\mathbf{x}^T]$, N^k and current image $\mathbf{X}_k$ at every step.

3.2 Mean and Covariance Matching

Given the statistics μ and $\boldsymbol{\Sigma}$ for input images of training dataset and the target statistics μ_0 and $\boldsymbol{\Sigma}_0$, we need to find a linear transformation to make the first and second order statistics of transformed pixel the same as target statistics. The pixel $\mathbf{x}$ is transformed as: $\mathbf{x}' = \mathbf{A}\mathbf{x} + \mathbf{b}$, where $\mathbf{A}$ is a 3×3 matrix and $\mathbf{b}$ is a 3-vector. We need to find proper $\mathbf{A}$ and $\mathbf{b}$ to satisfy $E[\mathbf{x}'] = \mu_0$ and $E[\mathbf{x}'\mathbf{x}'^T] - \mu_0^2 = \boldsymbol{\Sigma}_0$, then we can obtain the following conditions:

$$\begin{aligned} \mathbf{A}\mu + \mathbf{b} &= \mu_0 \\ \mathbf{A}\boldsymbol{\Sigma}\mathbf{A}^T &= \boldsymbol{\Sigma}_0 \end{aligned} \tag{3}$$

The solution for $\mathbf{A}$ and $\mathbf{b}$ are not unique under this conditions. There remain a family of solutions. Suppose the eigenvalue decomposition for $\boldsymbol{\Sigma}$ and $\boldsymbol{\Sigma}_0$ is $\boldsymbol{\Sigma} = \mathbf{U}\boldsymbol{\Lambda}\mathbf{U}^T$ and $\boldsymbol{\Sigma}_0 = \mathbf{U}_0\boldsymbol{\Lambda}_0\mathbf{U}_0^T$, Then we have

$$\begin{aligned} \mathbf{A} &= \mathbf{U}_0\boldsymbol{\Lambda}_0^{\frac{1}{2}}\mathbf{Q}\boldsymbol{\Lambda}^{-\frac{1}{2}}\mathbf{U}^T \\ \mathbf{b} &= \mu_0 - \mathbf{A}\mu \end{aligned} \tag{4}$$

where $\mathbf{Q}$ is any orthogonal matrix (i.e. $\mathbf{Q}\mathbf{Q}^T = \mathbf{I}$). Therefore, we can choose a proper orthogonal matrix $\mathbf{Q}$ to get a specific solution. The most two common choices for $\mathbf{Q}$ is $\mathbf{I}$ and $\mathbf{U}_0^T\mathbf{U}$, and their corresponding solution for $\mathbf{A}$ are $\mathbf{A} = \mathbf{U}_0\mathbf{\Lambda}_0^{\frac{1}{2}}\mathbf{\Lambda}^{-\frac{1}{2}}\mathbf{U}^T$ and $\mathbf{A} = \mathbf{U}_0\mathbf{\Lambda}_0^{\frac{1}{2}}\mathbf{U}_0^T\mathbf{U}\mathbf{\Lambda}^{-\frac{1}{2}}\mathbf{U}^T$, respectively. In our experiments, we use the second choice for $\mathbf{Q}$.

3.3   Transformation for Different Cameras

In order to reduce the difference of color distribution among different cameras, we use a linear transformation for the images from one camera to make color statistics the same as images from ImageNet. Suppose we have obtained the mean and covariance of the images from different cameras according to Eq. (1) and (2), and we use $\{\boldsymbol{\mu}_c\}_{c=1}^C$ and $\{\boldsymbol{\Sigma}_c\}_{c=1}^C$ to denote the color mean and covariance matrix of images from C cameras, and use $\boldsymbol{\mu}_I$ and $\boldsymbol{\Sigma}_I$ to denote the color mean and covariance matrix of image from ImageNet. Then we adopt the Eq. (4) to get the linear transformation parameters $\{\mathbf{A}\}_{c=1}^C$ and $\{\mathbf{b}\}_{c=1}^C$ for images from different cameras:

$$\mathbf{A}_c = \mathbf{U}_I\mathbf{\Lambda}_I^{\frac{1}{2}}\mathbf{U}_I^T\mathbf{U}_c\mathbf{\Lambda}_c^{-\frac{1}{2}}\mathbf{U}_c^T$$
$$\mathbf{b}_c = \boldsymbol{\mu}_I - \mathbf{A}_c\boldsymbol{\mu}_c, \quad c = 1, 2, ..., C, \tag{5}$$

where $\boldsymbol{\Sigma}_c = \mathbf{U}_c\mathbf{\Lambda}_c\mathbf{U}_c^T$ and $\boldsymbol{\Sigma}_I = \mathbf{U}_I\mathbf{\Lambda}_I\mathbf{U}_I^T$. Therefore, for a pixel $\mathbf{x}$ from the c-th camera, the input pixel for the backbone DNNs is $\mathbf{x}' = \mathbf{A}_c\mathbf{x} + \mathbf{b}_c$. After making the color statistics of images from all cameras the same as that of images from ImageNet, we also need to use the same normalization parameters (mean and variance of each channel) as that used in training ImageNet for input images. This normalization method can be viewed as simple linear transformation so it can be fused with color transformation. We use the diagonal matrix $\mathbf{A}_0 = \mathrm{Diag}\{\frac{1}{\sigma_r}, \frac{1}{\sigma_g}, \frac{1}{\sigma_b}\}$ and $\mathbf{b}_0 = [\mu_r, \mu_g, \mu_b]^T$ to denote the normalization transformation parameters. Then, the fused linear transformation for c-th camera changes to:

$$\mathbf{x}' = \mathbf{A}_c'\mathbf{x} + \mathbf{b}_c',$$
$$\mathbf{A}_c' = \mathbf{A}_0\mathbf{A}_c, \tag{6}$$
$$\mathbf{b}_c' = \mathbf{A}_0\mathbf{b}_c + \mathbf{b}_0.$$

We only need to compute and save the parameters $\mathbf{A}_c'$ and $\mathbf{b}_c'$ for each cameras, and it can work as a pre-processing step in network training.

3.4   Progressive Unsupervised Learning

Progressive unsupervised learning is an effective paradigm used in [21,45] to boost the performance of unsupervised person ReID. We first train a base network on the labeled source dataset, then we follow the training strategy in [21] and conduct the progressive training on target training set in an iterative manner. The overall framework can be seen in Fig. 3.

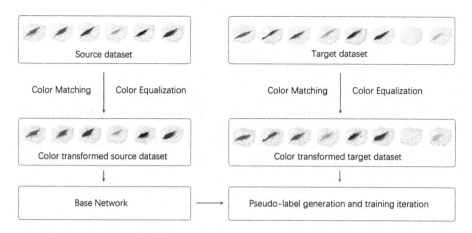

Fig. 3. Pipeline of our training framework. We use Market1501 (6 camera views) as source dataset, DukeMTMC (8 camera views) as target dataset in this figure. After training base network using transformed source data, pseudo-labels are generated from transformed target data with base network. Then progressive learning is applied to train the model in an iterative manner.

Base Network Training. We use ResNet50 as the backbone network for a fair comparison, as it is used by most of the state-of-the-art methods. We follow the training strategy and network structure in [45] to fine-tune on the ImageNet pre-trained model. We discard the last fully connected (FC) layer and add two FC layer. The output of the first FC layer is 2,048-dim, followed by batch normalization [46], ReLU. The output of the second FC layer is the identity number in the labeled training set. As mentioned in the previous section, we add a pre-processing step to make our model invariant to color statistic changes.

Progressive Learning. Inspired by previous ReID work [21,47], we adopt a clustering-training iterative strategy, and both global and local features are considered in the iterative training process. We denote the unlabeled image on the target training set to be I^i, after feeding the input image to the base network, the output feature could then be denoted X^i, which is a $H \times W \times C$ feature map. Besides global feature map X^i, we further split the X^i into upper body and lower body feature maps $X_{up}^i, X_{low}^i \in \mathbb{R}^{\frac{H}{2} \times \frac{W}{2} \times C}$. The feature maps are then average pooled to feature vector f_g^i, f_{up}^i and f_{low}^i. To keep the model consistency with the pre-trained model, we add a 2048-dim FC layer after f_g to get f_e.

After generating features of all target training set, we then apply DBSCAN [48] to cluster and generate pseudo-label y_g^i, y_{up}^i and y_{low}^i for each sample, respectively. Re-ranking [49] is also applied to generate a more reliable distance matrix. We use these pseudo-labels as supervised information to train the model on the target training set. We apply hard triplet loss function to fine-tune the model, and the formula can be represented as follows:

$$\mathcal{L}_t = \sum_{i \in P \times K} [\max \underbrace{\|f_a^i - f_p^i\|_2^2}_{\text{hardest positive}} - \overbrace{\|f_a^i - f_n^i\|_2^2}^{\text{hardest negative}} + m]_+ \tag{7}$$

where P is the identity number, K is the number of samples per identity, f_a^i represents anchor feature vector, f_p^i stands for positive feature vector, f_n^i stands for negative feature vector, m is the margin. This formula aims to make largest positive distance smaller than smallest negative distance by margin m. We apply hard triplet loss on both global and local features, the whole loss function can be represented as:

$$L = L_t(f_g, y_g) + L_t(f_{up}, y_{up}) + L_t(f_{low}, y_{low}) + L_t(f_e, y_g) \tag{8}$$

We also apply identity dictionary strategy proposed in [21] and randomly sample an identity in each cluster group as the identity agent. The pseudo-label of other samples would then be decided by the feature distance to the identity agent. This leads to new pseudo label set $y_{n-g}, y_{n-up}, y_{n-low}$. We apply the same hard triplet loss in Eq. 8 on these new labels. The overall loss function becomes:

$$\begin{aligned} L = &L_t(f_g, y_g) + L_t(f_{up}, y_{up}) + L_t(f_{low}, y_{low}) + L_t(f_e, y_g) \\ &+ L_t(f_g, y_{n-g}) + L_t(f_{up}, y_{n-up}) + L_t(f_{low}, y_{n-low}) + L_t(f_e, y_{n-g}) \end{aligned} \tag{9}$$

The clustering and training process is kept several times until iterations.

Fig. 4. Samples of color equalization augmentation of different views of Market1501. The first row are the originals, the second row are the images after color equalization. (Color figure online)

Color Equalization Augmentation. Color equalization is a simple yet efficient technique for image visual effect enhancement. It equalizes the image histogram and improves the contrast by effectively spreading out the most frequent intensity values, i.e., stretching out the intensity range of the image. In person ReID, the contrast of images is inconsistent among different camera views. Therefore, using equalization augmentation would ease the inconsistency and improve the generalization ability. The visual effect of color equalization can be seen from Fig. 4. As we can see, the images after color equalization are lighter and feel more constant among different views. Our implementation of color equalization augmentation is based on the Python Image Library (PIL)[1], which applies the library function *ImageOps.equalize()*. In all our experiments, we set the color equalization augmentation probability to 0.5.

4 Experiments

4.1 Implementation Details

Baseline Training. As described in Sect. 3.4, we first train a baseline model on the source dataset with the color transformation layer. We resize all the input images to 256×128. For data augmentation, we employ random cropping, flipping, random erasing [50], and our proposed color equalization. For hard triplet mining, in each mini-batch, we randomly selected P = 4 identities and sampled K = 8 images for each identity from the training set, so that the mini-batch size is 32. And in our experiment, we set the margin parameter to 0.5. During training, we use the Adam [51] with weight decay 0.0005 to optimize the parameters for 150 epochs. The initial learning rate is set to 3×10^{-4} and decays to 3×10^{-5} after 100 epochs.

Unsupervised Training. For unsupervised training, we follow the same data augmentation strategy and triplet loss setting. And we decrease the initial learning rate from 3×10^{-4} to 6×10^{-5} and change the training epoch from 150 to 70. Besides, the whole framework is trained for 30 iterations.

4.2 Ablation Study

Effectiveness of Camera-Aware Color Transformation. We investigate the influences of different normalization and color transformation strategy. The "Baseline" method applies the mean and standard deviation of ImageNet, which is used by most of the methods. As listed in Table 1, using domain-specific mean and deviation "MD" outperforms using ImageNet statistics by around 3–4% in mAP/top1 when transferred from DukeMTMC to Market1501. While camera-aware first-order normalization C_{first} improves 1.9% mAP and 1.8% top1 accuracy over "MD" when tested from D→M. This shows the effectiveness of camera-aware normalization, even though it is a simple first-order method, it can still largely boost the performance. Our proposed C_{second} achieves the best performance and outperforms other methods by a large margin. We use C to represent C_{second} for convenience in the experiments below.

---

[1] http://www.pythonware.com/products/pil/.

Table 1. Comparison of using different color transformation methods. "Baseline" denotes using ImageNet image statistics for normalization. "MD" stands for using mean and std for normalization. "C_{first}" stands for using each camera view's mean and standard deviation of source and target datasets for input normalization. "C_{second}" stands for using the proposed second-order camera-aware color transformation.

Method	DukeMTMC → Market1501				Market1501 → DukeMTMC			
	mAP	Top1	Top5	Top10	mAP	Top1	Top5	Top10
Baseline	20.3	46.5	65.4	72.4	15.9	29.0	45.2	52.3
Baseline + MD	23.1	50.1	67.0	73.8	16.8	29.9	45.3	50.9
Baseline + C_{first}	25.0	51.9	68.2	74.6	19.8	35.5	51.3	57.5
Baseline + C_{second}	30.6	58.2	74.0	80.1	21.9	38.5	55.1	62.3

In Table 2 we can see that with camera-aware color transformation, we improve the performance by 10.3% and 15.4% in mAP and rank-1 accuracy comparing to baseline when the model is transferred from DukeMTMC to Market1501. Similarly, when the model is trained on Market1501 and tested on DukeMTMC, the performance gain becomes 6.0% and 9.5% in mAP and rank-1 accuracy, respectively. Moreover, color transform keeps boosting the performance when combined with progressive learning. It can further improve the performance by 5.9% in mAP and 4.6% in rank-1 accuracy when transfer from DukeMTMC to Market1501, which show its strong adaptive ability.

Effectiveness of Equalization Augmentation. We conduct an ablation study to prove the effectiveness of equalization data augmentation in Table 2. This augmentation could relieve the lighting differences between different camera views. From Table 2, we can see that with the color equalization augmentation the performance is improved by 8.6% and 11.9% in mAP and top1 accuracy comparing to "Baseline" when the model is transferred from DukeMTMC to Market1501. When the model is trained on Market1501 and tested on DukeMTMC, the performance gain becomes 8.5% and 13.9% in mAP and top1 accuracy, respectively. Moreover, when we combine color equalization and camera-aware color transformation, the performance would further be improved by around 2% in top1 accuracy and 1−2% in mAP.

Effectiveness of Progressive Unsupervised Learning. We perform several ablation studies to prove the effectiveness of progressive unsupervised learning (PUL) as listed in Table 2. Specifically, comparing "Baseline + C + E" with "Baseline + C + E + P", we improve the performance by 35.5% and 28.4% in mAP and rank-1 accuracy when the model is transferred from DukeMTMC to Market1501. Similarly, when the model is trained on Market1501 and tested on DukeMTMC, the performance gain becomes 35.0% and 32.3% in rank-1 accuracy and mAP, respectively. Although the progressive unsupervised learning and

Table 2. Comparison of various methods on the target domains. When tested on DukeMTMC-reID, Market-1501 is used as the source and vice versa. "Baseline" means directly applying the source-trained model on the target domain. "Baseline+x" means using "x" method upon baseline model. "E" means trained with color equalization augmentation. "C" denotes camera-aware color transformation. "P" stands for progressive learning methods.

Method	DukeMTMC → Market1501				Market1501 → DukeMTMC			
	mAP	Top1	Top5	Top10	mAP	Top1	Top5	Top10
Baseline	20.3	46.5	65.4	72.4	15.9	29.0	45.2	52.3
Baseline + E	28.9	58.4	74.6	80.1	24.4	42.9	58.8	65.2
Baseline + C	30.6	58.2	74.0	80.1	21.9	38.5	55.1	62.3
Baseline + C + E	32.4	61.9	77.8	83.6	25.4	44.7	60.7	67.1
Baseline + P	62.0	82.0	92.7	94.9	54.9	71.8	82.9	86.0
Baseline + E + P	65.5	84.6	93.8	95.6	57.5	75.1	84.6	88.0
Baseline + C + E + P	67.9	86.6	94.5	96.9	60.4	76.0	85.0	88.9

direct transfer have a huge performance gap, our proposed method can constantly improve the performance under these two settings. With progressive learning, camera-aware color transformation and color equalization augmentation achieve the best overall performance.

4.3   Comparison with State-of-the-Arts

In this section, we compare the proposed Second-order Camera-aware Color Transformation (SCCT) with state-of-the-art unsupervised learning methods on Market1501, DukeMTMC in Table 3. SCCT outperforms existing approaches with a clear advantage. In particular, our model outperforms the best published method SSG [21] by almost 9.7% on mAP when testing on Market1501 and DukeMTMC-reID dataset.

Results on Market1501. On Market-1501, we compare our results with state-of-the-art methods including Bag-of-Words (BoW) [25], local maximal occurrence (LOMO) [52], UMDL [53], PUL [54] and CAMEL [55], PTGAN [18], SPGAN [56], TJ-AIDL [41], ARN [57], UDAP [45], MAR [58], PDA-Net [59], PAST [60], SBSGAN [61], CASCL [43] and SSG [21]. Methods that trained on target training set with clustering and pseudo-label (UDAP, PAST, SSG) always obtain higher results than other methods. Therefore, we show the performance of SCCT in two different settings. When tested under direct transfer setting, our SCCT-DIRECT outperforms many complicated state-of-the-art direct transfer methods including TJ_AIDL, SBSGAN, and HHL. TJ_AIDL use additional attribute label information from source data. SBSGAN use additional JPPNet to obtain foreground masks. While SCCT-DIRECT only apply linear camera-aware color transformation and color equalization augmentation. We believe if combined with SCCT, these methods would further boost performance. When comparing with progressive learning methods, SCCT-PUL achieves rank-1 accuracy = 86.6% and mAP = 67.9%, which outperforms unsupervised version SSG in [21] by 6.6% and 9.6%.

Results on DukeMTMC. A similar improvement can also be observed when we test it on the DukeMTMC dataset. Although the camera view discrepancy in DukeMTMC is not as large as Market1501, SCCT can still significantly improve the model performance over the Baseline. Specifically, we achieve mAP = 60.4%, top1 accuracy = 76.0%, top5 accuracy = 85.0% and top10 accuracy = 88.9% by unsupervised learning. Compared with the best unsupervised method, our result is 7.0%/3.0%/4.6%/5.7% higher on mAP and top1/top5/top10 accuracy. Therefore the superiority of our camera-aware color transformation methods with color equalization augmentation can be concluded.

Table 3. Comparison of proposed approach with state-of-the-arts unsupervised domain adaptive person re-ID methods on Market1501 and DukeMTMC dataset.

Method	DukeMTMC → Market1501				Market1501 → DukeMTMC			
	mAP	Top1	Top5	Top10	mAP	Top1	Top5	Top10
LOMO [52]	8.0	27.2	41.6	49.1	4.8	12.3	21.3	26.6
BOW [25]	14.8	35.8	52.4	60.3	8.3	17.1	28.8	34.9
UMDL [53]	12.4	34.5	52.6	59.6	7.3	18.5	31.4	37.4
PTGAN [18]	–	38.6	–	66.1	–	27.4	–	50.7
PUL [54]	20.5	45.5	60.7	66.7	16.4	30.0	43.4	48.5
SPGAN [56]	22.8	51.5	70.1	76.8	26.2	46.4	62.3	68.0
CAMEL [55]	26.3	54.5	–	–	–	–	–	–
SPGAN+LMP [56]	26.7	57.7	75.8	82.4	26.2	46.4	62.3	68.0
TJ_AIDL [41]	26.5	58.2	74.8	81.1	23.0	44.3	59.6	65.0
SBSGAN [61]	27.3	58.5	–	–	30.8	53.5	–	–
HHL [20]	31.4	62.2		84.0	27.2	46.9	61.0	66.7
CASCL [43]	35.5	65.4	80.6	37.8	86.2	59.3	73.2	77.8
ARN [57]	39.4	70.3	80.4	86.3	33.4	60.2	73.9	79.5
MAR [58]	40.0	67.7	81.9	–	48.0	67.1	79.8	–
ECN [19]	43.0	75.1	87.6	91.6	40.4	63.3	75.8	80.4
PDA-Net [59]	47.6	75.2	86.3	90.2	45.1	63.2	77.0	82.5
UDAP [45]	53.7	75.8	89.5	93.2	49.0	68.4	80.1	83.5
PAST [60]	54.6	78.4	–	–	54.3	72.4	–	–
SSG [21]	58.3	80.0	90.0	92.4	53.4	73.0	80.6	83.2
SCCT-DIRECT	32.4	61.9	77.8	83.6	25.4	44.7	60.7	67.1
SCCT-PUL	67.9	86.6	94.5	96.9	60.4	76.0	85.0	88.9

Table 4. Experiments on MSMT17 dataset. "Baseline" denotes using ImageNet image statistics for normalization. "C" stands for using the proposed second-order camera-aware color transformation. "E" means applying color equalization augmentation.

Method	DukeMTMC → MSMT17				Market1501 → MSMT17			
	mAP	Top1	Top5	Top10	mAP	Top1	Top5	Top10
Baseline	5.6	17.0	27.0	32.2	2.8	8.7	15.6	19.7
PTGAN [18]	3.3	11.8	–	27.4	2.9	10.2	–	24.4
ECN [19]	10.2	30.2	41.5	46.8	8.5	25.3	36.3	42.1
TAUDL [62]	12.5	28.4	–	–	–	–	–	–
UTAL [63]	13.1	31.4	–	–	–	–	–	–
Baseline + C	7.1	21.7	32.2	37.8	4.1	12.6	21.1	25.5
Baseline + E	12.1	33.8	48.0	54.0	7.2	21.8	33.8	39.4
SCCT-DIRECT	**13.2**	**37.8**	**51.2**	**57.0**	8.3	23.6	36.0	42.1

Results on MSMT17. We further validate the effectiveness of our proposed Second-order Camera-aware Color Transformation (SCCT) and color equalization augmentation on MSMT17 [18] dataset as listed in Table 4. Using color transformation can boost the performance by 1.5% on mAP and 4.7% on top1 accuracy comparing to the baseline model when transferring from DukeMTMC to MSMT17. Similarly, it improves 1.3% on mAP and 3.9% on top1 accuracy when transferring from Market1501 to MSMT17. Color equalization boosts the performance even larger on these datasets. On DukeMTMC to MSMT17, it improves the baseline method by 6.9% in mAP and 15.8% on top1 accuracy. On Market1501 to MSMT17, it surpasses baseline by 4.4% on mAP and 13.1% on top1. When color transformation and color equalization are combined, it achieves 13.2%/37.8% on DukeMTMC to MSMT17 and 8.3%/23.6 on Market1501 to MSMT17, which is very significant as it outperforms or achieves similar performances with many state-of-the-art methods (e.g. ECN [19], TAUDL [62], UTAL [63]) with simple image-level color transformation and augmentation.

5   Conclusions

In this work, we proposed camera-aware second-order color transformation for person ReID, which can reduce the discrepancy of source and target data caused by the input distribution, constantly improve performance on direct transfer setting and progressive learning settings. It is a novel input normalization method, which is often neglected by previous unsupervised person ReID methods. It is simple to implement and can be easily combined with many existing state-of-the-art methods. We also investigate the color equalization data augmentation under the unsupervised person ReID setting, which is very effective and can boost the generalization ability of the ReID model. Extensive experimental results demonstrate that the performance of our approach outperforms the state-of-the-arts by a clear margin.

Acknowledgements. This research is supported by the China NSFC grant (no. 61672446).

References

1. Gheissari, N., Sebastian, T.B., Hartley, R.: Person reidentification using spatiotemporal appearance. In: CVPR (2006)
2. Chen, W., Chen, X., Zhang, J., Huang, K.: Beyond triplet loss: a deep quadruplet network for person re-identification. In: CVPR (2017)
3. Sun, Y., Zheng, L., Deng, W., Wang, S.: SVDNet for pedestrian retrieval. In: ICCV (2017)
4. Zhao, L., Li, X., Wang, J., Zhuang, Y.: Deeply-learned part-aligned representations for person re-identification. In: ICCV (2017)
5. Varior, R.R., Haloi, M., Wang, G.: Gated siamese convolutional neural network architecture for human re-identification. In: Leibe, B., Matas, J., Sebe, N., Welling, M. (eds.) ECCV 2016. LNCS, vol. 9912, pp. 791–808. Springer, Cham (2016). https://doi.org/10.1007/978-3-319-46484-8_48
6. Varior, R.R., Shuai, B., Lu, J., Xu, D., Wang, G.: a siamese long short-term memory architecture for human re-identification. In: Leibe, B., Matas, J., Sebe, N., Welling, M. (eds.) ECCV 2016. LNCS, vol. 9911, pp. 135–153. Springer, Cham (2016). https://doi.org/10.1007/978-3-319-46478-7_9
7. Geng, M., Wang, Y., Xiang, T., Tian, Y.: Deep transfer learning for person re-identification. arXiv preprint arXiv:1611.05244 (2016)
8. Li, D., Chen, X., Zhang, Z., Huang, K.: Learning deep context-aware features over body and latent parts for person re-identification. In: CVPR (2017)
9. Zhao, H., et al.: Spindle Net: person re-identification with human body region guided feature decomposition and fusion. In: CVPR (2017)
10. Yi, D., Lei, Z., Li, S.Z.: Deep metric learning for practical person re-identification. arXiv preprint arXiv:1407.4979 (2014)
11. Shi, H., et al.: Embedding deep metric for person re-identification: a study against large variations. In: Leibe, B., Matas, J., Sebe, N., Welling, M. (eds.) ECCV 2016. LNCS, vol. 9905, pp. 732–748. Springer, Cham (2016). https://doi.org/10.1007/978-3-319-46448-0_44
12. Liao, S., Hu, Y., Zhu, X., Li, S.Z.: Person re-identification by local maximal occurrence representation and metric learning. In: CVPR (2015)
13. Jose, C., Fleuret, F.: Scalable metric learning via weighted approximate rank component analysis. In: Leibe, B., Matas, J., Sebe, N., Welling, M. (eds.) ECCV 2016. LNCS, vol. 9909, pp. 875–890. Springer, Cham (2016). https://doi.org/10.1007/978-3-319-46454-1_53
14. Song, H.O., Xiang, Y., Jegelka, S., Savarese, S.: Deep metric learning via lifted structured feature embedding. In: CVPR (2016)
15. Liao, S., Li, S.Z.: Efficient PSD constrained asymmetric metric learning for person re-identification. In: ICCV (2015)
16. Zheng, Z., Zheng, L., Yang, Y.: Pedestrian alignment network for large-scale person re-identification. In: CVPR (2017)
17. Zhang, Y., Li, X., Zhao, L., Zhang, Z.: Semantics-aware deep correspondence structure learning for robust person re-identification. In: IJCAI (2016)
18. Wei, L., Zhang, S., Gao, W., Tian, Q.: Person transfer GAN to bridge domain gap for person re-identification. In: Proceedings of the IEEE Conference on Computer Vision and Pattern Recognition, pp. 79–88 (2018)

19. Zhong, Z., Zheng, L., Luo, Z., Li, S., Yang, Y.: Invariance matters: exemplar memory for domain adaptive person re-identification. In: Proceedings of IEEE Conference on Computer Vision and Pattern Recognition (CVPR) (2019)
20. Zhong, Z., Zheng, L., Li, S., Yang, Y.: Generalizing a person retrieval model hetero- and homogeneously. In: Ferrari, V., Hebert, M., Sminchisescu, C., Weiss, Y. (eds.) ECCV 2018. LNCS, vol. 11217, pp. 176–192. Springer, Cham (2018). https://doi.org/10.1007/978-3-030-01261-8_11
21. Fu, Y., Wei, Y., Wang, G., Zhou, Y., Shi, H., Huang, T.S.: Self-similarity grouping: a simple unsupervised cross domain adaptation approach for person re-identification. In: Proceedings of the IEEE International Conference on Computer Vision, pp. 6112–6121 (2019)
22. Goodfellow, I., et al.: Generative adversarial nets. In: Advances in Neural Information Processing Systems, pp. 2672–2680 (2014)
23. Zhong, Z., Zheng, L., Zheng, Z., Li, S., Yang, Y.: Camera style adaptation for person re-identification. In: CVPR (2018)
24. Deng, J., Dong, W., Socher, R., Li, L.J., Li, K., Fei-Fei, L.: ImageNet: a large-scale hierarchical image database. In: CVPR (2009)
25. Zheng, L., Shen, L., Tian, L., Wang, S., Wang, J., Tian, Q.: Scalable person re-identification: a benchmark. In: CVPR (2015)
26. Zheng, Z., Zheng, L., Yang, Y.: Unlabeled samples generated by GAN improve the person re-identification baseline in vitro. In: CVPR (2017)
27. Chen, Y., Zhu, X., Gong, S.: Person re-identification by deep learning multi-scale representations. In: CVPR (2017)
28. Zhou, S., Wang, J., Shi, R., Hou, Q., Gong, Y., Zheng, N.: Large margin learning in set to set similarity comparison for person re-identification. IEEE Trans. Multimedia 20, 593–604 (2017)
29. Ahmed, E., Jones, M., Marks, T.K.: An improved deep learning architecture for person re-identification. In: CVPR (2015)
30. Li, W., Zhao, R., Xiao, T., Wang, X.: Deepreid: deep filter pairing neural network for person re-identification. In: CVPR (2014)
31. Wu, L., Shen, C., van der Hengel, A.: PersonNet: person re-identification with deep convolutional neural networks. arXiv preprint arXiv:1601.07255 (2016)
32. Hermans, A., Beyer, L., Leibe, B.: In defense of the triplet loss for person re-identification. arXiv preprint arXiv:1703.07737 (2017)
33. Cheng, D., Gong, Y., Zhou, S., Wang, J., Zheng, N.: Person re-identification by multi-channel parts-based CNN with improved triplet loss function. In: CVPR (2016)
34. Gretton, A., Borgwardt, K.M., Rasch, M.J., Schölkopf, B., Smola, A.: A kernel two-sample test. J. Mach. Learn. Res. 13, 723–773 (2012)
35. Sun, B., Feng, J., Saenko, K.: Return of frustratingly easy domain adaptation. In: Thirtieth AAAI Conference on Artificial Intelligence (2016)
36. Ganin, Y., Lempitsky, V.: Unsupervised domain adaptation by backpropagation. In: International Conference on Machine Learning, pp. 1180–1189 (2015)
37. Chen, C., et al.: HoMM: Higher-order moment matching for unsupervised domain adaptation, order 1, p. 20 (2020)
38. Sener, O., Song, H.O., Saxena, A., Savarese, S.: Learning transferrable representations for unsupervised domain adaptation. In: Advances in Neural Information Processing Systems, pp. 2110–2118 (2016)
39. Saito, K., Ushiku, Y., Harada, T.: Asymmetric tri-training for unsupervised domain adaptation. In: Proceedings of the 34th International Conference on Machine Learning-Volume 70, pp. 2988–2997. JMLR.org (2017)

40. Zhu, J.Y., Park, T., Isola, P., Efros, A.A.: Unpaired image-to-image translation using cycle-consistent adversarial networks. In: Proceedings of the IEEE International Conference on Computer Vision, pp. 2223–2232 (2017)
41. Wang, J., Zhu, X., Gong, S., Li, W.: Transferable joint attribute-identity deep learning for unsupervised person re-identification. In: Proceedings of the IEEE Conference on Computer Vision and Pattern Recognition, pp. 2275–2284 (2018)
42. Ye, M., Shen, J., Lin, G., Xiang, T., Shao, L., Hoi, S.C.: Deep learning for person re-identification: a survey and outlook. arXiv preprint arXiv:2001.04193 (2020)
43. Wu, A., Zheng, W.S., Lai, J.H.: Unsupervised person re-identification by camera-aware similarity consistency learning. In: Proceedings of the IEEE International Conference on Computer Vision, pp. 6922–6931 (2019)
44. Lan, X., Zhu, X., Gong, S.: Universal person re-identification (2019)
45. Song, L., et al.: Unsupervised domain adaptive re-identification: theory and practice. Pattern Recogn. **102**, 107173 (2020)
46. Ioffe, S., Szegedy, C.: Batch normalization: accelerating deep network training by reducing internal covariate shift (2015)
47. Fu, Y., et al.: Horizontal pyramid matching for person re-identification. Proc. AAAI Conf. Artif. Intell. **33**, 8295–8302 (2019)
48. Ester, M., Kriegel, H.P., Sander, J., Xu, X., et al.: A density-based algorithm for discovering clusters in large spatial databases with noise. KDD **96**, 226–231 (1996)
49. Zhong, Z., Zheng, L., Cao, D., Li, S.: Re-ranking person re-identification with k-reciprocal encoding. In: Proceedings of the IEEE Conference on Computer Vision and Pattern Recognition, pp. 1318–1327 (2017)
50. Zhong, Z., Zheng, L., Kang, G., Li, S., Yang, Y.: Random erasing data augmentation. arXiv preprint arXiv:1708.04896 (2017)
51. Kingma, D.P., Ba, J.: Adam: a method for stochastic optimization. arXiv preprint arXiv:1412.6980 (2014)
52. Liao, S., Hu, Y., Zhu, X., Li, S.Z.: Person re-identification by local maximal occurrence representation and metric learning. In: CVPR (2015)
53. Peng, P., et al.: Unsupervised cross-dataset transfer learning for person re-identification. In: Proceedings of the IEEE Conference on Computer Vision and Pattern Recognition, pp. 1306–1315 (2016)
54. Fan, H., Zheng, L., Yan, C., Yang, Y.: Unsupervised person re-identification: clustering and fine-tuning. ACM Trans. Multimedia Comput. Commun. Appl. (TOMM) **14**, 1–18 (2018)
55. Yu, H.X., Wu, A., Zheng, W.S.: Cross-view asymmetric metric learning for unsupervised person re-identification. In: Proceedings of the IEEE International Conference on Computer Vision, pp. 994–1002 (2017)
56. Deng, W., Zheng, L., Ye, Q., Kang, G., Yang, Y., Jiao, J.: Image-image domain adaptation with preserved self-similarity and domain-dissimilarity for person re-identification. In: Proceedings of the IEEE Conference on Computer Vision and Pattern Recognition, pp. 994–1003 (2018)
57. Li, Y.J., Yang, F.E., Liu, Y.C., Yeh, Y.Y., Du, X., Frank Wang, Y.C.: Adaptation and re-identification network: An unsupervised deep transfer learning approach to person re-identification. In: Proceedings of the IEEE Conference on Computer Vision and Pattern Recognition Workshops, pp. 172–178 (2018)
58. Yu, H.X., Zheng, W.S., Wu, A., Guo, X., Gong, S., Lai, J.H.: Unsupervised person re-identification by soft multilabel learning. In: Proceedings of the IEEE Conference on Computer Vision and Pattern Recognition, pp. 2148–2157 (2019)

59. Li, Y.J., Lin, C.S., Lin, Y.B., Wang, Y.C.F.: Cross-dataset person re-identification via unsupervised pose disentanglement and adaptation. In: Proceedings of the IEEE International Conference on Computer Vision, pp. 7919–7929 (2019)

60. Zhang, X., Cao, J., Shen, C., You, M.: Self-training with progressive augmentation for unsupervised cross-domain person re-identification. In: Proceedings of the IEEE International Conference on Computer Vision, pp. 8222–8231 (2019)

61. Huang, Y., Wu, Q., Xu, J., Zhong, Y.: SBSGAN: suppression of inter-domain background shift for person re-identification. In: Proceedings of the IEEE International Conference on Computer Vision, pp. 9527–9536 (2019)

62. Li, M., Zhu, X., Gong, S.: Unsupervised person re-identification by deep learning tracklet association. In: Ferrari, V., Hebert, M., Sminchisescu, C., Weiss, Y. (eds.) ECCV 2018. LNCS, vol. 11208, pp. 772–788. Springer, Cham (2018). https://doi.org/10.1007/978-3-030-01225-0_45

63. Li, M., Zhu, X., Gong, S.: Unsupervised tracklet person re-identification. IEEE Trans. Pattern Anal. Machine Intell. **42**, 1770–1782 (2019)

CS-MCNet: A Video Compressive Sensing Reconstruction Network with Interpretable Motion Compensation

Bowen Huang[1], Jinjia Zhou[2,3], Xiao Yan[1], Ming'e Jing[1], Rentao Wan[1], and Yibo Fan[1(✉)]

[1] State Key Laboratory of ASIC and System, Fudan University, Shanghai, China
fanyibo@fudan.edu.cn
[2] Graduate School of Science and Engineering, Hosei University, Tokyo, Japan
[3] JST, PRESTO, Tokyo, Japan

Abstract. In this paper, a deep neural network with interpretable motion compensation called CS-MCNet is proposed to realize high-quality and real-time decoding of video compressive sensing. Firstly, explicit multi-hypothesis motion compensation is applied in our network to extract correlation information of adjacent frames (as shown in Fig. 1), which improves the recover performance. And then, a residual module further narrows down the gap between reconstruction result and original signal. The overall architecture is interpretable by using algorithm unrolling, which brings the benefits of being able to transfer prior knowledge about the conventional algorithms. As a result, a PSNR of 22 dB can be achieved at 64x compression ratio, which is about 4% to 9% better than state-of-the-art methods. In addition, due to the feed-forward architecture, the reconstruction can be processed by our network in real time and up to three orders of magnitude faster than traditional iterative methods.

1 Introduction

Traditional image or video compression methods, such as JPEG and H.265, compress the data after the measurement. However, compressive sensing, firstly introduced by Candes, Tao and Donoho [1,2] in 2006, allows compression in the sensing process, *i.e.* sampling part of the signal instead of the entirety. It has been shown that if the target signal has transform sparse properties, *i.e.* being sparse in a transform domain, then it can be recovered from sample less than the Shannon-Nyquist sampling criterion requires [3]. Suppose the target signal is $x \in C^N$, CS incorporates the compression into acquisition with a measurement matrix $\Phi \in C^{M \times N}$, where $M << N$:

$$y = \Phi \cdot x . \tag{1}$$

Here y is the measurements.

© Springer Nature Switzerland AG 2021
H. Ishikawa et al. (Eds.): ACCV 2020, LNCS 12623, pp. 54–67, 2021.
https://doi.org/10.1007/978-3-030-69532-3_4

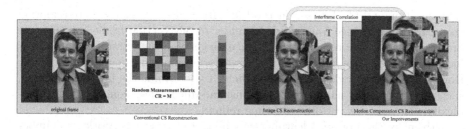

Fig. 1. *Video CS reconstruction with explicit multi-hypothesis motion compensation*: CS measurement is acquired with random measurement matrix and preliminary result is gotten by using image CS reconstruction. Multi-hypothesis motion compensation is added to extract correlation information of adjacent frames, which improves recover performance. The reconstruction can be processed in real time.

Even though traditional compression methods provides higher compression ratio and more mature system in some cases, the characteristic of simultaneous sensing and compression of compressive sensing requires very different encoder and decoder, which is of great importance to some specific areas, such as medical imaging systems, high frame rate video systems, and multimedia data compression.

The compression ratio CR can be defined as $CR = \frac{M}{N}$. CS reconstruction should be 'sparse', *i.e.* the original signal can be represented as $\hat{x} = \Psi \cdot x$, where Ψ is called the sparsity basis and $\hat{x}$ the sparse representation of x. While natural images and video are difficult to achieve true sparsity, compressive sensing allows for approximate sparsity as well. Besides, CS reconstruction should also obey restricted isometry property, or RIP [4,5]. It has been proved that RIP rule is equal to measurement basis Φ and sparsity basis Ψ being mutually incoherent [6]. Thus, random matrix is commonly chosen in CS measurement. In addition, structured random matrix (SRM) can also meet the requirements and provide additional benefits, such as preserving information or reducing computation and memory consumption (e.g., [7]).

1.1 Related Works

In the recent decades, many methods have been proposed to solve the CS reconstruction problem [8–11]. For image reconstruction of compressive sensing, the algorithm of traditional transformation (e.g., wavelets domain [10,12]) runs fast but with low accuracy. Methods that rely on complex sparsity, such as dictionary learning methods [13] generally have better reconstruction performance but lower computational speed. Furthermore, while most research efforts for image CS problems can be directly applied to video CS tasks, they fail to take advantage of the correlation between adjacent frames in a video sequence.

For video CS recovery, in [8], the authors use Gaussian mixture model (GMM) to recover high-frame-rate videos, and the reconstruction can be efficiently computed as an analytical solution. In [14], the authors propose a motion-compensation and block-based method MC-BCS-SPL, which estimate a motion vector from a reference frame and the under-reconstruction frame can then get prediction to improve recover performance. In general, these traditional methods focus on the design of different priors, transformations and sparsity constraints. However, these methods are usually difficult to determine the hyperparameters, such as thresholds or number of iterations, and due to their computational complexity, they can not perform real-time rebuild.

Driven by the powerful learning capabilities of neural networks, a number of DNN-based approaches have been applied [15–19]. In [19], the authors cast ISTA into deep network form and develop an effective strategy to solve the proximal mapping associated with the sparsity-inducing regularizer using nonlinear transforms. In [17], the authors propose a fully-connected neural network to reconstruct video temporal CS measurement, and a repetitive pattern measurement mask is proposed to make such a task practical. In [15], the authors propose a network named "CSVideoNet". The network combines a multi-rate CNN and a synthesizing RNN to improve the trade-off between compression ratio and spatial-temporal resolution of the reconstructed videos. Compared with iterative algorithms, these feed-forward methods significantly reduce time consumption. However, the structure of these networks is often empirically determined and is ambiguous as a black box, which brings difficulty in making targeted improvements.

To resolve the conflict between interpretability and speed of reconstruction, a technique called algorithm unrolling has been applied recently. The technique was proposed by Gregor et al. [20], and builds neural network by unfolding an iterative optimization algorithm to be a hierarchical architecture, which provides a principled framework by expressing traditional iterative algorithms as neural networks, and offers promise in developing interpretable network. There are several networks using algorithm unrolling to solve CS reconstruction [19,21], but they are developed for image CS tasks rather than specifically for video CS tasks.

In this work, we develop a network, called CS-MCNet, that attempts to use inter-frame information to improve the reconstruction quality of video CS measurements. By mapping the iterative algorithm MC-BCS-SPL into non-iterative neural network, all of CS-MCNet's block is designed to correspond to an iteration in MC-BCS-SPL. By end-to-end training, our network can learn all parameters efficiently.

1.2 Contribution

Our main contributions are summarized as follows. 1) We use neural network modules to replace the optimization steps in traditional model-based approaches and implement them in a simple form that is easy to realize quickly. 2) We propose a multi-hypothesis motion compensation structure. The module exploits the similarity between neighboring frames to improve the reconstruction quality. To the best of our knowledge, it is the first work that explicitly uses motion compensation for video CS reconstruction in deep neural network. 3) We employ a residual module in the network to further improve performance, and this structure also facilitates the training of deeper neural networks. With these improvements, our work outperforms previous work in terms of both reconstruction quality and computational cost.

2 Methodology

By taking advantage of the merits of model based and DNN-based CS methods, CS-MCNet maps the optimization steps into a deep network architecture consisting of a fixed number of stages, each of which is designed to correspond to one iteration in the MC-BCS-SPL algorithm. The overall architecture of CS-MCNet is shown in Fig. 2. The proposed CS-MCNet consists of an encoder (sensing matrix) and a decoder. The encoder performs simultaneous sampling and compression. The decoder consists of several stages, each of which is divided into three parts. Firstly, the decoder roughly recovers input measurements to get a preliminary result. Secondly, it get prediction from a single reference frame. Then the prediction is measured and subtracted from original measurements to get the residual. Thirdly, the residual measurements are recovered and the result is added to the prediction. The output is derived from combining the preliminary result and residual reconstruction linearly. We will introduce each module in the following subsections.

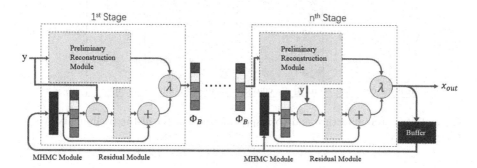

Fig. 2. The overall architecture of the proposed network. The input y is acquired from video frames by compressive sensing. The network is composed of several stages and the reconstruction is performed by three modules in each stage, which is corresponding to the blue, purple and pink modules in the figure. A buffer is designed to store recovery results of one frame and offer reference for the reconstruction of the next frame. (Color figure online)

2.1 Priliminary Reconstruction Module

The first hidden layer is a fully-connected layer that would provide 3D signal from 2D compressed measurements. Several papers have shown that CNNs can achieve superior performance on CS reconstruction problems compared with simple optimization-based algorithms. [16–18], thus we use CNN to get the preliminary reconstruction result. Typical CNN architectures used to do recognition, classification, and segmentation are not suitable to the reconstruction problem here. The goal of CNNs in our network is to retain as much detail as possible and need to recover pixels that do not exist based on known information. Therefore, we eliminated the pooling layer, which causes information loss.

To reduce the size of parameters and simplify the network architecture, we use video blocks as input and set the block size to 16×16. The convolutional layers, each of which is followed by a ReLU layer except for the final layer, are carefully designed to get amenable recovery performance. All feature maps are the same size as the reconstructed video block, and the number of feature maps is monotonically reduced. The detailed structure of the CNN is shown in Fig. 3. This process resembles the sparse coding stage in CS, where a subset of dictionary atoms are combined to form an estimation of the original input. To improve final reconstruction performance, we pre-train the CNN before training the whole CS-MCNet, since the path is long from the input to the output of the whole net and pre-training can help prevent the vanishing gradient problem [22].

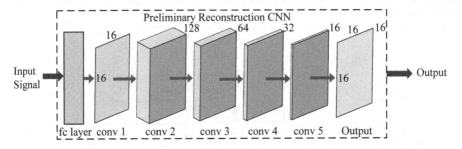

Fig. 3. Detailed architecture and corresponding parameter of the preliminary reconstruction CNN.

2.2 Multi-hypothesis Motion Compensation Module

Traditional video compression algorithms have long exploited motion compensation to improve video-coding quality [23, 24]; In consideration of bit rate at the encoder side, these techniques use single hypothesis in order to limit the amount of motion vector. However, this limitation doesn't exist since the motion compensation is all calculated at the decoder side of the system. Thus, multi-hypothesis motion compensation can be considered to combine all available best assumptions in the reference frame. A MH CS reconstruction can be represented as an optimal linear combination of all possible reference blocks:

$$w_{t,i} = arg \min_{w} ||x_{t,i} - H_{t,i}w||_2^2 . \tag{2}$$

$$\tilde{x}_{t,i} = H_{t,i} w_{t,i} . \tag{3}$$

Here, the subscript "t" and "i" represents the index of frame in the video and the index of block in the frame, and $H_{t,i}$ is a matrix of dimensionality $B^2 \times K$ consisted of rasterizations of the possible blocks within the search window in the reference frame, and $K = |H_{t,i}|$. In this context, $w_{t,i}$ represents the linear combination of the columns of $H_{t,i}$; The solution of this optimization can be calculated as a least-squares (LSQ) problem [25].

The proposed network in this paper uses MH motion compensation to improve the recovery performance. Unlike traditional optimization-based solutions to the LSQ problem, we use fully-connected layers to learn the optimal parameters. Due to the similarity of adjacent frames, this MH motion compensation module can be trained appropriately to produce accurate predictions of motion and the recovery quality can be improved by the aggregation of motion and spatial visual features.

To get the reference frame, we design a buffer to store the reconstructed video blocks, as shown in Fig. 2. For the sake of simplicity, we choose to do reconstruction after the reference frame is completely reconstructed. However, the search window actually only involves part of the reference frame, and therefore we can reduce the size of the buffer by carefully designing the rebuilding order. In [15], the authors use LSTM network to do temporal reference, which is similar to motion compensation. However with the experiment, we prove that the utilization of explicit motion compensation module outperforms the RNN based methods and decrease the model size simultaneously.

2.3 Residual Reconstruction Module

With the prediction of MH motion compensation, we introduce the residual reconstruction module to further narrow down the gap between $x_{reconstruction}$ and x. The output of residual learning is fused with the output of preliminary reconstruction module as the final result.

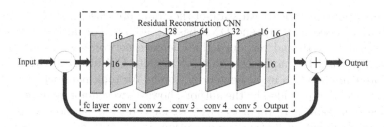

Fig. 4. Detailed architecture and corresponding parameter of the residual reconstruction module.

We get the residual signal d by measuring the result of MH motion compensation and subtracting it from the original measurements y,

$$d_i = y_i - \Phi_B x_{mc,i} . \tag{4}$$

According to [26], the convolutional layers in residual module could be easily trained to approximate the residual, most of which is zero. As shown in Fig. 4, the residual reconstruction module contains one fully-connected layer and five convolution layers. The fully-connected layer has the same function of recover 3D volume signal from 2D measurements as in preliminary reconstruction module. The rest has decreasing number of feature maps and holds the size of 16×16. All convolutional layers is followed by a ReLU layer except the last one.

2.4   Learning Algorithm

Given the training data pairs $\{x, x_{ref}\}_i$, CS-MCNet firstly gets measurements y_i with sensing matrix. Then y_i serves as input of the decoder and generates the reconstruction result. We wanted to reduce the discrepancy between the raw measurements and the MH motion compensation measurements, i.e. the residual signal. Therefore, the loss function for CS-MCNet is designed as follows:

$$L_{total}(\omega, b) = L_{err} + \lambda L_{mc} . \tag{5}$$

$$\begin{cases} L_{err} = \frac{1}{2N} \Sigma_i^T ||f(y_i; \omega, b) - x_i||_2^2 , \\ L_{mc} = \frac{1}{2N} \Sigma_i^T ||y_i - \Phi_B x_{mc,i}||_2^2 . \end{cases} \tag{6}$$

where λ is the scale factor to control the influence of motion compensation on the total loss. Determined by experiment, we set λ to be 0.5 during training to get the best performance.

We choose MSE to calculate the loss, which is a commonly used metric to quantitatively evaluate recovery quality. The proposed framework can also be adapted to other loss functions. Adam optimizer with default parameters is chosen to optimize the proposed network.

3   Experiment

We compare our methods with state-of-the-art approaches, including iterative optimization based methods and DNN based methods. For fairness, we set the block size of 16×16 and retrained the reference networks with our self-built dataset. It should be emphasized that we rewrote CSVideoNet with Pytorch, whose original code was implemented by Torch. We took parameters from the original model files provided by the authors, however we cannot guarantee that it will achieve the same performance as the original code. Furthermore, to prove the advantage of exploiting motion compensation, image specific methods are also included. Both noiseless and noise measurements are tested and we also discuss the performance of our proposed network under different network parameters (i.e. number of stages). Two metrics, peak signal-to-noise ration (PSNR) and structural similarity (SSIM) are used to evaluate the performance, and visualization of the results are provided.

3.1   Implementation Details

As there is no standard dataset designed for video CS, we use UCF-101 dataset [27] to build our own training dataset. UCF-101 dataset includes 13k clips and about 27 h of video, which is collected from YouTube and is divided into 101 action classes. We extract only the luminance component of the extracted frames and crop the central 160×160 patch from each frame. All of the patches are segmented into 16×16 non-overlapping blocks. We randomly choose video sequences from UCF-101 dataset and finally get around 300,000 pairs of data for training and validation in total.

Our model is implemented with PyTorch and all the experiments are performed on a workstation with an Intel Xeon CPU and a Nvidia GeForce RTX2080 GPU. Our networks are trained for 200 epochs with batch size of 400. We normalize the input pre-feature to zero mean and standard deviation one. We set the starting learning rate to 0.01 and divide the learning rate by 10 if the loss of the current epoch is greater than that of the previous epoch. Except for the last subsection, we use 4 cascaded stages in the following experiments.

3.2   Comparison with the State-of-the-Art

We compare the reconstruction performance of our proposed method with several reference work of CS reconstruction [8,11,14,15,17,19]. The summarized information about all baseline approaches is listed in Table 1. All the methods reconstruct video blocks from its CS measurements independently, and the result of average PSNR, SSIM and time consumption for each method on the test dataset is reported in Fig. 5. To save training time, all methods are tested under CR of 16. From the results we can observe that CS-MCNet outperforms the reference method in terms of metrics and time consumption. Compared with conventional image CS algorithm BCS-SPL, D-AMP, and video CS algorithm MC-BCS-SPL, GMM, our DNN-based CS-MCNet benefits from learnable parameters and feedforward architecture, and thus gets better reconstruction quality and uses less time. The similar DNN based methods DeepVideoCS, CSVideoCS and ISTANet either uses barely CNN or combines CNN and RNN to extract inexplicit motion features. In contrast to them, our work exploits explicit MH motion compensation, further improving the quality of the reconstruction and compressing the size of the model, which makes it easier and faster to train and deploy.

To further validate the advantages of using MH motion compensation, we do comparison with MC-BCS-SPL and ISTA under different CRs of 4,16 and 64. As shown in Table 2, CS-MCNet achieves relatively better performance, especially under high compression ratio. CS-MCNet outperforms MC-BCS-SPL both on reconstruction quality and time consumption, since its learnable parameters can be better optimized through end-to-end training, and GPU acceleration makes it three orders of magnitude faster than iterative methods. As for ISTANet, which also uses algorithm unrolling and has a similar residual block structure, the utilization of inter-frame information helps our network achieve better reconstruction quality, though the storage of reference frame requires extra storage space and time consumption.

Table 1. Classification and summary information for all reference methods and the proposed approach

Image CS	Model based	BCS-SPL [14]	Block based CS with smooth projected Landweber
		D-AMP [11]	Denoising-based approximate message passing
	DNN based	ISTANet [19]	CNN inspired by ISTA algorithm
Video CS	Model based	MC-BCS-SPL [14]	Motion compensation block based CS
		GMM [8]	Gaussian mixture model
	DNN based	DeepVideoCS [17]	Deep neural network with fully-connected layers
		CSVideoNet [15]	A multi-rate CNN and a synthesizing RNN
		CS-MCNet	Proposed approach

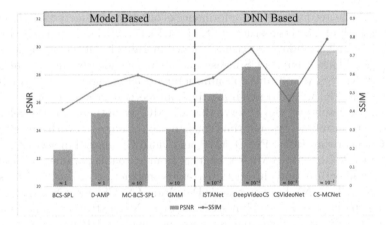

Fig. 5. Performance Comparison with different reference methods on test dataset. The time (at the bottom of the histogram) refers to the magnitude of the average time for reconstructing each frame.

Visual examples of some reference methods are shown in Fig. 6. The ground truth is also shown in Fig. 6. As we can see, CS-MCNet provides the best detail of selected methods and suffers minimal block effect. CS-MCNet produces sharper edges in the highlight areas and a more uniform image overall. This comparison demonstrates that inter-frame information is significant for video CS reconstruction, and the image CS approaches are not suitable for video tasks. Through further optimization, we believe that CS-MCNet has the potential to be applied on real-time reconstruction of high-frame-rate video CS.

Table 2. Performance comparison with MC-BCS-SPL [14] and ISTANet [19] under different CRs on test dataset.

CR	Metric	ISTANet [19]	MC-BCS-SPL [14]	*CS-MCNet:proposed*
4	PSNR	*33.851*	31.067	33.35
	SSIM	*0.953*	0.834	0.918
16	PSNR	26.618	26.141	*29.707*
	SSIM	0.583	0.436	*0.789*
64	PSNR	19.93	19.79	*21.45*
	SSIM	0.382	0.288	*0.528*

3.3 Reconstruction Under Noise

In this subsection, we investigate the performance of our proposed network in the presence of measurement noise. The measurement of CS usually involves noise in practice caused by devices, and the measurement model should now be modified as

$$y = \Phi \cdot x + n . \tag{7}$$

where n is the additive measurement noise.

We conduct experiment with input measurements contaminated by random Gaussian noise, and all other parameters remain the same as in the noiseless case. We test the performance at four level of SNR from 20 dB to 50 dB under CR of 16. The result is shown in Fig. 7. It can be observed that at different noise level, CS-MCNet can achieve stable reconstruction performance and outperform the reference methods consistently. It is worth emphasizing that we did not retrain the network with noise measurement and all the experiments in this subsection are implemented with noiseless model, which shows the robustness of our model under different measurement conditions. Besides, it is easy to combat with performance degradation under noise by cascading our network with a deep denoising architecture or other denoising algorithm.

3.4 Discussion

As described earlier, the number of stages of CS-MCNet corresponds to the number of iterations of the original algorithm. In this subsection, we mainly focuses on the structure parameter of CS-MCNet, *i.e.* the number of stages. From Table 3, we can find that as the number of stages increases from 2 to 4, the performance improves under different CRs. This can be explained by the fact that the deeper the neural network, the better its learning capacity. However, as the number of stages increases to 5, the performance deteriorates. We speculate that the reason is that while a deeper structure may help to fit the training data more accurately, it also makes it more difficult to train, resulting in an undertrained model. The training time increased slightly when the number of stages is less than 4 and increases rapidly when the number of stages is further

Fig. 6. Visual results and PSNR/SSIM metric of reconstructed frames of reference methods ISTANet [19], DeepVideoCS [17], CSVideoNet [15], MC-BCS-SPL [14]and the proposed approach. The original frames are also presented in the figure.

increased. For CS-MCNet with no more than 4 stages, the time used to train an epoch varies from 30 to 40 min with GPU acceleration, but for networks with 5 or more stages, it can take more than an hour. To strike a balance between the effectiveness of the reconstruction and the cost of training, we empirically decides to use CS-MCNet with 4 stages.

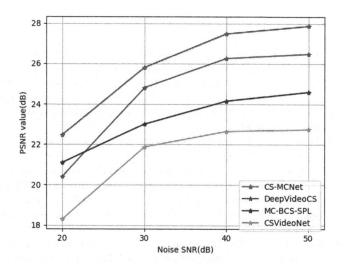

Fig. 7. Average PSNR over test dataset for several methods under different levels of measurement noise.

Table 3. Performance comparison of proposed approach with different number of stages.

CR	Metric	2 stages	3 stages	4 stages	5 stages
4	PSNR	32.776	32.892	*32.936*	32.656
	SSIM	0.904	0.905	0.909	*0.910*
16	PSNR	26.268	26.399	*26.834*	26.097
	SSIM	0.691	0.697	*0.698*	0.684
64	PSNR	21.312	21.412	*21.447*	21.359
	SSIM	0.379	*0.391*	0.382	0.386
Average	PSNR	26.864	26.862	*26.979*	26.797
	SSIM	0.658	*0.664*	0.663	0.659

4 Conclusion

Inspired by the MC-BCS-SPL algorithm, we use algorithmic unrolling to build a novel deep neural network to perform video compressive sensing reconstruction. Our proposed CS-MCNet has an interpretable multi-hypothesis motion compensation module that can exploit the correlation of neighboring frames in the video, which is important for improving reconstruction quality. The feedforward structure allows for fast CS reconstruction using GPU acceleration. CS-MCNet has been shown to outperform the reference method in terms of reconstruction quality and time consumption, and has the potential to be developed as a common framework for video CS applications. One direction of our future work is to integrate this network with video codec systems in general, and specifically on the task of bit rate control.

References

1. Candes, E.J., Tao, T.: Near-optimal signal recovery from random projections: universal encoding strategies? IEEE Trans. Inf. Theory **52**, 5406–5425 (2006)
2. Donoho, D.L.: Compressed sensing. IEEE Trans. Inf. Theory **52**, 1289–1306 (2006)
3. Duarte, M.F., Davenport, M.A., Takhar, D., Laska, J.N., Sun, T., Kelly, K.F., Baraniuk, R.G.: Single-pixel imaging via compressive sampling. IEEE Signal Process. Mag. **25**, 83–91 (2008)
4. Candes, E.J., Wakin, M.B.: An introduction to compressive sampling. IEEE Signal Process. Mag. **25**, 21–30 (2008)
5. Candès, E.J., Romberg, J.K., Tao, T.: Stable signal recovery from incomplete and inaccurate measurements. Commun. Pure Appl. Math. **59**, 1207–1223 (2006)
6. Baraniuk, R., Davenport, M.A., DeVore, R.A., Wakin, M.B.: A simple proof of the restricted isometry property for random matrices. Constr. Approx. **28**, 253–263 (2008)
7. Zhou, J., Zhou, J., Guo, L.: Angular intra prediction based measurement coding algorithm for compressively sensed image. In: 2018 IEEE International Conference on Multimedia Expo Workshops (ICMEW), pp. 1–6 (2018)
8. Yang, J., Yuan, X., Liao, X., Llull, P., Sapiro, G., Brady, D.J., Carin, L.: Gaussian mixture model for video compressive sensing. In: 2013 IEEE International Conference on Image Processing, pp. 19–23 (2013)
9. Daubechies, I., Defrise, M., De Mol, C.: An iterative thresholding algorithm for linear inverse problems with a sparsity constraint. Commun. Pure Appl. Math. **57**, 1413–1457 (2004)
10. He, L., Carin, L.: Exploiting structure in wavelet-based Bayesian compressive sensing. IEEE Trans. Signal Process. **57**, 3488–3497 (2009)
11. Metzler, C.A., Maleki, A., Baraniuk, R.G.: From denoising to compressed sensing. IEEE Trans. Inf. Theory **62**, 5117–5144 (2016)
12. Qu, X., et al.: Undersampled MRI reconstruction with patch-based directional wavelets. Magn. Reson. Imaging **30**, 964–977 (2012)
13. Zhan, Z., Cai, J., Guo, D., Liu, Y., Chen, Z., Qu, X.: Fast multiclass dictionaries learning with geometrical directions in MRI reconstruction. IEEE Trans. Biomed. Eng. **63**, 1850–1861 (2016)
14. Mun, S., Fowler, J.E.: Residual reconstruction for block-based compressed sensing of video. In: 2011 Data Compression Conference, pp. 183–192 (2011)
15. Xu, K., Ren, F.: Csvideonet: A real-time end-to-end learning framework for high-frame-rate video compressive sensing. In: 2018 IEEE Winter Conference on Applications of Computer Vision (WACV), pp. 1680–1688 (2018)
16. Yao, H., Dai, F., Zhang, S., Zhang, Y., Tian, Q., Xu, C.: DR2-Net: deep residual reconstruction network for image compressive sensing. Neurocomputing **359**, 483–493 (2019)
17. Iliadis, M., Spinoulas, L., Katsaggelos, A.K.: Deep fully-connected networks for video compressive sensing. Digit. Signal Proc. **72**, 9–18 (2018)
18. Kulkarni, K., Lohit, S., Turaga, P., Kerviche, R., Ashok, A.: ReconNet: non-iterative reconstruction of images from compressively sensed measurements. In: 2016 IEEE Conference on Computer Vision and Pattern Recognition (CVPR), pp. 449–458 (2016)
19. Zhang, J., Ghanem, B.: ISTA-Net: interpretable optimization-inspired deep network for image compressive sensing. In: 2018 IEEE/CVF Conference on Computer Vision and Pattern Recognition, pp. 1828–1837 (2018)

20. Gregor, K., LeCun, Y.: Learning fast approximations of sparse coding. In: Proceedings of the 27th International Conference on International Conference on Machine Learning, ICML 2010, Madison, WI, USA. Omnipress, pp. 399–406 (2010)
21. Yang, Y., Sun, J., Li, H., Xu, Z.: ADMM-CSNet: a deep learning approach for image compressive sensing. IEEE Trans. Pattern Anal. Mach. Intell. **42**, 521–538 (2020)
22. Erhan, D., Bengio, Y., Courville, A., Manzagol, P., Vincent, P., Bengio, S.: Why does unsupervised pre-training help deep learning? J. Mach. Learn. Res. **11**, 625–660 (2010)
23. Tekalp, A.M.: Digital Video Processing, 2nd edn. Prentice Hall Press, New York (2015)
24. Jain, J., Jain, A.: Displacement measurement and its application in interframe image coding. IEEE Trans. Commun. **29**, 1799–1808 (1981)
25. Tramel, E.W., Fowler, J.E.: Video compressed sensing with multihypothesis. In: 2011 Data Compression Conference, pp. 193–202 (2011)
26. He, K., Zhang, X., Ren, S., Sun, J.: Deep residual learning for image recognition. In: 2016 IEEE Conference on Computer Vision and Pattern Recognition (CVPR), pp. 770–778 (2016)
27. Soomro, K., Zamir, A.R., Shah, M.: UCF101: a dataset of 101 human actions classes from videos in the wild. ArXiv abs/1212.0402 (2012)

MCGKT-Net: Multi-level Context Gating Knowledge Transfer Network for Single Image Deraining

Kohei Yamamichi$^{(\boxtimes)}$ and Xian-Hua Han

Graduate School of Science and Technology for Innovation, Yamaguchi University,
1677-1 Yoshida, Yamaguchi City, Yamaguchi 753-8511, Japan
{a035vbu,hanxhua}@yamaguchi-u.ac.jp

Abstract. Rain streak removal in a single image is a very challenging task due to its ill-posed nature in essence. Recently, the end-to-end learning techniques with deep convolutional neural networks (DCNN) have made great progress in this task. However, the conventional DCNN-based deraining methods have struggled to exploit deeper and more complex network architectures for pursuing better performance. This study proposes a novel MCGKT-Net for boosting deraining performance, which is a naturally multi-scale learning framework being capable of exploring multi-scale attributes of rain streaks and different semantic structures of the clear images. In order to obtain high representative features inside MCGKT-Net, we explore internal knowledge transfer module using ConvLSTM unit for conducting interaction learning between different layers and investigate external knowledge transfer module for leveraging the knowledge already learned in other task domains. Furthermore, to dynamically select useful features in learning procedure, we propose a multi-scale context gating module in the MCGKT-Net using squeeze-and-excitation block. Experiments on three benchmark datasets: Rain100H, Rain100L, and Rain800, manifest impressive performance compared with state-of-the-art methods.

1 Introduction

With the rapid development of image acquisition technology, it has become possible to obtain more and more high-quality images than ever before and has witnessed major advances in various practical computer vision-based systems. However, the images captured under adverse weather conditions such as rain, haze, night have been greatly degraded and significantly affect the performance of the vision systems such as surveillance and autonomous driving [1]. Therefore, automatically recovering the underlying clean single rainy image, simply named as image deraining.

Traditional image deraining methods mainly exploit simple linear-mapping transformation motivated by the physical rainy model that the observed rainy image: $\mathbf{O}$ can be generally modeled as a linear sum of a rain-free clean image: $\mathbf{B}$

© Springer Nature Switzerland AG 2021
H. Ishikawa et al. (Eds.): ACCV 2020, LNCS 12623, pp. 68–83, 2021.
https://doi.org/10.1007/978-3-030-69532-3_5

and the rain streak: $\mathbf{R}$ [2,3]. The linear model as mathematical representation can be formulated as:

$$\mathbf{O} = \mathbf{B} + \mathbf{R} \tag{1}$$

Given Eq. (1), the deraining method aims at removing $\mathbf{R}$ from $\mathbf{O}$ to get $\mathbf{B}$. Since the number of the unknown variables in $\mathbf{B}$ and $\mathbf{R}$ are 2 times of the known ones in $\mathbf{O}$ and there are many solutions of $\mathbf{B}$, $\mathbf{R}$ for a given $\mathbf{O}$, this is naturally an ill-posed problem. For well solving this problem, previous methods [4–6] mainly focus on employing various hand-crafted priors for exploring the underlying structure of the latent clean image or the attribute of the rain streaks. However, to hammer out the proper prior for a specific image and a kind of rain streak remains to be an art. Recent approaches for single image deraining leverage deep learning to mitigate the dependence on the hand-crafted priors, and illustrate that the convolutional neural network (CNN [7,12,14]) itself can effectively capture the intrinsic characteristics of the latent clean images via learning strategy. In the deep learning-based scenario for single image deraining, various CNN models have been proposed and revolved to more and more complicated architectures for pursuing high performance. Although the deep learning-based approaches manifest significant improvement in single image deraining, there still exist some limitations. As mentioned above, the CNN models have progressed into much more complex and diverse architectures to boost the performance, and thus lead to difficulty for practical implementation and model training. In addition, most existing CNN models adopt a single-scale framework for feature representation, which rarely captures the underlying correlation of rain streaks across scales. Recently, authors in [8,9] exploited a multi-scale deep framework for image deraining. Unfortunately, these exploitations fail to make full use of the interactive correlation of multi-scale rain streaks and have complicated architectures with several subnets. Furthermore, the exiting CNN methods generally get to start training with the training pairs of the observed rainy images and their corresponding clean images from scratch and cannot exploit the knowledge existed in the already learned CNN models from the clean training images in other task domains such as image classification.

To handle with the above limitations, we propose a novel deraining network, called as multi-level context-gating knowledge transfer network: MCGKT-Net. The MCGKT-Net is based on the well-known U-Net architecture, which can be simply implemented and naturally a multi-scale learning framework. In order to exploit the correlation of the low-level features and high-level features in multi-scale encoder and decoder subnets of U-Net [10], we employ a ConvLSTM unit for interactively transferring the learned knowledge of two sides instead of directly duplicating the encoder's feature to the decoder side, called as internal knowledge transfer. Since training CNN model with rain-degraded images as input possibly leads to model deviation from optimal parameters, we advocate to transfer a part of knowledge (the shallow layer's parameters) hold in the learned CNN model with the clean training images in other task domains such as image classification, and reuse them in our proposed MCGKT-Net for boosting deraining performance, called as external knowledge transfer. Finally, we adopt squeeze-and-excitation block in multi-scale learned features of the decoder subnet for dynamically selecting the useful learned contexts for being inputted to the next scale, called as multi-scale context gating. Experiments on three benchmark datasets demonstrate the promising performance compared with the state-of-the-art methods on image deraining.

In summary, our main contributions are three-fold:

1. We present a simply-implemented and naturally multi-scale deraining network, which can effectively explore the multi-scale attributes of rain streak and different underlying semantic structures of the clean images;
2. We exploit the interactive learning between the same level features of encoder and decoder subnets for internal knowledge transfer and reuses the existed knowledge learned in other task domains for external knowledge transfer to boosting deraining performance;
3. We explore a multi-scale context gating module for dynamically selecting useful features of decoder subnet using squeeze-and-excitation block.

The rest of this paper is organized as follows. Section 2 surveys the related work including deep learning-based image deraining methods and multi-level learning networks. Section 3 presents the proposed MCGKT network for image deraining. Extensive experiments are conducted in Sect. 4 to compare the proposed MCGKT-Net with state-of-the-art image deraining methods on three benchmark datasets. The conclusion is given in Sect. 5.

2   Related Work

In the past decades, image deraining has been actively researched in the low-level computer vision community, and substantial improvements have been witnessed. This work mainly concentrates on the more challenge deraining from a single image. Here, we briefly survey the related work.

2.1   Single Image Deraining

Rain streaks removal from a single image is an extremely challenging task due to its ill-posed nature. Previous methods are mainly divided into two categories: optimization-based methods [15,17,18,25] and deep learning-based methods [19–21,30]. Optimization based methods usually formulate the deraining task as a mathematical model motivated by the fact that rainy images can be decomposed into a clean background image layer and a rain layer. To recover more robust clean image, the prior knowledge for characterizing the underlying structure of the latent clean image layer and the attribute of the rain layers has imposed on the formulated mathematical model as regularization term and employed optimization strategy for solving. Kang et al. [15] proposed to apply sparse coding to separate rain streaks from the high-frequency layer, while Luo et al. [16] explored a discriminative sparse coding framework for modeling image patches. The work by Chen et al. [17] and Chang et al. [18] leveraged the low-rank property of rain streaks for removing the decomposed rain layer based on low-rankness. Since the composite models [15, 17, 18] regularized by modeling the sparse and low-rank prior are insufficient in characterizing the decomposed layers, leading to limited deraining performance on diverse images. In addition, the explored priors (for example sparsity, low-rankness) on the previous approaches are hand-crafted, and to discover a proper prior for a specific image and a kind of rain type still remains be an art or requires comprehensive analysis for a specific rainy image. Recently, deep convolutional neural network has been widely applied to single image deraining, and validated that promising performance can be achieved [19–21, 30]. Fu et al. [19] first explored a three-layer convolutional network to predict clean image high-frequency component from its rain-contaminated counterpart, and further extended it to a 20-layer CNN structure by incorporating Residual-Block, called as deep detail network, for pursuing better performance [20]. Zhang et al. [30] presented a multi-stream dense network for joint rain density estimation and deraining. To generate more visually plausible deraining result, the same research group investigated a conditional generative adversarial network (GAN) for single image deraining [21], and proved to achieve visually high-quality reconstructions. In [35], a novel deep network architecture based on recurrent neural networks and squeeze-and-excitation context aggregation module (RESCAN) has been proposed and adaptively adjusted parameters for various rain streak layers. Fan et al. [23] proposed residual-guide network with recursive convolution module and multi-level supervision not only on the final results but also on the intermediate results progressively for predicting high-quality reconstruction. Wei et al. [24] proposed a semi-supervised image deraining network, while Ren et al. [36] focused on several factors including network architecture for integrating progressive ResNet and recurrent layers inside and cross stages, and loss functions, and provided a better and simpler baseline deraining network.

2.2 Multi-level Learning Network

It is known that a rainy image is possibly decomposed into the image layer and rain streak layer, which may consist of multiple layers, especially under heavy rain conditions. The rain streaks decomposed in multiple layers manifest intrinsically multi-scale attributes and some self-similarity properties within and across scales, which is prospected to boost the deraining performance via exploring the correlated information between and across multiple levels of rain layers. Most existing methods recur to deeper and more complex network architecture for pursuing better deraining performance but cannot make full use of the underlying correlation between and across different rain layers. Although, a few work [8, 9, 33] have been investigated to explore multiscale information for deraining from a single image, which mainly leverages multiple subnets (several mainstreams) for exploiting different scales, and lead to more complicated DCNN architectures. As we know that the convolutional encoder-decoder network itself is a multi-level learning architecture, where the encoder path learns feature representation evolved to large scale with the increased depth of the network while the decoder path attempts to recover the feature representation with more detailed structure (small scale) from the final output of the encoder with more semantic information and large context. Further, to retain more detail structures in the final prediction results, skip connection is usually used for duplicating the feature representation of the encoder path to the decoder side in the same level such as in U-Net [10], FCN [11]. Although the encoder-decoder network has also been adopted for image deraining [12–14], most existing methods cannot effectively exploit the correlation of the feature representations and compensate each other between the encoder and decoder paths. This study explores a novel and simple deraining network, called multi-level context gating knowledge transfer network (MCGKT-Net), which is based on the multi-level encoder-decoder network and investigates both internal and external knowledge transfer for boosting deraining performance.

3   The Proposed MCGKT-Net

The mainstream of our proposed MCGKT-Net follows the encoder-decoder network architecture, and multi-level feature representation can be learned in both encoder and decoder paths. To effectively explore the feature interaction and correlation between encoder and decoder paths, we propose to leverage backward ConvLSTM blocks instead of simple duplication, to transfer the semantic structure of the high-level features in the decoder path to the encoder side, and input the interactively learned features to the subsequent level of the decoder, called as internal knowledge transfer module (IKT). We further leverage a part of knowledge (the shallow layer's parameters) maintained in the learned CNN model with the clean training images in other task domains such as image classification for training the deraining model from a good initial state, called as external knowledge transfer module (EKT). In addition, to adaptively select more useful feature representations in the learning procedure, we exploit squeeze and excitation block (SE) to the multi-level features in the decoder path for constructing the multi-level context gating module (MLCG). Then the MCGKT-Net consists of the mainstream of the encoder-decoder architecture, the knowledge transfer module with IKT and EKT, and the MLCG module. The schematic concept of the proposed MCGKT-Net is shown in Fig. 1. Next, we would describe the different parts of the MCGKT-Net.

3.1   The Mainstream of the Encoder-Decoder Architecture

The mainstream of our used network architecture consists of two paths: encoder and decoder, and each path is divided into four blocks. Both encoder and decoder paths learn multi-level feature representations in the multiple blocks, where encoder employs MaxPooling layer with a 2 * 2 kernel for decreasing feature map size to half in both horizontal and vertical directions between blocks while decoder performs up-sampling for doubly recovering the feature map size between blocks. In each block of both encode and decoder, we implement it in 3 convolutional layers with 3 * 3 kernels following ReLU activation function.

The channel number of the learned feature maps block-wisely is doubled in the encoder while is halve in the decoder. Thus the architecture in the encoder path is same as the first 3 shallow layers of the popularly used VGGNet in different vision problems.

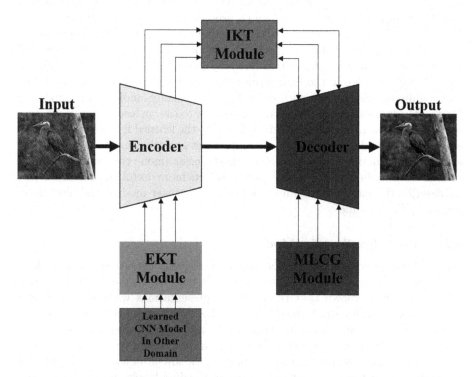

Fig. 1. Network architecture of MCGKT-Net. The abbreviations IKT, EKT and MLCG Module denote internal knowledge transfer, external knowledge transfer module, and multi-level context gating module, respectively.

Let's denotes the input and output of the $j - th$ block in the encoder path as $\mathbf{E}_i^j$, $\mathbf{E}_o^j$, and in the decoder path as $\mathbf{D}_i^j$, $\mathbf{D}_o^j$, respectively, the relation of the input and output of each block can be expressed as:

$$\mathbf{E}_o^j = f(\mathbf{E}_o^j, \theta_{E,i}), \ \mathbf{D}_o^j = f(\mathbf{D}_o^j, \theta_{D,i}) \qquad (2)$$

where $f(\cdot)$ represents the transformation operation of 3 convolutional layers with the learned parameters $\theta_{E,i}$ and $\theta_{D,i}$, respectively. The $j + 1 - th$ inputs in the encoder and the $j - 1 - th$ output in the decoder sides can be obtained from the $j - th$ outputs, and are expressed as:

$$\mathbf{E}_i^{j+1} = MP(\mathbf{E}_o^j), \ \mathbf{D}_i^{j-1} = UP(\mathbf{D}_o^j) \qquad (3)$$

where $MP(\cdot)$ and $UP(\cdot)$ denote the MaxPooling and up-sampling layer implemented between blocks, respectively. Then the mainstream of our encoder-decoder network can learn multi-level feature representations: $\mathbf{E}_i = [\mathbf{E}_i^1, \mathbf{E}_i^2, \mathbf{E}_i^3, \mathbf{E}_i^4]$ in the encoder and $\mathbf{D}_o = [\mathbf{D}_o^1, \mathbf{D}_o^2, \mathbf{D}_o^3, \mathbf{D}_o^4]$ in the decoder with different context information, where the encoder generates low-level features with more detail image structure while decoder results in high-level feature representation with more semantic information. The encoder-decoder architecture is very simple with the convolutional layer of small kernel size 3 * 3 and is prospected to be easily trained in different vision tasks. In this network, it is known that the outputs of the deeper blocks inherit from the shallow blocks of the decoder and all blocks of the encoder, and produce more semantic information but may lose detail structure. To maintain more detail structure in the final results, the existing encoder-decoder architecture in different vision tasks such as FCN, U-Net usually employ skip connection for directly duplicating the output of the encoder to the corresponding input sides in the decoder, which cannot effectively leverage the learned feature maps in both encoder and decoder paths. This study integrates several elementary modules for effectively interaction learning or knowledge transfer among the feature representations of the main network and adaptively selects more useful information. Next, we describe the integrated modules: knowledge transfer module and multi-level context gating module.

3.2 Knowledge Transfer Module

As described above, the simple feature reuse via skip connection cannot effectively fuse the learned feature representations in both encoder and decoder paths. In addition, it is known that the feature representations with more semantic information are gradually learned based on the former ones and inherit from the already learned features including those in the encoder. However, the feature representations with more semantic information in the decoder path cannot be back transferred to the encoder side for calibrating the low-level features. This study integrates a transfer module among the corresponding blocks in the encoder and decoder paths and conducts back transfer, called as internal knowledge transfer (IKT) module. Furthermore, we also aim at investigating the already learned knowledge in the released CNN models in other vision domains for aiding our deraining network training, called as external knowledge transfer (EKT) module.

IKT Module: In the conventional feature reuse with skip connection, the simple concatenate layer is used for fusing the output: $\mathbf{E}_o^j$ of the $j - th$ block in the encoder and the input: $\mathbf{D}_i^j$ of the $j - th$ block in the decoder as the real input instead of $\mathbf{D}_i^j$. To effectively transfer the learned semantic features in the decoder path for calibrating those in the encoder path, we consider the encoder's output: $\mathbf{E}_o^j$ and the decoder's input: $\mathbf{D}_i^j$ as a time sequence $[\mathbf{E}_o^j, \mathbf{D}_i^j]$ with two-time points, and employ a backward ConvLSTM ($BW\_ConvLSTM(\cdot)$) unit for learning more effective features from both paths, which can be formulated as:

$$\hat{\mathbf{D}}_i^j = BW\_ConvLSTM([\mathbf{E}_o^j, \mathbf{D}_i^j]) \qquad (4)$$

where $\mathbf{D}_i^j$ with semantic information is firstly inputted and the generated state in ConvLSTM calibrate the final output of $\mathbf{E}_o^j$ with more detailed structure.

The output: $\hat{\mathbf{D}}_i^j$ of $BW\_ConvLSTM(\cdot)$ is adopted as the input of the $j - th$ block in the decoder. With the ConvLSTM unit, it is prospected that the learned semantic features (knowledge) in the decoder side can be effectively transferred back to the encoder side, and results in high-level representative features inside the deraining network.

EKT Module: Most existing deep learning-based deraining methods usually train the network from a randomly initialized state, and cannot leverage knowledge of the pre-trained CNN models in other vision tasks such as image classification. However, to train a good generalization model with a huge amount of unknown parameters, a large dataset is necessary, which is very tough to gather a vast number of labeled data especially for the deraining scenario. This inspires the knowledge exploiting of a pre-trained CNN to a specific under-studying task, generally called as transfer learning, which requires the similar network structure for the specific task with the pre-trained CNN model. This study attempts to explore the knowledge in the pre-trained VGG family with Imagenet dataset to overcome the isolated learning paradigm for boosting the deraining performance. Although our encoder-decoder network has different architecture with the pre-trained VGG-Net models, there are partially same structures of the encoder path in our deraining network with the shallow layers in VGG-Net. Thus, we simply transfer the parameters of the pre-trained VGG-Net's shallow layers to the first 3 blocks of the encoder path while randomly initialize the remainder structure's parameters. Then we re-train the network inheriting somewhat knowledge from the pre-trained VGG models for adapting to the new deraining task.

3.3   Multi-level Context Gating Module

It is obvious that the network can obtain large amount of feature representations in different layers of multi-level blocks. However, not all learned features equivalently contribute to the subsequent extraction of high representative features and the final prediction. Recently, attention mechanism has been popularly explored to adaptively concentrate the more discriminated and effective features in the network training procedure. For example, motivated by the fact that different regions in the input may have various contributions to the final prediction such as in image classification, detection and segmentation, many work exploit the spatial attention via mutual enhancement with spatial correlation, and manifest significant improvement. Our goal aims at predicting all underlying pixel values from the rain-degraded input, and all regions should be indispensable for estimating the precise pixel values nearby. Thus, this study instead investigates the channel attention for dedicating to emphasize the channel with the underlying scene information. We suppose that the feature maps extracted by various convolutional kernels may correspond to some underlying scene layers or a part of rain layers, and propose to exploit explicit relationship between channels of the convolutional layers for gating context. We implement the context gating module via adaptively assigning a weight for each channel (channel attention) and then encoding the inputted raw feature maps.

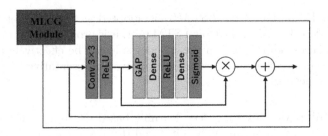

Fig. 2. The multi-level context gating module for MCGKT-Net.

The multi-level context gating (MLCG) module shown in Fig. 2, consists of two-part: squeeze and excitation (also called SE-block), and is employed on multi-level integrated feature maps $[\hat{\mathbf{D}}_i^1, \hat{\mathbf{D}}_i^2, \cdots, \hat{\mathbf{D}}_i^L]$ of the encoder and decoder paths, which are also the input of the decoder's blocks. The input feature maps to MLCG module are aggregated to generate channel contribution index by employing global average pooling (GAP) of the whole context of channels. Let's denote the input feature map to the $l-th$ MLCG module as $\hat{\mathbf{D}}_i^l = [\hat{\mathbf{d}}_{i,1}^l, \hat{\mathbf{d}}_{i,2}^l, \cdots, \hat{\mathbf{d}}_{i,C}^l]$, where $\hat{\mathbf{d}}_{i,c}^l \in \mathbb{R}^{W \times H}$, and the spatial squeeze (GAP) is formulated as:

$$s_c = f_{sq}(\hat{\mathbf{d}}_{i,c}^l) = \frac{1}{W \times H} \sum_h^H \sum_w^W \hat{\mathbf{d}}_{i,c}^l(h, w) \tag{5}$$

where $f_{sq}(\cdot)$ is the spatial squeeze function for compressing each two-dimensional feature map as a contribution index s_c, and $W \times H$ is the size of the $c-th$ channel feature map. Then, we employ excitation functions for capturing the channel-wise dependencies and non-linear interaction based on the global channel information $\mathbf{s} = [s_1, s_2, \cdots, s_C]$, which is implemented with two fully connected (FC) layers in the MLCG module. The first FC layer encodes the channel global vector $\mathbf{s}$ to a dimension-reduced vector with reduction ratio r, and the second FC layer encodes it back again to the dimension C as an excitation vector, which can be expressed:

$$z = f_{ex}(\mathbf{s}, \mathbf{W}) = \delta(\mathbf{W}_2 \sigma(\mathbf{W}_1 \mathbf{s})) \tag{6}$$

where $\mathbf{W}_1 \in \mathbb{R}^{\frac{C}{r} \times C}$ and $\mathbf{W}_2 \in \mathbb{R}^{C \times \frac{C}{r}}$ are the parameters of the first and second FC layers, respectively, $\sigma(\cdot)$ and $\delta(\cdot)$ refer ReLU and sigmoid activation functions. The final output of the MLCG module is generated as:

$$\tilde{\mathbf{d}}_{i,c}^l = f_{scale}(\hat{\mathbf{d}}_{i,c}^l, z_c) = z_c \hat{\mathbf{d}}_{i,c}^l \tag{7}$$

where f_{scale} denotes a channel-wise multiplication between the channel attention index z_c and the input feature map.

4   Experimental Results

In this section, we conduct extensive experiments to validate the effectiveness of the proposed multi-level context gating knowledge transfer network (MCGKT-

Net) for single image deraining. Comprehensive ablation study is given for demonstrating the effect of different modules.

4.1 Experimental Setting-Up

Implementation Details. We implement our MCGKT-Net using Keras with TensorFlow as backbend. In network training stage, we randomly sample image patches of size 224×224 from all images as training samples, and then train the network with epochs 500. We use Adam optimizer [26] with default parameters and batch size of 4. The learning rate is set as 2×10^{-4}.

Datasets. We evaluate MCGKT-Net on three public benchmark datasets:

Rain100H [27], Rain100L [27], and Rain800 [28]. Rain100L consists of 1800 training images and 200 test images, where the rainy images are synthesized with only one type of rain streaks while Rain100H has 1800 rainy/clean pairs as training images and 200 rainy/clean pairs as test, where the rainy images are synthesized with five directions of rain streaks. Rain800 has in total 800 images, where 700 rainy/clean pairs are as training samples and the remainders are as testing. The rainy images in Rain800 are created via adding rain streak to the clean images following the guidelines mentioned in [19], which aims at generating a diverse rainy dataset via adding various intensities and orientations of rain streak to different pixels. Some synthesized rainy images from all three datasets are shown Fig. 3 manifests that the rainy images in Rain100L and Rain100H have thick and clean line structure while the rain steaks in Rain800 are much thinner and arbitrarily discontinuous without any regulation.

Fig. 3. Example rainy images from Rain100H, Rain100L and Rain800 datasets.

Evaluation Metrics. We use two commonly metrics: i.e. peak signal to noise ratio (PSNR) and structure similarity index (SSIM [29]), which measures the image structure difference and is more consistent with human perceptual measure, to evaluate the deraining performance on all three datasets.

4.2 Comparison to the State-of-the-art Methods

We compare our proposed MCGKT-Net with the state-of-the-art deraining approaches, including semi-supervised transfer learning (SEMI) [24], density-aware deraining (DIDMDN) [30], simple deep convolutional network for image SR (SRCNN) [31], deep detail network (DDN) [20], image-to-image translation (pix2pix) [32], lightweight pyramid network (LPNet) [33], U-Net [10], uncertainty guided multi-scale residual learning (UMRL) [34], recurrent squeeze-and-excitation context aggregation net (RESCAN) [35], progressive deraining network (PreNet) [36]. Table 1 shows the quantitative measure on the three datasets. From Table 1, we can see that our methods can outperform almost methods. For providing visual comparison, Fig. 4 and 5 visualize the derained examples from Rain100L and Rain100H datasets using different methods, which manifests that our proposed MCGKT-Net can recover more clean images than other existing methods. Furthermore, we also provide the derained results on three real images in Fig. 6 using our proposed MCGKT-Net and several state-of-the-art methods.

Table 1. Average PSNR and SSIM comparison on the synthetic datasets Rain100H [27], Rain100L [27] and Rain800 [28]. Red and blue colors are used to indicate top 1st, 2nd performance.

Methods	Rain100H	Rain100L	Rain800
SEMI [24]	16.56/0.486	25.03/0.842	22.35/0.788
DIDMDN [30]	17.35/0.524	25.23/0.741	22.56/0.818
SRCNN [31]	18.29/0.612	32.63/0.936	25.10/0.823
DDN [20]	22.08/0.788	31.12/0.953	25.10/0.823
pix2pix [32]	21.96/0.679	29.20/0.886	–/–
LPNet [33]	23.16/0.801	33.61/0.958	22.21/0.789
U-Net [10]	23.28/0.741	30.97/0.921	26.28/0.826
UMRL [34]	24.91/0.810	31.98/0.955	24.37/0.819
RESCAN [35]	26.36/0.786	29.80/0.881	25.00/0.835
PreNet [36]	26.77/0.858	32.44/0.950	24.81/0.865
Ours	27.06/0.848	35.23/0.962	27.44/0.840

4.3 Ablation Studies

Our proposed MCGKT-Net is evolved from the baseline U-Net architecture, which is very simple and easy to be trained effectively. We integrated three modules: internal knowledge transfer (IKT), external knowledge transfer (EKT), and

Fig. 4. Deraining results of different methods on Rain100H.

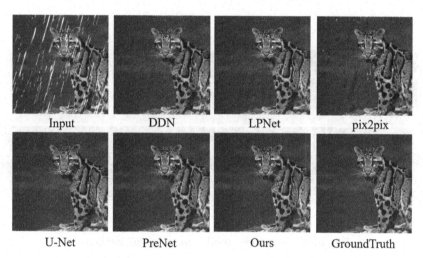

Fig. 5. Deraining results of different methods on Rain100L.

multi-level context gating (MLCG) modules into the baseline U-Net for higher representative feature learning. Therein EKT module adopted the pre-trained VGG models: VGG16 and VGG19. This section evaluates the effectiveness of the integrated modules on the baseline U-Net. Quantitative results on all three datasets are given in Table 2. It can be seen from Table 2 that the proposed MCGKT-Net manifests great superiority over the baseline U-Net and its incomplete versions not integrating all proposed modules. The results of the experiment with the addition of each of the three modules in the Rain800 are shown in Fig. 7. Integration of all modules surpasses the baseline by 3.78 dB, 4.26 dB, 1.16 dB for Rain100H, Rain100L, and Rain800, respectively.

Table 2. Quantitative results by different setups on the baseline U-Net model.

IKT Module		×	✓	×	×	×	✓	✓	✓
EKT Module(VGG19)		×	×	✓	×	×	✓	×	✓
EKT Module(VGG16)		×	×	×	✓	×	×	✓	×
MLCG Module		×	×	×	×	✓	×	×	✓
Rain100H	PSNR	23.28	24.61	26.77	26.45	24.92	27.03	26.82	27.06
	SSIM	0.7407	0.7837	0.8422	0.8393	0.7888	0.8475	0.8458	0.8477
Rain100L	PSNR	30.97	33.16	32.04	31.98	31.10	35.03	35.02	35.23
	SSIM	0.9210	0.9475	0.9231	0.9231	0.9131	0.9608	0.9606	0.9618
Rain800	PSNR	26.28	26.76	26.52	26.38	25.80	27.32	27.44	27.03
	SSIM	0.8269	0.8307	0.8422	0.8428	0.8190	0.8409	0.8402	0.8327

| Input | DDN | LPNet | Ours |

Fig. 6. The compared results on real rainy images.

From the results of Table 2, all integrated modules can improve the quantitative measures on both Rain100H and Rain100L datasets while the integration of the MLCG module on the Rain800 dataset decreases the quantitative metrics a little. From Fig. 3 as mentioned above that the rain streaks in Rain100H and Rain100L datasets exhibit some regular characteristics similar to the line structures with diverse directions while the rain streaks in the Rain800 dataset have no regular pattern most like un-regular noise. The intent of integrating the MLCG module is to adaptively emphasize and attenuate specific channels of features with some specific patterns and is expected to be oriented well to the existed rain steaks in the Rain100H and Rain100L datasets while be difficult to attenuate the noise-like rain streaks in the Rain800 dataset.

Fig. 7. Deraining results of ablation study on Rain800. Values below every image indicate PSNR value and SSIM [29] value, respectively.

5   Conclusion

In this paper, we proposed a multi-level context gating knowledge transfer network for the removal of rain streaks from a single image. Taking the possible multi-layer characteristic of the rain streak in mind, we used the encoder-decoder network architecture, which itself is a multi-scale structure for feature learning, as a baseline network, and integrated several simple modules for higher representative feature learning. We employed an internal knowledge transfer module for interactively learning between the features of the encoder and decoder paths and an external knowledge transfer module for effective reuse of the knowledge preserved in a pre-trained CNN model in other task domains. Further, we explored a multi-level context gating module for adaptively emphasizing useful feature channels and attenuating the channels related to rain layers. Experimental results demonstrated that our proposed MCGKT-Net gave promising deraining performance compared with the state-of-the-art methods.

Acknowledgement. This research was supported in part by the Grant-in Aid for Scientific Research from the Japanese Ministry for Education, Science, Culture and Sports (MEXT) under the Grant No. 20K11867.

References

1. Sultani, W., Chen, C., Shah, M.: Real-world anomaly detectionin surveillance videos. In: Proceedings of the IEEE Conference on Computer Vision and Pattern Recognition (CVPR), pp. 6479–6488 (2018)
2. Barnum, P.C., Narasimhan, S., Kanade, T.: Analysis of rain and snow in frequency space. Int. J. Comput. Vis. **86**(2), 256 (2010)
3. Xu, J., et al.: Star: a structure and texture aware retinex model. IEEE Trans. Image Process. **29**, 5022–5037 (2020)
4. Kang, L.-W., Lin, C.-W., Fu, Y.-H.: Automatic single-image-base drain streaks removal via image decomposition. IEEE Trans. Image Process. **21**(4), 1742–1755 (2012)

5. Li, Y., Tan, R.T., Guo, X., Lu, J., Brown, M.S.: Rain streak removal using layer priors. In: Proceedings of the IEEE Conference on Computer Vision and Pattern Recognition (CVPR), pp. 2736–2744 (2016)
6. He, K., Sun, J., Tang, X.: Single image haze removal using dark channel prior. IEEE Trans. Pattern Anal. Mach. Intell. **33**(12), 2341–2353 (2010)
7. Goodfellow, I., Bengio, Y., Courville, A.: Deep Learning, pp. 326–366. MIT Press, Cambridge (2016)
8. Zheng, Y., Yu, X., Liu, M., Zhang, S.: Residual multiscale based single image deraining. In: Conference on BMVC (2019)
9. Jiang, K., et al.: Multi-scale progressive fusion network for single image deraining. arXiv:2003.10985 (2020). http://arxiv.org/abs/2003.10985
10. Ronneberger, O., Fischer, P., Brox, T.: U-Net: convolutional networks for biomedical image segmentation. In: Navab, N., Hornegger, J., Wells, W.M., Frangi, A.F. (eds.) MICCAI 2015. LNCS, vol. 9351, pp. 234–241. Springer, Cham (2015). https://doi.org/10.1007/978-3-319-24574-4_28
11. Long, J., Shelhamer, E., Darrell, T.: Fully convolutional networks for semantic segmentation. In: Proceedings of the IEEE Conference on Computer Vision and Pattern Recognition (CVPR) (2015)
12. Du, Y., Xu, J., Zhen, X., Cheng, M., Shao, L.: Conditional variational image deraining. IEEE Trans. Image Process. **29**, 6288–6301 (2020). https://doi.org/10.1109/TIP.2020.2990606
13. Du, Y., Xu, J., Qiu, Q., Zhen, X., Zhang, L.: Variational image deraining. In: IEEE Winter Conference on Applications of Computer Vision (WACV), Snowmass Village, CO, USA, 2020, pp. 2395–2404 (2020). https://doi.org/10.1109/WACV45572.2020.9093393
14. Wang, G., Sun, C., Sowmya, A.: ErlNet: entangled representation learning for single image deraining. In: IEEE International Conference on Computer Vision (ICCV), October 2019
15. Kang, L.W., Lin, C.W., Fu, Y.H.: Automatic single image-based rain streaks removal via image decomposition. IEEE Trans. Image Process. **21**(4), 1742–1755 (2012)
16. Luo, Y., Xu, Y., Ji, H.: Removing rain from a single image via discriminative sparse coding. In: IEEE International Conference on Computer Vision (ICCV), pp. 3397–3405 (2015)
17. Chen, Y., Hsu, C.: A Generalized low-rank appearance model for spatio-temporally correlated rain streaks. In: IEEE International Conference on Computer Vision, Sydney, NSW 2013, pp. 1968–1975 (2013). https://doi.org/10.1109/ICCV.2013.247
18. Chang, Y., Yan, L., Zhong, S.: Transformed low-rank model for line pattern noise removal. IEEE International Conference on Computer Vision (ICCV), pp. 1726–1734 (2017)
19. Fu, X., Huang, J., Ding, X., Liao, Y., Paisley, J.: Clearing the skies: a deep network architecture for single-image rain removal. IEEE Trans. Image Process. **26**, 2944–2956 (2017)
20. Fu, X., Huang, J., Zeng, D., Huang, Y., Ding, X., Paisley, J.: Removing rain from single images via a deep detail network. In: Proceedings of the IEEE Conference on Computer Vision and Pattern Recognition (CVPR), pp. 1715–1723 (2017)
21. Zhang, H., Sindagi, V., Patel, V.M.: Image de-raining using a conditional generative adversarial network. arXiv preprint, arXiv:1701.05957 (2017)

22. Li, X., Wu, J., Lin, Z., Liu, H., Zha, H.: Recurrent squeezeand-excitation context aggregation net for single image deraining. In: European Conference on Computer Vision, pp. 262–277 (2018)

23. Fan, Z., Wu, H., Fu, X., Huang, Y., Ding, X.: Residual-guide network for single image deraining. In: Proceedings of the ACM Multimedia Conference, pp. 1751–1759. ACM (2018)

24. Wei, W., Meng, D., Zhao, Q., Xu, Z., Wu, Y.: Semi-supervised transfer learning for image rain removal. In: Proceedings of the IEEE Conference on Computer Vision and Pattern Recognition (CVPR), pp. 3877–3886 (2019)

25. Ren, D., Zuo, W., Zhang, D., Zhang, L., Yang, M.-H.: Simultaneous fidelity and regularization learning for image restoration. IEEE Trans. Pattern Anal. Mach. Intell. (2019)

26. Kingma, D., Ba, J.: Adam: a method for stochastic optimization. In: International Conference on Learning Representations (ICLR) (2015)

27. Yang, W., Tan, R.T., Feng, J., Liu, J., Guo, Z., Yan, S.: Deep joint rain detection and removal from a single image. In: Proceedings of the IEEE Conference on Computer Vision and Pattern Recognition (CVPR), pp. 1357–1366 (2017)

28. Zhang, H., Sindagi, V., Patel, V.M.: Image de-raining using a conditional generative adversarial network. arXiv e-prints, arXiv:1701.05957 (2017)

29. Wang, Z., Bovik, A.C., Sheikh, H.R., Simoncelli, E.P.: Image quality assessment: from error visibility to structural similarity. IEEE Trans. Image Process. **13**(4), 600–612 (2004)

30. Zhang, H., Patel, V.M.: Density-aware single image de-raining using a multi-stream dense network. In: Proceedings of the IEEE Conference on Computer Vision and Pattern Recognition (CVPR), pp. 695–704 (2018)

31. Dong, C., Loy, C.C., He, K., Tang, X.: Image super-resolution using deep convolutional networks. IEEE Trans. Pattern Anal. Mach. Intell. **38**(2), 295–307 (2016)

32. Isola, P., Zhu, J.-Y., Zhou, T., Efros, A.A.: Image-to-image translation with conditional adversarial networks. arXiv preprint arXiv:1611.07004 (2016)

33. Fu, X., Liang, B., Huang, Y., Ding, X., Paisley, J.: Lightweight pyramid networks for image deraining. arXiv preprint arXiv:1805.06173 (2018)

34. Yasarla, R., Patel, V.M.: Uncertainty guided multi-scale residual learning-using a cycle spinning CNN for single image de-raining. In: Proceedings of the IEEE Conference on Computer Vision and Pattern Recognition (CVPR), pp. 8405–8414 (2019)

35. Li, X., Wu, J., Lin, Z., Liu, H., Zha, H.: Recurrent squeeze-and-excitation context aggregation net for single image deraining. In: Ferrari, V., Hebert, M., Sminchisescu, C., Weiss, Y. (eds.) ECCV 2018. LNCS, vol. 11211, pp. 262–277. Springer, Cham (2018). https://doi.org/10.1007/978-3-030-01234-2_16

36. Ren, D., Zuo, W., Hu, Q., Zhu, P., Meng, D.: Progressive image deraining networks: a better and simpler baseline. In: Proceedings of the IEEE Conference on Computer Vision and Pattern Recognition, pp. 3937–3946 (2019)

Degradation Model Learning for Real-World Single Image Super-Resolution

Jin Xiao[1], Hongwei Yong[1,2], and Lei Zhang[1,2]([⊠])

[1] Department of Computing, The Hong Kong Polytechnic University,
Hung Hom, Hong Kong
{csjxiao,cshyong,cslzhang}@comp.polyu.edu.hk
[2] DAMO Academy, Alibaba Group, Hangzhou, China

Abstract. It is well-known that the single image super-resolution (SISR) models trained on those synthetic datasets, where a low-resolution (LR) image is generated by applying a simple degradation operator (e.g., bicubic downsampling) to its high-resolution (HR) counterpart, have limited generalization capability on real-world LR images, whose degradation process is much more complex. Several real-world SISR datasets have been constructed to reduce this gap; however, their scale is relatively small due to laborious and costly data collection process. To remedy this issue, we propose to learn a realistic degradation model from the existing real-world datasets, and use the learned degradation model to synthesize realistic HR-LR image pairs. Specifically, we learn a group of basis degradation kernels, and simultaneously learn a weight prediction network to predict the pixel-wise spatially variant degradation kernel as the weighted combination of the basis kernels. With the learned degradation model, a large number of realistic HR-LR pairs can be easily generated to train a more robust SISR model. Extensive experiments are performed to quantitatively and qualitatively validate the proposed degradation learning method and its effectiveness in improving the generalization performance of SISR models in practical scenarios.

1 Introduction

Single image super-resolution (SISR) aims to recover a high-resolution (HR) image from its low-resolution (LR) observation, which is a highly valuable technique for improving the resolution and quality of digital photography. As a typical ill-posed inverse problem, SISR has been widely studied during the past

L. Zhang—This work is supported by the Hong Kong RGC GRF grant (PolyU 152216/18E).

Electronic supplementary material The online version of this chapter (https://doi.org/10.1007/978-3-030-69532-3_6) contains supplementary material, which is available to authorized users.

H. Ishikawa et al. (Eds.): ACCV 2020, LNCS 12623, pp. 84–101, 2021.
https://doi.org/10.1007/978-3-030-69532-3_6

decades [1–6], yet it is still a challenging and active research topic. The traditional methods generally utilize powerful image priors [7–12] for SISR, and have made remarkable progresses. However these handcrafted image priors are limited in representing the complex image textures.

Benefitting from the rapid development and great success of deep convolutional neural networks (CNNs) [13], recently SISR has witnessed significant progresses by employing deep CNNs [14–24]. Most of the existing CNN based SISR models are trained on synthetic HR-LR image pairs, which are generated by applying a simple degradation model (e.g., bicubic downsampling) to the HR images [14,15,18,19,21,23,24]. However, the authentic HR to LR image degradation process is much more complicated than these simple uniform downsample operators. As a result, the SISR networks trained on such synthetic datasets have low generalization capability to real-world LR images, largely limiting their value in practical applications.

Efforts have been made to address the generalization problem of SISR models [16,25–27]. Zhang et al. [16] proposed to use multiple Gaussian kernels together with additive white Gaussian noise to increase the diversity of HR-LR pairs, yet the selection and combination of these kernels are very sensitive. Very recently, researchers have started to construct real-world datasets by using digital cameras to capture images of the same scene under different focal lengths [25–27]. Particularly, Cai et al. [27] carefully designed a registration algorithm to obtain pixel-wise aligned HR-LR image pairs. The so-called RealSR dataset enables supervised learning of SISR models, and the learned models demonstrate better performance than previous ones on real-world scenarios. However, constructing such datasets of real-world HR-LR pairs is laborious and costly, and the existing datasets of this kind [25–27] are all limited in number of image pairs, diversity of scenes and illuminating conditions. For example, the RealSR dataset contains only 559 scenes in total, limiting the generalization capability of trained SISR models to a wider range of scenarios.

While constructing real-world datasets of HR-LR image pairs, researchers have also proposed to learn the image degradation process from unpaired HR and LR images, and use the learned degradation model to generate HR-LR image pairs for SISR model learning [28–31]. All these methods employ the Generative Adversarial Network (GAN) [32] to learn the degradation process by differentiating the distribution between generated LR and real LR images. Unfortunately, training such a GAN with unpaired data is very difficult and may not converge to the desired result. Moreover, using a network to model the degradation from HR to LR images makes it hard to interpret the degradation process, ignoring some prior knowledge on the image formation.

In this paper, we model the image degradation process by using spatially variant degradation kernels instead of a network, and propose to learn this model from the HR-LR image pairs in the RealSR dataset instead of the unpaired HR and LR images. It is widely agreed in literature [1–3,16,33] that the LR image formation process can be formulated as first blurring the HR image with a degradation kernel, followed by downsampling and noise addition, while in real scenarios the degradation kernel is spatially variant, relating to the depth and local content in the scene. Clearly, the pixel-wise degradation kernels are the key to model the degradation process. One may propose to learn a network to directly map the HR image to LR image, or propose to learn a network to directly predict the pixel-wise degradation kernel. However, the learning space of those two proposals can be too big for modeling the degradation process, while they ignore the common knowledge of image degradation. Considering the fact that blurring kernels in an optical imaging system can be generally described as bell-shaped smooth functions [34], we argue that the plausible degradation kernels distribute in a small subspace, which can be approximated as a linear combination of a group of basis kernels. Therefore, we propose to learn a group of basis kernels as well as a weight prediction network to predict the combination coefficients at each pixel.

An end-to-end learning scheme is designed to learn the basis kernels and the weight prediction network from the RealSR dataset [27]. Once learned, our degradation model takes an HR image as input, predicts the spatially variant kernels at each location, and outputs the degraded LR image. In this way, we can easily generate a large amount of realistic HR-LR image pairs using the HR images on hand. Finally, we can train SISR models by using these synthetic yet realistic HR-LR pairs. Experimental results show that the trained SISR models achieve better generalization performance than the models trained only on the RealSR dataset, owing to the enlarged training data of realistic HR-LR image pairs. Our main contributions are summarized as follows:

- We propose to learn the LR image degradation process in a supervised manner from a set of real-world HR-LR image pairs. Specifically, we learn spatially variant degradation kernels by learning a group of basis kernels as well as a pixel-wise weights prediction network.
- By using the learned degradation model to generate realistic HR-LR image pairs, more robust SISR models can be trained, which exhibit higher generalization performance than previous SISR models and produce promising visual quality for real-world LR images.

2   Related Work

2.1   Single Image Super-Resolution

Single image super-resolution (SISR) is an active topic in low-level vision, and a plenty of works have been proposed in the past decades, including interpolation-based [35], model-based [10,12] and learning-based methods [14,15,17–21,23,24]. Traditional methods are usually limited in representing the complex image local structures, while the recently developed deep CNN have shown great advantages in image structure representation and consequently improved much the SISR performance [14,15,19,23,24,36]. For example, Kim et al. [15] employed the residual learning strategy to design the VDSR model with 20 convolutional layers. Liu et al. [19] proposed to utilize contextual information by exploiting the image non-locally correlation. Zhang *et al.* [23] proposed a very deep CNN with over 400 layers, and improved much the SISR performance. Despite the great success, most of the CNN based SISR models are trained on synthetic datasets, where the LR images are generated by applying simple operators such as bicubic downsampling to the HR images [14,15,17–21,23,24]. Unfortunately, the real-world image degradation process is far more complex than bicubic downsampling. Such a gap between synthetic data and real data makes the trained deep SISR models hardly be generalized to real-world LR images.

2.2 Real-World SISR

To solve the problem of real-world SISR, one intuitive way is to use a more complex degradation process to simulate LR images. Zhang *et al.* [16] proposed to use multiple Gaussian kernels with additive white Gaussian noise to simulate LR images, whereas the selection of suitable kernels is difficult and ad hoc for practical applications. Another recently popular solution is to employ the generative adversarial network (GAN) [32] with unsupervised learning. E.g., SRGAN [22] is proposed to utilize adversarial loss to improve the perceptual quality of images. While the GAN-based methods show some interesting results on SISR, their results are not stable and often exhibit some unnatural visual artifacts.

Instead of simulating HR-LR image pairs, recently efforts have been devoted to construct real-world SISR datasets. Qu *et al.* [37] proposed to use a beam splitter to acquire paired HR-LR images. Kóhler *et al.* [38] used hardware binning on camera sensor to generate LR images. However, these two datasets contain very limited scenes, 31 in [37] and 14 in [38]. Very recently, DSLR cameras have been used to construct real-world SISR datasets by capturing the same scene under different focal lengths. Chen *et al.* [26] collected 100 image pairs of printed postcards. Zhang *et al.* [25] constructed the SR-RGB dataset with 500 scenes, whereas the image pairs are not strictly aligned. To enable pairwise learning, an image registration algorithm is proposed in [27] to carefully handle the misalignment between HR and LR images caused in the data collection process. The so-called RealSR dataset contains a set of aligned real-world HR-LR image pairs, which allow direct pairwise training of SISR models. However, the collection and processing of such a dataset is laborious and costly, and the scale and diversity of RealSR dataset is relatively limited (559 scenes in total).

2.3 Degradation Model Learning

To diminish the domain gap between synthetic and real HR-LR image pairs, another line of work aims to learn the image degradation process and uses it to generate more realistic HR-LR image pairs. Bulat *et al.* [29] proposed to use a generator to learn how to degrade from HR to LR, and a discriminator to distinguish between synthetic LR and real LR images. Manuel *et al.* [28] further improved the generator to learn on image high frequency layers. However, training a GAN is very difficult and may not always converge to the desired result, and the above GAN based degradation learning methods do not exploit the prior knowledge of image formation process in an optical imaging system. In this paper, we model the image degradation process by spatially variant degradation kernels, and propose a supervised learning scheme to learn the degradation model from existing real-world SISR datasets.

3   The Proposed Method

In this section, we first formulate the LR image degradation model based on the real-world LR image formation process. We then present how to learn the pixel-wise degradation models. Finally, we present how to use the learned degradation models to generate realistic HR-LR datasets for training real-world SISR models.

3.1   Formulation of Image Degradation Model

Denote by $\mathbf{I}^H$ an HR image and by $\mathbf{I}^L$ its LR counterpart. In literature [1–3,16,33], the image degradation from an HR image to an LR image can be generally represented as

$$\mathbf{I}^L = (\mathbf{I}^H * \mathbf{k})\!\downarrow_d + \mathbf{v}, \tag{1}$$

where "$*$" is the convolution operator, $\mathbf{k}$ is the degradation kernel, $\downarrow_d$ is the downsampling operator, and $\mathbf{v}$ is the random observation noise. The goal of SISR is to recover the underlying HR image $\mathbf{I}^H$ given its LR observation $\mathbf{I}^L$.

Most of existing SISR works [14,15,18,19,21,23,24] assumes that the degradation kernel $\mathbf{k}$ is uniform, i.e., spatially invariant, over the whole image. Particularly, they apply the bicubic kernel to HR images to simulate the HR-LR image pairs, and then use those pairs to train SISR models. Whereas in real-world SISR problems, the degradation kernel is much more complex, correlating with the depth and local content of the scene [27]. Therefore, the degradation kernel is typically non-uniform and spatially variant. At each location (i, j), the kernel may vary, and we use $\mathbf{k}_{i,j}$ to denote the per-pixel degradation kernel. The spatially variant image degradation from HR to LR can be formulated as:

$$\mathbf{I}^L(i,j) = \mathbf{I}^H_{i,j} \odot \mathbf{k}_{i,j} + \mathbf{v}(i,j), \tag{2}$$

where $\mathbf{I}^H_{i,j}$ denotes a local image window centered at (i, j) with the same size as kernel $\mathbf{k}_{i,j}$, and "$\odot$" is the inner product operator.

From Eq. 2, one can see that the key to model the real-world image degradation process is how to predict the pixel-wise degradation kernel $\mathbf{k}_{i,j}$. One intuitive idea is to learn a CNN from the available HR-LR pairs (e.g., the RealSR dataset [27]) to predict the kernel $\mathbf{k}_{i,j}$; however, the learning space of a CNN can be too big for the kernels and the network can be over-fitted by the limited training data. On the other hand, the predicted kernel may have poor interpretability since they may not accord with our prior knowledge on the image degradation process (please refer to our ablation study in Sect. 4.3 for more discussions). It is commonly agreed that the degradation kernels in an optical imaging system can be generally described as bell-shaped smooth functions [34]. This means that the plausible degradation kernels are not arbitrary but actually fall into a small subspace, which can be spanned by a group of basis kernels. Denote by $\boldsymbol{\Phi} = \{\boldsymbol{\phi}, ..., \boldsymbol{\phi}_M\}$ the set of M basis kernels. We propose to approximate the pixel-wise degradation kernel $\mathbf{k}_{i,j}$ as a weighted combination of $\boldsymbol{\Phi}$ as follows:

$$\mathbf{k}_{i,j} \approx \sum\nolimits_{m=1}^{M} \mathbf{C}_{i,j}(m)\boldsymbol{\phi}_m, \tag{3}$$

where $\boldsymbol{\phi}_m$ is the mth basis kernel and $\mathbf{C}_{i,j}$ represents the combination weight vector at location (i, j). The above formulation constrains the kernels in a subspace which can be more easily learned, especially when the available training dataset (e.g., RealSR) is not very big.

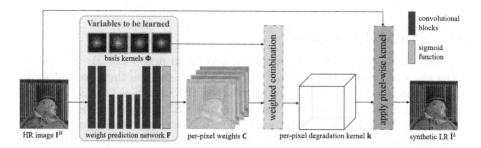

Fig. 1. Overview of the proposed approach for degradation model learning. A group of basis kernels $\boldsymbol{\Phi}$ are learned together with a weight prediction network $\mathbf{F}$, which are used to generate the pixel-wise degradation kernels. The LR image is obtained by applying the pixel-wise degradation kernels to the HR image.

3.2 Degradation Model Learning

From Eq. (3), one can see that the learning of pixel-wise kernels $\mathbf{k}_{i,j}$ is turned into the learning of basis kernels $\boldsymbol{\Phi}$ and the weight vectors $\mathbf{C}_{i,j}$. The basis kernels are global to all image regions, while the weights depend on the image local contents. We propose to use a network to predict the weights and learn it simultaneously with the basis kernels from some real-world HR-LR dataset.

Our degradation model learning (DML) approach is illustrated in Fig. 1. With the HR image $\mathbf{I}^H$ as input, a CNN $\mathbf{F}$ with parameters $\boldsymbol{\Theta}$ is learned to predict the weights, i.e., $\mathbf{C} = \mathbf{F}(\mathbf{I}^H|\boldsymbol{\Theta})$, where $\mathbf{C}$ is the set of weight vectors $\mathbf{C}_{i,j}$. The basis kernels $\boldsymbol{\phi}_m$ are also learned so that the kernels $\mathbf{k}_{i,j}$ can be predicted according to Eq. (3). The predicted degradation kernels are applied to the HR image $\mathbf{I}^H$ to output the predicted LR image, denoted by $\hat{\mathbf{I}}^L$. Suppose there are N pairs of HR-LR training images, the learning objective can be formulated as

$$\min_{\boldsymbol{\Phi},\boldsymbol{\Theta}} \sum\nolimits_{n=1}^{N} ||\hat{\mathbf{I}}_n^L - \mathbf{I}_n^L||_2^2. \tag{4}$$

We learn the basis kernels $\mathbf{\Phi}$ and weight prediction network $\mathbf{F}$ in an end-to-end manner by using the RealSR dataset [27].

We design the weight prediction network $\mathbf{F}$ following an encoder-decoder structure. It takes an HR image as input and outputs a weight vector at each location. To embrace large receptive field, we use a max pooling layer for feature down-sampling, and employ the bilinear upsampling layer to increase the feature resolution and ensure pixel-wise outputs. Convolutional layer with filters of size 3×3 is used, and ReLU is used as the activation function. To output the per-pixel weights, we use sigmoid function after the last convolutional layer for normalization. The whole network can be easily optimized by the SGD or ADAM optimizer. Examples of the learned kernels, the visualization of the predicted weight maps and more discussions will be provided in the ablation study (see Sect. 4.3).

3.3 SISR Model Learning

Once the basis kernels $\mathbf{\Phi}$ and the weight prediction network $\mathbf{F}$ are learned by using the DML approach presented in Sect. 3.2, we can use them to synthesize HR-LR image pairs by using a set of collected HR images as inputs. However, directly using the synthesized LR images to train SISR models is problematic. As described in Eqs. (1) and (2), the real-world LR images are usually corrupted by a certain amount of noise. However, the training objective in Eq. (4) encourages to generate a noise-free LR image since the random noise is hard to predict. If we use the synthesized clean LR images to train the SISR model and then apply the model to real-world noisy LR data, the noise will be exaggerated and lead to unpleasant visual artifacts.

To address this issue and further diminish the gap between synthetic and real LR images, we add random noise to the synthesized LR image $\hat{\mathbf{I}}_n^L$ according to the LR image formulation process described in Eq. (1). Without additional information on the imaging system (e.g., sensors, lens), we simply assume additive white Gaussian noise (AWGN) and empirically set the noise level as $\sigma = 5$.

Finally, we collect a set of high quality images as the HR set, and use the learned degradation model together with AWGN to generate synthetic yet realistic HR-LR image pairs. These image pairs are used to train the SISR model. In this paper, we adopt two representative SISR network architectures, a lightweight network VDSR [15] and a deeper network RCAN [23], to validate the proposed DML method.

4   Experimental Results

4.1   Experiment Setup

We carry out both quantitative and qualitative experiments to demonstrate the effectiveness of our proposed DML method for SISR model training. Considering that there are a few issues to be validated and explained, here we summarize how we set up the experiments for a better understanding of our work.

- In Sect. 4.2, we introduce the training dataset and the testing dataset in our experiments, as well as some implementation details of our algorithm.
- Section 4.3 conducts some ablation studies. First, we discuss the selection of the number of basis kernels in DML. Then we compare our DML with another two potential solutions to synthesize HR-LR pairs. One is to learn a CNN to directly map an HR image to an LR one, and another is to learn a CNN to predict the pixel-wise degradation kernel.
- In Sect. 4.4 we demonstrate that our DML can result in more robust real-world SISR performance. We first use the RealSR dataset [27], where aligned real-world HR-LR pairs are available so that PSNR/SSIM/LPIPS indices can be computed, to perform quantitative experiments. We then use other real-world data out of the training dataset to perform qualitative experiments, which are to demonstrate that our DML can improve the robustness and generalization performance of real-world SISR models.

4.2 Datasets and Implementation Details

Datasets. There are three types of datasets required to validate the performance of DML in degradation process learning and SISR model training.

- The first one is the RealSR [27] dataset (version 2), which contains aligned HR-LR image pairs of 559 scenes collected by two cameras with 3 zooming factors: ×2, ×3 and ×4. We follow [27] to split the RealSR dataset into 459 scenes for training and the remaining 100 for testing. We use the training part of this dataset to train our degradation model by the method described in Sect. 3.2, and use the testing part to quantitatively evaluate the performance of DML and its application to real-world SISR.
- Once the degradation model is learned, we can apply it to an HR image dataset to generate synthetic HR-LR pairs. We construct an HR dataset by combining the Flickr2K dataset [24] and Internet images, containing 3150 images in total. The Flickr2k dataset has 2650 high quality images of various scenes, whose resolution is mostly 1500 × 2000. To diminish the effect of compression artifacts, we downsample those Flickr2k images by a factor of 2 after Gaussian smoothing (with scale $\sigma = 1$). We also download 500 raw images of 4K resolution from [39], and then apply the PhotoShop CameraRaw tool to them so that uncompressed high quality RGB images of 4K resolution are obtained.
- The third dataset is to validate the effectiveness of DML for real-world SISR. We use the SR-RGB dataset [25] which consists of real-world LR images and their unaligned HR counterparts obtained by optical zoom of DSLR. Since the HR and LR images are not aligned, the PSNR/SSIM/LPIPS measures can not be calculated but the HR images can be used as references for visual comparison.

Implemention Details. We set the size of basis kernels to be learned as 15×15 for all zooming scales ×2, ×3, and ×4. The basis kernels are randomly initialized, and then normalized to have summation 1 for further updating. The weight prediction network is initialized using the Xavier initializer [40]. In the training of both DML and SISR networks, we convert the RGB images to YCbCr color space, and train or test on the Y channel. Images are cropped into 192×192 patches for training of all models. Left-right and up-down flips are used for data augmentation. The Adam optimizer [41] with the default parameter setting ($\beta_1 = 0.9$, $\beta_2 = 0.999$) is used as the optimizer. We train DML and SISR models using fixed learning rate of $1e^{-4}$ for 100K and 300K iterations, respectively. The batch size is set as 16 in DML training. As for SISR models, we adopt two representative network architectures: VDSR [15] and RCAN [23]. We implement RCAN with 100 convolutional layers. The batch size is set as 16 and 2, respectively, for training VDSR and RCAN models.

4.3   Ablation Study

We conduct ablation studies to investigate the following two issues of DML: (1) selection of the number of basis kernels in DML; and (2) comparison of DML with the other two potential HR-LR pair synthesis approaches. We train our DML and its variants on the training set (459 image pairs) of RealSR [27], and use the testing set of RealSR to evaluate the quality of generated LR images and the quality of super-resolved HR images. PSNR and SSIM are used as the quantitative metrics.

Table 1. Evaluation of the quality of generated LR images and super-resolved HR images by using the RealSR [27] dataset. The best and second results are highlighted in red and blue, respectively.

Method	Generated LR						Super-resolved HR					
	$\times 2$		$\times 3$		$\times 4$		$\times 2$		$\times 3$		$\times 4$	
	PSNR	SSIM	PSNR	SSIM	PSNR	SSIM	PSNR	SSIM	PSNR	SSIM	PSNR	SSIM
DML ($N{=}4$)	37.82	0.9862	36.46	0.9848	35.61	0.9840	33.23	0.9544	30.09	0.9150	28.50	0.8856
DML ($N{=}8$)	37.93	0.9864	36.54	0.9850	35.75	0.9842	33.32	0.9552	30.18	0.9157	28.60	0.8864
DML ($N{=}16$)	37.90	0.9863	36.51	0.9849	35.73	0.9841	33.28	0.9548	30.16	0.9153	28.58	0.8859
DirectNet	37.70	0.9864	36.33	0.9843	35.50	0.9838	33.13	0.9539	30.01	0.9144	28.42	0.8853
DirectKPN	37.77	0.9863	36.35	0.9844	35.56	0.9836	33.16	0.9545	30.06	0.9147	28.48	0.8860

Number of Basis Kernels. We first study the suitable number of basis kernels in our DML. By using the training part of the RealSR dataset, we learn $N = 4, 8, 16$ basis kernels and their associated weight predict networks. We then apply the learned models to the HR images in the testing part of the RealSR dataset to generate LR images. By comparing the synthesized and real LR images, we compute and list the PSNR/SSIM results in Table 1. One can see that by increasing the number from $N = 4$ to $N = 8$, better LR generation performances can be achieved, whereas the performance of using $N = 16$ basis kernels is slightly worse than $N = 8$. This means that the underlying degradation process can be well approximated by using $N = 8$ basis kernels.

We visualize the learned 8 basis kernels for different zooming factors in Fig. 2. One can see that with the increase of zooming factor from 2 to 4, the kernels becomes more dispersed and complex, which are in accordance with our common knowledge of image degradation process. We also visualize the basis coefficients predicted by our weight prediction network in Fig. 3. One can see that the learned network can adaptively assign different weights to the kernels according to the scene content and image local structure to generate realistic LR images.

Since our final goal is to improve the SISR performance via DML, it is also necessary to test the effect of N on the final SISR results. We apply the learned DML models to our collected HR image dataset (see Sect. 4.2) to synthesize 3150 HR-LR images pairs, which are then used to train a VDSR super-resolution model. By applying the trained VDSR model to the LR images in the RealSR testing set, we compute the PSNR/SSIM indices of the super-resolved HR images. Table 1 lists the results. One can see that $N = 8$ again achieves the best results for real-world SISR. Therefore, we set $N = 8$ for DML in our experiments.

Comparison with Other HR-LR Pair Synthesis Strategies. Besides the proposed DML, there are two other intuitive strategies to synthesize HR-LR image pairs. One is to learn a CNN that directly maps an HR image to an LR one, denoted as DirectNet, and the other is to learn a kernel prediction network [42] to predict the degradation kernel, denoted as DirectKPN. To validate the advantages of our proposed DML method, we implement these two strategies by using the same backbone (with the same hyper-parameters) of the weight prediction network in our DML for fair comparison. For DirectNet, we implement

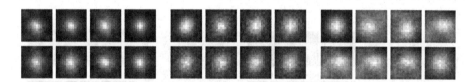

Fig. 2. Visualization of the learned degradation basis kernels by our DML ($N = 8$) model. The left, middle and right 4 columns represent the basis kernels for SR zooming factors ×2, ×3 and ×4, respectively.

Fig. 3. Visualization of the predicted combination weights of the basis kernels by our DML method for zooming factor ×2. The leftmost image is the input HR image, and the right 8 images visualize the predicted weights corresponding to each basis kernels (refer to Fig. 2 for the 8 kernels). The brighter intensity denotes larger weight. One can see that our weight prediction network can adaptively assign different weights according to the scene content and local structures.

it using the residual learning strategy [15] for better convergence. All the three
competitors are trained on the training set of RealSR [27], and tested on the
RealSR testing set. PSNR and SSIM are used as quantitative measures.

We first evaluate the performance of the three strategies on LR image generation. The results are listed in Table 1. One can see that DML performs constantly
better than DirectNet or DirectKPN on all the three zooming factors, with an
improvement of 0.23 dB and 0.20 dB in PSNR, respectively. This shows that
DML can generate more realistic LR images, owing to our proposed strategy of
learning basis kernels and predicting pixel-wise combination weights. Besides, it
is observed that DirectKPN performs slightly better than DirectNet. This shows
that by taking into account the image degradation process, better LR generation performance can be achieved by learning to predict pixel-wise kernels than
directly predicting LR image pixels.

We then evaluate their effectiveness on improving SISR. We apply the three
LR image generation models to the collected HR image dataset, synthesizing
3150 HR-LR images pairs by each model. We add small AWGN to those HR-LR
pairs (refer to Sect. 3.3 for details), and train three VDSR models. Finally, we
apply these three VDSR models to the LR images in the testing part of the
RealSR dataset, and obtain the super-resolved HR images. The PSNR/SSIM
results are listed in Table 1. One can see that the VDSR network trained on synthetic HR-LR pairs generated by our DML method, performs constantly better
(around $0.15dB$ in PSNR) than those trained on pairs generated by DirectNet or
DirectKPN. This validates the superiority of DML to DirectNet and DirectKPN
on improving SISR performance. Our DML method can generate realistic LR
images with a smaller gap to real-world LR images, therefore leading to better
SISR results than DirectNet and DirectKPN.

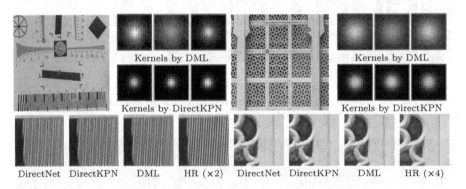

Fig. 4. Visualization of predicted degradation kernels by DML and DirectKPN. One
can see that the degradation kernels predicted by DML vary with the image local
content, whereas the kernels predicted by DirectKPN are simple and rather uniform
across the whole image. We also show the SISR results of the VDSR models trained
on the synthetic HR-LR pairs by DML, DirectNet and DirectKPN. One can see that
the model based on DML can recover more details with less artifacts.

We visualize the pixel-wise degradation kernels predicted by our DML and DirectKPN in Fig. 4 (note that DirectNet does not predict kernels). One can see that predicted degradation kernels by DML vary with the image local content, whereas the degradation kernels predicted by DirectKPN are simple and rather uniform across the whole image. This is probably because when we directly learn the pixel-wise degradation kernel, the solution space is too large so that DirectKPN can only converge to a simple solution, resulting in uniform kernels for an input image. In contrast, our DML strategy can effectively reduce the kernel space and thus result in a more robust adaptive degradation kernel prediction model. We also visualize the SISR results by the three degradation models in Fig. 4. It can be seen that our DML based SISR method exhibits better visual quality with more details and less artifacts.

4.4 Experiments on Real-World SISR

As discussed in the Introduction section, the goal of our DML is to synthesize realistic HR-LR image pairs to supplement the limited number of real-world HR-LR pairs so that more robust SISR models can be trained. To validate whether this goal is achieved by our DML method, in this section we use VDSR [15] (20 layers) and RCAN [23] (100 layers) as two representative SISR models to perform extensive SISR experiments. By using the HR image dataset we collected, we synthesized 3150 HR-LR pairs via the learned DML model, and denote this dataset by Syn-DML. Note that recently a GAN based HR-LR pair synthesis method called DSGAN [28] was developed. We finetuned this model on the RealSR dataset, and applied it to our HR image dataset to synthesize another dataset of HR-LR pairs, denoted by Syn-DSGAN. Therefore, we can train variants of VDSR/RCAN models by using: only RealSR, only Syn-DSGAN, only Syn-DML, the combination of RealSR and DSGAN, and the combination of RealSR and Syn-DML dataset, resulting in a total of 10 SISR models.

We evaluate the 10 VDSR/RCAN models on two real-world datasets. One is the testing set of RealSR [27]. Since the aligned HR-LR pair are available, we can compute the PSNR/SSIM/LPIPS indices to perform quantitative evaluation. Another is the SR-RGB dataset [25], which consists of many LR images and their unaligned HR counterparts. Qualitative visual comparisons can be made on it for the different SISR models. We would like to stress that the testing on the second dataset is more important (though qualitative) because it is independent of the RealSR dataset, part of whose samples are used to train the DML and VDSR/RCAN models. The testing results on the SR-RGB [25] dataset can more faithfully reflect the generalization capability of competing SISR models than those on the RealSR dataset.

Results on the RealSR Dataset [27]. We apply the competing VDSR/RCAN models to the testing set of RealSR, and the PSNR/SSIM/LPIPS indices are shown in Table 2. Note that LPIPS is a perceptual index that measures the perceptual quality of images (lower the better). We can have the following findings. First, the VDSR/RCAN models trained on Syn_DML achieve better LPIPS

Table 2. Evaluation of SISR performances on the RealSR [27] dataset by models trained using different training data. The best, second and third results for each SISR network architecture are highlighted in red, blue and yellow, respectively.

SISR model	Training dataset	LPIPS ↓			PNSR ↑			SSIM ↑		
		×2	×3	×4	×2	×3	×4	×2	×3	×4
VDSR	RealSR	0.141	0.224	0.291	33.60	30.53	28.92	0.957	0.919	0.887
	Syn-DSGAN	0.145	0.240	0.309	32.47	29.57	27.20	0.949	0.908	0.851
	Syn-DML	0.137	0.218	0.284	33.32	30.18	28.60	0.955	0.916	0.886
	RealSR+Syn-DSGAN	0.151	0.234	0.289	33.35	30.13	28.56	0.954	0.915	0.885
	RealSR+Syn-DML	0.124	0.198	0.267	33.50	30.37	28.86	0.957	0.918	0.889
RCAN	RealSR	0.141	0.227	0.283	33.91	30.86	29.26	0.960	0.924	0.896
	Syn-DSGAN	0.148	0.239	0.319	32.45	29.78	27.95	0.948	0.916	0.877
	Syn-DML	0.131	0.210	0.265	33.38	30.29	28.66	0.956	0.918	0.887
	RealSR+Syn-DSGAN	0.143	0.230	0.288	33.50	30.56	28.80	0.956	0.920	0.888
	RealSR+Syn-DML	0.123	0.195	0.242	33.73	30.61	28.99	0.958	0.921	0.891

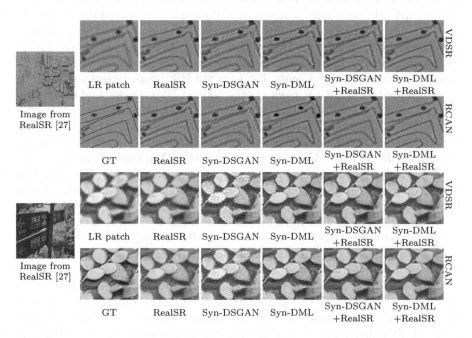

Fig. 5. Visual comparison of the competing SISR models on RealSR [27] dataset with SR scale ×4. The first and second rows of each example are super-resolved patches by VDSR and RCAN networks, respectively, which are trained on different training data.

score in all cases than the models trained on RealSR. This validates the effectiveness of our model in improving perceptual quality by synthesizing realistic HR-LR image pairs. Second, the VDSR/RCAN models trained on the Syn-DML

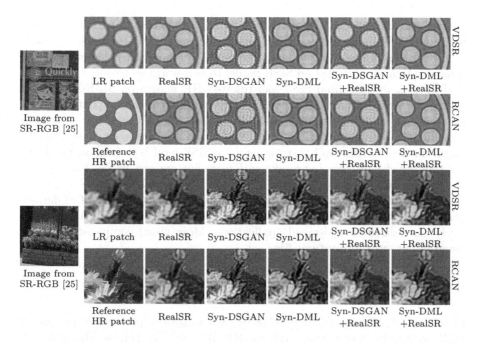

Fig. 6. Qualitative comparison of competing SISR methods on the SR-RGB [25] dataset with SR scale ×4. The first and second rows of each example show the results of VDSR and RCAN models, respectively, trained on different datasets.

dataset achieve comparable but slightly inferior PSNR/SSIM indices to the models trained on RealSR. This is not a surprise because the training and testing data for the latter model are from the same source. Third, SISR models trained on Syn-DML perform significantly better (about 1dB) than those trained on Syn-DSGAN, which demonstrates the superiority of our DML method to the GAN based DSGAN [28]. Last, by combining RealSR with the synthetic dataset for training, better quantitative results can be achieved than training using only synthetic dataset. Particularly, the VDSR model (×4) trained on RealSR+Syn-DML achieves even high SSIM scores than the model trained on RealSR.

In Fig. 5, we compare the visual quality of super-resolved HR images by the ten SISR models. One can see that models trained on Syn-DML and RealSR+Syn-DML can effectively recover more image details with more pleasant perceptual quality than the trained using only the RealSR dataset. In particular, the models trained on RealSR+Syn-DML achieve the best visual quality. This validates that our DML method can largely improve the generalization performance of real-world SISR models by synthesizing realistic HR-LR pairs for training.

Results on the SR-RGB Dataset [25]. The SR-RGB dataset contains real-world HR and LR images of the same scene, which are however not well aligned. Though it is hard to compute PSNR/SSIM metrics, the HR images in this dataset can be well used a reference for visual comparison of SISR methods. Since the SR-RGB dataset was constructed independently of the RealSR dataset by using different cameras and lens, the results can more fairly demonstrate the generalization capability of an SISR model to real-world scenarios.

In Fig. 6, we visualized the super-resolved HR images on SR-RGB dataset [25] by the ten VDSR/RCAN models trained on different training datasets. One can see that models trained on RealSR dataset can only moderately recover some details. Models trained on Syn-DSGAN produce severe artifacts. Benefitting from the enlarged realistic training data, SISR models trained on Syn-DML can produce visually pleasing results with more fine-grained details. Particularly, the models trained on combined RealSR+Syn-DML deliver the best perceptual quality of super-resolved HR images. The experiments on SR-RGB dataset demonstrate that the SISR models trained by our DML method can be effectively generalized to real-world applications. More visual comparisons can be found in our **supplementary file**.

5 Conclusions

In this paper we proposed to tackle the generalization problem of real-world SISR models by synthesizing realistic HR-LR pairs. To achieve this goal, we first learned an image degradation model from real-world HR-LR image pairs. Specifically, we learned a set of basis degradation kernels together with a weight prediction network. The degradation kernel at any location was estimated as the linear combination of the basis kernels using the weights predicted by the weight prediction network. The learned degradation model was then used to synthesize 3150 HR-LR image pairs covering various scenes for SISR model training. Our extensive analyses and experiments showed that the proposed degradation model learning method can effectively improve the generalization performance of SISR models to real-world applications.

References

1. Yang, C.-Y., Ma, C., Yang, M.-H.: Single-image super-resolution: a benchmark. In: Fleet, D., Pajdla, T., Schiele, B., Tuytelaars, T. (eds.) ECCV 2014. LNCS, vol. 8692, pp. 372–386. Springer, Cham (2014). https://doi.org/10.1007/978-3-319-10593-2_25
2. Park, S.C., Park, M.K., Kang, M.G.: Super-resolution image reconstruction: a technical overview. IEEE Sig. Process. Mag. **20**, 21–36 (2003)
3. Yang, W., Zhang, X., Tian, Y., Wang, W., Xue, J.H., Liao, Q.: Deep learning for single image super-resolution: a brief review. IEEE Trans. Multimedia **21**, 3106–3121 (2019)
4. Timofte, R., Agustsson, E., Van Gool, L., Yang, M.H., Zhang, L.: Ntire 2017 challenge on single image super-resolution: methods and results. In: Proceedings of the IEEE Conference on Computer Vision and Pattern Recognition Workshops, pp. 114–125 (2017)

5. Cai, J., Gu, S., Timofte, R., Zhang, L.: Ntire 2019 challenge on real image super-resolution: methods and results. In: Proceedings of the IEEE Conference on Computer Vision and Pattern Recognition Workshops (2019)
6. Lugmayr, A., et al.: Aim 2019 challenge on real-world image super-resolution: methods and results. In: 2019 IEEE/CVF International Conference on Computer Vision Workshop (ICCVW), pp. 3575–3583. IEEE (2019)
7. Mairal, J., Bach, F., Ponce, J., Sapiro, G., Zisserman, A.: Non-local sparse models for image restoration. In: 2009 IEEE 12th International Conference on Computer Vision, pp. 2272–2279. IEEE (2009)
8. Dong, W., Zhang, L., Shi, G., Li, X.: Nonlocally centralized sparse representation for image restoration. IEEE Trans. Image Process. **22**, 1620–1630 (2012)
9. Wang, S., Zhang, L., Liang, Y.: Nonlocal spectral prior model for low-level vision. In: Lee, K.M., Matsushita, Y., Rehg, J.M., Hu, Z. (eds.) ACCV 2012. LNCS, vol. 7726, pp. 231–244. Springer, Heidelberg (2013). https://doi.org/10.1007/978-3-642-37431-9_18
10. Gu, S., Zuo, W., Xie, Q., Meng, D., Feng, X., Zhang, L.: Convolutional sparse coding for image super-resolution. In: Proceedings of the IEEE International Conference on Computer Vision, pp. 1823–1831 (2015)
11. Yang, J., Wright, J., Huang, T.S., Ma, Y.: Image super-resolution via sparse representation. IEEE Trans. Image Process. **19**, 2861–2873 (2010)
12. Dong, W., Zhang, L., Shi, G., Wu, X.: Image deblurring and super-resolution by adaptive sparse domain selection and adaptive regularization. IEEE Trans. Image Process. **20**, 1838–1857 (2011)
13. Goodfellow, I., Bengio, Y., Courville, A.: Deep Learning. MIT Press, Cambridge (2016)
14. Dong, C., Loy, C.C., He, K., Tang, X.: Learning a deep convolutional network for image super-resolution. In: Fleet, D., Pajdla, T., Schiele, B., Tuytelaars, T. (eds.) ECCV 2014. LNCS, vol. 8692, pp. 184–199. Springer, Cham (2014). https://doi.org/10.1007/978-3-319-10593-2_13
15. Kim, J., Kwon Lee, J., Mu Lee, K.: Accurate image super-resolution using very deep convolutional networks. In: Proceedings of the IEEE Conference on Computer Vision and Pattern Recognition, pp. 1646–1654 (2016)
16. Zhang, K., Zuo, W., Zhang, L.: Learning a single convolutional super-resolution network for multiple degradations. In: Proceedings of the IEEE Conference on Computer Vision and Pattern Recognition, pp. 3262–3271 (2018)
17. Shi, W., et al.: Real-time single image and video super-resolution using an efficient sub-pixel convolutional neural network. In: Proceedings of the IEEE Conference on Computer Vision and Pattern Recognition, pp. 1874–1883 (2016)
18. Tai, Y., Yang, J., Liu, X.: Image super-resolution via deep recursive residual network. In: Proceedings of the IEEE Conference on Computer Vision and Pattern Recognition, pp. 3147–3155 (2017)
19. Liu, D., Wen, B., Fan, Y., Loy, C.C., Huang, T.S.: Non-local recurrent network for image restoration. In: Advances in Neural Information Processing Systems, pp. 1680–1689 (2018)
20. Dai, T., Cai, J., Zhang, Y., Xia, S.T., Zhang, L.: Second-order attention network for single image super-resolution. In: Proceedings of the IEEE Conference on Computer Vision and Pattern Recognition, pp. 11065–11074 (2019)
21. Zhang, Y., Tian, Y., Kong, Y., Zhong, B., Fu, Y.: Residual dense network for image super-resolution. In: Proceedings of the IEEE Conference on Computer Vision and Pattern Recognition, pp. 2472–2481 (2018)

22. Ledig, C., et al.: Photo-realistic single image super-resolution using a generative adversarial network. In: Proceedings of the IEEE Conference on Computer Vision and Pattern Recognition, pp. 4681–4690 (2017)
23. Zhang, Y., Li, K., Li, K., Wang, L., Zhong, B., Fu, Y.: Image Super-Resolution Using Very Deep Residual Channel Attention Networks. In: Ferrari, V., Hebert, M., Sminchisescu, C., Weiss, Y. (eds.) ECCV 2018. LNCS, vol. 11211, pp. 294–310. Springer, Cham (2018). https://doi.org/10.1007/978-3-030-01234-2_18
24. Lim, B., Son, S., Kim, H., Nah, S., Mu Lee, K.: Enhanced deep residual networks for single image super-resolution. In: Proceedings of the IEEE Conference on Computer Vision and Pattern Recognition Workshops, pp. 136–144 (2017)
25. Zhang, X., Chen, Q., Ng, R., Koltun, V.: Zoom to learn, learn to zoom. In: Proceedings of the IEEE Conference on Computer Vision and Pattern Recognition, pp. 3762–3770 (2019)
26. Chen, C., Xiong, Z., Tian, X., Zha, Z.J., Wu, F.: Camera lens super-resolution. In: Proceedings of the IEEE Conference on Computer Vision and Pattern Recognition, pp. 1652–1660 (2019)
27. Cai, J., Zeng, H., Yong, H., Cao, Z., Zhang, L.: Toward real-world single image super-resolution: a new benchmark and a new model. In: Proceedings of the IEEE International Conference on Computer Vision, pp. 3086–3095 (2019)
28. Fritsche, M., Gu, S., Timofte, R.: Frequency separation for real-world super-resolution. arXiv preprint arXiv:1911.07850 (2019)
29. Bulat, A., Yang, J., Tzimiropoulos, G.: To learn image super-resolution, use a GAN to learn how to do image degradation first. In: Ferrari, V., Hebert, M., Sminchisescu, C., Weiss, Y. (eds.) ECCV 2018. LNCS, vol. 11210, pp. 187–202. Springer, Cham (2018). https://doi.org/10.1007/978-3-030-01231-1_12
30. Han, Z., et al.: Unsupervised image super-resolution with an indirect supervised path. arXiv preprint arXiv:1910.02593 (2019)
31. Lugmayr, A., Danelljan, M., Timofte, R.: Unsupervised learning for real-world super-resolution. In: 2019 IEEE/CVF International Conference on Computer Vision Workshop (ICCVW), pp. 3408–3416. IEEE (2019)
32. Goodfellow, I., et al.: Generative adversarial nets. In: Advances in Neural Information Processing Systems, pp. 2672–2680 (2014)
33. Romano, Y., Isidoro, J., Milanfar, P.: RAISR: rapid and accurate image super resolution. IEEE Trans. Comput. Imaging 3, 110–125 (2016)
34. Chaudhuri, S.: Super-Resolution Imaging, vol. 632. Springer, Boston (2001). https://doi.org/10.1007/b117840
35. Zhang, L., Wu, X.: An edge-guided image interpolation algorithm via directional filtering and data fusion. IEEE Trans. Image Process. 15, 2226–2238 (2006)
36. Lai, W.S., Huang, J.B., Ahuja, N., Yang, M.H.: Deep Laplacian pyramid networks for fast and accurate super-resolution. In: Proceedings of the IEEE Conference on Computer Vision and Pattern Recognition, pp. 624–632 (2017)
37. Qu, C., Luo, D., Monari, E., Schuchert, T., Beyerer, J.: Capturing ground truth super-resolution data. In: 2016 IEEE International Conference on Image Processing (ICIP), pp. 2812–2816. IEEE (2016)
38. Köhler, T., Batz, M., Naderi, F., et al.: Bridging the simulated-to-real gap: benchmarking super-resolution on real data. Arxiv: 180906420 [Cs] (2018)
39. wesaturate: Photo sharing (2016). http://www.wesaturate.com
40. Glorot, X., Bengio, Y.: Understanding the difficulty of training deep feedforward neural networks. In: Proceedings of the Thirteenth International Conference on Artificial Intelligence and Statistics, pp. 249–256 (2010)

41. Kingma, D.P., Ba, J.: Adam: A method for stochastic optimization. arXiv preprint arXiv:1412.6980 (2014)
42. Mildenhall, B., Barron, J.T., Chen, J., Sharlet, D., Ng, R., Carroll, R.: Burst denoising with kernel prediction networks. In: Proceedings of the IEEE Conference on Computer Vision and Pattern Recognition. (2018) 2502–2510

Chromatic Aberration Correction Using Cross-Channel Prior in Shearlet Domain

Kunyi Li[iD] and Xin Jin[(✉)][iD]

Shenzhen International Graduate School, Tsinghua University, Shenzhen, China
li-ky19@mails.tsinghua.edu.cn, jin.xin@sz.tsinghua.edu.cn

Abstract. Instead of more expensive and complex optics, recent years, many researches are focused on high-quality photography using lightweight cameras, such as single-ball lens, with computational image processing. Traditional methods for image enhancement do not comprehensively address the blurring artifacts caused by strong chromatic aberrations in images produced by a simple optical system. In this paper, we propose a new method to correct both lateral and axial chromatic aberrations based on their different characteristics. To eliminate lateral chromatic aberration, cross-channel prior in shearlet domain is proposed to align texture information of red and blue channels to green channel. We also propose a new PSF estimation method to better correct axial chromatic aberration using wave propagation model, where F-number of the optical system is needed. Simulation results demonstrate our method can provide aberration-free images while there are still some artifacts in the results of the state-of-art methods. PSNRs of simulation results increase at least 2 dB and SSIM is on average 6.29% to 41.26% better than other methods. Real-captured image results prove that the proposed prior can effectively remove lateral chromatic aberration while the proposed PSF model can further correct the axial chromatic aberration.

1 Introduction

Modern camera lenses use a dozen of individual lens elements to minimize optical aberrations but it raises the cost and weight of cameras. Recent years, many researchers turn to much simpler optics such as single-chip lens [1], simple Fresnel lens [2] or the single-ball lens. However, there are still barriers to generate high-quality images with this kind of lightweight equipment. Chromatic aberration (CA) is one of the most severe problems. Because camera lenses have wavelength-dependent refractive indices, it is troublesome to make all color components converge to the same point [3,4]. This phenomenon often reflects at the edge areas of images. Usually, chromatic aberration can be divided into two categories: axial chromatic aberration (ACA) and lateral chromatic aberration (LCA). The former one may cause the effect of image blurring, which can be corrected by deconvolution, and the later one may cause geometric errors, which can be corrected by image processing [3].

© Springer Nature Switzerland AG 2021
H. Ishikawa et al. (Eds.): ACCV 2020, LNCS 12623, pp. 102–117, 2021.
https://doi.org/10.1007/978-3-030-69532-3_7

Traditional CA correction methods only focus on one chromatic aberration. Among those LCA correction methods, employing global warping is the most popular one [5]. These global warping methods need a pre-calibration process to estimate parameters. Noticing that CA mainly occurs near the edges, Kim B.K. et al. [6] proposed a method to detect and correct purple fringes using color information with large gradient magnitudes. Pixels in the detected purple fringing regions are desaturated to correct aberration. However, it only works for purple fringes but fails at other color fringes like green fringes. Kang H. et al. [7] developed a partial differential equation based on the study that the edges in the green channel are sharper than those in the red and blue channels. It matches the edges in the red and blue channels to green channel locally. Pi et al. [8] used a spatially variant model to match the gradient and intensity between the red or blue channels and the green channel at the edges. All these methods work well on LCA eliminating. However, without using PSF model of lens, the images are not able to correct ACA.

As for ACA correction, most of these methods choose to use PSFs to deconvolve the images. Schuler et al. [9] presented an aberration removal algorithm for a single lens in YUV color space, which results in a better image quality. He C. et al. [10] proposed a deblurring method using shearlet transform. The power of multiscale and multidirectional analysis and the ability of preserving details of images can be used to surpass the limitation of other methods. Instead of using PSFs for deconvolution, Hosseini et al. [11] proposed a method by convolving the blurry images with inversed PSFs to avoid iterative operation.

Heide F. et al. [1] introduced a convex cross-channel prior using normalized gradient information to correct both ACA and LCA. But it fails to work well on images with complex texture and severe aberrations, since it only uses vertical and horizontal gradient information.

As mentioned above, deconvolution methods with LCA correction priors can correct both two types of aberrations simultaneously, but they need the PSFs of lens. Thus, a proper PSF estimation is needed to acquire better image quality. PSF models are usually proposed by analyzing the statistic of different types of blurry and sharp images. In some circumstances, blur kernels are of parametric forms and these parameters can be estimated from blurry images including spectral methods [12] and edge-based methods [13]. Gokstorp et al. [14] employed the Gaussian function to approximate the blur kernel using a pair of sharp and defocused images. However, in common cases only blurry images are available. Oliveira et al. [15] presented an algorithm using the circular Radon transform. But it would fail for certain scenes because the frequency magnitudes are highly anisotropic. A General Gaussian model was proposed using edge detection and re-blur approach by Liu et al. [16]. It established a LUT between PSFs and parameters for further use. However, all of these methods were based on statistic models and ignored wave propagation characters.

In this paper, based on the distribution of color and texture information of images in RGB channels, we propose a robust aberration correction approach which corrects both LCA and ACA. Cross-channel prior in shearlet domain

(CC-SD prior) is introduced to align red and blue channels to green channel, the sharpest channel. Clear images are recovered and LCA is effectively suppressed. PSNR and SSIM have significant improvements in simulation results. Moreover, to deal with ACA in real-captured images, a more precise PSF estimation method based on wave propagation model is presented. Results demonstrate that CC-SD prior combined with wave propagation PSF model can remove LCA and ACA efficiently.

The rest of this paper is organized as follows. Section 2 presents analysis of color and texture information distribution and the CC-SD prior. Section 3 shows proposed PSF estimation model. Section 4 shows experimental results including simulations and real-captured images. Conclusion is drawn in Sect. 5.

2   Cross-Channel Prior in Shearlet Domain

In this section, we propose a new prior to deal with LCA, which takes edges from all direction into account and can handle much severer aberration. We start by demonstrating image restoration model and introducing the novel CC-SD prior to correct LCA. Then Alternating Direction Method of Multipliers (ADMM) is used to solve the minimization problem.

2.1   LCA Correction Model Using CC-SD Prior

Reconstructing the original image from blurry image can be carried out within the framework of image deconvolution. However, it is a well-known highly ill-posed problem because only blurry image is known. Regularization terms were introduced to constraint this problem. In general, many regularization methods lead to the following minimization function:

$$\min_{x} \|Hx - y\|_2^2 + \frac{\beta_1}{2} S(x) + \frac{\beta_2}{2} J(x), \tag{1}$$

where x denotes the recovered clear image. y is observed blurry image. The first term is called data fidelity term. H is the convolution operator related to spatially invariant PSF in matrix form. The second and third terms are regularization terms. $S(x)$ enforces a heavy-tailed distributed for gradients, like total-variation [17] or shearlet-regularization [10]. $J(x)$ implements a special constraint to correct LCA. β_1, β_2 are penalty factors which keep the compromise between the data fidelity term and the regularization terms.

The main idea of our proposed method is to align the image texture, like fringes, of red and blue channels to green channel. For red or blue channel, the regularization term $J(x)$ is defined as:

$$J(x) = \|T(x_G) - T(x)\|_2^2, \tag{2}$$

where x is latent red or blue channel image. $T(x)$ represents the texture information extracted from the red or blue channel. x_G is the green channel image

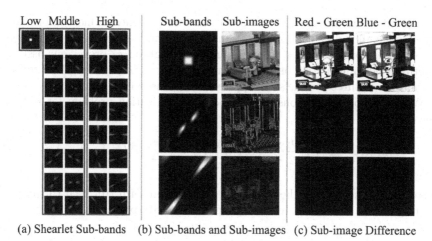

(a) Shearlet Sub-bands   (b) Sub-bands and Sub-images   (c) Sub-image Difference

Fig. 1. (a) Shearlet sub-bands in frequency domain. Images in blue, red and green rectangles are low-frequency, middle-frequency and high-frequency sub-bands, respectively. (b) Three sub-bands and their corresponding sub-images. First, second and last rows are images of one low-frequency, one middle-frequency and one high-frequency sub-bands and their corresponding sub-images, respectively. (c) Difference of sub-images between red/blue and green channel. The whiter the figures are, the larger difference is between two sub-images. (Color figure online)

recovered by an existing method, such as PSA method [10]. $T(x_G)$ represents the texture information extracted from green channel.

To extract texture information from images, instead of gradients which only use vertical and horizontal edge information, we apply shearlet transform [18–20] which is a multiscale and multidirectional analysis method. Shearlet transform of x can be implemented in frequency domain by component-wise multiplication:

$$SH_j(x) = \mathfrak{F}^{-1}(\hat{H}_j. * X), \tag{3}$$

where X denotes the Fourier transform of x and $\hat{H}_j$ is the frequency domain shearlet base of the jth sub-band. $.*$ denotes the component-wise multiplication operator. $\mathfrak{F}^{-1}(.)$ is the inverse Fourier transform operator. Shearlet transform decomposes the images into several sub-images in frequency domain, including one low frequency component and numbers of middle and high frequency components. The number of sub-bands depends on the shearlet level. Therefore, $T(x)$ can be written as:

$$T_i(x) = \mathfrak{F}^{-1}(\hat{H}_i. * X), \tag{4}$$

where $\hat{H}_i$ is the middle and high frequency sub-bands, $T_i(x)$ represents the corresponding sub-image of ith sub-band. Figure 1 shows the result of shearlet transform on an aberration-free image. Figure 1(a) demonstrates the sub-bands of a level 3 shearlet transform. These are filters of different frequency ranges and directions in frequency domain. Figure 1(b) shows three sub-bands and its corresponding sub-images. Low frequency sub-image contains most information of the image, including color information. Middle and high frequency sub-images are texture information of a selected direction. Figure 1(c) proves our assumption that color information only exists in low-frequency components and texture information of three channels are approximately the same.

With the above notations, the proposed optimization problem for red and blue channel is:

$$\min \|Hx - y\|_2^2 + \frac{\beta_1}{2} \sum_j \|\mathrm{SH}_j(x)\|_1 + \frac{\beta_2}{2} \sum_i \|\mathrm{T}_i(x_G) - \mathrm{T}_i(x)\|_2^2, \qquad (5)$$

where the second term is the shearlet-regularization term [10] used to suppress the ring effect. The third term is proposed CC-SD prior. β_1, β_2 are penalty factors.

2.2   Optimization Using ADMM

In this subsection, we use ADMM [21] to solve the optimization problem. To solve the L_1–norm simply, we introduce auxiliary variables f_i for each L_1-norm term. To avoid the inner iterations, another auxiliary variable u is employed for Hx. The corresponding augmented Lagrangian function is defined as:

$$\mathcal{L}(x, u, f; \mu, \xi, \gamma) \triangleq \frac{\alpha}{2}\|u - Hx\|_2^2 - < \mu, u - Hx > + \delta_\Omega(u) + \sum_j \|f_j\|_1$$

$$+ \frac{\beta_1}{2} \sum_j \|f_j - \mathrm{SH}_j(x)\|_2^2 - \sum_j < \xi_j, f_j - \mathrm{SH}_j(x) >$$

$$+ \frac{\beta_2}{2} \sum_i \|\mathrm{T}_i(x_G) - \mathrm{T}_i(x)\|_2^2 - \sum_i < \gamma_i, \mathrm{T}_i(x_G) - \mathrm{T}_i(x) >,$$

$$(6)$$

where f_i and u are auxiliary variables, and

$$\delta_\Omega(u) = \begin{cases} 0, & \text{if } u \in \Omega \triangleq \{u : \|u - y\|_2^2 \le c\} \\ +\infty, & \text{otherwise} \end{cases},$$

The inequality constraint is related to Morozov's discrepancy principle [22], $c = \tau n^2 \sigma^2$. σ^2 is the white noise variance of image. $\tau = -0.006 * BSNR + 1.09$, $BSNR = \log_{10}(\frac{\|y - mean(y)\|_2^2}{n^2 \sigma^2})$, μ, ξ_j, γ_i are Lagrange multipliers, $\alpha, \beta_1, \beta_2 \ge 0$ are penalty parameters. According ADMM, we can solve the following subproblems alternatively:

$$\begin{cases} x^{k+1} = \arg\min_x \dfrac{\alpha}{2}\|u^k - Hx - \dfrac{\mu^k}{\alpha_1}\|_2^2 + \dfrac{\beta_1}{2}\sum_j \|f_j^k - \mathrm{SH}_j(x) - \dfrac{\xi^k}{\beta_1}\|_2^2 \\ \qquad\qquad + \dfrac{\beta_2}{2}\sum_i \|\mathrm{T}_i(x_G) - \mathrm{T}_i(u) - \dfrac{\gamma^k}{\beta_2}\|_2^2 \\ f_j^{k+1} = \arg\min_{f_j} \|f_j\|_1 + \dfrac{\beta_1}{2}\|f_j - \mathrm{SH}_j(x^{k+1} - \dfrac{\xi_j^k}{\beta_1})\|_2^2 \\ u^{k+1} = \arg\min_u \delta_\Omega(u) + \dfrac{\alpha}{2}\|u - Hx^{k+1} - \dfrac{\mu^k}{\alpha}\|_2^2 \\ \mu^{k+1} = \mu^k - \alpha(u^{k+1} - Hx^{k+1}) \\ \xi_j^{k+1} = \xi^k - \beta_1(f_j^{k+1} - \mathrm{SH}_j(x^{k+1})) \\ \gamma_i^{k+1} = \gamma_i^k - \beta_2(\mathrm{T}_i(x_G) - \mathrm{T}_i(x)) \end{cases} \qquad (7)$$

The minimization subproblem with respect to x has three quadratic terms and can be solved through FFT and IFFT [17]. Subproblem respect to f_i can be expressed in the form of 1D soft-threshold shrinkage. And sub-problem with respect to u can be solved by He's method [10].

3   PSF Estimation Based on Wave Propagation

Previous section only focuses on LCA correction. In this section, we deal with ACA by proposing a new PSF estimation model for further deconvolution. The main influence of blurring reflects on edges. Therefore, the blurring degree of edges may determine parameters of PSF, like the shape and size. Here, we define a parameter called gradient ratio:

$$R = \frac{\nabla y}{\nabla y_1} = \frac{\nabla(h * x)}{\nabla(h * x * h_g(\sigma_0))} \qquad (8)$$

where y represents edge patches extracted from blurry image. y_1 represents a re-blurred edge patch using y convolve with a given Gaussian function. ∇ is the gradient operator. h is unknown PSF of the imaging system. Figure 2(a) and Fig. 2(b) illustrate the flow chart of the algorithm. First, edge detection is used. Figure 2(c) shows four templates for edge detection. Then, gradient ratio distribution R_0 of the blurry and re-blurred edges is computed [16] by $R_0 = \frac{\nabla y(0,0)}{\nabla y_1(0,0)}$. The remaining problem is to link R_0 with parameters of the unknown PSF h.

In the sub-sections, instead of only use the statistic model, wave propagation model is used to establish a LUT between R_0 and aberration parameters. Then, the computed R_0 can determine a unique PSF.

3.1   Wave Propagation Model

For any image system, aberrated pupil function is described as [23]:

$$\mathrm{P}(W_d, W_{040}; u, v) = \mathrm{circ}(\frac{\sqrt{u^2 + v^2}}{w_{XP}})\exp(-j\frac{2\pi}{\lambda}\mathrm{Sc}(W_d, W_{040}; \frac{u}{w_{XP}}, \frac{u}{w_{XP}})), \quad (9)$$

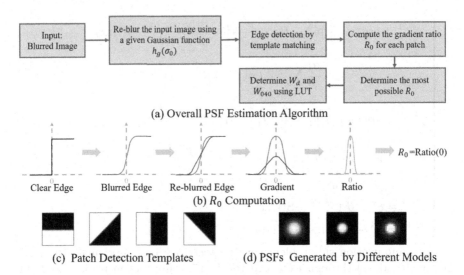

Fig. 2. (a) Flow chart of PSF estimation algorithm. (b) Flow chart of R_0 computation. (c) 4 templates for patch detection. (d) First column is a PSF generated by Gaussian model [22] where $\sigma_0 = (4, 2, 7)$. Second column is a PSF generated by General Gaussian model [15] where $\beta_0 = (1.9, 1.2, 2.2)$. Third column is a PSF generated by proposed model where $W_d = (-1, 0.5, 2)$ and $W_{040} = (0.4, 0.1, 0.5)$.(a) Flow chart of PSF estimation algorithm. (b) Flow chart of R_0 computation. (c) 4 templates for patch detection. (d) First column is a PSF generated by Gaussian model [22] where $\sigma_0 = (4, 2, 7)$. Second column is a PSF generated by General Gaussian model [15] where $\beta_0 = (1.9, 1.2, 2.2)$. Third column is a PSF generated by proposed model where $W_d = (-1, 0.5, 2)$ and $W_{040} = (0.4, 0.1, 0.5)$.

where $\mathrm{Se}(W_d, W_{040}; \frac{u}{w_{XP}}, \frac{v}{w_{XP}}) = W_d((\frac{u}{w_{XP}})^2 + (\frac{v}{w_{XP}})^2) + W_{040}((\frac{u}{w_{XP}})^2 + (\frac{v}{w_{XP}})^2)^2$ is Seidel Polynomials, which is used to describe aberrations for optical systems. W_d defines defocus aberration and W_{040} defines spherical aberration. u, v are physical coordinates of exit pupil. w_{XP} is the diameter of exit pupil. λ represents wavelength. And $\mathrm{circ}(X)$ is a circular function where $\mathrm{circ}(X) = 1$ if $X \leq 0.5$ and $\mathrm{circ}(X) = 0$ if $X > 0.5$. According to the computational Fourier optics [23], PSF of this image system can be written as

$$h_{WP}(W_d, W_{040}; u, v) = |\mathfrak{F}^{-1}\{P(W_d, W_{040}; -2\lambda w_{XP} f^{\#} f_U, -2\lambda w_{XP} f^{\#} f_V)\}|^2, \tag{10}$$

where $\mathfrak{F}^{-1}$ is inverse Fourier transform operator. $f^{\#}$ is F-number of the optical system, f_U, f_V is frequency of the senor plane, λ is wavelength. Figure 2(d) shows PSFs generated by different estimating models.

3.2 Establish the LUT Between W_d, W_{040} and R_0

PSF is assumed as spatially invariant. According to the gradient-based framework [24], the relationship between W_d, W_{040} and R_0 can be written as:

$$R_0 = \frac{\nabla y(0,0)}{\nabla y_1(0,0)} = \frac{\int_{-\infty}^{\infty} h_{WP}(W_d, W_{040}, 0, v) \, dv}{\int_{-\infty}^{\infty} h(W_d, W_{040}, \sigma_0, 0, v) \, dv} \tag{11}$$

where $h_{WP}(W_d, W_{040}, 0, v)$ denotes the magnitudes along the y-axis of blur kernel, and $h(W_d, W_{040}, \sigma_0, 0, v) = \iint_{-\infty}^{\infty} h_{WP}(W_d, W_{040}, u - \xi, v - \eta) h_g(\sigma_0, \xi, \eta) \, d\xi \, d\eta$. However, it is difficult to have an analytical solution among W_d, W_{040} and R_0, A LUT is pre-established by varying W_d and W_{040}, and corresponding R_0 can be calculated by Eq. (11). Using this LUT, Seidel parameters can be located by computing R_0 from blurry images. Then the PSF h can be reconstructed.

4 Experiments

In this section, we present experimental results including simulation results and real-captured images provided by our lens system which have severe optical aberrations. We apply the proposed method and make a comparison with other state-of-art methods. Codes of comparison methods are downloaded from GitHub provided by the authors.

4.1 Experiment Image Sets and Parameters Setting

Table 1. Computational Time (Seconds).

	IGM [8]	CC [1]	PSA [10]	IDBP [25]	TRI [26]	1Shot [11]	Proposed
Buildings	683	1668	674	787	/	/	**860**
Cars	689	1968	680	779	/	/	**854**
LEGO	687	1758	674	773	/	/	**857**
Windows	689	1974	680	763	/	/	**858**
LEGO	685	1570	677	1057	454	0.58	**862**
Taxi	692	1281	678	917	521	0.45	**865**
Workers	696	1944	676	946	456	0.25	**866**

Four simulation images and three captured images are tested. The size of each image is $720 * 720$. These images are suitable for illustrating the potential of proposed algorithm, because they possess abundant details.

Simulation images are captured by Sony ILCE 7 Mark 3 with Tamron 28–75 lens, one of the best commercial cameras, which can be regarded as aberration-free images. Images include one indoor scene, image LEGO, and three outdoor

(a) Single-ball lens system   (b) Estimated PSFs

Fig. 3. (a) Single-ball lens with a 4F system. The ball lens and sensor are shown in orange and red rectangles, respectively. (b) Estimated PSFs of single-ball lens system.

scenes. Image Buildings and image Cars have rich texture details. Image Windows shows a significant color bias. To get blurry images, we convolved each image in three channels with different blur kernel, as shown in Fig. 2(d).

Real-captured images are acquired from our sing-ball lens system, as shown in Fig. 3(a). Image Taxi shows a blue toy car while the wheel appears significant purple fringe. Image Workers suffers less chromatic aberration but still there is a green fringe on the face of the toy worker. Image LEGO is much vaguer which makes it more difficult to estimate PSF.

To balance the convergence speed and result performance, we set $\alpha = 10 * \beta_1, \beta_1 = \beta_2 = 1$ in the simulation process and $\alpha = 0.1 * \beta_1, \beta_1 = \beta_2 = 1$ in real-captured images process. For shearlet transform, ShearLab 3D toolbox is used and a shearlet level 3 is set. During PSF estimation process, we set $f^{\#} = 1.2$. W_d and W_{040} vary from -3 to 3 and 0.1 to 2 with an interval of 0.05, respectively, while we establish LUT. Experiments are tested on a PC with Intel® Core™ i7-9700 CPU 3.00GHz and 8GB RAM. Time consumption is shown in Table 1.

4.2 Comparison of Simulation Results

In this sub-section, we compared the proposed CC-SD prior with other 4 state-of-art methods, including methods which only use convex optimization, methods which only process deblurring, and methods which correct color fringes while deblurring. Pi et al. [8] presented a convex optimization method using intensity and gradient matchings (IGM). But it only corrects LCA. Heide F. et al. tried to align three channels by a Cross-Channel prior [1] while deblurring. The results of PSA method [10] demonstrate that our CC-SD prior indeed corrects the color misalign. IDBP [25] solves the inverse problems using off-the-shelf denoisers, which requires less parameter tuning. All algorithms in this sub-section were fed with the same PSFs for deconvolution, and ran until the per-iteration change fell below a given threshold. As for the evaluation criterion, PSNR and SSIM are shown in this section and visual performance is also considered. As for visual performance evaluation, we mainly focus on the sharpness and color consistency of edges.

Figure 4, 5, 6 and 7 demonstrate 4 different results. In each figure, sub-figure (a) is the original image, and sub-figure (b) is the blurry image. Three selected areas are magnified and fringes can be seen distinctly. Sub-figures (c) to (f) are

Table 2. PSNR (dB)/SSIM Comparison of Simulation result.

	Blurry	IGM [8]	CC [1]	PSA [10]	IDBP [25]	Proposed
Buildings	18.40/0.54	20.58/0.63	18.88/0.80	20.76/0.81	20.40/0.78	**24.64/0.89**
Cars	19.70/0.63	21.58/0.71	19.98/0.81	22.37/0.84	22.01/0.83	**25.11/0.90**
LEGO	24.46/0.88	26.48/0.92	24.25/0.88	29.28/0.96	28.48/0.95	**31.90/0.98**
Windows	19.09/0.66	20.81/0.73	19.39/0.82	21.44/0.95	21.08/0.85	**24.71/0.91**

recovered images using the state-of-art algorithms and sub-figure (g) is recovered image using our CC-SD prior.

Figure 4 shows a number of buildings. The result of IGM method shows the least color fringes, however it causes desaturation and image is still blurry. Since these details are small but rich, Cross-Channel method only recovers a sharper image but the color fringes are still existed. Our proposed algorithm presents a sharp image with almost none color fringe. Figure 5 shows a business street. There is a significant degradation on advertising boards after blurring. Among these recovery algorithms, our result is the most approximate one to the original image. In Fig. 6, our algorithm shows a better performance in sharpness and color consistency as well. Figure 7 displays a yellow wall with a white window, in which exists a distinct color bias. Due to advantage of CC-SD prior, color bias cannot interfere the performance of our algorithm. However, result of Cross-Channel Prior shows an obvious color shift. PSA and IDBP methods provide acceptable results but still with some purple fringes.

PSNR and SSIM of all methods is demonstrated in Table 2. Note that our algorithm consistently outperforms than others. Overall, the proposed method is able to reconstruct the textures and show more clear and clean edges than other approaches.

4.3   Comparison of Real-Captured Image Results

In this sub-section, all algorithms contain two steps, PSFs estimation and image deconvolution, except for IGM method. Proposed algorithm is compared with other 6 state-of-art methods. Cross-Channel Prior [1], PSA [10] and IDBP [25] were fed with the same PSFs estimated by proposed wave-propagation method. TRI [26] method uses the three segments of intensity prior which is motivated by that the blur process destroys the sparsity of intensity, and shrinks the distance between two distinct gray levels. 1ShotMaxPol [11] calculates the inversed PSF and convolves with images to avoid iterative process. The results of proposed prior without ACA correctionis are also present to show the effect of LCA and ACA correction, respectively.

For real-captured images, we only compared the visual performance of each methods. Figure 8, 9 and 10 demonstrate the captured blurry images and results using different methods. The corresponding estimated PSFs are shown in Fig. 3(b). Three different scenes were tested and a square area has been magnified to demonstrate details of results. Although some approaches may have

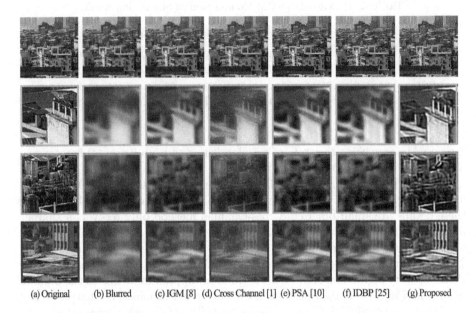

(a) Original   (b) Blurred   (c) IGM [8] (d) Cross Channel [1] (e) PSA [10]   (f) IDBP [25]   (g) Proposed

Fig. 4. Buildings. Full images and three selected areas marked by yellow, red and green rectangles respectively. (Color figure online)

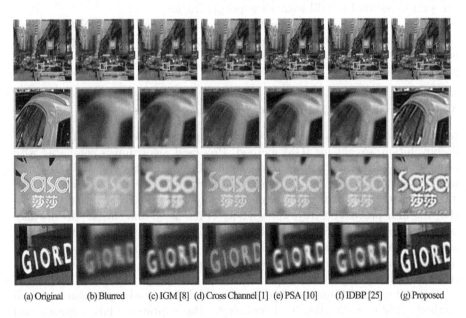

(a) Original   (b) Blurred   (c) IGM [8] (d) Cross Channel [1] (e) PSA [10]   (f) IDBP [25]   (g) Proposed

Fig. 5. Cars. Full images and three selected areas marked by yellow, red and green rectangles respectively. (Color figure online)

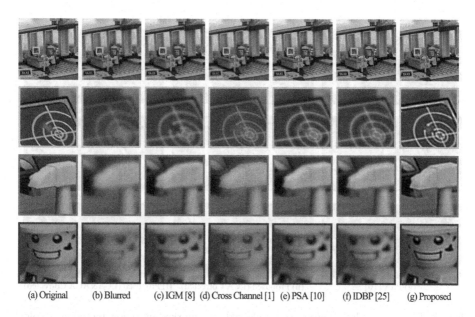

(a) Original   (b) Blurred   (c) IGM [8] (d) Cross Channel [1] (e) PSA [10]   (f) IDBP [25]   (g) Proposed

Fig. 6. LEGO. Full images and three selected areas marked by yellow, red and green rectangles respectively. (Color figure online)

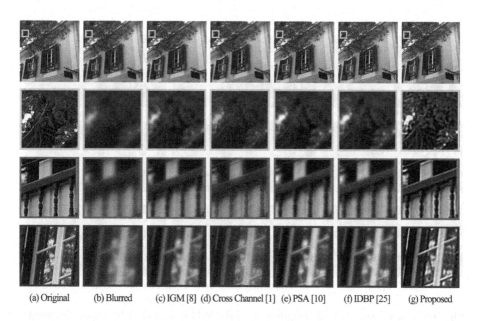

(a) Original   (b) Blurred   (c) IGM [8] (d) Cross Channel [1] (e) PSA [10]   (f) IDBP [25]   (g) Proposed

Fig. 7. Windows. Full images and three selected areas marked by yellow, red and green rectangles respectively. (Color figure online)

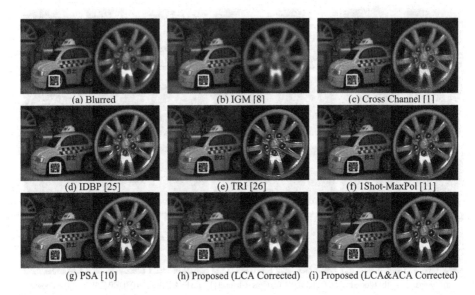

Fig. 8. Taxi. (a)–(i) Full images and a selected area marked by yellow rectangle. (Color figure online)

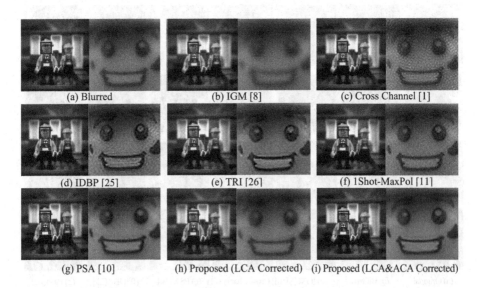

Fig. 9. Workers. (a)–(i) Full images and a selected area marked by yellow rectangle. (Color figure online)

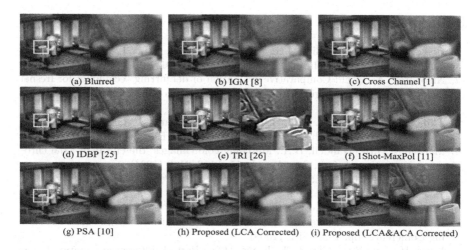

Fig. 10. LEGO. (a)–(i) Full images and a selected area marked by yellow rectangle. (Color figure online)

more clear edges, it may increase some artifacts as cost, such as ring effect and distinct noise. IGM method eliminates the color fringes effectively. The wheel of captured image has severe purple fringes. Figure 8(b) shows a totally chromatic-aberration-free but it is still blurry. Figure 8 and Fig. 9 have a certain degree of color deviation and affect the results of Cross-Channel method significantly. All results of TRI method have a sense of smear in images, as Fig. 10(e) shows. 1Shot-MaxPol method provides good quality of images but raises some regular unnatural texture and color fringes still can be seen. Results of PSA method show sharp images but contain color fringes. Results of LCA correction only, like Fig. 9(h), show chromatic-aberration-free images but they remain blurry. The proposed method produces both sharp images and correct images.

5   Conclusion

In the current study, a novel LCA correction method was conducted by introducing the cross-channel prior in shearlet domain. Employing the CC-SD prior while deconvolving, we corrected both LCA and ACA. Details can be preserved and image quality can be promoted by our method. Wave-propagation model for PSFs estimation was proposed to help deal with ACA in real-captured images. This model takes Seidel Polynomials into account and surpasses the limitation of statistic models. Experiments indicated that the proposed algorithm is competitive in PSNR, SSIM and visual performance.

Acknowledgment. The work was supported in part by National Natural Science Foundation of China (Grant No. 61827804 and 61991450).

References

1. Heide, F., Rouf, M., Hullin, M.B., Labitzke, B., Kolb, A.J.A.T.O.G.: High-quality computational imaging through simple lenses **32**, 1491–14914 (2013)
2. Nikonorov, A., et al.: Comparative evaluation of deblurring techniques for fresnel lens computational imaging. In: 2016 23rd International Conference on Pattern Recognition (ICPR), pp. 775–780 (2016)
3. Thibos, L.N., Bradley, A., Still, D.L., Zhang, X., Howarth, P.A.J.V.R.: Theory and measurement of ocular chromatic aberration. Vision. Res. **30**, 33–49 (1990)
4. Marimont, D.H., Wandell, B.A.: Matching color images: the effects of axial chromatic aberration. J. Opt. Soc. Am. A: **11**, 3113–3122 (1994)
5. Boult, T.E., Wolberg, G.: Correcting chromatic aberrations using image warping. In: CVPR, pp. 684–687 (1992)
6. Kim, B.K., Park, R.H.: Automatic detection and correction of purple fringing using the gradient information and desaturation. In: 2008 16th European Signal Processing Conference, pp. 1–5. IEEE (2008)
7. Kang, H., Lee, S.H., Chang, J., Kang, M.G.: Partial differential equation-based approach for removal of chromatic aberration with local characteristics. J. Electron. Imaging **19**, 033016 (2010)
8. Pi, L., Wang, W., Ng, M.: A spatially variant total variational model for chromatic aberration correction. J. Vis. Commun. Image Represent. **41**, 296–304 (2016)
9. Schuler, C.J., Hirsch, M., Harmeling, S., Schölkopf, B.: Non-stationary correction of optical aberrations. In: 2011 International Conference on Computer Vision, pp. 659–666. IEEE (2011)
10. He, C., Hu, C.H., Zhang, W.: Adaptive shearlet-regularized image deblurring via alternating direction method. In: 2014 IEEE International Conference on Multimedia and Expo (ICME), pp. 1–6. IEEE (2014)
11. Hosseini, M.S., Plataniotis, K.N.: Convolutional deblurring for natural imaging. IEEE Trans. Image Process. **29**, 250–264 (2019)
12. Bovik, A.C.: Handbook of Image and Video Processing. Academic Press, New York (2010)
13. Joshi, N., Szeliski, R., Kriegman, D.J.: PSF estimation using sharp edge prediction. In: 2008 IEEE Conference on Computer Vision and Pattern Recognition, pp. 1–8. IEEE (2008)
14. Gokstorp, M.: Computing depth from out-of-focus blur using a local frequency representation. In: Proceedings of 12th International Conference on Pattern Recognition, vol. 1, pp. 153–158. IEEE (1994)
15. Oliveira, J.P., Figueiredo, M.A., Bioucas-Dias, J.M.: Parametric blur estimation for blind restoration of natural images: linear motion and out-of-focus. IEEE Trans. Image Process. **23**, 466–477 (2013)
16. Liu, Y.Q., Du, X., Shen, H.L., Chen, S.J.: Estimating generalized gaussian blur kernels for out-of-focus image deblurring. IEEE Trans. Circuits Syst. Video Technol. (2020)
17. Wen, Y.W., Chan, R.H.: Parameter selection for total-variation-based image restoration using discrepancy principle. IEEE Trans. Image Process. **21**, 1770–1781 (2011)
18. Easley, G., Labate, D., Lim, W.Q.: Sparse directional image representations using the discrete shearlet transform. Appl. Comput. Harmonic Anal. **25**, 25–46 (2008)
19. Lim, W.Q.: The discrete shearlet transform: a new directional transform and compactly supported shearlet frames. IEEE Trans. Image Process. **19**, 1166–1180 (2010)

20. Kutyniok, G., Lim, W.Q., Reisenhofer, R.: Shearlab 3D: Faithful digital shearlet transforms based on compactly supported shearlets. ACM Trans. Math. Software (TOMS) **42**, 1–42 (2016)

21. Xie, S., Rahardja, S.: Alternating direction method for balanced image restoration. IEEE Trans. Image Process. **21**, 4557–4567 (2012)

22. Colton, D., Piana, M., Potthast, R.: A simple method using Morozov's discrepancy principle for solving inverse scattering problems. Inverse Prob. **13**, 1477 (1997)

23. Voelz, D.: Computational fourier optics: a matlab tutorial, Society of Photo-Optical Instrumentation Engineers (2011)

24. Zhuo, S., Sim, T.: Defocus map estimation from a single image. Pattern Recogn. **44**, 1852–1858 (2011)

25. Tirer, T., Giryes, R.: Image restoration by iterative denoising and backward projections. IEEE Trans. Image Process. **28**, 1220–1234 (2018)

26. Zhang, H., Wu, Y., Zhang, L., Zhang, Z., Li, Y.: Image deblurring using tri-segment intensity prior. Neurocomputing (2020)

Raw-Guided Enhancing Reprocess of Low-Light Image via Deep Exposure Adjustment

Haofeng Huang$^{(\boxtimes)}$, Wenhan Yang, Yueyu Hu, and Jiaying Liu

Peking University, Beijing, People's Republic of China
{huang6013,yangwenhan,huyy,liujiaying}@pku.edu.cn

Abstract. Enhancement of images captured in low-light conditions remains to be a challenging problem even with the advanced machine learning techniques. The challenges include the ambiguity of the ground truth for a low-light image and the loss of information during the RAW image processing. To tackle the problems, in this paper, we take a novel view to regard low-light image enhancement as an exposure time adjustment problem and propose a corresponding explicit and mathematical definition. Based on that, we construct a RAW-Guiding exposure time adjustment Network (RGNET), which overcomes RGB images' nonlinearity and RAW images' inaccessibility. That is, RGNET is only trained with RGB images and corresponding RAW images, which helps project nonlinear RGB images into a linear domain, simultaneously without using RAW images in the testing phase. Furthermore, our network consists of three individual sub-modules for unprocessing, reconstruction and processing, respectively. To the best of our knowledge, the proposed sub-net for unprocessing is the first learning-based unprocessing method. After the joint training of three parts, each pre-trained seperately with the RAW image guidance, experimental results demonstrate that RGNET outperforms state-of-the-art low-light image enhancement methods.

1 Introduction

Low-light environments lead to several kinds of degradations in imaging, including low visibility, intensive noise, color cast, *etc.* Modern digital cameras provide options to tackle the problem but all these options have their drawbacks. For example, high ISO leads to amplified noise, and long exposure time introduces blurring effects. Thus, there is a demand for enhancement methods to handle various degradation for images captured in low light conditions. Early attempts [1,2] focus on the adjustment of global illumination, *e.g.* histogram equalization. Later on, Retinex theory-based methods [3–5] decompose the image into reflectance and illumination layers, and adopt specially designed priors on these two layers for detail preservation and noise suppression.

Electronic supplementary material The online version of this chapter (https://doi.org/10.1007/978-3-030-69532-3_8) contains supplementary material, which is available to authorized users.

© Springer Nature Switzerland AG 2021
H. Ishikawa et al. (Eds.): ACCV 2020, LNCS 12623, pp. 118–133, 2021.
https://doi.org/10.1007/978-3-030-69532-3_8

Recent works [6–9] approach higher-fidelity enhancement of low-light images with learning-based methods, and they show promising performance on the tasks. Despite that, most of the learning-based methods need low/normal light image pairs for supervised training. However, in real applications, a smaller distortion between the reconstructed image and the only preset ground truth in the training set does not necessarily correspond to the enhancement performance, due to the mapping ambiguity (one normal-light image might correspond to several low-light images, and what "normal-light" is has not been appropriately defined as well).

Besides, there have also been works to improve the quality of images by adjusting the RAW image processing pipeline [10] or to unprocess the images for easier enhancement [11–13]. Because intensities in RAW images maintain the linear relationship with the number of photons captured by the sensor in the physical world, it facilitates the analysis and enhancement of the images. However, RAW representations are sometimes hard to obtain in real application scenarios (need to change the existing ISP systems in many scenarios). And such methods are usually designed for professional image processing on specific devices, e.g. digital single-lens reflex (DSLR) and other high-end cameras.

As in practical photography, expanding the exposure time in a steady shot significantly helps improve the Signal-to-Noise Ratio (SNR) and therefore enhances the image quality. Thus, in this paper, we define the low light enhancement task as to simulate the long exposure operation in image capture. It can practically result in adjusting the illumination and restore derivative degradation. We further utilize RAW signals in the training phase which are proportional to the exposure time with fixed settings. For that, we propose the RAW-Guiding exposure time adjustment Network (RGNET). RGNET is trained on processed RGB images and simultaneously takes RAW images as the guidance during the training phase, while it does not rely on any RAW images in real applications considering its unusualness. Experimental results show that our approach outperforms multiple state-of-the-art approaches both quantitatively and qualitatively. The contributions of this work are summarized as follows,

- We take a novel view of the low-light enhancement, and propose an explicit and mathematical definition of the task, i.e. a simulation of expanding the exposure time during the capturing. Exposure time adjustment can be formulated as solving the joint problem of illumination adjustment and the derivative degradation restoration. The illumination adjustment is handled by the amplifying RAW signals in linear style, and the enhancement network focuses on tackling the derivative degradation with the learning techniques.
- We propose the RAW-guiding exposure time adjustment network to enhance the quality of images captured in low-light conditions. During the training phase, the network is tuned with the guidance of the corresponding RAW images. And it achieves improved quality in the benchmark where the RAW images are not available.
- To the best of our knowledge, we are the first to adopt a learning-based unprocessing sub-network to facilitate the RAW-guiding low-light image enhancement pipeline. With the proposed sub-network and other enhancing components, the framework achieves state-of-the-art performance in the low-light image enhancement task.

2   Related Work

2.1   Traditional Methods

A traditional way to make dark images visible is stretc.hing the dynamic range of an image via manipulating the corresponding histogram, *i.e.*, HE [1], which applies the adjustment globally. With more side information and constraints, *e.g.* mean intensity preservation, HE-based methods [2,14,15] improve local adaptability of the enhancement. Some methods [16] regard the inverted low-light images as haze images, and enhance the visibility by dehazing, then the result is inverted back as the output. A wide range of methods [17,18] are carefully designed to depict desirable properties of images with statistical models *e.g.* based on imaging or visual perception guided models. Due to the lack of flexibility for the visual property, these methods basically fail in extreme low-light conditions.

Retinex model [19] is proposed to compute visual appearance at first, which is generally adopted in low-light image enhancement afterwards. The methods [3,4,20] decompose images into reflectance and illumination, then unique enhancement follows and enhanced results are combined into final outputs in designed style. Retinex-based methods generally assume that the images contain good representations of the scene content, do not model image noise and typically apply denoising as a post-process, but in fact, the severe noise in considered extreme low-light imaging affects decomposing part heavily [10].

2.2   Learning-Based Methods

Adopting deep-learning methods in low-light enhancement starts in 2017, and this branch's excellent performance and flexibility make it mainstream instead. Lore *et al.* [6] made the first efforts in using a deep auto-encoder named LLNet to perform enhancement and denoising. Then, various learning-based methods [8,9,21,22] are proposed. Among them, SICE [8] builds a dataset of low-contrast and good-contrast image pairs, making the discrimination learning of SICE enhancers possible. KinD [9] builds a network to decomposes images into two components inspired by the Retinex theory and adjust light levels arbitrarily. In addition, KinD proposes that no ground-truth real data exists for low light image enhancement. DeepUPE [21] constructs a network for enhancing underexposed photos and introduces intermediate illumination in it to associate the input with expected enhancement result. However, ignored by most methods, there stands a basic problem for low-light supervised learning and fair evaluation, *i.e.* what is the ground truth corresponding to a low-light image. An outstanding method trained to handle images in 10 lux illumination even totally fails to produce a visible result in 0.1 lux condition sometimes.

Moreover, there are RAW-based works for low light enhancement. SID [10] builds the first low-light RAW dataset and proposes a pipeline to directly produce normal-light sRGB images from low-light RAW files. With the similar considering, low light video enhancement methods [23,24] are constructed, providing low-light RAW videos. Nevertheless, RAW files' unusualness limits their generalization.

2.3   Datasets

As data-driven methods emerge, some datasets are collected for training and evaluations in low light enhancement. On the one hand, for convenience and to avoid misalignment, synthetic datasets [6,7] generate corresponding low-light images based on a certain strategy. On the other hand, synthetic style is highly coupled with the adopted strategy and constantly mismatches real-world data, therefore some datasets [8] capture real low/normal-light image pairs, which is accomplished by firmly fixing the camera and taking pictures with different camera settings, *e.g.* exposure. Among them, SID [10], DRV [23], SMOID [24] provide RAW files. Additionally, there are datasets [21,22] including both synthetic and real data to trade off and unpaired datasets [5] without ground truth.

Specific to exposure time adjustment task, RAW images are required to simulate the unprocess/process stages, whose meta-data records exposure time as a label for our method as well. Because DRV and SMOID serve for video enhancement, we adopt SID as the dataset for training and evaluation.

3   RAW-Guiding Exposure Time Adjustment Network

3.1   Motivation

As mentioned in Sect. 1, there is currently not an explicit and mathematical definition for what the corresponding ground truth is, given a low-light image. Naturally, the low light image enhancement problem is highly ill-posed. "There are a thousand Hamlets in a thousand people's eyes." There are different criteria for the best desirable lightness for different people or from different perspectives [9], which results in difficulties to evaluate the generalization performance of low light enhancement methods. To get rid of this dilemma, we treat the low light enhancement as a novel task, *i.e.* exposure time adjustment. That is, given an image and an exposure ratio, the corresponding ground truth is the image shot in the identical static scene with the same settings but the exposure time multiplied by the given ratio. Obviously, from this perspective, the low light enhancement is equivalent to amplifying the exposure time, which, as we will discuss below, has concise mathematical form and yields conveniences for a controllable and deterministic low light image enhancement process. In the following parts, Sect. 3.2 describes a simplified traditional image processing pipeline and Sect. 3.3 explains how RGNET is constructed based on this pipeline, as shown in Fig. 1.

3.2   RAW Image Pipeline

Modern digital cameras are equipped with mature image processing systems, proceeding the raw sensor data into a relatively less noisy and pleasant looking image. Because the specific processing systems are held by camera manufacturers as commercial secrets, we regard the related details, *i.e.* specific system design and parameter selection, as black boxes in our discussion. In spite of that, we describe a conventional image processing pipeline similar to [11], establish a

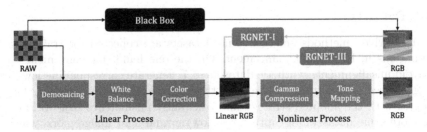

(a) Image Processing Stages

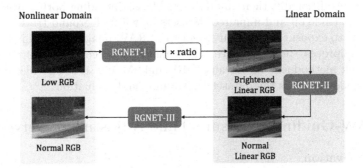

(b) RAW-Guiding Exposure Time Adjustment Network

Fig. 1. (a) The top path is a real camera image processing system, a black box in our discussion, and the lower path is a simplified conventional pipeline. The proposed RGNET-I and RGNET-III, simulate transformations between actual RGB and linear RGB. (b) The proposed method adopts three subnets to complete transformations and reconstruction in the linear domain.

concise mathematical model, and fully utilize the linear parts to bridge the gap between RAW and RGB. Note that, our designed deep network method follows the paradigm of the conventional image processing pipeline and however do not rely on the detailed knowledge of any specific system.

Shot and Read Noise. The noise model in RAW is undisturbed, without nonlinearity induced by the process. As a simple consensus, sensor noise in RAW comes from two sources, usually named shot noise and read noise [25]. With the fixed settings of aperture and ISO, the noise level λ_{read} and λ_{shot} of two kinds of noise are considered as constants and the mean value x is proportional to the exposure time. Specifically, shooting with the short exposure time in the low light environment, sensor data in RAW is formulated as follows[1],

$$y_s^{raw} \sim \mathcal{N}(\mu_s, \sigma_s^2) \tag{1}$$

---

[1] The real noise model in low light is clipped and more complex [26] but it does not impact our discussion.

with $\mu_s = x_s$, $\sigma_s^2 = \lambda_{read} + \lambda_{shot}x_s$. With the exposure time ratio γ, the corresponding long-exposure data, which is regarded to be noise-free by convention, can be represented as follows,

$$y_l^{raw} = x_l = \gamma x_s,\tag{2}$$

x, $y \in R^{m \times n \times 1}$. Therefore, the low light enhancement becomes a denoising task in the RAW domain with the brightened y_s^{raw} as follows,

$$y_b^{raw} = \gamma y_s^{raw} \sim \mathcal{N}(\mu_b, \sigma_b^2)\tag{3}$$

with $\mu_b = \gamma x_s$, $\sigma_b^2 = \gamma^2 \lambda_{read} + \gamma \lambda_{shot}(\gamma x_s)$. The subscript s denotes "with short exposure", l denotes for "with long exposure" and b denotes "brightened".

Demosaicing. Because the sensor only captures photons, imperceptible of the chromatic light, each pixel in a camera is covered by a colored filter which arranges in some patterns, *e.g.* R-G-G-B for Bayer. Demosaicing is the processing stage to reconstruct the full-size image with all three color channels. We simply split the R-G-G-B pattern into RGB channels with green channels averaged and employ bilinear interpolation to demosaic. For concise illustration, we view this stage as detail reconstruction and just modify shapes of x and y into $m \times n \times 3$.

White Balance and Color Correction. Owing to that the color temperature of the ambient light effects filtered sensor data, the camera adopts a white balance to simulate human eyes' adaptation, *i.e.* producing an image that appears under the normal illumination. This stage is proceeded with three channels multiplied by individual weights w_c ($c = r, g, b$), recorded in the RAW file. Note that the light metering process in low light environments is inaccurate, which leads to biases in those weights (denoted by $\widehat{w_c}$), which call for further calibration.

$$y_s^{wb} = y_s^{raw} * \widehat{W},$$
$$y_l^{wb} = y_l^{raw} * W,\tag{4}$$

with $\widehat{W} = [[[\widehat{w_r}, \widehat{w_g}, \widehat{w_b}]]]_{1 \times 1 \times 3}$ and $W = [[[w_r, w_g, w_b]]]_{1 \times 1 \times 3}$.

The following stage is color correction, during which the camera applies a 3×3 color correction matrix (CCM) to convert the camera color space to a required one, *i.e.* sRGB color space. The CCM M_{cc} can be obtained with the meta-data in RAW files.

$$y^{linear} = y^{cc}{}_{3 \times (m \times n)} = \begin{pmatrix} y_r^{cc} \\ y_g^{cc} \\ y_b^{cc} \end{pmatrix} = \begin{pmatrix} y_r^{wb} \\ y_g^{wb} \\ y_b^{wb} \end{pmatrix} M_{cc}.\tag{5}$$

For convenience, y^{cc} is also named y^{linear} and the procedure to transform y^{raw} into y^{linear} is called "linear process".

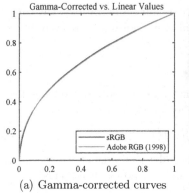

(a) Gamma-corrected curves   (b) brightened RGB

Fig. 2. (a) The Gamma-corrected curves based on the sRGB standard and Adobe RGB (1998) standard. (b) Brightened RGB images. The original image adopts sRGB-standard Gamma compression, and the left is brightened according to sRGB-standard Gamma function but the other uses Adobe RGB (1998) standard.

Gamma Compression and Tone Mapping. For the sake of human-vision pleasantness, nonlinear procedures follow, which usually consist of Gamma compression and tone mapping. We skip the details of both stages and simply define a function $\sigma(\cdot)$ to express the nonlinearity they introduce, named "nonlinear process".

$$y^{rgb} = \sigma(y^{cc}).\tag{6}$$

As shown in Fig. 2, without using an accurate Gamma compression (the right), it induces a huge gap between the brightened images although the two Gamma-corrected curves approach.[2] Apparently, the wrong brightened one mismatches the normal brightness.

3.3   Network Architecture

The proposed method, with a trade-off between the inaccessibility of RAW images in the testing phase (if we do no change the standard ISP process) and the expedience of adjusting exposure time in the linear domain, adopts RAW-Guiding exposure time adjustment Network (RGNET). RGNET is only trained with RGB images and RAW images, which helps project the nonlinear RGB images into a linear domain, simultaneously without the need of RAW images in the testing phase. Furthermore, considering the difficulty of totally inverting the process, RGNET exploits a linear process defined in Sect. 3.2 with RAW files' meta-data to bridge the gap between RGB images and RAW images, linearity kept. The specific architecture is shown in Fig. 3.

---

[2] Brightening follows the procedure of inverting the Gamma compression, multiplying by the ratio, applying Gamma compression.

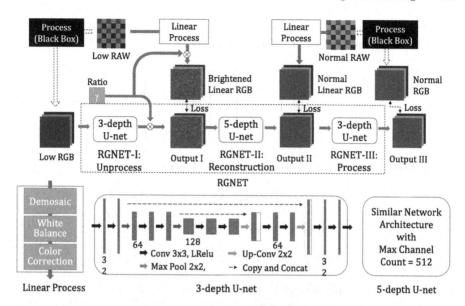

Fig. 3. The architecture of the proposed RAW-Guiding exposure time adjustment Network (RGNET). Fully utilizing the RAW file of low/normal light image, RGNET functionally implements unprocessing, reconstruction and processing, corresponding subnets named RGNET-I, RGNET-II and RGNET-III.

RGNET consists of three sub-modules: RGNET-I for unprocessing RGB images into a linear domain, RGNET-II for dealing with the amplified noise and color casting induced by the inaccurate white balance, RGNET-III for processing the enhanced results back into the nonlinear domain.

Note that as the pipeline introduce in Sect. 3.2 is a simplified one, the real processing systems may be different. With that being said, RGNET-I and RGNET-III not only simulate nonlinear stages but also aim to cope with the gap between linear stages real systems adopt and ours, *e.g.* different interpolation algorithms for demosaicing.

RGNET-I: Nonlinear Unprocess. As RGB images provide no relevant metadata about the pipeline, the traditional method [11] that converts the processed nonlinear RGB images into the linear ones is hand-crafted, which might not be consistent with the real applications. The inconsistency leads to inaccuracy of the estimation, which is further amplified simultaneously when data multiplies by the ratio, as shown in Fig. 2. Consequently, we employ an end-to-end convolutional neural network, *i.e.* a three-layer U-Net [27] to perform the task, which fits the function σ'.

More exactly, given the processed inputs y_s^{rgb} and linear targets y_s^{linear}, RGNET-I aims to output $\widehat{y}_s^{linear} = \widehat{\sigma}'(y_s^{rgb})$ after training.

RGNET-II: Normal-Light Image Reconstruction. Multiplied by the ratio, the brightened linear RGB images become:

$$y_s^{linear} \times \gamma = \begin{pmatrix} \gamma y_{s,r}^{cc} \\ \gamma y_{s,g}^{cc} \\ \gamma y_{s,b}^{cc} \end{pmatrix} = \begin{pmatrix} \widehat{w_r}\gamma y_{s,r}^{raw} \\ \widehat{w_g}\gamma y_{s,g}^{raw} \\ \widehat{w_b}\gamma y_{s,b}^{raw} \end{pmatrix} M_{cc}. \tag{7}$$

Comparison to the long-exposure linear RGB images

$$y_l^{linear} = \begin{pmatrix} y_{l,r}^{cc} \\ y_{l,g}^{cc} \\ y_{l,b}^{cc} \end{pmatrix} = \begin{pmatrix} w_r y_{l,r}^{raw} \\ w_g y_{l,g}^{raw} \\ w_b y_{l,b}^{raw} \end{pmatrix} M_{cc} = \begin{pmatrix} w_r \gamma x_{s,r} \\ w_g \gamma x_{s,g} \\ w_b \gamma x_{s,b} \end{pmatrix} M_{cc}, \tag{8}$$

and according to Eq. (3), RGNET-II targets to denoise with a noise level $\gamma^2 \lambda_{read}$ and $\gamma \lambda_{shot}$ and to correct the color casting introduced by inaccurate white balance $\widehat{W}$. Considering the convolution networks' effectivity in image/video denoising [28,29] and color correction [10,23], we employ a five-layer U-Net as RGNET-II. The fitted denoising and color restoration function is simply denoted as $f(\cdot)$.

Specifically, given brightened inputs $y_s^{linear} \times \gamma$ and long-exposure linear targets y_l^{linear}, RGNET-II targets to output $\widehat{y_l^{rgb}} = \widehat{f}(y_s^{linear} \times \gamma)$.

RGNET-III: Nonlinear Process. Convolution networks in image processing achieve superior performance and become a common choice [30–32], which provides firm reasons for us to employ an end-to-end CNN *i.e.* three-layer U-Net to model the nonlinear process, identical to RGNET-I.

To be exact, given the long-exposure linear input y_l^{linear} and the corresponding nonlinear RGB target y_l^{rgb}, RGNET-III outputs $\widehat{y_l^{rgb}} = \widehat{\sigma}(y_l^{linear})$.

To summarize, when put into the real application, the joint RGNET outputs the exposure time adjusted result: $\widehat{y_l^{rgb}} = \widehat{\sigma}(\widehat{f}(\widehat{\sigma'}(y_s^{rgb}) \times \gamma))$, RAW files absent.

4   Experiments

In this section, we first provide the details of the adopted dataset and implementation in Sect. 4.1, then demonstrate the superiority of the proposed method through experimental comparisons with traditional and learning-based methods in Sect. 4.2 and Sect. 4.3. The effectiveness of our designs is discussed in ablation studies in Sect. 4.4. More results and analysis (including an additional evaluation of RAW-based methods) are provided in the supplementary material.

Table 1. Quantitative results of traditional methods and ours. The bold value denotes the best result.

Method	PSNR	SSIM	VIF	NIQE
HE	5.90	0.028	0.095	28.27
BPDHE	10.67	0.072	0.051	18.64
Dehazing	12.81	0.103	0.077	25.79
MSR	10.04	0.070	0.116	32.24
MF	13.87	0.111	0.108	33.13
LIME	12.59	0.102	0.118	32.33
BIMEF	13.06	0.110	0.086	26.27
Ours	**28.42**	**0.880**	**0.139**	**15.23**

4.1 Training Details

We adopt the SID dataset [10] for training and evaluation[3], which includes 409 low/normal-light RAW image pairs, 280 pairs for training, 93 pairs for testing, and 36 pairs for validation.

In the training, we take the low-light and normal-light nonlinear RGB images (processed by Libraw) as inputs and ground truths, respectively, and employ RAW images as the side information guidance. The amplification factor is set to the ratio of exposure time. We use L_1 loss and Adam optimizer [33] for training. The learning rate is set to 10^{-4} and reduced to 10^{-5} after 2000 epochs. Each output of the subnet is clipped to $[0, 1]$. The batch size is set to 1 and patch-size to 512×512. All sub-modules are pre-trained independently and are converged in 2000–3000 epochs and the joint training lasts for 1000 epochs with learning rate 10^{-5}.

The entire network is trained on an Nvidia RTX 2080Ti GPU and Intel(R) Xeon(R) E5-2650 2.20GHz CPU using the Tensorflow framework. Due to the large spatial size of the testing image, cropping is implemented in testing.[4]

4.2 Comparison to Traditional Methods

We first compare our methods with several traditional methods including HE [1], Dehazing [16], MF [4], MSR [3], LIME [5], BIMEF [18], BPDHE [14].

The quantitative evaluation adopts full-reference metrics PSNR, SSIM [34], VIF [35], and a no-reference metric NIQE [36], results shown in Table 1. Considering, our RGNET outperforms traditional methods on the SID dataset.

Qualitative results are shown in Fig. 4. Conventional methods tend to brighten images uniformly, which easily leads to the under/over-exposure in some regions. Furthermore, extreme low-light environments of the SID dataset give rise to severe

---

[3] We use the Sony set, whose images are captured by Sony α7S II with a Bayer sensor.

[4] We crop 4256 × 2848 images into four 2128 × 1424 patches, and pad 200 pixels to reduce the blocking artifacts.

Fig. 4. Qualitative results of traditional methods and ours.

noise and color cast or insufficient illumination in the results. Specifically, Dehazing and BIMEF totally fail to enhance low-light images with a reasonable illumination level. HE, MF, MSR and LIME produce gray results owing to uniform brightening, and HE and BPDHE handle color biases improperly.

4.3 Comparison to Learning-Based Methods

We also evaluate the performance of state-of-the-art learning-based RGB low-light enhancement methods on the SID dataset, including LLNET [6], SICE [8], KinD [9] and DeepUPE [21].[5]

Due to extreme low-light imaging with severely limited illumination and short exposure time the SID dataset adopts, without using the ratio, these methods lead to under-exposure, as shown in Fig. 5. That further proves how absence of the definition of ground truths affects the generalization performance of methods in low light enhancement tasks. Excellent methods might totally fail only with the testing set changed. Specifically, DeepUPE fails to produce human visible outputs. KinD, LLNET and SICE's results are still not bright enough and these

---

[5] We choose the maximum brightening ratio ($\gamma = 5.0$) for KinD. Due to the GPU memory limit, the input resolution of SICE has to be small, so we down-sample the input images, perform SICE and up-sample results back into the original size.

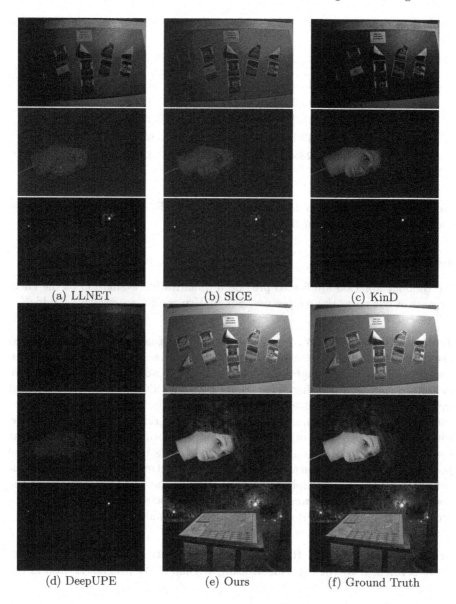

(a) LLNET   (b) SICE   (c) KinD

(d) DeepUPE   (e) Ours   (f) Ground Truth

Fig. 5. Qualitative results of learning-based methods and ours.

methods do not generate the bright regions of ground truth as shown at the top panel in Fig. 5. Besides, there still exists much noise in results and color cast is not properly dealt with as well, shown at the middle panel. All other methods reveal their scarcity handling moonlight cases, shown at the bottom panel.

The quantitative evaluation still adopts the same metrics as Sect. 4.2 and BLIINDS-II [37] is added, results shown in Table 2. Comprehensively, only using

Table 2. Quantitative results of learning-based methods and ours. The bold value denotes the best result.

Method	PSNR	SSIM	VIF	NIQE	BLIINDS-II
LLNET	14.21	0.221	0.047	18.02	52.46
SICE	14.26	0.366	0.011	16.89	49.53
KinD	13.35	0.109	0.048	17.73	47.66
DeepUPE	12.10	0.070	0.028	18.30	62.54
Ours	**28.42**	**0.880**	**0.139**	**15.23**	**18.38**

processed RGB images in the testing phase, our RGNET outperforms these learning-based methods on the SID dataset.

4.4 Ablation Study

We conduct ablation studies to provide a quantitative evaluation of the effectiveness of our network architecture. Summative results are shown as Table 3.

Training Without RAW. First, we consider the situation most learning-based low light enhancement methods are designed for, *i.e.* only making use of processed RGB low/normal-light pairs for training. We adopt a U-net architecture for end-to-end deep learning. The results have low SNR and, severely affected by the SID dataset's feature *i.e.* one ground truth for several low-light images with different illumination, enhanced images have serious artifacts. Apparently, without other labels, networks hardly dynamically brighten low-light images at variance. The MS-SSIM loss helps eliminate artifacts but induce a drop on the pixel-level full-reference metric PSNR. We try to stretch the histogram without extra labels *i.e.* multiplying by the ratio of the mean pixel value of the normal/low-light pair. However, the operation conflicts with the nonlinearity of processed RGB images so it doesn't display comparable performance.

Training with Original RAW. Then the necessity of linearly preprocessing RAW is revealed by the experiment using original RAW instead. A drop in the

Table 3. Ablation study. This table reports mean PSNR in each condition.

Condition	PSNR
w/o RAW	22.11
w/o RAW, adding MS-SSIM loss	21.88
w/o RAW, adjusting mean	24.27
With original RAW	28.17
Ours	**28.42**

Table 4. Controlled experiments on subnets. Note that different architectures require different inputs. RGNET-III's joint network is identical to the individual one.

Inputs	RGNET			PSNR	
	I	II	III	Individual	Joint
Low RGB	✓	✓	✓	26.06	28.42
Brightened linear RGB	×	✓	✓	27.91	28.50
Normal linear RGB	×	×	✓	42.68	42.68

score is predictable because the adopted linear process consists of basic stages included in most image processing pipelines therefore it bridges the gap between original RAW and processed RGB images which relieves the pressure to simulate the whole pipeline.

Controlled Experiments on Subnets. We further evaluate quantitative performance of proposed subnets as shown in Table 4. "individual" means directly testing after seperate pre-training of subnets and "joint" means testing after further joint training. The gap between them is owing to losing information for the following stages and error accumulation. Based on the result, RGNET-I and RGNET-III target nonlinear parts properly, which can be made out with a relatively little drop in PSNR between Table 4. Row. 1 and 2 and excellent PSNR score in Row. 3. The most challenging part is still reconstructing normal-light linear RGB from the brightened one affected by severe noise and biased color.

5 Conclusion

In this paper, we take a novel view to regard low light enhancement as exposure time adjustment and obtain an explicit and mathematical definition of this task. Based on that the proposed RGNET overcome RGB images' nonlinearity and RAW images' unusualness, and outperforms many RGB-based state-of-the-art approaches. Our network consists of three individual sub-modules for unprocessing, reconstruction and processing and it's the first attempt to adopt a learning-based unprocessing method for low light enhancement, which facilitates the end-to-end training of the whole designed pipeline. Our framework only needs access to the RAW image in the training process but can offer better results with that kind of information during the testing phase, therefore our results are guided by the RAW information but not rely on RAW input and the change of ISP process in the real applications.

Our future work is to extend the generalization of RGNET-I which, optimistically, handles the unprocessing task of various RGB images with different illumination and processing systems. Based on that, label-free training and evaluation are accessible, with a ratio of unprocessed linear normal/low-light images' intensity instead.

References

1. Pizer, S.M., Johnston, R.E., Ericksen, J.P., Yankaskas, B.C., Muller, K.E.: Contrast-limited adaptive histogram equalization: speed and effectiveness. In: Proceedings of Conference on Visualization in Biomedical Computing, pp. 337–345 (1990)
2. Abdullah-Al-Wadud, M., Kabir, M.H., Dewan, M.A.A., Chae, O.: A dynamic histogram equalization for image contrast enhancement. IEEE Trans. Consum. Electron. **53**, 593–600 (2007)
3. Jobson, D.J., Rahman, Z., Woodell, G.A.: A multiscale retinex for bridging the gap between color images and the human observation of scenes. IEEE Trans. Image Process. **6**, 965–976 (1997)
4. Fu, X., Zeng, D., Huang, Y., Liao, Y., Ding, X., Paisley, J.: A fusion-based enhancing method for weakly illuminated images. Sig. Process. **129**, 82–96 (2016)
5. Guo, X., Li, Y., Ling, H.: Lime: Low-light image enhancement via illumination map estimation. IEEE Trans. Image Process. **26**, 982–993 (2017)
6. Lore, K.G., Akintayo, A., Sarkar, S.: Llnet: a deep autoencoder approach to natural low-light image enhancement. Pattern Recogn. **61**, 650–662 (2017)
7. Shen, L., Yue, Z., Feng, F., Chen, Q., Liu, S., Ma, J.: MSR-net: low-light image enhancement using deep convolutional network. ArXiv e-prints (2017)
8. Cai, J., Gu, S., Zhang, L.: Learning a deep single image contrast enhancer from multi-exposure images. IEEE Trans. Image Process. **27**, 2049–2062 (2018)
9. Zhang, Y., Zhang, J., Guo, X.: Kindling the darkness: a practical low-light image enhancer. In: ACM International Conference on Multimedia (2019)
10. Chen, C., Chen, Q., Xu, J., Koltun, V.: Learning to see in the dark. In: Proceedings of the IEEE International Conference on Computer Vision and Pattern Recognition, pp. 3291–3300 (2018)
11. Brooks, T., Mildenhall, B., Xue, T., Chen, J., Sharlet, D., Barron, J.T.: Unprocessing images for learned raw denoising. In: Proceedings of the IEEE Int'l Conf. Computer Vision and Pattern Recognition, pp. 11028–11037 (2019)
12. Afifi, M., Abdelhamed, A., Abuolaim, A., Punnappurath, A., Brown, M.S.: Cie xyz net: unprocessing images for low-level computer vision tasks. arXiv preprint (2020)
13. Zamir, S.W., et al.: Cycleisp: Real image restoration via improved data synthesis. In: CVPR (2020)
14. Ibrahim, H., Pik Kong, N.S.: Brightness preserving dynamic histogram equalization for image contrast enhancement. IEEE Trans. Consum. Electron. **53**, 1752–1758 (2007)
15. Arici, T., Dikbas, S., Altunbasak, Y.: A histogram modification framework and its application for image contrast enhancement. IEEE Trans. Image Process. **18**, 1921–1935 (2009)
16. Dong, X., Wang, G., Pang, Y., Li, W., Wen, J., Meng, W., Lu, Y.: Fast efficient algorithm for enhancement of low lighting video. In: Proceedings of the IEEE International Conference on Multimedia and Expo, pp. 1–6 (2011)
17. Celik, T., Tjahjadi, T.: Contextual and variational contrast enhancement. IEEE Trans. Image Process. **20**, 3431–3441 (2011)
18. Ying, Z., Li, G., Gao, W.: A Bio-Inspired Multi-Exposure Fusion Framework for Low-light Image Enhancement. ArXiv e-prints (2017)
19. Land, E., McCann, J.: Lightness and retinex theory. J. Opt. Soc. Am. 1–11 (1971)

20. Jobson, D.J., Rahman, Z., Woodell, G.A.: Properties and performance of a center/surround retinex. IEEE Trans. Image Process. **6**, 451–462 (1997)
21. Wang, R., Zhang, Q., Fu, C.W., Shen, X., Zheng, W.S., Jia, J.: Underexposed photo enhancement using deep illumination estimation. In: Proceedings of the IEEE International Conference Computer Vision and Pattern Recognition (2019)
22. Wei*, C., Wang*, W., Yang, W., Liu, J.: Deep retinex decomposition for low-light enhancement. In: British Machine Vision Conference (2018)
23. Chen, C., Chen, Q., Do, M., Koltun, V.: Seeing motion in the dark. In: Proceedings of the IEEE International Conference on Computer Vision, pp. 3184–3193 (2019)
24. Jiang, H., Zheng, Y.: Learning to see moving objects in the dark. In: Proceedings of the IEEE International Conference on Computer Vision, pp. 7323–7332 (2019)
25. Hasinoff, S.W.: Photon, Poisson Noise, pp. 608–610. Springer, Boston (2014). https://doi.org/10.1007/978-0-387-31439-6
26. Abdelhamed, A., Lin, S., Brown, M.S.: A high-quality denoising dataset for smartphone cameras. In: Proceedings of the IEEE Conference on Computer Vision and Pattern Recognition (CVPR) (2018)
27. Ronneberger, O., Fischer, P., Brox, T.: U-Net: convolutional networks for biomedical image segmentation. In: Navab, N., Hornegger, J., Wells, W.M., Frangi, A.F. (eds.) MICCAI 2015. LNCS, vol. 9351, pp. 234–241. Springer, Cham (2015). https://doi.org/10.1007/978-3-319-24574-4_28
28. Burger, H., Schuler, C., Harmeling, S.: Image denoising: can plain neural networks compete with bm3d? In: 2012 IEEE Conference on Computer Vision and Pattern Recognition (2012)
29. Liu, P., Zhang, H., Zhang, K., Lin, L., Zuo, W.: Multi-level wavelet-CNN for image restoration. In: The IEEE Conference on Computer Vision and Pattern Recognition (CVPR) Workshops (2018)
30. Gharbi, M., Chaurasia, G., Paris, S., Durand, F.: Deep joint demosaicking and denoising. ACM Trans. Graph. **35**, 1–12 (2016)
31. Chen, Q., Xu, J., Koltun, V.: Fast image processing with fully-convolutional networks. In: The IEEE International Conference on Computer Vision (ICCV) (2017)
32. Yue, H., Cao, C., Liao, L., Chu, R., Yang, J.: Supervised raw video denoising with a benchmark dataset on dynamic scenes. In: IEEE Conference on Computer Vision and Pattern Recognition (2020)
33. Kingma, D.P., Ba, J.: Adam: a method for stochastic optimization. In: Bengio, Y., LeCun, Y. (eds.) 3rd International Conference on Learning Representations, ICLR 2015, San Diego, CA, USA, May 7–9, 2015, Conference Track Proceedings (2015)
34. Wang, Z., Bovik, A.C., Sheikh, H.R., Simoncelli, E.P.: Image quality assessment: from error visibility to structural similarity. IEEE Trans. Image Process. **13**, 600–612 (2004)
35. Sheikh, H.R., Bovik, A.C.: Image information and visual quality. IEEE Trans. Image Process. **15**, 430–444 (2006)
36. Mittal, A., Soundararajan, R., Bovik, A.C.: Making a "completely blind" image quality analyzer. IEEE Signal Process. Lett. **20**, 209–212 (2013)
37. Saad, M.A., Bovik, A.C., Charrier, C.: Blind image quality assessment: a natural scene statistics approach in the DCT domain. IEEE Trans. Image Process. **21**, 3339–3352 (2012)

Robust High Dynamic Range (HDR) Imaging with Complex Motion and Parallax

Zhiyuan Pu[1], Peiyao Guo[1], M. Salman Asif[2], and Zhan Ma[1]

[1] Nanjing University, Nanjing, China
{zhiyuanpu,peiyao}@smail.nju.edu.cn, mazhan@nju.edu.cn
[2] University of California, Riverside, CA, USA
sasif@ece.ucr.edu

Abstract. High dynamic range (HDR) imaging is widely used in consumer photography, computer game rendering, autonomous driving, and surveillance systems. Reconstructing ghosting-free HDR images of dynamic scenes from a set of multi-exposure images is a challenging task, especially with large object motion, disparity, and occlusions, leading to visible artifacts using existing methods. In this paper, we propose a Pyramidal Alignment and Masked merging network (PAMnet) that learns to synthesize HDR images from input low dynamic range (LDR) images in an end-to-end manner. Instead of aligning under/overexposed images to the reference view directly in pixel-domain, we apply deformable convolutions across multiscale features for pyramidal alignment. Aligned features offer more flexibility to refine the inevitable misalignment for subsequent merging network without reconstructing the aligned image explicitly. To make full use of aligned features, we use dilated dense residual blocks with squeeze-and-excitation (SE) attention. Such attention mechanism effectively helps to remove redundant information and suppress misaligned features. Additional mask-based weighting is further employed to refine the HDR reconstruction, which offers better image quality and sharp local details. Experiments demonstrate that PAMnet can produce ghosting-free HDR results in the presence of large disparity and motion. We present extensive comparative studies using several popular datasets to demonstrate superior quality compared to the state-of-the-art algorithms.

1   Introduction

Human visual system has astounding capabilities to capture natural scenes with high dynamic range [1]. In recent years, significant efforts have been made to develop specialized high dynamic range (HDR) imaging sensors, such as using beam splitters [2,3] or spatially varying exposed pixels [4]. Most common approaches for HDR imaging still rely on capturing and fusing multi-exposure images with cost-efficient, low dynamic range (LDR) sensors.

© Springer Nature Switzerland AG 2021
H. Ishikawa et al. (Eds.): ACCV 2020, LNCS 12623, pp. 134–149, 2021.
https://doi.org/10.1007/978-3-030-69532-3_9

The multi-exposure fusion schemes input a sequence of LDR images captured at different exposures and apply a variety of computational methods to construct ghosting-free HDR images. Images with different exposures can be captured in two possible options: (1) Using a single camera by adjusting its exposure over time to capture a set of images. (2) Using a camera array (e.g., in a multi-camera system) in which each camera is set to a different exposure to capture a set of images simultaneously. Images captured by the first approach often contain object motion, while the parallax effects are inevitable for multi-camera, multi-exposure setup alternatively. Thus, effectively removing artifacts caused by motion or parallax is the main challenge for high-quality, ghosting-free HDR imaging.

Over past several years, numerous efforts have been made to reduce the ghosting artifacts for HDR image generation. For example, the popular exposure bracketing-based weighted fusion is enhanced with motion detection and displaced pixel rejection [5,6] to alleviate motion-induced artifacts. Its performance, however, heavily depends on the accuracy of motion detection algorithm. On the other hand, alignment-before-merging schemes have been proposed to align input LDR images to a reference view, and then merge them altogether for HDR image reconstruction [7]. Inspired by recent advancements in deep neural networks, a large amount of learning-based approaches have also been introduced for HDR imaging. The method in [8] performs optical flow-based image alignment followed by a convolutional neural network (CNN)-based merging process. However, aligning images in pixel domain is often prone to the noisy or saturated pixels-induced misalignment, which leads to visible artifacts in final synthesized presentation. End-to-end learning-based approaches such as [9,10] without implicitly alignment directly feed LDR images into a network to reconstruct HDR images, failing to deal with scenarios with complex motion or large disparity.

In this work, we present a robust HDR imaging system along the alignment-before-merging direction, where *alignment* and *merging* network models are carefully designed to efficiently resolve the ghosting problem that arises due to temporal motion or spatial disparity-induced displacement. In *alignment* network, we use *feature-domain* processing to replace existing pixel-domain solutions, where a deformable convolution-based network is applied on three input LDR images to generate multiscale features for subsequent *pyramidal alignment*. Aligned features are then fed into a *merging network* for synthesizing the final HDR output. The merging process includes dilated dense blocks with squeeze-and-excitation (SE) attention modules and adaptive mask-based weighting by which feature redundancy and misalignment are efficiently removed. This scheme preserves local details and provides better image quality. Such feature-domain pyramidal alignment and masked merging networks (PAMnet) are trained in an end-to-end manner. Our experiments demonstrate that the proposed PAMnet can produce ghosting-free HDR images using inputs with complex motion and parallax. We compare our method against popular algorithms in [8–12], on various public test datasets, with superior reconstruction quality.

The main contributions are summarized below:

- We propose a deformable convolution-based pyramidal alignment network that uses multiscale image features for offset generation.
- We employ an attention optimized dense network to suppress misaligned features and fully utilize feature information for subsequent effective fusion using context-adaptive masks in the merging network.
- The pyramidal alignment and masked merging in feature domain can efficiently capture the complex displacements across LDR inputs induced by either temporal motion or spatial disparity for the HDR output with better image quality and richer local details. Extensive experiments and comparisons to the state-of-the-art algorithms have validated the superior efficiency of our proposed PAMnet, across a variety of test datasets.

2   Related Work

In this section, we will briefly review the existing approaches for multi-exposure based HDR reconstruction and deep learning methods for image registration related to this study.

2.1   Motion Handling Methods in HDR Reconstruction

Early works deal with camera motion and object motion to reconstruct ghosting-free HDR images. Previous approaches can be categorized into two classes depending on how to deal with object motion. The first class is based on motion detection. They detect moving pixels in the images which are rejected for final weighted HDR fusion, assuming that the images have been globally registered. The key to these methods is accurate motion detection. Yan *et al.* [5] formulate the object motion using a sparse representation. Lee *et al.* [6] propose to detect motion via rank minimization. However, these algorithms heavily depend on the effectiveness of motion detection and can not fully exploit the information of inputs.

The other class relies on the region alignment. Alignment-before-merging methods first align images of different exposures to the reference image, then merge them altogether to reconstruct the HDR image. The alignment is achieved through optical flow or patch match. Bogoni [7] registers local motion through estimating an optical flow field between each source image and a common reference image. Hu *et al.* [13] and Sen *et al.* [11] use patch-based methods to jointly optimize the alignment and reconstruction. These patch-based methods provide high robustness, but are time-consuming and may fail when there are large motions or large over-exposed regions in the reference image.

Recently, deep CNNs have offered significant performance improvement for many image reconstruction tasks. Kalantari *et al.* [8] firstly introduce neural networks in an alignment-before-merging pipeline to generate HDR images. Wu *et al.* [9] and Yan *et al.* [14] employ deep auto-encoder networks to translate multiple LDR images into a ghosting-free HDR image. Metzler *et al.* [15] and Sun *et al.* [16] jointly train an optical flow encoder and a CNN decoder to hallucinate the HDR content from a single LDR image. Choi *et al.* [17] suggest to reconstruct HDR videos using interlaced samples with joint sparse coding. Prabhakar *et al.* [18] propose a deep network that can handle arbitrary inputs, where they first align input images using optical flow and refinement network, then merge aggregated features. Yan *et al.* [10] utilize spatial attention mechanism to guide HDR merging, however, its principle is close to that of the motion detection based methods. The spatial attention cannot fully exploit the characteristics of image features. Instead, we propose a network with multiscale feature-based pyramidal alignment which is more flexible and robust in handling motion and disparity.

2.2 Multi-camera HDR Reconstruction

Alternatively, multi-camera system can be utilized for HDR imaging, in which two or more cameras are fixed on a rig with different exposure settings. Park *et al.* [19] utilize multi-exposed LDR images from a stereo camera for HDR merging, where they estimated the depth map with the help of superpixel and hole-filling, then fused the HDR image using a depth weighting map. Selmanovic *et al.* [20] generate stereoscopic HDR video using an HDR and an LDR camera where HDR content of the LDR view was enhanced with the reference of captured HDR data. Popovic *et al.* [21] produce panoramic HDR videos using a circular multi-camera system. Adjacent cameras share pixels with similar perspective but different exposures. Most multi-camera HDR solutions employ depth-based warping for HDR reconstruction and can generate HDR images of multiple views, while occlusion and overexposure often make accurate depth estimation difficult.

2.3 Deep Registration Networks

Special network structures have been developed to solve the alignment task, which allow complex inputs and are not limited to traditional alignment pipeline steps [22]. The spatial transformer network [23] predicts hyper parameters for global spatial transformations but cannot solve local object motions. Bert *et al.* [24] use filters generated dynamically based on the input to learn transformations such as translation and rotation. However, limited kernel size restricts the ability of dynamic filters in handling large motions. The deformable convolution [25] enhances the standard convolution with flexible offsets and enables free deformable receptive fields. For modeling unknown transformations (e.g., motion induced occlusion, etc.), we employ the deformable convolution for feature alignment.

3   Proposed Method

This section describes our network architecture in detail. Given a set of LDR images $(L_1, L_2, ..., L_k)$ that contain object and camera motion and are captured

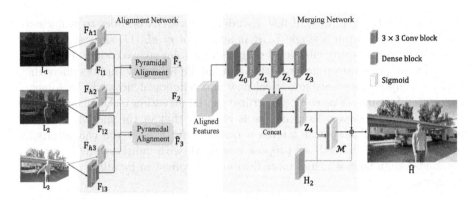

Fig. 1. PAMnet. The overall model includes a pyramidal alignment network and a merging network. Given input images with different exposures L_i, the alignment network first extracts image features at different scales (F_{li}, F_{hi}) and aligns them to the reference view. H_i denotes the gamma corrected L_i. Reference image features F_2 and the aligned features $\widehat{F}_i$ are then fed into the merging network to reconstruct HDR image $\widehat{H}$.

with different exposures, our goal is to reconstruct a ghosting-free HDR image $\widehat{H}$ at a specific reference view. We choose the middle exposure image as the reference image, that is, the image with the least number of underexposed or overexposed pixels. Using an image group (L_1, L_2, L_3) with three exposures as input, we set the middle exposure image L_2 as the reference image. We first convert the LDR images to corresponding HDR representations using gamma correction. Such gamma corrected images are closer to what we have perceived with our eyes [11]. The mapping operation can be written as

$$H_i = L_i^\gamma / t_i, \quad \text{for } i = 1, 2, 3, \tag{1}$$

where $\gamma = 2.2$ [26], t_i is the exposure time of the ith image L_i, and H_i denotes the mapped HDR domain image after gamma correction from the L_i.

As suggested in [8], LDR images can be used to detect the noisy or saturated regions (pixels), while the corresponding gamma corrected samples measure the content deviations from the reference image. As a result, we feed L_i and H_i together into our network. Note that image pre-alignment is not required in our approach. Pixel values of L_i, H_i and $\widehat{H}$ are all normalized to $[0, 1]$.

3.1   Approach Overview

Our network employs deformable convolution for image feature alignment, then merges the aligned features using dilated dense blocks with attention optimization. The deformable convolution estimates content-based offsets for adaptive receptive fields. As shown in Fig. 1, our network is composed of two subnetworks: feature alignment network and merging network.

The alignment network first extracts image features at different scales in LDR and HDR domain using convolution layers. Then reference and non-reference image pyramidal feature pairs are fed into separate pyramidal alignment modules. The modules take multi-scale image features in the HDR domain for offsets computation. Non-reference LDR and HDR domain image features are then aligned to the reference image features using corresponding offsets.

The merging network concatenates aligned image features in LDR and HDR domain as the input, and reconstructs HDR image by exploiting dilated dense residual blocks with SE connection and masked merging. Dilation rate d is enlarged in dense blocks to learn nonlocal information followed by the SE attention [27] to remove redundant information and alleviate misalignment. Finally, the HDR image is reconstructed through a weighted fusion using adaptive mask.

3.2 Pyramidal Alignment

Given the input (L_i, H_i), $i = 1, 2, 3$, the alignment network first extracts image features of different scales in LDR and HDR domain (F_{li}^s, F_{hi}^s), $i = 1, 2, 3$, $s = 1, 2$, where s denotes the number of scales. Considering the trade-off of network efficiency and capacity, pyramidal alignment module at 2 scales $(max(s)s = 2)$ is enough for strong performance, although a pyramidal alignment module with larger s has a stronger ability in dealing with large motions.

We use the deformable convolution [28] to align image features in a coarse-to-fine manner. Let w_k denotes convolution weight of the k-th location and let $p_k \in \{(-1, -1), (-1, 0), \ldots, (0, 1), (1, 1)\}$ denotes pre-specified offset. Set $K = 9$ for a 3×3 kernel convolution layer with dilation rate 1. For pixel $x(p_0)$ at position p_0, the pixel value after deformable convolution alignment is:

$$y(p_0) = \sum_{k=1}^{K} w_k \cdot x \left(p_0 + p_k + \Delta p_k \right) \cdot \Delta m_k . \tag{2}$$

where Δp_k and Δm_k are the learnable offset and modulation scalar for the k-th location. Δm_k and Δp_k are calculated with the same features, the computation of Δm_k is omitted in the following description for simplicity.

As shown in Fig. 2, we use image features in the HDR domain for offset computation which reduces the impact of different exposures. Learnable offsets are predicted from concatenated reference and i-th image features in HDR domain, then a deformable convolution layer aligns the source image features to the reference features:

$$\Delta p^s = ConvM \left([F_{hi}^s, F_{h2}^s] \right) . \tag{3}$$

$$\widehat{F}_i^s = Dconv \left([F_{li}^s, F_{hi}^s], \Delta p^s \right) . \tag{4}$$

where $ConvM$ denotes convolution layers, $\widehat{F}_i^s$ is the aligned feature of i-th input of scale s, $[\cdot, \cdot]$ is the concatenation operation, and $DConv$ is the deformable convolution. Let $\uparrow^2$ denotes the bilinear upsampling of scale factor 2, Δp^s and

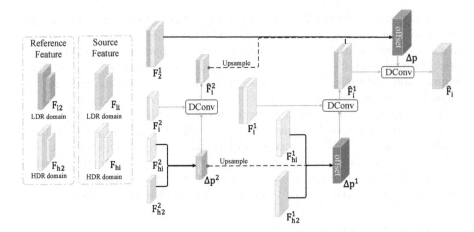

Fig. 2. Pyramidal alignment module architecture. The gray dotted frame on the left side of the figure shows the input features (yellow boxes indicate source features and green boxes indicate reference features), and the right side is the detailed alignment module structure. The alignment network uses HDR domain image features to compute offset, then align multi-scale features with the corresponding offsets. The aligned features $\widehat{F}_i^s$ and the final aligned feature after refinement $\widehat{F}_i$ are indicated by orange boxes. (Color figure online)

Δp^{s+1} refer to offset of scale s and $s+1$ separately. After obtaining the aligned feature of $i+1$-th scale, we further refine the alignment on a upper scale with deformable convolution:

$$\Delta p^s = ConvM\left(F_{hi}^s, F_{h2}^s, \Delta p^{s+1} \uparrow^2\right) \ . \tag{5}$$

Following the pyramidal feature alignment, an additional deformable convolution is introduced to improve details in the final aligned image feature $\widehat{F}_i$:

$$\Delta p = ConvM\left([F_2^1, F_i^1, F_i^2 \uparrow^2]\right) \ . \tag{6}$$

$$\widehat{F}_i = Dconv\left(F_i^1, \Delta p\right) \ . \tag{7}$$

Where Δp denotes the offset for refinement and $\widehat{F}_i$ is the final aligned feature. Previous works have validated the effect of coarse-to-fine spatial pyramidal alignment approach [29–31]. Taking advantage of the feature-based offset and pyramidal alignment, our alignment network can successfully handle parallax and complex motions, improving alignment accuracy with sub-pixel refinement. Besides, features in the HDR domain have higher brightness consistency. Consequently, we compute offsets with features in the HDR domain for better performance and less computation.

3.3 Merging Network

Inspired by the success of previous methods [10,32], we utilize residual dense blocks with SE connection [27] for feature merging. As shown in Fig. 1, the

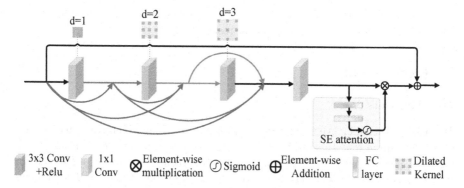

Fig. 3. Residual dense block with three dilated layers. squeeze-and-excitation (SE) attention module (the yellow box) is employed to remove redundant information and misalignment in channels. (Color figure online)

merging network takes the concatenated aligned features $F = [\widehat{F}_1, F_2, \widehat{F}_3]$ as input. Z_0 is obtained after a convolution layer, then feature maps Z_1, Z_2, Z_3 are generated by feeding Z_0 into 3 residual dense blocks. Concatenated feature maps produce Z_4 after several convolution layers and the sigmoid function. Finally, the HDR image $\widehat{H}$ is reconstructed with Z_4, H_2 and corresponding mask M_{merge}:

$$\mathcal{M} = \texttt{sigmoid}(ConvM([Z_4, H_2])) , \tag{8}$$

$$M_{refine}, M_{merge} = \texttt{split}(\mathcal{M}) , \tag{9}$$

$$\widehat{H} = M_{merge} \cdot (M_{refine} \cdot Z_4) + (1 - M_{merge}) \cdot H_2 . \tag{10}$$

The `split` operation splits the mask $\mathcal{M}$ in the shape of $(N, 4, H, W)$ into a 3-channel mask M_{refine} and 1-channel mask M_{merge}, of which the shape are $(N, 3, H, W)$ and $(N, 1, H, W)$ respectively.

Since dense connections may cause information redundancy, we apply SE connections in residual dense blocks which helps to remove redundancy. In addition, growing dilation rates are set in dense blocks to get larger receptive field for hallucinating details and misalignment elimination, as shown in Fig. 3.

3.4 Loss Function

Since HDR images are displayed after tone mapping, optimization in the tone mapped domain produces results with fewer artifacts in the dark regions than optimization in the HDR domain. We employ the μ-law for tone mapping as supposed in [8], which is formulated as:

$$T(H) = \frac{\log(1 + \mu H)}{\log(1 + \mu)} . \tag{11}$$

where μ is set to 5000. Denoting ground truth HDR image and predicted HDR image as H and $\widehat{H}$, the loss function can be defined as:

$$L(H, \widehat{H}) = \|T(H) - T(\widehat{H})\|_1 + \alpha \|\nabla T(H) - \nabla T(\widehat{H})\|_2 + \beta \|T(H) - T(Z_4)\|_1. \tag{12}$$

where $\alpha = 10, \beta = 0.5$, $\nabla T(H)$ denotes the gradient magnitude of image $T(H)$, $\|\cdot\|_1$ and $\|\cdot\|_2$ denote ℓ_1 and ℓ_2 norm, respectively.

4   Experiments

4.1   Datasets

Training Dataset. We train on Kalantari's dataset [8] which contains 74 samples for training and 15 samples for testing. Each sample includes ground truth HDR images and three LDR images with exposure biases of $\{-2, 0, +2\}$ or $\{-3, 0, +3\}$. The dataset has both indoor and outdoor scenes and all images are resized to 1000×1500.

Testing Dataset. Testing is performed on Kalantari's testset [8] which has 15 scenes with ground truth and a dataset without ground truth [11]. To verify the model's ability in handling parallax, we also test our model on the Middlebury dataset [33] which consists of sets of images of different views with three different exposures. We use scenes from Middlebury 2005 and Middlebury 2006 for testing, and choose image sets of 3 illuminations and 2 different reference views from each scene.

4.2   Implementation Details

Given training data, we first crop them into 256×256 patches with a stride of 128 to expand training set size. The crop is conducted on LDR images and corresponding HDR label. Random flipping, noise, and $90°$ rotation are applied on generated patches to avoid over-fitting. We use Adam optimizer [34] with $\beta_1 = 0.9$, $\beta_2 = 0.999$, learning rate $= 10^{-4}$ and set batch size as 8. We perform training for 160 epochs. In order to better train the deformable convolution based alignment module, we employ the learning rate warmup trick where the warmup epoch is set to 10. We implement our model using PyTorch [35] on NVIDIA GeForce GTX 1080 GPU, and we decrease the learning rate by a factor of 4 every 70 epochs.

Table 1. Quantitative comparison on Kalantari's Testset [8]. Red color indicates the best performance and blue color indicates the second-best result.

Methods	PSNR-L	PSNR-μ	SSIM-L	SSIM-μ	HDR-VDP-2
AHDR [10]	41.1782	43.7013	0.9857	0.9905	62.0521
Wu [9]	41.6593	41.9977	0.9860	0.9878	61.7981
Kalantari [8]	41.2200	42.7177	0.9829	0.9889	61.3139
Sen [11]	38.3425	40.9689	0.9764	0.9859	60.3463
Ours	41.6452	43.8487	0.9870	0.9906	62.5495

LDR images   low   refer   high   GT   ours   AHDR   Wu   Kalantari   Sen   HDRNet
  [10]   [9]   [8]   [11]   [12]

Fig. 4. Visual comparison using "Parking" from Kalantari's testset [8]. **Left**: input LDR images; **Upper Right**: HDR image reconstructed using proposed PAMnet; **Lower Right**: Zoomed-in patches of LDR images and HDR images. We choose the medium-exposure image as the reference. We show the results of the state-of-the-art HDR imaging algorithms, AHDR [10], Wu [9], Kalantari [8], Sen [11], and HDRNet [12]. The proposed PAMnet can produce high-quality HDR images even there are background saturation and large foreground motions.

4.3 Analysis of Single-Camera Case

We compare the proposed model with existing state-of-the-art methods on two datasets captured with single camera. We perform quantitative evaluations on Kalantari's testset [8] and qualitative assessments on dataset without ground truth [11]. We compare our model with the patch-based method [11], the single image enhancement method (HDRnet) [12], the flow alignment based method with a CNN merger [8], the UNet-based method [9] and the attention-guide method (AHDR) [10]. Note that we use a PyTorch [35] implementation of HDR-net which is trained on the same dataset as [12]. For other methods, we utilize the code and trained models provided by the authors for testing comparison.

We use metrics such as PSNR, SSIM, and HDR-VDP-2 for quantitative comparison. We compute PSNR and SSIM for images in linear domain (PSNR-L and SSIM-L) and images after the μ-law tone mapping (PSNR-μ, SSIM-μ). We also compute HDR-VDP-2 [36] for quantitative comparison. Quantitative evaluation on Kalantari's testset [8] can be found in Table 1. All values are averaged on 15 test scenes. The proposed PAMnet has better numerical performance than

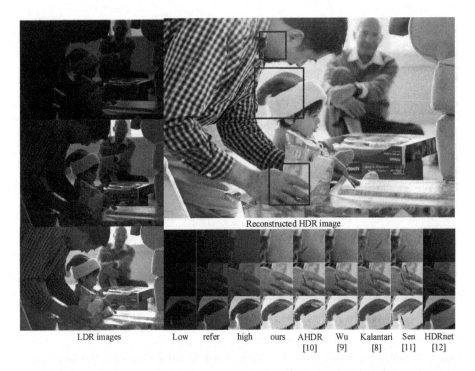

Reconstructed HDR image

LDR images   Low   refer   high   ours   AHDR   Wu   Kalantari   Sen   HDRnet
                                                  [10]   [9]   [8]   [11]   [12]

Fig. 5. Visual comparison using "Santas Little Helper" from Sen's dataset [11]. **Left**: input LDR images; **Upper Right**: HDR image reconstructed using proposed PAMnet; **Lower Right**: Zoomed-in patches of LDR images and HDR images. Our PAMnet produces HDR images with less noise and artifacts.

other methods. For the sake of fairness, the HDRnet [12] is not included in the quantitative comparison because it produces enhanced LDR images. Figure 4 and Fig. 5 compare our method with existing state-of-the-art methods. Sample of Fig. 4 contains saturated background and large foreground motion. AHDR [10] and method of Wu *et al.* [9] produce ghosting artifacts in occluded region. Method of Kalantari *et al.* [8] leaves artifacts caused by optical flow alignment. Patch-based method (Sen *et al.* [11]) cannot find the right corresponding patches in the saturated region and generates line dislocation and color blocks. HDRnet [12] can't recover details in the saturated region and perturbs the tone of the image. With task-oriented pyramidal alignment, our network can produce high-quality HDR images even there is large motion in the inputs. For samples with underexposed objects in the reference image (as shown in Fig. 5), most methods can't reconstruct artifacts-free face and hand. Method of Sen *et al.* [11] and Kalantari *et al.* [8] produce results with local abnormal color and noise. HDRnet [12] enhances the underexposed region but can't hallucinate all details in the dark areas. Local color inconsistency appears around the hat in results generated by AHDR [10] because the spatial attention mask can only suppress unwanted pixels rather than find corresponding useful pixels.

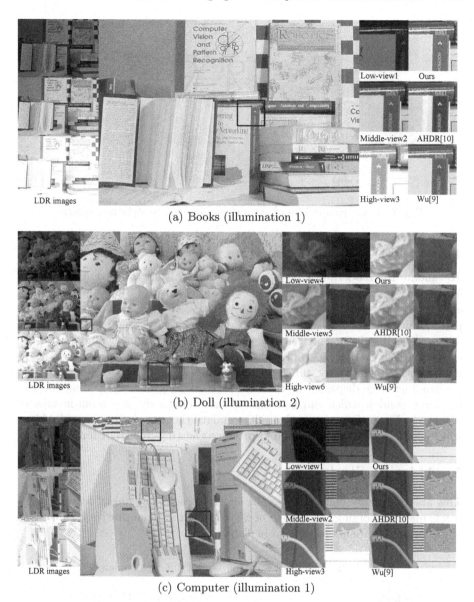

Fig. 6. Visual comparison on the Middlebury dataset [33]. **Left**: the input LDR images; **Middle**: the HDR image; **Right**: Zoomed-in patches of LDR images and HDR images. Our PAMnet can handle parallax (see zoomed-in patches) and produce ghosting-free HDR images.

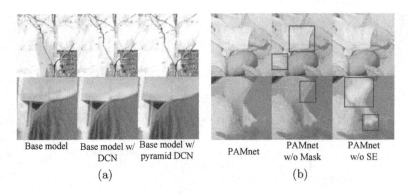

Base model   Base model w/   Base model w/   PAMnet   PAMnet
                   DCN   pyramid DCN   PAMnet   w/o Mask   w/o SE
                   (a)   (b)

Fig. 7. Visual comparison of network variants via modularized switch.

4.4 Analysis of Multi-camera Case

To validate the model's ability to handle parallax, we performed evaluation on Middlebury testset [33]. For each scene, we select a set of 3 images with different exposures as inputs. We choose the two models with the best quantitative performance on Kalantari's testset [8] to compare with ours on the Middlebury dataset [33]. Results on three scenes with different environment illumination are shown in Fig. 6. AHDR [10] suffers ghosting artifacts because the attention-based network which suppresses unhelpful pixel values before merging is not suitable for handling large disparity. Method of Wu *et al.* [9] produces gridding effect in the fused results, which can be observed more obviously in a zoom-in view of patches in Fig. 6. Experimental results validate the superiority of our PAMnet which can handle large parallax and produce ghosting-free HDR images.

5   Ablation Study

This ablation study demonstrates the effectiveness of pyramidal feature alignment, masked merging, and usage of SE connection. Quantitative comparisons of the network variants are shown in Table 2.

Table 2. Quantitative comparison of different models.

Methods	PSNR-L	PSNR-μ	SSIM-L	SSIM-μ
Base model	40.1189	41.9602	0.9841	0.9891
Base model w/ DCN	40.8987	42.3182	0.9863	0.9896
Base model w/ pyramidal DCN	41.4254	43.4087	0.9865	0.9900
PAMnet w/o SE	41.5191	43.5479	0.9865	0.9903
PAMnet w/o mask	41.4764	43.6738	0.9866	0.9901
PAMnet	41.6452	43.8487	0.9870	0.9906

Deformable Convolution-Based Pyramidal Alignment. The deformable convolution based feature alignment can better mitigate the ghosting problem caused by motion and parallax. We remove the pyramidal alignment, SE connection and masked merging from our PAMnet as the base model. As shown in Fig. 7 (a), model with deformable convolution generates fewer ghosting artifacts comparing with the base model. The model with pyramidal feature alignment can generate ghosting-free HDR images, and its ability to handle large motions is stronger than the model with only single scale feature alignment.

Masked Merging and SE Connection. Though model with pyramidal feature alignment can handle large motions, inaccurate alignment may introduce extra artifacts to the fused image. To suppress the misaligned features, we employ the SE attention [27] to the dense blocks of our network. The masked merging also helps to generate better results. As shown in Fig. 7 (b), the model without SE connection produces abnormal color in the second row while unnatural shadows and highlights arise in images generated by the model without masked merging (rectangle region). The full model with SE connection and masked merging can discard redundant information and inaccurate alignment, producing results with richer details and fewer artifacts.

6 Conclusion

In this paper, we propose a learned HDR imaging method that can handle complex object motion and large camera parallax. With pyramidal alignment and masked merging in feature domain, our method can produce high-quality HDR images in various scenarios having saturation, parallax, and occlusion in input data. Experiments validate that our model performs well on multi-exposure frames captured by both single-camera and multi-camera systems. We compare our method with existing state-of-the-art approaches on publicly available datasets and observe that our method offers significant improvement both objectively and subjectively. Our current work is exemplified using a fixed number of LDR images, but it is possibly extended to support an arbitrary number of images.

Acknowledgement. We are grateful for the constructive comments from anonymous reviewers.

References

1. Ledda, P., Santos, L.P., Chalmers, A.: A local model of eye adaptation for high dynamic range images. In: Proceedings of the 3rd International Conference on Computer Graphics, virtual Reality, Visualisation and Interaction in Africa, pp. 151–160 (2004)

2. Froehlich, J., Grandinetti, S., Eberhardt, B., Walter, S., Schilling, A., Brendel, H.: Creating cinematic wide gamut hdr-video for the evaluation of tone mapping operators and hdr-displays. In: Digital Photography X, vol. 9023. International Society for Optics and Photonics (2014)

3. Tocci, M.D., Kiser, C., Tocci, N., Sen, P.: A versatile HDR video production system. ACM Trans. Graphics (TOG) **30**, 1–10 (2011)

4. Nayar, S.K., Mitsunaga, T.: High dynamic range imaging: Spatially varying pixel exposures. In: Proceedings IEEE Conference on Computer Vision and Pattern Recognition. CVPR 2000 (Cat. No. PR00662), vol. 1, pp. 472–479. IEEE (2000)

5. Yan, Q., Sun, J., Li, H., Zhu, Y., Zhang, Y.: High dynamic range imaging by sparse representation. Neurocomputing **269**, 160–169 (2017)

6. Lee, C., Li, Y., Monga, V.: Ghost-free high dynamic range imaging via rank minimization. IEEE Signal Process. Lett. **21**, 1045–1049 (2014)

7. Bogoni, L.: Extending dynamic range of monochrome and color images through fusion. In: Proceedings 15th International Conference on Pattern Recognition. ICPR-2000, vol. 3. IEEE (2000)

8. Kalantari, N.K., Ramamoorthi, R.: Deep high dynamic range imaging of dynamic scenes. ACM Trans. Graph. **36**, 144–1 (2017)

9. Wu, S., Xu, J., Tai, Y.-W., Tang, C.-K.: Deep high dynamic range imaging with large foreground motions. In: Ferrari, V., Hebert, M., Sminchisescu, C., Weiss, Y. (eds.) ECCV 2018. LNCS, vol. 11206, pp. 120–135. Springer, Cham (2018). https://doi.org/10.1007/978-3-030-01216-8_8

10. Yan, Q., Gong, D., Shi, Q., Hengel, A.V.D., Shen, C., Reid, I., Zhang, Y.: Attention-guided network for ghost-free high dynamic range imaging. In: Proceedings of the IEEE Conference on Computer Vision and Pattern Recognition, pp. 1751–1760 (2019)

11. Sen, P., Kalantari, N.K., Yaesoubi, M., Darabi, S., Goldman, D.B., Shechtman, E.: Robust patch-based HDR reconstruction of dynamic scenes. ACM Trans. Graph. **31**, 203:1–203:11 (2012)

12. Gharbi, M., Chen, J., Barron, J.T., Hasinoff, S.W., Durand, F.: Deep bilateral learning for real-time image enhancement. ACM Trans. Graphics (TOG) **36**, 1–12 (2017)

13. Hu, J., Gallo, O., Pulli, K., Sun, X.: HDR deghosting: how to deal with saturation? In: Proceedings of the IEEE Conference on Computer Vision and Pattern Recognition, pp. 1163–1170 (2013)

14. Yan, Q., et al.: Deep HDR imaging via a non-local network. IEEE Trans. Image Process. **29**, 4308–4322 (2020)

15. Metzler, C.A., Ikoma, H., Peng, Y., Wetzstein, G.: Deep optics for single-shot high-dynamic-range imaging. In: Proceedings of the IEEE/CVF Conference on Computer Vision and Pattern Recognition, pp. 1375–1385 (2020)

16. Sun, Q., Tseng, E., Fu, Q., Heidrich, W., Heide, F.: Learning rank-1 diffractive optics for single-shot high dynamic range imaging. In: Proceedings of the IEEE/CVF Conference on Computer Vision and Pattern Recognition, pp. 1386–1396 (2020)

17. Choi, I., Baek, S.H., Kim, M.H.: Reconstructing interlaced high-dynamic-range video using joint learning. IEEE Trans. Image Process. **26**, 5353–5366 (2017)

18. Prabhakar, K.R., Arora, R., Swaminathan, A., Singh, K.P., Babu, R.V.: A fast, scalable, and reliable deghosting method for extreme exposure fusion. In: 2019 IEEE International Conference on Computational Photography (ICCP), pp. 1–8. IEEE (2019)

19. Park, W.J., Ji, S.W., Kang, S.J., Jung, S.W., Ko, S.J.: Stereo vision-based high dynamic range imaging using differently-exposed image pair. Sensors **17**, 1473 (2017)
20. Selmanovic, E., Debattista, K., Bashford-Rogers, T., Chalmers, A.: Enabling stereoscopic high dynamic range video. Sig. Process. Image Commun. **29**, 216–228 (2014)
21. Popovic, V., Seyid, K., Pignat, E., Çogal, Ö., Leblebici, Y.: Multi-camera platform for panoramic real-time HDR video construction and rendering. J. Real-Time Image Proc. **12**, 697–708 (2016)
22. Villena-Martinez, V., Oprea, S., Saval-Calvo, M., Azorin-Lopez, J., Fuster-Guillo, A., Fisher, R.B.: When deep learning meets data alignment: a review on deep registration networks (drns). arXiv preprint arXiv:2003.03167 (2020)
23. Jaderberg, M., Simonyan, K., Zisserman, A., et al.: Spatial transformer networks. In: Advances in neural information processing systems, pp. 2017–2025 (2015)
24. Jia, X., De Brabandere, B., Tuytelaars, T., Gool, L.V.: Dynamic filter networks. In: Advances in Neural Information Processing Systems, pp. 667–675 (2016)
25. Dai, J., et al.: Deformable convolutional networks. In: Proceedings of the IEEE International Conference on Computer Vision, pp. 764–773 (2017)
26. Poynton, C.: Digital video and HD: Algorithms and Interfaces. Elsevier (2012)
27. Hu, J., Shen, L., Sun, G.: Squeeze-and-excitation networks. In: Proceedings of the IEEE Conference on Computer Vision and Pattern Recognition, pp. 7132–7141 (2018)
28. Zhu, X., Hu, H., Lin, S., Dai, J.: Deformable convnets v2: more deformable, better results. arXiv preprint arXiv:1811.11168 (2018)
29. Ranjan, A., Black, M.J.: Optical flow estimation using a spatial pyramid network. In: Proceedings of the IEEE Conference on Computer Vision and Pattern Recognition, pp. 4161–4170 (2017)
30. Sun, D., Yang, X., Liu, M.Y., Kautz, J.: PWC-net: CNNs for optical flow using pyramid, warping, and cost volume. In: Proceedings of the IEEE Conference on Computer Vision and Pattern Recognition, pp. 8934–8943 (2018)
31. Wang, X., Chan, K.C., Yu, K., Dong, C., Change Loy, C.: EDVR: video restoration with enhanced deformable convolutional networks. In: Proceedings of the IEEE Conference on Computer Vision and Pattern Recognition Workshops (2019)
32. Zhang, Y., Tian, Y., Kong, Y., Zhong, B., Fu, Y.: Residual dense network for image super-resolution. In: Proceedings of the IEEE Conference on Computer Vision and Pattern Recognition, pp. 2472–2481 (2018)
33. Scharstein, D., Pal, C.: Learning conditional random fields for stereo. In: 2007 IEEE Conference on Computer Vision and Pattern Recognition, pp. 1–8. IEEE (2007)
34. Kingma, D.P., Ba, J.: Adam: a method for stochastic optimization. arXiv preprint arXiv:1412.6980 (2014)
35. Paszke, A., et al.: Automatic differentiation in pytorch (2017)
36. Mantiuk, R., Kim, K.J., Rempel, A.G., Heidrich, W.: HDR-VDP-2: a calibrated visual metric for visibility and quality predictions in all luminance conditions. ACM Trans. Graphics (TOG) **30**, 1–14 (2011)

Low-Light Color Imaging via Dual Camera Acquisition

Peiyao Guo[ID] and Zhan Ma[(✉)][ID]

Vision Lab, Nanjing University, Nanjing, China
peiyao@smail.nju.edu.cn, mazhan@nju.edu.cn

Abstract. As existing low-light color imaging suffers from the unrealistic color representation or blurry texture with a single camera setup, we are motivated to devise a dual camera system using a high spatial resolution (HSR) monochrome camera and another low spatial resolution (LSR) color camera for synthesizing the high-quality color image under low-light illumination conditions. The key problem is how to efficiently learn and fuse cross-camera information for improved presentation in such heterogeneous setup with domain gaps (e.g., color vs. monochrome, HSR vs. LSR). We have divided the end-to-end pipeline into three consecutive modularized sub-tasks, including the reference-based exposure compensation (RefEC), reference-based colorization (RefColor) and reference-based super-resolution (RefSR), to alleviate domain gaps and capture inter-camera dynamics between hybrid inputs. In each step, we leverage the powerful deep neural network (DNN) to respectively transfer and enhance the illuminative, spectral and spatial granularity in a data-driven way. Each module is first trained separately, and then jointly fine-tuned for robust and reliable performance. Experimental results have shown that our work provides the leading performance in synthetic content from popular test datasets when compared to existing algorithms, and offers appealing color reconstruction using real captured scenes from an industrial monochrome and a smartphone RGB cameras, in low-light color imaging application.

1 Introduction

Low-light color imaging is a challenging task which plays a vital role in auto driving, security surveillance, and professional photography. Insufficient illumination which may come from the under-exposure acquisition or low-light radiation, would lead to very low signal-to-noise ratio (SNR) and corresponding severely degraded imaging quality.

Classical histogram equalization or gamma correction [1–3] was applied to directly enhance the luminance component without taking the chrominance part into account. On the other hand, as suggested in Retinex theory [4], color image

Electronic supplementary material The online version of this chapter (https://doi.org/10.1007/978-3-030-69532-3_10) contains supplementary material, which is available to authorized users.

© Springer Nature Switzerland AG 2021
H. Ishikawa et al. (Eds.): ACCV 2020, LNCS 12623, pp. 150–167, 2021.
https://doi.org/10.1007/978-3-030-69532-3_10

could be represented by the product of its illuminance and reflectance map, where the reflectance map captures intrinsic "color" (spectral) information of the object under varying lighting conditions, and the illuminance component describes the energy intensity of light radiation. Thus, a number of explorations had been made to decompose the illuminance and reflectance components from observed images for synthesizing better image reconstruction at a different (e.g., higher) illumination condition, where these components can be represented with either hand-crafted [5,6] or learning-based [7–9] features. These works assumed the single camera setup in low-light condition. Though color image quality could be enhanced to some extent in this category, its reconstruction often suffered from the unrealistic color presentation, blurry texture, etc.

Recently, we have witnessed explosive advancements of multi-camera system, by which we can significantly improve the imaging capacity in various dimensions, such as gigapixel photography [10], high-speed video acquisition [11], light-field imaging [12], etc. Besides, as reported in neuronal science studies [13,14], rods are responsible for illumination changes, especially in low-light condition, without color perception (e.g., scotopic vision), while cones are mainly for color sensation (e.g., photopic vision). Especially, the human visual system exhibits higher sensitivity to luminance variations than to chrominance under low illumination condition, since rod cells are dominantly activated (e.g., much more than cones) in such scenario [15]. All above have motivated us to apply the heterogeneous dual camera setup for low-light color imaging, where one monochrome camera is used to mimic the rod cells for capturing the monochromic image at higher spatial resolution (HSR), and the other color camera emulates the cone cells by inputting the regular color image at lower spatial resolution (LSR). Note that without requiring the color filter arrays (CFA) such as the Bayer CFA [16], monochromic imaging often provides better energy preservation of light radiance that can be leveraged to enhance corresponding color image.

Recalling the color image decomposition in Retinex theory, we have attempted to apply cross-camera synthesis by transferring the colors captured via a LSR color camera to the monochromic image acquired with a HSR monochrome camera. Because of the domain gaps in the camera pair, e.g., LSR vs. HSR, color vs. monochrome, we have proposed to divide the entire task into three consecutive sub-tasks, i.e., reference-based exposure compensation (RefEC), reference-based colorization (RefColor), and reference-based super-resolution (RefSR). Herein, RefEC downscales the HSR monochromic image to the same size of the corresponding LSR color image, and transfers the illumination level from its downscaled version to brighten the LSR color image; while RefColor module resolves the parallax between HSR and LSR cameras, and migrates the brightened LSR image colors to downscaled HSR monochromic image; In the end, re-colored and downscaled HSR image is super-resolved with the guidance of the native HSR monochromic sample in RefSR for final output. All modules, i.e., RefEC, RefColor and RefSR, are implemented using stacked convolutions to efficiently characterize and learn the illumination-, spectrum (color)- and resolution-dependent dynamics between proposed hybrid inputs.

We first train each modularized component individually, and then fine-tune the end-to-end pipeline for robust and reliable low-light imaging.

Experimental results have demonstrated that our method shows leading performance in each task using popular datasets when compared with relevant algorithms. Simulations have also revealed appealing image reconstruction using camera-captured real scenes under low-light illumination conditions. Overall, main contributions of this work are summarized below:

- We are motivated to devise a dual camera system for low-light color imaging, where a HSR monochromic image and a LSR color image from respective cameras are synthesized for final enhanced color image under low-light illumination condition; Such heterogeneous camera setup is inspired by the non-uniform light responses of retinal rods and cones for luminance and chrominance.
- We have divided the entire system into three consecutive sub-tasks, i.e., RefEC, RefColor and RefSR, by implicitly enforcing the cross-camera reference to alleviate domain gaps and capture cross-camera dynamics (e.g., illumination, spectrum, spatial resolution) for synthesizing the final high-quality output.
- Our method shows competitive performance on both public datasets and the real captured scenes, promising the generalization in practical applications.

2   Related Work

This work is closely related to the multi-camera imaging, low-light image enhancement, colorization and super-resolution. A brief review is given below.

Multi-camera Imaging. As aforementioned, multi-camera system could significantly improve the imaging capacity by computationally synthesizing input sources for gigapixel photography, high-speed videography, light-fields, hyperspectral imaging, etc. Wang et al. [17] have proposed to register a pair of RGB and NIR-G-NUV image for addressing the motion blur and temporal delay of dark flash photography. Trinidad et al. [18] have applied an end-to-end feature fusion from multiple misaligned images for high-quality image generation in color transferring, high dynamic range imaging, texture restoration, etc. Dong et al. [19] have imposed a monochrome and color dual-lens setup to shoot high-quality color images. Recently, multi-camera system becomes a commodity and is widely adopted in mobile platforms for super-resolution [20,21], denoising [22] and quality enhancement [23].

Low-Light Image Enhancement. In this category, classical approaches include the histogram equalization (HE) and gamma correction [1,3]. However, they fail to retain the local details and suppress noise. Leveraging the characteristics of low-light image, dehazing model [24,25] assumes that the low-light image resembles the haze image after inversion, and Retinex model [8,9,26–29] decomposes the reflectance map from the observed image for synthesizing it at a higher illumination condition. For example, Wei et al. [29] reconstruct the

high-quality image with the decomposed reflectance map and enhanced illuminance map using an end-to-end learning approach. And Zhang *et al.* [8] assume
the histogram consistency after equalization for low-light image enhancement.
Besides, Guo *et al.* [30] impose a non-reference enhancement for dynamic range
adjustment via high-order polynomial function-based pixel-wise processing.

Colorization. Automatic colorization, scribble-based colorization and
exemplar-based colorization are the main types of colorization methods. Abundant automatic proposals [31–34] benefit from the supervised colorization training on large datasets. Scribble-based methods [35,36] focus on propagating local
user hints to the entire monochrome image. These methods are prone to produce
visual artifacts such as chromatic aberration since the color priors heavily depend
on the training dataset or user preference. Exemplar-based colorization provides
a similar reference for the input monochrome image from pixel [37] or semantic
level [38,39], to generate more plausible colors without manual effort. Dong *et
al.* [37] have utilized weighted average of colors of all potential pixels in the reference image to approximate correct color. He *et al.* [38] have proposed to use
VGG-19 feature of gray-scale image to measure the semantic similarity between
the reference and target image for color propagation while Zhang *et al.* [39]
have added contextual loss to semantically constrain the region re-sampling in
intra-colorization.

Super-Resolution. Super-resolution techniques have been widely utilized in
applications. Learning-based methods have been dominantly leveraged for single image super-resolution (SISR) because of its superior performance, such
as [40–42]. Recent explorations have then introduced another reference image
(e.g., often from an alternative camera or from a semantically similar scene) as
the prior to further improve SR performance. This is so-called Reference-based
super-resolution (refSR). CrossNet [12] and AWnet [11] use the refSR to generate high-quality images in light-fields imaging and high-speed videography.
Additionally, Yang *et al.* [43] suggest the SR improvement with finer texture
reconstruction by learning the semantic priors from the high-definition reference.

3 Method

3.1 Framework

Our system is generally shown in Fig. 1, where we input a HSR monochrome
image and another LSR color image for final HSR color image reconstruction.
To efficiently characterize the cross-domain variations (e.g., illumination, spectra and resolution) for better synthesis, we have divided the entire pipeline into
modularized RefEC, RefColor and RefSR consecutively. Each module is implemented with DNNs for massively exploiting the power of data-driven learning
methodology.

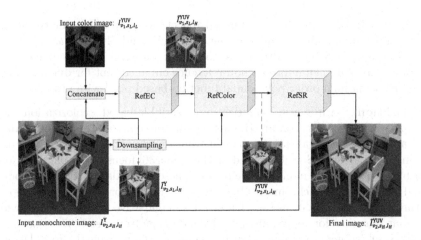

Fig. 1. Framework. A cascaded workflow inputs a HSR monochrome image and a LSR color image for final HSR color image reconstruction using modularized RefEC, RefColor and RefSR to characterize, learn and fuse cross-camera information (e.g., illumination, spectra, and resolution). The intermediate outputs are also provided using dash lines for step-wise illustration.

Let l be the light energy or illumination intensity, s as the spatial resolution, v as the viewpoint, and Y, U, V as respective color/spectral components[1]. The input LSR color image is formulated as $I^{YUV}_{v_1,s_L,l_L}$, while the HSR monochromic image from another camera is $I^{Y}_{v_2,s_H,l_H}$. Normally, monochrome camera offers better light radiance preservation with higher illumination intensity, and higher spatial resolution without Bayer sampling than corresponding color camera. Thus, we simply use subscripts H and L (a.k.a., high and low) to indicate the difference.

In low-light condition, it is an ill-posed problem to reconstruct high-quality color information from a single image due to insufficient exposure prior. Recent learning-based computational imaging [44] motivates us to fuse cross-camera characteristics for high-quality color image reconstruction under low-light illumination condition. Considering that the human visual system is less sensitive to the chrominance than the luminance component, we suggest to transfer the colors from a LSR color image to anther HSR monochrome image in a dual camera system. First, RefEC learns the light radiation level from downscaled monochromic image $I^{Y}_{v_2,\tilde{s}_L,l_H}$ that is the same size scale of $I^{YUV}_{v_1,s_L,l_L}$, and compensates $I^{YUV}_{v_1,s_L,l_L}$ to $\tilde{I}^{YUV}_{v_1,s_L,l_H}$ with brighter color; And in RefColor module, the color information is transferred from $\tilde{I}^{YUV}_{v_1,s_L,l_H}$ at v_1 to $I^{Y}_{v_2,\tilde{s}_L,l_H}$ at v_2 assuming that the similar luminance component shall have close chrominance intensity [37], resulting in $\tilde{I}^{YUV}_{v_2,s_L,l_H}$. Nevertheless, it often incurs the missing regions due to the parallax induced occlusion; Thus an additional post refinement block is included

---

[1] Here, Y and UV represent the luminance and chrominance components in YUV color space that is widely adopted in image/video applications.

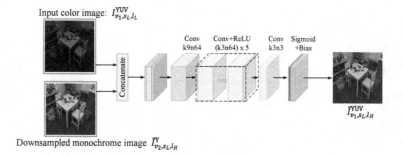

Input color image: $I^{YUV}_{v_1,s_L,l_L}$

Conv k9n64   Conv+ReLU (k3n64) x 5   Conv k3n3   Sigmoid +Bias

Concatenate

$\tilde{I}^{YUV}_{v_1,s_L,l_H}$

Downsampled monochrome image $I^{Y}_{v_2,s_L,l_H}$

Fig. 2. RefEC. k9n64 indicates a kernel size of 9×9 and a feature map channel number of 64. Similar conventions are applied to k3n64, k3n3.

in RefColor to improve warped chrominance components. Finally, $\tilde{I}^{YUV}_{v_2,s_H,l_H}$ is interpolated to native higher resolution as the raw HSR monochromic input, leading to the final output $\hat{I}^{YUV}_{v_2,s_H,l_H}$. Our pipeline stepwise learns and aggregates the dynamics of input LSR color and HSR monochromic images for robust and reliable reconstruction. More details are introduced in the following sections.

3.2   RefEC Net

Retinex Theory [4] is widely used in the image enhancement task to reconstruct real scenes. It assumes the captured color image I could be represented with the element-wise product of illuminance and reflectance map, denoted as below,

$$I = L \cdot R \tag{1}$$

Here, the illuminance map L describes the overall light condition which depends on light source, sensor quantum efficiency and integration time. (To distinguish the illuminance map here with the luma component in YUV color space, we describe the Y channel feature with the brightness or intensity.) The reflectance map R depicts the object's intrinsic color information which keeps constant in various light condition. Commonly, R consists of spectral components like RGB channels for color representation. When I denotes a monochrome image, the decomposition could be in the following form.

$$I = L \cdot \sum_{i \in C} R_i \tag{2}$$

According to Eq. (1), (2), to enhance the image which obtained with pool photon conversion, the L component of $\tilde{I}^{YUV}_{v_1,s_L,l_H}$ could draw on that of $I^{Y}_{v_2,\tilde{s}_L,l_H}$ which shares similar perspective. Inspired by the decomposition module in [7], we handle this problem with stacked CNN modules. Instead of separating exact illuminance and reflectance map, we directly obtain the predicted images following the reference's light condition.

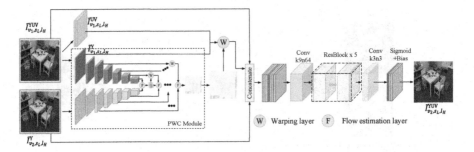

Fig. 3. RefColor. Resblock consists of a k3n64 convolutional layer followed by a batch norm and ReLU layer. PWCNet is used for flow-based color correlation measurement.

As shown in Fig. 2, the input of RefEC net is a dual color-monochrome image pair at the lower resolution, namely, $I^{YUV}_{v_1,s_L,l_L}$ and the downscaled $I^{Y}_{v_2,\tilde{s}_L,l_H}$ on the basis of $I^{Y}_{v_2,s_H,l_H}$. RefEC module is made up of one 9×9 and six 3×3 convolutional layers. Most convolutional layers are followed by a ReLU layer with the exception of the first and last ones. The first convolutional layer extracts features with a large receptive field. Successive layers exploit the non-linearity to establish high dimension characteristics. And a sigmoid function and constant bias follows the last convolutional layer to limit $\tilde{I}^{Y}_{v_1,s_L,l_H} \in [0,1]$ and $\tilde{I}^{UV}_{v_1,s_L,l_H} \in [-0.5, 0.5]$.

3.3   RefColor Net

The goal of the RefColor module is to colorize the coarse monochromic image $I^{Y}_{v_2,\tilde{s}_L,l_H}$ based on $\tilde{I}^{YUV}_{v_1,s_L,l_H}$. As the input dual pairs share the similar perspective, conventional methods commonly adopt hand-crafted features like Gabor features, SURF descriptors or DCT transformation [45,46] to perform a long match with spatial priors, while optical flow could quickly record pixel-level motion in frame prediction and stereo matching tasks [47–50]. Hence, we measure the color correlation based on the optical flow between $I^{Y}_{v_2,\tilde{s}_L,l_H}$ and $\tilde{I}^{Y}_{v_1,s_L,l_H}$. Here, we empirically take PWCNet [51] as optical flow estimation backbone due to its compact and efficient feature representations. Even though warping $\tilde{I}^{YUV}_{v_1,s_L,l_H}$ to the viewpoint v_2 could restore most color information, there are still no appropriate matches for some occluded areas. To fill these holes in the rough result, we add residual-block modules to fuse all reference images and predict each pixel's color information in an end-end way.

As illustrated in Fig. 3, the Y channel of $\tilde{I}^{YUV}_{v_1,s_L,l_H}$ and $I^{Y}_{v_2,\tilde{s}_L,l_H}$ are fed into PWCNet module for reference pixel prediction. To make the best of features at different granularity, PWCNet progressively links different pyramid-level features with the warping layer to estimate large displacement flow. The coarse-to-fine concept could weaken the effect of large parallax but there still exists some missing areas. After warping $\tilde{I}^{YUV}_{v_1,s_L,l_H}$ to v_2, the rough color map $\tilde{I}^{YUV}_{v_2,s_L,l_H}$ is fused with the monochrome image $I^{Y}_{v_2,\tilde{s}_L,l_H}$ and the referenced color image

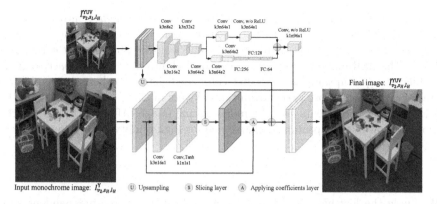

Fig. 4. RefSR. k3n8s2 indicates the convolutional layer with a kernel size of 3×3, a feature map channel number of 64 and a stride of 2. FC,256 denotes the full connection layer with the output channel size of 256. Most convolutional layers are followed by ReLU and the exceptions are clearly annotated. Slicing layer is a tri-linear interpolation operator considering space and intensity effect proposed in [53]. And in the applying coefficients layer, the monochrome image is element-wisely multiplied with the upsampled color coefficients.

$\tilde{I}^{YUV}_{v_1,s_L,l_H}$ through residual blocks to directly predict each pixel's color information $\tilde{I}^{YUV}_{v_2,s_L,l_H}$. Note that sigmoid activation and constant bias are also applied here to make the results follow the YUV space limitation.

3.4 RefSR Net

On the strength of convolution kernel's efficient feature representation, the coarse color information $\tilde{I}^{YUV}_{v_2,s_L,l_H}$ is obtained via transferring $\tilde{I}^{YUV}_{v_1,s_L,l_H}$'s chrominance to $I^{Y}_{v_2,\tilde{s}_L,l_H}$. To reconstruct the high-definition color images, we need to interpolate $\tilde{I}^{YUV}_{v_2,s_L,l_H}$ to the higher resolution. The HSR monochromic input $I^{Y}_{v_2,s_H,l_H}$ reserves the complete structure information which could suppress oversmooth effect in the chrominance interpolation although without color decomposition. Since the trainable slicing layer in [52] shows impressive performance in edge preservation, we take the similar network as HDRNet [52] to reconstruct finer chrominance information.

As shown in Fig. 4, RefSR net extracts color and structure representations from the LSR color image and HSR monochromic image respectively. Instead of directly interpolating $\tilde{I}^{YUV}_{v_2,s_L,l_H}$ with the guidance of $I^{Y}_{v_2,s_H,l_H}$ pixel by pixel, this module decomposes the scene's chrominance at the low resolution and then interpolates the color coefficients to the high resolution in a bilateral-grid upsampling way with the $I^{Y}_{v_2,s_H,l_H}$'s guidance. In the low-resolution branch, the input $\tilde{I}^{YUV}_{v_2,s_L,l_H}$ is firstly converted into the representation of multiple channels at lower resolution after cascaded convolutional layers' processing, which decides the channel granularity for successive bilateral grid. The following local and global stream take the surrounding pixels and the overall consistency into consideration and combine with each other for coarse color coefficients to alleviate large variations in the flat region. To reconstruct finer color coefficients at the high resolution, the HSR monochrome image is projected into the channel space to guide the bilateral-grid upsampling of coarse color coefficients. For better chrominance interpolation, we impose two convolutional layers in the UV space following the fusion of color coefficients and the monochrome image. Afterwards, we add the color residual to the upsampled coarse one for high-quality color images.

4   Experiments

We divide the low light image enhancement task into three independent subtasks. We randomly crop image patches from various datasets for different subtask. And in our task, the dual monochromic-color image pair is simulated via images at different specification as shown in Table 1. The input of our models are converted into the YUV color space [54] and the Y channel feature is chosen as the monochromic input. Besides, to imitate the capture noise in real scenes, various amount of noises to are added to both training and test image pairs as recommended in [55,56]. Due to the page limitation, we provide more training details in the supplementary.

Table 1. Details on the training data setup

Task	Datasets	Viewpoint	Scale	Light energy	numbers
RefEC	Middleburry2006	(v_1, v_2)	(s_L, s_L)	(l_L, l_H)	45K
RefColor	FlyingThings3D	(v_1, v_2)	(s_L, s_L)	(l_H, l_H)	26K
RefSR	DIV2K	(v_2, v_2)	(s_L, s_H)	(l_H, l_H)	15K
Overall	Middleburry2006	(v_1, v_2)	(s_L, s_H)	(l_L, l_H)	1596
Description	The parameters in $(\cdot, \cdot)$ denote the specification of input color and monochromic image respectively. (v_1, v_2) represents different viewpoints. s_L denotes the spatial resolution at 256×256 while $s_H = 1024 \times 1024$. l_L, l_H means different light energy obtained by different sensors. Here we leverage various exposure time to imitate light efficiency diversity between monochrome and color sensors [56]				

Moreover, we also evaluate our model in other datasets and compared with different proposals. Our work is also validated in the monochrome-color smartphone camera module. More details are shown in the following Sect. 4.2.

4.1   Implementation

Our framework is implemented in PyTorch on NVIDIA GTX1080 GPU. All models are optimized with Adam [57]. L1, MSE and Cosine similarity loss are used to supervise the information reconstruction in the YUV space. We pretrain three subtasks with different datasets and than finetune the whole pipeline with Middleburry2006 dataset for more robustness. L1 and Cosine similarity loss for refEC and refColor task at the lower resolution are beneficial to sharp details preservation. And MSE loss dominates in the refSR task for faster convergence. The initial learning rate (lr) of refEC and refSR module is set to $1e^{-4}$. As we exploit the officially pretrained PWCNet model for refColor module initialization, the lr for the gray correlation and refinement module decay from $1e^{-5}$ and $5e^{-5}$, respectively. Afterwards, we finetune the whole pipeline with batchsize = 24, lr = $5e^{-5}$ (except $1e^{-5}$ for the gray correlation module) based on each module's pretrained model. The weight ratio for L1 and Consine similarity is 1 and 0.1 for the finetune procedure.

4.2 Comparison

In this part, we compare our individually-trained modules with other public works in each subtask and then give the performance of the whole pipeline on the simulated and real-captured scenes. Further user study and ablation study are introduced in the supplementary.

RefEC. As the previous work introduced, low light image enhancement and histogram equalization (HE) both can adjust the image's intensity to the normal level. We pick up HE, Retinex Net [7], SSIE Net [8], Zero-DCE [30] methods as the reference result since we leverage different dimension information to handle this problem. Middleburry2014 [58] and S7 ISP Dataset [59] are chosen as test datasets which contain the indoor and outdoor underexposure cases. As shown in Table 2, our work shows great performance above other methods. Note that other methods only use a single frame to enhance image light condition and it is a tough problem to estimate good illumination level. Figure 5 presents qualitative results of these methods. HE only adjusts the brightness to uniformly distribute among the whole range and couldn't compensate for chroma information. Retinex net reconstructs sharp textures but loses realistic gloss on the captured surface. Based on Retinex Net, SSIE Net still suffers from the absence of realistic surface gloss even though it shows high brightness. Zero-DCE takes color constancy as well as local exposure into consideration for good reconstruction, but suffers from some ringing artifacts around the edge due to the smooth illuminance constraint. Our work exploits the monochromic image's illumination as the guidance to adjust the underexposure image to the normal light level, which preserves sharpness and compensate chrominance meanwhile. It is manifested via the increase on $PSNR_{UV}$ in contrast to the input. But the reconstructed highlight areas are relatively dim due to the global intensity consistency.

RefColor. In this task, we collect different proposals from automatic colorization [34] (IAIC), exemplar colorization [38] (DEC) and conventional image patch match [60] (PM) to illustrate our work. The test datasets consist of indoor and outdoor scenes from Middleburry2014 and Cityscapes [61]. Since the input

Table 2. Quantitative average results of exposure compensation models on Middleburry2014 and S7 ISP datasets.

Model	$PSNR_{YUV}$	$PSNR_{UV}$	MS-SSIM	$PSNR_{YUV}$	$PSNR_{UV}$	MS-SSIM
HE	15.1593	29.31	0.6991	20.7308	28.5491	0.858
Retinex Net [7]	17.74	24.51	0.719	20.58	25.689	0.76
SSIE Net [8]	16.5245	24.6488	0.8422	18.2423	22.1694	0.8473
Zero-DCE [30]	26.86	34.7532	0.9327	24.3149	32.7543	0.9271
Ours	33.38	38.45	0.981	26.81	32.97	0.95
input-label	17.301	29.42	0.655	14.99	28.64	0.700
Dataset	Middleburry2014			S7 ISP		

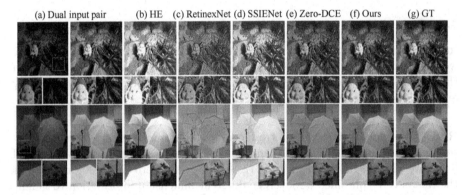

(a) Dual input pair   (b) HE   (c) RetinexNet (d) SSIENet (e) Zero-DCE   (f) Ours   (g) GT

Fig. 5. Qualitative results of different image enhancement algorithms: (a) are the input color image with low luminance and the reference monochrome image. (g) is the ground truth with normal luminance.

images are captured from different viewpoint, it imposes huge pressure to find the appropriate reference patch with global traversal, especially in the strong contrast region like the third scene in Fig. 6. The performance of automatic ICIA depends on the instance segmentation and it may fails to reconstruct colors when the instance is not accurately detected. DEC leverages semantic features to search the potential match in the reference. But this match may lose the awareness of the object structure and result in color distortion around the object boundary. In our work, Y channel features which preserve complete structure information are exploited to calculate the correlation between the target and reference image and shows better performance in colorizing details. However, similarly, when the gray channel correlation is not well measured, color bleeding will affect the colorization's quality (Table 3).

RefSR. There are many proposals in the field of the super resolution. The usage of deep learning benefits texture reconstruction in both single frame or multiple frame super resolution. Most of them show the impressive performance and we list some typical models like RCAN [42], TTSR [43] for the comparison. Here,

Table 3. Quantitative average results of colorization models on Middleburry2014 and Cityscapes datasets. We randomly choose 100 cases from Cityscapes dataset for test due to PM's low computation efficiency.

Model	$PSNR_{YUV}$	$PSNR_{UV}$	MS-SSIM	$PSNR_{YUV}$	$PSNR_{UV}$	MS-SSIM
PM [60]	29.6468	29.0148	0.9272	33.7849	35.6041	0.9796
IAIC [34]	28.8133	27.0774	0.9455	–	–	–
DEC [38]	37.0040	36.0793	0.9825	39.2985	38.7194	0.9927
Ours	41.0477	39.48	0.9924	42.1154	40.791	0.9968
Dataset	Middleburry2014			Cityscapes		

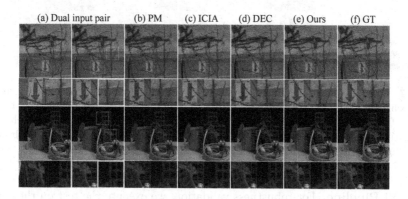

(a) Dual input pair   (b) PM   (c) ICIA   (d) DEC   (e) Ours   (f) GT

Fig. 6. Colorization results of different proposals.

Table 4. Quantitative results of super resolution models on City100 datasets.

Model	$PSNR_{YUV}$	$PSNR_{UV}$	MS-SSIM	$PSNR_{YUV}$	$PSNR_{UV}$	MS-SSIM
RCAN [42]	29.1734	38.226	0.8924	31.4657	36.3924	0.9099
TTSR-rec [43]	29.365	38.2135	0.8965	32.7906	35.4508	0.9234
Ours	40.52	39.066	0.9870	38.6833	37.0752	0.9755
Dataset	City100-iphone			City100-Nikon		

we use the captured low-high resolution image datasets City100 [62] to validate the models' performance. We adopt the pretrained model in their origin work to process the low resolution color image. Note that we use TTSR model which is trained with only reconstruction loss for higher quantitative performance and slice the test image into small patches as the input of TTSR due to GPU memory shortage. Table 4 demonstrates the results of various super resolution methods. In the sharp edges or stripe structure regions, RCAN's result is more blurry than others since it only takes the single low resolution frame as the input. It is also demonstrated that our proposal preserves more clear textures within color interpolation when compared to the information alignment with soft and hard attention mechanism in TTSR (Fig. 7).

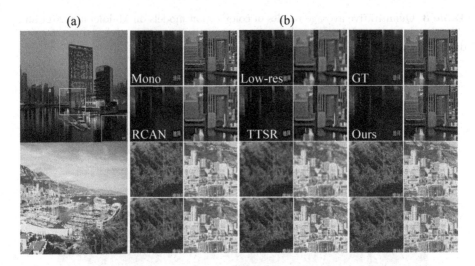

Fig. 7. Qualitative results of super resolution proposals: (a) represents the input monochrome image at the high resolution. And another color image is at the 14 × 14 scale of it. (b) illustrates the details of corresponding green and yellow patches in respectively, monochrome image, color image (×4 for display), ground truth, RCAN, TTSR and our method. (Color figure online)

Overall Pipeline. For robustness validation, we execute the test on the extra simulated datasets and some monochrome-color pairs captured via the dual cameras. We resize the image pairs of Middleburry2014 into 256 × 256 and the corresponding 1024 × 1024 scale. And in this simulated datasets, the average $PSNR_{YUV}$, $PSNR_{UV}$ and MS-SSIM of overall model reach to **38.604dB, 36.906dB** and **0.9804** respectively, while the corresponding performances of the cascaded separative model are 38.444dB, 36.816dB and 0.9802. Besides, we also use the monochrome-color industrial pair cameras and HuaweiP20 to capture the real scenes. In the industrial cameras case, we turn the aperture to the minimum (F = 16) and capture the objects in the normal light condition with the shutter speed of 30 ms. We pre-crop the captured images to generate the 4×-1× monochrome-color image pair. While in HuaweiP20 case, the smartphone automatic exposures with the only color or monochrome sensor. As shown in Fig. 8, our proposal successfully transfers the chrominance of the LSR image to the HSR monochromic image with the noise suppressed.

As we finally refine the overall enhancement in an end-to-end way with the only supervision of re-colored HSR monochromic image, performance on each subtask is affected by global optimization which is shown in Fig. 9, when compared with cascaded individually-trained models. And error accumulation becomes severe due to the cascaded mechanism, especially when color transfer fails from the color viewpoint to the monochrome viewpoint at the low resolution.

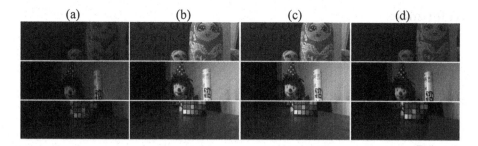

Fig. 8. The performance on the real scenes: Here, we only display partial regions due to space shortage. (a) denotes the LSR color image (×4 scale). (b) and (c) are the HSR monochromic image as well as its color reconstruction. (d) is the value-amplified LSR image for showing noise and blur (×4 scale).

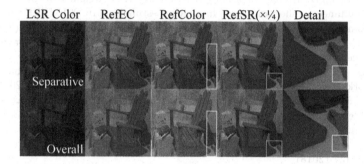

Fig. 9. The performance of the separative and overall model: In the overall model, the result of each subtask has obvious color aberration without hidden supervision but the final generation does well in details. We enlarge the green patch in 4th column to show the difference.

5   Conclusion

We present a cost-effective dual-camera system for low-light color imaging with a HSR monochromic camera and a LSR color one. Such end-to-end cross-camera synthesis is decomposed into consecutive reference-based exposure compensation, reference-based colorization and reference-based super resolution, by which we can effectively capture, learn and fuse hybrid inputs for high-quality color image with improved granularity of illumination, spectra and resolution. Extensive experiments using both synthetic images from public datasets and real captured scenes evidence that our work offers the encouraging low-light imaging efficiency with such dual camera setup.

Acknowledgement. We are grateful for the constructive comments from anonymous reviewers.

References

1. Pizer, S.M., et al.: Adaptive histogram equalization and its variations. Graph. Models Graph. Models Image Process. Comput. Vis. Graph. Image Process. **39**, 355–368 (1987)
2. Coltuc, D., Bolon, P., Chassery, J.M.: Exact histogram specification. IEEE Trans. Image Process. **15**, 1143–1152 (2006)
3. Ibrahim, H., Kong, N.S.P.: Brightness preserving dynamic histogram equalization for image contrast enhancement. IEEE Trans. Consum. Electron. **53**, 1752–1758 (2007)
4. Land, E.H.: The retinex theory of color vision. Sci. Am. **237**(6), 108–128 (1977)
5. Wang, S., Zheng, J., Hu, H.M., Li, B.: Naturalness preserved enhancement algorithm for non-uniform illumination images. IEEE Trans. Image Process. **22**, 3538–3548 (2013)
6. Fu, X., Zeng, D., Huang, Y., Zhang, X.P.S., Ding, X.: A weighted variational model for simultaneous reflectance and illumination estimation. In: 2016 IEEE Conference on Computer Vision and Pattern Recognition (CVPR), pp. 2782–2790 (2016)
7. Wei, C., Wang, W., Yang, W., Liu, J.: Deep retinex decomposition for low-light enhancement. arxiv abs/1808.04560 (2018)
8. Zhang, Y., Di, X.G., Zhang, B., Wang, C.: Self-supervised image enhancement network: training with low light images only. arxiv abs/2002.11300 (2020)
9. Wang, J., Tan, W., Niu, X., Yan, B.: RDGAN: retinex decomposition based adversarial learning for low-light enhancement. In: 2019 IEEE International Conference on Multimedia and Expo (ICME), pp. 1186–1191 (2019)
10. Brady, D.J., Pang, W., Li, H., Ma, Z., Tao, Y., Cao, X.: Parallel cameras. Optica **5**, 127–137 (2018)
11. Cheng, M., et al.: A dual camera system for high spatiotemporal resolution video acquisition. IEEE Trans. Pattern Anal. Mach. Intell. (2020)
12. Zheng, H., Ji, M., Wang, H., Liu, Y., Fang, L.: Crossnet: an end-to-end reference-based super resolution network using cross-scale warping. In: ECCV (2018)
13. Wikipedia contributors: Retina – Wikipedia, the free encyclopedia (2020). https://en.wikipedia.org/w/index.php?title=Retina&oldid=964207154. Accessed 30 June 2020
14. Morie, J., McCallum, K.: Handbook of Research on the Global Impacts and Roles of Immersive Media. Advances in Media, Entertainment, and the Arts. IGI Global (2019)
15. Robinson, S., Schmidt, J.: Fluorescent penetrant sensitivity and removability: what the eye can see, a fluorometer can measure. Mater. Eval. **42**, 1029–1034 (1984)
16. Bayer, B.E.: Color image array. US Patent 3971056 (1976)
17. Wang, J.J., Xue, T., Barron, J.T., Chen, J.: Stereoscopic dark flash for low-light photography. In: 2019 IEEE International Conference on Computational Photography (ICCP), pp. 1–10 (2019)
18. Trinidad, M.C., Martin-Brualla, R., Kainz, F., Kontkanen, J.: Multi-view image fusion. In: 2019 IEEE/CVF International Conference on Computer Vision (ICCV), pp. 4100–4109 (2019)
19. Dong, X., Li, W.: Shoot high-quality color images using dual-lens system with monochrome and color cameras. Neurocomputing **352**, 22–32 (2019)
20. Chu, X., Zhang, B., Ma, H., Xu, R., Li, J., Li, Q.: Fast, accurate and lightweight super-resolution with neural architecture search. arXiv preprint arXiv:1901.07261 (2019)

21. Wronski, B., et al.: Handheld multi-frame super-resolution. ACM Trans. Graph. (TOG) **38**, 1–18 (2019)
22. Godard, C., Matzen, K., Uyttendaele, M.: Deep burst denoising. In: Proceedings of the European Conference on Computer Vision (ECCV), pp. 538–554 (2018)
23. Ignatov, A., Van Gool, L., Timofte, R.: Replacing mobile camera ISP with a single deep learning model. In: Proceedings of the IEEE/CVF Conference on Computer Vision and Pattern Recognition Workshops, pp. 536–537 (2020)
24. Dong, X., et al.: Fast efficient algorithm for enhancement of low lighting video. In: ICME (2011)
25. Li, L., Wang, R., Wang, W., Gao, W.: A low-light image enhancement method for both denoising and contrast enlarging. In: 2015 IEEE International Conference on Image Processing (ICIP), pp. 3730–3734 (2015)
26. Kimmel, R., Elad, M., Shaked, D., Keshet, R., Sobel, I.: A variational framework for retinex. Int. J. Comput. Vision **52**, 7–23 (2004)
27. Fu, X., Zeng, D., Huang, Y., Ding, X., Zhang, X.P.S.: A variational framework for single low light image enhancement using bright channel prior. In: 2013 IEEE Global Conference on Signal and Information Processing, pp. 1085–1088 (2013)
28. Guo, X., Li, Y., Ling, H.: LIME: low-light image enhancement via illumination map estimation. IEEE Trans. Image Process. **26**, 982–993 (2017)
29. Wei, C., Wang, W., Yang, W., Liu, J.: Deep retinex decomposition for low-light enhancement. In: British Machine Vision Conference (2018)
30. Guo, C., et al.: Zero-reference deep curve estimation for low-light image enhancement. In: Proceedings of the IEEE Conference on Computer Vision and Pattern Recognition (CVPR), pp. 1780–1789 (2020)
31. Iizuka, S., Simo-Serra, E., Ishikawa, H.: Let there be color!: joint end-to-end learning of global and local image priors for automatic image colorization with simultaneous classification. ACM Trans. Graph. **35**, 110:1–110:11 (2016)
32. Zhang, R., Isola, P., Efros, A.A.: Colorful image colorization. In: ECCV (2016)
33. Zhao, J., Liu, L., Snoek, C.G.M., Han, J., Shao, L.: Pixel-level semantics guided image colorization. arxiv abs/1808.01597 (2018)
34. Su, J.W., Chu, H.K., Huang, J.B.: Instance-aware image colorization. In: IEEE Conference on Computer Vision and Pattern Recognition (CVPR) (2020)
35. Zhang, R., et al.: Real-time user-guided image colorization with learned deep priors. ACM Trans. Graph. **36**, 119:1–119:11 (2017)
36. Xiao, Y., Zhou, P., Zheng, Y.: Interactive deep colorization using simultaneous global and local inputs. In: ICASSP 2019-2019 IEEE International Conference on Acoustics, Speech and Signal Processing (ICASSP), pp. 1887–1891 (2019)
37. Dong, X., Li, W., Wang, X., Wang, Y.: Learning a deep convolutional network for colorization in monochrome-color dual-lens system. In: AAAI (2019)
38. He, M., Chen, D., Liao, J., Sander, P.V., Yuan, L.: Deep exemplar-based colorization. ACM Trans. Graph. (TOG) **37**, 1–16 (2018)
39. Zhang, B., et al.: Deep exemplar-based video colorization. In: 2019 IEEE/CVF Conference on Computer Vision and Pattern Recognition (CVPR), pp. 8044–8053 (2019)
40. Zhang, Y., Tian, Y., Kong, Y., Zhong, B., Fu, Y.: Residual dense network for image super-resolution. In: 2018 IEEE/CVF Conference on Computer Vision and Pattern Recognition, pp. 2472–2481 (2018)
41. Liu, D., Wen, B., Fan, Y., Loy, C.C., Huang, T.S.: Non-local recurrent network for image restoration. In: NeurIPS (2018)
42. Zhang, Y., Li, K., Li, K., Wang, L., Zhong, B., Fu, Y.: Image super-resolution using very deep residual channel attention networks. In: ECCV (2018)

43. Yang, F., Yang, H., Fu, J., Lu, H., Guo, B.: Learning texture transformer network for image super-resolution. In: CVPR (2020)
44. Barbastathis, G., Ozcan, A., Situ, G.: On the use of deep learning for computational imaging. Optica **6**, 921–943 (2019)
45. Ironi, R., Cohen-Or, D., Lischinski, D.: Colorization by example. In: Rendering Techniques, pp. 201–210. Citeseer (2005)
46. Gupta, R.K., Chia, A.Y.S., Rajan, D., Ng, E.S., Zhiyong, H.: Image colorization using similar images. In: Proceedings of the 20th ACM International Conference on Multimedia, pp. 369–378 (2012)
47. Liu, Z., Yeh, R.A., Tang, X., Liu, Y., Agarwala, A.: Video frame synthesis using deep voxel flow. In: Proceedings of International Conference on Computer Vision (ICCV) (2017)
48. Jiang, H., Sun, D., Jampani, V., Yang, M.H., Learned-Miller, E.G., Kautz, J.: Super slomo: high quality estimation of multiple intermediate frames for video interpolation. In: 2018 IEEE/CVF Conference on Computer Vision and Pattern Recognition, pp. 9000–9008 (2018)
49. Bao, W., Lai, W.S., Zhang, X., Gao, Z., Yang, M.H.: MEMC-Net: motion estimation and motion compensation driven neural network for video interpolation and enhancement. IEEE Trans. Pattern Anal. Mach. Intell. (2018)
50. Haris, M., Shakhnarovich, G., Ukita, N.: Space-time-aware multi-resolution video enhancement. In: IEEE Conference on Computer Vision and Pattern Recognition (CVPR) (2020)
51. Sun, D., Yang, X., Liu, M.Y., Kautz, J.: PWC-Net: CNNs for optical flow using pyramid, warping, and cost volume. In: 2018 IEEE/CVF Conference on Computer Vision and Pattern Recognition, pp. 8934–8943 (2018)
52. Gharbi, M., Chen, J., Barron, J.T., Hasinoff, S.W., Durand, F.: Deep bilateral learning for real-time image enhancement. ACM Trans. Graph. (TOG) **36**, 118 (2017)
53. Chen, J., Paris, S., Durand, F.: Real-time edge-aware image processing with the bilateral grid. ACM Trans. Graph. (TOG) **26**, 103-es (2007)
54. Wikipedia contributors: YUV – Wikipedia, the free encyclopedia (2020). https://en.wikipedia.org/w/index.php?title=YUV&oldid=962998638. Accessed 30 June 2020
55. Schechner, Y.Y., Nayar, S.K., Belhumeur, P.N.: Multiplexing for optimal lighting. IEEE Trans. Pattern Anal. Mach. Intell. **29**, 1339–1354 (2007)
56. Jeon, H.G., Lee, J.Y., Im, S., Ha, H., Kweon, I.S.: Stereo matching with color and monochrome cameras in low-light conditions. In: 2016 IEEE Conference on Computer Vision and Pattern Recognition (CVPR), pp. 4086–4094 (2016)
57. Kingma, D.P., Ba, J.: Adam: a method for stochastic optimization. CoRR abs/1412.6980 (2015)
58. Scharstein, D., et al.: High-resolution stereo datasets with subpixel-accurate ground truth. In: Jiang, X., Honegger, J., Koch, R. (eds.) GCPR 2014. LNCS, vol. 8753, pp. 31–42. Springer, Cham (2014). https://doi.org/10.1007/978-3-319-11752-2_3
59. Schwartz, E., Giryes, R., Bronstein, A.M.: DeepISP: toward learning an end-to-end image processing pipeline. IEEE Trans. Image Process. **28**, 912–923 (2019)
60. Welsh, T., Ashikhmin, M., Mueller, K.: Transferring color to greyscale images. In: Proceedings of the 29th Annual Conference on Computer Graphics and Interactive Techniques, pp. 277–280 (2002)

61. Cordts, M., et al.: The cityscapes dataset for semantic urban scene understanding. In: Proceedings of the IEEE Conference on Computer Vision and Pattern Recognition (CVPR) (2016)
62. Chen, C., Xiong, Z., Tian, X., Zha, Z.J., Wu, F.: Camera lens super-resolution. In: Proceedings of the IEEE Conference on Computer Vision and Pattern Recognition, pp. 1652–1660 (2019)

Frequency Attention Network: Blind Noise Removal for Real Images

Hongcheng Mo[1,2], Jianfei Jiang[1], Qin Wang[1(✉)], Dong Yin[2], Pengyu Dong[2], and Jingjun Tian[2]

[1] Shanghai Jiao Tong University, Shanghai 200240, China
{momo1689,qinqinwang}@sjtu.edu.cn
[2] Fullhan Research, Shanghai, China

Abstract. With outstanding feature extraction capabilities, deep convolutional neural networks (CNNs) have achieved extraordinary improvements in image denoising tasks. However, because of the difference of statistical characteristics of signal-dependent noise and signal-independent noise, it is hard to model real noise for training and blind real image denoising is still an important challenge problem. In this work we propose a method for blind image denoising that combines frequency domain analysis and attention mechanism, named frequency attention network (FAN). We adopt wavelet transform to convert images from spatial domain to frequency domain with more sparse features to utilize spectral information and structure information. For the denoising task, the objective of the neural network is to estimate the optimal solution of the wavelet coefficients of the clean image by nonlinear characteristics, which makes FAN possess good interpretability. Meanwhile, spatial and channel mechanisms are employed to enhance feature maps at different scales for capturing contextual information. Extensive experiments on the synthetic noise dataset and two real-world noise benchmarks indicate the superiority of our method over other competing methods at different noise type cases in blind image denoising.

1   Introduction

Image denoising is a very critical low-level task in computer vision, and the quality of the image has a significant impact on high-level tasks – image classification, semantic segmentation, object localization, instance segmentation. Image denoising is an ill-posed problem like a transcendental equation which is difficult to find a unique solution by reversing it but only by optimizing it. For a real-world noisy image, noise usually results from the interaction of photons of the image and electrons thermal movement when the sensor obtains the image signal, such as shot noise, dark current noise, quantification noise, etc [1,2]. During ISP pipeline, some nonlinear operations like demosaicking and gamma correction also change the noise distribution which makes real-world noise more sophisticated.

© Springer Nature Switzerland AG 2021
H. Ishikawa et al. (Eds.): ACCV 2020, LNCS 12623, pp. 168–184, 2021.
https://doi.org/10.1007/978-3-030-69532-3_11

For decades, methods of image denoising can be divided into two categories, model-driven and data-driven. One exact scheme of the first category is to find similar blocks by exploiting the correlations that exist in the image information itself and using these similar blocks to estimate the clean image [3–5]. Another direction is to exploit prior information based on the transformed domain by converting image signal to another domain for shrinkage like frequency domain. The noise is usually contained in the medium and high frequency information of the image due to the randomness and sparsity of the noise which causes the gradient of the image increases so that reasonable reconstruction of the medium and high frequency information can effectively remove noise [6, 7]. Recently, data-driven deep convolutional neural networks (CNNs) are increasingly applied on the image denoising task in that CNN can extract high-dimensional features of images and utilize them to restore clean images.

Deep CNN denoisers significantly improve image denoising performance on synthetic noise model [8–13] but tend to be over-fitted to the realistic noise model like additive white Gaussian noise (AWGN). When they are applied on the real-world denoising task, they are lack of the ability to eliminate both signal-dependent noise and signal-independent noise. Thus, real-world denoising is still a challenging task since noise distributions vary a lot in different scenes.

In this article, we tackle this issue by developing a frequency attention network (FAN) which combine frequency domain analysis and a deep CNN model for the image denoising task. From the perspective of Fourier, image transformation methods that can enhance the performance of the network are essentially to change the frequency domain information of the image to enhance the feature [14]. Motivated by this perspective and sensitivity of frequency components in human visual system (HVS) [15], we employ wavelet transform to extract the spectral information and structure information of images as the prior information of the network. The wavelet transform can preserve the structural information of the image and facilitate high-dimensional features for image restoration.

Flexibility and robustness are still significant problems for most denoising methods. [9,16] introduce the noise map to train denoising networks jointly which can provide more information to help extract image features and we adopt it to accelerate our network training. We combine spatial attention mechanism and channel attention mechanism to enhance the feature map for improving the feature extraction ability of the network and removing signal-dependent noise. At last, we explore the influence of different individual components of the network and different wavelet basis functions.

To sum up, the contributions of this paper are following:

- We proposed frequency attention networks (FAN) combining traditional signal processing methods and deep learning, which makes the method based on neural network with more interpretability from the perspective of frequency domain.
- We introduced the *Spatial-Channel Attention Block* which combines the spatial attention and channel attention mechanisms to enhance feature maps and help to better extract the main features of the image.

- We evaluate the effect of different wavelet basis functions on denoising performance and experiments show Haar wavelet with symmetry, orthogonality and compactly supported characteristics can achieve the best result.
- Experiments on synthetic noise datasets and real noise datasets respectively prove the superiority of our model compared with competing methods and can achieve state-of-the-art results.

2   Related Work

With the rapid development of convolutional neural networks in the field of computer vision, many researchers have proposed algorithms based on deep learning to solve low-level and high-level computer vision problems. Some combination of traditional methods and deep learning provides more comprehensive interpretability for neural networks. Next, we briefly describe representative methods of image denoising.

Traditional Denoising Methods: Noise images can be seen as the sum of clean signal and noise signal with their relationship usually expressed as $Y = X + n$. Towards employing high frequency characteristic of noise, image denoising methods on the different transform domains were widely proposed especially DCT [7,17] and wavelet transform [6,18]. Wavelet transform is a widely application method in signal processing, which uses the wavelet basis function as a filter to extract the frequency information of the image and then solve sub-band reconstruction coefficients in accordance with the desired expectation to obtain a denoised image. Based on images self-similar patches, it is effective to make full use of the structural information of the images themselves as prior information to approximate the optimal estimate clean patches through their statistical relationships involving CBM3D [19], NLM [3], NL-Bayes [5]. Another type of solution is to convert the image denoising task to a mathematical optimization problem based on the noise model and use decomposition or dictionary-based to solve it, such as low-rank model [20,21], sparse representation [22–24]. However, the main drawbacks of these algorithms are computationally expensive and time-consuming in that they need to be re-implemented for new coming images so that they are difficult in gaining wider access.

Deep CNN Denoiser: With the widespread use of deep convolutional networks in computer vision, deep CNN has also led to great performance on image denoising. DnCNN [8] is the first to introduce a residual network for denoising, allowing the network to learn the distribution of noise and then remove the noise to get the result. FFDNet [9] adopts downsampling, introducing noise map and orthogonalization to improve the speed, flexibility and robustness of the denoising network. CBDNet [16] adopts two-stage denoising strategy including estimating noise map and denoising, using asymmetric loss function for training. MWCNN [25] replaces the downsampling of UNet with wavelet transform to retain more information using orthogonalization. VDN [26] introduces variable inference to predict the noise distribution for denoising. CBDNet, MWCNN and

VDN all adopt UNet network [27] as their backbone which includes downsampling and can be operated for pixel-level tasks, with excellent results for image restoration task that require attention to pixel points.

An improvement for image denoising is to apply attention mechanisms for adapting to different regions. RIDNet [28] introduces enhancement attention modules to select essential features and use a residual on residual structure to build networks. KPN [29] utilizes the idea of non-local mean to train out filter windows and then use these filter cores for image reconstruction. [30] considers the deformable convolution to predict the distribution of filter kernels for obtaining good results. However, these networks are learned in spatial domain which are costly to learn and underutilize the frequency domain characteristics of the noise.

More recently, frequency domain learning has shown its potential to improve model efficiency and feature extraction capabilities. Both [31] and [?] employ DCT transformations to convert training data into the frequency domain while the front applied to image classification and the latter applied to image segmentation. For the image denoising task, the spectral information can reflect the relationship between noise and clean image signal in the frequency domain. Wavelet transform is commonly used to convert images to the frequency domain which preserves both the spatial structure information and the spectral information of the image at the same time. Thus, we propose our method based on the characteristic of wavelet transform and deep learning for blind image denoising.

3   Frequency Attention Network

This section presents our FAN consisting of data pre-processing, networks architecture and attention design. To begin with, we show FAN architecture including *Est-Net* and *De-net*. Then, we analysis the effects of wavelet transform characteristics on network performance. Finally, we introduce *Spatial-Channel Attention Block* used for feature map enhancement.

3.1   Network Architecture

Inspired by the observation that human visual system (HVS) is more sensitive to the spatial resolution of the luminance signal than that of the chrominance signal [32] and HVS has the varying sensitivity to different frequency components [15], we convert the image from the RGB color space to YCbCr color space for denoising.

As shown in Fig. 1, the network we designed contains two subnetworks including the noise estimation network and the denoising network. *Est-Net* takes the noisy image as input and estimates different noise level map for each channel. *Est-Net* is composed of five full-convolutional layers, each consisting of only the Conv and PReLU layers excluding the batch normalization layer and the pooling layer. The filter size is 3×3 and the feature map is set as 64. The noise map

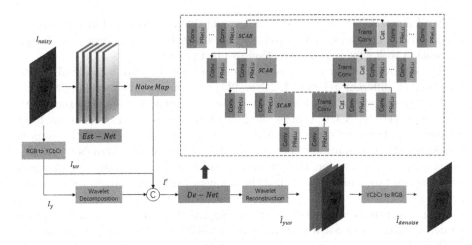

Fig. 1. Frequency attention network architecture

which can improve network flexibility and generalizability for different noise levels is also conductive to increase the convergence speed of the network because its redundancy can help to better extract image features. Given a training set $\{I_{noisy}, I_{gt}, \sigma_{gt}\}_{i=1}^{N}$, loss of the estimated noise map $\hat{\sigma}(I_{noisy})$ is defined as

$$\mathcal{L}_{map} = \frac{1}{N}\sum_{i=1}^{N} ||\hat{\sigma}(I_{noisy}) - \sigma_{gt}||_1 \tag{1}$$

where $|| \cdot ||_1$ denotes l_1 norm.

In the denoising network, the input RGB images are transformed to the YCbCr color space including luminance I_y and chroma I_{uv}. Considering the sensitivity of the human visual system to luminance, I_y is converted to the frequency domain by wavelet transform for reserving spectral information and structure information while I_{uv} stays original. We concatenate the processed data and noise map to get I' as input to the *De-Net* network which contains 4 encoder blocks and 3 decoder blocks and there is a skip connection to concatenate two blocks under the same scale.

The U-Net structure can use feature fusion at different resolutions to obtain better contextualized representations, but it will cause the loss of image details at high resolution when the network depth at each scale is consistent. Aim at retaining more details, we adopted variable depth design for *De-Net* where the numbers of residual convolutional blocks at different scales increase with the resolution to ensure that our network can obtain a stronger expressive ability. Besides, we add the SCAB module after each encoder for feature enhancement. For the denoised image $\hat{I}(I_{noisy})$, we define image loss of *De-Net* as

$$\mathcal{L}_{img} = \frac{1}{N}\sum_{i=1}^{N} ||\hat{I}(I_{noisy}) - I_{gt}||_1 \tag{2}$$

Finally, we obtain the complete denoised image by wavelet reconstruction and convert it to RGB color space. Given a training set $\{I_{noisy}, I_{gt}\}_{i=1}^N$, loss function of our networks is defined as

$$\mathcal{L}(\theta) = \mathcal{L}_{img} + \gamma\mathcal{L}_{map} \tag{3}$$

3.2 Wavelet Transform

Wavelet is an important tool for the analysis of unstable signals while the image as a 2D plane unstable signal is well suited for study with the wavelet. Wavelet transformation of one image decomposes the image into different sub-bands based on the frequency information and the processing of the medium and the high frequency sub-bands can result in noise removal. Two-dimensional wavelet decomposition of level j can be described as

$$f(x,y) = \sum_{j,m,n \in Z} a_{j,m,n}(k)\psi_{j,m,n}(x,y) \tag{4}$$

where $f(x)$ can be expanded into a linear combination of wavelet basis functions with $a_{j,m,n}(k)$ as the expansion factor and $\psi_{j,m,n}$ as the wavelet basis function. For FAN, reconstruction denoising result can be defined as following,

$$\hat{I}(I_{noisy}) = \sum_{k \in Z} W(a_k)\psi_k(I_{noisy}) \tag{5}$$

where $W(\cdot)$ refers to network output. It is difficult to deduce the expression relationship between $W(a_k)$ and a_k through mathematical theory but the optimal estimation of a_k can be obtained with the help of the nonlinear characteristics of the neural network and auxiliary noise map by deep learning to restore the image as close as possible to ground truth. Therefore, the learning objective of our neural network can be abstracted as the optimal solution to the wavelet coefficients.

Separable wavelets which is widely used for two-dimension wavelet transform generally use orthogonal wavelets and for discrete signal discrete orthogonal wavelets have completeness to retain all the energy of the image signal in the transformation process. Meanwhile, orthogonal wavelets can reduce the data correlation between different sub-bands. Therefore, using wavelet to transform the image into the frequency domain will not lose any information. Instead, it can use the frequency characteristics of the image signal in the frequency domain to help the deep convolutional network extract its nonlinear characteristics.

The wavelet transform includes discrete wavelet transform (DWT), stationary wavelet transform (SWT) and continuous wavelet transform (CWT) where CWT is the analysis of continuous signals, DWT and SWT are the analysis of discrete signals. The decompose transformation process of DWT and SWT is shown in the Fig. 2. SWT is also called unsampled wavelet transform, which can calculate the wavelet transform value point by point. The biggest difference between SWT and DWT is that SWT has translation invariance because

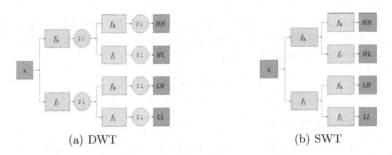

(a) DWT   (b) SWT

Fig. 2. Discrete wavelet transform and stationary wavelet transform

DWT performs downsampling operation during the calculation process which will cause the pseudo-Gibbs phenomena of reconstruction images. Meanwhile, SWT can make the decomposition result keep the same size as the original image to retain more prior information for network training and avoid information loss caused by the downsampling and upsampling operation of the chroma layer for ensuring the same size of the input and the output when we perform DWT on the luminance layer instead of the chroma layer.

3.3 Spatial-Channel Attention Block (SCAB)

Signal-independent noise can be easily filtered out from the wavelet sub-band through neural network learning, but signal-dependent noise is not easy to remove because of the high correlation between high-frequency signal and noise. In order to make full use of the inter-channel and inter-spatial relationships of the image, we used a *Spatial-Channel Attention Block* to extract the features in the convolutional stream. The schematic of SCAB is shown in Fig. 3. We extracted the distribution of noise levels through *Est-Net* and also characterized the structure information of noise which we can use spatial attention mechanism to refine features map of I_y. Meanwhile, we apply channel attention mechanism [33] on I_y to achieve the feature recalibration.

Spatial attention is used to extract the inter-spatial relationship of images. Non-local block [12,34] generates attention map through point-by-point calculation of the feature map, but this method has limitations on the size of the image and the calculation amount is large when the image size is too large. CBAM [35] uses GAP and GMP to utilize the full channel information which saves the amount of calculation while missing some feature information. We use a progressively expanding multi-layer convolution operation to obtain an effective tradeoff between model complexity and performance. Dilated convolution and expanding filter kernel size are adopted to increase the receptive field, and gradually decreasing channels reduce the computational complexity. At the same time, 1×1 convolution layers distributed between convolutional layers work to gather feature information in receptive fields of different ranges so as to calculate the dependency relationship on the feature map space.

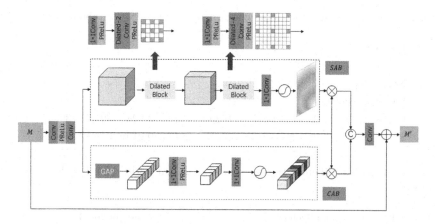

Fig. 3. Spatial-channel attention block

Channel attention utilizes the squeeze and excitation operation [33] to enhance the main features of the feature map based on the inter-channel relationship. For an input feature map $M \in \mathbb{R}^{1 \times 1 \times c}$, firstly generate the channel-by-channel statistics $d \in \mathbb{R}^{1 \times 1 \times c}$ through global pooling as the squeeze operation. This statistic expresses the entire image under this type of feature extraction convolution kernel global description. The excitation operation is used for fully capturing the dependencies between channels through two convolutional layers with the sigmoid gating and obtains activations $\hat{d} \in \mathbb{R}^{1 \times 1 \times c}$ as follow

$$\hat{d} = \sigma(W_2 \delta(W_1 \mathrm{GAP}(f_{in}))) \tag{6}$$

where δ refers to PReLU function and σ is sigmoid gating.

In the image restoration, the attention mechanism can be regarded as an extension of the classical method ideas on the neural network. Similar to the bilateral filter [36] which adopts the difference between the spatial domain and the value domain to calculate the weight of different locations for the central area, spatial attention mechanism can re-weight the feature map according to the location of the features and help the network learn where to be paid attention. Channel attention is the overall enhancement of different types of features, which emphasizes the features corresponding to edge information in order to achieve the effect of better retaining edges. The fusion of spatial and channel attention mechanisms can enhance the feature maps in the high dimension, which is conducive to smoothing the flat region and recovering the details of the texture region.

4 Experiments

In this section, we design various ablation study to demonstrate effectiveness of our strategy and evaluate performance by our method on synthetic and real noise datasets compared with previous outstanding methods. The code of our method is available at https://github.com/momo1689/FAN.

Table 1. Impact of each individual components (Test on SIDD validation dataset)

Wavelet		✓		✓	✓	✓	✓
SCAB			✓		✓	✓	✓
Noise Map	✓	✓	✓	✓		✓	✓
Variable Depth			✓	✓	✓		✓
PSNR (dB)	39.04	39.13	39.29	39.16	39.24	39.37	39.45
SSIM	0.9124	0.9139	0.9157	0.9144	0.9158	0.9172	0.9184

Table 2. Impact of different types of wavelet on real-world noise (SIDD validation dataset)

Wavelet	Haar	Daubechies				Biorthogonal		
		db2	db3	db4	db5	bior2.2	bior3.3	bior4.4
PSNR	39.45	39.36	39.25	39.17	39.10	39.39	39.35	39.26
SSIM	0.9184	0.9175	0.9163	0.9160	0.9157	0.9176	0.9173	0.9161

4.1 Implement Details

We employ SIDD real noise dataset and synthetic noise with as our training dataset, respectively. Each image is cropped to a size of $128*128*3$ as input, each epoch trained 96000 images and 50 epochs trained each time. We adopt Adam [37] as the optimizer with $\beta_1 = 0.9$, $\beta_2 = 0.999$ while we set initial learning rate as 2e-4 and adopt the cosine annealing strategy [38] with the final learning rate as 5e-10. The hyper-parameter γ is set as 0.2 both for real-noise and synthetic noise training.

4.2 Ablation Study

Table 1 shows our ablation study on the impact of different architectural components including wavelet transform, SCAB, noise map and variable depth when testing on the SIDD validation dataset.

Compared with the spatial domain image as input, the wavelet transform can simultaneously assemble frequency domain information and spatial structure information for learning and improves the network performance by 0.16 dB. Wavelet decomposition essentially regards the wavelet basis function as a filter to decompose the image into different frequency bands. This operation can also be learned by the neural network without wavelet transformation. However, the Haar wavelet with orthogonality, compactly supported and symmetry provides a certain prior constraint for the image to help the network pay attention to the frequency domain information of the image during training process.

In order to choose a better wavelet basis function for wavelet transform, we compare the performance of Haar, Daubechies and Biorthogonal wavelets on our proposed FAN and the result is shown on Table 2. Daubechies wavelet is a

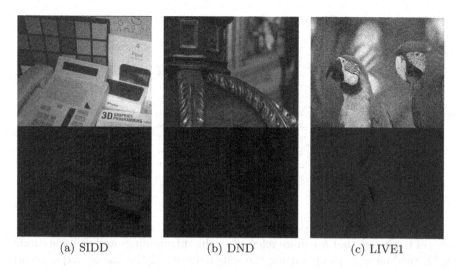

(a) SIDD   (b) DND   (c) LIVE1

Fig. 4. The noise map predicted by our FAN on SIDD, DND and LIVE1 dataset. The noisy image and noise map of one typical image of SIDD validation dataset, one of DND dataset and one of LIVE1 dataset with $\sigma = 50$.

continuous orthogonal compactly supported wavelet and suitable for whitening wavelet coefficients [39]. However, Daubechies wavelet is an asymmetric wavelet which will cause the phase distortion of images during wavelet reconstruction and the performance of Daubechies wavelet gets worse as the approximation order increases. In order to construct "linear phase" filters, biorthogonal wavelets are proposed to construct compactly supported symmetric wavelets [40]. Note that the biorthogonal wavelet does not perform better on the denoising task compared with Haar, which indicates that the strictly orthogonal wavelet basis function can decompose the image into an orthogonal space and is effective in eliminating the correlation of the image signal.

We also experiment on applying the wavelet decomposition of the chroma layer to concatenate that of the luminance layer as input and introducing the multi-resolution decomposition of wavelet for wavelet transform respectively and we observe these operations perform slightly worse than not using them. We conclude that chrominance noise is eventually greater than luminance noise and distributed in lower frequency band which results in insufficient separation of chromiannce noise. In the case of the same number of convolution kernels, increasing the width of the network input will affect the ability of the network to extract features and limit the denoising performance.

Furthermore, considering that the distribution of luminance noise and chrminance noise is inconsistent, we also train a FAN_{dual} with two *De-Nets* for the lumianance layer and the chroma layer respectively. However, the final observation is that FAN_{dual} and FAN achieve close denoising results on the test dataset while parameters of FAN_{dual} is almost twice that of FAN so that we still adopt FAN for testing.

Table 3. The PSNR (dB) results about AWGN removal of three datasets

Sigma	Datasets	CBM3D [19]	WNNM [20]	NCSR [23]	MWCNN [25]	DnCNN [8]	MemNet [10]	FFDNet [9]	VDN [26]	FAN (Ours)
$\sigma = 15$	LIVE1	33.08	31.70	31.46	32.33	33.72	33.84	33.96	33.94	**34.16**
	Set5	33.90	32.92	32.57	33.84	34.04	34.18	34.31	34.34	**35.01**
	CBSD68	32.89	31.27	30.84	31.86	33.87	33.76	33.85	33.90	**34.08**
$\sigma = 25$	LIVE1	30.39	29.15	29.05	31.56	31.23	31.26	31.37	31.50	**31.66**
	Set5	31.34	30.61	30.33	29.84	31.88	31.98	32.10	32.24	**32.59**
	CBSD68	30.13	28.62	28.35	29.41	31.22	31.17	31.21	31.35	**31.46**
$\sigma = 50$	LIVE1	27.13	26.07	26.06	26.86	27.95	27.99	28.10	28.36	**28.44**
	Set5	28.25	27.58	27.20	28.61	28.95	29.10	29.25	29.47	**29.51**
	CBSD68	26.94	25.86	25.75	26.54	27.91	27.91	27.95	28.19	**28.24**

We develop SCAB to make the network pay more attention to the main features of the image that are more relevant to the surroundings and to some extent SCAB module aims at enhancing the self-similarity of the image. Experiments also show that the attention module has achieve 0.32 dB improvement on the overall network.

For blind denoising tasks, the estimation of the noise level map can make the network adaptive to different scenes with various noise distribution and help the network adjust the ability of extract features to remove noise. Compared with no noise map, FAN with noise map can reach a faster convergence when training and better visual results. Figure 4 shows noise level map of real-world noise and synthetic noise predicted by our proposed FAN including a typical image of SIDD validation dataset, another of DND dataset and an image of LIVE1 with $\sigma = 50$. It can be seen that the noise intensity information in the predicted map of real-world noise is more hierarchical because of signal-dependent noise and signal-independent noise while noise map of synthetic noise has a smooth distribution in each channel.

4.3 Experiments on Synthetic Noise

We collect 4744 pictures from Waterloo Exploration Database [41] and cropped them into $N = 20 * 4744$ pictures with the size of $128 * 128 * 3$ for training. We adopt three common image restoration datasets as test datasets to evaluate the performance of different competing methods. There is still another challenge to make noise contribution of synthetic noise as close as real-noise and it is unfair to adopt one noise model for training when other methods train with another. Considering that most denoising algorithms use additive white Gaussian noise (AWGN) for the assumption of synthetic noise, in order to compare the different methods more fairly, our noise model is defined as following,

$$Y = X + n, n \sim \mathcal{N}(0, \sigma^2) \tag{7}$$

Table 3 lists the average PSNR results of different competing methods on three testing datasets and Fig. 5 shows some denoising results of different method

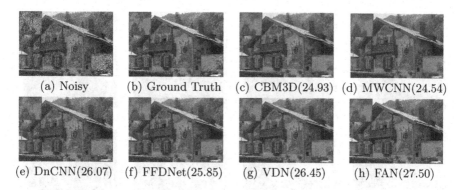

(a) Noisy   (b) Ground Truth   (c) CBM3D(24.93)   (d) MWCNN(24.54)

(e) DnCNN(26.07)   (f) FFDNet(25.85)   (g) VDN(26.45)   (h) FAN(27.50)

Fig. 5. Denoised results on one typical image in LIVE1 dataset with $\sigma = 50$ by different methods

Table 4. The comparison results of other methods on SIDD benchmark [43]

Method	DnCNN [8]	TNRD [44]	CBM3D [19]	NLM [3]	WNNM [20]	KSVD [22]	CBDNet [16]	CBDNet* [16]	RIDNet [28]	VDN [26]	FAN (Ours)
PSNR	23.66	24.73	25.65	26.75	25.78	26.88	33.28	38.68	38.71	39.26	**39.33**
SSIM	0.583	0.643	0.685	0.699	0.809	0.842	0.868	0.901	0.914	0.955	**0.956**

*Retrain with the SIDD dataset

on one typical images of CBSD68 dataset when $\sigma = 50$. From Table 3 and Fig. 5, it can be easily observed that: 1) Although the CBM3D based on self-similarity model is a stable traditional method, there are color artifact and left noise in the denoising results while most methods based on neural network performs better at this problem. 2) Some outstanding CNN denoisers like FFDNet easily over-smooth the images and are unable to preserve edge information while our proposed FAN can retain more details by variable depth design. 3) For noise in the flat regions, our model can also deal with it well because SWT can avoid the pseudo-Gibbs effect and make the image look more natural and real.

4.4 Experiments on Real-World Noise

We select two real noise datasets DND [42] and SIDD [43] to evaluate the denoising performance of FAN. DND collected 50 images from 50 scenes captured by four consumer cameras. The carefully post-processing of low-ISO images results in clean images, but it does not provide ground truth while PSNR/SSIM results of denoised images through the online server. SIDD is another real noise dataset which contains 320 image pairs of 10 scenes taken by 5 smartphones. Clean Images are obtained by a series of ISP pipeline processing performing on multiple images of the same scene. SIDD uses some unpublished image pairs as a test set for verifying the performance of the denoising algorithms online.

Table 4 lists the denoising performance of different competing methods shown on the SIDD benchmark. It can be seen that our FAN has obvious advantages compared of model-driven traditional denoising algorithm and data-driven neu-

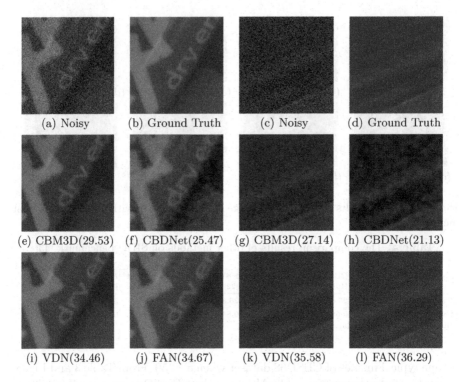

(a) Noisy   (b) Ground Truth   (c) Noisy   (d) Ground Truth

(e) CBM3D(29.53) (f) CBDNet(25.47) (g) CBM3D(27.14) (h) CBDNet(21.13)

(i) VDN(34.46)   (j) FAN(34.67)   (k) VDN(35.58)   (l) FAN(36.29)

Fig. 6. Denoised results (PSNR: dB) on two typical images in SIDD validation dataset by different methods

ral network denoising algorithm. In view of the fact that the noise type of CBD-Net training data is inconsistent with SIDD, for fairly we also compared the results of CBDNet training on the SIDD training set [26] and over 0.64 dB. Specially, FAN achieves 0.62 dB higher than RIDNet and 0.06 dB higher than VDN on the SIDD test dataset. As shown in Fig. 6, we compare our results with other competing algorithms. In the first example, our proposed FAN performs well in the smooth region and the color boundary distinction while avoiding speckled structures and chroma artifacts. For another example, the image denoised by VDN has lattice-like artifact on the upper and left sides while the denoising result of our FAN can maintain the spatial smoothness of the homogeneous regions and keep fine textural details.

Table 5 summarizes the quantitative comparison of different methods on DND benchmark. It is easy to be seen that our proposed FAN surpasses other methods, especially has a performance gain of 1.35 dB and 0.15 dB compared to CBDNet and RIDNet respectively. Figure 7 shows some visualizing results of the comparison between FAN and other competitive algorithms on DND benchmark. We can see that our FAN can make the image smoother and retain perceptually-pleasing texture details.

Table 5. The comparison results of other methods on DND benchmark [42]

Method	CBM3D [19]	WNNM [20]	KSVD [22]	MCWNNM [25]	FFDNet [9]	DnCNN+ [8]	TWSC [24]	CBDNet [16]	RIDNet [28]	VDN [26]	FAN (Ours)
PSNR	34.51	34.67	36.49	37.38	37.61	37.90	37.96	38.06	39.26	39.38	**39.41**
SSIM	0.8507	0.8507	0.8978	0.9294	0.9415	0.9430	0.9416	0.9421	**0.9528**	0.9518	0.9507

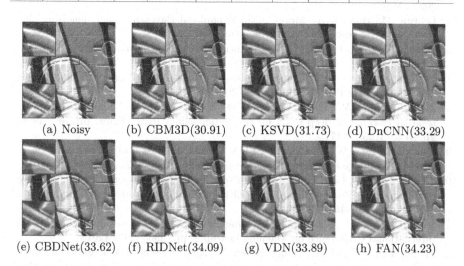

(a) Noisy   (b) CBM3D(30.91)   (c) KSVD(31.73)   (d) DnCNN(33.29)

(e) CBDNet(33.62)   (f) RIDNet(34.09)   (g) VDN(33.89)   (h) FAN(34.23)

Fig. 7. Denoised results (PSNR: dB) on one typical image in DND benchmark by different methods

5   Conclusion

In this paper, we propose frequency attention network for blind real noise removal which exploits spectral information and structural information of images and employ the attention mechanism to enhance the feature maps. Abundant ablation experiments indicate that Haar wavelet basis function which satisfies symmetry, orthogonality and compactly supported characteristics at the same time can achieve the best performance on our proposed FAN. Comprehensive evaluations on different noise distribution cases demonstrate the superiority and effectiveness of our method for image restoration tasks. Our method can also be implemented on other low-level tasks including super-resolution and deblurring.

References

1. Liu, C., Szeliski, R., Bing Kang, S., Zitnick, C.L., Freeman, W.T.: Automatic estimation and removal of noise from a single image. IEEE Trans. Pattern Anal. Mach. Intell. **30**, 299–314 (2007)
2. Wang, W., Chen, X., Yang, C., Li, X., Hu, X., Yue, T.: Enhancing low light videos by exploring high sensitivity camera noise. In: Proceedings of the IEEE International Conference on Computer Vision, pp. 4111–4119 (2019)

3. Buades, A., Coll, B., Morel, J.M.: A non-local algorithm for image denoising. In: 2005 IEEE Computer Society Conference on Computer Vision and Pattern Recognition (CVPR 2005), vol. 2, pp. 60–65. IEEE (2005)
4. Dabov, K., Foi, A., Katkovnik, V., Egiazarian, K.: Image denoising by sparse 3-D transform-domain collaborative filtering. IEEE Trans. Image Process. **16**, 2080–2095 (2007)
5. Lebrun, M., Buades, A., Morel, J.M.: A nonlocal Bayesian image denoising algorithm. SIAM J. Imaging Sci. **6**, 1665–1688 (2013)
6. Donoho, D.L., Johnstone, I.M.: Adapting to unknown smoothness via wavelet shrinkage. J. Am. Stat. Assoc. **90**, 1200–1224 (1995)
7. Yu, G., Sapiro, G.: DCT image denoising: a simple and effective image denoising algorithm. Image Process. On Line **1**, 292–296 (2011)
8. Zhang, K., Zuo, W., Chen, Y., Meng, D., Zhang, L.: Beyond a gaussian denoiser: residual learning of deep CNN for image denoising. IEEE Trans. Image Process. **26**, 3142–3155 (2017)
9. Zhang, K., Zuo, W., Zhang, L.: FFDNet: toward a fast and flexible solution for CNN-based image denoising. IEEE Trans. Image Process. **27**, 4608–4622 (2018)
10. Tai, Y., Yang, J., Liu, X., Xu, C.: MemNet: a persistent memory network for image restoration. In: Proceedings of the IEEE International Conference on Computer Vision, pp. 4539–4547 (2017)
11. Lehtinen, J., et al.: Noise2Noise: learning image restoration without clean data. In: International Conference on Machine Learning, pp. 2965–2974 (2018)
12. Zhang, Y., Li, K., Li, K., Zhong, B., Fu, Y.: Residual non-local attention networks for image restoration. In: International Conference on Learning Representations (2019)
13. Jia, X., Liu, S., Feng, X., Zhang, L.: FOCNet: a fractional optimal control network for image denoising. In: Proceedings of the IEEE Conference on Computer Vision and Pattern Recognition, pp. 6054–6063 (2019)
14. Yin, D., Lopes, R.G., Shlens, J., Cubuk, E.D., Gilmer, J.: A fourier perspective on model robustness in computer vision. In: Advances in Neural Information Processing Systems, pp. 13255–13265 (2019)
15. Kim, J., Lee, S.: Deep learning of human visual sensitivity in image quality assessment framework. In: Proceedings of the IEEE Conference on Computer Vision and Pattern Recognition, pp. 1676–1684 (2017)
16. Guo, S., Yan, Z., Zhang, K., Zuo, W., Zhang, L.: Toward convolutional blind denoising of real photographs. In: Proceedings of the IEEE Conference on Computer Vision and Pattern Recognition, pp. 1712–1722 (2019)
17. Foi, A., Katkovnik, V., Egiazarian, K.: Pointwise shape-adaptive DCT for high-quality denoising and deblocking of grayscale and color images. IEEE Trans. Image Process. **16**, 1395–1411 (2007)
18. Chang, S.G., Yu, B., Vetterli, M.: Adaptive wavelet thresholding for image denoising and compression. IEEE Trans. Image Process. **9**, 1532–1546 (2000)
19. Dabov, K., Foi, A., Katkovnik, V., Egiazarian, K.: Color image denoising via sparse 3D collaborative filtering with grouping constraint in luminance-chrominance space. In: 2007 IEEE International Conference on Image Processing, vol. 1, p. I-313. IEEE (2007)
20. Gu, S., Zhang, L., Zuo, W., Feng, X.: Weighted nuclear norm minimization with application to image denoising. In: Proceedings of the IEEE Conference on Computer Vision and Pattern Recognition, pp. 2862–2869 (2014)

21. Xu, J., Zhang, L., Zhang, D., Feng, X.: Multi-channel weighted nuclear norm minimization for real color image denoising. In: Proceedings of the IEEE International Conference on Computer Vision, pp. 1096–1104 (2017)
22. Aharon, M., Elad, M., Bruckstein, A.: K-SVD: an algorithm for designing overcomplete dictionaries for sparse representation. IEEE Trans. Signal Process. **54**, 4311–4322 (2006)
23. Dong, W., Zhang, L., Shi, G., Li, X.: Nonlocally centralized sparse representation for image restoration. IEEE Trans. Image Process. **22**, 1620–1630 (2012)
24. Xu, J., Zhang, L., Zhang, D.: A trilateral weighted sparse coding scheme for real-world image denoising. In: Proceedings of the European Conference on Computer Vision (ECCV), pp. 20–36 (2018)
25. Liu, P., Zhang, H., Zhang, K., Lin, L., Zuo, W.: Multi-level wavelet-CNN for image restoration. In: Proceedings of the IEEE Conference on Computer Vision and Pattern Recognition Workshops, pp. 773–782 (2018)
26. Yue, Z., Yong, H., Zhao, Q., Meng, D., Zhang, L.: Variational denoising network: toward blind noise modeling and removal. In: Advances in Neural Information Processing Systems, pp. 1688–1699 (2019)
27. Ronneberger, O., Fischer, P., Brox, T.: U-Net: convolutional networks for biomedical image segmentation. In: Navab, N., Hornegger, J., Wells, W.M., Frangi, A.F. (eds.) MICCAI 2015. LNCS, vol. 9351, pp. 234–241. Springer, Cham (2015). https://doi.org/10.1007/978-3-319-24574-4_28
28. Anwar, S., Barnes, N.: Real image denoising with feature attention. In: Proceedings of the IEEE International Conference on Computer Vision, pp. 3155–3164 (2019)
29. Mildenhall, B., Barron, J.T., Chen, J., Sharlet, D., Ng, R., Carroll, R.: Burst denoising with kernel prediction networks. In: Proceedings of the IEEE Conference on Computer Vision and Pattern Recognition, pp. 2502–2510 (2018)
30. Xu, X., Li, M., Sun, W.: Learning deformable kernels for image and video denoising. arxiv abs/1904.06903 (2019)
31. Gueguen, L., Sergeev, A., Kadlec, B., Liu, R., Yosinski, J.: Faster neural networks straight from JPEG. In: Advances in Neural Information Processing Systems, pp. 3933–3944 (2018)
32. Chou, C.H., Li, Y.C.: A perceptually tuned subband image coder based on the measure of just-noticeable-distortion profile. IEEE Trans. Circuits Syst. Video Technol. **5**, 467–476 (1995)
33. Hu, J., Shen, L., Sun, G.: Squeeze-and-excitation networks. In: Proceedings of the IEEE Conference on Computer Vision and Pattern Recognition, pp. 7132–7141 (2018)
34. Liu, D., Wen, B., Fan, Y., Loy, C.C., Huang, T.S.: Non-local recurrent network for image restoration. In: Advances in Neural Information Processing Systems, pp. 1673–1682 (2018)
35. Woo, S., Park, J., Lee, J.Y., So Kweon, I.: CBAM: convolutional block attention module. In: Proceedings of the European Conference on Computer Vision (ECCV), pp. 3–19 (2018)
36. Tomasi, C., Manduchi, R.: Bilateral filtering for gray and color images. In: Sixth International Conference on Computer Vision (IEEE Cat. No. 98CH36271), pp. 839–846. IEEE (1998)
37. Kingma, D.P., Ba, J.: Adam: a method for stochastic optimization. CoRR abs/1412.6980 (2015)
38. Loshchilov, I., Hutter, F.: SGDR: stochastic gradient descent with warm restarts. In: ICLR (2017)

39. Po, D.Y., Do, M.N.: Directional multiscale modeling of images using the contourlet transform. IEEE Trans. Image Process. **15**, 1610–1620 (2006)
40. Cohen, A., Daubechies, I., Feauveau, J.C.: Biorthogonal bases of compactly supported wavelets. Commun. Pure Appl. Math. **45**, 485–560 (1992)
41. Ma, K., et al.: Waterloo exploration database: new challenges for image quality assessment models. IEEE Trans. Image Process. **26**, 1004–1016 (2016)
42. Plotz, T., Roth, S.: Benchmarking denoising algorithms with real photographs. In: Proceedings of the IEEE Conference on Computer Vision and Pattern Recognition, pp. 1586–1595 (2017)
43. Abdelhamed, A., Lin, S., Brown, M.S.: A high-quality denoising dataset for smartphone cameras. In: Proceedings of the IEEE Conference on Computer Vision and Pattern Recognition, pp. 1692–1700 (2018)
44. Chen, Y., Pock, T.: Trainable nonlinear reaction diffusion: a flexible framework for fast and effective image restoration. IEEE Trans. Pattern Anal. Mach. Intell. **39**, 1256–1272 (2016)

Restoring Spatially-Heterogeneous Distortions Using Mixture of Experts Network

Sijin Kim[1], Namhyuk Ahn[1,2], and Kyung-Ah Sohn[1,2(✉)]

[1] Department of Computer Engineering, Ajou University, Suwon, South Korea
tlwlsdi0306@gmail.com, {aa0dfg,kasohn}@ajou.ac.kr
[2] Department of Artificial Intelligence, Ajou University, Suwon, South Korea

Abstract. In recent years, deep learning-based methods have been successfully applied to the image distortion restoration tasks. However, scenarios that assume a single distortion only may not be suitable for many real-world applications. To deal with such cases, some studies have proposed sequentially combined distortions datasets. Viewing in a different point of combining, we introduce a spatially-heterogeneous distortion dataset in which multiple corruptions are applied to the different locations of each image. In addition, we also propose a mixture of experts network to effectively restore a multi-distortion image. Motivated by the multi-task learning, we design our network to have multiple paths that learn both common and distortion-specific representations. Our model is effective for restoring real-world distortions and we experimentally verify that our method outperforms other models designed to manage both single distortion and multiple distortions.

1 Introduction

The image restoration task is a classic and fundamental problem in the computer vision field. It aims to generate a visually clean image from a corrupted observation. There exist various problems related to the image restoration such as super-resolution, denoising, and deblurring. For all such tasks, clean and distorted images are many-to-one mapping, so it is very challenging to develop an effective restoration algorithm. Despite the difficulties, image restoration has been actively investigated because it can be applied to various scenarios.

Recently, the performance of the image restoration methods has been significantly improved since the use of a deep learning-based approach. For example, in the super-resolution task, various methods [1–5] progressively push the performance by stacking more layers and designing novel modules. Likewise, other restoration tasks such as denoising [6–10] and deblurring [11–14] also enjoy the huge performance leap. However, most of the deep restoration models assume that the image is corrupted by a single distortion only (Fig. 1b), which may not be suitable for the real scenarios. In real-world applications, there can be mixed

---

S. Kim and N. Ahn—Indicates equal contribution.

© Springer Nature Switzerland AG 2021
H. Ishikawa et al. (Eds.): ACCV 2020, LNCS 12623, pp. 185–201, 2021.
https://doi.org/10.1007/978-3-030-69532-3_12

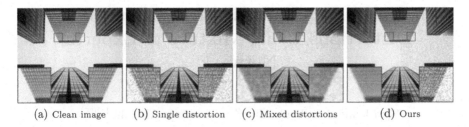

(a) Clean image   (b) Single distortion   (c) Mixed distortions   (d) Ours

Fig. 1. Comparison of three different image distortion assumptions. **(a)** Clean image. **(b)** Single distortion (Gaussian noise). Only one corruption is applied to the image. **(c)** Mixed distortions [15]. Multiple distortions corrupt the image in sequentially (Gaussian blur and Gaussian noise), but no variation on the spatial domain. **(d)** Our proposed spatially-variant distortion. Instead of mixing in sequentially, we *spatially* combine heterogeneous distortions (left: Gaussian blur, right: Gaussian noise).

or multiple distortions in one image such as JPEG artifact of the blurry image or a photo taken on a hazy and rainy day. To cope with such a multi-distortions scenario, some studies have proposed new datasets [15,16] and methods [17,18] recently. They generated combined distortion datasets by overlapping multiple distortions sequentially, which makes the assumption more realistic than the single distortion datasets (Fig. 1c).

Viewing in a different point of the multi-distortions, we introduce a spatially-heterogeneous distortion dataset (SHDD). In our dataset, distortions are applied in different regions of the image (Fig. 1d). This concept makes our dataset a proxy environment of the real-world applications such as multi-camera systems. For example, in the case where the images are acquired from various devices or post-processors, stitching these images may produce output that has different quality regions, thus degrading the recognition performance. Because of the nature of the spatial-heterogeneity, it is crucial to catch both *what* and *where* the corruptions are, unlike the existing multi-distortion datasets [15,16] which spread corruptions to the entire image. Recently, Ahn *et al.* [19] proposed a multi-distortion dataset similar to ours. However, corruptions of their dataset are spatially sparse thus may not be ideal to our potential applications (*i.e.* image stitching). In addition, their work is limited to recognizing the distortions.

To address the above requirements, we propose a mixture of experts with a parameter sharing network (MEPSNet) that effectively restores an image corrupted by the spatially-varying distortions. Motivated by the multi-task learning [21,22] and the mixture of experts [23], we build our network to have a multi-expert system (Fig. 2). With this approach, individual distortion can be treated as a single task, thus the model divides and distributes the task to appropriate experts internally. By doing so, experts are able to concentrate on restoring only the given single distortion. We experimentally observed that each expert learns a particular distortion distribution as well. Note that even though we build every expert to be identical, any type of the network design can be adapted thanks to the flexibility and modularity of our framework.

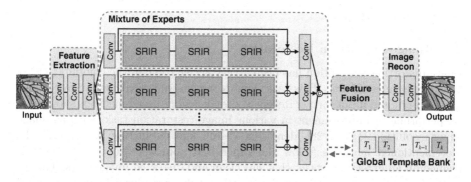

Fig. 2. Overview of the MEPSNet. Our network is composed of 1) feature extraction, 2) mixture of experts, 3) global template bank, 4) feature fusion, and 5) reconstruction modules. Here, SRIR denotes our proposed shared residual-in-residual block. ⓒ and ⊕ symbols are concatenation and element-wise addition operations, respectively. The mixture of experts unit has several pathways, each with multiple SRIR blocks. The parameters of all SRIRs are soft-shared through the global template bank [20]. (Color figure online)

However, naively constructing the sub-networks (experts) may limit the power of using MTL. Misra *et al.* [24] investigated the trade-offs amongst different combinations of the shared and the task-specific architectures and revealed that the performance mostly depends on the tasks, not on the proportion of the shared units. Based on the above investigation, they proposed a cross-stitch unit so that the network can learn an optimal combination of shared and task-specific representations. Following the analysis of Misra *et al.* [24], we use the soft parameter sharing [20] to guide experts to learn both shared and distortion-specific information effectively. In this approach, convolutional layers of the experts only contain the coefficient vector, not the entire weights and biases. Instead, these are stored in the global template bank thus layers adaptively generate their parameters by a linear combination between the coefficient vector and the templates. It allows each expert to grasp not only the characteristics of the individual distortions but also common representation from the various corruptions automatically. In addition, the number of the parameters is decoupled to the number of the experts and we can increase the experts only using negligible additional parameters. Our experiments show that MEPSNet outperforms other restoration methods including OWAN [17] which is specifically designed network to manage multiple distortions. We summarize our contributions as follows:

- We introduce a new image distortion restoration task and dataset (**SHDD**). It simulates the cases where the various distortions are applied to different locations of an image, a very common scenario in the real world.
- We propose a novel distortion restoration method, **MEPSNet**, which successfully restores the multiple corruptions by jointly adapting two motivations from the multi-task learning and the parameter sharing approach.
- Our proposed model shows significant improvement over other image restoration networks in spatially-heterogeneous distortion environments.

2   Related Work

2.1   Image Distortion Restoration

Image distortion restoration has been a very active topic in the computer vision field for decades [25,26]. This task aims to reconstruct a distortion-free image from a corrupted input image. Recently, deep learning-based methods show drastic performance improvement in various image restoration tasks such as image super-resolution [1,3,27,28], denoising [6–10], and deblurring [11–14]. All the aforementioned methods follow the supervised approach where the model is trained on an external dataset that has clean and distorted image pairs. Thanks to the high-complexity of the deep networks, such a training scheme is powerful if the volume of the training data is large enough. However, the performance is heavily deteriorated when the dataset size becomes small [29,30] or the dataset distributions between the training and testing are mismatched [31,32].

2.2   Multiple Image Distortion Restoration

In real-world applications, multiple distortions can damage entire images, or only the partial regions. Restoring such images using the model trained on a single distortion dataset may produce undesirable artifacts due to the mismatched distribution. To close the gap between the real and simulated data, recent studies have proposed new datasets [15,16,19] and methods [17,18] for multi-distortion restoration task. In their datasets, images are damaged with sequentially applied distortions [15,16] or only small parts of the image are corrupted [19]. To restore multiple distortions, Yu *et al.* [15] used the toolbox that has several distortion specialized tools. Then, the framework learns to choose the appropriate tool given the current image. Similarly, path-restore [18] and OWAN [17] adopt a multi-path approach so that the models dynamically select an appropriate pathway for each image regions or distortions. Although our method is also motivated by the multi-path scheme, we have two key differences. First, our proposed network is built for restoring spatially-varying distortions. Second, by cooperatively using a mixture of experts and parameter sharing strategies, we can achieve more advanced performance than the other competitors.

2.3   Multi-task Learning

Multi-task learning (MTL) guides a model to learn both common and distinct representations across different tasks [21,22]. One of the widely used approaches for MTL is combining a shared and task-specific modules [21]. Based on this work, numerous studies have been investigated the power of MTL in various tasks [24,33,34]. Among them Misra *et al.* [24] is one notable work; they proposed a cross-stitch unit to optimize the best combination settings for given tasks with a end-to-end training. Without this module, the optimal point depends on the tasks, and the searching process may become cumbersome. Hinted by this work, our network also learns to find the balance between the shared and the distortion-specific representations using the soft parameter sharing approach.

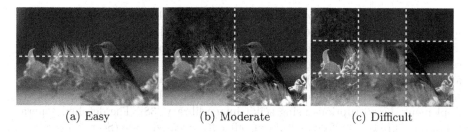

(a) Easy   (b) Moderate   (c) Difficult

Fig. 3. Examples of our proposed spatially-heterogeneous distortion dataset (SHDD). We separate our dataset into three levels (*easy, moderate,* and *difficult*) according to the number of the blocks in a single image. To generate a dataset, we first split image to sub-images using the virtual perforated line (divide phase) and corrupt each region with different distortions (distort phase). Best viewed on display.

3 Spatially-Heterogeneous Distortion Dataset

In this section, we introduce a novel spatially-heterogeneous distortion dataset (SHDD). Our proposed dataset is designed to simulate the scenario where the image is corrupted by spatially varying distortions. To implement this idea, we synthetically generate corrupted images using *divide-and-distort* procedure. That is, we divide clean images into the multiple blocks (divide), and corrupt each block with selected distortions (distort).

In *divide* phase, we split images according to the virtual horizontal or vertical lines (Fig. 3). These lines are randomly arranged so as to prevent the model from memorizing the position of the resulting regions. We create three levels of difficulties (easy, moderate, and difficult), by varying the number of split regions. The reason for creating a multi-level dataset is two-fold. First, we consider the relationship between the restoration hardness and the number of regions presented in a single image. Second, we would like to explore the robustness of the model by training on one level and evaluating it on others. In *distort* stage, we corrupt each block with randomly selected distortion. We use **1)** Gaussian noise, **2)** Gaussian blur, **3)** f-noise, **4)** contrast change, and **5)** identity (no distortion). Note that we include *identity* to the distortion pool. By including it, we can measure the generalizability of the model in depth since deep restoration methods tend to over-sharpen or over-smooth when the input is already of high-quality [30]. In addition, it simulates more realistic cases where the real-world scenarios suffer very often (*i.e.* stitching clean image to the corrupted ones).

We build our SHDD based on the DIV2K dataset [35]. It has 800 and 100 images for training and validation respectively. We use half of the DIV2K valid set as validation of the SHDD and the rest of half for testing. For each of the high-quality images, we generate 12 distorted images (training dataset: $9,600 = 800 \times 12$ images) to cover data samples as densely as possible since SHDD is inherently sparse due to the spatially-varying distortions. We set {easy, moderate, difficult}-levels by chopping each image {2, 3, 4}-times (Fig. 3).

The distortions used in our SHDD are carefully selected following the recent image distortion datasets [36, 37]. These reflect the real-world scenario, especially for image acquisition and registration stage. When applying the distortions, we randomly sample its strength from following ranges: **1)** [0.005, 0.02]-variances for Gaussian white noise, **2)** [1.0, 2.5]-variances for Gaussian blur, **3)** [6.0, 10.0]-scales for f-noise (pink noise), and **4)** [25.0, 40.0]-levels for contrast change. We implement the corruptions using scikit-image library [38]. The detailed generation procedure can be founded in our officially released code (Sect. 5.1).

4   Our Method

Our proposed *mixture of experts with a parameter sharing network* (MEPSNet) is composed of five parts: feature extraction, mixture of experts, template bank, feature fusion, and reconstruction blocks (Fig. 2). In Sect. 4.1, we show an overview of our proposed method. Then, we describe the multi-expert architecture and the feature fusion module in Sect. 4.2 and 4.3.

4.1   Model Overview

Let's denote $\mathbf{X}$ and $\mathbf{y}$ as a distorted and a clean image, respectively. Given the image $\mathbf{X}$, a feature extractor f_{ext} computes the intermediate feature $\mathbf{F}_0$ as:

$$\mathbf{F}_0 = f_{ext}(\mathbf{X}). \tag{1}$$

To extract informative features, the extraction module has multiple convolutional layers (we use three layers) and their dimensions are gradually expanded up to 256 unlike the recent image restoration methods [3,5]. We observed that the capacity of the extraction module makes the impact to the performance. We conjecture that it is due to the usage of multiple distortion-specialized experts (Sect. 4.2). With this concept, it is crucial to extract informative shared representation to encourage the individual experts concentrate solely on their own goal. Extracted intermediate feature $\mathbf{F}_0$ is then fed into the mixture of experts module which outputs a concatenated feature $\mathbf{F}_D$ as in below.

$$\mathbf{F}_D = \left[f_{exp}^k(\mathbf{F}_0) \right], \text{ for } k = 1 \dots N \tag{2}$$

Here, N is the number of experts, f_{exp} and [.] denote the expert branch and the channel-wise concatenation respectively. With this deep feature $\mathbf{F}_D$, we finally generate restored image $\hat{\mathbf{y}}$ by Eq. 3. To guide the reconstruction module to gather multiple information adequately, we attach the attentive feature fusion module f_{fuse} before the image reconstruction unit (Sect. 4.3).

$$\hat{\mathbf{y}} = f_{recon}(f_{fuse}(\mathbf{F}_D)). \tag{3}$$

We optimize our MEPSNet using a pixel-wise L_2 loss function. While several criteria for training restoration network have been investigated [39, 40], we observed that there is no performance gain of using other loss functions in our task. More detailed training setups are shown in Sect. 5.1.

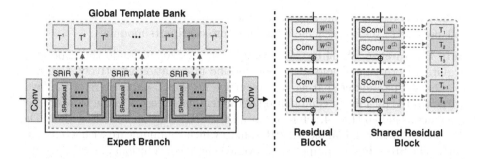

Fig. 4. Our proposed mixture of experts module. **(Left)** Expert branch with parameter sharing. Experts are shared using global template bank (other branches are omitted). In each pathw, there exist three shared residual-in-residual (SRIR) units which have several shared residual blocks. **(Right)** Comparison of the standard and our shared residual blocks. While convolutional layers of the standard block have their own parameters $\{W^{(1)}, \ldots, W^{(4)}\}$, ours only have coefficient. Instead, weights are adaptively generated using coefficients $\{\alpha^{(1)}, \ldots, \alpha^{(4)}\}$ and templates $\{T^1, \ldots, T^k\}$.

4.2 Mixture of Parameter Shared Experts

Mixture of Experts Module. In our network, this module is the key component to successfully restore heterogeneous distortions. As shown in Fig. 2, multiple branches, dubbed as *experts*, are positioned in between the feature extraction and the feature fusion blocks. Each expert has the same structure, which consists of three contiguous shared residual-in-residual (SRIR) units and few convolutional layers (green boxes in Fig. 2) that envelope the SRIR blocks. Following the prior works [3–5], we use a long skip connection to bridge across multiple intermediate features for stable training. The SRIR is composed of multiple residual blocks [3,41] as shown in Fig. 4 (left). We also employ additional shortcut connection between the residual blocks to further stabilize the training [5]. Note that the structure of the experts is not restricted to be identical; they could be the networks with different receptive fields [42] or disparate operations [17]. However, we choose to set all the experts to have same structure considering both the simplicity and the performance.

In contrast to the conventional mixture of experts [23], our experts module does not have an external gating network. Instead, distilled information adaptively selects their importance themselves by the self-attention scheme (Sect. 4.3). Since we do not attach additional gating mechanism, now the formulation of our mixture of experts module is related to the multi-branch networks [43,44]. However, we observed that the vanilla multi-branch network requires very careful tuning to stabilize the training and even shows degraded performance when we increase the number of the branches or the depths of each branch. We hypothesize that the degradation issue of using multi-branch system arises due to the *isolated branch* structure. That is, no bridge exists between the branches, thus experts (branches) learn all the representations on their own way without referring others. This is inefficient since some information are sufficient to be extracted once and shared to others. To mitigate such issue, we employ soft parameter sharing scheme to the mixture of experts module.

Soft Parameter Sharing. We use this scheme [20] to guide the experts in acquiring both shared and distortion-specific information effectively. Contrary to the hard parameter sharing (*i.e.* recursive network), parameters of the layer are generated by a linear combination of the template tensors in the bank. We set the bank as global (Fig. 4, left) so that all the SRIRs are shared altogether. The SRIR has shared residual blocks (SResidual) which communicate with a template bank. The SResidual is composed of several shared convolutional layers (SConv), and the parameters of the SConv are adaptively generated through the template bank (Fig. 4, right). In detail, a standard convolutional layer stores weights $W \in \mathbb{R}^{C_{in} \times C_{out} \times S \times S}$ (S is kernel size). In contrast, our SConv only contains a coefficient vector $\alpha \in \mathbb{R}^K$, where K is the number of templates in the bank. Instead, the global template bank holds all the weights as $\{\mathbf{T}_1, \ldots \mathbf{T}_K\}$ where $\mathbf{T}_k$ is the $[C_{in} \times C_{out} \times S \times S]$-dimensional tensor. By referring these templates, each layer generates their adaptive weight $\tilde{W}$ as

$$\tilde{W} = \sum_{j=1}^{K} \alpha_j \mathbf{T}_j. \tag{4}$$

Jointly using a parameter sharing and the mixture of experts provides two advantages: First, the number of the parameters is determined by the number of templates K, not the experts. Second, it improves the restoration performance compared to the model without a parameter sharing. In detail, we share the parameters not only within the experts but also between the branches. This allows every expert to jointly optimize the common representations from various distortions while each expert produces their specialized features. We can also interpret the benefit of the parameter sharing as in the multi-task learning literature. In a multi-task learning context, finding a good balance between the task-specific and the shared representations is cumbersome job and moreover, the optimal point depends on the tasks themselves [24]. To find the best combination without human-laboring, they share the intermediate representations using a cross-stitch unit [24]. Our approach has an analogous role and motivation to them but we tackle this issue using a parameter sharing scheme.

4.3   Attentive Feature Fusion

As described in Sect. 4.2, each expert branch generates their specific high-level features. Our attentive feature fusion module takes concatenated features $\mathbf{F}_D$, which is the output of the mixture of experts module, and fuses this information via channel-wise attention mechanism [5,45]. With given feature $\mathbf{F}_D \in \mathbb{R}^{C \times H \times W}$, we first apply global average pooling to make C-dimensional channel descriptor $\mathbf{F}_{CD} \in \mathbb{R}^C$ as in below.

$$\mathbf{F}_{CD} = \frac{1}{H \times W} \sum_{i=1}^{H} \sum_{j=1}^{W} \mathbf{F}_D(i,j), \tag{5}$$

where $\mathbf{F}_D(i, j)$ denotes the (y, x) position of the feature $\mathbf{F}_D$. With $\mathbf{F}_{CD}$, we calculate the scaling vector $\mathbf{S}$ using a two-layer network followed by a simple gating scheme. Then, $\mathbf{F}_F$ is produced by multiplying the scaling vector $\mathbf{S}$ and the feature $\mathbf{F}_D$ in a channel-wise manner via Eq. 6. Finally, the reconstruction block receives this feature and generates a restored image $\hat{\mathbf{y}}$.

$$\mathbf{S} = \sigma(W_2 \cdot \delta(W_1 \cdot \mathbf{F}_{CD})),$$
$$\mathbf{F}_F = \mathbf{S} \cdot \mathbf{F}_D. \tag{6}$$

Here, $\sigma(.)$ and $\delta(.)$ are sigmoid and ReLU respectively, and $\{W_1, W_2\}$ denotes the weight set of convolutional layers. With this attentive feature fusion module, diverse representations inside of the $\mathbf{F}_D$ are adaptively selected. Unlike ours, previous mixture of experts methods [23] generate attention vector using the external network. However, we observed that such design choice does not work well in our task. Related to the isolation issue of the vanilla multi-branch network, as described in Sect. 4.2, we suspect that isolated external gating network cannot judge how to select features from the multiple experts adequately. In contrast, our fusion module is based on the self-attention [5, 45, 46]. With this concept, attentive feature fusion unit is now closely linked to the main expert module so that is able to decide which feature to take or not more clearly.

5   Experiments

5.1   Implementation Details

We train all the models on moderate level of SHDD. The reason for using single level only for training is to measure the generalizability of the model by evaluating on unseen (easy and difficult) cases. In each training batch, 16 patches with a size of 80×80 are used as input. We train the model for 1.2M iterations using ADAM optimizer [47] with settings of $(\beta_1, \beta_2, \epsilon) = (0.9, 0.99, 10^{-8})$, and weight decay as 10^{-4}. We initialize the network parameters following He et al. [48]. The learning rate is initially set to 10^{-4} and halved 120K and 300K iterations. Unless mentioned, our network consists of three experts, each of which has three SRIRs. We choose the number of SResidual blocks in SRIR to 12 and the number of the templates K as 16. We release the code and dataset on https://github.com/SijinKim/mepsnet.

5.2   Comparison to the Other Methods

Baseline. We use following deep restoration methods: DnCNN [10], VDSR [2], OWAN [17] and RIDNet [6]. OWAN is proposed to restore multiple distortions while others are for a single distortion. We modify VDSR by stacking convolutional layers four times than the original ones to match the number of the parameters to the others. For OWAN and RIDNet, we use author's official code.

Fig. 5. Qualitative comparison of the MEPSNet and other restoration methods.

Table 1. Quantitative comparison (PSNR/SSIM) on SHDD in three levels to the deep learning-based restoration methods.

Method	Levels of SHDD		
	Easy	Moderate	Difficult
DnCNN [10]	25.29/0.7110	25.54/0.7354	26.70/0.7723
VDSR [2]	27.34/0.7709	25.73/0.7701	25.95/0.7760
OWAN [17]	30.95/0.9181	29.77/0.9112	29.27/0.9098
RIDNet [6]	34.19/0.9361	32.94/0.9317	32.30/0.9282
MEPSNet (ours)	**34.23/0.9369**	**33.47/0.9331**	**32.71/0.9284**

Table 2. Quantitative comparison (mAP) on object detection and semantic segmentation tasks. We use faster R-CNN [49] and mask R-CNN [33] to measure mAP for object detection and instance segmentation, respectively.

Task	Clean	Distorted	DnCNN	VDSR	OWAN	RIDNet	MEPSNet
Detection	40.2	26.4	26.8	25.6	28.6	**29.5**	**29.5**
Segmentation	37.2	24.4	24.8	23.6	26.5	27.4	**27.5**

Evaluation on SHDD. We compare the MEPSNet to the baselines on SHDD using pixel-driven metrics such as PSNR and SSIM. Table 1 shows the quantitative comparison on the different levels of the SHDD test set. In this benchmark, our proposed method consistently outperforms the others. For example, the performance gain of the MEPSNet in moderate level is +0.53 dB PSNR compared to the second best method, RIDNet. In addition, MEPSNet achieves the best performance on the unseen settings as well, and especially shows the superior PSNR on difficult level, +0.41 dB to the second best. It should be noted that OWAN [17] is also devised for the multi-distortion restoration. However, their performance is much lower than both ours and RIDNet. We conjecture that isolating all the operation layers and attention layer results in degraded performance. On the other hand, ours can fully enjoy the effect of using multi-route by sharing the parameters altogether. Figure 5 shows the qualitative results of our model. For the contrast change distortion (1st and 4th rows), the other methods create unpleasant spots (OWAN, RIDNet) or regions (DnCNN) while ours successfully reconstructs the original color. Similarly, MEPSNet effectively restores the other corruptions, such as f-noise (2nd row) or Gaussian blur (3rd row).

Evaluation on Image Recognition Tasks. To further compare the performance of our method, we use image recognition tasks: object detection and semantic segmentation. To be specific, we distort images of COCO dataset [50] with same protocols of SHDD. Then, we restore distorted images using the trained models on SHDD. We evaluate mean average precision (mAP) score using faster R-CNN [49] and mask R-CNN [33] for detection and segmentation respectively. As in Table 2, mAPs of the distorted images are significantly lower

Table 3. Ablation study. ME and PS denote the mixture of experts and parameter sharing, respectively. Using both modules dramatically improves the performance of the baseline and successfully suppressing the number of the parameters.

ME	PS	# Experts	# Params	PSNR/SSIM
		1	3.9M	29.36/0.8835
	✓	1	1.9M	33.55/0.9322
✓	✓	3	2.2M	34.29/0.9353
✓	✓	5	2.6M	**34.39/0.9362**

Table 4. Effect of the multi experts and parameter sharing under the layer constraint scenario. We force the number of the residual (or SResidual) blocks in entire mixture of experts module as 36. That is, expert has 36 blocks for single expert case (1st, 3rd rows), whereas 12 blocks for each when using three experts (2nd, 4th rows).

# Blocks	# Experts	PS	PSNR/SSIM
36	1		29.36/0.8835
	3		**32.21/0.9226**
	1	✓	33.55/0.9322
	3	✓	**33.78/0.9334**

than the clean cases. Restored results with our proposed MEPSNet show the best mAP than the other methods and RIDNet [6] is the only method comparable to ours.

5.3   Model Analysis

In this section, we dissect our proposed MEPSNet through the internal analysis. Unless mentioned, we set the MEPSNet to have three SRIRs each of which includes twelve SResidual blocks. We trained our model using 48×48 input patches.

Ablation Study. In Table 3, we analyze how the mixture of experts (ME) and the parameter sharing (PS) affect the restoration performance. First, using PS (2nd row) outperforms the baseline (1st row) by a huge margin only using half of the parameters. We hypothesize that the PS through the global template bank successfully guides the model to combine low- and high-level features internally. The advantages of combining the multiple features are also verified in recent restoration methods [4,51], and network with PS (via template bank) enjoy the fruitful results by an alternative implementation of the feature aggregating.

Simultaneously applying PS and ME additionally gives dramatic improvements (2nd vs. 3rd rows). Even though we triple the number of experts, the total number of parameters is marginally increased by only 15%, thanks to the parameter sharing scheme. Increasing the number of the experts to five (4th row)

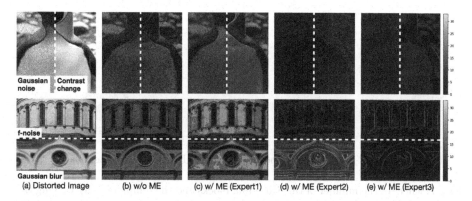

Fig. 6. Visualization of the extracted feature maps from the mixture of experts module. **(a)-upper** Distorted image by Gaussian noise (left) and contrast change (right). **(a)-lower** Distorted image by f-noise (top) and Gaussian blur (bottom). **(b)** Generated feature map of the single expert module, without mixture of experts. **(c–e)** Feature maps produces by three different experts when using multi-expert system.

further boosts the performance as well. However, unless we share the parameters, using five experts increases about 40% of the parameters compared to the single expert network due to the additional coefficients and extra burden to the fusion module. Considering the trade-off between the number of the parameters and the performance, we choose to use three experts for the final model.

To analyze the impact of the mixture of experts and parameter sharing more clearly, we conduct an experiment based on the layer constraint setting as in Table 4. In this scenario, the number of the residual (or SResidual) blocks in the entire mixture of experts module is fixed to 36. Without a multi-expert (1st, 3rd rows), models are three times deeper than the others (2nd, 4th rows). However, single expert models result in degraded performance than the multi-expert. It may contradict the recent trends of single distortion restoration task [3,5]: deeper network is better than the shallow one. Such a result may indicate that it is necessary to view multi-distortion restoration task on a different angle to the single distortion restoration literature.

Feature Visualization. Figure 6 shows the output feature map of the mixture of experts module. The model without a mixture of experts (Fig. 6b) struggles to recover all the distortions simultaneously while ours separates the role to each other (Fig. 6c–e). For example, expert 1 (c) produces coarse and large activations, implying that it mainly deals with contrast change and partially reduces the color tone of the f-noise and Gaussian noise. On the other hand, expert 2 (d) concentrates on recovering edges for the Gaussian blur. The expert 3 (e) also focuses on the primitives but finer elements than the expert 2.

Effect of the Number of Layers and Templates. In Fig. 7a, we fix the number of the experts to three and vary the number of the SResidual blocks for each of the expert. Not surprisingly, we can stack more layers without a sudden

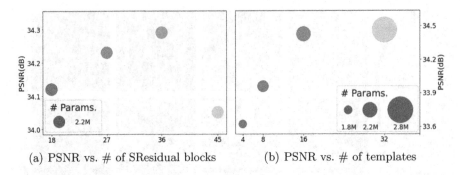

(a) PSNR vs. # of SResidual blocks   (b) PSNR vs. # of templates

Fig. 7. Effect of the number of the SResidual blocks and the templates. **(a)** Varying the number of the blocks of each expert. The number of the experts are fixed as three for all the cases. With parameter sharing, they all have similar parameters. **(b)** Increasing the number of the templates in the global bank from 4 to 32.

increase in the number of the parameters. The performances are consistently improved except the 45 blocks case may due to the unstable training of the extremely deep network. Increasing the number of the templates also gives the progressive gains as show in Fig. 7b. With diverse templates, layers can generate more complex and advanced weight combinations so that it is possible to restore complicated distortion patterns.

6   Conclusion

In this paper, we have presented the spatially-heterogeneous distortion dataset (SHDD) and the mixture of experts with a parameter sharing network (MEP-SNet) for effective distortion restoration. The proposed SHDD assumes the cases where the multiple corruptions are applied to the different locations. To appropriately handle the above scenario, our method is motivated by the analysis from the multi-task learning contexts [24]. By jointly utilizing the mixture of experts scheme [23] and the parameter sharing technique [20], MEPSNet outperforms the other image restoration methods on both the pixel-based metrics (PSNR and SSIM) and the indirect measures (image detection and segmentation). As future work, we plan to integrate the spatially-heterogeneous and the sequentially-combined distortions [15] concepts to further reduce the disparity between the simulated and the real-world environments.

Acknowledgement. This research was supported by the National Research Foundation of Korea grant funded by the Korea government (MSIT) (No. NRF-2019R1A2C1006608), and also under the ITRC (Information Technology Research Center) support program (IITP-2020-2018-0-01431) supervised by the IITP (Institute for Information & Communications Technology Planning & Evaluation).

References

1. Dong, C., Loy, C.C., He, K., Tang, X.: Learning a deep convolutional network for image super-resolution. In: Fleet, D., Pajdla, T., Schiele, B., Tuytelaars, T. (eds.) ECCV 2014. LNCS, vol. 8692, pp. 184–199. Springer, Cham (2014). https://doi.org/10.1007/978-3-319-10593-2_13

2. Kim, J., Kwon Lee, J., Mu Lee, K.: Accurate image super-resolution using very deep convolutional networks. In: Proceedings of the IEEE Conference on Computer Vision and Pattern Recognition, pp. 1646–1654 (2016)

3. Lim, B., Son, S., Kim, H., Nah, S., Mu Lee, K.: Enhanced deep residual networks for single image super-resolution. In: Proceedings of the IEEE Conference on Computer Vision and Pattern Recognition Workshops, pp. 136–144 (2017)

4. Ahn, N., Kang, B., Sohn, K.A.: Fast, accurate, and lightweight super-resolution with cascading residual network. In: Proceedings of the European Conference on Computer Vision (ECCV), pp. 252–268 (2018)

5. Zhang, Y., Li, K., Li, K., Wang, L., Zhong, B., Fu, Y.: Image super-resolution using very deep residual channel attention networks. In: Proceedings of the European Conference on Computer Vision (ECCV), pp. 286–301 (2018)

6. Anwar, S., Barnes, N.: Real image denoising with feature attention. In: Proceedings of the IEEE International Conference on Computer Vision, pp. 3155–3164 (2019)

7. Brooks, T., Mildenhall, B., Xue, T., Chen, J., Sharlet, D., Barron, J.T.: Unprocessing images for learned raw denoising. In: Proceedings of the IEEE Conference on Computer Vision and Pattern Recognition, pp. 11036–11045 (2019)

8. Burger, H.C., Schuler, C.J., Harmeling, S.: Image denoising: can plain neural networks compete with BM3D? In: 2012 IEEE Conference on Computer Vision and Pattern Recognition, pp. 2392–2399. IEEE (2012)

9. Zhang, K., Zuo, W., Zhang, L.: FFDNet: toward a fast and flexible solution for CNN-based image denoising. IEEE Trans. Image Process. **27**, 4608–4622 (2018)

10. Zhang, K., Zuo, W., Chen, Y., Meng, D., Zhang, L.: Beyond a gaussian denoiser: residual learning of deep CNN for image denoising. IEEE Trans. Image Process. **26**, 3142–3155 (2017)

11. Kumar, N., Nallamothu, R., Sethi, A.: Neural network based image deblurring. In: 11th Symposium on Neural Network Applications in Electrical Engineering, pp. 219–222. IEEE (2012)

12. Nah, S., Hyun Kim, T., Mu Lee, K.: Deep multi-scale convolutional neural network for dynamic scene deblurring. In: Proceedings of the IEEE Conference on Computer Vision and Pattern Recognition, pp. 3883–3891 (2017)

13. Zhang, J., et al.: Dynamic scene deblurring using spatially variant recurrent neural networks. In: Proceedings of the IEEE Conference on Computer Vision and Pattern Recognition, pp. 2521–2529 (2018)

14. Kupyn, O., Budzan, V., Mykhailych, M., Mishkin, D., Matas, J.: DeblurGAN: blind motion deblurring using conditional adversarial networks. In: The IEEE Conference on Computer Vision and Pattern Recognition (CVPR) (2018)

15. Yu, K., Dong, C., Lin, L., Change Loy, C.: Crafting a toolchain for image restoration by deep reinforcement learning. In: Proceedings of the IEEE Conference on Computer Vision and Pattern Recognition, pp. 2443–2452 (2018)

16. Liu, X., Suganuma, M., Luo, X., Okatani, T.: Restoring images with unknown degradation factors by recurrent use of a multi-branch network. arXiv preprint arXiv:1907.04508 (2019)

17. Suganuma, M., Liu, X., Okatani, T.: Attention-based adaptive selection of operations for image restoration in the presence of unknown combined distortions. In: Proceedings of the IEEE Conference on Computer Vision and Pattern Recognition, pp. 9039–9048 (2019)
18. Yu, K., Wang, X., Dong, C., Tang, X., Loy, C.C.: Path-restore: learning network path selection for image restoration. arXiv preprint arXiv:1904.10343 (2019)
19. Ahn, N., Kang, B., Sohn, K.A.: Image distortion detection using convolutional neural network. In: 2017 4th IAPR Asian Conference on Pattern Recognition (ACPR), pp. 220–225. IEEE (2017)
20. Savarese, P., Maire, M.: Learning implicitly recurrent CNNs through parameter sharing. arXiv preprint arXiv:1902.09701 (2019)
21. Caruana, R.: Multitask learning. Mach. Learn. **28**, 41–75 (1997)
22. Ruder, S.: An overview of multi-task learning in deep neural networks. arXiv preprint arXiv:1706.05098 (2017)
23. Jacobs, R.A., Jordan, M.I., Nowlan, S.J., Hinton, G.E.: Adaptive mixtures of local experts. Neural Comput. **3**, 79–87 (1991)
24. Misra, I., Shrivastava, A., Gupta, A., Hebert, M.: Cross-stitch networks for multi-task learning. In: Proceedings of the IEEE Conference on Computer Vision and Pattern Recognition, pp. 3994–4003 (2016)
25. Dabov, K., Foi, A., Katkovnik, V., Egiazarian, K.: Image denoising by sparse 3-D transform-domain collaborative filtering. IEEE Trans. Image Process. **16**, 2080–2095 (2007)
26. Roth, S., Black, M.J.: Fields of experts. Int. J. Comput. Vision **82**, 205 (2009)
27. Dong, C., Loy, C.C., Tang, X.: Accelerating the super-resolution convolutional neural network. In: Leibe, B., Matas, J., Sebe, N., Welling, M. (eds.) ECCV 2016. LNCS, vol. 9906, pp. 391–407. Springer, Cham (2016). https://doi.org/10.1007/978-3-319-46475-6_25
28. Ledig, C., et al.: Photo-realistic single image super-resolution using a generative adversarial network. In: Proceedings of the IEEE Conference on Computer Vision and Pattern Recognition, pp. 4681–4690 (2017)
29. Feng, R., Gu, J., Qiao, Y., Dong, C.: Suppressing model overfitting for image super-resolution networks. In: Proceedings of the IEEE Conference on Computer Vision and Pattern Recognition Workshops (2019)
30. Yoo, J., Ahn, N., Sohn, K.A.: Rethinking data augmentation for image super-resolution: a comprehensive analysis and a new strategy. arXiv preprint arXiv:2004.00448 (2020)
31. Guo, S., Yan, Z., Zhang, K., Zuo, W., Zhang, L.: Toward convolutional blind denoising of real photographs. In: Proceedings of the IEEE Conference on Computer Vision and Pattern Recognition, pp. 1712–1722 (2019)
32. Cai, J., Zeng, H., Yong, H., Cao, Z., Zhang, L.: Toward real-world single image super-resolution: a new benchmark and a new model. In: Proceedings of the IEEE International Conference on Computer Vision, pp. 3086–3095 (2019)
33. He, K., Gkioxari, G., Dollár, P., Girshick, R.: Mask R-CNN. In: Proceedings of the IEEE International Conference on Computer Vision, pp. 2961–2969 (2017)
34. Ma, J., Zhao, Z., Yi, X., Chen, J., Hong, L., Chi, E.H.: Modeling task relationships in multi-task learning with multi-gate mixture-of-experts. In: Proceedings of the 24th ACM SIGKDD International Conference on Knowledge Discovery & Data Mining, pp. 1930–1939 (2018)
35. Agustsson, E., Timofte, R.: NTIRE 2017 challenge on single image super-resolution: dataset and study. In: Proceedings of the IEEE Conference on Computer Vision and Pattern Recognition Workshops, pp. 126–135 (2017)

36. Zhang, R., Isola, P., Efros, A.A., Shechtman, E., Wang, O.: The unreasonable effectiveness of deep features as a perceptual metric. In: Proceedings of the IEEE Conference on Computer Vision and Pattern Recognition, pp. 586–595 (2018)
37. Ponomarenko, N., et al.: Image database TID2013: peculiarities, results and perspectives. Sig. Process. Image Commun. **30**, 57–77 (2015)
38. Van der Walt, S., et al.: Scikit-image: image processing in python. PeerJ **2**, e453 (2014)
39. Lai, W.S., Huang, J.B., Ahuja, N., Yang, M.H.: Deep laplacian pyramid networks for fast and accurate super-resolution. In: Proceedings of the IEEE Conference on Computer Vision and Pattern Recognition, pp. 624–632 (2017)
40. Dong, C., Loy, C.C., He, K., Tang, X.: Image super-resolution using deep convolutional networks. IEEE Trans. Pattern Anal. Mach. Intell. **38**, 295–307 (2015)
41. He, K., Zhang, X., Ren, S., Sun, J.: Deep residual learning for image recognition. In: Proceedings of the IEEE Conference on Computer Vision and Pattern Recognition, pp. 770–778 (2016)
42. Wang, Y., Tao, X., Qi, X., Shen, X., Jia, J.: Image inpainting via generative multi-column convolutional neural networks. In: Advances in Neural Information Processing Systems, pp. 331–340 (2018)
43. Ren, H., El-Khamy, M., Lee, J.: Image super resolution based on fusing multiple convolution neural networks. In: Proceedings of the IEEE Conference on Computer Vision and Pattern Recognition Workshops, pp. 54–61 (2017)
44. Du, X., El-Khamy, M., Lee, J., Davis, L.: Fused DNN: a deep neural network fusion approach to fast and robust pedestrian detection. In: 2017 IEEE Winter Conference on Applications of Computer Vision (WACV), pp. 953–961. IEEE (2017)
45. Hu, J., Shen, L., Sun, G.: Squeeze-and-excitation networks. In: Proceedings of the IEEE Conference on Computer Vision and Pattern Recognition, pp. 7132–7141 (2018)
46. Woo, S., Park, J., Lee, J.Y., So Kweon, I.: CBAM: convolutional block attention module. In: Proceedings of the European Conference on Computer Vision (ECCV), pp. 3–19 (2018)
47. Kingma, D.P., Ba, J.: Adam: a method for stochastic optimization. arXiv preprint arXiv:1412.6980 (2014)
48. He, K., Zhang, X., Ren, S., Sun, J.: Delving deep into rectifiers: surpassing human-level performance on imagenet classification. In: Proceedings of the IEEE International Conference on Computer Vision, pp. 1026–1034 (2015)
49. Ren, S., He, K., Girshick, R., Sun, J.: Faster R-CNN: towards real-time object detection with region proposal networks. In: Advances in Neural Information Processing Systems, pp. 91–99 (2015)
50. Lin, T.-Y., et al.: Microsoft COCO: common objects in context. In: Fleet, D., Pajdla, T., Schiele, B., Tuytelaars, T. (eds.) ECCV 2014. LNCS, vol. 8693, pp. 740–755. Springer, Cham (2014). https://doi.org/10.1007/978-3-319-10602-1_48
51. Tong, T., Li, G., Liu, X., Gao, Q.: Image super-resolution using dense skip connections. In: Proceedings of the IEEE International Conference on Computer Vision, pp. 4799–4807 (2017)

Color Enhancement Using Global Parameters and Local Features Learning

Enyu Liu$^{(\boxtimes)}$, Songnan Li, and Shan Liu

Tencent Media Lab, Shenzhen, China
{enyuliu,sunnysnli,shanl}@tencent.com

Abstract. This paper proposes a neural network to learn global parameters and extract local features for color enhancement. Firstly, the global parameters extractor subnetwork with dilated convolution is used to estimate a global color transformation matrix. The introduction of the dilated convolution enhances the ability to aggregate spatial information. Secondly, the local features extractor subnetwork with a light dense block structure is designed to learn the matrix of local details. Finally, an enhancement map is obtained by multiplying these two matrices. A novel combination of loss functions is formulated to make the color of the generated image more consistent with that of the target. The enhanced image is formed by adding the original image with an enhancement map. Thus, we make it possible to adjust the enhancement intensity by multiplying the enhancement map with a weighting coefficient. We conduct experiments on the MIT-Adobe FiveK benchmark, and our algorithm generates superior performance compared with the state-of-the-art methods on images and videos, both qualitatively and quantitatively.

1 Introduction

Color enhancement boosts the picture quality of an image or video by adjusting the global contrast, intensifying the local details, and generating more vivid colors. Due to low light, poor shooting equipment, bad weather conditions and other factors, the colors of images and videos may fade and distort, which seriously affect the visual quality. Using image processing software such as photoshop, many people like to manually modify image color to subjectively adjust the contrast, brightness, saturation, hue, exposure and etc. Different image contents need specific operations for maximize its visual quality. If all images are processed individually, it is time-consuming and the color coherence between adjacent video frames would be disrupted. For these reasons, color enhancement for both images and videos is a challenging and popular task in computer vision.

On the other hand, in the literature many algorithms have been developed to enhance colors automatically. The traditional algorithms [1,2] enhanced images

---

Electronic supplementary material The online version of this chapter (https://doi.org/10.1007/978-3-030-69532-3_13) contains supplementary material, which is available to authorized users.

H. Ishikawa et al. (Eds.): ACCV 2020, LNCS 12623, pp. 202–216, 2021.
https://doi.org/10.1007/978-3-030-69532-3_13

from the spatial domain or frequency domain by exploiting techniques, such as histogram equalization, retinex, and wavelet multi-scale transform. However, these methods cannot enhance image details effectively. Deep learning based methods are widely investigated for this task in recent years [3,4], which can achieve better performance compared with traditional methods. There are two mainstream methods: one is to learn the local features; the other is to estimate the global transformation parameters. For the method of learning local features, it is indeed effective to obtain good effects, but improper network design may cause flickering problems in videos, so postprocessing is needed to keep the brightness consistency between video frames. While for the method of estimating global parameters, compared with the method of learning local features, it can better maintain the consistency in video processing, but a global matrix may cause the inadequate enhancement of the local contrast, making the picture details in dark and bright regions less visible.

Therefore, we propose a novel deep model for tackling these problems, which obtains superior color enhancement effects by combining the global parameters and local features. The design of our network considers its practical applicability. The input can be of arbitrary resolution and the color enhancement intensity can be adjusted conveniently by tuning a single parameter. Estimating a global color transformation matrix as in [5] is appealing for its computational efficiency and the ability to coherently enhance the global contrast of adjacent video frames. And image details are also considered by learning local features.

1. In order to extract global parameters, a multi-branch network with multi-scale dilated convolution layers is proposed to enlarge the receptive field so as to get a more accurate global transformation matrix.
2. For extracting local features, a network with a light dense block is employed, which can strengthen the feature propagation and enhance the local contrast.
3. Considering both structure and color similarity, we propose a novel combination of loss functions, including a L2 loss in CIElab color space, a structure similarity (SSIM) loss, and an improved color loss.

Our algorithm can enhance the picture color and contrast both globally and locally. We conduct subjective and objective experiments to prove its superiority over the state-of-art methods. Furthermore, the proposed method can be applied on video, since it can effectively avoid flicker and maintain the color consistency of adjacent video frames.

2   Related Work

For color enhancement, many algorithms have been proposed to improve brightness, contrast and saturation. Converting to HSV color space is one of the effective approaches [6,7]. HSV represents hue, saturation and brightness respectively. The HSV space can subtly separate each feature, so it is more convenient to process each factor and obtain good enhancement results. However, a global enhancement may cause the loss of local details.

Example-based enhancement methods are also widely investigated. Wang et al. [8] proposed a method to discover mathematical relationships and to learn the nonlinear mappings of color and tone from a pair of corresponding images before and after adjustments. Lee et al. [9] presented an unsupervised algorithm by selecting several styles from subsets and transforming the color of the input into the style and tone of selected exemplars. However, selecting suitable example images and learning the mapping between inputs and example images are tricky and difficult problems.

The generative adversarial networks (GAN) based approach is able to achieve good results [4]. Hui et al. [10] designed lightweight local residual networks that can be applied on smartphone cameras. Specifically, transformation of teacher-student information is introduced to maintain the realism of the outputs. Chen et al. [11] proposed a global feature network, which used Wasserstein GAN (WGAN) to speed up the convergence. Two-way GANs exploited individual batch normalization layers for each generator which can adjust to their own distributions easily. Chai et al. [5] trained an unsupervised model which applied the cycle consistency of CycleGAN [12] and also employed individual batch normalization layers.

Deep reinforcement learning can be applied for this task as well. Park et al. [13] used reinforcement learning to give a guidance of several image enhancement operations, and a distort-recover scheme was proposed for unpaired images training. The advantage of these methods is that the unsupervised learning uses unpaired images for training which are more accessible than paired images. However, it is hard to converge, and is subject to color distortions.

Recently, investigation of using supervised CNN for color enhancement are thriving. Since training on matched pairs is more accurate and controllable, our algorithm also uses paired images for training. Chen et al. [14] proposed to use dilated convolution and individual batch normalization on a fully convolutional network to learn the mapping from the input to the output. Ignatov et al. [15] collected a dataset that consists of real photos captured from different cameras and trained an end-to-end network to generate the enhanced images for mobile devices. Huang et al. [3] proposed a range scaling layer based on UNet [16] to extract features at different resolutions so as to reduce the output artifacts. Isola et al. [4] also used UNet [16] to learn the mapping between the target and the input.

Rather than directly generating an enhanced image, there are approaches that use deep neural networks to predict intermediate color transformation matrices, which then are applied on the input image to produce the output [5,17]. Gharbi et al. [17] introduced the HDRNet which predicted the intermediate color transformation matrices in a low resolution bilateral grid, and then used bilateral slicing to up-sample the grid into the original resolution. Bianco et al. [18] proposed to predict the coefficients of local polynomial transformations that are applied to the input image to remove artistic photo filter. Based on previous research, Bianco et al. [19] later designed the novel CNN that estimates the coefficients to be used to the basis function (including polynomial, piecewise, cosine and radial) to get the color transformation. Afifi et al. [20] trained several pairs of incorrect white-balanced images and computed nonlinear color correction matrices that map the incorrect colors to the target, and finally their corresponding correctly white-balanced images are obtained by weighting multiple effects. Wang et al. [21] developed a network to predict a mapping between the input image and its illumination, and the input was combined with the illumination map for color enhancement. This method can successfully cover different photographic adjustments. Biano et al. [22] proposed to use two neural networks. One for a global tone enhancement, while the other for local adjustment to spatially align the input and the ground truth. Maron et al. [23] introduced a novel approach to automatically enhance images using learned parameters of three spatial filters. Chai et al. [5] presented a supervised model that used the CNN to predict color transformation parameters. And then the parameters are multiplied by the color basis vector for each pixel to get the enhanced RGB value.

3   Proposed Method

3.1   Overview

We develop our method based on [5] with modifications to enhance the output both globally and locally. Specifically, an enhancement map M is calculated by our neural network, and then the enhancement map is added on the input image to obtain the enhanced image. The process can be simply defined as:

$$O = M + I \tag{1}$$

where I is the input with RGB channels, O is the output, M is the enhancement map, $M \in \mathbb{R}^{w \times h \times 3}$, w and h are the width and height of the image. Furthermore, by using Eq. (2) which multiply M by a weighting factor, we can easily control the color enhancement intensity:

$$O = \alpha \cdot M + I \tag{2}$$

where α is the weighting coefficient. If $\alpha > 1$, the enhancement strength would be enlarged; if $0 < \alpha < 1$, the strength would be reduced. This coefficient can be adjusted according to different scenes or videos. In this paper, experiments are performed by setting $\alpha = 1$, which shows the original intensity learned from the training set. The calculation of the enhancement map consists of two parts. One is to estimate the matrix of the global parameters from the global parameters extractor subnetwork, which is defined as P. The input of P is I_{ds}, which is a downsampled version of the input image I. The output of P is a global color transformation matrix $\theta \in \mathbb{R}^{10 \times 3}$, so the inference process of P can be expressed as:

$$\theta_P = P(I_{ds}) \tag{3}$$

The structure of the global parameters extractor subnetwork P is elaborated in Sect. 3.2. The other part is to estimate the local features from the local features extractor subnetwork. We use F as the notation for this subnetwork. The input of F is defined as $I_F \in \mathbb{R}^{w \times h \times 10}$, which contains the quadratic color basis vectors of I. $p_F(x,y)$ is the quadratic color basis vector at coordinate (x,y) in I_F, and $p(x,y)$ represents RGB values at coordinate (x,y) in I, i.e., $p(x,y) = [R(x,y), G(x,y), B(x,y)]$. Thus, $p_F(x,y)$ can be defined as:

$$p_F(x,y) = [R(x,y), G(x,y), B(x,y), R(x,y)^2, G(x,y)^2, B(x,y)^2, \\ R(x,y) \cdot G(x,y), G(x,y) \cdot B(x,y), B(x,y) \cdot R(x,y), 1] \tag{4}$$

which is also used in [5,18], in order to make it easy to preserve the details in the input [18]. The output of the local feature extractor subnetwork F is $\theta_F \in \mathbb{R}^{w \times h \times 10}$, which has the same size as its input. The inference process of F can be expressed as:

$$\theta_F = F(I_F) \tag{5}$$

We elaborate on the structure of the local feature extractor subnetwork in Sect. 3.3. Finally, the enhancement map M is defined as:

$$M = \theta_P \theta_F = F(I_F)P(I_{ds}) \tag{6}$$

In order to make the structure and color of the output as close as possible to the ground truth, we propose a loss function which consists of three loss terms as to be described in Sect. 3.4. The overall architecture of our algorithm is shown in Fig. 1.

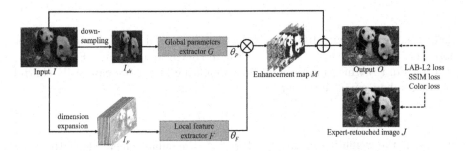

Fig. 1. The architecture of our color enhancement network.

3.2 Global Parameters Extractor Subnetwork

To extract the global parameters, we augment the multi-branch network of [5] with dilated convolution as shown in Fig. 2. The whole global parameters extractor subnetwork consists of five branches, and each branch has an identical structure.

Each branch consists of four parts, including feature extraction, context aggregation, feature extraction and parameter compression. Firstly, the input image is downsampled to $256 \times 256 \times 3$. The first layer consists of 5×5 filtering followed by Leaky Relu, and the second and third layers use 3×3 filter with stride 2. Every subsequent convolutional layer is followed by Batch Normalization and Leaky Relu.

Next, the $32 \times 32 \times 48$ feature map are expanded to $32 \times 32 \times 96$ after the context aggregation. Three dilated convolution layers are added in the middle of the architecture with a kernal size of 3×3, and the dilation rates of 1, 2 and 3 separately. The special combination of three dilation rates has been proved to be helpful and defined as the hybrid dilated convolution (HDC) framework [24]. It can amplify the receptive fields of the network, aggregate global information, and decrease the gridding issue produced by the normal dilated convolution operation.

After that, the $32 \times 32 \times 96$ feature maps are further convolved by 3×3 filters to generate a $8 \times 8 \times 192$ tensor. Finally, the dimensions of the parameters are compressed. An average pooling with a kernel size of 8 decreases the $8 \times 8 \times 192$ feature maps to a $1 \times 1 \times 192$ tensor, followed by a 1×1 filter, and two Leaky Relu layers. Subsequently the $1 \times 1 \times 192$ tensor is processed by two fully connected layers, a leaky relu and a softmax layer to generate a $1 \times 1 \times 30$ tensor. Since there are five identical branches, we obtain five $1 \times 1 \times 30$ tensors which are averaged and rearranged to generate the final 10×3 global color transformation matrix θ_P.

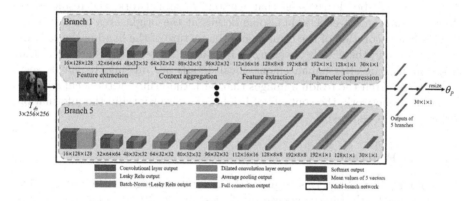

Fig. 2. The architecture of the global parameters extractor subnetwork.

3.3   Local Features Extractor Subnetwork

In order to extract features in different scales and overcome the vanishing gradient, deep neural networks with skip connections are proposed, such as UNet [4], ResNet [25] and DenseNet [26]. Empirically we adopt the DenseNet as the local feature extractor subnetwork. But unlike the original DenseNet which has three dense blocks, our neural network only uses one dense block. And the reason for adopting only one denseblock in our network is based on the following considerations: first is the complexity of the network, and the second is the small amount of datasets. An overly complex network may cause overfitting.

Here is a detailed description of the local features extractor subnetwork F, which is shown in Fig. 3. First, I_F goes through a convolutional layer to expand the dimensions of I_F. And then the matrix enters the dense block. In the dense block, a bottleneck [26] layer with kernel size 1×1 is used before a convolution with kernel size 3×3, which is proposed to fuse features in DenseNet [26]. Such combination loops 3 times, which is far less than the times of each dense block in DenseNet. Therefore, a light dense block is presented in our network. In a denseblock, the output of each 3×3 convolution is the concatenation of the inputs of all convolutional layers before and the output of this convolutional layer. Finally, the feature matrix goes through the translation layer with kernel size 1×1 to reduce dimension and obtain θ_F. Every subsequent convolutional layer is followed by Batch Normalization and Relu layers. These layers are not shown in Fig. 3, in order to illustrate the convolutional layers of our light dense block more clearly and make comparisons with alternative architectures more easily. In Sect. 4.3, we will analyze the selection and adjustment of our local features extractor subnetwork.

We compare the results of whether to use local features extractor subnetwork, in Fig. 4. When subnetwork is not used, $\theta_F = I_F$, the algorithm is similar to PCE [5]. It can be clearly seen that without F subnetwork, the results have obvious enhancement effects, but some details at the bright area are lost, such as the silver decoration of the camera and the texture of the hand in the red box in Fig. 4(a), and the details of ceiling in Fig. 4(b). These features are very clear in the input, but after enhancement, local details are missing. It can be seen much clearer from the residual images that with the utility of the local features extractor subnetwork, the contents of bright areas are kept and the information of dark areas is restored.

3.4   Loss Function

We combine three loss terms to make the generated image as close as possible to the ground truth. Firstly, we use the $\mathcal{L}_2$ loss in the CIElab color space which correlate better with the human perception of color differences than other color spaces, such RGB, XYZ, YUV and so on. CIElab was derived from CIEXYZ. And the intention behind CIElab was to create a space that can be computed via simple formulas from CIEXYZ space but is more perceptually uniform then CIEXYZ. I is the input with RGB channels, O is the output, J is the target, and O^{lab} is the output transformed into the CIElab color space, J^{lab} is the target transformed into the CIElab color space. The $\mathcal{L}_2$ loss term is given by:

$$\mathcal{L}_2 = \frac{1}{N} \sum_i \|O_i^{lab} - J_i^{lab}\|^2 \tag{7}$$

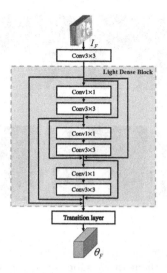

Fig. 3. The architecture of the local features extractor subnetwork.

N is the number of pixels, and i is the pixel index. We further add an color loss using the angular difference to measure the color similarity [21]. The RGB values of a pixel can be regarded as a 3D vector, and when two pixels are similar, the angle of the two RGB vectors approaches $0°$, and its cosine value is close to 1. Therefore, the cosine of the angle should be as close as possible to 1. The color loss is defined as:

$$\mathcal{L}_{colorloss} = \frac{1}{N}\sum_i 1 - \cos \angle (O_i, J_i) \tag{8}$$

Where $\angle(,)$ means the angle of two vectors.

Besides considering the color similarity, we also pay attention to the structure of the image by using a SSIM loss [27] as defined in Eq. (9):

$$\mathcal{L}_{SSIM} = 1 - SSIM(O_i, J_i) \tag{9}$$

Finally, the total loss is given by:

$$\mathcal{L} = \omega_1 \mathcal{L}_2 + \omega_2 \mathcal{L}_{colorloss} + \omega_3 \mathcal{L}_{SSIM} \tag{10}$$

where ω_1, ω_2, ω_3 are the weighting coefficients. The functionality of each loss function is analyzed in Sect. 4.2.

4 Experiments

4.1 Training Details

Training Datasets. MIT-Adobe FiveK [28] is a high-quality dataset for color enhancement containing a collection of five sets of retouched image pairs by

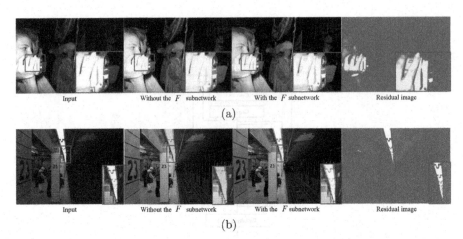

Fig. 4. The effects of the utilization of the local features extractor subnetwork. From left to right (1) Input (2) Without the F subnetwork (3) With the F subnetwork (4) Residual image. (Color figure online)

expert A/B/C/D/E. Like most previous methods [5,13,21], we select 5000 images retouched by Expert C as the ground truth. We randomly select 250 image pairs for validation and test, each including 125 pairs, and use the remaining 4750 images for training.

Experiment Setting. We train the proposed network using the Adam optimizer on a Nvidia Tesla P40 GPU with 24 GB of memory. The batch size is 20 and the base learning rate is 9×10^{-4}. The learning rate linearly decays to 2×10^{-6}, and the training stops at the 500th epoch. ω_1, ω_2, ω_3 in the loss function (11) are set to 1, 200, and 10 respectively. PSNR and SSIM are used to evaluate the performance of our algorithm. Higher PSNR and SSIM values indicate better performance. For features extractor subnetwork, the input channels of the dense block is 24, and the growthrate is set as 12.

4.2 Ablation Study

Dilated Convolution. Dilated convolution has the effect of expanding the receptive field. The specific role in the global parameters extractor subnetwork is further distinguished through the subjective effect. With dilated convolution, the details of the enhanced image are kept better. For example, in the red area of Fig. 5, without dilated convolution, the texture of the mountain is less visible.

Loss Function. $\mathcal{L}_2$ loss, SSIM loss, and the improved color loss are used in this paper. Generally, we found that using SSIM can enhance the overall image quality, but in some cases, as illustrated by Fig. 6, the color diversity becomes

(a) Input   (b) Without dilated convolution   (c) Proposed

Fig. 5. The texture of the mountain is clearer when using the dilated convolution.

more obvious. When using the improved color loss term, the color consistency can be improved, as shown in the fourth column of Fig. 6.

4.3   Alternative Architecture

For the local feature extractor network, we compare three different architectures. One of the structures is our proposed subnetwork F with the light dense block, which is illustrated in Sect. 3.3. Removing all of the skip connections in the light dense block, another structure is obtained, which is denoted as F'. For a fair comparison, the number of channels of each 3×3 convolutional layer matches that of the architecture. We also compare the setting that using the feature map $I_F = \theta_F$ directly without the local feature extractor subnetwork. The average MSEs of the validation set are shown in Table 1. It can be seen that the light dense block network has the lowest MSE and compared to F' it has a lower complexity, so we finally choose it as the local features extractor subnetwork in this paper.

Table 1. The average MSE values of different local feature extractor network.

Network structure	Without F	F'	Proposed
MSE	8.954	8.602	8.553

4.4   Comparison with the State-of-the-Art Methods

We compare our algorithm with eight state-of-the-art methods. There are six deep learning based methods, including HDRNet [17], Deep Photo Enhancer [11], Pix2pix [4], DPED [14], the supervised model in PCE [5] and RSGU [3]. For fair comparison, the same training set are used for these models. The other two methods are traditional algorithms, including NPEA [1] and SIRE [2].

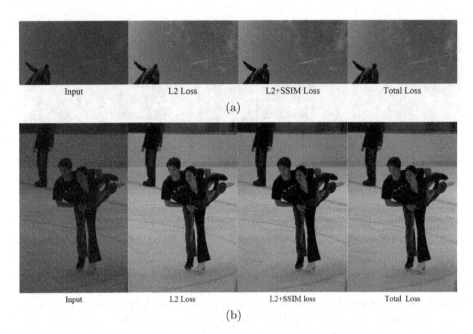

Fig. 6. Comparison with different loss functions. From left to right (1) Input (2) $\mathcal{L}_2$ loss only (3) $\mathcal{L}_2$+SSIM loss (4) Total loss.

Objective and Subjective Performance. Table 2 shows the PSNR and SSIM of different methods. We only compare with deep learning methods, because these methods need ground truth. While for traditional algorithms, the purpose is to recover more details and colors in dark or bright scenes, sometimes these results show more content, but they are far from Expert-retouched images, resulting in extremely low values of PSNR and SSIM. While for DPED, the pretraining model is used. Moreover, because the training set of DPED is inconsistent with the training set of our algorithm and other comparison methods. So it is unfair to compare these two indicators with DPED [14], NPEA [1], SIRE [2], which cannot reflect the real effect of these algorithms. With the same dataset, our algorithm exhibits the highest PSNR and SSIM values. The objective indexes of HDRNet [17] are the worst, while PCE [5] and Deep Photo Enhancer [11] are relatively better.

Subjective comparison is given in Fig. 7. It can be seen from the comparison that our algorithm can not only maintain and restore more details, but also have brighter colors and higher contrast. For example, the sky in Fig. 7(a), our method is bluer and more vivid, and the contrast of the mountain is higher; the enlarged part of the white flowers of our algorithm in Fig. 7(b) still maintains excellent details; the color and contrast of the squirrel and background in Fig. 7(c) are superior to the effect of other algorithms.

Table 2. Objective performance of the deep learning methods in comparison.

Method	PSNR	SSIM
HDRNet [17]	19.138	0.860
Deep photo enhancer [11]	23.486	0.935
Pix2pix [4]	20.581	0.890
PCE [5]	24.127	0.905
RSGU [3]	20.818	0.905
Proposed	**24.684**	**0.948**

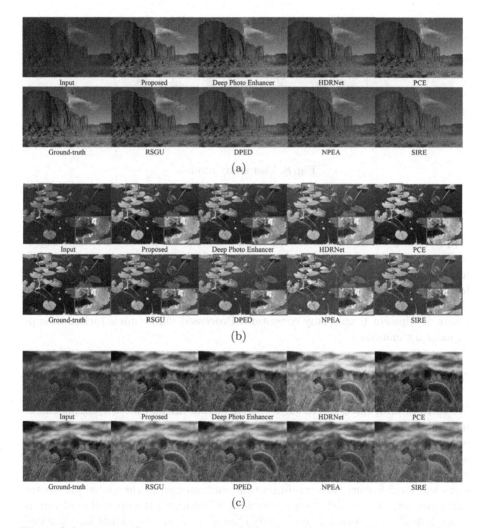

Fig. 7. Subjective quality comparisons with the state-of-the-art methods. From left to righ, from top to bottom (1) Input (2) Proposed (3) Deep Photo Enhancer (4) HDRNet (5) PCE (6) Expert (7) RSGU (8) DPED (9) NPEA (10) SIRE.

User Study. We conducted a user study and adopted pairwise comparisons with seven state-of-the-art methods, which included 20 images and 58 participants. We compared the paired results of our algorithm and the state-of-art method, and each set of images was compared 7 times. While testing, the paired-images were displayed side-by-side, allowing users to choose which one they prefer, according to colors and details of the image. The 20 images were randomly selected from our test set. The results of user study are shown in Fig. 8. Our algorithm is more frequently picked as the better one compared with other state-of-the-art methods.

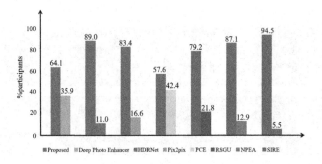

Fig. 8. User study results.

Application on Video. Our algorithm can also be applied on videos. Lightroom is a popular image processing software which can also process videos. We use the Lightroom Auto-Tune feature to enhance the images. We 4K videos from Youtube, and compared the enhancing performance of our algorithm and the lightroom. Our algorithm shows superior vivid results, and the enhanced colors of adjacent frames stay consistent. Processed videos are attached as supplementary materials.

5 Conclusion

We introduced a novel approach for color enhancement that the enhancement map is learned using an end-to-end neural network, and added to the input to obtain an enhanced image. The enhancement intensity can be adjusted by tuning a coefficient, predefined or automatically determined according to the image or video content. To generate the enhancement map, the extraction of global parameters and local features are two important components. In the global parameter extractor network, a multi-branch network is used, and the operation of multi-scale dilated convolution layers is introduced to aggregate global information. We also design a network with a light dense block that can help to enhance local contrasts. Furthermore, we present a new loss function, combining the improved color loss with a $\mathcal{L}_2$ loss and a SSIM loss. We conducted experiments to compare our algorithm with the state-of-art methods. Our algorithm shows superior performance evaluated by both objective metrics and a subjective user study.

References

1. Wang, S., Zheng, J., Hu, H., Li, B.: Naturalness preserved enhancement algorithm for non-uniform illumination images. IEEE Trans. Image Process. **22**, 3538–3548 (2013)
2. Fu, X., Liao, Y., Zeng, D., Huang, Y., Zhang, X.S., Ding, X.: A probabilistic method for image enhancement with simultaneous illumination and reflectance estimation. IEEE Trans. Image Process. **24**, 4965–4977 (2015)
3. Huang, J., et al.: Range scaling global U-Net for perceptual image enhancement on mobile devices. In: Proceedings of the European Conference on Computer Vision (ECCV), pp. 230–242 (2018)
4. Isola, P., Zhu, J.Y., Zhou, T., Efros, A.A.: Image-to-image translation with conditional adversarial networks. In: Proceedings of the IEEE Conference on Computer Vision and Pattern Recognition, pp. 1125–1134 (2017)
5. Chai, Y., Giryes, R., Wolf, L.: Supervised and unsupervised learning of parameterized color enhancement. In: The IEEE Winter Conference on Applications of Computer Vision, pp. 992–1000 (2020)
6. Veluchamy, M., Subramani, B.: Image contrast and color enhancement using adaptive gamma correction and histogram equalization. Optik **183**, 329–337 (2019)
7. Hassanpour, H., Samadiani, N.: A new image enhancement method considering both dynamic range and color constancy. Scientia Iranica **26**, 1589–1600 (2019)
8. Wang, B., Yu, Y., Xu, Y.Q.: Example-based image color and tone style enhancement. ACM Trans. Graph. (TOG) **30**, 1–12 (2011)
9. Lee, J.Y., Sunkavalli, K., Lin, Z., Shen, X., So Kweon, I.: Automatic content-aware color and tone stylization. In: Proceedings of the IEEE Conference on Computer Vision and Pattern Recognition, pp. 2470–2478 (2016)
10. Hui, Z., Wang, X., Deng, L., Gao, X.: Perception-preserving convolutional networks for image enhancement on smartphones. In: Proceedings of the European Conference on Computer Vision (ECCV), pp. 197–213 (2018)
11. Chen, Y.S., Wang, Y.C., Kao, M.H., Chuang, Y.Y.: Deep photo enhancer: unpaired learning for image enhancement from photographs with GANs. In: Proceedings of the IEEE Conference on Computer Vision and Pattern Recognition, pp. 6306–6314 (2018)
12. Zhu, J.Y., Park, T., Isola, P., Efros, A.A.: Unpaired image-to-image translation using cycle-consistent adversarial networks. In: Proceedings of the IEEE International Conference on Computer Vision, pp. 2223–2232 (2017)
13. Park, J., Lee, J.Y., Yoo, D., So Kweon, I.: Distort-and-recover: color enhancement using deep reinforcement learning. In: Proceedings of the IEEE Conference on Computer Vision and Pattern Recognition, pp. 5928–5936 (2018)
14. Ignatov, A., Kobyshev, N., Timofte, R., Vanhoey, K., Van Gool, L.: DSLR-quality photos on mobile devices with deep convolutional networks. In: Proceedings of the IEEE International Conference on Computer Vision, pp. 3277–3285 (2017)
15. Chen, Q., Xu, J., Koltun, V.: Fast image processing with fully-convolutional networks. In: Proceedings of the IEEE International Conference on Computer Vision, pp. 2497–2506 (2017)

16. Ronneberger, O., Fischer, P., Brox, T.: U-Net: convolutional networks for biomedical image segmentation. In: International Conference on Medical Image Computing and Computer-Assisted Intervention, pp. 234–241 (2015)

17. Gharbi, M., Chen, J., Barron, J.T., Hasinoff, S.W., Durand, F.: Deep bilateral learning for real-time image enhancement. ACM Trans. Graph. (TOG) **36**, 1–12 (2017)

18. Bianco, S., Cusano, C., Piccoli, F., Schettini, R.: Artistic photo filter removal using convolutional neural networks. J. Electron. Imaging **27**, 011004 (2017)

19. Bianco, S., Cusano, C., Piccoli, F., Schettini, R.: Learning parametric functions for color image enhancement. In: Tominaga, S., Schettini, R., Trémeau, A., Horiuchi, T. (eds.) CCIW 2019. LNCS, vol. 11418, pp. 209–220. Springer, Cham (2019). https://doi.org/10.1007/978-3-030-13940-7_16

20. Afifi, M., Price, B., Cohen, S., Brown, M.S.: When color constancy goes wrong: correcting improperly white-balanced images, pp. 1535–1544 (2019)

21. Wang, R., Zhang, Q., Fu, C.W., Shen, X., Zheng, W.S., Jia, J.: Underexposed photo enhancement using deep illumination estimation. In: Proceedings of the IEEE Conference on Computer Vision and Pattern Recognition, pp. 6849–6857 (2019)

22. Bianco, S., Cusano, C., Piccoli, F., Schettini, R.: Content-preserving tone adjustment for image enhancement. In: Proceedings of the IEEE Conference on Computer Vision and Pattern Recognition Workshops, pp. 1936–1943 (2019)

23. Moran, S., Marza, P., McDonagh, S., Parisot, S., Slabaugh, G.: DeepLPF: deep local parametric filters for image enhancement. In: Proceedings of the IEEE/CVF Conference on Computer Vision and Pattern Recognition, pp. 12826–12835 (2020)

24. Wang, P., et al.: Understanding convolution for semantic segmentation. In: 2018 IEEE Winter Conference on Applications of Computer Vision (WACV), pp. 1451–1460 (2018)

25. He, K., Zhang, X., Ren, S., Sun, J.: Deep residual learning for image recognition. In: Proceedings of the IEEE Conference on Computer Vision and Pattern Recognition, pp. 770–778 (2016)

26. Huang, G., Liu, Z., Van Der Maaten, L., Weinberger, K.Q.: Densely connected convolutional networks. In: Proceedings of the IEEE Conference on Computer Vision and Pattern Recognition, pp. 4700–4708 (2017)

27. Wang, Z., Simoncelli, E.P., Bovik, A.C.: Multiscale structural similarity for image quality assessment. In: The Thrity-Seventh Asilomar Conference on Signals, Systems & Computers, vol. 2, pp. 1398–1402 (2003)

28. Bychkovsky, V., Paris, S., Chan, E., Durand, F.: Learning photographic global tonal adjustment with a database of input/output image pairs. In: CVPR 2011, pp. 97–104 (2011)

An Efficient Group Feature Fusion Residual Network for Image Super-Resolution

Pengcheng Lei and Cong Liu$^{(\boxtimes)}$

School of Optical-Electrical and Computer Engineering, University of Shanghai for Science and Technology, 516 Jungong Road, Shanghai 200093, China
13027510953@163.com, congl2014@usst.edu.cn

Abstract. Convolutional neural networks (CNNs) have made great breakthrough in the field of image super-resolution (SR). However, most current methods are usually to improve their performance by simply increasing the depth of their network. Although this strategy can get promising results, it is inefficient in many real-world scenarios because of the high computational cost. In this paper, we propose an efficient group feature fusion residual network (GFFRN) for image super-resolution. In detail, we design a novel group feature fusion residual block (GFFRB) to group and fuse the features of the intermediate layers. In this way, GFFRB can enjoy the merits of the lightweight of the group convolution and the high-efficiency of the skip connections, thus achieving better performance compared with most current residual blocks. Experiments on the benchmark test sets show that our models are more efficient than most of the state-of-the-art methods.

1 Introduction

Single image super-resolution (SR) is a classical low-level computer vision problem that tries to restore a high-resolution (HR) image from a single low-resolution (LR) image. Since the reconstructed HR image contains rich details, SR techniques have been widely used in the field of image processing such as face authentication, public relations security monitoring and so on [1,2].

SR is an inherent ill-posed problem since a multiplicity of solutions exist for any given LR image. To solve this problem, numerous SR methods have been proposed, including interpolation-based methods [3], reconstruction-based methods [4] and learning-based methods [5,6]. In recent years, the convolutional neural network (CNN) based SR methods, with their powerful nonlinear expression ability, have achieved dramatic success in the field of image SR.

Since Dong et al. [7] firstly proposed a three-layer CNN (SRCNN) for image SR, a large number of CNN based methods have emerged. The early CNN based

Electronic supplementary material The online version of this chapter (https://doi.org/10.1007/978-3-030-69532-3_14) contains supplementary material, which is available to authorized users.

© Springer Nature Switzerland AG 2021
H. Ishikawa et al. (Eds.): ACCV 2020, LNCS 12623, pp. 217–233, 2021.
https://doi.org/10.1007/978-3-030-69532-3_14

SR methods used shallow networks (less than 10 layers) to learn the mapping function between LR and HR images, such as FSRCNN [8] and ESPCN [9]. Since He et al. [10] proposed ResNet to solve the convergence problem of deep networks, the SR methods began to grow in depth to improve the reconstruction accuracy. Kim et al. [11] utilized global residual learning to build a very deep network (VDSR, about 20 layers). Lim et al. [12] proposed an Enhanced Deep Residual Network (EDSR, about 60 layers), which used a stack of residual blocks to gradually recover the high frequency details from the LR inputs. Zhang et al. [13] further proposed a Residual Dense Network (RDN, about 150 layers), which employed dense connections in the residual block to extract abundant local features. Zhang et al. [14] proposed a Residual Channel Attention Network (RCAN). By using residual in residual (RIR) structure, the depth of the network reached 400 layers.

All the methods introduced above show excellent reconstruction performance by increasing the depth of their network, however, they all have a huge number of parameters and computations, which will put a high demand on the hardware resources. Considering that the SR method may be operated on a mobile device, the computing and storage resources of them are limited. A huge network will consume more hardware resources and result in longer inference time, which will seriously affect the user experience. Another time demanding scenario is video streaming data SR because it contains a large number of images and a huge network will affect the real-time performance of video image processing. Therefore, it is particularly important to design a more efficient and lightweight network.

2   Related Work

2.1   Lightweight Neural Network

Recent studies indicate that Skip connection, Recursive network and Group convolution are three widely used strategies in current lightweight SR networks. The details of them are introduced as follows.

(1) **Skip Connection.** Skip connection can enhance the information flow between different convolutional layers, thus improving the reconstruction accuracy. The most representative lightweight methods with this strategy are Mem-Net [15] and CARN [16]. MemNet designed a memory module to adaptively retain the useful information of different residual blocks. CARN employed the cascading mechanism to fuse the information among different residual blocks, thus building an efficient cascade residual network. However, the skip connections of these networks are only conducted between different residual blocks, thus the improvement of reconstruction accuracy is very limited.

(2) **Recursive Network.** Recursive network designs a recursive unit and makes the data pass the unit repeatedly thus building a more complex mapping function. Through parameter sharing between different recursive phases, this strategy reduces the model parameters effectively. The most representative recursive

networks are DRCN [17], DRRN [18], MemNet [15] and SRFBN [19]. Although these methods can achieve good performance with fewer parameters, they also have some problems: 1) Most of them upsample the LR image before CNN. 2) These methods usually use very deep networks to compensate for the performance degradation caused by parameter sharing. Both the two problems increase the time complexity of the network.

(3) **Group Convolution.** Group convolution groups the input feature maps and convolves them within each group. This strategy can reduce both the number of the parameters and the calculations of the model. AlexNet [20] firstly proposed the group convolution to solve the scarcity of hardware resources. MobileNet [21] designed a depthwise separable convolution network for mobile vision applications. In the field of image super-resolution, CARN-m [16] used this strategy to design a lightweight SR method for mobile devices. However, simply using group convolution to replace the traditional convolution will result in the decrease of the accuracy, so we need to combine it with some other strategies to build more efficient methods.

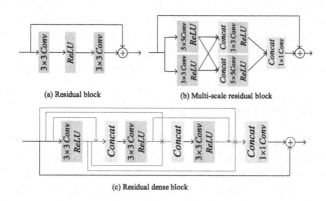

Fig. 1. The structure of current residual blocks: (a) Residual block, (b) Multi-scale residual block, (c) Residual dense block. The ⊕ operations are element-wise addition for residual learning.

2.2 Recent Residual Blocks

To design an efficient network, a good way is to design a more efficient residual block. In recent years, many efficient residual blocks have been proposed to improve the reconstruction accuracy. Lim et al. [12] proposed a residual block (RB, as shown in Fig. 1(a)) by removing the BN operation of SRResNet [22] and got higher reconstruction accuracy. RB is really concise and effective, but its utilization of local information is limited. To solve this problem, Zhang et al. [13] proposed a dense residual block (RDB, as shown in Fig. 1(c)), which designed dense skip connections to continuously fuse the features of the current layer with those features of the previous layers. This structure has powerful nonlinear capability to fully extract the local information. However, the dense connection also introduces a large number of parameters and computations, which is not desirable for lightweight networks. Li et al. [23] proposed a multi-scale residual block (MSRB, as shown in Fig. 1(b)), which used convolution kernels of different sizes $(3 \times 3, 5 \times 5)$ to adaptively detect the features in different scales. However, the 5×5 filters do not seem efficient in lightweight models.

To solve these problems, in this paper, we propose a Group Feature Fusion Residual Network (GFFRN) and its lightweight version GFFRN-L. Both the two models consist of a series of Group Feature Fusion Residual Blocks (GFFRB). GFFRB is a newly proposed residual block in this paper, which takes advantage of group convolution and skip connection to fully extract abundant local features. More details are shown in Sect. 3.

The main contributions are as follows: **(1)** We propose a novel group feature fusion residual block (GFFRB), which combines the advantages of both the lightweight of the group convolution and the high-efficiency of the skip connections, thus achieving better performance compared with most current residual blocks. **(2)** Based on GFFRB, we propose an efficient two-path group feature fusion residual network (GFFRN), which achieves higher efficiency compared with most state-of-the-art methods. **(3)** To further reduce the number of parameters and computations, we also propose a lightweight network GFFRN-L by reducing the depth and the width of GFFRN. The proposed GFFRN-L achieves the best performance among the models that have less than 1M parameters.

3 Proposed Method

In this section, we will introduce the details of the proposed GFFRN, GFFRN-L and GFFRB respectively. Let's denote I_{LR} and $\hat{I}_{HR}$ as the input and output of GFFRN respectively and both of them have C channels. We also denote $Conv(s, n)$ as a convolutional layer, where s represents the size of the filters and n represents the number of the filters.

3.1 Network Architecture of GFFRN

We first propose an efficient GFFRN for image SR. As shown in Fig. 2, GFFRN has two paths, e.t. a high-path and a low-path. The high-path of GFFRN has a powerful nonlinear ability, which uses multiple GFFRBs to restore the high-frequency information. It mainly consists of three parts: shallow feature extraction net (SFE-Net), deep feature extraction net (DFE-Net) and finally the upsampling and reconstruction net (Up&Recon-Net). The low-path has a relatively weak nonlinear ability, which uses a simple structure to restore the low-frequency information. The network structure of GFFRN is actually an improved version of WDSR [24]. Compared with WDSR, we mainly make improvements in two aspects. Firstly, we add a bottleneck layer [13,23] in the high-path to make our network fully utilize the hierarchical features. Secondly, we add a GFFRB in the low-path to properly enhance its feature extraction ability. Note that the

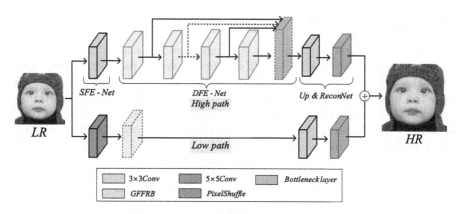

Fig. 2. The structure of the proposed group feature fusion residual network (GFFRN). The modules marked by the red dotted line represent the removed parts in GFFRN-L. GFFRN-L has the same structure with WDSR [24]. (Color figure online)

original WDSR only uses a 5×5 convolutional layer in the low-path to extract the low-frequency information.

In the high-path of GFFRN, the first part is SFE-Net and it uses one convolutional layer, $Conv(3, m)$, to extract shallow features and expand the number of channels from C to m, where m denotes the base channel number of the intermediate layers. The second part is DFE-Net and this part contains D GFFRBs and a bottleneck layer [13,23]. The third part is Up&ReconNet. It consists of $Conv(3, C \times s^2)$ and a sub-pixel convolutional layer in sequence, where $s = (2, 3, 4)$ denotes the upscaling factor. In the low-path of GFFRN, it mainly consists of a convolutional layer $Conv(5, m)$, a GFFRB and an Up&ReconNet. The final HR image can be obtained by

$$\widehat{I}_{HR} = f_{HP}(I_{LR}) + f_{LP}(I_{LR}), \tag{1}$$

where $f_{HP}(\cdot)$ and $f_{LP}(\cdot)$ denote the operations of the high-path and the low-path respectively.

Loss Function. We employ $L1$ loss to optimize the proposed network. Given a training set $\{I^i_{LR}, I^i_{HR}\}^N_{i=1}$, which contains N LR images and their corresponding HR images. We need to minimize the $L1$ loss function between the reconstructed image $\widehat{I}_{HR}$ and the ground truth image I_{HR}. $L1$ loss function is shown in Eq. 2.

$$L(\Theta) = \frac{1}{N} \sum_{i=1}^{N} \|\widehat{I}^i_{HR} - I^i_{HR}\|_1, \tag{2}$$

where Θ represents the parameters of proposed network.

3.2   Lightweight GFFRN (GFFRN-L)

To further reduce the number of the parameters and computations, we also propose a lightweight network GFFRN-L (Less than 1M parameters). GFFRN-L has the same structure with WDSR [24]. Compared with GFFRN, there are fewer residual blocks and channels. As shown in Fig. 2, the modules marked by red dotted line represent the removed components in GFFRN-L. By using these strategies, the number of parameters in GFFRN-L is reduced by 80% compared with GFFRN. More model details are shown in Sect. 4.2.

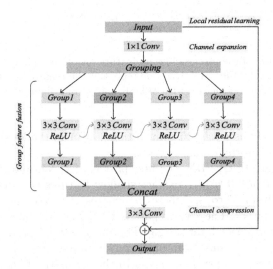

Fig. 3. The structure of the proposed group feature fusion residual block (GFFRB).

3.3   Group Feature Fusion Residual Block (GFFRB)

As mentioned above, current residual blocks have some drawbacks that cause them to be inefficient. Inspired by lightweight networks, we propose a more efficient group feature fusion residual block (GFFRB). As shown in Fig. 3, the GFFRB contains four parts: channel expansion layer, group feature fusion layer, channel compression layer and local residual learning. Next, we will describe the four parts in details.

Channel Expansion Layer. Wider network allows more information to pass through [24]. However, simply increasing the width of the network will increase the computation complexity quadratically. To avoid this problem, we utilize a relatively small base channel number ($m = 64$). When the feature enters GFFRB, we first use an efficient convolutional layer $Conv(1, m \times e)$ to expand the channels from m to $m \times e$, where e denotes the expansion factor. Let F_{d-1}

and F_d be the input and output of the d-th GFFRB respectively and both of them have m feature maps. This operation can be formulated as

$$F_E = f_{CE}(F_{d-1}), \tag{3}$$

where $f_{CE}(\cdot)$ denotes the convolutional layer, F_E denotes the feature maps after channel expansion.

Group Feature Fusion Layer. To further control the computations, inspired by group convolution, we divide the wide feature into four groups along the channel axis. However, different from the group convolution used in previous methods [16], we design a novel group feature fusion layer, which gradually fuses the features of the current group with the output features of the last group. The group feature fusion operations have two advantages: **1)** It increases both the depth and the width of the network with fewer parameters. **2)** The skip connections in different groups are more sparse than the skip connections in dense block, which can not only improve the utilization of local features, but also control the number of parameters. In detail, we firstly divide the F_E into 4 feature groups (G_1, G_2, G_3, G_4) and each group has $(gc = m \times e/4)$ channels, where gc denotes the number of channels in each group. Then we use skip connections and convolution operations to fuse the features between different groups. Finally, all the fused feature maps are concatenated together. These operations are formulated as follows.

$$\begin{cases} [G_1, G_2, G_3, G_4] = Grouping(F_E), \\ \quad G_{f1} = ReLU(f_{g1}(G_1)), \\ \quad G_{f2} = ReLU(f_{g2}([G_2, G_{f1}])), \\ \quad G_{f3} = ReLU(f_{g3}([G_3, G_{f2}])), \\ \quad G_{f4} = ReLU(f_{g4}([G_4, G_{f3}])), \\ \quad F_{fuse} = [G_{f1}, G_{f2}, G_{f3}, G_{f4}]. \end{cases} \tag{4}$$

$Grouping(\cdot)$ denotes the operation that averagely groups F_E into four groups in channel dimension. $f_{g1}(\cdot), f_{g2}(\cdot), f_{g3}(\cdot), f_{g4}(\cdot)$ denote the convolutional layers $Conv(3, gc)$ of the four groups. $G_{f1}, G_{f2}, G_{f3}, G_{f4}$ denote the fused feature maps of the four groups. $ReLU(\cdot)$ represents the ReLU activation function. F_{fuse} denotes the extracted features from the group feature fusion layer.

Channel Compression Layer. After the group feature fusion layer, we use one convolutional layer $Conv(3, m)$ to fuse the features of the four groups. This operation can further improve the utilization of the local multilevel features and compress the number of channels at the same time. It can be formulated as

$$F_C = f_{Comp}(F_{fuse}), \tag{5}$$

where $f_{Comp}(\cdot)$ denotes the convolutional layer, F_C denotes the feature maps after channel compression.

Local Residual Learning. This part we use the local residual learning to further improve the information flow. The final output of the d-th GFFRB can be obtained by

$$F_d = F_{d-1} + F_C. \tag{6}$$

4   Experimental Results

4.1   Datasets

In experiment, we apply DIV2K dataset [25] to train our models. This dataset is a newly-proposed high-quality image dataset, which contains 800 training images, 100 validation images and 100 test images. In the testing phase, we use five widely used benchmark datasets: Set5 [26], Set14 [27], BSDS100 [28], Urban100 [29] and Manga109 [30]. These datasets contain a variety of images, so they can fully validate our models.

4.2   Implementation and Training Details

Training Details. The training configurations of our models are similar to MSRN [23]. We use the images of 1–800 and 801–810 in DIV2K dataset as our training set and validation set respectively. The training data is augmented by random scaling, rotation and flipping. In the training phase, we randomly select 16000 RGB input patches ($C = 3$) of size 48×48 from all the LR images in every epoch. The batch size is set to 16, thus every epoch has 1000 iterations of back-propagation. The model is trained 800 epochs. The learning rate begins with 1×10^{-4} and is halved every 200 epochs. Our model is optimized by Adam [31] by setting $\beta 1 = 0.9$, $\beta 2 = 0.999$ and $\epsilon = 10^{-8}$. The network is programmed by Pytorch and the experiment is performed on a PC with an i9-9900k CPU, 32GB RAM, and a RTX 2080Ti GPU.

Model Details. The proposed GFFRN and GFFRN-L consist of a series of GFFRBs. In the high-path of GFFRN, the number of GFFRB D is set to 12 and the expansion factor e is set to 4. In the low-path of GFFRN, D is set to 1, e is set to 2. In GFFRN-L, D is set to 6, e is set to 2. The base channel number m of the two models are all set to 64.

4.3   Comparisons with State-of-the-Art Methods

In this section, we compare the proposed GFFRN and GFFRN-L with some other state-of-the-art SR methods including Bicubic [3], SRCNN [7], VDSR [11], DRRN [18], IDN [32], CARN [16], SRFBN-S [19], MSRN [23] and SRFBN [19]. In particular, GFFRN has the similar number of parameters to MSRN and GFFRN-L has the similar number of parameters to CARN. It should be noticed that GFFRN-L do not apply the multi-scale learning approach that used in

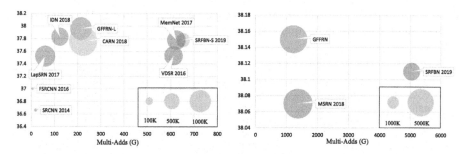

Fig. 4. Trade-off between accuracy vs. number of operations and parameters on Set5 ×2 dataset. The x-axis and the y-axis denote the Multi-Adds and PSNR, and the area of the circle represents the number of parameters. The Multi-Adds are computed by assuming that the resolution of HR image is 720p.

CARN because of the two-path network structure. The widely used image evaluation methods, peak signal-to-noise ratio (PSNR) and structural similarity index measure (SSIM), are used to evaluate the performance of the proposed methods. Furthermore, we also compare these models from other dimensions, including the number of parameters and computational complexity. Similar to CARN, we use the Multi-Adds to represent the computational complexity of the model and assume the HR image size to be 720p (1280 × 720) to calculate Multi-Adds. In Fig. 4, we compare our GFFRN and GFFRN-L against various state-of-the-art methods on the Set5 ×2 dataset. As shown in the figure, when considering three aspects of speed, accuracy and the number of parameters, the proposed GFFRN and GFFRN-L achieve the best performance.

Table 1 lists the experiment results of PSNR and SSIM obtained by using different methods. Here we only compare models that have roughly similar number of parameters as ours[1]. We first to analyse the performance of GFFRN-L. Compared with CARN, the proposed GFFRN-L achieves comparable results with fewer parameters and computations. Compared with IDN, GFFRN-L has twice as many parameters, but the benefits are also huge. GFFRN-L outperforms IDN by a margin of 0.1–0.5 PSNR on different benchmark test sets. Compared with SRFBN-S, the proposed GFFRN-L has fewer computations but gets higher reconstruction accuracy. Especially when the scaling factor is ×4, GFFRN-L obtains higher accuracy with only 5% computations of SRFBN-S. Secondly, we analyse the performance of GFFRN. Compared with MSRN, even with fewer parameters and computations, the proposed GFFRN outperforms it by a large margin on different benchmark test sets. SRFBN outperforms GFFRN, however, its benefits mainly come from the recursive structure, which introduces a huge number of computations. When the scaling factor is ×4, the calculations of SRFBN are more than 20 times of GFFRN, hence the SRFBN is inefficient in terms of computational complexity.

---

[1] Comparison of the larger models can be found in our supplementary material.

Table 1. Quantitative comparisons of state-of-the-art methods. Red and blue represent the best and the second best result respectively.

Scale	Model	Params	Multi-Adds	Set5	Set14	B100	Urban100	Manga109
2	Bicubic	—	—	33.69/0.9284	30.34/0.8675	29.57/0.8434	26.88/0.8438	30.82/0.9332
	SRCNN [7]	0.02M	19G	36.66/0.9542	32.42/0.9063	31.36/0.8879	29.50/0.8946	35.60/0.9663
	VDSR [11]	0.67M	612G	37.53/0.9587	33.03/0.9124	31.90/0.8960	30.76/0.9140	37.22/0.9750
	DRRN [18]	0.30M	6797G	37.74/0.9591	33.23/0.9136	32.05/0.8973	31.23/0.9188	37.60/0.9736
	IDN [32]	0.59M	124G	37.83/0.9600	33.30/0.9148	32.08/0.8985	31.27/0.9196	-/-
	CARN [16]	1.59M	224G	37.76/0.9590	33.52/0.9166	32.09/0.8978	31.51/0.9312	-/-
	SRFBN-S [19]	0.37M	653G	37.78/0.9597	33.35/0.9156	32.00/0.8970	31.41/0.9207	38.06/0.9757
	GFFRN-L(ours)	0.94M	215G	37.96/0.9603	33.51/0.9169	32.13/0.8992	31.91/0.9263	38.38/0.9766
	MSRN [23]	5.93M	1370G	38.07/0.9608	33.68/0.9184	32.22/0.9002	32.32/0.9304	38.64/0.9771
	SRFBN [19]	2.14M	5044G	38.11/0.9609	33.82/0.9196	32.29/0.9010	32.62/0.9328	39.08/0.9779
	GFFRN(ours)	5.32M	1226G	38.15/0.9610	33.84/0.9202	32.29/0.9010	32.57/0.9326	38.97/0.9777
3	Bicubic	—	—	30.41/0.8655	27.64/0.7722	27.21/0.7344	24.46/0.7411	26.95/0.8556
	SRCNN [7]	0.02M	19G	32.75/0.9090	29.28/0.8209	28.41/0.7863	26.24/0.7989	30.48/0.9117
	VDSR [11]	0.67M	612G	33.66/0.9213	29.77/0.8314	28.82/0.7976	27.14/0.8279	32.01/0.9340
	DRRN [18]	0.30M	6797G	34.03/0.9244	29.96/0.8349	28.95/0.8004	27.53/0.8378	32.42/0.9359
	IDN [32]	0.59M	55G	34.11/0.9253	29.99/0.8354	28.95/0.8013	27.42/0.8359	-/-
	CARN [16]	1.59M	119G	34.29/0.9255	30.29/0.8407	29.06/0.8034	27.38/0.8404	-/-
	SRFBN-S [19]	0.49M	788G	34.20/0.9255	30.10/0.8372	28.96/0.8010	27.66/0.8415	33.02/0.9404
	GFFRN-L(ours)	0.96M	98G	34.27/0.9263	30.29/0.8409	29.07/0.8039	28.03/0.8493	33.31/0.9429
	MSRN [23]	6.11M	627G	34.48/0.9276	30.40/0.8436	29.13/0.8061	28.31/0.8560	33.56/0.9451
	SRFBN [19]	2.83M	6024G	34.70/0.9292	30.51/0.8461	29.24/0.8084	28.73/0.8641	34.18/0.9481
	GFFRN(ours)	5.34M	546G	34.57/0.9286	30.46/0.8449	29.20/0.8077	28.54/0.8605	33.89/0.9470
4	Bicubic	—	—	28.43/0.8022	26.10/0.6936	25.97/0.6517	23.14/0.6599	24.89/0.7866
	SRCNN [7]	0.02M	19G	30.48/0.8628	27.49/0.7503	26.90/0.7101	24.52/0.7221	27.58/0.8555
	VDSR [11]	0.67M	612G	31.35/0.8838	28.01/0.7674	27.29/0.7251	25.18/0.7524	28.83/0.8870
	DRRN [18]	0.30M	6797G	31.68/0.8888	28.21/0.7720	27.38/0.7284	25.44/0.7638	29.18/0.8914
	IDN [32]	0.59M	31G	31.82/0.8903	28.25/0.7730	27.41/0.7297	25.41/0.7632	-/-
	CARN [16]	1.59M	91G	32.13/0.8937	28.60/0.7806	27.58/0.7349	26.07/0.7837	-/-
	SRFBN-S [19]	0.63M	983G	31.98/0.8923	28.45/0.7779	27.44/0.7313	25.71/0.7719	29.91/0.9008
	GFFRN-L(ours)	0.98M	56G	32.03/0.8934	28.54/0.7803	27.54/0.7347	25.94/0.7815	30.23/0.9050
	MSRN [23]	6.08M	377G	32.25/0.8958	28.63/0.7833	27.61/0.7377	26.22/0.7905	30.57/0.9103
	SRFBN [19]	3.63M	7466G	32.47/0.8983	28.81/0.7868	27.72/0.7409	26.60/0.8015	31.15/0.9160
	GFFRN(ours)	5.36M	309G	32.37/0.8974	28.70/0.7853	27.66/0.7394	26.38/0.7962	30.81/0.9132

Figure 8 presents some reconstructed images obtained by using these methods with different scaling factors. For image "img067", we observe that most of compared methods can not restore the complete line of the building. In contrast, our GFFRN restores a complete line, which is closer to the original HR image. For image "Belmondo", all the compared methods restore the words with noticeable artifacts and blurred edges. While, our GFFRN can recover clearer words. The same conclusions can be obtained by image "img034" and image "14802". This is mainly because of the powerful local feature extraction ability of the well-designed GFFRB.[2]

---

[2] More compared images can be found in our supplementary material.

4.4   Discussion

The most important contribution of this paper is the newly proposed group feature fusion residual block (GFFRB). Based on GFFRB, we design two efficient SR models GFFRN and GFFRN-L. To demonstrate the effectiveness of GFFRB, we have done a series of experiments on the two models. In addition, we also discuss the influence of the group feature fusion layer.

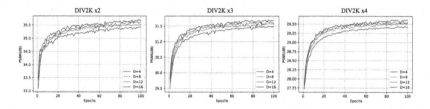

Fig. 5. Performance comparison of GFFRN with different number of GFFRBs.

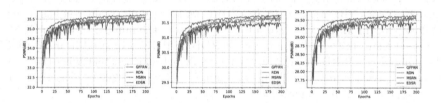

Fig. 6. Performance comparison of the models with different residual blocks.

Analysis of D. As we all know, increasing network depth can improve reconstruction accuracy. In order to verify the impact of the number of GFFRB on network, we have done a series of experiments. Here we mainly discuss the different numbers of GFFRB in GFFRN ($D = 4, 8, 12, 16$ respectively). For a quick verification, all the models of this subsection are trained 100 epochs (1×10^5 iterations) in the same environment. As shown in Fig. 5, the accuracy of GFFRN keeps raising with the increasing number of GFFRB. Although increasing the number of the GFFRB can improve the reconstruction accuracy, it also leads to a more complex network. By weighting the performance and the complexity of the network, we use 12 GFFRBs in the final model. Experiments shows that our final model outperforms MSRN [23] on all the benchmark test sets with fewer parameters and computations.

Table 2. Quantitative comparisons of state-of-the-art methods. All the models are trained 200 epoches (2×10^5 iterations) in the same environment. Red represents the best result.

Scale	Model	Params	Multi-Adds	Set5	Set14	B100	Urban100	Manga109
2	EDSR [12]	8.87M	2050G	37.81/0.9599	33.44/0.9158	32.04/0.8978	31.49/0.9225	37.94/0.9757
	MSRN [23]	5.93M	1370G	37.98/0.9605	33.49/0.9168	32.13/0.8990	31.88/0.9261	38.38/0.9765
	RDN [13]	5.70M	1310G	37.92/0.9603	33.51/0.9173	32.13/0.8995	31.96/0.9273	38.17/0.9764
	GFFRN(ours)	5.32M	1226G	38.03/0.9607	33.59/0.9175	32.18/0.8997	32.09/0.9282	38.47/0.9768
3	EDSR [12]	11.8M	1210G	34.10/0.9250	30.14/0.8389	28.97/0.8020	27.69/0.8428	32.83/0.9400
	MSRN [23]	6.11M	627G	34.33/0.9266	30.32/0.8423	29.08/0.8049	28.08/0.8509	33.36/0.9435
	RDN [13]	5.88M	603G	34.40/0.9274	30.34/0.8423	29.09/0.8047	28.13/0.8520	33.44/0.9439
	GFFRN(ours)	5.34M	546G	34.43/0.9274	30.37/0.8432	29.12/0.8059	28.24/0.8547	33.52/0.9448
4	EDSR [12]	11.23M	1060G	31.88/0.8909	28.43/0.7781	27.46/0.7323	25.72/0.7742	29.86/0.9000
	MSRN [23]	6.08M	377G	32.04/0.8933	28.56/0.7809	27.56/0.7352	26.02/0.7831	30.29/0.9055
	RDN [13]	5.86M	364G	32.09/0.8940	28.58/0.7820	27.58/0.7363	26.06/0.7851	30.39/0.9073
	GFFRN(ours)	5.36M	309G	32.20/0.8950	28.61/0.7827	27.60/0.7372	26.19/0.7894	30.53/0.9093

Efficiency Analysis of GFFRB. The GFFRB is the key component to establish our network. In this subsection, we compare it with some other widely used residual blocks, including the residual blocks (RB) used in EDSR [12], the residual dense block (RDB) used in RDN [13] and the multi-scale residual block (MSRB) used in MSRN [23]. For a fair comparison, the number of RB in EDSR decreased from 32 to 5. The number of RDB in RDN decreased from 16 to 4. The number of MSRB in MSRN is set to 8, which is consistent with the original paper. All the models of this subsection are trained 200 epochs (2×10^5 iterations) in the same environment.

Figure 6 presents the convergence curves obtained by using these models under different scaling factors. From the figure, we can see that compared with other models, the proposed GFFRN achieves the best performance. We also compare these models by quantitative indicators, including the number of parameters, the computational complexity and the performance on different benchmark test sets. As shown in Table 2, compared with other state-of-the-art methods, the proposed GFFRN gets the highest accuracy on all the benchmark test sets with the fewest parameters and calculations of all the methods. All of these experiments fully demonstrate that the proposed GFFRB is more efficient than most current residual blocks.

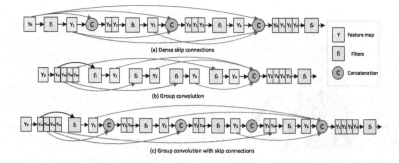

Fig. 7. Diagram the structural relations of Group convolution, Dense Skip Connections and Group feature fusion.

Table 3. Quantitative comparisons of the models that use different modules. Red represent the best result.

Scale	Model	Params	Set5	Set14	B100	Urban100	Manga109
2	Group Convolution	1.21M	38.00/0.9605	33.59/0.9177	32.14/0.8993	31.90/0.9264	38.46/0.9767
	Dense Skip Connections	1.77M	38.02/0.9606	33.61/0.9180	32.20/0.9000	32.21/0.9293	38.59/0.9770
	Group Feature Fusion	1.49M	38.04/0.9606	33.64/0.9182	32.19/0.8999	32.19/0.9293	38.64/0.9771

Ablation Studies on the Group Feature Fusion Layer. The novelty of the proposed GFFRN is the skip connections among different groups. Here we will analyse the effectiveness of this structure. In Fig. 7, we present the structure of dense skip connection, the structure of group convolution and the structure of the group feature fusion layer. Notably, Fig. 7(c) is the unfolded format of the group feature fusion layer in Fig. 3. From the figure, we can find that the structure of group feature fusion layer is the combination of the group convolution and the dense skip connection.

Next we will do some experiments to compare the efficiency of the three structures. We use 10 GFFRBs to conduct experiments. We replace the group feature fusion layer with dense connection and group convolution. For a fair comparison, the number of dense connection layer is set to 4 and the number of the group in group convolutional layer is set to 4. In Table 3, we use PSNR/SSIM to measure the accuracy of the reconstruction result, and the number of the parameters to measure the storage efficiency. We can see that the model with group convolution has the least parameters, but gets the poorest performance. When we add skip connections on the group convolution, the performance improves effectively. Compared with dense skip connections, our group feature fusion layer has fewer parameters, but achieves a comparable performance. This fully demonstrates the effectiveness of the skip connections among different groups.

Fig. 8. Visual comparison of different methods on different images.

5   Conclusions and Future Works

In this paper, we propose a novel group feature fusion residual block (GFFRB), which combines the group convolution with skip connection to fully fuse abundant local features. Experiments show that the well-designed GFFRB outperforms most current residual blocks. Based on GFFRB, we propose a two-path group feature fusion residual network (GFFRN). Experiments show that the proposed GFFRN achieves higher efficiency compared with most state-of-the-art methods. We also design a lightweight group feature fusion residual network (GFFRN-L), which achieves the best performance among the models that have less than 1M parameters.

Future works can be mainly explored from the following two aspects: (1) In this paper, we specify that the number of groups is 4. Future works can discuss the number of groups g to further improve the efficiency of GFFRB. (2) It would be worthwhile to try to apply the well-designed GFFRB to other computer vision tasks, such as image denoising and deblurring.

Funding. This research was supported by the National Natural Science Foundation of China under Grant No. 61703278.

References

1. Bilgazyev, E., Efraty, B., Shah, S.K., Kakadiaris, I.A.: Improved face recognition using super-resolution. In: 2011 International Joint Conference on Biometrics (IJCB) (2011)
2. Jian, M., Lam, K.M.: Simultaneous hallucination and recognition of low-resolution faces based on singular value decomposition. IEEE Trans. Circuits Syst. Video Technol. **25**, 1761–1772 (2015)
3. Lei, Z., Xiaolin, W.: An edge-guided image interpolation algorithm via directional filtering and data fusion. IEEE Trans. Image Process. **15**, 2226–2238 (2006)
4. Zeyde, R., Elad, M., Protter, M.: On single image scale-up using sparse-representations. In: Boissonnat, J.-D., et al. (eds.) Curves and Surfaces 2010. LNCS, vol. 6920, pp. 711–730. Springer, Heidelberg (2012). https://doi.org/10.1007/978-3-642-27413-8_47
5. Jianchao, Y., Zhaowen, W., Zhe, L., Scott, C., Thomas, H.: Coupled dictionary training for image super-resolution. IEEE Trans. Image Process. **21**, 3467–3478 (2012)
6. Fang, B., Huang, Z., Yong, L., Yong, W.: v-support vector machine based on discriminant sparse neighborhood preserving embedding. Pattern Anal. Appl. **20**, 1077–1089 (2017). https://doi.org/10.1007/s10044-016-0547-x
7. Dong, C., Loy, C.C., He, K., Tang, X.: Learning a deep convolutional network for image super-resolution. In: Fleet, D., Pajdla, T., Schiele, B., Tuytelaars, T. (eds.) ECCV 2014. LNCS, vol. 8692, pp. 184–199. Springer, Cham (2014). https://doi.org/10.1007/978-3-319-10593-2_13
8. Dong, C., Loy, C.C., Tang, X.: Accelerating the super-resolution convolutional neural network. In: Leibe, B., Matas, J., Sebe, N., Welling, M. (eds.) ECCV 2016. LNCS, vol. 9906, pp. 391–407. Springer, Cham (2016). https://doi.org/10.1007/978-3-319-46475-6_25

9. Shi, W., Caballero, J., Huszr, F., Totz, J., Wang, Z.: Real-time single image and video super-resolution using an efficient sub-pixel convolutional neural network. In: IEEE Conference on Computer Vision and Pattern Recognition (2016)
10. He K, Zhang X, R.S.E.A.: Deep residual learning for image recognition. In: Proceedings of the IEEE Conference on Computer Vision and Pattern Recognition (2015)
11. Kim, J., Lee, J.K., Lee, K.M.: Accurate image super-resolution using very deep convolutional networks. In: 2016 IEEE Conference on Computer Vision and Pattern Recognition (CVPR) (2016)
12. Lim, B., Son, S., Kim, H., Nah, S., Lee, K.M.: Enhanced deep residual networks for single image super-resolution. In: Proceedings of the IEEE Computer Vision and Pattern Recognition Workshops (2017)
13. Zhang, Y., Tian, Y., Kong, Y., Zhong, B., Fu, Y.: Residual dense network for image super-resolution. CoRR abs/1802.08797 (2018)
14. Zhang, Y., Li, K., Li, K., Wang, L., Zhong, B., Fu, Y.: Image super-resolution using very deep residual channel attention networks. In: European Conference on Computer Vision (ECCV) (2018)
15. Tai, Y., Yang, J., Liu, X., Xu, C.: Memnet: a persistent memory network for image restoration. In: 2017 IEEE International Conference on Computer Vision (ICCV) (2017)
16. Ahn, N., Sohn, K.B.: Fast, accurate, and lightweight super-resolution with cascading residual network. In: European Conference on Computer Vision (ECCV) (2018)
17. Kim, J., Lee, J.K., Lee, K.M.: Deeply-recursive convolutional network for image super-resolution. In: 2016 IEEE Conference on Computer Vision and Pattern Recognition (CVPR) (2016)
18. Tai, Y., Yang, J., Liu, X.: Image super-resolution via deep recursive residual network. In: 2017 IEEE Conference on Computer Vision and Pattern Recognition (CVPR) (2017)
19. Li, Z., Yang, J., Liu, Z., Yang, X., Jeon, G., Wu, W.: Feedback network for image super-resolution. CoRR abs/1903.09814 (2019)
20. Krizhevsky, A., Sutskever, I., Hinton, G.E.: Imagenet classification with deep convolutional neural networks. In: Neural Information Processing Systems, pp. 1097–1105 (2012)
21. Howard, A., et al.: Mobilenets: efficient convolutional neural networks for mobile vision applications (2017)
22. Ledig, C., et al.: Photo-realistic single image super-resolution using a generative adversarial network. arXiv: Computer Vision and Pattern Recognition (2016)
23. Li, J., Fang, F., Mei, K., Zhang, G.: Multi-scale residual network for image super-resolution. In: 2018 European Conference on Computer Vision (ECCV) (2018)
24. Yu, J., et al.: Wide activation for efficient and accurate image super-resolution. arXiv: Computer Vision and Pattern Recognition (2018)
25. Agustsson, E., Timofte, R.: Ntire 2017 challenge on single image super-resolution: dataset and study. In: The IEEE Conference on Computer Vision and Pattern Recognition (CVPR) Workshops (2017)
26. Bevilacqua, M., Roumy, A., Guillemot, C., Alberimorel, M.L.: Low-complexity single-image super-resolution based on nonnegative neighbor embedding. In: 2012 British Machine Vision Conference, pp. 1–10 (2012)

27. Li, T., Chang, K., Mo, C., Zhang, X., Qin, T.: Single image super resolution using local and non-local priors. In: Hong, R., Cheng, W.-H., Yamasaki, T., Wang, M., Ngo, C.-W. (eds.) PCM 2018. LNCS, vol. 11165, pp. 264–273. Springer, Cham (2018). https://doi.org/10.1007/978-3-030-00767-6_25

28. Arbelaez, P., Maire, M., Fowlkes, C.C., Malik, J.: Contour detection and hierarchical image segmentation. IEEE Trans. Pattern Anal. Mach. Intell. **33**, 898–916 (2011)

29. Huang, J., Singh, A., Ahuja, N.: Single image super-resolution from transformed self-exemplars. In: IEEE Conference on Computer Vision and Pattern Recognition, pp. 5197–5206 (2015)

30. Matsui, Y., Ito, K., Aramaki, Y., Yamasaki, T., Aizawa, K.: Sketch-based manga retrieval using manga109 dataset. Multimedia Tools Appl. **76**, 21811–21838 (2017). https://doi.org/10.1007/s11042-016-4020-z

31. Kingma, D., Ba, J.: Adam: a method for stochastic optimization. Computer Science (2014)

32. Hui, Z., Wang, X., Gao, X.: Fast and accurate single image super-resolution via information distillation network. In: IEEE Conference on Computer Vision and Pattern Recognition (2018)

Adversarial Image Composition with Auxiliary Illumination

Fangneng Zhan[1,2], Shijian Lu[1(✉)], Changgong Zhang[2], Feiying Ma[2],
and Xuansong Xie[2]

[1] Nanyang Technological University, Singapore, Singapore
{fnzhan,shijian.lu}@ntu.edu.sg
[2] Alibaba DAMO Academy, Hangzhou, China
{changgong.zcg,feiying.mfy}@alibaba-inc.com
xingtong.xxs@taobao.com

Abstract. Dealing with the inconsistency between a foreground object
and a background image is a challenging task in high-fidelity image composition. State-of-the-art methods strive to harmonize the composed
image by adapting the style of foreground objects to be compatible
with the background image, whereas the potential shadow of foreground
objects within the composed image which is critical to the composition
realism is largely neglected. In this paper, we propose an Adversarial
Image Composition Net (AIC-Net) that achieves realistic image composition by considering potential shadows that the foreground object projects
in the composed image. A novel branched generation mechanism is proposed, which disentangles the generation of shadows and the transfer of
foreground styles for optimal accomplishment of the two tasks simultaneously. A differentiable spatial transformation module is designed which
bridges the local harmonization and the global harmonization to achieve
their joint optimization effectively. Extensive experiments on pedestrian
and car composition tasks show that the proposed AIC-Net achieves
superior composition performance qualitatively and quantitatively.

1 Introduction

With the advances of deep neural networks (DNNs), image composition has
been attracting increasing attention as a typical approach for image synthesis,
augmented reality, etc. With a foreground object and a background image, a
direct combination tends to introduce unrealistic artifacts in the composed image
with various inconsistency in colors, illuminations, texture, etc. Several methods
have been proposed for harmonizing the foreground object and the background
image, including DNN-based image translation [1], local statistic transfer [2],
etc. On the other hand, existing methods typically simplify the harmonization
by solving the image consistency within the foreground object region only but
neglecting that realistic image composition goes far beyond that.

Specifically, a typical visual effect that is often associated with objects in
scenes is their projected shadows due to the 3D nature of the world. While

© Springer Nature Switzerland AG 2021
H. Ishikawa et al. (Eds.): ACCV 2020, LNCS 12623, pp. 234–250, 2021.
https://doi.org/10.1007/978-3-030-69532-3_15

embedding a foreground object into a background image for image composition, the shadow effects of the foreground object are critical which can significantly improve the realism of the composed image if handled properly. Due to various constraints in 2D images, such as complicated illuminations, losing of 3D information, etc., traditional computer vision methods are highly susceptible to failure for the task of high-fidelity shadow generation.

Foregrounds   Local Images   Harmonized Images   Global Images

Fig. 1. Given foreground objects and directly composed local images as shows in columns 1 and 2, the proposed AIC-Net disentangles the shadow generation and style transfer to produce realistic local harmonization as shown in column 3. With our spatial transformation module, the locally harmonized images in column 3 can be adapted and composed into the globally harmonized images as shown in column 4.

In this work, we design a novel Adversarial Image Composition Net (AIC-Net) that aims to achieve realistic image composition with adaptive shadow effects as illustrated in Fig. 1. AIC-Net adopts generative adversarial ideas to harmonize the foreground object within the background image and generates realistic shadow effects by learning from real shadows in natural images. It consists of local harmonization and global harmonization which are inter-connected and can be optimized jointly. We design a novel branched generation mechanism for high-fidelity local harmonization which disentangles the shadow generation and the style transfer of the foreground object for optimal accomplishment of two tasks simultaneously. An auxiliary illumination model is introduced to infer the illumination conditions of the background image such as lighting directions which help generate realistic shadows of the foreground object greatly. In addition, a differentiable spatial transformer is introduced to bridge the local region and the global background for joint optimization of the local and global harmonization. Two discriminators are employed where a local discriminator guides to learn style transfer and shadow generation of the foreground object and a global discriminator guide to learn global image harmonization.

The contributions of this work are three folds. First, we design an innovative AIC-Net that is capable of generating high-fidelity shadow of the foreground object adaptively. Second, we design a novel branched generation mechanism that disentangles the style transfer and shadow generation of the foreground object and accomplishes the two tasks optimally and simultaneously. Third, we design spatial transformer module (STM) that achieves joint optimization of local harmonization and global harmonization effectively.

2   Related Work

2.1   Image Composition and Harmonization

Image composition aims to generate new images by embedding foreground objects into background images [3–13]. GP-GAN [3] composes high-resolution images by leveraging Poisson blending [14]. [4] presents a spatial transformer GAN by inserting STNs into the generator. [15] describes a Compositional GAN that introduces a self-consistent composition-decomposition network. [16] proposes a model to distinguish natural photographs from automatically generated composite images. [17] proposes a generative adversarial network (GAN) architecture for automatic image composting with consideration of geometric, color and boundary consistency.

Image harmonization deals with the inconsistency between a foreground region and a background image for composition. Several methods have been proposed to adapt the appearance of the foreground object for image harmonization. For example, [18] matches contrast, texture, and blur by manipulating the scales of a pyramid decomposition of images. [19] studies image statistics that determine the realism of the composite images. [20] proposes a gradient domain to achieve composition which can prevent color bleeding without changing the boundary location. A number of deep-learning based image harmonization methods have also proposed in recent years. For example, [21] utilizes visual semantics to guide the process of replacement to generate realistic, artifact-free images with diverse styles. [2] achieves both spatial and inter-scale statistical consistency by carefully determining the local statistics to be transferred. [1] proposes an end-to-end deep convolutional neural network for image harmonization, which can capture both the context and semantic information of the composite images during harmonization. [17] combines a transformation network, a refinement network, a segmentation network and a pair of discriminator networks to achieve image composition via adversarial learning. Besides image harmonization, some work [16,22] focuses on the realism assessment of the composed images. [23] handles image harmonization through domain verification discriminator with the insight that the foreground needs to be translated to the same domain as background.

Illumination estimation is a classic computer vision problem and it is critical for achieving realistic lighting and shadows in image harmonization. Several deep learning based methods have been proposed to recover illumination from 2-dimensional RGB images [24–28].

2.2   Generative Adversarial Networks

GANs [29] have achieved great success in image generation from either existing images or random noises. Instead of manually selecting features and parameters, GAN generators learn an optimal mapping from random noise or existing images to synthesized images, while GAN discriminators differentiate the synthesized images from real ones via adversarial learning. Several GAN-based image synthesis methods have been reported in recent years. [30] introduces Laplacian pyramids that improve the quality of GAN-synthesized images greatly. [31] proposes an end-to-end trainable network for inserting an object instance mask into the semantic label map of an image. Other systems attempt to learning more reasonable potential features [32], exploring new training approach [33], visualizing GANs at the unit, object and scene level [34], etc. To expand the applicability, [13] generate shadow for augmented reality by modeling the mapping relation between the virtual object shadow and the real-world.

GAN-based image-to-image translation has been widely explored due to its wide applicability. CycleGAN [35] proposes a cycle-consistent adversarial network for realistic image-to-image translation. [36] investigates conditional adversarial networks for image-to-image translation. [37] adopts unsupervised learning to improve the realism of synthetic images using unlabelled real data. Other GANs [38–41] also achieve great performance in image-to-image translation.

3   Proposed Method

The proposed AIC-Net consists of local harmonization and global harmonization which are inter-connected and can be optimized jointly as illustrated in Fig. 2. Detailed network structures and training strategies will be presented in the following subsections.

3.1   Local Harmonization

The local harmonization is achieved by a local discriminator and a branched generation network which consists of a shadow branch and a texture branch as illustrated in Fig. 2. Given a background image (BG), a meaningful region within it is first selected for composition with a foreground object (FG). The selection of the meaningful region will be described in more details in *Experiment Setting*. We thus obtain a directly composed image (CI) x by embedding the foreground object into the selected region in the background image, as well as a foreground mask m_f by setting the foreground object pixels to 1 and the rest pixels in x to 0 as illustrated in Fig. 2

In local harmonization, the generator aims to transfer the style of the composed image and generate realistic object shadows concurrently. Although the two processes can be jointly handled through image-to-image translation, they have very different translation objectives and learn with distinct image-to-image mapping mechanisms. The concurrent learning of both degrades the translation severely as illustrated in 'W/o Branched Generation' in Fig. 3. We design

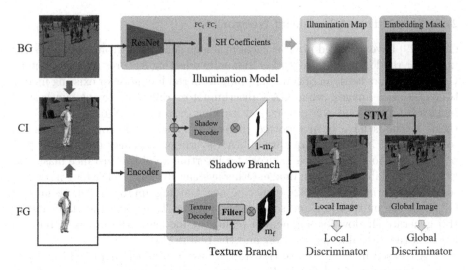

Fig. 2. The structure of the proposed AIC-Net: With a background image *BG* (with specified composition regions) and foreground object *FG* to be composed, a directly composed images *CI* can be derived directly. A shadow branch and a texture branch will learn to generate shadow and transfer the style of *CI* which produces a harmonized *Local Image*. A spatial transformer module (STM) then learns to compose the *Local Image* with the background image to produce a *Global Image*. An *Illumination Model* will predict SH coefficients which can be used to reconstruct an *Illumination Map* ('FC' denote fully connected layer). The *Local Image* will be concatenated with the *Illumination Map* to be distinguished by the *Local Discriminator*. The *Global Image* will be concatenated with an *Embedding Mask* to be distinguished by the *Global Discriminator*.

a novel branched generation strategy to disentangle style transfer and shadow generation for optimal image harmonization. As shown in Fig. 2, the generator has two branches that share the same Encoder. With a background image and a composed image as the input, the decoder in shadow branch strives to generate shadows in the composed image while the decoder in the texture branch strives to transfer the style of the composed image to be compatible with the background image.

Shadow Branch. To avoid synthesizing shadows with false directions as shown in 'W/o Illumination Model' in Fig. 3, we need to infer the global illumination information from the background images. In this work, we adopt a deep learning based method for illumination estimation. Specially, the ground truth of illumination map which is a panorama is represented by spherical harmonics (SH) coefficients [42], then a model with ResNet [43] as the backbone is adopt to regress the SH coefficients from the background images with limited field of view.

With the predicted SH coefficients, an illumination map M_s can reconstructed as follows:

$$M(s) = \sum_{i=1}^{M} SH_i * y_i(s) \tag{1}$$

where s is the spatial direction, M is the number of SH coefficients, y_i and SH_i are the i-th SH basis function and SH coefficients, respectively. We pre-train the illumination model on the Laval Indoor dataset [25] and [44] and fix the model weights while training AIC-Net.

The illumination model is able to infer the illumination from cues such as shadow existed in the background. Thus, the feature extracted by the illumination model contains rich information of shadow direction, size and intensity. In the shadow branch as shown in Fig. 2, we concatenate the feature extracted by the illumination model and the feature extracted by Encoder to integrate the shadow and illumination information into the shadow generation. The shadow decoder then strives to generate shadows with realistic shadow directions and styles in the local images. A binary mask $(1 - m_f)$ is applied to the output for integration with the texture branch. As the shadow branch may translate other regions beyond the shadow areas undesirably, we feed real images into the shadow branch to keep the non-shadow areas be the same with the input. The shadow branch will thus concentrate on the translation of potential shadow areas for realistic shadow generation. To drive the effective learning of shadow branch, the reconstructed illumination map will be combined with the locally harmonized image to be distinguished by the local discriminator.

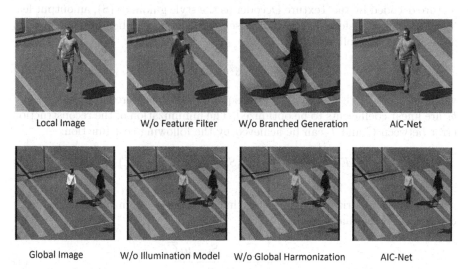

Fig. 3. Illustration of the proposed guided feature filter, branched generation, illumination model and global harmonization: The introduction of the branched generation and guided feature filter helps to suppress various artifacts and generate realistic shadows and foreground object in the local image. The illumination model helps to generate shadow with high-fidelity shadow styles and directions. The global harmonization helps to suppress artifacts and style discrepancy between the local and global images.

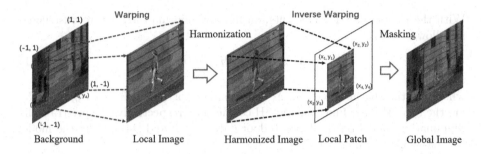

Fig. 4. Global harmonization: With a selected region in the background image, a homography matrix H can be estimated to transform the selected region to the local image. After the local harmonization, the harmonized local image can be transformed back to the background image by an inverse warping H^{-1}. A masking operation is followed to obtain the global image.

Texture Branch. The texture branch aims to translate the texture of the foreground region to be harmonious with the background image. As a normal GAN generator tends to over-translate the foreground region which often degrades the foreground features as illustrated in 'W/o Feature Filter' in Fig. 3, we introduce a guided feature filter to preserve the 'content features' while performing style transfer. Different from the guided image filter [45] which is conducted in image level, guided feature filter is conducted in the feature space to achieve flexible style transfer. With the foreground object as the content guidance (C) and the feature decoded by the Texture Decoder as the style guidance (S), an output feature (T) with transferred style but preserved contents can be obtained through a linear model as follows:

$$T_i = a_k C_i + b_k, \forall i \in \omega_k \tag{2}$$

where i is a pixel index and ω_k is a local square window centered at pixel k, a_k and b_k are linear coefficients to be optimized. The minimization of the reconstruction error between C and T can be achieved by the following cost function:

$$E(a_k, b_k) = \sum_{i \in \omega_k} ((a_k S_i + b_k - C_i)^2 + \epsilon a_k^2) \tag{3}$$

where ϵ is a regularization parameter that prevents a_k from being too large. It can be solved via linear regression:

$$a_k = \frac{\frac{1}{|\omega|} \sum_{i \in \omega_k} S_i - \mu_k \overline{C}_k}{\overline{\sigma}_k + \epsilon} \tag{4}$$

$$b_k = \overline{R}_k - a_k \mu_k \tag{5}$$

where μ_k and σ_k^2 are the mean and variance of S in ω_k, $|\omega|$ is the number of pixels in ω_k, and $\overline{C}_k = \frac{1}{|\omega|} \sum_{i \in \omega_k} C_i$ is the mean of C in ω_k. Then we can obtain the transferred feature T. A following convolution layer will finally generate images with transferred style. A binary mask m_f is applied to the output for further integration with the shadow branch. By denoting the outputs of the shadow branch and the texture branch by x_s and x_t, the locally harmonized image x_h can be obtained as follows:

$$x_h = x_t * m_f + x_s * (1 - m_f) \tag{6}$$

3.2 Global Harmonization

The harmonized local region should be consistent with global image regarding the image style especially the boundary of the local region in the global image, otherwise the global image will tend to present clearly artifacts as shown in 'W/o Global Harmonization' of Fig. 3 which should be addressed as well for high-fidelity global harmonization. We adopt a global discriminator to ensure the consistency in global harmonization. With real background image as the training reference, the global discriminator learns to distinguish the harmonized global image (Fake Global in Fig. 2) and real global images (Real Global in Fig. 2), driving the generator for generating harmonious shadows and an attention network for eliminating the style discrepancy and boundary artifacts. A spatial transformer module (STM) is designed to bridge the local image and global image to achieve joint optimization.

Spatial Transformer Module: The spatial transformer is a differentiable module that applies a homography to the local image as illustrated in Fig. 4. We denote the coordinates of the four vertices of the background image by $[(-1, 1),$ $(1, 1), (1, -1), (-1, -1)]$, and the coordinate of the four vertices of the selected region by $[(x1, y1), (x2, y2), (x3, y3), (x4, y4)]$ $(-1 < x_i < 1, -1 < y_i < 1, i = 1, 2, 3, 4)$. With four paired vertices, the homograhy H can be computed which applied STM to warp the selected region to the local image. Once the local image is harmonized, it can be warped back to the local region of the background image by using the inverse homography H_{-1} as illustrated in Fig. 4. A warping mask with the selected region as 1 and other regions as 0 can be obtained simultaneously. A globally harmonized image can thus be obtained by masking the local patch into the background image. Since the STM and the masking operation are both differentiable, the local harmonization and the global harmonization can be bridged for end-to-end joint optimization.

3.3 Adversarial Training

With a GAN-based structure, the network is trained through adversarial learning between a generator and two discriminators. For clarity purpose, we denote the *BG*, *CI* in Fig. 2 as X and x, the generator and the two branches *Shadow*

Branch and *Texture Branch* as G, G_s and G_t, **Global Discriminator** and **Local Discriminator** as D_G and D_L. The foreground mask is denoted as m_f, the real global and local images as Y and y. The **Embedding Mask** in real global images and harmonized global images as m_Y and m_X.

For the local harmonization, the shadow and texture branches strive to generate shadow and translate foreground that are denoted by $G_s(X, x)$ and $G_t(X, x)$, respectively. The local image x_h can thus be denoted by:

$$x_h = G_s(X, x) * (1 - m_f) + G_t(X, x) * m_f \tag{7}$$

The local discriminator tries to distinguish the local image while the generator tries to mislead the local discriminator. As we adopt Wasserstein GAN [33] objective for training, the local adversarial loss of the generator and local discriminator can be defined by:

$$L_{D_L} = E[D_L(x_h)] - E[D_L(y)] \tag{8}$$

$$L_{G_L} = -E[D_L(x_h)] \tag{9}$$

To ensure the irrelevant region keep unchanged and preserve more details of the original image, an identity loss is defined as follows:

$$L_{S_{idt}} = E[G(Y, y) - y] \tag{10}$$

For the global harmonization, the global discriminator will distinguish the pair of global image X_h and embedding mask m_X which drives the generator to generate consistent texture and suppress artifacts around the local image boundary. The global adversarial loss of the generator and the global discriminator can thus be defined by:

$$L_{D_G} = E[D_G(X_h, m_X)] - E[D_G(Y, m_Y)] \tag{11}$$

$$L_{G_G} = -E[D_G(X_h, m_X)] \tag{12}$$

The overall objective function for the generator is:

$$L_G = L_{G_L} + \lambda_G L_{G_G} + \lambda_{G_{idt}} L_{S_{idt}} \tag{13}$$

where $\lambda_G, \lambda_{G_{idt}}$ denote weights of global adversarial loss and generator identity loss respectively. The overall objective function for the discriminators is:

$$L_D = L_{D_L} + \lambda_{D_G} L_{D_G} \tag{14}$$

where λ_{D_G} denotes the weight of global adversarial loss for the discriminator. L_D and L_G drive the learning of the whole model alternately.

4 Experiment

4.1 Dataset

PRID 2011. [46] was created to evaluate person re-identification methods. The dataset consists of images extracted from multiple person trajectories recorded from two surveillance cameras.

WILDTRACK. [47] is multi-camera detection and tracking dataset of pedestrians in the wild, where the cameras' fields of view has large part overlap.

Penn-Fudan. [48] is an image database that was used for pedestrian detection evaluation as reported in [1]. The images are taken from scenes around campus and urban streets. The objects we are interested in these images are pedestrians. Each image will have at least one pedestrian.

UA-DETRAC. [49] dataset consists of 100 challenging video sequences captured from over 140 thousand frames of real-world traffic scenes. More than 1.2 million labeled bounding boxes of vehicles with information of occlusion, weather, vehicle category and truncation are annotated.

Cityscapes. [50] dataset focuses on semantic understanding of urban street scenes. It has street scenes from 50 cities and provides semantic segmentation of 30 classes. 3475 images are annotated with bounding boxes of persons.

ShapeNet. [51] is a large repository of 3D object models which index more than 3 million models of which 220 thousand are classified into 3,135 categories.

4.2 Experiment Setting

In the pedestrian harmonization experiment, 2000 background images are collected from [46] and [47] and 500 pedestrians are cropped from [48] as the foreground objects. In the car harmonization experiment, we collect the background images from [49] and [50] which contain images captured under different illumination conditions and viewpoints. Random horizontal flipping is applied to the background images to augment the training set. For the foreground images, 1000 3D car models from [51] are utilized to render 3000 car images in different views.

The local region to compose with the foreground object is derived by a simple mechanism. As the bounding boxes of the foreground objects are know, we first select a box region around an existed bounding box and the one with no overlap with other bounding boxes is selected as the local region.

The proposed method is implemented using the Tensorflow framework. The optimizer is Adadelta which employs adaptive learning rate. The model is trained in 100 thousand iterations with a batch size of 4. In addition, the network is trained on a workstation with an Intel Core i7-7700K CPU and a NVIDIA GeForce GTX 1080 Ti graphics card with 12 GB memory. All input images are resized to 256×256 in training.

Table 1. Comparison of harmonization methods with different metrics: 'Car' and 'Ped' denote the results of car and pedestrian synthesis respectively. 'Local' and 'Global' denote harmonized local and global images. 'MS' metric denotes the manipulation scores. For AMT user study, the number in each cell is the percentage of the harmonized images that are deemed as the most realistic by Turkers.

Metrics	CycleGAN		DeepIH		DeepPH		AdaIN		AIC-Net	
	Car	Ped	Car	Ped	Car	Ped	Car	Ped	Car	Ped
AMT(Local)	8%	4%	12%	11%	20%	23%	18%	17%	**42%**	**45%**
AMT(Global)	3%	1%	16%	15%	25%	24%	21%	22%	**41%**	**42%**
FID(Local)	115.1	131.6	136.2	151.4	99.1	103.3	88.7	97.2	**84.4**	**97.1**
FID(Global)	102.4	126.1	121.8	139.3	92.4	101.9	84.6	92.8	**72.2**	**89.6**
MS(Local)	0.69	0.70	0.75	0.74	0.72	0.73	0.69	0.71	**0.63**	**0.64**
MS(Global)	0.71	0.70	0.73	0.76	0.73	0.74	0.70	0.74	**0.62**	**0.62**

4.3 Experiment Analysis

Quantitative Analysis: The evaluation is performed through Frechet Inception Distance (FID) [52], Manipulation Score (MS) [17] and Amazon Mechanical Turk (AMT) study. For the evaluation with FID, the harmonized images are fed to the Inception network [53] trained on ImageNet [54], and the features from the layer before the last fully-connected layer are used to calculate the Fréchet Inception Distance. The Manipulation Score [17] is generated by a state-of-the-art manipulation detection algorithm [55] where a higher score indicates a higher possibility that the image is manipulated. For the AMT study which involves 10 users, we present a set of images (5 images by 5 methods) each time to the user to select the most realistic one. With 20 sets of presented images, an AMT score is derived by averaging the percentage of most realistic images as judged by the 10 users. 'Local' and 'Global' denote the results of locally and globally harmonized images respectively.

Table 1 compares the quality and realism of images processed by different harmonization methods. For the local harmonization, AIC-Net outperforms all compared methods with all metrics clearly as it harmonizes the foreground region and generates relevant shadow which improves the image realism significantly. The using of guided filter helps to preserve texture of high quality, thus obtaining the best FID scores. The spatial transformer module achieves the joint optimization of local and global harmonization, leading to best Manipulation score. CycleGAN can also synthesize shadows but the foreground region tends to be translated undesirably as it does not disentangle the shadow generation and style transfer processed. As DeepIH requires paired training images with semantic annotations, it performs terribly bad when paired training images are not available. As style transfer methods, DeepPH and AdaIN harmonize the foreground region successfully but all of them ignore the shadow generation completely. For the global harmonization, AIC-Net outperforms other methods by large margins as its joint optimization of local and global harmonization ensures consistent shadow and smooth local boundary. The lack of global harmonization leads to clear artifacts in the global image harmonized by CycleGAN. For DeepIH, DeepPH and AdaIN, there are not many artifacts but the lack of shadow and guided filter degrades the image realism and quality greatly. Normally, the global harmonized images present better score than local harmonized images as only small part of global image needs to be harmonized.

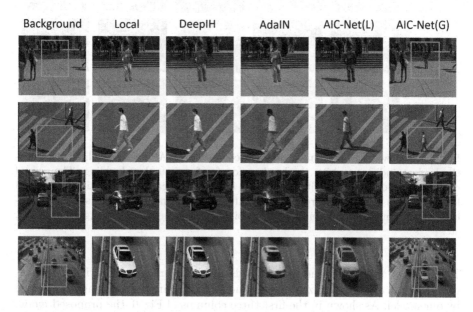

Fig. 5. Comparing AIC-Net with other harmonization methods: Images in col. 1 are background images with selected regions. Col. 2 shows directly composed local images. AIC-Net (L) and AIC-Net (G) show images after local and global harmonization.

Qualitative Analysis: We compare the images harmonized by different methods in Fig. 5, where AIC-Net (L) and AIC-Net (G) denote harmonization of local images and global images by our proposed AIC-Net. As Fig. 5 shows, DeepIH [1] can only achieve a slight translation and cannot generate any potential shadow, thus resulting in unrealistic harmonized images. The branched generation in AIC-Net disentangles the style transfer and shadow generation, leading to much more realistic image harmonization. The global discriminator in AIC-Net works better by driving the generator to remove the boundary artifacts. AdaIN [56] transfer the style of the foreground region to be harmonious with the background, but they do not handle shadow generation which leads to unrealistic composition. Besides, AdaIN is unable to preserve the texture quality of harmonized image due to the missing of guided filter.

To validate that the proposed model is able to generate various shadow adaptively, we tested the trained model in different environments as shown in Fig. 6.

Fig. 6. Shadow generation under different conditions by AIC-Net: The first row shows the background image with the local region for foreground embedding. The second row show the direct composition. Rows 3–4 show the local harmonization and global harmonization by AIC-Net, respectively. AIC-Net can generate various shadows adaptively conditioned on illumination, viewpoint and weather of the background image, etc.

The first two rows show the backgrounds and local images respectively, the last row shows locally harmonized images and globally harmonized images produced by our model. As shown in the first three columns of Fig. 6, the proposed model generates shadows conditioned on the existed shadow cases in the backgrounds. For background images without clearly shadow case as shown in the last two columns of Fig. 6, the proposed model is still able to synthesize realistic shadows conditioned on the feature extracted by the illumination model.

Ablation Study: We conducted an ablation study to evaluate the effectiveness of different technical designs in AIC-Net. As shown in Table 2, four variants of AIC-Net are designed including: 1) AIC-Net (WF) denotes AIC-Net without the guided feature filter; 2) AIC-Net (WB) denotes AIC-Net without using the branched generation mechanism; 3) AIC-Net (WS) denotes AIC-Net without incorporating the spatial transformer module; 4) AIC-Net(WI) denotes AIC-Net without illumination model. The evaluations are performed with three metrics including FID, MS and AMT study that involves 10 users. For AMT user study, a set of images (5 generated by AIC-Net and its four variants) are presented to each of 10 users who will choose the most realistic image. We presented 25 sets of harmonized images and the AMT score is derived by averaging the percentages of the most realistic images as judged by the 10 users. The scores of car and pedestrian experiments are averaged for each metric to obtain the final scores.

Table 2. We conduct ablation study with three metrics (FID, AMT, MS) to evaluate the quality of harmonized local and global images. AIC-Net (WF), AIC-Net (WB), AIC-Net (WS) and AIC-Net(WI) denote AIC-Net without the guided feature filter, without branched generation mechanism, without spatial transformer module and without illumination model respectively. For AMT user study, the percentage numbers represent how often the harmonized images in each category are classified as *most realistic* by Turkers. We average the FID, AMT and MS scores of car and pedestrian images as the final scores.

Methods	FID		AMT		MS	
	Local	Global	Local	Global	Local	Global
AIC-Net(WF)	115.5	106.1	14%	19%	0.72	0.70
AIC-Net(WB)	109.2	93.7	19%	20%	0.70	0.69
AIC-Net(WS)	98.5	92.1	21%	16%	0.73	0.71
AIC-Net(WI)	94.2	91.8	17%	18%	0.67	0.65
AIC-Net	90.8	81.8	29%	27%	0.63	**0.62**

As Table 2 shows, AIC-Net (WF) obtains clearly lower scores with all metrics as compared with the standard AIC-Net which shows the importance of guided feature filter in generating realistic image harmonization. AIC-Net (WB) also obtains lower scores than AIC-Net as the branched generation in AIC-Net disentangles the shadow generation and style transfer to produce more realistic local harmonization as shown in Fig. 3. For AIC-Net (WS), the scores for the global images are much lower than the other models, demonstrating the importance of the spatial transformer module which bridges the local and global harmonization to produce globally realistic harmonization. On the other hand, AIC-Net (WS) achieves similar scores which can be expected as both models are almost the same in local harmonization. AIC-Net (WI) present clearly drop of AMT score compared with standard AIC-Net, indicating the significance of illumination model for the generation of realistic shadow.

5   Conclusion

This paper presents AIC-Net, an end-to-end trainable network that harmonizes foreground objects and background images with adaptive and realistic shadow effects. A branched generation mechanism is designed to disentangle style transfer and shadow generation to produce high-fidelity local harmonization. An auxiliary illumination model is collaborated in shadow branch to achieve adaptive shadow generation. A spatial transformer module is introduced to bridge the local and global harmonization for joint optimization. The quantitative and qualitative experiments demonstrate the superior harmonization performance and wide adaptability of the proposed method. We will continue to study AIC-Net for image harmonization with shadow generation within more complicated illumination environments.

References

1. Tsai, Y.H., Shen, X., Lin, Z., Sunkavalli, K., Lu, X., Yang, M.H.: Deep image harmonization. In: CVPR (2017)
2. Luan, F., Paris, S., Shechtman, E., Bala, K.: Deep painterly harmonization. arXiv preprint arXiv:1804.03189 (2018)
3. Wu, H., Zheng, S., Zhang, J., Huang, K.: Gp-gan: towards realistic high-resolution image blending. arXiv:1703.07195 (2017)
4. Lin, C.H., Yumer, E., Wang, O., Shechtman, E., Lucey, S.: St-gan: spatial transformer generative adversarial networks for image compositing. In: CVPR (2018)
5. Zhan, F., Lu, S., Xue, C.: Verisimilar image synthesis for accurate detection and recognition of texts in scenes. In: ECCV, pp. 249–266 (2018)
6. Zhan, F., Huang, J., Lu, S.: Adaptive composition gan towards realistic image synthesis, vol. 1905, p. 04693 (2019)
7. Zhan, F., Xue, C., Lu, S.: Ga-dan: geometry-aware domain adaptation network for scene text detection and recognition. In: ICCV (2019)
8. Zhan, F., Zhu, H., Lu, S.: Scene text synthesis for efficient and effective deep network training. arXiv:1901.09193 (2019)
9. Zhan, F., Zhu, H., Lu, S.: Spatial fusion gan for image synthesis. In: CVPR (2019)
10. Zhan, F., Lu, S.: Esir: end-to-end scene text recognition via iterative image rectification. In: CVPR (2019)
11. Zhan, F., Lu, S., Zhang, C., Ma, F., Xie, X.: Towards realistic 3D embedding via view alignment. arXiv preprint arXiv:2007.07066 (2020)
12. Zhan, F., Lu, S., Xiao, A.: Spatial-aware gan for unsupervised person re-identification. arXiv preprint arXiv:1911.11312 (2019)
13. Liu, D., Long, C., Zhang, H., Yu, H., Dong, X., Xiao, C.: Arshadowgan: shadow generative adversarial network for augmented reality in single light scenes. In: CVPR (2020)
14. Pérez, P., Gangnet, M., Blake, A.: Poisson image editing. In: TOG, vol. 22 (2003)
15. Azadi, S., Pathak, D., Ebrahimi, S., Darrell, T.: Compositional gan: learning conditional image composition. arXiv:1807.07560 (2018)
16. Zhu, J.Y., Krähenbühl, P., Shechtman, E., Efros, A.A.: Learning a discriminative model for the perception of realism in composite images. In: ICCV (2015)
17. Chen, B.C., Kae, A.: Toward realistic image compositing with adversarial learning. In: CVPR (2019)
18. Sunkavalli, K., Johnson, M.K., Matusik, W., Pfister, H.: Multi-scale image harmonization. ACM Trans. Graph. (Proc. ACM SIGGRAPH) 29, 1–10 (2010)
19. Xue, S., Agarwala, A., Dorsey, J., Rushmeier, H.: Understanding and improving the realism of image composites. TOG 31, 1-10 (2012)
20. Tao, M.W., Johnson, M.K., Paris, S.: Error-tolerant image compositing. IJCV 103, 31–44 (2013). https://doi.org/10.1007/978-3-642-15549-9_3
21. Tsai, Y.H., Shen, X., Lin, Z., Sunkavalli, K., Yang, M.H.: Sky is not the limit: semantic-aware sky replacement. ACM Trans. Graph. (Proc. SIGGRAPH) 35, 1449 (2016)
22. Efros, J.F.L.A.A.: Using color compatibility for assessing image realism. In: ICCV (2007)
23. Cong, W., et al.: Dovenet: deep image harmonization via domain verification. In: CVPR (2020)
24. Lalonde, J.F., Efros, A.A., Narasimhan, S.G.: Estimating the natural illumination conditions from a single outdoor image. IJCV 98, 123–145 (2012). https://doi.org/10.1007/s11263-011-0501-8

25. Gardner, M.A., et al.: Learning to predict indoor illumination from a single image. In: SIGGRAPH Asia (2017)
26. Hold-Geoffroy, Y., Sunkavalli, K., Hadap, S., Gambaretto, E., Lalonde, J.F.: Deep outdoor illumination estimation. In: CVPR (2017)
27. Gardner, M.A., Hold-Geoffroy, Y., Sunkavalli, K., Gagné, C., Lalonde, J.F.: Deep parametric indoor lighting estimation. In: ICCV (2019)
28. Garon, M., Sunkavalli, K., Hadap, S., Carr, N., Lalonde, J.F.: Fast spatially-varying indoor lighting estimation. In: CVPR (2019)
29. Goodfellow, I.J., et al.: Generative adversarial networks. In: NIPS, pp. 2672–2680 (2014)
30. Denton, E., Chintala, S., Szlam, A., Fergus, R.: Deep generative image models using a Laplacian pyramid of adversarial networks. In: NIPS (2015)
31. Lee, D., Liu, S., Gu, J., Liu, M.Y., Yang, M.H., Kautz, J.: Context-aware synthesis and placement of object instances. In: NIPS (2018)
32. Chen, X., Duan, Y., Houthooft, R., Schulman, J., Sutskever, I., Abbeel, P.: Infogan: interpretable representation learning by information maximizing generative adversarial nets. In: NIPS (2016)
33. Arjovsky, M., Chintala, S., Bottou, L.: Wasserstein generative adversarial networks. In: ICML (2017)
34. Bau, D., et al.: Gan dissection: visualizing and understanding generative adversarial networks. In: ICLR (2019)
35. Zhu, J.Y., Park, T., Isola, P., Efros, A.A.: Unpaired image-to-image translation using cycle-consistent adversarial networks. In: ICCV (2017)
36. Isola, P., Zhu, J.Y., Zhou, T., Efros, A.A.: Image-to-image translation with conditional adversarial networks. In: CVPR (2017)
37. Shrivastava, A., Pfister, T., Tuzel, O., Susskind, J., Wang, W., Webb, R.: Learning from simulated and unsupervised images through adversarial training. In: CVPR (2017)
38. Zhu, J.Y., et al.: Toward multimodal image-to-image translation. In: NIPS (2017)
39. Azadi, S., Fisher, M., Kim, V., Wang, Z., Shechtman, E., Darrell, T.: Multi-content gan for few-shot font style transfer. In: CVPR (2018)
40. Park, T., Liu, M.Y., Wang, T.C., Zhu, J.Y.: Semantic image synthesis with spatially-adaptive normalization. In: CVPR (2019)
41. Liu, M.Y., et al.: Few-shot unsupervised image-to-image translation. arXiv:1905.01723 (2019)
42. Green, R.: Spherical harmonic lighting: the gritty details. In: Game Developers Conference (2003)
43. He, K., Zhang, X., Ren, S., Sun, J.: Deep residual learning for image recognition. In: CVPR (2016)
44. Cheng, D., Shi, J., Chen, Y., Deng, X., Zhang, X.: Learning scene illumination by pairwise photos from rear and front mobile cameras. In: Computer Graphics Forum (2018)
45. He, K., Sun, J., Tang, X.: Guided image filtering. In: Daniilidis, K., Maragos, P., Paragios, N. (eds.) ECCV 2010. LNCS, vol. 6311, pp. 1–14. Springer, Heidelberg (2010). https://doi.org/10.1007/978-3-642-15549-9_1
46. Hirzer, M., Beleznai, C., Roth, P.M., Bischof, H.: Person re-identification by descriptive and discriminative classification. In: Heyden, A., Kahl, F. (eds.) SCIA 2011. LNCS, vol. 6688, pp. 91–102. Springer, Heidelberg (2011). https://doi.org/10.1007/978-3-642-21227-7_9
47. Chavdarova, T., et al.: Wildtrack: a multi-camera HD dataset for dense unscripted pedestrian detection. In: CVPR (2018)

48. Wang, L., Shi, J., Song, G., Shen, I.: Object detection combining recognition and segmentation. In: Yagi, Y., Kang, S.B., Kweon, I.S., Zha, H. (eds.) ACCV 2007. LNCS, vol. 4843, pp. 189–199. Springer, Heidelberg (2007). https://doi.org/10.1007/978-3-540-76386-4_17

49. Wen, L., et al.: Ua-detrac: a new benchmark and protocol for multi-object detection and tracking. arXiv preprint arXiv:1511.04136 (2015)

50. Cordts, M., et al.: The cityscapes dataset for semantic urban scene understanding. In: CVPR (2016)

51. Chang, A.X., et al.: Shapenet: an information-rich 3D model repository. arXiv preprint arXiv:1512.03012 (2015)

52. Heusel, M., Ramsauer, H., Unterthiner, T., Nessler, B., Hochreiter, S.: Gans trained by a two time-scale update rule converge to a local nash equilibrium. In: NIPS (2017)

53. Szegedy, C., et al.: Going deeper with convolutions. In: CVPR (2015)

54. Deng, J., Dong, W., Socher, R., Li, L.J., Li, K., Fei-Fei, L.: Imagenet: a large-scale hierarchical image database. In: CVPR (2009)

55. Zhou, P., Han, X., Morariu, V.I., Davis, L.S.: Learning rich features for image manipulation detection. In: CVPR (2018)

56. Huang, X., Belongie, S.: Arbitrary style transfer in real-time with adaptive instance normalization. In: ICCV. (2017)

Overwater Image Dehazing via Cycle-Consistent Generative Adversarial Network

Shunyuan Zheng$^{(\boxtimes)}$, Jiamin Sun, Qinglin Liu, Yuankai Qi, and Shengping Zhang

School of Computer Science and Technology, Harbin Institute of Technology, Weihai 264209, China
sawyer0503@gmail.com, sunjiamin17@gmail.com

Abstract. In contrast to images taken on land scenes, images taken over water are more prone to degradation due to the influence of the haze. However, existing image dehazing methods are mainly developed for land scenes and perform poorly when applied to overwater images. To address this problem, we collect the first overwater image dehazing dataset and propose an OverWater Image Dehazing GAN (OWI-DehazeGAN). Due to the difficulties of collecting paired hazy and clean images, the dataset is composed of unpaired hazy and clean images taken over water. The proposed OWI-DehazeGAN learns the underlying style mapping between hazy and clean images in an encoder-decoder framework, which is supervised by a forward-backward translation consistency loss for self-supervision and a perceptual loss for content preservation. In addition to qualitative evaluation, we design an image quality assessment network to rank the dehazed images. Experimental results on both real and synthetic test data demonstrate that the proposed method performs superiorly against several state-of-the-art land dehazing methods.

Keywords: Image dehazing · Overwater image · Unpaired data · Generative adversarial networks

1 Introduction

Images of overwater scenes play an important role in human image galleries. However, these images are prone to degradation due to thick mist that are often appearing over lakes, rivers, and seas. Although numerous image dehazing methods have been developed [1–5], our experiments show that these methods perform far from satisfying since they are originally designed for land scene images, of which the data distribution differs significantly.

Hazy images are usually modeled as $I(x) = J(x)t(x) + A(1 - t(x))$, where $I(x)$ and $J(x)$ are the observed hazy image and the scene, respectively [6,7]. The symbol x denotes a pixel index, and A is the global atmospheric light. $t(\cdot)$ denotes the transmission map, which describes the portion of light that is not

© Springer Nature Switzerland AG 2021
H. Ishikawa et al. (Eds.): ACCV 2020, LNCS 12623, pp. 251–267, 2021.
https://doi.org/10.1007/978-3-030-69532-3_16

scattered and reaches the camera sensors. When the haze is homogeneous, $t(\cdot)$ can be defined as: $t(x) = e^{-\beta d(x)}$, where β is the scattering coefficient and $d(x)$ is the distance between objects and the camera.

(a) Input Hazy Image   (b) Cai [8]   (c) Yang [4]   (d) Ours

Fig. 1. Overwater image dehazing example. The proposed method generates more clear images compared to state-of-the-art methods.

Existing methods fall into two categories according to the type of features they used: methods based on hand-crafted features [1,2,9–12] or methods based CNN features [3–5,8,13–15]. The former generally focuses on estimating the global atmospheric light intensity and the transmission map, and hence their performance are susceptible to estimation errors of $A(\cdot)$ or $t(\cdot)$. To alleviate these limitations, the latter, which is based on CNNs [16] or Generative Adversarial Networks (GANs) [17], aims to directly estimate clean images in a data-driven scheme. Although promising dehazing results have been achieved, existing CNN- or GAN- based methods perform not well on overwater images as shown in Fig. 1b and 1c. Another issue is that existing image dehazing datasets [18–20] are dominated by land scenes.

In this paper, we address both the above mentioned issues. *First*, we construct a new dataset, named OverwaterHaze, specially for dehazing overwater images. Since collecting paired hazy and clear images is difficult and expensive, the OverwaterHaze dataset is composed of unpaired hazy and clean overwater images. *Second*, we propose an OverWater Image Dehazing GAN (OWI-DehazeGAN) inspired by CycleGAN [21] to directly recover clean images. Although the unpaired character challenges most of existing methods, we demonstrate that satisfying dehazing performance could be achieved by the proposed method.

Our contributions are summarized as follows:

- We create the first overwater image dehazing dataset, and we hope this dataset is able to facilitate the research in this field.
- We propose an OWI-DehazeGAN to dehaze overwater images, which is based on but performs superior to Cycle-GAN. The proposed network is able to utilize unpaired training data and preserve image details simultaneously.
- We propose an image quality assessment network to rank the generated dehazed images, which facilitates the comparison of different algorithms.

2   Related Work

2.1   Methods Based on Hand-Crafted Features

Many efforts have been devoted to image dehazing in the past decades based on hand-crafted features [1,2,9–12]. Tan *et al.* [9] propose a contrast maximizing approach using markov random fields (MRF) based on the observation that clean images have higher contrast than hazy ones. In [10] Tarel *et al.* propose a fast dehazing method by combining atmospheric veil inference, image restoration and smoothing tone mapping. Later, He *et al.* [11] estimate the transmission map by utilizing dark-channel prior (DCP). Meng *et al.* [12] explore the inherent boundary constraint on the transmission function. In order to recover depth information, Zhu *et al.* [1] propose a color attenuation prior (CAP) by creating a linear model on local priors. Different from previous methods that use various patch-based priors, Berman *et al.* [2] present a new image dehazing algorithm based on non-local prior so that a haze-free image is able to be well approximated by a few distinct colors.

While the afore-mentioned methods have achieved promising results, they perform far from satisfying when applied to overwater images. MRF [9] tends to produce over-saturated images. The enhanced images of FVR [10] often contain distorted colors and severe halos. DCP [11] does not work well when it comes to the sky regions, as the scene objects are similar to the atmospheric light.

2.2   Methods Based on CNN Features

Deep convolutional neural networks have shown promising success in various computer vision tasks. Cai *et al.* [8] propose an end-to-end DehazeNet with non-linear regression layers to estimate medium transmission. Instead of estimating the transmission map or the atmospheric light firstly, AOD-Net [15] predicts the haze-free images directly using a light-weight CNN. Proximal Dehaze-Net [4] attaches the advantages of traditional prior-based dehazing methods to deep learning technologies by incorporating the haze-related prior learning.

Since Goodfellow [17] proposed the GAN method in 2014, there have been many effective variants tailored to different computer vision tasks [21–23]. Motivated by the success of GANs in those regions, several GAN-based methods have been proposed for image dehazing. In [5], a Densely Connected Pyramid Dehazing Network (DCPDN) is proposed to jointly learn the transmission map, atmospheric light and dehazing result all together. Yang *et al.* [24] propose to loose the paired training constraint by introducing a disentanglement and reconstruction mechanism. Li *et al.* [13] design a solution based on a cGAN network [22] to directly estimate the clean image. Ren *et al.* [3] adopt an ensemble strategy to take advantage of information in white balance, contrast enhancing, and gamma correction images. Overall, these methods are trained on paired data, which is unsuitable for the proposed overwater image dehazing task, where only unpaired training data is available.

2.3   Image Dehazing Dataset

Image dehazing tasks profit from the continuous efforts for large-scale data. Several datasets [18–20] have been introduced for image dehazing.

MSCNN [14] and AOD-Net [15] utilize the indoor NYU2 Depth Database [25] and the Middlebury Stereo database [26] to synthesize hazy images using the known depth information. O-HAZE [19] is an outdoor scenes dataset, which is composed of pairs of real hazy and corresponding clean data. I-HAZE [19] is a dataset that contains 35 image pairs of hazy and corresponding ground-truth indoor images. Li *et al.* [20] have launched a new large-scale benchmark which is made up of synthetic and real-world hazy images, called Realistic Single Image Dehazing (RESIDE). However, most datasets are synthetic and not tailored to handling overwater image dehazing. Different from the above datasets, we collect a dataset containing real data which is specially for dehazing overwater images.

3   Proposed Method

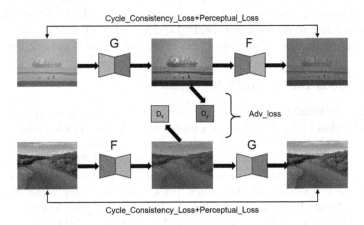

Fig. 2. The main architecture of the proposed OWI-DehazeGAN network. G and F denote generators, where $G : X \rightarrow Y$ generates clean images from hazy images and $F : Y \rightarrow X$ vice versa. D_x and D_y denote discriminators. Adversarial loss, cycle consistency loss and perceptual loss are employed to train the network.

Figure 2 shows the main architecture of the proposed OWI-DehazeGAN. Unlike traditional GANs, OWI-DehazeGAN consists of two generators (G and F) and two discriminators (D_x and D_y) in order to be trainable with unpaired training data. Specifically, generator G predicts clean images Y from hazy images X, and F vice versa. D_x and D_y distinguish hazy images and clean images, respectively. Below we provide more details about each component.

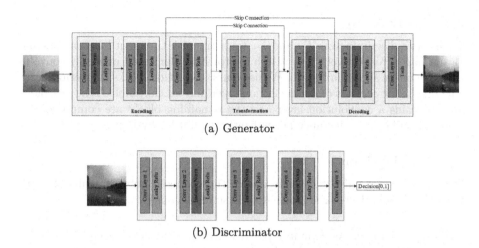

(a) Generator

(b) Discriminator

Fig. 3. Architecture of our generator and discriminator. The Generator consists of encoding, transformation, and decoding three parts.

3.1 Generator

We adopt the same structure for the two generators G and F. Both generators are divided into three parts: encoding, transformation, and decoding. The architecture of the generator is shown in Fig. 3a.

Encoding. The encoding module extracts image features by three convolution layers, which serve as down-sampling layers to decrease the resolution of the original input. Each convolution layer is followed by an instance normalization and a Leaky ReLU. Since image dehazing can be treated as a domain adaptation problem, instance normalization is more suitable than batch normalization.

Transformation. The transformation module translates information from one domain to another via nine ResNet blocks [27]. The ResNet block in our network contains two 3×3 convolution layers with the same number of filters. Due to the results of image dehazing need to retain the characteristics of the original image, the ResNet block is well suited to accomplish these transformations.

Decoding. The decoding module includes up-sampling operations and nonlinear mappings. There are several choices for upsampling, such as deconvolution [28], sub-pixel convolution [29] and resize convolution [30]. In order to reduce checker-board artifacts [30] caused by deconvolution or sub-pixel convolution, we use the resize convolution for decoding. Inspired by the success of U-Net [31], we introduce two symmetric skip connections to deliver information between encoding and decoding modules. Finally, images are recovered through convolution and tanh activation.

3.2 Discriminator

We use two discriminators D_x and D_y to distinguish the input hazy images and clean images, respectively. The discriminator is implemented in a fully convolution fashion, as shown in Fig. 3b. We use four convolution blocks in discriminator. The first block consists of a convolution layer and a Leaky ReLU, the last block only contains a convolution layer and the remaining blocks are composed of a convolution layer, an instance normalization and a Leaky ReLU.

3.3 Loss Function

We utilize three kinds of losses to enable the proposed network trainable with unpaired data and preserve image details simultaneously.

Adversarial Loss. As done in CycleGAN, we use the adversarial loss and the cycle consistency loss for unpaired training data. $x \in X$, $y \in Y$ are a hazy image and an unpaired clean image, respectively. For the generator G and discriminator D_y, the adversarial loss is formulated as:

$$L_{GAN}(G, D_y, x, y) = log(D_y(y)) + log(1 - D_y(G(x))) \tag{1}$$

Correspondingly, the constraint on generator F and its discriminator D_x is

$$L_{GAN}(F, D_x, x, y) = log(D_x(x)) + log(1 - D_x(F(y))) \tag{2}$$

However, the above losses are prone to unstable training and generating low quality images. To make the training more robust and achieve high quality images, we use a least squares loss [23] instead of the negative log likelihood objective [17]. Therefore, Eq. (1) and (2) are modified as:

$$L_{adv}(G, D_y, x, y) = \frac{1}{2} * [(D_y(G(x)) - 1)^2 + (D_y(y) - 1)^2 + D_y(G(x))^2] \tag{3}$$

$$L_{adv}(F, D_x, x, y) = \frac{1}{2} * [(D_x(F(y)) - 1)^2 + (D_x(x) - 1)^2 + D_x(F(y))^2] \tag{4}$$

And the final adversarial loss is denoted as:

$$L_{adv}(G, F, D_x, D_y) = L_{adv}(G, D_y, x, y) + L_{adv}(F, D_x, x, y) \tag{5}$$

Cycle Consistency Losss. CycleGAN introduces a cycle consistency loss to solve the problem that an adversarial loss alone cannot ensure the matching between the output distribution and the target distribution. For each image x, $F(G(x))$ is able to bring $G(x)$ back to the original image. Similarly, $G(F(y))$ is able to bring $F(y)$ back to the original image y. $F(G(x))$ is the cyclic image of input x, and $G(F(y))$ is the cyclic image of the original image y. To train generators G and F at the same time, the consistency loss includes two constraints: $F(G(x)) \approx x$, $G(F(y)) \approx y$. The cycle consistency loss is defined to calculate L1-norm between the input and the cyclic image for unpaired image dehazing:

$$L_{cyc}(G, F) = ||F(G(x)) - x||_1 + ||G(F(y)) - y||_1 \tag{6}$$

Perceptual Loss. We introduce perceptual loss to restrict the reconstruction of image details. Instead of measuring per-pixel difference between the images, perceptual loss is concerned with the distinction between feature maps, which comprises various aspects of content and perceptual quality. The perceptual loss is defined as:

$$L_{per}(G, F) = ||\theta(x) - \theta(F(G(x)))||_2^2 + ||\theta(y) - \theta(G(F(y)))||_2^2 \qquad (7)$$

Here, θ represents the feature maps which generated from the relu4_2 on pertained VGG-16 [32] network.

Objective Function. We define the loss as a weighted sum of previous losses:

$$L(G, F, D_x, D_y) = L_{adv}(G, F, D_x, D_y) + \lambda L_{cyc}(G, F) + \mu L_{per}(G, F) \qquad (8)$$

where coefficients λ and μ represent the weights of cycle consistency loss and perceptual loss, respectively. We found that giving an over-weight to perceptual loss may cause the instability of training process thus the weight of perceptual loss should be much less than the weight of cyclic consistency loss. We minimize the generators G, F and maximize the discriminators D_x, D_y in training process. The final objective function is:

$$< G^*, F^* > = \arg\min_{G,F} \max_{D_x, D_y} L(G, F, D_x, D_y) \qquad (9)$$

3.4 Dehazed Image Quality Assessment

In order to verify the effectiveness of the proposed OWI-DehazeGAN, we design a dehazed image quality assessment model based on natural image statistics and VGG network. Natural images are directly captured from natural scenes, so they have some natural properties. By making statistics on these properties, natural scene statistics (NSS [33]) of images can be obtained. NSS has been widely used in image quality assessment, especially no-reference image quality assessment.

In this paper, the NSS we use is mean subtracted contrast normalization (MSCN [34]) coefficients, which is used to normalize a hazy image. After normalization pixel intensities of haze-free by MSCN coefficient follow a Gaussian Distribution while pixel intensities of hazy images do not. The deviation of the distribution from an ideal bell curve is therefore a measure of the amount of distortion in the image. To calculate the MSCN Coefficients, the image intensity $I(i,j)$ at pixel (i,j) is transformed to the luminance $\widehat{I}(i,j)$. $\widehat{I}(i,j)$ is defined as:

$$\widehat{I}(i,j) = \frac{I(i,j) - \mu(i,j)}{\sigma(i,j) + C} \qquad (10)$$

where $\mu(i,j)$ and $\sigma(i,j)$ represent the local mean field and local variance field obtained by calculating the image using a gaussian window with a specific size. Local Mean Field μ is the Gaussian Blur of the input image. Local Variance

Field σ is the Gaussian Blur of the square of the difference between original image and μ. In case the denominator is zero, a constant C is added. When a dehazed image is normalized by MSCN coefficient, only the uniform appearance and the edge information are retained. Human eyes are very sensitive to edge information, so the normalized image is consistent with human vision.

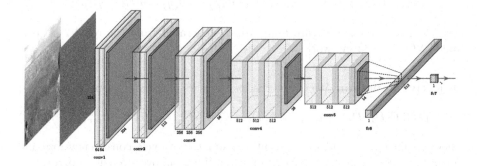

Fig. 4. Architecture of the proposed IQA model for dehazed images.

The proposed IQA model for dehazed images is consist of luminance normalization, feature extraction and regression of evaluation score. The dehazed images are firstly normalized by MSCN coefficient, which provides a good normalization of image luminance and does not have a strong dependence on the intensity of texture. Then a VGG-16 model is used to extract features for finally predicting an image quality score between 0 and 9 through two fully connected layers, whose units are 512 and 1 respectively. The architecture of the IQA model is shown in Fig. 4. The loss function of this IQA model is MAE. The loss is defined as:

$$loss_{IQA} = \frac{1}{N} \sum_{i=1}^{n} |y_i - y_i^*| \tag{11}$$

where N represents the number of images in the training set, y_i and y_i^* denote target data and output data, respectively. The optimization goal of the IQA model in the training phase is to minimize the average absolute error loss. Learning the mapping between dehazed images and corresponding Mean Opinion Scores (MOS [35]) is achieved by minimizing the loss between the predicted score y_i^* and the corresponding ground truth y_i.

4   Experiment

4.1   Dataset

We collect a real unpaired image dataset called OverwateHaze for image dehazing in overwater scenes. The training set consists of 4531 unpaired images, which are 2090 hazy images and 2441 clean images, all images are crawled from Google.

These training images are resized to 640×480. Figure 5 illustrates some examples of our dataset. There are three differences between the proposed dataset and the existing datasets: (1) The OverwaterHaze dataset is a large-scale natural dataset with hazy images and unpaired haze-free images, as the previous datasets are only composed of synthetic data; (2) The OverwaterHaze dataset is tailored to the task of overwater image dehazing, rather than focusing on indoor or outdoor scenes; (3) The proposed dataset is much more challenging because the regions of sky and water surface make up a large part of the image.

Fig. 5. Examples of the training set in OverwaterHaze dataset (best viewed in color). (a)–(f) Hazy images. (g)–(l) Clean images. (Color figure online)

In order to evaluate different image dehazing methods in overwater scene subjectively, we introduce a natural overwater testing set, which contains 127 challenging hazy images collected from overwater scenes. To quantitatively compare different image dehazing methods, we select 90 (30 images × 3 medium extinction coefficients β) overwater hazy images with corresponding ground-truth from the RESIDE OTS dataset [20]. We apply SSIM, PSNR and CIEDE2000 to the dehazed results on synthetic images. Based on the OverwaterHaze dataset, we compare our proposed method against several state-of-the-art dehazing methods in real and synthetic data, including: DCP [11], FVR [10], BCCR [12], CAP [1], DehazeNet [8], MSCNN [14], AOD-Net [15], dehaze-cGAN [13], Proximal Dehaze-Net [4], CycleGAN [21].

4.2 Experimental Settings

The input images of generators and discriminators are set to 256×256 during training. We use an Adam solver to optimize gradient with a learning rate of $2e-4$. The batch size is 1. The weights of cyclic consistency loss λ and perceptual loss μ are 10 and 0.0001, respectively. The coefficient a of Leaky ReLU is 0.2. The update proportion is 1 for generators G, F and discriminators D_x, D_y.

4.3   Qualitative Results on Real Images

Figure 6 shows an example of dehazing results of the proposed algorithm against the state-of-the-art methods. DCP [11] tends to overestimate the thickness of the haze and produce dark results (Fig. 6b). The dehazed images by FVR [10] and BCCR [12] have significant color distortions and miss most details as shown in Fig. 6c–6d. The best performer in the hand-crafted prior based methods is CAP [1], which generally reconstructs details of haze-free images. The deep learning based approach achieve comparable results, such as DehazeNet [8], MSCNN [14] and dehaze-cGAN [13]. But these results indicate that existing methods cannot handle overwater hazy images well. For example, the dehazed results by MSCNN and DehazeNet (Fig. 6f–6g) have a similar problem that tends to magnify the phenomenon of color cast and have some remaining haze. The illumination appears dark in the results of Proximal Dehaze-Net [4] and AOD-Net [15], as shown in Fig. 6h–6j. From Fig. 6k, CycleGAN [21] generates some pseudo-colors to a certain degree, which makes it quite different from the original colors. Meanwhile, its result generates extensive checkerboard artifacts in the sky regions. In contrast, the dehazed result by our method shown in Fig. 6l is visually pleasing in the mist condition.

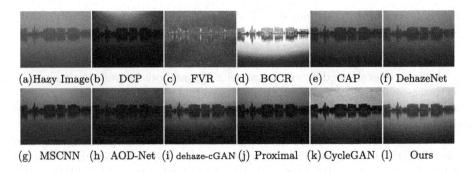

(a) Hazy Image (b)   DCP   (c)   FVR   (d)   BCCR   (e)   CAP   (f) DehazeNet

(g)   MSCNN   (h) AOD-Net (i) dehaze-cGAN (j) Proximal (k) CycleGAN (l)   Ours

Fig. 6. Real hazy images and corresponding dehazing results from several state-of-the-art methods (best viewed in color). (Color figure online)

4.4   Qualitative and Quantitative Results on Synthetic Images

We further conduct some experiments based on synthetic hazy images. Although the proposed method is trained on real unpaired data, we note that it can be applied for synthetic images as well. Figure 7 shows some dehazed images generated by various methods. Figure 7a shows the groundtruth as reference. As shown in Fig. 7b–7d, the results of DCP[11], FVR [10], and BCCR[12] have some distortions in colors or details. The dehazed results processed by CAP [1] (Fig. 7e), DehazeNet [8] (Fig. 7f), MSCNN [14] (Fig. 7g), AOD-Net [15] (Fig. 7h), dehaze-cGAN [13] (Fig. 7i), and Proximal Dehaze-Net [4] (Fig. 7j) are closer to groundtruth 7a than the results based on priors. However, there still exists some remaining haze as shown in Fig. 7e–7h. The result generated by CycleGAN [21] in Fig. 7k exists serious color cast and losses some color information. The dehazed result generated by our approach in Fig. 7l, by contrast, is visually close to the groundtruth image.

Table 1. Average PSNR, SSIM and, CIEDE2000 values of the dehazed results on the new synthetic dataset. The best result, the second result, and the third place result are represented by red, blue, and green, respectively.

	DCP	FVR	BCCR	CAP	DehazeNet	MSCNN	AOD-Net	dehaze-cGAN	Proximal	CycleGAN	Ours
SSIM	0.717	0.817	0.680	0.825	0.887	0.850	0.835	0.876	0.820	0.584	0.893
PSNR	14.57	16.56	13.92	19.50	23.27	20.55	19.33	22.77	17.79	18.31	24.93
CIEDE2000	14.92	11.71	15.35	9.37	6.23	7.81	9.11	6.51	10.14	11.5	5.98

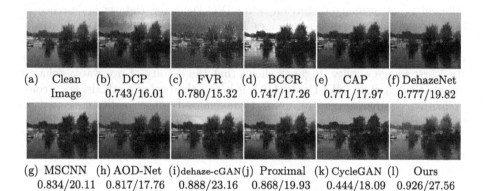

(a) Clean	(b) DCP	(c) FVR	(d) BCCR	(e) CAP	(f) DehazeNet
Image	0.743/16.01	0.780/15.32	0.747/17.26	0.771/17.97	0.777/19.82

(g) MSCNN	(h) AOD-Net	(i)dehaze-cGAN	(j) Proximal	(k) CycleGAN	(l) Ours
0.834/20.11	0.817/17.76	0.888/23.16	0.868/19.93	0.444/18.09	0.926/27.56

Fig. 7. Comparison in terms of SSIM/PSNR for different dehazing methods. (Color figure online)

An advantage of testing on synthetic data is able to objectively evaluate experimental results via SSIM, PSNR and CIEDE2000. Higher SSIM score indicates that the generated results are more consistent with human perception. PSNR forecasts the effectiveness of image dehazing, and CIEDE2000 presents that smaller scores indicate better color preservation. In Fig. 7, the SSIM and PSNR values also indicate that our method surpass other methods. From Table 1, our method get higher PSNR and SSIM. Remarkably, the SSIM and PSNR of our model are significantly better than CycleGAN.

4.5 Dehazed Images Ranking

The proposed IQA model for dehazed images is pre-trained on TID2013 [35] and then fine-tuned using the IVC Dehazing Dataset [18]. The TID2013 includes

Table 2. Comparison of dehazed image quality using four image quality assessment methods. The top three results are in red, blue, and green font, respectively.

	FADE ↓	SSEQ ↓	BLINDS-2 ↓	NIMA ↑
Ours	1.95	36.24	31.50	6.47
CAP	3.03	40.97	51.00	5.95
MSCNN	2.38	45.56	50.50	6.23
DehazeNet	3.11	42.49	49.50	6.12
Proximal-Dehaze	1.69	43.69	54.50	6.06
DCP	1.45	43.32	51.50	5.36
BCCR	1.17	45.76	48.50	6.08
FVR	2.67	41.71	48.00	4.86
AOD-Net	2.30	38.62	54.50	6.15

different types of image distortion, while IVC Dehazing Dataset is designed to evaluate the quality of dehazed images. Predicted scores are used to qualitatively rank photos as shown in Fig. 8. Ranking scores and the ranking are presented below each image, where '1' denotes the best visual perception and '10' for the worst image quality. Figure 8 shows that the quality of overwater dehazed images generated by OWI-DehazeGAN is better than other methods. For a comprehensive comparison, we also report the dehazed image quality measured by four typical image quality assessment methods in Table 2. The best results are shown in red font. Table 2 shows that the proposed method achieves the best performance in terms of almost all metrics.

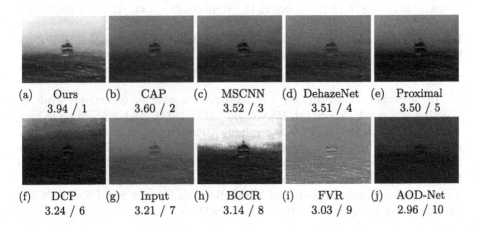

(a)　Ours　(b)　CAP　(c)　MSCNN　(d) DehazeNet　(e)　Proximal
3.94 / 1　3.60 / 2　3.52 / 3　3.51 / 4　3.50 / 5

(f)　DCP　(g)　Input　(h)　BCCR　(i)　FVR　(j)　AOD-Net
3.24 / 6　3.21 / 7　3.14 / 8　3.03 / 9　2.96 / 10

Fig. 8. Comparison via the proposed IQA model. Ranking scores and the ranking are shown below each image. (Color figure online)

5 Analysis and Discussion

5.1 Effect of Resize Convolution

In the decoding process of the generator, we use the resize convolution to increase the resolution of feature maps, rather than deconvolution or sub-pixel convolution. To better understand how the resize convolution contributes to our proposed method, we train three end-to-end networks with different upsample mode: (i) deconvolution, (ii) sub-pixel convolution, and (iii) resize convolution.

Figure 9 shows the results of three upsampling mode in our network. In comparison, the result of resize convolution is best viewed from the perspective of the human perception and retain more detailed information. From Fig. 9c, we observe plenty checkerboard pattern of artifacts caused by deconvolution. Although the sub-pixel convolution (Fig. 9d) can alleviate the 'checkerboard artifacts' to some extent, the result of sub-pixel convolution is rough and unsatisfying. Compared with the first two approaches, resize convolution recover most scene details and maintain the original colors. From Table 3, the introduced resize convolution gains higher PSNR, SSIM scores and a lower CIEDE2000 score than deconvolution and sub-pixel convolution, which indicate resize convolution can generate visually perceptible images.

Table 3. Average scores in terms of PSNR, SSIM, and CIEDE2000 for three upsampling convolutions on the synthetic test set of the OverwaterHaze dataset.

Average Metrics	SSIM	PSNR	CIEDE2000
Deconvolution	0.758	20.34	9.12
Sub-pixel Convolution	0.643	20.21	10.86
Resize Convolution	0.819	22.19	7.41

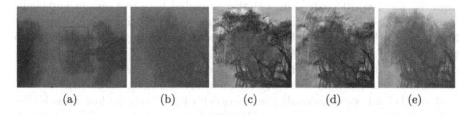

(a)   (b)   (c)   (d)   (e)

Fig. 9. Effectiveness of the proposed network with resize convolution. (a) and (b) are input hazy images. (b)–(e) are the zoom-in views. (c)–(e) are the dehazing results of deconvolution, sub-pixel convolution and resize convolution, respectively.

Table 4. Effect of perceptual loss in terms of SSIM, PSNR, and CIEDE2000.

Average Metrics	SSIM	PSNR	CIEDE2000
CycleGAN loss	0.819	22.19	7.41
CycleGAN loss+VGG loss	0.893	24.93	5.98

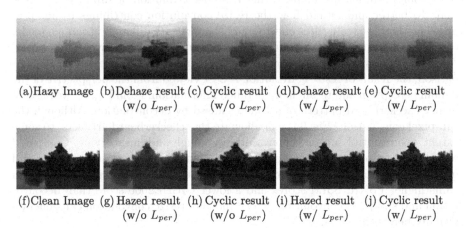

(a)Hazy Image (b)Dehaze result (c) Cyclic result (d)Dehaze result (e) Cyclic result
$\qquad$ (w/o L_{per}) (w/o L_{per}) (w/ L_{per}) (w/ L_{per})

(f)Clean Image (g) Hazed result (h) Cyclic result (i) Hazed result (j) Cyclic result
$\qquad$ (w/o L_{per}) (w/o L_{per}) (w/ L_{per}) (w/ L_{per})

Fig. 10. Comparison of dehazing with and without perceptual loss. (a)–(e) represents the generation direction of $X \rightarrow Y \rightarrow X$. (f)–(j) says the direction of formation is $Y \rightarrow X \rightarrow Y$. '(w/o L_{per})' denotes the network without perceptual loss, and '(w/ L_{per})' denotes the network with perceptual loss.

5.2   Effect of Perceptual Loss

To show the effectiveness of our loss function, we train an overwater image dehazing network without perceptual loss additionally. The result of a comparative experiment of dehazing with and without perceptual loss is shown in Fig. 10, the generated direction for images in the first row is $X \rightarrow G(x) \rightarrow F(G(x))$, the second row is the opposite of the first row $Y \rightarrow F(Y) \rightarrow G(F(Y))$. We can observe from the Fig. 10c, 10d, 10g, 10h that the estimated haze-free images and cyclic images lack fine details and the regions of the sky do not match with the input hazy image, which leads to the dehazed results containing halo artifacts when the perceptual loss is not used. Through the comparison of Fig. 10b and 10d we can also find that the perceptual loss is favorable for the reconstruction of the sky regions, which is very necessary for the overwater image dehazing.

From Table 4, we observe that our network with perceptual loss gains higher PSNR, SSIM scores and a lower CIEDE2000 score. Higher SSIM and PSNR scores suggest the proposed method with perceptual loss is consistent with human perception. Lower CIEDE2000 means the less color difference between dehazed image and groundtruth. The above experiments show that the proposed loss is effective for the overwater image dehazing task.

6   Conclusion

In this paper, we formulate an overwater image dehazing task, create the first overwater image dehazing dataset, and propose the OWI-DehazeGAN to dehaze overwater images. Compared to previous CNN-based methods which require paired training data, our OWI-DehazeGAN is able to be trained on unpaired images. Our method directly predicts clean images from hazy input bypassing to estimate transmission maps and global atmospheric lights. We utilize the perceptual loss and the resize convolution to preserve detailed textures and alleviate checkerboard artifacts. Extensive experiments demonstrate that our method produces superior results than most of the state-of-the-art dehazing methods.

Acknowledgement. This work was supported in part by National Natural Science Foundation of China (Nos. 61902092 and 61872112), Fundamental Research Funds for the Central Universities Grant No.HIT.NSRIF.2020005, and National Key Research and Development Program of China (Nos. 2018YFC0806802 and 2018YFC0832105).

References

1. Zhu, Q., Mai, J., Shao, L.: A fast single image haze removal algorithm using color attenuation prior. IEEE Trans. Image Process. **24**, 3522–3533 (2015)
2. Berman, D., treibitz, T., Avidan, S.: Non-local image dehazing. In: The IEEE Conference on Computer Vision and Pattern Recognition (CVPR), pp. 1674–1682 (2016)
3. Ren, W., et al.: Gated fusion network for single image dehazing. In: IEEE Conference on Computer Vision and Pattern Recognition, pp. 3253–3261 (2018)
4. Yang, D., Sun, J.: Proximal dehaze-net: a prior learning-based deep network for single image dehazing. In: The European Conference on Computer Vision (ECCV), pp. 729–746 (2018)
5. Zhang, H., Patel, V.M.: Densely connected pyramid dehazing network. In: The IEEE Conference on Computer Vision and Pattern Recognition (CVPR), pp. 3194–3203 (2018)
6. McCartney, E.J.: Optics of the Atmosphere: Scattering by Molecules and Particles, p. 421. Wiley, New York (1976)
7. Narasimhan, S.G., Nayar, S.K.: Chromatic framework for vision in bad weather. In: Proceedings IEEE Conference on Computer Vision and Pattern Recognition. CVPR 2000 (Cat. No. PR00662), vol. 1, pp. 598–605. IEEE (2000)
8. Cai, B., Xu, X., Jia, K., Qing, C., Tao, D.: Dehazenet: an end-to-end system for single image haze removal. IEEE Trans. Image Process. **25**, 5187–5198 (2016)
9. Tan, R.T.: Visibility in bad weather from a single image. In: 2008 IEEE Conference on Computer Vision and Pattern Recognition, pp. 1–8. IEEE (2008)
10. Tarel, J.P., Hautiere, N.: Fast visibility restoration from a single color or gray level image. In: 2009 IEEE 12th International Conference on Computer Vision, pp. 2201–2208. IEEE (2009)
11. He, K., Sun, J., Tang, X.: Single image haze removal using dark channel prior. IEEE Trans. Pattern Anal. Mach. Intell. **33**, 2341–2353 (2011)
12. Meng, G., Wang, Y., Duan, J., Xiang, S., Pan, C.: Efficient image dehazing with boundary constraint and contextual regularization. In: The IEEE International Conference on Computer Vision (ICCV), pp. 617–624 (2013)

13. Li, R., Pan, J., Li, Z., Tang, J.: Single image dehazing via conditional generative adversarial network. In: The IEEE Conference on Computer Vision and Pattern Recognition (CVPR), pp. 8202–8211 (2018)
14. Ren, W., Liu, S., Zhang, H., Pan, J., Cao, X., Yang, M.-H.: Single image dehazing via multi-scale convolutional neural networks. In: Leibe, B., Matas, J., Sebe, N., Welling, M. (eds.) ECCV 2016. LNCS, vol. 9906, pp. 154–169. Springer, Cham (2016). https://doi.org/10.1007/978-3-319-46475-6_10
15. Li, B., Peng, X., Wang, Z., Xu, J., Feng, D.: Aod-net: all-in-one dehazing network. In: Proceedings of the IEEE International Conference on Computer Vision, pp. 4770–4778 (2017)
16. Krizhevsky, A., Sutskever, I., Hinton, G.E.: Imagenet classification with deep convolutional neural networks. In: Advances in Neural Information Processing Systems, pp. 1097–1105 (2012)
17. Goodfellow, I., et al.: Generative adversarial nets. In: Advances in Neural Information Processing Systems, pp. 2672–2680 (2014)
18. Ma, K., Liu, W., Wang, Z.: Perceptual evaluation of single image dehazing algorithms. In: 2015 IEEE International Conference on Image Processing (ICIP), pp. 3600–3604. IEEE (2015)
19. Ancuti, C., Ancuti, C.O., Timofte, R., De Vleeschouwer, C.: I-HAZE: a dehazing benchmark with real hazy and haze-free indoor images. In: Blanc-Talon, J., Helbert, D., Philips, W., Popescu, D., Scheunders, P. (eds.) ACIVS 2018. LNCS, vol. 11182, pp. 620–631. Springer, Cham (2018). https://doi.org/10.1007/978-3-030-01449-0_52
20. Li, B., Ren, W., Fu, D., Tao, D., Feng, D., Zeng, W., Wang, Z.: Benchmarking single-image dehazing and beyond. IEEE Trans. Image Process. **28**, 492–505 (2019)
21. Zhu, J.Y., Park, T., Isola, P., Efros, A.A.: Unpaired image-to-image translation using cycle-consistent adversarial networks. In: The IEEE International Conference on Computer Vision (ICCV), pp. 2242–2251 (2017)
22. Mirza, M., Osindero, S.: Conditional generative adversarial nets. arXiv preprint arXiv:1411.1784 (2014)
23. Mao, X., Li, Q., Xie, H., Lau, R.Y., Wang, Z., Paul Smolley, S.: Least squares generative adversarial networks. In: Proceedings of the IEEE International Conference on Computer Vision, pp. 2794–2802 (2017)
24. Yang, X., Xu, Z., Luo, J.: Towards perceptual image dehazing by physics-based disentanglement and adversarial training. In: Thirty-Second AAAI Conference on Artificial Intelligence, pp. 7485–7492 (2018)
25. Silberman, N., Hoiem, D., Kohli, P., Fergus, R.: Indoor segmentation and support inference from RGBD images. In: Fitzgibbon, A., Lazebnik, S., Perona, P., Sato, Y., Schmid, C. (eds.) ECCV 2012. LNCS, vol. 7576, pp. 746–760. Springer, Heidelberg (2012). https://doi.org/10.1007/978-3-642-33715-4_54
26. Scharstein, D., Szeliski, R.: High-accuracy stereo depth maps using structured light. In: IEEE Computer Society Conference on Computer Vision and Pattern Recognition, 2003. Proceedings, vol. 1, pp. 195–202. IEEE (2003)
27. He, K., Zhang, X., Ren, S., Sun, J.: Deep residual learning for image recognition. In: Proceedings of the IEEE Conference on Computer Vision and Pattern Recognition, pp. 770–778 (2016)
28. Noh, H., Hong, S., Han, B.: Learning deconvolution network for semantic segmentation. In: Proceedings of the IEEE International Conference on Computer Vision, pp. 1520–1528 (2015)

29. Shi, W., et al.: Real-time single image and video super-resolution using an efficient sub-pixel convolutional neural network. In: The IEEE Conference on Computer Vision and Pattern Recognition (CVPR), pp. 1874–1883 (2016)

30. Odena, A., Dumoulin, V., Olah, C.: Deconvolution and checkerboard artifacts. Distill **1**, e3 (2016)

31. Ronneberger, O., Fischer, P., Brox, T.: U-Net: convolutional networks for biomedical image segmentation. In: Navab, N., Hornegger, J., Wells, W.M., Frangi, A.F. (eds.) MICCAI 2015. LNCS, vol. 9351, pp. 234–241. Springer, Cham (2015). https://doi.org/10.1007/978-3-319-24574-4_28

32. Simonyan, K., Zisserman, A.: Very deep convolutional networks for large-scale image recognition. arXiv preprint arXiv:1409.1556 (2014)

33. Ruderman, D.L.: The statistics of natural images. Netw. Comput. Neural Syst. **5**, 517–548 (2009)

34. Lark Kwon, C., Jaehee, Y., Alan Conrad, B.: Referenceless prediction of perceptual fog density and perceptual image defogging. IEEE Trans. Image Process. **24**, 3888–3901 (2015)

35. Ponomarenko, N., et al.: Color image database tid2013: peculiarities and preliminary results. In: European Workshop on Visual Information Processing (EUVIP), pp. 106–111. IEEE (2013)

Lightweight Single-Image Super-Resolution Network with Attentive Auxiliary Feature Learning

Xuehui Wang[1], Qing Wang[1], Yuzhi Zhao[2], Junchi Yan[3], Lei Fan[4], and Long Chen[1(✉)]

[1] School of Data and Computer Science, Sun Yat-sen University, Guangzhou, China
wangxh228@mail2.sysu.edu.cn, chenl46@mail.sysu.edu.cn
[2] City University of Hong Kong, Hong Kong, China
[3] Shanghai Jiao Tong University, Shanghai, China
[4] Northwestern University, Evanston, USA

Abstract. Despite convolutional network-based methods have boosted the performance of single image super-resolution (SISR), the huge computation costs restrict their practical applicability. In this paper, we develop a computation efficient yet accurate network based on the proposed attentive auxiliary features (A^2F) for SISR. Firstly, to explore the features from the bottom layers, the auxiliary feature from all the previous layers are projected into a common space. Then, to better utilize these projected auxiliary features and filter the redundant information, the channel attention is employed to select the most important common feature based on current layer feature. We incorporate these two modules into a block and implement it with a lightweight network. Experimental results on large-scale dataset demonstrate the effectiveness of the proposed model against the state-of-the-art (SOTA) SR methods. Notably, when parameters are less than 320k, A^2F outperforms SOTA methods for all scales, which proves its ability to better utilize the auxiliary features. Codes are available at https://github.com/wxxxxxxh/A2F-SR.

1 Introduction

Convolutional neural network (CNN) has been widely used for single image super-resolution (SISR) since the debut of SRCNN [1]. Most of the CNN-based SISR models [2–7] are deep and large. However, in the real world, the models often need to be run efficiently in embedded system like mobile phone with limited computational resources [8–13]. Thus, those methods are not proper for many practical SISR applications, and lightweight networks have been becoming an important way for practical SISR. Also, the model compression techniques can

Electronic supplementary material The online version of this chapter (https://doi.org/10.1007/978-3-030-69532-3_17) contains supplementary material, which is available to authorized users.

H. Ishikawa et al. (Eds.): ACCV 2020, LNCS 12623, pp. 268–285, 2021.
https://doi.org/10.1007/978-3-030-69532-3_17

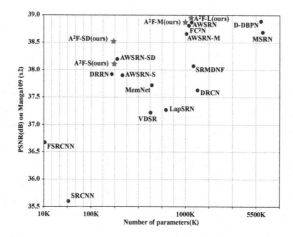

Fig. 1. Cost-effectiveness comparison between the proposed A^{2}F model variants (A^{2}F-S, A^{2}F-SD, A^{2}F-M, A^{2}F-L) with other methods on the Manga109 [19] on ×2 scale. The proposed models can achieve high PSNR with fewer parameters. Note that MSRN [20] and D-DBPN [21] are large models.

be used in lightweight architecture to further reduce the parameters and computation. However, before using model compression techniques (e.g. model pruning), it is time-consuming to train a large model and it also occupies more memory. This is unrealistic for some low budget devices, so CNN-based lightweight SISR methods become increasingly popular because it can be regarded as an image preprocessing or postprocessing instrument for other tasks [14–18].

One typical strategy is to reduce the parameters [22–25]. Moreover, the network architecture is essential for lightweight SISR models. Generally, methods of designing architectures can be categorized into two groups. One is based on neural architecture search. MoreMNA-S and FALSR [26,27] adopt the evolutionary algorithm to search efficient model architectures for lightweight SISR. The other is to design the models manually [28,29]. These methods all utilize features of previous layers to better learn the features of the current layer, which reflect that auxiliary features can boost the performance of lightweight models. However, these methods do not fully use all the features of previous layers, which possibly limits the performance.

Directly combining the auxiliary features with current features is conceptually problematic as features of different layers are often embedded in different space. Thus, we use the projection unit to project the auxiliary features to a common space that is suitable for fusing features. After projected to a common space, these projected features may not be all useful for learning features of the current layer. So we adopt the channel attention to make the model automatically assign the importance to different channels. The projection unit and channel attention constitute the proposed attentive auxiliary feature block.

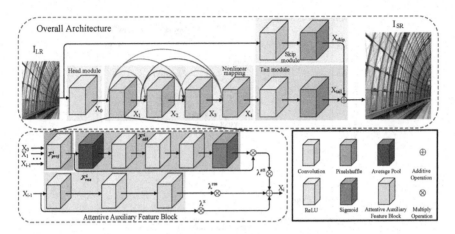

Fig. 2. The architecture of A^2F with 4 attentive auxiliary feature blocks. The architecture of A^2F with more attentive auxiliary feature blocks is similar. Note that 1×1 convolution kernel is used to project the auxiliary features and learn the importance of different channels of projected features. The convolution kernels elsewhere are all 3×3. The input is the LR image and the output is the predicted HR image. Pixelshuffle [24] is used to upsample the features to the high-resolution image with target size.

We term our model that consists of **A**ttentive **A**uxiliary **F**eature blocks as A^2F since it utilizes the auxilary features and the attention mechanism. Figure 1 gives the comparison between different models on Manga109 [19] dataset with a upscale factor of 2. As shown in Fig. 1, models of our A^2F family can achieve better efficiency than current SOTA methods [28,29]. Figure 2 describes the architecture of A^2F with four attentive auxiliary feature blocks. Our main contributions are given below:

- We handle the super resolution task from a new direction, which means we discuss the benefit brought by auxiliary features in the view of how to recover multi-frequency through different layers. Thus, we propose the attentive auxiliary feature block to utilize auxiliary features of previous layers for facilitating features learning of the current layer. The mainstay we use the channel attention is the dense auxiliary features rather than the backbone features or the sparse skip connections, which is different from other works.
- Compared with other lightweight methods especially when the parameters are less than 1000K, we outperform all of them both in PSNR and SSIM but have fewer parameters, which is an enormous trade-off between performance and parameters. In general, A^2F is able to achieve better efficiency than current state-of-the-art methods [28–30].
- Finally, we conduct a thorough ablation study to show the effectiveness of each component in the proposed attentive auxiliary feature block. We release our PyTorch implementation of the proposed method and its pretrained models together with the publication of the paper.

2   Related Work

Instead of powerful computers with GPU, embedded devices usually need to run a super resolution model. As a result, lightweight SR architectures are needed and have been recently proposed.

One pioneering work is SRCNN [1] which contains three convolution layers to directly map the low-resolution (LR) images to high-resolution (HR) images. Subsequently, a high-efficiency SR model named ESPCNN [24] was introduced, which extracts feature maps in LR space and contains a sub-pixel convolution layer that replaces the handcrafted bicubic filter to upscale the final LR map into the HR images. DRRN [25] also had been proposed to alleviate parameters by adopting recursive learning while increasing the depth. Then CARN [31] was proposed to obtain an accurate but lightweight result. It addresses the issue about heavy computation by utilizing the cascading mechanism for residual networks. More recently, AWSRN [28] was designed to decrease the heavy computation. It applies the local fusion block for residual learning. For lightweight network, it can remove redundancy scale branches according to the adaptive weights.

Feature fusion has undergone its tremendous progress since the ResNet [32] was proposed, which implies the auxiliary feature is becoming the crucial aspect for learning. The full utilization of the auxiliary feature was adopted in DenseNet [33]. The authors take the feature map of each former layer into a layer, and this alleviates the vanishing gradient problem. SR methods also make use of auxiliary features to improve performance, such as [2,7,25,34,35]. The local fusion block of AWSRN [28] consists of concatenated AWRUs and a LRFU. Each output of AWRUs is combined one by one, which means a dense connection for a block. A novel SR method called FC^{2}N was presented in [29]. A module named GFF was devised through implementing all skip connections by weighted channel concatenation, and it also can be considered as the auxiliary feature.

As an important technique for vision tasks, attention mechanism [36] can automatically determine which component is important for learning. Channel attention is a type of attention mechanism, which concentrates on the impact of each feature channel. SENet [37] is a channel attention based model in the image classification task. In the domain of SR, RCAN [7] had been introduced to elevate SR results by taking advantage of interdependencies among channels. It can adaptively rescale features according to the training target.

In our paper, auxiliaty features are not fully-dense connections, which indicates it is not dense in one block. We expect that each block can only learn to recover specific frequency information and provide auxiliary information to the next block. There are two main differences compared with FC^{2}N and AWSRN. One is that for a block of A^{2}F, we use the features of ALL previous blocks as auxiliary features of the current block, while FC^{2}N and AWSRN use the features of a FIXED number of previous blocks. The second is that we adopt channel attention to decide how to transmit different informations to the next block, but the other two works do not adopt this mechanism.

3 Proposed Model

3.1 Motivation and Overview

Our method is motivated by an interesting fact that many CNN based methods [3,29,31] can reconstruct the high frequency details from the low resolution images hierachically, which indicates that different layers learn the capacity of recovering multi-frequency information. However, stacking more layers increases the computation burden and higher frequency information is difficult to regain. So we aim to provide a fast, low-parameters and accurate method that can restore more high frequency details on the basis of ensuring the accuracy of low frequency information reconstruction. According to this goal, we have the following observations:

- To build a lightweight network, how to diminish parameters and the multiply operation is essential. Generally, we consider reducing the depth or the width of the network, performing upsampling operation at the end of the network and adopting small kernel to reach this target. It also brings a new issue that a shallow network (i.e. fewer layers and fewer channels in each layer) can not have an excellent training result due to the lower complexity of the model, which also can be considered as an under-fitting problem.
- For the limited depth and width of the network, feature reusing is the best way to solve the issue. By this way, the low-frequency information can be transmitted to the next layer easily and it is more useful to combine multi-level low-frequency features to obtain accurate high-frequency features. Thus, more features benefiting to recover high-frequency signal will circulate across the entire network. It will promote the capacity of learning the mapping function if the network is shallow.
- We also consider another problem that the impact of multi-frequency information should be different when used for the learning of high frequency features. As the depth of the layer becomes deeper, effective information of the last layer provided for current layer is becoming rarer, because the learning of high frequency features is more and more difficult. So how to combine the information of all the previous layers to bring an efficient result is important and it should be divided by the network.

Based on these observations, we design the model by reusing all features of the preceding layers and then concatenating them directly along channels like [33] in a block. Meanwhile, to reduce the disturbance brought by the redundant information when concatenating all of channels and adaptively obtain the multi-frequency reconstruction capability of different layers, we adopt the same-space attention mechanism in our model, which can avoid the situation that features from different space would cause extraodinary imbalance when computing the attention weight.

3.2 Overall Architecture

As shown in Fig. 2, the whole model architecture is divided into four components: head module, nonlinear mapping, skip module and tail module. Detailed configuration of each component can be seen in Table 1. We denote the low resolution and the predicted image as I_{LR} and I_{SR}, respectively. The input is first processed by the head module $\mathcal{F}_{head}$ to get the features x_0:

$$x_0 = \mathcal{F}_{head}(I_{LR}), \tag{1}$$

and $\mathcal{F}_{head}$ is just one 3×3 convolutional layer (Conv). We do not use 1×1 Conv in the first layer for it can not capture the spatial correlation and cause a information loss of the basic low frequency. The reason why we use a 3×3 Conv rather than a 5×5 Conv is twofold: a) 3×3 Conv can use fewer parameters to contribute to the lightweight of the network. b) It is not suitable to employ kernels with large receptive field in the task of super-resolution, especially for the first layer. Recall that each pixel in downsampled image corresponds to a mini-region in the original image. So during the training, large receptive field may introduce irrelevant information.

Then the nonlinear mapping which consists of L stacked attentive auxiliary feature blocks is used to further extract information from x_0. In the i_{th} attentive auxiliary feature block, the features x_i is extracted from all the features of the

Table 1. Configurations of the proposed method. We set $stride = 1$ for every convolutional operation to keep the same size in each layer. i indicates the i-th A^{2}F module and p means the scale factor. For the A^{2}F-SD model, we change the channels that are 32 in other models to 16 for each $\mathcal{F}$.

Function	Details	Kernel	Channels (Input, Output)
$\mathcal{F}_{head}$	Convolution	3×3	$(3, 32)$
$\mathcal{F}_{skip}$	Convolution	3×3	$(3, p*p*3)$
	PixelShuffle	–	–
$\mathcal{F}_{proj}^i$	Convolution	1×1	$(i*32, 32)$
$\mathcal{F}_{att}^i$	Adaptive AvgPool	–	–
	Convolution	1×1	$(32, 32)$
	ReLU	–	–
	Convolution	1×1	$(32, 32)$
	Sigmoid	–	–
$\mathcal{F}_{res}^i$	Convolution	3×3	$(32, 128)$
	ReLU	–	–
	Convolution	3×3	$(128, 32)$
$\mathcal{F}_{tail}$	Convolution	3×3	$(32, p*p*3)$
	PixelShuffle	–	–

previous blocks $x_0, x_1, x_2, ..., x_{i-1}$:

$$x_i = g^i_{AAF}(x_0, x_1, ..., x_{i-1}), \tag{2}$$

where g^i_{AAF} denotes attentive auxiliary feature block i.

After getting the features x_L from the last attentive auxiliary feature block, $\mathcal{F}_{tail}$, which is a 3×3 convolution layer followed by a pixelshuffle layer [24], is used to upsample x_L to the features x_{tail} with targe size:

$$x_{tail} = \mathcal{F}_{tail}(x_L). \tag{3}$$

We design this module to integrate the multi-frequency information produced by different blocks. It also correlates channels and spatial correlation, which is useful for pixelshuffle layer to rescale the image.

To make the mapping learning easier and introduce the original low frequency information to keep the accuracy of low frequency, the skip module $\mathcal{F}_{skip}$, which has the same component with $\mathcal{F}_{tail}$, is adopted to get the global residual information x_{skip}:

$$x_{skip} = \mathcal{F}_{skip}(I_{LR}). \tag{4}$$

Finally, the target I_{SR} is obtained by adding x_{skip} and x_{tail}:

$$I_{SR} = x_{tail} \oplus x_{skip}. \tag{5}$$

where $\oplus$ denotes the element-wise add operation.

3.3   Attentive Auxiliary Feature Block

The keypoint of the A^{2}F is that it adopts attentive auxiliary feature blocks to utilize all the usable features. Given features $x_0, x_1, ..., x_{i-1}$ from all previous blocks, it is improper to directly fuse with features of the current block because features of different blocks are in different feature spaces. Thus we need to project auxiliary features to a common-space that is suitable to be fused, which prevent features of different space from causing extraodinary imbalance for attention weights. In A^{2}F, 1×1 convolution layer $\mathcal{F}^i_{proj}$ is served as such a projection unit. The projected features of the i_{th} auxiliary block x^{proj}_i are obtained by

$$x^{proj}_i = \mathcal{F}^i_{proj}([x_0, x_1, ..., x_{i-1}]), \tag{6}$$

where $[x_0, x_1, ..., x_{i-1}]$ concatenates $x_0, x_1, ..., x_{i-1}$ along the channel. However, different channels of x^{proj}_i have different importance when being fused with features of current layer. Therefore, channel attention $\mathcal{F}^i_{att}$ is used to learn the importance factor of different channel of x^{proj}_i. In this way, we get the new features x^{att}_i by

$$x^{att}_i = \mathcal{F}^i_{att}(x^{proj}_i) \otimes x^{proj}_i, \tag{7}$$

where $\mathcal{F}^i_{att}$ consists of one average pooling layer, one 1×1 convolution layer, one ReLU layer, another 1×1 convolution layer and one sigmoid layer. The symbol

$\otimes$ means channel-wise multiplication. The block of WDSR_A [5] is adopted to get the features of current layer x_i^{res}:

$$x_i^{res} = \mathcal{F}_{res}^i(x_{i-1}), \tag{8}$$

where $\mathcal{F}_{res}^i$ consists of one 3×3 convolution layer, one ReLU layer and another 3×3 convolution layer. The output of i_{th} attentive auxiliary feature block x_i is given by:

$$x_i = \lambda_i^{res} \times x_i^{res} + \lambda_i^{att} \times x_i^{att} + \lambda_i^x \times x_{i-1}, \tag{9}$$

where λ_i^{res}, λ_i^{att} and λ_i^x are feature factors for different features like [28]. These feature factors will be learned automatically when training the model. Here we choose additive operation for it can better handle the situation that the λ_i^{att} of some auxiliary features is 0. If we concat channels directly, there will be some invalid channels which may increase the redundancy of the network. We can also reduce parameters by additive operation sin it does not expand channels.

4   Experiments

In this section, we first introduce some common datasets and metrics for evaluation. Then, we describe details of our experiment and analyze the effectiveness of our framework. Finally, we compare our model with state-of-the-art methods both in qualitation and quantitation to demonstrate the superiority of A²F. For more experiments please refer to the supplementary materials.

4.1   Dataset and Evaluation Metric

DIV2K dataset [38] with 800 training images is used in previous methods [28,29] for model training. When testing the performance of the models, Peak Signal to Noise Ratio (PSNR) and the Structural SIMilarity index (SSIM) [39] on the Y channel after converting to YCbCr channels are calculated on five benchmark datasets including Set5 [40], Set14 [41], B100 [42], Urban100 [43] and Manga109 [19]. We also adopt the LPIPS [44] as a perceptual metric to do comparison, which can avoid the situation that over-smoothed images may present a higher PSNR/SSIM when the performances of two methods are similar.

4.2   Implementation Details

Similar to AWSRN [28], we design four variants of A²F, denoted as A²F-S, A²F-SD, A²F-M and A²F-L. The channels of $\mathcal{F}_{res}^i$ in the attentive auxiliary feature block of A²F-S, A²F-M and A²F-L are set to {32,128,32} channels, which means the input, internal and output channel number of $\mathcal{F}_{res}^i$ is 32, 128, 32, respectively. The channels of $\mathcal{F}_{res}^i$ in the attentive auxiliary feature block of A²F-SD is set to {16,128,16}. For the A²F-SD model, we change all of the channels that are setted as 32 in A²F-S, A²F-M, A²F-L to 16. The number of the attentive auxiliary feature blocks of A²F-S, A²F-SD, A²F-M and A²F-L is 4, 8, 12, and 16, respectively. During the training process, typical data augmentation including horizontal flip, rotation and random rotations of 90°, 180°, 270° are used. The model is trained using Adam algorithm [45] with L1 loss. The initial value of λ_i^{res}, λ_i^{att} and λ_i^x are set to 1. All the code are developed using PyTorch on a machine with an NVIDIA 1080 Ti GPU.

4.3   Ablation Study

In this section, we first demonstrate the effectiveness of the proposed auxiliary features. Then, we conduct an ablation experiments to study the effect of essential components of our model and the selection of the kernel for the head component.

Effect of Auxiliary Features. To show the effect of auxiliary features, we plot the λ_i^{res}, λ_i^{att} and λ_{i-1}^x of each layer of each model in Fig. 3. As shown in Fig. 3, the value of λ_i^{att} are always bigger than 0.2, which reflects that the auxiliary features always play a certain role in generating the output features of the auxiliary features block. It can also be observed that in all the models of A^2F, the weight of x_i^{res} (i.e. λ_i^{res}) plays the most important role. The weight of x_{i-1} (i.e. λ_{i-1}^x) is usually larger than λ_i^{att}. However, for the more lightweight SISR models (i.e. A^2F-S and A^2F-SD), x_i^{att} becomes more and more important than x_{i-1} (i.e. λ_i^{att} becomes more and more larger than λ_{i-1}^x) as the number of layers increases. This reflects that auxiliary features may have great effects on the lightweight SISR models.

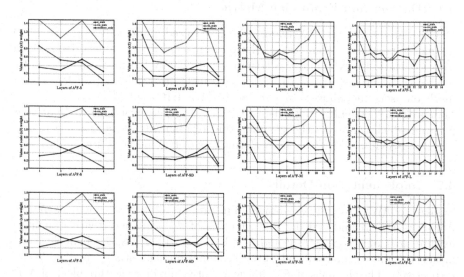

Fig. 3. The weight of λ_i^{res} (res_scale), λ_i^{att} (auxiliary_scale) and λ_{i-1}^x (x_scale) in different layers. From top to bottom are the results on the $\times 2$, $\times 3$, $\times 4$ tasks. From left to right are the results of models A^2F-S, A^2F-SD, A^2F-M and A^2F-L.

Table 2. Results of ablation study on the projection unit and the channel attention. PSNR is calculated on the super-resolution task with a scale factor of 2. PU means projection unit and CA means channel attention. "MP" in the model means more parameters.

Model	PU	CA	Param	MutiAdds	Set5	Set14	B100	Urban100	Manga109
BASELINE			1190K	273.9G	38.04	33.69	32.20	32.20	38.66
BASELINE-MP			1338K	308.0G	38.09	33.70	32.21	32.25	38.69
A^{2}F-L-NOCA	√		1329K	306.0G	38.08	33.75	32.23	32.39	38.79
A^{2}F-L-NOCA-MP	√		1368K	315.1G	38.09	33.77	32.23	32.35	38.79
A^{2}F-L	√	√	1363K	306.1G	**38.09**	**33.78**	**32.23**	**32.46**	**38.95**

Effect of Projection Unit and Channel Attention. To evaluate the performance of the projection unit and channel attention in the attentive auxiliary feature block, WDSR_A [5] with 16 layers is used as the BASELINE model. Then we drop the channel attention in the attentive auxiliary feature block and such model is denoted as A^{2}F-L-NOCA. To further prove the performance gain comes from the proposed attention module, we perform an experiment as follows: we increase the number of parameters of BASELINE and A^{2}F-L-NOCA, and we denote these models as BASELINE-MP and A^{2}F-L-NOCA-MP, where MP means more parameters. Table 2 shows that comparing the results of BASELINE, BASELINE-MP and A^{2}F-L-NOCA, we can find that projection unit with auxiliary features can boost the performance on all the datasets. Comparing the results of A^{2}F-L-NOCA, A^{2}F-L-NOCA-MP, A^{2}F-L, it can be found that channel attention in the attentive auxiliary feature block further improves the performance. Thus, we draw the conclusion that the projection unit and channel attention in the auxiliary can both better explore the auxiliary features. In our supplementary materials, we also do this ablation study on a challengeable case (i.e. A^{2}F-S for x4) to show that the good using of auxiliary features is especially important for shallow networks.

Table 3. Results of ablation study on different kernel size which is only used for head component. Note that other convolutional kernels are same.

Convolutional Kernel Selection						
Kernel	Parameters	Set5	Set14	B100	Urban100	Manga109
1×1	319.2K	32.00	28.46	27.46	25.78	30.13
$\mathbf{3 \times 3}$	**319.6K**	**32.06**	**28.47**	**27.48**	**25.80**	**30.16**
5×5	320.4K	32.00	28.45	27.48	25.80	38.13
7×7	321.6K	31.99	28.44	27.48	25.78	30.10

Kernel Selection for $\mathcal{F}_{head}$. We select different size of kernels in $\mathcal{F}_{head}$ to verify that 1×1 conv and large receptive field are not suitable for the head component. From Table 3, we can observe both of them have whittled the performance of the network. This result verifies the reasonability of our head component which has been introduced in Sect. 3.2

4.4   Comparison with State-of-the-Art Methods

We report an exhaustive comparative evaluation, comparing with several high performance but low parameters and multi-adds operations methods on five datasets, including FSRCNN [22], DRRN [25], FALSR [26], CARN [31], VDSR [2], MemNet [34], LapSRN [46], AWSRN [28], DRCN [23], MSRN [20], SRMDNF [47], SelNet [48], IDN [49], SRFBN-S [30] and so on. Note that we do not consider methods that have significant performance such as RDN [35], RCAN [7], EDSR [3] for they have nearly even more than 10M parameters. It is unrealistic to apply the method in real-world application though they have higher PSNR. But we provide a supplementary material to compare with these non-lightweight SOTAs. To ensure that parameters of different methods are at the same magnitude, we divide the comparison experiment on a single scale into multi-group according to different parameters. All methods including ours have been evaluated on ×2, ×3, ×4.

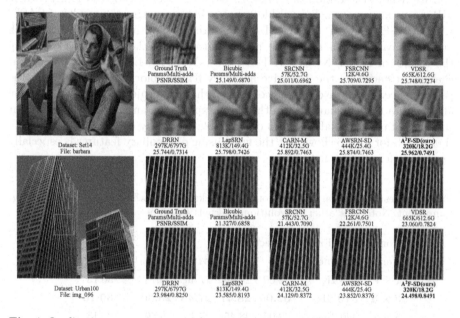

Fig. 4. Qualitative comparison over datasets for scale ×4. The red rectangle indicates the area of interest for zooming. Comparison for other two datasets can be seen supplementary material.

Table 4. Running time comparison with ×4 scale on Urban100 dataset. All of them are evaluated on the same mechine.

Model	Params	Multi-Adds	Running time(s)	PSNR
RCAN [7]	15590K	919.9G	0.8746	26.82
EDSR [3]	43090K	2896.3G	0.3564	26.64
D-DBPN [21]	10430K	685.7G	0.4174	26.38
SRFBN [30]	3631K	1128.7G	0.4291	26.60
SRFBN-S [30]	483K	132.5G	0.0956	25.71
VDSR [2]	665K	612.6G	0.1165	25.18
CARN-M [31]	412K	32.5G	0.0326	25.62
A²F-SD	**320K**	**18.2G**	**0.0145**	**25.80**
A²F-L	**1374K**	**77.2G**	**0.0324**	**26.32**

Qualitative Comparison. Qualitative comparison is shown in Fig. 4. We choose methods whose parameters are less than 1000k since we think high efficiency (low parameters) is essential. We can see that our method A²F-SD achieves better performance than others, which is represented through recovering more high-frequency information for the entire image. For the image barbara in Set14 (row 1 in Fig. 4), our method performs a clear difference between the blue area and the apricot area on the right top corner of the image. Compared with AWSRN-SD which is the second method in our table, our model removes more blur and constructs more regular texture on the right top corner of the image img096 of Urban100. We own this advantage to the sufficient using of auxiliary features of previous layers which incorporate multi-scale features in different convolution progress that might contain abundant multi-frequency information. While the attention mechanism conduces to the adaptive selection of different frequency among various layers.

Quantitative Comparison. Table 6 shows the detailed comparison results. Our models obtain a great trade-off between performance and parameters. In particular, when the number of parameters is less than 1000K, our model achieves the best result for arbitrary scales on each dataset among all of the algorithms. A²F-SD, which only has about 300K parameters, even shows better performance on a variety of datasets compared to DRCN that has nearly 1800K parameters. This proves the tremendous potential of A²F for real-world application. The high efficiency of A²F comes from the mechnism of sufficient fusion of former layers feature via the proposed attention scheme. Because we adopt 1×1 Conv and channel attention to select the appropriate features of former layers for fusing, which can help to reduce the number of layers in the network without sacrificing good performance. When the number of parameters is more than 1000K, A²F-L model also performs a SOTA result on the whole, although worse in some cases slightly. It is due to that they combine all features of former layers without considering whether they are useful, which cause a reduction to performance.

While compared to AWSRN-M and AWSRN, A^2F-M model has more advantage in trade-off since it has comparable PSNR and SSIM but only 1010K parameters that account for 63%, 80% of AWSRN and AWSRN-M, respectively.

4.5   Running Time and GFLOPS

We compare our model A^2F-SD and A^2F-L with other methods (both lightweight [2,30,31] and non-lightweight [3,7,21]) in running time to verify the high efficiency of our work in Table 4. Like [30], we evaluate our method on a same machine with four NVIDIA 1080Ti GPUs and 3.6 GHz Intel i7 CPU. All of the codes are official implementation. To be fair, we only use a single NVIDIA 1080Ti GPU for evaluation, and only contain codes that are necessary for testing an image, which means operations of saving images, saving models, opening log files, appending extra datas and so on are removed from the timing program.

To reduce the accidental error, we evaluate each method for four times on each GPU and calculate the average time as the final running time for a method. Table 4 shows that our models represent a significant surpass on running time for an image compared with other methods, even our A^2F-L model is three times faster than SRFBN-S [30] which has only 483K parameters with 25.71 PSNR. All of our models are highly efficient and keep being less comparable with RCAN [7] which are 60 and 27 times slower than our A^2F-SD, and A^2F-L model, respectively. This comparison result reflects that our method gets the tremendous trade-off between performance and running time and is the best choice for realistic applications.

We also calculate the GFLOPs based on the input size of 32×32 for several methods that can be comparable with A^2F in Table 5. We actually get high performance with lower GFLOPs both for our large and small models.

Table 5. The perceptual metric LPIPS on five datasets for scale ×4. The lower is better. We only choose methods that can be comparable with A^2F. All of the output SR images are provided officially.

Methods	Params	GFLOPs	Set5	Set14	B100	Urban100	Manga109
AWSRN [28]	1587K	1.620G	0.1747	0.2853	0.3692	0.2198	0.1058
AWSRN-SD [28]	444K	–	0.1779	0.2917	0.3838	0.2468	0.1168
CARN [31]	1592K	1.620G	0.1761	0.2893	0.3799	0.2363	–
CARN-M [31]	412K	0.445G	0.1777	0.2938	0.3850	0.2524	–
SRFBN-S [30]	483K	0.323G	0.1776	0.2938	0.3861	0.2554	0.1396
IMDN [50]	715K	0.729G	0.1743	0.2901	0.3740	0.2350	0.1330
A^2F-SD	320K	0.321G	0.1731	0.2870	0.3761	0.2375	0.1112
A^2F-L	1374K	1.370G	0.1733	0.2846	0.3698	0.2194	0.1056

4.6   Perceptual Metric

Perceptual metric can better reflect the judgment of image quality. In this paper, LPIPS [44] is chosen as the perceptual metric. From Table 5, our proposed model obtains superior results with high efficiency in most cases, which shows their ability of generating more realistic images.

Table 6. Evaluation on five datasets by scale ×2, ×3, ×4. Red and blue imply the best and second best result in a group, respectively.

Scale	Size Scope	Model	Param	MutiAdds	Set5	Set14	B100	Urban100	Manga109
x2	< 5 × 10²K	FSRCNN	12K	6G	37.00/0.9558	32.63/0.9088	31.53/0.8920	29.88/0.9020	36.67/0.9694
		SRCNN	57K	52.7G	36.66/0.9542	32.42/0.9063	31.36/0.8879	29.50/0.8946	35.74/0.9661
		DRRN	297K	6797G	37.74/0.9591	33.23/0.9136	32.05/0.8973	31.23/0.9188	37.92/0.9760
		A²F-SD(ours)	313k	71.2G	37.91/0.9602	33.45/0.9164	32.08/0.8986	31.79/0.9246	38.52/0.9767
		A²F-S(ours)	320k	71.7G	37.79/0.9597	33.32/0.9152	31.99/0.8972	31.44/0.9211	38.11/0.9757
		FALSR-B	326K	74.7G	37.61/0.9585	33.29/0.9143	31.97/0.8967	31.28/0.9191	-
		AWSRN-SD	348K	79.6G	37.86/0.9600	33.41/0.9161	32.07/0.8984	31.67/0.9237	38.20/0.9762
		AWSRN-S	397K	91.2G	37.75/0.9596	33.31/0.9151	32.00/0.8974	31.39/0.9207	37.90/0.9755
		FALSR-C	408K	93.7G	37.66/0.9586	33.26/0.9140	31.96/0.8965	31.24/0.9187	-
		CARN-M	412K	91.2G	37.53/0.9583	33.26/0.9141	31.92/0.8960	31.23/0.9193	-
		SRFBN-S	483K	-	37.78/0.9597	33.35/0.9156	32.00/0.8970	31.41/0.9207	38.06/0.9757
	< 10³K	IDN	552K	-	37.83/0.9600	33.30/0.9148	32.08/0.8985	31.27/0.9196	-
		VDSR	665K	612.6G	37.53/0.9587	33.03/0.9124	31.90/0.8960	30.76/0.9140	37.22/0.9729
		MemNet	677K	2662.4G	37.78/0.9597	33.28/0.9142	32.08/0.8978	31.31/0.9195	-
		LapSRN	813K	29.9G	37.52/0.9590	33.08/0.9130	31.80/0.8950	30.41/0.9100	37.27/0.9740
		SelNet	974K	225.7G	37.89/0.9598	33.61/0.9160	32.08/0.8984	-	-
		A²F-M(ours)	999k	224.2G	38.04/0.9607	33.67/0.9184	32.18/0.8996	32.27/0.9294	38.87/0.9774
	< 2 × 10³K	FALSR-A	1021K	234.7G	37.82/0.9595	33.55/0.9168	32.12/0.8987	31.93/0.9256	-
		MoreMNAS-A	1039K	238.6G	37.63/0.9584	33.23/0.9138	31.95/0.8961	31.24/0.9187	-
		AWSRN-M	1063K	244.1G	38.04/0.9605	33.66/0.9181	32.21/0.9000	32.23/0.9294	38.66/0.9772
		A²F-L(ours)	1363k	306.1G	38.09/0.9607	33.78/0.9192	32.23/0.9002	32.46/0.9313	38.95/0.9772
		AWSRN	1397K	320.5G	38.11/0.9608	33.78/0.9189	32.26/0.9006	32.49/0.9316	38.87/0.9776
		SRMDNF	1513K	347.7G	37.79/0.9600	33.32/0.9150	32.05/0.8980	31.33/0.9200	-
		CARN	1592K	222.8G	37.76/0.9590	33.52/0.9166	32.09/0.8978	31.92/0.9256	-
		DRCN	1774K	17974G	37.63/0.9588	33.04/0.9118	31.85/0.8942	30.75/0.9133	37.63/0.9723
	< 5 × 10³K	MSRN	5930K	1365.4G	38.08/0.9607	33.70/0.9186	32.23/0.9002	32.29/0.9303	38.69/0.9772
x3	< 10³K	FSRCNN	12K	5G	33.16/0.9140	29.43/0.8242	28.53/0.7910	26.43/0.8080	30.98/0.9212
		SRCNN	57K	52.7G	32.75/0.9090	29.28/0.8209	28.41/0.7863	26.24/0.7989	30.59/0.9107
		DRRN	297K	6797G	34.03/0.9244	29.96/0.8349	28.95/0.8004	27.53/0.8378	32.74/0.9390
		A²F-SD(ours)	316k	31.9G	34.23/0.9259	30.22/0.8395	29.01/0.8028	27.91/0.8465	33.29/0.9424
		A²F-S(ours)	324k	32.3G	34.06/0.9241	30.08/0.8370	28.92/0.8006	27.57/0.8392	32.86/0.9394
		AWSRN-SD	388K	39.5G	34.18/0.9273	30.21/0.8398	28.99/0.8027	27.80/0.8444	33.13/0.9416
		CARN-M	412K	46.1G	33.99/0.9236	30.08/0.8367	28.91/0.8000	27.55/0.8385	-
		AWSRN-S	477K	48.6G	34.02/0.9240	30.09/0.8376	28.92/0.8009	27.57/0.8391	32.82/0.9393
		SRFBN-S	483K	-	34.20/0.9255	30.10/0.8372	28.96/0.8010	27.66/0.8415	33.02/0.9404
		IDN	552K	-	34.11/0.9253	29.99/0.8354	28.95/0.8013	27.42/0.8359	-
		VDSR	665K	612.6G	33.66/0.9213	29.77/0.8314	28.82/0.7976	27.14/0.8279	32.01/0.9310
		MemNet	677K	2662.4G	34.09/0.9248	30.00/0.8350	28.96/0.8001	27.56/0.8376	-
	< 2 × 10³K	A²F-M(ours)	1003k	100.0G	34.50/0.9278	30.39/0.8427	29.11/0.8054	28.28/0.8546	33.66/0.9453
		AWSRN-M	1143K	116.6G	34.42/0.9275	30.32/0.8419	29.13/0.8059	28.26/0.8545	33.64/0.9450
		SelNet	1159K	120G	34.27/0.9257	30.30/0.8399	28.97/0.8025	-	-
		A²F-L(ours)	1367k	136.3G	34.54/0.9283	30.41/0.8436	29.14/0.8062	28.40/0.8574	33.83/0.9463
		AWSRN	1476K	150.6G	34.52/0.9281	30.38/0.8426	29.16/0.8069	28.42/0.8580	33.85/0.9463
		SRMDNF	1530K	156.3G	34.12/0.9250	30.04/0.8370	28.97/0.8030	27.57/0.8400	-
		CARN	1592K	118.8G	34.29/0.9255	30.29/0.8407	29.06/0.8034	28.06/0.8493	-
		DRCN	1774K	17974G	33.82/0.9226	29.76/0.8311	28.80/0.7963	27.15/0.8276	32.31/0.9328
	< 10⁴K	MSRN	6114K	625.7G	34.46/0.9278	30.41/0.8437	29.15/0.8064	28.33/0.8561	33.67/0.9456
x4	< 10³K	FSRCNN	12K	4.6G	30.71/0.8657	27.59/0.7535	26.98/0.7150	24.62/0.7280	27.90/0.8517
		SRCNN	57K	52.7G	30.48/0.8628	27.49/0.7503	26.90/0.7101	24.52/0.7221	27.66/0.8505
		DRRN	297K	6797G	31.68/0.8888	28.21/0.7720	27.38/0.7284	25.44/0.7638	29.46/0.8960
		A²F-SD(ours)	320k	18.2G	32.06/0.8928	28.47/0.7790	27.48/0.7373	25.80/0.7767	30.16/0.9038
		A²F-S(ours)	331k	18.6G	31.87/0.8900	28.36/0.7760	27.41/0.7305	25.58/0.7685	29.77/0.8987
		CARN-M	412K	32.5G	31.92/0.8903	28.42/0.7762	27.44/0.7304	25.62/0.7694	-
		AWSRN-SD	444K	25.4G	31.98/0.8921	28.46/0.7786	27.48/0.7368	25.74/0.7746	30.09/0.9024
		SRFBN-S	483K	132.5G	31.98/0.8923	28.45/0.7779	27.44/0.7313	25.71/0.7719	29.91/0.9008
		IDN	552K	-	31.82/0.8903	28.25/0.7730	27.41/0.7297	25.41/0.7632	-
		AWSRN	588K	37.7G	31.77/0.8893	28.35/0.7761	27.41/0.7304	25.56/0.7678	29.74/0.8982
		VDSR	665K	612.6G	31.35/0.8838	28.01/0.7674	27.29/0.7251	25.18/0.7524	28.83/0.8809
		MemNet	677K	2662.4G	31.74/0.8893	28.26/0.7723	27.40/0.7281	25.50/0.7630	-
		LapSRN	813K	149.4G	31.54/0.8850	28.19/0.7720	27.32/0.7280	25.21/0.7560	29.09/0.8845
	< 2 × 10³K	A²F-M(ours)	1010k	56.7G	32.28/0.8955	28.62/0.7828	27.58/0.7364	26.17/0.7892	30.57/0.9100
		AWSRN-M	1254K	72G	32.21/0.8954	28.65/0.7832	27.60/0.7368	26.15/0.7884	30.56/0.9093
		A²F-L(ours)	1374K	77.2G	32.32/0.8964	28.67/0.7839	27.62/0.7379	26.32/0.7931	30.72/0.9115
		SelNet	1417K	83.1G	32.00/0.8931	28.49/0.7783	27.44/0.7325	-	-
		SRMDNF	1555K	89.3G	31.96/0.8930	28.35/0.7770	27.49/0.7340	25.68/0.7730	-
		AWSRN	1587K	91.1G	32.27/0.8960	28.69/0.7843	27.64/0.7385	26.29/0.7930	30.72/0.9109
		CARN	1592K	90.9G	32.13/0.8937	28.60/0.7806	27.58/0.7349	26.07/0.7837	-
		DRCN	1774K	17974G	31.53/0.8854	28.02/0.7670	27.23/0.7233	25.14/0.7510	28.98/0.8816
	< 10⁴K	SRDenseNet	2015K	389.9K	32.02/0.8934	28.35/0.7770	27.53/0.7337	26.05/0.7819	-
		MSRN	6078K	349.8G	32.26/0.8960	28.63/0.7836	27.61/0.7380	26.22/0.7911	30.57/0.9103

5   Conclusion

In this paper, we propose a lightweight single-image super-resolution network called A^{2}F which adopts attentive auxiliary feature blocks to efficiently and sufficiently utilize auxiliary features. Quantitive experiment results demonstrate that auxiliary features with projection unit and channel attention can achieve higher PSNR and SSIM as well as perceptual metric LPIPS with less running time on various datasets. Qualitative experiment results reflect that auxiliary features can give the predicted image more high-frequency information, thus making the models achieve better performance. The A^{2}F model with attentive auxiliary feature block is easy to implement and achieves great performance when the number of parameters is less than 320K and the multi-adds are less than 75G, which shows that it has great potential to be deployed in practical applications with limited computation resources. In the future, we will investigate more measures to better fuse auxiliary features.

Acknowledgement. This work was supported in part by the National Key Research and Development Program of China under Grant 2018YFB1305002, in part by the National Natural Science Foundation of China under Grant 61773414, and Grant 61972250, in part by the Key Research and Development Program of Guangzhou under Grant 202007050002, and Grant 202007050004.

References

1. Dong, C., Loy, C.C., He, K., Tang, X.: Image super-resolution using deep convolutional networks. IEEE Trans. Pattern Anal. Mach. Intell. **38**, 295–307 (2015)
2. Kim, J., Kwon Lee, J., Mu Lee, K.: Accurate image super-resolution using very deep convolutional networks. In: Proceedings of the IEEE Conference on Computer Vision and Pattern Recognition, pp. 1646–1654 (2016)
3. Lim, B., Son, S., Kim, H., Nah, S., Mu Lee, K.: Enhanced deep residual networks for single image super-resolution. In: Proceedings of the IEEE Conference on Computer Vision and Pattern Recognition Workshops, pp. 136–144 (2017)
4. Tong, T., Li, G., Liu, X., Gao, Q.: Image super-resolution using dense skip connections. In: Proceedings of the IEEE International Conference on Computer Vision, pp. 4799–4807 (2017)
5. Yu, J., Fan, Y., Yang, J., Xu, N., Wang, Z., Wang, X., Huang, T.: Wide activation for efficient and accurate image super-resolution. arXiv preprint arXiv:1808.08718 (2018)
6. Zhang, K., Wang, B., Zuo, W., Zhang, H., Zhang, L.: Joint learning of multiple regressors for single image super-resolution. IEEE Signal Process. Lett. **23**, 102–106 (2015)
7. Zhang, Y., Li, K., Li, K., Wang, L., Zhong, B., Fu, Y.: Image super-resolution using very deep residual channel attention networks. In: Proceedings of the European Conference on Computer Vision (ECCV), pp. 286–301 (2018)
8. Chen, L., Zhan, W., Tian, W., He, Y., Zou, Q.: Deep integration: a multi-label architecture for road scene recognition. IEEE Trans. Image Process. **28**, 4883–4898 (2019)

9. Hsiao, P.-H., Chang, P.-L.: Video enhancement via super-resolution using deep quality transfer network. In: Lai, S.-H., Lepetit, V., Nishino, K., Sato, Y. (eds.) ACCV 2016. LNCS, vol. 10113, pp. 184–200. Springer, Cham (2017). https://doi.org/10.1007/978-3-319-54187-7_13

10. Peled, S., Yeshurun, Y.: Superresolution in MRI: application to human white matter fiber tract visualization by diffusion tensor imaging. J. Int. Soc. Magn. Resonan. Med. **45**, 29–35 (2001)

11. Shi, W., et al.: Cardiac image super-resolution with global correspondence using multi-atlas PatchMatch. In: Mori, K., Sakuma, I., Sato, Y., Barillot, C., Navab, N. (eds.) MICCAI 2013. LNCS, vol. 8151, pp. 9–16. Springer, Heidelberg (2013). https://doi.org/10.1007/978-3-642-40760-4_2

12. Valmadre, J., Bertinetto, L., Henriques, J., Vedaldi, A., Torr, P.H.: End-to-end representation learning for correlation filter based tracking. In: Proceedings of the IEEE Conference on Computer Vision and Pattern Recognition, pp. 2805–2813 (2017)

13. Zhang, L., Zhang, H., Shen, H., Li, P.: A super-resolution reconstruction algorithm for surveillance images. Sig. Process. **90**, 848–859 (2010)

14. Yang, X., Yan, J.: Arbitrary-oriented object detection with circular smooth label. In: Vedaldi, A., Bischof, H., Brox, T., Frahm, J.-M. (eds.) ECCV 2020. LNCS, vol. 12353, pp. 677–694. Springer, Cham (2020). https://doi.org/10.1007/978-3-030-58598-3_40

15. Chen, L., et al.: Surrounding vehicle detection using an FPGA panoramic camera and deep CNNs. IEEE Trans. Intell. Transp. Syst. **21**, 5110–5122 (2019)

16. Shen, W., Guo, Y., Wang, Y., Zhao, K., Wang, B., Yuille, A.L.: Deep differentiable random forests for age estimation. IEEE Trans. Pattern Anal. Mach. Intell. **43**, 404–419 (2019)

17. Yang, X., et al.: Scrdet: towards more robust detection for small, cluttered and rotated objects. In: Proceedings of the IEEE International Conference on Computer Vision, pp. 8232–8241 (2019)

18. Chen, L., Wang, Q., Lu, X., Cao, D., Wang, F.Y.: Learning driving models from parallel end-to-end driving data set. Proc. IEEE **108**, 262–273 (2019)

19. Matsui, Y., et al.: Sketch-based manga retrieval using manga109 dataset. Multimedia Tools Appl. **76**, 21811–21838 (2017). https://doi.org/10.1007/s11042-016-4020-z

20. Li, J., Fang, F., Mei, K., Zhang, G.: Multi-scale residual network for image super-resolution. In: Proceedings of the European Conference on Computer Vision (ECCV), pp. 517–532 (2018)

21. Haris, M., Shakhnarovich, G., Ukita, N.: Deep back-projection networks for super-resolution. In: Proceedings of the IEEE Conference on Computer Vision and Pattern Recognition, pp. 1664–1673 (2018)

22. Dong, C., Loy, C.C., Tang, X.: Accelerating the super-resolution convolutional neural network. In: Leibe, B., Matas, J., Sebe, N., Welling, M. (eds.) ECCV 2016. LNCS, vol. 9906, pp. 391–407. Springer, Cham (2016). https://doi.org/10.1007/978-3-319-46475-6_25

23. Kim, J., Kwon Lee, J., Mu Lee, K.: Deeply-recursive convolutional network for image super-resolution. In: Proceedings of the IEEE Conference on Computer Vision and Pattern Recognition, pp. 1637–1645 (2016)

24. Shi, W., et al.: Real-time single image and video super-resolution using an efficient sub-pixel convolutional neural network. In: Proceedings of the IEEE Conference on Computer Vision and Pattern Recognition, pp. 1874–1883 (2016)

25. Tai, Y., Yang, J., Liu, X.: Image super-resolution via deep recursive residual network. In: Proceedings of the IEEE Conference on Computer Vision and Pattern Recognition, pp. 3147–3155 (2017)
26. Chu, X., Zhang, B., Ma, H., Xu, R., Li, J., Li, Q.: Fast, accurate and lightweight super-resolution with neural architecture search. arXiv preprint arXiv:1901.07261 (2019)
27. Chu, X., Zhang, B., Xu, R., Ma, H.: Multi-objective reinforced evolution in mobile neural architecture search. arXiv preprint arXiv:1901.01074 (2019)
28. Wang, C., Li, Z., Shi, J.: Lightweight image super-resolution with adaptive weighted learning network. arXiv preprint arXiv:1904.02358 (2019)
29. Zhao, X., Liao, Y., Lfi, Y., Zhang, T., Zou, X.: Fc2n: fully channel-concatenated network for single image super-resolution. arXiv preprint arXiv:1907.03221 (2019)
30. Li, Z., Yang, J., Liu, Z., Yang, X., Jeon, G., Wu, W.: Feedback network for image super-resolution. In: Proceedings of the IEEE Conference on Computer Vision and Pattern Recognition, pp. 3867–3876 (2019)
31. Ahn, N., Kang, B., Sohn, K.A.: Fast, accurate, and lightweight super-resolution with cascading residual network. In: Proceedings of the European Conference on Computer Vision (ECCV), pp. 252–268 (2018)
32. He, K., Zhang, X., Ren, S., Sun, J.: Deep residual learning for image recognition. In: Proceedings of the IEEE Conference on Computer Vision and Pattern Recognition, pp. 770–778 (2016)
33. Huang, G., Liu, Z., Van Der Maaten, L., Weinberger, K.Q.: Densely connected convolutional networks. In: Proceedings of the IEEE Conference on Computer Vision and Pattern Recognition, pp. 4700–4708 (2017)
34. Tai, Y., Yang, J., Liu, X., Xu, C.: Memnet: a persistent memory network for image restoration. In: Proceedings of the IEEE International Conference on Computer Vision, pp. 4539–4547 (2017)
35. Zhang, Y., Tian, Y., Kong, Y., Zhong, B., Fu, Y.: Residual dense network for image super-resolution. In: Proceedings of the IEEE Conference on Computer Vision and Pattern Recognition, pp. 2472–2481 (2018)
36. Bahdanau, D., Cho, K., Bengio, Y.: Neural machine translation by jointly learning to align and translate. arXiv preprint arXiv:1409.0473 (2014)
37. Hu, J., Shen, L., Sun, G.: Squeeze-and-excitation networks. In: Proceedings of the IEEE Conference on Computer Vision and Pattern Recognition, pp. 7132–7141 (2018)
38. Agustsson, E., Timofte, R.: Ntire 2017 challenge on single image super-resolution: dataset and study. In: The IEEE Conference on Computer Vision and Pattern Recognition (CVPR) Workshops (2017)
39. Wang, Z., Bovik, A.C., Sheikh, H.R., Simoncelli, E.P.: Image quality assessment: from error visibility to structural similarity. IEEE Trans. Image Process. 13, 600–612 (2004)
40. Bevilacqua, M., Roumy, A., Guillemot, C., Alberi-Morel, M.L.: Low-complexity single-image super-resolution based on nonnegative neighbor embedding (2012)
41. Yang, J., Wright, J., Huang, T.S., Ma, Y.: Image super-resolution via sparse representation. IEEE Trans. Image Process. 19, 2861–2873 (2010)
42. Martin, D., Fowlkes, C., Tal, D., Malik, J., et al.: A database of human segmented natural images and its application to evaluating segmentation algorithms and measuring ecological statistics, ICCV Vancouver (2001)
43. Huang, J.B., Singh, A., Ahuja, N.: Single image super-resolution from transformed self-exemplars. In: Proceedings of the IEEE Conference on Computer Vision and Pattern Recognition, pp. 5197–5206 (2015)

44. Zhang, R., Isola, P., Efros, A.A., Shechtman, E., Wang., O.: The unreasonable effectiveness of deep features as a perceptual metric. In: Proceedings of the IEEE Conference on Computer Vision and Pattern Recognition, (2018)
45. Kingma, D.P., Ba, J.: Adam: a method for stochastic optimization. arXiv preprint arXiv:1412.6980 (2014)
46. Lai, W.S., Huang, J.B., Ahuja, N., Yang, M.H.: Deep Laplacian pyramid networks for fast and accurate super-resolution. In: Proceedings of the IEEE Conference on Computer Vision and Pattern Recognition, pp. 624–632 (2017)
47. Zhang, K., Zuo, W., Zhang, L.: Learning a single convolutional super-resolution network for multiple degradations. In: Proceedings of the IEEE Conference on Computer Vision and Pattern Recognition, pp. 3262–3271 (2018)
48. Choi, J.S., Kim, M.: A deep convolutional neural network with selection units for super-resolution. In: Proceedings of the IEEE Conference on Computer Vision and Pattern Recognition Workshops, pp. 154–160 (2017)
49. Hui, Z., Wang, X., Gao, X.: Fast and accurate single image super-resolution via information distillation network. In: Proceedings of the IEEE Conference on Computer Vision and Pattern Recognition, pp. 723–731 (2018)
50. Hui, Z., Gao, X., Yang, Y., Wang, X.: Lightweight image super-resolution with information multidistillation network. In: ACM Multimedia (2019)

Multi-scale Attentive Residual Dense Network for Single Image Rain Removal

Xiang Chen[1], Yufeng Huang[1(✉)], and Lei Xu[2]

[1] Shenyang Aerospace University, Shenyang 110136, China
cx@cvgpu.com, yufengh_sau@sina.com
[2] Shenyang Fire Science and Technology Research Institute of MEM,
Shenyang 110034, China
xulei@syfri.cn

Abstract. Single image deraining is an urgent yet challenging task since rain streaks severely degrade the image quality and hamper the practical application. The investigation on rain removal has thus been attracting, while the performances of existing deraining have limitations owing to over smoothing effect, poor generalization capability and rain intensity varies both in spatial locations and color channels. To address these issues, we proposed a Multi-scale Attentive Residual Dense Network called MARD-Net in end-to-end manner, to exactly extract the negative rain streaks from rainy images while precisely preserving the image details. The architecture of modified dense network can be used to exploit the rain streaks details representation through feature reuse and propagation. Further, the Multi-scale Attentive Residual Block (MARB) is involved in the dense network to guide the rain streaks feature extraction and representation capability. Since contextual information is very critical for deraining, MARB first uses different convolution kernels along with fusion to extract multi-scale rain features and employs feature attention module to identify rain streaks regions and color channels, as well as has the skip connections to aggregate features at multiple levels and accelerate convergence. The proposed method is extensively evaluated on several frequent-use synthetic and real-world datasets. The quantitative and qualitative results show that the designed framework performs better than the recent state-of-the-art deraining approaches on promoting the rain removal performance and preserving image details under various rain streaks cases.

1 Introduction

Images captured under outside conditions often affect by rain drops/streaks, which alter the image color and obstruct or distort content [1–3]. The visibility degradations and artifacts severely hinder the performance of computer vision tasks, like target detection [4], object tracking [5] and image recognition [6].

Xi. Chen and Y. Huang—Authors contributed equally to this work, listed alphabetically.

© Springer Nature Switzerland AG 2021
H. Ishikawa et al. (Eds.): ACCV 2020, LNCS 12623, pp. 286–300, 2021.
https://doi.org/10.1007/978-3-030-69532-3_18

Hence, rain removal has become an important preprocessing step and attracted much attention lately in the pattern recognition and computer vision [7–11].

In the recent years, various researches have been proposed for the single image deraining, and existing methods can be roughly divided into two categories: model-based and data-driven approaches [12]. The model-based methods can be further divided into filter-based and prior-based ones. Considering the single deraining as a signal filtering task, filter-based methods employ the edge preserving and physical properties filer to recover the rain-free images [7,9,10,13]. While the prior-based methods consider the deraining as an optimization question and apply handcrafted image prior to regularize the solution process, including discriminative sparse [9,14] Gaussian mixture model (GMM) [10] and low-rank representation [15]. Different from the model-based approaches, data-driven methods formulate deraining as a procedure of learning a non-linear function and find the proper parameters to map the rainy part into the background scene [16]. Motivated by the success of deep learning, the researchers model the mapping function with the convolution neural networks (CNN) or the Generative Adversarial Networks (GANs) [17]. The CNN methods directly get the deterministic mapping function from the rainy image to the clear background [3,18–21] and the GANs produce the deraining image inspired by their abilities on synthesizing visually appealing clean image [22].

Although effective in certain applications, the above methods suffer from several limitations. The rationality of model-based strategies refers to the subjective assumptions, and hence such learning schemes may not always adapt to diverse rainy conditions. The deep learning techniques neglect the intrinsic knowledge of rain, which make themselves easily trapped into the overfitting to training process. Most of the deraining methods generally fail to restore the structures and details, even yielding blurry background scenes. And it is difficult to get the derained image for a real-world rainy image, when the background and rain streaks merge with each other, especially in the heavy rain condition.

To address the mentioned issues, this paper conducts a Multi-scale Attentive Residual Dense Network called MARD-Net by leveraging the strong propagable capabilities of the dense network with advance residual blocks. The dense network provides a powerful capability to connect to all subsequent layers, from which the feature maps can be fully reused and smoothly transported to each layer. Multi-Scale Attention Residual Block (MARB) is introduced to better utilize multi-scale information and feature attention for improving the rain feature representation capability. Combing the features of different scales and layers, multi-scale manner is an efficient way to capture various rain streak components especially in the heavy rainy conditions. Reference to bright channel prior (BCP) [23] and the uneven distribution of rainy images, channel-wise and spatial attention mechanisms are involved in the MARB, since it helps the network to adjust the three-color channels respectively and identify the rainy region properly. We evaluate the proposed network on the public competitive benchmark synthetic and real-world datasets and the results significantly outperform the current outstanding methods on most of the deraining tasks.

In summary, our major contributions are summarized:

- We propose an end to end MARD-Net to address the single image deraining problem, which can effectively remove the rain streaks while well preserve the image details. The modified dense network is applied to boost the model performance via multi-level features reuse and maximum information flow between layers. It can reduce the loss of information transmission and vanishing-gradient, while fully utilizing the features of different layers to restore the details.
- To our knowledge, the Multi-Scale Attention Residual Block (MARB) is first constructed to improve the representation of rain streaks. The different convolution kernels along with fusion are employed to get multi-scale features for adapting the various rain cases. Then the feature attention module is applied to better extract the feature by using color channel and spatial information.
- Extensive experiments are carried out on six challenging datasets (4 synthetic and 2 real-world datasets). Our proposed network outperforms the state-of-the-art methods in visually and quantitatively comparisons. Furthermore, ablation studies have been provided to verify the rationality and necessity of important modules involved in our network.

2   Background and Related Work

An observed rainy image I can be generally modeled as a linear sum of a clean background B and a rain component R, which can be expressed by the formula as:

$$I = B + R \tag{1}$$

Based on the Eq. 1, deraining methods can be done either by removing R from I to get B or by directly estimating B from I. To make the deraining better be solved, various conventional methods adopted numerous prior models about rain or background to constrain the solution space [16]. Fu et al. [24] considered the image rain removal as a signal decomposition issue and performed the bilateral filter to decompose the low- frequency and high-frequency layers for getting the derained result. The discriminative sparse coding [9] was proposed to approximate the rain and background layers. To represent scales of rain and various orientations, Li et al. [10] employed the GMM based on patch priors for the rainy image to remove the rain streaks. These traditional methods usually make simple yet subjective hypotheses on the rain distribution and falling character, which work well only in some certain cases.

In recent years, numbers of deep learning based single image deraining approaches were proposed through constructing various networks [16]. Fu et al. [18] first designed the DerainNet for the image deraining, and further proposed Deep Detail Network (DDN) [3], which directly reduced the mapping range and removed the rain streak. Conditional GAN [25] was utilized to deal with the rain removal problem. Later, Qian et al. [26] introduced the attention mechanism into the GAN network, and tried to learn more about rain regions and their surrounding features. With the help of depth-guided attention mechanism, Hu [27] developed an end to end Depth-attentional Features network (DAF-Net) to estimate the rain-free image that formulated the attention to learn the feature and regressed a residual map. Zhang et al. [28] presented a multi-stream dense network combined with residual classifier process. In [29], Gated Context Aggregation Network (GCANet) was an end-to-end network, which try to restore the rain image from the gridding artifacts by adopting the smoothed dilation technique. The work of [20] offered a recurrent squeeze and excitation context aggregation net (RESCAN) to tackle the overlap layer in the rainy image. To handle with various rain scenes, Yang et al. [16] designed a multi-stage joint rain detection and estimate network (JORDER_E) and discussed the possible aspects as architecture and loss that effected on the deraining task. Lightweight Pyramid Networks (LPNet) [30] pursued a light-weighted pyramid to remove rain, so that the obtained network became simple and contained less parameters. In [19], the PReNet performed a stage-wise operation that repeatedly unfolded several Resblocks and a LSTM layer to effectively generate the rain-free images progressively. The work of [31], Spatial attentive network (SPANet) developed a spatial attention unit based on recurrent network and utilized a branch to capture the spatial details for removing rain in a local-to-global manner. However, most existing deraining researches do not notice the underlying connection of rain streaks across different scales and few attempts have been made to exploit the feature attention of the rainy image.

3 Proposed Method

The goal of this paper is to remove the rain, while maximally keeping the original structure and color in the image. We propose a Multi-scale Attentive Residual Dense Network (MARD-Net), including the overall network architecture, multi-scale attention residual block (MARB) and loss function.

3.1 Design of MARD-Net

We propose an end-to-end trainable MARD-Net that can take diverse rainy images as input and can well represent the rain steak feature through the MARB module. The overall architecture of MARD-Net is illustrated in Fig. 1. Based on the DenseNet framework, the proposed method ensures the maximum information flow through rain feature reuse, yielding condensed models that efficiently reduce the parameter numbers and are easy to be trained. Due to the different scales and shapes of rain streaks, it is an effective way that combining features from different scales and feature attention module to capture various rain streak components. In addition, skip connections are generally used in the residual block as they can aggregate features at multiple scales and accelerate the training process. Further, the MARB can better capture the feature with different scales and rain streak structure information, as discussed in the following parts.

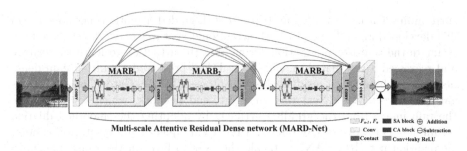

Fig. 1. The overall architecture of our proposed MARD-Net for image deraining. MARB is shown in Fig. 2. The goal of the MARD-Net is to estimate the clean image from the corresponding rainy image. The input of each layer consists of all preceding feature-maps and combines features by concatenating them. The blocks with same color share the same parameters.

3.2 Multi-scale Attention Residual Block (MARB)

Combining features at different scales effectively, multi-scale features have been widely employed to get a better information of the object and its surrounding context. In order to better solve the rain removal problem, an attention mechanism is introduced to strengthen the capability of extracting information, which is beneficial to improve the network performance and accuracy [32,33]. Inspired by these ideas, the MARB is applied to extract multi-scale features and guide to learn rain information effectively, as shown in Fig. 2.

The MARB can be described in detail mathematically. Referring to Fig. 2, the MARB is set to have an input feature of F_0 , which first passes through the different convolutional layer which sizes are 3×3 and 5×5 respectively, and its output is expressed as:

$$F_1^{3\times3} = f_{3\times3}(F_0; \eta_0^{3\times3}) \tag{2}$$

$$F_1^{5\times5} = f_{5\times5}(F_0; \eta_0^{5\times5}) \tag{3}$$

where $F_1^{n\times n}$ denotes the output of a convolution of size $n \times n$, $f_{n\times n}(\cdot)$ presents a convolution of size $n \times n$, and $\eta_0^{n\times n}$ means the hyperparameter of a convolution of size $n \times n$. The image features can be further extracted by the convolution layer of size 3×3 or 5×5 respectively.

$$F_2^{3\times3} = f_{3\times3}((F_1^{3\times3} + F_1^{5\times5}); \eta_1^{3\times3}) \tag{4}$$

$$F_2^{5\times5} = f_{5\times5}((F_1^{3\times3} + F_1^{5\times5}); \eta_1^{5\times5}) \tag{5}$$

where $F_2^{n\times n}$ denotes the output of a convolution layer of size $n \times n$ and $\eta_1^{n\times n}$ means the hyperparameter of a convolution layer of size $n \times n$. The activation functions for these convolution layers use Leaky-ReLU with $\alpha = 0.2$ as the activation function in general.

To further improve the network representation capabilities, MARB introduces the inter-layer multi-scale information fusion, which can integrate multi-scale information with the features of different scales. This structure guarantees

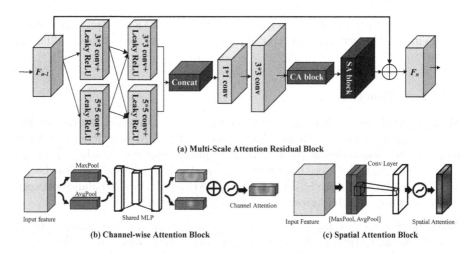

Fig. 2. (a) The architecture of our proposed Multi-Scale Attention Residual Block (MARB) consists the multi-scale residual blocks and the feature attention module. The feature module has two sequential sub-modules: channel-wise attention (CA) block (b) and spatial attention (SA) block (c).

that the input information can be propagated through all parameter layers, so that the MARB can learn the primary image features through different scales and features. To accelerate the training procedure, global skip connection is introduced among different MARB modules, which helps back-propagate gradient to update parameters. This skip connection can also propagate lossless information through the entire network directly, therefore it is useful for estimating the final derained image.

Rain density distribution patterns vary dramatically across different color channels, therefore the BCP prior [23], may be an effective way to get different weighted information for channel features. In [34], the research also finds that the channel-wise attention scheme with BCP can help the network better preserve the pixel brightness in derained images than previous methods, which treat different channels equally. Hence, the channel attention can capture the rain region and assist to extract important features. Meanwhile, the distributions of rain streaks are almost unevenly and may vary across different spatial locations. Therefore, the spatial attention may be also important to deal with rain region. Therefore, the spatial attention may be also important to deal with rain region. Multi-scale information fusion is achieved by using convolution layers of size 1×1 and 3×3, while channel-wise and spatial attention modules can also be introduced to improve feature fusion. We can reformulate the final output as:

$$F_{out} = sa(ca((f_{3\times3}(f_{1\times1}(C(F_2^{3\times3}, F_2^{5\times5}); \eta_2); \eta_3); \delta_0); \delta_1)) + F_0 \qquad (6)$$

where F_{out} denotes the output of the MARB, $sa(\cdot)$ and $ca(\cdot)$ indicate the spatial attention mechanism and channel attention mechanism, respectively, and

$\{\eta_2; \eta_3; \delta_0; \delta_1\}$ indicates the hyperparameters of the MARB output. This operation enables the network to better explore and reorganize features in different scales.

3.3 Loss Function

Mean squared error (MSE) is widely used as the loss function to evaluate the derained image and its corresponding ground truth. However, it usually leads to the blurry and over-smoothed of high-frequency textures, which do harm to remove the rain and restore the image content. To address the above drawbacks, we combine the MSE with SSIM as the proposed loss function to balance between image deraining and background structure preservation.

MSE Loss. Given an input rainy image I_i, the output rain-free image is $G(I_i)$ and the ground truth is J_i. Hence, a pixel-wise MSE loss can be defined as follows:

$$L_{MSE} = \frac{1}{HWC} \sum_{x=1}^{H} \sum_{y=1}^{W} \sum_{z=1}^{C} \|G(I_i) - J_i\|^2 \qquad (7)$$

where H, W and C represent height, width, and number of channels respectively.

SSIM Loss. SSIM is an important indicator to measure the structural similarity between two images [35], with the equation as follows:

$$SSIM(G(I), J) = \frac{2\mu_{G(I)}\mu_J + C_1}{\mu_{G(I)}^2 + \mu_J^2 + C_1} \cdot \frac{2\sigma_{G(I)}\sigma_J + C_2}{\sigma_{G(I)}^2 + \sigma_J^2 + C_2} \qquad (8)$$

where μ_x, σ_x^2 are the mean and the variance value of the image: x. The covariance of two images is σ_{xy}, C_1 and C_2 are constants value used to maintain equation stability. SSIM ranges from 0 to 1 and in the deraining issue the greater value means that the derained image are more similar to the ground truth image, so the SSIM loss can be defined as:

$$L_{SSIM} = 1 - SSIM(G(I), J) \qquad (9)$$

Total Loss. The total loss is defined by combing the MSE loss and the SSIM loss as follows:

$$L = L_{MSE} + \lambda L_{SSIM} \qquad (10)$$

where λ is the hyperparameter that can balance the weights between the MSE loss and SSIM loss. With the proper setting, the hybrid loss can keep the per-pixel similarity while preserving the global structures, which can help the rain removal model to obtain additional realistic derained images.

4   Experiments

In this section, we conduct comprehensive experiments to demonstrate the effectiveness of the proposed MARD-Net for image draining. Compared with the current state-of-the-art algorithms, the qualitative and quantitative analysis are carried out on the synthesized benchmark and real-world rainy datasets. In addition, ablation studies also perform to validate the effectiveness of our designed components.

4.1   Datasets and Performance Metrics

Datasets. We carry out experiments on four **synthetic benchmark datasets**: Rain100L [1], Rain100H [1], Rain12 [10] and Rain1400 [3], including rain streaks with various sizes, shapes and directions. With only one type of rain streaks, Rain100L contains 200 image pairs for training and the remaining 100 ones for evaluation. Compared with Rain100L, Rain100H is a dataset with 5 types of rain streak directions and consists of 1800 image pairs for training and 100 ones for testing. By training on Rain100L, like [19], Rain 12 is utilized to be a testing sample since it only includes 12 image pairs. With 14 types of streak orientations and magnitudes, Rain 1400 has 14000 rain synthetic images from 1000 clean images, where 12600 rainy images are selected as training data and the other 1400 ones are chosen for testing. **Real-world Datasets** are very important to evaluate the performance of deraining and two real-world datasets are involved for testing: the one with 185 real-world rainy images collected by [12], and the other with 34 images released by [36].

Performance Metrics. As the ground truths available for synthetic data, the rain removal method's performance can be evaluated on Peak Signal-to-Noise Ratio (PSNR in dB) and the Structural Similarity Index Measure (SSIM) [35]. The higher value of PSNR indicates better performance to remove rain streaks from the rainy image. The greater SSIM score nearest to 1 means that the two different images are more similar to each other. As no ground truth exits for real-world datasets, we may present the visual comparisons and zoom local parts for the real-world images.

4.2   Training Details

The detailed structure and parameter settings of the proposed model are given in Fig. 1 using Pytorch framework and the number of MARB is set to 8 to get a better result as discussed in the Ablation Studies part. Using Adam optimization [37] in the training process, its parameters can be set as followed: the learning rate is 1×10^{-3} and batch size is 32. Considering the loss function, the weight value of SSIM is set as $\lambda = 0.2$, empirically. We train the network for 100 epochs in total and reduce the learning rate by half every 25 epochs on a workstation with a NVIDIA Tesla V100 GPU (16 G). All subsequent experiments are performed with the same environment described in implementation details. To encourage more comparisons from the community, we will publicly release our codes on GitHub: https://github.com/cxtalk/MARD-Net.

4.3   Evaluation on Synthetic Datasets

In this section, we reveal the effective performance of our method by conducting a mass of experiments on frequent-used synthetic datasets: Rain100L, Rain100H, Rain1400 and Rain12. The proposed MARD-Net method is compared to five recent state deraining methods:GCANet [29], RESCAN [20], LPNet [30], SPANet [31] and PReNet [19]. All the methods use the source codes and default parameters specified published in the published literature. As the availability of ground truth in synthetic data, the results are evaluated using PSNR and SSIM. Table 1 shows the average evaluation criteria of each pairs of rain-free and deraining images with diverse and complicated rain types. From the table, the proposed method obtained the highest value of PSNR and SSIM in all synthetic datasets, which reflected the better robustness and generality of MARD-Net. The most notably increasing score in Rain100H and Rain1400 noted that our approach could properly remove the rain steaks and restore the image especially in the heavy rain as well as in the various rainy conditions.

Table 1. Quantitative results evaluate in term of average PSNR (dB) and SSIM on the synthesized benchmark datasets, including Rain100L, Rain100H, Rain1400 and Rain12. The best results are highlighted in bold. It is worth noting that the PSNR and SSIM are calculated in the RGB color space.

Datasets	Rain100L		Rain100H		Rain1400		Rain12	
Metrics	PSNR	SSIM	PSNR	SSIM	PSNR	SSIM	PSNR	SSIM
Input	26.89	0.8382	13.55	0.3785	25.24	0.8097	30.13	0.8553
GCANet	31.65	0.9325	23.80	0.8114	27.84	0.8406	30.76	0.8819
RESCAN	36.12	0.9691	28.88	0.8660	29.88	0.9053	36.43	0.9519
LPNet	33.39	0.9579	23.39	0.8208	26.45	0.8326	34.83	0.9568
SPANet	35.33	0.9694	25.11	0.8332	28.57	0.8913	35.85	0.9572
PReNet	37.41	0.9783	29.45	0.8980	30.73	0.9184	36.66	0.9618
Ours	**37.84**	**0.9814**	**30.19**	**0.9153**	**31.68**	**0.9215**	**36.88**	**0.9726**

In addition to the results by quantitative evaluation, we also provide visual observation derained images. Some corresponding pictures directly show visual difference in rain removal images, as particularly seen in Fig. 3 with crop and zoom in two local patch regions. As displayed, the GCANet leaves many rain streaks in the recovered images, especially in the heavy rain cases (Rain100H and Rain1400). The main drawbacks of RESCAN in the comparison show color degradation with different rain patterns (Rain1400) and there are still some streaks left after deraining. LPNet fails to remove the rain-streaks completely in the diverse rain pattern (Rain1400) and brings serious rain artifacts and blurred region to the derained image. Clearly, PReNet and SPANet, have the ability to remove most of rain streaks in different rain cases. However, by observing zoomed color boxes, we find that they lose some detailed information and lead to color degradation to a certain extent. In general, the proposed MARD-Net can successfully remove majority of rain in various rain patterns even in the heavy rain condition, and another benefit of our method is being good at preserving of color and detailed structure information similar to the ground truths.

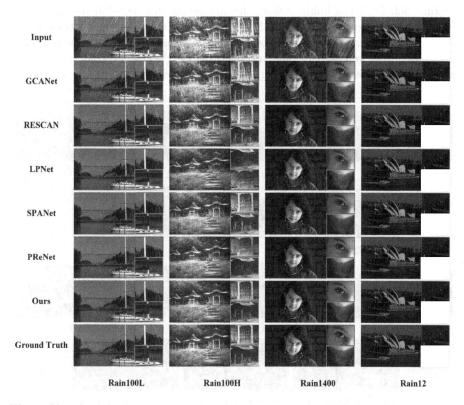

Fig. 3. Visual quality comparisons of all competing methods on synthetic datasets, including Rain100L, Rain100H, Rain1400 and Rain12. Zooming in the figure can provide a better look at the restoration quality. (Color figure online)

4.4 Evaluations on Real Rainy Images

To evaluate the effectiveness for practical use, we conduct a further comparison on the mentioned two real-world rainy datasets. Figure 4 demonstrates two real-world samples since the above one with various spatial information in the image space, while the other contains rich texture and content information. All the methods employ the pre-trained model trained on the same synthetic rainy datasets. Even though RESCAN, PReNet and SPANet achieve remarkable rain removal performance on synthetic datasets, all competing methods leave some rain streaks to a certain extent in various spatial space and complex content condition. Since objects far or near from the camera are mainly affected differently by the rain, our method significantly removes the majority of rain streaks by introducing multi-scale features and attention information. Due to the overfitting-to training-samples process [38] and loss of the spatial information, the competing methods fail to remove the rain steak with various spatial conditions, as seen in the above picture. With complex content information and texture details in the image below, the competing methods fail to remove the rain streaks on the road. Through the zoomed color boxes, we can see the obvious detail structure and information loss for derained results. Clearly, the proposed model performs well on deraining and restoring the details and color information with feature reuse and transferring in different scales and layers.

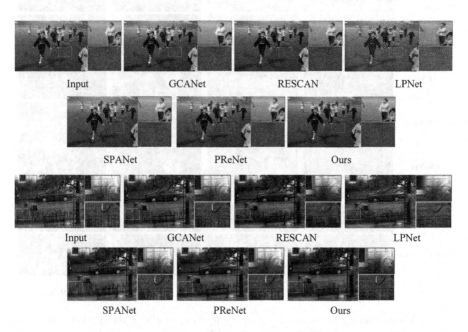

Fig. 4. Visual quality comparisons of all competing methods on real-world datasets. Zooming in the figure can provide a better look at the restoration quality.

4.5   Ablation Studies

We conduct the ablation study to explore the effectiveness of the parameters and configuration in our proposed network. All the studies are performed in the same environment by using the Rain100L dataset.

Multi-scale Attentive Residual Block Numbers

To study the influences of different numbers, we perform the experiments with different numbers of MARB to the proposed network. Specifically, MARB numbers N is set to $N \in \{2, 4, 6, 8, 10\}$ and the performances are illustrated in Table 2. As seen, increasing blocks can bring higher PSNR and SSIM values, while the value improvement is limited after $N = 8$ with extra time-consuming. Hence, 8 is chosen as our default setting to achieve the balance between effectiveness and efficiency.

Table 2. Ablation study on multi-scale attentive residual block (MARB) numbers. PSNR and SSIM results among different settings of MARD-Net on Rain100L dataset.

Block No.	$N = 2$	$N = 4$	$N = 6$	$N = 8$ (default)	$N = 10$
PSNR	34.84	35.50	36.79	**37.84**	37.86
SSIM	0.9635	0.9718	0.9786	**0.9814**	0.9810

Channel-Wise and Spatial Attention Modules

To further verify the effectiveness of feature attention modules, we conduct the studies with different variants of Multi-scale Residual Block. The baseline module is constructed by removing the channel-wise and spatial attention. As shown in Table 3, feature attention module is able to bring improvements in both PSNR and SSIM. The best performance is achieved by using the channel-wise and spatial attention both, with bringing a total gain of 1.89 dB over the baseline that verifies helpful to the task of rain removal.

Table 3. Ablation study on feature attention modules. PSNR and SSIM results among different decompositions on Rain100L dataset. The term "CA" and "SA" denote the channel-wise attention block and spatial attention block, respectively. It shows that the combination of all the designed components is the best.

	Baseline	CA	SA	SA+CA
PSNR	35.95	36.85	36.14	**37.84**
SSIM	0.9757	0.9785	0.9766	**0.9814**

Loss Function

We further investigate the impact of using the MSE and SSIM loss functions. In Table 4, the quantitative evaluations of different loss functions can be seen under the same conditions. We note that PSNR is a function of MSE, and SSIM focuses on structural similarity which is appropriate for preserving details. In this case, the quantitative performance measure of MSE and SSIM should favor the objective function that optimizes over this measure.

Table 4. Ablation study on loss functions. The results of different losses on Rain100L dataset.

	MSE	SSIM	MSE+SSIM
PSNR	36.71	35.93	**37.84**
SSIM	0.9671	0.9798	**0.9814**

5   Conclusion

In this paper, we present a novel Multi-scale Attentive Residual Dense Network named MARD-Net to handle the single image deraining problem. In MARD-Net, dense network is applied to explore the potential of network through feature reuse and fully information propagation. An innovative Multi-scale Attentive Residual Block is first utilized to identify and represent the rain streak features. Different convolution kernels along with progressive fusion are designed to explore the multi-scale rain patterns features. In addition, feature attention module is introduced to achieve the raining removal more adaptive in different color channels and spatial distribution. Extensive experiments on both frequent-use synthetic and real-world datasets demonstrate that the proposed MARD-Net achieves superior performance to the recent state deraining methods. In the future, we will further work on employing our network idea into semi/unsupervised scenarios and some other low-vision tasks.

References

1. Yang, W., Tan, R.T., Feng, J., Liu, J., Guo, Z., Yan, S.: Deep joint rain detection and removal from a single image. In: 2017 IEEE Conference on Computer Vision and Pattern Recognition (CVPR), pp. 1685–1694 (2017)
2. Yang, W., Tan, R.T., Feng, J., Guo, Z., Yan, S., Liu, J.: Joint rain detection and removal from a single image with contextualized deep networks. IEEE Trans. Pattern Anal. Mach. Intell. **42**, 1377–1393 (2020)
3. Fu, X., Huang, J., Zeng, D., Huang, Y., Ding, X., Paisley, J.: Removing rain from single images via a deep detail network. In: 2017 IEEE Conference on Computer Vision and Pattern Recognition (CVPR), pp. 1715–1723 (2017)
4. Ren, S., He, K., Girshick, R., Sun, J.: Faster r-CNN: towards real-time object detection with region proposal networks. IEEE Trans. Pattern Anal. Mach. Intell. **39**, 1137–1149 (2017)
5. Redmon, J., Farhadi, A.: Yolov3: an incremental improvement. arXiv preprint arXiv:1804.02767 (2018)
6. Simonyan, K., Zisserman, A.: Very deep convolutional networks for large-scale image recognition. In: ICLR 2015: International Conference on Learning Representations 2015 (2015)
7. Garg, K., Nayar, S.K.: Vision and rain. Int. J. Comput. Vis. **75**, 3–27 (2007). https://doi.org/10.1007/s11263-006-0028-6
8. Zhang, X., Li, H., Qi, Y., Leow, W., Ng, T.: Rain removal in video by combining temporal and chromatic properties. In: 2006 IEEE International Conference on Multimedia and Expo, pp. 461–464 (2006)

9. Luo, Y., Xu, Y., Ji, H.: Removing rain from a single image via discriminative sparse coding. In: 2015 IEEE International Conference on Computer Vision (ICCV), pp. 3397–3405 (2015)

10. Li, Y., Tan, R.T., Guo, X., Lu, J., Brown, M.S.: Rain streak removal using layer priors. In: 2016 IEEE Conference on Computer Vision and Pattern Recognition (CVPR), pp. 2736–2744 (2016)

11. Gu, S., Meng, D., Zuo, W., Zhang, L.: Joint convolutional analysis and synthesis sparse representation for single image layer separation. In: 2017 IEEE International Conference on Computer Vision (ICCV), pp. 1717–1725 (2017)

12. Li, S., et al.: Single image deraining: a comprehensive benchmark analysis. In: 2019 IEEE/CVF Conference on Computer Vision and Pattern Recognition (CVPR), pp. 3838–3847 (2019)

13. Xu, J., Zhao, W., Liu, P., Tang, X.: Removing rain and snow in a single image using guided filter. In: 2012 IEEE International Conference on Computer Science and Automation Engineering (CSAE), vol. 2, pp. 304–307 (2012)

14. Zhang, H., Patel, V.M.: Convolutional sparse and low-rank coding-based rain streak removal. In: 2017 IEEE Winter Conference on Applications of Computer Vision (WACV), pp. 1259–1267 (2017)

15. Chen, Y.L., Hsu, C.T.: A generalized low-rank appearance model for spatio-temporally correlated rain streaks. In: 2013 IEEE International Conference on Computer Vision, pp. 1968–1975 (2013)

16. Yang, W., Tan, R.T., Wang, S., Fang, Y., Liu, J.: Single image deraining: from model-based to data-driven and beyond. IEEE Trans. Pattern Anal. Mach. Intell. 1 (2020)

17. Goodfellow, I., et al.: Generative adversarial nets. In: Advances in Neural Information Processing Systems, vol. 27, pp. 2672–2680 (2014)

18. Fu, X., Huang, J., Ding, X., Liao, Y., Paisley, J.: Clearing the skies: a deep network architecture for single-image rain removal. IEEE Trans. Image Process. **26**, 2944–2956 (2017)

19. Ren, D., Zuo, W., Hu, Q., Zhu, P., Meng, D.: Progressive image deraining networks: a better and simpler baseline. In: 2019 IEEE/CVF Conference on Computer Vision and Pattern Recognition (CVPR), pp. 3937–3946 (2019)

20. Li, X., Wu, J., Lin, Z., Liu, H., Zha, H.: Recurrent squeeze-and-excitation context aggregation net for single image deraining. In: Proceedings of the European Conference on Computer Vision (ECCV), pp. 262–277 (2018)

21. Yang, W., Liu, J., Yang, S., Guo, Z.: Scale-free single image deraining via visibility-enhanced recurrent wavelet learning. IEEE Trans. Image Process. **28**, 2948–2961 (2019)

22. Shen, Y., et al.: Mba-raingan: multi-branch attention generative adversarial network for mixture of rain removal from single images. arXiv preprint arXiv:2005.10582 (2020)

23. Yan, Y., Ren, W., Guo, Y., Wang, R., Cao, X.: Image deblurring via extreme channels prior. In: 2017 IEEE Conference on Computer Vision and Pattern Recognition (CVPR), pp. 6978–6986 (2017)

24. Fu, Y.H., Kang, L.W., Lin, C.W., Hsu, C.T.: Single-frame-based rain removal via image decomposition. In: 2011 IEEE International Conference on Acoustics, Speech and Signal Processing (ICASSP), pp. 1453–1456 (2011)

25. Zhang, H., Sindagi, V., Patel, V.M.: Image de-raining using a conditional generative adversarial network. IEEE Trans. Circ. Syst. Video Technol. 1 (2019)

26. Qian, R., Tan, R.T., Yang, W., Su, J., Liu, J.: Attentive generative adversarial network for raindrop removal from a single image. In: 2018 IEEE/CVF Conference on Computer Vision and Pattern Recognition, pp. 2482–2491 (2018)
27. Hu, X., Fu, C.W., Zhu, L., Heng, P.A.: Depth-attentional features for single-image rain removal. In: 2019 IEEE/CVF Conference on Computer Vision and Pattern Recognition (CVPR), pp. 8022–8031 (2019)
28. Zhang, H., Patel, V.M.: Density-aware single image de-raining using a multi-stream dense network. In: 2018 IEEE/CVF Conference on Computer Vision and Pattern Recognition, pp. 695–704 (2018)
29. Chen, D., et al.: Gated context aggregation network for image dehazing and deraining. In: 2019 IEEE Winter Conference on Applications of Computer Vision (WACV), pp. 1375–1383 (2019)
30. Fu, X., Liang, B., Huang, Y., Ding, X., Paisley, J.: Lightweight pyramid networks for image deraining. IEEE Trans. Neural Netw. **31**, 1794–1807 (2020)
31. Wang, T., Yang, X., Xu, K., Chen, S., Zhang, Q., Lau, R.W.: Spatial attentive single-image deraining with a high quality real rain dataset. In: 2019 IEEE/CVF Conference on Computer Vision and Pattern Recognition (CVPR), pp. 12270–12279 (2019)
32. Liu, J., Gong, X.: Attention mechanism enhanced LSTM with residual architecture and its application for protein-protein interaction residue pairs prediction. BMC Bioinform. **20**, 1–11 (2019)
33. xu qin, zhilin wang, Bai, Y., Xie, X., Jia, H.: Ffa-net: feature fusion attention network for single image dehazing. In: AAAI 2020 : The Thirty-Fourth AAAI Conference on Artificial Intelligence, vol. 34, pp. 11908–11915 (2020)
34. Du, Y., Xu, J., Qiu, Q., Zhen, X., Zhang, L.: Variational image deraining. In: 2020 IEEE Winter Conference on Applications of Computer Vision (WACV), pp. 2406–2415 (2020)
35. Wang, Z., Bovik, A., Sheikh, H., Simoncelli, E.: Image quality assessment: from error visibility to structural similarity. IEEE Trans. Image Process. **13**, 600–612 (2004)
36. Li, S., Ren, W., Zhang, J., Yu, J., Guo, X.: Single image rain removal via a deep decomposition-composition network. Comput. Vis. Image Underst. **186**, 48–57 (2019)
37. Kingma, D.P., Ba, J.L.: Adam: a method for stochastic optimization. In: ICLR 2015: International Conference on Learning Representations 2015 (2015)
38. Wang, H., Li, M., Wu, Y., Zhao, Q., Meng, D.: A survey on rain removal from video and single image. arXiv preprint arXiv:1909.08326 (2019)

FAN: Feature Adaptation Network for Surveillance Face Recognition and Normalization

Xi Yin[1]([✉]), Ying Tai[2], Yuge Huang[2], and Xiaoming Liu[1]

[1] Michigan State University, East Lansing, USA
yinxi.whu@gmail.com, liuxm@cse.msu.edu
[2] Youtu Lab, Tencent, China
{yingtai,yugehuang}@tencent.com

Abstract. This paper studies face recognition (FR) and normalization in surveillance imagery. Surveillance FR is a challenging problem that has great values in law enforcement. Despite recent progress in conventional FR, less effort has been devoted to surveillance FR. To bridge this gap, we propose a Feature Adaptation Network (FAN) to jointly perform surveillance FR and normalization. Our face normalization mainly acts on the aspect of image resolution, closely related to face super-resolution. However, previous face super-resolution methods require paired training data with pixel-to-pixel correspondence, which is typically unavailable between real-world low-resolution and high-resolution faces. FAN can leverage both paired and unpaired data as we disentangle the features into identity and non-identity components and adapt the distribution of the identity features, which breaks the limit of current face super-resolution methods. We further propose a random scale augmentation scheme to learn resolution robust identity features, with advantages over previous fixed scale augmentation. Extensive experiments on LFW, WIDER FACE, QUML-SurvFace and SCface datasets have shown the effectiveness of our method on surveillance FR and normalization.

1 Introduction

Surveillance Face Recognition (FR) is a challenge and important problem, yet less studied. The performance on conventional benchmarks such as LFW [3] and IJB-A [4] have been greatly improved by state-of-the-art (SOTA) FR methods [5–7], which still suffer when applied to surveillance FR. One intuitive approach is to perform Face Super-Resolution (FSR) on surveillance faces to enhance facial details. However, existing FSR methods are problematic to handle surveillance faces, because they usually ignore the *identity* information and require *paired* training data. In fact, preserving identity information is more crucial for surveillance faces than recovering other information, e.g., background, Pose, Illumination, Expression (PIE).

In this work, we study surveillance FR and normalization. Specifically, given a surveillance face image, we aim to learn robust identity features for FR. Meanwhile, the features are used to generate a normalized face with enhanced facial

© Springer Nature Switzerland AG 2021
H. Ishikawa et al. (Eds.): ACCV 2020, LNCS 12623, pp. 301–319, 2021.
https://doi.org/10.1007/978-3-030-69532-3_19

LFW   SCface   WIDER FACE   QMUL-SurFace

Fig. 1. Visual results on 4 datasets. Vertically we show input in row 1 and our results in row 3. For LFW and SCface, we show the ground truth and gallery images in row 2. For WIDER FACE and QMUL-SurFace which do not have ground truth high-resolution images, we compare with two state-of-the-art SR methods: Bulat et al. [1] and FSRGAN [2] in row 2.

details and neutral PIE. Our normalization is performed mainly on the aspect of resolution. While sharing the same goal as traditional SR, it differs in removing the pixel-to-pixel correspondence between the original and super-resolved images, as required by traditional SR. Therefore, we term it as face *normalization*. For the same reason, we compare our work to previous FSR approaches, instead of prior normalization methods operating on pose [8], or expression [9]. To the best of our knowledge, this is the *first* work to study surveillance face normalization.

We propose a novel Feature Adaptation Network (FAN) to jointly perform face recognition and normalization, which has three advantages over conventional FSR. 1) Our joint learning scheme can benefit each other while most FSR methods do not consider the recognition task. 2) Our framework enables training with both paired and unpaired data while conventional SR methods only

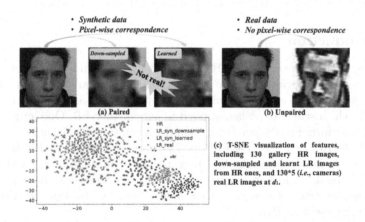

Fig. 2. Paired vs. unpaired data from SCface [10]. Synthetic paired data can be obtained by either down-sampling [2,11] or via a learned degradation mapping [1].

Table 1. Comparisons with previous state-of-the-art face super-resolution methods. Vis., Rec., Dis. and Frontal. indicate visualization, recognition, disentangled and frontalization, respectively. $A \to B$ refers to performing A first and then followed by B.

Method	FSRNet [2] (CVPR'18)	Bulat et al. [1] (ECCV'18)	S^2R^2 [19] (CVPR'08)	Wu et al. [13] (Arxiv'16)	SICNN [12] (ECCV'18)	FAN (Ours)
Deep model	√	√	×	√	√	√
Applications	Vis.	Vis.	Vis. & Rec.	Vis.& Rec.	Vis. & Rec	Vis. & Rec.
Pipeline	SR	SR	Features & SR→Rec.	SR→Rec.	SR→Rec.	Dis. Features→SR& Frontal.& Rec.
Scale factors	8	4	2/4	4	8	Random
Identity preserving	×	×	√	√	√	√
Scenarios	CelebA/Helen (Easy)	WIDER FACE (Hard)	MPIE/FRGC (Easy)	LFW/YTF (Medium)	LFW (Medium)	SCface/QMUL-SurFace/WIDER FACE (Hard)

support paired training. 3) Our method simultaneously improves the resolution and alleviates the background and PIE from real surveillance faces while conventional methods only act on the resolution. Examples in Fig. 1 demonstrate the superiority of FAN over SOTA FSR methods.

Our FAN consists of two stages. In the first stage, we adopt disentangled feature learning to learn both identity and non-identity features mainly from high-resolution (HR) images, which are combined as the input to a decoder for pixel-wise face recovering. In the second stage, we propose feature adaptation to further facilitate the feature learning from the low-resolution (LR) images, by approximating the feature distribution between the LR and HR identity encoders. There are two advantages to use FAN for surveillance FR and normalization. First, FAN focuses on learning disentangled identity features from LR images, which is better for FR than extracting features from super-resolved faces [8,12,13]. Second, our adaptation is performed in the disentangled identity feature space, which enables training with unpaired data without pixel-to-pixel correspondence. As shown in Fig. 2, the synthetic paired data used in prior works [1,2,11–16] cannot accurately reflect the difference between real LR and HR in-the-wild faces, which is also observed in [17].

Furthermore, to better handle surveillance faces with unknown and diverse resolutions, we propose a Random Scale Augmentation (RSA) method that enables the network to learn all kinds of scales during training. Prior FSR [2,11,18] methods either *artificially* generate the LR images from the HR ones by simple *downsampling*, or *learn* the degradation mapping via a Convolutional Neural Network (CNN). However, their common drawback is to learn reconstruction under *fixed* scales, which may greatly limit their applications to surveillance faces. In contrast, our RSA efficiently alleviates the constraint on scale variation.

In summary, the contributions of our work include:

- We propose a novel FAN to address surveillance face recognition and normalization, which is suitable for both paired and unpaired data.

- We integrate disentangled feature learning to learn identity and non-identity features, which helps achieve face normalization for visualization, and *identity preserving* for face recognition, simultaneously.
- We propose a random scale augmentation strategy in FAN to learn various scales during training, which addresses the unknown resolutions of surveillance faces.
- We achieve state-of-the-art performances on surveillance face datasets: WIDER FACE, QMUL-SurvFace and SCface, both quantitatively and qualitatively.

2   Related Work

Face Recognition. Face recognition is a long-standing topic in computer vision. The performance has improved substantially due to the success of CNNs and large training sets [20]. Most previous FR methods are focused on designing better loss functions to learn more discriminative features [5–7,21,22]. For example, Deng et al. [7] proposed ArcFace to introduce a margin in the angular space to make training more challenging and thus learn a more discriminative feature representation. Other methods are proposed to handle one or more specific variations in FR. For example, pose-invariant FR [8,23,24] has been widely studied as pose is one major challenge in FR. With recent advance in FR, the performance on conventional benchmarks like LFW [3], CFP [25], and IJB-A [4] are saturating.

However, most previous FR methods fail to achieve satisfactory performance on surveillance FR [26], which is a more challenging task that tackles unconstrained LR faces. To address surveillance FR, one common approach is to learn a unified feature space for LR and HR images [27,28]. Besides, face SR methods that preserve the identity information are another direction. E.g., Hennings-Yeomans et al. [19] incorporated face features based prior in SR. Wu et al. [13] integrated a FR net after a standard SR net, and jointly learned a deep model for face hallucination and recognition. More recently, Zhang et al. [12] defined a super-identity loss to measure the identity difference within the hypersphere identity metric space. Different from methods that performed recognition based on the recovered HR images [12,13], our method is more like [19] that firstly learns the features, but differs in three aspects: 1) Our *non-linear and compact* features learned from the deep CNNs are more powerful than the linear features in [12,13]. 2) Our FAN focuses on disentangled identity features and thus can fully leverage both paired and unpaired data. 3) Our FAN well handles LR *surveillance* faces.

Face Normalization. It is widely assumed in prior work [29–31] that the appearance of a face is influenced by two factors: identity and intra-class (or *non-identity*) variation. Normally face normalization is a general task of generating an identity-preserved face while removing other non-identity variation including

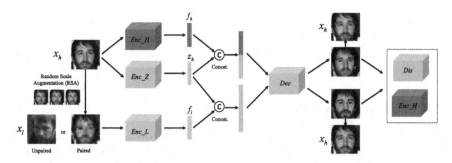

Fig. 3. Overview of FAN. Green parts represent disentangled feature learning in stage one, where dark green and light green are the two steps. First, *Enc_H* (dark green) is a HR identity encoder that is pre-trained and fixed. Second, *Enc_Z*, *Dec*, and *Dis* are trained for feature disentanglement. Orange parts represent the feature adaptation in stage two where a LR identity encoder is learned with all other models (green) fixed. (Color figure online)

pose, expression, illumination, and resolution. Most prior works of face normalization have focused on specifically removing pose variation, i.e., face frontalization [8,32,33], expression variation [9,34], or illumination variation [35]. Other works [9,36] perform pose and expression normalization. In contrast, our work mainly focuses on resolution normalization by enhancing facial details, which also handles PIE implicitly. Motivated by the disentanglement-based face recognition approaches [8,37], we incorporate disentangled feature learning for LR face normalization.

Our work is close to face SR. Early face SR work [38–40] adopt different types of machine learning algorithms. For example, Baker and Kanade [38] learned a prior on the spatial distribution of the image gradient for frontal faces. Yang et al. [39] assumed that facial landmarks can be accurately estimated from the LR face image, and incorporated the facial priors by using the mapping between specific facial components. Recently, deep CNN has shown its superiority for face SR. Zhou et al. [41] proposed a bi-channel CNN for faces with large appearance variations. Zhu et al. [42] super-resolved unaligned low-resolution faces in a task-alternating cascaded framework. More recently, several works [2,18] adopt Generative Adversarial Networks (GAN) to generate photo-realistic face images. However, the above methods ignore the identity information during training, which is essential for human perception [12] and downstream FR tasks. In contrast, our method jointly learns surveillance face recognition and normalization, which is based on the disentangled identity information. We compare with the most relevant FSR papers in Table 1.

3   Feature Adaptation Network

In this section, we first give an overview of FAN (Sect. 3.1) that consists of two stages. A feature disentanglement framework is introduced in Sect. 3.2, which aims to disentangle identity features with other factors of variations. Then we propose the feature adaptation with random scale augmentation in Sect. 3.3 to learn resolution-robust identity features from both paired and unpaired training data.

3.1 Framework Overview

The goals of our work are two-folds: 1) resolution-robust face recognition; 2) identity-preserved and resolution-enhanced face normalization. We propose to learn a disentangled representation to achieve both tasks. Performing face normalization from disentangled features enables identity supervision on both the disentangled features and the normalized faces, in contrast to previous SR work where identity supervision is only applied to the super-resolved faces. Such identity supervisions allow us to leverage real *unpaired* HR and LR faces without pixel correspondence. This is crucial for tackling surveillance scenario where paired images are usually unavailable in a large scale.

As shown in Fig. 3, our method consists of two stages: disentangled feature learning (green components) and feature adaptation (orange components). Feature disentanglement has been successfully applied to face recognition and face synthesis [8,43]. A disentangled representation is not only generative for face synthesis but also discriminative for face recognition. In this stage, we train our feature disentanglement framework with HR faces. A face image is encoded into identity and non-identity features, which are combined to generate the input image.

In the second stage, we fix all models in the disentanglement framework and perform feature adaptation with HR-LR input images that can be either *paired* or *unpaired*. A LR feature encoder is learned to extract discriminative identity features from LR faces. The disentanglement framework provides strong supervisions in the feature adaptation process. To achieve resolution-robust recognition, we propose Random Scale Augmentation (RSA) to overcome the drawbacks of fixed-scale SR in previous work [1,2].

3.2 Disentangled Feature Learning

Our feature disentanglement framework consists of five modules: an identity feature encoder Enc_H, a non-identity feature encoder Enc_Z, a decoder Dec, a linear classifier FC (omitted from Fig. 3 for clarity), and a discriminator Dis. To disentangle identity features from the non-identity variations, we perform a two-step feature disentanglement motivated by [37], but differs in three aspects.

In the first step, a state-of-the-art face recognition model is trained with HR and down-sampled LR images using standard softmax loss and m-L_2 regularization [44]. We denote the trained feature encoder as Enc_H, which remains fixed for all later stages to provide encoded identity features $\mathbf{f}_h = Enc\_H(\mathbf{x}_h)$ from a HR input $\mathbf{x}_h$. In the second step, we aim to learn non-identity features $\mathbf{z}_h = Enc\_Z(\mathbf{x}_h)$ by performing adversarial training and image reconstruction.

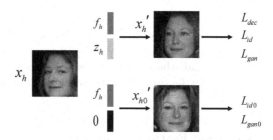

Fig. 4. Our feature disentanglement learning performs two kinds of reconstructions. Top row denotes the reconstruction from the identity and non-identity features where we supervise on both pixel domain reconstruction (L_{dec}) and feature level regularization (L_{id} and L_{gan}). Bottom row denotes the reconstruction from the identity features where only feature-level regularization are used.

The first difference to [37] is the loss for $\mathbf{z}_h$. [37] minimizes the identity classification loss, which we found to be unstable during training as it is unbounded. Instead, we propose to enforce the non-identity features to be evenly classified to all identities to make $\mathbf{z}_h$ identity *unrelated* [43].

$$L_z = ||FC(\mathbf{z}_h) - \mathbf{y}_z||_2^2, \tag{1}$$

where $\mathbf{y}_z = [\frac{1}{N_D}, \ldots, \frac{1}{N_D}] \in \mathbb{R}^{N_D}$ and N_D is the total number of identities in the training set. The gradient of this loss is used to update only Enc_Z but not FC.

The disentangled features are combined to generate a face image $\mathbf{x}_h' = Dec(\mathbf{f}_h, \mathbf{z}_h)$ with the goal of recovering the input: $L_{dec} = ||\mathbf{x}_h' - \mathbf{x}_h||_2^2$. As $\mathbf{f}_h$ is discriminative for face recognition, the non-identity components will be discarded from $\mathbf{f}_h$ in the first step. The reconstruction will encourage Enc_Z to encode non-identity features $\mathbf{z}_h$ that is complimentary to $\mathbf{f}_h$ in order to recover the input face.

The second difference to [37] is that we employ an identity similarity regularization and GAN-based discriminator loss to impose identity similarity and improve visual quality of the generated faces. Specifically, for identity loss we use Enc_H to extract features and regularize the feature distance: $L_{id} = ||Enc\_H(\mathbf{x}_h') - \mathbf{f}_h||_2^2$. For GAN-based discriminator loss, we use standard binary cross entropy classification loss that is omitted here for clarity.

The third difference to [37] is that we perform an additional reconstruction to generate a face image from the identity features alone: $\mathbf{x}_{h0}' = Dec(\mathbf{f}_h, \mathbf{0})$ where $\mathbf{0}$ represents a vector of 0 that is of the same dimension as $\mathbf{z}_h$. As the non-identity part is given as $\mathbf{0}$, we expect the generated face to be an identity-preserved and *normalized* face without variations in non-identity factors such as PIE. As there is no ground-truth target image, we impose identity and GAN loss respectively. This process is illustrated in Fig. 4.

The additional reconstruction has two benefits. First, it encourages the identity features alone to synthesize an identity-preserved face, which in turn prevents the non-identity features to encode identity information and results in better disentanglement. Second, the ability of *Dec* to reconstruct an identity-preserved face from the identity features alone is useful to enhancing facial details during inference (Sect. 3.3).

3.3 Paired and Unpaired Feature Adaptation

In the first stage, we have learned disentangled representation and image reconstruction from HR images. The reason to train *Dec* with HR only is to force *Dec* to generate HR images, which is the goal to enhance resolution for face normalization. However, this framework will not work well for LR inputs. Therefore, we propose a feature adaptation scheme to learn a LR Encoder *Enc_L* for LR face recognition and normalization. We aim to learn a feature extractor that works well for input faces with various resolutions.

Training with Paired Data. In conventional FSR, it is common to downsample the HR faces to LR versions with a few fixed scales and use the HR images to supervise FSR. Such methods cannot well handle the various resolutions in real-world surveillance imagery. To solve this issue, we propose Random Scale Augmentation (RSA). Given a HR input $\mathbf{x}_h \in \mathbb{R}^{N_h \times N_h}$, we down-sample the image to a random resolution to obtain $\mathbf{x}_l \in \mathbb{R}^{K \times K}$, where $K \in [N_l, N_h]$ and N_l is the lowest pixel resolution we care about (*e.g.* 8). We call the HR images and down-sampled LR counterparts as paired data as they have pixel-to-pixel correspondence.

Training with Unpaired Data. Unpaired data represents HR and LR face images from the same subject but do not have pixel-wise correspondence. As shown in Fig. 2, the distribution of paired data is very far away from that of unpaired data. However, conventional FSR cannot take advantage of such unpaired data. Fortunately, FAN can well handle such case as we conduct face normalization from the disentangled features. As shown in Fig. 3, FAN is suitable for both paired and unpaired training because it adapts the feature distributions between LR and HR images. We perform both feature-level and image-level similarity supervisions.

Specifically, given a LR face image $\mathbf{x}_l$ that is obtained from either random down-sampling or unpaired source, we resize $\mathbf{x}_l$ to the same dimension as $\mathbf{x}_h$ using bicubic interpolation. Then we use *Enc_L* to extract identity features $\mathbf{f}_l$, which is regularized to be similar to the disentangled features of the corresponding HR input image:

$$L_{enc} = ||Enc\_L(\mathbf{x}_l) - Enc\_H(\mathbf{x}_h)||_2^2. \tag{2}$$

This feature-level regularization adapts the features of LR images to the HR images in the disentangled feature space. The second regularization is defined in the recovered face image space. Recall that in the first stage *Dec* is trained

Table 2. Detailed training steps of FAN. The first stage (1.*) involves a two-step disentanglement learning process. The second stage (1.2) is the feature adaptation process.

Stage	Input	Training models	Fixed models
1.1	HR+LR	Enc_H	–
1.2	HR	Enc_Z, FC, Dec, Dis	Enc_H
2	HR+LR	Enc_L	Enc_H, Enc_Z, Dec, Dis

to generate a HR image from the identity and non-identity features of a HR input face. If Enc_L can encode identity-preserved features, such features can replace the original HR identity features $\mathbf{f}_h$ to recover the HR input face. Thus, we impose an image-level regularization:

$$L_{enc\_dec} = ||Dec(\mathbf{f}_l, Enc\_Z(\mathbf{x}_h)) - \mathbf{x}_h||_2^2. \tag{3}$$

As the non-identity features encoded from the HR image contributes to generating the output, the original HR can be used as the target for supervision. This formulation is fundamentally different to all previous face SR methods that cannot impose pixel-wise supervision from unpaired data.

Both feature-level and image-level regularization will enforce Enc_L to learn robust identity features $\mathbf{f}_l$. By varying the resolutions of the inputs, $\mathbf{f}_l$ is resolution robust. We also encourage the generated output to be realistic and identity preserving using the pre-trained discriminator Dis and Enc_H. The detailed training steps are summarized in Table 2. First, we train Enc_H using HR and down-sampled LR images in stage 1.1. Second, we train feature disentanglement using HR images only in stage 1.2 by fixing Enc_H. Third, we train Enc_L with all other models fixed in stage 2.

Inference. We extract identity features $\mathbf{f}_l = Enc\_L(\mathbf{x}_l)$ from a LR input for face recognition, and can further perform face normalization via $Dec(\mathbf{f}_l, \mathbf{0})$ by setting the non-identity component to $\mathbf{0}$. Thus we do not require HR images during inference.

4 Experiments

4.1 Implementation Details

Datasets. We conduct extensive experiments on several datasets including refined MS-Celeb-1M (MS1M) [7] for training, and LFW [3], SCface [10], QMUL-SurvFace [26] and WIDER FACE [45] for testing. Refined MS1M, a cleaned version of the original dataset [20], contains 3.8M images of 85K identities. For LFW, we down-sample the 6,000 face pairs to low resolution and adopt the standard evaluation protocol. SCface consists of HR (gallery) and LR (probe) face images of 130 subjects. Following [46], 50 subjects are used for fine-tuning and 80 subjects are for testing. We conduct face identification where HR images are used as the gallery set and LR images with different resolutions (captured at three distances: 4.2 m for d_1, 2.6 m for d_2 and 1.0 m for d_3) form the probe set. QMUL-SurvFace consists of very-low resolution face images captured under surveillance cameras, and is used for face verification.

Training Setting. Following [47], we use five facial landmarks (eye centers, nose tip and mouth corners) to align a face image to 128×128. We uniformly re-size the input LR images to a fixed size of 128×128 by bicubic interpolation, which makes our method suitable for the proposed RSA strategy. Our framework is implemented with the Torch7 toolbox [48]. Our Enc_H and Enc_L are based on ResNet-50 [49], Enc_Z, Dec, and Dis are similar to [8]. We train stages 1.1 and 1.2 with a learning rate of $2e^{-4}$ for 12 and 8 epochs respectively. Stage 2 is trained with a learning rate of $2e^{-5}$ for 6 epochs. We use Adam optimization [50]. For SCface experiments, we finetune Enc_L with refined-MS1M (*paired*) and SCface (*unpaired*) training set for $1,000$ iterations with a learning rate of $1e^{-5}$.

4.2   Ablation Study

Effects of Disentangled Feature Learning. First, we evaluate the effects of disentangled feature learning by visualizing the disentangled identity features $\mathbf{f}_h$ and non-identity features $\mathbf{z}_h$ through our trained Dec. As shown in Fig. 5, the fusing of $\mathbf{f}_h$ and $\mathbf{z}_h$ can successfully recover the original image. The identity features alone can generate an identity-preserved frontal face, while the PIE variations and background information are captured in the non-identity features. This suggests our framework effectively disentangles identity and non-identity features.

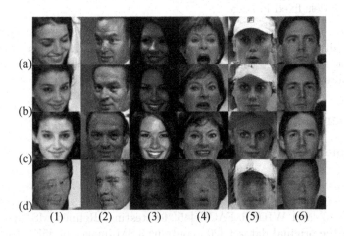

Fig. 5. Feature disentanglement visualization on LFW. We show input face $\mathbf{x}_h$ (a), reconstructed face from identity features $Dec(\mathbf{f}_h, \mathbf{0})$ (c), non-identity features $Dec(\mathbf{0}, \mathbf{z}_h)$ (d), and both (b). Feature disentanglement effectively normalizes faces in (c), and preserves pose (1, 2), illumination (3), expression (4), and occlusions (5, 6) in (d).

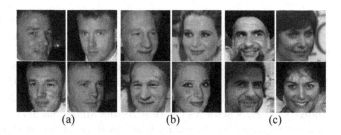

(a)   (b)   (c)

Fig. 6. Feature transfer visualization between two images of same subject (a) or different subjects (b, c). In each set of examples, the top row shows the original images and the bottom shows the transferred images. The transferred image keeps the source's (the above image) identity and the target's (the diagonal image) attributes.

Table 3. Face verification on super-resolved/normalized faces from LFW. The Enc_H achieves 99.5% on faces with the original resolutions.

Method	8× Acc./PSNR	RSA Acc./PSNR
Enc_H	86.6%/–	70.8%/–
VDSR (CVPR'16) + Enc_H	85.7%/26.63	69.4%/25.49
SRResNet (CVPR'17) + Enc_H	86.2%/27.46	68.6%/24.85
FSRNet (CVPR'18) + Enc_H	89.7%/28.27	69.4%/25.25
FSRGAN (CVPR'18) + Enc_H	86.7%/26.36	67.0%/23.94
FAN (*i.e.*, normalized image) + Enc_H	91.9%/–	76.8%/–
FAN (*i.e.*, Enc_L)	**95.2%/–**	**82.4%/–**

Our feature disentanglement framework can also be applied for feature transfer. Given two images from either the same or different subjects, our model generates identity features as $\mathbf{f}_{h_1}$, $\mathbf{f}_{h_2}$ and non-identity features as $\mathbf{z}_{h_1}$, $\mathbf{z}_{h_2}$. We perform feature transfer from one image to the other as: $Dec(\mathbf{f}_{h_1}, \mathbf{z}_{h_2})$ and $Dec(\mathbf{f}_{h_2}, \mathbf{z}_{h_1})$. Figure 6 shows some examples where our feature transfer can keep the original image's identity and change the attributes (PIE) accordingly.

Effects of Joint Learning. We conduct verification tests to demonstrate the effects of jointly learning both face recognition and normalization, compared with Enc_H that is only trained for face recognition, and state-of-the-art SR methods such as VDSR [51], SRResNet [52] and FSRNet/FSRGAN [2], that are only trained for face hallucination. With the standard verification protocol of LFW, we down-sample the 6,000 test pairs to 16 × 16 with a 8× scale factor, and upscale back to 128 × 128 via bicubic interpolation. Unlike [12] that retrains recognition network on the super-resolved images, we directly use Enc_H to evaluate the accuracy (*i.e.*, Acc.) of different face SR methods.

Since FAN handles face hallucination and frontalization simultaneously, it is not suitable to use pixel-wise evaluation metrics (*e.g.*, PSNR) to evaluate our method. Instead, we compare face verification performance. From the results in Table 3, we have three observations. 1) The recognition performance drops significantly when processing LR faces. 2) After incorporating SR methods, FSR-Net [2] achieves better verification (*i.e.*, Acc.) and SR (*i.e.*, PSNR) results than other SR methods. Our FAN achieves the best results among all SOTA SR methods. 3) It is more effective to learn identity features from LR input (Our Enc_L) than performing face hallucination and recognition on the normalized faces (Our normalized image + Enc_H).

Effects of Random Scale Augmentation. We further conduct tests to demonstrate the effects of our RSA strategy under the same experimental setting as the above study. The only difference is that we randomly down-sample the 6,000 test pairs to the resolution interval between 8×8 and 32×32, *i.e.*, the scale factors from $16\times$ to $4\times$. The extreme LR 8×8 and various/unknown resolutions existed in test images are more common than a larger and fixed resolution case. As shown in Table 3, we have three observations. 1) Since images with much lower resolutions (*e.g.*, 8×8) are evaluated, the baseline Enc_H is much lower than the $8\times$ case. 2) Since all of the SR methods are trained with specific scales (*e.g.*, $8\times$), they are not suitable for test images with varying resolutions. 3) Our FAN is much better than other methods in this case, which demonstrates the effects of RSA and our FAN is more practical in real-world scenarios.

4.3   Comparisons with SOTA Methods

In this section, we conduct extensive comparisons with SOTA methods both quantitatively and qualitatively. First, we show the hallucination ability of our method on recovering HR faces from heavily distorted faces on WIDER FACE [45]. Second, we demonstrate the ability for preserving the identity information via verification/identification comparisons on QMUL-SurFace [26] and SCface [10].

Comparisons on WIDER FACE. First, we qualitatively compare our FAN with CycleGAN [53], SRGAN [52], Wavelet-SRNet [54], FSRNet [2] and Bulat *et al.* [1] on WIDER FACE. Figure 7 illustrates the recovered images, where the results of the competitors are all imported directly from [1]. As we can see, both our FAN and [1] perform well on recovering valid faces in these cases. However, there are two differences between ours and the competitors. First, FAN is trained on refined-MS1M for joint face recognition and normalization, and we do **NOT** finetune our model with the WIDE FACE data, while the competitors are directly trained with $\sim 50K$ images from WIDER FACE. Second, FAN generates 128×128 HR images, while the competitors super-resolve to 64×64, a relatively **easier** task.

We further test our method on some heavily distorted images that [1] fails to recover meaningful HR faces, and show the results in Fig. 8. Thank to our

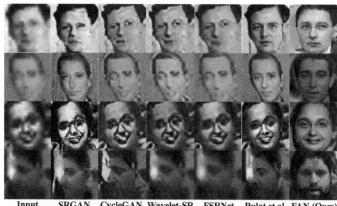

Input   SRGAN   CycleGAN   Wavelet-SR   FSRNet   Bulat et al.   FAN (Ours)

Fig. 7. Face SR/normalization on WIDER FACE.

Fig. 8. Face SR/normalization on heavily distorted images from WIDER FACE. Top: input images. Middle: Bulat *et al.* [1]. Bottom: our FAN (*i.e.*, $Dec(\mathbf{f}_l, \mathbf{0})$).

powerful encoder and decoder networks, even when dealing with extremely low-quality faces, our method still recovers valid faces that are much clear than [1]. It is an open question that whether we shall recover a face from a heavily distorted image. To address this issue, one could estimate the face quality and determine when normalization should be applied, which is not in the scope of our work or most prior face SR methods but a good direction for future work.

Comparisons on QMUL-Surv. QMUL-Surv includes very LR faces captured with surveillance cameras. It is a very challenging dataset as most of the faces are hardly visible. We compare our framework with SOTA face SR methods [2,51,52] to evaluate the performance on real world surveillance data. As shown in Fig. 9, previous works struggle to recover the high-frequency information from the input LR faces. In contrast, our FAN can consistently generate a high-quality frontal face that recovers identity information. In addition to this qualitative evaluation,

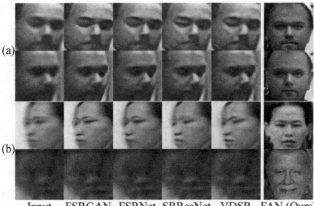

Input   FSRGAN   FSRNet   SRResNet   VDSR   FAN (Ours)

Fig. 9. Face SR/normalization on the verification set of QMUL-SurvFace.
(a): a face pair of the same subject. (b): a face pair of different subjects.

we also conduct face verification evaluation on the super-resolved/normalized face images. As shown in Table 4, our FAN performs better than previous SR methods. We have also evaluated the performance of using Enc_L to extract features directly from the LR inputs. The results in Table 4 indicates that it is more effective to learn features rather than performing super-resolution for LR face recognition, which is consistent with the observation in Table 3.

Comparisons on SCface. SCface defines face identification with unpaired HR and LR faces. It mimics the real-world surveillance watch-list problem, where the gallery contains HR faces and the probe consists of LR faces captured from surveillance cameras. The HR and LR images do not have correspondence in the pixel domain, which is difficult for previous face SR methods that requires pixel-level correspondence. It is not a problem for FAN as we regularize the model training in the disentangled feature space. Following [46], we conduct experiments on the daytime data only. The first 80 subjects are used for testing and the rest 50 subjects are for fine-tuning the second stage of our method. In addition to the unpaired HR and LR images in the training set, we also perform RSA to generate LR images from the HR images for model fine-tuning.

We mainly compare with DCR [46] as it achieved SOTA results on SCface. As far as we know, almost all SOTA face recognition methods have not evaluated on SCface. For fair comparison, we implemented ArcFace [7] using the same backbone and also finetuned on SCface training set. As shown in Table 5, our FAN achieves the best results among all other methods that are not finetuned on SCface. After finetuning on SCface with RSA, we achieve new SOTA results. Note that DCR proposed to use decoupled training that learns feature mapping for faces at *each* resolution, and the resolution information is assumed to be given in the testing stage. However, such resolution information is often unavailable in practice. Nevertheless, our method still outperforms DCR by a large margin even

Table 4. Face verification results on QMUL-Surv super-resolved faces evaluated with *Enc_H* except the last row.

Method	TAR(%)@FAR				AUC	Mean
	30%	10%	1%	0.1%		Acc (%)
VDSR [51]	61.03	35.32	8.89	3.10	71.02	65.64
SRResNet [52]	61.81	34.03	8.36	2.07	71.00	65.94
FSRNet [2]	59.92	33.10	7.84	1.93	70.09	64.96
FSRGAN [2]	56.03	30.91	8.45	2.66	67.93	63.06
FAN (norm. face)	62.31	36.64	11.89	**3.70**	71.66	66.32
FAN (*Enc_L*)	**71.30**	**44.59**	**12.94**	2.75	**76.94**	**70.88**

Table 5. Rank-1 performance of face identification on SCface testing set. '-FT' means fine-tuning with SCface training set. Most compared results are cited from [46] except ArcFace that we pretrained on refined MS1M.

Distance →	d1	d2	d3	Avg.
LDMDS [55]	62.7	70.7	65.5	66.3
LightCNN [56]	35.8	79.0	93.8	69.5
Center Loss [6]	36.3	81.8	94.3	70.8
ArcFace (ResNet50) [7]	48.0	92.0	**99.3**	79.8
LightCNN-FT	49.0	83.8	93.5	75.4
Center Loss-FT	54.8	86.3	95.8	79.0
ArcFace (ResNet50)-FT	67.3	93.5	98.0	86.3
DCR-FT [46]	73.3	93.5	98.0	88.3
FAN	62.0	90.0	94.8	82.3
FAN-FT (no RSA)	68.5	92.3	97.8	86.2
FAN-FT (no *Dec*)	73.0	94.0	97.8	88.3
FAN-FT	**77.5**	**95.0**	98.3	**90.3**

though we do **NOT** use the resolution information at the testing stage. From the gap between FAN-FT and FAN-FT (no RSA), we can see the effectiveness of RSA for surveillance FR. We also conducted ablative experiments by removing the *Dec*. No *Dec* means that we only perform feature-level similarity regularization in the second stage. The results of FAN-FT (no *Dec*) suggests that joint learning of face normalization can help feature learning for FR.

Figure 10 shows our face normalization results on SCface testing set. Our method can generate high-quality face images that recover the identity information from the input faces with various resolutions. The comparison between the results generated by *Enc_H* and *Enc_L* validates the effectiveness of feature adaptation in our second stage both quantitatively and qualitatively.

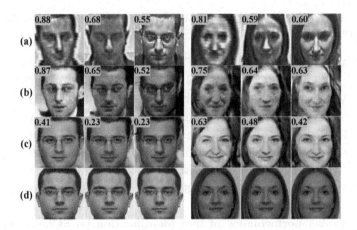

Fig. 10. Face normalization on SCface testing set. (a) input images at three resolutions. (b) normalized faces generated by Enc_H and Dec. (c) normalized faces generated by Enc_L and Dec. (d) HR gallery images. The number indicates the feature distance between the input/normalized face and the gallery HR face.

Time Complexity. Our framework adopts an encoder-decoder (*i.e.*, Enc_L and Dec) structure, it takes $\sim$0.011 s to extract *compact* identity features, and another $\sim$0.005 s to recover a 128×128 HR image on Titan X GPU, which is comparable to 0.012 s for FSRNet [2] on the same hardware, and much faster than 3.84 s for CBN [11], 8 min for [57] and 15 min for [58]. In general, compared with the SOTA methods, our FAN is a better choice in surveillance scenarios considering both visualization and recognition.

5   Conclusions

This paper proposes a Feature Adaptation Network (FAN) for surveillance face recognition and normalization. Despite the great improvement in face recognition and super-resolution, the applications in surveillance scenario is less studied. We aim to bridge this gap. FAN consists of two stages: feature disentanglement learning and feature adaptation. By first disentangling the face features into identity and non-identity components, it enables our adaptation network to impose both feature-level and image-level similarity regularizations. Such framework is suitable for both paired and unpaired training, which overcomes the limit by previous face SR methods that require paired training data. The proposed Random Scale Augmentation (RSA) is very effective in handling the various resolutions in surveillance imagery. We achieved SOTA face recognition and normalization results even from very low quality inputs.

References

1. Bulat, A., Yang, J., Tzimiropoulos, G.: To learn image super-resolution, use a GAN to learn how to do image degradation first. In: Ferrari, V., Hebert, M., Sminchisescu, C., Weiss, Y. (eds.) ECCV 2018. LNCS, vol. 11210, pp. 187–202. Springer, Cham (2018). https://doi.org/10.1007/978-3-030-01231-1_12
2. Chen, Y., Tai, Y., Liu, X., Shen, C., Yang, J.: FSRNet: end-to-End learning face super-resolution with facial priors. In: CVPR (2018)
3. Huang, G.B., Ramesh, M., Berg, T., Learned-Miller, E.: Labeled faces in the wild: a database for studying face recognition in unconstrained environments. Technical report 07–49, University of Massachusetts, Amherst (2007)
4. Klare, B.F., et al.: Pushing the frontiers of unconstrained face detection and recognition: Iarpa janus benchmark a. In: CVPR (2015)
5. Wang, H., Cosface: large margin cosine loss for deep face recognition. In: CVPR (2018)
6. Wen, Y., Zhang, K., Li, Z., Qiao, Yu.: A discriminative feature learning approach for deep face recognition. In: Leibe, B., Matas, J., Sebe, N., Welling, M. (eds.) ECCV 2016. LNCS, vol. 9911, pp. 499–515. Springer, Cham (2016). https://doi.org/10.1007/978-3-319-46478-7_31
7. Deng, J., Guo, J., Xue, N., Zafeiriou, S.: Arcface: additive angular margin loss for deep face recognition. In: CVPR (2019)
8. Tran, L., Yin, X., Liu, X.: Disentangled representation learning GAN for pose-invariant face recognition. In: CVPR (2017)
9. Zhu, X., Lei, Z., Yan, J., Yi, D., Li, S.Z.: High-fidelity pose and expression normalization for face recognition in the wild. In: CVPR (2015)
10. Grgic, M., Delac, K., Grgic, S.: SCface - surveillance cameras face database. Multimed. Tools Appl. **51**, 863–879 (2011)
11. Zhu, S., Liu, S., Loy, C.C., Tang, X.: Deep cascaded bi-network for face hallucination. In: Leibe, B., Matas, J., Sebe, N., Welling, M. (eds.) ECCV 2016. LNCS, vol. 9909, pp. 614–630. Springer, Cham (2016). https://doi.org/10.1007/978-3-319-46454-1_37
12. Zhang, K., et al.: Super-identity convolutional neural network for face hallucination. In: Ferrari, V., Hebert, M., Sminchisescu, C., Weiss, Y. (eds.) ECCV 2018. LNCS, vol. 11215, pp. 196–211. Springer, Cham (2018). https://doi.org/10.1007/978-3-030-01252-6_12
13. Wu, J., Ding, S., Xu, W., Chao, H.: Deep joint face hallucination and recognition. arXiv:1611.08091v1 (2016)
14. Tai, Y., Yang, J., Liu, X.: Image super-resolution via deep recursive residual network. In: CVPR. (2017)
15. Tai, Y., Yang, J., Liu, X., Xu, C.: MemNet: a persistent memory network for image restoration. In: ICCV (2017)
16. Rad, M.S., Bozorgtabar, B., Marti, U.V., Basler, M., Ekenel, H.K., Thiran, J.P.: SROBB: targeted perceptual loss for single image super-resolution. In: ICCV (2019)
17. Cai, J., Zeng, H., Yong, H., Cao, Z., Zhang, L.: Toward real-world single image super-resolution: a new benchmark and a new model. In: ICCV (2019)
18. Yu, X., Porikli, F.: Ultra-resolving face images by discriminative generative networks. In: Leibe, B., Matas, J., Sebe, N., Welling, M. (eds.) ECCV 2016. LNCS, vol. 9909, pp. 318–333. Springer, Cham (2016). https://doi.org/10.1007/978-3-319-46454-1_20

19. Hennings-Yeomans, P.H., Baker, S., Kumar, B.V.: Simultaneous super-resolution and feature extraction for recognition of low-resolution faces. In: CVPR (2008)
20. Guo, Y., Zhang, L., Hu, Y., He, X., Gao, J.: MS-Celeb-1M: a dataset and benchmark for large-scale face recognition. In: Leibe, B., Matas, J., Sebe, N., Welling, M. (eds.) ECCV 2016. LNCS, vol. 9907, pp. 87–102. Springer, Cham (2016). https://doi.org/10.1007/978-3-319-46487-9_6
21. Yin, B., Tran, L., Li, H., Shen, X., Liu, X.: Towards interpretable face recognition. In: ICCV. (2019)
22. Huang, Y., et al.: CurricularFace: adaptive curriculum learning loss for deep face recognition. In: CVPR (2020)
23. Yin, X., Liu, X.: Multi-task convolutional neural network for pose-invariant face recognition. IEEE Trans. Image Process. (TIP) **27**, 964–975 (2018)
24. Zhao, J., et al.: 3D-aided deep pose invariant face recognition. In: IJCAI (2018)
25. Sengupta, S., Chen, J.C., Castillo, C., Patel, V.M., Chellappa, R., Jacobs, D.: Frontal to profile face verification in the wild. In: WACV (2016)
26. Cheng, Z., Zhu, X., Gong, S.: Surveillance face recognition challenge. arXiv preprint arXiv:1804.09691 (2018)
27. Shekhar, S., Patel, V.M., Chellappa, R.: Synthesis-based recognition of low resolution faces. In: IJCB (2011)
28. Li, P., Brogan, J., Flynn, P.J.: Toward facial re-identification: experiments with data from an operational surveillance camera plant. In: BTAS (2016)
29. Belhumeur, P.N., Hespanha, J.P., Kriegman, D.J.: Eigenfaces vs. fisherfaces: recognition using class specific linear projection. IEEE Trans. Pattern Anal. Mach. Intell. **7**, 711–720(1997)
30. Susskind, J., Hinton, G., Memisevic, R., Pollefeys, M.: Modeling the joint density of two images under a variety of transformations. In: CVPR (2011)
31. Chen, D., Cao, X., Wang, L., Wen, F., Sun, J.: Bayesian face revisited: a joint formulation. In: Fitzgibbon, A., Lazebnik, S., Perona, P., Sato, Y., Schmid, C. (eds.) ECCV 2012. LNCS, vol. 7574, pp. 566–579. Springer, Heidelberg (2012). https://doi.org/10.1007/978-3-642-33712-3_41
32. Yin, X., Yu, X., Sohn, K., Liu, X., Chandraker, M.: Towards large-pose face frontalization in the wild. In: ICCV (2017)
33. Huang, R., Zhang, S., Li, T., He, R.: Beyond face rotation: Global and local perception gan for photorealistic and identity preserving frontal view synthesis. In: ICCV. (2017)
34. Amberg, B., Knothe, R., Vetter, T.: Expression invariant 3d face recognition with a morphable model. In: FG (2008)
35. Chen, W., Er, M.J., Wu, S.: Illumination compensation and normalization for robust face recognition using discrete cosine transform in logarithm domain. IEEE Transactions on Systems, Man, and Cybernetics, Part B (Cybernetics) 36 (2006) 458–466
36. Qian, Y., Deng, W., Hu, J.: Unsupervised face normalization with extreme pose and expression in the wild. In: CVPR (2019)
37. Hadad, N., Wolf, L., Shahar, M.: A two-step disentanglement method. In: CVPR (2018)
38. Baker, S., Kanade, T.: Hallucinating faces. In: FG (2000)
39. Yang, C.Y., Liu, S., Yang, M.H.: Structured face hallucination. In: CVPR (2013)
40. Kolouri, S., Rohde, G.K.: Transport-Based single frame super resolution of very low resolution face images. In: CVPR (2015)
41. Zhou, E., Fan, H., Cao, Z., Jiang, Y., Yin, Q.: Learning face hallucination in the wild. In: AAAI (2015)

42. Dong, C., Loy, C., He, K., Tang, X.: Image super-resolution using deep convolutional networks. IEEE Trans. Pattern Anal. Mach. Intell. (TPAMI) **38**, 295–307 (2016)

43. Liu, Y., Wei, F., Shao, J., Sheng, L., Yan, J., Wang, X.: Exploring disentangled feature representation beyond face identification. In: CVPR (2018)

44. Yin, X., Yu, X., Sohn, K., Liu, X., Chandraker, M.: Feature transfer learning for face recognition with under-represented data. In: CVPR (2019)

45. Yang, S., Luo, P., Loy, C., Tang, X.: Wider face: a face detection benchmark. In: CVPR (2016)

46. Lu, Z., Jiang, X., Kot, A.: Deep coupled resNet for low-resolution face recognition. IEEE Signal Process. Lett. **25**, 526–530 (2018)

47. Zhang, K., Zhang, Z., Li, Z., Qiao, Y.: Joint face detection and alignment using multitask cascaded convolutional networks. IEEE Signal Process. Lett. **23**, 1499–1503 (2016)

48. Collobert, R., Kavukcuoglu, K., Farabet, C.: Torch7: a matlab-like environment for machine learning. In: NIPS Workshop (2011)

49. He, K., Zhang, X., Ren, S., Sun, J.: Deep residual learning for image recognition. In: CVPR (2016)

50. Kingma, D.P., Ba, J.: Adam: a method for stochastic optimization. arXiv preprint arXiv:1412.6980 (2014)

51. Kim, J., Lee, J.K., Lee, K.M.: Accurate image super-resolution using very deep convolutional networks. In: CVPR (2016)

52. Ledig, C., et al.: Photo-realistic single image super-resolution using a generative adversarial network. In: CVPR (2017)

53. Zhu, J.Y., Park, T., Isola, P., Efros, A.A.: Unpaired image-to-image translation using cycle-consistent adversarial networks. In: ICCV (2017)

54. Huang, H., He, R., Sun, Z., Tan, T.: Wavelet-SRNet: a wavelet-based CNN for multi-scale face super resolution. In: ICCV (2017)

55. Yang, F., Yang, W., Gao, R., Liao, Q.: Discriminative multidimensional scaling for low-resolution face recognition. IEEE Signal Process. Lett. **25**, 388–392 (2018)

56. Wu, X., He, R., Sun, Z., Tan, T.: A light CNN for deep face representation with noisy labels. IEEE Trans. Inf. Forensics Secur. **13**, 2884–2896 (2018)

57. Liu, C., Shum, H.Y., Freeman, W.T.: Face hallucination: theory and practice. Int. J. Comput. Vis. (IJCV) **75**, 115–134 (2007)

58. Jin, Y., Bouganis, C.: Robust multi-image based blind face hallucination. In: CVPR (2015)

Human Motion Deblurring Using Localized Body Prior

Jonathan Samuel Lumentut, Joshua Santoso, and In Kyu Park[✉]

Department of Electrical and Computer Engineering, Inha University,
Incheon 22212, Korea
{jlumentut,22192280}@inha.edu, pik@inha.ac.kr

Abstract. In recent decades, the skinned multi-person linear model (SMPL) is widely exploited in the image-based 3D body reconstruction. This model, however, depends fully on the quality of the input image. Degraded image case, such as the motion-blurred issue, downgrades the quality of the reconstructed 3D body. This issue becomes severe as recent motion deblurring methods mainly focused on solving the camera motion case while ignoring the blur caused by human-articulated motion. In this work, we construct a localized adversarial framework that solves both human-articulated and camera motion blurs. To achieve this, we utilize the result of the restored image in a 3D body reconstruction module and produces a localized map. The map is employed to guide the adversarial modules on learning both the human body and scene regions. Nevertheless, training these modules straight-away is impractical since the recent blurry dataset is not supported by the 3D body predictor module. To settle this issue, we generate a novel dataset that simulates realistic blurry human motion while maintaining the presence of camera motion. By engaging this dataset and the proposed framework, we show that our deblurring results are superior among the state-of-the-art algorithms in both quantitative and qualitative performances.

1 Introduction

The task of restoring sharp and blur-free imaging becomes fundamental in computer vision works for the sake of ameliorating recent high-level tasks such as recognition or detection. The restoration of scene and object motion-blurred images are widely known as deblurring. This motion is represented by discrete representations of point-spread-function (PSF). The PSF is stored in a certain spatial window, known as blur kernel, for deconvolving the blurry image to its sharper version. The simplest way to do deblurring is to treat the scene motion as uniform. Krishnan et al. [1] introduce automatic regularization to estimate the correct blur kernel for optimization. However, in the real-world case, motion blurs variate along spatial region on the image. This happens due to the presence

---

Electronic supplementary material The online version of this chapter (https:// doi.org/10.1007/978-3-030-69532-3_20) contains supplementary material, which is available to authorized users.

© Springer Nature Switzerland AG 2021
H. Ishikawa et al. (Eds.): ACCV 2020, LNCS 12623, pp. 320–335, 2021.
https://doi.org/10.1007/978-3-030-69532-3_20

Fig. 1. Blurry images caused by both human and camera motions are restored using our approach.

of objects that are located at different depths on a scene. To solve this issue, Kim et al. [2] utilizes optical flow to obtain specific blur location to be restored accordingly. Since the rise of deep learning, the works of non-uniform deblurring are widely exploited. State-of-the-art work of Nah et al. [3] restored deblurred image directly without blur kernel estimation. Recently, the work of deblurring pursed inward with the goals of specific object restoration. The work of Shen et al. [4] introduces a semantic face mask to locally train the discriminators. The masks are generated from each specific human face part, such as eyes, nose, and mouth. Ren et al. [5] utilize human face prior for providing sharper deblurred face results. The human face prior is utilized in the deblurring layers by plugging the face identity and projected 3D rendered face directly in the network. On the other hand, Shen et al. [6] initiate the work of human deblurring. Their approach relies on the network's ability to recognize the rectangular human region that is provided from a sharp ground truth dataset.

In this work, we opt to focus on solving motion blur caused by human articulated and camera motions. Our work is amplified with the adversarial network that takes humans prior to focus on both human and scene regions themselves. To our best knowledge, this work is the first to apply such prior when it comes to deblurring. Training the network with recent human blur datasets [3,6] seems ineffective with our goal since they are mostly affected by camera motions. Therefore, we take the challenge of providing a novel blurry human dataset that considers both human and camera motions constraints. Human motion blur is mostly non-uniform since the articulated human motion is different between human joints. Thus, we provide a newly blurry human dataset that is generated from both camera and human motions. Then, we crafted the deblurring network that is joined with the 3D body reconstruction in an end-to-end fashion. The output of this generator, namely: the deblurred image and 3D reconstructed body, are utilized in the localized adversarial modules. This is learned via our generated attentional map that is part of our contribution.

In the experiments, we demonstrate our framework's performance using the blurry human dataset and achieve significant improvement in both quantitative and qualitative aspects. Visual results of our approach are demonstrated in Fig. 1. With the success of our work, we show that using the additional dataset and utilization of human prior in the deblurring modules, are learnable with generative adversarial network (GAN) approach. In summary, we describe our contributions as follows:

- We provide a learning based deblurring algorithm that utilizes human prior information from the remarkable body statistical model of SMPL [7].
- We propose, to our best knowledge, the first adversarial-based framework that is trained using localized regions that are extracted from humans and the scene's blurry locations.
- We present a novel way to synthesize blurry human motion dataset.

2   Related Works

Motion Deblurring. Early deblurring algorithms utilize the traditional way of firstly estimating the blur kernel. The kernel is used to deconvolve the blurry input in order to restore it back to a sharp image. Various regularization priors have been utilized for improving this approach [1,8]. These approaches further targeted multi-view imagings, such as the works of [9] in stereo and [10,11] in light field imaging. With the advancement of deep learning, various approaches are introduced. Nah et al. [3] proposes a multi-scale deep framework that shows deblurring robustness under various scales. Recently, the generative adversarial network (GAN) approach by [12] takes a particular interest in the deblurring field. State-of-the-art GAN deblurring is introduced by [13] that utilizes conditional GAN [14] with similar architecture to domain translation work [15]. This work is improved with the addition of multi-scale discriminators with more compact layers [16]. Recently, the work of human deblurring is introduced by [6], where a convolutional neural network is learned with the capability to find the human region in an image. However, they train the network by providing a non-precise human region since it is defined under a rectangular box.

Attention Modelling. The work of attention modeling is pioneered by [17] that provides a spatial transformer network to spatially warps specific feature regions during classification tasks. This study shows that localized attention is beneficial for a specific learning task. Pioneer work of [18] utilizes global and local regions in a GAN based framework to solve the traditional image inpainting method. Recently, the work of face de-occlusion that has the task of removing specific objects with inpainted pixels is done with the utilization of a local region of the human face in the discriminator [19]. Furthermore, face motion deblurring is shown to be improved when local face regions, such as forehead, eyes, nose, and mouth, are learned in the discriminators [4,5]. Following these trends, we introduced the utilization of the local human region to restore blurry images.

3D Body Reconstruction. In order to generate the human body region, a sophisticated model is needed. In recent years, a statistical model is introduced to represent a 3D virtual human body that is extracted from a single image. This state-of-the-art model is designed by [7] and widely known as SMPL. This model is constructed by mainly 2 parameters, namely: body pose (β) and shape (θ). The predicted outputs of SMPL are body vertices and joints. Kanazawa et al. [20] utilized deep learning approach that regresses image features for predicting those outputs. An additional discriminative network is added for distinguishing real

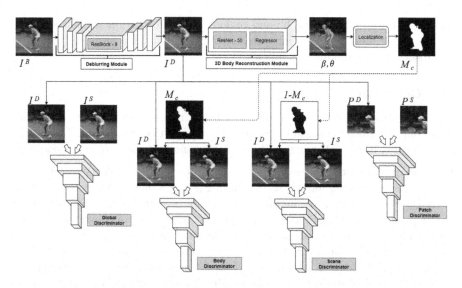

Fig. 2. The main architecture of our end-to-end framework. Blurry RGB image is fed through deblurring module where its output is processed through the 3D body reconstruction module to produce human body. Multiple discriminators improved the deblurring and predicted 3D body location results.

human and non-human body during learning. Their improved version of this work is done in the multi-frames (video) domain [21]. Recent work of [22] utilizes 2 images of the same person with different poses and views to generate the human body with colored textures. Both images are passed through the model of [20], and the textures from each view is used to complement each other.

Based on these works, we are motivated to utilize the body reconstruction model to generate our localized attention map. More precisely, this map defines the region of humans and its nearby blurry pixels. This map is regarded as prior information for the localization procedure in our adversarial framework.

3   Human and Scene Deblurring

Human articulated motion blur is a challenging task since the non-uniform blur differs much in certain parts of the human body in an image. This problem becomes severe with the addition of a camera motion blur. To tackle these issues, we define a framework that is constructed by generator and discriminator networks, as shown in Fig. 2. The generator is built with a concatenation of our deblurring model and the state-of-the-art 3D body prediction model. The key model of our framework is located in the discriminators, where they directly target the alleviation process of human and scene motion blur. Blur caused by human motion leaves distinguished trails on the blurry image. These trails are mostly located nearby the human region itself. Inversely, blurry scene regions can be captured outside the human region. This information is utilized in our discriminator modules. We elaborate on the details of our proposed generator and discriminator modules as follows.

3.1 Generator

The generator module of our framework has 2 main tasks, namely: predicting the deblurred image and estimating the 3D body vertices and joints. These tasks are described in the following modules: *deblurring* and *3D body reconstruction*.

Deblurring Module. In the first scheme, an input of RGB blurry image, I^B, is fed into the deblurring model. As shown in Fig. 2, the network receives an input of RGB blurry image, I^B. The image is initially passed through 3 convolutional blocks. The convolutional block is presented by a sequence of convolutional layer followed by instance normalization (IN) and $ReLU$ activation $(CONV \rightarrow IN \rightarrow ReLU)$. The stride of the first 2 and last 2 convolutional layers are 2. Thus the intermediate feature is downscaled to 4 times. This feature is propagated through 9 modified Residual Net blocks (ResBlocks) of [23]. Each block contains $CONV \rightarrow IN \rightarrow ReLU \rightarrow CONV \rightarrow IN$ with the final addition with input at the last layer without any dropout function. More details about the deblurring module architecture is informed in the supplementary material. The output of this deblurring module is a residual image and it is added with input image, I^B, to generate final deblurred output, I^D.

3D Body Reconstruction Module. 3D body prediction module is performed as an intermediator between the deblurring and the discriminative networks. This module benefits the performance of state-of-the-art work of [20] that uses a statistical model to predict the 3D human body. The statistic model is dubbed as SMPL [7] and is known for its capability to provide a high anatomic representation of the human body. With this model, a human body is defined by the shape (β) and pose (θ) parameters. Plugging these parameters into an SMPL function produces a renderable human body that contains 6890 vertices and 24 body joints. We utilize this model without its discriminator as in the original version [20] to balance our framework that has multiple adversarial modules. This module is utilized directly using the recent sophisticated weight of [20]. In our implementation, I^D is passed through a ResNet-50 feature extraction model and the regressor will generate features for predicting the SMPL output.

3.2 Discriminator

Besides the deblurring, our key contribution in the framework is the utilization of humans prior in the adversarial (discriminator) module. Our discriminator is trained to focus on learning a localized region. This is done by providing a specific attentional map that has the constraint of finding the local human region and its neighboring blurry region. We describe our approach in the following.

Human-Based Attention Map. An attention map is an approach of finding the local region of an image that provides useful information for the algorithm

Fig. 3. First-3: attention map from rendered shape. **Last-3**: localized attention map that is obtained from connected body joints and blurry-sharp edge differences. The application of localized map fully covers human's and its nearby blurry region. Subsequently, its reversed version covers the non-human region.

to learn. In this work, we show that omitting un-resourceful information such as the non-blurry region is beneficial. This information is penalized by a simple binary map with a value of 0. Instead of a generator, we utilized the map in the discriminator module as opposed to the approach of [6]. Our idea is motivated by several prevailing works such as [4,19] that utilizes face region from a 3D statistical face model [24]. Applying a similar idea by using the output of the 3D body reconstruction module seems like a direct application. However, it is worthy to wisely choose which information should be propagated. As known above, 2 main information is provided from the 3D body module, namely: Body vertices and joints. Utilizing body vertices have a major disadvantage as predicted shape might not fully cover the blurry human region as depicted in the first 3 columns of Fig. 3. This condition leaves us to the body joint prior option. First, the joint information from the predicted model contains only 24 coordinates that are far less than the vertices (6890), which is faster for training. Secondly, the body joint map can be connected to indicates favorable regions. Thus, we opt to connect the 24 body joint coordinates to visualize the human region. The result of this approach is dubbed as a line-joint (M_j) map and shown in the fourth column of Fig. 4. While connected body joint implies good exploration, the blurry region on the human body may not fully be covered. This is expressed in the first 3 columns of Fig. 3. We elaborate on the improvement of M_j to fully cover the blurry human region in the next region.

Localized Attention Map. To solve the previous issue, M_j is augmented with the difference of I^S and I^B maps. Since this approach is run on discriminator, I^S can be utilized. Following the basic computer vision technic, we firstly obtain the edges difference between I^S and I^B in both horizontal and vertical directions by a 3×3 Sobel filter, as shown in first and second columns of Fig. 4. The difference between horizontal and vertical edge maps is combined to produce the final map, M_b, of blurry edges, as shown in the third column of Fig. 4. However, M_b might appear in all regions on the image, although it is not nearby the human body. Thus, M_b is spatially limited with the position that corresponds to most-top, -bottom, -left, and -right of body joint. After cropped, the map is convolved with Maxpool function to do the hole-filling. Finally, this map is added with M_j to produce the combined map, M_c, which is shown in the fifth column of Fig. 4. As shown in the fourth column of Fig. 3, this map covers blur inside and

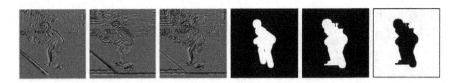

Fig. 4. First-3: Edge difference between blurry input and sharp ground truth in horizontal-vertical directions, and combined edge map from both directions. **Last-3:** Line joint map (M_j), localized map (M_c) for the body region, and reverse localized map ($1 - M_c$) for the scene region.

the nearby human body. M_c is termed as a localized attention map as it utilizes both human prior and blurry scene information. Scene's blurry region located outside M_c is also provided by reversing its value as $1 - M_c$.

Multiple Discriminator Networks. The discriminator networks act as the counter-learning process to the deblurring network in the generator scheme. Therefore, additional input, such as sharp (un-blurred) ground truth image, is utilized. In this module, deblurred and sharp ground truth images act as fake and real data distribution. Our adversarial networks are constructed by 4 discriminator modules, namely: global, body, scene, and patch discriminators, where each of them is assigned to solve specific tasks. Global and patch discriminators are utilized as a base framework that indicates no human prior. The utilization of M_c and $1 - M_c$ maps in the body and scene discriminators are regarded as our contribution to human prior. Discriminator networks' settings are provided in the supplementary material.

4   Optimization

In the initial stage, only the deblurring network is being trained without the human prior. Thus, only global and patch discriminators are included. During learning, the energy function is utilized to find the difference between the deblur output (I^D) and sharp ground truth image (I^S). At the first stage, we utilize perceptual loss that is calculated from L2 error between features of (I^D) and (I^S). These features are obtained from the convolution process of pre-trained VGG-19 network [25] until *conv3.3* layer. This approach is written in the following manner

$$L_{\mathbf{Deb}} = \frac{1}{b} \sum_i^b \gamma \|\Phi(I_i^S) - \Phi(I_i^D)\|^2 + (1 - \gamma)\|I_i^S - I_i^D\| \tag{1}$$

where Φ is the *conv3.3* function of VGG network and i represents each pixel in a set of batch multiplied by images spatial and channel size together (b). The γ value is a binary value. γ is set to 0 for final refinement using the L1 loss. For adversarial loss, we opt to utilize Least-squares GAN (LSGAN) [26]. The real and fake data probability losses are calculated by the average of discriminator scores upon real and fake results from the global and patch data, as:

$$L_{\mathbf{Real}} = \frac{0.5}{b} \sum_{i}^{b} (\Pi_{\mathbf{Glob}}(I_i^S) + \Pi_{\mathbf{Patch}}(P_i^S)); \tag{2}$$

$$L_{\mathbf{Fake}} = \frac{0.5}{b} \sum_{i}^{b} (\Pi_{\mathbf{Glob}}(I_i^D) + \Pi_{\mathbf{Patch}}(P_i^D)), \tag{3}$$

where $\Pi(\cdot)$ represents the discriminator function. Combining the equations above, the base LSGAN function of the discriminators and generator are defined by:

$$L_{\mathbf{Disc}} = 0.5 \times (\|L_{\mathbf{Real}} - 1\|^2 + \|L_{\mathbf{Fake}}\|^2); \tag{4}$$

$$L_{\mathbf{Gen}} = 100 \times L_{\mathbf{Deb}} + 0.5 \times (\|L_{\mathbf{Fake}} - 1\|^2). \tag{5}$$

In the next stage, we include the set of our contributions, namely: the body and scene discriminators. These discriminators are being trained with input data that is penalized by the generated mask from the 3D body predictor model. Thus, we define additional adversarial losses for the new discriminators. The real and fake data losses for the body and scene discriminators are calculated as follows:

$$L_{\mathbf{Real}}^* = \frac{0.5}{b} \sum_{i}^{b} (\Pi_{\mathbf{Body}}(M_c \odot I_i^S) + \Pi_{\mathbf{Scene}}((1 - M_c) \odot I_i^S)); \tag{6}$$

$$L_{\mathbf{Fake}}^* = \frac{0.5}{b} \sum_{i}^{b} (\Pi_{\mathbf{Body}}(M_c \odot I_i^D) + \Pi_{\mathbf{Scene}}((1 - M_c) \odot I_i^D)), \tag{7}$$

where M_c and $(1 - M_c)$ represent the body and scene masks that are used to piece-wisely penalized the images, respectively. This extension means that the total loss between real and fake data are calculated together, and written as:

$$L_{\mathbf{Real}}^{Tot} = 0.5 \times (L_{\mathbf{Real}} + L_{\mathbf{Real}}^*); L_{\mathbf{Fake}}^{Tot} = 0.5 \times (L_{\mathbf{Fake}} + L_{\mathbf{Fake}}^*). \tag{8}$$

Thus, the final discriminator and generator losses using 4 adversarial networks are simplified as:

$$L_{\mathbf{Disc}}^{Tot} = 0.5 \times (\|L_{\mathbf{Real}}^{Tot} - 1\|^2 + \|L_{\mathbf{Fake}}^{Tot}\|^2), \tag{9}$$

$$L_{\mathbf{Gen}}^{Tot} = 100 \times L_{\mathbf{Deb}} + 0.5 \times (\|L_{\mathbf{Fake}}^{Tot} - 1\|^2). \tag{10}$$

The constant parameters of 100 in $L_{\mathbf{Deb}}$ is used to balance the error score in generator while the value of 0.5 is an average constant for each LSGAN loss.

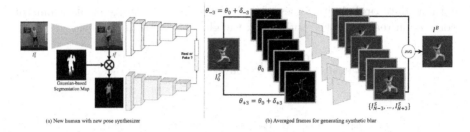

(a) New human with new pose synthesizer   (b) Averaged frames for generating synthetic blur

Fig. 5. Synthesizing the same human with a new pose is obtained by a neural network based algorithm. We provide additional discriminator to mask the human region for obtaining the sharp output of the synthesized pose. This process is done sequentially to produce multiple frames to be averaged for final blurry output.

5   Experiment Procedure

Another key factor of robust deep learning based algorithm is the quality of its datasets. As mentioned before, to handle the lack of a blurry human dataset, we propose our method. Our method generates a new human image with a new pose (I_k^S) at time-stamp k from the given initial image (I_0^S). I_0^S is extracted by employing the algorithm of [27]. We provide additional foreground discriminator, as shown in the left column of Fig. 5, to solve the unrealistic I_k^S result. This foreground prior information is obtained by the gaussian-based segmentation map to distinguish the human body and background pixels. This map is different from our approach as it is extracted from the sharp image I_0^S. For producing a blurry image, I^B, N frames of I_k^S are extracted and averaged. Each I_k^S has different pre-defined human pose θ_k. This pose is varied differently from θ_0 according to the change parameters, δ_k. The scene background is also translated to simulates camera motion. General visualization of our dataset generation approach is shown on the right column of Fig. 5. Details about the change parameters, synthesizer network, and its discriminators are provided in the supplementary material. Note that, our synthesized dataset is only used for training purpose and the images are collected from Leeds Sport Pose dataset [28]. The testing case of blurry human dataset are attained by averaging real blurry videos of InstaVariety dataset [21].

Before running the full experiments, an ablation study is performed to obtain the finest weight of our deblurring module. We divide the ablation procedure by 3 schemes: partial, full, and refined schemes. The partial scheme only includes Eqs. (1) for generator with $\gamma = 1$,   (4), and (5) for the discriminators. The full scheme includes whole equations with 4 discriminators in the discriminative modules. Both partial and full-schemes utilize the learning rate of 10^{-4}. The refined scheme has equal structures with the full scheme; however, the learning rate is reduced to 10^{-5} and γ is set to 0 to train on the L1 loss in Eq. (1). Each scheme is initially trained using GoPro dataset until 20K iterations and then our blurry human dataset is included until 65K iterations. Spatial augmentation is done during training with a size of 224×224. The Patch discriminator cropped

Ours-P   Ours-F   Ours-R

Fig. 6. Visual ablation results between our methods: *Ours-P*, *Ours-F*, and *Ours-R*.

Table 1. Quantitative comparisons on our blurry human test set between the deblurring algorithms. Ablation study is included to show the improvement of our methods. Last row indicates the performance of *Ours-R* approach.

Methods	[13]	[30]	[16]	*Ours-P*	*Ours-F*	*Ours-R*
SSIM	0.869	**0.901**	0.899	0.803	0.840	0.891
PSNR	33.29	34.93	35.25	33.07	34.56	**36.04**

the fake and real images into 80×80. Batch is set to 8 and the network is backpropagated using ADAM optimizer. The training is done in a TITAN RTX GPU for around 2.5 days for each scheme. Whole implementations are scripted using TensorFlow [29] framework.

6   Experimental Results

In the experiment section, we provide a comparison using our blurry human test set and general deblurring datasets. The general datasets are obtained from the test collections of GoPro [3] and recent HIDE [6] dataset. For comparison, we utilize recent state-of-the-art deblurring algorithms, precisely: DeblurGAN-V1 [13], Deep Hierarchical Multi Patch (DHMP) [30], and DeblurGAN-V2 [16],

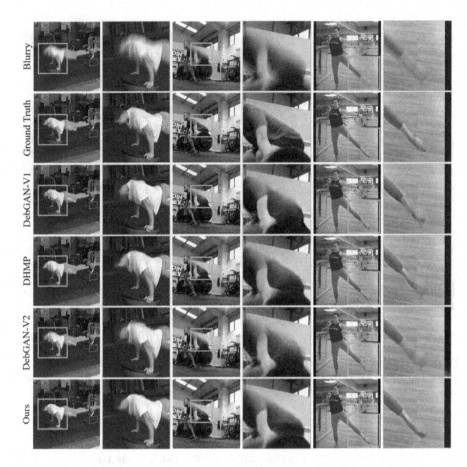

Fig. 7. Qualitative results between deblurring methods on our human blurry test set. Magnified images signify large motion blur on human region. Last row represents our refined (*Ours-R*) approach.

Table 2. Quantitative comparisons on GoPro test set [3] between the deblurring algorithms. Our method with refined approach (*Ours-R*) is used for the experiment.

Methods	[13]	[30]	[16]	*Ours-R*
SSIM	**0.958**	0.940	0.9340	0.805
PSNR	28.70	31.20	29.55	**32.51**

Table 3. Quantitative comparisons on HIDE test set [6] between the deblurring algorithms. Our method with refined approach (*Ours-R*) is used for the experiment.

Methods	[13]	[30]	[6]	[16]	*Ours-R*
SSIM	0.871	0.924	**0.931**	0.875	0.778
PSNR	24.51	29.09	28.89	26.61	**32.76**

Fig. 8. Qualitative results between deblurring methods on GoPro [3] test set. Last row represents our refined (*Ours-R*) approach.

that are publicly available. The metric of peak signal to noise ratio (PSNR) and structural similarity index (SSIM) are used in the calculation.

In the initial step, we provide ablation study on our approaches: partial (*Ours-P*), full (*Ours-F*), and refined (*Ours-R*) schemes. These schemes are tested in our blurry human test cases. The quantitative scores are shown in the last 3 columns of Table 1. Without the body prior, our method suffers from restoring the blurry region caused by human motion, as shown in the first column of Fig. 6. By providing full-scheme approach, that includes body prior, blurry human motion on the second column of Fig. 6 can be restored. However, this approach leaves artifact on the deblurred region caused by the mismatched size of deconvolution filter size when VGG loss is used. Thus, we refine this approach using L1 loss as described in Sect. 4. This strategy successfully restores the blurry human motion without artifact as shown in the third column of Fig. 6.

In the second step, we perform a comparison using the state-of-the-art methods using our blurry human dataset. The first 3 columns of Table 1 show the result of other methods. For fairness' sake, those algorithms are fine-tuned using our blurry human training set. It is clearly seen from Fig. 7 that our approach provides better visual results compared to others. Significant human motion blur, such in the case of the sixth column of Fig. 7, is hardly restored by other state-of-the-art methods. The main reason is that their methods are trained for deblurring camera motion cases only. However, in our case, we employ localized body prior information to train the deblurring network. This prior lets the network learn the blur caused by articulated human motion, which is different from general camera motion. Therefore, our method achieves superior performance in terms of qualitative. These results are also reflected in Table 1 as our approach (*Ours-R*) achieves the highest PSNR. Our method achieves a competitive SSIM score compared to the non-GAN method [30] since the GAN approach produces synthesized pixels during restoration.

In third step, we compare the deblurring algorithms with the GoPro dataset [3] that is widely known for benchmarking. In this case the GoPro dataset contains scene with and without humans and the total test set is 1111 images. The results in Table 2 show that our network able to outperforms previous deblurring methods. Note that our localized approach is done on image with single human in the middle during training. However, our deblurring network is fully-convolutional. Thus, multiple humans that present in the GoPro dataset, are well-deblurred using our method. Table 2 shows new record as *Ours-R* achieves the best score in terms of PSNR. Qualitative results are shown in Fig. 8. Our deblurring method that is trained for both camera and human motion blurs handles the blurry region eloquently by restoring some blurry scene's edges. Other methods show similar performance except in the case of restoring large blurry human motion. Second and fourth columns of Fig. 8 show magnified results of the blurry case when people are walking. These results clearly show that the articulated human motion is solved by our method with the more faithful result compared to others. Moreover, the blurry non-human region is also restored similarly compared to other state-of-the-art methods. This is achieved by our network as it is guided by the non-human region $(1 - M_c)$ during the optimization procedure. Best quantitative performance using this dataset is also achieved by our method, as shown in Table 2. For our final step, we also compare using the recent blurry dataset, known as HIDE [6], as they provide whole images with the presence of humans. Note that the HIDE dataset of [6] contains long-shot and close-up blurry human images, and most of the blur is caused by the scene motion. Our approach achieves the highest score in terms of PSNR compared to other methods, as shown in Table 3. Additional visual results are included in the material.

From these experiments, our method achieves state-of-the-art performance as it solves both camera and human articulated motion blurs. The human prior works well on guiding the discriminator, which eventually trains the deblurring generator on distinguishing human and non-human blurry regions.

7 Conclusion

While current deblurring methods perform well, most of them only focus on scene motion blur case. Human motion deblurring plays a crucial role in the recent computer vision's 3D body reconstruction task. In this paper, we explore several methods to handle human motion deblurring, specifically: we introduce localized body prior that guide the network to give more attention on the human region; we introduce adversarial framework from human prior that helps network on restoring blurred human and scene regions; and finally, we also introduce synthetic human motion blur dataset to train on the network. From experimental results, we show that our approach is able to reach state-of-the-art performance on both human and scene motion deblurring. We believe this exploration can be applied to various human-based image processing tasks.

Acknowledgement. This work was supported by Samsung Research Funding Center of Samsung Electronics under Project Number SRFCIT1901-06. This work was supported by Inha University Research Grant.

References

1. Krishnan, D., Tay, T., Fergus, R.: Blind deconvolution using a normalized sparsity measure. In: Proceedings of the IEEE Conference on Computer Vision and Pattern Recognition, pp. 233–240 (2011)
2. Kim, T.H., Lee, K.M.: Segmentation-free dynamic scene deblurring. In: Proceedings of the IEEE Conference on Computer Vision and Pattern Recognition, pp. 2766–2773 (2014)
3. Nah, S., Kim, T.H., Lee, K.M.: Deep multi-scale convolutional neural network for dynamic scene deblurring. In: Proceedings of the IEEE Conference on Computer Vision and Pattern Recognition, pp. 257–265 (2017)
4. Shen, Z., Lai, W.S., Xu, T., Kautz, J., Yang, M.H.: Deep semantic face deblurring. In: Proceedings of the IEEE Conference on Computer Vision and Pattern Recognition, pp. 8260–8269 (2018)
5. Ren, W., Yang, J., Deng, S., Wipf, D., Cao, X., Tong, X.: Face video deblurring using 3D facial priors. In: Proceedings of the IEEE International Conference on Computer Vision, pp. 9387–9396 (2019)
6. Shen, Z., et al.: Human-aware motion deblurring. In: Proceedings of the IEEE International Conference on Computer Vision, pp. 5571–5580 (2019)
7. Loper, M., Mahmood, N., Romero, J., Pons-Moll, G., Black, M.J.: SMPL: a skinned multi-person linear model. ACM Trans. Graph. **34**, 248:1–248:16 (2015)
8. Pan, J., Hu, Z., Su, Z., Yang, M.H.: Deblurring text images via L_0-regularized intensity and gradient prior. In: Proceedings of the IEEE Conference on Computer Vision and Pattern Recognition, pp. 2901–2908 (2014)

9. Sellent, A., Rother, C., Roth, S.: Stereo video deblurring. In: Leibe, B., Matas, J., Sebe, N., Welling, M. (eds.) ECCV 2016. LNCS, vol. 9906, pp. 558–575. Springer, Cham (2016). https://doi.org/10.1007/978-3-319-46475-6_35

10. Srinivasan, P.P., Ng, R., Ramamoorthi, R.: Light field blind motion deblurring. In: Proceedings of the IEEE Conference on Computer Vision and Pattern Recognition, pp. 2354–2362 (2017)

11. Lumentut, J.S., Kim, T.H., Ramamoorthi, R., Park, I.K.: Deep recurrent network for fast and full-resolution light field deblurring. IEEE Signal Process. Lett. **26**, 1788–1792 (2019)

12. Goodfellow, I., et al.: Generative adversarial nets. In: Advances in Neural Information Processing Systems, pp. 2672–2680 (2014)

13. Kupyn, O., Budzan, V., Mykhailych, M., Mishkin, D., Matas, J.: DeblurGAN: blind motion deblurring using conditional adversarial networks. In: Proceedings of the IEEE Conference on Computer Vision and Pattern Recognition, pp. 8183–8192 (2018)

14. Gulrajani, I., Ahmed, F., Arjovsky, M., Dumoulin, V., Courville, A.C.: Improved training of Wasserstein GANs. In: Advances in Neural Information Processing Systems, pp. 5767–5777 (2017)

15. Isola, P., Zhu, J.Y., Zhou, T., Efros, A.A.: Image-to-image translation with conditional adversarial networks. In: Proceedings of the IEEE Conference on Computer Vision and Pattern Recognition, pp. 5967–5976 (2017)

16. Kupyn, O., Martyniuk, T., Wu, J., Wang, Z.: DeblurGAN-v2: deblurring (orders-of-magnitude) faster and better. In: Proceedings of the IEEE International Conference on Computer Vision, pp. 8877–8886 (2019)

17. Jaderberg, M., Simonyan, K., Zisserman, A., Kavukcuoglu, K.: Spatial transformer networks. In: Advances in Neural Information Processing Systems, pp. 2017–2025 (2015)

18. Iizuka, S., Simo-Serra, E., Ishikawa, H.: Globally and locally consistent image completion. ACM Trans. Graph. **36**, 107:1–107:14 (2017)

19. Yuan, X., Park, I.K.: Face de-occlusion using 3D morphable model and generative adversarial network. In: Proceedings of the IEEE International Conference on Computer Vision, pp. 10061–10070 (2019)

20. Kanazawa, A., Black, M.J., Jacobs, D.W., Malik, J.: End-to-end recovery of human shape and pose. In: Proceedings of the IEEE Conference on Computer Vision and Pattern Recognition, pp. 7122–7131 (2018)

21. Kanazawa, A., Zhang, J.Y., Felsen, P., Malik, J.: Learning 3D human dynamics from video. In: Proceedings of the IEEE Conference on Computer Vision and Pattern Recognition, pp. 5614–5623 (2019)

22. Pavlakos, G., Kolotouros, N., Daniilidis, K.: Texturepose: supervising human mesh estimation with texture consistency. In: Proceedings of the IEEE International Conference on Computer Vision, pp. 803–812 (2019)

23. He, K., Zhang, X., Ren, S., Sun, J.: Deep residual learning for image recognition. In: Proceedings of the IEEE Conference on Computer Vision and Pattern Recognition, pp. 770–778 (2016)

24. Blanz, V., Vetter, T.: Face recognition based on fitting a 3D morphable model. IEEE Trans. Pattern Anal. Mach. Intell. **25**, 1063–1074 (2003)

25. Simonyan, K., Zisserman, A.: Very deep convolutional networks for large-scale image recognition. arXiv:1409.1556 (2014)

26. Mao, X., Li, Q., Xie, H., Lau, R.Y., Wang, Z., Paul Smolley, S.: Least squares generative adversarial networks. In: Proceedings of the IEEE International Conference on Computer Vision, pp. 2813–2821 (2017)

27. Balakrishnan, G., Zhao, A., Dalca, A.V., Durand, F., Guttag, J.: Synthesizing images of humans in unseen poses. In: Proceedings of the IEEE Conference on Computer Vision and Pattern Recognition, pp. 8340–8348 (2018)
28. Johnson, S., Everingham, M.: Clustered pose and nonlinear appearance models for human pose estimation. In: Proceedings of the British Machine Vision Conference, pp. 1–11. BMVA Press (2010)
29. Abadi, M., et al.: Tensorflow: a system for large-scale machine learning. In: 12th USENIX Conference on Operating Systems Design and Implementation, vol. 16, pp. 265–283 (2016)
30. Zhang, H., Dai, Y., Li, H., Koniusz, P.: Deep stacked hierarchical multi-patch network for image deblurring. In: Proceedings of the IEEE Conference on Computer Vision and Pattern Recognition, pp. 5978–5986 (2019)

Synergistic Saliency and Depth Prediction for RGB-D Saliency Detection

Yue Wang[1], Yuke Li[2], James H. Elder[3], Runmin Wu[4], Huchuan Lu[1(✉)], and Lu Zhang[1]

[1] Dalian University of Technology, Dalian, China
lhchuan@dlut.edu.cn
[2] UC Berkeley, Berkeley, USA
[3] York University, Toronto, Canada
[4] The University of Hong Kong, Hong Kong, China

Abstract. Depth information available from an RGB-D camera can be useful in segmenting salient objects when figure/ground cues from RGB channels are weak. This has motivated the development of several RGB-D saliency datasets and algorithms that use all four channels of the RGB-D data for both training and inference. Unfortunately, existing RGB-D saliency datasets are small, which may lead to overfitting and limited generalization for diverse scenarios. Here we propose a semi-supervised system for RGB-D saliency detection that can be trained on smaller RGB-D saliency datasets *without* saliency ground truth, while also make effective joint use of a large RGB saliency dataset with saliency ground truth together. To generalize our method on RGB-D saliency datasets, a novel prediction-guided cross-refinement module which jointly estimates both saliency and depth by mutual refinement between two respective tasks, and an adversarial learning approach are employed. Critically, our system does not require saliency ground-truth for the RGB-D datasets, which saves the massive human labor for hand labeling, and does not require the depth data for inference, allowing the method to be used for the much broader range of applications where only RGB data are available. Evaluation on seven RGB-D datasets demonstrates that even without saliency ground truth for RGB-D datasets and using only the RGB data of RGB-D datasets at inference, our semi-supervised system performs favorable against state-of-the-art fully-supervised RGB-D saliency detection methods that use saliency ground truth for RGB-D datasets at training and depth data at inference on two largest testing datasets. Our approach also achieves comparable results on other popular RGB-D saliency benchmarks.

Keywords: RGB-D saliency detection · Semi-supervised learning · Cross refinement · Adversarial learning

1 Introduction

Salient Object Detection (SOD) aims to accurately segment the main objects in an image at the pixel level. It is an early vision task important for downstream

© Springer Nature Switzerland AG 2021
H. Ishikawa et al. (Eds.): ACCV 2020, LNCS 12623, pp. 336–352, 2021.
https://doi.org/10.1007/978-3-030-69532-3_21

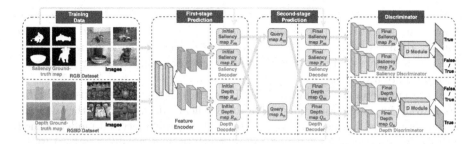

Fig. 1. Overview of our proposed method, including the first-stage prediction module, the second-stage prediction module, and our discriminator module. The input of our structure is RGB data only, and during testing, we only take RGB data from RGB-D saliency datasets to produce the saliency prediction with the Final Saliency map P.

tasks such as visual tracking [1], object detection [2], and image-retrieval [3]. Recently, deep learning algorithms trained on large ($>10K$ image) RGB datasets like DUTS [4] have substantially advanced the state of the art. However, the problem remains challenging when figure/ground contrast is low or backgrounds are complex.

It has been observed that in these cases depth information available from an RGB-D camera can be useful in segmenting the salient objects, which are typically in front of the background [5–12]. This has motivated the development of several small RGB-D saliency datasets [5,13–18] with pixel-level hand-labeled saliency ground-truth maps for training. In order to emphasize the value of depth information, these datasets were constructed so that segmentation based only on RGB channels is difficult due to similarities in colour, texture and 2D configural cues in figure and ground (Fig. 1). Note that algorithms trained on these datasets use all four channels of the RGB-D data for both training and inference.

Unfortunately, RGB-D images are much rarer than RGB images, and existing RGB-D saliency datasets are much smaller than existing RGB saliency datasets (several hundred vs ten thousand images), which might lead to overfitting and limited generalization for diverse scenarios. In theory, one could construct a much larger RGB-D dataset with hand-labeled saliency ground truth, but this would entail specialized equipment and an enormous amount of human labor. Moreover, the existing fully-supervised methods require the additional depth map as input during inference, which limits their applications and makes them be not suitable when only RGB data are available.

This raises the question: Is it possible to make joint use of large RGB saliency datasets with hand-labeled saliency ground truth, together with smaller RGB-D saliency datasets *without* saliency ground truth, for the problem of saliency detection on RGB-D datasets? This would allow us to recruit the massive hand-labeled RGB saliency datasets that already exist while facilitating the expansion of RGB-D training datasets, since hand-labeled saliency maps for these images is not required. Perhaps an even more interesting and ambitious question is: Can we train a semi-supervised system using these two disparate data sources such that it can perform accurate inference on the kinds of images found in RGB-D saliency datasets, *even when given only the RGB channels*? This would allow the system to be used in the much broader range of applications for which only RGB data are available.

However, the images found in RGB-D saliency datasets are statistically different from the images found in typical RGB saliency datasets since they contain more complicated background, how to make our semi-supervised model trained with RGB dataset and its saliency ground truth to be generalized well on RGB-D datasets without the saliency ground truth becomes the key challenge. To address this challenge, we propose our novel prediction-guided cross-refinement network with adversarial learning.

The system consists of three stages (Fig. 1). **Stage 1.** We build an initial prediction module with two branches: a saliency branch that takes RGB images from an RGB saliency dataset as input and is supervised with saliency ground truth; and a depth branch that takes RGB images from an RGB-D saliency dataset as input and is supervised with depth ground truth (i.e., the Depth data of the RGB-D images). **Stage 2.** Since in stage one, for each source dataset, only one branch is supervised, the statistical difference between two sources makes our initial model not generalize well on the unsupervised source, we propose our prediction-guided cross-refinement module as a bridge between two branches. The supervised branch contributes to the unsupervised one with extra information which promotes the generalization of our model. **Stage 3.** To further solve the distribution difference for two sources in this semi-supervised situation, we employ a discriminator module trained adversarially, which serves to increase the similarity in representations across sources.

Not only do we train our RGB-D saliency prediction model without the saliency ground truth from RGB-D datasets, we also do not need depth data at inference: the depth data of RGB-D images is used only as a supervisory signal during training. This makes our system usable not just for RGB-D data but for the wider range of applications where only RGB data are available. We evaluate our approach on seven RGB-D datasets and show that our semi-supervised method achieves comparable performance to the state-of-the-art fully-supervised methods, which, unlike our approach, use hand-labeled saliency ground truth for RGB-D datasets at training and use the depth data at inference.

In summary, we make two main contributions:

- We introduce a novel semi-supervised method with prediction-guided cross-refinement module and adversarial learning that effectively exploits large existing hand-labeled RGB saliency dataset, together with *unlabelled RGB-D data* to accurately predict saliency maps for RGB data from RGB-D saliency datasets. To the best of our knowledge, our paper is the first exploration of the semi-supervised method for RGB-D saliency detection.
- We show that, our semi-supervised method which does not use saliency ground truth for RGB-D datasets during training and uses only the RGB data at inference, performs favorable against existing fully-supervised meth-

ods that use saliency ground truth for RGB-D data at training and use the RGB data as well as depth data at inference on two largest RGB-D testing datasets (SIP and STEREO), and achieves comparable results on other popular RGB-D saliency benchmarks.

2   Related Work

Considering that it is still a challenge for the existing RGB saliency detections trained on RGB datasets tend to process images with complex scenarios, new RGB-D datasets with complex-scenario images and depth data are constructed to focus on this circumstance [5,13–17]. The spatial structure information provided by depth data can be of great help for saliency detection, especially for situations like lower contrast between foreground and background. Several methods focus on RGB-D saliency detection have been proposed to achieve better performance on images with complex scenarios.

In the early stage, approaches like [11,12,14,17,19,20] use traditional methods of hand-crafted feature representations, contextual contrast and spatial prior to extract information and predict saliency maps from both RGB data and depth data in an unsupervised way. [14] proposes the first large scale RGB-D benchmark dataset and a detection algorithm which combines depth information and appearance cues in a coupled manner. More recently, supervised CNN models that extract high-level content have been found beneficial to saliency detection for complex images. Methods based on CNN structures achieve better performance on RGB-D saliency detection [5–10,21,22]. [21] employs two CNN networks to deal with RGB and depth data separately, and fuses the two networks on prediction level to predict the final saliency map, while [22] fuses the two networks on feature level to predict the final saliency map. [5] applies the multi-scale recurrent attention network to combine features from RGB and depth data at multiple scales, which considers both global and local information.

However, the above methods suffer from two problems. First, RGB-D datasets are rarer and the number of images in the existing RGB-D datasets is much smaller, which makes the above methods may tend to be overfitting and perform limitedly for diverse situations. Build larger RGB-D datasets for training would require not only massive labor work on labeling the pixel-level ground-truth saliency maps, but also special equipment to collect depth data. Second, the above methods demand depth data in both training and inference processes, which limits the application of RGB-D saliency detection to images with both RGB data and depth data. In this paper, we propose our semi-supervised method with prediction-guided cross-refinement module and adversarial learning to predict saliency maps for RGB-D datasets. With the help of the existing RGB dataset and its saliency ground truth as well as our designed structure, we are able to train the saliency prediction model for RGB-D datasets *without accessing to their saliency ground truth*. Besides, by using depth data as an auxiliary task instead of input, it allows us to evaluate our model with only RGB data.

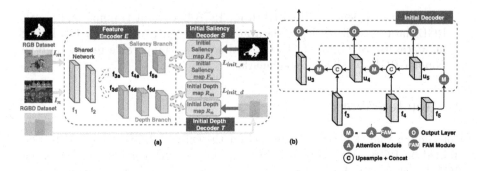

Fig. 2. (a) Illustration of our proposed first-stage initial prediction module. It outputs the initial saliency and depth prediction maps separately for both RGB and RGB-D datasets. (b) The detailed structure of our decoder, the saliency decoder and depth decoder apply the same structure.

3   Method

In this paper, we propose a novel semi-supervised approach for RGB-D saliency detection by exploiting small RGB-D saliency datasets without saliency ground truth, and large RGB saliency dataset with saliency ground truth. It contains three stages: a first-stage initial prediction module with two branches for saliency and depth tasks where each task is supervised with only one source dataset; a second-stage prediction-guided cross-refinement module which provides a bridge between the two branches for each source; and a third-stage discriminator module which further aligns representations from two sources. The overview of our proposed structure is shown in Fig. 1.

3.1   Prediction Module: The First Stage

The basic structure of our first stage prediction module showed in Fig. 2 consists of a feature encoder $\mathbf{E}$, an initial saliency decoder $\mathbf{S}$, and an initial depth decoder $\mathbf{T}$. Our $\mathbf{E}$ is based on a VGG19 [23] backbone, which extracts features at five levels. Both of our decoders $\mathbf{S}$ and $\mathbf{T}$ apply the same architecture using the last three levels of features from the encoder $\mathbf{E}$, similar to FCN [24]. To simultaneously perform two different tasks, our $\mathbf{E}$ is designed to have a two-branch structure for both saliency and depth feature representations. It has a common two-level root to constrain the model size by sharing weights on the first two levels, and it is followed by three separate layers for each branch encoding features that are passed to the respective decoders. In summary, our feature encoder $\mathbf{E}$ extracts 8 layers of features for each image: two features layers common to both saliency and depth $\{f_1, f_2\}$, three saliency-specific feature layers $\{f_{3s}, f_{4s}, f_{5s}\}$, and three depth-specific feature layers $\{f_{3d}, f_{4d}, f_{5d}\}$.

To further improve the prediction accuracy, we incorporate an extra attention module for features on each level for two decoders. We first introduce a very basic self-attention module from the non-local block [25], which is an implementation of the self-attention form in [26]. Given a query and a key-value pair, the attention function can be described as to learn a weighted sum of values with the compatibility function of the query and key. For self-attention module, query, key, and value are set to be the same, and the weighted sum output is:

$$u = W_z(\text{softmax}(f^T W_\theta^T W_\phi f)g(f)) + f \tag{1}$$

where f is the input feature, u is the weighted sum output. W_θ, W_ϕ, $g(\cdot)$ and W_z are the function for query, key, value and weight (See [25,26] for details).

For the highest-level feature f_5, we apply the idea of the above self-attention module (Eq. 1) which uses the f_5 itself as the query to obtain the output feature u_5. While for the feature from the other level f_L, $L \in \{4,3\}$, it first need to combine with a higher-level output u_{L+1} by the following common practice:

$$\tilde{f}_L = conv(\text{cat}(\text{UP}(u_{L+1}), f_L)) \tag{2}$$

where $L \in \{3,4\}$ indicates the level of feature, $\text{cat}(\cdot)$ is the concat function, $\text{UP}(\cdot)$ is the function for upsampling.

We also apply the attention module for the lower-level features. However, considering the fact that features on different levels are complementary to each other since they extract information in different resolutions, high-level features focus on global semantic information, and low-level features provide spatial details which may contain noises, we would like to select which fine details to pay attention to in low-level features with the global context. Therefore, the attention module we apply to lower-level features $\tilde{f}_L, L \in \{3,4\}$ are based on the highest-level feature u_5 to extract meaningful details for prediction. Based on the idea of Eq. 1, we replace the query with feature u_5 and form our feature-guided attention module. The overall feature-guided attention module is as follow:

$$u_L = \begin{cases} W_{z_L}(\text{softmax}(f_L^T W_{\theta_L}^T W_{\phi_L} f_L)g_L(f_L)) + f_L & L = 5 \\ W_{z_L}(\text{softmax}(u_5^T W_{\theta_L}^T W_{\phi_L} \tilde{f}_L)g_L(\tilde{f}_L)) + \tilde{f}_L & L \in \{4,3\} \end{cases} \tag{3}$$

where $\tilde{f}_L$ is the combined feature, and $u5$ is the updated feature on f_5.

Meanwhile, we also apply the FAM module [27] for all-level features. It is capable of reducing the aliasing effect of upsampling as well as enlarging the receptive field to improve the performance. We then apply three prediction layers on multi-level features $\{u_5, u_4, u_3\}$ and add the outputs together to form the initial prediction regarding the branch they belong to. The detailed architecture of our decoder is illustrated in Fig. 2(b).

Given an image I_m from RGB dataset with its saliency ground truth Y_m, and an image I_n from RGB-D dataset with its depth data Z_n, we can obtain their corresponding initial saliency and depth features $\{u_{3s}, u_{4s}, u_{5s}, u_{3d}, u_{4d}, u_{5d}\}_m$ and $\{u_{3s}, u_{4s}, u_{5s}, u_{3d}, u_{4d}, u_{5d}\}_n$ with the same encoder $\mathbf{E}$ and separate decoders $\mathbf{S}$, $\mathbf{T}$. The three levels of saliency features belong to image I_m will then be used to output its initial saliency maps F_m, while the three levels of depth features belong to image I_n will then be used to output its initial depth maps R_n. Since

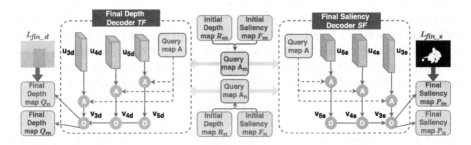

Fig. 3. Illustration of our proposed second-stage prediction module. It uses the initial saliency and depth prediction maps as the query to cross refine feature representations on both branches for RGB dataset and RGB-D dataset.

Y_m of I_m and Z_n of I_n are available, we can use them to calculate the losses of two initial maps to train our first stage prediction model:

$$\mathcal{L}_{init\_s}(\mathbf{E}, \mathbf{S}) = \mathcal{L}_{bce}(F_m, Y_m) \tag{4}$$

$$\mathcal{L}_{init\_d}(\mathbf{E}, \mathbf{T}) = \mathcal{L}_1(R_n, Z_n) \tag{5}$$

For the saliency branch, we calculate it using the binary cross-entropy loss $\mathcal{L}_{bce}$, and for the depth branch, we calculate it using the L1 loss $\mathcal{L}_1$. The overall architecture of our first-stage prediction is illustrated in Fig. 2.

3.2 Prediction Module: The Second Stage

In the first stage of our prediction module, the saliency and depth branch can only affect each other on the two shared layers in $\mathbf{E}$. Since $\mathbf{S}$ is only supervised with images from the RGB dataset and $\mathbf{T}$ is only supervised by images from the RGB-D dataset, these two decoders may not be generalized well on the unsupervised source datasets since the difference between RGB and RGB-D saliency datasets on distribution. However, we notice that the initial depth map R_n from RGB-D dataset which provides spatial structural information can be helpful for its saliency prediction, while the initial saliency map F_m from RGB dataset can be assisted to its depth prediction since it shows the location of the important objects which draw people's attention. Therefore, to enhance the generalization for our initial module on different source datasets, we come up with an idea of using a prediction-guided cross-refinement module as a bridge to transfer information between saliency and depth branch.

Here, we build our final saliency decoder $\mathbf{SF}$ and final depth decoder $\mathbf{TF}$, which use our designed prediction-guided method to cross refine the feature representations and initial maps from the first stage. Our prediction-guided cross-refinement method is based on the same idea of feature-guided attention module in Sect. 3.1. The detailed structure of our second stage prediction module is shown in Fig. 3.

In this stage, given features from two branches, $\{u_{3s}, u_{4s}, u_{5s}, u_{3d}, u_{4d}, u_{5d}\}$, the initial saliency map F as well as initial depth map R are used as the query

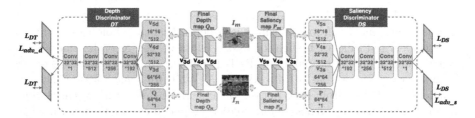

Fig. 4. Illustration of our discriminator module for adversarial learning. It has two parts, the discriminator DS deals with representations from the saliency branch, and the discriminator DT deals with representations from the depth branch.

in the attention module. We first concat F and R to form the query A since the initial F will also support the saliency branch itself to focus on the more informative spatial positions and channels in saliency representations and it is the same for R to our depth branch. And then we design a prediction-guided attention module with the following equation to update all the multi-level features from two branches.

$$v_L = W_{z n_L}(\mathrm{softmax}(A^T W_{\theta n_L}^T W_{\phi n_L} u_L) g_{n_L}(u_L)) + u_L \qquad (6)$$

where u_L represents the feature from the first stage and v_L is the updated feature, $L \in \{5,4,3\}$. All six features from one image $\{v_{3s}, v_{4s}, v_{5s}, v_{3d}, v_{4d}, v_{5d}\}$ will then be applied to new prediction layers specific to their tasks. For images from RGB dataset, we sum up three-level saliency outputs to get the final saliency predictions P_m, and then calculate the loss with saliency ground-truth Y_m by:

$$\mathcal{L}_{fin\_s}(\mathbf{E}, \mathbf{SF}, \mathbf{S}, \mathbf{T}) = \mathcal{L}_{bce}(P_m, Y_m) \qquad (7)$$

And for images from RGB-D dataset, we also sum up all three-level depth outputs to get the final depth predictions Q_n, and calculate the loss with depth ground-truth Z_n by:

$$\mathcal{L}_{fin\_d}(\mathbf{E}, \mathbf{TF}, \mathbf{S}, \mathbf{T}) = \mathcal{L}_1(Q_n, Z_n) \qquad (8)$$

3.3 Discriminator

Take the saliency branch as an example, in the first stage, the saliency prediction is only supervised by RGB saliency dataset. Even though we apply our feature-guided attention and FAM module, it can be only helpful for improving the performance for saliency detection on RGB saliency dataset itself. Due to the different distribution between RGB and RGB-D saliency datasets since images from RGB-D dataset contain more complicated background with similarities to the foreground in color and texture, the improvement on RGB dataset may also cause more noisy background to be detected as the salient region on RGB-D dataset by mistake (Fig. 5 from B to B+M). With extra depth information from RGB-D saliency dataset and the cross refinement module in our second stage, the information from the supervised depth branch is able to transfer to the unsupervised saliency branch for RGB-D dataset, the generalization ability of our saliency prediction model on RGB-D dataset can be enhanced, such as the first row in Fig. 5 from B+M to B+M+A. While for some images which are significantly different from RGB dataset on appearance and situations as the one in second row, the effectiveness of our prediction-guided cross-refinement module may be affected. To further generalize our saliency model on RGB-D dataset, we take advantage of the adversarial learning to narrow down the distance between the representations from RGB and RGB-D dataset by adding a discriminator module (Fig. 5 from B+M+A to Ours). It could also be equally applied to the depth branch, and the detail of our discriminator module is shown in Fig. 4.

The original idea of adversarial learning is used for Generative Adversarial Network (GAN) [28], which is to generate fake images from noise to look real. It is further used in domain adaptation for image classification [29,30], object detection [31,32] and semantic segmentation [33–36], where they train the model on source domain with easily obtained ground truth and generalize it to target domain without ground truth. The purpose of the domain adaptation is to solve the problem of domain shift due to image difference on appearance, textures, or style for two domains. The adversarial learning method uses the generator and discriminator modules to compete against each other to minimize the distance between distributions of representations on two domains, which is also suitable for our semi-supervised method to further improve its generalization ability.

Our discriminator module has two parts that respond to two task branches, discriminator **DS** is for the saliency branch, and discriminator **DT** is for the depth branch. These two discriminators are trained to distinguish representations from RGB and RGB-D dataset, and our two-stage prediction module is treated as the generator to fool the discriminators. The adversarial learning on generator and discriminators helps our prediction model to extract useful representations for saliency and depth tasks which can be generalized on both source datasets. Here, we align both latent feature representations and output prediction representations from the two datasets. For **DS**, since image I_m from RGB dataset have the saliency ground truth Y_m, we train **DS** so that the saliency feature representations $\{v_{3s}, v_{4s}, v_{5s}\}_m$ and output representation P_m can be classified as source domain label 0, while the representations $\{v_{3s}, v_{4s}, v_{5s}\}_n$ and P_n from image I_n in RGB-D dataset can be classified as target domain label 1. And we calculate the loss of **DS** by:

$$\mathcal{L}_{DS}(\mathbf{DS}) = \mathcal{L}_{bce}(\mathbf{DS}(v_{3s_m}, v_{4s_m}, v_{5s_m}, P_m), 0) \\ + \mathcal{L}_{bce}(\mathbf{DS}(v_{3s_n}, v_{4s_n}, v_{5s_n}, P_n), 1) \tag{9}$$

where $\mathcal{L}_{bce}$ is the binary cross-entropy domain classification loss since the output channel of our discriminator is 1. Meanwhile, instead of predicting one value for the whole image, we obtain a patch-level output corresponding to the patch-level representations, which allows the discriminator to predict different labels for each patch, in order to encourage the system to learn the diversity of factors that determine the generalization for each spatial position.

For **DT**, depth representations $\{v_{3d}, v_{4d}, v_{5d}\}_n$ and Q_n from image I_n are supervised by depth ground-truth data Z_n, so we train **DT** to classify its representations as source domain label 0, and classify representations $\{v_{3d}, v_{4d}, v_{5d}\}_m$ and Q_m from I_m as target domain label 1. The loss for **DT** is calculated by:

$$\mathcal{L}_{DT}(\mathbf{DT}) = \mathcal{L}_{bce}(\mathbf{DT}(v_{3d_n}, v_{4d_n}, v_{5d_n}, Q_n), 0)$$
$$+ \mathcal{L}_{bce}(\mathbf{DT}(v_{3d_m}, v_{4d_m}, v_{5d_m}, Q_m), 1) \tag{10}$$

To fool **DS**, our prediction model is trained to learn saliency representations $\{v_{3s}, v_{4s}, v_{5s}\}_n, P_n$ from I_n which can be classified as source domain in **DS**. The adversarial loss for saliency branch can be calculated as:

$$\mathcal{L}_{adv\_s}(\mathbf{E}, \mathbf{SF}, \mathbf{S}, \mathbf{T}) = \mathcal{L}_{bce}(\mathbf{DS}(v_{3s_n}, v_{4s_n}, v_{5s_n}, P_n), 0) \tag{11}$$

For **DT**, our prediction model is trained to learn depth representations $\{v_{3d}, v_{4d}, v_{5d}\}_m, Q_m$ from I_m which can be classified as source domain:

$$\mathcal{L}_{adv\_d}(\mathbf{E}, \mathbf{TF}, \mathbf{S}, \mathbf{T}) = \mathcal{L}_{bce}(\mathbf{DT}(v_{3d_m}, v_{4d_m}, v_{5d_m}, Q_m), 0) \tag{12}$$

3.4 Complete Training Loss

To summarize, the complete training process includes losses for our prediction model, which combines the initial saliency prediction loss for I_m (Eq. (4)), the initial depth prediction loss for I_n (Eq. (5)), the final saliency prediction loss for I_m (Eq. (7)), the final depth prediction loss for I_n (Eq. (8)), the adversarial loss of saliency branch for I_n (Eq. (11)), the adversarial loss of depth branch for I_m (Eq. (12)); and the losses for saliency and depth discriminators (Eq. (9), (10)),

$$\min_{\mathbf{DS}, \mathbf{DT}} \mathcal{L}_{DS} + \mathcal{L}_{DT} \tag{13}$$

$$\min_{\mathbf{E}, \mathbf{SF}, \mathbf{TF}, \mathbf{S}, \mathbf{T}} \lambda_s \mathcal{L}_{fin\_s} + \lambda_d \mathcal{L}_{fin\_d}$$
$$+ \lambda_{init} \lambda_s \mathcal{L}_{init\_s} + \lambda_{init} \lambda_d \mathcal{L}_{init\_d}$$
$$+ \lambda_{adv\_s} \mathcal{L}_{adv\_s} + \lambda_{adv\_d} \mathcal{L}_{adv\_d} \tag{14}$$

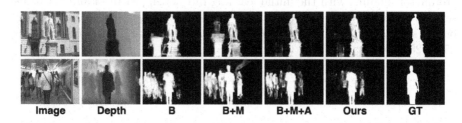

Image   Depth   B   B+M   B+M+A   Ours   GT

Fig. 5. Visual examples for ablation study. See Sect. 4.4 for the definition of each subset model.

4   Experiments

In this section, we evaluate our method and present the experimental results. First, we introduce the benchmark datasets and some implementation details of our network architecture. Then, we discuss the effectiveness of our method by comparison with the state-of-art methods and the ablation study.

4.1   Datasets and Evaluation Metrics

We evaluate our proposed method on seven widely used RGB-D saliency datasets including NJUD [13], NLPR [14], LFSD [15], STEREO [16], RGBD135 [17], SIP [18], and DUT-D [5]. To train our model, we use the DUTS [4], an RGB saliency dataset contains 10553 images with saliency ground truth for training the saliency branch. And for our depth branch, for a fair comparison, we use the selected 1485 NJUD images and 700 NLPR images as in [5] without saliency ground truth as our RGB-D training set. We then evaluate our model on 797 images in STEREO, 929 images in SIP (These two datasets contain the largest number of images for the test split); and other testing datasets including 100 images in LFSD, 135 images in RGBD135, 400 images in DUT-D testing set; as well as the remaining 500 testing images in NJUD, 300 testing images in NLPR.

For quantitative evaluation, we adopt four widely used evaluation metrics including F-measure (F_m) [37], mean absolute error (MAE) [38], S-measure (S_m) [39] and E-measure (E_m) [40]. In this paper, we report the average F-measure value as F_m which is calculated by the mean of the precision and recall. For MAE, the lower value indicates the method is better, while for all other metrics, the higher value indicates the method is better.

4.2   Implementation Details

We apply PyTorch for our implementation using two GeForce RTX 1080 Ti GPU with 22 GB memory. For our prediction model, we use VGG19 [23] pre-trained model as the backbone. And for the discriminator, we first apply one convolution layer for each input feature/prediction and concat the latent representations, then apply four convolution layers to output the one-channel classification result. We apply ADAM [41] optimizer for both two-stage prediction module and discriminator module, with the initial learning rate setting to 1e−4 and 5e−5. We set $\lambda_s = 1.75, \lambda_d = 1.0, \lambda_{init} = 0.2, \lambda_{adv\_s} = 0.002, \lambda_{adv\_d} = 0.001$ to focus more on the saliency branch and the second stage. All the input images are resized to 256×256 pixels.

Table 1. Results on different datasets. We highlight the best two result in each column in bold and italic.

	DUT-D				STEREO				SIP				RGBD135			
	MAE	F_m	S_m	E_m	MAE	F_m	S_m	E_m	MAE	F_m	S_m	E_m	MAE	F_m	S_m	E_m
DMRA	**0.048**	**0.883**	**0.887**	*0.930*	*0.047*	*0.868*	*0.886*	*0.934*	0.088	0.815	0.800	0.858	**0.030**	**0.867**	**0.899**	**0.944**
CPFP	0.100	0.735	0.749	0.815	0.054	0.827	0.871	0.902	*0.064*	0.819	*0.850*	0.899	0.038	0.829	0.872	*0.927*
TANet	0.093	0.778	0.808	0.871	0.059	0.849	0.877	0.922	0.075	0.809	0.835	0.894	0.046	0.795	0.858	0.919
MMCI	0.112	0.753	0.791	0.856	0.080	0.812	0.856	0.894	0.086	0.795	0.833	0.886	0.065	0.762	0.848	0.904
PCANet	0.100	0.760	0.801	0.863	0.061	0.845	0.880	0.918	0.071	*0.825*	0.842	*0.900*	0.050	0.774	0.843	0.912
CTMF	0.097	0.792	0.831	0.883	0.087	0.786	0.853	0.877	0.139	0.684	0.716	0.824	0.055	0.778	0.863	0.911
DF	0.145	0.747	0.729	0.842	0.142	0.761	0.763	0.844	0.185	0.673	0.653	0.794	0.131	0.573	0.685	0.806
DCMC	0.243	0.405	0.499	0.712	0.150	0.762	0.745	0.838	0.186	0.645	0.683	0.787	0.196	0.234	0.469	0.676
CDCP	0.159	0.633	0.687	0.794	0.149	0.681	0.727	0.801	0.224	0.495	0.595	0.722	0.120	0.594	0.709	0.810
Ours	*0.057*	*0.878*	*0.885*	**0.935**	**0.045**	**0.878**	**0.893**	**0.936**	**0.052**	**0.856**	**0.880**	**0.922**	*0.031*	*0.864*	*0.890*	*0.927*

4.3 Comparison with State-of-the-Art Methods

We compare our method with 9 state-of-the-art RGB-D saliency detection methods including 7 RGB-D deep learning methods: DMRA [5], CPFP [6], TANet [7], MMCI [8], PCANet [9], CTMF [21], DF [10], and 2 RGB-D traditional methods: DCMC [11], CDCP [12]. The performance of our method compared with the state-of-the-art methods on each evaluation metric is showed in Table 1 and Table 2. For a fair comparison, the saliency maps of the above methods we use are directly provided by authors, or predicted by their released codes. We apply the same computation of the evaluation metrics to all the saliency maps.

For all the listed latest RGB-D methods based on CNNs-based structure, they all require depth data as input for both training and inference, and they use RGB-D saliency ground-truth maps to train the model in a fully-supervised way. Therefore, they can achieve a good performance on all the datasets. For RGB-D traditional methods, they use manually designed cues to calculate the saliency prediction in an unsupervised way, and they perform worse compared with the CNN-based fully-supervised RGB-D methods. With the help of images and saliency ground-truth maps from RGB datasets, our semi-supervised method does not require access to any saliency ground-truth maps for images in RGB-D datasets during training, and we only require the RGB data without depth data at inference since we use the depth data as a supervisory signal during training.

The quantitative results show that, for the two largest testing SIP and STEREO datasets containing the largest number of images for testing, our semi-supervised method can achieve better results, which indicates that our method may generalize better on diverse scenario even without having access to saliency ground truth for RGB-D datasets. It can also demonstrate that useful information can be obtained from a larger RGB saliency dataset and generalized to RGB-D saliency datasets by our designed approach, despite that the images from these two source datasets have considerable difference on appearance since RGB-D datasets focus on images with more complicated background. For other datasets with a smaller number of images for testing such as DUT-D and RGBD135, we are also able to reach comparable results with DMRA which are better than

Table 2. Results on different datasets. We highlight the best two result in each column in bold and italic.

	LFSD				NJUD				NLPR			
	MAE	F_m	S_m	E_m	MAE	F_m	S_m	E_m	MAE	F_m	S_m	E_m
DMRA	**0.076**	**0.849**	**0.847**	**0.899**	**0.051**	**0.872**	**0.885**	**0.920**	**0.031**	**0.855**	**0.898**	**0.942**
CPFP	*0.088*	0.813	0.828	0.867	*0.053*	0.837	*0.878*	0.900	*0.038*	*0.818*	0.884	*0.920*
TANet	0.111	0.794	0.801	0.851	0.061	0.844	*0.878*	*0.909*	0.041	0.796	*0.886*	0.916
MMCI	0.132	0.779	0.787	0.840	0.079	0.813	0.859	0.882	0.059	0.730	0.856	0.872
PCANet	0.112	0.794	0.800	0.856	0.059	0.844	0.877	*0.909*	0.044	0.795	0.874	0.916
CTMF	0.120	0.781	0.796	0.851	0.085	0.788	0.849	0.866	0.056	0.724	0.860	0.869
DF	0.142	0.810	0.786	0.841	0.151	0.744	0.735	0.818	0.100	0.683	0.769	0.840
DCMC	0.155	0.815	0.754	0.842	0.167	0.715	0.703	0.796	0.196	0.328	0.550	0.685
CDCP	0.199	0.634	0.658	0.737	0.182	0.618	0.672	0.751	0.115	0.592	0.724	0.786
Ours	0.090	*0.823*	*0.830*	*0.879*	0.055	*0.852*	*0.878*	*0.909*	0.044	0.809	0.875	0.915

other methods. We may perform slightly worse on two specific datasets, NJUD and NLPR, since all other fully-supervised methods use the saliency ground-truth maps from these two datasets during training. However, we still manage to be comparable with the state-of-art methods on these two datasets. To better demonstrate the advantage of our method, we also present some qualitative saliency examples in Fig. 6.

4.4 Ablation Study

To demonstrate the impact of each component in our overall method, we conducted our ablation study by evaluating the following subset models:

1) B: Our baseline, a simple saliency detection model directly trained by RGB saliency dataset with only multi-level fusion in the first stage.

2) B + M: Only trained by RGB saliency dataset while adding the FAM module and our feature-guided attention module in the first stage.

3) B + M + A: Adding the depth branch trained by RGB-D saliency datasets and the second stage cross-refinement prediction with the prediction-guided attention module.

4) Ours: Our overall structure with the discriminator module.

Table 3. Ablation Study on our proposed method. We highlight the best result in each column in bold.

	NJUD				NLPR				STEREO			
	MAE	F_m	S_m	E_m	MAE	F_m	S_m	E_m	MAE	F_m	S_m	E_m
B	0.064	0.809	0.862	0.876	0.052	0.774	0.858	0.891	0.053	0.835	0.877	0.908
B+M	0.060	0.818	0.876	0.887	0.050	0.791	0.868	0.903	0.053	0.854	0.889	0.921
B+M+A	**0.055**	0.840	**0.878**	0.900	0.047	0.807	0.873	0.910	0.050	0.868	0.888	0.928
Ours	**0.055**	**0.852**	**0.878**	**0.909**	**0.044**	**0.809**	**0.875**	**0.915**	**0.045**	**0.878**	**0.893**	**0.936**

Our ablation study is evaluated on three RGB-D datasets and the result is showed in Table 3. We also include some visual examples in Fig. 5. It indicates that our baseline model B provides a good initial prediction with the saliency branch trained by the RGB dataset. By adding feature-guided attention module which helps to focus on more informative spatial positions and channels, and the FAM module which enlarges the receptive field, B+M further improves performance by helping saliency detection on RGB saliency dataset. However, the trained B+M module may not be generalized well on RGB-D saliency detection due to the different distribution between RGB and RGB-D saliency datasets. It may perform badly on images with more complicated background (Fig. 5).

To improve the generalization ability of our model on RGB-D datasets, we then add depth branch and the second-stage prediction-guided cross-refinement module to utilize depth data with spatial structure information for RGB-D images to form B+M+A module. To further help the generalization of our model on some images from RGB-D datasets which have significant difference with images from RGB dataset, we also add the discriminator module by adversarial learning to align the representations on two source datasets for each branch to form our final model. Table 3 also proves the effectiveness of each module.

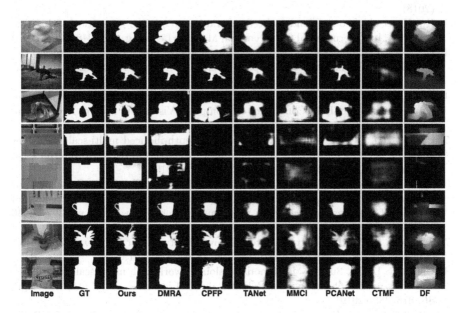

Fig. 6. Visual comparison of our method with the state-of-art methods.

5 Conclusions

In this paper, we propose a novel semi-supervised method for RGB-D saliency detection with a synergistic saliency and depth prediction way to deal with the small number of existing RGB-D saliency datasets without constructing a new dataset. It allows us to exploit larger existing hand-labeled RGB saliency datasets, avoid using saliency ground-truth maps from RGB-D datasets during training, and require only RGB data without depth data at inference. The system consists of three stages: a first-stage initial prediction module to train two separate branches for saliency and depth tasks; a second-stage prediction-guided cross-refinement module and a discriminator stage to further improve the generalization on RGB-D dataset by allowing two branches to provide complementary information and the adversarial learning. Evaluation on seven RGB-D datasets demonstrates the effectiveness of our method, by performing favorable against the state-of-art fully-supervised RGB-D saliency methods on two largest RGB-D saliency testing datasets, and achieves comparable results on other popular RGB-D saliency detection benchmarks.

References

1. Lee, H., Kim, D.: Salient region-based online object tracking. In: 2018 IEEE Winter Conference on Applications of Computer Vision (WACV), pp. 1170–1177. IEEE (2018)
2. Xu, K., et al.: Show, attend and tell: neural image caption generation with visual attention. In: International Conference on Machine Learning, pp. 2048–2057 (2015)
3. He, J., et al.: Mobile product search with bag of hash bits and boundary reranking. In: 2012 IEEE Conference on Computer Vision and Pattern Recognition, pp. 3005–3012. IEEE (2012)
4. Wang, L., et al.: Learning to detect salient objects with image-level supervision. In: Proceedings of the IEEE Conference on Computer Vision and Pattern Recognition, pp. 136–145 (2017)
5. Piao, Y., Ji, W., Li, J., Zhang, M., Lu, H.: Depth-induced multi-scale recurrent attention network for saliency detection. In: Proceedings of the IEEE International Conference on Computer Vision, pp. 7254–7263 (2019)
6. Zhao, J.X., Cao, Y., Fan, D.P., Cheng, M.M., Li, X.Y., Zhang, L.: Contrast prior and fluid pyramid integration for rgbd salient object detection. In: Proceedings of the IEEE Conference on Computer Vision and Pattern Recognition, pp. 3927–3936 (2019)
7. Chen, H., Li, Y.: Three-stream attention-aware network for RGB-D salient object detection. IEEE Trans. Image Process. 28, 2825–2835 (2019)
8. Chen, H., Li, Y., Su, D.: Multi-modal fusion network with multi-scale multi-path and cross-modal interactions for RGB-D salient object detection. Pattern Recogn. 86, 376–385 (2019)
9. Chen, H., Li, Y.: Progressively complementarity-aware fusion network for RGB-D salient object detection. In: Proceedings of the IEEE Conference on Computer Vision and Pattern Recognition, pp. 3051–3060 (2018)
10. Qu, L., He, S., Zhang, J., Tian, J., Tang, Y., Yang, Q.: RGBD salient object detection via deep fusion. IEEE Trans. Image Process. 26, 2274–2285 (2017)
11. Cong, R., Lei, J., Zhang, C., Huang, Q., Cao, X., Hou, C.: Saliency detection for stereoscopic images based on depth confidence analysis and multiple cues fusion. IEEE Signal Process. Lett. 23, 819–823 (2016)

12. Zhu, C., Li, G., Wang, W., Wang, R.: An innovative salient object detection using center-dark channel prior. In: Proceedings of the IEEE International Conference on Computer Vision Workshops, pp. 1509–1515 (2017)
13. Ju, R., Ge, L., Geng, W., Ren, T., Wu, G.: Depth saliency based on anisotropic center-surround difference. In: 2014 IEEE International Conference on Image Processing (ICIP), pp. 1115–1119. IEEE (2014)
14. Peng, H., Li, B., Xiong, W., Hu, W., Ji, R.: RGBD salient object detection: a benchmark and algorithms. In: Fleet, D., Pajdla, T., Schiele, B., Tuytelaars, T. (eds.) ECCV 2014. LNCS, vol. 8691, pp. 92–109. Springer, Cham (2014). https://doi.org/10.1007/978-3-319-10578-9_7
15. Li, N., Ye, J., Ji, Y., Ling, H., Yu, J.: Saliency detection on light field. In: Proceedings of the IEEE Conference on Computer Vision and Pattern Recognition, pp. 2806–2813 (2014)
16. Niu, Y., Geng, Y., Li, X., Liu, F.: Leveraging stereopsis for saliency analysis. In: 2012 IEEE Conference on Computer Vision and Pattern Recognition, pp. 454–461. IEEE (2012)
17. Cheng, Y., Fu, H., Wei, X., Xiao, J., Cao, X.: Depth enhanced saliency detection method. In: Proceedings of International Conference on Internet Multimedia Computing and Service, pp. 23–27 (2014)
18. Fan, D.P., et al.: Rethinking RGB-D salient object detection: models, datasets, and large-scale benchmarks. arXiv preprint arXiv:1907.06781 (2019)
19. Zhu, C., Li, G., Guo, X., Wang, W., Wang, R.: A multilayer backpropagation saliency detection algorithm based on depth mining. In: Felsberg, M., Heyden, A., Krüger, N. (eds.) CAIP 2017. LNCS, vol. 10425, pp. 14–23. Springer, Cham (2017). https://doi.org/10.1007/978-3-319-64698-5_2
20. Zhu, C., Li, G.: A three-pathway psychobiological framework of salient object detection using stereoscopic technology. In: Proceedings of the IEEE International Conference on Computer Vision Workshops, pp. 3008–3014 (2017)
21. Han, J., Chen, H., Liu, N., Yan, C., Li, X.: CNNs-based RGB-D saliency detection via cross-view transfer and multiview fusion. IEEE Trans. Cybern. 48, 3171–3183 (2017)
22. Zhu, C., Cai, X., Huang, K., Li, T.H., Li, G.: PDNet: prior-model guided depth-enhanced network for salient object detection. In: 2019 IEEE International Conference on Multimedia and Expo (ICME), pp. 199–204. IEEE (2019)
23. Simonyan, K., Zisserman, A.: Very deep convolutional networks for large-scale image recognition. In: ICLR (2015)
24. Shelhamer, E., Long, J., Darrell, T.: Fully convolutional networks for semantic segmentation. IEEE Trans. Pattern Anal. Mach. Intell. 39, 640–651 (2017)
25. Wang, X., Girshick, R., Gupta, A., He, K.: Non-local Neural Networks. In: Proceedings of the IEEE Conference on Computer Vision and Pattern Recognition, pp. 7794–7803 (2018)
26. Vaswani, A., et al.: Attention is all you need. In: Advances in Neural Information Processing Systems, pp. 5998–6008 (2017)
27. Liu, J.J., Hou, Q., Cheng, M.M., Feng, J., Jiang, J.: A simple pooling-based design for real-time salient object detection. In: Proceedings of the IEEE Conference on Computer Vision and Pattern Recognition, pp. 3917–3926 (2019)
28. Goodfellow, I., et al.: Generative adversarial nets. In: Advances in Neural Information Processing Systems, pp. 2672–2680 (2014)
29. Hu, L., Kan, M., Shan, S., Chen, X.: Duplex generative adversarial network for unsupervised domain adaptation. In: Proceedings of the IEEE Conference on Computer Vision and Pattern Recognition, pp. 1498–1507 (2018)

30. Zhang, Y., Tang, H., Jia, K., Tan, M.: Domain-symmetric networks for adversarial domain adaptation. In: Proceedings of the IEEE Conference on Computer Vision and Pattern Recognition, pp. 5031–5040(2019)

31. Chen, Y., Li, W., Sakaridis, C., Dai, D., Van Gool, L.: Domain adaptive faster R-CNN for object detection in the wild. In: Proceedings of the IEEE Conference on Computer Vision and Pattern Recognition, pp. 3339–3348 (2018)

32. Saito, K., Ushiku, Y., Harada, T., Saenko, K.: Strong-weak distribution alignment for adaptive object detection. In: Proceedings of the IEEE Conference on Computer Vision and Pattern Recognition, pp. 6956–6965 (2019)

33. Tsai, Y.H., Hung, W.C., Schulter, S., Sohn, K., Yang, M.H., Chandraker, M.: Learning to adapt structured output space for semantic segmentation. In: Proceedings of the IEEE Conference on Computer Vision and Pattern Recognition, pp. 7472–7481 (2018)

34. Luo, Y., Liu, P., Guan, T., Yu, J., Yang, Y.: Significance-aware information bottleneck for domain adaptive semantic segmentation. In: Proceedings of the IEEE International Conference on Computer Vision, pp. 6778–6787 (2019)

35. Luo, Y., Zheng, L., Guan, T., Yu, J., Yang, Y.: Taking a closer look at domain shift: category-level adversaries for semantics consistent domain adaptation. In: Proceedings of the IEEE Conference on Computer Vision and Pattern Recognition, pp. 2507–2516 (2019)

36. Vu, T.H., Jain, H., Bucher, M., Cord, M., Pérez, P.: Advent: adversarial entropy minimization for domain adaptation in semantic segmentation. In: Proceedings of the IEEE Conference on Computer Vision and Pattern Recognition, pp. 2517–2526 (2019)

37. Achanta, R., Hemami, S., Estrada, F., Susstrunk, S.: Frequency-tuned Salient Region Detection. In: 2009 IEEE Conference on Computer Vision and Pattern Recognition, pp. 1597–1604. IEEE (2009)

38. Borji, A., Cheng, M.M., Jiang, H., Li, J.: Salient object detection: a benchmark. IEEE Trans. Image Process. **24**, 5706–5722 (2015)

39. Fan, D.P., Cheng, M.M., Liu, Y., Li, T., Borji, A.: Structure-measure: a new way to evaluate foreground maps. In: Proceedings of the IEEE International Conference on Computer Vision, p. 4548–4557(2017)

40. Fan, D.P., Gong, C., Cao, Y., Ren, B., Cheng, M.M., Borji, A.: Enhanced-alignment measure for binary foreground map evaluation. arXiv preprint arXiv:1805.10421 (2018)

41. Kingma, D.P., Ba, J.: Adam: a method for stochastic optimization. In: ICLR (2015)

Deep Snapshot HDR Imaging Using Multi-exposure Color Filter Array

Takeru Suda, Masayuki Tanaka⑩, Yusuke Monno$^{(\boxtimes)}$⑩,
and Masatoshi Okutomi⑩

Tokyo Institute of Technology, Tokyo, Japan
tsuda@ok.sc.e.titech.ac.jp, {mtanaka,ymonno,mxo}@sc.e.titech.ac.jp

Abstract. In this paper, we propose a deep snapshot high dynamic range (HDR) imaging framework that can effectively reconstruct an HDR image from the RAW data captured using a multi-exposure color filter array (ME-CFA), which consists of a mosaic pattern of RGB filters with different exposure levels. To effectively learn the HDR image reconstruction network, we introduce the idea of luminance normalization that simultaneously enables effective loss computation and input data normalization by considering relative local contrasts in the "normalized-by-luminance" HDR domain. This idea makes it possible to equally handle the errors in both bright and dark areas regardless of absolute luminance levels, which significantly improves the visual image quality in a tone-mapped domain. Experimental results using two public HDR image datasets demonstrate that our framework outperforms other snapshot methods and produces high-quality HDR images with fewer visual artifacts.

1 Introduction

The dynamic range of a camera is determined by the ratio between the maximum and the minimum amounts of light that can be recorded by the image sensor at one shot. Standard digital cameras have a low dynamic range (LDR) and only capture a limited range of scene radiance. Consequently, they cannot capture a bright and a dark area outside the camera's dynamic range simultaneously. High dynamic range (HDR) imaging is a highly demanded computational imaging technique to overcome this limitation, which recovers the HDR scene radiance map from a single or multiple LDR images captured by a standard camera.

HDR imaging is typically performed by estimating a mapping from the sensor's LDR outputs to the scene radiance using multiple LDR images which are sequentially captured with different exposure levels [1]. Although this approach works for static situations, it is not suitable for dynamic scenes and video acquisition since the multiple images are taken at different times. Recent learning-based methods [2–4] have successfully reduced ghost artifacts derived from target motions between input LDR images. However, those methods are limited to small motions and the artifacts remain apparent for the areas with large motions, as shown in Wu's method [3] of Fig. 1.

Electronic supplementary material The online version of this chapter (https://doi.org/10.1007/978-3-030-69532-3_22) contains supplementary material, which is available to authorized users.

ⓒ Springer Nature Switzerland AG 2021
H. Ishikawa et al. (Eds.): ACCV 2020, LNCS 12623, pp. 353–370, 2021.
https://doi.org/10.1007/978-3-030-69532-3_22

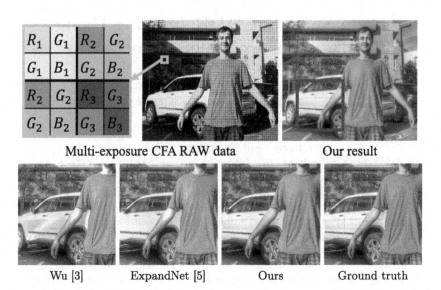

Fig. 1. Top: Examples of a multi-exposure CFA RAW data and an HDR image result by our framework. Bottom: Comparisons with state-of-the-art HDR imaging methods.

Some studies have used only a single LDR image to realize one-shot HDR imaging [5–7]. They essentially inpaint or hallucinate missing over- and under-exposed areas by exploiting an external database of LDR-HDR image pairs. Although this approach is free from ghost artifacts, it generates inpainting or hallucination artifacts for largely missing areas, as shown in ExpandNet [5] of Fig. 1, due to the lack of information in the missing areas.

As another one-shot approach, the methods based on a snapshot HDR sensor have also been investigated [8–11]. One way to realize a snapshot HDR sensor is to use a single image sensor with spatially varying exposure levels [10,11]. This can be achieved by using what we call a multi-exposure color filter array (ME-CFA), which consists of a mosaic pattern of RGB filters combined with neutral density filters with different attenuation levels. (see Fig. 1 for an example with three levels). The snapshot HDR sensor has the advantage of capturing multi-exposure information at one shot. Thus, it has great potential for HDR imaging of dynamic scenes and also HDR video acquisition without ghost and inpainting artifacts. However, HDR image reconstruction from the snapshot measurement includes two challenging problems: demosaicking (i.e., interpolation of missing RGB values) and HDR reconstruction (i.e., scene radiance estimation from LDR measurements). As we will show later, a simple combination of existing demosaicking/interpolation and HDR reconstruction methods cannot produce satisfactory results for this joint problem.

In this paper, we propose a novel deep snapshot HDR imaging framework that can effectively reconstruct an HDR image from the RAW data captured using an ME-CFA (see Fig. 1). In our framework, we introduce the key idea of luminance normalization and propose luminance-normalized network (LN-Net) that enables effective learning of HDR images in the luminance-normalized domain (LN domain).

In the training phase, we first train the network to generate tentatively interpolated LDR images, from which tentative HDR luminance is estimated. Then, we normalize the input ME-CFA RAW data and the corresponding ground-truth HDR image by the tentative HDR luminance. Finally, we train our main network (LN-Net) to reconstruct HDR images based on the pair of the RAW and the HDR image data in the LN domain. In the application phase, the HDR image is reconstructed through the learned two networks.

Our LN-Net mainly has two benefits. The first one is effective loss computation in the LN domain. The standard mean squared error (MSE) loss in the linear HDR domain has a problem of neglecting the errors in dark areas because they are quite small compared with the errors in bright areas. However, those errors in dark areas significantly affect the visual quality in a tone-mapped domain [12], which is commonly used to display HDR images. Based on this, some studies have computed the loss in a transformed domain, such as a log domain [6] and a global tone-mapped domain [2]. However, such signal-independent transformations do not reflect an actual signal component of each image. In contrast, by computing the loss in the LN domain, we can equally handle the errors in bright and dark areas by considering the actual luminance of each image.

The second benefit of LN-Net is effective input data normalization. In deep learning, the normalization of input data is important to extract effective features. Since a diverse range of scene radiance information is simultaneously encoded in the ME-CFA RAW data, we need to consider relative local contrasts, rather than absolute differences. Otherwise, features such as edges and textures in dark areas are prone to be ignored. In our LN-Net, by normalizing the input RAW data by the tentative luminance, we can naturally consider the relative local contrasts in both bright and dark areas regardless of absolute luminance.

Through the experiments using two public HDR image datasets, we validate the effectiveness of our framework by comparing it with other snapshot methods and current state-of-the-art HDR imaging methods using multiple LDR images. **Main Contributions** of this paper are summarized as below.

- We propose a novel deep learning framework that effectively solves the joint demosaicking and HDR reconstruction problem for snapshot HDR imaging.
- We propose the idea of luminance normalization that enables effective loss computation and input data normalization by considering relative local contrasts of each image.
- We demonstrate that our framework can outperform other snapshot methods and reconstruct high-quality HDR images with fewer visible artifacts.

2 Related Work

Multiple-LDR-Images-Based Methods have been studied for years. Their approaches include inverse radiometric function estimation [1], exposure fusion [13–15], patch-based [16,17], rank minimization-based [18,19], image alignment-based [20,21], and learning-based [2–4,22–24] methods. Although their performance has continuously been improved (see [17,25] for reviews), it is essentially difficult for multi-LDR-images-based methods to handle dynamic scenes with target or camera motions, resulting in ghost artifacts. Some methods have exploited a multi-camera/sensor system [26,27] for one-shot acquisition of multi-LDR images. However, they require image or sensor alignment, which is another challenging task.

Single-LDR-Image-Based Methods, also called inverse tone-mapping, have been actively studied in recent years. They train a mapping from a single-LDR image to an HDR image directly [5,6,28–30] or train a mapping to multiple LDR images intermediately, from which the HDR image is derived [7,31,32]. Although the single-LDR-image-based approach realizes one-shot HDR image acquisition, it is essentially difficult to reconstruct high-quality HDR images because there are no measurements obtained from different exposure levels.

Snapshot Methods are based on a snapshot HDR imaging system with spatially varying exposure levels [10,11]. Several hardware architectures or concepts have been proposed to realize a snapshot system, such as a coded exposure time [8,33,34], a coded exposure mask [35–37], a dual-ISO sensor [9,38–40], and what we call an ME-CFA, which consists of the mosaic of RGB filters combined with neutral density filters with different attenuation levels [10,11,41–45]. The snapshot systems have great potential for HDR imaging in dynamic situations since it enables one-shot acquisition of multi-exposure information. However, HDR image reconstruction from the snapshot measurements is very challenging due to the sparse nature of each color-exposure component.

Some existing snapshot methods based on an ME-CFA first convert the snapshot LDR measurements to the sensor irradiance domain. By doing this, the problem reduces to the demosaicking problem in the sensor irradiance domain, for which several probability-based [41,44] or learning-based [43] approaches have been proposed. However, this combined approach could not necessarily produce satisfactory results because the errors in the first step are propagated by the demosaicking step. Although some joint approach has also been proposed [10,11,42,45], it is limited to a specific ME-CFA pattern [10,11,45] or it only performs a limited over- and under-exposed pixels correction [42].

In this paper, different from existing methods, we propose a general and high-performance framework exploiting deep learning to jointly solve the demosaicking and the HDR reconstruction problems for snapshot HDR imaging using an ME-CFA.

3   Proposed Deep Snapshot HDR Imaging

3.1   Framework Overview

In this paper, we assume the ME-CFA pattern shown in Fig. 1, which consists of 4×4 regular pattern with three exposure levels, assuming the mosaic of

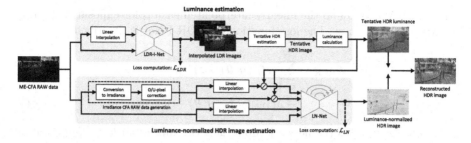

Fig. 2. Overview of our deep snapshot HDR imaging framework. It first estimates tentative HDR luminance and then estimates the HDR image in the luminance-normalized domain. The idea of luminance normalization enables to consider relative local contrasts in both bright and dark areas, regardless of the absolute luminance levels.

RGB filters combined with neutral density filters with three attenuation levels. Although our framework is general and not limited to this pattern, we use this because (i) it is based on the common Bayer pattern [46], similar to existing ME-CFA patterns [10,39], and (ii) it consists of three exposures, which are commonly used in recent HDR imaging studies [2,3]. Those two conditions make it possible to experimentally compare our framework with standard Bayer demosaicking methods [47,48] and also state-of-the-art HDR imaging methods using three LDR images [2,3].

Figure 2 shows the overview of our framework, which mainly consists of two parts: (i) luminance estimation and (ii) luminance-normalized HDR image estimation. The first part estimates tentative HDR luminance based on the interpolated LDR images by the learned LDR-interpolation-network (LDR-I-Net). Then, based on the tentative luminance, the second part estimates the luminance-normalized HDR image by the learned LN-Net. Each part is detailed in Subsect. 3.2 and 3.3, respectively. Finally, the HDR image is reconstructed by multiplying the tentative luminance and the estimated luminance-normalized HDR image.

Throughout this paper, we use the term "irradiance" or "sensor irradiance [1]" to represent the irradiance of the light reaching the image sensor after going through the camera's optical elements such as a lens. Because we assume a linear optical system as in [1,49], the sensor irradiance is assumed to be the same as scene radiance in this paper. We also assume linear responses between the sensor irradiance and pixel values because we process the RAW data, which typically have linear camera responses.

3.2   Luminance Estimation

In the luminance estimation, we first interpolate the missing RGB pixel values to generate interpolated LDR images. For this purpose, we train LDR-I-Net, for which we adopt the U-Net architecture [50]. The inputs of LDR-I-Net are the

ME-CFA RAW data and the linearly interpolated each color-exposure sample of the ME-CFA raw data. The loss function for LDR-I-Net is described as

$$\mathcal{L}_{\text{LDR}} = \sum_{k=1}^{N} ||\boldsymbol{f}_k(\boldsymbol{y};\boldsymbol{\theta}) - \boldsymbol{z}_k||_2^2$$
$$+ \lambda_{\text{LDR}}||\nabla \boldsymbol{f}_k(\boldsymbol{y};\boldsymbol{\theta}) - \nabla \boldsymbol{z}_k||_2^2, \tag{1}$$

where $\boldsymbol{y} = [\boldsymbol{x}; \boldsymbol{h}(\boldsymbol{x})]$ is the network input, $\boldsymbol{x}$ is the sub-mosaicked representation of the ME-CFA RAW data, as used in [51] (e.g., sparse 16-channel data for the $4{\times}4$ regular pattern), $\boldsymbol{h}()$ represents the linear interpolation for the sparse data, $\boldsymbol{f}_k(\boldsymbol{y};\boldsymbol{\theta})$ is the output of LDR-I-Net for k-th exposure LDR image, $\boldsymbol{\theta}$ represents the network weights, $\boldsymbol{z}_k$ is true k-th exposure LDR image, N is the number of exposure levels in the ME-CFA, ∇ represents the horizontal and the vertical derivative operators, and λ_{LDR} is a hyper-parameter. The second term, which we call the gradient term, evaluates the errors in the image gradient domain. In this paper, we empirically set to $\lambda_{\text{LDR}} = 1$ for the hyper-parameter. We will show the effectiveness of the gradient term by the ablation study in Subsect. 4.2. Note that the loss function of Eq. (1) evaluates the MSE in the LDR image domain, not in the HDR image domain. Thus, we use the standard MSE for loss computation.

Once we have interpolated LDR images, we apply Debevec's method [1] to the LDR images for tentative HDR image estimation. Then, tentative HDR luminance is derived as the maximum value of the RGB sensor irradiance values, which corresponds to the value (V) in the HSV color space. The tentative luminance can be formulated as

$$\hat{L}_i = \max_c \tilde{E}_i^{(c)}, \tag{2}$$
$$\tilde{\boldsymbol{E}} = \boldsymbol{R}(\boldsymbol{f}(\boldsymbol{y};\boldsymbol{\theta})), \tag{3}$$

where $\boldsymbol{f}(\boldsymbol{y};\boldsymbol{\theta})$ is the interpolated LDR images, $\boldsymbol{R}()$ represents the Debevec's HDR image estimation operation [1], $\tilde{\boldsymbol{E}}$ is the tentative HDR image estimated from the interpolated LDR images, $\tilde{E}_i^{(c)}$ is the estimated tentative sensor irradiance of c-th channel at i-th pixel in $\tilde{\boldsymbol{E}}$, and $\hat{L}_i$ is the tentative luminance of i-th pixel, where max operation is performed in a pixel-by-pixel manner.

3.3   Luminance-Normalized HDR Image Estimation

In the luminance-normalized HDR image estimation, we train LN-Net to reconstruct the HDR image in the luminance-normalized domain. The inputs of LN-Net are the sub-mosaicked representation of the ME-CFA RAW data, its sensor irradiance version as we will explain below, and linearly interpolated versions of them. The irradiance data is normalized by the tentative luminance to consider relative local contrasts regardless of the absolute luminance levels. We detail each process to train LN-Net below.

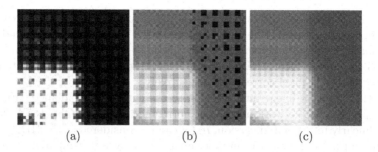

(a)   (b)   (c)

Fig. 3. Examples of (a) the ME-CFA RAW data in the LDR domain, (b) the irradiance CFA RAW data converted by Eq. (4), and (c) the irradiance CFA RAW data after the O/U-pixel correction.

We first convert the ME-CFA RAW data to the sensor irradiance domain as

$$\xi_{k,i} = \frac{x_i}{\rho_k \Delta t} \, , \tag{4}$$

where x_i is i-th pixel value of the ME-CFA RAW data, ρ_k is the attenuation factor for k-th exposure, Δt is the exposure time, and $\xi_{k,i}$ is the converted sensor irradiance of i-th pixel corresponding to k-th exposure. In the snapshot case using an ME-CFA, the attenuation factor ρ_k varies for each pixel according to the ME-CFA pattern, while the exposure time is constant for all pixels. Thus, in what follows, we set to $\Delta t = 1$, without loss of generality. Also, we call the irradiance data converted by Eq. (4) "irradiance CFA-RAW data", in which different exposure levels are already corrected by converting the ME-CFA RAW data to the sensor irradiance domain. Figure 3(a) and 3(b) show the examples of the ME-CFA RAW data and the converted irradiance CFA RAW data.

In the original ME-CFA RAW data, many pixels are over-exposed (saturated) or under-exposed (black-out) depending on the exposure level of each pixel compared to the scene radiance. Such over- or under-exposed pixels (what we denote as "O/U pixels") have no meaningful irradiance information even after the conversion by Eq. (4). Thus, we present an effective O/U-pixel correction method, which replaces the irradiance of an O/U pixel with the linearly interpolated value using adjacent lower- or higher-exposure irradiance samples. For example, the irradiance of an over-exposed pixel is corrected as

$$\hat{\xi}_{k,i} = \begin{cases} \xi_{k,i} & (\xi_{k,i} \leq \tau_{O,k}) \\ h_i(\boldsymbol{\xi}_{k-1}) & (\xi_{k,i} > \tau_{O,k}) \end{cases} \, , \tag{5}$$

where the suffix k represents k-th exposure, the suffix i represents i-th pixel, $\hat{\xi}_{k,i}$ is the irradiance after the over-exposed pixel correction, $\tau_{O,k}$ is the over-exposure threshold, $\boldsymbol{\xi}_{k-1}$ is the one-step lower-exposure sparse irradiance samples in the irradiance CFA RAW data, and $h_i(\boldsymbol{\xi}_{k-1})$ is i-th pixel value of the linearly interpolated irradiance of $\boldsymbol{\xi}_{k-1}$. We empirically set $0.995/(\rho_k \Delta t)$ to the over-exposure threshold $\tau_{O,k}$, where the range of the irradiance CFA RAW data is [0, 1]. This over-exposure correction is applied from the lower exposure data to the higher exposure data. The under-exposed pixel correction is performed in the same manner, where the under-exposure threshold is set to $\tau_{U,k} = 0.005/(\rho_k \Delta t)$. Figure 3(b) and 3(c) show the examples of the irradiance CFA RAW data before and after the O/U-pixel correction, respectively.

We then apply a linear interpolation to the corrected irradiance CFA RAW data to prepare the network input. The corrected irradiance CFA RAW data, $\hat{\boldsymbol{\xi}}$, and its linearly interpolated version, $\boldsymbol{h}(\hat{\boldsymbol{\xi}})$, can be considered as the HDR domain data, in which local contrasts in dark areas are very low compared with those in bright areas. Thus, we normalize the HDR domain data by the estimated tentative HDR luminance. This luminance normalization converts the absolute local contrasts to the relative local contrasts. We also use the LDR domain data of the sub-mosaicked ME-CFA RAW data $\boldsymbol{x}$ and its linearly interpolated version $\boldsymbol{h}(\boldsymbol{x})$. For these LDR domain data, we do not perform the luminance normalization because the range of the absolute local contrasts is limited. The input to LN-Net $\boldsymbol{\eta}$ is described as

$$\boldsymbol{\eta} = \left[\boldsymbol{x}, \boldsymbol{h}(\boldsymbol{x}), \hat{\boldsymbol{\xi}}/\hat{\boldsymbol{L}}, \boldsymbol{h}(\hat{\boldsymbol{\xi}})/\hat{\boldsymbol{L}}\right], \tag{6}$$

where $\hat{\boldsymbol{L}}$ is the tentative luminance, and the divide operation is performed in a pixel-by-pixel manner.

We then estimate the luminance-normalized HDR image by LN-Net, where we adopt the U-Net like network architecture [50]. The loss function of LN-Net is the MSE in the luminance-normalized HDR domain as follows.

$$\begin{aligned}\mathcal{L}_{\mathrm{LN}} = &\|\boldsymbol{g}(\boldsymbol{\eta};\boldsymbol{\psi}) - \boldsymbol{E}_{\mathrm{LN}}\|_2^2 \\ &+ \lambda_{\mathrm{LN}}\|\nabla\boldsymbol{g}(\boldsymbol{\eta};\boldsymbol{\psi}) - \nabla\boldsymbol{E}_{\mathrm{LN}}\|_2^2,\end{aligned} \tag{7}$$

where $\boldsymbol{g}(\boldsymbol{\eta};\boldsymbol{\psi})$ represents LN-Net which estimates the luminance-normalized HDR image, $\boldsymbol{\psi}$ is the weights for the network, $\boldsymbol{\eta}$ is the network input defined in Eq. (6), $\boldsymbol{E}_{\mathrm{LN}}$ is the luminance-normalized true HDR image, ∇ represents the horizontal and vertical gradient operator, and λ_{LN} is a hyper-parameter. In this paper, we empirically set to $\lambda_{\mathrm{LN}} = 1$ for the hyper-parameter. The luminance-normalized true HDR image is defined by

$$\boldsymbol{E}_{LN} = \boldsymbol{E}/\hat{\boldsymbol{L}}, \tag{8}$$

where $\boldsymbol{E}$ is the true HDR image and the divide operation is perform in a pixel-by-pixel manner. We finally reconstruct the final HDR image as

$$\hat{\boldsymbol{E}} = \hat{\boldsymbol{L}} \times \boldsymbol{g}(\boldsymbol{\eta};\boldsymbol{\psi}), \tag{9}$$

where the multiplying operation is performed in a pixel-by-pixel manner.

By substituting Eqs. (8) and (9) into Eq. (7), one can find that the loss function for LN-Net corresponds to the MSE normalized by the tentative luminance. In the proposed luminance-normalized HDR image estimation, the input and the output of the network are normalized by the luminance, which enables us to consider the relative local contrasts, rather than the absolute differences.

3.4 Network Architecture

In our framework, we use two networks: LDR-I-Net and LN-Net. In this paper, we adopt the U-Net architecture [50] for both networks, where the depth of the U-Net is five. Though, one can use any network architectures.

As mentioned above, the network inputs are a pair of the sparse sub-mosaicked data and the dense interpolated data. To adapt the data sparseness difference, we insert RAW data adaptation blocks as follows. The RAW data adaptation for the sparse data consists of a convolution layer with the ReLU activation whose kernel size is 7×7. The adaptation for the interpolated data is a convolution layer with the ReLU activation whose kernel size is 3×3. The outputs of both adaptations are concatenated and then fed into the network. We validate the effectiveness of the RAW data adaptation blocks in Subsect. 4.2. The detailed network architecture of the U-Net and the RAW data adaptation blocks are included in the supplemental material.

4 Experimental Results

4.1 Setups

Datasets. We used two public HDR image datasets for evaluating our framework: Funt's dataset [52] and Kalantari's dataset [2].

Funt's dataset consists of static scenes. We used this dataset for comparison with other snapshot methods. Although other static HDR datasets are available as listed in [29], we used Funt's dataset because it contains relatively a large number of HDR images (224 images) generated using the same camera. Each HDR image is generated by Debevec's method [1] using 9 LDR images with the exposure value (EV) set of $\{-4, -3, -2, -1, 0, 1, 2, 3, 4\}$.

Kalantari's dataset is recently used for evaluating dynamic scenes mainly with human motions. We used this dataset for comparison with state-of-the-art HDR imaging methods using a single or multiple LDR images. The dataset contains 89 dynamic scenes. For each scene, the ground-truth HDR image is generated using static LDR images taken with a reference human pose. In contrast, test LDR images are taken with a human motion including the reference pose. The EV set of $\{-2, 0, 2\}$ or $\{-3, 0, 3\}$ is used for the LDR image acquisition, where EV = 0 is used to take the test LDR image with the reference pose.

ME-CFA Data Simulation. We simulated the ME-CFA data from the above-mentioned HDR data, which is 32-bit RGBE image format. We first normalized each HDR data to $[0, 1]$ and scaled the normalized HDR data as $[0, 1]$, $[0, 4]$, and $[0, 16]$, according to the three exposure levels corresponding to the assumed EV set of $\{-2, 0, 2\}$. Then, we clipped each scaled data by $[0, 1]$ and quantized the clipped data by 8-bit depth. Finally, we sampled the quantized data according to the ME-CFA pattern to generate the mosaic ME-CFA data. By this data generation process, quantization errors were properly taken into account.

Table 1. Ablation study.

	CPSNR	G-CPSNR	L-CPSNR	HDR-VDP-2	LN-MSE
Ours (full version)	**48.57**	**41.94**	**40.38**	**80.57**	**0.0585**
Without luminance normalization	46.70	30.24	29.29	77.97	0.1289
Without O/U-pixel correction	42.30	36.60	34.45	78.51	0.0913
Without gradient term in the loss	41.76	36.14	35.76	65.41	0.4364
Without RAW data adaptation	46.19	39.45	37.77	78.16	0.0688

Training Setups. For Funt's dataset, we used randomly selected 13 images for testing and the rest 211 images for training. For Kalantari's dataset, we used the provided 15 test and 74 training images. In the training phase, we randomly sampled 32×32-sized patches from each training image set and randomly applied each of a horizontal flip, a vertical flip, and a swapping of horizontal and vertical axes (transpose) for data augmentation. The used optimizer is Adam [53], where the learning rate was set to 0.001 and the parameters (β_1, β_2) were set to $(0.9, 0.999)$. We performed 3,000 times mini-batch updates, where the mini-batch size was set to 32.

Evaluation Metrics. We used the following five metrics: color PSNR (CPSNR) in the linear HDR domain, CPSNR in the global tone-mapped domain (G-CPSNR), CPSNR in the local tone-mapped domain (L-CPSNR), HDR-VDP-2 [54], and luminance-normalized MSE (LN-MSE), which is the MSE normalized by the true luminance. We used the same global tone-mapping function as [2] for G-CPSNR and the MATLAB local tone-mapping function for L-CPSNR. For each dataset, the average metric value of all test images is presented for comparison. For subjective evaluation, we used a commercial software, Photomatix[1], to apply local tone-mapping for effective visualization.

4.2   Validation Study of Our Framework

We first evaluate the validity of our framework using Funt's dataset.

Ablation Study. Table 1 shows the result for the ablation study. We can observe that the case without the normalization by luminance (second row) presents much lower G-PSNR and L-CPSNR values compared with the cases with the normalization. This is because the cases without the normalization tend to neglect local contrasts in dark areas, which decreases the performance of both the subjective and the objective evaluation in the tone-mapped domains, where dark areas are significantly enhanced. We can also observe that the other proposed components certainly contribute to the performance improvements in all evaluated metrics.

---

[1] https://www.hdrsoft.com.

Table 2. Loss domain comparison.

Loss domain	CPSNR	G-CPSNR	L-CPSNR	HDR-VDP-2	LN-MSE
Linear HDR domain	47.63	38.42	36.25	78.96	0.0749
Global tone-mapped HDR domain	47.56	41.57	39.57	79.73	0.0609
Our luminance-normalized HDR domain	**48.57**	**41.94**	**40.38**	**80.57**	**0.0585**

Loss Domain Comparison. Table 2 shows the comparison of loss computation domains. The loss in the standard linear HDR domain presents lower G-CPSNR and L-CPSNR values because it tends to disregard the errors in dark areas. The loss in the global tone-mapped domain [2] improves the G-CPSNR and the L-CPSNR performance, respectively. The loss in our proposed luminance-normalized domain provides further better performance by considering the relative local contrasts.

The above two studies demonstrate the effectiveness of our framework with the luminance normalization that enables effective local contrast consideration.

4.3   Comparison with Other Methods

Compared Methods. To the best of our knowledge, there is no publicly available source code that is directly workable and comparable for the considered snapshot HDR imaging problem. Thus, we compared our framework with two combination frameworks as follows.

The first one is the demosaicking-based framework. It first converts the ME-CFA RAW data to the irradiance CFA RAW data and then applies an existing Bayer demosaicking method to the irradiance CFA RAW data. To generate the irradiance CFA RAW data, we applied the same processes as in Subsect. 3.3, including our proposed O/U-pixel correction since it was confirmed that our pixel correction significantly improves the numerical performance of existing methods. We used state-of-the-art interpolation-based (ARI [55]) and deep learning-based (Kokkions [48] and CDMNet [47]) demosaicking methods for comparison.

The second one is the LDR-interpolation-based framework. It first interpolates (up-samples) the sub-mosaicked ME-CFA RAW data by an existing super-resolution (SR) method with the scaling factor of 4 and then performs HDR reconstruction from the interpolated LDR images. We used existing competitive SR methods (ESRGAN [56], WDSR [57], and EDSR [58]) and our LDR-I-Net for SR and Debevec's method [1] for HDR reconstruction.

Results. Table 3 and Fig. 4 show the numerical and the visual comparisons using Funt's dataset. Table 3 demonstrates that our framework can provide the best performance in all metrics. In Fig. 4, we can observe that the demosaicking-based methods generate severe zipper artifacts (ARI and CDM-Net) or over-smoothed results (Kokkions), while the LDR-interpolation-based

Table 3. Comparison with two combination frameworks for snapshot HDR imaging.

Framework	Demosaicking/SR	CPSNR	G-CPSNR	L-CPSNR	HDR-VDP-2	LN-MSE
Demosaicking-based framework: Irradiance CFA RAW data generation → Demosaicking	ARI [55]	46.14	38.15	36.69	75.68	0.0712
	Kokkinos [48]	41.06	26.27	26.65	69.32	0.1840
	CDMNet [47]	46.32	38.37	37.12	58.00	0.0713
LDR-interpolation-based framework: LDR interpolation by SR → HDR reconstruction	ESRGAN [56]	30.66	25.21	21.87	53.55	0.2720
	WDSR [57]	35.75	30.97	29.32	60.16	0.3796
	EDSR [58]	39.19	32.57	29.95	66.04	0.1190
	LDR-I-Net	43.38	35.64	34.54	76.30	0.1030
Our deep snapshot HDR imaging framework		**48.57**	**41.94**	**40.38**	**80.57**	**0.0585**

Fig. 4. Visual comparisons on Funt's dataset.

methods (ESRGAN, WDSR, and EDSR) generate severe aliasing artifacts for the high-frequency area of the red box. Although LDR-I-Net provides comparable results for bright areas, it generates severe quantization artifacts in the dark area of the blue box, because it only learns LDR interpolation, but does not perform any learning for HDR reconstruction. In contrast, our framework can produce a better result with fewer visible artifacts, though slight artifacts still appear in the dark area. More results can be seen in the supplemental material.

4.4 Comparison with State-of-the-Art Methods Using a Single or Multiple LDR Images

Compared Methods. Using Kalantari's dataset, we next compare our snapshot framework with state-of-the-art HDR imaging methods using multiple LDR

Table 4. Comparison with state-of-the-art HDR imaging methods.

Input sources	Methods	CPSNR	G-CPSNR	L-CPSNR	HDR-VDP-2	LN-MSE
Multiple LDR images	Sen [17]	38.05	40.76	36.13	61.08	0.0389
	Kalantari [2]	41.15	**42.65**	**38.22**	64.57	**0.0306**
	Wu [3]	40.88	42.53	37.98	65.60	0.0338
Single LDR image (Second exposure)	HDRCNN [6]	12.92	14.13	34.80	54.48	4.1082
	DrTMO [31]	18.23	14.07	25.32	56.78	8.7912
	ExpandNet [5]	22.09	22.37	28.03	57.34	1.2923
ME-CFA RAW data	Ours	**41.43**	38.60	35.23	**66.59**	0.0832

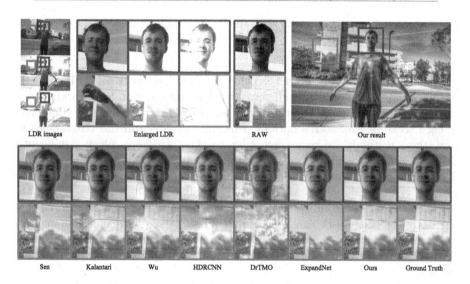

Fig. 5. Visual comparisons on Kalantari's dataset.

images (Sen [17], Kalantari [2], and Wu [3]) or a single LDR image (HDRCNN [6], DrTMO [31], and ExpandNet [5]). We used all three LDR images for the multi-LDR-based methods and the second-exposure LDR image for the single-LDR-based methods.

Results. Figure 5 shows the visual comparison. We can observe that the multi-LDR-based methods (Sen, Kalantari, and Wu) generate severe ghost artifacts in the red and the blue box areas, which are due to the head and the arm motions between input LDR images. The single-LDR-based methods (HDR-CNN, DrTMO, and ExpandNet) generate severe inpainting artifacts for the over-exposed areas in the input second-exposure LDR image. In contrast, our framework can reconstruct a visually pleasing result with much fewer visible artifacts. More results can be seen in the supplemental material.

Table 4 shows the numerical comparison. Our framework provides the highest score in CPSNR and HDR-VDP-2. In contrast, the multi-LDR-based methods

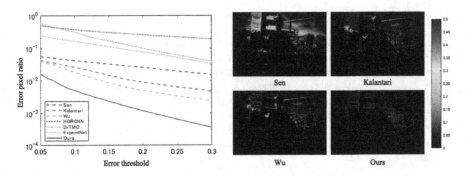

Fig. 6. Left: Comparison of the error pixel ratio. Right: Comparison of the error maps.

present better performance for the other metrics. This is because these methods have the benefit of having all three-exposure information for each pixel, and thus should provide better performance for static regions, which are dominant in each scene of Kalantari's dataset. However, as shown in the visual comparison, these methods are very susceptible to ghost artifacts, which significantly disturbs visual perception and makes the perceptual HDR-VDP-2 score lower. To quantitatively evaluate such significant artifacts, in Fig. 6, we evaluate the ratio of error pixels whose MSE of RGB irradiance values is larger than the threshold of the horizontal axis. From the result, we can clearly observe that our snapshot framework can generate the HDR image with much fewer error pixels. We also show the comparison of error maps, where the multi-LDR-based methods generate significant errors in the dynamic regions around the head and the arm.

4.5 Limitation

In our results, zipper artifacts still remain in some areas. This is because of the very challenging nature of snapshot HDR reconstruction with very sparse sampling of each color-exposure component and many saturated/blacked-out pixels. Furthermore, in the snapshot HDR problem, zipper artifacts may occur even for uniform areas without textures because of the differences of the quantization levels of three exposure images, meaning that converted sensor irradiance values in the uniform area do not match completely among the three exposure levels. To reduce the remaining zipper artifacts is our future work.

5 Conclusion

In this paper, we have proposed a novel deep learning-based framework that can effectively address the joint demosaicking and HDR reconstruction problem for snapshot HDR imaging using an ME-CFA. We have introduced the idea of luminance normalization that simultaneously enables effective loss computation and input data normalization to learn the HDR image reconstruction network by considering relative local image contrasts. Experimental results have demonstrated that our framework can produce HDR images with much fewer visual artifacts compared with other snapshot methods and also state-of-the-art HDR imaging methods using multiple LDR images. We provide the source code to reproduce our results at http://www.ok.sc.e.titech.ac.jp/res/DSHDR/index.html.

References

1. Debevec, P., Malik, J.: Recovering high dynamic range radiance maps from photographs. In: Proceedings of SIGGRAPH, pp. 1–10 (1997)
2. Kalantari, N.K., Ramamoorthi, R.: Deep high dynamic range imaging of dynamic scenes. ACM Trans. Graph. **36**(144), 1–12 (2017)
3. Wu, S., Xu, J., Tai, Y.-W., Tang, C.-K.: Deep high dynamic range imaging with large foreground motions. In: Ferrari, V., Hebert, M., Sminchisescu, C., Weiss, Y. (eds.) ECCV 2018. LNCS, vol. 11206, pp. 120–135. Springer, Cham (2018). https://doi.org/10.1007/978-3-030-01216-8_8
4. Yan, Q., et al.: Attention-guided network for ghost-free high dynamic range imaging. In: Proceedings of IEEE Conference on Computer Vision and Pattern Recognition (CVPR), pp. 1751–1760 (2019)
5. Marnerides, D., Bashford-Rogers, T., Hatchett, J., Debattista, K.: ExpandNet: a deep convolutional neural network for high dynamic range expansion from low dynamic range content. Comput. Graph. Forum **37**, 37–49 (2018)
6. Eilertsen, G., Kronander, J., Denes, G., Mantiuk, R.K., Unger, J.: HDR image reconstruction from a single exposure using deep CNNs. ACM Trans. Graph. **36**(178), 1–15 (2017)
7. Lee, S., An, G.H., Kang, S.J.: Deep chain HDRI: reconstructing a high dynamic range image from a single low dynamic range image. IEEE Access **6**, 49913–49924 (2018)
8. Cho, H., Kim, S.J., Lee, S.: Single-shot high dynamic range imaging using coded electronic shutter. Comput. Graph. Forum **33**, 329–338 (2014)
9. Choi, I., Baek, S.H., Kim, M.H.: Reconstructing interlaced high-dynamic-range video using joint learning. IEEE Trans. Image Process. **26**, 5353–5366 (2017)
10. Narasimhan, S.G., Nayar, S.K.: Enhancing resolution along multiple imaging dimensions using assorted pixels. IEEE Trans. Pattern Anal. Mach. Intell. **27**, 518–530 (2005)
11. Nayar, S.K., Mitsunaga, T.: High dynamic range imaging: spatially varying pixel exposures. In: Proceedings of IEEE Conference on Computer Vision and Pattern Recognition (CVPR), pp. 1–8 (2000)
12. Eilertsen, G., Mantiuk, R.K., Unger, J.: Real-time noise-aware tone mapping. ACM Trans. Graph. **34**(198), 1–15 (2015)
13. Ma, K., Duanmu, Z., Yeganeh, H., Wang, Z.: Multi-exposure image fusion by optimizing a structural similarity index. IEEE Trans. Comput. Imaging **4**, 60–72 (2017)
14. Ma, K., Li, H., Yong, H., Wang, Z., Meng, D., Zhang, L.: Robust multi-exposure image fusion: a structural patch decomposition approach. IEEE Trans. Image Process. **26**, 2519–2532 (2017)
15. Mertens, T., Kautz, J., Van Reeth, F.: Exposure fusion: a simple and practical alternative to high dynamic range photography. Comput. Graph. Forum **28**, 161–171 (2009)

16. Hu, J., Gallo, O., Pulli, K., Sun, X.: HDR deghosting: how to deal with saturation? In: Proceedings of IEEE Conferenc on Computer Vision and Pattern Recognition (CVPR), pp. 1163–1170 (2013)
17. Sen, P., Kalantari, N.K., Yaesoubi, M., Darabi, S., Goldman, D.B., Shechtman, E.: Robust patch-based HDR reconstruction of dynamic scenes. ACM Trans. Graph. **31**(203), 1–11 (2012)
18. Lee, C., Li, Y., Monga, V.: Ghost-free high dynamic range imaging via rank minimization. IEEE Signal Process. Lett. **21**, 1045–1049 (2014)
19. Oh, T.H., Lee, J.Y., Tai, Y.W., Kweon, I.S.: Robust high dynamic range imaging by rank minimization. IEEE Trans. Pattern Anal. Mach. Intell. **37**, 1219–1232 (2014)
20. Hasinoff, S.W., et al.: Burst photography for high dynamic range and low-light imaging on mobile cameras. ACM Trans. Graph. **35**(192), 1–12 (2016)
21. Kalantari, N.K., Ramamoorthi, R.: Deep HDR video from sequences with alternating exposures. Comput. Graph. Forum **38**, 193–205 (2019)
22. Prabhakar, K.R., Arora, R., Swaminathan, A., Singh, K.P., Babu, R.V.: A fast, scalable, and reliable deghosting method for extreme exposure fusion. In: Proceedings of IEEE Interntaional Conference on Computational Photography (ICCP), pp. 170–177 (2019)
23. Ram Prabhakar, K., Sai Srikar, V., Venkatesh Babu, R.: DeepFuse: a deep unsupervised approach for exposure fusion with extreme exposure image pairs. In: Proceedings of IEEE International Conference on Computer Vision (ICCV), pp. 4724–4732 (2017)
24. Yan, Q., et al.: Multi-scale dense networks for deep high dynamic range imaging. In: Proceedings of IEEE Winter Conference on Applications of Computer Vision (WACV), pp. 41–50 (2019)
25. Tursun, O.T., Akyüz, A.O., Erdem, A., Erdem, E.: The state of the art in HDR deghosting: a survey and evaluation. Comput. Graph. Forum **34**, 683–707 (2015)
26. Ogino, Y., Tanaka, M., Shibata, T., Okutomi, M.: Super high dynamic range video. In: Proc. of International Conference on Pattern Recognition (ICPR), pp. 4208–4213 (2016)
27. Tocci, M.D., Kiser, C., Tocci, N., Sen, P.: A versatile HDR video production system. ACM Trans. Graph. **30**(41), 1–9 (2011)
28. Yang, X., Xu, K., Song, Y., Zhang, Q., Wei, X., Lau, R.W.: Image correction via deep reciprocating HDR transformation. In: Proceedings of IEEE Conference on Computer Vision and Pattern Recognition (CVPR), pp. 1798–1807 (2018)
29. Moriwaki, K., Yoshihashi, R., Kawakami, R., You, S., Naemura, T.: Hybrid loss for learning single-image-based HDR reconstruction. arXiv preprint 1812.07134 (2018)
30. Kim, S.Y., Kim, D.-E., Kim, M.: ITM-CNN: learning the inverse tone mapping from low dynamic range video to high dynamic range displays using convolutional neural networks. In: Jawahar, C.V., Li, H., Mori, G., Schindler, K. (eds.) ACCV 2018. LNCS, vol. 11363, pp. 395–409. Springer, Cham (2019). https://doi.org/10.1007/978-3-030-20893-6_25
31. Endo, Y., Kanamori, Y., Mitani, J.: Deep reverse tone mapping. ACM Trans. Graph. **36**(177), 1–10 (2017)
32. Lee, S., An, G.H., Kang, S.-J.: Deep recursive HDRI: inverse tone mapping using generative adversarial networks. In: Ferrari, V., Hebert, M., Sminchisescu, C., Weiss, Y. (eds.) ECCV 2018. LNCS, vol. 11206, pp. 613–628. Springer, Cham (2018). https://doi.org/10.1007/978-3-030-01216-8_37

33. Gu, J., Hitomi, Y., Mitsunaga, T., Nayar, S.: Coded rolling shutter photography: flexible space-time sampling. In: Proceedings of IEEE International Conference on Computational Photography (ICCP), pp. 1–8 (2010)
34. Uda, S., Sakaue, F., Sato, J.: Variable exposure time imaging for obtaining unblurred HDR images. IPSJ Trans. Comput. Vis. Appl. **8**, 3:1–3:7 (2016)
35. Alghamdi, M., Fu, Q., Thabet, A., Heidrich, W.: Reconfigurable snapshot HDR imaging using coded masks and inception network. In: Proceedings of Vision, Modeling, and Visualization (VMV), pp. 1–9 (2019)
36. Nagahara, H., Sonoda, T., Liu, D., Gu, J.: Space-time-brightness sampling using an adaptive pixel-wise coded exposure. In: Proceedings of IEEE Conference on Computer Vision and Pattern Recognition Workshops (CVPRW), pp. 1834–1842 (2018)
37. Serrano, A., Heide, F., Gutierrez, D., Wetzstein, G., Masia, B.: Convolutional sparse coding for high dynamic range imaging. Comput. Graph. Forum **35**, 153–163 (2016)
38. Go, C., Kinoshita, Y., Shiota, S., Kiua, H.: Image fusion for single-shot high dynamic range imaging with spatially varying exposures. In: Proceedings of Asia-Pacific Signal and Information Processing Association Annual Summit and Conference (APSIPA ASC), pp. 1082–1086 (2018)
39. Hajisharif, S., Kronander, J., Unger, J.: Adaptive dualISO HDR reconstruction. EURASIP J. Image Video Process. **2015**, 1–13 (2015)
40. Heide, F., et al.: FlexISP: a flexible camera image processing framework. ACM Trans. Graph. **33**(231), 1–13 (2014)
41. Aguerrebere, C., Almansa, A., Delon, J., Gousseau, Y., Musé, P.: A Bayesian hyperprior approach for joint image denoising and interpolation, with an application to HDR imaging. IEEE Trans. Comput. Imaging **3**, 633–646 (2017)
42. Aguerrebere, C., Almansa, A., Gousseau, Y., Delon, J., Muse, P.: Single shot high dynamic range imaging using piecewise linear estimators. In: Proceedings of IEEE International Conference on Computational Photography (ICCP), pp. 1–10 (2014)
43. An, V.G., Lee, C.: Single-shot high dynamic range imaging via deep convolutional neural network. In: Proceedings of Asia-Pacific Signal and Information Processing Association Annual Summit and Conference (APSIPA ASC), pp. 1768–1772 (2017)
44. Rouf, M., Ward, R.K.: high dynamic range imaging with a single exposure-multiplexed image using smooth contour prior. In: Proceedings of IS&T International Symposium on Electronic Imaging (EI), vol. 440, pp. 1–6 (2018)
45. Cheng, C.H., Au, O.C., Cheung, N.M., Liu, C.H., Yip, K.Y.: High dynamic range image capturing by spatial varying exposed color filter array with specific demosaicking algorithm. In: Proceedings of IEEE Pacific Rim Conference on Communications, Computers and Signal Processing (PACRIM), pp. 648–653 (2009)
46. Bayer, B.E.: Color imaging array, US patent 3,971,065 (1976)
47. Cui, K., Jin, Z., Steinbach, E.: Color image demosaicking using a 3-stage convolutional neural network structure. In: Proceedings of IEEE International Conference on Image Processing (ICIP), pp. 2177–2181 (2018)
48. Kokkinos, F., Lefkimmiatis, S.: Deep image demosaicking using a cascade of convolutional residual denoising networks. In: Ferrari, V., Hebert, M., Sminchisescu, C., Weiss, Y. (eds.) Computer Vision – ECCV 2018. LNCS, vol. 11218, pp. 317–333. Springer, Cham (2018). https://doi.org/10.1007/978-3-030-01264-9_19
49. Grossberg, M.D., Nayar, S.K.: What is the space of camera response functions? In: Proceedings of IEEE Conference on Computer Vision and Pattern Recognition (CVPR), pp. 1–8 (2003)

50. Ronneberger, O., Fischer, P., Brox, T.: U-Net: convolutional networks for biomedical image segmentation. In: Navab, N., Hornegger, J., Wells, W.M., Frangi, A.F. (eds.) MICCAI 2015. LNCS, vol. 9351, pp. 234–241. Springer, Cham (2015). https://doi.org/10.1007/978-3-319-24574-4_28
51. Henz, B., Gastal, E.S., Oliveira, M.M.: Deep joint design of color filter arrays and demosaicing. Comput. Graphics Forum **37**, 389–399 (2018)
52. Funt, B., Shi, L.: The rehabilitation of MaxRGB. In: Proceedings of Color and Imaging Conference (CIC), pp. 256–259 (2010)
53. Kingma, D.P., Ba, J.: Adam: a method for stochastic optimization. arXiv preprint 1412.6980 (2014)
54. Mantiuk, R., Kim, K.J., Rempel, A.G., Heidrich, W.: HDR-VDP-2: a calibrated visual metric for visibility and quality predictions in all luminance conditions. ACM Trans. Graphics **30**(40), 1–13 (2011)
55. Monno, Y., Kiku, D., Tanaka, M., Okutomi, M.: Adaptive residual interpolation for color and multispectral image demosaicking. Sensors **17**(2787), 1–21 (2017)
56. Wang, X., et al.: ESRGAN: enhanced super-resolution generative adversarial networks. In: Leal-Taixé, L., Roth, S. (eds.) ECCV 2018. LNCS, vol. 11133, pp. 63–79. Springer, Cham (2019). https://doi.org/10.1007/978-3-030-11021-5_5
57. Fan, Y., Yu, J., Huang, T.S.: Wide-activated deep residual networks based restoration for BPG-compressed images. In: Proceedings of IEEE Conference on Computer Vision and Pattern Recognition workshops (CVPRW), pp. 2621–2624 (2018)
58. Lim, B., Son, S., Kim, H., Nah, S., Mu Lee, K.: Enhanced deep residual networks for single image super-resolution. In: Proceedings of IEEE Conference on Computer Vision and Pattern Recognition Workshops (CVPRW), pp. 1132–1140 (2017)

Deep Priors Inside an Unrolled and Adaptive Deconvolution Model

Hung-Chih Ko, Je-Yuan Chang, and Jian-Jiun Ding[✉]

National Taiwan University, Taipei, Taiwan
{r06942148,r07942158,jjding}@ntu.edu.tw

Abstract. Image deconvolution is an essential but ill-posed problem even if the degradation kernel is known. Recently, learning based methods have demonstrated superior image restoration quality in comparison to traditional methods which are typically based on empirical statistics and parameter adjustment. Though coming up with outstanding performance, most of the plug-and-play priors are trained in a specific degradation model, leading to inferior performance on restoring high-frequency components. To address this problem, a deblurring architecture that adopts (1) adaptive deconvolution modules and (2) learning based image prior solvers is proposed. The adaptive deconvolution module adjusts the regularization weight locally to well process both smooth and non-smooth regions. Moreover, a cascade made of image priors is learned from the mapping between intermediates thus robust to arbitrary noise, aliasing, and artifact. According to our analysis, the proposed architecture can achieve a significant improvement on the convergence rate and result in an even better restoration performance.

1 Introduction

Most of the pictures captured by hand-held devices are easily suffering from camera motion or out-of-focus which leads to blurry observed images. In general, the blurry observed image B is modeled as

$$B = I \otimes K + N \tag{1}$$

where $\otimes$ denotes convolution, I, K, and N refers to the latent clear image, the point spread function (PSF), and noise, respectively. Non-blind deblurring is to retrieve the clear image I when the PSF is already estimated from lens' parameters or motion sensors. Early approaches such as the Weiner filter [1] and the Richardson-Lucy algorithm [2,3] have become a mainstream in the past century; however, they may suffer from ringing artifacts or over-smoothness when dealing with severely interfered cases. In recent years, various image priors are widely adopted to serve as regularization terms in image deconvolution problems.

Electronic supplementary material The online version of this chapter (https://doi.org/10.1007/978-3-030-69532-3_23) contains supplementary material, which is available to authorized users.

© Springer Nature Switzerland AG 2021
H. Ishikawa et al. (Eds.): ACCV 2020, LNCS 12623, pp. 371–388, 2021.
https://doi.org/10.1007/978-3-030-69532-3_23

A good image prior not only promotes edge sharpness but also suppresses artifacts. In some early works like total variation (TV) [4] and hyper-Laplacian [5,6], the regularization term is formulated as a norm of derivative of intensities to encourage the gradient to approximate a heavy-tailed distribution. Alternative priors like K-SVD [7], Gaussian mixture model (GMM) [8] and Markov random field (MRF) [9] have provided spatial support for exploring latent image statistics. Despite coming up with practical solutions, most of the aforementioned methods still highly rely on empirical statistics and knowledge for parameter tuning.

Recently, with the successes in the field of computer vision, neural networks have been used for challenging image restoration tasks including image inpainting, denoising, and deblurring. Several image deblurring works based on discriminative models [10–17] or generative models [18,19] have demonstrated with superiority. Among learning based methods, [10,11,14–17] have focused on improving optimization process through the integration of deep learning networks, instead of conventional end-to-end training procedure. Despite of their surprising performance, models trained on specifically designated degradation $i.e.$ a fixed noise level are typically exploited to handle intermediate results within optimization. Therefore, it is inevitable to result in a limited performance when suffering from arbitrary noise or artifacts.

To address this problem, an unrolled deconvolution network (UDN) is proposed. Different from most of the existing works which aim to optimize an image prior within a narrow degradation domain, we further improve the half-quadratic splitting (HQS) [20] optimization process and encourage those priors to be learned from arbitrary intermediate outputs as well as aliasing which possibly emerges. Therefore, UDN can implicitly learn image priors during optimization and be more robust to severely degraded cases.

We also note that conventional deconvolution within HQS may have ignored the spatial variety in an image. When set parameters globally, it can lead the restored image to be over-smoothed in some region and under-smoothed in the others. To address this problem, we establish the adaptive deconvolution module (ADM) which is essentially composed of a small set of convolution layers for edge detection and determines the parameters adaptively. With the aid of increased capacity via the UDN, the models are expected to learn corresponding artifacts possibly different from the conventional scheme. We have combined the results of ADM and UDN by a simple and intuitive way that ensures both smoothness and detail are successfully preserved.

Through our analysis, the proposed methods have outperformed other existing works in PSNR and SSIM. Especially, when suffering from significant noise, the high-frequency components are successfully restored, which is not observed in other works. Furthermore, since the proposed UDN optimizes the image priors within intermediates, a great improvement on the convergence rate is achieved. It leads to a more efficient and faster restoration process.

2   Related Works

In the field of computer vision, non-blind deconvolution has long been an issue that featured with an ill-posed nature. The design on image prior is typically inferred from a Maximum a Posteriori (MAP) perspective which have been widely adopted for inverse problems; the prior always matter during the optimization on a MAP-based objective function. Among those early works, most of the priors are designed by empirical statistics on natural images. For example, TV regularization [4] and hyper-Laplacian prior [5,6] have shown success on capturing the heavy-tailed gradient distribution that usually failed when using Gaussian priors. Alternatives like mixture of Laplacians [21] and Gaussians [22] are adopted to approximate the gradient sparsity prior with the increased generality; and a content-aware local gradient prior [23] has also been emphasized to handle the spatial variety. Most of the works are solved by gradient descent, the alternating direction method of multiplier (ADMM) [24], or HQS [20], so that an inevitable increment on computation loads is expected due to the iterative process.

Other learning based methods like [9,25] has adopted fields of experts (FoE) to approximate the heavy-tailed gradient distribution by learned filters that capture local image statistics and further extended by cascade of shrinkage fields (CSF) [26], regression tree based models [27] and trainable non-linear reaction diffusion (TNRD) [28]. GMM are also developed to fit the image natures like expected patch log-likelihood (EPLL) [8] and its extended version which resorts multi-scale patch-pyramid modeling [29] for performance gains; this kind of works have demonstrated a powerful capacity on noise or blur removal. However, although patch-based methods achieve good results, solving these problems are usually time-consuming as well.

More recently, discriminative models [10–17] have shown significant improvement on restoration quality. An early work that using multi-layer perceptron (MLP) [12] can successfully remove the corresponding artifacts appeared after deconvolution by estimating clear images from an initial estimation by Gaussian prior. A convolution neural network (CNN) [13] model that based on the knowledge of kernel decomposition is trained to suppress various outliers like saturation, boundary effect or compression artifacts. However, both methods require fine-tune over each specific kernel, thus limited by a loss of generality.

Some of the works have decoupled image restoration problem into optimizing data fidelity term and regularization term, so that simpler subproblems are yielded. These methods named as plug-and-play frameworks [30,31] have exploited the concepts from variable splitting techniques like ADMM and HQS, and demonstrated a flexibility on handling various restoration tasks. Started from this concept, some frameworks integrated with deep learning models have been proposed [11,14,15,17,18] since it is regraded that models trained on pairs of degraded and latent images can learn the image priors implicitly.

A Fourier deconvolution network (FDN) [11] and a fully convolutional neural network (FCN) [14] are proposed to reduce noise after each deconvolution stage by learning CNN-based priors in gradient domain. A GMM-based method [32] learns a data fidelity term from intermediate results within cascaded shrinkage function models, and a work [17] proposes to simultaneously learn fidelity and regularization term in a task-driven manner. These methods are dedicated for aliasing removal in non-blind deconvolution cases. On the other hand, some of the works have handled these problems in a more generalized perspective. Image restoration CNN (IRCNN) [15] is composed of a set of learned CNN denoisers that can be plugged into the HQS optimization framework [5,33]. A denoising prior driven network [34] is proposed for a variety of restoration tasks. A CNN-based model is trained in an adversarial way [18] to encourage the optimal solution lies into natural image domain.

As noted in [10], most of the plugged-in learning based models which learn independently to the form of degradation are adopted to handle those tasks within intermediate optimization process. Although with increased flexibility, the learned priors cannot always react accurately to arbitrary perturbation lasted in the intermediates. For example, the denoising prior is originally trained to remove noise with homogenous power spectrum. However, as iterative deconvolution is applied to a blurry observation, the power spectrum among the outputs is expected to be more heterogenous, which is possibly out of the learned mappings. Besides, [29] has found several learning based methods are biased toward smoothness since the dominance of smooth gradient within natural images, so that the retrieval of coherent high frequency details remains an important challenge. In our investigation on non-blind deblurring, although IRCNN [15] generates outstanding performance for assessment, the restored images have lost a lot of details.

Basically, our proposed work has followed a HQS optimization framework. We first reformulate the deconvolution stage with adaptation (ADM), which only requires neglectable increment on computation complexity. Secondly, a fully convolutional network was proposed to unroll the HQS optimization. The rationale is to enlarge the learning domain with intermediate results, so that the priors can learned to handle the arbitrary deformation within optimization.

3   Unrolled Deconvolution Network

The proposed work is based on HQS optimization for a MAP-based problem that aims to estimate the latent clear image $\hat{I}$ from blurry observed image B by maximizing the posterior probability $P(.)$

$$\hat{I} = \arg\max_I P(I|B,K) = \arg\max_I P(B|I,K)P(I) \tag{2}$$

where $P(B|I,K)$ models the conditional probability distribution of B given I and K and $P(I)$ is the prior for latent clear images. The overall function can be solved in a negative log-likelihood scheme as both of the residual of blurry observation to clear image and the prior term are modeled as Gaussian distributions that can be used to measure the penalty. The objective function derived from (2) can be

$$\hat{I} = \arg\min_{I} \frac{1}{2\sigma_d^2} \|B - I \otimes K\|_2^2 + \frac{1}{2\sigma_p^2} \Phi(I) \tag{3}$$

$$= \arg\min_{I} \frac{1}{2} \|B - I \otimes K\|_2^2 + \frac{\lambda}{2} \Phi(I) \tag{4}$$

where the first term is the data fidelity and the second is the image prior term denoted as $\Phi(I)$. Note that $\lambda = \sigma_d^2/\sigma_p^2$, where the constant σ_d^2 and σ_p^2 are the variances of data term and prior term originated from the Gaussian modeling and can be reduced to a weight on prior term λ that controls the trade-off between fidelity and regularization. Under the HQS optimization scheme, an auxiliary variable Z is introduced to (3) to decouple I from concurrent minimization so that the objective problem becomes

$$\arg\min_{I,Z} \frac{1}{2} \|B - I \otimes K\|_2^2 + \frac{\beta}{2} \|I - Z\|_2^2 + \frac{\lambda}{2} \Phi(Z) \tag{5}$$

where β is a weight that controls the penalty on the fidelity between Z and I. According to the alternating minimization algorithm [5,33], the optimization process can be separated into I and Z subproblems described in (6) and (7), respectively. β is increased over iterations to encourage convergence.

$$\hat{I} = \arg\min_{I} \frac{1}{2} \|B - I \otimes K\|_2^2 + \frac{\beta}{2} \|I - Z\|_2^2 \tag{6}$$

$$\hat{Z} = \arg\min_{Z} \frac{\beta}{2} \|I - Z\|_2^2 + \frac{\lambda}{2} \Phi(Z) \tag{7}$$

As a quadratic regularized least-squared problem, (6) exists a FFT-based closed-form solution. On the other hand, although the solution of (7) is dependent to arbitrary image priors $\Phi(.)$, it can be reduced to the following equation, which is equivalent to the denoising problem with $\sigma = \sqrt{\lambda/\beta}$ described in the CNN-based image restoration algorithms in [15,34]:

$$\hat{Z} = \arg\min_{Z} \frac{1}{2(\sqrt{\lambda/\beta})^2} \|I - Z\|_2^2 + \frac{1}{2} \Phi(Z) \tag{8}$$

Hence, as a plug-and-play scheme, the CNN is designed to learn the prior implicitly and benefits the optimization process.

3.1 Adaptive Deconvolution Module

Look back into the I subproblem in (6), we have noted that the essence of β is to balance (a) the fidelity between restored I and observed B and (b) the fidelity of restored I and auxiliary variable Z which is derived from the prior-regulated subproblem (7). Actually, β poses significant influence on restored image quality. In most of the conventional methods, the value is preset empirically or complied with some rules according to the noise level. However, inferior performance can be observed on cases of unnatural images or those interfered with extremely high noise level. Besides, the weight is typically applied in a global manner so that it may have ignored the spatial variety over the entire images.

By intuition, as the value of β is set large, the solution is forced to comply with Z which is a prior-regulated solution, such that a smoothed outcome is expected. On the other hand, when β is set small, since the regularization is diminished, the solution is expected to be closed to that derived from direct inverse filter, which behaves well on restoring high-frequency components but as a trade-off, it also becomes easier to suffer from noise and other artifacts.

We have shown a simulation result in Fig. 1. When deconvolving with a smaller β, the noise becomes dominant while preserves more fine structures, as shown in Fig. 1(b, d). When β is larger, the noise is apparently suppressed with a loss of details, as shown in Fig. 1(a, c). Therefore, β can be set smaller in edge regions to better approximate the steep gradient in ground truth. On the other hand, β can be set larger at flat regions since it demonstrates a good ability for smoothness. Therefore, instead of setting β to be a global scalar, a spatially varying weight is expected to achieve a better performance.

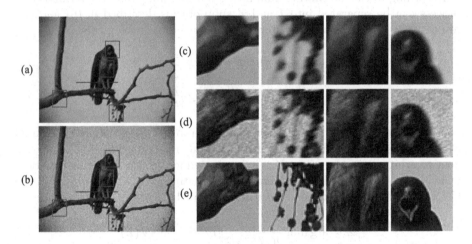

Fig. 1. Deconvolution results. The parameter β adopted in (a) is five-fold larger than that in (b). (c) and (d) are patches corresponding to (a) and (b), respectively. (e) the ground truth. (Color fgure online)

If we formulate β in (6) as a 2-d spatially varying matrix, one can suffer from difficulties when calculating the closed-form solution. The cause is ascribed to the element-wised multiplication out of the quadratic term lasting convolving operation when solving by FFT. Although it is still possible to solve patch by patch and extend the weight into a Toeplitz matrix for convolution, it seems not practical to implement.

Instead, we propose the ADM, an approximated version with spatially varying weights. To be specific, we solve I in two different fidelity weights and aggregate two solutions by an edge awareness criterion such that

$$I(\hat{x}) = \begin{cases} I_{\widehat{edge}}(x), & \text{when } Z(x) \in edge. \\ I_{\widehat{\sim edge}}(x), & \text{when } otherwise. \end{cases} \tag{9}$$

where x denotes the pixel index and $\hat{I}_n$ is defined as

$$I_{\{\widehat{edge,\sim edge}\}} = \mathcal{F}^{-1}\left(\frac{\mathcal{F}(k)^*\mathcal{F}(B) + \beta_{\{edge,\sim edge\}}\mathcal{F}(Z)}{\mathcal{F}(k)\mathcal{F}(k)^* + \beta_{\{edge,\sim edge\}}} \right) \tag{10}$$

where the two weights follow a linear relationship $\beta_{edge} = \alpha\beta_{\sim edge}$ and we set $0 < \alpha < 1$, $\beta_{\sim edge} = \beta$; β is determined as described in Sect. 3.2. The implementation detail about edge awareness criterion and determination rule for hyperparameters are included in supplementary material.

In practice, Z which is the optimal solution in (7) is sent to the edge detector to provide a binary edge map. α is set in an exponentially descending sequence over iterations since the noise component is usually dominant at early iterations, we regard to encourage the detail preservation in a gradual manner. An edge awareness criterion in (9) is established by a conventional multi-scaled Gaussian-smoothed edge detector. The rationale of Gaussian smoothness is also under the consideration of false detection of noise components as edges. Multi-scaling is designed to increase the detection capacity on edges with various scales.

The comparison on native deconvolution and the ADM is displayed in Table 1. At early stages, the ADM does not achieve a better result as most of the regions are dominated by the amplified noise. When optimization closes to convergence, we surprisingly find ADM leads to a better approximation to the ground truth, especially for some of the spike-liked signals, so that a better solution with lower MSE is achieved (refer to signal visualization in supplementary material). Another evidence is provided in Fig. 2 which records the PSNR of outputs from I and Z subproblems. In I subproblem, though ADM has larger MSE at first, it converges to a more optimal solution than native. On the other hand, in Z subproblem, an apparent performance gain is shown within almost all stages.

In summary, we have found the potential of adaptive deconvolution to retain detailed structures. Although an inferior result can be found in a single deconvolution stage, the performance between two methods are pulled apart as the

Table 1. The corresponding mean squared error (MSE) over iterations for two 1D signals indicated in the red lines in Fig. 1(a, b). The bold numbers indicate lower MSE.

Native/ADM(10^{-3})	$i = 1$	$i = 10$	$i = 20$	$i = 30$
Signal-1	**17.428**/18.695	3.241/**2.937**	2.752/**2.346**	2.634/**2.146**
Signal-2	**13.587**/14.589	**3.825**/3.933	4.128/**3.789**	4.295/**3.794**

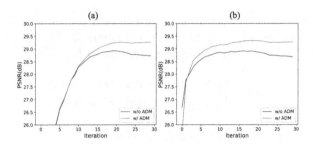

Fig. 2. The convergence process between native deconvolution and ADM on PSNR evaluation for the output of (a) I subproblem and (b) Z subproblem.

HQS iteration goes on. A possible rationale to this is the incorporation of high-frequency components *i.e.* the detailed structures has suppressed the over-smoothing effect usually found in the late iterations. Furthermore, the restoration is achieved in an accumulative manner, so that even a slight change in HQS loop can result in totally different performance in the end.

3.2   Learning Image Priors

The proposed UDN is consisted of a number of ADM and Z submodule pairs. The architecture of Z submodule is illustrated in Fig. 3(a) and the overall structure of UDN is sketched in Fig. 3(b). The Z submodules are designed to remove the corresponding noise and artifacts inferred from previous modules. The CNN architecture is basically inspired by the idea from IRCNN [15], but additional skip connections between dilated convolutional layers are introduced, since we find them beneficial for training stability and performance, especially for a deeply stacked scheme like UDN.

   Note that the ADM is essentially a learning-free module that only requires presetting on β at each layer. In fact, β is determined implicitly by an afore-mentioned relationship $\sigma = \sqrt{\lambda/\beta}$. The denoising level σ is set exponentially decreasing from 49 to 5 among iterations. We also find $\lambda \propto \sigma_d^2$ by assuming the variance between latent image to prior is unique among all cases so that λ is related to the squared initial perturbed noise level. Hence, β is set increasing with iterations to encourage the tendency to a regularized solution.

   In this paper, the number of pairs inside the UDN is set 8 and 10. While excluding the non-parametric ADMs and batch normalization layers, this model is composed of either $8 \times 7 = 56$ or $10 \times 7 = 70$ layers which easily lead to difficulties to train. However, with all kernels composed of size 3×3 that enlarges the receptive field without parameter overhead and additional skip connections, the gradient of loss can successfully back-propagate to optimize layers.

   During training, rather to train the overall model in a simple end-to-end manner, we regard the intermediates after pair of ADM and Z submodule still provide reasonable information for image restoration. Thus, we encourage these intermediates to approximate the ground truth by setting the loss function as

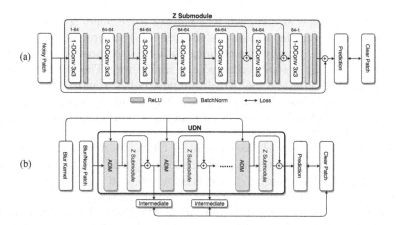

Fig. 3. (a) Training scheme and structure of Z submodule. p-DConv denotes p-dilated convolution. (b) Training scheme and structure of UDN (with ADM integration)

$$loss = \sum_n w_n \|\hat{I}_n - I\|_2^2, w_n = \frac{\beta_n}{\sum_n \beta_n} \qquad (11)$$

where $\hat{I}_n$ denotes the restoration after n-th ADM and Z submodule pair, and β_n denotes the preset value on n-th ADM. We have noted β which is an exponentially ascending sequence that complied with an intuitive to put more emphasis on the latter outputs rather than the former, so that it is used as a normalized weighting term over corresponding loss. An advantage derived is a more penetrated structure that the gradient of loss can easily propagate for parameter optimization. During inference, the final output is restored from the last layer. In this scheme, the Z submodule is expected to learn from the mapping between intermediates $\hat{I}_n$ and optimal ADM input $\hat{Z}_n$. Although with the reduction of flexibility described in existing plug-and-play manner, the learned image priors in Z submodules can accurately reflect to the interior mappings and lead to an efficient convergence and restoration quality.

4   Experiments

To generate the training data $\{(I_i, B_i, K_i)\}_{i=1}^M$, we crop 400 grayscale images selected from BSD500 dataset [35] of 64×64 with striding and augment with horizontal and vertical flip to prevent over-repetitiveness, then simulate 200 linear motion kernels of 25×25 with their length uniformly sampled from 5 to 25 at any orientation. The blurry image is synthesized by convolving full images with kernels and introducing additive Gaussian noise term from $N(0, \sigma^2)$. After that, 8-bit quantization is applied and the pixel values are clipped in range $[0, 255]$.

The blurry images are cropped into patches corresponding to that of clean ones, and those near the boundaries are excluded to prevent restoring from missing information. Finally, the training dataset is composed of 69600 triplets in total. Two testing sets are generated in a similar way. The first is synthesized by convolving Set14 dataset [36] which composed of 14 standard testing images with 8 blur kernels from Levin *et al.* [37]. The second is generated from Sun *et al.* dataset [38] which consists of 80 high-resolution images and 8 estimated kernels from Pan *et al.* dataset [39].

To optimize the network parameters in UDN, an Adam optimizer [40] is adopted by setting initial step at 10^{-3}; the learning rate is halved at 5-th, 15-th and 25-th epoch. The mini-batch size is set to 96, and trained by PyTorch1.0 [41] and Nvidia 2080Ti GPU for 50 epochs (about 15 h).

In addition, we have merged the outputs of ADM and UDN as a final restoration result. Based on the empirical observation that ADM provides enhanced details with smooth structures and UDN performs well on restoring high-frequency components, we combine two outputs in frequency domain by linear combination with a Gaussian mask (see detail description in the supplementary material).

For the following, we utilize a numerical image quality assessment (IQA) with other methods, including a patch-based learning method (EPLL) [8], non-local mean filter based method (DEB-BM3D) [42] and its modified version (IDD-BM3D) [43], and MLP [12], FCN [14], FDN [11] and IRCNN [15]. Among these methods, EPLL, DED-BM3D and IDD-BM3D are categorized into traditional state-of-the-arts that do not rely on the neural networks. The remaining methods are neural network based, e.g.. FCN, FDN and IRCNN are proposed at a similar period, all of these methods are CNN-based and derived from different concepts. The reason that we do not compare our works with those traditional prior-based methods like Krishnan *et al.* [5] or Pan *et al.* [39] is due to the difficulties of setting optimal hyperparameters, so that we cannot ensure these methods reach their best performance. For evaluation fairness, all of the methods are reproduced from their referenced code, as well as the pretrained models. The code corresponds to this paper is released[1].

4.1   Non-blind Deconvolution on Synthesized Datasets

We demonstrate several visualization examples on the BSD500 dataset [35] in exclusive of training patches that convolves with generated linear kernels with additive noise level at 1%, 3%, and 5%, to better discriminate the restoration performance and the robustness of algorithms. More visual and experimental results are included in the supplementary material.

For low noise level conditions, either when $\sigma = 1\%$ or $\sigma = 3\%$, IDD-BM3D shows apparently better results among traditional state-of-the-arts and even surpasses some of the deep learning based methods. In Fig. 4, some of the learning based methods like MLP, FCN and FDN suffer from obvious ringing

---

[1] https://github.com/angry77cat/DeepPriorUDN_ADM.

artifacts near the edge regions. In comparison, IRCNN and proposed methods can successfully preserve the details and structures without aliasing. The latter restores even more high frequency components; for example, displayed in the yellow block, so that the overall PSNR is better than the others. In Fig. 5, IDD-BM3D demonstrates a powerful restoration quality that not only outperforms traditional methods but also shows a competitive performance to some of the learning based methods. We also find that due to the over-smoothness, IRCNN has lost a lot of high-frequency components like the details originally existed in the red or yellow blocks, such that the performance is even worse than a patch-based method IDD-BM3D. Our model demonstrates even better performance on retrieving fine textures lies in the red and yellow blocks that is hard to be aware of in the blurred image. Besides, the restored structures in blue blocks are the most precise among all methods. In Fig. 6, where the noise level is increased to 5%, the FDN owns a powerful restoration quality that surpass all other methods excluding our proposal. We find the aliasing and over-smoothness that usually appear in learning based models can deteriorate the performance significantly. On the other hand, the proposed model has successfully restored the textures in the yellow block which is inappreciable in the blurry observation.

We also numerically evaluate aforementioned 2 testing datasets and summarize quantitative results in Table 2 and Table 3. Complying to our visualization results, the proposed ADM + UDN model generally demonstrates the best performance over the others. Such a surpassing image quality is found at a wide range of perturbed noise level from 1% to 10%, showing the robustness of our proposed models. It is worth to note that the increment on performance are generally proportional to the noise level which implies the significance of restoration quality.

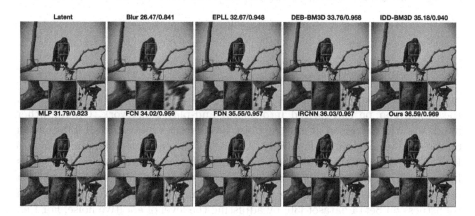

Fig. 4. Visual comparison on the images at $\sigma = 1\%$.

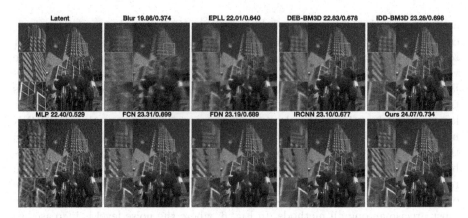

Fig. 5. Visual comparison on the images at $\sigma = 3\%$.

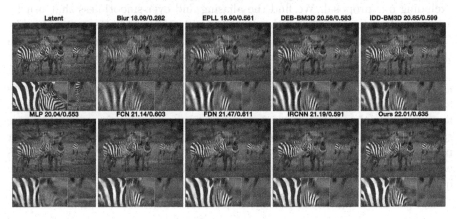

Fig. 6. Visual comparison on the images at $\sigma = 5\%$.

4.2   Noise Robustness

Since the ADM acting as a modified deconvolution plugin benefits convergence, the model can be categorized into a plug-and-play framework. On the other hand, the UDNs trained at specific noise levels retrieve more detail information on the sacrifice of training flexibility. As most of the end-to-end training schemes lead to inferior performance when handling different circumstances, the UDNs have shown robustness to a wide range of noise that significantly outperform other models that trained in an end-to-end manner as well. We evaluate such robustness on Set14 dataset [36] by adjusting the level of additive noise. For Fig. 7(b-d), it is worth noting that the ADMs acting as additional plugins have globally improved the restoration quality compared to IRCNN, which demonstrates comprehensive improvements by our proposed adaptive deconvolution.

As shown in a comparison in Fig. 7(a), the UDN trained at a high noise level shows significant improvements at low noise level at which other models

Table 2. Comparison on the Set14 dataset [36]. N/A denotes the absence of corresponding pretrained models in referenced code and bold numbers indicate the best performance.

σ	IQA	EPLL	DEB-BM3D	IDD-BM3D	MLP	FCN	FDN	IRCNN	Ours
1%	PSNR	28.40	30.89	31.76	30.56	29.48	30.02	31.57	**31.87**
	SSIM	0.845	0.854	0.879	0.848	0.860	0.862	0.876	**0.884**
3%	PSNR	25.43	26.95	27.79	25.53	26.68	27.16	27.63	**28.32**
	SSIM	0.725	0.744	0.765	0.637	0.758	0.759	0.760	**0.787**
5%	PSNR	23.96	25.29	26.00	24.33	25.30	25.88	25.97	**26.83**
	SSIM	0.663	0.689	0.705	0.657	0.706	0.710	0.697	**0.733**
10%	PSNR	22.12	23.39	23.80	23.53	N/A	N/A	23.99	**24.48**
	SSIM	0.581	0.614	0.625	0.614	N/A	N/A	0.624	**0.649**

Table 3. Comparison on the Sun *et al.* dataset [38]. N/A denotes the absence of corresponding pretrained models in referenced code and bold numbers indicate the best performance.

σ	IQA	EPLL	DEB-BM3D	IDD-BM3D	MLP	FCN	FDN	IRCNN	Ours
1%	PSNR	30.53	31.93	32.65	31.58	31.30	31.42	32.45	**33.00**
	SSIM	0.867	0.871	0.887	0.858	0.877	0.885	0.880	**0.901**
3%	PSNR	27.46	27.86	28.73	26.48	28.37	28.51	28.59	**29.43**
	SSIM	0.749	0.747	0.775	0.707	0.779	0.783	0.759	**0.806**
5%	PSNR	26.08	26.37	27.08	26.20	26.94	27.28	27.11	**27.97**
	SSIM	0.689	0.690	0.714	0.691	0.729	0.735	0.704	**0.753**
10%	PSNR	24.43	24.77	25.22	25.20	N/A	N/A	25.34	**26.18**
	SSIM	0.622	0.629	0.642	0.641	N/A	N/A	0.640	**0.684**

originally trained. When comparing with other plug-and-play models[2], the UDNs do not always outperform IRCNN but generally achieve better performance when perturbed by significant noise like Fig. 7(d) shows. Such a surprising observation has implied a flexibility for a model trained at a specific degradation domain, which is not observed in existing deblurring methods like FDN [11] and FCN [14].

4.3   Convergence Efficiency and Runtime Comparison

A good portion of deconvolution methods are based on iterative algorithms, for example, the iterative shrinkage-thresholding algorithm (ISTA) [44], the fast ISTA (FISTA) [45], and alternating direction method of multipliers (ADMM) [46] are useful algorithms for image restoration. Similarly, an important concern is whether the proposed models benefit the convergence efficiency compared to others. We take a close look into an image deconvolution case sampled from

---

[2] FDN is trained at various noise levels ranged from 0.1 to 12.75 (5%).

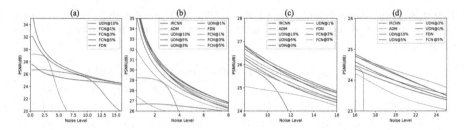

Fig. 7. Comparison on noise robustness for (a) models trained at specific noise levels and (b-d) includes IRCNN and ADM at different noise levels. @ denotes the model trained at which noise level.

the BSD500 dataset [35] and the Levin *et al.* dataset [37] and the PSNR is evaluated at each iteration shown in Fig. 8. One can observe the ADM has benefited the restoration performance especially when the noise level is high. In other words, by deconvolving adaptively, the restoration process can converge to a better solution. Furthermore, the UDN not only reaches the best result but also achieves even more faster convergence speed.

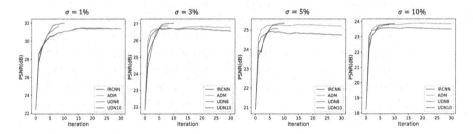

Fig. 8. Comparison on the convergence efficiency and the performance of optimal solution.

We also compare the runtime. All of the compared methods are implemented by PyTorch1.0 [41] package along with IntelCore i9-9900KF CPU@3.60 GHz, 64 GB RAM, and Nvidia 2080Ti GPU. Since the originally released code of IRCNN [15] was implemented in Matlab, a PyTorch version is implemented. It is worth noting that the ADM is essentially an edge detector that only accompanied by several convolutional operations. Therefore, it can be parallelized by GPU acceleration. As shown in Table 4, the runtime of the ADM is inevitably longer than that of the IRCNN; however, such overhead can be reduced in fold when handling high-resolution images. On the other hand, with the advantage of fast convergence, the runtime of the UDN8, which composed of 8 pairs of the ADM and Z submodules, is only 1/3 of that of the IRCNN.

Table 4. Runtime (in second) comparison.

Size	IRCNN	ADM	UDN8	UDN10
256×256	0.115	0.361	0.049	0.066
512×512	0.385	0.703	0.131	0.175
1024×1024	1.543	2.194	0.489	0.645

5 Conclusions

In this paper, we propose two learning based methods that are competitive to state-of-the-arts. The first approach is based on the success of incorporating MAP framework with CNN. As a solution to prevent over-smoothness which is usually found in CNN priors, a simple but useful plugin, ADM, is introduced without apparent increment on computation complexity. We have successfully alleviated over-smoothness and improved image quality for a wide range of noise perturbation. The second framework, UDN, is started from a concept to elaborate the great capacity of deep learning model to optimize the iterative optimization process in a gradient descent manner. Thus, a more effective optimization process is observed, which implies significantly less inference time. Furthermore, despite being trained at a specific noise level, UDN has demonstrated robustness for handling a wide range of cases and encouraged detail preservation. We further combine the outputs of two methods in frequency domain, leading to outstanding performance in evaluation benchmarks.

References

1. Wiener, N.: Extrapolation, Interpolation, and Smoothing of Stationary Time Series. The MIT Press, Cambridge (1964)
2. Lucy, L.B.: An iterative technique for the rectification of observed distributions. Astron. J. **79**, 745 (1974)
3. Richardson, W.H.: Bayesian-based iterative method of image restoration. J. Opt. Soc. Am. **62**, 55–59 (1972)
4. Rudin, L.I., Osher, S., Fatemi, E.: Nonlinear total variation based noise removal algorithms. Physica D **60**, 259–268 (1992)
5. Krishnan, D., Fergus, R.: Fast image deconvolution using hyper-Laplacian priors. In: Advances in Neural Information Processing Systems, pp. 1033–1041 (2009)
6. Levin, A., Fergus, R., Durand, F., Freeman, W.T.: Image and depth from a conventional camera with a coded aperture. ACM Trans. Graph. **26**, 70-es (2007)
7. Aharon, M., Elad, M., Bruckstein, A.: K-SVD: an algorithm for designing overcomplete dictionaries for sparse representation. IEEE Trans. Signal Process. **54**, 4311–4322 (2006)
8. Zoran, D., Weiss, Y.: From learning models of natural image patches to whole image restoration. In: International Conference on Computer Vision, pp. 479–486 (2011)
9. Roth, S., Black, M.J.: Fields of experts. Int. J. Comput. Vis. **82**, 205 (2009)

386 H.-C. Ko et al.

10. Gong, D., Zhang, Z., Shi, Q., Hengel, A.V.D., Shen, C., Zhang, Y.: Learning an optimizer for image deconvolution. arXiv preprint arXiv:1804.03368 (2018)
11. Kruse, J., Rother, C., Schmidt, U.: Learning to push the limits of efficient FFT-based image deconvolution. In: IEEE International Conference on Computer Vision, pp. 4586–4594 (2017)
12. Schuler, C.J., Christopher Burger, H., Harmeling, S., Scholkopf, B.: A machine learning approach for non-blind image deconvolution. In: IEEE Conference on Computer Vision and Pattern Recognition, pp. 1067–1074 (2013)
13. Xu, L., Ren, J.S., Liu, C., Jia, J.: Deep convolutional neural network for image deconvolution. In: Advances in Neural Information Processing Systems, pp. 1790–1798 (2014)
14. Zhang, J., Pan, J., Lai, W.S., Lau, R.W., Yang, M.H.: Learning fully convolutional networks for iterative non-blind deconvolution. In: IEEE Conference on Computer Vision and Pattern Recognition, pp. 3817–3825 (2017)
15. Zhang, K., Zuo, W., Gu, S., Zhang, L.: Learning deep CNN denoiser prior for image restoration. In: IEEE Conference on Computer Vision and Pattern Recognition, pp. 3929–3938 (2017)
16. Nan, Y., Ji, H.: Deep learning for handling kernel/model uncertainty in image deconvolution. In: IEEE Conference on Computer Vision and Pattern Recognition, pp. 2388–2397 (2020)
17. Ren, D., Zuo, W., Zhang, D., Zhang, L., Yang, M.H.: Simultaneous fidelity and regularization learning for image restoration. IEEE Trans. Pattern Analysis Mach. Intell. **43**(1), 284–299 (2019)
18. Rick Chang, J., Li, C.L., Poczos, B., Vijaya Kumar, B., Sankaranarayanan, A.C.: One network to solve them all-solving linear inverse problems using deep projection models. In: IEEE International Conference on Computer Vision, pp. 5888–5897 (2017)
19. Ren, D., Zhang, K., Wang, Q., Hu, Q., Zuo, W.: Neural blind deconvolution using deep priors. In: IEEE Conference on Computer Vision and Pattern Recognition, pp. 3341–3350 (2020)
20. Geman, D., Yang, C.: Nonlinear image recovery with half-quadratic regularization. IEEE Trans. Image Process. **4**, 932–946 (1995)
21. Levin, A., Weiss, Y.: User assisted separation of reflections from a single image using a sparsity prior. IEEE Trans. Pattern Anal. Mach. Intell. **29**, 1647–1654 (2007)
22. Fergus, R., Singh, B., Hertzmann, A., Roweis, S.T., Freeman, W.T.: Removing camera shake from a single photograph. ACM Trans. Graph. 787–794 (2006)
23. Cho, T.S., Joshi, N., Zitnick, C.L., Kang, S.B., Szeliski, R., Freeman, W.T.: A content-aware image prior. In: IEEE Conference on Computer Vision and Pattern Recognition, pp. 169–176 (2010)
24. Goldstein, T., O'Donoghue, B., Setzer, S., Baraniuk, R.: Fast alternating direction optimization methods. SIAM J. Imaging Sci. **7**, 1588–1623 (2014)
25. Roth, S., Black, M.J.: Fields of experts: A framework for learning image priors. In: IEEE Conference on Computer Vision and Pattern Recognition, vol. 2, pp. 860–867 (2005)
26. Schmidt, U., Roth, S.: Shrinkage fields for effective image restoration. In: IEEE Conference on Computer Vision and Pattern Recognition, pp. 2774–2781 (2014)
27. Schmidt, U., Rother, C., Nowozin, S., Jancsary, J., Roth, S.: Discriminative non-blind deblurring. In: IEEE Conference on Computer Vision and Pattern Recognition, pp. 604–611 (2013)

28. Chen, Y., Pock, T.: Trainable nonlinear reaction diffusion: a flexible framework for fast and effective image restoration. IEEE Trans. Pattern Anal. Mach. Intell. **39**, 1256–1272 (2016)

29. Sun, L., Cho, S., Wang, J., Hays, J.: Good image priors for non-blind deconvolution. In: Fleet, D., Pajdla, T., Schiele, B., Tuytelaars, T. (eds.) ECCV 2014. LNCS, vol. 8692, pp. 231–246. Springer, Cham (2014). https://doi.org/10.1007/978-3-319-10593-2_16

30. Venkatakrishnan, S.V., Bouman, C.A., Wohlberg, B.: Plug-and-play priors for model based reconstruction. In: IEEE Global Conference on Signal and Information Processing, pp. 945–948 (2013)

31. Chan, S.H., Wang, X., Elgendy, O.A.: Plug-and-play ADMM for image restoration: fixed-point convergence and applications. IEEE Trans. Comput. Imaging **3**, 84–98 (2016)

32. Dong, J., Pan, J., Sun, D., Su, Z., Yang, M.-H.: Learning data terms for non-blind deblurring. In: Ferrari, V., Hebert, M., Sminchisescu, C., Weiss, Y. (eds.) ECCV 2018. LNCS, vol. 11215, pp. 777–792. Springer, Cham (2018). https://doi.org/10.1007/978-3-030-01252-6_46

33. Wang, Y., Yang, J., Yin, W., Zhang, Y.: A new alternating minimization algorithm for total variation image reconstruction. SIAM J. Imaging Sci. **1**, 248–272 (2008)

34. Dong, W., Wang, P., Yin, W., Shi, G., Wu, F., Lu, X.: Denoising prior driven deep neural network for image restoration. IEEE Trans. Pattern Anal. Mach. Intell. **41**, 2305–2318 (2018)

35. Arbelaez, P., Maire, M., Fowlkes, C., Malik, J.: Contour detection and hierarchical image segmentation. IEEE Trans. Pattern Anal. Mach. Intell. **33**, 898–916 (2010)

36. Zeyde, R., Elad, M., Protter, M.: On single image scale-up using sparse-representations. In: International Conference on Curves and Surfaces, pp. 711–730 (2010)

37. Levin, A., Weiss, Y., Durand, F., Freeman, W.T.: Understanding and evaluating blind deconvolution algorithms. In: IEEE Conference on Computer Vision and Pattern Recognition, pp. 1964–1971 (2009)

38. Sun, L., Cho, S., Wang, J., Hays, J.: Edge-based blur kernel estimation using patch priors. In: IEEE International Conference on Computational Photography, pp. 1–8 (2013)

39. Pan, J., Lin, Z., Su, Z., Yang, M.H.: Robust kernel estimation with outliers handling for image deblurring. In: IEEE Conference on Computer Vision and Pattern Recognition, pp. 2800–2808 (2016)

40. Kingma, D.P., Ba, J.: Adam: a method for stochastic optimization. arXiv preprint arXiv:1412.6980 (2014)

41. Paszke, A., et al.: Pytorch: an imperative style, high-performance deep learning library. In: Advances in Neural Information Processing Systems, pp. 8024–8035 (2019)

42. Dabov, K., Foi, A., Katkovnik, V., Egiazarian, K.: Image restoration by sparse 3d transform-domain collaborative filtering. In: SPIE Image Processing: Algorithms and Systems VI, vol. 6812, 681207(2008)

43. Danielyan, A., Katkovnik, V., Egiazarian, K.: Bm3d frames and variational image deblurring. IEEE Trans. Image Process. **21**, 1715–1728 (2011)

44. Bioucas-Dias, J.M., Figueiredo, M.A.: A new twist: two-step iterative shrinkage/thresholding algorithms for image restoration. IEEE Trans. Image Process. **16**, 2992–3004 (2007)

45. Beck, A., Teboulle, M.: A fast iterative shrinkage-thresholding algorithm for linear inverse problems. SIAM J. Imaging Sci. **2**, 183–202 (2009)
46. Boyd, S., Parikh, N., Chu, E., Peleato, B., Eckstein, J., et al.: Distributed optimization and statistical learning via the alternating direction method of multipliers. Found. Trends Mach. Learn. **3**, 1–122 (2011)

Motion and Tracking

Adaptive Spatio-Temporal Regularized Correlation Filters for UAV-Based Tracking

Libin Xu[1], Qilei Li[2], Jun Jiang[3], Guofeng Zou[1], Zheng Liu[4],
and Mingliang Gao[1($\boxtimes$)]

[1] School of Electrical and Electronic Engineering, Shandong University
of Technology, Zibo 255000, China
mlgao@sdut.edu.cn
[2] School of Electronics and Information Engineering, Sichuan University,
Chengdu 610065, China
[3] School of Computer Science, Southwest Petroleum University,
Chengdu 610500, China
[4] Faculty of Applied Science, The University of British Columbia,
Vancouver, BC V1V 1V7, Canada

Abstract. Visual tracking on unmanned aerial vehicles (UAVs) has
enabled many new practical applications in computer vision. Meanwhile,
discriminative correlation filter (DCF)-based trackers have drawn great
attention and undergone remarkable progress due to their promising performance and efficiency. However, the boundary effect and filter degradation remain two challenging problems. In this work, a novel Adaptive Spatio-Temporal Regularized Correlation Filter (ASTR-CF) model
is proposed to address these two problems. The ASTR-CF can optimize
the spatial regularization weight and the temporal regularization weight
simultaneously. Meanwhile, the proposed model can be effectively optimized based on the alternating direction method of multipliers (ADMM).
Experimental results on DTB70 and UAV123@10fps benchmarks have
proven the superiority of the ASTR-CF tracker compared to the state-
of-the-art trackers in terms of both accuracy and computational speed.

Keywords: UAV tracking · Correlation filter · Spatio-temporal
regularization

1 Introduction

The advance of visual tracking has provided UAV with the intriguing capability
for various practical applications. Differing from the generic tracking, UAV-based
tracking poses new challenges to the tracking problem, *e.g.*, rapid changes in

Electronic supplementary material The online version of this chapter (https://
doi.org/10.1007/978-3-030-69532-3_24) contains supplementary material, which is
available to authorized users.

scale and perspective, limited pixels in the target region, and multiple similar disruptors [1].

Recently, discriminative correlation filter (DCF)-based trackers brought the performance of tracking into a new level [2–6]. One of the prominent merits that highlights the DCF-based trackers is that DCF is efficient in the training and detection stage as they can be transferred into the Fourier domain and operated in element-wise multiplication, which is of significance for the real-time tracking. However, it is still challenging to achieve high-performance tracking for an arbitrary object in unconstrained scenarios. The main obstacles include spatial boundary effect and temporal filter degeneration [6].

Learning DCF in the frequency domain comes at the high cost of learning from circularly shifted examples of the foreground target, thus it produces the unwanted boundary effects. This dilemma has been alleviated to some extent with additional pre-defined spatial constraints on filter coefficients. For example, Danelljan et al. [7] introduced the Spatially Regularized Discriminative Correlation Filters (SRDCF) to mitigate boundary effects. With the coefficient spatially penalized according to their distance to the center, the tracker is expected to focus on information near the center. Galoogahi et al. [8] multiplied the filter directly with a binary matrix to generate real positive and negative samples for model training. The aforementioned two spatial constraints are widely used in the subsequent research works [9–11].

The appearance model of most DCF-based trackers is updated via a linear interpolation approach and it cannot adapt to ubiquitous appearance change, leading to filter degradation inevitably. Some attempts are made to tackle the problem of filter degradation, e.g., training set management [12–14], temporal restriction [15,16], tracking confidence verification [17,18] and over-fitting alleviation [19]. Among them, the temporal regularization is proven to be an effective way.

In this work, the problems of boundary effect and filter degradation are solved by the proposed adaptive spatio-temporal regularized correlation filters (ASTR-CF). Meanwhile, the ASTR-CF is applied to real-time UAV target tracking. We compared our approach with state-of-the-art trackers on DTB70 and UAV123-@10fps benchmarks. The results demonstrate that ASTR-CF outperforms state-of-the-art trackers in terms of accuracy and computational speed.

2   Related Work

Despite the great success of DCF in visual tracking, it remains a challenge to achieve high performance tracking for an arbitrary object in unconstrained scenarios due to the intrinsic problems of spatial boundary effect and temporal filter degradation [15]. To solve these problems, spatial regularization and temporal regularization are introduced to the DCF framework successively.

2.1 Spatial Regularization

Learning DCF in the frequency domain produces unwanted boundary effects which reduce the tracking performance [7,15]. To alleviate the boundary effect problem, SRDCF [7] stimulates the interest in spatial regularization which allocates more energy for the central region of a filter using a predefined spatial weighting function. A similar idea has been pursued through pruning the training samples or learned filters with a predefined mask [20–22]. A common characterization of the approaches above is that they are all based on a fixed spatial regularization pattern, decreasing the ambiguity emanating from the background and resulting in a relatively large search window for tracking. Different from the aforementioned approaches, Dai *et al.* [11] proposed an Adaptive Spatially Regularized Correlation Filters (ASRCF) model, which could estimate an object-aware spatial regularization and obtain more reliable filter coefficients during the tracking process.

2.2 Spatio-temporal Regularization

Most of DCF-based trackers updated the appearance model via a linear interpolation approach, but it cannot adapt to ubiquitous appearance changes. To address this problem, Li *et al.* [15] introduced a temporal regularization module to SRDCF and incorporated both spatial and temporal regularization into DCF. The improved version, named as STRCF, is a rational approximation of the full SRDCF formulation on multiple training images, and can also be exploited for simultaneous DCF learning and model updating. Although STRCF has achieved competent performance, it remains two limitations. **(i)** The fixed spatial regularization failing to address appearance variation in the unforeseeable aerial tracking scenarios. **(ii)** The unchanged temporal penalty strength μ (set as 15 in [15]) is not general in all kinds of situations.

In this work, a novel Adaptive Spatio-Temporal Regularized Correlation Filters (ASTR-CF) model was proposed to estimate an object-aware spatial regularization and context-aware temporal regularization. The overall procedure of the tracking process is shown in Fig. 1. Meanwhile, the ADMM algorithm is directly introduced to solve the ASTR-CF model making it more generic.

3 ASTR-CF

3.1 Objective Function of ASTR-CF

CF: The original multi-channel CF model in the spatial domain aims to minimize the following objective function [4],

$$E(\mathbf{H}) = \frac{1}{2}\left\|\mathbf{y} - \sum_{k=1}^{K}\mathbf{x}^k * \mathbf{h}^k\right\|_2^2 + \frac{1}{2}\sum_{k=1}^{K}\left\|\mathbf{h}^k\right\|_2^2. \tag{1}$$

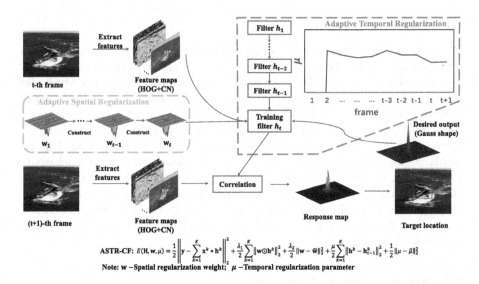

Note: w —Spatial regularization weight; μ —Temporal regularization parameter

Fig. 1. Tracking framework based on the proposed ASTR-CF. In the training stage, a training patch is cropped at the estimated location of the target at the t-th frame. We extract the feature (HOG [23] and Color Names [24]) maps combined with prior filters and $\mathbf{w}$ to train the current filter. At the $(t+1)$-th frame, the trained filter is used to produce a response map, based on which the target is located.

Here, $\mathbf{x}^k \in \mathbb{R}^{T \times 1}(k = 1, 2, 3, \dots, K)$ and $\mathbf{h}^k \in \mathbb{R}^{T \times 1}(k = 1, 2, 3, \dots, K)$ denote the extracted feature with length T in the t-th frame and filter trained in the t-th frame respectively. The vector $\mathbf{y} \in \mathbb{R}^{T \times 1}$ is the desired response (*i.e.*, the Gaussian-shaped ground truth) and $*$ denotes the convolution operator. $\mathbf{H} = \left[\mathbf{h}^1, \mathbf{h}^2, \dots, \mathbf{h}^K\right]$ is the matrix representing the filters from all the K channels.

The original CF model suffers from periodic repetitions on boundary positions caused by circulant shifted samples, which inevitably degrades the tracking performance. To solve this problem, several spatial constraints have been introduced to alleviate unexpected boundary effects. The representative methods are SRDCF [7] and STRCF [15].

SRDCF: The SRDCF method [7] introduces a spatial regularization to penalize the filter coefficients with respect to their spatial locations and the objective function is formulated as,

$$E(\mathbf{H}) = \frac{1}{2}\left\| \mathbf{y} - \sum_{k=1}^{K} \mathbf{x}^k * \mathbf{h}^k \right\|_2^2 + \frac{1}{2}\sum_{k=1}^{K}\left\| \widetilde{\mathbf{w}} \odot \mathbf{h}^k \right\|_2^2. \tag{2}$$

Here, $\widetilde{\mathbf{w}}$ is a negative Gaussian-shaped spatial weight vector to make the learned filters have a high response around the center of the tracked object. However, although SRDCF is effective in suppressing the adverse boundary effects, it also increases the computational burden due to the following two reasons. **(i)** The failure of exploiting circulant matrix structure. **(ii)** The large linear equations and Gauss-Seidel solver. More implementation details are refer to [7].

STRCF: The STRCF model [15] introduces a spatial-temporal regularized module to CF and the objective function is formulated as,

$$E(\mathbf{H}) = \frac{1}{2} \left\| \mathbf{y} - \sum_{k=1}^{K} \mathbf{x}^k * \mathbf{h}^k \right\|_2^2 + \frac{1}{2} \sum_{k=1}^{K} \left\| \widetilde{\mathbf{w}} \odot \mathbf{h}^k \right\|_2^2 + \frac{\mu}{2} \sum_{k=1}^{K} \left\| \mathbf{h}^k - \mathbf{h}_{t-1}^k \right\|_2^2. \quad (3)$$

Here, $\mathbf{x}^k \in \mathbb{R}^{T \times 1}(k = 1, 2, 3, \ldots, K)$ is the extracted feature with length T in frame t. $\mathbf{h}^k, \mathbf{h}_{t-1}^k \in \mathbb{R}^{T \times 1}(k = 1, 2, 3, \ldots, K)$ denote the filter of the t-th channel trained in the k-th and $(t-1)$-th frame respectively. As for regularization, the spatial regularization parameter $\widetilde{\mathbf{w}}$ is imitated from SRDCF [7] to decrease boundary effect, and temporal regularization (the third term in Eq. (3)), is firstly proposed to restrict filter's variation by penalizing the difference between the current and previous filters.

However, as aforementioned, the spatial regularization and temporal penalty strength of STRCF [15] are fixed. Therefore, it fails to address the appearance variation in the unforeseeable aerial tracking scenarios.

Our Objective Function: Motivated by the discussions above, we propose a novel ASTR-CF method to learn effective multi-channel CFs, and our objective function is defined as follows,

$$\begin{aligned} E(\mathbf{H}, \mathbf{w}, \mu) = &\frac{1}{2} \left\| \mathbf{y} - \sum_{k=1}^{K} \mathbf{x}^k * \mathbf{h}^k \right\|_2^2 + \left(\frac{\lambda_1}{2} \sum_{k=1}^{K} \left\| \mathbf{w} \odot \mathbf{h}^k \right\|_2^2 + \frac{\lambda_2}{2} \| \mathbf{w} - \widetilde{\mathbf{w}} \|_2^2 \right) \\ &+ \left(\frac{\mu}{2} \sum_{k=1}^{K} \left\| \mathbf{h}^k - \mathbf{h}_{t-1}^k \right\|_2^2 + \frac{1}{2} \| \mu - \tilde{\mu} \|_2^2 \right). \end{aligned} \quad (4)$$

Here, the first term is the ridge regression term that convolves the training data $\mathbf{X} = \left[\mathbf{x}^1, \mathbf{x}^2, \ldots, \mathbf{x}^K \right]$ with the filter $\mathbf{H} = \left[\mathbf{h}^1, \mathbf{h}^2, \ldots, \mathbf{h}^K \right]$ to fit the Gaussian-distributed ground truth $\mathbf{y}$. The second term introduces an adaptive spatial regularization on the filter $\mathbf{H}$. The spatial weight $\mathbf{w}$ requires to be optimized to approximate a reference weight $\widetilde{\mathbf{w}}$. This constraint introduces prior information on $\mathbf{w}$ and avoids model degradation. λ_1 and λ_2 are the regularization parameters of the second terms. The third term introduces an adaptive temporal regularization, where $\tilde{\mu}$ and μ denote the reference and optimized context-aware temporal regularization parameter respectively [6]. $\tilde{\mu}$ is denoted as ,

$$\tilde{\mu} = \frac{\zeta}{1 + \log \left(\nu \| \mathbf{\Pi} \|_2 + 1 \right)}, \quad \| \mathbf{\Pi} \|_2 \le \phi. \quad (5)$$

Here, $\mathbf{\Pi} = \left[\left| \Pi^1 \right|, \left| \Pi^2 \right|, \cdots \left| \Pi^T \right| \right]$ denotes the response variations. ζ and ν denote hyper parameters.

3.2   Optimization of ASTR-CF

We express the objective function *i.e.*, Eq. (4), in the frequency domain using Parseval's theorem, and convert it into the equality constrained optimization form,

$$
E(\mathbf{H}, \widehat{\mathbf{G}}, \mathbf{w}, \mu) = \frac{1}{2} \left\| \widehat{\mathbf{y}} - \sum_{k=1}^{K} \widehat{\mathbf{x}}^k \odot \widehat{\mathbf{g}}^k \right\|_2^2 + \frac{\lambda_1}{2} \sum_{k=1}^{K} \left\| \mathbf{w} \odot \mathbf{h}^k \right\|_2^2
$$
$$
+ \frac{\lambda_2}{2} \left\| \mathbf{w} - \widetilde{\mathbf{w}} \right\|_2^2 + \frac{\mu}{2} \sum_{k=1}^{K} \left\| \widehat{\mathbf{g}}^k - \widehat{\mathbf{g}}_{t-1}^k \right\|_2^2 + \frac{1}{2} \| \mu - \widetilde{\mu} \|_2^2,
$$

$$
s.t., \widehat{\mathbf{g}}^k = \sqrt{T} \mathbf{F} \mathbf{h}^k, \ k = 1, \dots, K.
$$

(6)

Here, $\widehat{\mathbf{G}} = [\widehat{\mathbf{g}}^1, \widehat{\mathbf{g}}^2, \dots, \widehat{\mathbf{g}}^K] \left(\widehat{\mathbf{g}}^k = \sqrt{T} \mathbf{F} \mathbf{h}^k, k = 1, 2, \dots, K \right)$ is an auxiliary variable matrix. The symbol $\wedge$ denotes the discrete Fourier transform form of a given signal, and $\mathbf{F}$ is the orthonormal $T \times T$ matrix of complex basis vectors to map any T dimensional vectorized signal into the Fourier domain. The model in Eq. (6) is bi-convex, and can be minimized to obtain a local optimal solution using ADMM [25]. The augmented Lagrangian form of Eq. (6) can be formulated as,

$$
L(\mathbf{H}, \widehat{\mathbf{G}}, \mathbf{w}, \mu, \widehat{\mathbf{V}}) = E(\mathbf{H}, \widehat{\mathbf{G}}, \mathbf{w}, \mu) + \frac{\gamma}{2} \sum_{k=1}^{K} \left\| \widehat{\mathbf{g}}^k - \sqrt{T} \mathbf{F} \mathbf{h}^k \right\|_2^2
$$
$$
+ \sum_{k=1}^{K} \left(\widehat{\mathbf{v}}^k \right)^{\mathrm{T}} \left(\widehat{\mathbf{g}}^k - \sqrt{T} \mathbf{F} \mathbf{h}^k \right).
$$

(7)

Here, $\mathbf{V}$ is the Lagrange multiplier, and $\widehat{\mathbf{V}}$ is the corresponding Fourier transform. By introducing $\mathbf{s}^k = \frac{1}{\gamma} \mathbf{v}^k$, the optimization of Eq. (7) is equivalent to solving,

$$
L(\mathbf{H}, \widehat{\mathbf{G}}, \mathbf{w}, \mu, \widehat{\mathbf{S}}) = E(\mathbf{H}, \widehat{\mathbf{G}}, \mathbf{w}, \mu) + \frac{\gamma}{2} \sum_{k=1}^{K} \left\| \widehat{\mathbf{g}}^k - \sqrt{T} \mathbf{F} \mathbf{h}^k + \widehat{\mathbf{s}}^k \right\|_2^2.
$$

(8)

Then, the ADMM algorithm is adopted by alternately solving the following subproblems.

Subproblem H: If $\widehat{\mathbf{G}}, \mathbf{w}, \mu$ and $\widehat{\mathbf{S}}$ are given, the optimal $\mathbf{H}^*$ can be obtained as,

$$
\mathbf{h}^{k*} = \underset{\mathbf{h}^k}{\mathrm{argmin}} \left\{ \frac{\lambda_1}{2} \left\| \mathbf{w} \odot \mathbf{h}^k \right\|_2^2 + \frac{\gamma}{2} \left\| \widehat{\mathbf{g}}^k - \sqrt{T} \mathbf{F} \mathbf{h}^k + \widehat{\mathbf{s}}^k \right\|_2^2 \right\}
$$
$$
= \left[\lambda_1 \mathbf{W}^{\mathrm{T}} \mathbf{W} + \gamma T \mathbf{I} \right]^{-1} \gamma T \left(\mathbf{g}^k + \mathbf{s}^k \right)
$$
$$
= \frac{\gamma T \left(\mathbf{g}^k + \mathbf{s}^k \right)}{\lambda_1 (\mathbf{w} \odot \mathbf{w}) + \gamma T}.
$$

(9)

Here, $\mathbf{W} = \mathrm{diag}\,(\mathbf{w}) \in \mathbb{R}^{T \times T}$. Equation (9) shows that the solution of $\mathbf{h}^k$ merely requires the element-wise multiplication and the inverse fast Fourier transform (*i.e.*, $\mathbf{g}^k = \frac{1}{\sqrt{T}}\mathbf{F}^{\mathrm{T}}\widehat{\mathbf{g}}^k$ and $\mathbf{s}^k = \frac{1}{\sqrt{T}}\mathbf{F}^{\mathrm{T}}\widehat{\mathbf{s}}^k$).

Subproblem $\widehat{\mathbf{G}}$: If $\mathbf{H}$, $\mathbf{w}$, μ, and $\widehat{\mathbf{S}}$ are given, the optimal $\widehat{\mathbf{G}}^*$ can be estimated by solving the optimization problem as,

$$
\widehat{\mathbf{G}}^* = \underset{\widehat{\mathbf{G}}}{\mathrm{argmin}} \left\{ \frac{1}{2} \left\| \mathbf{y} - \sum_{k=1}^{K} \widehat{\mathbf{x}}^k \odot \widehat{\mathbf{g}}^k \right\|_2^2 + \frac{\mu}{2} \sum_{k=1}^{K} \left\| \widehat{\mathbf{g}}^k - \widehat{\mathbf{g}}_{t-1}^k \right\|_2^2 \right.
$$
$$
\left. + \frac{\gamma}{2} \sum_{k=1}^{K} \left\| \widehat{\mathbf{g}}^k - \sqrt{T}\mathbf{F}\mathbf{h}^k + \widehat{\mathbf{s}}^k \right\|_2^2 \right\}. \tag{10}
$$

However, it is difficult to optimize Eq. (10) due to its high computation complexity. Thus, we consider processing on all channels of each pixel to simplify our formulation written by,

$$
\mathcal{V}_j^*(\widehat{\mathbf{G}}) = \underset{\mathcal{V}_j(\widehat{\mathbf{G}})}{\mathrm{argmin}} \left\{ \frac{1}{2} \left\| \widehat{\mathbf{y}}_j - \mathcal{V}_j(\widehat{\mathbf{X}})^{\mathrm{T}} \mathcal{V}_j(\widehat{\mathbf{G}}) \right\|_2^2 + \frac{\mu}{2} \left\| \mathcal{V}_j(\widehat{\mathbf{G}}) - \mathcal{V}_j\left(\widehat{\mathbf{G}}_{t-1}\right) \right\|_2^2 \right.
$$
$$
\left. + \frac{\gamma}{2} \left\| \mathcal{V}_j(\widehat{\mathbf{G}}) + \mathcal{V}_j(\widehat{\mathbf{S}}) - \mathcal{V}_j(\sqrt{T}\mathbf{F}\mathbf{H}) \right\|_2^2 \right\}. \tag{11}
$$

Here, $\mathcal{V}_j(\widehat{\mathbf{X}}) \in \mathbb{C}^{K \times 1}$ denotes the values of all K channels of $\widehat{\mathbf{X}}$ on pixel j, $(j = 1, 2, \ldots, T)$. Then, the analytical solution of Eq. (11) can be obtained as,

$$
\mathcal{V}^*(\widehat{\mathbf{G}}) = \frac{1}{\mu + \gamma} \left[\mathbf{I} - \frac{\mathcal{V}_j(\widehat{\mathbf{X}}) \mathcal{V}_j(\widehat{\mathbf{X}})^{\mathrm{T}}}{\mu + \gamma + \mathcal{V}_j(\widehat{\mathbf{X}})^{\mathrm{T}} \mathcal{V}_j(\widehat{\mathbf{X}})} \right] \rho, \tag{12}
$$

here,

$$
\rho = \mathcal{V}_j(\widehat{\mathbf{X}}) \widehat{\mathbf{y}}_j + \mu \left[\mathcal{V}_j\left(\widehat{\mathbf{G}}_{t-1}\right) \right] + \gamma \left[\mathcal{V}_j(\sqrt{T}\mathbf{F}\mathbf{H}) - \mathcal{V}_j(\widehat{\mathbf{S}}) \right]. \tag{13}
$$

The derivation of Eq. (12) uses the Sherman Morrsion formula,

$$
\left(\mathbf{A} + \mathbf{u}\mathbf{v}^{\mathrm{T}}\right)^{-1} = \mathbf{A}^{-1} - \frac{\mathbf{A}^{-1}\mathbf{u}\mathbf{v}^{\mathrm{T}}\mathbf{A}^{-1}}{1 + \mathbf{v}^{\mathrm{T}}\mathbf{A}^{-1}\mathbf{u}}. \tag{14}
$$

Here, $\mathbf{u}$ and $\mathbf{v}$ are two column vectors and $\mathbf{u}\mathbf{v}^{\mathrm{T}}$ is a rank-one matrix.

Solving $\mathbf{w}$: If $\mathbf{H}$, $\widehat{\mathbf{G}}$, μ and $\widehat{\mathbf{S}}$ are fixed, the closed-form solution regrading $\mathbf{w}$ can be determined as,

$$
\mathbf{w}^* = \underset{\mathbf{w}}{\mathrm{argmin}} \left\{ \frac{\lambda_1}{2} \sum_{k=1}^{K} \left\| \mathbf{w} \odot \mathbf{h}^k \right\|_2^2 + \frac{\lambda_2}{2} \left\| \mathbf{w} - \widetilde{\mathbf{w}} \right\|_2^2 \right\}
$$
$$
= \left[\lambda_1 \sum_{k=1}^{K} \left(\mathbf{N}^k\right)^{\mathrm{T}} \mathbf{N}^k + \lambda_2 \mathbf{I} \right]^{-1} \lambda_2 \widetilde{\mathbf{w}} \tag{15}
$$
$$
= \frac{\lambda_2 \widetilde{\mathbf{w}}}{\lambda_1 \sum_{k=1}^{K} \mathbf{h}^k \odot \mathbf{h}^k + \lambda_2 \mathbf{I}}.
$$

Here, $\mathbf{N}^k = \mathrm{diag}\left(\mathbf{h}^k\right) \in \mathbb{R}^{T \times T}$.

Solving μ: Given other variables $\mathbf{H}$, $\widehat{\mathbf{G}}$, $\mathbf{w}$, and $\widehat{\mathbf{S}}$, the optimal solution of μ can be determined as,

$$
\begin{aligned}
\mu^* &= \underset{\mu}{\mathrm{argmin}}\left\{\frac{\mu}{2}\sum_{k=1}^{K}\left\|\widehat{\mathbf{g}}^k - \widehat{\mathbf{g}}_{t-1}^k\right\|_2^2 + \frac{1}{2}\|\mu - \tilde{\mu}\|_2^2\right\} \\
&= \tilde{\mu} - \frac{1}{2}\sum_{k=1}^{K}\left\|\widehat{\mathbf{g}}^k - \widehat{\mathbf{g}}_{t-1}^k\right\|_2^2.
\end{aligned}
\tag{16}
$$

Lagrangian Multiplier Update: We update Lagrangian multipliers as,

$$
\widehat{\mathbf{S}}^{i+1} = \widehat{\mathbf{S}}^i + \gamma^i\left(\widehat{\mathbf{G}}^{i+1} - \widehat{\mathbf{H}}^{i+1}\right).
\tag{17}
$$

Here, i and $i+1$ denote the iteration index. The step size regularization constant γ takes the form of $\gamma^{i+1} = \min\left(\gamma_{\max}, \beta\gamma^i\right)$ ($\beta = 10, \gamma_{\max} = 10000$). By iteratively solving the five subproblems above, we can optimize our objective function effectively and obtain the optimal filter $\widehat{\mathbf{G}}$, object-aware spatial regularization weight $\mathbf{w}$ and context-aware temporal regularization parameter μ in frame t. Then $\widehat{\mathbf{G}}$ is used for detection in frame $t+1$.

3.3 Target Localization

The location of the target can be determined in the Fourier domain as,

$$
\widehat{\mathcal{R}}_t = \sum_{k=1}^{K}\widehat{\mathbf{x}}^k \odot \widehat{\mathbf{g}}_{t-1}^k.
\tag{18}
$$

Here, $\mathcal{R}_t$ and $\widehat{\mathcal{R}}_t$ denote the response map and its Fourier transform. After obtaining the response map, the optimal location can be obtained based on the maximum response.

4   Experimental Results

In this section, we demonstrate the effectiveness of our tracker on DTB70 [26] and UAV123@10fps [27] datasets among the current state-of-the-art trackers. We use the same evaluation criteria on the two benchmarks.

The experiments of tracking performance evaluation are conducted using MATLAB R2017a on a PC with an i7-8700K processor (3.7 GHz), 32 GB RAM, and an NVIDIA GTX 1080Ti GPU. For the hyper-parameters of our tracker, we set $\lambda_1 = 1, \lambda_2 = 0.001, \nu = 2 \times 10^{-5}$, and $\zeta = 13$. The threshold of ϕ is 3000, and the ADMM iteration is set to 4.

4.1   Quantitative Evaluation

DTB70: The DTB70 dataset [26] contains 70 difficult UAV image sequences, primarily addressing the problem of severe UAV motion. In addition, various cluttered scenes and objects with different sizes as well as aspect ratios are included. We compare our tracker with 12 state-of-the-art trackers, including trackers using hand-crafted features (*i.e.*, AutoTrack [6], BACF [8], DAT [28], DSST [29], ECO-HC [12], KCF [4], SRDCF [7], and STRCF [15]), using deep feature-based or pretrained deep architecture-based trackers (*i.e.*, ASRCF [11], IBCCF [30], UDT+ [31], and MDNet [32]). To make a fair comparison, the publicly available codes or results provided by the original authors are employed.

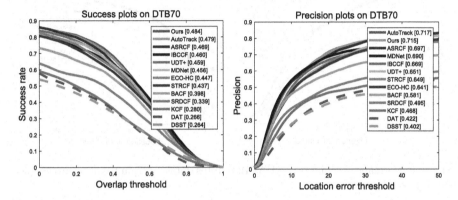

Fig. 2. Comparison of the success rate and precision plots with the state-of-the-art trackers on DTB70 dataset [26]. The numbers in the legend indicate the representative AUC for success plots and precisions at 20 pixels for precision plots.

We evaluate the trackers based on One Pass Evaluation (OPE) rule [33], and two measures are used for evaluation, namely success rate and precision. The success rate can display the percentage of situations when the overlap between the estimated bounding box and the ground truth is greater than different thresholds, and Area under the curve (AUC) is utilized for ranking. Precision can demonstrate the percentage of scenarios when the distance between the estimated bounding box and ground truth one is smaller than different thresholds, and the score at 20 pixels is used for ranking. Figure 2 depicts both the success rate and precision of different trackers. Overall, the proposed tracker achieves the best result with an AUC score of 0.484 among all the other trackers. For the distance precision, the proposed ASTR-CF outperforms most of the competing trackers except for AutoTrack [6]. It is noteworthy that the proposed tracker surpasses its counterpart SRDCF [7] and STRCF [15] by 22% and 6.6%, respectively. What's more, only with hand-crafted features, our tracker outperforms deep feature-based trackers (ASRCF [11], and IBCCF [30]) and pre-trained deep architecture-based trackers (MDNet [32], and UDT+ [31]).

UAV123@10fps: The UAV123@10fps dataset [27] is a temporarily down-sampled version of the UAV123 [27]. It increases the tracing challenge compared with the original UAV123 [27] because the displacements of the moving objects become bigger. Nine state-of-the-art trackers, *i.e.*, AutoTrack [6], BACF [8], DSST [29], ECO-HC [12], MEEM [34], SRDCF [7], STRCF [15], Struck [35], MUSTer [36] are implemented for comparison. The comparative results are depicted in Fig. 3. One can see that the proposed tracker outperforms all the other state-of-the-art trackers in terms of both success rate and precision.

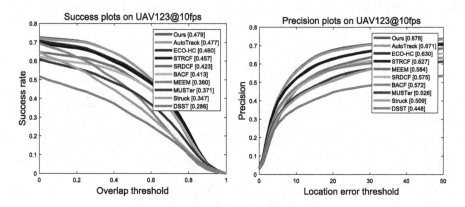

Fig. 3. Performance evaluation on UAV123@10fps dataset [27] in terms of success plots and precision plots.

Figure 4 shows the overlap success plots of different trackers on 6 attributes, *e.g.*, illumination variation, partial occlusion, viewpoint changes, fast motion, scale variation, and low resolution. Our tracker achieves the best performance in all these attributes. This is mainly attributed to the proposed adaptive spatio-temporal regularization, in which the adaptive temporal regularization enables the learned filter to perform more robust to occlusion while adapting well to large appearance variation. Meanwhile, the learned filters focus on the reliable features of the tracked object, it can alleviate the effects of unexpected noises within the object region by introducing adaptive spatial regularization. *More attribute-based evaluations can be seen in the supplementary material.*

Finally, we perform qualitative evaluations of different trackers on several video sequences. For a clearer visualization, we exhibit the results of ASTR-CF and 4 state-of-the-art trackers, *i.e.*, AutoTrack [6], STRCF [15] ECO-HC [12], and BACF [8]. The tracking results on 6 video sequences are shown in Fig. 5. One can note that the proposed ASTR-CF performs favorably against the state-of-the-art hand-crafted trackers.

Overall Performance Evaluation: Average performance of the top-5 CPU-based trackers on DTB70 dataset [26] and UAV123@10fps dataset [27] are summarized in Table 1. One can see that the proposed tracker performs the best in

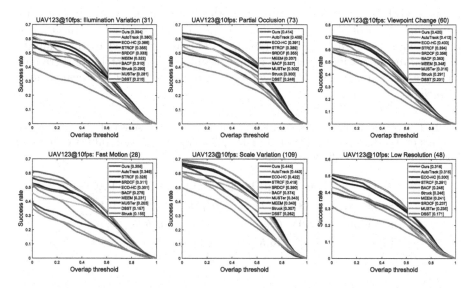

Fig. 4. Evaluation of different trackers with 6 attributes on the UAV123@10fps dataset [27]. Success plot can display the percentage of situations when the overlap between estimated bounding boxes and ground truth one is greater than different thresholds. Area under curve (AUC) is utilized for ranking.

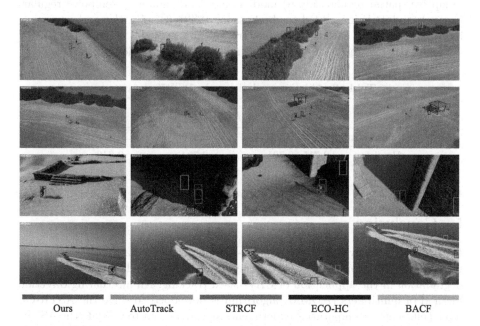

Fig. 5. Qualitative comparison of our approach with state-of-the-art trackers on the group2_2, group2_3, person1_s, and wakeboard5 sequences.

terms of both success rate and precision. Meanwhile, it has a second fast computational speed of 55.5fps, only slower than AutoTrack (56.5fps). However, it is two times faster than STRCF (25.3fps). This is attributed to the adaptive temporal regularization which can reduce meaningless and detrimental training on contaminated samples. *More detailed results can be found in supplementary materials.*

Table 1. Average accuracy and computational speed comparisons of top-5 CPU-based trackers on DTB70 [26] and UAV123@10fps [27]. The best three results are shown in bold, italic, and bold italic fonts, respectively.

Tracker	Ours	AutoTrack	ECO-HC	STRCF	BACF
Success rate	**0.481**	*0.478*	*0.455*	0.450	0.408
Precision	**0.691**	*0.687*	0.634	*0.635*	0.575
FPS	*55.5*	**56.5**	47.7	25.3	*48.1*

4.2 Ablation Study

To validate the effectiveness, our tracker is compared to itself with different modules enabled. The overall evaluation is presented in Table 2. With ASR (adaptive spatial regularization) module and ATR (adaptive temporal regularization) module being added to the baseline (STRCF [15]), the performance is improved smoothly. Besides, our final tracker improves the baseline method by 4.7% and 6.6% in terms of success rate and precision criterion, respectively.

Table 2. Ablation analysis on the DTB70 dataset.

Tracker	Ours	Baseline+ATR	Baseline+ASR	Baseline
Success rate	0.484	0.480	0.476	0.437
Precision	0.715	0.701	0.704	0.649

5   Conclusion

In this study, a novel Adaptive Spatio-Temporal Regularized Correlation Filter (ASTR-CF) is proposed to solve the problems of boundary effect and filter degradation in the application of UAV-based tracking. An alternating direction method of multipliers (ADMM) algorithm is developed to solve the ASTR-CF model efficiently. Comparative experiments are carried out to validate the ASTR-CF model. Experimental results demonstrate that the proposed ASTR-CF outperforms the state-of-the-art trackers in terms of both accuracy and computational speed.

References

1. Zhang, W., Song, K., Rong, X., Li, Y.: Coarse-to-fine UAV target tracking with deep reinforcement learning. IEEE Trans. Autom. Sci. Eng. **16**, 1522–1530 (2019)
2. Danelljan, M., Häger, G., Khan, F.S., Felsberg, M.: Discriminative scale space tracking. IEEE Trans. Pattern Anal. Mach. Intell. **39**, 1561–1575 (2016)
3. Bolme, D.S., Beveridge, J.R., Draper, B.A., Lui, Y.M.: Visual object tracking using adaptive correlation filters. In: CVPR (2010)
4. Henriques, J.F., Caseiro, R., Martins, P., Batista, J.: High-speed tracking with kernelized correlation filters. IEEE Trans. Pattern Anal. Mach. Intell. **37**, 583–596 (2015)
5. Bertinetto, L., Valmadre, J., Golodetz, S., Miksik, O., Torr, P.H.: Staple: complementary learners for real-time tracking. In: CVPR (2016)
6. Li, Y., Fu, C., Ding, F., Huang, Z., Lu, G.: Autotrack: towards high-performance visual tracking for uav with automatic spatio-temporal regularization. In: CVPR (2020)
7. Danelljan, M., Hager, G., Khan, F.S., Felsberg, M.: Learning spatially regularized correlation filters for visual tracking. In: ICCV (2015)
8. Galoogahi, H.K., Fagg, A., Lucey, S.: Learning background-aware correlation filters for visual tracking. In: ICCV (2017)
9. Zhou, Y., Han, J., Yang, F., Zhang, K., Hong, R.: Efficient correlation tracking via center-biased spatial regularization. IEEE Trans. Image Process. **27**, 6159–6173 (2018)
10. Guo, Q., Han, R., Feng, W., Chen, Z., Wan, L.: Selective spatial regularization by reinforcement learned decision making for object tracking. IEEE Trans. Image Process. **29**, 2999–3013 (2020)
11. Dai, K., Wang, D., Lu, H., Sun, C., Li, J.: Visual tracking via adaptive spatially-regularized correlation filters. In: CVPR (2019)
12. Danelljan, M., Bhat, G., Khan, F.S., Felsberg, M.: Eco: efficient convolution operators for tracking. In: CVPR (2017)
13. Danelljan, M., Hager, G., Shahbaz Khan, F., Felsberg, M.: Adaptive decontamination of the training set: a unified formulation for discriminative visual tracking. In: CVPR (2016)
14. Lukezic, A., Vojir, T., CehovinZajc, L., Matas, J., Kristan, M.: Discriminative correlation filter tracker with channel and spatial reliability. Int. J. Comput. Vis. **126**, 671–688 (2018)
15. Li, F., Tian, C., Zuo, W., Zhang, L., Yang, M.: Learning spatial-temporal regularized correlation filters for visual tracking. In: CVPR (2018)
16. Li, Y., Fu, C., Huang, Z., Zhang, Y., Pan, J.: Keyfilter-aware real-time UAV object tracking. arXiv preprint arXiv:2003.05218 (2020)
17. Wang, M., Liu, Y., Huang, Z.: Large margin object tracking with circulant feature maps. In: CVPR (2017)
18. Fu, C., Huang, Z., Li, Y., Duan, R., Lu, P.: Boundary effect-aware visual tracking for UAV with online enhanced background learning and multi-frame consensus verification. arXiv preprint arXiv:1908.03701 (2019)
19. Sun, Y., Sun, C., Wang, D., He, Y., Lu, H.: Roi pooled correlation filters for visual tracking. In: CVPR (2019)
20. Gu, X., Xu, X.: Accurate mask-based spatially regularized correlation filter for visual tracking. J. Electron. Imaging **26**, 013002 (2017)

21. Kang, B., Chen, G., Zhou, Q., Yan, J., Lin, M.: Visual tracking via multi-layer factorized correlation filter. IEEE Signal Process. Lett. **26**, 1763–1767 (2019)
22. Sun, C., Wang, D., Lu, H., Yang, M.H.: Learning spatial-aware regressions for visual tracking. In: CVPR (2018)
23. Dalal, N., Triggs, B.: Histograms of oriented gradients for human detection. In: CVPR (2005)
24. Danelljan, M., Khan, F.S., Felsberg, M., v. d. Weijer, J.: Adaptive color attributes for real-time visual tracking. In: CVPR (2014)
25. Boyd, S., Parikh, N., Chu, E.: Distributed Optimization and Statistical Learning Via the Alternating Direction Method of Multipliers. Now Publishers Inc., Boston (2011)
26. Li, S., Yeung, D.Y.: Visual object tracking for unmanned aerial vehicles: a benchmark and new motion models. In: AAAI (2017)
27. Mueller, M., Smith, N., Ghanem, B.: A benchmark and simulator for UAV tracking. In: Leibe, B., Matas, J., Sebe, N., Welling, M. (eds.) ECCV 2016. LNCS, vol. 9905, pp. 445–461. Springer, Cham (2016). https://doi.org/10.1007/978-3-319-46448-0_27
28. Possegger, H., Mauthner, T., Bischof, H.: In defense of color-based model-free tracking. In: CVPR (2015)
29. Danelljan, M., Häger, G., Khan, F., Felsberg, M.: Accurate scale estimation for robust visual tracking. In: BMVC (2014)
30. Li, F., Yao, Y., Li, P., Zhang, D., Zuo, W., Yang, M.: Integrating boundary and center correlation filters for visual tracking with aspect ratio variation. In: ICCVW (2017)
31. Wang, N., Song, Y., Ma, C., Zhou, W., Liu, W., Li, H.: Unsupervised deep tracking. In: CVPR (2019)
32. Nam, H., Han, B.: Learning multi-domain convolutional neural networks for visual tracking. In: CVPR (2016)
33. Wu, Y., Lim, J., Yang, M.H.: Object tracking benchmark. IEEE Trans. Pattern Anal. Mach. Intell. **37**, 1834–1848 (2015)
34. Zhang, J., Ma, S., Sclaroff, S.: MEEM: robust tracking via multiple experts using entropy minimization. In: Fleet, D., Pajdla, T., Schiele, B., Tuytelaars, T. (eds.) ECCV 2014. LNCS, vol. 8694, pp. 188–203. Springer, Cham (2014). https://doi.org/10.1007/978-3-319-10599-4_13
35. Hare, S., Saffari, A., Torr, P.H.S.: Struck: structured output tracking with kernels. In: ICCV (2011)
36. Hong, Z., Chen, Z., Wang, C., Mei, X., Prokhorov, D., Tao, D.: Multi-store tracker (muster): a cognitive psychology inspired approach to object tracking. In: CVPR (2015)

Goal-GAN: Multimodal Trajectory Prediction Based on Goal Position Estimation

Patrick Dendorfer$^{(\boxtimes)}$ ⑩, Aljoša Ošep ⑩, and Laura Leal-Taixé ⑩

Technical University Munich, Munich, Germany
{patrick.dendorfer,aljosa.osep,leal.taixe}@tum.de

Abstract. In this paper, we present Goal-GAN, an interpretable and end-to-end trainable model for human trajectory prediction. Inspired by human navigation, we model the task of trajectory prediction as an intuitive two-stage process: (i) goal estimation, which predicts the most likely target positions of the agent, followed by a (ii) routing module which estimates a set of plausible trajectories that route towards the estimated goal. We leverage information about the past trajectory and visual context of the scene to estimate a multi-modal probability distribution over the possible goal positions, which is used to sample a potential goal during the inference. The routing is governed by a recurrent neural network that reacts to physical constraints in the nearby surroundings and generates feasible paths that route towards the sampled goal. Our extensive experimental evaluation shows that our method establishes a new state-of-the-art on several benchmarks while being able to generate a realistic and diverse set of trajectories that conform to physical constraints.

1 Introduction

Modeling human motion is indispensable for autonomous systems that operate in public spaces, such as self-driving cars or social robots. Safe navigation through crowded scenes and collision prevention requires awareness not only of the present position but also of the future path of all moving objects. Human trajectory prediction is particularly challenging since pedestrian trajectories depend primarily on their intention – and the destination of a pedestrian is inherently unknown to the external observer. Consider the example of a pedestrian reaching a crossroad such as the one depicted in Fig. 1. Based solely on past observations, we cannot infer the future path of the pedestrian: turning right, left, or going straight, are all equally likely outcomes.

For this reason, a powerful prediction model should be able to capture the *multimodality* of this task, *i.e.*, forecast trajectories that cover the distinctive modes present in the scene. Furthermore, it should produce a *diverse* set of the paths within each mode, reflecting inherent uncertainty in walking style, velocity, and different strategies for obstacle avoidance.

To capture the stochastic nature of trajectory prediction, state-of-the-art methods leverage generative the power of variational autoencoders (VAEs) [1–3]

© Springer Nature Switzerland AG 2021
H. Ishikawa et al. (Eds.): ACCV 2020, LNCS 12623, pp. 405–420, 2021.
https://doi.org/10.1007/978-3-030-69532-3_25

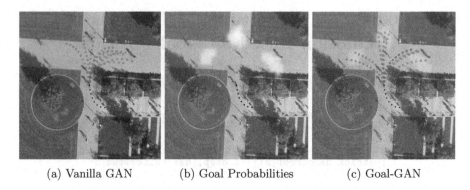

(a) Vanilla GAN   (b) Goal Probabilities   (c) Goal-GAN

Fig. 1. Visual comparison between predictions of our proposed Goal-GAN and a vanilla GAN. In contrast to the baseline, our proposed model covers all three modes and predicts diverse and feasible trajectories by explicitly estimating realistic goals.

and/or generative adversarial networks (GANs) [4–6] to predict a set of trajectories for every observation.

While generative methods are widely used to generate diverse outputs, they are unable to explicitly capture the inherent multimodality of pedestrian trajectories. Often, these methods generate highly diverse trajectories but tend to neglect the physical structure of the environment. The resulting trajectories are not necessarily feasible, and often do not fully cover multiple possible directions that a pedestrian can take (Fig. 1a). A more natural way of capturing all feasible directions is to first determine an intermediate goal sampled from a distribution of plausible positions, as shown in Fig. 1b. In the second step, the model generates the trajectories reaching the sampled positions (Fig. 1c). While social interactions among agents [4–7] and local scene interaction have been extensively studied, there are almost no methods tackling the challenge of explicitly learning the inherent multimodal distribution of pedestrian trajectories.

In this paper, we aim to bridge this gap and explicitly focus on the under-explored problem of generating diverse multimodal trajectories that conform to the physical constraints. Influenced by recent studies on human navigation [8] we propose an end-to-end trainable method that separates the task of trajectory prediction into two stages. First, we estimate a posterior over possible goals, taking into account the dynamics of the pedestrian and the visual scene context, followed by the prediction of trajectories that route towards these estimated goals. Therefore, trajectories generated by our model take both local scene information and past motion of the agent explicitly into account. While the estimated distribution of possible goal positions reflects the multimodality in the scene, the routing module reacts to local obstacles and generates diverse and feasible paths. We ensure diversity and realism of the output trajectories by training our network in a generative adversarial setup.

In summary, our main **contribution** is three-fold: (i) we propose Goal-GAN, a two-stage end-to-end trainable trajectory prediction method inspired by human navigation, which separates the prediction task into goal position estimation and routing. (ii) To this end, we design a novel architecture that explicitly estimates an interpretable probability distribution of future goal positions and allows us to sample from it. Using the Gumbel Softmax trick [9] enables us to train the network through the stochastic process. (iii) We establish a new state-of-the-art on several public benchmarks and qualitatively demonstrate that our method predicts realistic end-goal positions together with plausible trajectories that route towards them. The code for Goal-GAN[1] is publicly available.

2   Related Work

Several methods focus on modelling human-human [4,7], human-space interactions [2,10,11], or both [5]. Recent methods leverage generative models to learn a one-to-many mapping, that is used to sample multimodal future trajectories.

Trajectory Prediction. Helbing and Molar introduced the Social Force Model (SFM) [12], a physics-based model, capable of taking agent-agent and agent-space interactions into account. This approach was successfully applied in the domain of multi-object tracking [13–16]. Since then, data-driven models [4,7,17–19] have vastly outperformed physics-based models. Encoder-decoder based methods [2,7] leverage recurrent neural networks (RNNs) [20] to model the temporal evolution of the trajectories with long-short term memory (LSTM) units [21]. These deterministic models cannot capture the stochastic nature of the task, as they were trained to minimize the L_2 distance between the prediction and the ground truth trajectories. This often results in implausible, average-path trajectories.

Recent methods [11,22] focus on human-space interactions using bird-view images [5] and occupancy grids [10,23] to predict trajectories that respect the structural constraints of the scene. Our method similarly leverages bird-eye views. However, we use visual information to explicitly estimate feasible and interpretable goal positions, that can, in turn, be used to explicitly sample end-goals that ease the task of future trajectory estimation.

Generative Models for Trajectory Prediction. Recent works [4–6] leverage generative models to sample diverse trajectories rather than just predicting a single deterministic output. The majority of methods either use variational autoencoders (VAEs) [2,3,11,24–27] or generative adversarial networks (GANs) [4–6,28,29]. Social GAN (S-GAN) [4] uses a discriminator to learn the distribution of socially plausible paths. Sadeghian *et al.* [5] extend the model to human-environment interactions by introducing a soft-attention [30] mechanism. GANs have shown promising results for the task of trajectory prediction, but tend to suffer from mode collapse. To encourage the generator to produce more diverse predictions, [1] uses a best-of-many sampling approach during training while [6] enforces the network to make use of the latent noise vector in combination with BicycleGAN [31] based training. While producing trajectories with high variance, many trajectories are not realistic, and a clear division between

---

[1] https://github.com/dendorferpatrick/GoalGAN.

different feasible destinations (reflecting inherent multi-modality of the inherent task) is not clear. To account for that, we take inspiration from prior work conditioning the trajectory prediction on specific target destinations.

Goal-Conditioned Forecasting. In contrast to the aforementioned generative models that directly learn a one-to-many mapping, several methods propose two-stage prediction approaches. Similarly to ours, these methods predict first the final (goal) position, followed by trajectory generation that is conditioned on this position. Early work of [32] models the distribution over possible destinations using a particle filter [33] while other approaches [34] propose a Bayesian framework that estimates both, the destination point together with the trajectory. However, these purely probabilistic approaches are highly unstable during training. The Conditional Generative Neural System (CGNS) [35] uses variational divergence minimization with soft-attention [30] and [36] presents a conditional flow VAE that uses a conditional flow-based prior to effectively structured sequence prediction. These models condition their trajectory generator on initially estimated latent codes but do not explicitly predict a goal distribution nor sample an explicit goal position. Most recently, [37] proposes P2TIRL that uses a maximum entropy inverse reinforcement learning policy to infer goal and trajectory plan over a discrete grid. P2TRL assigns rewards to future goals that are learned by the training policy which is slow and computationally expensive. In contrast, we directly learn the multimodal distribution over possible goals using a binary cross-entropy loss between the (discrete) probability distribution estimate and the ground truth goal position. This makes our work the first method (to the best of our knowledge) that directly predicts an explicit (and discrete) probability distribution for multimodal goals and is efficiently end-to-end trainable.

3   Problem Definition

We tackle the task of predicting the future positions of pedestrians, parametrized via x and y coordinates in the 2D ground plane. As input, we are given their past trajectory and visual information of the scene, captured from a bird-view.

We observe the trajectories $X_i = \{(x_i^t, y_i^t) \in \mathbb{R}^2 | t = 1, \ldots, t_{obs} \}$ of N currently visible pedestrians and a top-down image I of the scene, observed at the timestep t_{obs}. Our goal is to predict the future positions $Y_i = \{(x_i^t, y_i^t) \in \mathbb{R}^2 | t = t_{obs} + 1, \ldots, t_{pred}\}$.

In the dataset, we are only given one future path for t_{obs} – in particular, the one that was observed in practice. We note that multiple distinctive trajectories could be realist for this observed input trajectory. Our goal is, given the input past trajectory X_i, to generate $k \in \{1, \ldots, K\}$ multiple future samples $\hat{Y}_i^k$ for all pedestrians $i \in \{1, \ldots, N\}$. These should cover all feasible modes and be compliant with the physical constraints of the scene.

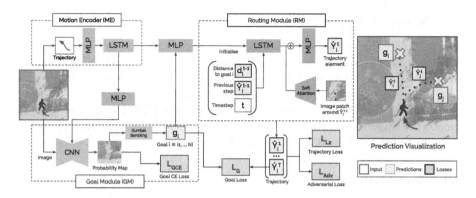

Fig. 2. Overview of Model Architecture: Our model consists of three components: 1) Motion Encoder, 2) Goal Module, and the 3) Routing Module. The Goal Module combines the dynamic features of the Motion Encoder and the scene information to predict a final goal g. The Routing Module generates the future trajectory while taking into account the dynamic features and the estimated goal. During inference, we generate multiple trajectories i by sampling goals from the estimated goal probability map.

4   Goal-GAN

When pedestrians walk through public spaces, they aim to reach a predetermined goal [8], which depends on their intentions and the scene context. Once the goal is set, humans route to their final destination while reacting to obstacles or other pedestrians along their way. This observation motivates us to propose a novel two-stage architecture for trajectory prediction that first estimates the end-goal position and then generates a trajectory towards the estimated goal. Our proposed Goal-GAN consists of three key components, as shown in Fig. 2.

- *Motion Encoder (ME):* extracts the pedestrians' dynamic features recursively with a long short-term memory (LSTM) unit capturing the speed and direction of motion of the past trajectory.
- *Goal Module (GM):* combines visual scene information and dynamic pedestrian features to predict the goal position for a given pedestrian. This module estimates the probability distribution over possible goal (target) positions, which is in turn used to sample goal positions.
- *Routing Module (RM):* generates the trajectory to the goal position sampled from the GM. While the goal position of the prediction is determined by the GM, the RM generates feasible paths to the predetermined goal and reacts to obstacles along the way by using visual attention.

Figure 2 shows an overview of our model. In the following sections, we motivate and describe the different components in detail.

4.1 Motion Encoder (ME)

The past trajectory of a pedestrian is encoded into the Motion Encoder (ME), which serves as a dynamic feature extractor to capture the speed and direction of the pedestrian, similarly to [4,7]. Each trajectory's relative displacement vectors $(\Delta x_i^t, \Delta y_i^t)$ are embedded into a higher dimensional vector e^t with a multi-layer perceptron (MLP). The output is then fed into an LSTM, which is used to encode the trajectories. The hidden state of the LSTM, h_{ME}, is used by the other modules to predict the goal and to decode the trajectory for each pedestrian.

4.2 Goal Module (GM)

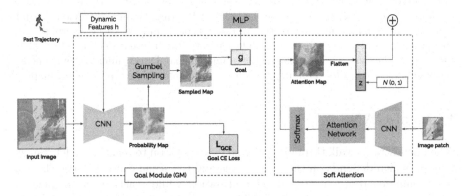

Fig. 3. Goal Module (GM) and Soft Attention (SA). The Goal Module samples a goal coordinate g while the soft attention assigns attention scores to spatial positions.

In our work, we propose a novel Goal Module (GM). The Goal Module combines visual and dynamic features of the pedestrian to estimate a distribution of possible end goals. As can be seen in Fig. 1, the scene dictates the distinctive modes for possible trajectories. Here, the pedestrian can go left, right, or straight. The Goal Module is responsible for capturing all the possible modes and predicting a final goal position, *i.e.*, choosing one of the three options.

Architecture. In order to estimate the goal distribution, the network assesses the visual scene and the dynamics of the pedestrian. The visual scene is represented as an RGB image (or a semantic map) of size $H \times W$, captured from a bird-eye view. This image is input to the goal module.

The scene image is passed through an encoder-decoder CNN network with skip connections similar to [38]. Before the decoder, the scene image features in the bottleneck layer are concatenated with the motion features h_{ME} from the Motion Encoder. Intuitively, the CNN decoder should analyze both the past trajectory and the scene to estimate the future target positions – goals. The module outputs a probability distribution that reflects the multimodal directions for a given input trajectory and scene.

Training through Sampling. The CNN decoder outputs a score map $\alpha = (\alpha_1, \alpha_2, \ldots, \alpha_n)$ for which each α_i reflects the probability of a particular cell being the end-goal location of the agent.

The discrete probability distribution α is used to sample an end-goal by using the Gumbel-Softmax-Trick [9]. This allows us to sample a discrete distribution over possible goal locations while being able to backpropagate the loss through the stochastic process. The resulting two-dimensional goal position g is sampled randomly from the 2D grid representing the scene,

Goal Sampling vs. Soft Attention. A major novelty of our work is the Goal Module that replaces soft attention [30] to process the scene contextual information [5,11]. Both approaches are illustrated in Fig. 3. A soft attention module assigns attention scores to spatially relevant positions based on the visual CNN features. In [5], the attention values are combined with random noise and fed to the trajectory decoder to generate scene-aware multimodal trajectories. However, this often leads to unsatisfying results when the network simply ignores the spatial attention scores or has difficulties combining the attention values with the noise to capture all modes in the scene.

We argue that the attention module is useful when predicting the route towards a goal (as we show in Sect. 4.3), as it encourages the feasibility of the predicted trajectories. However, the model that solely relies on soft visual attention mechanism tends to generate trajectories that do not capture the multimodal nature of the task, as illustrated in Sect. 1. Furthermore, in Sect. 5, we experimentally confirm that stochasticity of the task is reflected better when sampling from the learned probability distribution, produced by our Goal Module, compared to merely relying on noise injection.

We can directly train the module for the goal position estimation using the Gumbel Softmax trick [9], in combination with the standard cross-entropy loss, which is directly applied to the estimated goal distribution based on the observed (final) position of the ground truth trajectories. We emphasize that we do not use nor need any other data than what is provided in the standard training set.

During the inference, we simply sample the goal from the learned probability distribution and pass it to the decoder. This significantly eases the task for the decoder, as the Goal Module already assesses the visual surroundings and only passes a low dimensional input into the routing module.

4.3   Routing Module (RM)

The Routing Module (see Fig. 2) is the third component of our method. It combines the dynamic features and the global goal estimate to generate the final trajectory prediction. The RM consists of an LSTM network, a visual soft attention network (ATT), and an additional MLP layer that combines the attention map with the output of the LSTM iteratively at each timestep.

First, we forward the goal estimate embedding e_g and the object dynamics embedding h_{ME} (given by the motion encoder, ME) to an MLP to initialise the hidden state h_{RM}^0 of the RM.

Then, we recursively estimate predictions for the future time steps. To this end, the LSTM in the RM obtains three inputs: the previous step prediction $\hat{Y}^{t-1}$, the remaining distance to the estimated goal $d_{t-1} = g - \hat{Y}^{t-1}$ and the current scalar timestep value t.

To assess the traversability of the local surroundings, we apply soft attention [30] on the image patch centered around the current position of the pedestrian. As shown in the Fig. 3, we combine the output of the LSTM with the attention map F^t to predict the next step $\hat{Y}^t$. The visual attention mechanism allows the RM to react to obstacles or other nearby structures. Finally, we use both the dynamic and visual features to predict the final prediction $\hat{Y}^t$.

4.4 Generative Adversarial Training

In our work, we use a Generative Adversarial Network (GAN) to train our trajectory generator to output realistic and physically feasible trajectories. The GAN consists of a Generator and Discriminator network competing in a two-player min-max game. While the generator aims at producing feasible trajectories, the discriminator learns to differentiate between real and fake samples, i.e., feasible and unfeasible trajectories. Adversarial training is necessary because, in contrast to prediction accuracy, it is not possible to formulate a differential loss in a closed mathematical form that captures the concept of feasibility and realism of the generated trajectories.

The discriminator network consists of an LSTM network that encodes the observed trajectory X. This encoding is used to initialize the second LSTM that processes the predicted trajectory Y together with visual features (obtained from the CNN network, that encodes the image patch centered around the current position) at each time step. Finally, the last hidden state of the LSTM_{pred} is used for the final output of the discriminator.

4.5 Losses

For training our Goal-GAN we use multiple losses addressing the different modules of our model. To encourage the generator to predict trajectories, that are closely resembling the ground truth trajectories, we use a best-of-many [1] distance loss $\mathcal{L}_{L2} = \min_k \|Y - \hat{Y}^{(k)}\|_2$ between our predictions $\hat{Y}$ and the ground truth Y. As an adversarial loss, we employ the *lsgan* [39] loss:

$$\mathcal{L}_{Adv} = \frac{1}{2}\mathbb{E}\left[(D(X,Y) - 1)^2\right] + \frac{1}{2}\mathbb{E}\left[D(X,\hat{Y})^2\right], \tag{1}$$

due to the fact, the original formulation [28] using a classifier with sigmoid cross-entropy function potentially leads to the vanishing gradient problem.

To encourage the network to take into account the estimated goal positions for the prediction, we propose a goal achievement losses $\mathcal{L}_G$ that measures the L_2 distance between the goal prediction g and the actual output $\hat{Y}^{t_{pred}}$,

$$\mathcal{L}_G = \|g - \hat{Y}^{t_{pred}}\|_2. \tag{2}$$

In addition, we use a cross-entropy loss

$$\mathcal{L}_{GCE} = -\log(p_i),\qquad(3)$$

where p_i is the probability that is predicted from the Goal Module for the grid cell i corresponding to the final ground-truth position. The overall loss is the combination of the partial losses weighted by λ:

$$\mathcal{L} = \lambda_{Adv}\,\mathcal{L}_{Adv} + \mathcal{L}_{L2} + \lambda_G\,\mathcal{L}_G + \lambda_{GCE}\,\mathcal{L}_{GCE}.\qquad(4)$$

5   Experimental Evaluation

In this section, we evaluate our proposed Goal-GAN on three standard datasets used to assess the performance of pedestrian trajectory prediction models: ETH [40], UCY [41] and Stanford Drone Dataset (SDD) [19]. To assess how well our prediction model can cover different possible modes (splitting future paths), we introduce a new, synthetically generated scene.

We compare our method with several state-of-the-art methods for pedestrian trajectory prediction and we qualitatively demonstrate that our method produces multi-modal, diverse, feasible, and interpretable results.

Evaluation Measures. We follow the standard evaluation protocol and report the prediction accuracy using Average Displacement Error (ADE) and Final Displacement Error (FDE). Both measures are computed using the L_2 distance between the prediction and ground truth trajectories. The generative models are tested on these metrics with a $N-K$ variety loss [1,4,5]. As in the previous work [7,19], we observe 8 time steps (3.2 s) and predict the future 12 time steps (4.8 s) simultaneously for all pedestrians in the scene.

Visual Input and Coordinates. As in [5], we use a single static image to predict trajectories in a given scene. We transform all images into a top-down view using the homography transformation provided by the respective datasets. This allows us to perform all predictions in real-world coordinates.

5.1   Benchmark Results

In this section, we compare and discuss our method's performance against state-of-the-art on ETH [40], UCY [41] and SDD [19] datasets.

Datasets. ETH [40] and UCY datasets [41] contain 5 sequences (ETH:2, UCY: 3), recorded in 4 different scenarios. All pedestrian trajectories are converted into real-world coordinates and interpolated to obtain positions every 0.4 s. For training and testing, we follow the standard leave-one-out approach, where we train on 4 datasets and test on the remaining one. The Stanford Drone Dataset (SDD) [19] consists of 20 unique video sequences captured at the Stanford University campus. The scenes have various landmarks such as roundabouts, crossroads, streets, and sidewalks, which influence the paths of pedestrians. In our experiments, we follow the train-test-split of [42] and focus on pedestrians.

Table 1. Quantitative results for ETH [40] and UCY [41] of Goal-GAN and baseline models predicting 12 future timesteps. We report ADE and FDE in meters.

Dataset	Baseline						Ours
	S-LSTM [7]	S-GAN [4]	S-GAN-P [4]	SoPhie [5]	S-BiGAT [6]	CGNS [35]	Goal GAN
K	1	20	20	20	20	20	20
ETH	1.09/2.35	0.81/1.52	0.87/1.62	0.70/1.43	0.69/1.29	0.62/1.40	**0.59/118**
HOTEL	0.79/1.76	0.72/1.61	0.67/1.37	0.76/1.67	0.49/1.01	0.70/0.93	**0.19/0.35**
UNIV	0.67/1.40	0.60/1.26	0.76/1.52	0.54/1.24	0.55/1.32	**0.48**/1.22	0.60/**1.19**
ZARA1	0.47/1.00	0.34/0.69	0.35/0.68	**0.30**/0.63	**0.30**/0.62	0.32/**0.59**	0.43/0.87
ZARA2	0.56/1.17	0.42/0.84	0.42/0.84	0.38/0.78	0.36/0.75	0.35/0.71	**0.32/0.65**
AVG	0.72/1.54	0.58/1.18	0.61/1.21	0.54/1.15	0.48/1.00	0.49/0.97	**0.43/0.85**

Baselines. We compare our model to several published methods. S-LSTM [7] uses a LSTM encoder-decoder network with social pooling. S-GAN [4] leverages a GAN framework and S-GAN-P [4] uses max-pooling to model social interactions. SoPhie [5] extends the S-GAN model with a visual and social attention module, and Social-BiGAT [6] uses a BicycleGAN [43] based training. DESIRE [2] is an inverse optimal control based model, that utilizes generative modeling. CARNet [11] is a physically attentive model. The Conditional Generative Neural System (CGNS) [35] uses conditional latent space learning with variational divergence minimization to learn feasible regions to produce trajectories. CF-VAE [36] leverages a conditional normalizing flow-based VAE and P2TIRL [37] uses a grid-based policy learned with maximum entropy inverse reinforcement learning policy. As none of the aforementioned provide publicly available implementation, we outline the results reported in the respective publications.

ETH and UCY. We observe a clear trend – the generative models improve the performance of the deterministic approaches, as they are capable of sampling a diverse set of trajectories. Compared to other generative models, Goal-GAN achieves state-of-the-art performance with an overall decrease of the error of nearly 15% compared to *S-BiGAT* and *CGNS*. While *SoPhie* and *S-BiGAT* also use visual input, these models are unable to effectively leverage this information to discover the dominant modes for the trajectory prediction task, thus yielding a higher prediction error. It has to be pointed out that Goal-GAN decreases the average FDE by 0.12 m compared to the current state-of-the-art method. We explain the drastic increase in performance with our new Goal Module as we can cover the distribution of all plausible modes and are therefore able to generate trajectories lying close to the ground truth.

Stanford Drone Dataset. We compare our model against other baseline methods on the SDD and report ADE and FDE in pixel space. As it can be seen in Table 2, Goal-GAN achieves state-of-the-art results on both metrics, ADE and FDE. Comparing Goal-GAN against the best non-goal-conditioned method, *SoPhie*, Goal-GAN decreases the error by 25%. This result shows clearly the merit of having a two-stage process of predicting a goal estimate over standard generator methods using only soft attention modules but does not explicitly condition their model on a future goal. Further, it can be understood that multimodal trajectory predictions play a major role in the scenes of the SDD. Also, Goal-GAN exceeds all other goal-conditioned methods and is on par with P2TIRL (which was not yet published during the preparation of this work).

Table 2. Quantitative results for the Stanford Drone Dataset (SDD) [19] of Goal-GAN and baseline models predicting 12 future timesteps. We report ADE and FDE in pixels.

	Baseline								Ours
	S-LSTM [7]	S-GAN [4]	CAR-NET [11]	DESIRE [2]	SoPhie [5]	CGNS [35]	CF-VAE [36]	P2TIRL [37]	Goal GAN
K	1	20	20	20	20	20	20	20	20
ADE	57.0	27.3	25.7	19.3	16.3	15.6	12.6	12.6	**12.2**
FDE	31.2	41.4	51.8	34.1	29.4	28.2	22.3	22.1	**22.1**

5.2 Assessing Multimodality of Predictions on Synthetic Dataset

In this section, we conduct an additional experiment using synthetically generated scenarios to study the multimodality of the predictions. We compare the performance of Goal-GAN against two vanilla GAN baselines, with and without visual soft attention [30]. The synthetic dataset allows us to explicitly control multimodality and feasibility of the (generated) ground truth trajectories, as the other datasets do not provide that information.

Dataset. We generate trajectories using the Social Force Model [12] in the *hyang 4* scene of the SDD dataset [19]. To ensure the feasibility of the generated trajectories, we use a two-class (manually labeled) semantic map, that distinguishes between feasible (walking paths) from unfeasible (grass) areas. We simulate 250 trajectories approaching and passing the two crossroads in the scene.

Additional Evaluation Measures. In addition to ADE and FDE, we follow [26,44] to measure the multimodality of the distribution of generated trajectories. Here we evaluate the negative log-likelihood (NLL) of the ground truth

Table 3. Quantitative results on our synthetic dataset. We show results obtained by a GAN baseline [4] and different versions of our Goal-GAN model, predicting 12 future time steps. We report ADE, FDE, F (feasibility) and MC (mode coverage) for $k = 10$ sampled trajectories for each scene. We also report the negative log-likelihood (NLL) of the ground truth trajectory computed with the KDE (Kernel Density Estimate), following [26].

Model	Loss	ADE ↓	FDE ↓	F ↑	MC ↑	NLL ↓
GAN w/o visual	$\mathcal{L}_{L2} + \mathcal{L}_{Adv}$	0.70	1.49	59.94	78.51	4.54
GAN w visual	$\mathcal{L}_{L2} + \mathcal{L}_{Adv}$	0.68	1.27	66.51	85.12	4.47
Goal-GAN	$\mathcal{L}_{GCE} + \mathcal{L}_{G}$	2.09	1.27	76.78	88.22	**3.76**
Goal-GAN	$\mathcal{L}_{L2} + \mathcal{L}_{GCE} + \mathcal{L}_{G}$	0.62	1.20	85.05	89.27	3.90
Goal-GAN w/o GST	$\mathcal{L}_{L2} + \mathcal{L}_{Adv} + \mathcal{L}_{GCE} + \mathcal{L}_{G}$	0.84	1.45	76.84	86.27	4.18
Goal-GAN (full model)	$\mathcal{L}_{L2} + \mathcal{L}_{Adv} + \mathcal{L}_{GCE} + \mathcal{L}_{G}$	**0.55**	**1.01**	**89.47**	**92.48**	3.88

trajectories using a Kernel Density Estimate (KDE) from the sampled trajectories at each prediction timestep. In addition, we define a new mode coverage (MC) metric. For each scene, MC assesses if at least one of the k generated trajectories $\hat{y}$ reaches the final position of the ground truth final up to a distance of 2 m:

$$\text{MC} = \frac{1}{n} \sum_i^n S\left(\hat{\mathbf{y}}_i\right) \text{ with } S\left(\hat{\mathbf{y}}\right) = \begin{cases} 1 & \text{if } \exists k, \ \|\hat{y}^k - y\|_2 < 2m \\ 0 & \text{else.} \end{cases} \tag{5}$$

To evaluate the feasibility of the trajectories, we report the ratio of trajectories lying inside the feasible area $\mathcal{F}$, i.e., predictions staying on the path:

$$\text{F} = \frac{1}{n} \sum_{i,k}^n f\left(\hat{y}_i^k\right) \text{ with } f\left(\hat{y}\right) = \begin{cases} 1 & \text{if } \hat{y} \in \mathcal{F} \\ 0 & \text{else.} \end{cases} \tag{6}$$

Results. As can be seen in Table 3, the vanilla GAN baseline [4] that is not given access to the visual information, yields ADE/FDE of 0.70/1.49, respectively. Adding visual information yields a performance boost (0.68/1.27), however, it is still not able to generate multimodal and feasible paths. When we add our proposed goal module (Goal-GAN) and train it using our full loss, we observe a large boost of performance w.r.t. multimodality (7.36 increase in terms of MC) and feasibility (10.26 increase in terms of F). To ablate our model, we train our network using different loss components, incentivizing the network to

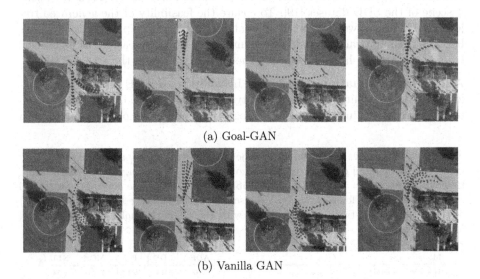

(a) Goal-GAN

(b) Vanilla GAN

Fig. 4. Visualisation of multiple generated trajectories (orange) for past trajectory (black) on the synthetic dataset. We compare the output of our Goal-GAN against the performance of the vanilla GAN using visual attention for $t_{pred} = 12$. For Goal-GAN, the yellow heatmap corresponds to the goal probability map. (Color figure online)

train different modules of the network. A variant of our model, trained only with goal achievement loss $\mathcal{L}_G$ and adversarial loss $\mathcal{L}_{Adv}$ can already learn to produce multimodal trajectories (MC of 88.22), however, yields a high ADE error of 2.09. The addition of L_2 loss $\mathcal{L}_{L2}$ significantly increases the accuracy of the predictions (1.47 reduction in ADE), and at the same time, increases the quality and feasibility (8.26 increase in F), of the predictions. This confirms that our proposed goal module, which explicitly models the distribution over the future goals, is vital for accurate and realistic predictions. Furthermore, we note that the performance drastically drops if we train the full model without the Gumbel-Softmax Trick (GST) (see Sect. 4.2) which seems to be crucial for stable training, enabling the loss back-propagation through the stochastic sampling process in the Goal Module.

5.3 Qualitative Evaluation

In this section, we visually inspect trajectories, generated by our model, and assess the quality of the predictions.

Synthetic Dataset: In Fig. 4 we visualize trajectories of the synthetic dataset for our proposed Goal-GAN (top) and the vanilla GAN baseline [4] (bottom). Next to the predicted trajectories (orange circles), we display the probability distribution (yellow heatmap) of goal positions, estimated by the Goal Module. As shown in Fig. 4, Goal-GAN predicts a diverse set of trajectories routing to specific estimated modes. Here, we observe that Goal-GAN outputs an interpretable probability distribution that allows us to understand where the model "sees" the dominant modes in the scene. Comparing the quality of the predictions, we can demonstrate that Goal-GAN produces distinct modes while the GAN baseline tends to instead span its trajectory over a wider range leading to unfeasible paths.

(a) Hotel   (b) Zara 2   (c) Hyang 4   (d) Coupa 1

Fig. 5. Visualisation of generated trajectories (orange circles) and estimated global goal probabilities (yellow heatmap). The figures show that the model interacts with the visual context of the scene and ensures feasibility predictions. (Color figure online)

Real Data: Furthermore, we present qualitative results of the datasets ETH/UCY and SDD in Fig. 5. The two figures show predictions on the *Hotel*

((Fig. 5a) and *Zara 2* ((Fig. 5b) sequences. Our model assigns high probability to a large area in the scene as in *Hotel* sequence, as several positions could be plausible goals. The broad distribution ensures that we generate diverse trajectories when there are no physical obstacles. Note that the generated trajectories do not only vary in direction but also in terms of speed. In *Zara 2*, the model recognizes the feasible area on the sidewalk and predicts no probability mass on the street or in the areas covered by the parked cars. In the scene *Hyang 4* SDD dataset, we observe that the model successfully identifies that the pedestrian is walking on the path, assigning a very low goal probability to the areas, overgrown by the tree. This scenario is also presented successfully with synthetic data which shows that we can compare the results of the synthetic dataset to the behavior of real data. The trajectories shown for *Coupa 1* demonstrate that the model generates solely paths onto concrete but avoids predictions leading towards the area of the tree.

6 Conclusion

In this work, we present Goal-GAN, a novel two-stage network for the task of pedestrian trajectory prediction. With the increasing interest in the interpretability of data-driven models, Goal-GAN allows us to comprehend the different stages iduring the prediction process. This is an alternative to the current generative models, which use a latent noise vector to encourage multimodality and diversity of the trajectory predictions. Our model achieves state-of-the-art results on the ETH, UCY, and SDD datasets while being able to generate multimodal, diverse, and feasible trajectories, as we experimentally demonstrate.

References

1. Bhattacharyya, A., Schiele, B., Fritz, M.: Accurate and diverse sampling of sequences based on a "best of many" sample objective. In: Conference on Computer Vision and Pattern Recognition (2018)
2. Lee, N., Choi, W., Vernaza, P., Choy, C.B., Torr, P.H., Chandraker, M.: Desire: distant future prediction in dynamic scenes with interacting agents. In: Conference on Computer Vision and Pattern Recognition (2017)
3. Felsen, P., Lucey, P., Ganguly, S.: Where will they go? predicting fine-grained adversarial multi-agent motion using conditional variational autoencoders. In: European Conference on Computer Vision (2018)
4. Gupta, A., Johnson, J., Fei-Fei, L., Savarese, S., Alahi, A.: Social GAN: socially acceptable trajectories with generative adversarial networks. In: Conference on Computer Vision and Pattern Recognition (2018)
5. Sadeghian, A., Kosaraju, V., Sadeghian, A., Hirose, N., Rezatofighi, H., Savarese, S.: Sophie: an attentive GAN for predicting paths compliant to social and physical constraints. In: Conference on Computer Vision and Pattern Recognition (2019)
6. Kosaraju, V., Sadeghian, A., Martín-Martín, R., Reid, I., Rezatofighi, H., Savarese, S.: Social-BiGAT: multimodal trajectory forecasting using bicycle-gan and graph attention networks. In: Neural Information Processing Systems (2019)

7. Alahi, A., Goel, K., Ramanathan, V., Robicquet, A., Fei-Fei, L., Savarese, S.: Social LSTM: human trajectory prediction in crowded spaces. In: Conference on Computer Vision and Pattern Recognition (2016)

8. Bellmund, J.L.S., Gärdenfors, P., Moser, E.I., Doeller, C.F.: Navigating cognition: spatial codes for human thinking. Science (2018)

9. Jang, E., Gu, S., Poole, B.: Categorical Reparameterization with Gumbel-Softmax. arXiv e-prints (2016) arXiv:1611.01144

10. Ridel, D.A., Deo, N., Wolf, D.F., Trivedi, M.M.: Scene compliant trajectory forecast with agent-centric spatio-temporal grids. IEEE Robotics Autom Lett (2020)

11. Sadeghian, A., Legros, F., Voisin, M., Vesel, R., Alahi, A., Savarese, S.: CAR-Net: clairvoyant attentive recurrent network. In: European Conference on Computer Vision (2018)

12. Helbing, D., Molnár, P.: Social force model for pedestrian dynamics. Phys. Rev. E (1995)

13. Scovanner, P., Tappen, M.: Learning pedestrian dynamics from the real world. In: International Conference on Computer Vision (2009)

14. Pellegrini, S., Ess, A., Schindler, K., van Gool, L.: You'll never walk alone: modeling social behavior for multi-target tracking. In: International Conference on Computer Vision (2009)

15. Yamaguchi, K., Berg, A., Ortiz, L., Berg, T.: Who are you with and where are you going? In: Conference on Computer Vision and Pattern Recognition (2011)

16. Leal-Taixé, L., Pons-Moll, G., Rosenhahn, B.: Everybody needs somebody: modeling social and grouping behavior on a linear programming multiple people tracker. In: International Conference on Computer Vision Workshop (2011)

17. Leal-Taixé, L., Fenzi, M., Kuznetsova, A., Rosenhahn, B., Savarese, S.: Learning an image-based motion context for multiple people tracking. In: Conference on Computer Vision and Pattern Recognition (2014)

18. Milan, A., Rezatofighi, S.H., Dick, A., Reid, I., Schindler, K.: Online multi-target tracking using recurrent neural networks. In: International Conference on Computer Vision (2017)

19. Robicquet, A., Sadeghian, A., Alahi, A., Savarese, S.: Learning social etiquette: human trajectory understanding in crowded scenes. In: European Conference on Computer Vision (2016)

20. E. Rumelhart, D., E. Hinton, G., J. Williams, R.: Learning representations by back propagating errors. Nature (1986)

21. Hochreiter, S., Schmidhuber, J.: Long short-term memory. Neural Computation (1997)

22. Hiroaki, M., Tsubasa Hirakawa, T.Y., Fujiyoshi, H.: Path predictions using object attributes and semantic environment. In: International Conference on Computer Vision Theory and Applications (2019)

23. Hong, J., Sapp, B., Philbin, J.: Rules of the road: predicting driving behavior with a convolutional model of semantic interactions. In: Conference on Computer Vision and Pattern Recognition (2019)

24. Kingma, D.P., Welling, M.: Auto-encoding variational bayes. In: International Conference on Learning Representations (2014)

25. Deo, N., Trivedi, M.M.: Multi-modal trajectory prediction of surrounding vehicles with maneuver based LSTMS. In: Intelligent Vehicles Symposium (2018)

26. Ivanovic, B., Pavone, M.: The trajectron: probabilistic multi-agent trajectory modeling with dynamic spatiotemporal graphs. In: International Conference on Computer Vision (2019)

27. Rhinehart, N., McAllister, R., Kitani, K., Levine, S.: Precog: Prediction conditioned on goals in visual multi-agent settings. In: International Conference on Computer Vision (2019)
28. Goodfellow, I., et al.: Generative adversarial nets. In: Neural Information Processing Systems (2014)
29. Amirian, J., Hayet, J.B., Pettré, J.: Social ways: learning multi-modal distributions of pedestrian trajectories with gans. In: Conference on Computer Vision and Pattern Recognition Workshop (2019)
30. Xu, K., et al.: Show, attend and tell: Neural image caption generation with visual attention. In: International Conference on Machine Learning (2015)
31. Zhu, J.Y., et al.: Toward multimodal image-to-image translation. In: Neural Information Processing Systems (2017)
32. Rehder, E., Kloeden, H.: Goal-directed pedestrian prediction. In: International Conference on Computer Vision Workshop (2015)
33. Thrun, S., Burgard, W., Fox, D.: Probabilistic Robotics (Intelligent Robotics and Autonomous Agents). The MIT Press, Cambridge (2005)
34. Best, G., Fitch, R.: Bayesian intention inference for trajectory prediction with an unknown goal destination. In: International Conference on Intelligent Robots and Systems (2015)
35. Li, J., Ma, H., Tomizuka, M.: Conditional generative neural system for probabilistic trajectory prediction. In: International Conference on Intelligent Robots and Systems (2019)
36. Bhattacharyya, A., Hanselmann, M., Fritz, M., Schiele, B., Straehle, C.N.: Conditional flow variational autoencoders for structured sequence prediction. In: Neural Information Processing Systems (2019)
37. Deo, N., Trivedi, M.M.: Trajectory forecasts in unknown environments conditioned on grid-based plans. arXiv e-prints (2020) arXiv:2001.00735
38. Ronneberger, O., Fischer, P., Brox, T.: U-Net: convolutional networks for biomedical image segmentation. In: International Conference on Medical Image Computing and Computer Assisted Intervention (2015)
39. Mao, X., Li, Q., Xie, H., Lau, R.Y.K., Wang, Z., Smolley, S.P.: Least squares generative adversarial networks. In: International Conference on Computer Vision (2016)
40. Pellegrini, S., Ess, A., Gool, L.V.: Improving data association by joint modeling of pedestrian trajectories and groupings. In: European Conference on Computer Vision (2010)
41. Lerner, A., Chrysanthou, Y., Lischinski, D.: Crowds by example. Comput. Graph. Forum (2007)
42. Sadeghian, A., Kosaraju, V., Gupta, A., Savarese, S., Alahi, A.: Trajnet: Towards a benchmark for human trajectory prediction. arXiv preprint (2018)
43. Isola, P., Zhu, J.Y., Zhou, T., Efros, A.A.: Image-to-image translation with conditional adversarial networks. In: Conference on Computer Vision and Pattern Recognition (2016)
44. Thiede, L.A., Brahma, P.P.: Analyzing the variety loss in the context of probabilistic trajectory prediction. In: International Conference on Computer Vision (2019)

Self-supervised Sparse to Dense Motion Segmentation

Amirhossein Kardoost[1](), Kalun Ho[1,2,3], Peter Ochs[4],
and Margret Keuper[1]

[1] Data and Web Science Group, University of Mannheim, Mannheim, Germany
kardoostamirhossein@gmail.com
[2] Fraunhofer Center Machine Learning, Sankt Augustin, Germany
[3] Fraunhofer ITWM, Competence Center HPC, Kaiserslautern, Germany
[4] Mathematical Optimization Group, Saarland University, Saarbrcken, Germany

Abstract. Observable motion in videos can give rise to the definition of objects moving with respect to the scene. The task of segmenting such moving objects is referred to as motion segmentation and is usually tackled either by aggregating motion information in long, sparse point trajectories, or by directly producing per frame dense segmentations relying on large amounts of training data. In this paper, we propose a self supervised method to learn the densification of sparse motion segmentations from single video frames. While previous approaches towards motion segmentation build upon pre-training on large surrogate datasets and use dense motion information as an essential cue for the pixelwise segmentation, our model does not require pre-training and operates at test time on single frames. It can be trained in a sequence specific way to produce high quality dense segmentations from sparse and noisy input. We evaluate our method on the well-known motion segmentation datasets FBMS59 and DAVIS$_{16}$.

1 Introduction

The importance of motion for visual learning has been emphasized in recent years. Following the Gestalt principle of common fate [1], motion patterns within an object are often more homogeneous than its appearance, and therefore provide reliable cues for segmenting (moving) objects in a video. Motion segmentation is the task of segmenting motion patterns. This is in contrast to semantic segmentation, where one seeks to assign pixel-wise class labels in an image. Thus, for motion segmentation, we need motion information and at least two frames to be visible in order to distinguish between motion segments. Ideally, such motion patterns separate meaningful objects., e.g. an object moving w.r.t. the scene (refer to Fig. 1). To illustrate the importance of motion segmentation, consider an autonomous driving scenario. A first step to classify potential danger caused by the presence of a possibly static object, e.g., a parking car, is the knowledge about its mobility. Unknowingly waiting for the observation that the door of the parking car suddenly opens may be too late to avoid an accident. The speed of the autonomously driving vehicle must be adjusted based on the mobility

© Springer Nature Switzerland AG 2021
H. Ishikawa et al. (Eds.): ACCV 2020, LNCS 12623, pp. 421–437, 2021.
https://doi.org/10.1007/978-3-030-69532-3_26

Fig. 1. Motion segmentation example is provided for frames 1 and 160 of the "horses01" sequence (with their ground-truth motion segmentation) in the FBMS59 [2] dataset. Due to the reason that the person and the horse are moving together and have the same motion pattern, they are assigned the same motion label (blue color). (Color figure online)

and danger of other objects. While models for the direct prediction of pixel-wise motion segmentations are highly accurate [3,4], they can only take very limited account of an objects motion history.

In this paper, we propose a model to produce high quality dense segmentations from sparse and noisy input (i.e. *densification*). It can be trained in a sequence specific way using sparse motion segmentations as training data, i.e. the densification model can be trained in a self-supervised way. Our approach is based on sparse (semi-dense) motion trajectories that are extracted from videos via optical flow (Fig. 2, center). Point trajectory based motion segmentation algorithms have proven to be robust and fast [2,5–10]. By a long term analysis of a whole video shot at once by the means of such trajectories, even objects that are static for most of the time and only move for few frames can be identified, i.e. the model would not "forget" that a car has been moving, even after it has been static for a while. The same argument allows articulated motion to be assigned to a common moving object.

In our approach we use object annotations that are generated using established, sparse motion segmentation techniques [5]. We also propose an alternative, a GRU-based multicut model, which allows to learn the similarity between the motion of two trajectories and potentially allows for a more flexible application. In both cases, the result is a sparse segmentation of video sequences, providing labels only for points lying on the original trajectories, e.g. every 8 pixels (compare Fig. 2). From such sparse segmentations, pixel-wise segmentations can be generated by variational methods [2]. In order to better leverage the consistency within the video sequences, we propose to train sequence specific densification models using only the sparse motion segmentations as labels.

Specifically, we train a U-Net like model [11] to predict dense segmentations from given images (Fig. 2), while we only have sparse and potentially noisy labels given by the trajectories. The training task can thus be interpreted as a label densification. Yet, the resulting model does not need any sparse labels at test time but can generalize to unseen frames.

In contrast to end-to-end motion segmentation methods such as e.g. [4], we are not restricted to binary labels but can distinguish between different motion

Fig. 2. Exemplary multi-label motion segmentation results showing *(left)* the image and its sparse *(middle)* and dense *(right)* segmentation. The sparse segmentation is produced by [5] and the dense segmentation is the result of the proposed model.

patterns belonging to different objects and instances per image and only require single images to be given at test time. Also, in contrast to such approaches, our model does not rely on the availability of large surrogate datasets such as ImageNet [12] or FlyingChairs [13] for pre-training but can be trained directly on the sequences from for example the FBMS59 [2] and DAVIS$_{16}$ [14] datasets.

To summarize, we make the following contributions:

- We provide an improved affinity graph for motion segmentation in the minimum cost multicut framework using a GRU-model. Our model generates a sparse segmentation of motion patterns.
- We utilize the sparse and potentially noisy motion segmentation labels to train a U-Net model to produce class agnostic and dense motion segmentation. Sparse motion labels are not required during prediction.
- We provide competitive video object segmentation and motion segmentation results on the FBMS59 [2] and DAVIS$_{16}$ [14] datasets.

2   Related Work

Our goal is to learn to segment moving objects based on their motion pattern. For efficiency and robustness, we focus on point trajectory based techniques as initial cues. Trained in a sequence specific way, our model can be used for label *densification*. We therefore consider in the following related work in the areas *motion segmentation* and *sparse to dense labeling*.

2.1   Motion Segmentation

Common end-to-end trained CNN based approaches to motion segmentation are based on single frame segmentations from optical flow [3,4,15–17]. Tokmakov et al. [3,4] make use of large amounts of synthetic training data [13] to learn the concept of object motion. Further, [4] combine these cues with an ImageNet [12] pre-trained appearance stream and achieve long-term temporal consistency by using a GRU optimized on top. They learn a binary video segmentation and distinguish between static and moving elements. Siam et al. [17] use a single convolutional network to model motion and appearance cues jointly for autonomous driving. A frame-wise classification problem is formulated in [16] to detect motion saliency in videos. In [15] for each frame multiple figure-ground segmentations are produced based on motion boundaries. A moving objectness detector trained on image and motion fields is used to rank the segment candidates. Methods like [18,19] approach the problem in a probabilistic way. In [18] the camera motion is subtracted from each frame to improve the training. Variational formulations based on optical flow are used in [19,20], where [20] employ a strong geometric model. Addressing motion segmentation is different than object segmentation, as in motion segmentation, different motion patterns are segmented, which makes connected objects seem as one object if they move together with the same motion pattern. As an example, we refer to the example of a person riding a horse (Fig. 1). As long as they move together they will be considered as same object while in object segmentation we deal with two separate objects, this makes our method different than object segmentation approaches [21–23].

A different line of work relies on point trajectories for motion segmentation. Here, long-term motion information is first used to establish sparse but coherent motion segments over time. Dense segmentations are usually generated in a post-processing step such as [2]. However, in contrast to end-to-end CNN motion segmentation approaches, trajectory based methods have the desirable property to directly handle multiple motion pattern segmentations. While in [5,6] the partitioning of trajectories into motion segments uses the minimum cost multicut problem, other approaches employ sparse subspace clustering [24] or spectral clustering and normalized cuts [25–27]. In this setting, a model selection is needed to determine the final number of segments. In contrast, the minimum cost multicut formulation allows for a direct optimization of the number of components via repulsive cost.

Our GRU approach uses the same graph construction policy as [5] for motion segmentation while the edge costs are assigned using a Siamese (also known as twin) gated recurrent network. The Siamese networks [28] are metric learning approach used to provide a comparison between two different inputs. Similar trajectory embeddings have been used in [29] to predict a pedestrians future walking direction. For motion segmentation, we stick to the formulation as a minimum cost multicut problem [5].

2.2   Sparse to Dense Labeling

While the trajectory based motion segmentation methods can propagate object information through frames, they produce sparse results. Therefore, specific methods, e.g. [2,30] are needed to produce dense results. A commonly used densification approach is the variational framework of Ochs et al. [2]. In this approach the underlying color and boundary information of the images are used for the diffusion of the sparsely segmented trajectory points, which sometimes leaks the pixel labels to unwanted regions, e.g. loosely textured areas of the image. Furthermore, [31] address the densification problem using Gabriel graphs as per frame superpixel maps. Gabriel edges bridge the gaps between contours using geometric reasoning. However, super-pixel maps are prone to neglect fine structure of the underlying image and leads to low segmentation quality.

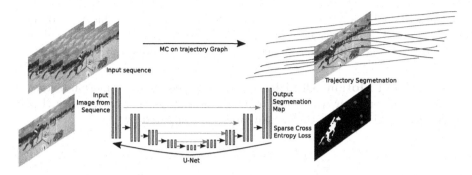

Fig. 3. Sparsely segmented trajectories are produced by minimum cost multicuts (MC) either with our Siamese-GRU model or simple motion cues as in [5] (top). The sparsely labeled points are used to train the U-Net model (bottom). At test time, U-Net model can produce dense segmentations without requiring any sparse labels as input.

Our method benefits from trajectory based methods for producing a sparse multi-label segmentation. A sparsely trained U-Net [11] produces dense results for each frame purely from appearance cues, potentially specific for a scene or sequence.

3 Proposed Self-supervised Learning Framework

We propose a self-supervised learning framework for sparse-to-dense segmentation of the sparsely segmented point trajectories. In another words, a U-Net model is trained from sparse annotations to estimate dense segmentation maps (Sect. 3.2). The sparse annotations can be provided either with some potentially unsupervised state-of-the-art trajectory segmentation methods [5] or our proposed Siamese-GRU model.

3.1 Annotation Generation

Point trajectories are generated from optical flow [7]. Each point trajectory corresponds to the set of sub-pixel positions connected through consecutive frames using the optical flow information. Such point trajectories are clustered by the minimum cost multicut approach [32] (aka. correlation clustering) with respect to their underlying motion model estimated (i) from a translational motion model or (ii) from a proposed Siamese GRU network.

Point Trajectories are spatio-temporal curves represented by their frame-wise sub-pixel-accurate (x,y)-coordinates. They can be generated by tracking points using optical flow by the method of Brox et al. [7]. The resulting trajectory set aims for a minimal target density (e.g. one trajectory in every 8 pixels). Trajectories are initialized in some video frame and end when the point cannot be tracked reliably anymore, e.g. due to occlusion. In order to achieve the desired density, possibly new trajectories are initialized throughout the video. Using trajectories brings the benefit of accessing the object motion in prior frames.

Translational Motion Affinities can be assigned based on motion distances of each trajectory pair with some temporal overlap [5]. For trajectories A and B, the frame-wise motion distance at time t is computed by

$$d_t(A, B) = \frac{\|\partial_t A - \partial_t B\|}{\sigma_t}. \tag{1}$$

It solely measures in-plane translational motion differences, normalized by the variation of the optical flow σ_t (refer to [2] for more information). The $\partial_t A$ and $\partial_t B$ represent the partial derivatives of A and B with respect to the time dimension.

The overall motion distance of a pair of trajectories A and B is computed by maximum pooling over their joint life-time,

$$d^{motion}(A, B) = \max_t d_t(A, B) \tag{2}$$

Color and spatial cues are added in [5] for robustness. Instead of using translational motion affinities we propose a Siamese Gated Recurrent Units (GRUs) based model to provide affinities between the trajectory pairs.

Siamese Gated Recurrent Units (GRUs) can be used to learn trajectory affinities by taking trajectory pairs as input. The proposed network consists of two legs with shared weights, where in our model each leg consists of a GRU model which takes a trajectory as input. Specifically, for two trajectories A and B, the ∂A and ∂B (partial derivative of the trajectories with respect to the time dimension) on the joint life-time of the trajectories are given to each leg of the Siamese-GRU model. The partial derivatives represent their motion information, while no information about their location in image coordinates is provided. The motion cues are embedded by the GRU network, i.e. the hidden units are gathered for each time step. Afterwards, the difference between two embedded motion vectors $embed_{\partial A}$ and $embed_{\partial B}$ is computed as

$$d_{(embed_{\partial A}, embed_{\partial B})} = \sum_{i=1}^{h} (embed_{\partial Ai} - embed_{\partial Bi})^2, \tag{3}$$

where h denotes the number of hidden units for each time step. The result of Eq. (3) is a vector which is consequently given to two fully connected layers and the final similarity value is computed by a Sigmoid function. Therefore, for each pair of trajectories given to the Siamese [28] GRU network, it provides a measure of their likelihood to belong to the same motion pattern.

The joint life-time of the two trajectories could in practice be different from pair to pair and the GRU network requires a fixed number of time steps as input (N). This problem is dealt as follows:

If the joint life-time of the two trajectories is less than N, each trajectory is padded with its respective final partial derivative value in the intersection part. Otherwise, when the joint life-time has more than N time steps, the time step t with maximum motion distance, similar to Eq. (2), is determined for the entire lifetime,

$$t_{A,B} = \arg\max_t d_t(A, B). \tag{4}$$

The trajectory values are extracted before and after t so that the required number of time steps N is reached. The reason for doing this is that the important part of the trajectories are not lost. Consider a case where an object does not move in the first x frames and starts moving from frame $x + 1$, the most important information will be available around frames x and $x + 1$ and it is better not to lose such information by cutting this part out.

In our approach, the frame-wise Euclidean distance of trajectory embeddings (extracted from the hidden units) of the GRU model is fed to a fully connected layer for dimensionality reduction and passed to a Sigmoid function for classification into the classes 0 (same label - pair of trajectories belong to the same motion pattern) or 1 (different label - pair of trajectories belong to different motion pattern) using a mean squared error (MSE) loss.

To train the Siamese-GRU model two labels are considered for each pair of trajectories, label 0 where the trajectory pair correspond to the same motion pattern and label 1 otherwise (the trajectories belong to different motion patterns). To produce the ground-truth labeling to train the Siamese-GRU model, a subset of the edges in the produced graph $G = (V, E)$ by the method of Keuper et al. [5] are sampled (information about the graph is provided in the next paragraph). For each edge, which corresponds to a pair of trajectories, we look into each trajectory and its label in the provided ground-truth segmentation. We only take those trajectories which belong to exactly one motion pattern in the provided ground-truth. Some trajectories change their labels while passing through frames which are considered as unreliable. Furthermore, the same amount of edges with label 0 (same motion pattern) and label 1 (different motion pattern) are sampled to have a balanced training signal. At test time, costs for each edge E in graph $G = (V, E)$ are generated by the trained Siamese-GRU network.

Trajectory Clustering yields a grouping of trajectories according to their modeled or learned motion affinities. We formalize the motion segmentation problem as minimum cost multicut problem [5]. It aims to optimally decompose a graph $G = (V, E)$, where trajectories are represented by nodes in V and their affinities define costs on the edges E. In our approach the costs are assigned using the Siamese-GRU model.

While the multicut problem is APX-hard [33], heuristic solvers [34–38] are expected to provide practical solutions. We use the Kernighan Lin [34] implementation of [39]. This solver is proved to be practically successful in motion segmentation [5,6], image decomposition and mesh segmentation [35] scenarios.

3.2 Deep Learning Model for Sparse to Dense Segmentation

We use the sparse motion segmentation annotated video data as described in Sect. 3.1 for our deep learning based sparse-to-dense motion segmentation model. Specifically, the training data consist of input images (video frames) or edge maps and their sparse motion segmentations, which we use as annotations. Although, the loss function only applies at the sparse labels, the network learns to predict dense segmentations.

Deep Learning Model. We use a U-Net [11] type architecture for dense segmentation, which is known for its high quality predictions in tasks such as semantic segmentation [40–42]. A U-Net is an encoder-decoder network with skip connections. During encoding, characteristic appearance properties of the input are extracted and are learnt to be associated with objectness. In the decoding phase, the extracted properties are traced back to locations causing the observed effect, while details from the downsampling phase are taken into account to ease the localisation (see Fig. 3 for details). The output is a dense (pixel-wise) segmentation of objects, i.e., a function $u\colon \Omega \to \{1,\dots,K\}$, where Ω is the image domain and K is the number of classes which corresponds to number of trajectory labels. This means that, after clustering the trajectories each cluster takes a label and overall we have class-agnostic motion segmentation of sparse trajectories. Such labels are only used during training.

Loss Function. The U-Net is trained via the Binary Cross Entropy (BCE) and Cross Entropy (CE) loss function for the single and multiple object case, respectively. As labels are only present at a sparse subset of pixels, the loss function is restricted to those pixels. Intuitively, since the label locations where the loss is evaluated are unknown to the network, it is forced to predict a label at every location. (A more detailed discussion is provided below.)

Dense Predictions with Sparse Loss Functions. At first glance, a sparse loss function may not force the network to produce a meaningful dense segmentation. Since trajectories are generated according to a simple deterministic criterion, namely extreme points of the local structure tensor [7], the network could internally reproduce this generation criterion and focus on labeling such points only. Actually, we observed exactly the problematic behaviour mentioned above, and, therefore, suggest variants for the learning process employing either RGB images or (deterministic) Sobel edge maps [43] as input. One remedy is to alleviate the local structure by smoothing the input RGB-image, making it harder for the network to pick up on local dominant texture and to stimulate the usage of globally extracted features that can be associated with movable object properties.

Conditional Random Filed (CRF) Segmentation Refinement. To build the fine-grained segmentation maps from the blurred images, we employ Conditional Random Fields (CRF): We compare

- the fully connected pre-trained CRF layer (dense-CRF) [44], with parameters learnded from pixel-level segmentation [45] and
- a CRFasRNN [46] model which we train using the output of our U-Net model as unaries on our same sparse annotations. To generate a training signal even in case the U-Net output perfectly fits the sparse labels, we add Gaussian noise to the unaries.

Discussion: Sparse Trajectories Vs. Dense Segmentation. The handling of sparse labels could be avoided if dense unsupervised motion segmentations were given. Although, in principle, dense trajectories can be generated by the motion segmentation algorithm, the clustering algorithm does not scale linearly with the number of trajectories and the computational cost explodes. Instead of densely tracking pixels throughout the video, a frame-wise computationally affordable densification step, for example based on variational or inpainting strategies [2], could be used. However, some sparse labels might be erroneous, an issue that can be amplified by the densification. Although some erroneous labels can also be corrected by [2], especially close to object boundaries, we observed that the negative effect prevails when it comes to learning from such unsupervised annotations. Moreover, variational methods often rely on local information to steer the propagation of label information in the neighborhood. In contrast, the U-Net architecture can incorporate global information and possibly objectness properties to construct its implicit regularization.

4   Experiments

We evaluate the performance of the proposed models on the two datasets DAVIS$_{16}$ [14] and FBMS59 [2], which contain challenging video sequences with high quality segmentation annotations of moving objects.

4.1   Datasets and Implementation Details

Datasets. The DAVIS$_{16}$ dataset [14] is produced for high-precision binary object segmentation tracking of rigidly and non-rigidly moving objects. It contains 30 train and 20 validation sequences. The pixel-wise binary ground truth segmentation is provided per frame for each sequence. The evaluation metrics are Jaccard index (also known as Intersection over Union) and F-measure. Even though this dataset is produced for object segmentation, it is commonly used to evaluate motion segmentation because only one object is moving in each sequence which makes the motion pattern of the foreground object to be different from the background motion.

Table 1. The trajectories are segmented by 1. the method of Keuper et al. [5] and 2. our Siamese-GRU model. The densified results are generated based on 1. the method of Ochs et al. [2] and 2. the proposed U-Net model. The results are provided for the validation set of DAVIS$_{16}$.

Traj. Se.g. method	Densification method	Jaccard index
Keuper et al. [5]	Ochs et al. [2]	55.3
Keuper et al. [5]	U-Net model (ours)	58.5
Siamese-GRU (ours)	Ochs et al. [2]	57.7
Siamese-GRU (ours)	U-Net model (ours)	**66.2**

The FBMS59 [2] dataset is specifically designed for motion segmentation and consists of 29 train and 30 test sequences. The sequences cover camera shaking, rigid/non-rigid motion as well as occlusion/dis-occlusion of single and multiple objects with ground-truth segmentations given for a subset of the frames. We evaluate precision, recall and F-measure.

Implementation Details. Our Siamese-GRU model with 2 hidden units ($h = 2$, Eq. 3) and experimentally selected 25 time steps ($N = 25$, for more information refer to Sect. 3.1) is trained for 3 epochs, a batch size of 256 and a learning rate of 0.001 where the trajectories are produced by large displacement optical flow (LDOF) [47] at 8 pixel sampling on the training set of DAVIS$_{16}$ [14].

We employ two different strategies of using the sparse motion segmentations of the resulting trajectories as labels, depending whether we face binary (DAVIS$_{16}$) or multi-label (FBMS59) problems. In case of single label, the most frequent trajectory label *overall frames* and second most frequent label *per frame* are considered as background and foreground, respectively. For multi-label cases, the most frequent class-agnostic labels are selected, i.e. we take only those labels which are frequent enough compared to the other labels.

Our U-Net model is trained in a sequence specific way. Such model can be used for example for label densification and is trained using color and edge-map data with a learning rate of 0.01 and batch size of 1 for 15 epochs. The overall train and prediction process takes around (maximally) 30 min per sequence on a NVIDIA Tesla V100 GPU. The CRFasRNN [46] is trained with learning rate of 0.0001, batch size 1 and 10 epochs with 5 and 10 inference iterations at train and test time, respectively.

4.2 Sparse Trajectory Motion-Model

We first evaluate our GRU model for sparse motion segmentation on the validation set of DAVIS$_{16}$ [14]. Therefore, we produce, in a first iteration, densified segmentations using the variational approach from [2]. The results are given in Table 1 (line 3) and show an improvement over the motion model from Keuper et al. [5] by 2% in Jaccard index. In the following experiments on DAVIS$_{16}$, we thus use sparse labels from our Siamese GRU approach.

Table 2. Sparse Motion Segmentation trained on DAVIS$_{16}$ (all seq.) and evaluated on FBMS59 (train set). We compare to [5] and their variant only using motion cues.

	Precision	Recall	F-measure	#of extracted objs.
Keuper et al. [5] (motion cues)	83.88	69.97	76.30	20
Keuper et al. [5] (full)	83.69	73.17	**78.07**	**27**
Siamese-GRU (ours - transfer)	81.01	70.07	75.14	24

Knowledge Transfer. Next, we investigate the generalization ability of this motion model. We evaluate the DAVIS$_{16}$-trained GRU-model on the train set of FBMS59 [2]. Results are given in Table 2. While this model performs below the hand-tuned model of [5] on this dataset, results are comparable, especially considering that our GRU model does not use color information. In further experiments on FBMS59, we use sparse labels from [5].

4.3   Dense Segmentation of Moving Objects

Next, we evaluate our self-supervised dense segmentation framework with sequence specific training on the color images as well as edge maps on the validation set of DAVIS$_{16}$ [14]. Table 1 shows that this model, trained on the GRU based labels, outperforms the model trained on the motion models from [5] as well as the densification of Ochs et al. [2] by a large margin. Table 3 (top) provides a comparison between different versions of our model, the densification model of Ochs et al. [2], and the per-frame evaluation of Tokmakov et al. [3] on DAVIS$_{16}$. [3] use large amounts of data for pre-training. Their better performing model variants require optical flow and full sequence information to be given at test time. Our results based on RGB and edge maps are better than those solely using edge maps. We also compare the different CRF versions:

- pre-trained dense-CRF [44],
- our trained CRFasRNN [46] model trained per sequence *(CRF-per-seq)*,
- CRFasRNN [46] trained on all frames in the train set of DAVIS$_{16}$ *(CRF-general)* with sparse labels

All CRF versions improve the F-measure. The CRF-general performs on par with dense-CRF by only using our sparse labels for training. See Fig. 4 and Fig. 5 for qualitative results of our model on DAVIS$_{16}$ [14] and FBMS59 [2] datasets, respectively. We show on par performance with the layered optimization approach by [20] in DAVIS$_{16}$ with Jaccard's index of 68.3 versus *ours:* 67.1.

Partly Trained Model. We further evaluate how well our model works for video frames for which no sparse labels are given during training. Please note that, throughout the sequences, the appearance of an object can change drastically. In Table 3 (bottom), we report results for the sequence specific U-Net model + *CRF-general* trained on the first 50%, 70% and 90% of the frames and

Table 3. Evaluation of self supervised training on sequences from DAVIS$_{16}$ validation and comparison with other methods is provided. Effect of adding color information (RGB) to the edge maps (sobel) is studied (*ours*) and comparison between (pretrained) dense-CRF (*dense*), CRF-per-seq (*per-seq*) and CRF-general (*general*) is provided (for different versions of CRF refer to 4.3). We studied the effect of our best model while training it only on 50%, 70% and 90% of the frames in the last three rows.

	% of frames	Jaccard index	F-measure
Variational [2]	100	57.7	57.1
Appearance + GRU [3]	100	59.6	-
Sobel + *dense*	100	62.6	54.0
Sobel + RGB (*ours*)	100	61.3	49.0
Ours + *dense*	100	**67.1**	60.2
Ours + *per-seq*	100	66.2	60.3
Ours + *general*	100	66.2	**62.1**
Ours + *general*	50	59.6	50.4
Ours + *general*	70	62.3	53.5
Ours + *general*	90	63.4	55.4

Table 4. We evaluate our densification method on FBMS59 (train) using sparse motion segmentations from Keuper et al. [5]. The sparse trajectories are produced with different flow estimation methods (LDOF [47] and FlowNet2 [48]) and densified with our proposed U-Net model (using edge maps (sobel) and color information (RGB) (*ours*)). Further, we study on different CRF methods, (pretrained) dense-CRF (*dense*) and CRF-general (*general*). For more details about different versions of CRF refer to Sect. 4.3.

	Precision	Recall	F-measure
Ochs et al. [2]	85.31	68.70	76.11
Lao et al. [20]	90.04	65.09	76.02
LDOF + *ours* + *dense*	89.35	67.67	77.01
FlowNet2 + *ours* + *dense*	89.59	68.29	**77.56**
FlowNet2 + *ours* + *general*	89.27	68.20	77.33

evaluated on the remaining frames. While there is some loss in Jaccard's index compared to the model evaluated on seen frames (above), the performance only drops slightly as smaller portions of the data are used for training.

Fig. 4. Exemplary single-label motion segmentation results showing the five frames and their sparse and dense segmentation for two different sequences, generated using the proposed U-Net model. The images are from the sequences on the validation set of DAVIS$_{16}$ [14] dataset.

Densification on FBMS59. Next, we evaluate our sequence specific model for label densification on FBMS59 [2]. We study on two different variants of optical flow (FlowNet2 [48] and Large Displacement Optical Flow (LDOF) [47]) for trajectory generation and sparse motion segmentation [5]. The results in Table 4 show that the proposed approach outperforms the approach of Ochs et al. [2] as well as the geometric, layered optimization approach by [20]. Improved optical flow leads to improved results overall. The different CRF versions do not provide significantly different results.

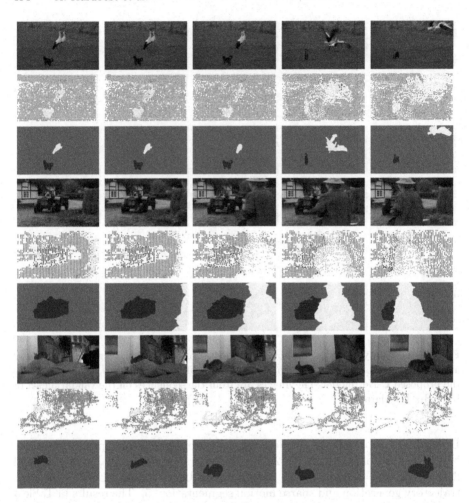

Fig. 5. Exemplary single- and multi-label motion segmentation results showing the image and its sparse results as well as dense segmentation for five frames in three different sequences, generated using the proposed U-Net model. The images are from the FBMS59 [2] dataset. Segmentations with fine details are produced even when training labels were scarce, notice how scarce the labels are for "rabbit" images in the 8th row. White areas are parts without any label.

5   Conclusion

In this paper, we have addressed the segmentation of moving objects from single frames. To that end, we proposed a GRU-based trajectory embedding to produce high quality sparse segmentations automatically. Furthermore, we closed the gap between sparse and dense results by providing a self-supervised U-Net model trained on sparse labels and relying only on edge maps and color information. The trained model on sparse points provides single and multi-label dense segmentations. The proposed approach generalizes to unseen sequences from FBMS59 and DAVIS$_{16}$ and provides competitive and appealing results.

Acknowledgment. We acknowledge funding by the DFG project KE 2264/1-1 and thank the NVIDIA Corporation for the donation of a Titan Xp GPU.

References

1. Koffka, K.: Principles of Gestalt Psychology. Hartcourt Brace Jovanovich, NewYork (1935)
2. Ochs, P., Malik, J., Brox, T.: Segmentation of moving objects by long term video analysis. IEEE TPAMI **36**, 1187–1200 (2014)
3. Tokmakov, P., Alahari, K., Schmid, C.: Learning video object segmentation with visual memory. In: ICCV (2017)
4. Tokmakov, P., Alahari, K., Schmid, C.: Learning motion patterns in videos. In: CVPR (2017)
5. Keuper, M., Andres, B., Brox, T.: Motion trajectory segmentation via minimum cost multicuts. In: IEEE International Conference on Computer Vision (ICCV) (2015)
6. Keuper, M.: Higher-order minimum cost lifted multicuts for motion segmentation. In: The IEEE International Conference on Computer Vision (ICCV) (2017)
7. Brox, T., Malik, J.: Object segmentation by long term analysis of point trajectories. In: European Conference on Computer Vision (ECCV). Lecture Notes in Computer Science, Springer (2010)
8. Fragkiadaki, K., Zhang, W., Zhang, G., Shi, J.: Two-granularity tracking: mediating trajectory and detection graphs for tracking under occlusions. In: ECCV (2012)
9. Shi, F., Zhou, Z., Xiao, J., Wu, W.: Robust trajectory clustering for motion segmentation. In: ICCV (2013)
10. Rao, S.R., Tron, R., Vidal, R., Yi Ma: Motion segmentation via robust subspace separation in the presence of outlying, incomplete, or corrupted trajectories. In: 2008 IEEE Conference on Computer Vision and Pattern Recognition, pp. 1–8 (2008)
11. Ronneberger, O., Fischer, P., Brox, T.: U-Net: convolutional networks for biomedical image segmentation. In: Navab, N., Hornegger, J., Wells, W.M., Frangi, A.F. (eds.) MICCAI 2015. LNCS, vol. 9351, pp. 234–241. Springer, Cham (2015). https://doi.org/10.1007/978-3-319-24574-4_28
12. Deng, J., Dong, W., Socher, R., Li, L.J., Li, K., Fei-Fei, L.: ImageNet: a large-scale hierarchical image database. In: CVPR09 (2009)
13. Dosovitskiy, A., et al.: Flownet: learning optical flow with convolutional networks. In: IEEE International Conference on Computer Vision (ICCV) (2015)
14. Perazzi, F., Pont-Tuset, J., McWilliams, B., Van Gool, L., Gross, M., Sorkine-Hornung, A.: A benchmark dataset and evaluation methodology for video object segmentation, pp. 724–732 (2016)
15. Maczyta, L., Bouthemy, P., Meur, O.: CNN-based temporal detection of motion saliency in videos. Pattern Recognition Letters **128** (2019)

16. Fragkiadaki, K., Arbelaez, P., Felsen, P., Malik, J.: Learning to segment moving objects in videos, pp. 4083–4090 (2015)
17. Siam, M., Mahgoub, H., Zahran, M., Yogamani, S., Jagersand, M., El-Sallab, A.: Modnet: motion and appearance based moving object detection network for autonomous driving. In: 2018 21st International Conference on Intelligent Transportation Systems (ITSC), pp. 2859–2864 (2018)
18. Bideau, P., Learned-Miller, E.: It's moving! a probabilistic model for causal motion segmentation in moving camera videos. In: Leibe, B., Matas, J., Sebe, N., Welling, M. (eds.) ECCV 2016. LNCS, vol. 9912, pp. 433–449. Springer, Cham (2016). https://doi.org/10.1007/978-3-319-46484-8_26
19. Cremers, D.: A variational framework for image segmentation combining motion estimation and shape regularization. In: Proceedings of the 2003 IEEE Computer Society Conference on Computer Vision and Pattern Recognition. CVPR'03, Washington, DC, USA, IEEE Computer Society, pp. 53–58 (2003)
20. Lao, D., Sundaramoorthi, G.: Extending layered models to 3d motion. In: ECCV (2018)
21. Hu, Y.T., Huang, J.B., Schwing, A.: In: Unsupervised Video Object Segmentation Using Motion Saliency-Guided Spatio-Temporal Propagation: 15th EuropeanConference, Munich, Germany, 8-14 September 2018, Proceedings, Part I, pp. 813–830 (2018)
22. Tsai, Y.H., Yang, M.H., Black, M.J.: Video segmentation via object flow. In: IEEE Conference on Computer Vision and Pattern Recognition (CVPR) (2016)
23. Papazoglou, A., Ferrari, V.: Fast object segmentation in unconstrained video. In: 2013 IEEE International Conference on Computer Vision, pp. 1777–1784 (2013)
24. Elhamifar, E., Vidal, R.: Sparse subspace clustering. In: ICCV (2013)
25. Ochs, P., Brox, T.: Higher order motion models and spectral clustering. In: IEEE International Conference on Computer Vision and Pattern Recognition (CVPR) (2012)
26. Jianbo, S., Malik, J.: Motion segmentation and tracking using normalized cuts. In: Sixth International Conference on Computer Vision (IEEE Cat. No.98CH36271), pp. 1154–1160 (1998)
27. Fragkiadaki, K., Shi, J.: Detection free tracking: exploiting motion and topology for segmenting and tracking under entanglement. In: CVPR (2011)
28. Chopra, S., Hadsell, R., LeCun, Y.: Learning a similarity metric discriminatively, with application to face verification. In: 2005 IEEE Computer Society Conference on Computer Vision and Pattern Recognition (CVPR'05). vol. 1, pp. 539–546 (2005)
29. Bhattacharyya, A., Fritz, M., Schiele, B.: Long-term on-board prediction of people in traffic scenes under uncertainty (2018)
30. Müller, S., Ochs, P., Weickert, J., Graf, N.: Robust interactive multi-label segmentation with an advanced edge detector. In: Rosenhahn, B., Andres, B. (eds.) GCPR 2016. LNCS, vol. 9796, pp. 117–128. Springer, Cham (2016). https://doi.org/10.1007/978-3-319-45886-1_10
31. Shi, J.: Video segmentation by tracing discontinuities in a trajectory embedding. In: Proceedings of the 2012 IEEE Conference on Computer Vision and Pattern Recognition (CVPR). CVPR 2012, Washington, DC, USA, IEEE Computer Society, pp. 1846–1853 (2012)
32. Andres, B., et al.: Globally optimal closed-surface segmentation for connectomics. In: ECCV (2012)
33. Bansal, N., Blum, A., Chawla, S.: Correlation clustering. Machine Learning 56, 89–113 (2004)

34. Kernighan, B.W., Lin, S.: An efficient heuristic procedure for partitioning graphs. The Bell Syst. Technical J. **49**, 291–307 (1970)
35. Keuper, M., Levinkov, E., Bonneel, N., Lavoue, G., Brox, T., Andres, B.: Efficient decomposition of image and mesh graphs by lifted multicuts. In: IEEE International Conference on Computer Vision (ICCV) (2015)
36. Beier, T., Andres, B., Köthe, U., Hamprecht, F.A.: An efficient fusion move algorithm for the minimum cost lifted multicut problem. In: ECCV (2016)
37. Kardoost, A., Keuper, M.: Solving minimum cost lifted multicut problems by node agglomeration. In: Jawahar, C.V., Li, H., Mori, G., Schindler, K. (eds.) ACCV 2018. LNCS, vol. 11364, pp. 74–89. Springer, Cham (2019). https://doi.org/10.1007/978-3-030-20870-7_5
38. Bailoni, A., Pape, C., Wolf, S., Beier, T., Kreshuk, A., Hamprecht, F.: A generalized framework for agglomerative clustering of signed graphs applied to instance segmentation (2019)
39. Keuper, M., Andres, B., Brox, T.: Motion trajectory segmentation via minimum cost multicuts. In: ICCV (2015)
40. Siam, M., Gamal, M., Abdel-Razek, M., Yogamani, S., Jagersand, M.: Rtseg: real-time semantic segmentation comparative study. In: 2018 25th IEEE International Conference on Image Processing (ICIP), pp. 1603–1607 (2018)
41. Siam, M., Elkerdawy, S., Jagersand, M., Yogamani, S.: Deep semantic segmentation for automated driving: Taxonomy, roadmap and challenges. In: 2017 IEEE 20th International Conference on Intelligent Transportation Systems (ITSC), pp. 1–8 (2017)
42. Fu, J., Liu, J., Wang, Y., Zhou, J., Wang, C., Lu, H.: Stacked deconvolutional network for semantic segmentation. IEEE Transactions on Image Processing (2019)
43. Kanopoulos, N., Vasanthavada, N., Baker, R.L.: Design of an image edge detection filter using the sobel operator. IEEE J. Solid-State circ. **23**, 358–367 (1988)
44. Krähenbühl, P., Koltun, V.: Efficient inference in fully connected CRFS with gaussian edge potentials. CoRR abs/1210.5644 (2012)
45. Chen, L.C., Papandreou, G., Kokkinos, I., Murphy, K., Yuille, A.L.: Semantic image segmentation with deep convolutional nets and fully connected CRFS. In: ICLR (2015)
46. Zheng, S., et al.: Conditional random fields as recurrent neural networks. In: International Conference on Computer Vision (ICCV) (2015)
47. Brox, T., Bregler, C., Malik, J.: Large displacement optical flow. In: IEEE International Conference on Computer Vision and Pattern Recognition (CVPR) (2009)
48. Ilg, E., Mayer, N., Saikia, T., Keuper, M., Dosovitskiy, A., Brox, T.: Flownet 2.0: evolution of optical flow estimation with deep networks. In: IEEE Conference on Computer Vision and Pattern Recognition (CVPR) (2017)

Recursive Bayesian Filtering for Multiple Human Pose Tracking from Multiple Cameras

Oh-Hun Kwon, Julian Tanke$^{(\boxtimes)}$, and Juergen Gall

University of Bonn, Bonn, Germany
ohkwon@uni-bonn.de, {tanke,gall}@iai.uni-bonn.de

Abstract. Markerless motion capture allows the extraction of multiple 3D human poses from natural scenes, without the need for a controlled but artificial studio environment or expensive hardware. In this work we present a novel tracking algorithm which utilizes recent advancements in 2D human pose estimation as well as 3D human motion anticipation. During the prediction step we utilize an RNN to forecast a set of plausible future poses while we utilize a 2D multiple human pose estimation model during the update step to incorporate observations. Casting the problem of estimating multiple persons from multiple cameras as a tracking problem rather than an association problem results in a linear relationship between runtime and the number of tracked persons. Furthermore, tracking enables our method to overcome temporary occlusions by relying on the prediction model. Our approach achieves state-of-the-art results on popular benchmarks for 3D human pose estimation and tracking.

1 Introduction

Markerless motion capture [1–9] has many applications in sports [10,11] and surveillance [12]. Utilizing multiple calibrated cameras extends the field of view, allows to resolve ambiguities such as foreshortening and occlusions, and provides accurate 3D estimates. However, challenges still remain: large crowds and close interactions result in heavy occlusions which severely degrade the 3D tracking performance. Furthermore, most recent works [3–5,9] cast multiple 3D human pose estimation from multiple camera views as an association problem where extracted 2D pose features have to be matched across views and across time. This way, the time complexity grows quadratic [9] or even exponential [4,5] with the number of tracked individuals, making tracking of large numbers of persons impractical.

In this work we cast the problem of estimating multiple persons from multiple calibrated cameras as a tracking problem where each person is individually tracked using the well-known recursive Bayesian filtering method [13]. Individually tracking each person results in a linear relationship between time complexity and the number of persons in the scene. Furthermore, utilizing a tracking framework enables us to retain plausible poses even under temporary heavy occlusion. Last but not least, the Bayesian framework allows us to quantify uncertainty.

© Springer Nature Switzerland AG 2021
H. Ishikawa et al. (Eds.): ACCV 2020, LNCS 12623, pp. 438–453, 2021.
https://doi.org/10.1007/978-3-030-69532-3_27

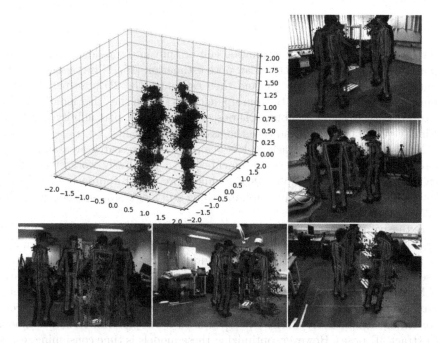

Fig. 1. Probabilistic representation for 3D pose tracking. The black points represent 3D pose predictions from the prediction step while the colored skeletons represent the pose samples after the update step. Notice that both representations model uncertainty. The final pose is the black skeleton at the center of each person.

Recursive Bayesian filtering naturally lends itself for human pose tracking from multiple cameras. It models an underlying process $z_{1:T}$, which we are interested in but which we cannot directly observe. Instead, at each time step t we receive observations o_t which are related to z_t. Bayesian filtering provides us with tools to form our best guess about z_t given the observations $o_{1:t}$. For 3D human pose tracking, the unobserved hidden state z_t represents the 3D pose at time t while the observation o_t represents the camera input at time t for all cameras. Bayesian filtering utilizes a prediction step, which forecasts the current estimate in time, and an update step, which incorporates current observations into the prediction. To model uncertainty we utilize a sample-based approach for z_t. For the prediction step we build on recent advancements in 3D human motion anticipation [14] and utilize a sequence-to-sequence model. During the update step we process all samples in z_t and make use of importance sampling, similar to the particle filter [13]. In order to reduce the number of required particles, we combine it with an optimization step to find good 3D poses. Our method achieves state-of-the-art results on common multiple person multi-camera pose estimation and tracking benchmarks.

2   Related Work

Methods for 2D human pose estimation can be split into top-down and bottom-up approaches. Top-down 2D human pose estimation [15,16] first estimates 2D bounding boxes for each person and then estimates the 2D pose per detected human on a fixed resolution. Bottom-up methods [17] on the other hand estimate features that assist in assembling 2D poses. For example, part affinity fields [17] estimate vector fields that indicate the association of joints.

Multi-person 2D pose tracking has been an active research area and recent works achieved tremendous advancements [16,18–21]. Early works focused on solving spatio-temporal graphs [18,19] while more recent approaches [16,20,21] showed that utilizing a greedy graph matching still yields state-of-the-art results while being much faster.

Extensive progress has been made in estimating 3D poses from monocular views [22–26]. For example, the problem of inferring 3D human poses from single images is split into estimating a 2D human pose and then regressing a 3D pose [22]. However, these methods do not generalize well to unconstrained data.

Multiple 3D human pose estimation from multiple views can be cast as a matching problem where poses or joints have to be matched across views for accurate triangulation. Early works [3,6–8] utilized a 3D pictorial structure model to extract 3D poses. However, optimizing these models is time consuming, especially when applied to multiple persons, due to the large state space. When many camera views are available, a voting mechanism [27] can be employed - assuming persons are visible in most camera views. Recently, a simple baseline [9] was proposed which independently extracts 2D poses for each view and greedily matches them using geometric cues. Furthermore, they utilize Gaussian smoothing across time to introduce temporal information. While this method is simple and fast, it suffers from an early commitment to 2D pose matches. This may lead to different predictions based on the processing order of the cameras. Dong et al. [5] solve the correspondence problem of 2D poses per camera utilizing a top-down 2D pose estimator [28] for each view. They match 2D poses across views using geometric and appearance cues solved with convex optimization with cycle-consistency constrains. While this works well when persons are easy to differentiate, e.g. when full-body poses are visible, it can result in incorrect matches in more complex scenes. Zhang et al. [4] formulate cross-view matching and temporal tracking as a 4D association graph, similar to early works in 2D pose tracking [19].

To facilitate tracking, Bayesian filtering [13] is often utilized. While linear methods such as linear quadratic estimation are well-understood they restrict the model too much for tracking complex 3D human poses. Representing the distribution of poses as a set of 3D pose samples, also known as particle filter, offers more flexibility. However, due to the high dimensionality of 3D poses additional optimization steps are typically required [29–31]. In this work we show that a simple heuristic can be utilized.

In recent years deep neural networks have been used to anticipate 3D human poses from motion capture data. Holden et al. [32] show that autoencoders can be

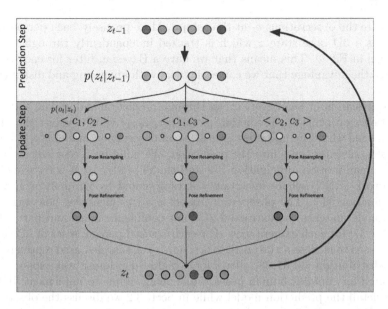

Fig. 2. Tracking procedure for tracking a single person z with a set of three cameras c_1, c_2 and c_3. The prediction step forecast z_{t-1} from time $t-1$ to t. In the update step each pose sample gets assigned an importance weight independently for each camera pair. The importance weights are calculated using the observations o_t at time t. We then resample for each camera pair relative to the total number of samples and refine the poses using pose refinement. Finally, we concatenate the sub-samples for each camera pair and obtain our prediction for z_t.

utilized to learn a human motion manifold. Bütepage et al. [33] extend this idea by embedding the skeletal hierarchy structure of the data into the model. Similarly, structural RNNs [34] encode the hierarchy utilizing RNNs. The Encoder-Recurrent-Decoder (ERD) [35] auto-regressively forecasts human motion by utilizing an encoder-decoder structure for modeling human poses and an LSTM for temporal modelling while Martinez et al. [14] introduce a sequence-to-sequence architecture for human motion forecasting.

Monte-Carlo Dropout sampling [36] places a Bernoulli distribution over the weights of a neural network. This way one can generate multiple samples using different dropout masks to represent the model uncertainty.

3 Method

In this work we formulate the problem of estimating and tracking multiple 3D human poses from multiple calibrated cameras as a recursive Bayesian filter where the hidden states z_t represent the 3D human poses and where the camera images are the observations o_t at time step t. More precisely, each person in the scene has a 3D pose state z which is tracked independently through time, as described in Fig. 2. This means that we have a Bayesian filter for each person. This has the advantage that we can easily deal with appearing and disappearing persons.

A Bayesian filter recursively cycles through prediction and update steps. The prediction step utilizes a prediction model $p(z_t|z_{t-1})$ which evolves the hidden state in time while the update step utilizes an observation model $p(o_t|z_t)$ which integrates measurements into the prediction. We build on recent advancements in 3D human motion anticipation [14] and model $p(z_t|z_{t-1})$ as a recurrent neural network (RNN) where uncertainty is represented by Dropout as Bayesian approximation [36]. The observation model $p(o_t|z_t)$ measures how well a 3D pose sample matches the extracted 2D joint confidence maps and part affinity fields [17,37] for each camera view. For each tracked person, a set of 3D sample poses is used to represent the posterior $p(z_t|o_{1...t})$. A sample-based representation of the distribution [30,31,38] allows for a highly non-linear state space, which is required for complex human poses, while being simple to implement. In Sect. 3.1 we detail the prediction model while in Sect. 3.2 we discuss the observation model. The initialization procedure for $p(z_1|o_1)$ of each person is explained in Sect. 3.3. Finally, Sect. 3.4 explains how point samples can be obtained for each frame t from the estimated posterior $p(z_t|o_1 \ldots o_t)$.

3.1   Prediction Step

The prediction model $p(z_t|z_{t-1})$ evolves the pose state of a single tracked person in time - without taking any observation into account. The pose state z_t of a person encompasses possible 3D poses which we make tractable by representing them as a fixed set of 3D pose samples. A sample is made up of 14 3D joints.

We represent $p(z_t|z_{t-1})$ as GRU [14] and we inject uncertainty by utilizing Dropout during training and inference at the final linear layer that extracts z_t. Dropout is crucial to generate a diverse set of forecast poses which we will discuss in our ablation studies. As z_{t-1} is represented as a list of 3D pose samples, we apply the forecast for each sample independently with an independent hidden layer for the GRU for each sample. This way, z_t and z_{t-1} will be represented by the same number of samples while samples will be sufficiently varied due to the independent forecasting. For brevity, we define this as:

$$z_t, h_t = \mathrm{GRU}(z_{t-1}, h_{t-1}) \tag{1}$$

where z_t, h_t, z_{t-1} and h_{t-1} are 3D pose samples and GRU hidden states, respectively.

The 3D poses in z are in a global coordinate frame which is defined by the calibrated cameras. We transform the 3D poses into a standardized coordinate frame before forecasting. Here, the center hip joint of the poses in z_{t-1} are set as the origin and the poses are rotated along the z axis[1] such that the left and right

---

[1] Assuming z axis points upwards.

hip joints align to the y axis and such that the 3D pose faces forward along the x axis. More formally, we apply the following transformation to each 3D pose

$$\hat{\mathbf{x}}_j = R^{(t-1)} \left(\mathbf{x}_j - \mathbf{x}_{\text{hiproot}}^{(t-1)}\right) \forall j \in J \tag{2}$$

where J represents all joints that make up a 3D pose and where $\mathbf{x}_j$ represents the j-th joint as 3D point in global coordinate space and where $\hat{\mathbf{x}}_j$ represents the same joint in normalized coordinates. The hip root joint of the pose at time $t-1$ is defined as $\mathbf{x}_{\text{hiproot}}^{(t-1)}$ and the rotation to forward-face the pose at $t-1$ is defined as

$$R^{(t-1)} = \begin{bmatrix} \cos\theta & \sin\theta & 0 \\ -\sin\theta & \cos\theta & 0 \\ 0 & 0 & 1 \end{bmatrix} \tag{3}$$

$$\theta = \text{atan2}\left(y_{\text{righthip}}^{(t-1)} - y_{\text{lefthip}}^{(t-1)}, x_{\text{righthip}}^{(t-1)} - x_{\text{lefthip}}^{(t-1)}\right) \tag{4}$$

where $x_{\text{righthip}}^{(t-1)}$, $x_{\text{lefthip}}^{(t-1)}$, $y_{\text{righthip}}^{(t-1)}$ and $y_{\text{lefthip}}^{(t-1)}$ represent the x and y coordinate of the right hip and left hip, respectively. After forecasting a pose, the original position and orientation in global coordinates can be recovered by applying the transformation

$$\mathbf{x}_j = R^{(t-1)^T} \hat{\mathbf{x}}_j + \mathbf{x}_{\text{hiproot}}^{(t-1)} \ \forall j \in J. \tag{5}$$

The prediction model is trained with motion capture data from the Human3.6M [39] and the CMU mocap database [40] where we select 14 joints that the two datasets have in common. We utilize Adam with learning rate 0.001 and optimize over the Huber loss. The number of hidden units for the GRU is set to 2048. The dropout rate is set to 50% and a weight decay of 10^{-8} is added. We set the framerate to 25 Hz and 30 Hz, respectively, which is similar to the framerate used in the evaluation datasets.

3.2 Update Step

To obtain the posterior $p(z_t|o_{1,...,t})$ for a single tracked person we need to incorporate the observations o_t into the predictions z_t obtained from the prediction model. For each camera we utilize Openpose [17] to extract part confidence maps and part affinity fields, similar to other multi-person multi-camera 3D pose estimation methods [4,9]. We then calculate importance weights for each sample pose in z_t and then re-sample z_t based on the weights. To prevent poses that are visible in many camera views to be over-represented over poses that are visible in less cameras and to tackle false-positive detections caused by occlusion, we sample the importance weight for each camera pair independently - for all samples. The weight is calculated as follows:

$$w_{v,s} = \frac{\Phi(v,s)}{\sum_{\hat{s}}^{z_t} \Phi(v,\hat{s})} \tag{6}$$

where v represents a camera pair and where s represents a single 3D pose sample from z_t. We normalize by the scores of all samples $\hat{s}$ in z_t. The unnormalized weight $\Phi(\cdot, \cdot)$ is calculated as follows:

$$\Phi(v, s) = \prod_{l \in L} \sqrt{\sum_{c \in v} \phi(c, l, s)^2} + \epsilon \qquad (7)$$

where L represents all limbs of a pose, as described in Openpose [17]. Each camera pair v consists of two different camera views c. The score $\phi(\cdot, \cdot, \cdot)$ is calculated using part affinity fields paf_c and confidence maps conf_c, which are obtained from Openpose [17], for a given camera c:

$$\phi(c, l, s) = \left(\int_{u=0}^{u=1} \max\left(0, \text{paf}_c(s, l, u)\right) \, du \right) \prod_{j \in l} \text{conf}_c(s, j) \qquad (8)$$

where $\text{paf}_c(s, l, u)$ calculates the dot product between the part affinity field for limb l and the projected limb from s, linearly interpolated by u. $\text{conf}_c(s, j)$ calculates the confidence score for the joint j of sample s for camera c. Finally, we resample z_t for each camera pair a subset of particles to obtain the same number of initial samples as shown in Fig. 2. As sampling procedure we use stochastic universal sampling.

In practice, the state space of a 3D pose is prohibitively large for a sample-based representation. However, we utilize a simple yet effective heuristic optimization called joint refinement to keep the number of samples low while obtaining accurate results. For each joint of a sample, we sample additional joint positions from a normal distribution centered at the joint. We then take the joint position with the highest confidence map score. In our ablation study we show that this significantly improves the results while it allows the numbers of samples for each person to be low.

3.3   Initialization Step

(a) Heatmap   (b) Projected Samples   (c) Output

Fig. 3. Input and output of the confidence subtraction network. The input is composed of a confidence map (a) extracted by [17] for a specific joint and projected points (b) of that joint for the tracked person. The network removes the part of the heatmap that corresponds to the tracked person.

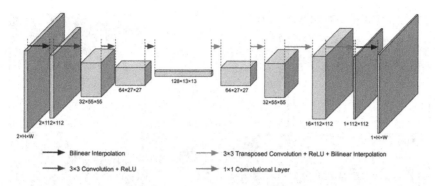

Fig. 4. Fully convolutional architecture for the confidence map subtraction network.

To facilitate multi-person 3D pose tracking, a set of currently tracked persons is kept which are all independently tracked using the prediction (Sect. 3.1) and update (Sect. 3.2) step. However, at each time step we have to check whether one or more untracked persons have entered the 3D recording volume and generate new tracks accordingly. To do so, we first remove currently tracked persons from the confidence maps for each camera using a confidence subtraction network. To remove a tracked person from a confidence map, we project the joints of all samples of that person for the given frame to that camera view (see Fig. 3 (b)). We then pass the projected points as well as the confidence map to the confidence subtraction network which will return an updated confidence map without the peak of the tracked person. Figure 3 shows an example while Fig. 4 details the network structure. We repeat this procedure for all tracked persons and for all camera views.

Once all tracked persons are removed from the confidence maps, we find the remaining local maxima and triangulate them pairwise if both points are close to their respective epipolar line as in [9]. To reduce the number of redundant points, we apply agglomerative hierarchical clustering with threshold ϵ_j and use the mean point of the clusters. We then build a set of 3D pose candidates by greedily matching joints based on the part affinity fields [17]. We also drop limbs that have unreasonable length. Each pose candidate is then scored using Eq. (7), where v contains all camera views, and the 3D pose with the highest score is selected for the new track.

As a person track is represented as a list of 3D pose samples, we utilize a stochastic generation function $z \leftarrow g(\cdot)$ which takes as input the previously selected best 3D pose candidates and generates a set of 3D pose samples z that represent the distribution of the newly generated track. Once the pose samples are generated the person can be tracked using the prediction and update steps. The new pose is removed from the confidence maps and the initialization procedure is repeated until no further person tracks are found.

Fig. 5. Qualitative results from the Campus [6,41] (top row) and Shelf [6] (bottom row) dataset.

Fig. 6. Qualitative results showing the first three hd-cameras of the CMU Panoptic studio [42].

We model g as a three-layer feed-forward Bayesian neural network [36] which takes as input a pose vector and outputs a pose vector. As a person might only be partially visible g also fills in missing joints. This is facilitated by adding a binary vector to the input pose vector which indicates if a joint is missing. As dropout is utilized during inference, g generates a diverse set of 3D pose samples. The network is trained with motion capture data from Human3.6M [39] and from the CMU mocap database [40], similar to Sect. 3.1. During training, random joints are removed from the pose to encourage the model to fill in missing joints. The model has three layers with 2048 hidden units each and is optimized over the Huber loss using SGD with a learning rate of 0.001, weight decay of 10^{-6} and dropout of 75%.

3.4   Inference

Using multiple samples to represent a 3D pose allows for robust tracking. However, when extracting 3D poses a final single pose is required. To obtain a final pose from z_t for a tracked person at frame t, we calculate the weighted average for all samples using Eq. (6) where v contains all cameras.

Table 1. Quantitative comparison with state-of-the-art methods using percentage of correctly estimated parts (PCP) on the Campus and Shelf datasets. *A1* to *A3* represent the three actors while the number in parentheses represents the number of ground-truth frames. We report both actor-wise (*aAvg*) as well as global average (*gAvg*) PCP. Models utilizing temporal information are marked with + while appearance information is marked with *. As our method is probabilistic, we report results as mean ± standard deviation, which is calculated over 10 runs using different random seeds.

	Campus					Shelf				
	A1(48)	A2(188)	A3(136)	aAvg	gAvg	A1(279)	A2(37)	A3(161)	aAvg	gAvg
Belagiannis et al. [6]	82.01	72.43	73.72	76.05	74.14	66.05	64.97	83.16	71.39	71.75
+Belagiannis et al. [7]	83.00	73.00	78.00	78.00	76.12	75.00	67.00	86.00	76.00	78.09
Belagiannis et al. [43]	93.45	75.65	84.37	84.49	81.14	75.26	69.68	87.59	77.51	79.00
Ershadi-Nasab et al. [3]	94.18	92.89	84.62	90.56	90.03	93.29	75.85	94.83	87.99	92.46
Dong et al. [5]	97.40	90.10	89.40	92.30	90.79	97.20	79.50	96.50	91.07	95.59
*Dong et al. [5]	97.60	93.30	98.00	96.30	95.57	98.80	94.10	97.80	96.90	98.10
+Tanke et al. [9]	98.00	91.00	98.00	95.67	94.46	99.21	93.51	97.14	96.62	98.07
+Zhang et al. [4]	-	-	-	-	-	99.00	96.20	97.60	97.60	98.31
+Ours	97.35 ± 0.40	93.44 ± 0.04	97.43 ± 0.18	96.07 ± 0.13	95.40 ± 0.07	99.49 ± 0.06	95.81 ± 0.37	97.83 ± 0.00	97.71 ± 0.13	98.64 ± 0.05

4 Experiments

4.1 Quantitative Comparison

We provide a quantitative comparison to recent state-of-the-art methods using the Campus [6,41] as well as the Shelf [6] dataset. Qualitative results on this datasets can be seen in Fig. 5. As metric we use percentage of correct parts (PCP) in 3D [10] and we adopt the head position alignment utilized in [5] as well as the temporal Gaussian smoothing described in [9]. Furthermore, we report PCP averaged over the actors (aAvg) and PCP averaged over the actors weighted by the number of visible frames (gAvg), which was first discussed in [43]. Weighting by the number of visible frames (gAvg) provides a more accurate measure as it does not overemphasize actors which appear only in very few frames. Table 1 presents our results. For the Shelf dataset we achieve state-of-the-art results while we achieve highly competitive results on the Campus dataset. We argue that the top-down pose estimation model and the appearance model of [5] are beneficial when the full bodies are visible and the scenes are relatively uncluttered, as it is the case with the Campus dataset (Fig. 5 top row). However, in more complex scenes where bodies are only partially visible and with large background clutter and occlusions, such as Shelf, the appearance model does not help as much. Here, temporal information is crucial to recover from occlusions.

Table 2. Tracking scores MOTA [44], precision and recall for sequence 160422_ultimatum1 of the CMU Panoptic Studio [42].

Method	MOTA	Precision	Recall	MOTA	Precision	Recall
	Average			Nose		
Tanke et al. [9]	0.82	91.0	91.1	0.84	91.7	91.8
Ours	**0.87**	**93.3**	**94.1**	**0.94**	**96.6**	**97.5**
	Left Wrist			Right Wrist		
Tanke et al. [9]	0.82	**91.2**	91.3	0.86	**93.0**	93.1
Ours	**0.83**	91.1	**91.9**	0.86	92.6	**93.4**
	Left Foot			Right Foot		
Tanke et al. [9]	0.81	90.5	90.6	0.77	88.6	88.7
Ours	**0.90**	**94.6**	**95.5**	**0.84**	**91.5**	**92.3**

4.2 Tracking

For evaluating the tracking performance of our method, we utilize the MOTA [44] score as well as precision and recall. We cannot evaluate tracking on the Shelf or Campus dataset as some of the ground-truth annotations are missing, which results in a large number of false positives. Instead we evaluate on the CMU Panoptic studio [42], which utilizes the same human pose keypoints [45] as our method and which provides unique identifiers for each person in the scene. We use the sequence 160422_ultimatum1 from frames 300 to 1300 as in [9] since it contains different interacting persons that enter and leave the scene. A sample scene can be seen in Fig. 6. To ensure occlusions, we utilize only the first three hd-cameras and we consider a track as correct if its prediction is within 10 cm of the ground-truth. For measuring the tracking accuracy, we utilize the nose, left/right wrist and left/right foot. Our results are presented in Table 2. We observe that our model significantly outperforms [9] for feet and nose since these keypoints are for some frames only visible in one camera as shown in Fig. 6. Our method can recover these cases.

4.3 Ablation

Our ablation results are presented in Table 3. Removing tracking and only using the pose initialization algorithm described in Sect. 3.3 at each frame results in very strong results for the Shelf dataset while the performance drops significantly for the Campus dataset. The reason for this is that the pose initialization works better when multiple views are present (5 for Shelf, 3 for Campus) while tracking helps when a person is temporally visible in only one or two views. Removing pose resampling during the update step and instead using a fixed set of samples for each camera pair results in a significant performance drop. One of the biggest factors for the strong performance of our method is the joint refinement as the

Table 3. Ablation study using percentage of correctly estimated parts (PCP) on the Campus and Shelf datasets. *A1* to *A3* represent the three actors while the number in parentheses represents the number of ground-truth frames. We report both actor-wise (*aAvg*) as well as global average (*gAvg*) PCP.

	Campus					Shelf				
	A1(48)	A2(188)	A3(136)	aAvg	pAvg	A1(279)	A2(37)	A3(161)	aAvg	pAvg
only Pose Initialization	91.85 ± 1.33	92.94 ± 0.22	69.96 ± 0.95	84.92 ± 0.68	84.40 ± 0.46	99.51 ± 0.14	94.03 ± 0.83	97.69 ± 0.05	97.07 ± 0.31	98.47 ± 0.13
w/o Pose Resampling	87.29 ± 7.86	90.57 ± 0.33	88.27 ± 5.43	88.71 ± 3.74	89.31 ± 2.62	97.47 ± 1.10	88.95 ± 1.40	97.83 ± 0.09	94.75 ± 0.70	96.93 ± 0.70
w/o Joint Refinement	47.33 ± 24.53	74.78 ± 14.91	57.52 ± 5.16	59.88 ± 11.89	64.93 ± 9.81	90.96 ± 1.95	73.11 ± 5.39	91.89 ± 1.92	85.32 ± 2.24	89.89 ± 1.27
w/o Pose Prediction	70.56 ± 12.91	82.93 ± 6.40	73.19 ± 5.22	75.56 ± 4.23	77.77 ± 4.01	99.16 ± 0.04	65.22 ± 11.09	97.73 ± 0.03	87.37 ± 3.70	96.04 ± 0.86
Pose Prediction: $\mathcal{N}(0, 0.01^2)$	75.83 ± 27.52	80.84 ± 6.47	70.49 ± 10.29	75.72 ± 11.99	76.41 ± 8.38	99.12 ± 0.04	69.24 ± 12.09	97.71 ± 0.04	88.69 ± 4.03	96.33 ± 0.94
Pose Prediction: w/o dropout	90.42 ± 0.73	92.12 ± 0.12	97.28 ± 0.15	93.27 ± 0.27	93.79 ± 0.15	99.29 ± 0.04	94.78 ± 1.09	97.76 ± 0.00	97.28 ± 0.37	98.43 ± 0.09
Joint Refinement: Gradient Ascent	96.15 ± 0.10	92.34 ± 0.11	97.13 ± 0.22	95.21 ± 0.07	94.58 ± 0.12	99.40 ± 0.05	93.92 ± 0.68	97.80 ± 0.03	97.04 ± 0.23	98.43 ± 0.07
Proposed	97.35 ± 0.40	93.44 ± 0.04	97.43 ± 0.18	96.07 ± 0.13	95.40 ± 0.07	99.49 ± 0.06	95.81 ± 0.37	97.83 ± 0.00	97.71 ± 0.13	98.64 ± 0.05

sample-based representation of 3D poses does not permit enough samples to accurately represent such high dimensional data. Removing the pose prediction model and just utilizing a zero velocity model also results in a significant performance loss. Replacing the zero-velocity model with a normal distribution for pose prediction does not significantly improve the results. Replacing the heuristic joint refinement algorithm described in Sect. 3.2 with a gradient ascent based algorithm results in a slight performance drop. We argue that the local optimization gets stuck in local optima while the heuristic can jump over them and find even better pose configurations.

4.4 Parameters

The effects of the hyperparameters are shown in Fig. 7. The Dropout rates of both the prediction model and the initialization model g are determined to obtain a reasonable approximation of uncertainty. If it is too small, the uncertainty is underestimated. For large values, the generated samples are too diverse, making the approach inefficient. The number of pose samples is important to ensure a sufficient representation of the pose distribution. However, a too high number of pose samples impedes sometimes the discovery of newly appearing persons and thus degrades the overall quality of the results. The distance threshold ϵ_j of the hierarchical clustering for merging joints influences the quality of the triangulated 3D joint positions to initialize poses. While a high value ϵ_j merges

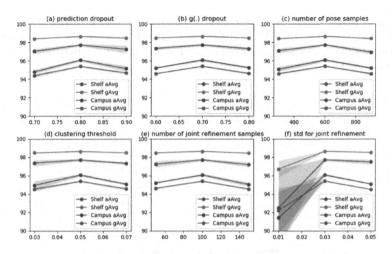

Fig. 7. Evaluation of hyperparameters. PCP is evaluated while varying the hyperparameters. With each setting, the experiments are performed 10 times. The solid line indicates the mean value of the PCP and the colored area is the coverage determined by the standard deviation. (a) The dropout rate of the prediction model. (b) The dropout rate of the model $g(\cdot)$. (c) The number of pose samples. (d) Distance parameter to merge joints using the hierarchical clustering. (e) The number of samples for joint refinement. (f) Standard deviation for joint refinement.

3D joints of different persons, more redundant 3D joints would remain with a lower threshold. Using many samples for joint refinement encourages that each joint is located in regions with high part confidences. When the number is too large, it reduces the variety of the samples which weakens the tracking quality. Similarly, a high standard deviation for the joint refinement allows to search a large 3D space for each joint. If it is too large, the joints might move to the wrong position.

4.5   Runtime Analysis

In Table 4 we compare the runtime of the approach [9] with our approach on the same machine, using an Intel Core i7-7700 3.60 GHz and a Nvidia GeForce 1080ti. We evaluate the runtime on the Shelf dataset, which uses five cameras and which has 2, 3 or 4 persons in the scene. Both [9] and our method are implemented in Python, utilizing the output of the official OpenPose [17] implementation which processes an image in 35 ms. While our approach needs more time than [9] for two actors, the runtime scales better as the number of actors increases. While the runtime of [9] increases quadratically as the number of actors increases, our approach requires 26 ms for each additional actor, i.e. the runtime increases linearly as the number of actors increases.

Table 4. Time analysis for the Shelf dataset with respect to the number of actors. The time for the prediction and update steps of our method are measured with 300 sampled 3D poses per person and 50 sampled points for joint refinement.

	2 Actors	3 Actors	4 Actors
Tanke et al. [9]	0.023 s	0.045 s	0.104 s
Ours	0.062 s	0.088 s	0.114 s

5 Conclusion

In this paper we have presented a novel tracking algorithm based on the well-known recursive Bayesian filtering framework and on recent advancements in 2D human pose estimation and 3D human motion anticipation. Our approach tracks multiple persons, initializes newly appearing persons, and recovers occluded joints. Our approach achieves state-of-the-art results for 3D human pose estimation as well as for 3D human pose tracking. In the future our approach could be extended using an appearance model similar to [5]. Furthermore, we could include a smoothing step which would improve 3D pose predictions backwards through time, utilizing the model uncertainty.

Acknowledgment. The work has been funded by the Deutsche Forschungsgemeinschaft (DFG, German Research Foundation) under Germany's Excellence Strategy - EXC 2070–390732324, GA 1927/8-1, and the ERC Starting Grant ARCA (677650).

References

1. Liu, Y., Stoll, C., Gall, J., Seidel, H.P., Theobalt, C.: Markerless motion capture of interacting characters using multi-view image segmentation. In: Conference on Computer Vision and Pattern Recognition (2011)
2. Liu, Y., Gall, J., Stoll, C., Dai, Q., Seidel, H.P., Theobalt, C.: Markerless motion capture of multiple characters using multiview image segmentation. In: Transactions on Pattern Analysis and Machine Intelligence (2013)
3. Ershadi-Nasab, S., Noury, E., Kasaei, S., Sanaei, E.: Multiple human 3d pose estimation from multiview images. Multimedia Tools and Applications (2018)
4. Zhang, Y., An, L., Yu, T., Li, X., Li, K., Liu, Y.: 4D association graph for real-time multi-person motion capture using multiple video cameras. In: Conference on Computer Vision and Pattern Recognition (2020)
5. Dong, J., Jiang, W., Huang, Q., Bao, H., Zhou, X.: Fast and robust multi-person 3D pose estimation from multiple views. In: Conference on Computer Vision and Pattern Recognition (2019)
6. Belagiannis, V., Amin, S., Andriluka, M., Schiele, B., Navab, N., Ilic, S.: 3D pictorial structures for multiple human pose estimation. In: Conference on Computer Vision and Pattern Recognition (2014)
7. Belagiannis, V., Wang, X., Schiele, B., Fua, P., Ilic, S., Navab, N.: Multiple human pose estimation with temporally consistent 3D pictorial structures. In: European Conference on Computer Vision (2014)

8. Belagiannis, V., Amin, S., Andriluka, M., Schiele, B., Navab, N., Ilic, S.: 3d pictorial structures revisited: Multiple human pose estimation. Transactions on Pattern Analysis and Machine Intelligence (2016)

9. Tanke, J., Gall, J.: Iterative greedy matching for 3d human pose tracking from multiple views. In: German Conference on Pattern Recognition (2019)

10. Burenius, M., Sullivan, J., Carlsson, S.: 3d pictorial structures for multiple view articulated pose estimation. In: Conference on Computer Vision and Pattern Recognition (2013)

11. Kazemi, V., Burenius, M., Azizpour, H., Sullivan, J.: Multi-view body part recognition with random forests. In: British Machine Vision Conference (2013)

12. Zheng, L., Shen, L., Tian, L., Wang, S., Wang, J., Tian, Q.: Scalable person re-identification: a benchmark. In: International Conference on Computer Vision (2015)

13. Särkkä, S.: Bayesian Filtering and Smoothing. Cambridge University Press, Cambridge (2013)

14. Martinez, J., Black, M.J., Romero, J.: On human motion prediction using recurrent neural networks. In: Conference on Computer Vision and Pattern Recognition (2017)

15. Newell, A., Yang, K., Deng, J.: Stacked hourglass networks for human pose estimation. In: European Conference on Computer Vision (2016)

16. Xiao, B., Wu, H., Wei, Y.: Simple baselines for human pose estimation and tracking. In: European conference on Computer Vision (2018)

17. Cao, Z., Simon, T., Wei, S.E., Sheikh, Y.: Realtime multi-person 2D pose estimation using part affinity fields. In: Conference on Computer Vision and Pattern Recognition (2017)

18. Insafutdinov, E., et al.: Arttrack: articulated multi-person tracking in the wild. In: Conference on Computer Vision and Pattern Recognition (2017)

19. Iqbal, U., Milan, A., Gall, J.: Posetrack: joint multi-person pose estimation and tracking. In: Conference on Computer Vision and Pattern Recognition (2017)

20. Doering, A., Rafi, U., Leibe, B., Gall, J.: Multiple human pose estimation with temporally consistent 3d pictorial structures. In: European Conference on Computer Vision (2020)

21. Doering, A., Iqbal, U., Gall, J.: Joint flow: temporal flow fields for multi person tracking. In: British Machine Vision Conference (2018)

22. Martinez, J., Hossain, R., Romero, J., Little, J.J.: A simple yet effective baseline for 3d human pose estimation. In: International Conference on Computer Vision (2017)

23. Iqbal, U., Doering, A., Yasin, H., Krüger, B., Weber, A., Gall, J.: A dual-source approach for 3d human pose estimation from single images. Computer Vision and Image Understanding (2018)

24. Iqbal, U., Molchanov, P., Breuel Juergen Gall, T., Kautz, J.: Hand pose estimation via latent 2.5 d heatmap regression. In: European Conference on Computer Vision (2018)

25. Kostrikov, I., Gall, J.: Depth sweep regression forests for estimating 3d human pose from images. In: British Machine Vision Conference (2014)

26. Mehta, D., et al.: Single-shot multi-person 3d pose estimation from monocular RGB. In: International Conference on 3D Vision (2018)

27. Joo, H., et al.: Panoptic studio: a massively multiview system for social interaction capture. Transactions on Pattern Analysis and Machine Intelligence (2017)

28. Chen, Y., Wang, Z., Peng, Y., Zhang, Z., Yu, G., Sun, J.: Cascaded pyramid network for multi-person pose estimation. In: Conference on Computer Vision and Pattern Recognition (2018)
29. Deutscher, J., Reid, I.: Articulated body motion capture by stochastic search. Int. J. Comput. Vis. (2005)
30. Gall, J., Rosenhahn, B., Brox, T., Seidel, H.P.: Optimization and filtering for human motion capture. Int. J. Comput. Vis. (2010)
31. Yao, A., Gall, J., Gool, L.V., Urtasun, R.: Learning probabilistic non-linear latent variable models for tracking complex activities. In: Advances in Neural Information Processing Systems (2011)
32. Holden, D., Saito, J., Komura, T.: A deep learning framework for character motion synthesis and editing. Transactions on Graphics (2016)
33. Bütepage, J., Black, M.J., Kragic, D., Kjellstrom, H.: Deep representation learning for human motion prediction and classification. In: Conference on Computer Vision and Pattern Recognition (2017)
34. Jain, A., Zamir, A.R., Savarese, S., Saxena, A.: Structural-RNN: deep learning on spatio-temporal graphs. In: Conference on Computer Vision and Pattern Recognition (2016)
35. Fragkiadaki, K., Levine, S., Felsen, P., Malik, J.: Recurrent network models for human dynamics. In: International Conference on Computer Vision (2015)
36. Gal, Y., Ghahramani, Z.: Dropout as a bayesian approximation: representing model uncertainty in deep learning. In: International Conference on Machine Learning (2016)
37. Cao, Z., Hidalgo Martinez, G., Simon, T., Wei, S., Sheikh, Y.A.: Openpose: real-time multi-person 2d pose estimation using part affinity fields. In: Transactions on Pattern Analysis and Machine Intelligence (2019)
38. Muñoz-Salinas, R., Medina-Carnicer, R., Madrid-Cuevas, F.J., Carmona-Poyato, A.: Particle filtering with multiple and heterogeneous cameras. In: Pattern Recognition (2010)
39. Ionescu, C., Papava, D., Olaru, V., Sminchisescu, C.: Human3.6m: large scale datasets and predictive methods for 3d human sensing in natural environments. Transactions on Pattern Analysis and Machine Intelligence (2014)
40. CMU Mocap Database. http://mocap.cs.cmu.edu/ (0)
41. Fleuret, F., Berclaz, J., Lengagne, R., Fua, P.: Multicamera people tracking with a probabilistic occupancy map. Pattern Analysis and Machine Intelligence (2007)
42. Joo, H., Liu, H., Tan, L., Gui, L., Nabbe, B., Matthews, I., Kanade, T., Nobuhara, S., Sheikh, Y.: Panoptic studio: A massively multiview system for social motion capture. In: International Conference on Computer Vision (2015)
43. Belagiannis, V., Amin, S., Andriluka, M., Schiele, B., Navab, N., Ilic, S.: 3d pictorial structures revisited: multiple human pose estimation. Transactions on Pattern Analysis and Machine Intelligence (2015)
44. Bernardin, K., Elbs, A., Stiefelhagen, R.: Multiple object tracking performance metrics and evaluation in a smart room environment. In: International Workshop on Visual Surveillance (2006)
45. Lin, T.Y., et al.: Microsoft coco: common objects in context. In: European Conference on Computer Vision (2014)

Adversarial Refinement Network for Human Motion Prediction

Xianjin Chao[1]($\boxtimes$)(iD), Yanrui Bin[2](iD), Wenqing Chu[3], Xuan Cao[3], Yanhao Ge[3],
Chengjie Wang[3], Jilin Li[3], Feiyue Huang[3], and Howard Leung[1](iD)

[1] City University of Hong Kong, Hong Kong, China
xjchao2-c@my.cityu.edu.hk, howard@cityu.edu.hk
[2] Key Laboratory of Image Processing and Intelligent Control, School of Artificial
Intelligence and Automation, Huazhong University of Science and Technology,
Wuhan, China
yrbin@hust.edu.cn
[3] Tencent Youtu Lab, Shanghai, China
{wenqingchu,marscao,halege,jasoncjwang,jerolinli,garyhuang}@tencent.com

Abstract. Human motion prediction aims to predict future 3D skeletal sequences by giving a limited human motion as inputs. Two popular methods, recurrent neural networks and feed-forward deep networks, are able to predict rough motion trend, but motion details such as limb movement may be lost. To predict more accurate future human motion, we propose an Adversarial Refinement Network (ARNet) following a simple yet effective coarse-to-fine mechanism with novel adversarial error augmentation. Specifically, we take both the historical motion sequences and coarse prediction as input of our cascaded refinement network to predict refined human motion and strengthen the refinement network with adversarial error augmentation. During training, we deliberately introduce the error distribution by learning through the adversarial mechanism among different subjects. In testing, our cascaded refinement network alleviates the prediction error from the coarse predictor resulting in a finer prediction robustly. This adversarial error augmentation provides rich error cases as input to our refinement network, leading to better generalization performance on the testing dataset. We conduct extensive experiments on three standard benchmark datasets and show that our proposed ARNet outperforms other state-of-the-art methods, especially on challenging aperiodic actions in both short-term and long-term predictions.

1 Introduction

Given the observed human 3D skeletal sequences, the goal of human motion prediction is to predict plausible and consecutive future human motion which convey abundant clues about the person's intention, emotion and identity.

Electronic supplementary material The online version of this chapter (https://doi.org/10.1007/978-3-030-69532-3_28) contains supplementary material, which is available to authorized users.

H. Ishikawa et al. (Eds.): ACCV 2020, LNCS 12623, pp. 454–469, 2021.
https://doi.org/10.1007/978-3-030-69532-3_28

Effectively predicting the human motion plays an important role in wide visual computing applications such as human-machine interfaces [1], smart surveillance [2], virtual reality [3], healthcare applications [4], autonomous driving [5] and visual human-object tracking [6]. However, predicting plausible future human motion is a very challenging task due to the non-linear and highly spatial-temporal dependencies of human body parts during movements [7]. Considering the time-series property of human motion sequence, recent deep learning based methods formulated the human motion prediction task as a sequence-to-sequence problem and achieved remarkable progresses by using chain-structured Recurrent Neural Networks (RNNs) to capture the temporal dependencies frame-by-frame among motion sequence. However, recent literature [8] indicated that the chain-structured RNNs suffer from error accumulation in temporal modeling and deficiency in spatial dynamic description, leading to problems such as imprecise pose and mean pose in motion prediction.

Feed-forward deep networks [9] are regarded as alternative solutions for human motion prediction task by learning rich representation from all input motion sequences at once. The holistic reasoning of the human motion sequences leads to more consecutive and plausible predictions than chain-structured RNNs.

Unfortunately, current feed-forward deep networks adopt singe-stage architecture and tend to generate the predicted motion coarsely thus yielding unsatisfactory performance, especially for complex aperiodic actions (e.g., Direction or Greeting in H3.6m dataset). The reason is that it is difficult to guide the network to focus more on detailed information when directly predicting the future human motion from limited input information.

To address the above issues, we propose a novel Adversarial Refinement Network (ARNet) which resorts to a coarse-to-fine framework. We decompose the human motion prediction problem into two stages: coarse motion prediction and finer motion refinement. By joint reasoning of the input-output space of the coarse predictor, we achieve to take both the historical motion sequences and coarse future prediction as input not just one-sided information to polish the challenging human motion prediction task. The coarse-to-fine design allows the refinement module to concentrate on the complete motion trend brought by the historical input and coarse prediction, which are ignored in previous feed-forward deep networks used for human motion prediction.

Given different actions performed by diverse persons fed to the refinement network in training and testing, the coarse prediction results tend to be influenced by generalization error, which makes it difficult for the refinement network to obtain the fine prediction robustly. We therefore enhance the refinement network with adversarial error distribution augmentation. During training, we deliberately introduce the error distribution by learning through the adversarial mechanism among different subjects based on the coarse prediction. In testing, our cascaded refinement network alleviates the prediction error from the coarse predictor resulting in a finer prediction. Our adversarial component acts as regularization to let our network refine the coarse prediction well. Different from the previous work [10] which casts the predictor as a generator and introduces discriminator to validate the prediction results, our adversarial training strategy aims to generate error distribution which acts as implicit regularization for better refinement instead of directly generating the skeleton data as prediction. The error augmentation is achieved by a pair of adversarial learning based generator and discriminator.

Consequently, the proposed ARNet achieves state-of-the-art results on several standard human motion prediction benchmarks over diverse actions categories, especially over the complicated aperiodic actions as shown in Fig. 2.

Our contributions are summarized as follows:

- We propose a coarse-to-fine framework to decompose the difficult prediction problem into coarse prediction task and refinement task for more accurate human motion prediction.
- We design an adversarial learning strategy to produce reasonable error distribution rather than random noise to optimize the refinement network.
- The proposed method is comprehensively evaluated on multiple challenging benchmark datasets and outperforms state-of-the-art methods especially on complicated aperiodic actions.

2   Related Work

2.1   Human Motion Prediction

With the emergence of large scale open human motion capture (mocap) datasets, exploring different deep learning architectures to improve human motion prediction performance on diverse actions has become a new trend. Due to the inherent temporal-series nature of motion sequence, the chain-structured Recurrent Neural Networks (RNNs) are natively suitable to process motion sequences. The Encoder-Recurrent-Decoder (ERD) model [11] simultaneously learned the representations and dynamics of human motion. The spatial-temporal graph is later employed in [12] to construct the Structural-RNNs (SRNN) model for human motion prediction. The residual connections in RNN model (RRNN) [13] helped the decoder model prior knowledge of input human motion. Tang et al. [8] adopted the global attention and Modified Highway Unit (MHU) to explore motion contexts for long-term dependencies modeling. However, these chain-structured RNNs suffer from either frozen mean pose problems or unnatural motion in predicted sequences because of the weakness of RNNs in both long-term temporal memory and spatial structure description. Feed-forward deep network as an emerging framework has shown the superiority over chain-structured RNNs. Instead of processing input frame by frame like chain-structured RNNs, feed-forward deep networks feed all the frames at once, which is a promising alternative for feature extraction to guarantee the integrity and smoothness of long-term temporal information in human motion prediction [8]. In this paper, our ARNet is on the basis of feed-forward deep network.

2.2   Prediction Refinement

Refinement approaches learn good feature representation from the coarse results in output space and infer the precise location of joints in a further step by recovering from the previous error, which have achieved promisingly improvement in human pose related work. Multi-stage refinement network [14] associated the coarse pose estimation and refinement in one go to improve the accuracy of 3D human pose estimation by jointly processing the belief maps of 2D joints and projected 3D joints as the inputs to the next stage. Cascaded Pyramid Network (CPN) [15] introduced refinement after the pyramid feature network for sufficient context information mining to handle the occluded and invisible joints estimation problems. Another trend of refinement mechanism performed coarse pose estimation and refinement separately. PoseRefiner [16] refined the given pose estimation by modelling hard pose cases. Posefix [17] proposed an independent pose refinement network for arbitrary human pose estimator and refined the predicted keypoints based on error statistics prior. Patch-based refinement [18] utilised the retain fine details from body part patches to improve the accuracy of 3D pose estimation. In contrast to the previous work, we further adopt the benefits of refinement network to deal with the problems in 3D human motion prediction via a creative coarse-to-fine manner.

2.3   Adversarial Learning

Inspired by the minimax mechanism of Generative Adversarial Networks (GANs) [19], adversarial learning has been widely adopted to train neural networks [20–22]. Several attempts have been proposed to perform data augmentation in the way of adversarial learning, which mainly rely on the pixel manipulation through image synthesis [23] or a serious of specific image operations [24]. The adversarial learning based data augmentation shows powerful potential for model performance improvement. In [25], the results of image recognition achieved promising improvement due to the image synthesis data augmentation. In human motion prediction, [10] adopted a predictor with two discriminators to keep the fidelity and continuity of human motion predicted sequences by adversarial training. In this work, we introduce an online data augmentation scheme in the motion space to improve generalization and optimize the refinement network.

3   Methodology

3.1   Overall Framework

The overall framework of our ARNet is shown in Fig. 1. The coarse-to-fine module consists of a coarse predictor $\mathcal{P}$ and a refinement network $\mathcal{R}$. In the context of human motion prediction, given N frames of observed human motion at once, the coarse predictor $\mathcal{P}$ aims to forecast the following T frames of human motion. The input human motion sequences $X = \{x_1, x_2, ..., x_n\}$ are first fed into the predictor $\mathcal{P}$ to obtain coarse future human motion $Y = \{y_1, y_2, ..., y_n\}$, where

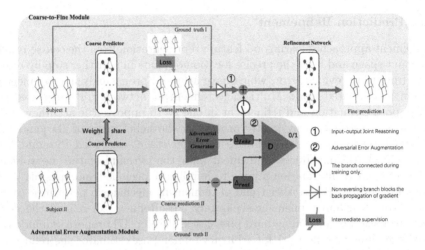

Fig. 1. The overall framework of our ARNet. The proposed coarse-to-fine module consists of coarse predictor and refinement network as shown in the top part. The bottom part illustrates the dedicated adversarial error augmentation module which consists of coarse predictor with a pair of error generator and discriminator. The observed human motion sequence of Subject I and Subject II are separately fed to the weight-shared coarse predictors to obtain corresponding coarse human motion prediction. Then the generator in the adversarial error augmentation module adopts the coarse prediction of Subject I as the conditional information to generate fake motion error of Subject II in an adversarial manner. After that, the augmented error distribution and the real coarse prediction are both utilised to optimize the refinement network for fine human motion prediction

$x_i, y_i \in \mathbb{R}^K$ are K dimensional joint features represented as exponential map of joint angle in each frame. Then in the adversarial error augmentation module, we adopt a pair of generator and discriminator to produce fake motion error calculated from the coarse prediction from a person (subject I) and the real motion error from another person (subject II) as the conditional information for the next stage fine prediction.

During training, we deliberately introduce the error distribution by learning through the adversarial mechanism among different subjects based on the coarse prediction. In testing, our cascaded refinement network alleviates the prediction error from the coarse predictor resulting in a finer prediction.

3.2   Refinement Network

Given the input motion sequence, we adopt a Graph Convolutional Network (GCN) [26,27], a popular feed-forward deep network which is specialized in dealing with the graph structured data, to initially model the spatial-temporal dependencies among the human poses and obtain the coarse human motion prediction. We construct a K nodes graph $G = (V, E)$, where $V = \{v_i | i = 1, ..., K\}$

denotes the node set and $E = \{e_{i,j} | i, j = 1, ..., K\}$ denotes the edge set. The main idea of Graph Convolutional Network is that, each d dimensional node representations $H_v^l \in \mathbb{R}^d$ is updated by feature aggregation of all its neighbors defined by the weighted adjacency matrix $A^l \in \mathbb{R}^{K \times K}$ on the l-th Graph Convolutional layer. Therefore, the spatial structure relationships between the nodes could be fully encoded and the l-th Graph Convolution layer outputs a $K \times d$ matrix $H^{l+1} \in \mathbb{R}^d$:

$$H^{l+1} = \sigma(A^l H^l W^l) \tag{1}$$

where $\sigma(\cdot)$ denotes an activation function and $W^l \in \mathbb{R}^{d \times \hat{d}}$ denotes the trainable weight matrix. The network architecture of our predictor is similar to [9], which is the state-of-the-art feed-forward baseline on human motion prediction.

In order to improve the human motion prediction performance in a further step, we construct a coarse-to-fine framework, which cascades N-stage refinement network on top of the preliminary predictor, to process the complete future information of the output from human motion predictor iteratively. Given the input human motion sequences H_I, we initially obtain the coarse human motion prediction sequences $H_P = f_p(H_I)$ from the preliminary predictor and forward the fusion of historical and future sequences as the inputs to the refinement network. As a result, we output the final refined human motion prediction sequences by error correction of initially coarse prediction $H_R = f_r(H_P + H_I)$.

3.3   Adversarial Learning Enhanced Refinement Network

Considering that the human motion sequences collected by different actors in datasets contain variations, especially for complicated aperiodic actions, various error scenarios will occur. To improve the error-correction ability and robustness of our refinement network, we additionally introduce an adversarial learning mechanism to generate challenging error cases which are fed to the refinement network together with the coarse prediction. We randomly choose 1 person's actions sequences (Subject II) from the 6 subjects' actions sequences in the training dataset and feed it to the predictor in another branch to get the independent coarse prediction sequences for every epoch as shown in Fig. 1. Then the real error is able to be computed from this person's coarse prediction sequences and the corresponding ground-truth. To augment this person's error cases to the other 5 people, we utilise a generator that produces fake human motion error to fool the discriminator. The discriminator constantly tries to distinguish between real error cases and fake error cases so as to transfer different persons' error to other subjects in the mocap dataset. This augmentation provides rich error cases as input to our refinement network, leading to better generalization performance on the testing dataset.

We train the networks following the standard GAN pipeline. During training, the adversarial error generator generates error bias which will be added on the coarse prediction and then fed to refinement network. The adversarial refinement network effectively learns from the coarse prediction with adversarial error augmentation. During testing, the coarse prediction without added error is fed directly to the adversarial refinement network and get finer prediction as final results.

3.4 Training Loss

In this section, we describe the training loss functions for different modules. Notably, in order to achieve joint reasoning of the input-output space of the coarse predictor, our ARNet defines the loss function in predictor and refinement network separately to achieve simultaneous supervision. Following [9], we optimize the coarse predictor network parameters with the mean-squared loss, which is denoted as the prediction loss $\mathcal{L}_\mathcal{P}$. Suppose K is the number of joints in each frame, N is the number of input frames and T is the number of predicted frames, then $\mathcal{L}_\mathcal{P}$ can be written as:

$$\mathcal{L}_\mathcal{P} = \frac{1}{(N+T)K} \sum_{n=1}^{N+T} \sum_{k=1}^{K} ||h'_{k,n} - h_{k,n}|| \tag{2}$$

where $h_{k,n}$ and $h'_{k,n}$ respectively represent the ground-truth and predicted joint k in frame n.

For the refinement network to produce the refined human motion sequences, we also adopt the mean-squared loss to optimize the network parameters. The mean-squared loss $\mathcal{L}_\mathcal{R}$ can be written as:

$$\mathcal{L}_\mathcal{R} = \frac{1}{(N+T)K} \sum_{n=1}^{N+T} \sum_{k=1}^{K} ||h''_{k,n} - h_{k,n}|| \tag{3}$$

where $h_{k,n}$ indicates the ground-truth joint in frame n, $h''_{k,n}$ is the refined corresponding joint. Our refiner is trained by minimizing the loss function.

The goal of our refinement network is to refine the coarse human motion prediction by utilizing the sequence-level refinement with the adversarial learning based error distribution augmentation. We utilise the minimax mechanism of adversarial loss to train the GAN:

$$\mathcal{L}_\mathcal{D} = \boldsymbol{E}[log\mathcal{D}(\delta_{real})] + \boldsymbol{E}[log(1 - \mathcal{D}(\mathcal{G}(\delta_{fake}))] \tag{4}$$

$$\mathcal{L}_\mathcal{G} = \boldsymbol{E}[log(1 - \mathcal{D}(\mathcal{G}(\delta_{fake}))] \tag{5}$$

where $\mathcal{L}_\mathcal{D}$ denotes the discriminator loss, $\mathcal{L}_\mathcal{G}$ is the generator loss, and $\boldsymbol{\delta}$ represents the error distribution.

In summary, we gather the predictor and refinement network together to train the whole network in an end-to-end way. As we adopt the adversarial refinement network behind the coarse predictor, the objective function consists of two parts:

$$\mathcal{L} = \mathcal{L}_\mathcal{P} + s * \mathcal{L}_\mathcal{R} \tag{6}$$

where $\mathcal{L}_\mathcal{P}$ denotes the prediction loss, $\mathcal{L}_\mathcal{R}$ denotes the refinement loss, and the number of refinement stage s used in our adversarial refinement network will be shown in the ablation studies.

4   Experiments

4.1   Datasets and Evaluation Metrics

H3.6m Dataset. Human 3.6 Million (H3.6m) dataset [28] is the largest and most challenging mocap dataset which has 15 different daily actions performed by 7 males and females, including not only simple periodic actions such as walking and eating, but also complex aperiodic actions such as discussion and purchase. Following previous methods [9,29], the proposed algorithm is trained on subject 1, 6, 7, 8, 9, 11 and tested on subject 5. There are 25 frames per second and each frame consists of a skeleton of 32 joints. Except for removing the global translations and rotations, some of the joints that do not move (*i.e.*, joints that do not bend) will be ignored as previous work [9].

CMU-Mocap Dataset. To be more convincing, we also conduct experiments on the CMU-Mocap dataset [29]. In order to achieve fair comparisons, we employ the same experimental settings as [9,29], including the pre-processing, data representation and training/testing splits.

3DPW Dataset. Recently, the 3D Pose in the Wild dataset (3DPW) [30] is released which contains around 51k frames with 3D annotations. The dataset is challenging as the scenarios are composed of indoor and outdoor activities. We follow [9,30] to split the dataset for comparable experimental results.

Evaluation Metrics. In order to make fair and comprehensive comparisons with previous work, we adopt the Mean Angle Error (MAE) between the predicted frames and the ground-truth frames in the angle space as the quantitative evaluation and visualize the prediction as the qualitative evaluation, which are the common evaluation metrics in human motion prediction [9].

4.2   Implementation Details

The proposed algorithm is implemented on Pytorch [31] and trained on a NVIDIA Tesla V100 GPU. We adopted the Adam [32] optimizer to train our model for about 50 epochs. The learning rate was set to 0.002 and the batch size was 256. To tackle the long-term temporal memory problems, we encode the complete time series by using Discrete Cosine Transform (DCT) [33] and discard the high-frequency jittering to maintain complete expression and smooth consistency of temporal domain information [9] at one time.

4.3   Quantitative Comparisons

We conduct quantitative comparisons on three human mocap datasets including H3.6m, 3DPW and CMU-Mocap between our ARNet and the state-of-the-art baselines. For fair comparisons with previous work [9,10,13,29,34], we feed 10 frames as inputs to predict the future 10 frames (400 ms) for short-term prediction and the future 25 frames (1000 ms) for long-term prediction.

Table 1. Short-term (80 ms, 160 ms, 320 ms, 400 ms) human motion prediction measured in mean angle error (MAE) over 15 actions on H3.6m dataset

Milliseconds	Walking				Eating				Smoking				Discussion			
	80	160	320	400	80	160	320	400	80	160	320	400	80	160	320	400
Zero-velocity [13]	0.39	0.68	0.99	1.15	0.27	0.48	0.73	0.86	0.26	0.48	0.97	0.95	0.31	0.67	0.94	1.04
Residual sup. [13]	0.28	0.49	0.72	0.81	0.23	0.39	0.62	0.76	0.33	0.61	1.05	1.15	0.31	0.68	1.01	1.09
convSeq2Seq [29]	0.33	0.54	0.68	0.73	0.22	0.36	0.58	0.71	0.26	0.49	0.96	0.92	0.32	0.67	0.94	1.01
Retrospec [34]	0.28	0.45	0.62	0.68	0.21	0.34	0.53	0.68	0.26	0.50	0.96	0.93	0.29	0.64	0.90	0.96
AGED [10]	0.22	0.36	0.55	0.67	0.17	**0.28**	0.51	0.64	0.27	0.43	**0.82**	0.84	0.27	0.56	**0.76**	**0.83**
LTraiJ [9]	**0.18**	**0.31**	**0.49**	0.56	**0.16**	0.29	0.50	0.62	**0.22**	**0.41**	0.86	**0.80**	**0.20**	**0.51**	0.77	0.85
ARNet (Ours)	**0.18**	**0.31**	**0.49**	**0.55**	**0.16**	**0.28**	**0.49**	**0.61**	**0.22**	0.42	0.86	0.81	**0.20**	**0.51**	0.81	0.89
Milliseconds	Direction				Greeting				Phoning				Posing			
	80	160	320	400	80	160	320	400	80	160	320	400	80	160	320	400
Zero-velocity [13]	0.39	0.59	0.79	0.89	0.54	0.89	1.30	1.49	0.64	1.21	1.65	1.83	0.28	0.57	1.13	1.37
Residual sup. [13]	0.26	0.47	0.72	0.84	0.75	1.17	1.74	1.83	0.23	0.43	0.69	0.82	0.36	0.71	1.22	1.48
convSeq2Seq [29]	0.39	0.60	0.80	0.91	0.51	0.82	1.21	1.38	0.59	1.13	1.51	1.65	0.29	0.60	1.12	1.37
Retrospec [34]	0.40	0.61	0.77	0.86	0.52	0.86	1.26	1.43	0.59	1.11	1.47	1.59	0.26	0.54	1.14	1.41
AGED [10]	**0.23**	**0.39**	**0.63**	**0.69**	0.56	0.81	1.30	1.46	**0.19**	**0.34**	**0.50**	**0.68**	0.31	0.58	1.12	1.34
LTraiJ [9]	0.26	0.45	0.71	0.79	0.36	0.60	0.95	1.13	0.53	1.02	1.35	1.48	0.19	0.44	1.01	1.24
ARNet (Ours)	**0.23**	0.43	0.65	0.75	**0.32**	**0.55**	**0.90**	**1.09**	0.51	0.99	1.28	1.40	**0.17**	**0.43**	**0.97**	**1.20**
Milliseconds	Purchases				Sitting				Sitting Down				Taking Photo			
	80	160	320	400	80	160	320	400	80	160	320	400	80	160	320	400
Zero-velocity [13]	0.62	0.88	1.19	1.27	0.40	1.63	1.02	1.18	0.39	0.74	1.07	1.19	0.25	0.51	0.79	0.92
Residual sup. [13]	0.51	0.97	1.07	1.16	0.41	1.05	1.49	1.63	0.39	0.81	1.40	1.62	0.24	0.51	0.90	1.05
convSeq2Seq [29]	0.63	0.91	1.19	1.29	0.39	0.61	1.02	1.18	0.41	0.78	1.16	1.31	0.23	0.49	0.88	1.06
Retrospec [34]	0.59	0.84	1.14	1.19	0.40	0.64	1.04	1.22	0.41	0.77	1.14	1.29	0.27	0.52	0.80	0.92
AGED [10]	0.46	0.78	1.01	**1.07**	0.41	0.76	1.05	1.19	0.33	0.62	0.98	1.10	0.23	0.48	0.81	0.95
LTraiJ [9]	0.43	0.65	1.05	1.13	0.29	0.45	**0.80**	**0.97**	0.30	**0.61**	0.90	1.00	0.14	0.34	0.58	0.70
ARNet (Ours)	**0.36**	**0.60**	**1.00**	1.11	**0.27**	**0.44**	0.80	**0.97**	**0.29**	0.61	**0.87**	**0.97**	**0.13**	**0.33**	**0.55**	**0.67**
Milliseconds	Waiting				Walking Dog				Walking Together				Average			
	80	160	320	400	80	160	320	400	80	160	320	400	80	160	320	400
Zero-velocity [13]	0.34	0.67	1.22	1.47	0.60	0.98	1.36	1.50	0.33	0.66	0.94	0.99	0.40	0.78	1.07	1.21
Residual sup. [13]	0.28	0.53	1.02	1.14	0.56	0.91	1.26	1.40	0.31	0.58	0.87	0.91	0.36	0.67	1.02	1.15
convSeq2Seq [29]	0.30	0.62	1.09	1.30	0.59	1.00	1.32	1.44	0.27	0.52	0.71	0.74	0.38	0.68	1.01	1.13
Retrospec [34]	0.33	0.65	1.12	1.30	0.53	0.87	1.16	1.33	0.28	0.52	0.68	0.71	0.37	0.66	0.98	1.10
AGED [10]	0.24	0.50	1.02	**1.13**	0.50	0.81	1.15	**1.27**	0.23	0.41	0.56	0.62	0.31	0.54	0.85	0.97
LTraiJ [9]	0.23	0.50	0.91	1.14	0.46	0.79	1.12	1.29	0.15	0.34	**0.52**	**0.57**	0.27	0.51	0.83	0.95
ARNet (Ours)	**0.22**	**0.48**	**0.90**	1.13	**0.45**	**0.78**	1.11	1.27	**0.13**	**0.33**	0.53	0.58	**0.25**	**0.49**	**0.80**	**0.92**

Short-Term Prediction on H3.6m. H3.6m is the most challenging dataset for human motion prediction. Table 1 shows the quantitative comparisons for short-term human motion prediction between our ARNet and a series of baselines including Zero-velocity [13], RRNN [13], convSeq2Seq [29], Retrospec [34], AGED [10] and LTraiJ [9] on H3.6m dataset. We computed the mean angle error (MAE) on 15 actions by measuring the euclidean distance between the ground-truth and prediction at 80 ms, 160 ms, 320 ms, 400 ms for short-term evaluation. The results in bold show that our method outperforms both of the state-of-the-art chain-structured baseline AGED and the feed-forward baseline LTraiJ.

Compared with the state-of-the-art feed-forward baseline LTraiJ [9], in Table 1, the proposed ARNet clearly outperforms the feed-forward baseline LTraiJ on average for short-term human motion prediction. Different from LTraiJ which adopts the single-stage predictor without refinement network, our ARNet obtains better performance especially on aperiodic actions (e.g. Directions, Greeting, Phoning and so on). It is difficult to model this type of actions which involved multiple small movements and high acceleration during human motion especially at the end of human limbs. In addition, due to the stable change of periodic behavior, the traditional feed-forward deep network can also achieve competitive results on periodic actions (such as walking, eating and smoking), but we note that our ARNet further improves the accuracy of prediction. The results validate that the coarse-to-fine design enables our ARNet to correct the error joints in human motion prediction and outperform the existing feed-forward baseline on almost all actions.

Compared with the state-of-the-art chain-structured baseline AGED [10], which utilises chain-structured RNNs as the predictor with two different discriminators, our ARNet still outperforms it on almost all action categories for short-term human motion prediction within 400 ms as shown in Table 1. The results show the superiority of our ARNet over the best performing chain-structured methods for short-term human motion prediction tasks.

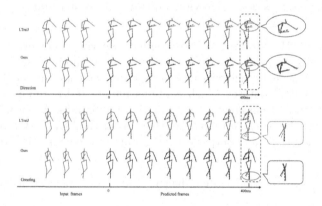

Fig. 2. Visual comparisons for short-term human motion prediction on H3.6m dataset. We compare our proposed ARNet with the state-of-the-art feed-forward baseline LTraiJ [9] which is the best performing method for short-term prediction (400 ms). The left few frames represent the input human motion sequence. From top to bottom, we show the final predictions obtained by the feed-forward baseline LTraiJ represented as green-purple skeletons and our proposed ARNet represented as red-blue skeletons respectively on two challenging a period actions (e.g., Direction and Greeting). Marked in red circles, our predictions better match the ground-truth shown as the gray dotted skeletons (Color figure online)

Table 2. Long-term (560 ms, 1000 ms) human motion prediction on H3.6m dataset

Milliseconds	Walking		Eating		Smoking		Discussion		Average	
	560	1000	560	1000	560	1000	560	1000	560	1000
Zero-velocity [13]	1.35	1.32	1.04	1.38	1.02	1.69	1.41	1.96	1.21	1.59
Residual sup. [13]	0.93	1.03	0.95	1.08	1.25	1.50	1.43	1.69	1.14	1.33
AGED [10]	0.78	0.91	0.86	**0.93**	1.06	**1.21**	**1.25**	**1.30**	0.99	**1.09**
Retrospec [34]	NA	0.79	NA	1.16	NA	1.71	NA	1.72	NA	1.35
LTraiJ [9]	**0.65**	**0.67**	0.76	1.12	0.87	1.57	1.33	1.70	0.90	1.27
ARNet (Ours)	**0.65**	0.69	**0.72**	1.07	**0.86**	1.51	**1.25**	1.68	**0.88**	1.24

Long-Term Prediction on H3.6m. Additionly, we also quantitatively evaluate the long-term prediction performance of our proposed ARNet at 560 ms and 1000 ms as shown in Table 2. The results measured in MAE demonstrate that our method still outperforms the state-of-art feed-forward baseline LTraiJ [9] in long-term human motion prediction on almost action categories as shown in bold. Nevertheless, the MAE of the chain-structured AGED [10] is lower than ours in 1000 ms. We will further examine the results by visualizing the motion sequences obtained by our proposed ARNet and the chain-structured baseline AGED in the later section to provide a qualitative comparison.

3DPW and CMU-Mocap. We also conduct experiments on other two human mocap datasets to prove the robustness of our method. Table 3 shows that our method consistently achieves promising improvements compared with other baselines on 3DPW dataset which contains indoor and outdoor activities for both short-term and long-term human motion predictions. As for CMU-Mocap dataset, the results in Table 4 illustrate that our method has better performance on almost action types and outperforms the state-of-the-art methods on average.

Table 3. Short-term and long-term human motion predictions on 3DPW dataset

Milliseconds	200	400	600	800	1000
Residual sup. [13]	1.85	2.37	2.46	2.51	2.53
convSeq2Seq [29]	1.24	1.85	2.13	2.23	2.26
LTraiJ [9]	0.64	**0.95**	1.12	1.22	1.27
ARNet (Ours)	**0.62**	**0.95**	**1.11**	**1.20**	**1.25**

4.4 Qualitative Visualizations

Short-Term Prediction on H3.6m. To evaluate our method qualitatively, we firstly visualize the representative comparisons on Directions and Greeting

Table 4. Short-term and long-term human motion predictions on CMU-Mocap dataset

Milliseconds	Basketball					Basketball Signal					Directing Traffic				
	80	160	320	400	1000	80	160	320	400	1000	80	160	320	400	1000
Residual sup. [13]	0.50	0.80	1.27	1.45	1.78	0.41	0.76	1.32	1.54	2.15	0.33	0.59	0.93	1.10	2.05
convSeq2Seq [29]	0.37	0.62	1.07	1.18	1.95	0.32	0.59	1.04	1.24	1.96	0.25	0.56	0.89	1.00	2.04
LTraiJ [9]	0.33	0.52	0.89	**1.06**	**1.71**	0.11	0.20	0.41	0.53	1.00	0.15	0.32	0.52	0.60	2.00
ARNet (Ours)	**0.31**	**0.48**	**0.87**	1.08	**1.71**	**0.10**	**0.17**	**0.35**	**0.48**	**1.06**	**0.13**	**0.28**	**0.47**	**0.58**	**1.80**
Milliseconds	Jumping					Running					Soccer				
	80	160	320	400	1000	80	160	320	400	1000	80	160	320	400	1000
Residual sup. [13]	0.33	0.50	0.66	0.75	1.00	0.29	0.51	0.88	0.99	1.72	0.56	0.88	1.77	2.02	2.4
convSeq2Seq [29]	**0.28**	**0.41**	**0.52**	**0.57**	**0.67**	0.26	0.44	0.75	0.87	1.56	0.39	0.6	1.36	1.56	2.01
LTraiJ [9]	0.33	0.55	0.73	0.74	0.95	0.18	0.29	0.61	0.71	1.40	0.31	0.49	1.23	1.39	1.80
ARNet (Ours)	0.30	0.50	0.60	0.61	0.72	**0.16**	**0.26**	**0.57**	**0.67**	**1.22**	**0.29**	**0.47**	1.21	**1.38**	**1.70**
Milliseconds	Walking					Washwindow					Average				
	80	160	320	400	1000	80	160	320	400	1000	80	160	320	400	1000
Residual sup. [13]	0.35	0.47	0.60	0.65	0.88	0.30	0.46	0.72	0.91	1.36	0.38	0.62	1.02	1.18	1.67
convSeq2Seq [29]	0.35	0.44	0.45	0.50	0.78	0.30	0.47	0.80	1.01	1.39	0.32	0.52	0.86	0.99	1.55
LTraiJ [9]	0.33	0.45	0.49	0.53	0.61	0.22	0.33	0.57	0.75	1.20	0.25	0.39	0.68	0.79	1.33
ARNet (Ours)	**0.32**	**0.41**	**0.39**	**0.41**	**0.56**	**0.20**	**0.27**	**0.51**	**0.69**	**1.07**	**0.23**	**0.37**	**0.65**	**0.77**	**1.29**

which belong to challenging aperiodic actions in H3.6m dataset as shown in Fig. 2. Given 10 observed frames for each action as motion seeds, which are represented as green-purple skeletons at the left part, we compare our ARNet represented as red-blue skeletons with the best quantitatively performing feed-forward baseline LTraiJ [9] shown as green-purple skeletons for short-term prediction (400 million seconds) as illustrated in Table 1. The dotted rectangles mark that our predictions better match the ground-truth which is represented as gray dotted skeletons. The qualitative comparison further demonstrates that our ARNet possesses the ideal error-correction ability to generate high-quality prediction, especially for the joints at the end of body which contain multiple small movements on aperiodic actions.

Long-Term Prediction on H3.6m. Figure 3 visualizes the comparisons between chain-structured baselines RRNN [13] and AGED [13] on Phoning, which belongs to aperiodic actions in H3.6m dataset for long-term prediction (4 s). As marked by the red rectangles, our proposed ARNet is still able to predict the motion dynamics when the RRNN converges to mean pose. Meanwhile, the AGED drifts away on the foot joints compared with the ground-truth. The visualised results demonstrate that our ARNet outperforms the chain-structured baselines in long-term prediction.

5 Ablation Studies

5.1 Different Components in Our ARNet

In order to verify the effectiveness of the different components in our model, we perform comprehensive ablation studies as shown in Table 5. Specifically, we

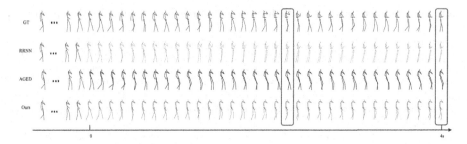

Fig. 3. Visual comparisons for long-term human motion prediction on H3.6m dataset. From top to bottom, we show the corresponding ground-truth shown in grey skeletons, the final predictions obtained by RRNN [13], AGED [10] and our approach on Phoning which belongs to the aperiodic action. The left gray skeletons represent the input motion sequences. Marked in red rectangles, the baseline RRNN converges to mean pose and the baseline AGED drifts away on the foot joints compared with the ground-truth. Our ARNet generates more accurate long-term human motion prediction relatively. Best viewed in color with zoom (Color figure online)

Table 5. Ablation study for refined model design and adversarial training strategy. We compared the results measured in MAE of our model with the 1-stage CoarseNet, the 2-stage CoarseNet without future information as refinement and the 2-stage RefineNet with traditional training strategy on H3.6m dataset

Milliseconds	Direction						Posing						Greeting					
	80	160	320	400	560	1000	80	160	320	400	560	1000	80	160	320	400	560	1000
1-stage CoarseNet	0.26	0.45	0.71	0.79	0.88	1.29	0.19	0.44	1.01	1.24	1.44	1.64	0.36	0.60	0.95	1.13	1.51	1.70
2-stage CoarseNet	0.25	0.45	0.67	0.78	0.88	1.30	0.19	0.46	1.01	1.26	1.42	1.68	0.34	0.60	0.94	1.11	1.66	1.92
2-stage RefineNet	0.25	0.44	0.67	0.77	0.86	1.27	0.19	0.43	0.99	1.23	1.42	1.63	0.34	0.58	0.92	1.10	1.49	1.63
ARNet	**0.23**	**0.43**	**0.65**	**0.75**	**0.85**	**1.23**	**0.17**	**0.43**	**0.97**	**1.20**	**1.41**	**1.60**	**0.31**	**0.55**	**0.90**	**1.08**	**1.46**	**1.56**

Milliseconds	Greeting						Phoning						Average (on 15 actions)					
	80	160	320	400	560	1000	80	160	320	400	560	1000	80	160	320	400	560	1000
1-stage CoarseNet	0.36	0.60	0.95	1.13	1.51	1.70	0.53	1.02	1.35	1.48	1.45	1.68	0.27	0.51	0.83	0.95	1.18	1.59
2-stage CoarseNet	0.34	0.60	0.94	1.11	1.66	1.92	0.53	1.02	1.34	1.48	1.58	1.98	0.27	0.52	0.83	0.95	1.20	1.61
2-stage RefineNet	0.34	0.58	0.94	1.10	1.48	1.64	0.52	1.01	1.33	1.46	1.42	1.65	0.27	0.50	0.82	0.94	1.17	1.58
ARNet	**0.31**	**0.55**	**0.90**	**1.08**	**1.46**	**1.56**	**0.50**	**0.99**	**1.28**	**1.40**	**1.41**	**1.60**	**0.25**	**0.49**	**0.80**	**0.92**	**1.16**	**1.57**

compare our ARNet with three baselines: the 1-stage CoarseNet, the 2-stage CoarseNet without future information as refinement and the 2-stage RefineNet with future information and traditional training strategy. The 1-stage CoarseNet denotes that there only exists single coarse predictor module without other components in the whole framework. We utilize the LTraiJ network [9] as our coarse predictor. Due to the coarse-to-fine 2-stage structure of our ARNet, the inference time of our ARNet is 56.2 ms, which is slightly longer than the 45.4 ms of 1-stage CoarseNets on GPU V100. Moreover, another baseline is the 2-stage CoarseNet without future information refinement, which increase the number of layers by simply cascading two 1-stage CoarseNets, utilise the same training strategy as the single coarse predictor by back-propagating the gradient all the way to the beginning. Although the parameters of our ARNet is same as the 2-stage CoarseNet which is twice that of 1-stage CoarseNets, the results show that stacking multi-layers with traditional training strategy fails to improve the performance in a further step and even achieved worse prediction due to over-fitting occurred in stacked feed-forward deep network. Then, the 2-stage RefineNet without adversarial error augmentation leads to improvement over the previous two baselines. Our adversarial refinement network shows the superior performance compared with single-stage model, 2-stage model without refinement and refinement network without adversarial training strategy.

5.2   Multi-stage Analysis

We also evaluate the impact of number of stages adopted in our adversarial refinement model by calculating the MAE over 15 actions. The foregoing results in the Table 6 indicate that the 2-stage refined model design, in general, utilising the output space of previous stage, is simple enough to learn the rich representation and achieves superior results in most cases. The reason is that concatenating more than 2 stages refinement module faces up over-fitting problems and fails to further improve the human motion prediction performance. Taking the efficiency and simplicity into account, we employ the 2-stage adversarial refinement network as the final model design.

Table 6. Ablation study of adversarial refinement network with different number of stages. We compared the results measured in MAE on H3.6m dataset

Milliseconds	Direction						Posing						Greeting					
	80	160	320	400	560	1000	80	160	320	400	560	1000	80	160	320	400	560	1000
2-stage	**0.23**	**0.43**	**0.65**	**0.75**	0.85	**1.23**	**0.17**	**0.43**	**0.97**	**1.20**	**1.41**	**1.60**	**0.31**	0.55	0.90	**1.08**	**1.46**	**1.56**
3-stage	0.25	0.46	0.64	0.75	**0.84**	1.50	0.18	0.44	1.00	1.25	1.71	2.64	0.32	**0.54**	**0.89**	1.12	1.52	1.75
4-stage	0.25	0.46	0.68	0.77	1.02	1.70	0.19	0.46	1.05	1.28	1.86	3.03	0.33	0.56	0.93	1.15	1.56	1.82

Milliseconds	Greeting						Phoning						Average (on 15 actions)					
	80	160	320	400	560	1000	80	160	320	400	560	1000	80	160	320	400	560	1000
2-stage	**0.31**	0.55	0.90	**1.08**	**1.46**	**1.56**	**0.50**	**0.99**	**1.28**	**1.40**	**1.41**	**1.60**	**0.25**	**0.49**	**0.80**	**0.92**	**1.16**	**1.57**
3-stage	0.32	**0.54**	**0.89**	1.12	1.52	1.75	0.52	1.02	1.36	1.45	1.49	1.80	0.25	0.49	0.83	0.95	1.17	1.58
4-stage	0.33	0.56	0.93	1.15	1.56	1.82	0.52	0.99	1.33	1.48	1.49	1.76	0.27	0.50	0.83	0.95	1.17	1.58

6   Conclusions

In this paper, we introduce an Adversarial Refinement Network (ARNet) to forecast more accurate human motion sequence in a coarse-to-fine manner. We adopt a refinement network behind the single-stage coarse predictor to generate finer human motion. Meanwhile, we utilise an adversarial learning strategy to enhance the generalization ability of the refinement network. Experimental results on the challenging benchmark H3.6m, CMU-Mocap and 3DPW datasets show that our proposed ARNet outperforms the state-of-the-art approaches in both short-term and long-term predictions especially on the complex aperiodic actions. Our adversarial refinement network shows promising potential for feedforward deep network to deal with rich representation in a further step on other areas.

Acknowledgement. The work described in this paper was supported by grants from City University of Hong Kong(Project No. 9220077 and 9678139).

References

1. Koppula, H.S., Saxena, A.: Anticipating human activities for reactive robotic response. In: IROS (2013)
2. Saquib Sarfraz, M., Schumann, A., Eberle, A., Stiefelhagen, R.: A pose-sensitive embedding for person re-identification with expanded cross neighborhood re-ranking. In: CVPR (2018)
3. Elhayek, A., Kovalenko, O., Murthy, P., Malik, J., Stricker, D.: Fully automatic multi-person human motion capture for VR applications. In: Bourdot, P., Cobb, S., Interrante, V., kato, H., Stricker, D. (eds.) EuroVR 2018. LNCS, vol. 11162, pp. 28–47. Springer, Cham (2018). https://doi.org/10.1007/978-3-030-01790-3_3
4. Yuminaka, Y., Mori, T., Watanabe, K., Hasegawa, M., Shirakura, K.: Non-contact vital sensing systems using a motion capture device: medical and healthcare applications. In: Key Engineering Materials (2016)
5. Paden, B., Čáp, M., Yong, S.Z., Yershov, D., Frazzoli, E.: A survey of motion planning and control techniques for self-driving urban vehicles. IEEE Transactions on intelligent vehicles 1, 33–35 (2016)
6. Gong, H., Sim, J., Likhachev, M., Shi, J.: Multi-hypothesis motion planning for visual object tracking. In: ICCV (2011)
7. Wang, J.M., Fleet, D.J., Hertzmann, A.: Gaussian process dynamical models for human motion. IEEE Trans. Pattern Anal. Mach. Intell. **30**, 283–298 (2007)
8. Tang, Y., Ma, L., Liu, W., Zheng, W.: Long-term human motion prediction by modeling motion context and enhancing motion dynamic. In: IJCAI (2018)
9. Mao, W., Liu, M., Salzmann, M., Li, H.: Learning trajectory dependencies for human motion prediction. In: ICCV (2019)
10. Gui, L.Y., Wang, Y.X., Liang, X., Moura, J.M.: Adversarial geometry-aware human motion prediction. In: ECCV (2018)
11. Fragkiadaki, K., Levine, S., Felsen, P., Malik, J.: Recurrent network models for human dynamics. In: ICCV (2015)
12. Jain, A., Zamir, A.R., Savarese, S., Saxena, A.: Structural-RNN: deep learning on spatio-temporal graphs. In: CVPR (2016)
13. Martinez, J., Black, M.J., Romero, J.: On human motion prediction using recurrent neural networks. In: CVPR (2017)
14. Tome, D., Russell, C., Agapito, L.: Lifting from the deep: convolutional 3D pose estimation from a single image. In: Proceedings of the IEEE Conference on Computer Vision and Pattern Recognition, pp. 2500–2509 (2017)
15. Chen, Y., Wang, Z., Peng, Y., Zhang, Z., Yu, G., Sun, J.: Cascaded pyramid network for multi-person pose estimation. In: Proceedings of the IEEE Conference on Computer Vision and Pattern Recognition, pp. 7103–7112 (2018)
16. Fieraru, M., Khoreva, A., Pishchulin, L., Schiele, B.: Learning to refine human pose estimation. In: CVPR-W (2018)
17. Moon, G., Chang, J.Y., Lee, K.M.: Posefix: model-agnostic general human pose refinement network. In: CVPR (2019)
18. Wan, Q., Qiu, W., Yuille, A.L.: Patch-based 3D human pose refinement. arXiv preprint arXiv:1905.08231 (2019)
19. Goodfellow, I., et al.: Generative adversarial nets. In: NIPS (2014)

20. Deng, K., Fei, T., Huang, X., Peng, Y.: IRC-GAN: introspective recurrent convolutional GAN for text-to-video generation. In: IJCAI (2019)
21. Balaji, Y., Min, M.R., Bai, B., Chellappa, R., Graf, H.P.: Conditional GAN with discriminative filter generation for text-to-video synthesis. In: IJCAI (2019)
22. Vankadari, M., Kumar, S., Majumder, A., Das, K.: Unsupervised learning of monocular depth and ego-motion using conditional patchgans. In: IJCAI (2019)
23. Chu, W., Hung, W.C., Tsai, Y.H., Cai, D., Yang, M.H.: Weakly-supervised caricature face parsing through domain adaptation. In: ICIP (2019)
24. Zhang, X., Wang, Q., Zhang, J., Zhong, Z.: Adversarial autoaugment. In: ICLR (2020)
25. Frid-Adar, M., Klang, E., Amitai, M., Goldberger, J., Greenspan, H.: Gan-based data augmentation for improved liver lesion classification (2018)
26. Kipf, T.N., Welling, M.: Semi-supervised classification with graph convolutional networks (2017)
27. Yan, S., Xiong, Y., Lin, D.: Spatial temporal graph convolutional networks for skeleton-based action recognition. In: Thirty-Second AAAI Conference on Artificial Intelligence (2018)
28. Ionescu, C., Papava, D., Olaru, V., Sminchisescu, C.: Human3.6m: large scale datasets and predictive methods for 3D human sensing in natural environments. TPAMI 36, 1325–1339 (2014)
29. Li, C., Zhang, Z., Lee, W.S., Lee, G.H.: Convolutional sequence to sequence model for human dynamics. In: CVPR (2018)
30. von Marcard, T., Henschel, R., Black, M., Rosenhahn, B., Pons-Moll, G.: Recovering accurate 3D human pose in the wild using imus and a moving camera. In: ECCV (2018)
31. Paszke, A., et al.: Automatic differentiation in pytorch. In: NIPS-W (2017)
32. Kingma, D.P., Ba, J.: adam: a method for stochastic optimization. arXiv preprint arXiv:1412.6980 (2014)
33. Akhter, I., Sheikh, Y., Khan, S., Kanade, T.: Nonrigid structure from motion in trajectory space. In: NIPS (2009)
34. Dong, M., Xu, C.: On retrospecting human dynamics with attention. In: IJCAI (2019)

Semantic Synthesis of Pedestrian Locomotion

Maria Priisalu[1]([envelope]), Ciprian Paduraru[2,3], Aleksis Pirinen[1],
and Cristian Sminchisescu[1,3,4]

[1] Department of Mathematics, Faculty of Engineering, Lund University,
Lund, Sweden
{maria.priisalu,aleksis.pirinen,cristian.sminchisescu}@math.lth.se
[2] The Research Institute of the University of Bucharest (ICUB), Bucharest, Romania
ciprian.paduraru@fmi.unibuc.ro
[3] Institute of Mathematics of the Romanian Academy, Bucharest, Romania
[4] Google Research, Lund, Sweden

Abstract. We present a model for generating 3d articulated pedestrian locomotion in urban scenarios, with synthesis capabilities informed by the 3d scene semantics and geometry. We reformulate pedestrian trajectory forecasting as a structured reinforcement learning (RL) problem. This allows us to naturally combine prior knowledge on collision avoidance, 3d human motion capture and the motion of pedestrians as observed e.g. in Cityscapes, Waymo or simulation environments like Carla. Our proposed RL-based model allows pedestrians to accelerate and slow down to avoid imminent danger (e.g. cars), while obeying human dynamics learnt from in-lab motion capture datasets. Specifically, we propose a hierarchical model consisting of a semantic trajectory policy network that provides a distribution over possible movements, and a human locomotion network that generates 3d human poses in each step. The RL-formulation allows the model to learn even from states that are seldom exhibited in the dataset, utilizing all of the available prior and scene information. Extensive evaluations using both real and simulated data illustrate that the proposed model is on par with recent models such as S-GAN, ST-GAT and S-STGCNN in pedestrian forecasting, while outperforming these in collision avoidance. We also show that our model can be used to plan goal reaching trajectories in urban scenes with dynamic actors.

1   Introduction

Pedestrian trajectory prediction is an important sub-problem for safe autonomous driving. Recent 3d traffic datasets [1–6] focus on bounding box detection and prediction of cars and pedestrians. Bounding boxes are popular since they provide information on the location and velocity of the travelling object, and are relatively well suited to model cars, but neglect the detailed motion cues present in pedestrian

---

Electronic supplementary material The online version of this chapter (https://doi.org/10.1007/978-3-030-69532-3_29) contains supplementary material, which is available to authorized users.

© Springer Nature Switzerland AG 2021
H. Ishikawa et al. (Eds.): ACCV 2020, LNCS 12623, pp. 470–487, 2021.
https://doi.org/10.1007/978-3-030-69532-3_29

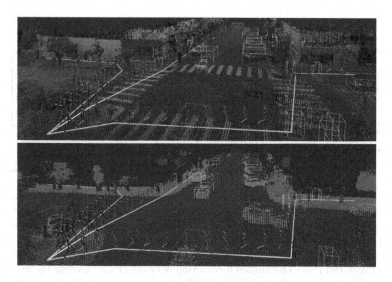

Fig. 1. Pedestrian trajectories and poses generated by our agent on a Waymo scene. RGB and semantic pointclouds of the scene are shown in the top and bottom images, respectively. A local neighborhood of these pointclouds are observed by the agent. Coloured lines on the ground show different trajectories taken by the agent when initialized with varying agent histories, cf. Sect. 2.2. The agent crosses the roads without collisions. Cars and other pedestrians in the scene are shown as positioned in the first frame and are surrounded by bounding boxes for clarity. (Color figure online)

posture. Pedestrian poses compactly model posture and motion cues and have been shown effective in pedestrian intent prediction [7–9]. However, to our knowledge there exists no large-scale datasets with ground truth annotations of pedestrian poses in traffic. Moreover, most previous work in pedestrian pose modelling has been performed without spatial reasoning [7,9] or using action-conditioned human models [8]. In contrast, we formulate pedestrian synthesis as a 3d scene reasoning problem that is constrained by human dynamics and where the generated motion must follow the scene's 3d geometric and semantic properties as seen in Fig. 1. To impose human dynamics, the articulated pose trajectories are conditioned on the current and past poses and velocities.

Specifically, we propose a *semantic pedestrian locomotion* (SPL) agent, a hierarchical articulated 3d pedestrian motion generator that conditions its predictions on both the scene semantics and human locomotion dynamics. Our agent first predicts the next trajectory location and then simulates physically plausible human locomotion to that location. The agent explicitly models the interactions with objects, cars and other pedestrians surrounding it, as seen in Fig. 2. We develop two different pedestrian locomotion generators – one without any restrictions that can roll forward from a given starting location, and one which is additionally conditioned on a target location. The former is useful for simulating generic pedestrian motion in traffic situations, while the latter can be used to control the simulation target, for example when generating high-risk scenarios. Moreover, our model can be used to augment existing traffic datasets with articulated poses. For example, the 3d poses generated by the SPL agent can

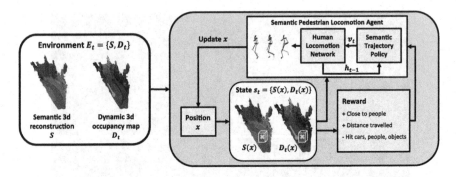

Fig. 2. Semantic pedestrian locomotion (SPL) agent and framework. The 3d environment $E_t = \{S, D_t\}$ consists of a semantic map S of static objects and a dynamic occupancy map D_t of cars and people at time t (shown as blue and green trajectories, ellipsoids indicate the positions at time t). The agent observes a top-view projection of a local crop (yellow box) of E_t. A velocity v_t is sampled from the semantic trajectory policy network (STPN). The human locomotion network (HLN) models the articulated movement of the step v_t. Note that the STPN observes pose information via the previous hidden state h_{t-1} from the HLN. In training, a reward evaluating the subsequent state is given to the agent. (Color figure online)

be used to produce dense pedestrian predictions by applying a pose conditioned human mesh such as SMPL [10]. Augmented pedestrians can then be produced in semantic segmentation masks by projecting the dense pedestrian mesh onto the image plane. RGB images can be augmented similarly, but this may additionally require a photorealistic style transfer similar to [11,12]. Alternatively, LiDAR augmentations can be generated by sampling [13] from the dense bodies.

Learning to synthesize pedestrian motion is difficult, since the diversity among expert pedestrian trajectories is often limited in the training data, especially for high-risk scenarios. A trajectory generation model trained via imitation learning is unlikely to act reliably in situations that are not present in the training data. This implies e.g. that such an agent will likely behave poorly in near collision scenarios, as these are not present in existing datasets. Recent work on generative adversarial imitation learning (GAIL) [14] has recently gained popularity within trajectory forecasting [15–18] since it models the data distribution rather than cloning expert behaviour. GAIL is an inverse RL method where a policy tries to mimic the experts and the reward function aims to discriminate policy trajectories from expert trajectories. However, as for behaviour cloning, GAIL cannot learn reliable behaviour in situations that are highly different from those available in the training data, since the discriminator will in such cases be able to trivially distinguish between generated and expert trajectories.

To allow our SPL agent to learn also from states outside the training set, in Sect. 2 we pose the trajectory forecasting problem in the framework of reinforcement learning (RL). We extrapolate the learning signal with an optima-preserving reward signal that additionally involves prior knowledge to promote e.g. collision avoidance. We adapt the RL policy sampling process to simultaneously optimize the trajectory forecasting loss and maximize the reward.

Moreover, our analysis in Sect. 2 can be used to adapt any trajectory forecasting model into a robust articulated pedestrian synthesis model. By sampling initial positions of the agent in different locations, all of the spatio-temporal data in the driving dataset can be utilized. Because we train on a large number of different spatial locations and in near-collision scenarios, our motion synthesis model learns to generate plausible trajectories even in states that are far from expert trajectories such as near-collision scenarios. In summary, our contributions are as follows:

- We propose an articulated 3d pedestrian motion generator that conditions its predictions on both the scene semantics and human locomotion dynamics. The model produces articulated pose skeletons for each step along the trajectory.
- We propose and execute a novel training paradigm which combines the sample-efficiency of behaviour cloning with the open-ended exploration of the full state space of reinforcement learning.
- We perform extensive evaluations on Cityscapes, Waymo and CARLA and show that our model matches or outperforms existing approaches in three different settings: i) for pedestrian forecasting; ii) for pedestrian motion generation; and iii) for goal-directed pedestrian motion generation.

1.1 Related Work

In pedestrian trajectory forecasting, social interactions of pedestrians have been modelled with different GAN-based approaches [19,20], by social graphs [21–23], by recurrent networks [24,25] and by temporal convolutions [26,27]. Differently from us, these approaches only model the social interactions of pedestrians and ignore cars and obstacles. An attention model is used by [28] to forecast pedestrian trajectory given environmental features and GAN-based social modelling that neglects cars. Differently from [19–28] we utilize a locomotion model and therefore do not need to learn human dynamics from scratch. All of the mentioned supervised models in pedestrian forecasting can in principle be trained with our proposed methodology (cf. Sect. 2) to extend to unobserved states.

Our model does not rely on action detection (e.g. "walking" or "standing") of the expert dataset for trajectory forecasting, as opposed to action conditioned intention detection networks [8,29] and motion forecasting models [30,31]. Instead the pedestrian's future trajectory is conditioned on its past trajectory. A benefit of our approach is thus that it avoids dealing with temporal ambiguities associated with action detection. Recently it has been shown that pedestrian future augmentation can improve pedestrian forecasting features [32]. Our generator produces articulated 3d trajectories on real data, and in comparison to [33] we do not require the recreation of the full dataset in a simulation environment. We note that the goal-reaching version of our model could be utilized with a goal proposal method [34] to provide multiple future augmentations to data.

Human synthesis models for still images [11,18,35–37] aim to synthesize poses in semantically and geometrically plausible ways in images, and have no temporal modelling, but could be used to initialize the SPL's pose trajectories. The works [36,37] model likely locations for humans in images. The models in [11,18,35] synthesize pedestrians with 3d models, but do this only in static scenes. Similar to us, the affordance model of [38] explicitly incorporates 3d scene semantics to propose plausible human poses, but only for static scenes. Synthetic videos are generated in [39] by cropping humans from sample videos and pasting them into target videos followed by visual smoothing with a GAN, but this approach does not guarantee semantic plausibility.

The majority of 3d human pose forecasting models concentrate on predicting future poses given only the past pose history [40–42]. In [43] human pose futures are predicted on a static dataset by forecasting a trajectory, to which poses are fitted by a transformer network. Differently from our work the reasoning is performed in 2d which leads to geometrically implausible failure cases. [44] forecast pedestrian motion by combining a pose predicting GRU [45] with social pooling and a 2d background context layer. Both [43,44] are not readily applicable to driving datasets as they lack modelling of cars and require access to high quality 2d human poses which are in general hard to obtain in driving datasets.

2   Methodology

The pedestrian trajectory forecasting problem on a dataset $\mathcal{D}$ of pedestrian trajectories can be formulated as follows. Let $x_0, \ldots, x_t, x_{t+1}, \ldots x_T$ be a pedestrian trajectory[1] of length T in $\mathcal{D}$. Given the trajectory $x_0, \ldots, x_t$ up to timestep t we would like to predict the pedestrian's position in the next timestep $x_{t+1} = x_t + v_t$, where v_t is the step taken by the pedestrian from x_t to x_{t+1}. Each position x_t is associated with a state s_t, described in detail in Sect. 2.1, that includes the pedestrian's past trajectory and other relevant scene information at position x_t. We denote the density function of the random variable v_t conditioned on s_t as $p(v_t|s_t)$. The prediction task is to estimate $p(v_t|s_t)$ by a parametric function $p_\Theta(v_t|s_t)$ where the step forecast is $\hat{v}_t = \max_{v_t} p_\Theta(v_t|s_t)$. The maximum likelihood estimate of the model parameters Θ is then given by

$$\Theta^* = \arg\max_\Theta \log \mathcal{L}(\Theta|\mathcal{D}) = \arg\max_\Theta \sum_\mathcal{D} \sum_{t=0}^{T-1} \log p_\Theta(v_t|s_t) \qquad (1)$$

From the RL perspective on the other hand, an agent has an initial position x_0 and takes steps by sampling from a parametric policy: $v_t \sim \pi_\Theta(v_t|s_t)$. After taking a step v_t the agent finds itself in a new location $x_{t+1} = x_t + v_t$ and in training receives a reward $R(s_t, v_t)$. The objective is to find a policy π_Θ that maximizes the expected cumulative reward,

$$J(\Theta) = \mathbb{E}_{\pi_\Theta} \left[\sum_{t=0}^{T-1} R(s_t, v_t) \right] \qquad (2)$$

---

[1] The x_t are 2d locations in the movement plane.

Comparing the RL perspective with the standard forecasting formulation, we first note that $\pi_\Theta(v_t|s_t) = p_\Theta(v_t|s_t)$. Furthermore, the optima of (1) is unchanged if it is multiplied by a function $R(s_t, v_t)$ that obtains its maximum at all $(s_t, v_t) \in \mathcal{D}$, i.e. on the expert trajectories. Thus, assuming that the actions taken by the pedestrians in $\mathcal{D}$ are optimal in the reward function R, we can rewrite the maximum likelihood objective (1) as a Monte Carlo estimate of the policy gradient objective [46], sampled from the expert trajectories $(s_t, v_t) \in \mathcal{D}$:

$$\Theta^* = \arg\max_\Theta \sum_{\mathcal{D}} \sum_{t=0}^{T-1} \log \pi_\Theta(v_t|s_t) R(s_t, v_t) \tag{3}$$

We can now unify the policy gradient objective (3) and the supervised objective (1) by sampling respectively from $(\tilde{s}_t, \tilde{v}_t) \sim \pi_\Theta$ and $(s_t, v_t) \in \mathcal{D}$. Optimizing (3) while sampling from both the expert trajectories and the current parametric policy equates to iteratively optimizing the policy gradient objective and the maximum likelihood objective. Thus we have shown that (1) can be rewritten as a policy gradient objective assuming a reward function that obtains its optima on $\mathcal{D}$. In Sect. 2.4 we construct a reward function that fulfills this criteria.

By posing the supervised learning problem of pedestrian trajectory forecasting as an RL problem, the detailed human dynamics model HLN becomes part of the observable environment dynamics and does not need to be modelled explicitly in the trajectory prediction model π_Θ. This is a natural way of combining accurate human motion models trained on in-laboratory motion capture data [47,48] with trajectories available in autonomous driving datasets [1–6].

In the following subsections we present our SPL agent, which performs human 3d motion synthesis within two modules. First a semantic pedestrian locomotion network (STPN) samples a step v_t based on s_t, and then a human locomotion network (HLN) generates realistic body joint movements to the next position x_{t+1}. The HLN is first trained in a supervised fashion (see Sect. 2.3). Then the STPN and HLN modules are combined, and the STPN is trained by alternating[2] between sampling from expert trajectories and from arbitrary states, following the objective (3). Figure 2 provides an overview of the SPL model.

2.1 States and Actions

The agent acts in the voxelized 3d environment $E_t = \{S, D_t\}$ over the time horizon $\{0, \ldots, T\}$, where E_t is a 3d pointcloud reconstruction of a scene with resolution 20 cm × 20 cm × 20 cm. The reconstruction E_t consists of stationary objects S and a dynamic occupancy map D_t of moving objects. Specifically, the dynamic occupancy map marks the timestamps of voxel occupancies by other pedestrians and cars (in separate channels) in the time horizon $\{0, \ldots, T\}$. For past timesteps $0 - t$ the dynamic occupancy map contains the past trajectories of cars and pedestrians, while a constant velocity model is used to predict the future $t + 1, \ldots, T$. Further details of D_t are in the supplement. Each 3d point in

---

[2] See details of the alternating training in the supplement.

E_t is described by a semantic label l and an RGB-color label c. We let $E_t(x_t) = \{S(x_t), D_t(x_t)\}$ denote a 5 m × 5 m × 1.8 m rectangular 3d crop of E_t centered at the agent's current position x_t and touching the ground.

The agent's state at time t consists of its external semantic state s_t and the internal locomotion state l_t. The external semantic state is defined as

$$s_t = \{E_t^{2d}(x_t), v_{t-N}, \ldots, v_{t-1}, d_v, h_{t-1}\} \tag{4}$$

where $E_t^{2d}(x_t)$ is a top-view projection of $E_t(x_t)$, $v_{t-N}, \ldots, v_{t-1}$ constitute the agent's movement history for the past $N = 12$ timesteps, d_v is the displacement[3] to the closest vehicle, and h_{t-1} is the hidden layer of the HLN (cf. Sect. 2.3) which informs about the agent's posture, pose and acceleration. The locomotion state

$$l_t = \{x_{t-M}, \ldots, x_{t-1}, x_t, g_{t-M}, \ldots g_{t-1}, g_t, j_t, i_t, x_{t+1}, |v_t|\} \tag{5}$$

consists of the past positions $x_{t-M}, \ldots, x_{t-1}$ of the agent ($M = 11$), the current position x_t, the past gait characteristics $g_{t-M}, \ldots, g_{t-1}$, the next step's gait g_t, the joint positions and velocities j_t and i_t, the next trajectory position $x_{t+1} = x_t + v_t$, and the speed $|v_t|$. The gait characteristic g_t is a binary vector indicating if the agent is standing, walking or jogging and is regressed from $|v_t|$. The joint positions j_t are the 3d positions of the root-joint centered 30 BVH joints of the CMU motion capture data [49].

2.2 Semantic Trajectory Policy Network (STPN)

The STPN is a neural network that parametrizes $\pi_\Theta(v_t|s_t)$, the velocity distribution of the agent in position x_t with state s_t. We factorize $\pi_\Theta(v_t|s_t)$ into a Gaussian distribution over speed $|v_t|$, and a multinomial distribution over discretized unit directions u_t. Since the agent is acting and observing the world in a regular voxel grid, the movement directions are discretized into the eight directions North (N), North-East (NE) and so on: N, NE, E, SE, S, SW, W, NW, as well as a no-move action. After the velocity v_t is sampled, the agent's next position x_{t+1} is given by the HLN in Sect. 2.3. The new position is often close to $x_t + v_t$ but could be adjusted by the HLN to ensure physical plausibility.

The policy $\pi_\Theta(v_t|s_t)$ is parameterized by a neural network, consisting of a convolutional features extractor, an agent history encoder and two parallel fully connected (FC) layers. The convolutional features extractor consists of two convolutional layers of size $(2, 2, 1)$ with ReLU activations and max pooling. The agent history encoder is a 32-unit LSTM [50] that extracts a temporal feature vector f_t from the agent's past trajectory $v_{t-N}, \ldots, v_{t-1}$. The parallel FC layers both receive[4] as input the convolutional features, the temporal features f_t, the displacement vector d_t and the hidden state[5] h_{t-1} of the HLN. The previous unit direction u_{t-1} is added as a prior to the output of the first FC layer,

---

[3] This is comparable to a pedestrian being aware of cars in its vicinity.

[4] The goal-directed agent additionally includes the direction to the goal at this stage.

[5] The previous hidden state is used, as the HLN is executed after the STPN.

and the result is then fed through a softmax activation to output a probability distribution over the unit directions $\boldsymbol{u}_t$. The second FC layer is activated by the sigmoid function which is scaled with the maximal speed 3 m/s to produce μ_t, the mean of the normal distribution that models the speed taken at time t. Hence $|\boldsymbol{v}_t| \sim \mathcal{N}(\mu_t, \sigma)$, where σ is exponentially decreased from 2 to 0.1 in training. Finally, the sampled velocity $\boldsymbol{v}_t$ is given by $\boldsymbol{v}_t = |\boldsymbol{v}_t|\boldsymbol{u}_t$.

2.3 Human Locomotion Network (HLN)

The HLN produces 3d body joint positions to take a step $\boldsymbol{v}_t$ from $\boldsymbol{x}_t$. The HLN is adapted from [51] with the addition of a velocity regression layer that estimates $\boldsymbol{g}_t$ in (5) from $\boldsymbol{v}_t$. Network weights are learnt following the data and procedure in [51]. The HLN is a phase function network that is conditioned on the walking phase of the body at time t, where the phase varies from 0 to 2π for a full cycle from the right foot touching the ground until the next occurrence of the right foot touching the ground. The HLN regresses $\boldsymbol{j}_{t+1}, \boldsymbol{i}_{t+1} = h(\boldsymbol{l}_t)$, i.e. the joint positions $\boldsymbol{j}_{t+1}$ and velocities $\boldsymbol{i}_{t+1}$, conditioned on the current state $\boldsymbol{l}_t$ (see Sect. 2.1).

The next position $\boldsymbol{x}_{t+1}$ of the agent is set to the plane coordinates of the pelvis joint in $\boldsymbol{j}_{t+1}$ at timestep $t+1$ (the agent is not allowed to move through objects). The HLN architecture consist of three fully connected layers with 512 hidden units per layer and an exponential rectified linear function [52] as the activation function. The last hidden layer $\boldsymbol{h}_t$ is observed by the STPN in the next timestep, informing it of the agent's current posture. Network weights are trained for different walking phases by augmenting surface curvature for constant feet to ground distances from motion capture data as reported in [51].

2.4 Reward Signal

In training the agent's state is evaluated by the reward function $R_t = R(\boldsymbol{x}_t, \boldsymbol{v}_t)$ at each step. We wish to estimate the optimal policy $\pi_{\Theta^*}(\boldsymbol{v}_t|\boldsymbol{s}_t)$ that maximizes the total expected reward. The reward function is designed so that its maximal value occurs on the expert trajectories, as discussed in Sect. 2. A reward $R_d = 1$ is given for visiting a pedestrian trajectory in the dataset $\mathcal{D}$, otherwise $R_d = 0$. The reward is given only for newly visited locations to promote the agent to move. We also encourage the agent to move close to positions where pedestrians tend to appear. To approximate a pedestrian density map from $\mathcal{D}$ we apply an exponential kernel on the trajectory locations in $\mathcal{D}$, i.e.

$$R_k(\boldsymbol{x}_t, \boldsymbol{v}_t) = \log\left\{ \frac{1}{b} \sum_{\boldsymbol{x}^i \in D} \sum_{t'=0}^{T} \exp\{-\|\boldsymbol{x}_{t'}^i - \boldsymbol{x}_{t+1}\|\} \right\} \tag{6}$$

where b is the bandwidth (we set $b = 0.0001$) and the sum is over all pedestrian trajectory positions $\boldsymbol{x}^i$ in the dataset $\mathcal{D}$. We gather the terms that encourage the agent to stay near trajectories in $\mathcal{D}$ as $R_{ped}(\boldsymbol{x}_t, \boldsymbol{v}_t) = R_k(\boldsymbol{x}_t, \boldsymbol{v}_t) + R_d(\boldsymbol{x}_t, \boldsymbol{v}_t)$.

Fig. 3. Several 1-min trajectories of our SPL-goal agent reaching its goal location in orange (maximum distance to goal: 120 m) on the CARLA test set. Car, person and agent trajectories are shown in blue, green and red respectively. *Left:* Agent sharply but safely crossing the street to reach a goal. *Middle:* Agent safely crossing the street as no cars are approaching. *Right:* Agent safely moving along the pavement when given a goal on the road. The shortest path to the goal would involve walking on the road for a longer amount of time, so the agent balances its desire to reach the goal with the risk of being on the road. (Color figure online)

To penalize collisions, let R_v, R_p and R_s be negative indicator functions that are active if the agent collides with vehicles, pedestrians and static objects, respectively. The terms are gathered as $R_{coll}(\boldsymbol{x}_t, \boldsymbol{v}_t) = R_v(\boldsymbol{x}_t, \boldsymbol{v}_t) + R_p(\boldsymbol{x}_t, \boldsymbol{v}_t) + R_s(\boldsymbol{x}_t, \boldsymbol{v}_t)$. Note that $R_{ped}(\boldsymbol{x}_t, \boldsymbol{v}_t)$ is only given when $R_p(\boldsymbol{x}_t, \boldsymbol{v}_t) = 0$.

To encourage smooth transitions between the exhibited poses and to penalize heavy effort motions, we penalize the average yaw ϕ (in degrees) of the joints in the agent's lower body as $R_\phi(\boldsymbol{x}_t, \boldsymbol{v}_t) = \max(\min(\phi - 1.2, 0), 2.0)$. Thus the full reward[6] is $R(\boldsymbol{x}_t, \boldsymbol{v}_t) = R_{coll}(\boldsymbol{x}_t, \boldsymbol{v}_t) + R_{ped}(\boldsymbol{x}_t, \boldsymbol{v}_t) + R_\phi(\boldsymbol{x}_t, \boldsymbol{v}_t)$.

When the agent is given a goal location, every step taken towards the goal should provide a reward for the improvement made relative to the initial goal distance. Thus, given a goal location $\boldsymbol{x}_g$ we define

$$R_g(\boldsymbol{x}_t, \boldsymbol{v}_t) = \begin{cases} 1 & \text{if } \|\boldsymbol{x}_{t+1} - \boldsymbol{x}_g\| < \epsilon \\ 1 - \frac{\|\boldsymbol{x}_{t+1} - \boldsymbol{x}_g\|}{\|\boldsymbol{x}_t - \boldsymbol{x}_g\|} & \text{otherwise} \end{cases} \tag{7}$$

where ϵ defines the distance from the goal location to the agent center.[7] The full reward[8] of the goal reaching agent is $R(\boldsymbol{x}_t, \boldsymbol{v}_t) = R_{coll}(\boldsymbol{x}_t, \boldsymbol{v}_t) + R_{ped}(\boldsymbol{x}_t, \boldsymbol{v}_t) + R_\phi(\boldsymbol{x}_t, \boldsymbol{v}_t) + R_g(\boldsymbol{x}_t, \boldsymbol{v}_t)$. Note that the goal-driven reward does not necessarily reach its optima on expert trajectories, as the it is not assumed that $\boldsymbol{x}_g \in \mathcal{D}$.

2.5 Policy Training

With a finite sequence length T, a large number of states are in practice unreachable for the agent with an initial location $\boldsymbol{x}_0$. However, thanks to the RL reformulation the agent can be initialized in any location. By regularly choosing

---

[6] Each term weighted with the respective weights, $\lambda_v = 1$, $\lambda_p = 0.1$, $\lambda_s = 0.02$, $\lambda_k = 0.01$, $\lambda_d = 0.01$, $\lambda_\phi = 0.001$.

[7] We set $\epsilon = 20\sqrt{2}$ cm, i.e. the agent must overlap the goal area.

[8] The weights except for $\lambda_v = 2$, $\lambda_g = 1$ are the same. The fraction term of R_g is weighted by 0.001.

Fig. 4. Subsampled pose sequence in a Waymo test scene, showing the SPL agent walking behind a car (indicated with an orange 3d bounding box) to avoid a collision, and then returning to the crosswalk. A zoomed out view of the scene at the beginning of the agent's trajectory is shown in the top left. (Color figure online)

information dense x_0, the number of samples needed to learn critical behaviours such as collision avoidance can be reduced, and thus the agent is initialized in front of cars, near pedestrians, randomly, on pavement and on pedestrians. Agents are trained in Tensorflow [53] using Adam [54] with a batch size of 30 trajectories, learning rate of 10^{-3}, and a discount rate of 0.99.

3 Experiments

The proposed pedestrian motion generation agent is evaluated on both simulated and real data, with and without target goals. The goal-free and goal-directed agents are denoted SPL and SPL-goal, respectively. Since the human locomotion network (HLN) described in Sect. 2.3 imposes realistic human dynamic constraints, we present all results with the HLN performing joint transformations along the trajectories. We compare SPL with the following methods:

- *Behaviour cloning (BC)* is an imitation learning baseline. BC is trained with the same network structure as SPL, but by only sampling from $\mathcal{D}$, i.e. max-likelihood forecasting. The same hyperparameters as for SPL are used.
- *Constant velocity (CV)* models pedestrian motion with a constant velocity, which as shown in [55] is surprisingly effective in many cases. When initialized on a pedestrian it continues with the last step velocity of that pedestrian. When initialized elsewhere, a Gaussian with $\mu = 1.23$ and $\sigma = 0.3$ (same as [56]) is used to estimate speed and the direction is drawn at random.
- *S-GAN* is the Social-GAN [19] used for pedestrian forecasting.
- *S-STGCNN* (*S-STG* in tables) the Social Spatio-Temporal Graph Convolutional Neural Network [23], a pedestrian trajectory forecasting network.
- *ST-GAT* is the Spatial-Temporal Graph Attention Network [22], another recent pedestrian trajectory forecasting network.

- *CARLA-simulated (GT)* are the pedestrians simulated in CARLA, here considered ground truth. These pedestrians follow hand-designed trajectories.

S-GAN, S-STGCNN and ST-GAT are trained with default hyperparameters from the official implementations. We compare SPL-goal with the following:

- *Goal direction (GD)* takes the shortest Euclidean path to the goal.
- *Collision avoidance with deep RL (CADRL)* [57] walks towards the goal location while avoiding moving objects around itself. CADRL is a learning based model for collision avoidance with dynamic obstacles.

3.1   Datasets

Simulated Data from CARLA. The CARLA package [58] is a simulator for autonomous driving. RGB images, ground truth depth, 2d semantic segmentations and bounding boxes of pedestrians and cars are collected from the simulator at 17 fps. Town 1 is used to collect training and validation sets, with 37 and 13 scenes, respectively. The test set consists of 37 scenes from Town 2.

Fig. 5. Multiple SPL-goal agent trajectories generated from the same initial position in Cityscapes. The agent can be seen reaching different goals (marked by crosses). The agent chooses to walk on pavement when nearby.

3D Reconstructions from Cityscapes. This dataset [59] consists of on-board stereo videos captured in German cities. The videos are 30 frames long with a frame rate of 17 fps (video length: 1.76 s). We use GRFP [60] to estimate the semantic segmentation of all frames. The global reconstructions are computed by COLMAP [61] assuming a stereo rig with known camera parameters. The density of the dense reconstructions from COLMAP varies; an example reconstruction can be seen in Fig. 5. Cars and people are reconstructed frame-by-frame from PANnet [62] 2d bounding boxes and instance level segmentation masks. Triangulation is used to infer 3d positions from 2d bounding boxes. The dataset consists of 200 scenes; 100 for training, 50 for validation and 50 for testing.

LiDAR Waymo. The Waymo dataset [2] consist of 200 frame 10 Hz LiDAR 3d scans, traffic agent trajectories and RGB images in 5 directions from the top of a data gathering car. We subsample a dataset of the 100 most pedestrian dense scenes in 50 m radius to the collecting car. We use 70, 10 and 20 scenes for training, validation and testing, respectively. The images are segmented by [63] and the semantic labels are mapped to the 3d scans by the mapping between LiDAR and cameras provided by the Waymo dataset.

3.2 Training and Evaluation Details

In CARLA and Waymo the training sequence length is 30 timesteps, and in testing 300 timesteps ($\approx$17 s). The agents are trained for 20 epochs, 10 of which are STPN-pretraining without the HLN, and 10 of which are further refinements with the HLN attached (cf. Sect. 2.2 and Sect. 2.3). Agents tested on Cityscapes are first trained on CARLA for 10 epochs and refined on Cityscapes for 22 epochs. Agents that are given a goal are trained with a sequence length of 10 timesteps for the first 5 epochs, after which the sequence length is increased to 30. The SPL-goal agents are refined from the weights of goal-free SPL agent that

Table 1. *Left:* Evaluation of pedestrian motion generation with 17s rollouts on the CARLA test set. The SPL (goal-free) agent is compared to the behaviour cloning (BC), constant velocity (CV) heuristics, as well as to to S-GAN [19], ST-GAT [22] and S-STG(CNN) [23]. The average of five different starting scenarios is shown (on pedestrian, random, close to a car, near a pedestrian, or on pavement). Our SPL agent collides with objects and people (f_o) and cars (f_v) less frequently than any other method, while travelling (d) only slightly shorter than ST-GAT. *Right:* Our SPL-goal agent outperforms or matches the goal direction (GD) heuristic and CADRL in success rate (f_s), while colliding much less (f_v, f_o).

	SPL	BC	CV	S-GAN	ST-GAT	S-STG		f_o	f_v	f_s
f_o	**0.02**	0.03	0.13	0.14	0.14	0.02	**SPL-goal**	0.09	0.01	**0.78**
f_v	**0.07**	0.13	0.16	0.16	0.15	0.12	**CADRL**	0.24	0.08	0.75
d	7.0	1.6	3.7	5.1	**7.9**	0.47	**GD**		0.14	0.07	**0.78**

Table 2. *Left:* Average displacement error (m) for pedestrian forecasting on CARLA and Waymo. Our SPL agent receives the second lowest forecasting error on both datasets. The ST-GAT outperforms SPL on the CARLA dataset but yields the worst results on the Waymo dataset. On the Waymo dataset our SPL and BC models outperform the others with a large margin. *Right:* Our SPL agent avoids more collisions ($f_o + f_v$), walks further (d) and stays more on pavements (f_p) than ground truth simulated pedestrians (GT) on CARLA. The SPL agent is initialized on the same positions as the simulated pedestrians.

	SPL	BC	S-GAN	ST-GAT	S-STG		f_o	f_v	d	f_p
CARLA	0.11	0.22	0.16	**0.09**	0.12	**SPL**	0.00	0.0	17.0	**0.46**
WAYMO	0.06	**0.03**	0.11	0.13	0.11	**GT**	0.08	0.0	16.0	0.35

was trained on CARLA, with the addition of a feature indicating the direction to the goal. Each test scene is evaluated for 10 episodes with different spatial and agent history initializations to compute mean metrics.

3.3   Results

Evaluation metrics are adapted from the benchmark suite of CARLA and are:

- f_o, average frequency of collisions with static objects and pedestrians;
- f_v, average frequency of collisions with vehicles;
- d, average Euclidean distance (in meters) between agent's start and end location in episodes;
- f_p, average frequency of the agent being on pavements;
- f_s, success rate in reaching a goal (only applicable for goal reaching agents).

CARLA. Table 1 (left) shows that our SPL agent generates long trajectories and yields significantly fewer collisions than the compared methods. The SPL average trajectory length 7.0 m is 11% less than the furthest travelling ST-GAT of 7.9 m, but the SPL agent collides 53% less with vehicles and 86% less with objects and pedestrians. As shown in Table 2 (right), SPL even outperforms the CARLA-simulated (GT) trajectories in collision avoidance, and learns to stay on the sidewalk more, despite GT being the experts. To show the effect on the loss (1) of training on states outside of the expert trajectories, we compute the average negative log-likelihood loss (NLL) with respect to expert trajectories on the test set for the STPN module of SPL and of the BC baseline, obtaining losses of 0.009 and 0.013, respectively. The lower NLL of STPN indicates that training on states outside the expert trajectories provides more informative features and a model that acts more similar to ground truth data (i.e. expert trajectories). Finally, the SPL agent obtains the second lowest one-step trajectory forecasting error, or average displacement error (ADE), as seen in Table 2 (left).

Table 3. *Left:* The SPL agent has learnt to avoid collisions with cars and pedestrians significantly better than BC, CV, S-GAN, ST-GAT and S-STG(CNN) on the Waymo data. *Right:* SPL-goal outperforms CADRL and GD on all metrics on Cityscapes. SPL-goal can reach goals while avoiding cars even in noisy scenes.

	SPL	BC	CV	S-GAN	ST-GAT	S-STG		f_o	f_v	f_s
f_o	**0.07**	0.16	0.22	0.60	0.71	0.15	**SPL-goal**	0.23	0.03	0.71
f_v	**0.03**	0.06	0.10	0.26	0.12	0.07	**CADRL**	0.28	0.10	0.70
d	1.4	**4.0**	1.2	2.9	2.5	0.34	**GD**	0.28	0.09	0.70

To the right in Table 1 the SPL-goal agent is compared to CADRL and to the goal direction (GD) heuristic when given a goal at a distance of 6 m. Our SPL-goal agent achieves a slightly higher success rate (f_s) than CADRL while being on par with GD. Moreover, SPL-goal is significantly better at avoiding collisions with cars, people and obstacles than the compared methods. In Fig. 3, the SPL-goal agent can be seen safely crossing streets to reach its goals.

Cityscapes. The 3d reconstructions of moving objects in the Cityscapes data can be noisy due to errors in depth estimation in frame-by-frame reconstruction, as well as noise in bounding boxes and semantic segmentation. Therefore the goal reaching task is harder in Cityscapes than in CARLA. Agents are initialized on pavement, near cars or randomly. The SPL-goal agent outperforms the GD heuristic and CADRL in collision avoidance as seen in Table 3 (right). Sample trajectories of our agent can be seen in Fig. 5.

Waymo. In Table 3 (left), our SPL agent, BC, CV, S-GAN, ST-GAT and ST-GCNN are evaluated on 4 second trajectories. The SPL agent is significantly better at collision avoidance than any other model that is only trained on expert pedestrian trajectories. It should be noted that the collision-aware SPL agent travels slower than BC to avoid collisions, which results in shorter trajectories on average. However SPL's trajectories are three times longer than S-STG(CNN) with half of the collisions. The SPL model has the second lowest ADE after BC (which shares SPL's architecture) on the Waymo dataset as seen in Table 2 (left). The SPL model is the only model to perform well on trajectory forecasting on both simulated and real data, while outperforming all models in collision avoidance. Qualitative examples of the SPL agent (without goals) are shown in Fig. 1, Fig. 6 and frame-by frame car avoidance in Fig. 4.

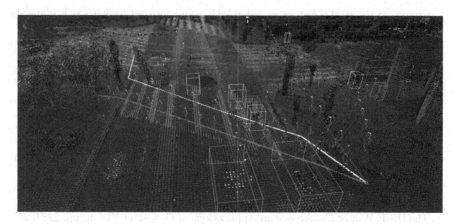

Fig. 6. SPL agent trajectories on the Waymo dataset, showing the pedestrian taking a number of different paths depending on how the agent history is initialized (cf. Sect. 2.2). Cars and other pedestrians are indicated with 3d bounding boxes.

4   Conclusions

We have introduced a novel hierarchical 3d pedestrian locomotion generation model, based on explicit 3d semantic representations of the scene and 3d pedestrian locomotion model. By training the generator with a unified reward and likelihood maximization objective, the model learns to forecast well on both real and simulated data, while outperforming even expert trajectories in collision avoidance. More generally, our formulation can be used to adapt or refine any maximum likelihood-based trajectory forecasting method to simultaneously handle collision avoidance and forecasting. Our formulation also enables the use of articulated human models to enforce human dynamics on the trajectory forecasting model. Finally, the proposed pedestrian motion generator can also be refined to plausibly navigate among other pedestrians and traffic to specific goals. Future work includes studying finer grained agent-scene interactions, for example modelling traffic signs, crossroads, and other relevant objects in urban scenes.

Acknowledgments. This work was supported by the European Research Council Consolidator grant SEED, CNCS-UEFISCDI PN-III-P4-ID-PCE-2016-0535 and PCCF-2016-0180, the EU Horizon 2020 Grant DE-ENIGMA, and the Swedish Foundation for Strategic Research (SSF) Smart Systems Program.

References

1. Chang, M.F., et al.: Argoverse: 3d tracking and forecasting with rich maps. In: CVPR (2019)
2. Sun, P., et al.: Scalability in perception for autonomous driving: Waymo open dataset (2019)
3. Caesar, H., et al.: nuScenes: a multimodal dataset for autonomous driving. In: CVPR (2020)
4. Behley, J., et al.: SemanticKITTI: a dataset for semantic scene understanding of lidar sequences. In: ICCV (2019)
5. Huang, X., et al.: The apolloscape dataset for autonomous driving. In: CVPR Workshops (2018)
6. Kesten, R., et al.: Lyft level 5 AV dataset 2019, vol. 2, p. 5 (2019). https.level5.lyft.com/dataset
7. Mangalam, K., Adeli, E., Lee, K.H., Gaidon, A., Niebles, J.C.: Disentangling human dynamics for pedestrian locomotion forecasting with noisy supervision. In: The IEEE Winter Conference on Applications of Computer Vision, pp. 2784–2793 (2020)
8. Mínguez, R.Q., Alonso, I.P., Fernández-Llorca, D., Sotelo, M.Á.: Pedestrian path, pose, and intention prediction through Gaussian process dynamical models and pedestrian activity recognition. IEEE Trans. Intell. Transp. Syst. **20**, 1803–1814 (2018)
9. Rasouli, A., Kotseruba, I., Tsotsos, J.K.: Pedestrian action anticipation using contextual feature fusion in stacked RNNs. arXiv preprint arXiv:2005.06582 (2020)

10. Bogo, F., Kanazawa, A., Lassner, C., Gehler, P., Romero, J., Black, M.J.: Keep it SMPL: automatic estimation of 3D human pose and shape from a single image. In: Leibe, B., Matas, J., Sebe, N., Welling, M. (eds.) ECCV 2016. LNCS, vol. 9909, pp. 561–578. Springer, Cham (2016). https://doi.org/10.1007/978-3-319-46454-1_34

11. Zanfir, M., Oneata, E., Popa, A.I., Zanfir, A., Sminchisescu, C.: Human synthesis and scene compositing. In: AAAI, pp. 12749–12756 (2020)

12. Wang, M., et al.: Example-guided style-consistent image synthesis from semantic labeling. In: The IEEE Conference on Computer Vision and Pattern Recognition (CVPR) (2019)

13. Cheng, S., et al.: Improving 3d object detection through progressive population based augmentation. arXiv preprint arXiv:2004.00831 (2020)

14. Ho, J., Ermon, S.: Generative adversarial imitation learning. In: NIPS (2016)

15. Rhinehart, N., Kitani, K.M., Vernaza, P.: R2p2: a reparameterized pushforward policy for diverse, precise generative path forecasting. In: ECCV (2018)

16. Li, Y.: Which way are you going? Imitative decision learning for path forecasting in dynamic scenes. In: Proceedings of the IEEE/CVF Conference on Computer Vision and Pattern Recognition (CVPR) (2019)

17. van der Heiden, T., Nagaraja, N.S., Weiss, C., Gavves, E.: SafeCritic: collision-aware trajectory prediction. In: British Machine Vision Conference Workshop (2019)

18. Zou, H., Su, H., Song, S., Zhu, J.: Understanding human behaviors in crowds by imitating the decision-making process. ArXiv abs/1801.08391 (2018)

19. Gupta, A., Johnson, J., Fei-Fei, L., Savarese, S., Alahi, A.: Social GAN: socially acceptable trajectories with generative adversarial networks. In: CVPR (2018)

20. Kosaraju, V., Sadeghian, A., Martín-Martín, R., Reid, I., Rezatofighi, H., Savarese, S.: Social-BiGAT: multimodal trajectory forecasting using bicycle-GAN and graph attention networks. In: NeurIPS (2019)

21. Zhang, L., She, Q., Guo, P.: Stochastic trajectory prediction with social graph network. CoRR abs/1907.10233 (2019)

22. Huang, Y., Bi, H., Li, Z., Mao, T., Wang, Z.: STGAT: modeling spatial-temporal interactions for human trajectory prediction. In: The IEEE International Conference on Computer Vision (ICCV) (2019)

23. Mohamed, A., Qian, K., Elhoseiny, M., Claudel, C.: Social-STGCNN: a social spatio-temporal graph convolutional neural network for human trajectory prediction. In: IEEE/CVF Conference on Computer Vision and Pattern Recognition (CVPR) (2020)

24. Alahi, A., Goel, K., Ramanathan, V., Robicquet, A., Li, F., Savarese, S.: Social LSTM: human trajectory prediction in crowded spaces. In: CVPR (2016)

25. Lee, N., Choi, W., Vernaza, P., Choy, C.B., Torr, P.H., Chandraker, M.: Desire: distant future prediction in dynamic scenes with interacting agents. In: CVPR (2017)

26. Luo, W., Yang, B., Urtasun, R.: Fast and furious: real time end-to-end 3d detection, tracking and motion forecasting with a single convolutional net. In: CVPR (2018)

27. Zhao, T., et al.: Multi-agent tensor fusion for contextual trajectory prediction. In: CVPR (2019)

28. Sadeghian, A., Kosaraju, V., Sadeghian, A., Hirose, N., Rezatofighi, H., Savarese, S.: SoPhie: an attentive GAN for predicting paths compliant to social and physical constraints. In: CVPR (2019)

29. Malla, S., Dariush, B., Choi, C.: Titan: future forecast using action priors. In: CVPR (2020)

30. Tanke, J., Weber, A., Gall, J.: Human motion anticipation with symbolic label. CoRR abs/1912.06079 (2019)
31. Liang, J., Jiang, L., Niebles, J.C., Hauptmann, A.G., Fei-Fei, L.: Peeking into the future: predicting future person activities and locations in videos. In: CVPR (2019)
32. Liang, J., Jiang, L., Murphy, K., Yu, T., Hauptmann, A.: The garden of forking paths: towards multi-future trajectory prediction. In: CVPR (2020)
33. Liang, J., Jiang, L., Hauptmann, A.: SimAug: learning robust representations from 3d simulation for pedestrian trajectory prediction in unseen cameras. arXiv preprint arXiv:2004.02022 (2020)
34. Makansi, O., Cicek, O., Buchicchio, K., Brox, T.: Multimodal future localization and emergence prediction for objects in egocentric view with a reachability prior. In: CVPR (2020)
35. Zhang, Y., Hassan, M., Neumann, H., Black, M.J., Tang, S.: Generating 3d people in scenes without people. In: Proceedings of the IEEE/CVF Conference on Computer Vision and Pattern Recognition, pp. 6194–6204 (2020)
36. Hong, S., Yan, X., Huang, T.S., Lee, H.: Learning hierarchical semantic image manipulation through structured representations. In: Advances in Neural Information Processing Systems, pp. 2708–2718 (2018)
37. Chien, J.T., Chou, C.J., Chen, D.J., Chen, H.T.: Detecting nonexistent pedestrians. In: CVPR (2017)
38. Li, X., Liu, S., Kim, K., Wang, X., Yang, M.H., Kautz, J.: Putting humans in a scene: learning affordance in 3d indoor environments. In: Proceedings of the IEEE Conference on Computer Vision and Pattern Recognition, pp. 12368–12376 (2019)
39. Lee, D., Pfister, T., Yang, M.H.: Inserting videos into videos. In: Proceedings of the IEEE Conference on Computer Vision and Pattern Recognition, pp. 10061–10070 (2019)
40. Wang, B., Adeli, E., Chiu, H.K., Huang, D.A., Niebles, J.C.: Imitation learning for human pose prediction. In: 2019 IEEE/CVF International Conference on Computer Vision (ICCV), pp. 7123–7132 (2019)
41. Wei, M., Miaomiao, L., Mathieu, S., Hongdong, L.: Learning trajectory dependencies for human motion prediction. In: ICCV (2019)
42. Du, X., Vasudevan, R., Johnson-Roberson, M.: Bio-LSTM: a biomechanically inspired recurrent neural network for 3-d pedestrian pose and gait prediction. IEEE Robot. Autom. Lett. **4**, 1501–1508 (2019)
43. Cao, Z., Gao, H., Mangalam, K., Cai, Q.-Z., Vo, M., Malik, J.: Long-term human motion prediction with scene context. In: Vedaldi, A., Bischof, H., Brox, T., Frahm, J.-M. (eds.) ECCV 2020. LNCS, vol. 12346, pp. 387–404. Springer, Cham (2020). https://doi.org/10.1007/978-3-030-58452-8_23
44. Adeli, V., Adeli, E., Reid, I., Niebles, J.C., Rezatofighi, H.: Socially and contextually aware human motion and pose forecasting. IEEE Robot. Autom. Lett. **5**, 6033–6040 (2020)
45. Chung, J., Gulcehre, C., Cho, K., Bengio, Y.: Empirical evaluation of gated recurrent neural networks on sequence modeling. arXiv preprint arXiv:1412.3555 (2014)
46. Williams, R.J.: Simple statistical gradient-following algorithms for connectionist reinforcement learning. Mach. Learn. **8**, 229–256 (1992)
47. Hodgins, J.: CMU graphics lab motion capture database (2015)
48. Ionescu, C., Papava, D., Olaru, V., Sminchisescu, C.: Human3. 6m: large scale datasets and predictive methods for 3d human sensing in natural environments. IEEE Trans. Pattern Anal. Mach. Intell. **36**, 1325–1339 (2013)
49. Joo, H., et al.: Panoptic studio: a massively multiview system for social motion capture. In: ICCV (2015)

50. Hochreiter, S., Schmidhuber, J.: Long short-term memory. Neural Comput. **9**, 1735–1780 (1997)
51. Holden, D., Komura, T., Saito, J.: Phase-functioned neural networks for character control. ACM Trans. Graph. **36**, 42:1–42:13 (2017)
52. Clevert, D.A., Unterthiner, T., Hochreiter, S.: Fast and accurate deep network learning by exponential linear units (elus). arXiv preprint arXiv:1511.07289 (2015)
53. Abadi, M., et al.: Tensorflow: a system for large-scale machine learning. In: 12th USENIX Symposium on Operating Systems Design and Implementation, OSDI 2016, Savannah, GA, USA, November 2–4, 2016 (2016)
54. Kingma, D.P., Ba, J.: Adam: a method for stochastic optimization. In: ICLR (2015)
55. Schöller, C., Aravantinos, V., Lay, F., Knoll, A.: What the constant velocity model can teach us about pedestrian motion prediction. IEEE Robot. Autom. Lett. **5**, 1696–1703 (2020)
56. Chandra, S., Bharti, A.K.: Speed distribution curves for pedestrians during walking and crossing. Procedia-Soc. Behav. Sci. **104**, 660–667 (2013)
57. Everett, M., Chen, Y.F., How, J.P.: Motion planning among dynamic, decision-making agents with deep reinforcement learning. In: IROS (2018)
58. Dosovitskiy, A., Ros, G., Codevilla, F., Lopez, A., Koltun, V.: CARLA: an open urban driving simulator. In: CoRL (2017)
59. Cordts, M., et al.: The cityscapes dataset for semantic urban scene understanding. In: CVPR (2016)
60. Nilsson, D., Sminchisescu, C.: Semantic video segmentation by gated recurrent flow propagation. In: CVPR (2018)
61. Schonberger, J.L., Frahm, J.M.: Structure-from-motion revisited. In: CVPR (2016)
62. Liu, S., Qi, L., Qin, H., Shi, J., Jia, J.: Path aggregation network for instance segmentation. In: CVPR (2018)
63. Zhou, B., et al.: Semantic understanding of scenes through the ADE20K dataset. IJCV **127**, 302–321 (2018)

Betrayed by Motion: Camouflaged Object Discovery via Motion Segmentation

Hala Lamdouar$^{(\boxtimes)}$, Charig Yang, Weidi Xie, and Andrew Zisserman

Visual Geometry Group, University of Oxford, Oxford, UK
{lamdouar,charig,weidi,az}@robots.ox.ac.uk
http://www.robots.ox.ac.uk/~vgg/data/MoCA

Abstract. The objective of this paper is to design a computational architecture that discovers camouflaged objects in videos, specifically by exploiting motion information to perform object segmentation. We make the following three contributions: (i) We propose a novel architecture that consists of two essential components for breaking camouflage, namely, a differentiable registration module to align consecutive frames based on the background, which effectively emphasises the object boundary in the difference image, and a motion segmentation module with memory that discovers the moving objects, while maintaining the object permanence even when motion is absent at some point. (ii) We collect the first large-scale Moving Camouflaged Animals (MoCA) video dataset, which consists of over 140 clips across a diverse range of animals (67 categories). (iii) We demonstrate the effectiveness of the proposed model on MoCA, and achieve competitive performance on the unsupervised segmentation protocol on DAVIS2016 by only relying on motion.

Keywords: Camouflage breaking · Motion segmentation

1 Introduction

We consider a fun yet challenging problem of breaking animal camouflage by exploiting their motion. Thanks to years of evolution, animals have developed the ability to hide themselves in the surrounding environment to prevent being noticed by their prey or predators. Consider the example in Fig. 1a, discovering the fish by its appearance can sometimes be extremely challenging, as the animal's texture is indistinguishable from its background environment. However, when the fish starts moving, even very subtly, it becomes apparent from the motion, as shown in Fig. 1c. Having the ability to segment objects both in still images, where this is possible, and also from motion, matches well to the two-stream hypothesis in neuroscience. This hypothesis suggests that the human visual cortex consists of two different processing streams: the ventral stream that performs recognition, and the dorsal stream that processes motion [1], providing strong cues for visual attention and detecting salient objects in the scene.

In recent years, computer vision research has witnessed tremendous progress, mainly driven by the ability of learning effective representations for detecting,

© Springer Nature Switzerland AG 2021
H. Ishikawa et al. (Eds.): ACCV 2020, LNCS 12623, pp. 488–503, 2021.
https://doi.org/10.1007/978-3-030-69532-3_30

(a) t-th frame.   (b) (t+1)-th frame.   (c) Optical flow.

Fig. 1. Two consecutive frames from the camouflage dataset, with a bounding box denoting the salient object. When the object starts moving, even subtly, we are able to detect it more easily, as shown, in the computed optical flow.

segmenting and classifying objects in *still images*. However, the assumption that objects can be well-segmented by their appearance alone is clearly an oversimplification; that is to say, if we draw an analogy from the two-stream hypothesis, the computer vision systems trained on images can only mimic the function of the ventral stream. The goal of this paper is to develop a computational architecture that is able to process motion representations for breaking camouflage, *e.g.* by taking optical flow (Fig. 1c) as input, and predicting a segmentation mask for the animal of interest.

Unfortunately, simply relying on motion will not solve our problem completely, as, *first*, optical flow estimation itself remains extremely challenging and is under active research. In practice, modern optical flow estimation techniques provide a fairly good indication of rough object motion, but not fine-grained details, *e.g.* the exact shape of the objects and their contours. To compensate for the missing details, we propose to use a differentiable registration module for aligning consecutive frames, and use the difference of the registered images as auxiliary information to determine the exact contour; *Second*, if the motion stops at certain points in the video sequence, then a memory module is required to maintain the object permanence, as is done in [2], *i.e.* to capture the idea that objects continue to exist even when they cannot be seen explicitly in the motion representation.

Another main obstacle encountered when addressing the challenging task of camouflage breaking is the limited availability of benchmarks to measure progress. In the literature, there is a Camouflaged Animals video dataset, released by Bideau *et al.* [3], but this has only 9 clips on 6 different kinds of animals (about 840 frames). To overcome this limitation, we collect a **Mo**ving **C**amouflaged **A**nimal dataset, termed **MoCA**, which consists of 141 video sequences (37K frames), depicting 67 kinds of camouflaged animals moving in natural scenes. Both temporal and spatial annotations are provided in the form of tight bounding boxes on every 5th frame and the rest are linearly interpolated.

To summarize, in this paper, we make the following contributions: *First*, we propose a novel architecture with two essential components for breaking camouflage, namely, a differentiable registration module to align the background (regions other than the camouflaged animal) of consecutive frames, which effectively highlights the object boundary in the difference image, and a motion segmentation module with memory that discovers moving objects, while maintaining the object permanence even when motion is absent at some point. *Second*, we collect the first large-scale video camouflage benchmark (MoCA), which we release to the community for measuring progress on camouflage breaking and object tracking. *Third*, we demonstrate the effectiveness of the proposed model on MoCA, outperforming the previous video segmentation approaches using motion. In addition, we also benchmark on DAVIS2016, achieving competitive performance on the unsupervised segmentation protocol despite using only motion. Note that, DAVIS2016 is fundamentally different from MoCA, in the sense that the objects are visually distinctive from the background, and hence motion may not be the most informative cue for segmentation.

2   Related Work

Our work cuts across several areas of research with a rich literature, we can only afford to review some of them here.

Video Object Segmentation [2–23] refers to the task of localizing objects in videos with pixel-wise masks. In general, two protocols have recently attracted an increasing interest from the vision community [4,5], namely unsupervised video object segmentation (**unsupervised VOS**), and semi-supervised video object segmentation (**semi-supervised VOS**). The former aims to automatically separate the object of interest (usually the most salient one) from its background in a video sequence; and the latter aims to re-localize one or multiple targets that are specified in the first frame of a video with pixel-wise masks. The popular methods to address the unsupervised VOS have extensively relied on a combination of appearance and motion cues, *e.g.* by clustering trajectories [6,7], or by using two stream networks [2,8–10]; or have purely used appearance [14,22,24,25]. For semi-supervised VOS, prior works can roughly be divided into two categories, one is based on mask propagation [11–16], and the other is related to few shot learning or online adaptation [17–19].

Camouflage Breaking [3,26] is closely related to the unsupervised VOS, however, it poses an extra challenge, as the object's appearance from *still image* can rarely provide any evidence for segmentation, *e.g.* boundaries. As such, the objects or animals will only be apparent when they start to move. In this paper, we are specifically interested in this type of problem, *i.e.* breaking the camouflage in a class-agnostic manner, where the model takes no prior knowledge of the object's category, shape or location, and is asked to discover the animal with pixel-wise segmentation masks whenever they move.

Image Registration/Alignment is a long-standing vision problem with the goal of transferring one image to another with as many pixels in correspondence as possible. It has been applied to numerous applications such as video stabilization, summarization, and the creation of panoramic mosaics. A comprehensive review can be found in [27,28]. In general, the pipeline usually involves both correspondence estimation and transformation estimation. Traditionally, the alignment methods apply hand-crafted features, *e.g.* SIFT [29], for keypoint detection and matching in a pair of images, and then compute the transformation matrix by solving a linear system. To increase the robustness of the geometric transformation estimation, RANdom SAmple Consensus (RANSAC) [30] is often adopted. In the deep learning era, researchers have constructed differentiable architectures that enable end-to-end optimization for the entire pipeline. For instance, [31] proposed a differentiable RANSAC by relaxing the sparse selection with a soft-argmax operation. Another idea is to train a network with binary classifications on the inliers/outliers correspondences using either ground truth supervision or a soft inlier count loss, as in [32–35], and solve the linear system with weighted least squares.

3   A Video Registration and Segmentation Network

At a high level, we propose a novel computational architecture for breaking animal camouflage, which *only* considers motion representation as input, *e.g.* optical flow, and produces the segmentation mask for the moving objects. Specifically, as shown in Fig. 2, the model consists of two modules: (i) a differentiable registration module for aligning consecutive frames, and computing the *difference* image to highlight the fine-grained detail of the moving objects, *e.g.* contours and boundaries (Sect. 3.2); and (ii) a motion segmentation network, which takes optical flow together with the difference image from the registration as input, and produces a detailed segmentation mask (Sect. 3.3).

3.1   Motion Representation

In this paper, we utilise optical flow as a representation of motion. Formally, consider two frames in a video sequence, I_t and I_{t+1}, each of dimension $\mathbb{R}^{H \times W \times 3}$, the optical flow is defined as the displacement field $F_{t \to t+1} \in \mathbb{R}^{H \times W \times 2}$ that maps each pixel from I_t to a corresponding one in I_{t+1}, such that:

$$I_t(\mathbf{x}) = I_{t+1}(\mathbf{x} + F_{t \to t+1}(\mathbf{x})), \tag{1}$$

where $\mathbf{x}$ represents the spatial coordinates (x, y) and F represents the vector flow field in both horizontal and vertical directions. In practice, we use the pretrained PWCNet [36] for flow estimation, some qualitative examples can be found in Fig. 1 and Fig. 5.

3.2   Differentiable Registration Module

One of the main challenges of segmentation with optical flow is the loss of rich fine-grained details due to motion approximations. In order to recover the sharp contours of the objects under motion, we seek a low level RGB signal which ideally suppresses the background and highlights the object's boundaries.

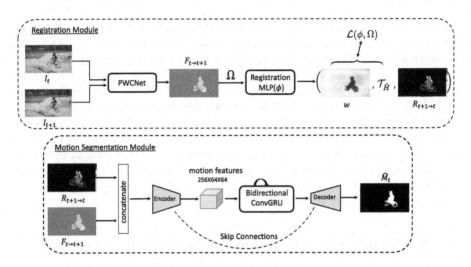

Fig. 2. Architecture overview. The proposed architecture is composed of two different modules, namely registration and motion segmentation.

In this paper, we use the image difference between consecutive frames after camera motion compensation. To this end, a reasonable assumption to make is that the foreground object undergoes an independent motion with respect to the global transformation of the background. We propose a differentiable registration module for estimating this transformation, which we approximate with a homography ($\mathcal{T}_{\hat{H}}$) between consecutive frames, and then compute the *difference* image after alignment ($R_{t+1\to t} = |\mathcal{T}_{\hat{H}}(I_{t+1}) - I_t|$), which will provide cues for the animal contours.

The key here is to train a registration module that accepts a set of correspondences obtained from the consecutive frames, outputs an homography transformation matrix (H), and an inlier weight map (w), which, ideally, acts like a RANSAC process, and has 1's for every background pixel, and 0's for every foreground pixel (moving object's). In this paper, we parametrize the registration module with Multiple Layer Perceptrons (MLPs), *i.e.* $[H, w] = \phi(\{p_s, p_t\}; \theta_r)$, where $p_s \in \mathcal{R}^{mn\times2}$ denotes the spatial coordinates of all pixels (normalized within the range $[-1, 1]$) in the source image, and their corresponding position in the target image ($p_t \in \mathcal{R}^{mn\times2}$), based on the computed optical flow, and θ_r are the trainable parameters.

Homography Transformation. In order to be self-contained, we summarise here the homography computation. Mathematically, a homography transformation ($\mathcal{T}_H$) maps a subset of points $\mathcal{S}_s$ from the source image to a subset of points $\mathcal{S}_t$ in the target image; in our case, the source and target images refer to I_{t+1} and I_t respectively:

$$\forall p_i{}^s \in \mathcal{S}_s, \ \exists p_i{}^t \in \mathcal{S}_t \quad p_i{}^t = \mathcal{T}_H(p_i{}^s) = \alpha_i H p_i{}^s, \tag{2}$$

where H is the matrix associated with the homography transformation $\mathcal{T}_H$ with 8 degrees of freedom, and α_i a non-zero scalar. This formulation can be expressed using homogeneous coordinates of $p_i{}^s$ and $p_i{}^t$ as:

$$\begin{pmatrix} x_i{}^t \\ y_i{}^t \\ 1 \end{pmatrix} = \alpha_i H \begin{pmatrix} x_i{}^s \\ y_i{}^s \\ 1 \end{pmatrix}. \tag{3}$$

Using the standard Direct Linear Transform (DLT) [27], the previous equation can be written as:

$$A\, vec(H) = \mathbf{0}, \tag{4}$$

where $vec(H) = \begin{pmatrix} h_{11} & h_{12} & h_{13} & h_{21} & h_{22} & h_{23} & h_{31} & h_{32} & h_{33} \end{pmatrix}^T$ is the vectorised homography matrix and A the data matrix. The homography H can therefore be estimated by solving such over-complete linear equation system. For more details on the DLT computation, refer to the extended ArXiv version of this paper.

Training Objective. In order to train the registration module $(\phi(\cdot; \theta_r))$, we can optimize:

$$\mathcal{L} = \frac{1}{\sum w} \sum_{\Omega} w \cdot ||\mathcal{T}_H(p_s) - p_t||_2 + R(w), \tag{5}$$

where Ω refers to all the pixels on the mn grid. Note that, the homography $\mathcal{T}_H$ transformation in this case can be solved with a simple weighted least square (WLS) and differentiable SVD [33] for parameter updating. To avoid trivial solution, where the weight map can be full of zeros that perfectly minimize the loss, we add a regularization term $(R(w))$, that effectively encourages as many inliers as possible:

$$R(w) = -\gamma \sum_{p \in \Omega} l_p - \frac{1}{mn} \sum_{\Omega} \{l_p \cdot \log(w) + (1 - l_p) \cdot \log(1 - w)\}, \tag{6}$$

$$\text{where} \quad l_p = \sigma\{(\epsilon - ||\mathcal{T}_H(p_s) - p_t||_2)/\tau\}.$$

In our training, $\gamma = 0.05$, $\tau = 0.01$, $\epsilon = 0.01$ and $m = n = 64$. The first term in $R(w)$ (l_p) refers to a differentiable inlier counting [32,34]. The rest of the terms aim to minimize the binary cross-entropy at each location of the inlier map, as in [37], forcing the predictions to be classified as inlier (1's) or outlier (0's).

3.3   Motion Segmentation Module

After introducing the motion representation and registration, we consider a sequence of frames from the video, $I \in \mathcal{R}^{T \times 3 \times H \times W}$, where the three channels refer to a concatenation of the flow (2 channels) and difference image (1 channel). For simplicity, here we use a variant of UNet [38] with the bottleneck feature maps being recurrently processed.

Specifically, the **Encoder** of the segmentation module will independently process the current inputs, ending up with motion features of $\mathcal{R}^{T \times 256 \times 64 \times 64}$, where $T, 256, 64, 64$ refer to the number of frames, number of channels, height, and width respectively. After the Encoder, the **memory module** (a bidirectional convGRU [39] is used in our case) operates on the motion features, updating them by aggregating the information from time steps in both directions. The **Decoder** takes the updated motion features, and produces an output binary segmentation mask, *i.e.* foreground vs background. The Motion Segmentation Module is trained with pixelwise binary cross-entropy loss.

This completes the descriptions of the two individual modules used in the proposed architectures. Note that the entire model is trained together as it is end-to-end differentiable.

4   MoCA: A New Moving Camouflaged Animal Dataset

One of the main obstacles encountered when addressing the challenging task of camouflage breaking is the limited availability of datasets. A comparison of existing datasets in Table 1. Bideau *et al.* published the first Camouflaged Animals video dataset with only 9 clips, and Le *et al.* proposed the CAMO dataset with only single image camouflage, and therefore not suitable for our video motion segmentation problem.

To overcome this limitation, we collect the **M**oving **C**amouflaged **A**nimal dataset, termed **MoCA**, which consists of 141 video sequences depicting various camouflaged animals moving in natural scenes. We include the PWC-Net optical flow for each frame and provide both spatial annotations in the form of bounding boxes and motion labels every 5-th frame with the rest linearly interpolated.

4.1   Detailed Statistics

MoCA contains 141 video sequences collected from YouTube, at the highest available resolution, mainly 720×1280, and sampled at 24 fps. A total of 37250 frames spanning 26 min. Each video represents a continuous sequence depicting one camouflaged animal, ranging from 1.0 to 79.0 s. The distribution of the video lengths is shown in Fig. 3a. The dataset is labelled with a bounding box in each

Table 1. Statistics for recent camouflage breaking datasets; "# Clips" denotes the number of clips in the dataset; "# Images" denotes the number of frames or images in the dataset; "# Animals" denotes the number of different animal categories in the dataset; "Video" indicates whether videos are available.

Datasets	# Clips	# Images	# Animals	Video
Camouflaged Animals [40]	9	839	6	✓
CAMO [26]	0	1250	80	✗
MoCA (ours)	141	37K	67	✓

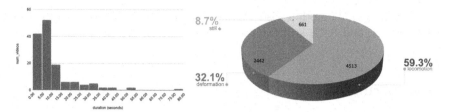

(a) Distribution of video lengths.   (b) Distribution of motion labels.

Fig. 3. Statistics for the Moving Camouflaged Animals (MoCA) dataset. In (a), the x-axis denotes the video duration, and the y-axis denotes the number of video sequences. (b) the distribution of frames according to their motion types (still, deformation and locomotion), see text for the detailed definitions.

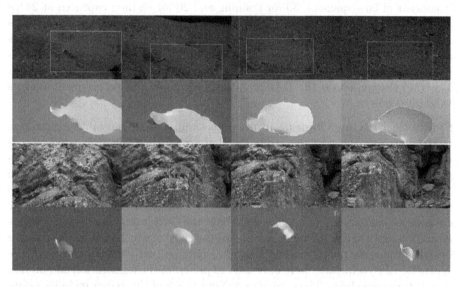

Fig. 4. Example sequences from the Moving Camouflaged Animals (MoCA) dataset with their corresponding optical flows.

frame, as well as a motion label for the type of motion. While annotating the data, we distinguish three types of motion:

- **Locomotion:** when the animal engages in a movement that leads to a significant change of its location within the scene *e.g.* walking, running, climbing, flying, crawling, slithering, swimming, *etc.*
- **Deformation:** when the animal engages in a more delicate movement that only leads to a change in its pose while remaining in the same location *e.g.* moving a part of its body.
- **Static:** when the animal remains still.

As shown in Fig. 3b, motion wise, the dataset contains 59.3% locomotion, 32.1% deformations, and 8.7% still frames. Examples from the dataset are shown in Fig. 4.

5 Experiments

In this section, we detail the experimental setting used in this paper, including the datasets, evaluation metrics, baseline approaches and training details.

5.1 Datasets

DAVIS2016 refers to the Densely Annotated VIdeo Segmentation dataset [41]. It consists of 50 sequences, 30 for training and 20 for testing, captured at 24 fps and provided at two resolutions. We use the 480p version in all experiments. This dataset has the advantage that accurate pixelwise ground truth segmentations are provided, 3,455 annotations in total, as well as spanning a variety of challenges, such as occlusions, fast-motion, non-linear deformation and motion-blur. We train the model on the DAVIS 2016 training set and report results on its validation splits.

Synthetic Moving Chairs. In order to train the differentiable registration module properly, we use video sequences that are synthetically generated. Specifically, we use the 3D-rendered objects from the Flying Chairs dataset as foreground, and take random images from YouTube-VOS as background. We then apply rigid motions, *e.g.* homographies, to the background, and simulate an independent motion for the foreground object. Note that, with such a synthetic dataset, we have complete information about the background homography transformation, optical flow, inlier maps, and object masks, which enables us to better initialise the registration module before training on real video sequences. These synthetic video sequences were only used to pre-train the registration and motion segmentation modules. The extended ArXiv version of this paper includes example images.

Evaluation Metrics. Depending on the benchmark dataset used, we consider two different evaluation metrics. For **DAVIS2016**, we follow the standard protocol for unsupervised video object segmentation proposed in [41], namely, the mean region similarity $\mathcal{J}$, which is the intersection-over-union (IOU) of the prediction and ground truth; and mean contour accuracy $\mathcal{F}$, which is the F-measure defined on contour points from the prediction and the ground truth. For **MoCA**, as we only have the bounding box annotations, we define the metric as the IOU between the groundtruth box and the minimum box that includes the predicted segmentation mask. Note that, we follow the same protocol used in Bideau *et al.* [3], meaning, we only evaluate the segmentation of the animals under locomotion or deformation (*not* in static frames).

5.2   Baselines

We compare with five previous state-of-the-art approaches [2, 10, 22, 23, 42]. In [2], Tokmakov *et al.*, the LVO method uses a two-stream network for motion segmentation, where the motion stream accepts optical flow as input via a MPNet [42] architecture, and the appearance stream uses an RGB image as input. Similar to ours, a memory module is also applied to recurrently process the frames. A more recent approach [10] adapts the Mask-RCNN architecture to motion segmentation, by leveraging motion cues from optical flow as a bottom-up signal for separating objects from each other, and combines this with appearance evidence for capturing the full objects. For fair comparison across methods, we use the same optical flow computed from PWCNet for all the flow-based methods. To this end, we re-implement the original MPNet [42], and train on the synthetic FT3D dataset [43]. For LVO [2], we also re-train the pipeline on DAVIS2016. For Seg-det [10] and Seg-track [10], we directly replace the flows from Flownet2 [44] with the ones from PWCNet in the model provided by the authors. In all cases, our re-implemented models outperform or match the performance reported in the original papers. In addition, we also compare our method to AnchorDiff [22] and COSNet [23], both approaches have been trained for unsupervised video object segmentation with only RGB video clips, and show very strong performance on DAVIS.

5.3   Training and Architecture Details

Registration Module. We adopt the architecture of [37], which is MLPs with 12 layer residual blocks. We first train the registration module on the Synthetic Moving Chairs sequences described in Sect. 5.1, for $10K$ iterations using an Adam optimizer with a weight decay of 0.005 and a batch size of 4. For a more stable training, we use a lower learning rate, *i.e.* 5×10^{-5}, avoiding the ill-conditioned matrix in the SVD.

Motion Segmentation Module. We adopt a randomly initialized ResNet-18. Frame-wise segmentation is trained from scratch on the synthetic dataset, together with the pre-trained registration module. We further include the bidirectional ConvGRU and finetune the whole pipeline on DAVIS 2016, with each sequence of length 11, batch size of 2, for a total of $25K$ iterations. For all trainings, we use frames with a resolution of $\mathcal{R}^{256 \times 256 \times 3}$.

6   Results

In this section, we first describe the performance of our model and previous state-of-the-art approaches on the new MoCA dataset, and then compare segmentation performance on the DAVIS2016 benchmark.

Table 2. Mean Intersection Over Union on MoCA for the different motion type subsets. "All_Motion" refers to the overall performance

Input	Model	RGB	Flow	Register	Memory	Locomotion	Deform	All_Motion
Flow	MPNet [42]	×	✓	×	✓	21.3	**23.5**	22.2
	Ours-A	×	✓	×	✓	31.3	17.8	27.6
	Ours-B	×	✓	MLP	×	29.9	15.6	25.5
	Ours-C	×	✓	MLP	✓	**47.8**	20.7	**39.4**
	Ours-D	×	✓	RANSAC	✓	42.9	19.2	35.8
RGB	AnchorDiff [22]	✓	×	×	×	30.9	29.4	30.4
	COSNet [23]	✓	×	×	×	35.9	35.1	36.2
Both	LVO [2]	✓	✓	×	✓	30.6	34.9	30.6
	Seg-det [10]	✓	✓	×	×	16.9	18.7	17.9
	Seg-track [10]	✓	✓	×	×	29.9	32.2	30.2
	Ours-E	✓	✓	MLP	✓	**45.0**	**38.0**	**42.4**

6.1   Results on the MoCA Benchmark

We summarise all the quantitative results in Table 2 and discuss them in the following sections. In Fig. 5, we illustrate the effect of the differentiable registration and Fig. 6 shows examples of the overall segmentation method.

Effectiveness of Registration/Alignment. To demonstrate the usefulness of the differentiable registration module, we carry out an ablation study. By comparing ours-A (without registration), ours-D (registration using RANSAC) and Ours-C (registration using our trainable MLPs), it is clear that the model with trainable MLPs for alignment helps to improve both the animal discovery on video sequences with locomotion and deformation, outperforming ours-A (without registration) and ours-D (RANSAC).

In Fig. 5 we visualise the results from the registration module, *e.g.* the inlier map, difference image before alignment (second last row) and after alignment (last row). It is clear that the difference images computed after alignment are able to ignore the background, and successfully highlight the boundary of the moving objects, *e.g.* the wheels of the bicycle from the first column.

Effectiveness of Memory. Comparing model-B (without memory) and model-C (with memory), the only difference lies on whether the frames are processed individually or recurrently. As shown by the results, a significant boost is obtained with the help of the memory module (25.5 vs. 39.4 on All_Motion), showing its effectiveness.

Comparison to Baselines and Previous Approaches. From Table 2, we make the following observations: *First*, when comparing with MPNet [42], which also processes optical flow, our model demonstrates a superior performance on All_Motion (39.4 vs 22.2), and an even larger gap on Locomotion, showing the usefulness of image registration and memory modules; *Second*, as expected, the state-of-the-art unsupervised video segmentation approaches relying on appearance (RGB image as input), *e.g.* AnchorDiff [22] and COSNet [23], tend to

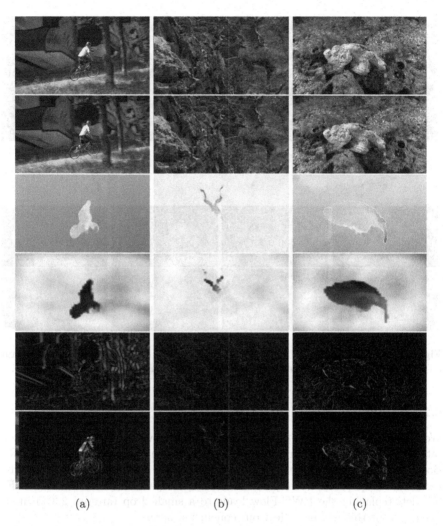

Fig. 5. Registration results from (a) the validation set of DAVIS 2016; and (b)(c) MoCA. From top to bottom: frame t, frame $t + 1$, Forward PWCNet optical flow, inlier weights (background pixels are shown as gray or white), image difference without alignment, aligned image difference.

struggle on this camouflage breaking task, as the animals often blend with the background, and appearance then does not provide informative cues for segmentation, emphasising the importance of motion information (by design) in this dataset; *Third*, when we adopt a two-stream model, *i.e.* extend the architecture with a Deeplabv3-based appearance model, and naively average the prediction from appearance and flow models, the performance can be further boosted from 39.4 to 42.4, significantly outperforming all the other two-stream competitors, *e.g.* LVO [2], Seg-det and Seg-seg [10].

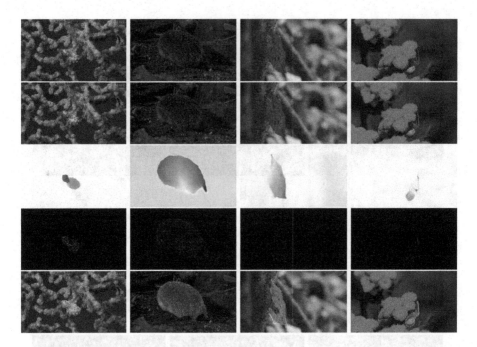

Fig. 6. Motion segmentation results on MoCA. From top to bottom: frame t, frame $t + 1$, PWCNet optical flow, aligned image difference, moving object segmentation.

6.2 Results on DAVIS2016 Benchmark

We compare to previous approaches on the Unsupervised Video Object Segmentation protocol. In all experiments, we *do not* use any post-processing *e.g.* CRF. Both our re-trained MPNet and LVO model outperform the original reported results in the papers, which guarantees a fair comparison with their model. For Seg-det, replacing the PWC-Flow leads to a small drop (around 2.3%) in the mean $\mathcal{J}$, but this will not affect our conclusion here.

As shown in Table 3, when compared with MPNet which also take flow-only input, our model (ours-C) outperforms it on all metrics by a large margin. Note that, the DAVIS benchmark is fundamentally different from MoCA, as the approaches only relying on appearance are very effective [22], indicating that the objects in the DAVIS sequences can indeed be well-identified by the appearance, and motion is not playing the dominant role as it is in MoCA. This can also be observed from the results for Seg-det, Seg-track, AnchorDiff and COSNet, which show significantly stronger performance on DAVIS than on MoCA. Given this difference, our flow-based architecture still shows very competitive performance. Moreover, when we extend our model with an RGB appearance stream, we do observe a performance boost, but since our appearance model has only been finetuned on the DAVIS training set (30 training sequences), the two stream (ours-E) is not comparable with other models trained with more segmentation data.

Table 3. Results on the validation set of DAVIS 2016.

Measure		Flow-based		RGB-based		Two-stream			
		MPNet [42]	**Ours-C**	AD [22]	COSNet [23]	LVO [2]	[10]-det	[10]-track	**Ours-E**
$\mathcal{J}$	Mean	60.3	**65.3**	**80.3**	77.6	69.8	**76.8**	75.8	69.9
	Recall	69.9	**77.3**	90.0	**91.4**	83.8	84.8	81.8	**85.3**
$\mathcal{F}$	Mean	58.7	**65.1**	**79.3**	77.5	70.1	**77.8**	76.1	70.3
	Recall	64.3	**74.7**	84.7	**87.4**	84.3	**91.3**	88.7	82.9

7   Conclusions

To summarise, in this paper we consider the problem of breaking animal camouflage in videos. Specifically, we propose a novel and effective architecture with two components: a differentiable registration module to highlight object boundaries; and a motion segmentation module with memory that discovers moving regions. As future work, we propose to improve the architecture from two aspects: *First*, building more effective memory module for handling longer video sequences, for example, a Transformer [45]. *Second*, for objects that are only partially moving, RGB appearance is required to get the sense of objectness, therefore a future direction is to explore RGB inputs, for both visual-matching-based registration and appearance features.

Acknowledgements. This research was supported by the UK EPSRC CDT in AIMS, Schlumberger Studentship, and the UK EPSRC Programme Grant Seebibyte EP/M013774/1.

References

1. Goodale, M.A., Milner, A.D.: Separate visual pathways for perception and action. Trends Neurosci. **15**, 20–25 (1992)
2. Tokmakov, P., Schmid, C., Alahari, K.: Learning to segment moving objects. IJCV **127**, 282–301 (2019)
3. Bideau, P., Learned-Miller, E.: A detailed rubric for motion segmentation. arXiv preprint arXiv:1610.10033 (2016)
4. Pont-Tuset, J., Perazzi, F., Caelles, S., Arbeláez, P., Sorkine-Hornung, A., Gool, L.V.: The 2017 Davis challenge on video object segmentation. arXiv preprint arXiv:1704.00675 (2017)
5. Xu, N., et al.: YouTube-VOS: a large-scale video object segmentation benchmark. In: Proceedings of ECCV (2018)
6. Brox, T., Malik, J.: Object segmentation by long term analysis of point trajectories. In: Daniilidis, K., Maragos, P., Paragios, N. (eds.) ECCV 2010. LNCS, vol. 6315, pp. 282–295. Springer, Heidelberg (2010). https://doi.org/10.1007/978-3-642-15555-0_21
7. Ochs, P., Brox, T.: Object segmentation in video: a hierarchical variational approach for turning point trajectories into dense regions. In: Proceedings of ICCV (2011)
8. Papazoglou, A., Ferrari, V.: Fast object segmentation in unconstrained video. In: Proceedings of ICCV (2013)

9. Jain, S.D., Xiong, B., Grauman, K.: FusionSeg: learning to combine motion and appearance for fully automatic segmentation of generic objects in videos. In: Proceedings of CVPR (2017)

10. Dave, A., Tokmakov, P., Ramanan, D.: Towards segmenting anything that moves. In: ICCV Workshop on Holistic Video Understanding (2019)

11. Oh, S.W., Lee, J.Y., Xu, N., Kim, S.J.: Video object segmentation using space-time memory networks. In: Proceedings of ICCV (2019)

12. Voigtlaender, P., Chai, Y., Schroff, F., Adam, H., Leibe, B., Chen, L.C.: FEELVOS: fast end-to-end embedding learning for video object segmentation. In: Proceedings of CVPR (2019)

13. Vondrick, C., Shrivastava, A., Fathi, A., Guadarrama, S., Murphy, K.: Tracking emerges by colorizing videos. In: ECCV (2018)

14. Wang, W., Lu, X., Shen, J., Crandall, D.J., Shao, L.: Zero-shot video object segmentation via attentive graph neural networks. In: Proceedings of ICCV (2019)

15. Lai, Z., Xie, W.: Self-supervised learning for video correspondence flow. In: Proceedings of BMVC (2019)

16. Lai, Z., Lu, E., Xie, W.: MAST: a memory-augmented self-supervised tracker. In: Proceedings of CVPR (2020)

17. Maninis, K.K., et al.: Video object segmentation without temporal information. IEEE Trans. Pattern Anal. Mach. Intell. **41**, 1515-1530 (2018)

18. Voigtlaender, P., Leibe, B.: Online adaptation of convolutional neural networks for video object segmentation. arXiv (2017)

19. Caelles, S., Maninis, K.K., Pont-Tuset, J., Leal-Taixé, L., Cremers, D., Van Gool, L.: One-shot video object segmentation. In: Proceedings of CVPR (2017)

20. Fragkiadaki, K., Zhang, G., Shi, J.: Video segmentation by tracing discontinuities in a trajectory embedding. In: Proceedings of CVPR (2012)

21. Keuper, M., Andres, B., Brox, T.: Motion trajectory segmentation via minimum cost multicuts. In: Proceedings of ICCV (2015)

22. Yang, Z., Wang, Q., Bertinetto, L., Bai, S., Hu, W., Torr, P.H.: Anchor diffusion for unsupervised video object segmentation. In: Proceedings of ICCV (2019)

23. Xiankai, L., Wenguan, W., Chao, M., Jianbing, S., Ling, S., Fatih, P.: See more, know more: unsupervised video object segmentation with co-attention Siamese networks. In: Proceedings of CVPR (2019)

24. Koh, Y.J., Kim, C.S.: Primary object segmentation in videos based on region augmentation and reduction. In: Proceedings of CVPR (2017)

25. Fan, D.P., Wang, W., Cheng, M.M., Shen, J.: Shifting more attention to video salient object detection. In: Proceedings of CVPR (2019)

26. Le, T.N., Nguyen, T.V., Nie, Z., Tran, M.T., Sugimoto, A.: Anabranch network for camouflaged object segmentation. CVIU **184**, 45–56 (2016)

27. Hartley, R.I., Zisserman, A.: Multiple View Geometry in Computer Vision, 2nd edn. Cambridge University Press, Cambridge (2004). ISBN:0521540518

28. Szeliski, R.: Image alignment and stitching: a tutorial. Technical report MSR-TR-2004-92 (2004)

29. Lowe, D.: Object recognition from local scale-invariant features. In: Proceedings of ICCV, pp. 1150–1157 (1999)

30. Fischler, M.A., Bolles, R.C.: Random sample consensus: a paradigm for model fitting with applications to image analysis and automated cartography. Commun. ACM **24**, 381–395 (1981)

31. Brachmann, E., et al.: DSAC-differentiable RANSAC for camera localization. In: Proceedings of CVPR (2017)

32. Brachmann, E., Rother, C.: Learning less is more-6d camera localization via 3d surface regression. In: Proceedings of CVPR (2018)
33. Ranftl, R., Koltun, V.: Deep fundamental matrix estimation. In: Proceedings of ECCV (2018)
34. Rocco, I., Arandjelovic, R., Sivic, J.: End-to-end weakly-supervised semantic alignment. In: Proceedings of CVPR (2018)
35. Brachmann, E., Rother, C.: Neural-guided RANSAC: learning where to sample model hypotheses. In: Proceedings of ICCV (2019)
36. Sun, D., Yang, X., Liu, M.Y., Kautz, J.: PWC-Net: CNNs for optical flow using pyramid, warping, and cost volume. In: Proceedings of CVPR (2018)
37. Yi, K.M., Trulls, E., Ono, Y., Lepetit, V., Salzmann, M., Fua, P.: Learning to find good correspondences. In: Proceedings of CVPR (2018)
38. Ronneberger, O., Fischer, P., Brox, T.: U-Net: convolutional networks for biomedical image segmentation. In: Navab, N., Hornegger, J., Wells, W.M., Frangi, A.F. (eds.) MICCAI 2015. LNCS, vol. 9351, pp. 234–241. Springer, Cham (2015). https://doi.org/10.1007/978-3-319-24574-4_28
39. Ballas, N., Yao, L., Pal, C., Courville, A.: Delving deeper into convolutional networks for learning video representations. In: Proceedings of ICLR (2016)
40. Bideau, P., Learned-Miller, E.: It's moving! a probabilistic model for causal motion segmentation in moving camera videos. In: Leibe, B., Matas, J., Sebe, N., Welling, M. (eds.) ECCV 2016. LNCS, vol. 9912, pp. 433–449. Springer, Cham (2016). https://doi.org/10.1007/978-3-319-46484-8_26
41. Perazzi, F., Pont-Tuset, J., McWilliams, B., Van Gool, L., Gross, M., Sorkine-Hornung, A.: A benchmark dataset and evaluation methodology for video object segmentation. In: Proceedings of CVPR (2016)
42. Tokmakov, P., Alahari, K., Schmid, C.: Learning motion patterns in videos. In: Proceedings of CVPR (2017)
43. Mayer, N., et al.: A large dataset to train convolutional networks for disparity, optical flow, and scene flow estimation. In: Proceedings of CVPR (2016)
44. Ilg, E., Mayer, N., Saikia, T., Keuper, M., Dosovitskiy, A., Brox, T.: FlowNet 2.0: evolution of optical flow estimation with deep network. In: Proceedings of CVPR (2017)
45. Vaswani, A., et al.: Attention is all you need. In: NIPS (2017)

Visual Tracking by TridentAlign
and Context Embedding

Janghoon Choi[1]([✉]), Junseok Kwon[2], and Kyoung Mu Lee[1]

[1] ASRI, Department of ECE, Seoul National University, Seoul, South Korea
{ultio791,kyoungmu}@snu.ac.kr
[2] School of CSE, Chung-Ang University, Seoul, South Korea
jskwon@cau.ac.kr

Abstract. Recent advances in Siamese network-based visual tracking methods have enabled high performance on numerous tracking benchmarks. However, extensive scale variations of the target object and distractor objects with similar categories have consistently posed challenges in visual tracking. To address these persisting issues, we propose novel TridentAlign and context embedding modules for Siamese network-based visual tracking methods. The TridentAlign module facilitates adaptability to extensive scale variations and large deformations of the target, where it pools the feature representation of the target object into multiple spatial dimensions to form a feature pyramid, which is then utilized in the region proposal stage. Meanwhile, context embedding module aims to discriminate the target from distractor objects by accounting for the global context information among objects. The context embedding module extracts and embeds the global context information of a given frame into a local feature representation such that the information can be utilized in the final classification stage. Experimental results obtained on multiple benchmark datasets show that the performance of the proposed tracker is comparable to that of state-of-the-art trackers, while the proposed tracker runs at real-time speed. (Code available on https://github.com/JanghoonChoi/TACT).

1 Introduction

Visual tracking, which has practical applications such as automated surveillance, robotics, and image stabilization, is one of the fundamental problems among the fields under computer vision research. Given initial target bounding box coordinates along with the first frame of a video sequence, visual tracking algorithms aim to precisely locate the target object in the subsequent frames of the video. Tracking algorithms are designed to successfully track targets under various circumstances such as scale change, illumination change, occlusion, deformation, and motion blur.

Electronic supplementary material The online version of this chapter (https://doi.org/10.1007/978-3-030-69532-3_31) contains supplementary material, which is available to authorized users.

H. Ishikawa et al. (Eds.): ACCV 2020, LNCS 12623, pp. 504–520, 2021.
https://doi.org/10.1007/978-3-030-69532-3_31

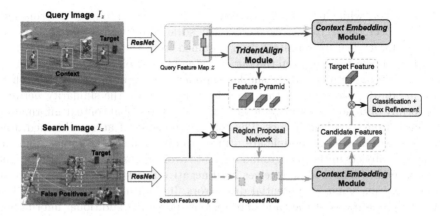

Fig. 1. Overview of the proposed visual tracking framework. Our tracker incorporates the TridentAlign module, which generates a feature pyramid representation of the target that can be utilized for better scale adaptability of the RPN. Moreover, the context embedding module modulates the locally pooled features to incorporate the global context information of a given frame, which encourages the discrimination of the target object from false positives.

Along with the wide application of convolutional neural networks (CNNs) to various computer vision tasks [1–3], recent advances in Siamese network-based visual tracking methods [4–7] have advantages in performance and speed owing to the scalability of the network and elimination of online updates. However, most existing Siamese trackers are still designed and trained for short-term tracking scenarios [8,9] with strong assumptions of motion smoothness and gradual scale change. In order to impose these assumptions, most trackers assume a small search region around the target and penalize large displacements using hand-crafted window functions. This makes the tracker susceptible to error accumulation and drift due to erroneous localizations, leading to lower performance in numerous long-term tracking scenarios [10–12] in which smoothness assumptions are no longer valid. To alleviate these problems, recent Siamese trackers have adopted full-frame search [13,14], so that the target location can be recovered after the out-of-frame disappearance, at the cost of computation time and with sub-real-time speeds. Although a full-frame search can be effective for re-detecting the target, it is susceptible to distractors with appearances similar to that of the target owing to the lack of temporal consistency and global context modeling. Diverse scale variations of the target can also lead to failed re-detection because the target feature representation has a fixed spatial dimension that may fail to represent the wide spatial variation of the target object.

In this paper, we propose a novel real-time visual tracking algorithm to address the aforementioned issues by incorporating the TridentAlign and context embedding modules into our tracking framework, where our region proposal network (RPN) is inspired by the success of recent object detectors. We incorporate the anchor-free FCOS [15] detector head in our RPN to minimize the number of parameters while maximizing the flexibility with regard to large deformations in the aspect ratio. To further enforce the scale adaptiveness of the RPN, we use the target feature representation obtained from the TridentAlign module, which pools the features from the target region to multiple spatial dimensions to form a feature pyramid, where similar approaches have been shown to be effective in [16–19]. Moreover, rather than focusing only on the similarity between the locally obtained features, we make full use of the global context information obtained from the given frames. The context-embedded features obtained from the context embedding module are utilized to discriminate the target from the distractor objects in the background region to avoid choosing false-positives. The context embedding module receives hard negative features pooled from a given frame that encompasses potential distractors. It then modulates the local feature representations of the candidate regions, providing additional information on global context.

We compare our method to other Siamese network-based trackers on large-scale visual tracking datasets LaSOT [10], OxUvA [12], TrackingNet [11], and GOT-10k [20] thereby demonstrating performance comparable to that of state-of-the-art trackers. Moreover, our proposed modules require minimal computational overhead, and our tracker is able to run at real-time speed. Our overall tracking framework is shown in Fig. 1.

2   Related Work

CNN-Based Trackers: Conventional online visual tracking algorithms solve the tracking problem via tracking-by-detection, where they attempt to locate the target inside a search region by finding the position where the classifier produces the highest similarity/classification score to that of the target. Given the powerful representation capabilities of CNNs, recent trackers use CNNs for feature representation and classification. One early CNN-based tracker [21] used the feature representation obtained from the denoising autoencoder network. In MDNet [22], VGG [23] features with multi-task training are used, and this tracker is accelerated to real-time speed in [24] by using ROIAlign [25]. Correlation filter-based trackers [26,27] are also widely used on top of pretrained deep features. Notable approaches include the use of the continuous convolutional operator for the fusion of multi-resolution CNN features [28,29], spatially regularized filters [30], the fusion of deep and shallow features [31], and group feature selection [32].

Siamese Network-Based Trackers: Siamese network-based trackers have gained attention owing to their simplicity and high performance. SiamFC [4] proposed a fully convolutional end-to-end approach to visual tracking, enabling increased speed and accuracy, in which correlation filter can be also trained on top of the feature map [33]. SiamRPN [5] added RPN in the final stage for more accurate localization and size estimation, and DaSiamRPN [34] improved the discriminability of the network by adding negative pairs during training to rule out distractors. Both [6] and [7] employed deeper and wider backbone networks based on [2] and [35] with extensive experimental analysis to achieve further performance gains. Other notable approaches include the use of a dynamic network with a transformation learning model [36], pattern detection for local structure-based prediction [37], and cascaded region proposal for progressive refinement [38]. Recently, noteworthy methods have been proposed to improve the discriminability of the network by performing adaptation at test-time. Particularly, [39] and [40] used gradient information obtained during tracking to update the target representation. Moreover, [41] used a learned update module to obtain the updated accumulated template. An optimization-based model predictor is used in [42] to predict the classifier weights.

Context-Aware Trackers: Conventional visual tracking algorithms treat all candidate regions in the search image independently. They perform tracking by choosing the candidate region with the highest similarity score to the target, where other candidate regions have no influence on this decision process. Online adaptation-based approaches partially address this issue by updating the tracker with previously obtained self-labeled training examples at test-time [22,40,42]; however, the possibility of error accumulation and drift persists. Several tracking approaches take a broader context area into consideration [43,44]. Particularly, [43] employs a context-aware network in the initial adaptation process to choose an expert autoencoder that is used throughout the online tracking process. Furthermore, [44] proposed a generic context-aware correlation filter learning scheme that can add contextual information for better background suppression. Nevertheless, the context modeling in these approaches is still limited to a fixed spatial region around the target, which lacks the global context information of all the possible distractors in a given scene.

Long-Term Trackers: With growing interest on long-term visual tracking tasks and more benchmarks becoming available to the public [10,12,45], tracking algorithms focused on solving long-term tracking scenarios have emerged. Long-term visual tracking problems are typically defined as problems involving the tracking of a target object in a relatively long (*e.g.*, >1 min) video sequence, during which the target may disappear for a brief period [12]. The main challenge of long-term tracking tasks is recovering the target after its disappearance or a tracking failure. To solve this problem, [34,46] attempted to expand the search area when the confidence value falls below a predefined threshold. Moreover, [13,14] performed a full-frame search without any locality assumption. Our approach shares some similarities with [13], but it differs significantly in these aspects: (1) We use the proposed TridentAlign module to construct a feature pyramid representation of the target for improved scale adaptability and part-based predictions in the region proposal stage, whereas [13] pools the target feature into a 1×1 kernel, losing spatial information; (2) Our tracker introduces the context embedding module, which employs hard negative features obtained from potential distractors as contextual information, and the local feature representations can be modulated accordingly during tracking. In contrast, [13] only uses local features without any consideration of the context, which makes it susceptible to distractors; (3) Our tracker runs at a real-time speed of 57 fps with a ResNet-18 backbone and 42 fps with a ResNet-50 backbone. It thus achieves higher performance on LaSOT [10] with a significantly lighter backbone network (ResNet-18) and is approximately 9 times faster than the model proposed in [13], which uses a significantly deeper backbone network (ResNet-50).

3   Proposed Method

Inspired by two-stage object detection networks [3,16,17], our framework largely includes two stages: the region proposal stage and classification stage. Given a pair of input RGB images, that is, the query image (initial frame) I_z and search image (current frame) I_x along with the shared backbone network $\varphi(\cdot)$, the respective feature maps $z = \varphi(I_z)$ and $x = \varphi(I_x)$ are obtained and then passed to the RPN. In the region proposal stage, the RPN generates proposals for target region-of-interest (RoIs) in the search image, given the target information obtained from the query image. Subsequently, in the classification stage, the classifier performs binary classification on the ROI proposals obtained in the previous stage, with a positive result indicating the target region and a negative indicating the background region. Figure 1 shows the overall flow of the proposed method.

In the following subsections, we provide more detailed explanations of the proposed TridentAlign module used in the region proposal stage and context embedding module used in the classification stage. Then, we describe the online tracking procedure for our approach.

3.1   Region Proposal with Scale Adaptive TridentAlign

The initial target bounding box coordinates and input feature maps are given as $z, x \in \mathbb{R}^{h \times w \times c}$, where the channel dimension of the input feature maps are reduced from the original outputs of the ResNet backbone by employing 1×1 conv layers. Using these feature maps, the TridentAlign module performs multiple ROIAlign [25] operations on z with varying spatial dimensions to obtain target feature representations $z_i \in \mathbb{R}^{s_i \times s_i \times c}$, where s_i is the spatial dimension of the pooled features. These features form a feature pyramid denoted as $Z = \{z_1, z_2, ..., z_K\}$, where K is the total number of features in the feature pyramid. Then, the depth-wise cross-correlation between search feature map x and each target feature z_i in the feature pyramid Z is calculated as

$$\hat{x}_i = x \circledast z_i, \tag{1}$$

where $\circledast$ denotes the depth-wise cross-correlation operator with zero padding. As a result, each $\hat{x}_i \in \mathbb{R}^{h \times w \times c}$ is obtained for the corresponding z_i and is concatenated along the channel dimension to form the multi-scale correlation map $[\hat{x}_1, \hat{x}_2, ..., \hat{x}_K] = \hat{x} \in \mathbb{R}^{h \times w \times Kc}$. The correlation map is then refined as in $f_{att}(\hat{x}) \in \mathbb{R}^{h \times w \times c}$ using a self-attention block analogous to that employed in [47]. In this self-attention block, the adaptive channel and spatial attention weights are applied to focus on a specific position and target scale, followed by a 1×1 conv layer, thereby reducing the channel dimension back to c.

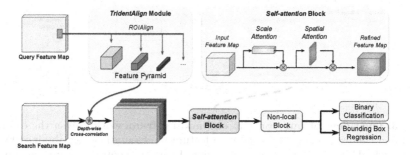

Fig. 2. Overview of the proposed region proposal network. The feature pyramid representation of the target is constructed using our TridentAlign module, wherein each feature undergoes a depth-wise cross-correlation operation with the search feature map. The correlated feature maps are concatenated along the channel dimension; here, a self-attention block is used to focus more on a certain spatial area with a certain target scale. Followed by a non-local block [48] and binary classification/bounding box regression branches, ROI can be obtained.

With the refined correlation map, we use the detection head module employed in [15], where each branch outputs binary classification labels and bounding box regression values. For a single location (i, j) inside the output map, classification labels $p_{i,j}$ with bounding box regression values $t_{i,j}$ are predicted from the respective branches. At training stage, if a location (i, j) is inside the ground-truth (GT) target bounding box, it is considered a positive sample and we assign the GT label $c_{i,j}^* = 1$ and GT regression target $t_{i,j}^* = (l^*, t^*, r^*, b^*)$, where l^*, t^*, r^*, and b^* are the distances from (i, j) to the four sides (left, top, right, bottom) of the bounding box, respectively. For negative samples, we assign $c_{i,j}^* = 0$. To train the overall RPN, we use the same loss as the one used in [15]:

$$L_{rpn}(\{p_{i,j}\}, \{t_{i,j}\}) = \frac{1}{N_{pos}} \sum_{i,j} L_{cls}(p_{i,j}, c_{i,j}^*) + \frac{\lambda}{N_{pos}} \sum_{i,j} \mathbf{1}_{\{c_{i,j}^* > 0\}} L_{reg}(t_{i,j}, t_{i,j}^*),$$

$$(2)$$

where N_{pos} is the number of positive samples, L_{cls} is the focal loss [17], and L_{reg} is the linear IoU loss. The loss is summed over all locations of the output map, and L_{reg} is only calculated for positive samples. Subsequently, a non-maximum suppression (NMS) operation is performed to obtain the top N candidate ROIs. The overall architecture of the RPN is illustrated in Fig. 2.

3.2 Classification with Context-Embedded Features

Given the candidate ROIs obtained from the preceding region proposal stage, ROIAlign operations are performed on the search feature map x to obtain a set of candidate features $X = \{x_1, x_2, ..., x_N\}$, where each $x_i \in \mathbb{R}^{s \times s \times c}$ with N candidate regions. Using all of the candidate features in X to generate the global context information, we aim to modulate each feature x_i to obtain the context-embedded feature $\tilde{x}_i \in \mathbb{R}^{s \times s \times c}$. First, element-wise maximum and averaging operations are

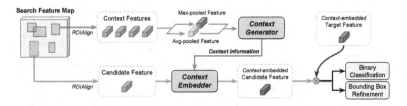

Fig. 3. Overview of our context embedding framework. Given the candidate ROI and context regions, the respective feature representations are obtained by performing ROIAlign operations on each region. Using the context features, max-pooled and average-pooled features are obtained via element-wise maximum and averaging operations. The context generator receives these features to generate the global context information, which the context embedder embeds into the candidate features. Finally, the context-embedded candidate feature can be compared with the context-embedded target features for binary classification and bounding box refinement.

performed over all features in X to obtain max-pooled and average-pooled features, which are concatenated along the channel dimension as $x_{cxt} \in \mathbb{R}^{s \times s \times 2c}$. Then, inside the context embedding module, context generator $g_1(\cdot)$ receives x_{cxt} to generate the global context information, and context embedder $g_2(\cdot)$ receives both the candidate feature x_i and context information from g_1 to generate the context-embedded feature $\tilde{x}_i$. The overall context embedding scheme is illustrated in Fig. 3. For our context generator and embedder design, we test 4 variants: (1) simple concatenation, (2) simple addition, (3) CBAM [47], and (4) FILM [49] based modules. The details of each variant are listed in Table 1.

For the simple concatenation-based module (Table 1(1)), x_{cxt} is directly used as context information and the context embedder g_2 receives $[x_i, x_{cxt}]$ as input, where $[\cdot, \cdot]$ denotes concatenation along the channel dimension. In the simple addition-based module (Table 1(2)), context information is generated in a form of additive modulation δ, which is added to the original candidate feature x_i. For the CBAM-based module (Table 1(3)), context information is generated and applied to x_i as channel attention m_c and spatial attention m_s. Finally, the FILM-based module (Table 1(4)) modulates x_i by applying an affine transformation with coefficients γ and β.

Table 1. Variants of the context embedding module. We test 4 possible implementations of the context embedding module. For 3-layer CNNs, we use 1×1 kernels with output channels set to c, followed by ReLU activation.

	Generator $g_1(x_{cxt})$		Embedder $g_2(g_1(x_{cxt}), x_i)$
	Type	Output	Operation
(1) Simple concat.	Identity	$x_{cxt} \in \mathbb{R}^{s \times s \times 2c}$	3-layer CNN, $g_2([x_i, x_{cxt}])$
(2) Simple add.	3-layer CNN	$\delta \in \mathbb{R}^{s \times s \times c}$	$x_i + \delta$
(3) CBAM-based	3-layer CNN	$m_c \in \mathbb{R}^{1 \times 1 \times c}, m_s \in \mathbb{R}^{s \times s \times 1}$	$(x_i \otimes m_c) \otimes m_s$
(4) FILM-based	3-layer CNN	$\gamma, \beta \in \mathbb{R}^{s \times s \times c}$	$\gamma \otimes x_i + \beta$

Algorithm 1: TACT

Input   : Tracking sequence of length L, $\{I^1, I^2, ..., I^L\}$
          Initial target bounding box coordinates
Output: Target bounding box coordinates for each frame

 # Initialization at $t = 1$
Compute query feature map $z = \varphi(I^1)$ for initial frame I^1
Build target feature pyramid Z from z using TridentAlign
Using same z as search feature map; obtain candidate features using RPN
Obtain context-embedded target feature $\tilde{z}_0$

 # For later frames in tracking sequence
for $t = 2$ *to* L **do**
  Compute search feature map $x = \varphi(I^t)$ for frame I^t
  Using Z and x, obtain ROIs with candidate features X using RPN
  For every $x_i \in X$, calculate context-embedded feature $\tilde{x}_i$ to form $\tilde{X}$
  Compute $\tilde{x}_i \otimes \tilde{z}_0$ for every $\tilde{x}_i \in \tilde{X}$
  For every ROI, obtain softmax classification scores and box refinement
  values
  Choose refined ROI with highest classification score as output
end

Finally, each context-embedded candidate feature $\tilde{x}_i$ is compared with the context-embedded target feature $\tilde{z}_0 \in \mathbb{R}^{s \times s \times c}$ by element-wise multiplication as in $\tilde{x}_i \otimes \tilde{z}_0$. Binary classification and bounding box refinement operations are subsequently performed. For every $\tilde{x}_i$, a classification label c_i and refined bounding box coordinates t_i are obtained. At training stage, the GT classification label $c_i^* = 1$ is assigned to candidate boxes with $\text{IoU}(t_i, t_i^*) > \tau_p$, where t_i^* is the GT box coordinates, and $c_i^* = 0$ is assigned to candidate boxes with $\text{IoU}(t_i, t_i^*) < \tau_n$. In our experiments, we use $(\tau_p, \tau_n) = (0.5, 0.4)$. To train our context embedding module and classifier, we minimize the loss function given as

$$L_{det}(\{c_i\}, \{t_i\}) = \frac{1}{N_{pos}} \sum_i L_{cls}(c_i, c_i^*) + \frac{\lambda}{N_{pos}} \sum_i \mathbf{1}_{\{c_i^* > 0\}} L_{reg}(t_i, t_i^*), \quad (3)$$

where the loss functions L_{cls} and L_{reg} are the same as those in Eq. (2).

3.3 TridentAlign and Context Embedding Tracker

Herein, we propose **Trident**Align and **C**ontext embedding **T**racker (**TACT**). The overall tracking procedure is organized and shown as Algorithm 1. The tracking process is purposely made simple to achieve real-time speed. Furthermore, our tracking algorithm performs a full-frame search for every frame without any motion smoothness assumption based on the previous positions of the target; therefore, it is possible to run our tracker on a batch of multiple frames of offline videos. Increasing the batch size from 1 to 8 results in a large boost in tracking speed: we obtain $57 \rightarrow 101$ fps with the ResNet-18 backbone and $42 \rightarrow 65$ fps with the ResNet-50 backbone.

4   Experiments

In this section, we specify the implementation details and the experimental setup, then we compare the performance of our proposed tracking algorithm with that of other approaches on four large-scale tracking benchmarks, namely LaSOT [10], OxUvA [12], TrackingNet [11], and GOT-10k [20]. We also perform ablation experiments for the individual components to further analyze the effectiveness of our proposed method.

4.1   Implementation Details

Parameters: We resized the input images to 666×400, where original aspect ratio is preserved by adding zero-padding to the right or bottom side of the images. We used ResNet-18 and ResNet-50 [2] as the backbone feature extractor network, followed by 1×1 conv layers, where the channel dimension of the output features was set to $c = 256$. We reduced the stride of the last residual block to 1 to obtain feature maps with a size of 42×25. Regarding the RPN stage, the TridentAlign module generates a feature pyramid of size $K = 3$ with spatial dimensions $s_i \in \{3, 5, 9\}$. A total of $N = 64$ ROI proposal boxes are obtained via NMS with an overlap threshold value of 0.9. In the subsequent classification stage, the spatial dimension of the pooled candidate features obtained by ROIAlign was set to $s = 5$.

Training Data: To train the model, we used training splits of the ImageNetVID [50], YouTubeBB [51], GOT-10k [20], and LaSOT [10] datasets, and pairs of query and search images are uniformly sampled from the video sequences in these datasets. When sampling an image pair, a video sequence was chosen randomly where the probability of choosing a certain dataset is proportional to its total size. For a sampled image pair, we performed random data augmentation such as horizontal flips and the addition of gaussian noise, blurring, and color jitter. The bounding box coordinates were also randomly augmented by $\pm 1\%$ of their original width/height.

Training Details: We optimized the sum loss functions $L = L_{rpn} + L_{det}$, where the losses are given in Eq. (2) and Eq. (3) with $\lambda = 1$. We used the Adam [52] optimizer with a batch size of four pairs to train our network. The learning rate was set to 10^{-4}, and the weight decay coefficient was set to 10^{-5}. For initialization, we used pretrained weights from the ResNet architectures, and during training, we freeze the weights of the residual blocks, except for the last block. We first trained the network for 2×10^6 iterations without the context embedding module and decayed the learning rate by a factor of 0.5 halfway. Then, we added the context embedding module and trained the network for another 10^6 iterations with a learning rate of 10^{-5}. We allocated an initial burn-in phase of 10^4 iterations, during which only the RPN was trained. In this way, we prevent negative candidate ROIs from overwhelming the classification stage, which can stabilize the training process. Our model was implemented in Python using the PyTorch [53] library. For run-time measurements, we run and time our model on a single Nvidia RTX 2080Ti GPU.

Table 2. Comparison on the **LaSOT** test set.

	TACT-18	TACT-50	GlobalTrack [13]	ATOM [54]	DiMP-50 [42]	SiamRPN++ [6]	DASiam [34]	SPLT [55]	MDNet [22]	Ocean [56]	SiamFC [4]	CFNet [33]
AUC	0.556	0.575	0.521	0.518	0.569	0.496	0.448	0.426	0.397	0.560	0.336	0.275
Precision	0.583	0.607	0.529	0.506	-	0.491	0.427	0.396	0.373	0.566	0.339	0.259
Norm. precision	0.628	0.660	0.599	0.576	0.650	0.569	-	0.494	0.460	-	0.420	0.312
FPS	57	42	6	30	43	35	110	25.7	0.9	25	58	43

Table 3. Comparison on the **OxUvA** test set.

(%)	TACT-50	GlobalTrack [13]	SPLT [55]	MBMD [57]	DASiam$_{LT}$ [34]	EBT [58]	SiamFC$_{+R}$ [4]	SINT [59]	LCT [46]	TLD [60]	MDNet [22]	ECO-HC [29]
MaxGM	70.9	60.3	62.2	54.4	41.5	28.3	45.4	32.6	39.6	43.1	34.3	31.4
TPR	80.9	57.4	49.8	60.9	68.9	32.1	42.7	42.6	29.2	20.8	47.2	39.5
TNR	62.2	63.3	77.6	48.5	0.0	0.0	48.1	0.0	53.7	89.5	0.0	0.0

4.2   Quantitative Evaluation

Evaluation Datasets and Metrics: We evaluated our tracker (hereafter denoted as TACT) on test sets including four large-scale visual tracking benchmark datasets: LaSOT [10], OxUvA [12], TrackingNet [11], and GOT-10k [20]. The parameters were fixed for all benchmarks and experiments. LaSOT and OxUvA are long-term tracking benchmarks whose average sequence length is longer than 1 min, whereas TrackingNet and GOT-10k have shorter sequences but include a larger number of sequences with more various classes of objects.

The **LaSOT** [10] dataset is a large-scale and long-term tracking dataset consisting of 1,400 long-term sequences with an average sequence length of 2,512 frames (83 s), which are annotated with the bounding box coordinates of the target object. We evaluated our tracker on the test set that includes 280 sequences under a one-pass evaluation setting, where the performance metrics are the area-under-curve (AUC) of the success plot, location precision, and normalized precision. The **OxUvA** [12] dataset is used to evaluate long-term tracking performance where its development and test sets have 200 and 166 sequences, respectively, with an average length of 4,260 frames (142 s). In addition to evaluating the accuracy of the predicted boxes, the tracker must also report whether the target is present/absent in a given frame. The performance metric is the maximum geometric mean (MaxGM) over the true positive rate (TPR) and the true negative rate (TNR). **TrackingNet** [11] is a large-scale dataset of more than 30,000 videos collected from YouTube, of which 511 are included in the test set. Similar to the other benchmarks, it uses precision, normalized precision, and the AUC of the success plot as performance metrics. **GOT-10k** [20] is a tracking dataset focused on the one-shot experiment setting in which the training and test sets have disjoint object classes. It contains 10,000 videos of which 420 are used as the test set. Trackers are evaluated by calculating the success rate (SR, with threshold values 0.5 and 0.75) and average overlap (AO) value.

Table 4. Comparison on the **TrackingNet** test set.

(%)	TACT-18	TACT-50	GlobalTrack [13]	ATOM [54]	DiMP-50 [42]	SiamRPN++ [6]	DASiam [34]	UPDT [31]	MDNet [22]	SiamFC [4]	CFNet [33]	ECO [29]
Precision	70.1	70.8	65.6	64.8	68.7	69.4	59.1	55.7	56.5	53.3	53.3	49.2
Norm. precision	78.4	78.8	75.4	77.1	80.1	80.0	73.3	70.2	70.5	66.6	65.4	61.8
Success	73.4	74.0	70.4	70.3	74.0	73.3	63.8	61.1	60.6	57.1	57.8	55.4

Table 5. Comparison on the **GOT-10k** test set.

(%)	TACT-18	TACT-50	ATOM [54]	DiMP-50 [42]	SiamMask [61]	Ocean [56]	CFNet [33]	SiamFC [4]	GOTURN [62]	CCOT [28]	ECO [29]	CF2 [63]	MDNet [22]
$SR_{0.50}$	64.8	69.5	63.4	71.7	58.7	72.1	40.4	35.3	37.5	32.8	30.9	29.7	30.3
$SR_{0.75}$	44.7	47.7	40.2	49.2	36.6	-	14.4	9.8	12.4	10.7	11.1	8.8	9.9
AO	55.9	57.8	55.6	61.1	51.4	61.1	37.4	34.8	34.7	32.5	31.6	31.5	29.9

Comparison to Other Trackers: We evaluated our proposed tracker on the LaSOT test set and provide the results in Table 2, where we denote our tracker with the ResNet-18 backbone as **TACT-18** and that with the ResNet-50 backbone as **TACT-50**. Both variants of TACT outperform other recent ResNet backbone-based trackers, which are GlobalTrack [13], ATOM [54], SiamRPN++ [6], and SPLT [55]. Moreover, our tracker runs faster than these algorithms, at real-time speed. To further test the long-term tracking capabilities of TACT, we evaluated our tracker on the OxUvA test set and show the results in Table 3. To predict the presence/absence of the target, we simply used a threshold value of 0.95. Output confidence scores below the given threshold were considered to indicate absence of the target. The results show that our tracker outperforms other long-term tracking algorithms in terms of the MaxGM and TPR metrics by a substantial margin, even when compared to GlobalTrack [13] and SPLT [55], which are trackers specifically designed for long-term tracking applications.

We also evaluated TACT on the relatively short-term and large-scale tracking benchmarks, which are TrackingNet and GOT-10k. The evaluation results for TrackingNet are shown in Table 4, where both variants of TACT exhibit competitive results in terms of the precision and success rate metrics, outperforming most trackers. Furthermore, Table 5 shows that the proposed method also obtains consistent results with regard to the comparison performed on GOT-10k: both variants of TACT were able to demonstrate high performance on all metrics. Even without any temporal smoothness assumptions or manual parameter tuning, TACT was able to achieve superior performance on the short-term tracking datasets compared to that of conventional trackers that are focused on short-term tracking applications.

To analyze the effectiveness of our proposed TridentAlign and context embedding modules, we show the success plots for eight different challenge attributes of the LaSOT dataset in Fig. 4. TACT achieved substantial performance improvements on the attributes of aspect ratio change, deformation, rotation, and scale variation. Compared to other full-frame search-based tracker GlobalTrack, TACT performed better by a large margin owing to its TridentAlign module, which facilitates robustness to scale variations and large deformations of the

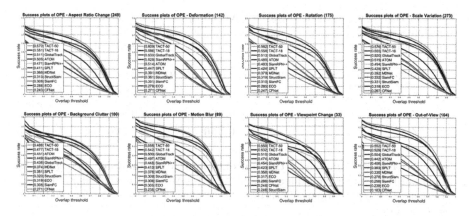

Fig. 4. Success plots for eight challenge attributes of the LaSOT dataset

target. Moreover, GlobalTrack only considers local features without any global context information; therefore, it is more prone to being affected by distractors similar to the target as shown in the background clutter plots, with inferior performance to that of ATOM and SiamRPN++. Using our context embedding module, robustness to background clutter can be reinforced via the global context modeling and embedding scheme. TACT also shows improvements with regard to the motion blur, viewpoint change, and out-of-view attributes owing to its full-frame search based design, which allows it to successfully recover from prolonged out-of-frame target disappearances and brief drifts.

In Fig. 5, we present qualitative results produced by GlobalTrack, ATOM, SiamRPN++, SPLT, MDNet, and TACT-50 for selected videos from the LaSOT dataset. The results show that TACT successfully tracks the target despite challenging conditions such as large deformation in *kite-6*, occlusion in *fox-5*, and background clutter in *bicycle-9* and *skateboard-19*, whereas the other trackers fail. For additional attribute plots and qualitative results for other videos from the LaSOT dataset, please refer to the attached supplementary document and video.

4.3   Ablation Study

To provide more in-depth analysis of and insight into the proposed TACT, we performed additional ablation experiments for the individual components. For the following experiments, we used the test set of the LaSOT dataset and the success plot AUC metric to compare the performance of different variants of TACT.

Component-Wise Ablation: To validate the contribution of each individual component to the performance gain, we compared different variants of TACT by adding or removing the proposed modules. Table 6 shows the results of the ablation analysis on individual components for both TACT-18 and TACT-50.

Table 6. Ablation analysis of individual components. Adding each component contributes to consistent performance gains over the baseline model. As a performance measure, the AUC of the success plot on the LaSOT test set is shown.

TridentAlign	Context embedding	AUC (TACT-18)	AUC (TACT-50)
✗	✗	0.535	0.552
✓	✗	0.545	0.564
✓	✓	**0.556**	**0.575**

Table 7. Ablation analysis of the context embedding module. Among possible variants of the context embedding module, the FILM-based module shows the best performance. As a performance measure, the AUC of the success plot for the LaSOT test set is shown.

	No context	Simple concat.	Simple add.	CBAM-based	FILM-based
AUC (TACT-18)	0.545	0.532	0.552	0.551	**0.556**

Starting from the variants without the TridentAlign or context embedding modules, adding each component consistently improves the performance of both TACT-18 and TACT-50, which validates the effectiveness of our proposed approach. Our proposed TridentAlign and context embedding modules contribute to +2.1% and +2.3% to the performance gains of TACT-18 and TACT-50, respectively. All models were trained under the same settings using the same training datasets until convergence.

Variants of the Context Embedding Module: We test four possible designs for the context embedding module, as introduced in Table 1. For the experiments, we started from a baseline model of TACT-18, which was trained without the context embedding module. Then, we added the context embedding module on top of the baseline model and trained the final model for additional iterations (as specified in Sect. 4.1). Table 7 shows the results for different variants of the context embedding module. Among all variants, the FILM-based module shows the highest performance gain followed by the simple addition-based module and the CBAM-based module. In contrast, the simple concatenation-based module degrades the performance. These results are somewhat consistent with other affine transform-based feature-wise transformation methods utilized in previous literature [49], where its multiplicative and additive operations provide adequate conditioning information for a given feature without hampering the discriminability of the original feature space.

Fig. 5. Qualitative Results on LaSOT. Tracking results for the sequences *kite-6*, *zebra-17*, *fox-5*, *bicycle-9*, *giraffe-10*, and *skateboard-19*. The color of the bounding box denotes a specific tracker. Yellow numbers on the top-left corner indicate frame indexes. (Color figure online)

5 Conclusion

In this paper, we proposed a novel visual tracking method that aims to deal with large scale variations and deformations of the target while improving its discriminability by utilizing the global context information of the surroundings. Built upon a two-stage object detection framework, our proposed TACT incorporates the TridentAlign and context embedding modules to overcome the limitations of conventional tracking algorithms. The TridentAlign module constructs a target feature pyramid that encourages the adaptability of the tracker to large scale variations and deformations by fully utilizing the spatial information of the target. The context embedding module generates and embeds the global context information of a given frame into a local feature representation for improved discriminability of the target against distractor objects. The proposed modules are designed efficiently such that the overall framework can run at a real-time speed. Experimental results on four large-scale visual tracking benchmarks validate the strong performance of the TACT on long-term and short-term tracking tasks, achieving improved performance on challenging scenarios.

Acknowledgments. This work was supported by IITP grant funded by the Ministry of Science and ICT of Korea (No. 2017-0-01780).

References

1. Krizhevsky, A., Sutskever, I., Hinton, G.E.: ImageNet classification with deep convolutional neural networks. In: NIPS (2012)
2. He, K., Zhang, X., Ren, S., Sun, J.: Deep residual learning for image recognition. In: CVPR (2016)
3. Ren, S., He, K., Girshick, R., Sun, J.: Faster R-CNN: towards real-time object detection with region proposal networks. In: NIPS (2015)
4. Bertinetto, L., Valmadre, J., Henriques, J.F., Vedaldi, A., Torr, P.H.: Fully-convolutional Siamese networks for object tracking. arXiv preprint arXiv:1606.09549 (2016)
5. Li, B., Yan, J., Wu, W., Zhu, Z., Hu, X.: High performance visual tracking with Siamese region proposal network. In: CVPR (2018)
6. Li, B., Wu, W., Wang, Q., Zhang, F., Xing, J., Yan, J.: SiamRPN++: evolution of Siamese visual tracking with very deep networks. In: CVPR (2019)
7. Zhang, Z., Peng, H.: Deeper and wider Siamese networks for real-time visual tracking. In: CVPR (2019)
8. Wu, Y., Lim, J., Yang, M.H.: Object tracking benchmark. IEEE TPAMI **37**, 1834–1848 (2015)
9. Čehovin, L., Leonardis, A., Kristan, M.: Visual object tracking performance measures revisited. IEEE TIP **25**, 1261–1274 (2016)
10. Fan, H., et al.: LaSOT: a high-quality benchmark for large-scale single object tracking. In: CVPR (2019)
11. Müller, M., Bibi, A., Giancola, S., Alsubaihi, S., Ghanem, B.: TrackingNet: a large-scale dataset and benchmark for object tracking in the wild. In: Ferrari, V., Hebert, M., Sminchisescu, C., Weiss, Y. (eds.) ECCV 2018. LNCS, vol. 11205, pp. 310–327. Springer, Cham (2018). https://doi.org/10.1007/978-3-030-01246-5_19
12. Valmadre, J., et al.: Long-term tracking in the wild: a benchmark. In: ECCV (2018)
13. Huang, L., Zhao, X., Huang, K.: GlobalTrack: a simple and strong baseline for long-term tracking. In: AAAI (2019)
14. Voigtlaender, P., Luiten, J., Torr, P.H., Leibe, B.: Siam R-CNN: visual tracking by re-detection. In: CVPR (2020)
15. Tian, Z., Shen, C., Chen, H., He, T.: FCOS: fully convolutional one-stage object detection. In: ICCV (2019)
16. He, K., Zhang, X., Ren, S., Sun, J.: Spatial pyramid pooling in deep convolutional networks for visual recognition. IEEE TPAMI **37**, 1904–1916 (2015)
17. Lin, T.Y., Goyal, P., Girshick, R., He, K., Dollár, P.: Focal loss for dense object detection. In: ICCV (2017)
18. Li, Y., Chen, Y., Wang, N., Zhang, Z.: Scale-aware trident networks for object detection. In: ICCV (2019)
19. Hariharan, B., Arbeláez, P., Girshick, R., Malik, J.: Hypercolumns for object segmentation and fine-grained localization. In: CVPR (2015)
20. Huang, L., Zhao, X., Huang, K.: GOT-10k: a large high-diversity benchmark for generic object tracking in the wild. IEEE TPAMI 1 (2019). https://doi.org/10.1109/tpami.2019.2957464
21. Wang, N., Yeung, D.Y.: Learning a deep compact image representation for visual tracking. In: NIPS (2013)
22. Nam, H., Han, B.: Learning multi-domain convolutional neural networks for visual tracking. In: CVPR (2015)

23. Simonyan, K., Zisserman, A.: Very deep convolutional networks for large-scale image recognition. arXiv preprint arXiv:1409.1556 (2014)
24. Jung, I., Son, J., Baek, M., Han, B.: Real-time MDNet. In: Ferrari, V., Hebert, M., Sminchisescu, C., Weiss, Y. (eds.) ECCV 2018. LNCS, vol. 11208, pp. 89–104. Springer, Cham (2018). https://doi.org/10.1007/978-3-030-01225-0_6
25. He, K., Gkioxari, G., Dollár, P., Girshick, R.: Mask R-CNN. In: ICCV (2017)
26. Henriques, J.F., Caseiro, R., Martins, P., Batista, J.: High-speed tracking with kernelized correlation filters. IEEE TPAMI **37**, 583–596 (2015)
27. Bolme, D.S., Beveridge, J.R., Draper, B.A., Lui, Y.M.: Visual object tracking using adaptive correlation filters. In: CVPR (2010)
28. Danelljan, M., Robinson, A., Shahbaz Khan, F., Felsberg, M.: Beyond correlation filters: learning continuous convolution operators for visual tracking. In: Leibe, B., Matas, J., Sebe, N., Welling, M. (eds.) ECCV 2016. LNCS, vol. 9909, pp. 472–488. Springer, Cham (2016). https://doi.org/10.1007/978-3-319-46454-1_29
29. Danelljan, M., Bhat, G., Khan, F., Felsberg, M.: ECO: efficient convolution operators for tracking. In: CVPR (2017)
30. Danelljan, M., Hager, G., Shahbaz Khan, F., Felsberg, M.: Convolutional features for correlation filter based visual tracking. In: ICCV Workshop (2015)
31. Bhat, G., Johnander, J., Danelljan, M., Shahbaz Khan, F., Felsberg, M.: Unveiling the power of deep tracking. In: ECCV (2018)
32. Xu, T., Feng, Z.H., Wu, X.J., Kittler, J.: Joint group feature selection and discriminative filter learning for robust visual object tracking. In: ICCV (2019)
33. Valmadre, J., Bertinetto, L., Henriques, J., Vedaldi, A., Torr, P.H.S.: End-to-end representation learning for correlation filter based tracking. In: CVPR (2017)
34. Zhu, Z., Wang, Q., Li, B., Wu, W., Yan, J., Hu, W.: Distractor-aware Siamese networks for visual object tracking. In: ECCV (2018)
35. Szegedy, C., et al.: Going deeper with convolutions. In: CVPR (2015)
36. Guo, Q., Feng, W., Zhou, C., Huang, R., Wan, L., Wang, S.: Learning dynamic Siamese network for visual object tracking. In: ICCV (2017)
37. Zhang, Y., Wang, L., Qi, J., Wang, D., Feng, M., Lu, H.: Structured Siamese network for real-time visual tracking. In: Ferrari, V., Hebert, M., Sminchisescu, C., Weiss, Y. (eds.) ECCV 2018. LNCS, vol. 11213, pp. 355–370. Springer, Cham (2018). https://doi.org/10.1007/978-3-030-01240-3_22
38. Fan, H., Ling, H.: Siamese cascaded region proposal networks for real-time visual tracking. In: CVPR (2019)
39. Li, P., Chen, B., Ouyang, W., Wang, D., Yang, X., Lu, H.: GradNet: gradient-guided network for visual object tracking. In: ICCV (2019)
40. Choi, J., Kwon, J., Lee, K.M.: Deep meta learning for real-time target-aware visual tracking. In: ICCV (2019)
41. Zhang, L., Gonzalez-Garcia, A., Weijer, J.V.D., Danelljan, M., Khan, F.S.: Learning the model update for Siamese trackers. In: ICCV (2019)
42. Bhat, G., Danelljan, M., Gool, L.V., Timofte, R.: Learning discriminative model prediction for tracking. In: ICCV (2019)
43. Choi, J., et al.: Context-aware deep feature compression for high-speed visual tracking. In: CVPR (2018)
44. Mueller, M., Smith, N., Ghanem, B.: Context-aware correlation filter tracking. In: CVPR (2017)
45. Moudgil, A., Gandhi, V.: Long-term visual object tracking benchmark. In: Jawahar, C.V., Li, H., Mori, G., Schindler, K. (eds.) ACCV 2018. LNCS, vol. 11362, pp. 629–645. Springer, Cham (2019). https://doi.org/10.1007/978-3-030-20890-5_40

46. Ma, C., Yang, X., Zhang, C., Yang, M.H.: Long-term correlation tracking. In: CVPR (2015)
47. Woo, S., Park, J., Lee, J.-Y., Kweon, I.S.: CBAM: convolutional block attention module. In: Ferrari, V., Hebert, M., Sminchisescu, C., Weiss, Y. (eds.) ECCV 2018. LNCS, vol. 11211, pp. 3–19. Springer, Cham (2018). https://doi.org/10.1007/978-3-030-01234-2_1
48. Wang, X., Girshick, R., Gupta, A., He, K.: Non-local neural networks. In: CVPR (2018)
49. Perez, E., Strub, F., De Vries, H., Dumoulin, V., Courville, A.: FILM: visual reasoning with a general conditioning layer. In: AAAI (2018)
50. Russakovsky, O., et al.: ImageNet large scale visual recognition challenge. IJCV **115**, 211–252 (2015)
51. Real, E., Shlens, J., Mazzocchi, S., Pan, X., Vanhoucke, V.: YouTube-BoundingBoxes: a large high-precision human-annotated data set for object detection in video. In: CVPR (2017)
52. Kingma, D., Ba, J.: Adam: a method for stochastic optimization. ICLR (2015)
53. Paszke, A., et al.: PyTorch: an imperative style, high-performance deep learning library. In: NeurIPS (2019)
54. Danelljan, M., Bhat, G., Khan, F.S., Felsberg, M.: ATOM: accurate tracking by overlap maximization. In: CVPR (2019)
55. Yan, B., Zhao, H., Wang, D., Lu, H., Yang, X.: 'Skimming-perusal' tracking: a framework for real-time and robust long-term tracking. In: ICCV (2019)
56. Zhang, Z., Peng, H., Fu, J., Li, B., Hu, W.: Ocean: object-aware anchor-free tracking. In: Vedaldi, A., Bischof, H., Brox, T., Frahm, J.-M. (eds.) ECCV 2020. LNCS, vol. 12366, pp. 771–787. Springer, Cham (2020). https://doi.org/10.1007/978-3-030-58589-1_46
57. Zhang, Y., Wang, D., Wang, L., Qi, J., Lu, H.: Learning regression and verification networks for long-term visual tracking. arXiv preprint arXiv:1809.04320 (2018)
58. Zhu, G., Porikli, F., Li, H.: Beyond local search: tracking objects everywhere with instance-specific proposals. In: CVPR (2016)
59. Tao, R., Gavves, E., Smeulders, A.W.: Siamese instance search for tracking. In: CVPR (2016)
60. Kalal, Z., Mikolajczyk, K., Matas, J.: Tracking-learning-detection. IEEE TPAMI **34**, 1409–1422 (2011)
61. Wang, Q., Zhang, L., Bertinetto, L., Hu, W., Torr, P.H.: Fast online object tracking and segmentation: a unifying approach. In: CVPR (2019)
62. Held, D., Thrun, S., Savarese, S.: Learning to track at 100 FPS with deep regression networks. In: Leibe, B., Matas, J., Sebe, N., Welling, M. (eds.) ECCV 2016. LNCS, vol. 9905, pp. 749–765. Springer, Cham (2016). https://doi.org/10.1007/978-3-319-46448-0_45
63. Ma, C., Huang, J.B., Yang, X., Yang, M.H.: Hierarchical convolutional features for visual tracking. In: ICCV (2015)

Leveraging Tacit Information Embedded in CNN Layers for Visual Tracking

Kourosh Meshgi[1(✉)], Maryam Sadat Mirzaei[1], and Shigeyuki Oba[2]

[1] RIKEN Center for Advanced Intelligence Project (AIP), Tokyo, Japan
kourosh.meshgi@riken.jp
[2] Graduate School of Informatics, Kyoto University, Kyoto, Japan

Abstract. Different layers in CNNs provide not only different levels of abstraction for describing the objects in the input but also encode various implicit information about them. The activation patterns of different features contain valuable information about the stream of incoming images: spatial relations, temporal patterns, and co-occurrence of spatial and spatiotemporal (ST) features. The studies in visual tracking literature, so far, utilized only one of the CNN layers, a pre-fixed combination of them, or an ensemble of trackers built upon individual layers. In this study, we employ an adaptive combination of several CNN layers in a single DCF tracker to address variations of the target appearances and propose the use of style statistics on both spatial and temporal properties of the target, directly extracted from CNN layers for visual tracking. Experiments demonstrate that using the additional implicit data of CNNs significantly improves the performance of the tracker. Results demonstrate the effectiveness of using style similarity and activation consistency regularization in improving its localization and scale accuracy.

1 Introduction

Discovering new architectures for deep learning and analyzing their properties, have resulted in a rapid expansion in computer vision, along with other domains. Deep learning has been introduced to visual tracking in different forms, mostly to provide features for established trackers based on correlation filters [1], particle filters [2,3] and detector-based trackers [4]. Deep features extracted by fully-connected layers of CNN are shown to be adequately generic to be used for a variety of computer vision tasks, including tracking [5]. Further studies revealed that convolutional layers are even more discriminative, semantically meaningful and capable of learning structural information [6]. However, the direct use of CNNs to perform tracking is complicated because of the need to re-train the classifier with the stream of target appearances during tracking, the diffusion of background information into template [7], and "catastrophic forgetting" of previous appearance in the face of extreme deformations and occlusions [8].

Early studies in the use of deep learning in tracking utilized features from autoencoders [9,10] and fully-connected layers of pre-trained (CNN-based)

© Springer Nature Switzerland AG 2021
H. Ishikawa et al. (Eds.): ACCV 2020, LNCS 12623, pp. 521–538, 2021.
https://doi.org/10.1007/978-3-030-69532-3_32

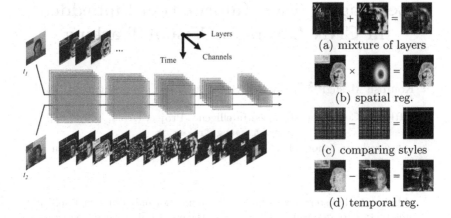

(a) mixture of layers

(b) spatial reg.

(c) comparing styles

(d) temporal reg.

Fig. 1. When presented with a sequence of images, CNN neurons are activated in a particular way, involving information about the spatial, semantic, style and transformations of the target. **(a)** Combining information from different layers balances the amount of spatial and semantic information, **(b)** spatial weighting of the response would discard most of the background discratction, **(c)** changes of the co-activations of neurons (measured by Gram matrices) for different subsequent images indicate style changes of the target (the plot is exaggeratedly enhanced for visibility), and **(d)** changes in the activations of the neurons themselves signals the appearance transformations and pose changes (in shallower layers) or alteration of semantic contents.

object detector [11], but later the layers were used to serve as features balancing the abstraction level needed to localize the target [12], provide ST relationship between the target and its background [13], combine spatial and temporal features [14,15], and generate probability maps for the tracker [16]. Recently trackers employ other deep learning approaches such as R-CNN for tracking-by-segmentation [17], Siamese Networks for template similarity measuring [18–21], GANs to augment positive samples [22,23], and CNN-embeddings for self-supervised image coloring and tracking [24]. However, the tacit information in pre-trained CNNs including information between layers, within layers, and activation patterns across the time axis are underutilized (Fig. 1).

Different layers of CNNs provide different levels of abstraction [25], and it is known that using multiple layers of CNNs can benefit other tasks such as image classification [26]. Such information was used as a coarse-to-fine sifting mechanism in [12], as a tree-like pre-defined combination of layers with fixed weights and selective updating [8], as the features for different trackers in an ensemble tracker [27], or in a summation over all layers as uniform features [28]. However, direct adaptive fusion of these features in a single tracker that can address different object appearances is still missing in the literature.

CNN stores information not only between layers but within layers in different channels, each representing a different filter. These filters may respond to different visual stimuli. The shallower layers have a Gabor-like filter response

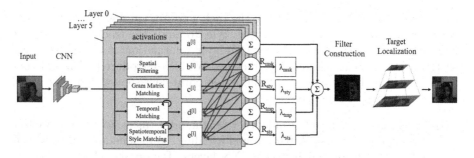

Fig. 2. Schematic of the proposed tracker. Given the input image, the activations of different layers of CNN are processed independently and its spatial irregularities, style mismatches, temporal inconsistencies and ST pattern changes compared to the template are calculated. These errors are then adaptively fused with that of other layers to form the regularization terms R_x. The final filter is then constructed and used in the baseline DCF tracker that uses multi-scale matching to find the position and scale of the target in the input image. The weights of different error terms are then updated in reverse proportion of their contribution in total error of each level.

[29] whereas in the deeper layers, they respond to angles, color patterns, simple shapes, and gradually highly complex stimuli like faces [25]. The co-occurring patterns within a layer, activate two or more different channels of the layer. Such co-incidental activations are often called style in the context of neural style transfer (NST), and different approaches are proposed to measure the similarity between two styles [30,31]. The loss functions for NST problem can serve as the similarity index for two objects (e.g., in the context of image retrieval [32]).

Most of the current CNN-based techniques use architectures with 2D convolutions to achieve different invariances to the variations of the images. Meanwhile, the invariance to transformations in time is of paramount importance for video analysis [33]. Modeling temporal information in CNNs has been tackled by applying CNNs on optical flow images [34], reformulating R-CNNs to exploit the temporal context of the images [35] or by the use of separate information pathways for spatial and temporal pathways [36,37]. Motion-based CNNs typically outperform CNN representations learned from images for tasks dealing with dynamic target, e.g. action recognition [33]. In these approaches, a CNN is applied on 3-channel optical flow image [38], and different layers of such network provide different variances toward speed and the direction of the target's motion [39]. In visual tracking, deep motion features provide promising results [40]. However, this requires the tracker to fuse the information from two different CNN networks (temporal+spatial) [37], and their inconsistency hinders a meaningful layer-wise fusion and only the last layers of temporal CNN are used for tracking [40].

Contributions: We propose an adaptive fusion of different CNN layers in a tracker to combine high spatial resolution of earlier layers for precise localization, and semantic information of deeper layers to handle large appearance changes and alleviate model drift. We utilize the tacit information between each layer's channels at several timepoints, i.e., the style, to guide the tracker. To our best knowledge, this is the first use of within-layer information of CNNs especially spatial and ST co-activations for tracking. We also introduced temporal constraint helps to better preserve target's temporal consistency, suppress jitter, and promote scale adaptation.

(i) We propose an intuitive adaptive weight adjustment to tune the effect of components (spatial, background avoiding, co-incidental, temporal, and ST) both within and between CNN layers. Temporal and style regs are typically complementary: target changes are punished by a reduction in activation and style similarity, big changes are punished by spatial reg and style keep track of the target. Employing multiple layers not only gives different realization of details-semantics trade-off [12], but also provides richer statistics compared to one layer. We incorporate different regularization terms on CNN layers using only one feed-forward pass on an arbitrary pre-trained CNN, with no change to its architecture or CNN block design (e.g. ST block as in [41]) and no additional computation (e.g., compute optical flow).

(ii) We introduce a Gram-based style matching in our tracker to capture style alterations of the target. The style matching exploits the co-activation patterns of the layers and improves the localization accuracy of the target and provides complementary information to the baseline which relies on spatial matching.

(iii) We introduce the temporal coherence regularization to the tracker by monitoring activations of each layer through the course of tracking, to enhance tracker's movement speed and direction invariance, adaptation to different degrees of changes in the target appearance, stability, and scale tuning.

(iv) Our system is tested on various public datasets and considering the simplicity of our baseline (SRDCF [7]) we obtained results on par with many sophisticated trackers. The results shed light on the hidden information within CNN layers, that is the goal of this paper. The layer-fusion, style-matching, and temporal regularization component of the proposed tracker is further shown to advance the baseline significantly and outperformed the state-of-the-art.

It should be noted that our proposed method differs with HDT [27], CCOT [28] and ECO [42] that also integrates the multi-layer deep features by considering them in the continuous domain. Here, we employed a pre-trained CNN for object detection task, simplified the need to deal with different dimensions of convolutional layers by maintaining the consistency between layers while isolating them to make an ensemble of features (rather than an ensemble of trackers in [27]). Additionally, we proposed style and temporal regularization that can be incorporated into Conjugate Gradient optimization of C-COT [28], ADMM optimization of BACF [43] and Gauss-Newton optimization of ECO [42].

2   Method

We propose a tracker that adaptively fuse different convolutional layers of a pre-trained CNN into a DCF tracker. The adaptation is inspired by weight tuning of the different tracker components as well as the scale-aware update of [44]. As Fig. 2 illustrates, we incorporated spatial regularization (a multi-layer extension of [1]), co-incidental regularization (which matches style between the candidate patch and historical templates), temporal regularization (that ensures a smooth alteration of the activations in normal condition), and ST regularization that captures the change patterns of spatial features.

2.1   Discriminative Correlation Filter Tracker

The DCF framework utilizes the properties of circular correlation to efficiently train and apply a classifier in a sliding window fashion [45]. The resulting classi-fier is a correlation filter applied to the image, similar to conv layers in a CNN.

A set of example patches x_τ are sampled at each frame $\tau = 1, \ldots, t$ to train the discriminative correlation filer f_t, where t denotes the current frame. The patches are all of the same size (conveniently, the input size of the CNN) centered at the estimated target location in each frame. We define feature x_τ^k as the output of channel k at a convolutional layer in the CNN. With this notion, the tracking problem is reduced to learn a filter f_t^k for each channel k, that minimizes the L^2-error between the responses S_{f_t} on samples x_τ and the desired filter form y_k:

$$\epsilon = \sum_{\tau=1}^{t} \alpha_\tau ||S(f_t, x_\tau) - y_\tau||^2 + \lambda ||f_t||^2 \tag{1}$$

where $S(f_t, x_\tau) = f_t \star x_\tau$ in which the $\star$ denotes circular correlation generalized to multichannel signals by computing inner products. The desired correlation output y_τ is set to a Gaussian function with the peak placed at the target center location [46]. A weight parameter λ controls the impact of the filter size regularization term, while the weights α_τ determine the impact of each sample.

To find an approximate solution of Eq. (1), we use the online update rule of [44]. At frame t, the numerator g_t and denominator $\hat{h}_t$ of the discrete Fourier transformed (DFT) filter $\hat{f}_t$ are updated as,

$$\hat{g}_t^k = (1 - \gamma)\hat{g}_{t-1}^k + \gamma \overline{\hat{y}_t}.\hat{x}_t^k \tag{2a}$$

$$\hat{h}_t^k = (1 - \gamma)\hat{h}_{t-1}^k + \gamma \left(\sum_{k'=1}^{n_C} \overline{\hat{x}_t^{k'}}.\hat{x}_t^{k'} + \lambda \right) \tag{2b}$$

in which the 'hat' denotes the 2D DFT, the 'bar' denotes complex conjugation, '.' denotes pointwise multiplication, $\gamma \in [0, 1]$ is learning rate and n_C is the number of channels. Next, the filter is constructed by a point-wise division $\hat{f}_t^k = \hat{h}_t^k / \hat{g}_t^k$.

To locate the target at frame t, a sample patch s_t is extracted at the previous location. The filter is applied by computing the correlation scores in the Fourier domain $\mathscr{F}^{-1}\left\{ \sum_{k'=1}^{n_C} \overline{\hat{f}_{t-1}^{k'}}.\hat{s}_t^{k'} \right\}$, in which $\mathscr{F}^{-1}$ denotes the inverse DFT.

2.2   Incorporating Information of CNN Layers

Here, we extend the DCF tracker with a weighted sum of multiple CNN layers $l \in \mathcal{L}$ with dimensions $n_W^{[l]} \times n_H^{[l]} \times n_C^{[l]}$. We embed spatial focus, style consistency, temporal coherency, and ST style preserving terms as regularizations.

$$\epsilon = \sum_{\tau=1}^{t} \alpha_\tau \left(\sum_{l \in \mathcal{L}} a_t^{[l]} ||S(f_t^{[l]}, x_\tau) - y_\tau||^2 + \sum_{x \in \{\mathrm{msk,sty,tmp,sts}\}} \lambda_x R_x(f_t, x_\tau) \right) \quad (3)$$

where the desired filter form for all layers $l \in \mathcal{L}$, $\mathcal{A}_t = \{a_t^{[l]}\}$ is the activation importance of the layers l, and $\Lambda = \{\lambda_{\mathrm{msk}}, \lambda_{\mathrm{sty}}, \lambda_{\mathrm{tmp}}, \lambda_{\mathrm{sts}}\}$ are the regularization weights for tracker components.

2.3   Regularizing the Filter

We embed five different regularizations to push the resulting filter toward ideal form given the features of the tracker. To localize the effect of features a mask reg R_{msk} is used, to penalize the style mismatches between target and the template, co-incidental reg R_{sty} is employed, to push temporal consistency of the target and smoothness of tracking, the temporal reg R_{tmp} is proposed, and to punish abrupt ST changes, the ST style reg R_{sts} is introduced.

Mask Component. To address the boundary problems induced by the periodic assumption [7] and minimizing the effect of background [47] we use mask regularization to penalize filter coefficients located further from object's center:

$$R_{\mathrm{msk}}(f_t, x_\tau) = \sum_{l \in \mathcal{L}} b_t^{[l]} \sum_{k=1}^{n_C^{[l]}} ||\mathbf{w}.f_t^{k,[l]}||^2 \quad (4)$$

in which $\mathbf{w} : \{1, \ldots, n_W^{[l]}\} \times \{1, \ldots, n_H^{[l]}\} \to [0,1]$ is the spatial penalty function, and $\mathcal{B}_t = \{b_t^{[l]}\}$ is the spatial importances of the layers. We use Tikhonov reg. similar to [7] as $\mathbf{w}$ smoothly increase with distance from the target center.

Co-incidental Component. CNN activations may suffer from extreme target deformations, missing information in the observation (e.g. due to partial occlusions) and complex transformations (e.g. out-of-plane rotations). On the other hand, Gram-based description of a CNN layer encodes the second order statistics of the set of CNN filter responses and tosses spatial arrangements [48]. Although, this property may lead to some unsatisfying results in NST domain, it is desired in the context of visual tracking as a complement for raw activations.

$$R_{\mathrm{sty}}(f_t, x_\tau) = c_{\mathrm{norm}} \sum_{l \in \mathcal{L}} c_t^{[l]} ||G^{[l]}(f_t) - G^{[l]}(f_\tau)||_F^2 \quad (5)$$

where $\mathcal{C}_t = \{c_t^{[l]}\}$ is the layers' co-incidental importance, $c_{\text{norm}} = \sum_{l \in \mathcal{L}} c_t^{[l]} = (2n_H^{[l]} n_W^{[l]} n_C^{[l]})^{-2}$ as normalizing constant and $||.||_F^2$ is the Frobenios norm operator and $G^{[l]}(.)$ is the cross-covariance of activations in layer l, the Gram matrix:

$$G_{kk'}^{[l]} = \sum_{i=1}^{n_H^{[l]}} \sum_{j=1}^{n_W^{[l]}} q_{ijk}^{[l]} q_{ijk'}^{[l]} \tag{6}$$

where $q_{ijk}^{[l]}$ is the activation of neuron in (i,j) of channel k in layer l. The Gram matrix captures the correlation of activations across different channels of layer l, indicating the frequency of co-activation of features of a layer. It is a second-degree statistics of the network activations, that captures co-occurrences between neurons, known as "style" in spatial domain. Style information encodes input patterns, which in lowest form is considered as the texture, known to be useful for tracking [49]. The patterns of deeper layers contain higher levels of co-occurrences, such as the relation of the body-parts and shape-color.

Temporal Component. This term is devised to ensure the smoothness of activation alterations of CNNs, which means to see the same features in the same positions of the input images, and punish big alterations in the target appearance, which may happen due to misplaced sampling window. Another benefit of this term is to prefer bounding boxes which include all of the features and therefore improve the scale adaptation ($\mathcal{D}_t = \{d_t^{[l]}\}$):

$$R_{\text{tmp}}(f_t, x_\tau) = \sum_{l \in \mathcal{L}} d_t^{[l]} ||S(f_t^{[l]}, x_\tau) - S(f_t^{[l]}, x_{\tau-1})||^2 \tag{7}$$

Spatiotemporal Style Component. To capture the style of target's ST changes, the style of the spatial patterns in consecutive frames is compared. It promotes the motion smoothness of the spatial features, and monitors the style in which each features evolve throughout the video ($\mathcal{E}_t = \{e_t^{[l]}\}$):

$$R_{\text{sts}}(f_t, x_\tau) = \sum_{l \in \mathcal{L}} e_t^{[l]} ||G^{[l]}(f_\tau) - G^{[l]}(f_{\tau-1})||_F^2 \tag{8}$$

Model Update. Extending filter update equations (Eq. 2) to handle multiple layers is not trivial. It is the importance weights $\mathcal{A}_t, \ldots, \mathcal{E}_t$, that provides high degree of flexibility for the visual tracker to tailor its use of different layers (i.e., their activations, styles, spatial, temporal, and spatitemporal coherences) to the target. As such, we use a simple yet effective way of adjusting the weights, considering the effect of the layer they represent among all the layers. Here, we denote $\tilde{z}_t^{[l]}$ as the portion of error in t caused by layer l among all layers $\mathcal{L}$:

$$z_{t+1}^{[l]} = 1 - \frac{\eta + \tilde{z}_t^{[l]}}{\eta + \sum_{l' \in \mathcal{L}} \tilde{z}_t^{[l']}} \quad , \text{where } z_t \in \{a_t, b_t, c_t, d_t, e_t\} \tag{9}$$

in which η is a small constant and error terms $\tilde{z}_t^{[l]}$ are defined as follows:

$$\tilde{a}_t^{[l]} = ||S(f_t^{[l]}, x_t) - y_t||^2 \tag{10a}$$

$$\tilde{b}_t^{[l]} = a_t^{[l]} \tilde{a}_t^{[l]} + \sum_{k=1}^{n_C^{[l]}} ||w.f_t^{k,[l]}||^2 \tag{10b}$$

$$\tilde{c}_t^{[l]} = a_t^{[l]} \tilde{a}_t^{[l]} + b_t^{[l]} \tilde{b}_t^{[l]} + ||G^{[l]}(f_t) - G^{[l]}(f_{t-1})||_F^2 \tag{10c}$$

$$\tilde{d}_t^{[l]} = a_t^{[l]} \tilde{a}_t^{[l]} + b_t^{[l]} \tilde{b}_t^{[l]} + c_t^{[l]} \tilde{c}_t^{[l]} + ||S(f_t^{[l]}, x_t) - S(f_t^{[l]}, x_{t-1})||^2 \tag{10d}$$

$$\tilde{e}_t^{[l]} = a_t^{[l]} \tilde{a}_t^{[l]} + b_t^{[l]} \tilde{b}_t^{[l]} + c_t^{[l]} \tilde{c}_t^{[l]} + d_t^{[l]} \tilde{d}_t^{[l]} + ||G^{[l]}(f_t) - G^{[l]}(f_{t-1})||_F^2 \tag{10e}$$

In the update phase, first, $\tilde{a}_t$ is calculated that represents the reconstruction error. Plugged into Eq. (9) (which is inspired by AdaBoost), a_{t+1} is obtained. a_t for layer l is the weight of reconstruction error of this layer compared to the other layers, which is weighted by its importance $\tilde{a}_t$. Next, the weighted reconstruction error is added to the raw mask error to give the $\tilde{b}_t$. This is, in turn, used to calculate the weight of the mask error in this layer. This process is repeated for coincidental error, temporal component, and ST component. The errors of each layer are also accumulated to update the weight of the next. Hence, the network won't rely on the style information of a layer with large reconstruction error, etc. The same holds for ST co-occurrences.

Optimization and Target Localization. Following [7], we used the Gauss-Seidel iterative approach to compute filter coefficients. The cost can be effectively minimized in Fourier domain due to the sparsity of DFT coefficients after regularizations. Image patch with the minimum error of Eq. (3) is a target candidate and target scale is estimated by applying the filter at multiple resolutions. The maximum filter response corresponds to the target's location and scale.

2.4   Implementation Details

We used VGG19 network consisting of 16 convolutional and 5 max-pooling layers, as implemented in MatConvNet [50] and pre-trained on the ImageNet dataset for the image classification. To be constistant with [1] and [30], we used the conv layers after the pooling. We also added the input as Layer 0 which enables the tracker to benefit from NCC tracking, hence $\mathcal{L} = \{\text{input, conv1\_1, conv2\_1, conv3\_1, conv4\_1, conv5\_1}\}$. In our implementation, $\sum_{l \in \mathcal{L}} a_t^{[l]}, \ldots, e_t^{[l]} = 1$, regularization weights Λ are determined with cross-validation on YouTubeBB [51] and are fixed for all the experiments, others parameters are similar to [1].

3   Experiments

We take a step-by-step approach to first prove that adding co-incidental and temporal regularization to the baseline improves the tracking performance, and then show that combining multiple layers can improve the tracking performance significantly. We also show that the regularization based on activation, style, and temporal coherence is helpful only if proper importance parameters are selected for different layers. Then we discuss the effect of different regularization terms on the performance of the tracker in different scenarios. Finally, we compare our proposed algorithm with the state-of-the-art and discuss its merits and demerits. For this comparison, we used success and precision plots and PASCAL metric ($IoU > 0.50$) over OTB50 [52]. For each frame, the area of the estimated box divided by the area of the annotation is defined as *scale ratio*, and its average and standard deviation represents the scale adaptation and jitteriness of a tracker.

For the comparisons, we use OTB100 [53], UAV123 [54], LaSot [55], GOT-10K [71] and TrackingNet [72] with success and precision indexes and VOT2015 [56] and VOT2018 [57] using accuracy, robustness, and expected average overlap (EAO).[1] We have developed our tracker with Matlab using MatConvNet and C++ and on a Nvidia RTX2080 GPU, we achieved the speed of 53.8 fps.

3.1   The Effects of Regularization on Single Layer

In this experiment, we study the effect of proposed regularizations on different CNN layers, used as the features in our baseline tracker, the single layer Deep-DCF using Eq. (1). Mask regularization (Eq. (4)) as MR, proposed co-incidental (CR, Eq. (5)), temporal (TR, Eq. (7)) and ST (SR, (8)) are then progressively added to the baseline tracker to highlight their contribution in the overall tracker performance (all importance weights are fixed to 1).

Table 1. The effectiveness of regularizations with single layer of CNN with success rate $IoU > 0.50$. Here, we benchmarked baseline (B) with mask (MR), co-incidental (CR), temporal (TR), and ST style (SR) regularizations on OTB50 [52].

Layer (l)	L0	L1	L2	L3	L4	L5
B	46.2	62.3	57.4	53.9	52.9	56.3
B + MR	**49.5**	65.1	60.0	56.4	55.0	58.5
B + CR	45.1	61.9	57.5	57.4	55.1	58.4
B + TR	45.8	62.2	57.9	55.6	54.0	57.8
B + MR + CR	46.2	62.7	59.0	55.9	54.8	58.3
B + MR + CR + TR	47.5	64.3	**60.1**	57.3	57.5	**62.8**
B + MR + CR + TR + SR	48.1	**64.7**	**60.1**	58.3	58.2	62.0

Layer-Wise Analysis: Table 1 shows that the activations of features in the shallower layer of CNN generally yields better tracking compared to the deeper

---

[1] For more info see http://ishiilab.jp/member/meshgi-k/ccnt.html.

layers, except L5 which according to [1] contains high-level object-specific features. Shallower layers encodes more spatial information while accommodating a certain degree of invariance in target matching process. Contrarily, deeper layers ignore the perturbations of the appearance and perform semantic matching.

Mask Reg: Results shows that the use of mask regularization for tracking improve the tracking performance around 2.1–3.3%, where shallower layers benefit more from such regularization.

Style Reg: The style information (CR) generally improves the tracking, especially in deeper layers which the activations are not enough to localize the target. However, when applied to shallower layers, especially input image, the style information may be misleading for the tracker which is aligned with the observation of Gatys et al. [30].

Temporal Reg: Deeper layers enjoys temporal regularization more. This is due to the fact that changes in activations in deeper layers signals semantic changes in the appearance, such as misalignment of the window to the target, partial or full occlusions or unaccounted target transformations such as out-of-plane rotations. In contrary, the changes in shallower layers come from minor changes in the low-level features (e.g. edges) that is abundant in the real-world scenarios, and using only this regularization for shallow layers is not recommended.

Spatiotemporal Reg: Using this regularization on top of temporal regularization, often improves the accuracy of the tracking since non-linear temporal styles of the features cannot be always handled using temporal reg.

All Regularizations: The combination of MR and CR terms, especially helps the tracking using deeper layers and starting from L2 it outperforms both MR and CR regularizations. The combination of all regularization terms proved to be useful for all layers, improving tracking accuracy by 2–6% compared to baseline.

Feature Interconnections: Feature interconnections can be divided into *(i)* spatial-coincidental (when two features have high filter responses at the same time), *(ii)* spatial-temporal (a feature activates in a frame), *(iii)* spatial-ST style (a feature coactivates with a motion feature), *(iv)* style-temporal (coupled features turns on/off simultaneously), *(v)* style-ST style (coupled features moves similarly), temporal-ST style (a features starts/stops moving). The features are designed to capture different aspects of the object's appearance and motion; they are sometimes overlapping. Such redundancy improves tracking, with more complex features improving semantics of tracking, and low-level features improving the accuracy of the localization.

3.2   Employing Multiple Layers of CNN

To investigate different components of the proposed tracker, we prepared several ablated versions and compared them in Table 2. Three settings have been considered for the importance weights: *uniform weights, random weights,* and *optimized weights based on the model update* (Eq. (9)). The random initial weights were

Table 2. The effect of using multiple CNN layers with various importance weight strategies. This is based on the success rate ($IoU > 0.50$) on OTB50. Last column presents the speed of the ablated trackers (+ model update) compared to baseline (%).

Model update	Uniform	Random	Proposed	Speed (%)
B ($\mathcal{B}_t = \mathcal{C}_t = \mathcal{D}_t = \mathcal{E}_t = 0$)	66.8	64.4	**79.2**	100.0
B + MR ($\mathcal{C}_t = \mathcal{D}_t = \mathcal{E}_t = 0$)	67.3	66.4	**81.7**	95.2
B + CR ($\mathcal{B}_t = \mathcal{D}_t = \mathcal{E}_t = 0$)	69.1	69.9	**82.8**	83.1
B + TR ($\mathcal{B}_t = \mathcal{C}_t = \mathcal{E}_t = 0$)	67.3	67.0	**81.1**	98.4
B + MR + CR ($\mathcal{D}_t = \mathcal{E}_t = 0$)	68.3	72.6	**85.9**	80.8
B + MR + CR + TR ($\mathcal{E}_t = 0$)	69.0	73.0	**86.5**	78.0
B + MR + CR + TR + SR	69.2	73.3	**86.9**	78.7

Table 3. Scale adaptation obtained by proposed regularizations on OTB-100 measured by the mean of estimate-to-real scale ratio and its standard deviation (jitter).

Tracker	B	B + MR	B + CR	B + TR	B + MR + TR	B + MR + CR + TR	ALL
Avg. ratio	92.2	93.1	93.3	93.8	93.3	94.2	**94.7**
Jitter	8.17	7.13	5.81	2.66	5.11	2.40	**2.35**

generated for each time t (summed up to 1), and the experiment was repeated five times and averaged. By adding each regularization term, the speed of the tracker degrades, therefore, we added the ratio of the custom tracker speed to the baseline (first row) in the last column. *Uniform weighting* keeps reg. weights fixed and equal during tracking, *random weighting* assigns random weights to different components of each layer and our *proposed* AdaBoost-inspired weighting penalizes components proportional to their contribution in the previous mistakes.

Comparing Model Update Schemes: Table 2 shows that with the use of proposed model update, different components of the tracker may collaborate to improve the overall performance of the tracker when combining different layers. However, uniform weights for all parameters (equal to $|\mathcal{L}|^{-1}$) cannot provide much improvement compared to the single layer DeepDCF, especially when compared to the L1 column of Table 1. Interestingly, random weights outperform uniform weights when applied to style regularization, which shows that not all layers contain equivalently useful co-incidental information.

Multiple Layers: By comparing each row of the Table 2 with the corresponding row of Table 1, the effect of combining different layers is evident. Comparing the first rows shows the advantage of combining layers without using any regularization. Uniform weights for the layers raise the performance only by 4.5% (all layers vs. L1), whereas the proposed fusion can boost the combination performance up to 16.9%. This is a recurring pattern for other rows that show the benefit of the layer combination for activations, as well as regularization terms.

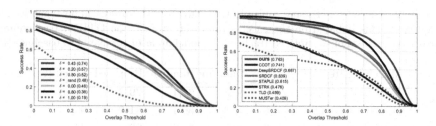

Fig. 3. (left) The activation vs. style trade-off for the custom tracker on OTB50. While $\delta \to 1$ puts too much emphasize on the style, $\delta = 0$ overemphasizes on the activations. (middle) Performance comparison of trackers on OTB100 using success plot.

Applying Different Reg: Similar to the case of single layers, regularization multiple layers is also effective. In case of uniform weights, using CR outperforms MR + CR which indicates that without proper weight adjustment, different regularization cannot be effectively stacked in the tracker. Therefore, it is expected that the proposed adaptive weight can handle this case, as table shows.

3.3 Scale Adaptation

The proposed style and temporal regs, tend to discard candidates with mismatching scale due to style and continuity inconsistencies. Additionally, temporal reg tend to reduce the jittering of the position and scale. Table 3 demonstrates the proposed tracker with multi-layers of CNN, adaptive weights and different regs.

3.4 Activation vs. Style

As seen in NST literature [30,31], various amount of focus on the content image and style image yields different outcomes. In tracking, however, the accuracy provides a measure to balance this focus. We conducted an experiment to see the effect of the regularization weights λ_{sty} on the tracking performance. Hence, we set $\lambda_{sty} = \delta$ while disabling spatial and temporal regularizers. Figure 3-left depicts the success plot for several δ and the optimal value δ^* (via annealing and cross-validation on OTB-50, with proposed model update for layers in $\mathcal{L}$).

3.5 Preliminary Analysis

We compared our tracker with TLD [58], STRUKK [59], MEEM [60], MUSTer [61], STPL [62], CMT [63], SRDCF [7], dSRDCF [64] and CCOT [28].

Attribute Analysis: We use partial subsets of OTB50 [52] with a distinguishing attribute to evaluate the tracker performance under different situations. Table 4 shows the superior performance of the algorithm, especially in handling deformations (by adaptive fusion of deep and shallow layers of CNN) and background clutter (by spatial and style reg.) and motion (by temporal reg.).

Table 4. Quantitative evaluation of trackers (top) using average success on OTB50 [52] for different tracking challenges; (middle) success and precision rates on OTB100 [53], estimated-on-real scale ratio and jitter; (bottom) robustness and accuracy on VOT2015 [56]. The ***first***, **second** and *third* best methods are shown in color.

		TLD	STRUCK	MEEM	MUSTer	STAPLE	SRDCF	dSRDCF	CCOT	Ours
OTB50	Illumination	0.48	0.53	0.62	*0.73*	0.68	0.70	0.71	**0.75**	*0.80*
	Deformation	0.38	0.51	0.62	*0.69*	**0.70**	0.67	0.67	*0.69*	*0.78*
	Occlusion	0.46	0.50	0.61	0.69	0.69	0.70	*0.71*	**0.76**	*0.79*
	Scale Changes	0.49	0.51	0.58	0.71	0.68	0.71	*0.75*	**0.76**	*0.82*
	In-plane Rot.	0.50	0.54	0.58	0.69	0.69	0.70	**0.73**	*0.72*	*0.80*
	Out-of-plane Rot.	0.48	0.53	0.62	*0.70*	0.67	0.69	*0.70*	**0.74**	*0.81*
	Out-of-view	0.54	0.52	0.68	*0.73*	0.62	0.66	0.66	**0.79**	*0.81*
	Low Resolution	0.36	0.33	0.43	0.50	0.47	0.58	*0.61*	**0.70**	*0.74*
	Background Clutter	0.39	0.52	0.67	**0.72**	0.67	0.70	*0.71*	0.70	*0.78*
	Fast Motion	0.45	0.52	0.65	0.65	0.56	0.63	*0.67*	**0.72**	*0.78*
	Motion Blur	0.41	0.47	0.63	0.65	0.61	0.69	*0.70*	**0.72**	*0.78*
	Average Success	0.49	0.55	0.62	*0.72*	0.69	0.70	0.71	**0.75**	*0.80*
OTB100	Average Success	0.46	0.48	0.65	0.57	0.62	0.64	*0.69*	**0.74**	*0.76*
	Average Precision	0.58	0.59	0.62	0.74	0.73	0.71	*0.81*	**0.85**	*0.85*
	IoU > 0.5	0.52	0.52	0.62	0.65	0.71	0.75	*0.78*	**0.88**	*0.86*
	Average Scale	116.4	134.7	112.1	-	110.8	88.5	*101.8*	**94.0**	*93.7*
	Jitter	8.2	8.7	8.2	-	5.9	*4.1*	4.9	**3.8**	*2.3*
VOT	Accuracy	-	0.47	0.50	0.52	0.53	**0.56**	0.53	*0.54*	*0.76*
	Robustness	-	1.26	1.85	2.00	1.35	1.24	*1.05*	**0.82**	*0.65*

OTB100 & VOT2015: Figure 3 (right) and Table 4 presents the success and precision plots of our tracker along with others. Data shows that proposed algorithm has superior performance, less jitter, decent robustness and comparable localization and scale adaptation.

3.6 Comparison with State-of-the-Art

Deep Trackers: We compared our tracker against recent deep trackers on OTB100, including ECO [42], ATOM [65], VITAL [23], HDT [66], YCNN [15], MDNet [67], dSTRCF [68], STResCF [41], CBCW [69], SiamFC [19], SiamRPN [20], SiamRPN++ [21], SINT++ [22], and DiMP [70]. Table 5 shows that although our proposed tracker has some issues in accurate localization, it has a superior overall performance and success rate in handling various scenarios.

The experiments revealed that the proposed tracker is resistant to target abrupt or extensive target changes. Temporal and ST features in our method monitor the inconsistency in target appearance and style, co-occurrence features in different levels of abstraction provide different levels of robustness to target changes (from low-frequency features to the high-level features such as object part relations. The dynamic weighting enables the tracker to have the flexibility to resort to more abstract feature when the target undergoes drastic changes, and ST features handle abnormalities such as temporal occlusion and deformations.

Recent Public Datasets: Our method is compared with recent state-of-the-art methods in VOT2018 [57], UAV123 [54], LaSOT [55], GOT-10K [71] and TrackingNet [72] datasets (Tables 6, 7, 8 and 9). The results are better than SiamRPN++ in VOT2018 and UAV123, and VITAL in LaSOT, despite using a

Table 5. Evaluation of deep trackers on OTB100 [53] using success rate and precision.

	ECO	ATOM	VITAL	HDT	YCNN	MDNet	dSTRCF	STResCF	CBCW	SiFC	SiRPN	SiRPN++	SINT++	Ours
Avg. Succ	**0.69**	0.66	0.68	0.65	0.60	0.67	0.68	0.59	0.61	0.59	0.63	**0.69**	0.57	*0.76*
Avg. Prec	*0.91*	-	*0.91*	0.84	0.84	**0.90**	-	0.83	0.81	0.78	*0.85*	*0.91*	0.76	*0.85*
$IoU > \frac{1}{2}$	0.74	*0.86*	0.79	0.68	0.74	**0.85**	0.77	0.76	0.76	0.76	0.80	*0.83*	0.78	*0.86*

Table 6. Evaluation on VOT2018 by the means of EAO, robustness and accuracy.

	STURCK	MEEM	STAPLE	SRDCF	CCOT	SiamFC	ECO	SiamRPN	SiamRPN++	ATOM	Ours
EAO	0.097	0.192	0.169	0.119	0.267	0.188	0.280	0.383	*0.414*	*0.401*	**0.408**
Accuracy	0.418	0.463	0.530	0.490	0.494	0.503	0.484	*0.586*	**0.600**	*0.590*	0.586
Robustness	1.297	0.534	0.688	0.974	0.318	0.585	*0.276*	*0.276*	**0.234**	*0.204*	0.281

Table 7. Evaluation on LaSOT with protocol I (testing on all videos) and protocol II (training on given videos and testing on the rest). We get better results with dataset's own videos as training due to lare training set and matching domain.

	STAPLE	SRDCF	SiamFC	SINT	MDNet	ECO	BACF	VITAL	ATOM	SiamRPN++	DiMP	Ours
(I) Accuracy	0.266	0.271	0.358	0.339	0.413	0.340	0.277	0.412	*0.515*	0.496	*0.596*	0.521
(I) Robustness	0.231	0.227	0.341	0.229	**0.374**	0.298	0.239	*0.372*	-	-	-	*0.411*
(II)Accuracy	0.243	0.245	0.336	0.314	**0.397**	0.324	0.259	*0.390*	-	-	-	*0.507*
(II)Robustness	0.239	0.219	0.339	0.295	**0.373**	0.301	0.239	*0.360*	-	-	-	*0.499*

Table 8. Evaluation on UAV123 by success rate and precision. Our algorithm is having difficulty with small/low resolution targets.

	TLD	STRUCK	MEEM	STAPLE	SRDCF	MUSTer	ECO	ATOM	SiamRPN	SiamRPN++	DiMP	Ours
Success	0.283	0.387	0.398	0.453	0.473	0.517	0.399	*0.650*	0.527	0.613	*0.653*	0.651
Precision	0.439	0.578	0.627	-	0.676	-	0.591	-	*0.748*	**0.807**	-	*0.833*

Table 9. Benchmarking on TrackingNet and GOT-10k

		ECO	DaSiam-RPN	ATOM	SiamRPN++	DiMP	SiamMask	D3S	SiamFC++	SiamRCNN	ours
T-Net	Prec.	0.492	0.591	0.648	0.694	0.687	*0.733*	-	0.705	*0.800*	**0.711**
	N-Prec.	0.618	0.733	0.771	0.800	*0.801*	0.664	-	0.800	*0.854*	**0.810**
	Success	0.554	0.638	0.703	0.733	0.740	**0.778**	-	*0.754*	*0.812*	0.752
GOT10k	AO	0.316	0.417	0.556	0.518	*0.611*	0.514	*0.597*	0.595	-	**0.601**
	SR 0.75	0.111	0.149	0.402	0.325	*0.492*	0.366	*0.462*	**0.479**	-	0.479
	SR 0.5	0.309	0.461	0.635	0.618	*0.717*	0.587	0.676	**0.695**	-	*0.685*

pre-trained CNN. This method benefits from multi-layer fusion, adaptive model update, and various regularization. Comparing the results of the benchmark with ATOM, SiamRPN++ and DIMP showed that just using convolutional layers and using the underlying features is not enough to perform a high-level tracking. Having a deeper network (ResNet-18 in ATOM and ResNet-50 in DiMP) and having auxiliary branches (region proposal in SiamRPN, IOU prediction in ATOM, and model prediction in DIMP) are two main differences between our method and the SotA. However, the proposed method offers insight about extra features to be used in tracking, such as co-occurrence features that are embedded in all CNNs ready to be exploited. Further, good performance on specific datasets (e.g., UAV123) demonstrates that these features can support different object types and contexts.

4   Conclusion

We proposed a tracker that exploits various CNN statistics including activations, spatial data, co-occurrences within a layer, and temporal changes and patterns between time slices. It adaptively fuses several CNN layers to negate the demerits of each layer with merits of others. It outperformed recent trackers in various experiments, promoting the use of spatial and temporal style in tracking. Our regularizations can be used with other CNN-based methods.

References

1. Danelljan, M., Hager, G., Shahbaz Khan, F., Felsberg, M.: Convolutional features for correlation filter based visual tracking. In: Proceedings of the IEEE International Conference on Computer Vision Workshops, pp. 58–66 (2015)
2. Wang, L., Liu, T., Wang, G., Chan, K.L., Yang, Q.: Video tracking using learned hierarchical features. IEEE TIP **24**, 1424–1435 (2015)
3. Zhang, T., Xu, C., Yang, M.H.: Multi-task correlation particle filter for robust object tracking. In: CVPR, vol. 1 (2017)
4. Hong, S., You, T., Kwak, S., Han, B.: Online tracking by learning discriminative saliency map with convolutional neural network. In: International Conference on Machine Learning, pp. 597–606 (2015)
5. Sharif Razavian, A., Azizpour, H., Sullivan, J., Carlsson, S.: CNN features off-the-shelf: an astounding baseline for recognition. In: CVPRW, pp. 806–813 (2014)
6. Cimpoi, M., Maji, S., Vedaldi, A.: Deep convolutional filter banks for texture recognition and segmentation. arXiv preprint arXiv:1411.6836 (2014)
7. Danelljan, M., Hager, G., Shahbaz Khan, F., Felsberg, M.: Learning spatially regularized correlation filters for visual tracking. In: ICCV 2015, pp. 4310–4318 (2015)
8. Nam, H., Baek, M., Han, B.: Modeling and propagating CNNs in a tree structure for visual tracking. arXiv preprint arXiv:1608.07242 (2016)
9. Wang, N., Yeung, D.Y.: Learning a deep compact image representation for visual tracking. In: NIPS, pp. 809–817 (2013)
10. Zhou, X., Xie, L., Zhang, P., Zhang, Y.: An ensemble of deep neural networks for object tracking. In: 2014 IEEE International Conference on Image Processing (ICIP), pp. 843–847. IEEE (2014)
11. Fan, J., Xu, W., Wu, Y., Gong, Y.: Human tracking using convolutional neural networks. IEEE Trans. Neural Networks **21**, 1610–1623 (2010)
12. Ma, C., Huang, J.B., Yang, X., Yang, M.H.: Hierarchical convolutional features for visual tracking. In: ICCV, pp. 3074–3082 (2015)
13. Zhang, K., Liu, Q., Wu, Y., Yang, M.: Robust visual tracking via convolutional networks without training. IEEE TIP **25**, 1779–1792 (2016)
14. Zhu, Z., Huang, G., Zou, W., Du, D., Huang, C.: UCT: learning unified convolutional networks for real-time visual tracking. In: ICCVW, pp. 1973–1982 (2017)
15. Chen, K., Tao, W.: Once for all: a two-flow convolutional neural network for visual tracking. IEEE CSVT **28**(12), 3377–3386 (2018)
16. Wang, N., Li, S., Gupta, A., Yeung, D.Y.: Transferring rich feature hierarchies for robust visual tracking. arXiv preprint arXiv:1501.04587 (2015)
17. Drayer, B., Brox, T.: Object detection, tracking, and motion segmentation for object-level video segmentation. arXiv preprint arXiv:1608.03066 (2016)

18. Tao, R., Gavves, E., Smeulders, A.W.: Siamese instance search for tracking. In: CVPR, pp. 1420–1429 (2016)
19. Bertinetto, L., Valmadre, J., Henriques, J.F., Vedaldi, A., Torr, P.H.S.: Fully-convolutional Siamese networks for object tracking. In: Hua, G., Jégou, H. (eds.) ECCV 2016. LNCS, vol. 9914, pp. 850–865. Springer, Cham (2016). https://doi.org/10.1007/978-3-319-48881-3_56
20. Li, B., Yan, J., Wu, W., Zhu, Z., Hu, X.: High performance visual tracking with Siamese region proposal network. In: CVPR 2018, pp. 8971–8980 (2018)
21. Li, B., Wu, W., Wang, Q., Zhang, F., Xing, J., Yan, J.: SiamRPN++: evolution of siamese visual tracking with very deep networks. In: CVPR 2019, pp. 4282–4291 (2019)
22. Wang, X., Li, C., Luo, B., Tang, J.: Sint++: robust visual tracking via adversarial positive instance generation. In: Proceedings of the IEEE Conference on Computer Vision and Pattern Recognition, pp. 4864–4873 (2018)
23. Song, Y., et al.: Vital: visual tracking via adversarial learning. In: CVPR (2018)
24. Vondrick, C., Shrivastava, A., Fathi, A., Guadarrama, S., Murphy, K.: Tracking emerges by colorizing videos. In: ECCV (2018)
25. Zeiler, M.D., Fergus, R.: Visualizing and understanding convolutional networks. In: Fleet, D., Pajdla, T., Schiele, B., Tuytelaars, T. (eds.) ECCV 2014. LNCS, vol. 8689, pp. 818–833. Springer, Cham (2014). https://doi.org/10.1007/978-3-319-10590-1_53
26. Liu, L., Shen, C., van den Hengel, A.: The treasure beneath convolutional layers: cross-convolutional-layer pooling for image classification. In: CVPR, pp. 4749–4757 (2015)
27. Qi, Y., Zhang, S., Qin, L., Huang, Q., Yao, H., Lim, J., Yang, M.H.: Hedging deep features for visual tracking. PAMI 41(5), 1116–1130 (2018)
28. Danelljan, M., Robinson, A., Shahbaz Khan, F., Felsberg, M.: Beyond correlation filters: learning continuous convolution operators for visual tracking. In: Leibe, B., Matas, J., Sebe, N., Welling, M. (eds.) ECCV 2016. LNCS, vol. 9909, pp. 472–488. Springer, Cham (2016). https://doi.org/10.1007/978-3-319-46454-1_29
29. Bovik, A.C., Clark, M., Geisler, W.S.: Multichannel texture analysis using localized spatial filters. PAMI 12, 55–73 (1990)
30. Gatys, L.A., Ecker, A.S., Bethge, M.: Image style transfer using convolutional neural networks. In: CVPR, pp. 2414–2423 (2016)
31. Johnson, J., Alahi, A., Fei-Fei, L.: Perceptual losses for real-time style transfer and super-resolution. In: Leibe, B., Matas, J., Sebe, N., Welling, M. (eds.) ECCV 2016. LNCS, vol. 9906, pp. 694–711. Springer, Cham (2016). https://doi.org/10.1007/978-3-319-46475-6_43
32. Matsuo, S., Yanai, K.: CNN-based style vector for style image retrieval. In: Proceedings of the 2016 ACM on International Conference on Multimedia Retrieval, pp. 309–312. ACM (2016)
33. Varol, G., Laptev, I., Schmid, C.: Long-term temporal convolutions for action recognition. PAMI 40, 1510–1517 (2018)
34. Gkioxari, G., Malik, J.: Finding action tubes. In: CVPR, pp. 759–768 (2015)
35. Chao, Y.W., Vijayanarasimhan, S., Seybold, B., Ross, D.A., Deng, J., Sukthankar, R.: Rethinking the faster R-CNN architecture for temporal action localization. In: CVPR, pp. 1130–1139 (2018)
36. Simonyan, K., Zisserman, A.: Two-stream convolutional networks for action recognition in videos. In: NIPS, pp. 568–576 (2014)
37. Zhu, Z., Wu, W., Zou, W., Yan, J.: End-to-end flow correlation tracking with spatial-temporal attention. CVPR 42, 20 (2017)

38. Dosovitskiy, A., et al.: FlowNet: learning optical flow with convolutional networks. In: Proceedings of the IEEE International Conference on Computer Vision, pp. 2758–2766 (2015)
39. Feichtenhofer, C., Pinz, A., Wildes, R.P., Zisserman, A.: What have we learned from deep representations for action recognition? Connections **19**, 29 (2018)
40. Gladh, S., Danelljan, M., Khan, F.S., Felsberg, M.: Deep motion features for visual tracking. In: ICPR, pp. 1243–1248. IEEE (2016)
41. Zhu, Z., et al.: STResNet_cf tracker: the deep spatiotemporal features learning for correlation filter based robust visual object tracking. IEEE Access **7**, 30142–30156 (2019)
42. Danelljan, M., Bhat, G., Khan, F.S., Felsberg, M.: ECO: efficient convolution operators for tracking. In: CVPR (2017)
43. Galoogahi, H.K., Fagg, A., Lucey, S.: Learning background-aware correlation filters for visual tracking. arXiv preprint arXiv:1703.04590 (2017)
44. Danelljan, M., Häger, G., Khan, F., Felsberg, M.: Accurate scale estimation for robust visual tracking. In: BMVC. BMVA Press (2014)
45. Henriques, J.F., Caseiro, R., Martins, P., Batista, J.: Exploiting the circulant structure of tracking-by-detection with kernels. In: Fitzgibbon, A., Lazebnik, S., Perona, P., Sato, Y., Schmid, C. (eds.) ECCV 2012. LNCS, vol. 7575, pp. 702–715. Springer, Heidelberg (2012). https://doi.org/10.1007/978-3-642-33765-9_50
46. Bolme, D.S., Beveridge, J.R., Draper, B.A., Lui, Y.M.: Visual object tracking using adaptive correlation filters. In: CVPR 2010, pp. 2544–2550. IEEE (2010)
47. Jepson, A.D., Fleet, D.J., El-Maraghi, T.F.: Robust online appearance models for visual tracking. PAMI **25**(10), 1296–1311 (2003)
48. Berger, G., Memisevic, R.: Incorporating long-range consistency in CNN-based texture generation. In: ICLR (2017)
49. Wiyatno, R.R., Xu, A.: Physical adversarial textures that fool visual object tracking. In: Proceedings of the IEEE International Conference on Computer Vision, pp. 4822–4831 (2019)
50. Vedaldi, A., Lenc, K.: MatConvNet: convolutional neural networks for MATLAB. In: Proceedings of the 23rd ACM International Conference on Multimedia, pp. 689–692. ACM (2015)
51. Real, E., Shlens, J., Mazzocchi, S., Pan, X., Vanhoucke, V.: YouTube-BoundingBoxes: a large high-precision human-annotated data set for object detection in video. In: CVPR 2017, pp. 5296–5305 (2017)
52. Wu, Y., Lim, J., Yang, M.H.: Online object tracking: a benchmark. In: CVPR 2013, pp. 2411–2418. IEEE (2013)
53. Wu, Y., Lim, J., Yang, M.H.: Object tracking benchmark. PAMI **37**(9), 1834–1848 (2015)
54. Mueller, M., Smith, N., Ghanem, B.: A benchmark and simulator for UAV tracking. In: Leibe, B., Matas, J., Sebe, N., Welling, M. (eds.) ECCV 2016. LNCS, vol. 9905, pp. 445–461. Springer, Cham (2016). https://doi.org/10.1007/978-3-319-46448-0_27
55. Fan, H., et al.: LaSOT: a high-quality benchmark for large-scale single object tracking. In: CVPR 2019 (2019)
56. Kristan, M., et al.: The visual object tracking VOT2015 challenge results. In: ICCVw 2015, pp. 1–23 (2015)
57. Kristan, M., et al.: The sixth visual object tracking VOT2018 challenge results. In: ECCV 2018 (2018)
58. Kalal, Z., Mikolajczyk, K., Matas, J.: Tracking-learning-detection. PAMI **34**, 1409–1422 (2012)

59. Hare, S., Saffari, A., Torr, P.H.: Struck: structured output tracking with kernels. In: ICCV 2011 (2011)
60. Zhang, J., Ma, S., Sclaroff, S.: MEEM: robust tracking via multiple experts using entropy minimization. In: Fleet, D., Pajdla, T., Schiele, B., Tuytelaars, T. (eds.) ECCV 2014. LNCS, vol. 8694, pp. 188–203. Springer, Cham (2014). https://doi. org/10.1007/978-3-319-10599-4_13
61. Hong, Z., Chen, Z., Wang, C., Mei, X., Prokhorov, D., Tao, D.: Multi-store tracker (muster): a cognitive psychology inspired approach to object tracking. In: CVPR 2015, pp. 749–758 (2015)
62. Bertinetto, L., Valmadre, J., Golodetz, S., Miksik, O., Torr, P.H.: Staple: complementary learners for real-time tracking. In: CVPR, pp. 1401–1409 (2016)
63. Meshgi, K., Oba, S., Ishii, S.: Active discriminative tracking using collective memory. In: MVA 2017 (2017)
64. Danelljan, M., Hager, G., Shahbaz Khan, F., Felsberg, M.: Convolutional features for correlation filter based visual tracking. In: ICCVW, pp. 58–66 (2015)
65. Danelljan, M., Bhat, G., Khan, F.S., Felsberg, M.: ATOM: accurate tracking by overlap maximization. In: CVPR 2019, pp. 4660–4669 (2019)
66. Qi, Y., et al.: Hedged deep tracking. In: CVPR, pp. 4303–4311 (2016)
67. Nam, H., Han, B.: Learning multi-domain convolutional neural networks for visual tracking. In: CVPR, pp. 4293–4302 (2016)
68. Li, F., et al.: Learning spatial-temporal regularized correlation filters for visual tracking. In: CVPR 2018 (2018)
69. Zhou, Y., et al.: Efficient correlation tracking via center-biased spatial regularization. IEEE TIP **27**, 6159–6173 (2018)
70. Bhat, G., Danelljan, M., Gool, L.V., Timofte, R.: Learning discriminative model prediction for tracking. In: Proceedings of the IEEE International Conference on Computer Vision, pp. 6182–6191 (2019)
71. Huang, L., Zhao, X., Huang, K.: GOT-10k: a large high-diversity benchmark for generic object tracking in the wild. IEEE TPAMI (2019). https://doi.org/10.1109/ TPAMI.2019.2957464
72. Muller, M., Bibi, A., Giancola, S., Alsubaihi, S., Ghanem, B.: TrackingNet: a large-scale dataset and benchmark for object tracking in the wild. In: ECCV 2018 (2018)

A Two-Stage Minimum Cost Multicut Approach to Self-supervised Multiple Person Tracking

Kalun Ho[1,2,3(✉)], Amirhossein Kardoost[3], Franz-Josef Pfreundt[1,2], Janis Keuper[4], and Margret Keuper[3]

[1] Fraunhofer Center Machine Learning, Sankt Augustin, Germany
kalun.ho@itwm.fhg.de
[2] CC-HPC, Fraunhofer ITWM, Kaiserslautern, Germany
[3] Data and Web Science Group, University of Mannheim, Mannheim, Germany
[4] Institute for Machine Learning and Analytics, Offenburg University, Offenburg, Germany

Abstract. Multiple Object Tracking (MOT) is a long-standing task in computer vision. Current approaches based on the tracking by detection paradigm either require some sort of domain knowledge or supervision to associate data correctly into tracks. In this work, we present a self-supervised multiple object tracking approach based on visual features and minimum cost lifted multicuts. Our method is based on straightforward spatio-temporal cues that can be extracted from neighboring frames in an image sequences without supervision. Clustering based on these cues enables us to learn the required appearance invariances for the tracking task at hand and train an AutoEncoder to generate suitable latent representations. Thus, the resulting latent representations can serve as robust appearance cues for tracking even over large temporal distances where no reliable spatio-temporal features can be extracted. We show that, despite being trained without using the provided annotations, our model provides competitive results on the challenging MOT Benchmark for pedestrian tracking.

1 Introduction

The objective of multiple object tracking is to find a trajectory for each individual object of interest in a given input video. Specific interest has been devoted to the specific task of multiple person tracking [1–5]. Most successful approaches follow the *Tracking-By-Detection* paradigm. First, an object (pedestrian) detector is used in order to retrieve the position of each person within each frame. Secondly, the output detections of same persons across video frames are associated over space and time in order to form unique trajectories. Since objects might get

Electronic supplementary material The online version of this chapter (https://doi.org/10.1007/978-3-030-69532-3_33) contains supplementary material, which is available to authorized users.

H. Ishikawa et al. (Eds.): ACCV 2020, LNCS 12623, pp. 539–557, 2021.
https://doi.org/10.1007/978-3-030-69532-3_33

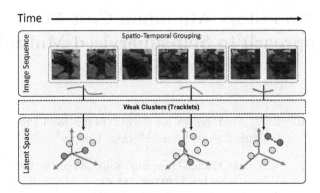

Fig. 1. Given an image sequence, many data associations can be made reliably from pure spatio-temporal cues such as the intersection over union of bounding boxes. These associations are injected into a convolutional AutoEncoder to enforce detections with the same, spatio-temporally determined label to be close to one-another in the latent space. Thus, the learned appearance features will generalize over viewpoint and pose variations.

occluded during the video sequence or the detector might simply fail on some examples, successful approaches are usually based not solely on spatial but also on appearance cues. These are learned from annotated data, for example using Siamese networks for person re-identification [4].

Motivation. Supervised approaches for person re-identification require large amounts of sequence specific data in order to achieve good performance. For this reason, multiple object tracking benchmarks such as MOT [6] are providing a training sequence recorded in a sufficiently similar setting for every test sequence. The results of our experiments in Table 1 confirm this dependency and show the high variance in the quality of supervised approaches, depending on the data used for training. The standard approach to solve this problem is to incorporate additional annotated training data. For example, [7,8] showed that additional data is key to improving the overall tracking performance.

Thus, publicly available, annotated training data currently seems not to be sufficient for training reliable person re-identification networks. Furthermore, recording and labeling sufficient data in a setting close to a final test scenario usually comes at a high price. Hence, the need for methods with a low amount of supervision becomes obvious and motivates us to propose a multiple object tracking method based on self-supervision.

While self-supervised learning methods [9] have been successfully exploited in other vision tasks [10–15], a direct application to tracking is non-trivial: Learning suitable object appearance metrics for object tracking in a self-supervised way is challenging since, compared to classical clustering problems, visual features of the same person may change over time due to pose and viewpoint changes and partial occlusion. Other issues, such as frequent and long range full occlusion or background noises, makes pedestrian tracking even more challenging.

Table 1. Results for training with one training sequence using *GT annotations* (Specifically, we mine GT tracklets from the detections with IoU > 0.5 with the GT as e.g. done in [16].) for the tracklet generation, and evaluating on other training sequences with different viewpoints and resolutions. This table shows the relative MOTA changes for non-matching sequences on MOT17, FRCNN in comparison to the baseline (bold). Columns represent the training sequence, rows the test sequence. The tracking performance heavily depends on the employed training data and can become unstable across domains.

		Train (Supervised)						
		MOT-02	MOT-04	MOT-05	MOT-09	MOT-10	MOT-11	MOT-13
	MOT-02	**100.0**	−0.3	−0.3	−19.2	−9.1	−12.5	−9.5
	MOT-04	0.0	**100.0**	0.0	−19.3	−4.9	−11.5	−4.9
	MOT-05	−0.6	−1.2	**100.0**	−3.2	−5.1	−3.4	−5.1
Test	MOT-09	−0.2	−0.4	−0.2	**100.0**	−2.9	−0.5	−2.5
	MOT-10	0.8	0.6	1.2	0.6	**100.0**	0.6	0.4
	MOT-11	0.0	−0.2	−0.2	0.2	−1.2	**100.0**	−1.4
	MOT-13	0.4	−1.1	−0.4	−3.8	−0.8	−2.7	**100.0**

In this paper, we propose an approach for learning appearance features for multiple object tracking without utilizing human annotations of the data. Our approach is based on two observations: I) given an image sequence, many data associations can be made reliably from pure spatio-temporal cues such as the intersection over union (IoU) of bounding boxes within one frame or between neighboring frames. II) Resulting tracklets, carry important information about the variation of an object's appearance over time, for example by changes of the pose or viewpoint. In our model, we cluster the initial data based on simple spatial cues using the recently successful minimum cost multicut approach [3]. The resulting clustering information is then injected into a convolutional AutoEncoder to enforce detections with the same, spatio-temporally determined label to be close to one-another in the latent space (see Fig. 1). Thus, the resulting latent data representation is encoding not only the pure object appearance, but also the expected appearance variations within one object ID. Distances between such latent representations can serve to re-identify objects even after long temporal distances, where no reliable spatio-temporal cues could be extracted. We use the resulting information in the minimum cost lifted multicut framework, similar to the formulation of Tang [4], whose method is based on Siamese networks trained in a fully supervised way.

To summarize, our contributions are:

- We present an approach for multiple object tracking, including long range connections between objects, which is completely supervision-free in the sense that no human annotations of person IDs are employed.
- We propose to inject spatio-temporally derived information into convolutional AutoEncoder in order to produce a suitable data embedding space for multiple object tracking.

– We evaluate our approach on the challenging MOT17 benchmark and show competitive results without using training annotations.

The rest of the paper is structured as follows: Section 2 discusses the related work on multiple object tracking. Our self-supervised approach on multiple object tracking is explained in Sect. 3. In Sect. 4, we show the tracking performance of the proposed method in the MOT Benchmark [6] and conclude in Sect. 5.

2   Related Work

Multiple Object Tracking. In Multiple Object Tracking according to the *Tracking by Detection* paradigm, the objective is to associate detections of individual persons, which may have spatial or temporal changes in the video. Thus re-identification over a long range remains a challenging task. Multiple object tracking by linking bounding box detections (*tracking by detection*) was studied, e.g., in [1,17–22,22–24]. These works solve the combinatorial problem of linking detections over time via different formulations e.g. via integer linear programming [25,26], MAP estimation [17], CRFs [27], continuous optimization [18] or dominant sets [28]. In such approaches, the pre-grouping of detections into tracklets or non-maximum suppression are commonly used to reduce the computational costs [1,19–23,29,30]. For example Zamir et al. [1] use generalized minimum clique graphs to generate tracklets as well as the final object trajectories. Non-maximum suppression also plays a crucial role in disjoint path formulations, such as [17,26,31]. In the work of Tang et al. [3], local pairwise features based on DeepMatching are used to solve a multicut problem. The affinity measure is invariant to camera motion and thus makes it reliable for short term occlusions. An extension of this work is found in [4], where additional long range information is included. By introducing a lifted edge in the graph, an improvement of person re-identification has been achieved. Similarly, [32] uses lifted edges as an extension to the disjoint path problem. [33] exploits the tracking formulation using a Message Passing Networks (MPNs). In [34], low-level point trajectories and the detections are combined to jointly solve a co-clustering problem, where dependencies are established between the low-level points and the detections. Henschel et al. [35] solves the multiple object tracking problem by incorporating additional head detection to the full body detection while in [36], they use a body and joint detector to improve the quality of the provided noisy detections from the benchmark. Other works that treat Multiple Object Tracking as a graph-based problem can be found in [2,37–39] and [1]. In contrast, [40] introduces a tracklet-to-tracklet method based on a combination of Deep Neural Networks, called *Deep Siamese Bi-GRU*. The visual appearance of detections are extracted with CNNs and RNNs in order to generate a tracklet of individuals. These tracklets are then split and reconnected such that occluded persons are correctly re-identified. The framework uses spatial and temporal information from the detector to associate the tracklets. The approach in [41] exploits the bounding box information by learning from detectors first and combined with a re-identification model trained on a siamese network. While the state of the art approaches in MOT17 Challenge are all based on supervised learning [35,42–44], there are similar works in [45–47], which attempt to solve person re-identification (ReID) problems in an unsupervised manner.

Self-supervised learning aims to generate pseudo labels automatically from a pretext task, and then employs these labels to train and solve for the actual downstream task. This is especially useful when no labeled data is available. Thus self-supervised approaches can be applied to many specific real-world problems. An extensive review of recent methods is presented in [48]. For instance [49] uses a motion-based approach to obtain labels to train a convolutional neural network for semantic segmentation problems. Another work on self-supervision based on motion can be found in [11] The idea of Doersch et al. [50] is to predict the position of eight spatial configurations given an image pair. In [51] semantic inpainting task is solved using a context encoder to predict missing pixels of an image. Hendrycks et al. [12] use a self-supervised method to improve the robustness of deep learning models. Lee et al. [52] propose an approach to improve object detection by recycling the bounding box labels while Ye et al. [53] use a progressive latent model to learn a customized detector based on spatio-temporal proposals.

3   AutoEncoder-Based Multicut Approach

The proposed approach is based on the idea to learn, from simple spatial data associations between object detections in image sequences, which appearance variations are to be expected within one object for the task of multiple object tracking. An overview of our workflow implementing this idea is given in Fig. 2.

Stage 1. The object detection bounding boxes are extracted along with their spatial information such that spatial correspondences between detections in neighboring frames can be computed. Based on these simple spatial associations, detections can be grouped into tracklets in order to obtain cluster labels using clustering approaches such as correlation clustering, also referred to as minimum cost multicuts [54].

Stage 2. A convolutional AutoEncoder is trained to learn the visual features of detections. The objective is to learn a latent space representation which can serve to match the same object in different video frames. Thus, the information about spatial cluster labels from the first stage is used as the centroid of latent features. Distances between latent representations of data samples and their centroids are minimized in the convolutional AutoEncoder using a clustering loss.

Lastly, the data are transformed into the latent space of the trained AutoEncoder to extract pairwise appearance distances which are expected to encode the desired invariances. Such pairwise appearance distances are used to not only provide additional grouping information between nearby detections, but also for

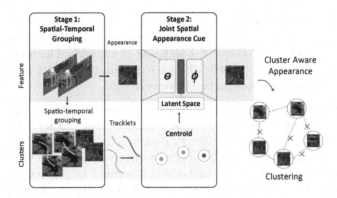

Fig. 2. Summary of our approach in two steps: 1. First, weak cluster labels (tracklets) are obtained from spatio-temporal vicinity using minimum cost multicuts [56]. 2. Then, visual features are learned by an AutoEncoder, with an additional data association loss within the tracklets. The AutoEncoder provides a stable appearance embedding while the additional loss forces detections within one tracklet to have similar embeddings. This facilitates to extract affinities between detections to compute the final tracking with re-identification using lifted multicuts [4].

detections with long temporal distance. The final detection grouping is computed using minimum cost lifted multicuts [55].

This section is divided into three subsections: Section 3.1 describes the minimum cost (lifted) multicut approach employed for obtaining the initial spatial cluster labels (e.g. tracklets), as well as for the generation of the final tracking result. Section 3.2 describes the feature learning process using a convolutional AutoEncoder and cluster labels, and Sect. 3.3 describes the computation of the joint spatial and appearance metrics used in the final data association step within the minimum cost lifted multicut framework.

3.1 Multicut Formulation

We follow Tang [4] and phrase the multiple target tracking problem as a graph partitioning problem, more concretely, as a minimum cost (lifted) multicut problem. This formulation can serve as well for an initial tracklet generation process, which will help us to inject cues learned from spatial information into the appearance features, as it can be used to generate the final tracking result using short- and long-range information between object detections.

Minimum Cost Multicut Problem. We assume, we are given an undirected graph $G = (V, E)$, where nodes $v \in V$ represent object detections and edges $e \in E$ encode their respective spatio-temporal connectivity. Additionally, we are given real valued costs $c : E \to \mathbb{R}$ defined on all edges. Our goal is to determine *edge* labels $y : E \to \{0, 1\}$ defining a graph decomposition such that every partition of the graph corresponds to exactly one object track (or tracklet). To infer such an edge labeling, we can solve instances of the minimum cost multicut problem with respect to the graph G and costs c, defined as follows [54,56]:

$$\min_{y \in \{0,1\}^E} \sum_{e \in E} c_e y_e \tag{1}$$

$$s.t. \quad \forall C \in cycles(G) \quad \forall e \in C : y_e \leq \sum_{e' \in C \setminus \{e\}} y_{e'} \tag{2}$$

Here, the objective is simply to cut those edges with negative costs c_e such that the resulting cut is a decomposition of the graph. This condition is formalized by the cycle inequalities in Eq. (2), which make sure that, for every cycle in G, if one of its edges is cut, so is at least one other. Thus, no two nodes can remain connected via some path of the graph if an edge is cut between them along any other path. In [56], it was shown to be sufficient to enforce Eq. (2) on all *chordless* cycles, i.e. all cycles.

Typically, if cut probabilities between pairs of nodes are available, the costs are computed using the *logit* function $logit(p) = \log \frac{p}{1-p}$ to generate positive and negative costs. With these costs set appropriately, the optimal solution of minimum cost multicut problems not only yields an optimal cluster assignment but also estimates the number of clusters (e.g. objects to track) automatically.

While the plain minimum cost multicut problem has shown good performance in multiple object tracking scenarios with only short range information available [3], the cost function actually has a rather limited expressiveness. In particular, when we want to add connectivity cues between temporally distant bounding boxes, we can only do so by inserting a direct edge into the graph. This facilitates solutions that directly connect such distant nodes even if this link is not justified by any path through space and time. This limitation is alleviated by the formulation of minimum cost *lifted* multicuts [55].

Minimum Cost Lifted Multicut Problem. For a given, undirected graph $G = (V, E)$ and an additional edge set $F \subseteq \binom{V}{2} \setminus E$ and any real valued cost function $c : E \cup F \to \mathbb{R}$, the 01 linear program written below is an instance of the *Minimum Cost Lifted Multicut Problem (LMP)* w.r.t. G, F and c [55]:

$$\min_{y \in Y_{EF}} \sum_{e \in E \cup F} c_e y_e \tag{3}$$

with $Y_{EF} \subseteq \{0,1\}^{E \cup F}$ the set of all $y \in \{0,1\}^{E \cup F}$ with

$$\forall C \in cycles(G) \ \forall e \in C : \ y_e \leq \sum_{e' \in C \setminus \{e\}} y_{e'} \tag{4}$$

$$\forall vw \in F \ \forall P \in vw\text{-paths}(G) : \ y_{vw} \leq \sum_{e \in P} y_e \tag{5}$$

$$\forall vw \in F \; \forall C \in vw\text{-cuts}(G) : 1 - y_{vw} \leq \sum_{e \in C}(1 - y_e) \tag{6}$$

The above inequalities Eq. (4) make sure that, as before, the resulting edge labeling is actually inducing a decomposition of G. Equation (5) enforces the same constraints on cycles involving edges from F, i.e. so called *lifted* edges, and Eq. (6) makes sure that nodes that are connected via a lifted edge $e \in F$ are connected via some path along original edges $e' \in E$ as well. Thus, this formulation allows for a generalization of the cost function to include long range information without altering the set of feasible solutions.

Optimization. The minimum cost multicut problem (1) as well as the minimum lifted multicut problem (3) are NP-hard [57] and even APX-hard [54,58]. Nonetheless, instances have been solved within tight bounds, e.g. in [59] using a branch-and-cut approach. While this can be reasonably fast for some, easier problem instances, it can take arbitrarily long for others. Thus, primal heuristics such as the one proposed in [55] or [60] are often employed in practice and show convincing results in various scenarios [4,55,61,62].

Spatio-temporal Tracklet Generation. Since the proposed approach is self-supervised in a sense that no annotated labels from the dataset are used in the training process, it is challenging to effectively learn such probabilities. To approach this challenge, we first extract reliable point matches between neighboring frames using DeepMatching [63] as done before e.g. in [3,4,34]. Instead of learning a regression model on features derived from the resulting point matches, we simply assume that the intersection over union (IoU) of retrieved matched within pairs of detections (denoted by IoU_{DM}) is an approximation to the true IoU. Thus, when $\text{IoU}_{\text{DM}} > 0.7$, we can be sure we are looking at the same object in different frames. While this rough estimation is not suitable in the actual tracking task since it clearly over-estimates the cut probability, it can be used to perform a pre-grouping of detections that definitely belong to the same person. The computation of pairwise cut probabilities used in the lifted multicut step for the final tracking task is described in Sect. 3.3.

3.2 Deep Convolutional AutoEncoder

A convolutional AutoEncoder takes an input image, compresses it into a *latent space* and reconstructs it with the objective to learn meaningful features in an unsupervised manner. It consists of two parts: the encoder $f_\theta(.)$ and a decoder $g_\phi(.)$, where θ and ϕ are trainable parameters of the encoder and decoder, respectively. For a given input video, there are in total n detections $x_i \in X_{i=1}^n$, the objective is to find a meaningful encoding z_i, where the dimension of z_i is much lower than x_i. The used convolutional AutoEncoder first maps the input data into a latent space Z with a non-linear function $f_\theta : X \to Z$, then decodes Z

to its input with $g_\phi : Z \to X$. The encoding and reconstruction is achieved by minimizing the following loss equation:

$$\min_{\theta,\phi} \sum_{i=1}^{N} L(g(f(x_i)), x_i) \tag{7}$$

where L is the least-squared loss $L(x, y) = \|x - y\|^2$. Similar to the work of [64], we add an additional clustering term to minimize the distance between learned features and their cluster center $\tilde{c}_i$ from the spatio-temporal tracklet labels.

$$\min_{\theta,\phi} \sum_{i=1}^{N} L(g(f(x_i)), x_i)\lambda + L(f(x_i), \tilde{c}_i)(1 - \lambda) \tag{8}$$

The parameter $\lambda \in [0, 1]$ balances between reconstruction and clustering loss. When choosing $0 < \lambda < 1$, the reconstruction part (Eq. (7)) can be considered to be a data-dependent regularization for the clustering. To compute the centroid c_i, the whole dataset is passed through the AutoEncoder once:

$$\tilde{c}_i = \frac{1}{N} \sum_{i=1}^{N} f(x_i) \tag{9}$$

We use a deep AutoEncoder with five convolutional and max-pooling layers for the encoder and five up-convolutional and upsample layers for the decoder, respectively. Furthermore, batch normalization is applied on each layer and initialized using Xavier Initialization [65]. The input image size is halved after each layer while the number of filters are doubled. The size of latent space is set to 32. The input layer takes a colored image with dimension 128×128 in width and height and we applied ReLu activation functions on each layer.

3.3 AutoEncoder-Based Affinity Measure

We use the trained AutoEncoder to estimate the similarity of two detections x_i and x_j of a video sequence based on the Euclidean distance in the latent space:

$$d_{i,j} = \|f(x_i) - f(x_j)\| \tag{10}$$

Figure 3 shows the nearest neighbor of a selected frame t (left box marked in red) from the sequence MOT17-09 and frame $t+5 \cdot k$. The example illustrates that the location of detections with the same ID are close to one another in the latent space even over a long distance of up to 40 frames. Yet, false positives can appear. The example also shows that change in appearance affects the AutoEncoder distance, further denoted d_{AE}. For instance in the first row, frame 1 and frame 6 are very similar due to the same detection position of the person within the bounding box as well as the direction the girl is looking to. At frame 41, the girl (in Fig. 3) slightly turned towards another person. Although the correct nearest neighbour was retrieved, the distance d_{AE} almost doubled (in blue: distance 4.83

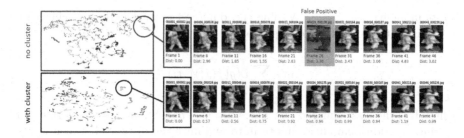

Fig. 3. Nearest neighbor of the query detection (left most detection) within 46 frames with a step size of 5 frames of the sequence MOT17-09-SDP without (top) and with (bottom) the self-supervised clustering loss. Without this loss, the detections on the girl are spread over several clusters and a false association is made by the nearest neighbor. These mistakes are corrected by the clustering loss. (Color figure online)

compared to 2.96 at frame 6). Another observation is that the position of the bounding box influences the latent space distance. Such behavior easily allows for false positive associations. In the second row, in the first detection from the left (frame 5), the detection of the person is slightly shifted to the left. At frame 15, 20 or 25, the position is slightly zoomed and d_{AE} increases. Yet, it is overall more stable and less false positive associations are made.

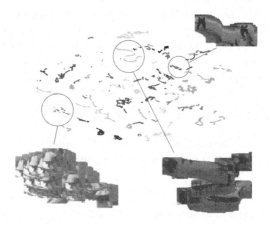

Fig. 4. TSNE Visualization of the latent space of the trained AutoEncoder for the sequence MOT17-04 FRCNN. The colors represent the assigned person IDs. As the appearance changes for example due to pose changes, the latent representations vary smoothly. (Color figure online)

Visualization of Latent Space. Figure 4 shows the TSNE-Visualization [66] of the latent space from the sequence MOT17-04-FRCNN. Our proposed

AutoEncoder learned the visual features without supervision. The different colors represent the cluster labels. As shown in the example circled on the bottom left, similar looking persons are very closed to one another in the latent space: The sitting person in white shirt and the lady, wearing a white shirt (example in bottom left). The visualization also shows that the same person may change the appearance over time (example on the bottom right). In the latent space, the *snake*-like shape may indicate that the viewpoint or pose of a person may have changed over time, causing a continuous appearance change. When standing still, the change is minimal, which is also observed in the example on the top right corner. While for nearby frames, we can compute pairwise cues based on the distance between latent feature representation (d_{AE}), as well as on spatial cues (IoU$_{DM}$), spatial information can not be used to associate detections over longer temporal distances. However, to facilitate the re-identification of objects after being fully or partly occluded, such long-range information is needed. In these cases, we have to purely rely on the learned latent space distance d_{AE}. The distance is directly cast to a binary logistic regression to compute the cut probability of the respective edge in graph G. The label that is used for the regression comes from the DeepMatching IoU. If IoU$_{DM}(x_i, x_j) < T_{low}$ for a threshold T_{low}, x_i and x_j most certainly belong to different objects. If IoU$_{DM}(x_i, x_j) > T_{high}$ for a different threshold T_{high}, they are very likely to match. Formally, we estimate a probability $p_e \in [0,1]$ between two detections using a feature vector $f^{(e)}$ by regressing the parameters β of a logistic function:

$$p_e = \frac{1}{1 + \exp(-\langle \beta, f^{(e)} \rangle)} \tag{11}$$

Thus, the costs c_e can intuitively be computed by the logit. To robustly estimate these probabilities, we set T_{low} and T_{high} most conservatively to 0.1 and 0.7, respectively. From this partial, purely spatially induced labeling, we can estimate cut probabilities for all available features combinations, i.e. possible combinations of IoU$_{DM}$ and d_{AE} within nearby frames and only d_{AE} for distant frames.

4   Experiments and Results

We evaluate the proposed method on the MOT17 Benchmark [6] for multiple person tracking. The dataset consists of 14 sequences, divided into train and test sets with 7 sequences each. For all sequences, three different detection sets are provided, from the detectors SDP [67], DPM [68] and FRCNN [69], thus yielding 21 sequences in both data splits. While SDP and FRCNN provide reliable detections, the performance of the DPM detector is relatively noise and many detections are show poor localization.

The settings between the training and testing scenes are very similar such as moving/static camera, place of recording or view angle, such that learning-based methods usually train on the most similar training sequence for every

Table 2. Tracking Performance using different features on the MOT17 Training Dataset. The third column refers to the frame distance over which bounding boxes are connected in the graph. d_{AE} represents the AutoEncoder latent space distance while d_{AE+C} includes the clustering term, respectively. Our proposed approach includes lifted edges [4] between frames of distance 10, 20 and 30.

No	Features	Distance	MOTA	MOTP	IDs	MT	ML	FP	FN
1	IoU$_{DM}$	1–3	47.2	83.8	3,062	311	657	7,868	167,068
2	d_{AE}	1–3	35.2	83.9	4,378	138	743	10,213	203,868
3	d_{AE+C}	1–3	37.6	84.0	3,830	162	745	8,951	197,308
4	Combined (1 + 2)	1–3	49.4	83.5	1,730	381	593	7,536	161,057
5	Combined (1 + 3)	1–3	49.4	83.4	1,713	380	594	7,786	161,084
6	IoU$_{DM}$	1–5	47.2	83.5	2,731	337	642	12,195	163,055
7	d_{AE}	1–5	35.8	84.2	4,623	129	755	6,867	204,697
8	d_{AE+C}	1–5	35.2	83.9	4,378	138	743	10,213	203,868
9	Combined (6 + 7)	1–5	49.7	83.3	1,567	389	578	9,067	158,788
10	Combined (6 + 8)	1–5	49.8	83.3	1,569	388	580	8,869	158,715
11	**Proposed**	**1–5**	**50.2**	**83.3**	**1,458**	**391**	**582**	**8,466**	**157,936**

Table 3. Tracking result compared to other methods on the MOT17 dataset. The best performance is marked in bold.

Sequence	Method	**MOTA**	MOTP	IDs	MT	ML	FP	FN
Lif_T [32]	Supervised	**60.5**	78.3	1,189	27.0	33.6	**14,966**	**206,619**
MPNTrack [33]	Supervised	58.8	**78.6**	**1,185**	**28.8**	**33.5**	17,413	213,594
eHAF17 [71]	Supervised	51.8	77.0	1,834	23.4	37.9	33,212	**236,772**
AFN17 [72]	Supervised	51.5	77.6	2,593	20.6	35.5	22,391	248,420
jCC [34]	Supervised	51.2	75.9	1,802	20.9	37.0	25,937	247,822
Proposed	Self-Supervised	48.1	76.7	2,328	17.7	39.8	17,480	272,602

test sequence. For the evaluation, we use the standard CLEAR MOTA metric [70]. We reported Tracking Accuracy (MOTA), Precision (MOTP), number of identity switches (IDs), mostly tracked trajectories ratio (MT) and mostly lost trajectories (ML).

Implementation Details. Our implementation is based on the Tensorflow Deep Learning Framework. We use a convolutional AutoEncoder in order to extract features by optimizing the Eq. (8). Thus no pre-training or any other ground truth is required. Furthermore, our pre-processing step is only limited to extracting the provided detections from all sequences and resizing them to the corresponding size of the AutoEncoder input layer. Thus the detections from the MOT17 dataset are directly fed to the AutoEncoder. For each sequence from the dataset (MOT17-01 to MOT17-14 with the detector SDP, FRCNN and DPM), one individual model is trained with the same setup and training parameters. However, it is important to note that the number of detections for each individual person varies significantly: while some pedestrians are staying in the scene for a long time, others are passing by quickly out of the scene. This results different cluster sizes. To balance this, randomized batches of detections are applied during the training, where each batch contains only images from one single frame. This way, one iteration of training contains only detections from unique persons. The initial learning rate is set to $\alpha = 0.001$ and decays exponentially by a factor of 10 over time. The balancing parameter between reconstruction and clustering loss is set to $\lambda = 0$ at the beginning in order to first learn the visual features of the video sequences. After five epochs, the cluster information is included in the training, e.g. λ is set to 0.95 to encode the appearance variations from the spatio-temporal clusters into the latent space of the AutoEncoder.

From Clusters to Tracklets. To transform detection clusters into actual tracks, we follow the procedure proposed in [3], i.e. from all detections within one cluster, we select the one with the best detection score pre frame. Clusters containing less than 5 detections are completely removed and gaps in the resulting tracklets are filled using bilinear interpolation.

4.1   Ablation Study

We investigated feature setups in the minimum cost multicut framework. The cut probability between pairs of nodes are computed using a logistic regression function. Adding new features directly affects the edge cost between pairs thus resulting in different clustering performances. Here, we investigate the extent to which our proposed appearance model improves the tracking performance.

Comparison of Different Setups. Table 2 shows the evaluated setups and the resulting tracking performance scores. The column *Features* lists the added features to the logistic regression model. The temporal distances over which bounding boxes are connected in the graph are marked in the column *Distances*. The tracking accuracy of experiment 1 and 6, which uses IoU_{DM} only, is 47.2%. Experiment $2 + 3$ and $7 + 8$ compare the different AutoEncoder models: the Euclidean distance (d_{AE}) from the AutoEncoder latent space is computed in order to estimate the similarity of each pair detections. Here, d_{AE} denotes the latent space distance before adding the clustering loss while d_{AE+C} denotes the distance after training of the AutoEncoder with the clustering loss, i.e. our proposed appearance method.

Best Performance with Proposed Method. The benefit from using the clustering loss on the model training is obvious: for both distances (1–3 and 1–5 frames), the performance is significantly higher. For distance 1–3, d_{AE+C} has a tracking accuracy of 37.6 compared to d_{AE} (35.2) and for distance 1–5, the MOTA scores are 35.2 and 35.8 for d_{AE+C} and d_{AE}, respectively. Although the scores are lower than using IoU_{DM}, combining them both together increases the performance further. This is shown in experiment $4 + 5$ and $9 + 10$, where the best score is achieved with in experiment 10 (proposed method). We also observe that the number of identity switches (IDs) is reduced with our setup. Finally, we add lifted long range edges and solve the resulting minimum cost lifted multicut problems on G. Our best performance is achieved using the setup of experiment 11 with a MOTA of 50.2% using all model components.

Table 4. Tracking results on the recent MOT20 dataset. Our proposed method is closed to the current state-of-the-art method given the fact that ours is based on self-supervised learning.

Sequence	Method	**MOTA**	MOTP	IDs	MT	ML	FP	FN
SORT20 [73]	Supervised	**42.7**	78.5	**4,470**	**16.7**	**26.2**	**27,521**	**264,694**
Proposed	Self-Supervised	41.8	**78.6**	5,918	15.9	27.0	28,341	266,672

4.2 Results

Tracking Performance on Test Data. Here, we present and discuss our final tracking results on the MOT17 test dataset. Compared to the performance on the training dataset, the MOTA score of our proposed approach is slightly lower (Training: 50.2% vs. Testing: 48.1%), which is within the observed variance between different sequences, neglecting excessive parameter tuning. The best performance is achieved in conjunction with the SDP-detector while the performance on the noisier DPM detections are weaker (detailed tables are provided in the supplementary material). While supervised approaches can also train their models w.r.t. the overlap of provided detections with the ground truth and thus compensate for poor detector quality, our self-supervised approach depends on reasonable object detections.

Comparison with Other Tracking Approaches. We compare our method with five other reported tracking methods Lif_T [32], MPNTrack [33], eHAF17 [71], AFN17 [72] and jCC [34]. We consider a tracking method as supervised when ground truth data is used (for example label data for learning a regression function) or if any pre-trained model is included in the approach. Table 3 gives an overview of the scores in different metrics that is being evaluated. The best on each category is marked in bold.

When comparing more closely the average MOTA scores we achieve per detector over all sequences, our proposed method reaches 46.9% on the SDP detector while [41] reach 47.1%. For a state-of-the-art detector, our method performs thus competitive with supervised one. Yet, on the noisy DPM detections, our approach is outperformed by 10% (49.0 [41] vs. 34.3 (Ours)), decreasing the total average significantly.

Evaluation on MOT20. We evaluated our approach on the recent MOT20 dataset. The current state-of-the-art method [73] achieves a MOTA score of 42.7% while ours 41.8% (see Table 4).

5   Conclusion

We present a two stage approach towards tracking of multiple persons without the supervision by human annotations. First, we group the data based on their spatial-temporal features to obtain weak clusters (tracklets). Combining the visual features learned from an AutoEncoder with these tracklets, we are able to automatically create robust appearance cues enabling multiple person tracking over a long distance. The result of our proposed method achieves a tracking accuracy of 48.1% and 41.8% on the MOT17 and MOT20 benchmark, respectively.

Acknowledgement. Margret Keuper and Amirhossein Kardoost receive funding from the German Research Foundation (KE 2264/1-1).

References

1. Roshan Zamir, A., Dehghan, A., Shah, M.: GMCP-tracker: global multi-object tracking using generalized minimum clique graphs. In: Fitzgibbon, A., Lazebnik, S., Perona, P., Sato, Y., Schmid, C. (eds.) ECCV 2012. LNCS, vol. 7573, pp. 343–356. Springer, Heidelberg (2012). https://doi.org/10.1007/978-3-642-33709-3_25
2. Henschel, R., Leal-Taixé, L., Cremers, D., Rosenhahn, B.: Improvements to Frank-wolfe optimization for multi-detector multi-object tracking. arXiv preprint arXiv:1705.08314 (2017)
3. Tang, S., Andres, B., Andriluka, M., Schiele, B.: Multi-person tracking by multicut and deep matching. In: Hua, G., Jégou, H. (eds.) ECCV 2016. LNCS, vol. 9914, pp. 100–111. Springer, Cham (2016). https://doi.org/10.1007/978-3-319-48881-3_8
4. Tang, S., Andriluka, M., Andres, B., Schiele, B.: Multiple people tracking by lifted multicut and person reidentification. In: Proceedings of the IEEE Conference on Computer Vision and Pattern Recognition, pp. 3539–3548 (2017)
5. Luo, W., et al.: Multiple object tracking: a literature review. arXiv preprint arXiv:1409.7618 (2014)
6. Milan, A., Leal-Taixé, L., Reid, I., Roth, S., Schindler, K.: MOT16: a benchmark for multi-object tracking. arXiv:1603.00831 [cs] (2016) arXiv: 1603.00831
7. Yoon, Y.C., Boragule, A., Song, Y.M., Yoon, K., Jeon, M.: Online multi-object tracking with historical appearance matching and scene adaptive detection filtering. In: 2018 15th IEEE International Conference on Advanced Video and Signal Based Surveillance (AVSS), pp. 1–6. IEEE (2018)
8. Feng, W., Hu, Z., Wu, W., Yan, J., Ouyang, W.: Multi-object tracking with multiple cues and switcher-aware classification. arXiv preprint arXiv:1901.06129 (2019)
9. Kolesnikov, A., Zhai, X., Beyer, L.: Revisiting self-supervised visual representation learning. In: Proceedings of the IEEE Conference on Computer Vision and Pattern Recognition, pp. 1920–1929 (2019)
10. Pathak, D., Girshick, R., Dollár, P., Darrell, T., Hariharan, B.: Learning features by watching objects move. In: CVPR (2017)
11. Mahendran, A., Thewlis, J., Vedaldi, A.: Cross pixel optical-flow similarity for self-supervised learning. In: Jawahar, C.V., Li, H., Mori, G., Schindler, K. (eds.) ACCV 2018. LNCS, vol. 11365, pp. 99–116. Springer, Cham (2019). https://doi.org/10.1007/978-3-030-20873-8_7

12. Hendrycks, D., Mazeika, M., Kadavath, S., Song, D.: Using self-supervised learning can improve model robustness and uncertainty. In: Advances in Neural Information Processing Systems, pp. 15637–15648 (2019)
13. Ye, Q., et al.: Self-learning scene-specific pedestrian detectors using a progressive latent model, pp. 2057–2066 (2017)
14. Lee, W., Na, J., Kim, G.: Multi-task self-supervised object detection via recycling of bounding box annotations. In: The IEEE Conference on Computer Vision and Pattern Recognition (CVPR) (2019)
15. Vondrick, C.M., Shrivastava, A., Fathi, A., Guadarrama, S., Murphy, K.: Tracking emerges by colorizing videos (2018)
16. Leal-Taixé, L., Canton-Ferrer, C., Schindler, K.: Learning by tracking: siamese CNN for robust target association. In: Proceedings of the IEEE Conference on Computer Vision and Pattern Recognition Workshops, pp. 33–40 (2016)
17. Pirsiavash, H., Ramanan, D., Fowlkes, C.C.: Globally-optimal greedy algorithms for tracking a variable number of objects. In: CVPR (2011)
18. Andriyenko, A., Schindler, K., Roth, S.: Discrete-continuous optimization for multi-target tracking. In: CVPR (2012)
19. Huang, C., Wu, B., Nevatia, R.: Robust object tracking by hierarchical association of detection responses. In: Forsyth, D., Torr, P., Zisserman, A. (eds.) ECCV 2008. LNCS, vol. 5303, pp. 788–801. Springer, Heidelberg (2008). https://doi.org/10.1007/978-3-540-88688-4_58
20. Andriluka, M., Roth, S., Schiele, B.: Monocular 3d pose estimation and tracking by detection. In: CVPR (2010)
21. Fragkiadaki, K., Zhang, W., Zhang, G., Shi, J.: Two-granularity tracking: mediating trajectory and detection graphs for tracking under occlusions. In: Fitzgibbon, A., Lazebnik, S., Perona, P., Sato, Y., Schmid, C. (eds.) ECCV 2012. LNCS, vol. 7576, pp. 552–565. Springer, Heidelberg (2012). https://doi.org/10.1007/978-3-642-33715-4_40
22. Henschel, R., Leal-Taixe, L., Rosenhahn, B.: Efficient multiple people tracking using minimum cost arborescences. In: GCPR (2014)
23. Tang, S., Andriluka, M., Schiele, B.: Detection and tracking of occluded people. IJCV **110**, 58–69 (2014)
24. Henschel, R., Leal-Taixé, L., Cremers, D., Rosenhahn, B.: Improvements to Frank-Wolfe optimization for multi-detector multi-object tracking. CoRR abs/1705.08314 (2017)
25. Shitrit, H.B., Berclaz, J., Fleuret, F., Fua, P.: Tracking multiple people under global appearance constraints. In: ICCV (2011)
26. Wang, X., Türetken, E., Fleuret, F., Fua, P.: Tracking interacting objects optimally using integer programming. In: Fleet, D., Pajdla, T., Schiele, B., Tuytelaars, T. (eds.) ECCV 2014. LNCS, vol. 8689, pp. 17–32. Springer, Cham (2014). https://doi.org/10.1007/978-3-319-10590-1_2
27. Kumar, R., Charpiat, G., Thonnat, M.: Multiple object tracking by efficient graph partitioning. In: Cremers, D., Reid, I., Saito, H., Yang, M.-H. (eds.) ACCV 2014. LNCS, vol. 9006, pp. 445–460. Springer, Cham (2015). https://doi.org/10.1007/978-3-319-16817-3_29
28. Tesfaye, Y.T., Zemene, E., Pelillo, M., Prati, A.: Multi-object tracking using dominant sets. IET Comput. Vis. **10**, 289–297 (2016)
29. Wojek, C., Roth, S., Schindler, K., Schiele, B.: Monocular 3D scene modeling and inference: understanding multi-object traffic scenes. In: Daniilidis, K., Maragos, P., Paragios, N. (eds.) ECCV 2010. LNCS, vol. 6314, pp. 467–481. Springer, Heidelberg (2010). https://doi.org/10.1007/978-3-642-15561-1_34

30. Wojek, C., Walk, S., Roth, S., Schindler, K., Schiele, B.: Monocular visual scene understanding: understanding multi-object traffic scenes. IEEE TPAMI **35**, 882–897 (2013)

31. Chari, V., Lacoste-Julien, S., Laptev, I., Sivic, J.: On pairwise costs for network flow multi-object tracking. 2015 IEEE Conference on Computer Vision and Pattern Recognition (CVPR), pp. 5537–5545 (2015)

32. Hornakova, A., Henschel, R., Rosenhahn, B., Swoboda, P.: Lifted disjoint paths with application in multiple object tracking. arXiv preprint arXiv:2006.14550 (2020)

33. Brasó, G., Leal-Taixé, L.: Learning a neural solver for multiple object tracking. In: Proceedings of the IEEE/CVF Conference on Computer Vision and Pattern Recognition, pp. 6247–6257 (2020)

34. Keuper, M., Tang, S., Andres, B., Brox, T., Schiele, B.: Motion segmentation & multiple object tracking by correlation co-clustering. IEEE Trans. Pattern Anal. Mach. Intell. **42**, 140–153 (2018)

35. Henschel, R., Leal-Taixé, L., Cremers, D., Rosenhahn, B.: Fusion of head and full-body detectors for multi-object tracking. In: Computer Vision and Pattern Recognition Workshops (CVPRW) (2018)

36. Henschel, R., Zou, Y., Rosenhahn, B.: Multiple people tracking using body and joint detections. In: Proceedings of the IEEE Conference on Computer Vision and Pattern Recognition Workshops (2019)

37. Keuper, M., Levinkov, E., Bonneel, N., Lavoué, G., Brox, T., Andres, B.: Efficient decomposition of image and mesh graphs by lifted multicuts. In: Proceedings of the IEEE International Conference on Computer Vision, pp. 1751–1759 (2015)

38. Keuper, M., Tang, S., Zhongjie, Y., Andres, B., Brox, T., Schiele, B.: A multi-cut formulation for joint segmentation and tracking of multiple objects. arXiv preprint arXiv:1607.06317 (2016)

39. Kumar, R., Charpiat, G., Thonnat, M.: Multiple object tracking by efficient graph partitioning. In: Cremers, D., Reid, I., Saito, H., Yang, M.-H. (eds.) ACCV 2014. LNCS, vol. 9006, pp. 445–460. Springer, Cham (2015). https://doi.org/10.1007/978-3-319-16817-3_29

40. Ma, C., et al.: Trajectory factory: tracklet cleaving and re-connection by deep siamese bi-GRU for multiple object tracking. arXiv preprint arXiv:1804.04555 (2018)

41. Bergmann, P., Meinhardt, T., Leal-Taixe, L.: Tracking without bells and whistles. arXiv preprint arXiv:1903.05625 (2019)

42. Kim, C., Li, F., Ciptadi, A., Rehg, J.M.: Multiple hypothesis tracking revisited. In: Proceedings of the IEEE International Conference on Computer Vision, pp. 4696–4704 (2015)

43. Sheng, H., Chen, J., Zhang, Y., Ke, W., Xiong, Z., Yu, J.: Iterative multiple hypothesis tracking with tracklet-level association. IEEE Trans. Circuits Syst. Video Technol. **29**, 3660–3672 (2018)

44. Chen, J., Sheng, H., Zhang, Y., Xiong, Z.: Enhancing detection model for multiple hypothesis tracking. In: Conference on Computer Vision and Pattern Recognition Workshops, pp. 2143–2152 (2017)

45. Li, M., Zhu, X., Gong, S.: Unsupervised person re-identification by deep learning tracklet association. In: Ferrari, V., Hebert, M., Sminchisescu, C., Weiss, Y. (eds.) ECCV 2018. LNCS, vol. 11208, pp. 772–788. Springer, Cham (2018). https://doi.org/10.1007/978-3-030-01225-0_45

46. Lv, J., Chen, W., Li, Q., Yang, C.: Unsupervised cross-dataset person re-identification by transfer learning of spatial-temporal patterns. In: Proceedings of the IEEE Conference on Computer Vision and Pattern Recognition, pp. 7948–7956 (2018)
47. Karthik, S., Prabhu, A., Gandhi, V.: Simple unsupervised multi-object tracking. arXiv preprint arXiv:2006.02609 (2020)
48. Jing, L., Tian, Y.: Self-supervised visual feature learning with deep neural networks: a survey. arXiv preprint arXiv:1902.06162 (2019)
49. Pathak, D., Girshick, R., Dollár, P., Darrell, T., Hariharan, B.: Learning features by watching objects move. In: Proceedings of the IEEE Conference on Computer Vision and Pattern Recognition, pp. 2701–2710 (2017)
50. Doersch, C., Gupta, A., Efros, A.A.: Unsupervised visual representation learning by context prediction. In: Proceedings of the IEEE International Conference on Computer Vision, pp. 1422–1430 (2015)
51. Pathak, D., Krahenbuhl, P., Donahue, J., Darrell, T., Efros, A.A.: Context encoders: Feature learning by inpainting. In: Proceedings of the IEEE Conference on Computer Vision and Pattern Recognition, pp. 2536–2544 (2016)
52. Lee, W., Na, J., Kim, G.: Multi-task self-supervised object detection via recycling of bounding box annotations. In: Proceedings of the IEEE Conference on Computer Vision and Pattern Recognition, pp. 4984–4993 (2019)
53. Ye, Q., et al.: Self-learning scene-specific pedestrian detectors using a progressive latent model. In: Proceedings of the IEEE Conference on Computer Vision and Pattern Recognition, pp. 509–518 (2017)
54. Demaine, E.D., Emanuel, D., Fiat, A., Immorlica, N.: Correlation clustering in general weighted graphs. Theoret. Comput. Sci. **361**, 172–187 (2006)
55. Keuper, M., Levinkov, E., Bonneel, N., Lavoue, G., Brox, T., Andres, B.: Efficient decomposition of image and mesh graphs by lifted multicuts. In: ICCV (2015)
56. Chopra, S., Rao, M.: The partition problem. Math. Program. **59**, 87–115 (1993)
57. Bansal, N., Blum, A., Chawla, S.: Correlation clustering. Mach. Learn. **56**, 89–113 (2004)
58. Horňáková, A., Lange, J.H., Andres, B.: Analysis and optimization of graph decompositions by lifted multicuts. In: ICML (2017)
59. Andres, B., et al.: Globally optimal closed-surface segmentation for connectomics. In: Fitzgibbon, A., Lazebnik, S., Perona, P., Sato, Y., Schmid, C. (eds.) ECCV 2012. LNCS, vol. 7574, pp. 778–791. Springer, Heidelberg (2012). https://doi.org/10.1007/978-3-642-33712-3_56
60. Beier, T., Kroeger, T., Kappes, J., Kothe, U., Hamprecht, F.: Cut, glue, & cut: a fast, approximate solver for multicut partitioning. In: CVPR (2014)
61. Insafutdinov, E., Pishchulin, L., Andres, B., Andriluka, M., Schiele, B.: DeeperCut: a deeper, stronger, and faster multi-person pose estimation model. In: Leibe, B., Matas, J., Sebe, N., Welling, M. (eds.) ECCV 2016. LNCS, vol. 9910, pp. 34–50. Springer, Cham (2016). https://doi.org/10.1007/978-3-319-46466-4_3
62. Kardoost, A., Keuper, M.: Solving minimum cost lifted multicut problems by node agglomeration. In: ACCV 2018, 14th Asian Conference on Computer Vision, Perth, Australia (2018)
63. Revaud, J., Weinzaepfel, P., Harchaoui, Z., Schmid, C.: Deep convolutional matching. CoRR abs/1506.07656 (2015)
64. Yang, B., Fu, X., Sidiropoulos, N.D., Hong, M.: Towards k-means-friendly spaces: simultaneous deep learning and clustering. arXiv preprint arXiv:1610.04794 (2016)

65. Glorot, X., Bengio, Y.: Understanding the difficulty of training deep feedforward neural networks. In: Proceedings of the Thirteenth International Conference on Artificial Intelligence and Statistics, pp. 249–256 (2010)

66. Maaten, L.v.d., Hinton, G.: Visualizing data using t-sne. J. Mach. Learn. Res. **9**, 2579–2605 (2008)

67. Yang, F., Choi, W., Lin, Y.: Exploit all the layers: fast and accurate CNN object detector with scale dependent pooling and cascaded rejection classifiers. In: Proceedings of the IEEE Conference on Computer Vision and Pattern Recognition, pp. 2129–2137 (2016)

68. Felzenszwalb, P.F., Girshick, R.B., McAllester, D., Ramanan, D.: Object detection with discriminatively trained part-based models. IEEE Trans. Pattern Anal. Mach. Intell. **32**, 1627–1645 (2010)

69. Ren, S., He, K., Girshick, R., Sun, J.: Faster R-CNN: towards real-time object detection with region proposal networks. In: Advances in Neural Information Processing Systems, pp. 91–99 (2015)

70. Leal-Taixé, L., Milan, A., Reid, I., Roth, S., Schindler, K.: Motchallenge 2015: towards a benchmark for multi-target tracking. arXiv:1504.01942 (2015)

71. Sheng, H., Zhang, Y., Chen, J., Xiong, Z., Zhang, J.: Heterogeneous association graph fusion for target association in multiple object tracking. IEEE Trans. Circuits Syst. Video Technol. **29**, 3269–3280 (2018)

72. Shen, H., Huang, L., Huang, C., Xu, W.: Tracklet association tracker: an end-to-end learning-based association approach for multi-object tracking. arXiv preprint arXiv:1808.01562 (2018)

73. Bewley, A., Ge, Z., Ott, L., Ramos, F., Upcroft, B.: Simple online and realtime tracking. In: 2016 IEEE International Conference on Image Processing (ICIP), pp. 3464–3468. IEEE (2016)

Learning Local Feature Descriptors
for Multiple Object Tracking

Dmytro Mykheievskyi, Dmytro Borysenko, and Viktor Porokhonskyy[(⊠)]

Samsung R&D Institute Ukraine (SRK),
57 L'va Tolstogo Street, Kyiv 01032, Ukraine
{d.mykheievsk,d.borysenko,v.porokhonsk}@samsung.com

Abstract. The present study aims at learning class-agnostic embedding, which is suitable for Multiple Object Tracking (MOT). We demonstrate that the learning of local feature descriptors could provide a sufficient level of generalization. Proposed embedding function exhibits on-par performance with its dedicated person re-identification counterparts in their target domain and outperforms them in others. Through its utilization, our solutions achieve state-of-the-art performance in a number of MOT benchmarks, which includes CVPR'19 Tracking Challenge.

1 Introduction

Multiple Object Tracking (MOT) problem has been receiving considerable attention from the computer vision community due to its significance to a number of practical tasks, such as scene understanding [1], activity recognition [2], behavior analysis [3], etc. Over the past few years, MOT solutions have gained considerable performance improvement [4–6] partially due to the advance in Object Detection. Namely, detectors rapidly progressed from Ada-Boost-based solutions, such as ACF detector [7], to CNN-based ones [8–12]. While the former are capable of returning bounding boxes with the fixed aspect ratio for a single category, the latter successfully deal with multiple categories and arbitrarily shaped objects. This progress was started by the invention of a two-stage detector [11]. It was further stimulated by the introduction of a single-stage paradigm [10] and consequent competition between the two [8,9,12]. The invention of Feature Pyramid Network (FPN) [13], backbone efficiency improvement [14,15], Regression Cascades [16], Deformable Convolutions [17,18] also resulted in considerable accuracy gains. This progress was one of the main reasons why Detection-Based Tracking (DBT), which is also known as tracking-by-detection, has become the dominating paradigm in MOT domain [19]. It essentially breaks MOT problem into the following sub-tasks: detection, embedding function application to the image area corresponding to each detect, and data association. Making the detection stage independent of the remaining two, DBT facilitates the adoption

Electronic supplementary material The online version of this chapter (https://doi.org/10.1007/978-3-030-69532-3_34) contains supplementary material, which is available to authorized users.

H. Ishikawa et al. (Eds.): ACCV 2020, LNCS 12623, pp. 558–575, 2021.
https://doi.org/10.1007/978-3-030-69532-3_34

of modern detectors. In its turn, any gain in Multiple Object Detection Accuracy (MODA) strongly positively affects the main MOT metrics [19–21], such as Multiple Object Tracking Accuracy (MOTA), via False Positive (FP) and False Negative (FN) counts.

At the same time, contemporary DBT solutions do not live up to the full potential of their detection stage. In particular, most of them keep relying on embeddings learned with single category datasets, thus making the scope of the entire solution restricted to that single category. Moreover, the choice of categories themselves is quite limited as long as the public datasets [5,6,22–24] are concerned. The main two options are pedestrians and vehicles. Even though a few DBT solutions have managed to keep their scope up with the scope of the corresponding detector, so far all of them are associated with costly compromises. For example, SORT [20] became applicable to multiple categories via the sacrifice of appearance information. Relying solely on the intersection-over-union (IoU) between considered detects at the data association stage obviously reduces its accuracy and limits the applicability. Quite an opposite path was taken by Wang et al. [25], who proposed to Jointly learn the Detection and Embedding (JDE) model in a multi-task manner so that the detector and embedding could deal with the same set of categories. However, such simultaneous training requires ID annotation to be available throughout the corresponding dataset. Besides the batch formation procedure for embedding learning, in this case, is expected to be less flexible compared to a devoted one.

All in all, a wide application of contemporary DBT solutions in practice is somewhat impeded by either the necessity of specific dataset creation or their compromised accuracy and applicability. Due to the former factor, the tracking of arbitrary objects (e.g. animals, robots, biological cells, etc.) becomes prohibitively expensive for the vast majority of applications.

Perhaps, the most radical solution to the problem of restricted DBT scope would be the utilization of class-agnostic embedding functions. Among tentative candidates for this role, one could mention Learned Local Features Descriptors (LLFD) [26–29]. While corresponding embedding functions shall obviously be sensitive to object appearance, to the best of our knowledge their utilization for object representation has not been reported. Indeed, there are a few factors that make such endeavor questionable. In the first place, the representation of objects in the case of LLFD could hardly correspond to the conventional one. Namely, the objective of typical DBT embedding function is to produce compact and separable object manifolds, when the loss formulation is adopted from metric learning [30]. The same loss combined with a different sampling approach in the case of LLFD is expected to result in extended and non-separable manifolds. At the same time, one could argue that visually similar samples, even if attributed to different manifolds, would tend to get mapped close to each other in the metric space. Along with the gradual evolution of object appearance observed in typical MOT setting, such property could potentially serve as a trade-off for lost manifold compactness and separability. Next, susceptibility to background variation and/or occlusions is another point of concern. Finally, the discriminative capability of LLFD may suffer from a rather low resolution of its input.

As the nature of listed above concerns calls for an empirical approach, in this study we report our rather successful results of LLFD utilization for Multiple Object Tracking. In addition, we discuss the essential features of object representation, which corresponds to the employed embedding. Finally, the aspects, which turn out to have a positive impact on its efficiency, are indicated.

The paper is organized in the following way: the second section is dedicated to related work. Section 3 is devoted to the preparation of our DBT MOT solution, which takes into account the object representation expected from LLFD. In particular, we consider the necessary adjustments, which ameliorate embedding function performance. Among them are the resolution of input patches, preserving color information, etc. For the sake of reproducibility, the details on the detector and the association stage are provided as well. In the following section, our MOT solution is evaluated and compared with other methods. In Sect. 5, the properties of the proposed embedding function are discussed.

2 Related Work

The two approaches to embedding learning, which are relevant to our study, are the following: person re-identification (Re-ID) and learned local feature descriptors. While being similar in some aspects, they exhibit a conceptual difference regarding the criteria, according to which given two samples are treated as such that belong to the same category or, in other words, could form a positive sample pair during training. In the case of person Re-ID, image patches representing a given category have to depict the same object. The difference in object appearance in these patches remains disregarded during the label assignment. In the case of LLFD, however, the appearance of samples affects label assignment in a more profound manner. Namely, it is required that the patches ascribed to a given category depict the same pattern. At the same time, it could be viewed from different perspectives and/or under various lighting conditions [26,31]. Typically each such pattern represents the vicinity of a particular local keypoint. Due to their nature, the patterns normally do not possess any specific boundary. As a consequence, the patterns extend right to the borders of corresponding patches. This is another important difference from the case of person Re-ID, where the image patches serving as training samples depict objects with well-defined boundaries. And these boundaries rarely extend to the patch borders. Some other aspects of these two approaches are summarized below.

2.1 Embedding Learning: Person Re-ID

Let us consider some person Re-ID aspects, which are relevant to MOT problem. While several approaches are being used in this domain the solutions applied to MOT task usually rely on metric learning. The employed backbone topologies vary from those adopted from classification domain to the specifically designed ones, as e.g. OSNet [32]. ResNet-50 [14] became de facto the standard option in the former case. Out of several representation options, global features turn out to be the most popular in DBT paradigm [19]. Successful solution tend to benefit from attention utilization [30,33,34]. Multi-scale feature learning is another topic of active research, which is approached explicitly by e.g. OSNet [32].

As far as training data are concerned, it is worth mentioning the following factors. There is a number of widely used image and video datasets, see Ref. [30] for an extensive list. Some of them are restricted to cropped patches, while others contain entire scenes. The annotation quality depends on whether a manual or automatic method was employed. The latter may include the application of Object Detectors (OD), trackers, and Re-ID solutions. However, even in the former case, the noise rate remains non-negligible [30]. Occlusions are quite frequent due to the scene and objects nature.

2.2   Embedding Learning: Local Feature Descriptors

Due to this task nature, it is desirable to start with the description of public datasets. Among the most influential options in this area are UBC PhotoTour [31] and HPatches [26]. Despite being introduced in 2007, UBC PhotoTour provides a sufficient amount of data for CNN training. Being a patch-based dataset it contains more than 10^6 grayscale patches extracted from three scenes. The patches represent image areas around local keypoints. The positive samples correspond to the matching keypoints. Recently introduced HPatches [26] addresses several limitations inherent in UBC PhotoTour, such as scarce diversity with respect to data, tasks, and the type of features. In particular, it consists of 116 sequences containing 6 RGB images each. These sequences form two groups: 59 sequences with significant viewpoint change and 57 with illumination change. In addition to the extracted grayscale patches, the dataset includes the set of original images in RGB format as well as the homography matrices representing the transformation between the images belonging to the same sequence.

The necessity to process numerous features per image imposes certain limitations on the network topologies. For this reason, specific lightweight CNN topologies find use in this domain. In recent years fully convolutional 7 layer CNN design of L2-Net [28] has been enjoying broad utilization [27,35–38].

Since the training task is usually formulated as a metric learning problem, a lot of effort is being invested into the following two directions: formulation of more efficient loss function; and rising the proportion of so-called hard training samples. The former activity is mainly related to modifying the triplet loss. The latter deals with the fact that a fair portion of randomly formed triplets tends to satisfy the objective function right away. Balntas *et al.* [29] approach this problem by means of the anchor swap, also known as hard-negative sampling within the triplet. In HardNet [27] the hardest-in batch sampling strategy was proposed. In this case, triplet loss reads

$$L_t = \frac{1}{N} \sum_{i=1}^{N} \max \left\{ \left\| x_i - x_i^+ \right\|_2 + 1 - \min_{j \neq i} \left\| x_i - x_j \right\|_2, 0 \right\}, \tag{1}$$

where $(x_i, x_i^+)_{i=1...N}$ designate descriptors corresponding to a set of N positive pairs. Each pair originates from the same local keypoint. This method gained broad recognition [35,36] due to its straightforward implementation and lack of side-effects. As examples of triplet loss modification, it is worthwhile to mention the following. Zhang *et al.* [39] proposed a regularization term named Global Orthogonal Regularization in order to achieve a more uniform distribution of embedding vectors over the unit hypersphere. The authors of SOS-Net [36] put forward an additional term named Second-Order Similarity aimed at improving cluster compactness in the metric space. In terms of Eq. 1, the net loss function, in this case, assumes the next form

$$L = L_t + \frac{1}{N} \sum_{i=1}^{N} \sqrt{\sum_{j \neq i, j \in c_i}^{N} \left(\|x_i - x_j\|_2 - \|x_i^+ - x_j^+\|_2 \right)^2}, \qquad (2)$$

where

$$c_j = \left\{ x_i \in KNN\left(x_j\right) \vee x_i^+ \in KNN\left(x_j^+\right) \right\} \qquad (3)$$

with $KNN\left(x_i\right)$ being a set of k nearest neighbors in the euclidean space.

3   ODESA-Based Tracker

In order to assess the applicability of LLFD for MOT problem we prepare a DBT solution, which accounts for the peculiarities in corresponding object representation, and test its performance with relevant benchmarks. Regarding these peculiarities, we make the following assumptions. Gradual appearance evolution of objects observed between adjacent frames in a typical MOT environment being combined with local descriptor capability to relate similar patterns is expected to produce object manifolds that evolve in the metric space in a non-abrupt manner. At longer time scales, certain objects may exhibit drastic changes in appearance. Thus corresponding manifolds could likely become quite extended. Periodic motion potentially could produce closed "trajectories" in the metric space. Also, the embedding derived from LLFD is assumed to exhibit better discrimination properties, if color information is preserved. This assumption is based on much lower probability to encounter lighting condition variations in a MOT environment compared to e.g. the case of image retrieval, where LLFD are typically find use. We also assume them to benefit from higher resolution of input patches. To distinguish the embeddings that were modified according to our assumptions from their LLFD origin, we will refer to them, hereafter, as Object DEscriptor that is Smooth Appearance-wise (ODESA).

The rest of this section is devoted to the description of our DBT solution, which in many aspects turns out to be similar to DeepSORT [40]. The subsections devoted to its components are ordered in accordance with DBT processing flow.

3.1   Object Detector

The main objective for detector design was to obtain a competitive solution constructed from the building blocks reported elsewhere [11, 13–16, 18, 41].

Table 1. Ablation analysis of object detector components. R101, X101, Cascade, DCN, GCB, Libra stand for ResNet-101, ResNeXt-101, Cascade R-CNN, Deformable ConvNets v2, Global Context Block, and specific Libra R-CNN components, respectively. mAP (Mod) represents the mean Average Precision value for Moderate KITTI split.

R101 [14]	X101 [15]	Cascade [16]	DCN [18]	GCB [41]	Libra [44]		FP ↓	FN ↓	MODA ↑	mAP(Mod) ↑
✓							**685**	2500	86.77	89.88
	✓						967	2113	87.20	**90.05**
	✓	✓				Car	857	2021	88.04	90.00
	✓	✓	✓	✓			876	1876	88.50	89.92
	✓	✓	✓	✓	✓		774	**1671**	**89.84**	89.87
✓							1162	2723	65.03	82.91
	✓						**787**	3019	65.74	78.40
	✓	✓				Pedestrian	843	2809	67.13	78.83
	✓	✓	✓	✓			934	2658	67.67	**85.69**
	✓	✓	✓	✓	✓		1018	**2447**	**68.81**	85.61

In particular, the component implementations of MMDetection repository [42] were reused. KITTI Tracking Benchmark [4] was considered as the main target.

The two-stage detector based on Faster R-CNN [11] was taken as the starting point. ResNet-101 [14] and ResNeXt-101 [15] pre-trained on ImageNet [43] were opted for the backbone. The following components were utilized as extension options: FPN [13], Regression Cascades [16], the deformable convolution [18], and Global Context Blocks (GCB) [41]. Also, IoU-balanced Sampling, Balanced Feature Pyramid, and Balanced L1 Loss of Libra R-CNN [44] were considered.

For experiments conducted on KITTI dataset [22], separate detectors were prepared for *Car* and *Pedestrian* targets. 7481 training images for the detection task were divided into a *trainset* of 4418 images and a *local validation* set of 3063 images so that the former does not contain any samples from 21 training sequences for the tracking task. 4418 KITTI images were supplemented with a sub-set from BDD [45] dataset, where 4975 suitable images were selected. Each detector was configured to output two categories. These were either *Car* and *Van* or *Pedestrian* and *Cyclist*. Such a configuration helps to get better accuracy.

The models were trained using SGD optimizer with momentum 0.9 and weight decay 10^{-4}. The learning rate was set to linearly increase from 3×10^{-4} to 10^{-2} over the initial 500 warm-up training steps. The resulting rate was used for 15 epochs. Finally, it was set to 10^{-3} for the last 10 epochs. The training was performed with a batch size of 16 on 8 GPUs. As augmentation, we applied multi-scale training and random horizontal flips. During evaluation and inference, the input images were resized to bring the shorter side to 700 pixels with preserved aspect ratio. The results of detector evaluation on 21 KITTI tracking train sequences are presented in Table 1.

3.2 ODESA Embedding

The topology of CNN adopted for ODESA models, which is depicted in Fig. 1, was derived from L2-Net [28]. The modifications are related to adopting multi-channel input and the increase of input patch resolution.

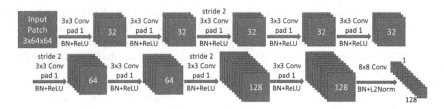

Fig. 1. CNN topology of ODESA(HSV64/128) model. The last seven convolutions correspond to L2-Net. The three layers introduced at the beginning reduce the lateral dimension of feature maps to 32×32, which is the standard size of LLFD input patch.

For training, we utilize exclusively the data from HPatches dataset [26]. In particular, the original set of RGB images and corresponding homography matrices were used as the starting point for patch extraction. By conducting this procedure by ourselves we obtained a set of patches with preserved color information. The original set is accessible in the grayscale format only. And to the best of our knowledge, the corresponding keypoint parameters are not publicly available. As for the patch extraction routine itself, we followed the procedure of Ref. [26]. The random transformations of keypoints with respect to their position, scale, and orientation were reproduced as well. Unless explicitly stated otherwise, they were applied before projecting keypoints into related images in order to simulate the detection noise. As it will be discussed later these transformations significantly affect embedding properties. Single intentional modification of the patch extraction routine concerned with the choice of local keypoint detectors. Namely, as an alternative to the original option, i.e. a combination of Difference of Gaussian, Hessian-Hessian, and Harris-Laplace[1] the following learnable Keypoint Detectors were considered: LF-Net [47] and D2-Net [48]. Hereafter, the former will be referred to as HandCrafted Keypoint Detectors (HCKD).

The loss function of Eq. 2 was used with the default settings from Ref. [36]. SGD optimizer with the momentum value of 0.9 and the weight decay of 10^{-4} was used. The learning rate was configured to decrease linearly from the initial value of 0.1 to zero over 20 epochs. Xavier [49] weight initialization method was employed. The batch size was set to 512. Random horizontal flips were used.

The embedding model for our tracking solution was selected via the validation procedure described in Ref. [25]. Essentially this routine estimates True Positive Rate at a given value of False Acceptance Rate (TPR@FAR) for a retrieval task set on a combination of person Re-ID datasets [24,50,51]. The results of such validation are presented in Table 2. As long as the range of FAR values from 10^{-4} to 10^{-1} is concerned, about every next entry in Table 2 shows a gradual improvement of TPR. In particular, the increase of input patch resolution from 32×32 to 64×64 results in higher performance. The patch sizes beyond 64×64 do not bring any considerable improvement. This observation indicates that the upscaling of training patches from their original size of 65×65 pixels

---

[1] Corresponding VLFeat [46] implementations were employed similarly to Ref. [26].

Table 2. Embedding validation results obtained according to the routine described in Ref. [25] on a set of public person Re-ID datasets. The model name in the first column refers to the color space and the size of square input patch in pixels. A number of person Re-ID and LLFD models were added to serve as a reference.

Model	Keypoint detector	Embedding size	TPR@FAR, % ↑						
			10e−6	10e−5	10e−4	0.001	0.01	0.05	0.1
GRAY32	HCKD	128	7.08	11.30	18.48	31.32	52.47	70.38	78.67
GRAY32	D2-Net [48]	128	7.18	11.46	18.80	31.82	52.60	71.10	79.59
GRAY64	D2-Net [48]	128	**7.79**	**12.35**	19.74	32.75	53.72	72.24	80.38
RGB64	LF-Net [47]	128	5.35	10.91	20.14	35.13	60.29	79.25	86.59
RGB64	D2-Net [48]	128	4.79	10.65	19.45	35.85	61.62	80.21	87.33
HSV32	D2-Net [48]	128	5.06	10.93	20.51	36.78	61.78	80.27	87.30
HSV64	D2-Net [48]	128	4.76	12.01	**21.81**	**37.34**	62.37	80.87	87.87
HSV64	D2-Net [48]	512	4.65	10.59	20.70	36.37	**63.67**	**81.35**	**87.95**
SOSNet [36]	HPatches [26]	128	7.31	10.79	16.38	27.05	47.88	66.92	75.60
OSNet [32]	–	512	3.23	5.98	11.35	22.46	44.76	70.01	81.45
HACNN [33]	–	1024	2.96	11.10	20.21	33.46	54.34	74.43	83.93

could be the limiting factor here. The datasets obtained by means of the learned keypoint detectors [47,48] permit to learn models, which consistently outperform the combination of hand-crafted keypoint detectors. The color information appears to be beneficial for this particular dataset. As will be shown later, the same conclusion holds for MOT datasets as well. We assume that this observation is related to limited changes in lighting conditions in typical person Re-ID or MOT scenes. HSV color space consistently outperforms other checked options, such as LAB, YUV, HLS, etc. Finally, the embedding dimensionality increase beyond 128 brings only moderate performance gains. The extended version of Table 2 is provided in the supplementary material.

3.3   Data Association Stage

The Hungarian algorithm [52] was employed to perform the association between incoming detects and known tracks. The appearance of each detect was reflected by a single embedding vector x_j of dimensionality k. The manifolds $\mathcal{H}_i = \{x_t\}_{t=1}^{D}$ containing up to D_{max} most recent embedding vectors, which were linked to each other in the past, represented the known tracks. Keeping in mind our assumptions about the non-compact nature of ODESA object representation and gradual appearance evolution, in the most general case we calculate the assignment matrix in the following way

$$c_{i,j} = (1 - \lambda) \, min \left\{ \frac{1}{2} \sqrt{\sum_k \left(x_t^k - x_j^k \right)^2} \mid x_t \in \mathcal{H}_i \right\} + \lambda \left(1 - IoU \left(i, j \right) \right). \quad (4)$$

Here each matrix element is represented by the normalized weighted sum of two terms. The first one reflects the distance in the metric space between j-th detect and its closest element of i-th manifold. The second one depends on the IoU value between the same detect and the most recent element from the considered manifold. In other words, such cost formulation promotes association with the closest manifold. Due to the second term, the association with the most recent manifold element may get an additional boost. λ values were kept up to 0.1 in all cases, where IoU was used in combination with the appearance information.

In order to incorporate motion information, we used the Mahalanobis gate. It was based on possible object location predicted by the Kalman filter [53,54] as described in DeepSORT [40]. The association was regarded as permitted, i.e. $b_{i,j} = 1$, on condition that Mahalanobis gating got passed and its final cost turned out to be smaller than the threshold value τ:

$$b_{i,j} = \mathbb{1}\left[c_{i,j} \leq \tau\right]. \tag{5}$$

Comparing our data association stage with those reported elsewhere [19,20,40], one could notice that it does not contain any unique components. The single requirement to it, which follows from the assumed object representation, is related to the criterion of visual similarity estimation. The expectations regarding considerable manifold extent make the minimal distance the simplest and, at the same time, quite a reasonable choice. By applying this or similar criterion, about any DBT solution could be adjusted to the utilization of LLDF or ODESA-like embeddings. On condition that the same ID restoration after object re-appearance is of interest, the utilization of larger D_{max} values makes an obvious sense. In our experiments, we kept $D_{max} \leq 100$, as further increases were not related to any accuracy gains. Such settings are also quite usual in DBT solutions [19,40].

4   Results

The evaluation results for our tracking solution on the testset of KITTI Tracking Benchmark [4] are presented in Table 3 along with the top-performing submissions. In this particular case, the following settings were applied: the Kalman filter was switched off, D_{max} was set to 1, and λ in Eq. 4 was equal to 0.1. HSV64/128 model was employed as the embedding function. It is evident from this table that our trackers achieve state-of-the-art performance in both leaderboards. They outperform other methods according to MODA metric while demonstrating reasonable ID Switch (IDs) counts. In order to make direct comparison between ODESA and a number of embeddings that often find use in MOT domain our DBT solution was adjusted to accept the latter as alternative options. In this case, the influence of the detection and data association stages becomes separated. The results are summarized in Table 4. Here each entry corresponds to the case, where the model listed in the first column was employed in our DBT solution as the embedding function. All person Re-ID models were trained on Market-1501 [58] dataset, which is a common practice for MOT solutions. The remaining models were trained on HPatches [26]. The detects employed for these experiments correspond to the detector entries, which achieve the highest MODA values for a given target in Table 1. Let us consider IDs count, which appears to be more discriminative compared to Fragmentation

Table 3. Top-performing solutions from KITTI Tracking Benchmark leaderboards. (The leaderboard state corresponds to July 7, 2020.) MOTA is the main evaluation criterion.

Target	Method	TP ↑	FP ↓	FN ↓	MODA ↑	IDs ↓	FRAG ↓	MOTA ↑
Car	TuSimple [55]	34'322	705	3'602	87.48	293	501	86.62
	IWNCC	34'146	571	3'819	87.24	130	521	86.86
	EagerMOT	32'858	1'209	3'173	87.26	31	472	87.17
	FG-3DMOT	34'052	611	3'491	88.07	**20**	**117**	88.01
	RE3T	34'991	785	3'005	88.98	31	193	88.89
	CenterTrack	**36'562**	849	2'666	89.78	116	334	89.44
	ODESA (Our)	36'258	451	2'887	**90.29**	90	501	**90.03**
Pedestrian	3D-TLSR	13'767	**942**	9'606	54.44	100	835	54.00
	CenterTrack	15'351	2'196	8'047	55.75	**95**	**751**	55.34
	VV_team	15'640	2'366	7'757	56.27	201	1'131	55.40
	Quasi-Dense [56]	14'925	1'284	8'460	57.91	254	1'121	56.81
	TuSimple [55]	14'936	1'192	8'359	58.74	138	818	58.15
	HWFD	17'296	1'302	6'159	67.77	116	918	67.27
	ODESA (Our)	**17'516**	991	**5'791**	**70.70**	191	1'070	**69.88**

Table 4. Comparison with state-of-the-art person Re-ID embeddings on 21 KITTI tracking training sequences for *Car* and *Pedestrian* targets. The association is restricted solely to visual similarity, i.e. $\lambda = 0$ in Eq. 4.

Method	Car				Pedestrian			
	MODA ↑	IDs ↓	FRAG ↓	MOTA ↑	MODA ↑	IDs ↓	FRAG ↓	MOTA ↑
SOSNet [36]	89.84	47	304	89.65	68.81	98	540	67.93
HardNet++ [27]		43	298	89.66		93	537	67.97
OSNet [32]		65	317	89.57		**78**	**523**	**68.11**
MLFN [57]		57	312	89.61		88	532	68.02
HACNN [33]		50	305	89.63		81	525	68.08
AGW [30]		51	308	89.63		81	522	68.08
ODESA(GRAY64/128)		**31**	**288**	**89.71**		88	530	68.02
ODESA(HSV64/128)		35	292	89.70		84	527	68.05
ODESA(HSV64/512)		40	296	89.69		81	525	68.08

(FRAG). Our most universal target-wise model, which is HSV64/128, with 84 IDs is about 8% behind OSNet [32]. The latter with 78 switches turns out to be the best-performing embedding for *Pedestrian* target. At the same time HACNN [33], which has the lowest IDs count for *Car* target, is outperformed by the same ODESA model by 43%. Also for both targets, our models show consistently lower IDs counts compared to the contemporary LLFD models represented by Hard-Net++ [27] and SOSNet [36]. These results are also consistent with the retrieval experiments summarized in Table 2. ODESA achieves such accuracy level while operating with smaller input patches, shorter embedding vector, and exhibiting faster inference time compared to the person Re-Id models.[2]

For further validation, our ODESA-based tracking solution was adjusted to the conditions of CVPR'2019 Tracking Challenge [59]. The modifications

---

[2] See the processing time comparison in the supplementary material.

Table 5. The results of the top-performing solutions from CVPR19 Tracking Challenge Leaderboard. MOTA serves as the main evaluation criterion.

Method	MOTA ↑	IDF1 ↑	FP ↓	FN ↓	IDs ↓	FRAG ↓
IITB_trk[2]	45.5	43.6	23'931	278'042	3'002	5'478
Aaron[2]	46.5	46.6	40'676	256'671	**2'315**	**2'968**
V_IOU [61]	46.7	46.0	33'776	261'964	2'589	4'354
DD_TAMA19 [62]	47.6	48.7	38'194	252'934	2'437	3'887
TracktorCV [60]	51.3	47.6	**16'263**	253'680	2'584	4'824
ODESA[1] (Our)	**54.9**	**52.7**	24'609	225'292	2'614	4'322
ODESA[2] (Our)	54.8	52.2	33'814	**215'572**	3'750	5'493

accounted for the requirement of relying exclusively on the set of public detects. In particular, we prepared a detector based on ResNet-101 [14], FPN [13], and Regression Cascade [16] using the training protocol described in Sect. 3.1. RPN [11] block was then stripped from the detector. Its output was replaced with either the items from the public set of detects, which correspond to earlier frames, or the detects derived from them in the manner described in Ref. [60]. However, no data association was performed at this point. HSV64/128 was employed as the embedding function. The history depth D_{max} was set to 100. The matching was performed in two stages. At the first one λ in Eq. 4 was set to zero. It accounted for about 97% of the associations. At the second one λ was set to 1 and the Kalman filter was turned off. The results of our two submissions, which differ solely by the rejection routine settings at the detect refinement stage, are presented in Table 5. Both show comparable performance, while the last table entry turned out to be the challenge winner.

The videos representing the output of our tracker for the benchmarks mentioned above have been made available for visual inspection.

5   Discussion

5.1   ODESA Object Representation

Let us check the assumptions which were made at the beginning of Sect. 3 about the object representation expected from ODESA. For this purpose, we utilize ALOI [63] dataset. It contains the images for 1000 objects taken on a rotating stage every 5° against a uniform background. Due to such restricted angle increment, each set of images could be regarded as representing gradual appearance evolution. Uniform background and absent occlusions also help to model a simplified version of MOT environment. A few samples from ALOI dataset are depicted in the top row of Fig. 2. For each object, a set of 72 embedding vectors was extracted by HSV64/128 model. t-SNE projections for corresponding manifolds are shown in Fig. 2(a), where the original ALOI object number to color correspondence is provided as well. Our assumption about the non-compact

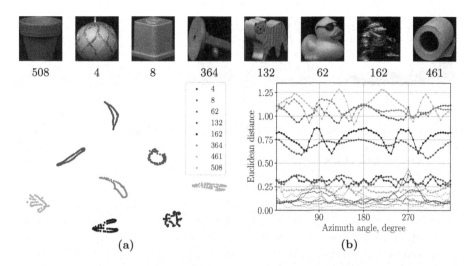

Fig. 2. Object mapping into the metric space for ODESA(HSV64/128) model. (a) t-SNE projection for all embedding vectors corresponding to the objects depicted at the top. (b) (*Solid*) and (*dashed lines*) represent the distances from a given sample embedding vector to its furthest element of the same manifold and its two closest angle-wise neighbors halved, respectively. Best viewed in color. (Color figure online)

nature of ODESA object representation can be readily checked via the estimation of the corresponding manifold extent. Due to ODESA embedding vector normalization, i.e. projection to the unit hypersphere, the maximal extent is limited to the value of two. It can be deduced from the solid lines in Fig. 2(b), which represent the distance from the embedding vector corresponding to a given azimuth angle to its most distant member of the same manifold. These curves indicate that for one of the examined objects the maximal extent exceeds the value of 1.25. At the same time, rather compact manifolds could also be observed, on condition that the appearance of objects does not vary much within considered set of images. This is the case of objects #508, 4, and 8. The distribution of the object manifold extent across the entire ALOI dataset is shown in Fig. 4 for HardNet++ and HSV64/128 models. This figure confirms that for the majority of objects the extent is significant, thus validating our initial assumption. It is also worthwhile to note that while t-SNE projection does not reflect the manifold extent, together with the solid lines in Fig. 2(b) it is indicative of the symmetry exhibited by the objects #8, 132, 162, and 461.

To estimate the manifold continuity, the average distance from each embedding vector to its two closest angle-wise neighbors was calculated. It is shown in Fig. 2(b) by the dashed lines as a function of azimuth angle. We assume that rotation by 5° shall not affect the object appearance significantly. Therefore, any discontinuity is expected to manifest itself as a sharp peak in such a curve. Our data indicate that the distance to neighbors is rather uniformly distributed and scales with the manifold extent. The former conclusion is also supported by

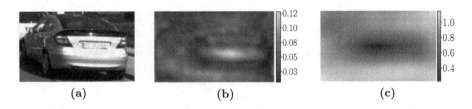

Fig. 3. The influence of occlusions and the bounding box misalignment on embedding vector: (a) image patch, (b) D_o, and (c) D_m as the function of δx and δy. The occluder size s amounts 10% of the patch height h. Best viewed in color. (Color figure online)

the t-SNE projection. These observations are rather supportive of our assumption about the non-abrupt nature of ODESA mapping. The utilization of color information tends to scale down the manifold extent, as shown in Fig. 4, and the distance between the angle-wise neighbors. The evolution of these properties from LLFD to ODESA models is discussed in the supplementary material.

5.2 Sensitivity to Occlusions, Background and Detection Noise

In Sect. 1, we mentioned the factors which cast doubts on LLFD utilization as global object features. A few of them are related to the nature of object bounding boxes. Namely, they usually contain a certain amount of background, could be occluded and could deviate from the ground truth shape and position due to the detection noise. The first two factors do not take place in LLFD domain. The sensitivity of ODESA models to them could be estimated by examining the influence of an occlusion applied in the sliding window manner. As a measure of such influence, one could use the distance between the embedding vector corresponding to the original patch $P(x, y, h, w)$ and those originating from occluded ones. Such distance could be calculated as the function of the occluder position

$$D_o(\delta x, \delta y) = \| f(P(x, y, h, w)) - f(P(x, y, h, w) \odot T_{\delta x, \delta y}(O(x, y, s, s))) \|_2,$$
(6)

where $f(\cdot)$ - embedding function, $\odot$ designate pixel-wise replacement operation, $T_{\delta x, \delta y}$ is a translation operation, $O(x, y, s, s)$ - the square occluding patch of size s filled with noise. An example of such estimation is shown in Fig. 3, where (a) depicts the image area within the ground truth bounding box, (b) contains $D_o(\delta x, \delta y)$. In this case, the occluder size s amounted as much as 10% of the patch height h. Figure 3(b) indicates that the modification of the patch periphery does not result in any considerable displacement of embedding vectors in the metric space. At the same time, the central part of the patch plays a rather significant role. Figure 5 represents our attempt to generalize these conclusions. It shows D_o averaged over 198 and 149 detects from KITTI dataset belonging to pedestrian and car categories, respectively. The detects of the highest resolution with unique IDs were selected for this purpose. To eliminate the aspect ratio, scale, and D_o magnitude differences, at first, relative D_o for individual detects

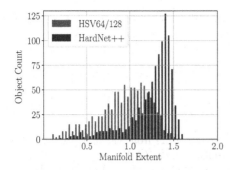
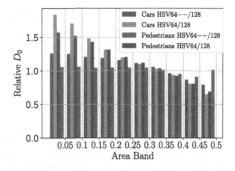

Fig. 4. Distribution of manifold extent across the entire ALOI dataset for HSV64/128 and HardNet++ models.

Fig. 5. Relative $D_o(\delta x, \delta y)$ averaged over a number of detects from KITTI dataset for HSV64/128 and HSV64--/128 models.

was calculated. Then the patch area was split into 10 bands. Each band was limited to the area between adjacent rectangles resulted from the bounding box scaling with a decrement of 5% height- and width-wise. Finally, the relative intensity was averaged over each band across all detects and shown in Fig. 5. This procedure was performed for HSV64/128 and HSV64--/128 models. The latter was learned while the random patch transformations and flips were both turned off. The data from Fig. 5 indicate that these options contribute to making the embedding models considerably less susceptible to the patch periphery.

Finally, the influence of the detection noise could be estimated by examining the embedding vector displacement due to the bounding box misalignment with its ground truth position

$$D_m(\delta x, \delta y) = \| f(P(x, y, h, w)) - f(P(x + \delta x, y + \delta y, h, w)) \|_2. \quad (7)$$

An example of $D_m(\delta x, \delta y)$ produced by means of HSV64/128 model is shown in Fig. 3(c). The corresponding distribution of distances is quite shallow for $(\delta x, \delta y)$ values up to about 20% of the bounding box size. The displacement values tend to grow as the misalignment increases. Such a picture appears to be typical for the majority of examined samples. Figure 3(c) indicates that ODESA models, as well as LLFD ones, could put up with a certain level of the detection noise. In the supplementary material, we indicate that the random patch transformations applied during dataset preparation [26] have a profound effect on $D_m(\delta x, \delta y)$. By controlling their strength, one could either get a model with a better generalization or higher discriminative capability.

6 Conclusions

Our study shows that starting with LLFD it is possible to derive a class-agnostic embedding function, which being deployed as a part of DBT solution is capable of achieving competitive results in MOT domain. It produces meaningful object manifolds with predictable properties. Corresponding object representation turns out to be compatible with the association stages of contemporary DBT solutions. For this reason, ODESA could be readily deployed with about any DBT solution.

References

1. Grant, J.M., Flynn, P.J.: Crowd scene understanding from video: a survey. ACM Trans. Multimedia Comput. Commun. Appl. **13**, 1–23 (2017)
2. Choi, W., Savarese, S.: A unified framework for multi-target tracking and collective activity recognition. In: Fitzgibbon, A., Lazebnik, S., Perona, P., Sato, Y., Schmid, C. (eds.) ECCV 2012. LNCS, vol. 7575, pp. 215–230. Springer, Heidelberg (2012). https://doi.org/10.1007/978-3-642-33765-9_16
3. Hu, W., Tan, T., Wang, L., Maybank, S.: A survey on visual surveillance of object motion and behaviors. IEEE Trans. Syst. Man Cybern. Part C (Appl. Rev.) **34**, 334–352 (2004)
4. Geiger, A., Lenz, P., Urtasun, R.: Are we ready for autonomous driving? The KITTI vision benchmark suite. In: Conference on Computer Vision and Pattern Recognition (CVPR) (2012)
5. Milan, A., Leal-Taixé, L., Reid, I., Roth, S., Schindler, K.: MOT16: a benchmark for multi-object tracking. arXiv preprint arXiv:1603.00831 (2016)
6. Wen, L., et al.: UA-DETRAC: a new benchmark and protocol for multi-object detection and tracking. arXiv preprint arXiv:1511.04136 (2015)
7. Dollár, P., Appel, R., Belongie, S., Perona, P.: Fast feature pyramids for object detection. IEEE Trans. Pattern Anal. Mach. Intell. **36**, 1532–1545 (2014)
8. He, K., Gkioxari, G., Dollár, P., Girshick, R.B.: Mask R-CNN. arXiv preprint arXiv:1703.06870 (2017)
9. Li, Y., Qi, H., Dai, J., Ji, X., Wei, Y.: Fully convolutional instance-aware semantic segmentation. In: The IEEE Conference on Computer Vision and Pattern Recognition (CVPR) (2017)
10. Liu, W., et al.: SSD: single shot multibox detector. arXiv preprint arXiv:1512.02325 (2015)
11. Ren, S., He, K., Girshick, R.B., Sun, J.: Faster R-CNN: towards real-time object detection with region proposal networks. arXiv preprint arXiv:1506.01497 (2015)
12. Tan, M., Pang, R., Le, Q.: EfficientDet: scalable and efficient object detection. arXiv preprint arXiv:1911.09070 (2019)
13. Lin, T., Dollár, P., Girshick, R.B., He, K., Hariharan, B., Belongie, S.J.: Feature pyramid networks for object detection. arXiv preprint arXiv:1612.03144 (2016)
14. He, K., Zhang, X., Ren, S., Sun, J.: Deep residual learning for image recognition. arXiv preprint arXiv:1512.03385 (2015)
15. Xie, S., Girshick, R.B., Dollár, P., Tu, Z., He, K.: Aggregated residual transformations for deep neural networks. arXiv preprint arXiv:1611.05431 (2016)
16. Cai, Z., Vasconcelos, N.: Cascade R-CNN: high quality object detection and instance segmentation. arXiv preprint arXiv:1906.09756 (2019)
17. Dai, J., et al.: Deformable convolutional networks. arXiv preprint arXiv:1703.06211 (2017)
18. Zhu, X., Hu, H., Lin, S., Dai, J.: Deformable ConvNets V2: More deformable, better results. arXiv preprint arXiv:1811.11168 (2018)

19. Luo, W., et al.: Multiple object tracking: A literature review. arXiv preprint arXiv:1409.7618v4 (2017)
20. Bewley, A., Ge, Z., Ott, L., Ramos, F., Upcroft, B.: Simple online and realtime tracking. In: 2016 IEEE International Conference on Image Processing (ICIP), pp. 3464–3468 (2016)
21. Yu, F., Li, W., Li, Q., Liu, Yu., Shi, X., Yan, J.: POI: multiple object tracking with high performance detection and appearance feature. In: Hua, G., Jégou, H. (eds.) ECCV 2016. LNCS, vol. 9914, pp. 36–42. Springer, Cham (2016). https://doi.org/10.1007/978-3-319-48881-3_3
22. Geiger, A., Lenz, P., Stiller, C., Urtasun, R.: Vision meets robotics: the KITTI dataset. Int. J. Robot. Res. (IJRR) **32**, 1231–1237 (2013)
23. Gray, D., Brennan, S., Tao, H.: Evaluating appearance models for recognition, reacquisition, and tracking. In: IEEE International Workshop on Performance Evaluation for Tracking and Surveillance, Rio de Janeiro (2007)
24. Zheng, L., Zhang, H., Sun, S., Chandraker, M., Tian, Q.: Person re-identification in the wild. arXiv preprint arXiv:1604.02531 (2016)
25. Wang, Z., Zheng, L., Liu, Y., Wang, S.: Towards real-time multi-object tracking. arXiv preprint arXiv:1909.12605v1 (2019)
26. Balntas, V., Lenc, K., Vedaldi, A., Mikolajczyk, K.: HPatches: a benchmark and evaluation of handcrafted and learned local descriptors. In: CVPR (2017)
27. Mishchuk, A., Mishkin, D., Radenovic, F., Matas, J.: Working hard to know your neighbor's margins: Local descriptor learning loss. arXiv preprint arXiv:1705.10872 (2017)
28. Tian, Y., Fan, B., Wu, F.: L2-Net: Deep learning of discriminative patch descriptor in Euclidean space. In: The IEEE Conference on Computer Vision and Pattern Recognition (CVPR), pp. 6128–6136 (2017)
29. Balntas, V., Edgar Riba, D.P., Mikolajczyk, K.: Learning local feature descriptors with triplets and shallow convolutional neural networks. In: Richard, C., Wilson, E.R.H., Smith, W.A.P. (eds.) Proceedings of the British Machine Vision Conference (BMVC), pp. 119.1–119.11. BMVA Press (2016)
30. Ye, M., Shen, J., Lin, G., Xiang, T., Shao, L., Hoi, S.C.H.: Deep learning for person re-identification: a survey and outlook. arXiv preprint arXiv:2001.04193 (2020)
31. Winder, S., Brown, M.: Learning local image descriptors. In: CVPR (2007)
32. Zhou, K., Yang, Y., Cavallaro, A., Xiang, T.: Omni-scale feature learning for person re-identification. In: ICCV (2019)
33. Li, W., Zhu, X., Gong, S.: Harmonious attention network for person re-identification. arXiv preprint arXiv:1802.08122 (2018)
34. Song, C., Huang, Y., Ouyang, W., Wang, L.: Mask-guided contrastive attention model for person re-identification. In: The IEEE Conference on Computer Vision and Pattern Recognition (CVPR) (2018)
35. Keller, M., Chen, Z., Maffra, F., Schmuck, P., Chli, M.: Learning deep descriptors with scale-aware triplet networks. In: The IEEE Conference on Computer Vision and Pattern Recognition (CVPR) (2018)
36. Tian, Y., Yu, X., Fan, B., Wu, F., Heijnen, H., Balntas, V.: SOSNet: second order similarity regularization for local descriptor learning. In: CVPR (2019)
37. Zhang, L., Rusinkiewicz, S.: Learning local descriptors with a CDF-based dynamic soft margin. In: International Conference on Computer Vision (ICCV) (2019)
38. Zhang, X.Y., Zhang, L., Zheng, Z.Y., Liu, Y., Bian, J.W., Cheng, M.M.: AdaSample: adaptive sampling of hard positives for descriptor learning. arXiv preprint arXiv:1911.12110 (2019)

39. Zhang, X., Yu, F.X., Kumar, S., Chang, S.F.: Learning spread-out local feature descriptors. arXiv preprint arXiv:1708.06320 (2017)
40. Wojke, N., Bewley, A., Paulus, D.: Simple online and realtime tracking with a deep association metric. In: 2017 IEEE International Conference on Image Processing (ICIP), pp. 3645–3649. IEEE (2017)
41. Cao, Y., Xu, J., Lin, S., Wei, F., Hu, H.: GCNet: non-local networks meet squeeze-excitation networks and beyond. arXiv preprint arXiv:1904.11492 (2019)
42. Chen, K., et al.: MMDetection: Open MMLab detection toolbox and benchmark. arXiv preprint arXiv:1906.07155 (2019)
43. Russakovsky, O., et al.: ImageNet large scale visual recognition challenge. arXiv preprint arXiv:1409.0575 (2014)
44. Pang, J., Chen, K., Shi, J., Feng, H., Ouyang, W., Lin, D.: Libra R-CNN: towards balanced learning for object detection. arXiv preprint arXiv:1904.02701 (2019)
45. Yu, F., et al.: BDD100K: a diverse driving video database with scalable annotation tooling. arXiv preprint arXiv:1805.04687 (2018)
46. Vedaldi, A., Fulkerson, B.: VLFeat: an open and portable library of computer vision algorithms (2008)
47. Ono, Y., Trulls, E., Fua, P., Yi, K.M.: LF-Net: learning local features from images. arXiv preprint arXiv:1805.09662 (2018)
48. Dusmanu, M., et al.: D2-Net: a trainable CNN for joint detection and description of local features. arXiv preprint arXiv:1905.03561 (2019)
49. Glorot, X., Bengio, Y.: Understanding the difficulty of training deep feedforward neural networks. In: Teh, Y.W., Titterington, D.M. (eds.) AISTATS. Volume 9 of JMLR Proceedings, pp. 249–256. JMLR.org (2010)
50. Dollár, P., Wojek, C., Schiele, B., Perona, P.: Pedestrian detection: a benchmark. In: The IEEE Conference on Computer Vision and Pattern Recognition (CVPR) (2009)
51. Xiao, T., Li, S., Wang, B., Lin, L., Wang, X.: Joint detection and identification feature learning for person search. In: The IEEE Conference on Computer Vision and Pattern Recognition (CVPR) (2017)
52. Kuhn, H.W.: The Hungarian method for the assignment problem. Naval Res. Logist. Q. 2, 83–97 (1955)
53. Kalman, R.: A new approach to linear filtering and prediction problems. J. Basic Eng. 82, 35–45 (1960)
54. Welch, G., Bishop, G.: An Introduction to the Kalman filter. University of North Carolina at Chapel Hill, Chapel Hill (1995)
55. Choi, W.: Near-online multi-target tracking with aggregated local flow descriptor. In: Proceedings of the IEEE International Conference on Computer Vision, pp. 3029–3037 (2015)
56. Pang, J., Qiu, L., Chen, H., Li, Q., Darrell, T., Yu, F.: Quasi-dense instance similarity learning. arXiv:2006.06664 (2020)
57. Chang, X., Hospedales, T.M., Xiang, T.: Multi-level factorisation net for person re-identification. arXiv preprint arXiv:1803.09132 (2018)
58. Zheng, L., Shen, L., Tian, L., Wang, S., Wang, J., Tian, Q.: Scalable person re-identification: a benchmark. In: IEEE International Conference on Computer Vision (2015)
59. Dendorfer, P., et al.: CVPR19 tracking and detection challenge: how crowded can it get? arXiv preprint arXiv:1906.04567 (2019)
60. Bergmann, P., Meinhardt, T., Leal-Taixé, L.: Tracking without bells and whistles. arXiv preprint arXiv:1903.05625 (2019)

61. Bochinski, E., Eiselein, V., Sikora, T.: High-speed tracking-by-detection without using image information. In: International Workshop on Traffic and Street Surveillance for Safety and Security at IEEE AVSS 2017, Lecce, Italy (2017)

62. Yoon, Y., Kim, D.Y., Yoon, K., Song, Y., Jeon, M.: Online multiple pedestrian tracking using deep temporal appearance matching association. arXiv preprint arXiv:1907.00831 (2019)

63. Geusebroek, J.M., Burghouts, G.J., Smeulders, A.W.M.: ALOI: Amsterdam library of object images. Int. J. Comput. Vis. **61**(1), 103–112 (2005)

VAN: Versatile Affinity Network for End-to-End Online Multi-object Tracking

Hyemin Lee(iD), Inhan Kim(iD), and Daijin Kim$^{(\boxtimes)}$(iD)

Department of Computer Science and Engineering, POSTECH, Pohang, Korea
{lhmin,kiminhan,dkim}@postech.ac.kr

Abstract. In recent years, tracking-by-detection has become the most popular multi-object tracking (MOT) method, and deep convolutional neural networks (CNNs)-based appearance features have been successfully applied to enhance the performance of candidate association. Several MOT methods adopt single-object tracking (SOT) and handcrafted rules to deal with incomplete detection, resulting in numerous false positives (FPs) and false negatives (FNs). However, a separately trained SOT network is not directly adaptable because domains can differ, and handcrafted rules contain a considerable number of hyperparameters, thus making it difficult to optimize the MOT method. To address this issue, we propose a versatile affinity network (VAN) that can perform the entire MOT process in a single network including target specific SOT to handle incomplete detection issues, affinity computation between target and candidates, and decision of tracking termination. We train the VAN in an end-to-end manner by using event-aware learning that is designed to reduce the potential error caused by FNs, FPs, and identity switching. The proposed VAN significantly reduces the number of hyperparameters and handcrafted rules required for the MOT framework and successfully improves the MOT performance. We implement the VAN using two baselines with different candidate refinement methods to demonstrate the effects of the proposed VAN. We also conduct extensive experiments including ablation studies on three public benchmark datasets: 2D MOT2015, MOT2016, and MOT2017. The results indicate that the proposed method successfully improves the object tracking performance compared with that of baseline methods, and outperforms recent state-of-the-art MOT methods in terms of several tracking metrics including MOT accuracy (MOTA), identity F1 score (IDF1), percentage of mostly tracked targets (MT), and FP.

Keywords: Multi-object tracking · Multiple-target tracking · Visual object tracking · Target association · Similarity learning

1 Introduction

Multi-object tracking (MOT) is a core problem in computer vision and appears in various fields, such as video surveillance, human–computer interaction, and

© Springer Nature Switzerland AG 2021
H. Ishikawa et al. (Eds.): ACCV 2020, LNCS 12623, pp. 576–593, 2021.
https://doi.org/10.1007/978-3-030-69532-3_35

autonomous driving. In recent years, tracking-by-detection has become the most popular MOT method. This method associates external detection results with targets to construct object trajectories [1–6]. The main operation in tracking-by-detection is the computation of affinity scores between targets and detection candidates. Many researchers have attempted to utilize various types of information to compute the affinity, such as appearance features, motion features, and location features. Deep convolutional neural networks (CNNs) have been successfully applied to MOT methods to significantly improve the extraction of useful features for candidate associations to mitigate the identity-switching problem. CNNs for MOT are designed to identify targets in place of handcrafted similarity measures for computing the similarity between targets and candidates [7–10]. However, despite the benefits of CNNs, MOT methods still suffer from incomplete detection, leading to numerous false positives (FPs) and false negatives (FNs) that can even make it impossible to associate targets with candidates. One potential solution to this problem is to include supplementary candidates for incomplete detection. Several MOT methods generate additional candidates to complement missing candidates by predicting potential locations using motion models and independent single-object tracking (SOT) [10–14].

However, utilizing SOT for MOT prediction involves two problems. First, the integration of SOT is not straightforward because scores generated from SOT are not compatible with the affinity values between targets and candidates. Therefore, the integration of SOT requires additional handcrafted rules and hyperparameters that are difficult to be optimized. Additionally, a separately trained SOT does not guarantee optimal MOT accuracy because SOT is primarily designed to discriminate between targets and their surrounding backgrounds, leading to drift issues relative to other targets. Second, the additional candidate may cause another FPs if it is not carefully generated. SOT can worsen this FP problem if the target is initialized with the FP candidate and is not terminated immediately. In this case, SOT continuously tracks the FP, thereby increasing the FP until the tracking is terminated with a certain rule; this phenomenon is called ghost tracking.

To address these issues, we propose a versatile affinity network (VAN) that can perform the entire MOT process in a single network including target-specific SOT to handle incomplete detection, affinity computation between target candidates, and decision of tracking termination. This process is performed by making the SOT prediction scores compatible with the affinity values between targets and candidates. We trained the VAN in an end-to-end manner by using event-aware learning that is designed to reduce the potential error caused by FNs, FPs, and tracking termination. The proposed VAN significantly reduced the effort required to tune hyperparameters and did not require handcrafted rules for integrating the SOT and decision of tracking termination. The overall process of proposed method is illustrated in Fig. 1.

We performed extensive experiments to validate the effectiveness of the proposed method by using three public benchmark datasets: 2D MOT2015, MOT2016, and MOT2017 [15]. The proposed method outperformed existing

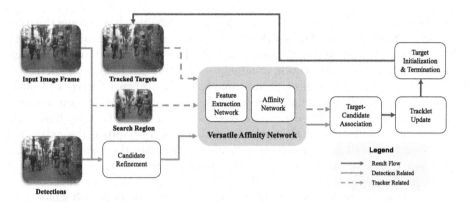

Fig. 1. Overview of a tracking method based on the proposed VAN.

state-of-the-art online MOT methods in terms of various metrics including MOT accuracy (MOTA), identity F1 score (IDF1), percentage of mostly tracked targets (MT), and FNs. Additionally, we performed experiments to conduct ablation studies on a validation set by comparing a baseline method to variants of the proposed method to clarify how the proposed VAN improves tracking performance.

The main contributions of this study are as follows.

- We propose a novel VAN that is designed to perform the entire MOT process including SOT, affinity computation used to associate candidates, and decision of tracking termination.
- We train the VAN in an end-to-end manner by using event-aware learning that is designed to reduce the potential error caused by FNs, FPs, and tracking termination.
- We perform extensive experiments to demonstrate and verify that the proposed method improves the tracking performance.

2   Related Work

In recent years, the tracking-by-detection framework has become the most common MOT method. This framework solves an MOT problem as a detection association problem [1–6]. The core principle of tracking-by-detection is the association method and features used to compute the affinity between targets. Early MOT methods focused on the association method and used various optimization algorithms to solve the association problem.

Offline trackers can utilize all frame information to determine a trajectory [16–18]. Therefore, they can use a global optimization method such as network flow [19–22], the Hungarian method [23,24], and multiple hypothesis tracking [25,26]. Offline trackers typically provide higher performance compared to online trackers. However, their application is limited because they cannot run in real-time. In contrast, online trackers can only utilize current and past frames. As an association is computed in every frame, linear assignment is frequently used to associate targets [7,13,27,28]. Compared with offline trackers, online trackers tend to focus more on the features used to compute the affinity between targets.

In the recent studies on MOT, various features have been proposed to associate targets with candidates. These features can be categorized into three types, i.e., appearance, motion, and location. Affinity is defined using different combinations of these three features. [29] uses the location of candidates combined with neighbor, while other methods, such as [4,9], combine appearance features with motion features.

The MOT methods developed in recent years have achieved success by utilizing deep CNNs, and they are designed to replace the conventional handcrafted affinity function to calculate the similarity between detection candidates. Certain methods [8,10,12] use deep features to associate candidates and long short-term memory (LSTM) [29,30] to enhance discrimination features by utilizing temporal information. Recurrent neural networks (RNNs) are adopted to associate targets with candidates [9]. Owing to the use of large-scale datasets to re-identify the targets, CNN features can discriminate targets in various environments, such as occlusion, scale change, and reappearance. Recently, the authors of [31] adopt the classification and regression networks from an object detector and propose the regression-based tracking method that only utilizes object candidates as region proposals.

Even though deep CNNs successfully associate targets with candidates, the MOT problem remains difficult to solve owing to incomplete detections, which cause false alarms and false negatives. Even if an association is perfect, a missing target cannot be associated with any candidate if there are no suitable candidates. To address this problem, some MOT methods, such as [10–13,18], adopt SOT to overcome missing detection using SOT prediction as a complementary candidate. [11] uses a correlation-filter-based tracker [32] to achieve high speeds and utilizes SOT scores in a candidate decision process. CNN feature-based single object trackers, such as [33], are directly used in [10]. [12,13] regard all detections as SOT candidates and develop an SOT module inside a framework. These approaches use a single object tracker to generate additional candidates, particularly for finding lost targets. However, SOT and MOT are not fully integrated; thus, the affinity network and single object trackers are generally trained independently.

Even though single object trackers can reduce false negatives, directly extending an SOT algorithm to an MOT problem is not straightforward because the former is mainly designed to discriminate a target from its surrounding background. In addition, as mentioned in Sect. 1, an SOT algorithm that exhibits high performance in an SOT task does not ensure high performance in an MOT task. Our method uses a VAN to compute the entire affinity scores for both SOT and MOT association task. This network naturally integrates SOT into an MOT association task by sharing target affinity, and as a result, the association becomes intuitive and tracking performance is improved.

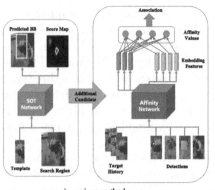 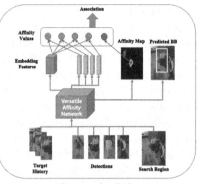

a) previous method   b) proposed method

Fig. 2. Differences between methods using SOT: a) method with independent SOT and affinity networks, and b) proposed method with a versatile affinity network.

3   Proposed Method

3.1   Overview

In every frame, the proposed MOT method takes an image frame, detections, and target trajectories as inputs. First, detection candidates are refined to filter FP candidates by using two-class classifiers. The remaining candidates, previously tracked targets, and corresponding search regions are then passed through the VAN. In the feature extraction network, detection candidates and tracked targets with corresponding search regions are processed and CNN features are obtained. The extracted features can be reused in all tracking processes.

In an affinity network, target features, including initial appearance features and temporal features, are correlated with search regions and detection candidates to compute affinity scores. Based on the affinity score matrix, targets and candidates including SOT results are associated using an optimization algorithm, new target is initialized, and the target that disappears is terminated. Figure 1 shows the overall process of the proposed method.

3.2   Candidate Refinement

False positive candidates are a critical problem in MOT because they generate continuous false trajectories when they are initialized as new targets, making association extremely difficult. These false positive candidates can be filtered by applying an additional classifier, as discussed in [31,34]. The authors of [34] adopted the feature extraction portion of a region-based fully convolutional network (R-FCN) detector [35] with SqueezeNet [36] as a backbone network. Their classifier uses entire image frames for feature extraction and the detection candidates in a single frame share a feature map. The feature maps corresponding to each detection candidate are classified into two classes: background and object.

The authors of [31] utilized the classification network of Faster R-CNN [37] with ResNet-101 [38] as a backbone network. Because the candidate refinement process can be viewed as part of the detection problem, we separate the performance gains from this process and implement our method using two algorithms as baseline trackers. Our method follows the same candidate refinement method and models used in [31,34] to determine the pure contributions of our proposed VAN. Two baseline methods discussed above are denoted as RFCN and FRCNN respectively.

In our proposed method, the set of detection candidates in a t-th frame is denoted as $D_t = \{d_t\}$, where each detection is denoted as $d_t = \{d_t^x, d_t^y, d_t^w, d_t^h\}$. The features of an input image frame I_t are extracted using the backbone network. The classification scores corresponding to each candidate are calculated by applying ROI pooling with a softmax function in the final layer to filter candidates with scores lower than a threshold. Finally, non-maximum suppression (NMS) is applied based on the classification scores and remaining candidates are fed into the next step.

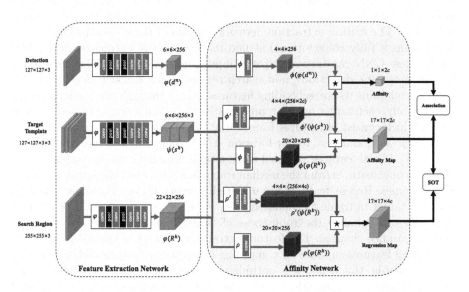

Fig. 3. VAN architecture. The feature extraction network shares layers and the template branch consists of different association layers for reflecting temporal features and anchors. The outputs of SOT branch are an affinity map and regression value map, whereas the output of the association branch is a single affinity value.

3.3   Versatile Affinity Network

In this subsection, we describe the proposed tracking framework based on the VAN and the overall network architecture. Tracking methods using SOT, such as those in [11–13,18], typically derive predictions from previous frames utilizing SOT. SOT results are then considered as candidates and affinity calculation is performed by a different network (Fig. 2a). In this type of framework, the affinity computed by the SOT network cannot be directly used in the association step. Even if the calculated affinity is used, an additional cost function must be employed to make the scores obtained from SOT compatible with the affinity network. In the proposed method, all candidates share affinity values, regardless of whether they are detection candidates or candidates from SOT prediction. SOT prediction results can be directly adopted in the association and target management step. Therefore, additional hyperparameter tuning and heuristic rules are not required (see Fig. 2b).

The basic structure of the VAN follows that of the Siamese CNN proposed in [39]. In our versatile network, SOT uses classification and regression branches, whereas the affinity task only utilizes a classification branch. At t-th frame, the network takes an image frame I_t, a set pf previously tracked target trajectories from the previous frame $S^{(t-1)}$, and a set of detection candidates D_t as inputs. The image patches extracted from the target and detection candidate locations are resized to 127×127 pixels, and the search region for SOT is resized to 255×255 pixels. The feature extraction network consists of three convolutional layers and retains a fully convolutional structure. The feature extraction network of the Siamese CNN can take any size of input and shares all weights for inputs, including targets, detections, and search regions. Each tracked target s_t^k inside set $S^{(t)}$ maintains its corresponding features, $\varphi(s_t)$, through the tracking phase. Additionally, each target has its representative temporally concatenated features $\psi(s_t)$, which consist of features from initial target location $\varphi(s_1)$, intermediate location $\varphi(s_m)$, and very recent location $\varphi(s_t)$ where the intermediate location $m = [\frac{t+1}{2}]$. Initial features are fixed when a target is initialized, and intermediate features come features from the median frame index between the initial and most recent frames. Recent features are updated at every frame. Therefore, the k-th tracking target in frame t is denoted as $s_t = \{s_t^x, s_t^y, s_t^w, s_t^h, \varphi(s_t), \psi(s_t)\}$. This structure can enhance the robustness of target features, to handle occlusion and appearance changes. The feature extraction network is trained to generate embedding features suitable for comparing target features to candidate features. In other words, this network is optimized for computing correct affinity scores between targets and candidates. The size of the search region is twice that of each target's bounding box and the search region is denoted as R. To predict new locations using SOT from frames $t-1$ to t, the features of the search regions corresponding to each tracked target are extracted. Simultaneously, the features of detection candidates are also extracted. In summary, in the feature extraction phase, we extract feature set $\varphi(s^k)$, $\varphi(R^k)$ and $\varphi(d^n)$, where k and n are the indexes of the targets and detection candidates, respectively.

The representative features of a target and corresponding features from the search region pass through the affinity network to generate an affinity map and regression results, which are used to predict the next location of each target. The features from a target s_k and its corresponding search region R_k are fed through the affinity layer and regression layer. We denote the output of the affinity layer as $\phi(\cdot)$ for the detection and search regions, and $\phi'(\cdot)$ for the temporally concatenated target template. The correlation operation is denoted as $\star$. The features $\phi'(\psi(s^k))$ and $\phi(\varphi(R^k))$ are used to calculate an affinity map A_k as follows:

$$A_k = \phi'(\psi(s^k)) \star \phi(\varphi(R^k)). \tag{1}$$

Among the affinity values, the best value corresponds to the predicted location for the next frame. This value is used in the association procedure. The regression value corresponding to the best location is applied to the current bounding box and the box is refined. The regression value indicates the normalized distance between the anchors and ground truth in the form of $\{dx, dy, dw, dh\}$. The regression map is calculated as follows:

$$E_k = \rho'(\psi(s^k)) \star \rho(\varphi(R^k)). \tag{2}$$

where the regression layers for the target template and the search region are denoted as $\rho'(\cdot)$ and $\rho(\cdot)$ respectively.

The detection features, $\varphi(d_t)$, pass through the affinity layer with target features and resulting in a $1 \times 1 \times 2c$ vector, where c is the number of anchors. The affinity between a single target s_k and detection d_n is calculated as

$$a_{nk} = \phi'(\psi(s^k)) \star \phi(\varphi(d^n)). \tag{3}$$

Because the purpose of the affinity network is to compare a target bounding box to a detection, we apply the softmax function across the channel to generate normalized affinity values. Among the resulting $1 \times 1 \times c$ affinity values, we only use the maximum value. The VAN computes the affinity values between all potential pairs of targets and detection candidates. In this manner, the network enables a tracker to perform both SOT and MOT associations. The network architecture and pipeline for this process were illustrated in Fig. 3.

3.4   Event-Aware Training

To train the proposed VAN, we utilized large-scale datasets containing ID information corresponding to each target to sample target and candidate pairs. The network is trained using the combination of classification loss and regression loss as proposed in [39]. We extracted target-candidate pairs from the YouTube-BB, ImageNet-VID, 2D MOT2015, and MOT2017 training sets. We randomly selected two frames from video sequences at 0 to 10 frame intervals and extracted positive samples with $IoU > 0.6$ and negative samples with $IoU < 0.4$ to make the network generalization power relative to the ground truth. Among selected two frames, target templates for temporally concatenated features are selected based on the ground truth with random perturbations.

Additionally, to make the network to have ability to discriminate the target with other candidate, we use event-aware training strategy motivated by distractor-aware training proposed in [40]. We designed the event-aware training suitable for MOT task to reduce the potential error caused by FNs, FPs, and tracking termination. To obtain semantically meaningful samples, we generated samples by using simulation trackers. The simulation trackers were pretrained using classical sampling technique. We ran the tracker with detection candidates, and calculated the affinity of whole target-candidate pairs. We decided the targets and candidates pairs included in a given event situation by using ground-truth assignments and extract sample pairs for preventing the situation. The event comprises three categories: false negative, false positive, and tracking termination. First, we extracted the negative pairs from two targets which has different identity (Fig. 4b). To extract the hard negative samples (distractors), we chose the candidate that had highest affinity except the true assignment. The FP could be reduced by degrading the SOT score if the SOT is initialized with FP candidate. We extracted the negative pairs from FP target generated during simulation (Fig. 4d). Also, the termination of track could arise another FP. Then, we explicitly cropped the negative pairs when the tracking was terminated by occlusion or exiting (Fig. 4c). These samples enabled the VAN to decide whether the tracking is terminated or not. Finally, the FN could be reduced by training the network elaborately using plenty of positive pairs within same identities (Fig. 4a).

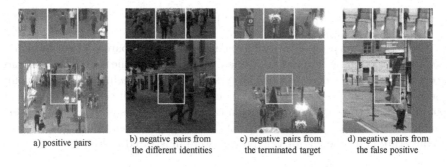

a) positive pairs
b) negative pairs from the different identities
c) negative pairs from the terminated target
d) negative pairs from the false positive

Fig. 4. Example of strategies to extract sample pairs for event-aware training.

3.5 Candidate Association

We associate targets and candidates by using the affinity values calculated in the previous section. We do not calculate affinity values for all possible pairs of targets and candidates because doing so would have been computationally expensive. We limit the possible change in targets (e.g., location and size). We calculate the affinity for pairs that satisfy this limitation and assign infinite negative affinity to other pairs. In this study, we apply different detailed tracking managements for each baseline methods.

For the RFCN baseline, we predict target locations using SOT and add the score to the affinity matrix. To prevent the SOT result being matched with other target, we assign infinite negative affinity to pairs that have different identity. Next, we compute the affinities for all potential target-candidate pairs, assign candidates only to the activated target using the Hungarian algorithm [24]. If the target is not associated with any candidate, and the SOT score is low, we deactivate this target. During this process, the SOT can naturally supplement missing detections without arising ghost tracking. Deactivated targets can associated with the remaining detection results for re-activation when these targets reappear on next frame.

For the FRCNN baseline, all targets are used to predict the next target based on SOT using the VAN. Targets are deactivated if the SOT score is not sufficient or the classification score is low. The affinity values for pairs of only deactivated targets and detection candidates are calculated using the VAN. If there exist additional matching, and the affinity is sufficiently high, a deactivated target is reactivated and is updated using the associated candidate location. The VAN is able to substitute the regression, classification, and reID module of the baseline tracker.

After all associations are completed, the remaining candidates that have no associations with any targets and exhibit low affinity value with all targets are added to the tracker and activated as new targets.

4 Experiments

We conducted several experiments to determine the effectiveness of the proposed VAN on three MOT benchmark datasets: 2D MOT2015, MOT2016, and MOT2017 [15]. The results of other trackers and the proposed method were evaluated using the official MOT challenge benchmark score board[1].

4.1 Implementation Details

The proposed method was implemented using PyTorch and tested on a workstation with a 6-core Intel i7@3.60 GHz CPU and NVIDIA Titan Xp GPU. We used an R-FCN architecture with SqueezeNet as the backbone network for the RFCN baseline and the Faster R-CNN detector with ResNet-101 as a backbone network for the FRCNN baseline. We followed the same tracking management strategy for both baselines, excluding the core tracking steps. The minimum threshold value for filtering candidates was set to 0.4. The VAN was implemented based on the Siamese CNNs [39] and the three convolutional layers of AlexNet [41] is utilized for feature extraction. The VAN was trained using stochastic gradient descent over 90 epochs with a learning rate of ranging from 10^{-2} to 10^{-6}. We generated training pairs from the YouTube-BB, ImageNet-VID, 2D MOT2015, and MOT2017 training sets with sets of two random frames extracted at intervals

---

[1] https://motchallenge.net.

between 0 and 10 frames. The target template images were resized to 127×127 pixels and the search regions were resized to 255×255 pixels. We concatenated the initial features, recent features, and intermediate features of each targets to reflect the temporal attention of targets. In the initial frames, the intermediate and recent features were cloned from the initial features. For both baselines, the classification threshold for target initialization were set to 0.3 and the maximum lost time for termination is set to 30 frames. We limited the possible change of location as 1/10 of the diagonal length of the frame, and the possible size change as 1/3 of the previous target size.

4.2   Evaluation on MOT Benchmarks

The proposed method was evaluated on the 2D MOT2015, MOT2016, and MOT2017 test datasets using on an official website. We adopted the CLEAR MOT metrics [42] to evaluate the performance of the tracker on the MOT datasets and compare it with other state-of-the-art trackers. The representative metric was multiple object tracking accuracy (MOTA), which reflects the false negatives (FN), false positives (FP), and identity switches (IDS). Other metrics are also reported, including identity F1 scores (IDF1), percentage of mostly tracked targets (MT), mostly lost targets (ML). We implement two version of trackers corresponding to the baseline approach which are denoted as VAN(RFCN) and VAN(FRCNN) respectively.

The 2D MOT2015 test dataset consists of 11 video sequences obtained from various scene with ACF detection results. The tracking performance evaluated on 2D MOT2015 test dataset are listed in Table 1. Note that in case of [34], we evaluated the results ourselves because there are no official results on 2D MOT2015 dataset. The MOT2016 test dataset contains 7 videos that are entirely disjoint with the training set with DPM detection results. The results obtained for the MOT2016 test dataset are reported in Table 2. The MOT2017 test dataset contains the same video sequences as the MOT2016 dataset, but different detections are provided. This dataset focuses on evaluating trackers based on various detection results. Three types of detectors are used in this dataset: DPM, SDP, and Faster-RCNN. The results for the MOT2017 test dataset are listed in Table 3. We evaluated the proposed tracker using the same network model and hyperparameters throughout the testing process.

Compared to the baseline methods, the proposed VAN exhibits significant improvements on every benchmark datasets. The proposed method also achieves excellent results in terms of MOTA, ML, and FN compared to existing state-of-the-art MOT methods, even offline methods that can utilize global optimization. In particular, our method significantly reduces the FN by integrating SOT prediction into the association step. The experimental results demonstrate the excellent performance of the proposed VAN.

We simply extended our method for comparisons with an offline method by using trajectory interpolation to complement the missing part of the trajectory by using neighbor frames. This method was denoted as VAN-off; it achieves higher performance than the online version.

Table 1. Tracking Performance on the 2D MOT2015 benchmark test set. Best in bold.

Type	Method	MOTA↑	IDF1↑	MT↑	ML↓	FP↓	FN↓	IDS↓
Offline	JPDA_m [43]	23.8	33.8	5.0	58.1	6373	40084	**365**
	R1TA [44]	24.3	24.1	5.5	46.6	6644	38582	1271
	SCNN [8]	29.0	34.3	8.5	48.4	**5160**	37798	639
	MHT_DAM [26]	32.4	45.3	16.0	43.8	9064	32060	435
	JMC [45]	35.6	45.1	23.2	39.3	10580	28508	457
	VAN-off	**47.4**	**49.5**	**24.0**	**26.8**	6044	**25164**	1087
Online	SCEA [28]	29.1	37.2	8.9	47.3	6060	36912	604
	MDP [13]	30.3	44.7	13.0	38.4	9717	32422	680
	AMIR [29]	37.6	46.0	15.8	26.8	7933	29397	1026
	AP [7]	38.5	47.1	8.7	37.4	**4006**	33203	586
	KCF [11]	38.9	44.5	16.6	31.6	7321	29501	720
	Base (RFCN) [34]	33.1	44.3	9.1	46.2	6806	36226	615
	VAN (RFCN)	34.7	45.9	10.5	47.8	6907	32698	**540**
	Base (FRCNN) [31]	44.1	46.7	18.0	**26.2**	6477	**26577**	1318
	VAN (FRCNN)	**46.0**	**48.3**	**19.3**	28.4	4531	27340	1280

4.3 Ablation Study

We performed additional experiments to conduct ablation studies by using various versions of the proposed tracker to determine which modules affect tracking performance. The experiments for the ablation studies were performed on a subset of the MOT2017 training dataset that was not used in training phase because the corresponding testing dataset did not provide ground truth labels for validation. We implemented five variants of each baseline tracker. The baseline tracker follows the existing MOT method without using SOT. The Base+SOT directly utilizes the SOT [39] and generates additional candidates for missing targets. Even when using SOT results without any fine tuning, the tracking performance of the RFCN baseline was improved. Note that the performance of Base+SOT for FRCNN baseline was degraded because this baseline uses a well-trained regression network for object detection, which has better performance than the raw SOT. Next, we trained the SOT module to improve the discrimination ability for the MOT datasets by training the networks using extra MOT datasets following the training approach of [39] while preserving the baseline association method. This approach is denoted as Base+TSOT in Table 4. This approach exhibits additional performance gains compared to the method directly using SOT. To demonstrate the effect of event-aware training and VAN architecture itself, we trained the proposed VAN without using event-aware learning strategy. Further, tracking termination were performed using existing methods. We denote this version as VAN-EA. This result shows the effectiveness of architecture of VAN itself to perform SOT and affinity computation. Finally, we utilized the proposed method. The VAN reduced the effort required to tune the hyperparameter and could significantly reduce FN and IDS with help of event-aware learning. These ablation studies prove that the proposed VAN and event-aware learning is a promising solution for MOT problems.

Table 2. Tracking Performance on the MOT2016 benchmark test set. Best in bold.

Type	Method	MOTA↑	IDF1↑	MT↑	ML↓	FP↓	FN↓	IDS↓
Offline	MHT_DAM [26]	45.8	46.1	16.2	43.2	6412	91758	590
	NOMT [46]	46.4	53.3	**18.3**	41.4	9753	87565	**359**
	LMP [47]	48.8	51.3	18.2	40.1	6654	86245	481
	eTC [48]	49.2	56.1	17.3	40.3	8400	83702	606
	HCC [49]	49.3	50.7	17.8	39.9	5333	86795	391
	NOTA [50]	49.8	55.3	17.9	37.7	7248	83614	616
	VAN-off	**57.3**	**57.5**	**24.8**	**33.9**	**3845**	**73489**	550
Online	oICF [51]	43.2	49.3	11.3	48.5	6651	96515	**381**
	STAM [12]	46.0	50.0	14.6	43.6	6895	91117	473
	DMAN [10]	46.1	**54.8**	17.4	42.6	7909	89874	532
	AMIR [29]	47.2	46.3	14.0	41.6	2681	92856	774
	KCF [11]	48.8	47.2	15.8	38.1	5875	86567	906
	Base (RFCN) [34]	47.6	50.9	15.2	38.3	9253	85431	792
	VAN (RFCN)	48.9	53.2	15.2	**36.2**	9987	82427	838
	Base (FRCNN) [31]	54.4	52.5	19.0	36.9	3280	**79149**	682
	VAN (FRCNN)	**54.6**	54.2	**19.4**	**36.2**	**2307**	79895	619

Table 3. Tracking Performance on the MOT2017 benchmark test set. Best in bold.

Type	Method	MOTA↑	IDF1↑	MT↑	ML↓	FP↓	FN↓	IDS↓
Offline	IoU17 [52]	45.5	39.4	15.7	40.5	19993	281643	5988
	EDMT [53]	50.0	51.3	21.6	36.3	32279	247297	2264
	TLMHT [54]	50.6	56.5	17.6	43.4	22213	255030	**1407**
	MHT_DAM [26]	50.7	47.2	20.8	36.9	22875	252889	2314
	JCC [55]	51.2	54.5	20.9	37.0	25937	247822	1802
	FWT [56]	51.3	47.6	21.4	35.2	24101	247921	2648
	VAN-off	**57.4**	**57.9**	**26.3**	**33.7**	14316	**224064**	1788
Online	PHD_GSDL [57]	48.0	49.6	17.1	35.6	23199	265954	3988
	AM_ADM [58]	48.1	52.1	13.4	39.7	25061	265495	2214
	DMAN [10]	48.2	**55.7**	19.3	38.3	26218	263608	2194
	HAM_SADF [58]	48.3	51.1	17.1	41.7	20967	269038	**1871**
	FAMNet [14]	52.0	48.7	19.1	33.4	14138	253616	5318
	Base(RFCN) [34]	50.9	52.7	17.5	35.7	24069	250768	2474
	VAN (RFCN)	52.0	53.9	**20.2**	33.4	31275	**237004**	2817
	Base(FRCNN) [31]	53.5	52.3	19.5	36.6	12201	248047	2072
	VAN (FRCNN)	**55.2**	54.2	20.0	35.5	**8522**	241848	2220

Table 4. Ablation study of various tracker versions on the MOT2017 benchmark validation set.

Base	Method	MOTA↑	IDF1↑	MT↑	ML↓	FP↓	FN↓	IDS↓
RFCN	Base	60.0	61.1	25.6	27.1	**1864**	42504	605
	Base+SOT	61.2	53.9	31.1	23.4	4092	38341	1099
	Base+TSOT	62.7	55.9	32.2	23.1	3503	37561	813
	VAN-EA	63.6	63.5	31.1	24.7	3057	37225	**539**
	VAN	**64.2**	**63.7**	**33.5**	**21.2**	3618	**35906**	685
FRCNN	Base	67.7	68.0	40.4	17.4	**803**	35055	368
	Base+SOT	63.6	62.9	42.3	16.7	4844	33414	2676
	Base+TSOT	66.6	66.5	39.0	17.3	1253	35704	520
	VAN-EA	68.6	69.2	43.5	17.2	1320	33578	322
	VAN	**69.1**	**70.7**	**44.3**	**16.6**	1671	**32656**	**305**

5   Conclusions

We proposed a novel MOT method using a VAN to perform the entire MOT process in a single network including SOT, affinity computation, and target management. During the tracking process, the results of target-specific SOT prediction and detection candidates are associated with targets by sharing network weights and compatible affinity values obtained from a unified network. The proposed method exhibited remarkable performance on several MOT benchmarks, making it a promising solution for MOT problems.

Acknowledgement. This work was supported by Institute of Information & communications Technology Planning & Evaluation(IITP) grant funded by the Korea government(MSIT) (No. 2014-0-00059, Development of Predictive Visual Intelligence Technology), (No. 2017-0-00897, Development of Object Detection and Recognition for Intelligent Vehicles) and (No. 2018-0-01290, Development of an Open Dataset and Cognitive Processing Technology for the Recognition of Features Derived From Unstructured Human Motions Used in Self-driving Cars).

References

1. Bae, S.H., Yoon, K.J.: Robust online multi-object tracking based on tracklet confidence and online discriminative appearance learning. In: Proceedings of the IEEE Conference on Computer Vision and Pattern Recognition, pp. 1218–1225 (2014)
2. Berclaz, J., Fleuret, F., Turetken, E., Fua, P.: Multiple object tracking using k-shortest paths optimization. IEEE Trans. Pattern Anal. Mach. Intell. **33**, 1806–1819 (2011)
3. Brendel, W., Amer, M., Todorovic, S.: Multiobject tracking as maximum weight independent set. In: CVPR 2011, IEEE, pp. 1273–1280 (2011)

4. Leal-Taixé, L., Fenzi, M., Kuznetsova, A., Rosenhahn, B., Savarese, S.: Learning an image-based motion context for multiple people tracking. In: Proceedings of the IEEE Conference on Computer Vision and Pattern Recognition, pp. 3542–3549 (2014)
5. Lenz, P., Geiger, A., Urtasun, R.: Followme: Efficient online min-cost flow tracking with bounded memory and computation. In: Proceedings of the IEEE International Conference on Computer Vision, pp. 4364–4372 (2015)
6. Milan, A., Schindler, K., Roth, S.: Multi-target tracking by discrete-continuous energy minimization. IEEE Trans. Pattern Anal. Mach. Intell. **38**, 2054–2068 (2015)
7. Chen, L., Ai, H., Shang, C., Zhuang, Z., Bai, B.: Online multi-object tracking with convolutional neural networks. In: 2017 IEEE International Conference on Image Processing (ICIP), IEEE, pp. 645–649 (2017)
8. Leal-Taixé, L., Canton-Ferrer, C., Schindler, K.: Learning by tracking: Siamese CNN for robust target association. In: Proceedings of the IEEE Conference on Computer Vision and Pattern Recognition Workshops, 33–40 (2016)
9. Milan, A., Rezatofighi, S.H., Dick, A., Reid, I., Schindler, K.: Online multi-target tracking using recurrent neural networks. In: Thirty-First AAAI Conference on Artificial Intelligence (2017)
10. Zhu, J., Yang, H., Liu, N., Kim, M., Zhang, W., Yang, M.H.: Online multi-object tracking with dual matching attention networks. In: Proceedings of the European Conference on Computer Vision (ECCV), pp. 366–382 (2018)
11. Chu, P., Fan, H., Tan, C.C., Ling, H.: Online multi-object tracking with instance-aware tracker and dynamic model refreshment. In: 2019 IEEE Winter Conference on Applications of Computer Vision (WACV), IEEE, pp. 161–170 (2019)
12. Chu, Q., Ouyang, W., Li, H., Wang, X., Liu, B., Yu, N.: Online multi-object tracking using cnn-based single object tracker with spatial-temporal attention mechanism. In: Proceedings of the IEEE International Conference on Computer Vision, pp. 4836–4845 (2017)
13. Xiang, Y., Alahi, A., Savarese, S.: Learning to track: Online multi-object tracking by decision making. In: Proceedings of the IEEE International Conference on Computer Vision, pp. 4705–4713 (2015)
14. Chu, P., Ling, H.: Famnet: Joint learning of feature, affinity and multi-dimensional assignment for online multiple object tracking. In: Proceedings of the IEEE International Conference on Computer Vision, pp. 6172–6181 (2019)
15. Milan, A., Leal-Taixé, L., Reid, I., Roth, S., Schindler, K.: Mot16: a benchmark for multi-object tracking. arXiv preprint arXiv:1603.00831 (2016)
16. Kim, H.-U., Kim, C.-S.: CDT: cooperative detection and tracking for tracing multiple objects in video sequences. In: Leibe, B., Matas, J., Sebe, N., Welling, M. (eds.) ECCV 2016. LNCS, vol. 9910, pp. 851–867. Springer, Cham (2016). https://doi.org/10.1007/978-3-319-46466-4_51
17. Pirsiavash, H., Ramanan, D., Fowlkes, C.C.: Globally-optimal greedy algorithms for tracking a variable number of objects. In: CVPR 2011, IEEE, pp. 1201–1208 (2011)
18. Yan, X., Wu, X., Kakadiaris, I.A., Shah, S.K.: To track or to detect? An ensemble framework for optimal selection. In: Fitzgibbon, A., Lazebnik, S., Perona, P., Sato, Y., Schmid, C. (eds.) ECCV 2012. LNCS, vol. 7576, pp. 594–607. Springer, Heidelberg (2012). https://doi.org/10.1007/978-3-642-33715-4_43

19. Dehghan, A., Modiri Assari, S., Shah, M.: GMMCP tracker: globally optimal generalized maximum multi clique problem for multiple object tracking. In: Proceedings of the IEEE Conference on Computer Vision and Pattern Recognition, pp. 4091–4099 (2015)

20. Leal-Taixé, L., Pons-Moll, G., Rosenhahn, B.: Everybody needs somebody: modeling social and grouping behavior on a linear programming multiple people tracker. In: IEEE International Conference on Computer Vision Workshops (ICCV workshops). IEEE 2011, pp. 120–127 (2011)

21. Roshan Zamir, A., Dehghan, A., Shah, M.: GMCP-Tracker: global multi-object tracking using generalized minimum clique graphs. In: Fitzgibbon, A., Lazebnik, S., Perona, P., Sato, Y., Schmid, C. (eds.) ECCV 2012. LNCS, vol. 7573, pp. 343–356. Springer, Heidelberg (2012). https://doi.org/10.1007/978-3-642-33709-3_25

22. Zhang, L., Li, Y., Nevatia, R.: Global data association for multi-object tracking using network flows. In: 2008 IEEE Conference on Computer Vision and Pattern Recognition, IEEE, pp. 1–8 (2008)

23. Huang, C., Wu, B., Nevatia, R.: Robust object tracking by hierarchical association of detection responses. In: Forsyth, D., Torr, P., Zisserman, A. (eds.) ECCV 2008. LNCS, vol. 5303, pp. 788–801. Springer, Heidelberg (2008). https://doi.org/10.1007/978-3-540-88688-4_58

24. Munkres, J.: Algorithms for the assignment and transportation problems. J. Soc. Ind. Appl. Math. **5**, 32–38 (1957)

25. Chu, P., Pang, Yu., Cheng, E., Zhu, Y., Zheng, Y., Ling, H.: Structure-aware rank-1 tensor approximation for curvilinear structure tracking using learned hierarchical features. In: Ourselin, S., Joskowicz, L., Sabuncu, M.R., Unal, G., Wells, W. (eds.) MICCAI 2016. LNCS, vol. 9900, pp. 413–421. Springer, Cham (2016). https://doi.org/10.1007/978-3-319-46720-7_48

26. Kim, C., Li, F., Ciptadi, A., Rehg, J.M.: Multiple hypothesis tracking revisited. In: Proceedings of the IEEE International Conference on Computer Vision, pp. 4696–4704 (2015)

27. Fagot-Bouquet, L., Audigier, R., Dhome, Y., Lerasle, F.: Online multi-person tracking based on global sparse collaborative representations. In: 2015 IEEE International Conference on Image Processing (ICIP), IEEE, pp. 2414–2418 (2015)

28. Hong Yoon, J., Lee, C.R., Yang, M.H., Yoon, K.J.: Online multi-object tracking via structural constraint event aggregation. In: Proceedings of the IEEE Conference on Computer Vision and Pattern Recognition, pp. 1392–1400 (2016)

29. Sadeghian, A., Alahi, A., Savarese, S.: Tracking the untrackable: Learning to track multiple cues with long-term dependencies. In: Proceedings of the IEEE International Conference on Computer Vision, pp. 300–311 (2017)

30. Kim, C., Li, F., Rehg, J.M.: Multi-object tracking with neural gating using bilinear LSTM. In: Proceedings of the European Conference on Computer Vision (ECCV), pp. 200–215 (2018)

31. Bergmann, P., Meinhardt, T., Leal-Taixe, L.: Tracking without bells and whistles. In: Proceedings of the IEEE International Conference on Computer Vision, pp. 941–951 (2019)

32. Henriques, J.F., Caseiro, R., Martins, P., Batista, J.: High-speed tracking with kernelized correlation filters. IEEE Trans. Pattern Anal. Mach. Intell. **37**, 583–596 (2014)

33. Danelljan, M., Bhat, G., Shahbaz Khan, F., Felsberg, M.: Eco: Efficient convolution operators for tracking. In: Proceedings of the IEEE Conference on Computer Vision and Pattern Recognition, pp. 6638–6646 (2017)

34. Long, C., Haizhou, A., Zijie, Z., Chong, S.: Real-time multiple people tracking with deeply learned candidate selection and person re-identification. In: ICME, vol. 5, p. 8 (2018)

35. Dai, J., Li, Y., He, K., Sun, J.: R-fcn: Object detection via region-based fully convolutional networks. In: Advances in Neural Information Processing Systems, pp. 379–387 (2016)

36. Iandola, F.N., Han, S., Moskewicz, M.W., Ashraf, K., Dally, W.J., Keutzer, K.: Squeezenet: alexnet-level accuracy with 50x fewer parameters and < 0.5 MB model size. arXiv preprint arXiv:1602.07360 (2016)

37. Ren, S., He, K., Girshick, R., Sun, J.: Faster R-CNN: towards real-time object detection with region proposal networks. In: Advances in Neural Information Processing Systems, pp. 91–99 (2015)

38. He, K., Zhang, X., Ren, S., Sun, J.: Deep residual learning for image recognition. In: Proceedings of the IEEE Conference on Computer Vision and Pattern Recognition, pp. 770–778 (2016)

39. Li, B., Yan, J., Wu, W., Zhu, Z., Hu, X.: High performance visual tracking with siamese region proposal network. In: Proceedings of the IEEE Conference on Computer Vision and Pattern Recognition, pp. 8971–8980 (2018)

40. Zhu, Z., Wang, Q., Li, B., Wu, W., Yan, J., Hu, W.: Distractor-aware siamese networks for visual object tracking. In: Proceedings of the European Conference on Computer Vision (ECCV), pp. 101–117 (2018)

41. Krizhevsky, A., Sutskever, I., Hinton, G.E.: Imagenet classification with deep convolutional neural networks. In: Advances in neural information processing systems, pp. 1097–1105 (2012)

42. Bernardin, K., Stiefelhagen, R.: Evaluating multiple object tracking performance: the clear mot metrics. J. Image Video Process. **2008**, 1 (2008)

43. Hamid Rezatofighi, S., Milan, A., Zhang, Z., Shi, Q., Dick, A., Reid, I.: Joint probabilistic data association revisited. In: Proceedings of the IEEE International Conference on Computer Vision, pp. 3047–3055 (2015)

44. Shi, X., Ling, H., Pang, Y., Hu, W., Chu, P., Xing, J.: Rank-1 tensor approximation for high-order association in multi-target tracking. Int. J. Comput. Vision, **127** pp. 1–21 (2019)

45. Keuper, M., Tang, S., Zhongjie, Y., Andres, B., Brox, T., Schiele, B.: A multi-cut formulation for joint segmentation and tracking of multiple objects. arXiv preprint arXiv:1607.06317 (2016)

46. Choi, W.: Near-online multi-target tracking with aggregated local flow descriptor. In: Proceedings of the IEEE International Conference on Computer Vision, pp. 3029–3037 (2015)

47. Tang, S., Andriluka, M., Andres, B., Schiele, B.: Multiple people tracking by lifted multicut and person re-identification. In: Proceedings of the IEEE Conference on Computer Vision and Pattern Recognition, pp. 3539–3548 (2017)

48. Wang, G., Wang, Y., Zhang, H., Gu, R., Hwang, J.N.: Exploit the connectivity: Multi-object tracking with trackletnet. In: Proceedings of the 27th ACM International Conference on Multimedia, pp. 482–490 (2019)

49. Ma, L., Tang, S., Black, M.J., Van Gool, L.: Customized multi-person tracker. In: Jawahar, C.V., Li, H., Mori, G., Schindler, K. (eds.) ACCV 2018. LNCS, vol. 11362, pp. 612–628. Springer, Cham (2019). https://doi.org/10.1007/978-3-030-20890-5_39

50. Chen, L., Ai, H., Chen, R., Zhuang, Z.: Aggregate tracklet appearance features for multi-object tracking. IEEE Signal Process. Lett. **26**, 1613–1617 (2019)

51. Kieritz, H., Becker, S., Hübner, W., Arens, M.: Online multi-person tracking using integral channel features. In: 2016 13th IEEE international conference on advanced video and signal based surveillance (AVSS), IEEE, pp. 122–130 (2016)
52. Bochinski, E., Eiselein, V., Sikora, T.: High-speed tracking-by-detection without using image information. In: 2017 14th IEEE International Conference on Advanced Video and Signal Based Surveillance (AVSS), IEEE, pp. 1–6 (2017)
53. Chen, J., Sheng, H., Zhang, Y., Xiong, Z.: Enhancing detection model for multiple hypothesis tracking. In: Proceedings of the IEEE Conference on Computer Vision and Pattern Recognition Workshops, pp. 18–27 (2017)
54. Sheng, H., Chen, J., Zhang, Y., Ke, W., Xiong, Z., Yu, J.: Iterative multiple hypothesis tracking with tracklet-level association. IEEE Trans. Circuits Syst. Video Technol. 29(2), 3660–3672 (2018)
55. Keuper, M., Tang, S., Andres, B., Brox, T., Schiele, B.: Motion segmentation & multiple object tracking by correlation co-clustering. IEEE Trans. Pattern Anal. Mach. Intell. 42, 142–153 (2018)
56. Henschel, R., Leal-Taixe, L., Cremers, D., Rosenhahn, B.: Fusion of head and full-body detectors for multi-object tracking. In: Proceedings of the IEEE Conference on Computer Vision and Pattern Recognition Workshops, pp. 1428–1437 (2018)
57. Fu, Z., Feng, P., Naqvi, S.M., Chambers, J.A.: Particle phd filter based multi-target tracking using discriminative group-structured dictionary learning. In: 2017 IEEE International Conference on Acoustics, Speech and Signal Processing (ICASSP), IEEE, pp. 4376–4380 (2017)
58. Yoon, Y.c., Boragule, A., Song, Y.m., Yoon, K., Jeon, M.: Online multi-object tracking with historical appearance matching and scene adaptive detection filtering. In, : 15th IEEE International Conference on Advanced Video and Signal Based Surveillance (AVSS). IEEE 2018, pp. 1–6 (2018)

COMET: Context-Aware IoU-Guided Network for Small Object Tracking

Seyed Mojtaba Marvasti-Zadeh[1,2,3]([✉])(iD), Javad Khaghani[1](iD),
Hossein Ghanei-Yakhdan[2](iD), Shohreh Kasaei[3](iD), and Li Cheng[1](iD)

[1] University of Alberta, Edmonton, Canada
{mojtaba.marvasti,khaghani,lcheng5}@ualberta.ca
[2] Yazd University, Yazd, Iran
hghaneiy@yazd.ac.ir
[3] Sharif University of Technology, Tehran, Iran
kasaei@sharif.edu

Abstract. We consider the problem of tracking an unknown small target from aerial videos of medium to high altitudes. This is a challenging problem, which is even more pronounced in unavoidable scenarios of drastic camera motion and high density. To address this problem, we introduce a context-aware IoU-guided tracker (COMET) that exploits a multitask two-stream network and an offline reference proposal generation strategy. The proposed network fully exploits target-related information by multi-scale feature learning and attention modules. The proposed strategy introduces an efficient sampling strategy to generalize the network on the target and its parts without imposing extra computational complexity during online tracking. These strategies contribute considerably in handling significant occlusions and viewpoint changes. Empirically, COMET outperforms the state-of-the-arts in a range of aerial view datasets that focusing on tracking small objects. Specifically, COMET outperforms the celebrated ATOM tracker by an average margin of 6.2% (and 7%) in precision (and success) score on challenging benchmarks of UAVDT, VisDrone-2019, and Small-90.

1 Introduction

Aerial object tracking in real-world scenarios [1–3] aims to accurately localize a model-free target, while robustly estimating a fitted bounding box on the target region. Given the wide variety of applications [4,5], vision-based methods for flying robots demand robust aerial visual trackers [6,7]. Generally speaking, aerial visual tracking can be categorized into videos captured from low-altitudes and medium/high-altitudes. Low-altitude aerial scenarios look at medium or large

---

S. M. Marvasti-Zadeh and J. Khaghani—Equal contribution.

Electronic supplementary material The online version of this chapter (https://doi.org/10.1007/978-3-030-69532-3_36) contains supplementary material, which is available to authorized users.

H. Ishikawa et al. (Eds.): ACCV 2020, LNCS 12623, pp. 594–611, 2021.
https://doi.org/10.1007/978-3-030-69532-3_36

Fig. 1. Examples to compare low-altitudes and medium/high-altitudes aerial tracking. The first row represents the size of most targets in UAV-123 [10] dataset, which captured from 10–30 m. However, some examples of small object tracking scenarios in UAVDT [2], VisDrone-2019 [1], and Small-90 [11] datasets are shown in last two rows. Note that Small-90 has been incorporated small object videos of different datasets such as UAV-123 [10], OTB [12], and TC-128 [13].

objects in surveillance videos with limited viewing angles. However, tracking a target in aerial videos captured from medium- (30–70 m) and high-altitudes (>70 m) has recently introduced extra challenges, including tiny objects, dense cluttered background, weather condition, wide aerial view, severe camera/object motion, drastic camera rotation, and significant viewpoint change [1,2,8,9]. In most cases, it is arduous even for humans to track tiny objects in the presence of complex background as a consequence of limited pixels of objects. Figure 1 compares the two main categories of aerial visual tracking. Most objects in the first category (captured from low-altitude aerial views (10–30 m)) are medium/large-sized and provide sufficient information for appearance modeling. The second one aims to track targets with few pixels involving complicated scenarios.

Recent state-of-the-art trackers cannot provide satisfactory results for small object tracking since strategies to handle its challenges have not been considered. Besides, although various approaches have been proposed for small object detection [14–16], there are limited methods to focus on aerial view tracking. These trackers [17–21] are based on the *discriminative correlation filters* (DCF) that have inherent limitations (e.g., boundary effect problem), and their performances are not competitive with modern trackers. Besides, they cannot consider aspect ratio change despite being a critical characteristic for aerial view tracking. Therefore, the proposed method will narrow the gap between modern visual trackers with aerial ones. Tracking small objects involves major difficulties comprising lacking sufficient target information to distinguish it from background or distractors, much more possibility of locations (i.e., accurate localization requirement), and limited knowledge according to previous efforts. Motivated by the issues and also recent advances in small object detection, this paper proposes a *Context-aware iOu-guided network for sMall objEct Tracking* (COMET). It exploits a multitask two-stream network to process target-relevant information at various scales and focuses on salient areas via attention modules. Given a rough estimation of target location by an online classification network [22], the proposed network simultaneously predicts *intersection-over-union* (IoU) and *normalized center location error* (CLE) between the estimated *bounding boxes* (BBs) and target. Moreover, an effective proposal generation strategy is proposed, which helps the network to learn contextual information. By using this strategy, the proposed network effectively exploits the representations of a target and its parts. It also leads to a better generalization of the proposed network to handle occlusion and viewpoint change for small object tracking from medium- and high-altitude aerial views.

The contributions of the paper are summarized as the following two folds.

1) Offline Proposal Generation Strategy: In offline training, the proposed method generates limited high-quality proposals from the reference frame. The proposed strategy provides context information and helps the network to learn target and its parts. Therefore, it successfully handles large occlusions and viewpoint changes in challenging aerial scenarios. Furthermore, it is just used in offline training to impose no extra computational complexity for online tracking.

2) Multitask Two-Stream Network: COMET utilizes a multitask two-stream network to deal with challenges in small object tracking. First, the network fuses aggregated multi-scale spatial features with semantic ones to provide rich features. Second, it utilizes lightweight spatial and channel attention modules to focus on more relevant information for small object tracking. Third, the network optimizes a proposed multitask loss function to consider both accuracy and robustness.

Extensive experimental analyses are performed to compare the proposed tracker with state-of-the-art methods on the well-known benchmarks, namely, UAVDT [2], VisDrone-2019 [1], Small-90 [11], and UAV-123 [10]. The results demonstrate the effectiveness of COMET for small object tracking purposes.

The rest of the paper is organized as follows. In Sect. 2, an overview of related works is briefly outlined. In Sect. 3 and Sect. 4, our approach and empirical evaluation are presented. Finally, the conclusion is summarized in Sect. 5.

2   Related Work

In this section, focusing on two-stream neural networks, modern visual trackers are briefly described. Also, aerial visual trackers and some small object detection methods are summarized.

2.1   Generic Object Tracking on Surveillance Videos

Two-stream networks (a generalized form of *Siamese neural networks* (SNNs)) for visual tracking were interested in *generic object tracking using regression networks* (GOTURN) [23], which utilizes offline training of a network without any online fine-tuning during tracking. This idea continued by *fully-convolutional Siamese networks* (SiamFC) [24], which defined the visual tracking as a general similarity learning problem to address limited labeled data issues. To exploit both the efficiency of the *correlation filter* (CF) and CNN features, CFNet [25] provides a closed-form solution for end-to-end training of a CF layer. The work of [26] applies triplet loss on exemplar, positive instance, and negative instance to strengthen the feedback of back-propagation and provide powerful features. These methods could not achieve competitive performance compared with well-known DCF methods (e.g., [27,28]) since they are prone to drift problems; However, these methods provide beyond real-time speed.

As the baseline of the well-known Siamese trackers (e.g., [29–33]), the *Siamese region proposal network* (SiamRPN) [34] formulates generic object tracking as local one-shot learning with bounding box refinement. *Distractor-aware Siamese RPNs* (DaSiamRPN) [29] exploits semantic backgrounds, distractor suppression, and local-to-global search region to learn robust features and address occlusion and out-of-view. To design deeper and wider networks, the SiamDW [30] has investigated various units and backbone networks to take full advantage of state-of-the-art network architectures. *Siamese cascaded RPN* (CRPN) [31] consists of multiple RPNs that perform stage-by-stage classification and localization. SiamRPN++ method [33] proposes a ResNet-driven Siamese tracker that not only exploits layer-wise and depth-wise aggregations but also uses a spatial-aware sampling strategy to train a deeper network successfully. SiamMask tracker [32] benefits bounding box refinement and class agnostic binary segmentation to improve the estimated target region.

Although the mentioned trackers provide both desirable performance and computational efficiency, they mostly do not consider background information and suffer from poor generalization due to lacking online training and update strategy. The ATOM tracker [22] performs classification and target estimation tasks with the aid of an online classifier and an offline IoU-predictor, respectively. First, it discriminates a target from its background, and then, an IoU-predictor refines the generated proposals around the estimated location. Similarly and based on a model prediction network, the DiMP tracker [35] learns a robust target model by employing a discriminative loss function and an iterative optimization strategy with a few steps.

Despite considerable achievements on surveillance videos, the performance of modern trackers is dramatically decreased on videos captured from medium- and high-altitude aerial views; The main reason is lacking any strategies to deal with small object tracking challenges. For instance, the limited information of a tiny target, dense distribution of distractors, or significant viewpoint change leads to tracking failures of conventional trackers.

2.2   Detection/Tracking of Small Objects from Aerial View

In this subsection, recent advances for small object detection and also aerial view trackers will be briefly described.

Various approaches have been proposed to overcome shortcomings for small object detection [14]. For instance, *single shot multi-box detector* (SSD) [36] uses low-level features for small object detection and high-level ones for larger objects. *Deconvolutional single shot detector* (DSSD) [37] increases the resolution of feature maps using deconvolution layers to consider context information for small object detection. *Multi-scale deconvolutional single shot detector for small objects* (MDSDD) [38] utilizes several multi-scale deconvolution fusion modules to enhance the performance of small object detection. Also, [39] utilizes multi-scale feature concatenation and attention mechanisms to enhance small object detection using context information. SCRDet method [40] introduces SF-Net and MDA-Net for feature fusion and highlighting object information using attention modules, respectively. Furthermore, other well-known detectors (e.g., YOLO-v3 [41]) exploit the same ideas, such as multi-scale feature pyramid networks, to alleviate their poor accuracy for small objects.

On the other hand, developing specific methods for small object tracking from aerial view is still in progress, and there are limited algorithms for solving existing challenges. Current trackers are based on *discriminative correlation filters* (DCFs), which provide satisfactory computational complexity and intrinsic limitations such as the inability to handle aspect ratio changes of targets. For instance, *aberrance repressed correlation filter* [17] (ARCF) proposes a cropping matrix and regularization terms to restrict the alteration rate of response map. To tackle boundary effects and improve tracking robustness, *boundary effect-aware visual tracker* (BEVT) [18] penalizes the object regarding its location, learns background information, and compares the scores of following response maps. Keyfilter-aware tracker [20] learns context information and avoids filter corruption by generating key-filters and enforcing a temporal restriction. To improve the quality of training set, *time slot-based distillation algorithm* [19] (TSD) adaptively scores historical samples by a cooperative energy minimization function. It also accelerates this process by discarding low-score samples. Finally, the AutoTrack [21] aims to learn a spatio-temporal regularization term automatically. It exploits local-global response variation to focus on trustworthy target parts and determine its learning rate. The results of these trackers are not competitive to the state-of-the-art visual trackers (e.g., Siam-based trackers [32,33], ATOM [22], and DiMP [35]). Therefore, the proposed method aims to narrow the gap between modern visual trackers and aerial view tracking methods, exploring small object detection advances.

3   Our Approach

A key motivation of COMET is to solve the issues discussed in Sect. 1 and Sect. 2 by adapting small object detection schemes into the network architecture for tracking purposes. The graphical abstract of proposed offline training and online tracking is shown in Fig. 2. The proposed framework mainly consists of an offline proposal generation strategy and a two-stream multitask network, which consists of lightweight individual modules for small object tracking. Also, the proposed proposal generation strategy helps the network to learn a generalized target model, handle occlusion, and viewpoint change with the aid of context information. This strategy is just applied to offline training of the network to avoid extra computational burden in online tracking. This section presents an overview of the proposed method and a detailed description of the main contributions.

3.1 Offline Proposal Generation Strategy

The eventual goal of proposal generation strategies is to provide a set of candidate detection regions, which are possible locations of objects. There are various category-dependent strategies for proposal generation [36,42,43]. For instance, the IoU-Net [43] augments the ground-truth instead of using *region proposal networks* (RPNs) to provide better performance and robustness to the network. Also, the ATOM [22] uses a proposal generation strategy similar to [43] with a modulation vector to integrate target-specific information into its network.

Motivated by IoU-Net [43] & ATOM [22], an offline proposal generation strategy is proposed to extract context information of target from the reference frame. The ATOM tracker generates N target proposals from the test frame $(\mathcal{P}_{t+\varsigma})$, given the target location in that frame $(\mathcal{G}_{t+\varsigma})$. Jittered ground-truth locations in offline training produce the target proposals. But, the estimated locations achieved by a simple two-layer classification network will be jittered in online tracking. The test proposals are generated according to $IoU_{Gt+\varsigma} \triangleq IoU(\mathcal{G}_{t+\varsigma}, \mathcal{P}_{t+\varsigma}) \geqslant \mathcal{T}_1$. Then, a network is trained to predict IoU values (IoU_{pred}) between $\mathcal{P}_{t+\varsigma}$ and object, given the BB of the target in the reference frame ($\mathcal{G}_t$). Finally, the designed network in the ATOM minimizes the mean square error of $IoU_{G_{t+\varsigma}}$ and IoU_{pred}.

In this work, the proposed strategy also provides target patches with background supporters from the reference frame (denoted as $\mathcal{P}_t$) to solve the challenging problems of small object tracking. Besides $\mathcal{G}_t$, the proposed method exploits $\mathcal{P}_t$ just in offline training. Using context features and target parts will assist the proposed network (Sect. 3.2) in handling occlusion and viewpoint change

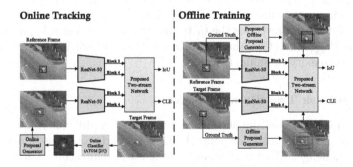

Fig. 2. Overview of proposed method in offline training and online tracking phases.

Algorithm 1 : Offline Proposal Generation

Notations: Bounding box $\mathcal{B}$ ($\mathcal{G}_{t+\varsigma}$ for a test frame or $\mathcal{G}_t$ for a reference frame), IoU threshold $\mathcal{T}$ ($\mathcal{T}_1$ for a test frame or $\mathcal{T}_2$ for a reference frame), Number of proposals $\mathbb{N}$ (N for a test frame or $(N/2) - 1$ for a reference frame), Iteration number (ii), Maximum iteration (max_{ii}), A Gaussian distribution with zero-mean ($\mu = 0$) and randomly selected variance Σ_r ($\mathcal{N}$), Bounding box proposals generated by a Gaussian jittering $\mathcal{P}$ ($\mathcal{P}_{t+\varsigma}$ for a test frame or $\mathcal{P}_t$ for a reference frame)

Input: $\mathcal{B}, \mathcal{T}, \mathbb{N}, \Sigma_r, max_{ii}$
Output: $\mathcal{P}$
for $i = 1 : \mathbb{N}$ **do**
$\quad$ $ii = 0,$
$\quad$ **do**
$\quad\quad$ $\mathcal{P}[i] = \mathcal{B} + \mathcal{N}(\mu, \Sigma_r),$
$\quad\quad$ $ii = ii + 1,$
$\quad$ **while** $(IoU(\mathcal{B}, \mathcal{P}[i]) < \mathcal{T})$ *and* $(ii < max_{ii})$;
end
return $\mathcal{P}$

---

problems for small objects. For simplicity, we will describe the proposed offline proposal generation strategy with the process of IoU-prediction. However, the proposed network predicts both IoU and *center location error* (CLE) of test proposals with target, simultaneously.

An overview of the process of offline proposal generation for IoU-prediction is shown in Algorithm 1. The proposed strategy generates $(N/2) - 1$ target proposals from the reference frame, which are generated as $IoU_{Gt} \triangleq IoU(\mathcal{G}_t, \mathcal{P}_t) \geqslant \mathcal{T}_2$. Note that it considers $\mathcal{T}_2 > \mathcal{T}_1$ to prevent drift toward visual distractors. The proposed tracker exploits this information (especially in challenging scenarios involving occlusion and viewpoint change) to avoid confusion during target tracking. The $\mathcal{P}_t$ and $\mathcal{G}_t$ are passed through the reference branch of the proposed network, simultaneously (Sect. 3.2). In this work, an extended modulation vector has been introduced to provide the representations of the target and its parts into the network. That is a set of modulation vectors that each vector encoded the information of one reference proposal. To compute IoU-prediction, the features of the test patch should be modulated by the features of the target and its parts. It means that the IoU-prediction of N test proposals is computed per each reference proposal. Thus, there will be $N^2/2$ IoU predictions. Instead of computing $N/2$ times of N IoU-predictions, the extended modulation vector allows the computation of $N/2$ groups of N IoU-predictions at once. Therefore, the network predicts $N/2$ groups of IoU-predictions by minimizing the mean square error of each group compared to $IoU_{Gt+\varsigma}$. During online tracking, COMET does not generate $\mathcal{P}_t$ and just uses the $\mathcal{G}_t$ to predict one group of IoU-predictions for generated $\mathcal{P}_{t+\varsigma}$. Therefore, the proposed strategy will not impose extra computational complexity in online tracking.

3.2 Multitask Two-Stream Network

Tracking small objects from aerial view involves extra difficulties such as clarity of target appearance, fast viewpoint change, or drastic rotations besides existing tracking challenges. This part aims to design an architecture that handles the problems of small object tracking by considering recent advances in small object detection. Inspired by [22,39,40,43,44], a two-stream network is proposed (see

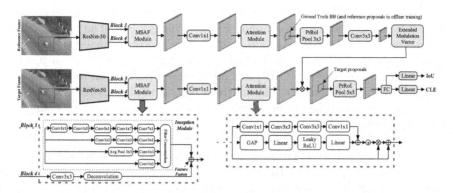

Fig. 3. Overview of proposed two-stream network. MSAF denotes multi-scale aggregation and fusion module, which utilizes the InceptionV3 module in its top branch. For deconvolution block, a 3 × 3 kernel with a stride of 2, input padding of 1, dilation value of 1, and output padding of 1 is used. After each convolution/fully-connected block, batch normalization and leaky ReLU are applied. Extended modulation vector allows COMET to learn targets and their parts in offline training. Also, the fully-connected block, global average pooling block, and linear layer are denoted as the FC, GAP, and linear, respectively.

Fig. 3), which consists of multi-scale processing and aggregation of features, the fusion of hierarchical information, spatial attention module, and channel attention module. Also, the proposed network seeks to maximize the IoU between estimated BBs and the object while it minimizes their location distance. Hence, it exploits a multitask loss function, which is optimized to consider both the accuracy and robustness of the estimated BBs. In the following, the proposed architecture and the role of the main components are described.

The proposed network has adopted ResNet-50 [45] to provide backbone features for reference and test branches. Following small object detection methods, features from block3 and block4 of ResNet-50 are just extracted to exploit both spatial and semantic features while controlling the number of parameters [14,40]. Then, the proposed network employs a *multi-scale aggregation and fusion module* (MSAF). It processes spatial information via the InceptionV3 module [46] to perform factorized asymmetric convolutions on target regions. This low-cost multi-scale processing helps the network to approximate optimal filters that are proper for small object tracking. Also, semantic features are passed through the convolution and deconvolution layers to be refined and resized for feature fusion. The resulted hierarchical information is fused by an element-wise addition of the spatial and semantic feature maps. After feature fusion, the number of channels is reduced by 1 × 1 convolution layers to limit the network parameters. Exploring multi-scale features helps the COMET for small objects that may contain less than 0.01% pixels of a frame.

Next, the proposed network utilizes the *bottleneck attention module* (BAM) [44], which has a lightweight and simple architecture. It emphasizes target-related spatial and channel information and suppresses distractors and redundant information, which are common in aerial images [40]. The BAM includes channel attention, spatial attention, and identity shortcut connection branches. In this work, the SENet [47] is employed as the channel attention branch, which uses *global average pooling* (GAP) and a multi-layer perceptron to find the optimal combination of channels. The spatial attention module utilizes dilated convolutions to increase the receptive field. Lastly, the identity shortcut connection helps for better gradient flow.

After that, the proposed method generates proposals from the test frame. Also, it uses the proposed proposal generation strategy to extract the BBs from the target and its parts from the reference frame in offline training. These generated BBs are applied to the resulted feature maps and fed into a *precise region of interest* (PrRoI) pooling layer [43], which is differentiable w.r.t. BB coordinates. The network uses a convolutional layer with a 3×3 kernel to convert the PrRoI output to target appearance coefficients. Target coefficients are expanded and multiplied with the features of a test patch to merge the information of the target and its parts into the test branch. That is, applying target-specific information into the test branch by the extended modulation vector. Then, the test proposals ($\mathcal{P}_{t+\varsigma}$) are applied to the features of the test branch and fed to a 5×5 PrRoI pooling. Finally, the proposed network simultaneously predicts IoU and CLE of test proposals by optimizing a multitask loss function as $\mathcal{L}_{Net} = \mathcal{L}_{IoU} + \lambda \mathcal{L}_{CLE}$, where the $\mathcal{L}_{IoU}$, $\mathcal{L}_{CLE}$, and λ represent the loss function for IoU-prediction head, loss function for the CLE-prediction head, and balancing hyper-parameter for loss functions, respectively. By denoting i-th IoU- and CLE-prediction values as $IoU^{(i)}$ and $CLE^{(i)}$, the loss functions are defined as

$$\mathcal{L}_{IoU} = \frac{1}{N} \sum_{i=1}^{N} (IoU_{G_{t+\varsigma}}^{(i)} - IoU_{pred}^{(i)})^2, \tag{1}$$

$$\mathcal{L}_{CLE} = \begin{cases} \frac{1}{N} \sum_{i=1}^{N} \frac{1}{2}(CLE_{G_{t+\varsigma}}^{(i)} - CLE_{pred}^{(i)})^2 & |(CLE_{G_{t+\varsigma}}^{(i)} - CLE_{pred}^{(i)}| < 1 \\ \frac{1}{N} \sum_{i=1}^{N} |(CLE_{G_{t+\varsigma}}^{(i)} - CLE_{pred}^{(i)})| - \frac{1}{2} & otherwise \end{cases}, \tag{2}$$

where the $CLE_{G_{t+\varsigma}} = (\Delta x_{G_{t+\varsigma}}/width_{G_{t+\varsigma}}, \Delta y_{G_{t+\varsigma}}/height_{G_{t+\varsigma}})$ is the normalized distance between the center location of $\mathcal{P}_{t+\varsigma}$ and $\mathcal{G}_{t+\varsigma}$. For example, $\Delta x_{G_{t+\varsigma}}$ is calculated as $x_{G_{t+\varsigma}} - x_{P_{t+\varsigma}}$. Also, the CLE_{pred} (and IoU_{pred}) represents the predicted CLE (and the predicted IoU) between BB estimations ($\mathcal{G}_{t+\varsigma}$) and target, given an initial BB in the reference frame. In offline training, the proposed network optimizes the loss function to learn how to predict the target BB from the pattern of proposals generation.

In online tracking, the target BB from the first frame (similar to [22, 32–34]) and also target proposals in the test frame passes through the network. As a result, there is just one group of CLE-prediction as well as IoU-prediction to avoid more computational complexity. In this phase, the aim is to maximize the IoU-prediction of test proposals using the gradient ascent algorithm and also to minimize its CLE-prediction using the gradient descent algorithm. Algorithm 2 describes the process of online tracking in detail. This algorithm shows how the

---

Algorithm 2 : Online Tracking

Notations: Input sequence ($\mathcal{S}$), Sequence length (T), Current frame (t), Rough estimation of bounding box ($\mathcal{B}_t^e$), Generated test proposals ($\mathcal{B}_t^p$), Concatenated bounding boxes ($\mathcal{B}_t^c$), Bounding box prediction ($\mathcal{B}_t^{pred}$), Step size (β), Number of refinements (n), Online classification network ($\text{Net}_{online}^{ATOM}$), Scale and center jittering ($Jitt$) with random factors, Network predictions (IoU and CLE)

Input: $\mathcal{S} = \{I_0, I_1, ..., I_T\}$, $\mathcal{B}_0 = \{x_0, y_0, w_0, h_0\}$

Output: $\mathcal{B}_t^{pred}$, $t \in \{1, ..., T\}$

for $t = 1 : T$ do

    $\mathcal{B}_t^e = \text{Net}_{online}^{ATOM}(I_t)$

    $\mathcal{B}_t^p = Jitt(\mathcal{B}_t^e)$

    $\mathcal{B}_t^c = Concat(\mathcal{B}_t^e, \mathcal{B}_t^p)$

    for $i = 1 : n$ do

        $IoU, CLE = \text{FeedForward}(I_0, I_t, \mathcal{B}_0, \mathcal{B}_t^c)$

        $\mathbf{grad}_{\mathcal{B}_t^c}^{IoU} = [\frac{\partial IoU}{\partial x}, \frac{\partial IoU}{\partial y}, \frac{\partial IoU}{\partial w}, \frac{\partial IoU}{\partial h}]$

        $\mathcal{B}_t^c \leftarrow \mathcal{B}_t^c + \beta \times [\frac{\partial IoU}{\partial x}.w, \frac{\partial IoU}{\partial y}.h, \frac{\partial IoU}{\partial w}.w, \frac{\partial IoU}{\partial h}.h]$

        $\mathbf{grad}_{\mathcal{B}_t^c}^{CLE} = [\frac{\partial CLE}{\partial x}, \frac{\partial CLE}{\partial y}, \frac{\partial CLE}{\partial w}, \frac{\partial CLE}{\partial h}]$

        $\mathcal{B}_t^c \leftarrow \mathcal{B}_t^c - \beta \times [\frac{\partial CLE}{\partial x}.w, \frac{\partial CLE}{\partial y}.h, \frac{\partial CLE}{\partial w}, \frac{\partial CLE}{\partial h}]$

    end

    $\mathcal{B}_t^{K \times 4} \leftarrow$ Select K best $\mathcal{B}_t^c$ w.r.t. IoU-scores

    $\mathcal{B}_t^{pred} = Avg(\mathcal{B}_t^{K \times 4})$

end

return $\mathcal{B}_t^{pred}$

---

inputs are passed through the network, and BB coordinates are updated based on scaled back-propagated gradients. While the IoU-gradients are scaled up with BB sizes to optimize in a log-scaled domain, just x and y coordinates of test BBs are scaled up for CLE-gradients. It experimentally achieved better results compared to the scaling process for IoU-gradients. The intuitive reason is that the network has learned the normalized location differences between BB estimations and target BB. That is, the CLE-prediction is responsible for accurate localization, whereas the IoU-prediction determines the BB aspect ratio. After refining the test proposals ($N = 10$ for online phase) for $n = 5$ times, the proposed method selects the $K = 3$ best BBs and uses the average of these predictions based on IoU-scores as the final target BB.

4   Empirical Evaluation

In this section, first, the proposed method is compared with the baseline ATOM [22] on the test sets of large-scale LaSOT [48] and GOT-10k [49] datasets. Then, as the main aim, the proposed tracker is evaluated on state-of-the-art benchmarks for small object tracking from aerial view: VisDrone-2019-test-dev [1], UAVDT [2], and Small-90 [11]. Although the Small-90 dataset includes the challenging videos of the UAV-123 dataset with small objects, the experimental results on the UAV-123 [10] dataset (low-altitude UAV dataset (10–30 m)) are also presented. However, the UAV-123 dataset lacks varieties in small objects, camera motions, and real scenes [9]. Moreover, traditional tracking datasets do not consist of challenges such as tiny objects, significant viewpoint changes, camera motion, and high density from aerial views. For these reasons and our focus on tracking small objects on videos captured from medium- & high-altitudes, the

Table 1. Ablation analysis of COMET considering different components and feature fusion operations on UAVDT dataset.

Metric	COMET	A1	A2	A3	A4	A5
Precision	88.7	87.2	85.2	83.6	88	85.3
Success	81	78	76.9	73.5	80.4	77.2

proposed tracker (COMET) is evaluated on related benchmarks to demonstrate the motivation and major effectiveness for small object tracking.

The employed datasets include various attributes, namely *background clutter* (BC), *illumination variation* (IV), *scale variation* (SV), *camera motion* (CM), *object motion* (OM), *small object* (SO), *object blur* (OB), *large occlusion* (LO), *long-term tracking* (LT), *aspect ratio change* (ARC), *fast motion* (FM), *partial occlusion* (POC), *full occlusion* (FOC), *low resolution* (LR), *out-of-view* (OV), *similar objects* (SOB), *deformation* (DEF), *motion blur* (MB), *rotation* (ROT), and *viewpoint change* (VC). Experiments have been conducted three times, and the average results are reported. The trackers are compared in terms of precision [12], success (or *success rate* (SR)) [12,49], *normalized area-under-curve* (AUC), and *average overlap* (AO) [49] metrics by standard benchmarks with default thresholds. Also, codes & experimental results are publicly available on github.com/VisualTrackingVLL. In the following, implementation details, ablation analyses, and state-of-the-art comparisons are presented.

4.1 Implementation Details

For offline proposal generation, hyper-parameters are set to $N = 16$ (test proposals number, $(N/2) = 8$ (seven reference proposal numbers plus reference ground-truth)), $\mathcal{T}_1 = 0.1$, $\mathcal{T}_2 = 0.8$, $\lambda = 4$, and image sample pairs randomly selected from videos with a maximum gap of 50 frames ($\zeta = 50$). Flipping and color jittering are used for data augmentation of the reference patch. The values for IoU and CLE are normalized to the range of $[-1, 1]$.

The maximum iteration number max_{ii} for proposal generation is 200 for reference proposals and 20 for test proposals. The weights of the backbone network are frozen, and other weights are initialized using [50]. The training splits are extracted from the official training set (protocol II) of LaSOT [48], training set of GOT-10K [49], NfS [51], and training set of VisDrone-2019 [1] datasets. Moreover, the validation splits of VisDrone-2019 and GOT-10K datasets have been used in the training phase. To train in an end-to-end fashion, the ADAM

Table 2. Overall & attribute-based evaluations on the test sets of LaSOT & GOT-10k.

Tracker	LaSOT (AUC metric)															GOT-10k		
	Overall	*IV*	*POC*	*DEF*	*MB*	*CM*	*ROT*	*BC*	*VC*	*SV*	*FOC*	*FM*	*OV*	*LR*	*ARC*	*AO*	*$SR_{0.5}$*	*$SR_{0.75}$*
COMET	54.2	57.8	50	56.2	53.2	57.5	53.5	48.7	51.1	53.9	46.3	44.2	46.2	46.8	52.2	59.6	70.6	44.9
ATOM	51.8	56.1	48.3	51.4	49.7	56.4	48.9	45.1	47.4	51.5	42.8	43.3	44.2	44.7	50.5	55.6	63.4	40.2

optimizer [52] is used with an initial learning rate of 10^{-4}, weight decay of 10^{-5}, and decay factor 0.2 per 15 epochs. The proposed network trained for 60 epochs with a batch size of 64 and 64000 sampled videos per epoch. Also, the proposed tracker has been implemented using PyTorch, and the evaluations performed on an Nvidia Tesla V100 GPU with 16 GB RAM. Finally, the parameters of the online classification network are set as the ATOM [22].

4.2   Ablation Analysis

A systematic ablation study on individual components of the proposed tracker has been conducted on the UAVDT dataset [9] (see Table 1). It includes three different versions of the proposed network consisting of the networks without 1) "CLE-head", 2) "CLE-head and reference proposals generation", and 3) "CLE-head, reference proposals generation, and attention module", referred to as A1, A2, and A3, respectively. Moreover, two other different feature fusion operations have been investigated, namely features multiplication (A4) and features concatenation (A5), compared to the element-wise addition of feature maps in the MSAF module (see Fig. 3).

   These experiments demonstrate the effectiveness of each component on tracking performance, while the proposed method has achieved 88.7% and 81% in terms of precision and success rates, respectively. According to these results, the attention module, reference proposal generation strategy, and CLE-head have improved the average of success and precision rates up to 2.5%, 1.55%, and 2.25%, respectively. Besides, comparing results of feature fusion operations demonstrate that the element-wise addition has provided the average of precision and success rates up to 0.65% and 3.6% compared to A4 and A5, respectively. Also, the benefit of feature addition previously has been proved in other methods such as [22]. Finally, the proposed tracker is compared with the baseline tracker [22] on the test sets of two large-scale generic object tracking benchmarks, namely LaSOT [48] and GOT-10k [49]. Table 2 demonstrates that the COMET also considerably improves the performance of the ATOM [22] on traditional visual tracking datasets.

4.3   State-of-the-Art Comparison

For quantitative comparison, COMET is compared with state-of-the-art visual trackers including AutoTrack [21], ATOM [22], DiMP-50 [35], PrDiMP-50 [53], Ocean-online [54], SiamRPN++ [33], SiamMask [32], DaSiamRPN [29], SiamDW [30], CREST [55], MDNet [56], PTAV [57], ECO [28], and MCPF [58] on aerial

Table 3. Average speed (FPS) of state-of-the-art trackers on UAVDT dataset.

	COMET	ATOM	SiamRPN++	DiMP-50	SiamMask	ECO	PrDiMP-50
Speed	24	30	32	33	42	35	22

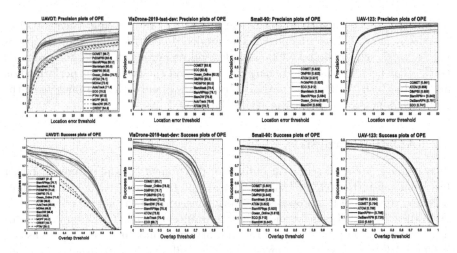

Fig. 4. Overall precision and success comparisons of the proposed method (COMET) with state-of-the-art tracking methods on UAVDT, VisDrone-2019-test-dev, Small-90, and UAV-123 datasets.

Table 4. Attribute-based comparison in terms of accuracy metric on UAVDT dataset [First , second , and third methods are shown in color].

Tracker	BC	CM	OM	SO	IV	OB	SV	LO	LT
COMET	83.8	86.1	90.6	90.9	88.5	87.7	90.2	79.6	96
ATOM	70.1	77.2	73.4	80.6	80.8	74.9	73	66	91.7
SiamRPN++	74.9	75.9	80.4	83.5	89.7	89.4	80.1	66.6	84.9
SiamMask	71.6	76.7	77.8	86.7	86.4	86	77.3	60.1	93.8
DiMP-50	71.1	80.3	75.8	81.4	84.3	79	76.1	68.6	100
PrDiMP-50	74.4	79.7	82.7	84.1	83.8	83.1	84.7	98.6	73.2
Ocean-online	69.7	72.3	76.2	83.2	87.8	85.6	74.5	83.3	62.5

Table 5. Attribute-based comparison in terms of AUC metric on VisDrone-2019-test-dev dataset [First , second , and third methods are shown in color].

Tracker	Overall	ARC	BC	CM	FM	FOC	IV	LR	OV	POC	SOB	SV	VC
COMET	64.5	64.2	43.4	62.6	64.9	56.7	65.5	41.8	75.9	62.1	42.8	65.8	70.4
ATOM	57.1	52.3	36.7	56.4	52.3	48.8	63.3	31.2	63	51.9	35.6	55.4	61.3
SiamRPN++	59.9	58.9	41.2	58.7	61.8	55.1	63.5	36.4	69.3	58.8	39.6	59.9	67.8
DiMP-50	60.8	54.5	40.6	60.6	62	55.8	63.6	32.7	62.4	56.8	39.8	59.7	66
SiamMask	58.1	57.8	38.5	57.2	60.8	49	56.6	46.5	67.5	52.9	37	59.4	65.1
PrDiMP-50	59.8	58.6	41.1	58	57.5	57	64.2	31.8	67.7	61.2	37.4	58.3	66.8
Ocean-online	59.4	61.1	46.3	59.2	55.3	53	56.6	47.7	66.8	53.4	45.8	62.1	65.3

tracking datasets. Figure 4 shows the achieved results in terms of precision and success plots [12]. According to these results, COMET outperforms top-performing visual trackers on three available challenging small object tracking

Fig. 5. Qualitative comparison of proposed COMET tracker with state-of-the-art tracking methods on S1202, S0602, and S0801 video sequences from UAVDT dataset (top to bottom row, respectively).

datasets (i.e., UAVDT, VisDrone-2019-test-dev and Small-90) as well as the UAV-123 dataset. For instance, COMET has outperformed the SiamRPN++ and DiMP-50 trackers by 4.4% and 3.2% in terms of average precision metric, and 3.3% and 3% in terms of average success metric on all datasets, respectively. Besides, it outperforms the PrDiMP and Ocean-online up to 3.3% and 5.4% in average precision metric, and 3.6% and 5.3% in average success metric on the small object tracking datasets. Compared to the baseline ATOM tracker, COMET has improved the average precision rate up to 10.6%, 7.2% and 0.8%, while it increased the average success rate up to 11.2%, 7.1% and 2.9% on the UAVDT, VisDrone-2019-test-dev and Small-90 datasets, respectively. Although COMET slightly outperforms ATOM on the UAV-123 (see Fig. 1), it achieved up to 6.2% and 7% improvements compared to it in terms of average precision and success metrics on small object tracking datasets.

These results are mainly owed to the proposed proposal generation strategy and effective modules, which makes the network focus on relevant target (and its parts) information and context information. Furthermore, COMET runs at 24 *frame-per-second* (FPS), while the average speeds of other trackers on the referred machine are indicated in Table 3. This satisfactory speed has been originated from considering different proposal generation strategies for offline & online procedures and employing lightweight modules in the proposed architecture. The COMET has been evaluated according to various attributes of small object tracking scenarios to investigate its strengths and weaknesses. Table 4 and Table 5 present the attribute-based comparison of visual trackers. These tables demonstrate that the COMET can successfully handle challenging scenarios for small object tracking purposes. For instance, compared to the DiMP-50, SiamRPN++, SiamMask, PrDiMP & Ocean-online, COMET achieves improvements up to 9.5%, 7.4%, 4.5%, 1.8% & 7.7% for small object attribute, and 4.4%, 2.6%, 5.3%, 3.6% & 5.1% for viewpoint change attribute, respectively. While the performance still can be improved based on IV, OB, LR, LO, and LT attributes,

COMET outperforms the ATOM by a margin up to 7.7%, 12.8%, 10.6%, 13.6%, and 4.3% on these attributes, respectively.

The qualitative comparisons of visual trackers are shown in Fig. 5, in which the videos have been selected for more clarity. According to the first row of Fig. 5, COMET successfully models small objects on-the-fly considering complicated aerial view scenarios. Also, it provides promising results when the aspect ratio of target significantly changes. Examples of occurring out-of-view and occlusion are shown in the next rows of Fig. 5. By considering target parts and context information, COMET properly handles these problems existing potential distractors.

5   Conclusion

A context-aware IoU-guided tracker proposed that includes an offline reference proposal generation strategy and a two-stream multitask network. It aims to track small objects in videos captured from medium- and high-altitude aerial views. First, an introduced proposal generation strategy provides context information for the proposed network to learn the target and its parts. This strategy effectively helps the network to handle occlusion and viewpoint change in high-density videos with a broad view angle in which only some parts of the target are visible. Moreover, the proposed network exploits multi-scale feature aggregation and attention modules to learn multi-scale features and prevent visual distractors. Finally, the proposed multitask loss function accurately estimates the target region by maximizing IoU and minimizing CLE between the predicted box and object. Experimental results on four state-of-the-art aerial view tracking datasets and remarkable performance of the proposed tracker demonstrate the motivation and effectiveness of proposed components for small object tracking purposes.

References

1. Du, D., Zhu, P., Wen, L., Bian, X., Ling, H., et al.: VisDrone-SOT2019: the vision meets drone single object tracking challenge results. In: Proceedings of ICCVW (2019)
2. Du, D., et al.: The unmanned aerial vehicle benchmark: object detection and tracking. In: Proceedings of ECCV, pp. 375–391 (2018)
3. Marvasti-Zadeh, S.M., Cheng, L., Ghanei-Yakhdan, H., Kasaei, S.: Deep learning for visual tracking: a comprehensive survey. IEEE Trans. Intell. Trans. Syst. 1–26 (2021). https://doi.org/10.1109/TITS.2020.3046478
4. Bonatti, R., Ho, C., Wang, W., Choudhury, S., Scherer, S.: Towards a robust aerial cinematography platform: localizing and tracking moving targets in unstructured environments. In: Proceedings of IROS, pp. 229–236 (2019)
5. Zhang, H., Wang, G., Lei, Z., Hwang, J.: Eye in the sky: drone-based object tracking and 3D localization. In: Proceedings of Multimedia, pp. 899–907 (2019)
6. Du, D., Zhu, P., et al.: VisDrone-SOT2019: the vision meets drone single object tracking challenge results. In: Proceedings of ICCVW (2019)

7. Zhu, P., Wen, L., Du, D., Bian, X., Hu, Q., Ling, H.: Vision meets drones: past, present and future (2020)
8. Zhu, P., Wen, L., Du, D., et al.: VisDrone-VDT2018: the vision meets drone video detection and tracking challenge results. In: Proceedings of ECCVW, pp. 496–518 (2018)
9. Yu, H., Li, G., Zhang, W., et al.: The unmanned aerial vehicle benchmark: object detection, tracking and baseline. Int. J. Comput. **128**(5), 1141–1159 (2019)
10. Mueller, M., Smith, N., Ghanem, B.: A benchmark and simulator for UAV tracking. In: Leibe, B., Matas, J., Sebe, N., Welling, M. (eds.) ECCV 2016. LNCS, vol. 9905, pp. 445–461. Springer, Cham (2016). https://doi.org/10.1007/978-3-319-46448-0_27
11. Liu, C., Ding, W., Yang, J., et al.: Aggregation signature for small object tracking. IEEE Trans. Image Process. **29**, 1738–1747 (2020)
12. Wu, Y., Lim, J., Yang, M.: Object tracking benchmark. IEEE Trans. Pattern Anal. Mach. Intell. **37**, 1834–1848 (2015)
13. Liang, P., Blasch, E., Ling, H.: Encoding color information for visual tracking: algorithms and benchmark. IEEE Trans. Image Process. **24**, 5630–5644 (2015)
14. Tong, K., Wu, Y., Zhou, F.: Recent advances in small object detection based on deep learning: a review. Image Vis. Comput. **97**, 103910 (2020)
15. LaLonde, R., Zhang, D., Shah, M.: ClusterNet: detecting small objects in large scenes by exploiting spatio-temporal information. In: Proceedings of CVPR (2018)
16. Bai, Y., Zhang, Y., Ding, M., Ghanem, B.: SOD-MTGAN: small object detection via multi-task generative adversarial network. In: Proceedings of ECCV (2018)
17. Huang, Z., Fu, C., Li, Y., Lin, F., Lu, P.: Learning aberrance repressed correlation filters for real-time UAV tracking. In: Proceedings of IEEE ICCV, pp. 2891–2900 (2019)
18. Fu, C., Huang, Z., Li, Y., Duan, R., Lu, P.: Boundary effect-aware visual tracking for UAV with online enhanced background learning and multi-frame consensus verification. In: Proceedings of IROS, pp. 4415–4422 (2019)
19. Li, F., Fu, C., Lin, F., Li, Y., Lu, P.: Training-set distillation for real-time UAV object tracking. In: Proceedings of ICRA, pp. 1–7 (2020)
20. Li, Y., Fu, C., Huang, Z., Zhang, Y., Pan, J.: Keyfilter-aware real-time UAV object tracking. In: Proceedings of ICRA (2020)
21. Li, Y., Fu, C., Ding, F., Huang, Z., Lu, G.: AutoTrack: towards high-performance visual tracking for UAV with automatic spatio-temporal regularization. In: Proceedings of IEEE CVPR (2020)
22. Danelljan, M., Bhat, G., Khan, F.S., Felsberg, M.: ATOM: accurate tracking by overlap maximization. In: Proceedings of CVPR (2019)
23. Held, D., Thrun, S., Savarese, S.: Learning to track at 100 FPS with deep regression networks. In: Leibe, B., Matas, J., Sebe, N., Welling, M. (eds.) ECCV 2016. LNCS, vol. 9905, pp. 749–765. Springer, Cham (2016). https://doi.org/10.1007/978-3-319-46448-0_45
24. Bertinetto, L., Valmadre, J., Henriques, J.F., Vedaldi, A., Torr, P.H.S.: Fully-convolutional siamese networks for object tracking. In: Hua, G., Jégou, H. (eds.) ECCV 2016. LNCS, vol. 9914, pp. 850–865. Springer, Cham (2016). https://doi.org/10.1007/978-3-319-48881-3_56
25. Valmadre, J., Bertinetto, L., Henriques, J., Vedaldi, A., Torr, P.H.: End-to-end representation learning for correlation filter based tracking. In: Proceedings of IEEE CVPR, pp. 5000–5008 (2017)
26. Dong, X., Shen, J.: Triplet loss in Siamese network for object tracking. In: Proceedings of ECCV, pp. 472–488 (2018)

27. Danelljan, M., Robinson, A., Khan, F.S., Felsberg, M.: Beyond correlation filters: learning continuous convolution operators for visual tracking. In: Proceedings of ECCV, pp. 472–488 (2016)

28. Danelljan, M., Bhat, G., Shahbaz Khan, F., Felsberg, M.: ECO: efficient convolution operators for tracking. In: Proceedings of IEEE CVPR, pp. 6931–6939 (2017)

29. Zhu, Z., Wang, Q., Li, B., Wu, W., Yan, J., Hu, W.: Distractor-aware Siamese networks for visual object tracking. In: Proceedings of ECCV, pp. 103–119 (2018)

30. Zhang, Z., Peng, H.: Deeper and wider Siamese networks for real-time visual tracking (2019)

31. Fan, H., Ling, H.: Siamese cascaded region proposal networks for real-time visual tracking (2018)

32. Wang, Q., Zhang, L., Bertinetto, L., Hu, W., Torr, P.H.: Fast online object tracking and segmentation: a unifying approach. In: Proceedings of IEEE CVPR (2019)

33. Li, B., Wu, W., Wang, Q., Zhang, F., Xing, J., Yan, J.: SiamRPN++: evolution of Siamese visual tracking with very deep networks. In: Proceedings of IEEE CVPR (2019)

34. Li, B., Yan, J., Wu, W., Zhu, Z., Hu, X.: High performance visual tracking with Siamese region proposal network. In: Proceedings of IEEE CVPR, pp. 8971–8980 (2018)

35. Bhat, G., Danelljan, M., Gool, L.V., Timofte, R.: Learning discriminative model prediction for tracking. In: Proceedings of IEEE ICCV (2019)

36. Liu, W., et al.: SSD: single shot MultiBox detector. In: Proceedings of ECCV, pp. 21–37 (2016)

37. Fu, C., Liu, W., Ranga, A., Tyagi, A., Berg, A.: DSSD: deconvolutional single shot detector (2017)

38. Cui, L., et al.: MDSSD: multi-scale deconvolutional single shot detector for small objects (2018)

39. Lim, J.S., Astrid, M., Yoon, H.J., Lee, S.I.: Small object detection using context and attention (2019)

40. Yang, X., et al.: SCRDet: towards more robust detection for small, cluttered and rotated objects. In: Proceedings IEEE ICCV (2019)

41. Redmon, J., Farhadi, A.: YOLOv3: an incremental improvement (2018)

42. Girshick, R., Donahue, J., Darrell, T., Malik, J.: Rich feature hierarchies for accurate object detection and semantic segmentation. In: Proceedings of IEEE CVPR, pp. 580–587 (2014)

43. Jiang, B., Luo, R., Mao, J., Xiao, T., Jiang, Y.: Acquisition of localization confidence for accurate object detection. In: Proceedings of IEEE ECCV, pp. 816–832 (2018)

44. Park, J., Woo, S., Lee, J.Y., Kweon, I.S.: BAM: bottleneck attention module. In: Proceedings of BMVC, pp. 147–161 (2018)

45. He, K., Zhang, X., Ren, S., Sun, J.: Deep residual learning for image recognition. In: Proceedings of IEEE CVPR, pp. 770–778 (2016)

46. Szegedy, C., Vanhoucke, V., Ioffe, S., Shlens, J., Wojna, Z.: Rethinking the inception architecture for computer vision. In: Proceedings of CVPR, pp. 2818–2826 (2016)

47. Hu, J., Shen, L., Albanie, S., Sun, G., Wu, E.: Squeeze-and-excitation networks. IEEE Trans. Pattern Anal. Mach. Intell. **42**(8), 2011–2023 (2020). https://doi.org/10.1109/TPAMI.2019.2913372

48. Fan, H., et al.: LaSOT: a high-quality benchmark for large-scale single object tracking. In: Proceedings of IEEE CVPR (2019)

49. Huang, L., Zhao, X., Huang, K.: GOT-10k: a large high-diversity benchmark for generic object tracking in the wild. IEEE Trans. Pattern Anal. Mach. Intell. 1 (2019). https://doi.org/10.1109/TPAMI.2019.2957464

50. He, K., Zhang, X., Ren, S., Sun, J.: Delving deep into rectifiers: surpassing human-level performance on ImageNet classification. In: Proceedings of ICCV, pp. 1026–1034 (2015)

51. Galoogahi, H.K., Fagg, A., Huang, C., Ramanan, D., Lucey, S.: Need for speed: a benchmark for higher frame rate object tracking. In: Proceedings of IEEE ICCV, pp. 1134–1143 (2017)

52. Kingma, D.P., Ba, J.: ADAM: a method for stochastic optimization. In: Proceedings of ICLR (2014)

53. Danelljan, M., Gool, L.V., Timofte, R.: Probabilistic regression for visual tracking. In: Proceedings of IEEE CVPR (2020)

54. Zhang, Z., Peng, H., Fu, J., Li, B., Hu, W.: Ocean: object-aware anchor-free tracking. In: Proceedings of ECCV (2020)

55. Song, Y., Ma, C., Gong, L., Zhang, J., Lau, R.W., Yang, M.H.: CREST: convolutional residual learning for visual tracking. In: Proceedings of ICCV, pp. 2574–2583 (2017)

56. Nam, H., Han, B.: Learning multi-domain convolutional neural networks for visual tracking. In: Proceedings of IEEE CVPR, pp. 4293–4302 (2016)

57. Fan, H., Ling, H.: Parallel tracking and verifying. IEEE Trans. Image Process. **28**, 4130–4144 (2019)

58. Zhang, T., Xu, C., Yang, M.H.: Multi-task correlation particle filter for robust object tracking. In: Proceedings of IEEE CVPR, pp. 4819–4827 (2017)

Adversarial Semi-supervised
Multi-domain Tracking

Kourosh Meshgi$^{(\boxtimes)}$ and Maryam Sadat Mirzaei

RIKEN Center for Advanced Intelligence Project (AIP), Tokyo, Japan
{kourosh.meshgi,maryam.mirzaei}@riken.jp

Abstract. Neural networks for multi-domain learning empowers an effective combination of information from different domains by sharing and co-learning the parameters. In visual tracking, the emerging features in shared layers of a multi-domain tracker, trained on various sequences, are crucial for tracking in unseen videos. Yet, in a fully shared architecture, some of the emerging features are useful only in a specific domain, reducing the generalization of the learned feature representation. We propose a semi-supervised learning scheme to separate domain-invariant and domain-specific features using adversarial learning, to encourage mutual exclusion between them, and to leverage self-supervised learning for enhancing the shared features using the unlabeled reservoir. By employing these features and training dedicated layers for each sequence, we build a tracker that performs exceptionally on different types of videos.

1 Introduction

Multi-task learning (MTL) is a branch of supervised learning that strives to improve the generalization of the regression or classification task by leveraging the domain-specific information contained in the training signals of related tasks [1]. MTL has been investigated in various applications of machine learning, from natural language processing [2] and speech recognition [3] to computer vision [4]. The tasks can be defined as applying the same model on different data (aka multi-domain learning, MDL) [5,6], or on various problems [7]. In NN-based MDL, different domains share a set of parameters, which means more training data for the shared feature space, faster training, and better generalization by averaging inherent noise of different domains [8].

MDNet [5] introduced this form of learning into a visual tracking problem, in which different video sequences are considered as different domains to learn from, and the task is defined as a foreground-background separation. This method, however, suffers from several setbacks: *(i)* this model captures domain-independent representation from different domains with a fully-shared (FS) network (Fig. 1(a)). Such an architecture is unable to exclude the domain-specific features from the shared space, and either ignores them (underfit) or includes them in shared representation (overfit). In the former case, the training tries to compensate by non-optimally change the shared feature space. In contrast, in

© Springer Nature Switzerland AG 2021
H. Ishikawa et al. (Eds.): ACCV 2020, LNCS 12623, pp. 612–630, 2021.
https://doi.org/10.1007/978-3-030-69532-3_37

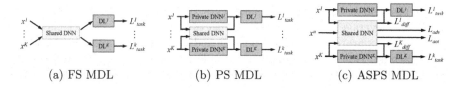

(a) FS MDL   (b) PS MDL   (c) ASPS MDL

Fig. 1. Different methods for obtaining shared representations using multi-domain learning (MDL). Panel (c) depicts our proposed architecture, Adversarial Semi-supervised Private-Shared (ASPS) MTL including adversarial, mutual exclusion, and self-supervised signals that promote the learning task.

the latter, the learned feature in the shared space is merely useful for one or a few domains, wasting the model capacity for an inferior representation learning [9]. Therefore, training on one domain inevitably hurts other domains and hinders the emergence of diverse shared features; *(ii)* a shallow network is selected to avoid vanishing gradients, enabling training with limited number of annotated videos, assuming that tracking is relatively easier than object classification and requires less number of layers, and *(iii)* the learned representation does not consider the patterns of the target motion.

To address these issues, we proposed a private-shared (PS) MDL architecture that separates the domain-specific and domain-invariant (shared) features to disentangle the training on different domains and allow for learning an effective, shared feature representation (Fig. 1(b)). However, experiments show that PS architecture by itself is not enough to prevent domain-specific features from creeping into the share space [10]. Therefore, we proposed to have a virtual discriminator to predict which domain introduces the feature to the shared space. In a GAN-style optimization, we encourage the shared space to have only domain-independent features. We also introduced a regularization term to penalize redundancy in different feature spaces. To deal with the limited number of annotated video sequences, we employ self-supervised learning in which another virtual classifier using shared feature space is constructed to detect the playback direction (i.e., playing forward and backward) to enforce shared feature space to learn low-level features as well as semantics (Fig. 1(c)). The use of both supervised and unsupervised videos improves the discriminative power of shared feature space, as shown with the experiments. Further, we employed ST-ResNets [11] to learn spatiotemporal features, addressing the vanishing gradients, and separating domain-specific motion patterns from the shared ones. Finally, the learned features are used in a custom-made tracking-by-detection method to asses its transferability and effectiveness. In general we *(i)* propose deep private-shared (PS) MTL architecture for tracking, *(ii)* propose adversarial training for PS-MTL, *(iii)* integrate semi-supervised and self-supervised training in a single MTL framework, *(iv)* enforce learning spatiotemporal features in multi-domain tracking, using self-supervision and a backbone network capable of doing that, and *(v)* propose SUS-based hard negative batch mining, and *(vi)* conducted extensive ablation, design choice, and performance experiments.

The problem at hand is closely similar to [12], which tries to perform domain adaptation, leverage multiple datasets with overlapping but distinct class sets, and tries to separate labeled and non-labeled data using multi-domain adversarial learning. However, we explicitly divide features into shared and specific groups, to obtain features that generalize well and push out the specific features that reveal the originating domain in a GAN-style setup.

2   Related Works

Deep Visual Tracking. Early studies in the use of deep learning in tracking utilized features from autoencoders [13,14] and fully-connected layers of pretrained (CNN-based) object detector [15]. Still, later the CNN layers themselves were used to serve as features that balance the abstraction level needed to localize the target [16], to provide a spatiotemporal relationship between the target and its background [17], to combine spatial and temporal aspects of tracking [18,19], and to generate probability maps for the tracker [20]. Recently the tracking studies pay attention to other deep learning approaches including the use of R-CNN for tracking-by-segmentation [21], Siamese Networks for similarity measuring [22–25] and GANs to augment positive samples [26,27].

Most of the current CNN-based techniques use architectures with 2D convolutions to achieve different invariances to the variations of the images. Meanwhile, the invariance to transformations in time is of paramount importance for video analysis [28]. Modeling temporal information in CNNs has been tackled by applying CNNs on optical flow images [29], reformulating R-CNNs to exploit the temporal context of the images [30] or by the use of separate information pathways for spatial and temporal pathways [31,32]. Motion-based CNNs typically outperform CNN representations learned from images for tasks dealing with dynamic target, e.g., action recognition [28]. In these approaches, a CNN is applied on a 3-channel optical flow image [33], and different layers of such network provide different variances toward speed and the direction of the target's motion [34]. In visual tracking, deep motion features provide promising results [35], which requires the tracker to fuse the information from two different CNN networks, a temporal and a spatial [32]. However, due to the difficulties in fusing these two streams, some researchers use only the motion features [35].

Deep Multi-Task/Domain Learning. When used with deep learning, MTL models tend to share the learned parameters across different tasks either by *(i)* hard parameter sharing [1] that the hidden layers are shared between all tasks, while task-specific ones are fine-tuned for each task, or by *(ii)* soft parameter sharing, where each task has its parameters, and the distance between the parameters of the model is then regularized to encourage the parameters to be similar using, e.g., ℓ_1 norm [36] or trace norm [37].

In the hard parameter sharing architectures, shared parameters provide a global feature representation, while task-specific layers further process these features or provide a complementary set of features suitable for a specific task. Some MTL approaches are based on the intuition that learning easy tasks is the

Fig. 2. Some of features in MDNet are activated for a few sequences containing a particular motion pattern or appearance and wastes the capacity of shared feature space. Domain-specific features emerged in shared space (left) motion features maximally activated by motion pattern in `Joggling` (right) appearance feature maximally activated by `FaceOcc1` due to the book cover (visualized using [34] and [52]).

prerequisite for learning more complex ones [8], hence put tasks in hierarchies [38–40] or try to automatically group similar tasks to dynamically form shared layers [41]. When training a multi-task learner, training each task normally increases the task's accuracy (fine-tuning) and, at the same time, provides more information for the shared representation that affects the accuracy of the rest of the tasks (generalization). Balancing the fine-tuning-generalization trade-off has been the subject of several studies. Kendall et al. [42] adjusts tasks' relative weights in the loss function in proportion to the task uncertainty, [43] divides the feature space into task-specific and shared spaces and later employs adversarial learning to encourage shared feature space to contain more common and less task-specific information [6], and [44] proposed orthogonality constraints to punish redundancy between shared and task layers. In line with this, learning through hints [45] trains a network to predict the most important features. To leverage correlations of different problems in MTL, the tasks could be adversarial [10], provide hints or attention for a main task [46,47], use a shared memory [48], explicitly perform representation learning for a more complex task [49], facilitate training for a quickly-plateauing main task [50], or learn a shared unsupervised representation [51]. It can be helpful to learn the relations between tasks to enable efficient transfer learning between them [7].

Self-supervised Learning. Self-supervised learning refers to a learning problem from unlabeled that is framed as a supervised learning problem by using proxy tasks on behalf of the main learning objective. Supervised learning algorithms are used to solve an alternate or pretext task, the result of which is a model or representation that can be used in the solution of the original (actual) modeling problem [53], e.g., by masking a known word in a sentence and trying to predict it [54]. Common examples of self-supervised learning in computer vision is to make colorful images grayscale and have a model to predict a color representation (colorization) [55], removing blocks of the image and have a to model predict the missing parts (inpainting) [56], or rotating an image by random multiples of 90° and predict if the image has the correct rotation [57]. Self-supervised learning extracts additional information from video sequences by exploiting the natural structure in them to use as labels for proxy learning problems. Such information may derive from low-level physics (e.g., gravity), high-level events (e.g., shooting the ball in a soccer match), and artificial cues (e.g., camera motion) [56,58]. The video sequence order [59], video colorization [60], and video direction [58] have been explored as the pretext task to learn video representations. For this purpose, CNNs are more suitable to learn representations compared to autoencoders [61].

3   Proposed Tracker

This section describes the architecture of the proposed Adversarial Semi-supervised Multi-Domain (ASMD) tracker. We consider multi-domain (domain:= video) learning to share the acquired knowledge from one sequence to another. First, we explore the private-shared MDL framework that provides both domain-specific and shared features for the tracking-by-detection. The network architecture of private and shared modules to capture spatiotemporal features and their training is discussed next. To avoid redundancy and loss of generalization in the shared layers, we introduce adversarial regularization and orthogonality constraint into the MDL training (Fig. 3). Further, to boost the performance of the MDL, the shared representation is intermittently trained using unlabeled videos (Fig. 4).

3.1   Private-Shared Multi-domain Learning

In FS-MDL (Fig. 1(a)), all of the domains share the features extracted by a shared set of layers. Such an idea has been explored in MDNet tracker [5], which assume that all features extracted for one domain is useful for other domains. This model ignores that some features are domain-dependent and may not be useful for other domains. Such features are maximally activated for one or very few domains (i.e., video sequences) while having low activation for others. Figure 2 illustrates some examples of such domain-specific features. On the other hand, PS-MDL [6] divides the feature space of each domain into a domain-invariant part that is shared among all domains, and a domain-specific part. As Fig. 1(b) depicts, each domain has its own set of features, that together with the shared features (i.e., concatenated with them), forms the domain features.

3.2   Network Architecture

We used a modified Spatiotemporal ResNet [11] for our private and shared networks. The first layer of motion stream is altered to have $2L = 10$ filter channels to operate on the horizontal and vertical optical flow stack of 5 frames. To establish the correspondence between the object and its motion, a residual link connects two streams for each ResNet block. The network receives 224×224 input and reduces it to 7×7 via global average pooling (GAP) (Fig. 3). The depth of the networks in MDNet [5] is kept low, however, with the use of ResNet blocks instead of ConvNet here, the network can be significantly deeper.

For each domain the shared features (i.e., concatenation of appearance and motion streams of shared layer) are concatenated with the domain-specific features, followed by two fully connected layers with 128 units and a binary classification fully-connected layer with softmax cross-entropy loss. The network is

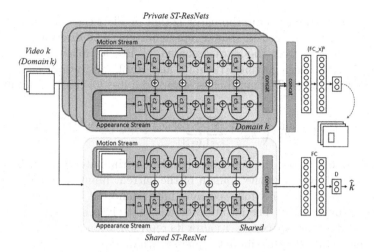

Fig. 3. The architecture of the proposed Private-Shared Multi-Domain Network, which consists of one shared and K modified ST-ResNet domain-specific. For domain $k \in \{1..K\}$, the feature space consists of shared features and the corresponding domain-specific features, and the final fully connected layer calculated the classification score of the input patch from video k for a foreground-background classification.

trained to minimize the cross-entropy of the predicted label and the true label of all target candidates for all domains. The loss is computed as:

$$L_{dom} = \sum_{k=1}^{K} \alpha_k L_{track}\left(\hat{y}^{(k)}, y^{(k)}\right) \tag{1}$$

where α_k is the weight of domain k and $L_{track}\left(\hat{y}^{(k)}, y^{(k)}\right)$ is defined in Eq. (6).

3.3 Adversarial Representation Learning

PS-MDL dissects the representation for each domain into a domain-specific and shared feature spaces but does not guarantee that shared feature space does not include domain-specific features and vice versa. To encourage the shared feature space to include more common information between domains yet has no domain-specific ones, we proposed to use adversarial training. Adversarial training became very popular after the seminal work of Goodfellow et al. [62]. This approach sets up a min-max between networks in which a network G tries to fool the other (D) by generating better samples (i.e., closer to real data distribution), and the other excels in distinguishing the generated data (P_G) from the real ones (P_{data}), by optimizing

$$\ell = \min_{G} \max_{D}\left(\mathbb{E}_{x \sim P_{data}}[\log D(x)] + \mathbb{E}_{z \sim p(z)}[\log(1 - D(G(z)))]\right) \tag{2}$$

We propose an adversarial loss function for our MDL-based tracking. The goal is to encourage the shared space to be free from domain-specific knowledge.

Therefore, we introduce a discriminator D that predicts the domain k only from the features that emerged in shared representation. The discriminator in each iteration is created from the learned shared ST-ResNet followed by three fully connected layers, each having 512 units and ReLU activation, and a K unit softmax output layer. The multi-class adversarial loss [6] can be formulated as

$$L_{adv} = \min_{\theta_s} \left(\max_{\theta_D} \left(\sum_{k=1}^{K} \sum_{i=1}^{N_k} \delta_i^k \log \left[D_{\theta_D} \left(\mathbb{E}(\mathbf{x}^{(k)}) \right) \right] \right) \right) \tag{3}$$

in which θ_D and θ_S are the parameters of the discriminator D and shared layer respectively, δ_i^k indicates the domain of the current input i, and $\mathbb{E}(\mathbf{x})$ denotes shared representation of $\mathbf{x}$ followed by 2 fully connected layers and just before the discriminator layer. The intuition here is that given a sample from domain k, the shared feature space tries to alter its representation to better discriminate the sample, while the discriminator guesses which domain is the sample from. If the learned feature helps the discriminator to find the domain, it includes some domain-specific knowledge [63], and the defined loss L_{adv} punishes this representation. It should be noted that L_{adv} ignores the label $y^{(k)}$ of the input $\mathbf{x}^{(k)}$, allowing for unsupervised training of the shared layer, which is essential to realize the semi-supervised training of the network.

A drawback of the PS-MDL is that the domain-specific and shared feature space may not be mutually exclusive, and redundant domain-invariant features may emerge in both [64]. To alleviate this, inspired by [44], we compare the activations of the private and shared networks, and penalize the high co-activations of the corresponding neurons that are likely to encode a similar latent feature,

$$L_{dif} = \sum_{k=1}^{K} \left\| (\mathbf{f}^s)^T \mathbf{f}^k \right\|_F^2 \tag{4}$$

in which $\mathbf{f}^s$ and $\mathbf{f}^k$ are shared and domain-specific feature vectors (i.e., last layer neuron activations) for a given input and $\|.\|_F^2$ denoted the Frobenius norm.

3.4   Self-supervised Representation Learning

To enrich the share representation, we want to leverage the structure of the video data to use them as labels for closely related proxy problems that can be solved with the current shared architecture. We select the video direction (forward or backward) as a proxy learning task that is compatible with this architecture.

The order of the frames in a natural video contains spatiotemporal clues about the way objects move. The order of the frames can provide a trivial label for a proxy classification task: to classify if the movie as played in the natural direction or backward. During this task, the network learns spatiotemporal features, which is useful for other tasks such as video understanding, action recognition, and object tracking. Therefore, we select random clips from our dataset, randomly invert the order of some of them, and give them to our network to classify. This helps the features to emerge in the shared layers of our network.

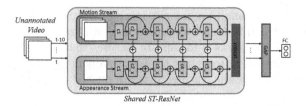

Fig. 4. Self-supervised network using shared ST-ResNet layers, a global average pooling layer, and an output layer to classify "arrow of time" in the 10-frame input clip.

To pull out this task, we draw 10-frame samples from annotated sequences as well as numerous unlabeled videos in YouTubeBB [65] dataset, randomly reverse their order (to augment the data with negative samples), and feed them to the shared ST-ResNet. The extracted features are then aggregated similar to [58] using a GAP layer, and a binary cross-entropy output layer computes the final arrow-of-time loss L_{aot} for the forward-backward classification (Fig. 4).

3.5   Semi-supervised MDL Training

The final loss function of the tracker can be written as

$$L = L_{dom} + \lambda_1 L_{adv} + \lambda_2 L_{dif} + \lambda_3 L_{aot} \qquad (5)$$

in which $\lambda_1, \lambda_2, \lambda_3$ are hyper-parameters. This network is periodically trained on labeled and unlabeled videos such that after every 100 supervised iterations, 1000 unsupervised iterations are conducted.

Supervised. For the supervised multi-domain learning, we collect 50 positive samples and 200 negative samples for each frame such that each positive sample has at least 70% overlap with the target ($IoU \geq 0.7$), and negative samples have $IoU \leq 0.5$). For multi-domain representation learning, the network is trained for 1M iterations with learning rate 0.0001 for ST-ResNets and 0.001 for FC layers on GOT10K dataset [66] and its grayscale version. The networks are trained using backpropagation through gradient reversal layer [10] to assist the minimax optimization. For each iteration, five random 10-frame clip and another five with reversed frame-order are extracted for L_{aot}.

Unsupervised. We also conduct 10M iteration of unsupervised training on 240k videos of the YouTubeBB dataset. Again in each iteration, five random 10-frame clips and another five reversed one is extracted from the input video to provide the L_{aot}, and the learning rate for ST-ResNet is set to 0.00001.

4   Online Tracking

After learning the shared features, the private branches are discarded, and 3 new FC layers and a binary softmax output layer is used for every new sequence.

During tracking (test time), no domain-specific network is used/trained. All of FC layers (after shared features) are randomly initialized and trained on-the-fly. The goal of private networks is to capture features that are not captured by the shared network (by trying to overfit the input sequence), introduce them to the feature pool, and receive the features that are pushed out of the shared pool.

4.1   Tracking-by-Detection

For each test sequence, the final FC layers convert the domain-specific and shared feature for all n samples of each T_k frame of video sequence k into classification score $\hat{y} \in [0,1]$, trained by minimizing the cross-entropy of the sample's label $y \in \{0,1\}$ and the score, by applying SGD on the loss

$$L_{track}(\hat{y}^{(k)}, y^{(k)}) = -\frac{1}{nT_k} \sum_{t=1}^{T_k} \sum_{j=1}^{n} y_t^{j(k)} \log\left(\hat{y}_t^{j(k)}\right) \tag{6}$$

while the shared layers are kept frozen during tracking. This is important to avoid over-fitting to the video sequence [5] and for computational efficiency. After training on the first annotated frame of the sequence, n samples are extracted from each frame t following a Gaussian distribution around the last known target position. The samples are classified using the shared features and dedicated FC layers, and the sample with highest classification score is considered as the new target location. To find a tight bounding box around the target, the target candidates (i.e., score > 0.5) are used in bounding box regression similar to [67].

To update the tracker, a dual-memory [68] is employed in which the network is updated every Δ^s frames (short-memory) with all positive and selected negative samples between t and $t - \Delta^s$. In the long run, the network is likely to forget the initial samples (especially those obtained from user), thus the network is updated every Δ^l frames ($\Delta^l \gg \Delta^s$) with the all previous target estimations (if score > 0.5) and the most uncertain negative sample (score $\to 0.5$).

4.2   Stochastic Universal Negative Mining

In visual tracking, negative examples (samples) comes from (i) background, or (ii) occluders, distractors and patches that has small overlap with the target. To identify such negative examples, hard negative mining [69] explicitly predict examples' labels and selects misclassified examples (i.e., false positives). Hard minibatch mining [5] selects random subsets of negative examples and selects ones with the lowest classification score as the negative training examples without the need to the examples' labels.

To keep the focus on the hard negatives while keeping the diversity of the negative samples, we borrowed a stochastic universal sampling (SUS) technique [70] from genetic algorithms to select negative training examples via repeated random sampling based on the classification score of the example (Fig. 5). This technique gives weaker members of the negative example pool (according to their score) a chance to be chosen to represent different parts of the background in the classifier.

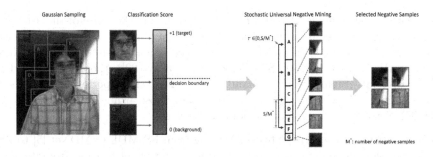

Fig. 5. Stochastic universal sampling to select negative examples for retraining. Using a comb-like ruler, SUS starts from a random real number, and chooses next candidates from the rest of negative examples, preventing the examples with the highest scores to saturate the selection space. S is the sum of negative samples' classification scores.

4.3   Implementation Details

This framework contains several sets of parameters. The tracking parameters including the number of positive and negative samples during train and test time, the covariance of the sampling from each frame, and the parameters of the bounding box regression are kept similar to MDNet [5]. The update intervals are set to $\Delta^s = 15$ and $\Delta^l = 50$. On the MDL side, all domains are equally weighted $\alpha_k = 1/K$, and regularization hyper-parameters are tuned on GOT10K and YouTubeBB datasets via a grid search in $\lambda_i \in [0.01, 0.1]$ and kept fixed through test-time trackings/experiments. Final values are 0.08,0.01,0.6 for $\lambda_{1..3}$.

The FC layers of tracker during the test are trained on the first (annotated) frame for 30 iterations with the learning rate of 0.0001 for hidden layers and 0.001 for the softmax layer. To update the classifier, the learning rate is increased to 0.0003 and 0.003 for hidden and output FC layers for ten iterations, with mini-batches composed of 32 positive and 96 SUS-sampled negatives out of 1024 available negative examples. The tracker is implemented in Matlab using Mat-ConvNet [72] and ST-ResNet Github Repos, and runs around 5.18 fps on Intel Core i7 @ 4.00 GHz with Nvidia V100 GPU.

5   Experiment

In a series of experiments using OTB50 dataset [73], the effect of the MDL architecture and the network used in it, and the proposed negative minibatch mining are investigated. An ablation study is conducted to clarify the contributions of each component in the tracker. Finally, the performance of the tracker on recent challenging datasets such as OTB-100 [74], LaSOT [75], UAV123 [76], TrackingNet [77], and VOT-2018 [78] is benchmarked against the state-of-the-art trackers. For this comparison, we have used success and precision plots, where their area under curve provides a robust metric for comparing tracker performances [73]. We also compare all the trackers by the success rate at the conventional thresholds of 0.50 ($IoU > \frac{1}{2}$) [73]. For the state-of-the-art comparisons, the results are averaged for five different runs using the original semi-supervised training (*cf* Sect. 3.5). The tracker is compared with latest trackers (DiMP [79], ATOM [80], STResCF [81], CBCW [82]), those with bounding box regression (SiamRPN [24], SiamRPN++ [25]), those performing adversarial learning (VITAL [27], SINT++ [26]), and those using MTL (MDNet [5], RT-MDNet [83]) as well as other popular trackers.

Multi-domain Learning Model. Moving from FS-MDL in MDNet [5] to PS-MDL enables the model to separate the domain-invariant features from domain-specific ones. Adversarial and mutual-exclusion regularizations encourage this effect. The proposed adversarial training cannot operate on the fully-shared architecture of MDNet. Additionally, MDNet's backbone (VGG-M) is unable to learn spatiotemporal features, thus ineffective for our self-supervised learning.

Table 1 presents five variations for the MDL architecture *(i)* vanilla FS (different from MDNet), that uses only a fully shared ST-ResNet, *(ii)* PS, that uses a task-specific ST-ResNet for each domain on top of the shared ST-ResNet, *(iii)* PS+dif, that adds L_{dif} to the PS variation, *(iv)* APS-, that adds L_{adv} to the PS variation, and *(v)* APS that uses both L_{adv} and L_{dif} for the network. All variations are **only** trained with supervised data for 200k iterations, and regularization weights are tuned by 5-fold cross-validation for each case. Using PS-MDL without regularizations is not always beneficial, but using both in APS significantly improves the learning performance.

Table 1. Comparison of MDL models with 200k iterations of *supervised* training on GOT10K [66] and tested OTB-50. We also retrained MDNet on this dataset for the same number of iterations ($\star$). The *first*, **second** and **third** best methods are highlighted.

	FS	MDNet*	PS	PS+dif	APS-	APS
Average success	0.62	**0.67**	0.59	0.41	*0.71*	*0.73*
Average precision	0.73	**0.76**	0.70	0.55	*0.80*	*0.81*
$IoU > \frac{1}{2}$	0.67	**0.71**	0.61	0.45	*0.74*	*0.76*

Backbone Network. We tested our tracker with different backbone architecture such as MDNet-style VGG-M, Two Stream ConvNets with convolutional fusion [84], TwoStream ResNets with late fusion, Spatiotemporal ConvNet [85] and SpatioTemporal ResNets [11]. Table 2 shows that similar to the action recognition domain [11], Spatiotemporal ResNets yields the best results for our intended tasks using to residual connections that enables learning the difference of sequences [54]. Notice the big jump between single-stream and two-stream architectures that is partly because the arrow-of-time self-supervised training is mostly beneficial to train the motion stream.

Table 2. Comparison of backbone networks with 200k iterations of supervised training on OTB-50 (1S: single stream, 2S: two-stream, ST: spatiotemporal).

	1S Conv [5]	2S Conv [84]	2S Res	ST Conv [85]	ST Res [11]
Avg Succ	0.64	0.69	0.67	0.63	*0.73*
Avg Prec	0.71	0.77	0.77	0.71	*0.81*
$IoU > \frac{1}{2}$	0.66	0.70	0.69	0.66	*0.76*

Table 3. Comparison of negative minibatch selection for tracking on OTB-50.

	RAND	GRDY	HMM [5]	SUNM (**ours**)
Average success	0.72	0.61	0.77	*0.80*
Average precision	0.81	0.69	0.89	*0.88*
$IoU > \frac{1}{2}$	0.75	0.67	0.87	*0.93*

Table 4. Comparison of the transferability of learned representations with different versions of the proposed framework as well as the pre-training on ILSRVC-2012 action recognition task for leave-one-out evaluation. For each video sequence of OTB50, 49 is used for semi-supervised training, and the remaining video is used for tracking, and the average of the success and precision of the tracker is reported in the table.

	PRE	LOO-FS	LOO-PS	LOO-APS	LOO-ASPS
Avg Succ	0.41	**0.70**	0.67	*0.72*	*0.78*
Avg Prec	0.52	**0.76**	0.72	*0.80*	*0.85*
$IoU > \frac{1}{2}$	0.46	*0.79*	0.70	*0.79*	*0.87*

Negative Minibatch Selection. To select representative negative samples from the pool, and to avoid model drift by insufficiently sampling from critical distractors and occluder, we proposed stochastic universal negative mining (SUNM). Table 3 shows the effectiveness of this method compared to a random selection of negative samples (RAND), hard minibatch mining (HMM) [5], and a greedy selection of the most uncertain negative examples (GRDY).

Shared Knowledge Transfer. To test the transferability of the learned representation, we design a leave-on-out experiment on OTB50 dataset, in which out of 50 unique sequences in this dataset, we train the MDL on 49 of them for training, and the remaining one for testing. We use only 100k supervised and 10M unsupervised iterations, and the shared layer is frozen during tracking (LOO-ASPS). This process is repeated for three ablated versions of the proposed model, *(i)* with fully-shared architecture (LOO-FS), *(ii)* with the private-shared model with no regularization (LOO-PS), and *(iii)* without unsupervised iterations (LOO-APS), all trained with 100k supervised iterations. We also set the parameters of shared layers with the ILSRVC-2012 pre-trained network (PRE). Table 4 shows that even FS-MDL in the LOO setting outperforms the tracker

Table 5. Quantitative evaluation of trackers under different visual tracking challenges of OTB50 [73] using AUC of success plot and their overall precision.

Attribute	TLD [86]	STRK [87]	TGPR [88]	MEEM [89]	MUSTer [90]	STAPLE [91]	CMT [92]	SRDCF [93]	CCOT [94]	MDNet [5]	Ours
Illumination variation	0.48	0.53	0.54	0.62	0.73	0.68	0.73	0.70	**0.75**	*0.76*	*0.80*
Deformation	0.38	0.51	0.61	0.62	0.69	**0.70**	0.69	0.67	0.69	*0.73*	*0.74*
Occlusion	0.46	0.50	0.51	0.61	0.69	0.69	0.69	0.70	*0.76*	0.75	*0.81*
Scale variation	0.49	0.51	0.50	0.58	0.71	0.68	0.72	0.71	**0.76**	*0.78*	*0.82*
In-plane rotation	0.50	0.54	0.56	0.58	0.69	0.69	**0.74**	0.70	0.72	*0.75*	*0.78*
Out-of-plane rotation	0.48	0.53	0.54	0.62	0.70	0.67	0.73	0.69	**0.74**	*0.76*	*0.80*
Out-of-view (Shear)	0.54	0.52	0.44	0.68	0.73	0.62	0.71	0.66	*0.79*	*0.79*	*0.84*
Low resolution	0.36	0.33	0.38	0.43	0.50	0.47	0.55	0.58	**0.70**	*0.72*	*0.71*
Background clutter	0.39	0.52	0.57	0.67	**0.72**	0.67	0.69	0.70	0.70	*0.76*	*0.77*
Fast motion	0.45	0.52	0.46	0.65	0.65	0.56	0.70	0.63	**0.72**	*0.73*	*0.78*
Motion blur	0.41	0.47	0.44	0.63	0.65	0.61	0.65	0.69	**0.72**	*0.72*	*0.78*
Avg. Succ	0.49	0.55	0.56	0.62	0.72	0.69	0.72	0.70	**0.75**	*0.76*	*0.80*
Avg. Prec	0.60	0.66	0.68	0.74	0.82	0.76	0.83	0.78	**0.84**	*0.85*	*0.88*
$IoU > 0.5$	0.59	0.64	0.66	0.75	0.86	0.82	0.83	0.83	**0.90**	*0.93*	*0.93*

Table 6. Quantitative evaluation on OTB100 using success rate and precision.

	dSRDCF [95]	CCOT [94]	BACF [96]	dSTRCF [97]	STResCF [81]	CBCW [82]	ECO [98]	SiamRPN [24]	SiamRPN++ [25]	SINT++ [26]	VITAL [27]	MDNet [5]	RT-MDNet [83]	ATOM [80]	DiMP [79]	Ours
Avg. Succ↑	*0.69*	0.68	0.62	0.68	0.59	0.61	*0.69*	0.63	*0.69*	0.57	0.68	0.67	0.65	0.66	0.68	*0.73*
Avg. Prec↑	0.81	0.85	0.82	–	0.83	0.81	*0.91*	0.85	*0.91*	0.76	*0.91*	0.90	0.88	–	0.89	*0.91*
$IoU > \frac{1}{2}$	0.78	*0.88*	0.77	0.77	0.76	0.76	–	0.80	0.83	0.78	0.75	0.80	0.79	*0.86*	0.87	*0.88*

Table 7. Evaluation on VOT2018 by expected avg overlap, robustness and accuracy.

	STURCK [87]	MEEM [89]	STAPLE [91]	SRDCF [93]	CCOT [94]	SiamFC [23]	ECO [98]	SiamRPN [24]	SiamRPN++ [25]	ATOM [80]	DiMP [79]	Ours
EAO↑	0.097	0.192	0.169	0.119	0.267	0.188	0.280	0.383	0.414	0.401	*0.440*	*0.427*
Acc↑	0.418	0.463	0.530	0.490	0.494	0.503	0.484	0.586	*0.600*	0.590	**0.597**	*0.604*
Rob↓	1.297	0.534	0.688	0.974	0.318	0.585	0.276	0.276	0.234	**0.204**	*0.153*	*0.169*

made with pre-training for the action recognition task. PS-MDL with regularization but without unsupervised iterations outperform FS-MDL, however, when unsupervised training is used, such distinction becomes more apparent. In summary, it is shown that the full treatment yields better results due to multi-task learning (PRE<LOO-FS), adversarial training (LOO-PS<LOO-FS<LOO-SPS), and self-supervised training (LOO-APS<LOO-ASPS).

Tracking Challenges Analysis. Table 5 presents the performance of the proposed tracker under challenging subsets of OTB50. The results reveal that using proposed PS-MTL architecture as well as the semi-supervised training scheme almost improved every aspect of the tracker compared to the baseline (MDNet). This improvement is more significant for occlusions, out-of-view and motion challenges due to the usage of spatiotemporal features in the tracker.

Evaluation on OTB-100. We benchmarked the tracker against the competing trackers on OTB100 [74] as presented in Table 6. In comparison with trackers who perform BB regression, those using adversarial learning, and the state-of-the-art in the tracking, our proposed tracker shows better performance.

Evaluation on VOT-2018. Table 7 shows the comparison of our method with the competing algorithms on 60 challenging videos of VOT-2018 [78].

Table 8. Evaluation on LaSOT with protocol I (testing on all videos) and protocol II (training on given videos and testing on the rest). We get better results with dataset's own videos as training due to large training set and matching domain.

	STAPLE [91]	SRDCF [93]	SiamFC [23]	SINT [22]	ECO [98]	BACF [96]	SiamRPN++ [25]	VITAL [27]	MDNet [5]	ATOM [80]	DiMP [79]	Ours
(I) Acc↑	0.266	0.271	0.358	0.339	0.340	0.277	0.496	0.412	0.413	0.515	0.569	0.554
(I) Rob↑	0.231	0.227	0.341	0.229	0.298	0.239	–	0.372	0.374	–	–	0.487
(II)Acc↑	0.243	0.245	0.336	0.314	0.324	0.259	–	0.390	0.397	–	–	0.499
(II)Rob↑	0.239	0.219	0.339	0.295	0.301	0.239	–	0.360	0.373	–	–	0.495

Table 9. Evaluation on UAV123 by success rate and precision.

	STRUCK [87]	MEEM [89]	STAPLE [91]	SRDCF [93]	MUSTer [90]	ECO [98]	CCOT [94]	SiamRPN [24]	SiamRPN++ [25]	MDNet [5]	RT-MDNet [83]	ATOM [80]	DiMP [79]	Ours
Succ↑	0.387	0.398	0.453	0.473	0.517	0.522	0.513	0.527	0.613	0.528	0.528	0.643	0.654	0.655
Prec↑	0.578	0.627	0.666	0.676	0.391	0.591	–	0.748	0.807	–	0.772	0.856	0.858	0.793

Table 10. Evaluation on TrackingNet by precision, normalized precision, and success.

	ECO [98]	SiamFC [23]	CFNet	MDNet [5]	DaSiam-RPN [99]	ATOM [80]	SiamRPN++ [25]	DiMP [79]	Ours
Precision	0.492	0.533	0.533	0.565	0.591	0.648	0.694	0.687	0.687
Norm. Prec	0.618	0.666	0.654	0.705	0.733	0.771	0.800	0.801	0.802
Success (AUC)	0.554	0.571	0.578	0.606	0.638	0.703	0.733	0.740	0.741

Evaluation on LaSOT [75]. In phase I, our tracker is trained on the GOT10K dataset for 1M supervised iterations and on YouTubeBB [65] for 10M unsupervised iterations. As showed in Table 8, our proposed algorithm obtained the best results compared to state-of-the-art trackers when tested on all 1400 video sequences of LaSOT. Protocol II brings an even more interesting challenge, that limits the training data to the given 1120 videos, and test the trained trackers on the remaining 280 sequences of the dataset. Using the given training videos, we conduct 1M supervised and 10M unsupervised training. The shared layer obtained a significant improvement compared to the MDNet and the state-of-the-art, which can be attributed to the abundance of labeled data, and the close distributions of training and test data, essential for unsupervised training.

Evaluation on UAV123. The result in Table 9 suggest that the shared feature space is good enough to surpass the state-of-the-art trackers for tracking in this dataset, but not good enough to obtain a high success score. In this regard, we conducted an additional experiment by 5-fold cross validating the network trained for 100K supervised iterations and 1M unsupervised iteration for each fold (we ensured that each fold has exactly 4 of the 20 longer videos of the dataset, called UAV20L subset). The average success score for this task on UAV123 reaches 0.655 that is almost 7.8% improvement compared to the generally trained version of the proposed tracker (on GOT10K and YouTubeBB).

Evaluation on TrackingNet. Table 10 shows our results on the TrackingNet test set [77] (511 videosh) that is comparable to the SOTA approaches.

6　Conclusion

We proposed a semi-supervised private-shared MDL to learn the domain-invariant and domain-specific features, push the domain-specific features out of the shared feature space using an adversarial regularization, and use the direction of video playing as a proxy learning task to further train the shared representation using unannotated videos. We then proposed a tracker that classifies the target from the background for each video that uses the learned feature representation. The results of the demonstrate the superior performance of the proposed tracker compared to the state-of-the-art. Our next step is to tailor our adversarial learning and global search for long-term tracking as proposed in [100,101].

References

1. Caruana, R.: Multitask learning: a knowledge-based source of inductive bias (1993)
2. Collobert, R., Weston, J.: A unified architecture for natural language processing: deep neural networks with multitask learning. In: ICML2008, pp. 160–167. ACM (2008)
3. Deng, L., Hinton, G., Kingsbury, B.: New types of deep neural network learning for speech recognition and related applications: an overview. In: ICASSP 2013, pp. 8599–8603. IEEE (2013)
4. Girshick, R.: Fast R-CNN. In: ICCV 2015, pp. 1440–1448 (2015)
5. Nam, H., Han, B.: Learning multi-domain convolutional neural networks for visual tracking. In: CVPR 2016
6. Liu, P., Qiu, X., Huang, X.: Adversarial multi-task learning for text classification. In: ACL 2017, pp. 1–10 (2017)
7. Roshan Zamir, A., Sax, A., Shen, W., Guibas, L.J., Malik, J., Savarese, S.: Taskonomy: disentangling task transfer learning. In: CVPR 2018, pp. 3712–3722 (2018)
8. Ruder, S.: An overview of multi-task learning in deep neural networks. arXiv preprint arXiv:1706.05098 (2017)
9. Bengio, Y., Courville, A., Vincent, P.: Representation learning: a review and new perspectives. PAMI **35**, 1798–1828 (2013)
10. Ganin, Y., Lempitsky, V.: Unsupervised domain adaptation by backpropagation. In: ICML 2015, pp. 1180–1189 (2015)
11. Feichtenhofer, C., Pinz, A., Wildes, R.: Spatiotemporal residual networks for video action recognition. In: NIPS 2016, pp. 3468–3476 (2016)
12. Sebag, A.S., Heinrich, L., Schoenauer, M., Sebag, M., Wu, L., Altschuler, S.: Multi-domain adversarial learning. In: ICLR 2019 (2019)
13. Wang, N., Yeung, D.Y.: Learning a deep compact image representation for visual tracking. In: NIPS, pp. 809–817 (2013)
14. Zhou, X., Xie, L., Zhang, P., Zhang, Y.: An ensemble of deep neural networks for object tracking. In: 2014 IEEE International Conference on Image Processing (ICIP), pp. 843–847. IEEE (2014)
15. Fan, J., Xu, W., Wu, Y., Gong, Y.: Human tracking using convolutional neural networks. IEEE Trans. Neural Networks **21**, 1610–1623 (2010)
16. Ma, C., Huang, J.B., Yang, X., Yang, M.H.: Hierarchical convolutional features for visual tracking. In: ICCV 2015, pp. 3074–3082 (2015)

17. Zhang, K., Liu, Q., Wu, Y., Yang, M.: Robust visual tracking via convolutional networks without training. IEEE TIP **25**, 1779–1792 (2016)
18. Zhu, Z., Huang, G., Zou, W., Du, D., Huang, C.: UCT: learning unified convolutional networks for real-time visual tracking. In: ICCVw, pp. 1973–1982 (2017)
19. Chen, K., Tao, W.: Once for all: a two-flow convolutional neural network for visual tracking. IEEE CSVT **28**, 3377–3386 (2018)
20. Wang, N., Li, S., Gupta, A., Yeung, D.Y.: Transferring rich feature hierarchies for robust visual tracking. arXiv (2015)
21. Drayer, B., Brox, T.: Object detection, tracking, and motion segmentation for object-level video segmentation. arXiv preprint arXiv:1608.03066 (2016)
22. Tao, R., Gavves, E., Smeulders, A.W.: Siamese instance search for tracking. In: CVPR, pp. 1420–1429 (2016)
23. Bertinetto, L., Valmadre, J., Henriques, J.F., Vedaldi, A., Torr, P.H.S.: Fully-convolutional Siamese networks for object tracking. In: Hua, G., Jégou, H. (eds.) ECCV 2016. LNCS, vol. 9914, pp. 850–865. Springer, Cham (2016). https://doi.org/10.1007/978-3-319-48881-3_56
24. Li, B., Yan, J., Wu, W., Zhu, Z., Hu, X.: High performance visual tracking with Siamese region proposal network. In: CVPR 2018 (2018)
25. Li, B., Wu, W., Wang, Q., Zhang, F., Xing, J., Yan, J.: SiamRPN++: evolution of Siamese visual tracking with very deep networks. In: CVPR 2019 (2019)
26. Wang, X., Li, C., Luo, B., Tang, J.: SINT++: Robust visual tracking via adversarial positive instance generation. In: CVPR 2018 (2018)
27. Song, Y., et al.: VITAL: visual tracking via adversarial learning. In: CVPR (2018)
28. Varol, G., Laptev, I., Schmid, C.: Long-term temporal convolutions for action recognition. PAMI **40**, 1510–1517 (2018)
29. Gkioxari, G., Malik, J.: Finding action tubes. In: CVPR, pp. 759–768 (2015)
30. Chao, Y.W., Vijayanarasimhan, S., Seybold, B., Ross, D.A., Deng, J., Sukthankar, R.: Rethinking the faster R-CNN architecture for temporal action localization. In: CVPR 2018, pp. 1130–1139 (2018)
31. Simonyan, K., Zisserman, A.: Two-stream convolutional networks for action recognition in videos. In: NIPS, pp. 568–576 (2014)
32. Zhu, Z., Wu, W., Zou, W., Yan, J.: End-to-end flow correlation tracking with spatial-temporal attention. In: CVPR, vol. 42, p. 20 (2017)
33. Dosovitskiy, A., et al.: FlowNet: learning optical flow with convolutional networks. In: ICCV 2015, pp. 2758–2766 (2015)
34. Feichtenhofer, C., Pinz, A., Wildes, R.P., Zisserman, A.: What have we learned from deep representations for action recognition? Connections **19**, 29 (2018)
35. Gladh, S., Danelljan, M., Khan, F.S., Felsberg, M.: Deep motion features for visual tracking. In: ICPR, pp. 1243–1248. IEEE (2016)
36. Duong, L., Cohn, T., Bird, S., Cook, P.: Low resource dependency parsing: cross-lingual parameter sharing in a neural network parser. In: ACL-IJCNLP 2015, pp. 845–850 (2015)
37. Yang, Y., Hospedales, T.M.: Trace norm regularised deep multi-task learning. In: ICLR 2017 (2017)
38. Søgaard, A., Goldberg, Y.: Deep multi-task learning with low level tasks supervised at lower layers. In: ACL 2016, pp. 231–235 (2016)
39. Hashimoto, K., Tsuruoka, Y., Socher, R., et al.: A joint many-task model: growing a neural network for multiple NLP tasks. In: EMNLP 2017, pp. 1923–1933 (2017)
40. Sanh, V., Wolf, T., Ruder, S.: A hierarchical multi-task approach for learning embeddings from semantic tasks. In: AAAI 2019, vol. 33, pp. 6949–6956 (2019)

41. Liu, S., Pan, S.J., Ho, Q.: Distributed multi-task relationship learning. In: ACM SIGKDD 2017, pp. 937–946. ACM (2017)
42. Kendall, A., Gal, Y., Cipolla, R.: Multi-task learning using uncertainty to weigh losses for scene geometry and semantics. In: CVPR 2018, pp. 7482–7491 (2018)
43. Liu, P., Qiu, X., Huang, X.: Recurrent neural network for text classification with multi-task learning. arXiv preprint arXiv:1605.05101 (2016)
44. Bousmalis, K., Trigeorgis, G., Silberman, N., Krishnan, D., Erhan, D.: Domain separation networks. In: NIPS 2016, pp. 343–351 (2016)
45. Abu-Mostafa, Y.S.: Learning from hints in neural networks. J. Complex. **6**, 192–198 (1990)
46. Yu, J., Jiang, J.: Learning sentence embeddings with auxiliary tasks for cross-domain sentiment classification. In: EMNLP 2016, pp. 236–246 (2016)
47. Caruana, R.: Multitask learning. Machine Learn. **28**, 41–75 (1997)
48. Liu, P., Qiu, X., Huang, X.: Deep multi-task learning with shared memory for text classification. In: EMNLP 2016 (2016)
49. Rei, M.: Semi-supervised multitask learning for sequence labeling. In: ACL 2017, pp. 2121–2130 (2017)
50. Bingel, J., Søgaard, A.: Identifying beneficial task relations for multi-task learning in deep neural networks. In: ACL 2015, pp. 164–169 (2017)
51. Doersch, C., Zisserman, A.: Multi-task self-supervised visual learning. In: ICCV 2017, pp. 2051–2060 (2017)
52. Zeiler, M.D., Fergus, R.: Visualizing and understanding convolutional networks. In: Fleet, D., Pajdla, T., Schiele, B., Tuytelaars, T. (eds.) ECCV 2014. LNCS, vol. 8689, pp. 818–833. Springer, Cham (2014). https://doi.org/10.1007/978-3-319-10590-1_53
53. Kolesnikov, A., Zhai, X., Beyer, L.: Revisiting self-supervised visual representation learning. arXiv preprint arXiv:1901.09005 (2019)
54. Devlin, J., Chang, M.W., Lee, K., Toutanova, K.: BERT: pre-training of deep bidirectional transformers for language understanding. arXiv preprint arXiv:1810.04805 (2018)
55. Zhang, R., Isola, P., Efros, A.A.: Colorful image colorization. In: Leibe, B., Matas, J., Sebe, N., Welling, M. (eds.) ECCV 2016. LNCS, vol. 9907, pp. 649–666. Springer, Cham (2016). https://doi.org/10.1007/978-3-319-46487-9_40
56. Doersch, C., Gupta, A., Efros, A.A.: Unsupervised visual representation learning by context prediction. In: ICCV 2015, pp. 1422–1430 (2015)
57. Gidaris, S., Singh, P., Komodakis, N.: Unsupervised representation learning by predicting image rotations. arXiv preprint arXiv:1803.07728 (2018)
58. Wei, D., Lim, J.J., Zisserman, A., Freeman, W.T.: Learning and using the arrow of time. In: CVPR 2018, pp. 8052–8060 (2018)
59. Misra, I., Zitnick, C.L., Hebert, M.: Shuffle and learn: unsupervised learning using temporal order verification. In: Leibe, B., Matas, J., Sebe, N., Welling, M. (eds.) ECCV 2016. LNCS, vol. 9905, pp. 527–544. Springer, Cham (2016). https://doi.org/10.1007/978-3-319-46448-0_32
60. Vondrick, C., Shrivastava, A., Fathi, A., Guadarrama, S., Murphy, K.: Tracking emerges by colorizing videos. In: Ferrari, V., Hebert, M., Sminchisescu, C., Weiss, Y. (eds.) ECCV 2018. LNCS, vol. 11217, pp. 402–419. Springer, Cham (2018). https://doi.org/10.1007/978-3-030-01261-8_24
61. Li, H., Li, Y., Porikli, F.: Deeptrack: learning discriminative feature representations online for robust visual tracking. IEEE TIP **25**, 1834–1848 (2016)
62. Goodfellow, I., et al.: Generative adversarial nets. In: NIPS 2014, pp. 2672–2680 (2014)

63. Ben-David, S., Blitzer, J., Crammer, K., Kulesza, A., Pereira, F., Vaughan, J.W.: A theory of learning from different domains. Machine Learn. **79**, 151–175 (2010)
64. Jia, Y., Salzmann, M., Darrell, T.: Factorized latent spaces with structured sparsity. In: NIPS 2010, pp. 982–990 (2010)
65. Real, E., Shlens, J., Mazzocchi, S., Pan, X., Vanhoucke, V.: Youtube-Boundingboxes: a large high-precision human-annotated data set for object detection in video. In: CVPR 2017, pp. 5296–5305 (2017)
66. Huang, L., Zhao, X., Huang, K.: Got-10k: a large high-diversity benchmark for generic object tracking in the wild. PAMI (2019)
67. Girshick, R., Donahue, J., Darrell, T., Malik, J.: Rich feature hierarchies for accurate object detection and semantic segmentation. In: CVPR 2014, pp. 580–587 (2014)
68. Meshgi, K., Oba, S., Ishii, S.: Efficient diverse ensemble for discriminative co-tracking: supplementary material. In: CVPR (2018)
69. Sung, K.K., Poggio, T.: Example-based learning for view-based human face detection. PAMI **20**, 39–51 (1998)
70. Baker, J.E.: Reducing bias and inefficiency in the selection algorithm. In: Proceedings of the Second International Conference on Genetic Algorithms (1987)
71. Lewis, D.D., Catlett, J.: Heterogeneous uncertainty sampling for supervised learning. In: ICML 1994, pp. 148–156 (1994)
72. Vedaldi, A., Lenc, K.: MatConvNet: convolutional neural networks for Matlab. In: Proceedings of the 23rd ACM International Conference on Multimedia, pp. 689–692. ACM (2015)
73. Wu, Y., Lim, J., Yang, M.H.: Online object tracking: a benchmark. In: CVPR 2013, pp. 2411–2418. IEEE (2013)
74. Wu, Y., Lim, J., Yang, M.H.: Object tracking benchmark. PAMI **37**, 1834–1848 (2015)
75. Fan, H., et al.: LaSOT: a high-quality benchmark for large-scale single object tracking. In: CVPR 2019 (2019)
76. Mueller, M., Smith, N., Ghanem, B.: A benchmark and simulator for UAV tracking. In: Leibe, B., Matas, J., Sebe, N., Welling, M. (eds.) ECCV 2016. LNCS, vol. 9905, pp. 445–461. Springer, Cham (2016). https://doi.org/10.1007/978-3-319-46448-0_27
77. Müller, M., Bibi, A., Giancola, S., Alsubaihi, S., Ghanem, B.: TrackingNet: a large-scale dataset and benchmark for object tracking in the wild. In: Ferrari, V., Hebert, M., Sminchisescu, C., Weiss, Y. (eds.) ECCV 2018. LNCS, vol. 11205, pp. 310–327. Springer, Cham (2018). https://doi.org/10.1007/978-3-030-01246-5_19
78. Kristan, M., et al.: The sixth visual object tracking VOT2018 challenge results. In: Leal-Taixé, L., Roth, S. (eds.) ECCV 2018. LNCS, vol. 11129, pp. 3–53. Springer, Cham (2019). https://doi.org/10.1007/978-3-030-11009-3_1
79. Bhat, G., Danelljan, M., Gool, L.V., Timofte, R.: Learning discriminative model prediction for tracking. In: ICCV 2019 (2019)
80. Danelljan, M., Bhat, G., Khan, F.S., Felsberg, M.: ATOM: accurate tracking by overlap maximization. In: CVPR 2019 (2019)
81. Zhu, Z., et al.: STResNet_cf tracker: the deep spatiotemporal features learning for correlation filter based robust visual object tracking. IEEE Access **7**, 30142–30156 (2019)
82. Zhou, Y., et al.: Efficient correlation tracking via center-biased spatial regularization. TIP **27**, 6159–6173 (2018)

83. Jung, I., Son, J., Baek, M., Han, B.: Real-time MDNet. In: Ferrari, V., Hebert, M., Sminchisescu, C., Weiss, Y. (eds.) ECCV 2018. LNCS, vol. 11208, pp. 89–104. Springer, Cham (2018). https://doi.org/10.1007/978-3-030-01225-0_6

84. Feichtenhofer, C., Pinz, A., Zisserman, A.: Convolutional two-stream network fusion for video action recognition. In: CVPR 2016 (2016)

85. Karpathy, A., Toderici, G., Shetty, S., Leung, T., Sukthankar, R., Fei-Fei, L.: Large-scale video classification with convolutional neural networks. In: CVPR 2014 (2014)

86. Kalal, Z., Mikolajczyk, K., Matas, J.: Tracking-learning-detection. PAMI **34**, 1409–1422 (2012)

87. Hare, S., Saffari, A., Torr, P.H.: Struck: structured output tracking with kernels. In: ICCV 2011 (2011)

88. Gao, J., Ling, H., Hu, W., Xing, J.: Transfer learning based visual tracking with Gaussian processes regression. In: Fleet, D., Pajdla, T., Schiele, B., Tuytelaars, T. (eds.) ECCV 2014. LNCS, vol. 8691, pp. 188–203. Springer, Cham (2014). https://doi.org/10.1007/978-3-319-10578-9_13

89. Zhang, J., Ma, S., Sclaroff, S.: MEEM: Robust tracking via multiple experts using entropy minimization. In: Fleet, D., Pajdla, T., Schiele, B., Tuytelaars, T. (eds.) ECCV 2014. LNCS, vol. 8694, pp. 188–203. Springer, Cham (2014). https://doi.org/10.1007/978-3-319-10599-4_13

90. Hong, Z., Chen, Z., Wang, C., Mei, X., Prokhorov, D., Tao, D.: Multi-store tracker (muster): a cognitive psychology inspired approach to object tracking. In: CVPR 2015

91. Bertinetto, L., Valmadre, J., Golodetz, S., Miksik, O., Torr, P.H.: Staple: complementary learners for real-time tracking. In: CVPR 2016, pp. 1401–1409 (2016)

92. Meshgi, K., Oba, S., Ishii, S.: Active discriminative tracking using collective memory. In: MVA 2017

93. Danelljan, M., Hager, G., Shahbaz Khan, F., Felsberg, M.: Learning spatially regularized correlation filters for visual tracking. In: ICCV 2015, pp. 4310–4318 (2015)

94. Danelljan, M., Robinson, A., Shahbaz Khan, F., Felsberg, M.: Beyond correlation filters: learning continuous convolution operators for visual tracking. In: Leibe, B., Matas, J., Sebe, N., Welling, M. (eds.) ECCV 2016. LNCS, vol. 9909, pp. 472–488. Springer, Cham (2016). https://doi.org/10.1007/978-3-319-46454-1_29

95. Danelljan, M., Hager, G., Shahbaz Khan, F., Felsberg, M.: Convolutional features for correlation filter based visual tracking. In: ICCVw, pp. 58–66 (2015)

96. Kiani Galoogahi, H., Fagg, A., Lucey, S.: Learning background-aware correlation filters for visual tracking. In: ICCV 2017

97. Li, F., et al.: Learning spatial-temporal regularized correlation filters for visual tracking. In: CVPR 2018 (2018)

98. Danelljan, M., Bhat, G., Khan, F.S., Felsberg, M.: ECO: efficient convolution operators for tracking. In: CVPR (2017)

99. Zhu, Z., Wang, Q., Li, B., Wu, W., Yan, J., Hu, W.: Distractor-aware Siamese networks for visual object tracking. In: Ferrari, V., Hebert, M., Sminchisescu, C., Weiss, Y. (eds.) ECCV 2018. LNCS, vol. 11213, pp. 103–119. Springer, Cham (2018). https://doi.org/10.1007/978-3-030-01240-3_7

100. Wang, X., Yang, R., Sun, T., Luo, B.: Learning target-aware attention for robust tracking with conditional adversarial network. In: BMVC, p. 131 (2019)

101. Huang, L., Zhao, X., Huang, K.: GlobalTrack: a simple and strong baseline for long-term tracking. AAAI (2020)

Tracking-by-Trackers with a Distilled and Reinforced Model

Matteo Dunnhofer$^{(\boxtimes)}$ (ID), Niki Martinel (ID), and Christian Micheloni (ID)

Machine Learning and Perception Lab, University of Udine, Udine, Italy
{matteo.dunnhofer,niki.martinel,christian.micheloni}@uniud.it

Abstract. Visual object tracking was generally tackled by reasoning independently on fast processing algorithms, accurate online adaptation methods, and fusion of trackers. In this paper, we unify such goals by proposing a novel tracking methodology that takes advantage of other visual trackers, offline and online. A compact student model is trained via the marriage of knowledge distillation and reinforcement learning. The first allows to transfer and compress tracking knowledge of other trackers. The second enables the learning of evaluation measures which are then exploited online. After learning, the student can be ultimately used to build (i) a very fast single-shot tracker, (ii) a tracker with a simple and effective online adaptation mechanism, (iii) a tracker that performs fusion of other trackers. Extensive validation shows that the proposed algorithms compete with real-time state-of-the-art trackers.

1 Introduction

Visual object tracking corresponds to the persistent recognition and localization –by means of bounding boxes– of a target object in consecutive video frames. This problem comes with several different challenges including object occlusion and fast motion, light changes, and motion blur. Additionally, real-time constraints are often posed by the many practical applications, such as video surveillance, behavior understanding, autonomous driving, and robotics.

In the past, the community has proposed solutions emphasizing different aspects of the problem. Processing speed was pursued by algorithms like correlation filters [1–5] or offline methods such as siamese convolutional neural networks (CNNs) [6–12]. Improved performance was attained by online target adaptation methods [13–17]. Higher tracking accuracy and robustness were achieved by methods built on top of other trackers [18–22]. All these characteristics belong to an optimal tracker but they were studied one independently from the other. The community currently lacks a general framework to tackle them jointly. In this view, a single model should be able to (i) track an object in a fast way, (ii) implement simple and effective online adaptation mechanisms, (iii) apply decision-making strategies to select tracker outputs.

Electronic supplementary material The online version of this chapter (https://doi.org/10.1007/978-3-030-69532-3_38) contains supplementary material, which is available to authorized users.

© Springer Nature Switzerland AG 2021
H. Ishikawa et al. (Eds.): ACCV 2020, LNCS 12623, pp. 631–650, 2021.
https://doi.org/10.1007/978-3-030-69532-3_38

It is a matter of fact that a large number of tracking algorithms has been produced so far, with different principles exploited. Preliminary solutions were based on mean shift algorithms [23], key-point [24] or part-based methods [25,26], or SVM learning [27]. Later, correlation filters gained popularity thanks to their fast processing times [1–5]. Since more recently, CNNs have been exploited to extract efficient image features. This kind of representation has been included in deep regression networks [6,7], online tracking-by-detection methods [13,14], solutions that treat visual tracking as a reinforcement learning (RL) problem [28–33], CNN-based discriminative correlation filters [15–17,34], and in siamese CNNs [8–10,12,35,36]. Other methods tried to take advantage of the output produced by multiple trackers [18–22]. Thus, one can imagine that different trackers incorporate different knowledge, and this may constitute a valuable resource to leverage during tracking.

Lately, the knowledge distillation (KD) framework [37] was introduced in the deep learning panorama as paradigm for, among the many [38–41], knowledge transferring between models [42] and model compression [43–45]. The idea boils down into considering a student model and one or more teacher models to learn from. Teachers explicit their knowledge through demonstrations on a never seen before transfer set. Through specific loss functions, the student is set to learn a task by matching the teachers' output and the ground-truth labels. As visual tracking requires fast and accurate methods, KD can be a valuable tool to transfer the tracking ability of more accurate teacher trackers to more compact and faster student ones. However, the standard setup of KD does not provide methods to exploit teachers online, but just offline. This makes this methodology unsuitable for tracking, which has been shown to benefit from both offline and online methods [15–17,28,32]. In contrast to such an issue, RL techniques offer established methodologies to optimize not only policies but also policy evaluation functions [46–50], which are then used to extract decision strategies. Along with this, RL also gives the possibility to maximize arbitrary and non-differentiable performance measures, and thus more tracking oriented objectives can be defined.

For the aforementioned motivations, the contribution of this paper is a novel tracking methodology where a student model exploits off-the-shelf trackers offline and online (tracking-by-trackers). The student is first trained via an effective strategy that combines KD and RL. After that, the model's compressed knowledge can be used interchangeably depending on the application's needs. We will show how to exploit the student in three setups which result in, respectively, (i) a fast tracker (TRAS), (ii) a tracker with a simple online mechanism (TRAST), and (iii) a tracker capable of expert tracker fusion (TRASFUST). Through extensive evaluation procedures, it will be demonstrated that each of the algorithms competes with the respective state-of-the-art class of trackers while performing in real-time.

2   Related Work

Visual Tracking. Here we review the trackers most related to ours. The network architecture implemented by the proposed student model takes inspiration from GOTURN [6] and RE3 [7]. These regression-based CNNs were shown to capture the target's motion while performing very fast. However, the learning strategy employed optimizes parameters just for coordinate difference. Moreover, great amount of data is needed to make such models achieve good accuracy. In contrast, our KD-RL-based method offers parameter optimization for overlap maximization and extracts previously acquired knowledge from other trackers requiring less labeled data. Online adaptation methods like discriminative model learning [13,14,51] or discriminative correlation filters [15–17] have been studied extensively to improve tracking accuracy. These procedures are time-consuming and require particular assumptions and careful design. We propose a simple online update strategy where an off-the-shelf tracker is used to correct the performance of the student model. Our method does not make any assumption on such tracker, and thus it can be freely selected to adapt to application needs. Present fusion models exploit trackers in the form of discriminative trackers [18], CNN feature layers [52], correlation filters [53] or out-of-the-box tracking algorithms [19–22]. However, such models work just online and do not take advantage of the great amount of offline knowledge that expert trackers can provide. Furthermore, they are not able to track objects without them. Our student model addresses these issues thanks to the decision making strategy learned via KD and RL.

KD and RL. We review the learning strategies most related to ours. KD techniques have been used for transferring knowledge between teacher and student models [37,54], where the supervised learning setting was employed more [38–40,42] than the setup that uses RL [55,56]. In the context of computer vision, KD was employed for action recognition [57,58], object detection [43,59], semantic segmentation [60,61], person re-identification [62]. In the visual tracking panorama, KD was explored in [63,64] to compress, CNN representations for correlation filter trackers and siamese network architectures, respectively. However, these works offer methods involving teachers specifically designed as correlation filter and siamese trackers, and so cannot be adapted to generic-approach visual trackers as we propose in this paper. Moreover, to the best of our knowledge, no method mixing KD and RL is currently present in the computer vision literature. Our learning procedure is also related to the strategies that use deep RL to learn tracking policies [28,29,31,32,65]. Our formulation shares some characteristics with such methods in the markov decision process (MDP) definition, but our proposed learning algorithm is different as no present method leverages on teachers to learn the policy.

3 Methodology

The key point of this paper is to learn a simple and fast student model with versatile tracking abilities. KD is used for transferring the tracking knowledge of off-the-shelf trackers to a compressed model. However, as both offline and online strategies are necessary for tracking [16,17,28,32], we propose to augment the

KD framework with an RL optimization objective. RL techniques deliver unified optimization strategies to directly maximize a desired performance measure (in our case the overlap between prediction and ground-truth bounding boxes) and to predict the expectation of such measure. We use the latter as base for an online evaluation and selection strategy. Put in other words, combining KD and RL lets the student model extract a tracking policy from teachers, improve it, and express its quality through an overlap-based objective.

3.1   Preliminaries

Given a transfer set of videos $\mathcal{D} = \{\mathcal{V}_0, \cdots, \mathcal{V}_{|\mathcal{D}|}\}$, we consider the j-th video $\mathcal{V}_j = \{F_t \in \mathcal{I}\}_{t=0}^{T_j}$ as a sequence of frames F_t, where $\mathcal{I} = \{0, \cdots, 255\}^{w \times h \times 3}$ is the space of RGB images. Let $b_t = [x_t, y_t, w_t, h_t] \in \mathbb{R}^4$ be the t-th bounding box defining the coordinates of the top left corner, and the width and height of the rectangle that contains the target object. At time t, given the current frame F_t, the goal of the tracker is to predict b_t that best fits the target in F_t. We formally consider the student model as $\mathbf{s} : \mathcal{I} \to \mathbb{R}^4 \times \mathbb{R}$ that is a function which outputs the relative motion between b_{t-1} and b_t, and the performance evaluation v_t, when inputted with frame F_t. Similarly, we define the set of tracking teachers as $\mathbf{T} = \{\mathbf{t} : \mathcal{I} \to \mathbb{R}^4\}$ where each $\mathbf{t}$ is a function that, given a frame image, produces a bounding box estimate for that frame.

3.2   Visual Tracking as an MDP

In our setting, $\mathbf{s}$ is treated as an artificial agent which interacts with an MDP defined over a video $\mathcal{V}_j$. The interaction happens through a temporal sequence of states $s_1, s_2, \cdots, s_t \in \mathcal{S}$, actions $a_1, a_2, \cdots, a_t \in \mathcal{A}$ and rewards $r_1, r_2, \cdots, r_t \in [-1, 1]$. In the t-th frame, the student is provided with the state s_t and outputs the continuous action a_t which consists in the relative motion of the target object, i.e. it indicates how its bounding box, which is known in frame $t - 1$, should move to enclose the target in the frame t. a_t is rewarded by the measure of its quality r_t. We refer this interaction process as the episode E_j, which dynamics are defined by the MDP $M_j = (\mathcal{S}, \mathcal{A}, r, f)$.

States. Every $s_t \in \mathcal{S}$ is defined as a pair of image patches obtained by cropping F_{t-1} and F_t using b_{t-1}. Specifically, $s_t = \rho(F_{t-1}, F_t, b_{t-1}, c)$, where $\rho(\cdot)$ crops the frames F_{t-1}, F_t within the area of the bounding box $b'_{t-1} = [x'_{t-1}, y'_{t-1}, c \cdot w_{t-1}, c \cdot h_{t-1}]$ that has the same center coordinates of b_{t-1} but which width and height are scaled by c. By selecting $c > 1$, we can control the amount of additional image context information to be provided to the student.

Actions and State Transition. Each $a_t \in \mathcal{A}$ consists in a vector $a_t = [\Delta x_t, \Delta y_t, \Delta w_t, \Delta h_t] \in [-1, 1]^4$ which defines the relative horizontal and vertical translations ($\Delta x_t, \Delta y_t$, respectively) and width and height scale variations

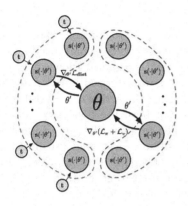

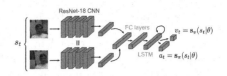

Fig. 2. The student architecture is composed by two branches of convolutional layers (gray boxes) with shared weights followed by, two fully-connected layers (orange boxes), an LSTM layer (in green) and two parallel fully connected layers for the prediction of v_t and a_t respectively. (Color figure online)

Fig. 1. Scheme of the proposed KD-RL-based learning framework. S students interact independently with M_j. After each E_j done, a copy θ' of the shared weights θ is sent to each one. Every t_{max} steps each student send the computed gradients to apply an update on θ. The distilling students (highlighted by the orange dashed contour) extract knowledge from teachers $\mathbf{t}$ by optimizing $\mathcal{L}_{\text{dist}}$. Autonomous students (circled with the blue dashed contour) learn an autonomous tracking policy by optimizing jointly $\mathcal{L}_\pi$ and $\mathcal{L}_v$. (Color figure online)

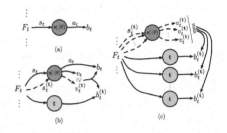

Fig. 3. Visual representation showing how the student and teachers are employed in the proposed trackers at every frame F_t. (a) represents TRAS, (b) TRAST, and (c) TRASFUST.

($\Delta w_t, \Delta h_t$, respectively) that have to be applied to b_{t-1} to predict b_t. The latter step is obtained through $\psi : \mathcal{A} \times \mathbb{R}^4 \to \mathbb{R}^4$.[1] After performing a_t, the student moves through f from s_t to s_{t+1} which is defined as the pair of cropped images obtained from F_t and F_{t+1} using b_t.

Reward. The reward function expresses the quality of a_t taken at s_t and it is used to feedback the student. Our reward definition is based on the Intersection-over-Union (IoU) metric computed between b_t and the ground-truth bounding box, denoted as g_t, i.e.,

$$\text{IoU}(b_t, g_t) = (b_t \cap g_t)/(b_t \cup g_t) \in [0, 1]. \tag{1}$$

At every interaction step t, the reward is formally defined as

$$r_t = r(b_t, g_t) = \begin{cases} \omega\left(\text{IoU}(b_t, g_t)\right) & \text{if } \text{IoU}(b_t, g_t) \geq 0.5 \\ -1 & \text{otherwise} \end{cases} \tag{2}$$

with $\omega(z) = 2(\lfloor z \rfloor_{0.05}) - 1$ that floors to the closest 0.05 digit and shifts the input range from $[0, 1]$ to $[-1, 1]$.

---

[1] Please refer to Appendix A.1 for the definition of $\psi(\cdot)$.

3.3 Learning Tracking from Teachers

The student s is first trained in an offline stage. Through KD, knowledge is transferred from $\mathbf{T}$ to $\mathbf{s}$. By means of RL, such knowledge is improved and the ability of evaluating its quality is also acquired. All the gained knowledge will be used for online tracking. We implement $\mathbf{s}$ as a parameterized function $\mathbf{s}(s_t|\theta)$: $\mathcal{S} \to \mathcal{A} \times \mathbb{R}$ that given s_t outputs at the same time the action a_t and state-value v_t. In RL terms, $\mathbf{s}$ maintains representations of both the policy $\mathbf{s}_\pi : \mathcal{S} \to \mathcal{A}$ and the state value $\mathbf{s}_v : \mathcal{S} \to \mathbb{R}$ functions. The proposed learning framework, which is depicted in Fig. 1, provides a single offline end-to-end learning stage. S students are distributed as parallel and independent learning agents. Each one owns a set of learnable weights θ' that are used to generate experience by interacting with M_j. The obtained experience, in the form of $\nabla_{\theta'}$, is used to update asynchronously a shared set of weights θ. After ending E_j, each student updates its θ' by copying the values of the currently available θ. The entire procedure is repeated until convergence. This learning architecture follows the recent trends in RL that make use of distributed algorithms to speed up the training phase [50,66,67]. We devote half of the students, which we refer to as distilling students, in acquiring knowledge from the teachers' tracking policy. The other half, called autonomous students, learn to track by interacting with M_j autonomously.

Distilling Students. Each distilling student interacts with M_j by observing states, performing actions and receiving rewards just as an autonomous student. However, to distill knowledge independently from the teachers' inner structure, we propose the student to learn from the actions of $\mathbf{t} \in \mathbf{T}$, which are executed in parallel. In particular, $\mathbf{t}$ is exploited every t_{max} steps with the following loss function

$$\mathcal{L}_{\text{dist}} = \sum_{i=1}^{t_{max}} |a_t^{(\mathbf{t})} - \mathbf{s}_\pi(s_t|\theta')| \cdot m_i, \tag{3}$$

which is the L1 loss between the actions performed by the student and the actions $a_t^{(\mathbf{t})} = \phi(b_t^{(\mathbf{t})}, b_{t-1})$ that the teacher would take to move the student's bounding box b_{t-1} into the teacher's prediction $b_t^{(\mathbf{t})}$.[2] At every t, $\mathbf{t}$ is selected as

$$\mathbf{t} \in \mathbf{T} : \text{IoU}(b_t^{(\mathbf{t})}, g_t) = \max_{\mathbf{t} \in \mathbf{T}} \text{IoU}(b_t^{(\mathbf{t})}, g_t) \tag{4}$$

as we would like to learn always from the best teacher. The absolute values are multiplied by $m_i \in \{0, 1\}$. Each of these is computed along the interaction and determines the status in which $\mathbf{s}$ performed worse than $\mathbf{t}$ ($m_i = 1$) or better ($m_i = 0$) in terms of the rewards $r(s_t, a_t)$ and $r(s_t, a_t^{(\mathbf{t})})$. The whole Eq. (3) is similar to what proposed in [43] for KD from bounding-box predictions of object detectors. However, here we provide a temporal formulation of such objective and

---

[2] Please refer to Appendix A.1 for the definition of $\phi(\cdot)$.

we swap the L2 loss with the L1, which was shown to work better for regression-based trackers [6,7]. By optimizing Eq. (3), the weights θ are changed only if the student's performance is lower than the performance of the teacher. In this way, we make the teacher transferring its knowledge by suggesting actions only in bad performing cases. In the others, we let the student free to follow its current tracking policy since it is superior.

Autonomous Students. The learning process performed by the autonomous students follows the standard RL method for continuous control [68]. Each student interacts with M_j for a maximum of t_{max} steps. At each step t, the students sample actions from a normal distribution $\mathcal{N}(\mu, \sigma)$, where the mean is defined as the student's predicted action, $\mu = \mathbf{s}_\pi(s_t|\theta')$, and the standard deviation is obtained as $\sigma = |\mathbf{s}_\pi(s_t|\theta') - \phi(g_t, b_{t-1})|$ (which is the absolute value of the difference between the student's action and the action that obtains, by shifting b_{t-1}, the ground-truth bounding box g_t). Intuitively, $\mathcal{N}$ shrinks when a_t is close to the ground-truth action $\phi(g_t, b_{t-1})$, reducing the chance of choosing potential wrong actions when approaching the correct one. On the other hand, when a_t is distant from $\phi(g_t, b_{t-1})$, $\mathcal{N}$ spreads letting the student explore more. The students also predict $v_t = \mathbf{s}_v(s_t|\theta)$ which is the cumulative reward that the student expects to receive from s_t to the end of the interaction. Since the proposed reward definition is a direct measure of the IoU occurring between the predicted and the ground-truth bounding boxes, $\mathbf{s}_v(s_t|\theta)$ gives an estimate of the total amount of IoU that $\mathbf{s}$ expects to obtain from state s_t on wards. Thus, this function can be exploited as a future-performance evaluator. After t_{max} steps of interaction, the gradient to update the shared weights θ is built as

$$\nabla_{\theta'}(\mathcal{L}_\pi + \mathcal{L}_v) \tag{5}$$

$$\mathcal{L}_\pi = -\sum_{i=1}^{t_{max}} \log \mathbf{s}_\pi(s_i|\theta')\big(r_i + \gamma \mathbf{s}_v(s_{i+1}|\theta') - \mathbf{s}_v(s_i|\theta')\big) \tag{6}$$

$$\mathcal{L}_v = \sum_{i=1}^{t_{max}} \frac{1}{2}\big(R_i - \mathbf{s}_v(s_i|\theta')\big)^2, R_i = \sum_{k=1}^{i} \gamma^{k-1} r_k \tag{7}$$

where (6) is the policy loss and (7) is the value loss. These definitions follow the standard advantage actor-critic objective [48].

To further facilitate and improve the learning, a curriculum learning strategy [69] is built for each parallel student. During learning, the length of the interaction is increased as $\mathbf{s}$ performs better than $\mathbf{T}$. Details are given in Appendix A.2.

3.4   Student Architecture

The architecture used to maintain the representation of both the policy $\mathbf{s}_\pi$ and the state value $\mathbf{s}_v$ functions, which is pictured in Fig. 2, is simple and presents a structure similar to the one proposed in [6,7]. The network gets as input two image patches that pass through two ResNet-18 based [38] convolutional branches that share weights. The feature maps produced by the branches are first linearized, then concatenated together and finally fed to two consecutive fully connected layers with ReLU activations. After that, features are given to an LSTM [70] layer. Both the fully connected layers and the LSTM are composed of 512 neurons. The output of the LSTM is ultimately fed to two separate fully connected heads, one that outputs the action $a_t = \mathbf{s}_\pi(s_t|\theta)$ and the other that outputs the value of the state $v_t = \mathbf{s}_v(s_t|\theta)$.

3.5   Tracking After Learning

After the learning process, the student $\mathbf{s}(\cdot|\theta)$ is ready to be used for tracking. Here we describe three different ways in which $\mathbf{s}(\cdot|\theta)$ can be exploited:

1. the student's learned policy $\mathbf{s}_\pi(s_t|\theta)$ is used to predict bounding boxes b_t independently from the teachers. We call this setting TRAS (TRAcking Student).
2. the learned policy $\mathbf{s}_\pi(s_t|\theta)$ and value function $\mathbf{s}_v(s_t|\theta)$ are used to, respectively, predict b_t and evaluate $\mathbf{s}$ and $\mathbf{t} \in \mathbf{T}$ tracking behaviors, in order to correct the former's performance. We refer to this setup as TRAST (TRAcking Student and Teacher).
3. the learned state-value function $\mathbf{s}_v(s_t|\theta)$ is used to evaluate the performance of the pool of teachers $\mathbf{T}$ in order to choose the best $b_t^{(t)}$ and perform tracker fusion. We call this setup TRASFUST (TRAcking by Student FUSing Teachers).

In the following, we provide more details about the three settings. For a better understanding, the setups are visualized in Fig. 3.

TRAS. In this setting, each tracking sequence $\mathcal{V}_j$, with target object outlined by g_0, is considered as M_j described in Sect. 3.2. States s_t are extracted from frames F_{t-1}, F_t, actions are performed by means of the student's learned policy $a_t = \mathbf{s}_\pi(s_t|\theta)$ and are used to output the bounding boxes $b_t = \psi(a_t, b_{t-1})$. This setup is fast as it requires just a forward pass through the network to obtain a bounding box prediction.

TRAST. In this setup, the student makes use of the learned $\mathbf{s}_\pi(s_t|\theta)$ to predict b_t and $\mathbf{s}_v(s_t|\theta)$ to evaluate its running tracking quality and the one of $\mathbf{t} \in \mathbf{T}$ which is run in parallel. In particular, at each time step t, $v_t = \mathbf{s}_v(s_t|\theta)$ and $v_t^{(t)} = \mathbf{s}_v(s_t^{(t)}|\theta)$ are obtained as performance evaluation for $\mathbf{s}$ and $\mathbf{t}$ respectively. The teacher state is obtained as $s_t^{(t)} = \rho(F_{t-1}, F_t, b_{t-1}^{(t)}, c)$. By comparing the two expected returns, TRAST decides if to output the student's or the teacher's bounding box. More formally, if $v_t \geq v_t^{(t)}$ then $b_t := \psi(a_t, b_{t-1})$ otherwise $b_t := b_t^{(t)}$. This assignment has the side effect of correcting the tracking behaviour of the student as, at the successive time step, the previously known bounding

Table 1. Teacher-based statistics of the transfer set.

Teachers	$\beta = 0.5$			$\beta = 0.6$			$\beta = 0.7$			$\beta = 0.8$			$\beta = 0.9$		
	# traj	AO	$|\mathcal{D}|$	# traj	AO	$|\mathcal{D}|$	# traj	AO	$|\mathcal{D}|$	# traj	AO	$|\mathcal{D}|$	# traj	AO	$|\mathcal{D}|$
T_K	1884	0.798	9225	1097	0.836	5349	439	0.873	2122	73	0.914	356	0	0.0	0
T_M	1600	0.767	7859	781	0.808	3831	216	0.851	1052	18	0.898	86	0	0.0	0
T_E	2754	0.808	13526	1659	0.843	8122	720	0.879	3507	160	0.915	773	1	0.954	4
T_S	3913	0.829	19259	2646	0.854	12997	1447	0.878	7080	431	0.908	2097	9	0.947	42
T_P	4519	0.840	22252	3092	0.863	15195	1698	0.887	8307	496	0.915	2414	10	0.948	46

box becomes the previous prediction of the teacher. Thus, the online adaption consists in a very simple procedure that evaluates t's performance to eventually pass control to it. Notice that, at every t, the execution of t is independent from s as the second does not need the first to finish because the evaluations are done based on the predictions given at $t - 1$. Hence, the executions of the two can be put in parallel, with the overall speed of TRAST resulting is the lowest between the one of s and t.

TRASFUST. In this tracking setup, just the student's learned state-value function $\mathbf{s}_v(s_t|\theta)$ is exploited. At each step t, teachers $t \in \mathbf{T}$ are executed following their standard methodology. States $s_t^{(t)} = \rho(F_{t-1}, F_t, b_{t-1}^{(t)}, c) \, \forall t \in \mathbf{T}$ are obtained. The performance evaluation of the teachers is obtained through the student as $v_t^{(t)} = \mathbf{s}_v(s_t^{(t)}|\theta)$. The output bounding box is selected as $b_t = b^{(t')}$ by considering the teacher t' that achieves the highest expected return, i.e.

$$t' \in \mathbf{T} \, : \, v_t^{(t')} = \max_{t \in \mathbf{T}} v_t^{(t)}. \tag{8}$$

This procedure consists in fusing sequence-wise the predictions of $\mathbf{T}$ and, similarly as for TRAST, the execution of teachers and student can be put in parallel. In such setting, the speed of TRASFUST results in the lowest between the ones of s and of each $t \in \mathbf{T}$.

4   Experimental Results

4.1   Experimental Setup

Teachers. The tracking teachers selected for this work are KCF [2], MDNet [13], ECO [15], SiamRPN [9], ATOM [16], and DiMP [17], due to their established popularity in the visual tracking panorama. Moreover, since they tackle visual tracking by different approaches, they can provide knowledge of various quality. In experiments, we considered exploiting single teacher or a pool of teachers. In particular, the following sets of teachers were examined $\mathbf{T}_K = \{\texttt{KCF}\}, \mathbf{T}_M = \{\texttt{MDNet}\}, \mathbf{T}_E = \{\texttt{ECO}\}, \mathbf{T}_S = \{\texttt{SiamRPN}\}, \mathbf{T}_A = \{\texttt{ATOM}\}, \mathbf{T}_D = \{\texttt{DiMP}\}, \mathbf{T}_P = \{\texttt{KCF}, \texttt{MDNet}, \texttt{ECO}, \texttt{SiamRPN}\}$.

Transfer Set. The selected transfer set was the training set of GOT-10k dataset [71], due to its large scale. Just $\mathbf{T}_K, \mathbf{T}_M, \mathbf{T}_E, \mathbf{T}_S$ were used for offline learning, as none of these was trained on this dataset. This is an important point because unbiased examples of the trackers' behavior should be exploited to train the student. Moreover, predictions that exhibit meaningful knowledge should be retained. Therefore, we filtered out all the videos $\mathcal{V}_j$ which teacher predictions did not satisfy $\text{IoU}(b_t^{(t)}, g_t) > \beta$ for all $t \in \{1, \ldots, T_j\}$. We considered $\beta = 0.5$ as minimum threshold for a prediction to be considered positive, and we then varied β among 0.6, 0.7, 0.8, 0.9 for more precise predictions. To produce more training samples, videos, and filtered trajectories were split in five randomly indexed sequences of 32 frames and bounding boxes, similarly as done in [7]. In Table 1 a summary of $\mathcal{D}$ is presented. The number of positive trajectories, the average overlap (AO) [71] on the transfer set, and the total number of sequences $|\mathcal{D}|$ are reported per teacher and per β.

Benchmarks and Performance Measures. We performed performance evaluations on the GOT-10k test set [71], UAV123 [72], LaSOT [73], OTB-100 [74] and VOT2019 [75] datasets. These offer videos of various nature and difficulty, and are all popular benchmarks in the visual tracking community. The evaluation protocol used for GOT-10k is the one-pass evaluation (OPE) [74], along with the metrics: AO, and success rates (SR) with overlap thresholds 0.50 and 0.75. For UAV123, LaSOT, and OTB-100 the OPE method was considered with the area-under-the-curve (AUC) of the success and precision plot, referred to as success score (SS) and precision scores (PS) respectively [74]. Evaluation on VOT2019 is performed in terms of expected average overlap (EAO), accuracy (A), and robustness (R) [76]. Further details about the benchmarks are given in Appendix B.

Implementation Details. The image crops of s_s were resized to $[128 \times 128 \times 3]$ pixels and standardized by the mean and standard deviation calculated on the ImageNet dataset [77]. The ResNet-18 weights were pre-trained for image classification on the same dataset [77]. The image context factor c was set to 1.5. The training videos were processed in chunks of 32 frames. At test time, every 32 frames, the LSTM's hidden state is reset to the one obtained after the first student prediction (i.e. $t = 1$), following [7]. Due to hardware constraints, a maximum of $S = 24$ training students were distributed on 4 NVIDIA TITAN V GPUs of a machine with an Intel Xeon E5-2690 v4 @ 2.60 GHz CPU and 320 GB of RAM. The discount factor γ was set to 1. The length of the interaction before an update was defined in $t_{max} = 5$ steps. The Radam optimizer [78] was employed and the learning rate for both distilling and autonomous students was set to 10^{-6}. A weight decay of 10^{-4} was also added to $\mathcal{L}_{\text{dist}}$ as regularization term. To control the magnitude of the gradients and stabilize learning, $(\mathcal{L}_\pi + \mathcal{L}_v)$ was multiplied by 10^{-3}. The student was trained until the validation performance on the GOT-10k validation set stopped improving. Longest trainings took around

Table 2. Performance of the proposed trackers. Results of removing some components of our methodology are also reported. Best values, per contribution, are highlighted in red. Please check the online version of this paper for colors.

Contribution	GOT-10k			UAV123		LaSOT		OTB-100	
	AO	$SR_{0.50}$	$SR_{0.75}$	SS	PS	SS	PS	SS	PS
TRAS-GT	0.444	0.495	0.286	0.483	0.616	0.331	0.271	0.438	0.581
TRAS-KD-GT	0.448	0.499	0.305	0.491	0.630	0.354	0.298	0.448	0.606
TRAS-KD	0.422	0.481	0.239	0.494	0.634	0.340	0.276	0.457	0.635
TRAS-no-curr	0.474	0.547	0.307	0.501	0.644	0.385	0.323	0.447	0.600
TRAS	0.484	0.556	0.326	0.515	0.655	0.386	0.330	0.481	0.644
TRAST-no-curr	0.530	0.630	0.347	0.602	0.770	0.484	0.464	0.595	0.794
TRAST	0.531	0.626	0.345	0.603	0.773	0.490	0.470	0.604	0.818
TRASFUST-no-curr	0.506	0.599	0.278	0.627	0.819	0.496	0.484	0.665	0.879
TRASFUST	0.519	0.616	0.287	0.628	0.823	0.510	0.505	0.660	0.890

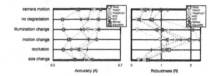

Fig. 4. Visual example of how TRAST relies effectively on the teacher, passing control to $\mathbf{T_S}$ and saving the simple student (TRAS) from the drift.

Fig. 5. Analysis of the accuracy (A) and robustness (R) on VOT2019 over different classes of tracking sequences.

10 days. The speed of the parallel setups of TRAST and TRASFUST was computed by considering the speed of the slowest tracker (student or teacher) plus an overhead. Code was implemented in Python and is available here[3]. Source code publicly available was used to implement the teacher trackers. Default configurations were respected as much as possible. For a fair comparison, we report the results of such implementations, that have slightly different performance than stated in the original papers.

4.2 Results

In the following sections, when not specified, the three tracker setups regard the student trained using $\mathbf{T_P}$ and $\beta = 0.5$, paired with $\mathbf{T_S}$ in TRAST, and managing $\mathbf{T_P}$ in TRASFUST.

General Remarks. In Table 2 the performance of TRAS, TRAST, TRASFUST are reported, while the performances of the teachers are presented

---

[3] https://github.com/dontfollowmeimcrazy/vot-kd-rl.

Table 3. Performance of the proposed trackers while considering different teacher setups for training and tracking. Best results per tracker are highlighted in red, second-best in blue. Please check the online version of this paper for colors.

	Training Teachers	Tracking Teachers	GOT-10k			UAV123		LaSOT		OTB-100		FPS
			AO	$SR_{0.50}$	$SR_{0.75}$	SS	PS	SS	PS	SS	PS	
TRAS	T_K	-	0.371	0.418	0.178	0.464	0.598	0.321	0.241	0.390	0.524	90
	T_M	-	0.414	0.473	0.214	0.462	0.606	0.336	0.262	0.390	0.545	
	T_E	-	0.422	0.484	0.232	0.507	0.652	0.357	0.286	0.422	0.567	
	T_S	-	0.441	0.499	0.290	0.517	0.646	0.377	0.310	0.447	0.599	
	T_P	-	0.484	0.556	0.326	0.515	0.655	0.386	0.330	0.481	0.644	
TRAST	T_K	T_K	0.390	0.440	0.191	0.526	0.682	0.388	0.319	0.495	0.660	90
	T_M	T_M	0.452	0.521	0.223	0.572	0.776	0.433	0.386	0.569	0.793	5
	T_E	T_E	0.491	0.571	0.249	0.580	0.768	0.442	0.397	0.583	0.786	15
	T_S	T_S	0.532	0.632	0.354	0.605	0.779	0.485	0.457	0.601	0.806	40
	T_P	T_K	0.469	0.541	0.297	0.562	0.727	0.422	0.376	0.560	0.760	90
	T_P	T_M	0.494	0.573	0.302	0.604	0.798	0.466	0.431	0.596	0.815	5
	T_P	T_E	0.521	0.607	0.307	0.606	0.795	0.456	0.419	0.608	0.822	15
	T_P	T_S	0.531	0.626	0.345	0.603	0.773	0.490	0.470	0.604	0.818	40
	T_P	T_A	0.557	0.640	0.393	0.634	0.823	0.513	0.488	0.623	0.838	20
	T_P	T_D	0.604	0.708	0.469	0.647	0.837	0.545	0.524	0.643	0.865	25
TRASFUST	T_P	$T_K \cup T_M$	0.317	0.319	0.105	0.493	0.720	0.396	0.372	0.666	0.901	5
	T_P	$T_M \cup T_E$	0.384	0.398	0.131	0.563	0.791	0.422	0.392	0.701	0.931	5
	T_P	$T_E \cup T_S$	0.526	0.624	0.305	0.634	0.815	0.507	0.500	0.670	0.877	15
	T_P	$T_A \cup T_D$	0.617	0.729	0.490	0.679	0.873	0.576	0.574	0.692	0.895	20
	T_P	$T_M \cup T_E \cup T_S$	0.517	0.615	0.294	0.633	0.823	0.513	0.504	0.682	0.897	5
	T_P	T_P	0.519	0.616	0.287	0.628	0.823	0.510	0.505	0.660	0.890	5

in the first six rows of Table 5. TRAS results in a very fast method with good accuracy. Combining KD and RL results in the best performance, outperforming the baselines that use for training just the ground-truth (TRAS-GT), KD and ground-truth (TRAS-KD-GT), and just KD (TRAS-KD). We did not report the performance of **s** trained only by RL because convergence was not attained due to the large state and action spaces. Benefiting the teacher during tracking is an effective online procedure. Indeed, TRAST improves TRAS by 24% on average, and a qualitative example of the ability to pass control to the teacher is given in Fig. 4. The performance of TRASFUST confirms the student's evaluation ability. This is the most accurate and robust tracker thanks to the effective fusion of the underlined trackers. Overall, all three trackers show balanced performance across the benchmarks, thus demonstrating good generalization. No use of the curriculum learning strategy (TRAS-no-curr, TRAST-no-curr, TRASFUST-no-curr) slightly decreases the performance of all. In Fig. 5 the performance of the trackers is reported for different classes of sequences of VOT2019, while in Fig. 7 some qualitative examples are presented.[4] These results demonstrate the effectiveness of our methodology and that the proposed student model respects, respectively, the goals (i), (ii), (iii) introduced in Sect. 1.

---

[4] For more, please see https://youtu.be/uKtQgPk3nCU.

Impact of Teachers. In Table 3 the performance of the proposed trackers in different student-teacher setups is reported. The general trend of the three trackers reflects the increasing tracking capabilities of the teachers. Indeed, on every considered benchmark, the tracking ability of the student increases as a stronger teacher is employed. For TRAST, this is also proven by Fig. 6 (a), where we show that better teachers are exploited more. Moreover, using more than one teacher during training leads to superior tracking policies and to better exploitation of them during tracking. Although in general student models cannot outperform their teachers due to their simple and compressed architecture [79], TRAS and TRAST show such behavior on benchmarks where teachers are weak. Using two teachers during tracking is the best TRASFUST configuration, as in this setup it outperforms the best teacher by more than 2% on all the considered benchmarks. When weaker teachers are added to the pool, the performance tends to decrease, suggesting a behavior similar to the one pointed out in [21]. Part of the error committed by TRAST and TRASFUST on benchmarks like OTB-100 and VOT2019 is explained by Fig. 8. In situations of ambiguous ground-truth, such trackers make predictions that are qualitatively better but quantitatively worse. TRAST and TRASFUST show to be unbiased to the training teachers, as their capabilities generalize also to T_A and T_D which are not exploited during training. In Table 4 we present the performance of the proposed trackers while considering different quality of teacher actions. Increasing the quality, thus reducing the number of videos, results in decreasing the performance of all three trackers. The loss is not significant between $\beta = 0.5$ and $\beta = 0.7$, while considering more precise actions, TRAS suffers majorly, suggesting that more data is a key factor for an autonomous tracking policy. Interestingly, TRAST and TRASFUST are able to perform tracking even if the student is trained with limited training

Table 4. Results of the proposed trackers considering T_P's increasingly better predictions. Best values, per tracker, are highlighted in red, second-best in blue. Please check the online version of this paper for colors.

	Tracker	GOT-10k			UAV123		LaSOT		OTB-100	
		AO	$SR_{0.50}$	$SR_{0.75}$	SS	PS	SS	PS	SS	PS
$\beta = 0.5$	TRAS	0.484	0.556	0.326	0.515	0.655	0.386	0.330	0.481	0.644
	TRAST	0.532	0.632	0.354	0.605	0.779	0.485	0.457	0.601	0.806
	TRASFUST	0.519	0.616	0.287	0.628	0.823	0.510	0.505	0.660	0.890
$\beta = 0.6$	TRAS	0.426	0.488	0.244	0.481	0.609	0.343	0.277	0.452	0.617
	TRAST	0.518	0.616	0.326	0.599	0.768	0.475	0.452	0.608	0.809
	TRASFUST	0.507	0.599	0.295	0.639	0.827	0.514	0.510	0.683	0.901
$\beta = 0.7$	TRAS	0.404	0.449	0.231	0.430	0.552	0.334	0.260	0.390	0.522
	TRAST	0.513	0.603	0.310	0.594	0.766	0.478	0.456	0.586	0.781
	TRASFUST	0.507	0.599	0.289	0.638	0.827	0.513	0.505	0.675	0.894
$\beta = 0.8$	TRAS	0.326	0.344	0.155	0.387	0.489	0.243	0.170	0.323	0.414
	TRAST	0.505	0.598	0.297	0.592	0.764	0.457	0.426	0.589	0.774
	TRASFUST	0.494	0.575	0.260	0.624	0.815	0.494	0.482	0.672	0.888
$\beta = 0.9$	TRAS	0.140	0.070	0.014	0.064	0.045	0.086	0.019	0.132	0.104
	TRAST	0.471	0.541	0.250	0.547	0.697	0.445	0.409	0.574	0.746
	TRASFUST	0.403	0.425	0.169	0.534	0.743	0.401	0.374	0.626	0.836

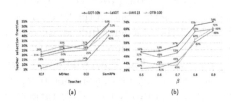

(a)   (b)

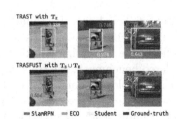

Fig. 6. Per benchmark fractions of predictions attributed to **t** in the TRAST setup.

Fig. 7. Qualitative examples of the proposed trackers.

Fig. 8. Behaviour of TRAST and TRASFUST with ambiguous ground-truths. In the presented frames, TRAST selects the bounding box predicted by the student, while TRASFUST to one given by $\mathbf{T_S}$. Those outputs are qualitative better but have much less IoU (quantified by the colored numbers) with respect to g_t. This impacts the overall quantitative performance.

samples. The plot (b) in Fig. 6 confirms that the student relies effectively to its teacher, as the latter's output is selected more often as **s** loses performance.

Running the student takes just 11 ms on our machine. TRAS performs at 90 FPS. The speed of TRAST and TRASFUST depends on the chosen teacher and varies between 5 and 40 FPS, as shown in Table 3. In parallel setups, TRAST and TRASFUST run in real-time if the teachers do so.

State of the Art Comparison. In Table 5 we report the results of the proposed trackers against the state-of-the-art. In the following comparisons, we consider the results of the best configurations proposed in the above analysis.

TRAS outperforms GOTURN and RE3 which employ a similar DNN architecture but different learning strategies. On GOT-10k and LaSOT it also surpasses the recent GradNet and ROAM, and GCT on UAV123. TRAST outperforms ATOM and SiamCAR on GOT-10k, UAV123, LaSOT, while losing little performance to DiMP. The performance is better than RL-based trackers [28,31,32] on UAV123 and comparable on OTB-100. Finally, TRASFUST outperforms all the trackers on all the benchmarks (where the pool $\mathbf{T_E} \cup \mathbf{T_S}$ was used). Remarkable results are obtained on UAV123 and OTB-100, with SS of 0.679 and 0.701 and PS of 0.873 and 0.931, respectively. Large improvement is achieved over all the methodologies that include expert trackers in their methodology.

Table 5. Performance of the proposed trackers (in the last block of rows) in comparison with the the state-of-the-art. First block of rows reports the performance of the selected teachers; second block shows generic-approach tracker performance; third presents trackers that exploit experts or perform fusion. Best results are highlighted in red, second-best in blue. Please check the online version of this paper for colors.

Tracker	GOT-10k			UAV123		LaSOT		OTB-100		VOT2019			FPS
	AO	$SR_{0.50}$	$SR_{0.75}$	SS	PS	SS	PS	SS	PS	EAO	A	R	
KCF [2]	0.203	0.177	0.065	0.331	0.503	0.178	0.166	0.477	0.693	0.110	0.441	1.279	105
MDNet [13]	0.299	0.303	0.099	0.489	0.718	0.397	0.373	0.673	0.909	0.151	0.507	0.782	5
ECO [15]	0.316	0.309	0.111	0.532	0.726	0.324	0.301	0.668	0.896	0.262	0.505	0.441	15
SiamRPN [9]	0.508	0.604	0.308	0.616	0.785	0.508	0.492	0.649	0.851	0.259	0.554	0.572	43
ATOM [16]	0.556	0.634	0.402	0.643	0.832	0.516	0.506	0.660	0.867	**0.292**	0.603	**0.411**	20
DiMP [17]	**0.611**	**0.717**	0.492	**0.653**	**0.839**	**0.570**	**0.569**	0.681	0.888	0.379	0.594	0.278	25
GOTURN [6]	0.347	0.375	0.124	0.389	0.548	0.214	0.175	0.395	0.534	-	-	-	100
RE3 [7]	-	-	-	0.514	0.667	0.325	0.301	0.464	0.582	0.152	0.458	0.940	150
ADNet [28]	-	-	-	-	-	-	-	0.646	0.880	-	-	-	3
ACT [32]	-	-	-	0.415	0.636	-	-	0.625	0.859	-	-	-	30
DRL-IS [31]	-	-	-	-	-	-	-	0.671	0.909	-	-	-	10
SiamRPN++ [10]	-	-	-	0.613	0.807	0.496	-	**0.696**	**0.914**	0.285	**0.599**	0.482	35
GCT [80]	-	-	-	0.508	0.732	-	-	0.648	0.854	-	-	-	50
GradNet [81]	-	-	-	-	-	0.365	0.351	0.639	0.861	-	-	-	80
SiamCAR [82]	0.569	0.670	0.415	0.614	0.760	0.507	0.510	-	-	-	-	-	52
ROAM [83]	0.436	0.466	0.164	-	-	0.368	0.390	0.681	0.908	-	-	-	13
MEEM [18]	0.253	0.235	0.068	0.392	0.627	0.280	0.224	0.566	0.830	-	-	-	10
HMMTxD [22]	-	-	-	-	-	-	-	-	-	0.163	0.499	1.073	–
HDT [52]	-	-	-	-	-	-	-	0.562	0.844	-	-	-	10
Zhu et al. [84]	-	-	-	-	-	-	-	0.587	0.788	-	-	-	36
Li et al. [53]	-	-	-	-	-	-	-	0.621	0.864	-	-	-	6
TRAS	0.484	0.556	0.326	0.515	0.655	0.386	0.330	0.481	0.644	0.131	0.400	1,020	90
TRAST	0.604	0.708	0.469	0.647	0.837	0.545	0.524	0.643	0.865	0.203	0.517	0.693	25
TRASFUST	0.617	0.729	**0.490**	0.679	0.873	0.576	0.574	0.701	0.931	0.266	0.592	0.597	20

5 Conclusions

In this paper, a novel methodology for visual tracking is proposed. KD and RL are joined in a novel framework where off-the-shelf tracking algorithms are employed to compress knowledge into a CNN-based student model. After learning, the student can be exploited in three different tracking setups, TRAS, TRAST and TRASFUST, depending on application needs. An extensive validation shows that the proposed trackers TRAS and TRAST compete with the state-of-the-art, while TRASFUST outperforms recently published methods and fusion approaches. All trackers can run in real-time.

Acknowledgements. This work is supported by the ACHIEVE-ITN project.

References

1. Bolme, D.S., Beveridge, J.R., Draper, B.A., Lui, Y.M.: Visual object tracking using adaptive correlation filters. In: IEEE Conference on Computer Vision and Pattern Recognition, pp. 2544–2550. IEEE (2010)

2. Henriques, J.F., Caseiro, R., Martins, P., Batista, J.: High-speed tracking with kernelized correlation filters. IEEE Trans. Pattern Anal. Mach. Intell. **37**, 583–596 (2015)

3. Danelljan, M., Hager, G., Khan, F.S., Felsberg, M.: Discriminative scale space tracking. IEEE Trans. Pattern Anal. Mach. Intell. **39**, 1561–1575 (2017)

4. Bertinetto, L., Valmadre, J., Golodetz, S., Miksik, O., Torr, P.H.: Staple: complementary learners for real-time tracking. In: IEEE Conference on Computer Vision and Pattern Recognition. Volume 2016-Dec., pp. 1401–1409 (2016)

5. Lukežič, A., Vojíř, T., Čehovin Zajc, L., Matas, J., Kristan, M.: Discriminative correlation filter tracker with channel and spatial reliability. Int. J. Comput. Vision **126**, 671–688 (2018)

6. Held, D., Thrun, S., Savarese, S.: Learning to track at 100 fps with deep regression networks. In: European Conference on Computer Vision. Volume abs/1604.0. (2016)

7. Gordon, D., Farhadi, A., Fox, D.: Re 3: Real-time recurrent regression networks for visual tracking of generic objects. IEEE Robot. Autom Lett. **3**, 788–795 (2018)

8. Bertinetto, L., Valmadre, J., Henriques, J.F., Vedaldi, A., Torr, P.H.S.: Fully-convolutional Siamese networks for object tracking. In: Hua, G., Jégou, H. (eds.) ECCV 2016. LNCS, vol. 9914, pp. 850–865. Springer, Cham (2016). https://doi.org/10.1007/978-3-319-48881-3_56

9. Li, B., Yan, J., Wu, W., Zhu, Z., Hu, X.: High performance visual tracking with Siamese region proposal network. In: IEEE Conference on Computer Vision and Pattern Recognition, pp. 8971–8980. IEEE (2018)

10. Li, B., Wu, W., Wang, Q., Zhang, F., Xing, J., Yan, J.: SIAMRPN++: evolution of Siamese visual tracking with very deep networks. In: IEEE Conference on Computer Vision and Pattern Recognition 2019-June, pp. 4277–4286 (2019)

11. Zhu, Z., Wang, Q., Li, B., Wu, W., Yan, J., Hu, W.: Distractor-aware Siamese networks for visual object tracking. In: Ferrari, V., Hebert, M., Sminchisescu, C., Weiss, Y. (eds.) ECCV 2018. LNCS, vol. 11213, pp. 103–119. Springer, Cham (2018). https://doi.org/10.1007/978-3-030-01240-3_7

12. Zhang, Z., Peng, H.: Deeper and wider Siamese networks for real-time visual tracking. In: IEEE Conference on Computer Vision and Pattern Recognition (2019)

13. Nam, H., Han, B.: Learning multi-domain convolutional neural networks for visual tracking. In: IEEE Conference on Computer Vision and Pattern Recognition 2016-Decem, pp. 4293–4302 (2016)

14. Jung, I., Son, J., Baek, M., Han, B.: Real-time MDNet. In: Ferrari, V., Hebert, M., Sminchisescu, C., Weiss, Y. (eds.) ECCV 2018. LNCS, vol. 11208, pp. 89–104. Springer, Cham (2018). https://doi.org/10.1007/978-3-030-01225-0_6

15. Danelljan, M., Bhat, G., Khan, F.S., Felsberg, M.: ECO: efficient convolution operators for tracking. In: IEEE Conference on Computer Vision and Pattern Recognition (2017)

16. Danelljan, M., Bhat, G., Khan, F.S., Felsberg, M.: ATOM: accurate tracking by overlap maximization. In: IEEE Conference on Computer Vision and Pattern Recognition (2019)

17. Bhat, G., Danelljan, M., Van Gool, L., Timofte, R.: Learning discriminative model prediction for tracking. In: Proceedings of the IEEE/CVF International Conference on Computer Vision (2019)

18. Zhang, J., Ma, S., Sclaroff, S.: MEEM: robust tracking via multiple experts using entropy minimization. In: Fleet, D., Pajdla, T., Schiele, B., Tuytelaars, T. (eds.) ECCV 2014. LNCS, vol. 8694, pp. 188–203. Springer, Cham (2014). https://doi.org/10.1007/978-3-319-10599-4_13

19. Yoon, J.H., Kim, D.Y., Yoon, K.-J.: Visual tracking via adaptive tracker selection with multiple features. In: Fitzgibbon, A., Lazebnik, S., Perona, P., Sato, Y., Schmid, C. (eds.) ECCV 2012. LNCS, vol. 7575, pp. 28–41. Springer, Heidelberg (2012). https://doi.org/10.1007/978-3-642-33765-9_3

20. Wang, N., Yeung, D.Y.: Ensemble-based tracking: aggregating crowdsourced structured time series data. In: 31st International Conference on Machine Learning, ICML 2014. vol. 4, pp. 2807–2817 (2014)

21. Bailer, C., Pagani, A., Stricker, D.: A superior tracking approach: building a strong tracker through fusion. In: Fleet, D., Pajdla, T., Schiele, B., Tuytelaars, T. (eds.) ECCV 2014. LNCS, vol. 8695, pp. 170–185. Springer, Cham (2014). https://doi.org/10.1007/978-3-319-10584-0_12

22. Vojir, T., Matas, J., Noskova, J.: Online adaptive hidden Markov model for multi-tracker fusion. Comput. Vis. Image Underst. **153**, 109–119 (2016)

23. Comaniciu, D., Ramesh, V., Meer, P.: Real-time tracking of non-rigid objects using mean shift. In: IEEE Conference on Computer Vision and Pattern Recognition, vol. 2, pp. 142–149 (2000)

24. Maresca, M.E., Petrosino, A.: MATRIOSKA: a multi-level approach to fast tracking by learning. In: Petrosino, A. (ed.) ICIAP 2013. LNCS, vol. 8157, pp. 419–428. Springer, Heidelberg (2013). https://doi.org/10.1007/978-3-642-41184-7_43

25. Čehovin, L., Kristan, M., Leonardis, A.: Robust visual tracking using an adaptive coupled-layer visual model. IEEE Trans. Pattern Anal. Mach. Intell. **35**, 941–953 (2013)

26. Nam, H., Hong, S., Han, B.: Online graph-based tracking. In: Fleet, D., Pajdla, T., Schiele, B., Tuytelaars, T. (eds.) ECCV 2014. LNCS, vol. 8693, pp. 112–126. Springer, Cham (2014). https://doi.org/10.1007/978-3-319-10602-1_8

27. Hare, S., et al.: Struck: structured output tracking with kernels. IEEE Trans. Pattern Anal. Mach. Intell. **38**, 2096–2109 (2016)

28. Yun, S., Choi, J., Yoo, Y., Yun, K., Choi, J.Y.: Action-decision networks for visual tracking with deep reinforcement learning. In: IEEE Conference on Computer Vision and Pattern Recognition, vol. 2017-Janua., pp. 1349–1358. IEEE (2017)

29. Supancic, J., Ramanan, D.: Tracking as online decision-making: learning a policy from streaming videos with reinforcement learning. In: Proceedings of the IEEE International Conference on Computer Vision 2017-Octob, pp. 322–331 (2017)

30. Choi, J., Kwon, J., Lee, K.M.: Real-time visual tracking by deep reinforced decision making. Comput. Vis. Image Underst. **171**, 10–19 (2018)

31. Ren, L., Yuan, X., Lu, J., Yang, M., Zhou, J.: Deep reinforcement learning with iterative shift for visual tracking. In: Ferrari, V., Hebert, M., Sminchisescu, C., Weiss, Y. (eds.) ECCV 2018. LNCS, vol. 11213, pp. 697–713. Springer, Cham (2018). https://doi.org/10.1007/978-3-030-01240-3_42

32. Chen, B., Wang, D., Li, P., Wang, S., Lu, H.: Real-time 'Actor-Critic' tracking. In: Ferrari, V., Hebert, M., Sminchisescu, C., Weiss, Y. (eds.) ECCV 2018. LNCS, vol. 11211, pp. 328–345. Springer, Cham (2018). https://doi.org/10.1007/978-3-030-01234-2_20

33. Dunnhofer, M., Martinel, N., Foresti, G.L., Micheloni, C.: Visual tracking by means of deep reinforcement learning and an expert demonstrator. In: Proceedings of The IEEE/CVF International Conference on Computer Vision Workshops (2019)

34. Danelljan, M., Robinson, A., Shahbaz Khan, F., Felsberg, M.: Beyond correlation filters: learning continuous convolution operators for visual tracking. In: Leibe, B., Matas, J., Sebe, N., Welling, M. (eds.) ECCV 2016. LNCS, vol. 9909, pp. 472–488. Springer, Cham (2016). https://doi.org/10.1007/978-3-319-46454-1_29

35. Wang, Q., Zhang, L., Bertinetto, L., Hu, W., Torr, P.H.S.: Fast online object tracking and segmentation: a unifying approach. In: IEEE Conference on Computer Vision and Pattern Recognition(2019)
36. Dunnhofer, M., et al.: Siam-U-Net: encoder-decoder Siamese network for knee cartilage tracking in ultrasound images. Med. Image Anal. **60**, 101631 (2020)
37. Hinton, G., Vinyals, O., Dean, J.: Distilling the knowledge in a neural network. In: Deep Learning Workshop NIPS 2014 (2014)
38. He, K., Zhang, X., Ren, S., Sun, J.: Deep residual learning for image recognition. In: IEEE Conference on Computer Vision and Pattern Recognition, vol. 2016-Decem., pp. 770–778 (2016)
39. Tang, Z., Wang, D., Zhang, Z.: Recurrent neural network training with dark knowledge transfer. In: IEEE International Conference on Acoustics, Speech and Signal Processing, vol. 2016-May, pp. 5900–5904 (2016)
40. Li, Y., Yang, J., Song, Y., Cao, L., Luo, J., Li, L.J.: Learning from noisy labels with distillation. In: Proceedings of the IEEE International Conference on Computer Vision, vol. 2017-Octob., pp. 1928–1936 (2017)
41. Phuong, M., Lampert, C.H.: Distillation-based training for multi-exit architectures. In: Proceedings of the IEEE/CVF International Conference on Computer Vision (2019)
42. Geras, K.J., et al.: Blending LSTMs into CNNs (2015)
43. Chen, G., Choi, W., Yu, X., Han, T., Chandraker, M.: Learning efficient object detection models with knowledge distillation. In: Advances in Neural Information Processing Systems, vol. 2017-Decem., pp. 743–752 (2017)
44. Howard, A.G., et al.: MobileNets: efficient convolutional neural networks for mobile vision applications (2017)
45. Polino, A., Pascanu, R., Alistarh, D.: Model compression via distillation and quantization. In: International Conference on Learning Representations, International Conference on Learning Representations, ICLR (2018)
46. Watkins, C.J.C.H., Dayan, P.: Q-learning. Mach. Learn. **8**, 279–292 (1992)
47. Konda, V.R., Tsitsiklis, J.N.: Actor-critic algorithms. In: Advances in Neural Information Processing Systems (2000)
48. Sutton, R.S., McAllester, D., Singh, S., Mansour, Y.: Policy gradient methods for reinforcement learning with function approximation. In: Advances in Neural Information Processing Systems, 1057–1063 (2000)
49. Mnih, V., et al.: Playing atari with deep reinforcement learning. CoRR abs/1312.5 (2013)
50. Mnih, V., et al.: Asynchronous methods for deep reinforcement learning. In: 33rd International Conference on Machine Learning, ICML 2016, vol. 4, pp. 2850–2869 (2016)
51. Kalal, Z., Mikolajczyk, K., Matas, J.: Tracking-learning-detection. IEEE Trans. Pattern Anal. Mach. Intell. **34**, 1409–1422 (2012)
52. Qi, Y., et al.: Hedged deep tracking. In: IEEE Conference on Computer Vision and Pattern Recognition, vol. 2016-Decem., pp. 4303–4311 (2016)
53. Li, Z., Wei, W., Zhang, T., Wang, M., Hou, S., Peng, X.: Online multi-expert learning for visual tracking. IEEE Trans. Image Process. **29**, 934–946 (2019)
54. Bucilă, C., Caruana, R., Niculescu-Mizil, A.: Model compression. In: Proceedings of the ACM SIGKDD International Conference on Knowledge Discovery and Data Mining, vol. 2006, pp. 535–541 (2006)
55. Rusu, A.A., et al.: Policy distillation. In: 4th International Conference on Learning Representations, ICLR 2016 (2016)

56. Parisotto, E., Ba, J., Salakhutdinov, R.: Actor-mimic deep multitask and transfer reinforcement learning. In: 4th International Conference on Learning Representations, ICLR 2016, International Conference on Learning Representations, ICLR (2016)

57. Garcia, N.C., Morerio, P., Murino, V.: Modality distillation with multiple stream networks for action recognition. In: Ferrari, V., Hebert, M., Sminchisescu, C., Weiss, Y. (eds.) ECCV 2018. LNCS, vol. 11212, pp. 106–121. Springer, Cham (2018). https://doi.org/10.1007/978-3-030-01237-3_7

58. Wang, X., Hu, J.F., Lai, J., Zhang, J., Zheng, W.S.: Progressive teacher-student learning for early action prediction. In: Computer Vision and Pattern Recognition (CVPR), pp. 3556–3565 (2019)

59. Shmelkov, K., Schmid, C., Alahari, K.: Incremental learning of object detectors without catastrophic forgetting. In: Proceedings of the IEEE International Conference on Computer Vision, vol. 2017-Octob., pp. 3420–3429 (2017)

60. Liu, Y., Chen, K., Liu, C., Qin, Z., Luo, Z., Wang, J.: Structured knowledge distillation for semantic segmentation. In: IEEE Conference on Computer Vision and Pattern Recognition, pp. 2599–2608 (2019)

61. He, T., Shen, C., Tian, Z., Gong, D., Sun, C., Yan, Y.: Knowledge adaptation for efficient semantic segmentation. In: IEEE Conference on Computer Vision and Pattern Recognition, pp. 578–587 (2019)

62. Wu, A., Zheng, W.S., Guo, X., Lai, J.H.: Distilled person re-identification: towards a more scalable system. In: IEEE Conference on Computer Vision and Pattern Recognition, pp. 1187–1196 (2019)

63. Wang, N., Zhou, W., Song, Y., Ma, C., Li, H.: Real-time correlation tracking via joint model compression and transfer. IEEE Trans. Image Process. **29**, 6123–6135 (2020)

64. Liu, Y., Dong, X., Lu, X., Khan, F.S., Shen, J., Hoi, S.: Teacher-students knowledge distillation for Siamese trackers (2019)

65. Meshgi, K., Mirzaei, M.S., Oba, S.: Long and short memory balancing in visual co-tracking using q-learning. In: 2019 IEEE International Conference on Image Processing (ICIP), pp. 3970–3974 (2019)

66. Nair, A., et al.: Massively parallel methods for deep reinforcement learning (2015)

67. Espeholt, L., et al.: IMPALA: scalable distributed Deep-RL with importance weighted actor-learner architectures. In: 35th International Conference on Machine Learning, ICML 2018, vol. 4, pp. 2263–2284 (2018)

68. Sutton, R.S., Barto, A.G.: Reinforcement Learning: An Introduction, 2nd edn. MIT Press, Cambridge (2018)

69. Bengio, Y., Louradour, J., Collobert, R., Weston, J.: Curriculum learning. In: 26th International Conference on Machine Learning, ICML 2009, New York, New York, USA, pp. 1–8. ACM Press (2009)

70. Hochreiter, S., Schmidhuber, J.: Long short-term memory. Neural Comput. **9**, 1735–1780 (1997)

71. Huang, L., Zhao, X., Huang, K.: GOT-10k: a large high-diversity benchmark for generic object tracking in the wild. IEEE Trans. Pattern Anal. Mach. Intell. 1 (2019)

72. Mueller, M., Smith, N., Ghanem, B.: A benchmark and simulator for UAV tracking. In: Leibe, B., Matas, J., Sebe, N., Welling, M. (eds.) ECCV 2016. LNCS, vol. 9905, pp. 445–461. Springer, Cham (2016). https://doi.org/10.1007/978-3-319-46448-0_27

73. Fan, H., et al.: LaSOT: a high-quality benchmark for large-scale single object tracking. In: IEEE Conference on Computer Vision and Pattern Recognition (2019)

74. Wu, Y., Lim, J., Yang, M.H.: Online object tracking: a benchmark. In: IEEE Conference on Computer Vision and Pattern Recognition, pp. 2411–2418. IEEE Computer Society (2013)
75. Kristan, M., et al.: The seventh visual object tracking VOT2019 challenge results. In: Proceedings of the IEEE/CVF International Conference on Computer Vision Workshops (2019)
76. Kristan, M., et al.: A novel performance evaluation methodology for single-target trackers. IEEE Trans. Pattern Anal. Mach. Intell. **38**, 2137–2155 (2016)
77. Deng, J., Dong, W., Socher, R., Li, L.J., Li, K., Fei-Fei, L.: ImageNet: a large-scale hierarchical image database. In: IEEE Conference on Computer Vision and Pattern Recognition, pp. 248–255. IEEE (2009)
78. Liu, L., et al.: On the variance of the adaptive learning rate and beyond (2019)
79. Cho, J.H., Hariharan, B.: On the efficacy of knowledge distillation. In: Proceedings of the IEEE International Conference on Computer Vision, vol. 2019-Octob., Institute of Electrical and Electronics Engineers Inc., pp. 4793–4801 (2019)
80. Gao, J., Zhang, T., Xu, C.: Graph convolutional tracking. In: IEEE Conference on Computer Vision and Pattern Recognition, no. 1, pp. 4649–4659 (2019)
81. Li, P., Chen, B., Ouyang, W., Wang, D., Yang, X., Lu, H.: GradNet: gradient-guided network for visual object tracking. In: Proceedings of the IEEE/CVF International Conference on Computer Vision (2019)
82. Guo, D., Wang, J., Cui, Y., Wang, Z., Chen, S.: SiamCAR: Siamese fully convolutional classification and regression for visual tracking. In: IEEE/CVF Conference on Computer Vision and Pattern Recognition (2020)
83. Yang, T., Xu, P., Hu, R., Chai, H., Chan, A.B.: ROAM: recurrently optimizing tracking model. In: IEEE/CVF Conference on Computer Vision and Pattern Recognition (2020)
84. Zhu, Y., Wen, J., Zhang, L., Wang, Y.: Visual tracking with dynamic model update and results fusion. In: Proceedings - International Conference on Image Processing, pp. 2685–2689. IEEE Computer Society (2018)

Motion Prediction Using Temporal Inception Module

Tim Lebailly[1] ⓘ, Sena Kiciroglu[1] ⓘ, Mathieu Salzmann[1,2] ⓘ, Pascal Fua[1] ⓘ,
and Wei Wang[1,3(✉)] ⓘ

[1] CVLab EPFL, Lausanne, Switzerland
{tim.lebailly,sena.kiciroglu,mathieu.salzmann,
pascal.fua,wei.wang}@epfl.ch
[2] ClearSpace, Ecublens, Switzerland
[3] University of Trento, Trento, Italy

Abstract. Human motion prediction is a necessary component for many applications in robotics and autonomous driving. Recent methods propose using sequence-to-sequence deep learning models to tackle this problem. However, they do not focus on exploiting different temporal scales for different length inputs. We argue that the diverse temporal scales are important as they allow us to look at the past frames with different receptive fields, which can lead to better predictions. In this paper, we propose a Temporal Inception Module (TIM) to encode human motion. Making use of TIM, our framework produces input embeddings using convolutional layers, by using different kernel sizes for different input lengths. The experimental results on standard motion prediction benchmark datasets Human3.6M and CMU motion capture dataset show that our approach consistently outperforms the state of the art methods.

1 Introduction

Human motion prediction is an essential component for a wide variety of applications. For instance, in the field of robotics, robots working closely with humans require an internal representation of the current and future human motion to navigate around them safely [1]. Autonomous driving is another important use case where cars need to forecast pedestrian motion accurately to avoid accidents [2,3]. Other applications such as sports tracking also heavily use these forecasting methods for better performances [4].

In order to achieve high accuracy motion prediction, we show that the encoding of the body joint trajectories (i.e., sequence of 3D joint locations) is key. In [5] this is achieved by representing each trajectory using its Discrete Cosine Transform (DCT) coefficients [6], a technique previously used to encode human motion for human pose estimation [7,8]. However, we show that we can gain a large boost in accuracy by using a network to encode the trajectories at multiple temporal scales. In particular, inspired by the Inception Module of [9], we have created a "Temporal Inception Module", which uses various size convolutional kernels to filter the trajectory at different temporal scales for different input

ⓒ Springer Nature Switzerland AG 2021
H. Ishikawa et al. (Eds.): ACCV 2020, LNCS 12623, pp. 651–665, 2021.
https://doi.org/10.1007/978-3-030-69532-3_39

sizes. This allows the network have different receptive fields in the temporal domain.

Following [5,10], the backbone of our prediction architecture is based on a graph convolutional network (GCN) [11] which is a high capacity feed-forward model. As input to the GCN, Mao *et al.* [5] transform time sequences of joint locations from the 10 past frames into a DCT representation. Moreover, they demonstrate that more frames from past do not help to boost the performance. In our paper we show that by looking at the trajectory at a multiple temporal scale, more frames from the past actually do help to further improve the performance, which is especially true for long-term future motion prediction. Therefore, instead of using the DCT coefficients of the trajectory as the input to the GCN, we use an encoder module to produce the input embeddings at multiple temporal scales.

Our key idea lies in the fact that recently seen frames hold more relevant information for the prediction of the near future frames than older ones that are far away from the current frame. Therefore by having many smaller kernels that look specifically at recent frames we are able to place more emphasis on the recent frames. This is especially useful for short-term prediction. Nevertheless, for long-term future frame prediction, the older frames also become important as they are able to describe the high-level motion patterns. For instance, for a walking motion which contains the pattern of moving left and right legs in turn, the most recently seen frames only contain the motion of one leg, rather than the cyclic motion of both legs. These high-level motion patterns are usually lower frequency signals. Incorporating this prior knowledge in the encoding of the trajectory allows us to keep local features of the recently seen frames while also keeping the high-level motion pattern for older frames. This inductive bias gives us a boost in accuracy.

In summary, our contributions are twofold:

- We introduce the Temporal Inception Module (TIM), which allows the network to view the motion trajectory at different temporal scales which leads to better performance.
- We present our action-agnostic end to end trainable pipeline combining TIM and GCN which can be trained once to handle all actions evaluated.

We demonstrate our results on the Human 3.6M [12] and CMU Motion Capture[1] datasets, where we achieve state-of-the-art performance. Qualitative results are shown in Fig. 1 and 4. Our code is publicly available at https://github.com/tileb1/motion-prediction-tim.

2 Related Work

The inherent complexity of human motions has driven research towards deep learning models which rely on very large motion capture datasets [13]. Before

---

[1] Available at http://mocap.cs.cmu.edu/.

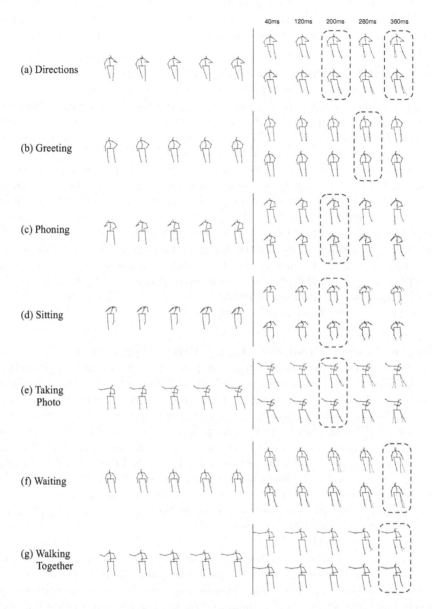

Fig. 1. Qualitative comparison between (DCT+GCN) [5] (red) and ours (blue) on H3.6M predicting up to 400 ms. The ground truth is superimposed faintly in black on top of both methods. Poses on the left are the conditioning ground truth and the rest are predictions. We observe that our predictions closely match the ground truth poses. We have highlighted some of our best predictions with green bounding boxes. (Color figure online)

the deep learning era, analytical models of human motion have been developed by restricting the human motions to simpler or cyclic trajectories like walking [14,15]. However, these models do not generalize well to more complex motions.

Human Motion Prediction Using RNNs. Recurrent neural networks (RNN) are standard architectures for modelling time-series data. Since the work of Fragkiadaki *et al.* [16], RNNs have been widely used for human motion forecasting. Jain *et al.* develop S-RNN [17], which transforms spatio-temporal graphs to a feedforward mixture of RNNs in order to model human motion. Ghosh *et al.* [18] propose the Dropout Autoencoder LSTM (DAE-LSTM) to synthesize long-term realistic looking motion sequences. However the low capacity of the RNN makes it less adequate for high dimensional time-series data like human motion. For instance, Martinez *et al.* [19] has shown that RNNs have problems with discontinuity of the predicted sequence at the last seen frame as well as a prediction that converges towards the mean pose of the ground-truth data for long-term predictions. They counter this by adding a residual connection so that the network is made to only predict the residual motion of the subject. More recently, Wang *et al.* [20] propose a Generative Adversarial Imitation Learning (GAIL) approach for motion prediction. Using GAIL, they iteratively train RNN based policy generator and critic networks.

Human Motion Prediction Using Other Approaches. There have also been various other architectures proposed for human motion prediction. Bütepage *et al.* [21] present several fully-connected encoder-decoder models that aim to encode different properties of the data. One of the models is a time-scale convolutional encoder where they consider different size filters for the input, but not on different length inputs as we propose in our Time Inception Module. In [22], conditional variational autoencoder (CVAE) are used to probabilistically model, predict and generate future motions. They extend their probabilistic approach to also incorporate hierarchical action labels in [23]. Aliakbarian *et al.* [24] also perform motion generation and prediction by encoding their inputs using a CVAE. They are able to generate diverse motions by randomly sampling and perturbing the conditioning variables.

Closest to our work are Li *et al.* [25] and Mao *et al.* [5]. Li *et al.* use a convolutional neural network for motion prediction, they produce separate short-term and long-term embeddings. Our Temporal Inception Module also uses convolution operations to produce input embeddings. However our kernel sizes are selected adaptively, and we use the inception module only to capture temporal dependencies within one joint coordinate's trajectory. The dependencies between several trajectories is learned in a separate step through the GCN. Mao *et al.* [5] exploit the graph-like relationship between joints and demonstrate the uses of a GCN for motion prediction. The data undergoes a DCT transformation before being fed to the network, in order to encode the temporal-dependencies within the sequence. Since our embedding strategy also encodes temporal-dependencies, we make use of a similar GCN architecture for the prediction network.

Inception Module. The Inception Module was first introduced by Szegedy *et al.* [9], used for the task of object detection and classification. Since then different designs have been proposed [26] and it has been adapted to a large variety of tasks including human pose estimation [27], action recognition [28–30], road segmentation [31], single image super-resolution [32], and object recognition [33]. To the best of our knowledge, we are the first to attempt to modify inception modules for generating input embeddings for motion prediction.

3   Methodology

The main encoding methods that have been widely used to represent human motion are 3D joint positions and Euler angle representation. Euler angle representation suffers from ambiguities: two different sets of angles can represent the same pose, which can lead to needlessly over-penalizing predictions. Recent approaches have tried to solve this by changing the encoding to quaternions instead of Euler angles [34]. For the sake of simplicity, our work is solely based on 3D-joint positions. As such, our data consists of time-sequences of skeletons where each skeleton is encoded as a stack of the 3D encoding of its individual body joints.

Let us now define our task. We are given input sequence of K joint trajectories across time, $\mathbf{X}_{-M:-1} = [\mathbf{X}^0_{-M:-1}, \cdots, \mathbf{X}^k_{-M:-1}, \cdots, \mathbf{X}^{K-1}_{-M:-1}]$, where $k \in \{0, 1, \cdots, K-1\}$ represents a Cartesian coordinate value of a joint. Moreover, each joint trajectory $\mathbf{X}^k_{-M:-1} = [\mathbf{X}^k_{-M}, \mathbf{X}^k_{-M+1}, \cdots, \mathbf{X}^k_{-1}]$ is a series of M past joint positions which have already been observed, where $\mathbf{X}^k_i$ represents a joint coordinate at time index i. We aim to predict the poses in the next T frames, $\mathbf{X}_{0:T-1}$. Negative time indices therefore belong to the observed sequence and positive time indices belong to the prediction. For simplicity, we refer to the trajectory of a joint coordinate as "joint trajectory" throughout this paper.

The overall framework converts the input human motion $\mathbf{X}_{-M:-1}$ into embeddings using our temporal inception module (TIM). These embeddings are then fed to the graph convolutional network (GCN) in order to produce the residual motion. The framework is depicted in detail in Fig. 2. The details of the TIM and GCN are introduced below.

3.1   Temporal Inception Module

Our main contribution, the Temporal Inception Module (TIM) is illustrated in Fig. 3. This module is used to obtain embeddings $\mathbf{E}^k$ of the input motion $\mathbf{X}_{-M:-1}$ for each $k \in \{0, 1, \cdots, K-1\}$ joint coordinate.

TIM takes as input a single joint trajectory $\mathbf{X}^k_{-M_J:-1}$ with the length M_J. Then the subsequence sampling block nested in TIM samples the long motion sequence into multiple sequences with different lengths M_j ($M_j > M_i$ if $j > i$).

For example, in our implementation, we consider two different input sizes $M_1 = 5$ and $M_2 = 10$ where the past motion the inception module sees

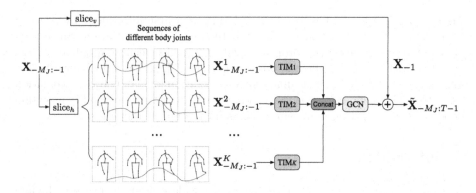

Fig. 2. Overview of the whole framework making use of multiple TIMs. Using the slice$_h$ operator, we split the input across different joint coordinates. The joint trajectories are fed into the TIMs to produce the embedding, which is then used by the GCN to obtain the residual motion predictions. Using the slice$_v$ operator, separate the most recently seen frame $\mathbf{X}_{-1}$, which is broadcasted to all timestamps and summed with the residual GCN results for the final prediction.

are $\mathbf{X}_{-M_1:-1}$ and $\mathbf{X}_{-M_2:-1}$ respectively. Each input goes through several 1D-convolutions with different sized kernels. The inception module is used to adaptively determine the weights corresponding to these convolution operations.

Each subsequence $\mathbf{X}^k_{-M_j:-1}$ has its unique convolutional kernels whose sizes are proportional to the length M_j. In other words, we have smaller kernel size for shorter subsequences and larger kernel size for longer subsequences. The intuition is as follows. Using a smaller kernel size allows us to effectively preserve the detailed local information. Meanwhile, for a longer subsequence, a larger kernel is capable of extracting higher-level patterns which depend on multiple time indices. This allows us to process the motion at different temporal scales.

All convolution outputs are then concatenated into one embedding $\mathbf{E}^k$ which has the desired features matching our inductive bias i.e. local details for recently seen frames and a low-frequency information for older frames.

More formally, we have

$$\mathbf{E}^k_j = \text{concat}(C_{S^j_1}(\mathbf{X}^k_{-M_j:-1}), C_{S^j_2}(\mathbf{X}^k_{-M_j:-1}), \cdots, C_{S^j_L}(\mathbf{X}^k_{-M_j:-1})) \qquad (1)$$

followed by

$$\mathbf{E}^k = \text{concat}(\mathbf{E}^k_1, \mathbf{E}^k_2, \cdots, \mathbf{E}^k_J) \qquad (2)$$

where $C_{S^j_l}$ is a 1D-convolution with filter size S^j_l. The embeddings for each joint trajectory $\mathbf{E}^k$ are then used as input feature vector for the GCN. An overview of the global framework is illustrated in Fig. 2.

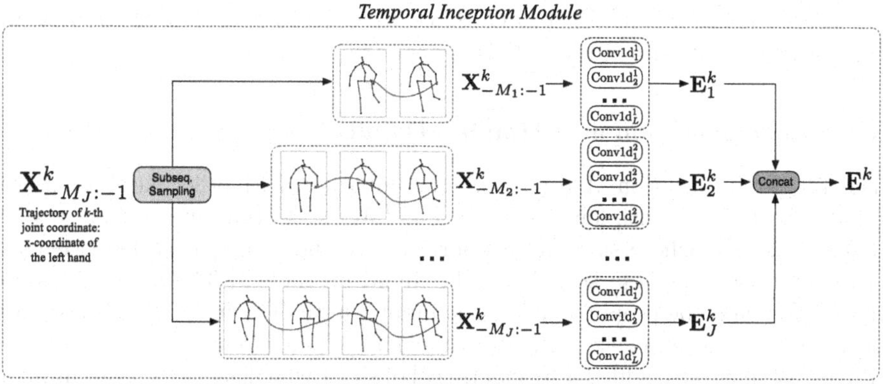

Temporal Inception Module

Fig. 3. Overview of the Temporal Inception Module (TIM). TIM processes each joint coordinate k separately, expressed as a superscript in this figure. The subseq sampling block splits a 1D input sequence into J subsequences, each of length M_j. The Conv1d$_l^j$ block corresponds to a 1D convolution operator with kernel size S_l^j. The results of the convolutions are concatenated to form the embeddings of each subsequence $\mathbf{E}_j^k$, which are concatenated again to form the input embeddings $\mathbf{E}^k$ to the GCN.

3.2 Graph Convolutional Network

For the high capacity feed-forward network, we make use of a graph convolutional neural network as proposed by Mao et al. [5]. This network is currently a state-of-the-art network for human motion prediction from separate time embeddings of each body joint. This makes it very well suited for our task. As shown in their previous work, using the kinematic tree of the skeleton as predefined weight adgency matrix is not optimal. Instead, a separate adgency matrix is learned for each layer.

Following the notation of [5], we model the skeleton as a fully connected set of K nodes, represented by the trainable weighted adjacency matrix $\mathbf{A}^{K \times K}$. The GCN consists of several stacked graph convolutional layers, each performing the operation

$$\mathbf{H}^{(p+1)} = \sigma(\mathbf{A}^{(p)}\mathbf{H}^{(p)}\mathbf{W}^{(p)}) \tag{3}$$

where $\mathbf{W}^{(p)}$ is the set of trainable weights of layer p, $\mathbf{A}^{(p)}$ is the learnable adgency matrix of layer p, $\mathbf{H}^{(p)}$ is the input to layer p, $\mathbf{H}^{(p+1)}$ is the output of layer p (and input to layer $p+1$) and $\sigma(\cdot)$ is an activation function.

The GCN receives as input the embeddings $\mathbf{E}$ produced by the multiple TIMs and regresses the residual motion which is later summed up with the most recently seen human pose $\mathbf{X}_{-1}$ to produce the entire motion sequence,

$$\tilde{\mathbf{X}}_{-M_J:T-1} = G(\mathbf{E}) + \mathbf{X}_{-1} \tag{4}$$

where the GCN is denoted as G. Since $\tilde{\mathbf{X}}_{0:T-1}$ is a subset of $\tilde{\mathbf{X}}_{-M_J:T-1}$, we thus predict the future motion. This is depicted in Fig. 2.

3.3 Implementation and Training Details

The Temporal Inception Module used for comparison with other baselines uses 2 input subsequences with lengths $M_1 = 5$ and $M_2 = 10$. Both are convolved with different kernels whose sizes are proportional to the subsequence input length. A detailed view of these kernels can be found in Table 1. The kernel sizes are indeed chosen to be proportional to the input length. The number of kernels are decreased as the kernel size increases to avoid putting too much weight on older frames. We have also added a special kernel of size 1 which acts as a pass-through. This leaves us with an embedding $\mathbf{E}^k$ of size 223 ($12\cdot4+9\cdot3+9\cdot8+7\cdot6+6\cdot4+1\cdot10$) for each joint coordinate $k \in \{0, 1, \cdots, K-1\}$ which are fed to the GCN. For more details on the GCN architecture, we refer the reader to [5].

Table 1. Detailed architecture of Temporal Inception Module used to compare with baselines.

Subsequence input length (M_j)	Number of kernels	Kernel size
5	12	2
5	9	3
10	9	3
10	7	5
10	6	7
10	1	1

The whole network (TIM + GCN) is trained end to end by minimizing the Mean Per Joint Position Error (MPJPE) as proposed in [12]. This loss is defined as

$$\frac{1}{K(M_J + T)} \sum_{t=-M_J}^{T-1} \sum_{i=1}^{I} ||\mathbf{p}_{i,t} - \hat{\mathbf{p}}_{i,t}||^2 \tag{5}$$

where $\hat{\mathbf{p}}_{i,t} \in \mathbb{R}^3$ is the prediction of the i-th joint at time index t, $\mathbf{p}_{i,t}$ is the corresponding ground-truth at the same indices and I is the number of joints in the skeleton ($3 \times I = K$ as the skeletons are 3D). Note that the loss sums over negative time indices which belong to the observed sequence as it adds an additional training signal.

It is trained for 50 epochs with a learning-rate decay of 0.96 every 2 epochs as in [5]. One pass takes about 75 ms on an NVIDIA Titan X (Pascal) with a batch-size of 16.

4   Evaluation

We evaluate our results on two benchmark human motion prediction datasets: Human3.6M [12] and CMU motion capture dataset. The details of the training/testing split of the datasets are shown below, followed by the experimental result analysis and ablation study.

4.1   Datasets

Human3.6M. Following previous works on motion prediction [17,35], we use 15 actions performed by 7 subjects for training and testing. These actions are *walking, eating, smoking, discussion, directions, greeting, phoning, posing, purchases, sitting, sitting down, taking photo, waiting, walking dog and walking together*. We also report the average performance across all actions. The 3D human pose is represented using 32 joints. Similar to previous work, we remove global rotation and translation and testing is performed on the same subset of 8 sequences belonging to Subject 5.

CMU Motion Capture. The CMU Motion Capture dataset contains challenging motions performed by 144 subjects. Following previous related work's training/testing splits and evaluation subset [25], we report our results across eight actions: *basketball, basketball signal, directing traffic, jumping, running, soccer, walking, and washwindow*, as well as the average performance. We implement the same preprocessing as the Human3.6M dataset, *i.e.*, removing global rotation and translation.

Baselines. We select the following baselines for comparison: Martinez *et al.* (Residual sup.) in order to compare against the well known method using RNNs [19], Li *et al.* (convSeq2Seq) as they also encode their inputs using convolution operations [25] and Mao *et al.* (DCT+GCN) [5] to demonstrate the gains of using TIM over DCT for encoding inputs. We are unable to compare to the also recent work of [20] and [24] due to them reporting results only in joint angle representation and not having code available for motion prediction so far.

4.2   Results

In our results (*e.g.*, Tables 1, 2, 3 and 5), for the sake of robustness we report the average error over 5 runs for our own method. We denote our method by "Ours $(5 - 10)$" since our final model takes as input subsequences of lengths $M_1 = 5$ and $M_2 = 10$.

   We report our short-term prediction results on Human3.6M in Table 2. For the majority of the actions and on average we achieve a lower error than the state-of-the-art (SOTA). Our qualitative results are shown in Fig. 1.

   Our long-term predictions on Human3.6M are reported in Table 3. Here we achieve an even larger boost in accuracy, especially for case of 1000 ms. We

Table 2. Short-term prediction test error of 3D joint positions on H3.6M. We outperform the baselines on average and for most actions.

Name	Walking [ms]				Eating [ms]				Smoking [ms]				Discussion [ms]			
	80	160	320	400	80	160	320	400	80	160	320	400	80	160	320	400
Residual sup. [19]	23.8	40.4	62.9	70.9	17.6	34.7	71.9	87.7	19.7	36.6	61.8	73.9	31.7	61.3	96.0	103.5
convSeq2Seq [25]	17.1	31.2	53.8	61.5	13.7	25.9	52.5	63.3	11.1	21.0	33.4	38.3	18.9	39.3	67.7	75.7
DCT + GCN [5]	**8.9**	**15.7**	**29.2**	**33.4**	8.8	18.9	39.4	47.2	7.8	14.9	25.3	**28.7**	9.8	22.1	**39.6**	**44.1**
Ours (5 − 10)	9.3	15.9	30.1	34.1	**8.4**	**18.5**	**38.1**	**46.6**	**6.9**	**13.8**	**24.6**	29.1	**8.8**	**21.3**	40.2	45.5

Directions [ms]				Greeting [ms]				Phoning [ms]				Posing [ms]			
80	160	320	400	80	160	320	400	80	160	320	400	80	160	320	400
36.5	56.4	81.5	97.3	37.9	74.1	139.0	158.8	25.6	44.4	74.0	84.2	27.9	54.7	131.3	160.8
22.0	37.2	59.6	73.4	24.5	46.2	90.0	103.1	17.2	29.7	53.4	61.3	16.1	35.6	86.2	105.6
12.6	24.4	**48.2**	**58.4**	14.5	30.5	74.2	89.0	**11.5**	20.2	**37.9**	**43.2**	9.4	23.9	66.2	82.9
11.0	**22.3**	48.4	59.3	**13.7**	**29.1**	**72.6**	**88.9**	**11.5**	**19.8**	38.5	44.4	**7.5**	**22.3**	**64.8**	**80.8**

Purchases [ms]				Sitting [ms]				Sitting Down [ms]				Taking Photo [ms]			
80	160	320	400	80	160	320	400	80	160	320	400	80	160	320	400
40.8	71.8	104.2	109.8	34.5	69.9	126.3	141.6	28.6	55.3	101.6	118.9	23.6	47.4	94.0	112.7
29.4	54.9	82.2	93.0	19.8	42.4	77.0	88.4	17.1	34.9	66.3	77.7	14.0	27.2	53.8	66.2
19.6	**38.5**	**64.4**	**72.2**	10.7	24.6	50.6	62.0	11.4	**27.6**	56.4	67.6	6.8	**15.2**	**38.2**	**49.6**
19.0	39.2	65.9	74.6	**9.3**	**22.3**	**45.3**	**56.0**	**11.3**	28.0	**54.8**	**64.8**	**6.4**	15.6	41.4	53.5

Waiting [ms]				Walking Dog [ms]				Walking Together [ms]				Average [ms]			
80	160	320	400	80	160	320	400	80	160	320	400	80	160	320	400
29.5	60.5	119.9	140.6	60.5	101.9	160.8	188.3	23.5	45.0	71.3	82.8	30.8	57.0	99.8	115.5
17.9	36.5	74.9	90.7	40.6	74.7	116.6	138.7	15.0	29.9	54.3	65.8	19.6	37.8	68.1	80.2
9.5	22.0	**57.5**	73.9	32.2	58.0	102.2	122.7	**8.9**	**18.4**	35.3	44.3	12.1	25.0	51.0	61.3
9.2	**21.7**	55.9	**72.1**	29.3	56.4	99.6	119.4	**8.9**	18.6	35.5	44.3	**11.4**	**24.3**	**50.4**	**60.9**

attribute this to the large kernel sizes we have set for input length 10, which allows the network to pick up the underlying higher-level patterns in the motion. We validate this further in our ablation study. We present our qualitative results in Fig. 4.

Our predictions on the CMU motion capture dataset are reported in Table 4. Similar to our results on Human3.6M, we observe that we outperform the state-of-the-art. For all timestamps except for 1000 ms, we show better performance than the baselines. We observe that both our and Mao *et al.*'s [5] high capacity GCN based models are outperformed by convSeq2Seq [25], a CNN based approach. Since the training dataset of CMU-Mocap is much smaller compared to H36M, this leads to overfitting for high-capacity networks such as ours. However, this is not problematic for short-term predictions, as in that case it is not as crucial for the model to be generalizable. We do however outperform Mao *et al.*'s results for the 1000 ms prediction which makes use of the same backbone GCN as us. We observe that on average and for many actions, we outperform the baselines for the 80, 160, 320 and 400 ms.

4.3 Ablation Study

The objective of this section is twofold.

- First, we inquire the effect of choosing a kernel size proportional to the input size M_j;
- Second, we inquire the effect of the varying length input subsequences.

Both results are shown in Fig. 5, where the version name represents the set $\{M_j : j \in \{1, 2, \cdots, J\}\}$ of varying length subsequences.

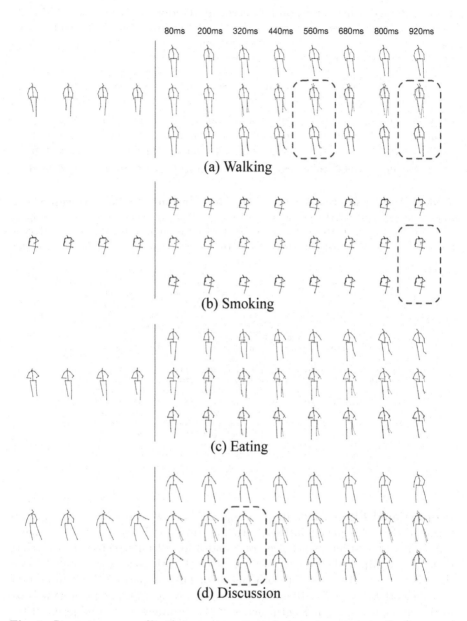

80ms   200ms   320ms   440ms   560ms   680ms   800ms   920ms

(a) Walking

(b) Smoking

(c) Eating

(d) Discussion

Fig. 4. Long-term qualitative comparison between ground truth (top row) (DCT+GCN) [5] (middle) and ours (bottom row) on H3.6M predicting up to 1000 ms. The ground truth is superimposed faintly on top of both methods. Poses on the left are the conditioning ground truth and the rest are predictions. We observe that our predictions closely match the ground truth poses, though as expected, the error increases as the time index increases. We have highlighted some of our best predictions with green bounding boxes. (Color figure online)

Table 3. Long-term prediction test error of 3D joint positions on H3.6M. We outperform the baselines on average and on almost every action. We have also found that we can have an even higher accuracy for 1000 ms in our ablation study, where we show the effect of adding another input subsequence of length $M_j = 15$.

Name	Walking [ms]		Eating [ms]		Smoking [ms]		Discussion [ms]		Average [ms]	
	560	1000	560	1000	560	1000	560	1000	560	1000
Residual sup. [19]	73.8	86.7	101.3	119.7	85.0	118.5	120.7	147.6	95.2	118.1
convSeq2Seq [25]	59.2	71.3	66.5	85.4	42.0	67.9	84.1	116.9	62.9	85.4
DCT + GCN [5]	42.3	51.3	**56.5**	**68.6**	**32.3**	**60.5**	70.5	103.5	50.4	71.0
Ours (5 − 10)	**39.6**	**46.9**	56.9	**68.6**	33.5	61.7	**68.5**	**97.0**	**49.6**	**68.6**

Table 4. Prediction test error of 3D joint positions on CMU-Mocap. For all timestamps except for 1000 ms, we demonstrate better performance than the baselines. Our model performs better in this case for short term predictions. We observe that on average and for many actions, we surpass the baselines for the 80, 160, 320 and 400 ms.

Name	Basketball [ms]					Basketball Signal [ms]					Directing Traffic [ms]				
	80	160	320	400	1000	80	160	320	400	1000	80	160	320	400	1000
Residual sup [19].	18.4	33.8	59.5	70.5	106.7	12.7	23.8	40.3	46.7	77.5	15.2	29.6	55.1	66.1	127.1
convSeq2Seq [25]	16.7	30.5	53.8	64.3	**91.5**	8.4	16.2	30.8	37.8	76.5	10.6	20.3	38.7	48.4	**115.5**
DCT+GCN [5]	14.0	25.4	49.6	61.4	106.1	3.5	6.1	11.7	**15.2**	**53.9**	7.4	15.1	31.7	42.2	152.4
Ours (5 − 10)	**12.7**	**22.6**	**44.6**	**55.6**	102.0	**3.0**	**5.6**	**11.6**	15.5	57.0	**7.1**	**14.1**	**31.1**	**41.4**	138.3

Jumping [ms]					Running [ms]					Soccer [ms]				
80	160	320	400	1000	80	160	320	400	1000	80	160	320	400	1000
36.0	68.7	125.0	145.5	195.5	15.6	19.4	31.2	36.2	43.3	20.3	39.5	71.3	84	129.6
22.4	44.0	87.5	106.3	**162.6**	14.3	16.3	18.0	20.2	27.5	12.1	21.8	41.9	52.9	**94.6**
16.9	34.4	76.3	96.8	164.6	25.5	36.7	39.3	39.9	58.2	11.3	**21.5**	44.2	55.8	117.5
14.8	**31.1**	**71.2**	**91.3**	163.5	24.5	37.0	39.9	41.9	62.6	**11.2**	22.1	45.1	58.1	122.1

Walking [ms]					Washwindow [ms]					Average [ms]				
80	160	320	400	1000	80	160	320	400	1000	80	160	320	400	1000
8.2	13.7	21.9	24.5	32.2	8.4	15.8	29.3	35.4	61.1	16.8	30.5	54.2	63.6	96.6
7.6	12.5	23.0	27.5	49.8	8.2	15.9	32.1	39.9	58.9	12.5	22.2	40.7	49.7	84.6
7.7	11.8	19.4	23.1	40.2	5.9	11.9	30.3	40.0	79.3	11.5	20.4	37.8	46.8	96.5
7.1	**11.1**	19.9	**22.8**	39.3	5.9	12.3	32.1	42.6	80.4	10.8	19.5	**36.9**	46.2	95.7

Proportional Filter Size. In our design of TIM, we chose filter sizes proportional to the subsequence input length M_j. In Table 5, we observe the effects of setting a "constant kernel size" of 2 and 3 for all input subsequences. Note that we also adjust the number of filters such that the size of the embedding is the more or less the same for both cases, for fair comparison. We can observe that for both versions $5 - 10$ and $5 - 10 - 15$, having a proportional kernel size to the subsequence input length increases the accuracy for the majority of the actions and this brings better performance on average. Therefore, our empirical results match our intuition that using larger filters for longer length inputs that look back further into the past helps by capturing higher-level motion patterns which yield embeddings of better quality.

Varying Length Input Subsequences. The goal of having the Temporal Inception Module is to sample subsequences of different length M_j which, once processed, yield embeddings with different properties. Embeddings of longer input sequences contain higher level information of the motion (lower frequencies), whereas embeddings of shorter input sequences would contain higher spatial resolution and higher frequency information of the short-term future motion. We expect our model to perform better on very long term prediction of 1000 ms prediction the bigger M_J is. As can be seen from Table 5, we also observe that there is unfortunately a trade-off to be made between aiming for very long term predictions (1000 ms) or shorter term predictions (560 ms). The 5−10−15 model yields higher accuracy than the 5−10 model on 1000 ms and performs worse on 560 ms predictions. This matches our intuition since the 5−10−15 model is trained to place more emphasis on the high-level motion pattern and is therefore tuned for very long term predictions at 1000 ms.

Note that we obtain even better performance for very long-term prediction with the 5−10−15 model compared with the 5−10 model which has already outperformed the baselines in Table 3.

Table 5. Effect of the kernel size and subsequence lengths M_j on the framework performance for long-term prediction on H3.6M. We observe that proportional kernel sizes on average yield better performance. We also observe that including the input subsequence with length $M_j = 15$ allows us to look back further into the past, boosting the predictions of the furthest timestamp evaluated, 1000 ms.

Version	Walking [ms]		Eating [ms]		Smoking [ms]		Discussion [ms]		Average [ms]	
	560	1000	560	1000	560	1000	560	1000	560	1000
5-10 (proportional kernel size)	39.6	46.9	56.9	68.6	**33.5**	**61.7**	**68.5**	97.0	**49.6**	68.6
5-10 (constant kernel size)	**38.4**	45.6	56.9	68.5	34.9	63.8	73.2	100.1	50.8	69.5
5-10-15 (proportional kernel size)	43.3	43.1	**45.8**	**65.2**	36.4	62.9	97.1	**94.6**	55.7	**66.5**
5-10-15 (constant kernel size)	42.8	**41.6**	47.1	66.0	36.6	63.2	98.3	96.6	56.2	66.9

5   Conclusion and Future Work

The task of human motion prediction has gained more attention with the rising popularity of autonomous driving and human-robot interaction. Currently, deep learning methods have made much progress, however, none has focused on utilizing different length input sequences seen at different temporal scales to learn more powerful input embeddings which can benefit the prediction. Our Temporal Inception Module allows us to encode various length input subsequences at different temporal scales and achieves state-of-the-art performance.

There are many different settings of the Temporal Inception Module to be explored, such as the effects of strided convolutions, allowing for sampling of the input sequence at different rates. The Temporal Inception Module could also be adapted to other applications, such as action recognition. Using longer input subsequences with larger kernels could also be of use for long-term motion generation. We believe these could be interesting avenues for future work and provide further performance gains in their respective fields.

References

1. Gui, L., Zhang, K., Wang, Y., Liang, X., Moura, J.M.F., Veloso, M.: Teaching robots to predict human motion. In: International Conference on Intelligent Robots and Systems, pp. 562–567 (2018)
2. Habibi, G., Jaipuria, N., How, J.P.: Context-aware pedestrian motion prediction in urban intersections. arxiv (2018)
3. Fan, Z., Wang, Z., Cui, J., Davoine, F., Zhao, H., Zha, H.: Monocular pedestrian tracking from a moving vehicle. In: Asian Conference on Computer Vision Workshops, pp. 335–346 (2012)
4. Kiciroglu, S., Rhodin, H., Sinha, S.N., Salzmann, M., Fua, P.: ActiveMoCap: optimized viewpoint selection for active human motion capture. In: Conference on Computer Vision and Pattern Recognition (2020)
5. Mao, W., Liu, M., Salzmann, M., Li, H.: Learning trajectory dependencies for human motion prediction. In: International Conference on Computer Vision (2019)
6. Ahmed, N., Natarajan, T., Rao, K.R.: Discrete cosine transform. IEEE Trans. Comput. **C-23**, 90–93 (1974)
7. Lin, J., Lee, G.H.: Trajectory space factorization for deep video-based 3D human pose estimation. In: British Machine Vision Conference (2019)
8. Huang, Y., et al.: Towards accurate marker-less human shape and pose estimation over time. In: International Conference on 3D Vision (2017)
9. Szegedy, C., et al.: Going deeper with convolutions. In: Conference on Computer Vision and Pattern Recognition, pp. 1–9 (2015)
10. Li, M., Chen, S., Zhao, Y., Zhang, Y., Wang, Y., Tian, Q.: Dynamic multiscale graph neural networks for 3D skeleton based human motion prediction. In: Conference on Computer Vision and Pattern Recognition (2020)
11. Bruna, J., Zaremba, W., Szlam, A., Lecun, Y.: Spectral networks and locally connected networks on graphs. In: International Conference on Learning Representations (2014)
12. Ionescu, C., Papava, I., Olaru, V., Sminchisescu, C.: Human3.6M: large scale datasets and predictive methods for 3D human sensing in natural environments. IEEE Trans. Pattern Anal. Mach. Intell. **36**(7), 1325–1339 (2014)
13. Goodfellow, I., Bengio, Y., Courville, A.: Deep Learning. MIT Press, Cambridge (2016)
14. Ormoneit, D., Sidenbladh, H., Black, M., Hastie, T.: Learning and tracking cyclic human motion. In: Advances in Neural Information Processing Systems, pp. 894–900 (2001)
15. Urtasun, R., Fua, P.: 3D human body tracking using deterministic temporal motion models. In: Pajdla, T., Matas, J. (eds.) ECCV 2004. LNCS, vol. 3023, pp. 92–106. Springer, Heidelberg (2004). https://doi.org/10.1007/978-3-540-24672-5_8
16. Fragkiadaki, K., Levine, S., Felsen, P., Malik, J.: Recurrent network models for human dynamics. In: International Conference on Computer Vision (2015)
17. Jain, A., Zamir, A., adn Saxena, S.S.A.: Structural-RNN: deep learning on spatio-temporal graphs. In: Conference on Computer Vision and Pattern Recognition (2016)
18. Ghosh, P., Song, J., Aksan, E., Hilliges, O.: Learning human motion models for long-term predictions. In: International Conference on 3D Vision (2017)
19. Martinez, J., Black, M., Romero, J.: On human motion prediction using recurrent neural networks. In: Conference on Computer Vision and Pattern Recognition (2017)

20. Wang, B., Adeli, E., Chiu, H.K., Huang, D.A., Niebles, J.C.: Imitation learning for human pose prediction. In: International Conference on Computer Vision, pp. 7123–7132 (2019)
21. Butepage, J., Black, M., Kragic, D., Kjellstrom, H.: Deep representation learning for human motion prediction and classification. In: Conference on Computer Vision and Pattern Recognition (2017)
22. Bütepage, J., Kjellström, H., Kragic, D.: Anticipating many futures: online human motion prediction and generation for human-robot interaction. In: International Conference on Robotics and Automation, pp. 1–9 (2018)
23. Bütepage, J., Kjellström, H., Kragic, D.: Predicting the what and how - a probabilistic semi-supervised approach to multi-task human activity modeling. In: 2019 IEEE/CVF Conference on Computer Vision and Pattern Recognition Workshops (CVPRW), pp. 2923–2926 (2019)
24. Aliakbarian, S., Saleh, F.S., Salzmann, M., Petersson, L., Gould, S.: A stochastic conditioning scheme for diverse human motion prediction. In: Conference on Computer Vision and Pattern Recognition (2020)
25. Li, C., Zhang, Z., Lee, W.S., Lee, G.H.: Convolutional sequence to sequence model for human dynamics. In: Conference on Computer Vision and Pattern Recognition (2018)
26. Szegedy, C., Vanhoucke, V., Ioffe, S., Shlens, J., Wojna, Z.: Rethinking the inception architecture for computer vision. In: Conference on Computer Vision and Pattern Recognition, pp. 2818–2826 (2016)
27. Liu, W., Chen, J.J., Li, C., Qian, C., Chu, X., Hu, X.: A cascaded inception of inception network with attention modulated feature fusion for human pose estimation. In: American Association for Artificial Intelligence Conference (2018)
28. Cho, S., Foroosh, H.: Spatio-temporal fusion networks for action recognition. In: Asian Conference on Computer Vision (2018)
29. Hussein, N., Gavves, E., Smeulders, A.: Timeception for complex action recognition. In: Conference on Computer Vision and Pattern Recognition, pp. 254–263 (2019)
30. Yang, C., Xu, Y., Shi, J., Dai, B., Zhou, B.: Temporal pyramid network for action recognition. In: Conference on Computer Vision and Pattern Recognition, pp. 588–597 (2020)
31. Doshi, J.: Residual inception skip network for binary segmentation. In: 2018 IEEE/CVF Conference on Computer Vision and Pattern Recognition Workshops (CVPRW), pp. 206–2063 (2018)
32. Shi, W., Jiang, F., Zhao, D.: Single image super-resolution with dilated convolution based multi-scale information learning inception module. In: International Conference on Image Processing, pp. 977–981 (2017)
33. Alom, M.Z., Hasan, M., Yakopcic, C., Taha, T.M., Asari, V.K.: Improved inception-residual convolutional neural network for object recognition. Neural Comput. Appl. 32(1), 279–293 (2018). https://doi.org/10.1007/s00521-018-3627-6
34. Pavllo, D., Grangier, D., Auli, M.: Quaternet: a quaternion-based recurrent model for human motion. In: British Machine Vision Conference (2018)
35. Martinez, J., Hossain, R., Romero, J., Little, J.: A simple yet effective baseline for 3D human pose estimation. In: International Conference on Computer Vision (2017)

A Sparse Gaussian Approach
to Region-Based 6DoF Object Tracking

Manuel Stoiber[1,2] (iD), Martin Pfanne[1] (iD), Klaus H. Strobl[1] (iD),
Rudolph Triebel[1,2(✉)] (iD), and Alin Albu-Schäffer[1,2] (iD)

[1] German Aerospace Center (DLR), 82234 Wessling, Germany
{manuel.stoiber,rudolph.triebel}@dlr.de
[2] Technical University of Munich (TUM), 80333 Munich, Germany

Abstract. We propose a novel, highly efficient sparse approach to region-based 6DoF object tracking that requires only a monocular RGB camera and the 3D object model. The key contribution of our work is a probabilistic model that considers image information sparsely along correspondence lines. For the implementation, we provide a highly efficient discrete scale-space formulation. In addition, we derive a novel mathematical proof that shows that our proposed likelihood function follows a Gaussian distribution. Based on this information, we develop robust approximations for the derivatives of the log-likelihood that are used in a regularized Newton optimization. In multiple experiments, we show that our approach outperforms state-of-the-art region-based methods in terms of tracking success while being about one order of magnitude faster. The source code of our tracker is publicly available (https://github.com/DLR-RM/RBGT).

1 Introduction

Tracking a rigid object and estimating its 6DoF pose is an essential task in computer vision that has a wide range of applications, from robotics to augmented reality. The aim is to estimate both the rotation and translation of an object relative to the camera from consecutive image frames. Typical challenges include partial occlusions, object ambiguities, appearance changes, motion blur, background clutter, and real-time requirements. To address those issues, many approaches have been proposed. Based on surveys [1,2], as well as recent developments, methods are typically differentiated by their use of key-points, explicit edges, template images, deep learning, depth information, and image regions.

While methods based on key-points [3,4] are very popular, rich texture is required, which limits the range of suitable objects. This is also the case for template-based approaches [5,6]. Methods that use explicit edges [7–9], while more suitable for texture-less objects, have the disadvantage of struggling with

---

Electronic supplementary material The online version of this chapter (https://doi.org/10.1007/978-3-030-69532-3_40) contains supplementary material, which is available to authorized users.

H. Ishikawa et al. (Eds.): ACCV 2020, LNCS 12623, pp. 666–682, 2021.
https://doi.org/10.1007/978-3-030-69532-3_40

Fig. 1. Example of the optimization process for the *ape* object on the *RBOT* dataset [19]. The outermost images display a rendered overlay before and after the optimization. The images in the middle visualize pixel-wise posteriors that describe the probability of a pixel belonging to the background. White pixels indicate $p_b = 1$. Also, the images show orange correspondence lines that converge toward the final pose with decreasing scale s. High probabilities for the contour position are illustrated in red. Notice that during the operation of the tracker, pixel-wise posteriors are only calculated along lines. (Color figure online)

background clutter. Deep-learning-based approaches [10–12] have also been used but are either computationally expensive or do not reach state-of-the-art results. Another recent development are methods that use depth cameras [13–16], which provide good results but depend heavily on depth image quality. Because of their capability to track texture-less objects in cluttered scenes, using only a monocular RGB camera, region-based methods [17–21] have become increasingly popular. However, while they reach state-of-the-art results, most methods feature computationally expensive, dense formulations that hardly run in real-time.

To overcome this issue, we propose a novel, sparse approach to region-based 6DoF object tracking that is based on correspondence lines (see Fig. 1). Also, we prove that the developed probabilistic model follows a Gaussian distribution and use this information in a regularized Newton optimization. Finally, in multiple experiments on the *RBOT* dataset [19], we show that our algorithm outperforms state-of-the-art methods both in terms of runtime and tracking success.

2   Related Work

In general, region-based methods differentiate between a foreground area that corresponds to the object and a background area. To model the membership of each pixel, differences in image statistics, such as color, are used. Based on the 3D geometry of the object, the goal is to find the pose that best explains the two regions. While early approaches [22,23] treated segmentation and pose tracking as independent problems that are solved sequentially, [24] combined both stages to increase tracking robustness. Building on this approach and including the pixel-wise posterior membership suggested by [17,25] developed *PWP3D*, a real-time capable algorithm that uses a level-set pose embedding.

Based on the concepts of *PWP3D*, multiple enhancements to incorporate additional information, extend the segmentation model, or improve efficiency were suggested. To fuse depth information, [26] added a term based on the *Iterative Closest Point (ICP)* approach to the energy function. Another method, introduced by [18], maximizes the probability of a model that tightly couples region and depth information. Recently, methods that incorporate texture information were suggested by both [21] and [27]. To better handle occlusion, learning-based object segmentation was proposed by [28]. The incorporation of orientation information from an inertial sensor was presented by [29]. To improve the segmentation model, [30] introduced a boundary term to consider spatial distribution regularities of pixels. Another approach, that was inspired by [31], proposed the use of local appearance models [32]. The idea was later enhanced with the development of temporally consistent local color histograms [19,33]. The most recent method introduced by [20], which is based on [27], uses polar-based region partitioning and edge-based occlusion detection to further improve tracking.

With respect to efficiency, enhancements such as a hierarchical rendering approach with Levenberg-Marquardt optimization [29], a simplified signed distance function [21], or a Gauss-Newton approach [19] were suggested. Another idea by [26] suggests to precompute contour points and use a sparse calculation of the energy function along rays. Starting from those ideas, this work focuses on the development of a highly efficient, sparse approach to region-based tracking. To keep complexity at a minimum, we use the global segmentation model of *PWP3D* and do not consider additional information. Notice, however, that our formulation is general enough to incorporate most of the discussed ideas.

3   Probabilistic Model

In this section, basic mathematical concepts are defined. This is followed by an introduction to our sparse probabilistic model. Finally, we extend this model and develop a discrete scale-space formulation to improve computational efficiency.

3.1   Preliminaries

In this work, 3D model points are defined by $\boldsymbol{X}_i = \begin{bmatrix} X_i\ Y_i\ Z_i \end{bmatrix}^\top \in \mathbb{R}^3$ or the corresponding homogeneous form $\widetilde{\boldsymbol{X}}_i = \begin{bmatrix} X_i\ Y_i\ Z_i\ 1 \end{bmatrix}^\top$. We denote a color image by $\boldsymbol{I}\colon \boldsymbol{\Omega} \to \{0,\ldots,255\}^3$, with the image domain $\boldsymbol{\Omega} \subset \mathbb{R}^2$. The RGB values $\boldsymbol{y}_i$ at image coordinate $\boldsymbol{x}_i = \begin{bmatrix} x_i\ y_i \end{bmatrix}^\top \in \mathbb{R}^2$ are described by $\boldsymbol{y}_i = \boldsymbol{I}(\boldsymbol{x}_i)$. To project a 3D model point into an undistorted image, we use the pinhole camera model

$$\boldsymbol{x}_i = \boldsymbol{\pi}(\boldsymbol{X}_i) = \begin{bmatrix} \frac{X_i}{Z_i} f_x + p_x \\ \frac{Y_i}{Z_i} f_y + p_y \end{bmatrix}, \tag{1}$$

with f_x and f_y the focal lengths and p_x and p_y the principal point coordinates for the directions x and y given in pixels.

To describe the relative pose between the model reference frame M and the camera reference frame C, we use the homogeneous matrix $_\text{C}\boldsymbol{T}_\text{M}$ and calculate

$$_\text{C}\widetilde{\boldsymbol{X}}_i = {}_\text{C}\boldsymbol{T}_\text{M}{}_\text{M}\widetilde{\boldsymbol{X}}_i = \begin{bmatrix} _\text{C}\boldsymbol{R}_\text{M} & _\text{C}\boldsymbol{t}_\text{M} \\ \boldsymbol{0} & 1 \end{bmatrix} {}_\text{M}\widetilde{\boldsymbol{X}}_i, \tag{2}$$

with $_{\mathrm{C}}\widetilde{\boldsymbol{X}}_i$ a 3D model point represented in the camera reference frame C, $_{\mathrm{M}}\widetilde{\boldsymbol{X}}_i$ a 3D model point represented in the model reference frame M, $_{\mathrm{C}}\boldsymbol{R}_{\mathrm{M}} \in \mathbb{SO}(3)$ the rotation matrix for the transformation from M to C, and $_{\mathrm{C}}\boldsymbol{t}_{\mathrm{M}} \in \mathbb{R}^3$ the translation vector for the transformation from M to C.

For small rotations, the angle-axis representation, which is a minimal representation, is used. With the exponential map, the rotation matrix writes as

$$\boldsymbol{R} = \exp([\boldsymbol{r}]_\times) = \boldsymbol{I} + [\boldsymbol{r}]_\times + \frac{1}{2!}[\boldsymbol{r}]_\times^2 + \frac{1}{3!}[\boldsymbol{r}]_\times^3 + ...,\tag{3}$$

where $[\boldsymbol{r}]_\times$ represents the skew-symmetric matrix of $\boldsymbol{r} \in \mathbb{R}^3$. Linearizing Eq. (3), by neglecting higher-order terms of the series expansion, the linear variation of a 3D model point represented in the camera reference frame C is described by

$$_{\mathrm{C}}\widetilde{\boldsymbol{X}}_i^+ = \begin{bmatrix} _{\mathrm{C}}\boldsymbol{R}_{\mathrm{M}} & _{\mathrm{C}}\boldsymbol{t}_{\mathrm{M}} \\ \boldsymbol{0} & 1 \end{bmatrix} \begin{bmatrix} \boldsymbol{I} + [\boldsymbol{\theta}_{\mathrm{r}}]_\times & \boldsymbol{\theta}_{\mathrm{t}} \\ \boldsymbol{0} & 1 \end{bmatrix} {}_{\mathrm{M}}\widetilde{\boldsymbol{X}}_i,\tag{4}$$

with the variated model point $_{\mathrm{C}}\widetilde{\boldsymbol{X}}_i^+$, the rotational variation $\boldsymbol{\theta}_{\mathrm{r}} \in \mathbb{R}^3$, and the translational variation $\boldsymbol{\theta}_{\mathrm{t}} \in \mathbb{R}^3$. In general, variated variables that depend on the full variation vector $\boldsymbol{\theta}^\top = \begin{bmatrix} \boldsymbol{\theta}_{\mathrm{r}}^\top & \boldsymbol{\theta}_{\mathrm{t}}^\top \end{bmatrix}$ are indicated by a plus operator. Notice that it is more natural to variate a model point in the reference frame M instead of C since the object is typically moved significantly more than the camera.

3.2   General Formulation

In contrast to most state-of-the-art algorithms, we do not compute a joint probability over the entire image. Instead, inspired by *RAPID* [7], we introduce a sparse model where the probability is only calculated along a small set of entities that we call correspondence lines. Note that the name is motivated by the term *correspondence points* used in *ICP*, since we also first define correspondences and then optimize with respect to them. A correspondence line is described by a center $\boldsymbol{c}_i = \begin{bmatrix} c_{xi} & c_{yi} \end{bmatrix}^\top \in \mathbb{R}^2$ and a normal vector $\boldsymbol{n}_i = \begin{bmatrix} n_{xi} & n_{yi} \end{bmatrix}^\top \in \mathbb{R}^2$, with $\|\boldsymbol{n}_i\|_2 = 1$. Both values are defined by projecting a 3D contour point $\boldsymbol{X}_i$ and an associated vector normal to the contour $\boldsymbol{N}_i$ into the image. With the distance $r \in \mathbb{R}$ from the center, pixels on the line are described by rounding as follows

$$\boldsymbol{x}_{\mathrm{cli}}(r) = \lfloor \boldsymbol{c}_i + r\,\boldsymbol{n}_i + \boldsymbol{0.5} \rfloor.\tag{5}$$

Once a correspondence line is established, and pixels have been defined, it remains fixed. During the pose variation in 6DoF, the projected difference Δc_i^+ from the unmoved center $\boldsymbol{c}_i$ to the variated model point $_{\mathrm{C}}\boldsymbol{X}_i^+$ is calculated as

$$\Delta c_i^+ = \boldsymbol{n}_i^\top \left(\boldsymbol{\pi}(_{\mathrm{C}}\boldsymbol{X}_i^+) - \boldsymbol{c}_i \right).\tag{6}$$

A visualization of a correspondence line with Δc_i^+ is shown in Fig. 2.

We now adopt the segmentation model of [25] and use color histograms to estimate the probability distributions for the foreground and background in the

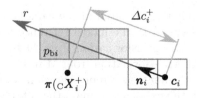

Fig. 2. Correspondence line defined by a center $\boldsymbol{c}_i$ and a normal vector $\boldsymbol{n}_i$, with selected pixels and the projected difference Δc_i^+ from $\boldsymbol{c}_i$ to the variated point $_{\mathrm{C}}\boldsymbol{X}_i^+$. The color intensity in red indicates the magnitude of the pixel-wise posterior $p_{\mathrm{b}i}$ for each pixel. (Color figure online)

RGB color space. For each pixel on the correspondence line and associated color $\boldsymbol{y}_i(r) = \boldsymbol{I}(\boldsymbol{x}_{\mathrm{cli}}(r))$, we use those distributions to calculate pixel-wise posteriors

$$p_{ji}(r) = \frac{p(\boldsymbol{y}_i(r)|m_j)}{p(\boldsymbol{y}_i(r)|m_{\mathrm{f}}) + p(\boldsymbol{y}_i(r)|m_{\mathrm{b}})}, \quad j \in \{\mathrm{f}, \mathrm{b}\}, \tag{7}$$

with m_{f} and m_{b} the foreground and background model, respectively. Based on *PWP3D* [17], we finally develop a probabilistic formulation. It describes how well a pose dependent contour model, which uses smoothed step functions to model uncertainty in the contour location, explains the calculated pixel-wise posteriors

$$p(\boldsymbol{D}_i|\boldsymbol{\theta}) \propto \prod_{r \in \mathcal{R}_i} \Big(h_{\mathrm{f}}(r - \Delta c_i^+)p_{\mathrm{f}i}(r) + h_{\mathrm{b}}(r - \Delta c_i^+)p_{\mathrm{b}i}(r) \Big), \tag{8}$$

with $\boldsymbol{D}_i$ the data specific to a single correspondence line, $\mathcal{R}_i$ a set of distances r from the line center to pixel centers that ensures that every pixel along the line appears exactly once, and h_{f} and h_{b} the smoothed step functions for foreground and background, which will be specified in Sect. 4.1. Finally, assuming n_{cl} independent correspondence lines, the full likelihood can be calculated as

$$p(\boldsymbol{D}|\boldsymbol{\theta}) \propto \prod_{i=1}^{n_{\mathrm{cl}}} p(\boldsymbol{D}_i|\boldsymbol{\theta}). \tag{9}$$

3.3   Discrete Scale-Space Formulation

In order to improve computational efficiency, we develop a discrete scale-space formulation that allows the combination of multiple pixels into segments and the precomputation of h_{f} and h_{b} (see Fig. 3). Real-numbered values, like the distances in $\mathcal{R}_i$, which depend on both the angle and the center of the correspondence line, are projected into a discrete space that is scaled according to

$$r_{\mathrm{s}} = (r - \Delta r_i)\frac{\bar{n}_i}{s}, \quad \Delta c_{\mathrm{s}i}^+ = (\Delta c_i^+ - \Delta r_i)\frac{\bar{n}_i}{s}, \tag{10}$$

with $s \in \mathbb{N}^+$ the scale that describes the number of pixels combined into a segment, $\bar{n}_i = \max(|n_{xi}|, |n_{yi}|)$ the normal component that projects a correspondence line to the closest horizontal or vertical coordinate, and $\Delta r_i \in \mathbb{R}$ a

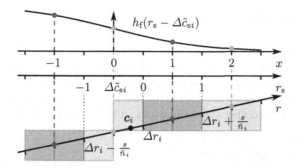

Fig. 3. Example of the relation between the unscaled space r along the correspondence line, the discretized scale-space r_s, and the space x of the smoothed step functions h_f and h_b. Neighboring pixels combined into segments are visualized by the same color. Δr_i was chosen such that the center $r_s = 0$ lies on a defined location on the border between two segments. Blue and yellow dots indicate precalculated values of h_f and segment centers. Dashed vertical lines connecting those dots highlight that $\Delta \tilde{c}_{si}$ has to be chosen such that precalculated values are aligned with segment centers. (Color figure online)

distance from the correspondence line center $\boldsymbol{c}_i$ to a defined segment location. Notice that while, in theory, arbitrary values can be chosen for Δr_i, it is typically chosen to point either to the closest center or border of a segment.

Based on Eq. (8), we write the likelihood function in scale-space as follows

$$p(\boldsymbol{D}_i|\Delta \tilde{c}_{si}) \propto \prod_{r_s \in \mathcal{R}_s} \Big(h_f(r_s - \Delta \tilde{c}_{si})p_{sfi}(r_s) + h_b(r_s - \Delta \tilde{c}_{si})p_{sbi}(r_s) \Big), \qquad (11)$$

with $\mathcal{R}_s$ a set of distances to segment centers that ensures that every segment along the correspondence line appears exactly once, $\Delta \tilde{c}_{si}$ a discretized projected difference value that ensures the alignment with precomputed values of h_f and h_b, and p_{sfi} and p_{sbi} segment-wise posteriors. Assuming pixel-wise independence, we define segment-wise posteriors similar to pixel-wise posteriors as

$$p_{sji}(r_s) = \frac{\prod\limits_{r \in \mathcal{S}(r_s)} p(\boldsymbol{y}_i(r)|m_j)}{\prod\limits_{r \in \mathcal{S}(r_s)} p(\boldsymbol{y}_i(r)|m_f) + \prod\limits_{r \in \mathcal{S}(r_s)} p(\boldsymbol{y}_i(r)|m_b)}, \quad j \in \{f, b\}, \qquad (12)$$

where $\mathcal{S}$ is a set-valued function that maps r_s to a set of values r that describe the s closest pixel centers of a segment. Note that pixel-wise independence is a well-established approximation that avoids ill-defined assumptions about spatial distribution regularities and is close enough to reality to ensure good results.

Due to a limited number of precalculated values for h_f and h_b, the likelihood function in Eq. (11) can only be evaluated at discrete values $\Delta \tilde{c}_{si}$. To approximate the likelihood for arbitrary $\boldsymbol{\theta}$ and corresponding Δc_{si}^+, the upper and lower neighboring discretized values $\Delta \tilde{c}_{si}^+$ and $\Delta \tilde{c}_{si}^-$ are used to linearly interpolate

$$p(\boldsymbol{D}_i|\boldsymbol{\theta}) \propto (\Delta \tilde{c}_{si}^+ - \Delta c_{si}^+)p(\boldsymbol{D}_i|\Delta \tilde{c}_{si}^-) + (\Delta c_{si}^+ - \Delta \tilde{c}_{si}^-)p(\boldsymbol{D}_i|\Delta \tilde{c}_{si}^+). \qquad (13)$$

4   Optimization

In the following section, a novel mathematical proof is derived to find functions h_f and h_b that ensure that the likelihood follows a Gaussian distribution. This is followed by a description of the regularized Newton method that is used to optimize the likelihood. Finally, we define the required gradient and Hessian and discuss how to find robust approximations in the presence of noise.

4.1   Gaussian Equivalence

In general, Newton optimization yields particularly good results for Gaussian distributions. In the case of a perfect normal distribution, where the application of the logarithm leads to a quadratic function, the algorithm converges in a single step. To improve convergence, we thus try to find smoothed step functions h_f and h_b that ensure that the developed likelihood function follows a normal distribution. Please note that only the main concepts of the proof are covered in this section. A detailed version is provided in the supplementary material.

To make the problem tractable, a contour at the correspondence line center and perfect segmentation are assumed. This results in simple unit step functions for pixel-wise posteriors. Also, the smoothed step functions h_f and h_b are restricted to sum to one and to be symmetric. Consequently, we define

$$h_f(x) = 0.5 - f(x), \quad h_b(x) = 0.5 + f(x), \tag{14}$$

where $f(x)$ is an odd function that lies within the interval $[-0.5, 0.5]$ and that fulfills $\lim_{x \to \infty} f(x) = 0.5$ and $\lim_{x \to -\infty} f(x) = -0.5$. Finally, we assume infinitesimally small pixels to write the likelihood from Eq. (8) in continuous form

$$p(\mathcal{D}_i|\boldsymbol{\theta}) \propto \exp\left(\int_{r=-\infty}^{\infty} \ln\left(h_f(r - \Delta c_i^+)p_{fi}(r) + h_b(r - \Delta c_i^+)p_{bi}(r) \right) dr \right). \tag{15}$$

Using the assumption of perfect pixel-wise posteriors, one is able to simplify

$$p(\mathcal{D}_i|\boldsymbol{\theta}) \propto \exp\left(\int_{x=-\infty}^{-\Delta c_i^+} \ln\left(h_f(x) \right) dx + \int_{x=-\Delta c_i^+}^{\infty} \ln\left(h_b(x) \right) dx \right). \tag{16}$$

To eliminate constant scaling terms and the integral, we apply the logarithm and use Leibniz's rule for differentiation under the integral to calculate the first-order derivative with respect to Δc_i^+. This is then factorized using Eq. (14)

$$\frac{\partial \ln\left(p(\mathcal{D}_i|\boldsymbol{\theta}) \right)}{\partial \Delta c_i^+} = -\ln\left(h_f(-\Delta c_i^+) \right) + \ln\left(h_b(-\Delta c_i^+) \right) \tag{17}$$

$$= 2 \tanh^{-1}\left(2f(-\Delta c_i^+) \right). \tag{18}$$

Finally, equality is enforced for the first-order derivative of the logarithm of both

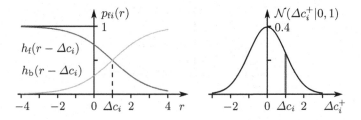

Fig. 4. Example of the relation between our smoothed step functions h_f and h_b and the normal distribution of Δc_i^+ for $s_h = 1$. The graph on the left shows perfect pixel-wise posterior probabilities p_{fi} for the foreground and smoothed step functions for a specific projected difference Δc_i. The graph on the right displays the corresponding normal distribution for all values of Δc_i^+. The probability value for Δc_i is depicted in red. (Color figure online)

the likelihood in Eq. (18) and the normal distribution $\mathcal{N}(\Delta c_i^+|0, s_h)$. Knowing that for the normal distribution one obtains $-s_h^{-1}\Delta c_i^+$, we solve for f and use Eq. (14) to find the following expressions for the smoothed step functions

$$h_f(x) = \frac{1}{2} - \frac{1}{2} \tanh\left(\frac{x}{2s_h}\right), \quad h_b(x) = \frac{1}{2} + \frac{1}{2} \tanh\left(\frac{x}{2s_h}\right), \qquad (19)$$

where s_h is at the same time the slope parameter for the smoothed step functions and the variance of the designed likelihood function.

Since equality is enforced for the first-order derivatives of the logarithms, the original functions can only differ by a constant scaling factor, and we can write

$$p(\mathcal{D}_i|\boldsymbol{\theta}) \propto \mathcal{N}(\Delta c_i^+|0, s_h). \qquad (20)$$

An example of the relation between the smoothed step functions and the resulting normal distribution is shown in Fig. 4. In summary, the proof shows that with the derived smoothed step functions, we attain a probabilistic model that follows a Gaussian distribution. Although assumptions, such as perfect pixel-wise posteriors and infinitesimally small pixels, are not an exact description of reality, experiments demonstrate that, with the constructed probabilistic model, we achieve excellent convergence for the used regularized Newton optimization.

4.2 Regularized Newton Method

To maximize the likelihood, we estimate the variation vector and iteratively update the pose. For a single iteration, the variation vector is calculated using Newton optimization with Tikhonov regularization as follows

$$\hat{\boldsymbol{\theta}} = \left(-\boldsymbol{H} + \begin{bmatrix} \lambda_r \boldsymbol{I}_3 & \boldsymbol{0} \\ \boldsymbol{0} & \lambda_t \boldsymbol{I}_3 \end{bmatrix}\right)^{-1} \boldsymbol{g}, \qquad (21)$$

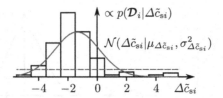

Fig. 5. Example showing normalized values of a noisy discrete likelihood $p(\mathcal{D}_i|\Delta\tilde{c}_{si})$ and the normal distribution $\mathcal{N}(\Delta\tilde{c}_{si}|\mu_{\Delta\tilde{c}_{si}}, \sigma^2_{\Delta\tilde{c}_{si}})$ that approximates that likelihood. The red line indicates a threshold for the probability values. To avoid errors from image noise and invalid pixel-wise posteriors, for values below this threshold, the normal distribution is used in the calculation of partial derivatives of the log-likelihood. (Color figure online)

where $\boldsymbol{g}$ and $\boldsymbol{H}$ are the gradient vector and the Hessian matrix defined as

$$\boldsymbol{g}^{\top} = \frac{\partial}{\partial\boldsymbol{\theta}} \ln\left(p(\boldsymbol{D}\mid\boldsymbol{\theta})\right)\Big|_{\boldsymbol{\theta}=0}, \quad \boldsymbol{H} = \frac{\partial^2}{\partial\boldsymbol{\theta}^2} \ln\left(p(\boldsymbol{D}\mid\boldsymbol{\theta})\right)\Big|_{\boldsymbol{\theta}=0}, \tag{22}$$

and λ_{r} and λ_{t} the regularization parameters for rotation and translation, respectively. Using the log-likelihood has the advantage that scaling terms vanish and products turn into summations. Finally, the pose can be updated according to

$$_{\mathrm{C}}\boldsymbol{T}_{\mathrm{M}} = {}_{\mathrm{C}}\boldsymbol{T}_{\mathrm{M}} \begin{bmatrix} \exp([\hat{\boldsymbol{\theta}}_{\mathrm{r}}]_{\times})\,\hat{\boldsymbol{\theta}}_{\mathrm{t}} \\ \boldsymbol{0} & 1 \end{bmatrix}. \tag{23}$$

Notice that due to the exponential map, no orthonormalization is necessary. By iteratively repeating the process, we are now able to estimate the optimal pose.

4.3   Gradient and Hessian Approximation

Using the chain rule, the gradient vector and Hessian matrix can be defined as

$$\boldsymbol{g}^{\top} = \sum_{i=1}^{n_{\mathrm{cl}}} \frac{\partial\ln\left(p(\boldsymbol{D}_i\mid\boldsymbol{\theta})\right)}{\partial\Delta c_{si}^+} \frac{\partial\Delta c_{si}^+}{\partial_{\mathrm{C}}\boldsymbol{X}_i^+} \frac{\partial_{\mathrm{C}}\boldsymbol{X}_i^+}{\partial\boldsymbol{\theta}}\Big|_{\boldsymbol{\theta}=0}, \tag{24}$$

$$\boldsymbol{H} \approx \sum_{i=1}^{n_{\mathrm{cl}}} \frac{\partial^2\ln\left(p(\boldsymbol{D}_i\mid\boldsymbol{\theta})\right)}{\partial\Delta c_{si}^{+2}} \left(\frac{\partial\Delta c_{si}^+}{\partial_{\mathrm{C}}\boldsymbol{X}_i^+} \frac{\partial_{\mathrm{C}}\boldsymbol{X}_i^+}{\partial\boldsymbol{\theta}}\right)^{\top} \left(\frac{\partial\Delta c_{si}^+}{\partial_{\mathrm{C}}\boldsymbol{X}_i^+} \frac{\partial_{\mathrm{C}}\boldsymbol{X}_i^+}{\partial\boldsymbol{\theta}}\right)\Big|_{\boldsymbol{\theta}=0}. \tag{25}$$

Notice that since the first-order partial derivative of the log-likelihood becomes zero when the optimization reaches the maximum, second-order partial derivatives for Δc_{si}^+ and $_{\mathrm{C}}\boldsymbol{X}_i^+$ are neglected. Omitting the plus operator for variables evaluated at $\boldsymbol{\theta} = 0$ and using Eq. (4), (6), and (10), we calculate

$$\frac{\partial_{\mathrm{C}}\boldsymbol{X}_i^+}{\partial\boldsymbol{\theta}}\Big|_{\boldsymbol{\theta}=0} = {}_{\mathrm{C}}\boldsymbol{R}_{\mathrm{M}} \begin{bmatrix} -[_{\mathrm{M}}\boldsymbol{X}_i]_{\times} & \boldsymbol{I} \end{bmatrix}, \tag{26}$$

$$\left.\frac{\partial \Delta c_{si}^+}{\partial_C X_i^+}\right|_{\theta=0} = \frac{\bar{n}_i}{s}\frac{1}{_C Z_i^2}\begin{bmatrix} n_{xi}f_{xC}Z_i & n_{yi}f_{yC}Z_i & -n_{xi}f_{xC}X_i - n_{yi}f_{yC}Y_i \end{bmatrix}. \quad (27)$$

For the first-order partial derivative of the log-likelihood, two cases are distinguished. If the normalized values of $p(\mathbf{D}_i|\Delta\tilde{c}_{si}^+)$ and $p(\mathbf{D}_i|\Delta\tilde{c}_{si}^-)$ are above a defined threshold, we assume that they are reliable and, based on Eq. (13), write

$$\left.\frac{\partial \ln\left(p(\mathbf{D}_i \mid \boldsymbol{\theta})\right)}{\partial \Delta c_{si}^+}\right|_{\theta=0} \approx \frac{p(\mathbf{D}_i|\Delta\tilde{c}_{si}^+) - p(\mathbf{D}_i|\Delta\tilde{c}_{si}^-)}{(\Delta\tilde{c}_{si}^+ - \Delta c_{si})p(\mathbf{D}_i|\Delta\tilde{c}_{si}^-) + (\Delta c_{si} - \Delta\tilde{c}_{si}^-)p(\mathbf{D}_i|\Delta\tilde{c}_{si}^+)}. \quad (28)$$

If one value is below the threshold, the knowledge that $p(\mathbf{D}_i \mid \Delta\tilde{c}_{si})$ follows a normal distribution is used. The distribution can be estimated using the mean $\mu_{\Delta\tilde{c}_{si}}$ and the standard deviation $\sigma_{\Delta\tilde{c}_{si}}$ calculated from $p(\mathbf{D}_i \mid \Delta\tilde{c}_{si})$ (see Fig. 5). Consequently, the first-order partial derivative can be approximated by

$$\left.\frac{\partial \ln\left(p(\mathbf{D}_i \mid \boldsymbol{\theta})\right)}{\partial \Delta c_{si}^+}\right|_{\theta=0} \approx -\frac{1}{\sigma_{\Delta\tilde{c}_{si}}^2}\left(\Delta c_{si} - \mu_{\Delta\tilde{c}_{si}}\right). \quad (29)$$

For the second-order partial derivative, we always use the approximation

$$\left.\frac{\partial^2 \ln\left(p(\mathbf{D}_i \mid \boldsymbol{\theta})\right)}{\partial \Delta c_{si}^{+2}}\right|_{\theta=0} \approx -\frac{1}{\sigma_{\Delta\tilde{c}_{si}}^2}. \quad (30)$$

The approximations ensure that our partial derivatives maintain a global view of the distribution and that they are robust in the presence of image noise and invalid pixel-wise posteriors. Also, notice that distinguishing between the two cases allows the first-order derivative to direct the optimization toward the actual maximum while remaining stable for small, inaccurate probability values.

5 Implementation

For the proposed method, 3D points and normal vectors from the contour of the model are required. To ensure computational efficiency, we take an approach similar to [16] and precompute template views that store the required information. The 3D model of an object is thereby rendered from 2562 different viewpoints that are placed on the vertices of a geodesic grid with a distance of 0.8 m to the object center. For each rendering, we randomly sample $n_{cl} = 200$ points from the object contour. Based on those coordinates, 3D model points and associated normal vectors are reconstructed. In addition, we compute continuous distances for the foreground and background, where the corresponding regions are not interrupted by the other. Starting from a coordinate, those distances are measured along the normal vector. For each view, the data is then stored together with a direction vector $_M \boldsymbol{v}_i \in \mathbb{R}^3$ that points from the camera to the model center.

Each tracking step starts either from the previous pose or an initial pose provided by a 3D object detection pipeline. Based on this pose, we first retrieve the template view i_t that is closest to the direction in which the object is located

$$i_t = \arg\max_{i \in \{1,\dots,2562\}} ({}_M\boldsymbol{v}_i^\top {}_M\boldsymbol{R}_{CC}\boldsymbol{t}_M). \tag{31}$$

Model points and normal vectors from the template view are then projected into the image plane to define correspondence lines. For the probabilistic model, a continuous foreground and background on each side of the contour are required. We thus scale precomputed continuous distances according to the current camera distance and scale s and reject correspondence lines with a continuous distance below 8 segments. After that, each distribution $p(\boldsymbol{D}_i \mid \Delta \tilde{c}_{si})$ is calculated for 11 discrete values $\Delta \tilde{c}_{si} \in \{-5, -4, \dots, 5\}$. The distance Δr_i is thereby chosen to be minimal such that the distribution center at $\Delta c_{si}^+ = 0$ is closest to the correspondence line center $\boldsymbol{c}_i$. For the smoothed step functions, 10 precomputed values corresponding to $x \in \{-4.5, -3.5, \dots, 4.5\}$ are used. Both h_f and h_b are defined using a slope of $s_h = 1.3$. Notice that with this slope, the smallest considered value is $h_f(4.5) = 0.03$. Values smaller than that are neglected since, in general, they do not contribute significantly to the overall distribution.

Following the calculation of the distributions, 2 iterations of the regularized Newton method are performed. Both the gradient and Hessian are recomputed for each iteration. As threshold for the normalized values of $p(\boldsymbol{D}_i|\Delta \tilde{c}_{si}^+)$ and $p(\boldsymbol{D}_i|\Delta \tilde{c}_{si}^-)$, we use 0.01. Also, we check if the standard deviation $\sigma_{\Delta \tilde{c}_{si}}$ is above the theoretical minimum $\sqrt{s_h}$. If it is smaller, due to the limited number of values considered in the distribution, it is set to $\sqrt{s_h}$. Similarly, the magnitude of the first-order derivative of the log-likelihood in Eq. (28) is limited by the theoretical maximum $10/s_h$. For the regularization, we use $\lambda_r = 5000$ and $\lambda_t = 500000$.

To find the final pose, the process is repeated 7 times, starting each time with the retrieval of a new template view. The first and second iterations use a scale of $s = 5$ and $s = 2$, respectively. For all other iterations, the scale is set to $s = 1$. Examples of different scales are shown in Fig. 1. The specified scales have the effect that in the first iteration a large area with low resolution is considered while short lines with high resolution are used in later iterations.

Once the final pose is estimated, the color histograms, that correspond to the probability distributions $p(\boldsymbol{y}|m_f)$ and $p(\boldsymbol{y}|m_b)$, are updated. The RGB color space is thereby discretized with 32 equidistant bins in each dimension, leading to a total of 32768 values. For the calculation, correspondence lines are established. Pixels along the line are then assigned to either the foreground or background, depending on which side of the center they are. Starting with an offset of 2 pixels, the first 10 pixels are used in both directions. Based on [25], we allow for online adaptation of the foreground and background statistical model as follows

$$p_t(\boldsymbol{y}|m_i) = \alpha_i p_t(\boldsymbol{y}|m_i) + (1 - \alpha_i)p_{t-1}(\boldsymbol{y}|m_i), \quad i \in \{f, b\}, \tag{32}$$

where $\alpha_f = 0.1$ and $\alpha_b = 0.2$ are the learning rates for the foreground and background, respectively. The update ensures that effects such as changes in illumination or in the background are considered. For the initialization, we directly use the computed histograms instead of blending them with previous values.

To take into account known occlusions, a renderer that generates occlusion masks for the rejection of correspondence lines is implemented. It only uses a fourth of the camera resolution to ensure computational efficiency. Also, the silhouette of each object is dilated by 1 pixel in the mask domain to consider uncertainty in the object pose. Finally, to reject occluded correspondence lines, the algorithm checks if the center c_i falls on the mask of another object.

6   Evaluation

In the following, we first introduce the *Region-Based Object Tracking (RBOT)* dataset [19] and describe the conducted experiments. Our results are then compared to the state of the art in region-based tracking [19,20,27,33]. Finally, based on an ablation study in the supplementary material, we discuss the essential aspects of our method. To ensure reproducibility, we provide the source code on *GitHub*[1]. Also, for visualization, we added a video in the supplementary material that illustrates the *RBOT* dataset, our approach, and the experiments. In addition, multiple real-world sequences are available on our project site[2].

Fig. 6. Overview of all objects in the *RBOT* dataset [19]. Objects from the *LINEMOD* dataset [34] and *Rigid Pose* dataset [35] are marked with * and °, respectively.

6.1   Experiments

The *RBOT* dataset consists of a collection of eighteen objects (see Fig. 6): twelve from the *LINEMOD* dataset [34], five from the *Rigid Pose* dataset [35], and one from its creators. For each object, four sequences exist. Each sequence consists of 1001 semi-synthetic monocular images with a resolution of 640 × 512 pixels. Objects were rendered into real-world images, recorded from a hand-held camera that moves around a cluttered desk scene (see Fig. 1). To simulate motion blur, a 3 × 3 Gaussian kernel was applied. The first sequence features a *regular* version with a static point light source. The second, *dynamic light*, variant simulates

---

[1] https://github.com/DLR-RM/RBGT.

[2] https://rmc.dlr.de/rm/staff/manuel.stoiber/accv2020.

simultaneous motion of the camera and object. For the third sequence, Gaussian *noise* and dynamic lighting were added. Finally, the fourth sequence features an additional squirrel object that leads to *occlusion* by orbiting around the first object. It also includes dynamic lighting. In all sequences, objects move along the same trajectories. The ground-truth pose is given by the rotation matrix $_{C}\boldsymbol{R}_{M_{gt}}(t_k)$ and the translation vector $_{C}\boldsymbol{t}_{M_{gt}}(t_k)$ for $k \in \{0, \ldots, 1000\}$.

The evaluation is conducted on a computer with an *Intel Xeon E5-1630 v4* CPU and a *Nvidia Quadro P600* GPU. All experiments are performed exactly as in [19], with the translational and rotational error calculated as

$$e_t(t_k) = \|_{C}\boldsymbol{t}_M(t_k) - _{C}\boldsymbol{t}_{M_{gt}}(t_k)\|_2, \tag{33}$$

$$e_r(t_k) = \cos^{-1}\left(0.5\left(\operatorname{trace}(_{C}\boldsymbol{R}_M(t_k)^\top {_{C}\boldsymbol{R}_{M_{gt}}}(t_k)) - 1\right)\right). \tag{34}$$

Starting from an initialization with the ground-truth pose at t_0, the tracker runs automatically until either the recorded sequence ends or tracking was unsuccessful. A pose is considered successful if both $e_t(t_k) < 5\,\text{cm}$ and $e_r(t_k) < 5°$. Otherwise, the tracker is re-initialized with the ground-truth pose at t_k. For the *occlusion* sequence, we differentiate between two variants. In the first, only the main object is tracked, and occlusions are considered as *unmodeled*. In the second, both objects are tracked, and occlusions are *modeled* using occlusion masks. Notice that, while the occluding object is re-initialized if tracking is unsuccessful, it is not considered in the evaluation of the tracking success.

6.2   Results

In Table 1, we compare the success rates of state-of-the-art methods to our proposed approach. Note that [27] and [20] do not support the *modeled occlusion* scenario. The results show that our approach outperforms the competition in almost all cases by a large margin. Only for very few cases, [19] or [20] produce better results. With respect to the average success rates, our method consistently achieves about seven percentage points more than [20], which previously performed best on the *RBOT* dataset. The superior tracking success is especially interesting since, in contrast to the competition, we do not use advanced segmentation models. Assuming that localized appearance models provide better segmentation, this represents a major disadvantage.

With respect to the remaining failure cases, we notice that there are mainly two causes. One challenge are local ambiguities, where the object silhouette is very similar in the vicinity of a particular pose. Naturally, in such cases, there is not enough information to converge to the correct pose. Another problem arises if large regions in the background contain colors that are also present in the object. Depending on how well the pose is constrained, this might perturb the final result. Together with the requirements that the 3D model has to be known and that frame-to-frame motion should not exceed the area covered by correspondence lines, these are the natural limitations of our algorithm.

Table 1. Tracking success rates of [19, 20, 27, 33], and our method, featuring all variants of the *RBOT* dataset. The best values are highlighted in bold numbers.

Method	Ape	Soda	Vise	Soup	Camera	Can	Cat	Clown	Cube	Driller	Duck	Egg Box	Glue	Iron	Candy	Lamp	Phone	Squirrel	Average
Regular																			
[33]	62.1	30.5	95.8	66.2	61.6	81.7	96.7	89.1	44.1	87.7	74.9	50.9	20.2	68.4	20.0	92.3	64.9	98.5	67.0
[19]	85.0	39.0	**98.9**	82.4	79.7	87.6	95.9	93.3	78.1	**93.0**	86.8	74.6	38.9	81.0	46.8	**97.5**	80.7	99.4	79.9
[27]	82.6	40.1	92.6	85.0	82.8	87.2	98.0	92.9	81.3	84.5	83.3	76.2	56.1	84.6	57.6	90.5	82.6	95.6	80.8
[20]	88.8	41.3	94.0	85.9	86.9	89.0	98.5	93.7	83.1	87.3	86.2	78.5	58.6	86.3	57.9	91.7	85.0	96.2	82.7
Us	**96.4**	**53.2**	98.8	**93.9**	**93.0**	**92.7**	**99.7**	**97.1**	**92.5**	92.5	**93.7**	**88.5**	**70.0**	**92.1**	**78.8**	95.5	**92.5**	**99.6**	**90.0**
Dynamic light																			
[33]	61.7	32.0	94.2	66.3	68.0	84.1	96.6	85.8	45.7	88.7	74.1	56.9	29.9	49.1	20.7	91.5	63.0	98.5	67.0
[19]	84.9	42.0	99.0	81.3	84.3	88.9	95.6	92.5	77.5	**94.6**	86.4	77.3	52.9	77.9	47.9	**96.9**	81.7	99.3	81.2
[27]	81.8	39.7	91.5	85.1	84.2	88.9	98.1	90.7	79.7	87.4	81.6	73.1	51.7	75.9	53.4	88.8	78.6	95.6	79.0
[20]	89.7	40.2	92.7	86.5	86.6	89.2	98.3	93.9	81.8	88.4	83.9	76.8	55.3	79.3	54.7	88.7	81.0	95.8	81.3
Us	**96.5**	**54.6**	**99.1**	**93.9**	**93.1**	**94.7**	**99.5**	**97.0**	**93.0**	93.4	**93.3**	**92.6**	**74.9**	**91.0**	**79.2**	95.6	**89.8**	**99.5**	**90.6**
Noise																			
[33]	55.9	35.3	75.4	67.4	27.8	10.2	94.3	33.4	8.6	50.9	76.3	2.3	2.2	18.2	11.4	36.6	31.3	93.5	40.6
[19]	77.5	44.5	**91.5**	82.9	51.7	38.4	95.1	69.2	24.4	64.3	88.5	11.2	2.9	46.7	32.7	57.3	44.1	96.6	56.6
[27]	80.5	35.0	80.9	85.5	58.4	53.5	96.7	65.9	38.2	71.8	85.8	29.7	17.0	59.3	34.8	61.1	60.8	93.6	61.6
[20]	79.3	35.2	82.6	86.2	65.1	56.9	96.9	67.0	37.5	75.2	85.4	35.2	18.9	63.7	35.4	**64.6**	66.3	93.2	63.6
Us	**91.9**	**53.3**	90.2	**92.6**	**67.9**	**59.3**	**98.4**	**80.6**	**43.5**	**78.1**	**92.5**	**44.0**	**31.3**	**72.3**	**62.0**	59.9	**71.7**	**98.3**	**71.5**
Unmodeled occlusion																			
[33]	55.2	29.9	82.4	56.9	55.7	72.2	87.9	75.7	39.6	78.7	68.1	47.1	26.2	35.6	16.6	78.6	50.3	77.6	57.5
[19]	80.0	42.7	91.8	73.5	76.1	81.7	89.8	82.6	68.7	86.7	80.5	67.0	46.6	64.0	43.6	88.8	66.2	86.2	73.3
[27]	77.7	37.3	87.1	78.7	74.6	81.0	93.8	84.3	73.2	83.7	77.0	66.4	48.6	70.8	49.6	85.0	73.8	90.6	74.1
[20]	83.9	38.1	92.4	81.5	81.3	85.5	**97.5**	88.9	76.1	87.5	81.7	72.7	52.5	77.2	53.9	88.5	79.3	92.5	78.4
Us	**90.8**	**51.7**	**95.9**	**88.5**	**88.0**	**90.5**	96.9	**91.6**	**87.1**	**90.3**	**86.4**	**85.6**	**65.8**	**87.0**	**72.7**	**91.2**	**84.0**	**97.0**	**85.6**
Modeled occlusion																			
[33]	60.3	31.0	94.3	64.5	67.0	81.6	92.5	81.4	43.2	89.3	72.7	51.6	28.8	53.5	19.1	89.3	62.2	96.7	65.5
[19]	82.0	42.0	95.7	81.1	78.7	83.4	92.8	87.9	74.3	91.7	84.8	71.0	49.1	73.0	46.3	90.9	76.2	96.9	77.7
Us	**95.0**	**53.8**	**97.8**	**92.4**	**90.6**	**93.5**	**99.1**	**96.3**	**91.5**	**92.6**	**90.9**	**91.3**	**70.5**	**91.8**	**77.2**	**93.7**	**87.0**	**99.0**	**89.1**

For the average runtime, we measure 1.04 ms. The only exception is the *modeled occlusion* scenario, which features two objects and requires to render occlusion masks. For this scenario, we obtain an average execution time of 7.41 ms. In comparison, [19, 27, 33], and [20] report average runtimes of 12.5 ∼ 33.3 ms, 15.5 ∼ 21.8 ms, 47.0 ms, and 41.2 ms, respectively. While experiments were performed on different computers, the significantly lower execution time demonstrates our method's computational efficiency. Also, our algorithm only utilizes a single CPU core and, except for the *modeled occlusion* variant, does not rely on a GPU. In contrast, the competition always requires a GPU. We thus conclude that, with less computational resources, our method is approximately one order of magnitude faster while achieving significantly better tracking success.

6.3 Essential Aspects

Based on an ablation study that is presented in the supplementary material, in the following, we want to highlight essential aspects that contribute to our excellent results. Regarding computational efficiency, the biggest performance gain is associated with our sparse formulation that considers fewer pixels. In addition, we simply measure the projected distance along correspondence lines instead of calculating a two-dimensional signed distance function over the entire image. Also, with our discrete scale-space formulation, we are able to both combine multiple pixels and use precomputed values for the smoothed step functions.

Concerning tracking success, one essential aspect is the adopted Tikhonov regularization, which constrains the optimization relative to the previous pose. Also, due to the one-dimensionality of our correspondence lines and the developed discrete scale-space implementation, multiple probability values along lines can be sampled in reasonable time. This allows the calculation of sound derivatives that maintain a global view of the distribution. Together with the derived smoothed step functions, that ensure Gaussian properties, a realistic gradient and Hessian are provided to the regularized Newton optimization.

7 Conclusion

In this work, we presented a novel, sparse approach to region-based 6DoF object tracking. On the *RBOT* dataset, we showed that our algorithm outperforms state-of-the-art region-based methods by a considerable margin, both with respect to tracking success and computational efficiency. Because of its general formulation, it is easy to conceive future methods that extend our approach with other developments in region-based tracking. Potential directions include the implementation of more advanced segmentation models or the incorporation of additional information such as depth or texture. In addition, by proving that our probabilistic model follows a Gaussian distribution, we provided a solid foundation for sound uncertainty estimation based on the Hessian matrix.

References

1. Lepetit, V., Fua, P.: Monocular Model-Based 3D Tracking of Rigid Objects: A Survey. Foundations and Trends in Computer Graphics and Vision, vol. 1 (2005)
2. Yilmaz, A., Javed, O., Shah, M.: Object tracking: a survey. ACM Comput. Surv. **38**, 13 (2006)
3. Rosten, E., Drummond, T.: Fusing points and lines for high performance tracking. In: IEEE International Conference on Computer Vision, vol. 2, pp. 1508–1515 (2005)
4. Wagner, D., Reitmayr, G., Mulloni, A., Drummond, T., Schmalstieg, D.: Real-time detection and tracking for augmented reality on mobile phones. IEEE Trans. Visual Comput. Graphics **16**, 355–368 (2010)
5. Lucas, B.D., Kanade, T.: An iterative image registration technique with an application to stereo vision. In: Proceedings of the 7th International Joint Conference on Artificial Intelligence, vol. 2, pp. 674–679 (1981)
6. Baker, S., Matthews, I.: Lucas-Kanade 20 years on: a unifying framework. Int. J. Comput. Vision **56**, 221–255 (2004)
7. Harris, C., Stennett, C.: RAPID - a video rate object tracker. In: Proceedings of the British Machine Vision Conference, pp. 15:1–15:6 (1990)
8. Wuest, H., Stricker, D.: Tracking of industrial objects by using CAD models. J. Virtual Reality Broadcast. **4** (2007)
9. Seo, B., Park, H., Park, J., Hinterstoisser, S., Ilic, S.: Optimal local searching for fast and robust textureless 3D object tracking in highly cluttered backgrounds. IEEE Trans. Visual Comput. Graphics **20**, 99–110 (2014)

10. Garon, M., Lalonde, J.F.: Deep 6-DOF tracking. IEEE Trans. Visual Comput. Graphics **23**, 2410–2418 (2017)
11. Crivellaro, A., Rad, M., Verdie, Y., Yi, K.M., Fua, P., Lepetit, V.: Robust 3D object tracking from monocular images using stable parts. IEEE Trans. Pattern Anal. Mach. Intell. **40**, 1465–1479 (2018)
12. Li, Y., Wang, G., Ji, X., Xiang, Y., Fox, D.: DeepIM: deep iterative matching for 6D pose estimation. In: European Conference on Computer Vision, pp. 695–711 (2018)
13. Newcombe, R.A., et al.: KinectFusion: real-time dense surface mapping and tracking. In: IEEE International Symposium on Mixed and Augmented Reality, pp. 127–136 (2011)
14. Choi, C., Christensen, H.I.: RGB-D object tracking: a particle filter approach on GPU. In: IEEE/RSJ International Conference on Intelligent Robots and Systems, pp. 1084–1091 (2013)
15. Krull, A., Michel, F., Brachmann, E., Gumhold, S., Ihrke, S., Rother, C.: 6-DOF model based tracking via object coordinate regression. In: Asian Conference on Computer Vision, pp. 384–399 (2015)
16. Tan, D.J., Navab, N., Tombari, F.: Looking beyond the simple scenarios: combining learners and optimizers in 3D temporal tracking. IEEE Trans. Visual Comput. Graphics **23**, 2399–2409 (2017)
17. Prisacariu, V.A., Reid, I.D.: PWP3D: real-time segmentation and tracking of 3D objects. Int. J. Comput. Vision **98**, 335–354 (2012)
18. Ren, C.Y., Prisacariu, V.A., Kähler, O., Reid, I.D., Murray, D.W.: Real-time tracking of single and multiple objects from depth-colour imagery using 3D signed distance functions. Int. J. Comput. Vision **124**, 80–95 (2017)
19. Tjaden, H., Schwanecke, U., Schömer, E., Cremers, D.: A region-based Gauss-Newton approach to real-time monocular multiple object tracking. IEEE Trans. Pattern Anal. Mach. Intell. **41**, 1797–1812 (2018)
20. Zhong, L., Zhao, X., Zhang, Y., Zhang, S., Zhang, L.: Occlusion-aware region-based 3D pose tracking of objects with temporally consistent polar-based local partitioning. IEEE Trans. Image Process. **29**, 5065–5078 (2020)
21. Liu, Y., Sun, P., Namiki, A.: Target tracking of moving and rotating object by high-speed monocular active vision. IEEE Sens. J. **20**, 6727–6744 (2020)
22. Rosenhahn, B., Brox, T., Weickert, J.: Three-dimensional shape knowledge for joint image segmentation and pose tracking. Int. J. Comput. Vision **73**, 243–262 (2007)
23. Schmaltz, C., Rosenhahn, B., Brox, T., Weickert, J.: Region-based pose tracking with occlusions using 3D models. Mach. Vis. Appl. **23**, 557–577 (2012)
24. Dambreville, S., Sandhu, R., Yezzi, A., Tannenbaum, A.: Robust 3D pose estimation and efficient 2D region-based segmentation from a 3D shape prior. In: European Conference on Computer Vision, pp. 169–182 (2008)
25. Bibby, C., Reid, I.: Robust real-time visual tracking using pixel-wise posteriors. In: European Conference on Computer Vision, pp. 831–844 (2008)
26. Kehl, W., Tombari, F., Ilic, S., Navab, N.: Real-time 3D model tracking in color and depth on a single CPU core. In: IEEE Conference on Computer Vision and Pattern Recognition, pp. 465–473 (2017)
27. Zhong, L., Zhang, L.: A robust monocular 3D object tracking method combining statistical and photometric constraints. Int. J. Comput. Vision **127**, 973–992 (2019)
28. Zhong, L., et al.: Seeing through the occluders: robust monocular 6-DOF object pose tracking via model-guided video object segmentation. IEEE Robot. Autom. Lett. **5**(4), 5159–5166 (2020)

29. Prisacariu, V.A., Kähler, O., Murray, D.W., Reid, I.D.: Real-time 3D tracking and reconstruction on mobile phones. IEEE Trans. Visual Comput. Graphics **21**, 557–570 (2015)

30. Zhao, S., Wang, L., Sui, W., Wu, H., Pan, C.: 3D object tracking via boundary constrained region-based model. In: IEEE International Conference on Image Processing, pp. 486–490 (2014)

31. Lankton, S., Tannenbaum, A.: Localizing region-based active contours. IEEE Trans. Image Process. **17**, 2029–2039 (2008)

32. Hexner, J., Hagege, R.R.: 2D–3D pose estimation of heterogeneous objects using a region based approach. Int. J. Comput. Vision **118**, 95–112 (2016)

33. Tjaden, H., Schwanecke, U., Schomer, E.: Real-time monocular pose estimation of 3D objects using temporally consistent local color histograms. In: IEEE International Conference on Computer Vision, pp. 124–132 (2017)

34. Hinterstoisser, S., et al.: Model based training, detection and pose estimation of texture-less 3D objects in heavily cluttered scenes. In: Asian Conference on Computer Vision, pp. 548–562 (2013)

35. Pauwels, K., Rubio, L., Dîaz, J., Ros, E.: Real-time model-based rigid object pose estimation and tracking combining dense and sparse visual cues. In: IEEE Conference on Computer Vision and Pattern Recognition, pp. 2347–2354 (2013)

Modeling Cross-Modal Interaction in a Multi-detector, Multi-modal Tracking Framework

Yiqi Zhong[1]($\boxtimes$), Suya You[2], and Ulrich Neumann[1]

[1] University of Southern California, Los Angeles, CA 90007, USA
{yiqizhon,uneumann}@usc.edu
[2] US Army Research Laboratory, Playa Vista, CA 90094, USA
suya.you.civ@mail.mil

Abstract. Different modalities have their own advantages and disadvantages. In a tracking-by-detection framework, fusing data from multiple modalities would ideally improve tracking performance than using a single modality, but this has been a challenge. This study builds upon previous research in this area. We propose a deep-learning based tracking-by-detection pipeline that uses multiple detectors and multiple sensors. For the input, we associate object proposals from 2D and 3D detectors. Through a cross-modal attention module, we optimize interaction between the 2D RGB and 3D point clouds features of each proposal. This helps to generate 2D features with suppressed irrelevant information for boosting performance. Through experiments on a published benchmark, we prove the value and ability of our design in introducing a multi-modal tracking solution to the current research on Multi-Object Tracking (MOT).

1 Introduction

Multi-object tracking (MOT) is a crucial task in many fields including robotics and autonomous driving. As different sensors (e.g., RGB camera, LiDAR, radar) get increasingly used together, the multi-modal MOT starts to attract research attention. The introduction of multi-modal solutions helps to better accomplish MOT tasks in a lot of ways. One benefit is that multiple sensors increase the diversity of object representations, which provides higher association reliability across objects from different timestamps.

In this study, we focus on the combined use of LiDAR and RGB camera sensors in MOT. Prior works on multi-modal MOT have explored better strategies of multi-modal feature fusion for boosting tracking performance. They, however, overlook the interaction between features of different modality, which could have provided rich information. For example, the 2D representation of a partially occluded vehicle would inevitably contain a certain amount of irrelevant information of other objects in the scene; however, the 3D representation is able to easily distinguish the vehicle from other objects. In this situation, we may introduce

H. Ishikawa et al. (Eds.): ACCV 2020, LNCS 12623, pp. 683–699, 2021.
https://doi.org/10.1007/978-3-030-69532-3_41

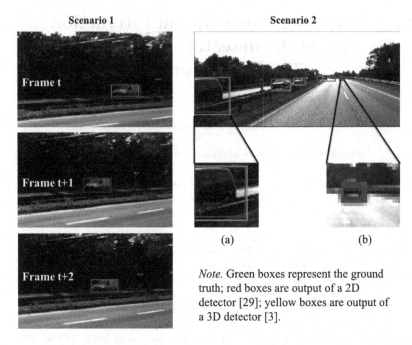

Note. Green boxes represent the ground truth; red boxes are output of a 2D detector [29]; yellow boxes are output of a 3D detector [3].

Fig. 1. Possible failure cases of single-detector methods for tracking. Scenario 1 shows three consecutive frames from the KITTI dataset. Even on the same object, a detector would make inconsistent detection decisions across frames. Hence, tracking failure may occur if only one detector is used. Scenario 2 demonstrates some typical limitations of 2D/3D detectors: the 2D detector failed to detect the partially visible object (a); the 3D detector failed to detect the small object (b). (Color figure online)

3D features to interact with 2D features to suppress irrelevant signals. Following this thread, we propose a new feature fusion strategy. In our proposed method, features of different modalities are extracted separately before they fully interact with each other through a cross-modal attention module which is described in Sect. 3.3. The interaction-aware features are then used for inter-frame proposals association.

Tracking often relies on detection. Multi-modal trackers in previous research usually require a detector to offer object proposals. The detector can be either 2D, 3D, or multi-modal. Different types of detectors have their own advantages and disadvantages: 2D detector has a higher precision but is sensitive to lighting conditions and occlusion; whereas 3D detector excels at handling occlusions but has high false alarm rates. Figure 1 shows two scenarios where the tracker may fail if we only use one type of detector. Intuitively, a multi-modal detectors should enable 2D and 3D features to complement each other's weaknesses. However, recent multi-modal detectors like [1,2] surprisingly do not outperform current SOTA 3D detector such as PointPillar [3] or PV-RCNN [4]. It appears that the community is still exploring an appropriate way to adopt the multi-modal setting in detection tasks. Hence, we propose the present study, which may be the first to associate multiple single-modal detectors in one tracking task. The cardinal challenge of our pipeline is how to reorganize proposals from multiple detectors in order to simultaneously retain merits and suppress demerits of each modality. To tackle this challenge, we design a classification module to re-classify raw proposals. We provide detailed explanations in Sect. 3.2.

Our work contributes to the current literature on MOT in three aspects.

1. Propose a novel cross-modal attention module to explicitly embed interaction between different modalities in feature fusion process;
2. Yield more robust tracking performance by associating object proposals from multiple single-modal detectors;
3. Conduct experiments to compare with published benchmarks, proving the value and potential of our proposed framework.

2   Related Work

2.1   Multi-object Tracking

As we stated above, tracking often relies on detection. This type of tracking method is known as the tracking-by-detection paradigm [5]. It takes object proposals from out-of-shell detectors as the input, and then associates the proposals to produce trajectories of each object of interest. The performance of this type of tracker, hence, is highly associated with the quality of detection results. In this section, we review seminal works on the tracking-by-detection paradigm.

A tracking-by-detection paradigm breaks down into two steps, feature extraction and data association. Feature extraction usually refers to the procedure of extracting features from each object proposal. Data association is correlating the features of proposals from different timestamps in order to discover proposals that belong to the same object. Based on proposals of the same object, the trajectory of each object is then generated.

Image based trackers (e.g. [6–8]) extract features from cropped image patches, which are defined by the 2D bounding boxes that the detectors produce. For LiDAR based methods [9,10], the LiDAR points inside every proposed 3D bounding box also take part in the feature extraction procedure. More recently, a few works [11,12] have raised the concept of 2D and 3D based multi-modal trackers. Trackers of this kind fuse the features from two modalities using different strategies. For instance, [12] directly concatenates the 2D and 3D features for later use to maintain the information from each modality. In comparison, [11] sums up features from two modalities and inputs them to a self-attention fusion module to generate the final feature. Similar to [11], we adopt an attention mechanism for feature fusion. However, instead of self-attention, we introduce a cross-modal attention module that allows 3D features to help generate attention masks for corresponding 2D features. In this way, our module makes use of the interaction-aware features from multiple modalities.

In addition to the data extraction step, the data association step has also been widely explored. Many strategies are almost equally popular as of today, including Hungarian assignments [13], particle filtering [14], and min-cost flow [15,16]. More recently, [17] explained a simpler method that exploits the regression head of a detector to perform temporal realignment of object bounding boxes, and their method achieved SOTA performance. In this paper, we follow [16] to apply adjacency matrix learning within the min-cost flow framework.

2.2 Cross-Modal Attention Mechanism

In this work, we propose a cross-modal attention mechanism that involves 2D image and 3D LiDAR information. As the usage of multi-modal information becomes increasingly popular, the attention mechanism starts to be used for matching and/or fusing features from different modalities, e.g, 2D image and text, videos and audios. We survey the existing cross-modal attention module designs in this subsection.

Several recent works [18,19] have introduced attention-based methods to fuse cross-modal information such as depth and color image, and they show promising results in the object detection task. Research to date has tested the adaptivity of these attention mechanisms in fusing 2D and 2.5D domains. Nevertheless, to the best of our knowledge, few works have explored cross-modal attention mechanisms that handle 2D and real 3D (e.g. point cloud) domains.

Besides the works mentioned above, we also notice that the concept of cross-modal attention has become well-liked in the community of image-text matching. For example, [20–22] propose several solutions to bridge the gap between different modalities. Among these three papers, [20,21] divide the image into different regions and then relate each region to the work in a text. Through this method, two-dimensional data is reduced to one-dimensional data which aligns with text modality. By comparison, [22] directly embeds both modalities into one-dimensional features, and then it applies attention mechanism at the feature level.

Apart from image-text matching, research also covers other tasks and different combinations of modalities. [23] comes up with a multi-level self-attention based method capturing the long-range dependencies between linguistic and visual contexts for image segmentation; [24] designs a hierarchical attention-based architecture to align audio and video information.

Among all works discussed so far, we are especially inspired by [20–22] from the image-text matching community. Thus, we adopt the idea of dimension reduction. We project 3D to 2D, generating a sparse depth map that not only maintains the 3D information but also naturally correlates to the image by spatial correspondence.

3 Approach

In this paper, we design a deep-learning based Multi-detector, multi-modal tracking framework. The whole pipeline is shown in Fig. 2. The framework follows

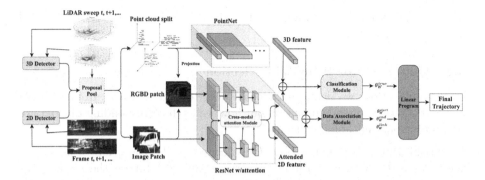

Fig. 2. Pipeline overview

a tracking-by-detection paradigm. It solves data association as a min-cost flow problem. The goal of this framework is to collaborate the information from multiple sensors and multiple different types of detectors in such a paradigm.

3.1 Pipeline Overview

Following the tracking-by-detection paradigm, our pipeline takes the detector-produced object proposals as the input. Then we extract the 2D image patch and the 3D point cloud split from their respective sensor data based on the localization information in the proposals. Afterwards, we use PointNet [25] to extract the proposals' 3D features from their corresponding point cloud splits and ResNet to extract 2D features from each image patch. The differences between our work and the previous works are (1) we collect object proposals from different types of object detectors; and (2) during 2D feature extraction, the 3D information gets involved to generate an attention mask as the guidance. We explain the details about how we operate these two novel ideas in Sect. 3.2 and Sect. 3.3. After feature extraction, we concatenate 3D features with the attended 2D features to yield the final feature for each proposal. Once all proposals obtain their final features, the classification module re-evaluates each proposal's score of being an object of interest. This module is especially important because when proposals are collected from multiple detectors, the false positive rate would inflate as the number of the total proposals increases. The classification module helps validate the input proposals for a better tracking performance. Besides the classification module, the data association module infers the affinity matrix, the start and end scores in the min-cost flow graph. This partition of the pipeline is similar to the previous work [11,26,27]. We skip the module details here and introduce its functionality in Sect. 3.4.

The whole framework is trained in an end-to-end manner using a multi-task loss. We use cross entropy loss for the classification module and the L2 loss for the data association module. The overall loss function is as follows:

$$L = \alpha L_{cls} + \beta L_{ds}, \tag{1}$$

where α and β are hyper-parameters to balance two losses. α is set to 2 and β is 1 in our experiments.

3.2   Multi-detector Proposal Collection

In this subsection, we define a proposal pool to collect results from multiple detectors, and we provide details about how we fetch corresponding raw data of proposals from multi-modal signals.

Proposal Pool. A proposal pool P is defined as the collection of all object proposals of t consecutive frames. We run every detector on the sequence of frames one at a time, and we collect the object proposals of each frame in the proposal pool P. In practice, we let $t = 2$. The proposal pool is denoted as $P = \{p_1, p_2, ..., p_N\}$, where N is the size of P and p_i is the ith proposal in P. We parameterize p_i as $p_i = (x_i, y_i, w_i, h_i)$, where x_i and y_i represent the coordinates of the 2D bounding box's center while w_i and h_i represent its width and height. Meanwhile, proposals from different detectors may occasionally overlap. To tackle this challenge, we conduct a non-maximum suppression procedure to re-organize P to avoid redundant proposals in P during its later use. In our experiment, we define two proposals as identical when their intersection over union (IoU) is larger than 0.5.

Preparation for Feature Extraction. Object proposals in the present study, in the form of 2D bounding boxes in P, enable us to extract 2D modality data from RGB cameras and 3D modality data from LiDAR sensors. For the RGB camera data, we crop their corresponding image patches from each image frame which will be used for the later 2D feature extraction. We use ResNet101 [28] as the backbone in 2D feature extraction.

As for the LiDAR data, since we use mixed types of detectors, the detector output does not necessarily contain the 3D bounding box information of a proposal. Without 3D bounding boxes, we would be unable to extract the precise point cloud split of each proposal. In response to this challenge, [29] makes a valuable attempt where they predict 3D bounding boxes according to 2D bounding boxes. However, we decide not to incorporate their system into our existing pipeline in consideration of optimal efficiency. In lieu of 3D bounding boxes, we use frustums projected from 2D bounding boxes, as inspired by [11]. [11] shows that the point cloud split in frustums can have comparable performance to that cropped from 3D bounding boxes in tracking tasks. In our framework, we project frustums from 2D bounding boxes with the help of calibration information. We use frustums to fetch the corresponding 3D point cloud split from LiDAR data of each proposal for later 3D feature extraction. After we fetch the point cloud split, we use PointNet [25] for 3D point cloud feature extraction.

3.3   Cross-Modal Attention Module

In this work, we propose a cross-modal attention module where 3D features interact with 2D features to guide the refinement of the latter.

Motivation. The attention mechanism [30] helps machine learning procedures to focus on certain aspects of data specific to a given task context. In a tracking task, attention should aim at the most discriminative sub-regions. If the attention mechanism can successfully tell the system "where to look at", the system can overcome the distraction from irrelevant information that is especially cumbersome to handle in 2D tracking application. Without extra information, however, it is not straightforward for 2D features to figure out a solution by themselves to distinguish objects of interest from noises, despite some attempts of a self-attention design such as [31]. Hence, we consider using 3D features to help guide the generation of attended 2D features.

Challenge and Solution. There is a dimensional gap between 3D and 2D information. In previous works that have explored the cross-modal attention module design [20,22], when the feature dimensions are different for different modalities, researchers usually choose to reduce the dimension of the higher-dimensional modality to make the cross-modal interaction more natural. Inspired by [20,22], we consider to reduce the dimension of LiDAR information to sparse depth maps by projecting 3D point cloud to 2D. Given a point cloud point v, the transformation matrix between LiDAR device and the camera T_{cam}, the rotation matrix R and the translation T of the camera as well as the corresponding 2D image coordinates with the depth value o can be calculated as:

$$o = TRT_{cam}v^T \tag{2}$$

In this way, we are able to transform a point cloud split to a 2D sparse depth map.

To suppress the negative impact from this sparsity, we perform the following two steps. First, we assign the neighbors of every projected point o the same depth value as o. The neighboring area is defined as a σ kernel centering around o. We choose $\sigma = 10$ pixel width in this work. Second, we concatenate the projected sparse depth map with its corresponding RGB image patch. In practice, we extract the proposal's point cloud split using generated frustum for all proposals regardless of their sources being 2D or 3D detectors. Figure 3 shows several example pairs of image patch and its corresponding masked version, where the yellow mask signals that depth values is available in that area. The figure also shows that the areas with depth values are highly correlated with the exact location of the object of interests in the image patch.

Implementation. We denote the input image patch of proposal i as I_i and the corresponding RGB with sparse depth patch as D_i. We adopt ResNet [28] as the backbone for our feature extractors and add cross-model attention heads after every pooling operation. In our experiment, we use different feature extractors for I_i and D_i to avoid the extracted features getting too similar so that it will not hurt the performance of the attention heads. We denote the extracted feature at scale l as f_I^l and f_D^l respectively. The attention operation is expressed as:

$$Att^l(f_I^l) = softmax(Q(f_D^l)K(f_D^l)^T)V(f_I^l), \tag{3}$$

Fig. 3. Samples of image patch with its corresponding projected point cloud. One yellow small patch in the second row represents a projected 3D point and its neighbors. (Color figure online)

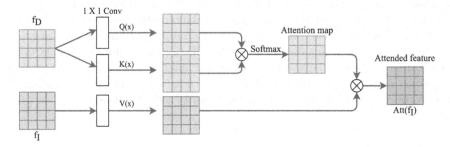

Fig. 4. Cross-modal attention head visual demonstration

where Q, K, and V are implemented as linear projection. The visual demonstration is Fig. 4. We concatenate the attended feature $Att^l(f_I^l)$ at all scales and use the concatenated features in the classification and data association module. However, we posit that the attention of the input features should be different for different tasks. To confirm our hunch, we conduct ablation studies to see if by generating task-aware attended features, we can improve the module's final performance. Please see details in Sect. 4.4.

3.4 Linear Programming Formulation

Based on the detection results from two consecutive frames t and $t+1$, we obtain a set of object proposals $P = \{p_1, p_2, ..., p_N\}$. We follow the model formulation that [16] proposes to introduce four types of binary variables: for each p_j, x_j^{true} indicates if proposal p_j is a true positive; x_j^{start} and x_j^{end} encode if p_j is the start node or the end node of the link; $x_{j,k}^{link}$ represents if there is a link between p_j and p_k.

In our pipeline, x_j^{true} is relatively more important among these four binary variables, as well as more important in our study than in previous works where x_j^{true} only functions as a validation for the detection results. This is because previous works are based on a single detector; hence, x_j^{true} in previous works acts similarly to each proposal's classification score that is already decided by the detector. Without drawing upon additional information, there is limited room for single-detector based tracking frameworks to correct the decisions made by the detector. In our pipeline, in comparison, the proposals are from different detectors of different data modalities. This setting adds a large amount of extra information to the classification module. A multi-detector and multi-modality approach is especially promising if we consider this: cases that a single-modality detector finds confusing may not be as confusing for another single-modality detector. When information from different detectors and modalities are jointly used for classification, we are able to optimize task performance.

We obtain x_j^{true} through the classification module. Other threes variables are estimated by data association module. For notation convenience, the four variables formulate a vector $x = (x^{true}, x^{start}, x^{end}, x^{link})$. Then, as [16] suggests, we formulate the tracking problem as a linear program:

$$\underset{x}{\text{maximize}} \quad \Theta_W(P)x$$
$$\text{subject to} \quad Ax \leq 0, \ x \in \{0, 1\}^{|x|} \tag{4}$$

In the above equation, $\Theta_W(P)$ is the cost of assigning each random variables and $Ax = 0$ is the constraints of the assignment. The constraints here can be described in natural languages as: (1) a proposal cannot be linked to a detection belonging to the same frame; and (2) if a proposal is a true positive, it has to be either linked to another detection in the previous frame or the start of a new trajectory.

4 Experiment

4.1 Dataset

We conducted experiments on the KITTI tracking benchmark [32] which consists of 21 training sequences and 29 test sequences. In our experiments, we further split the 21 training sequences into 10 and 11 sequences, respectively for the purposes of training and validation following the setting of [11]. The training set has 3,975 total frames and the validation set 3,945 frames. KITTI contains data collected by both 2D and 3D sensors and sensor calibration information. Hence, we were able to crop corresponding multi-modal data for each proposal given its bounding box location. Following the KITTI benchmark setting, we computed the Intersection over Union (IoU) between every output proposal and the entire ground truth bounding boxes. In occasions where a proposal identifies a ground truth bounding box as having yielded the largest IoU among all and where the IoU is greater than 0.5, we assigned the GT box ID to this proposal. We used the same IoU threshold of 0.5 during non-maximum suppression when we re-organized the proposal pool.

4.2   Metrics

Besides the precision and recall that evaluate the detection results, we evaluated our tracking performance using tracking metrics CLEARMOT, MTPTML, identity swit-ches, and fragmentations following the KITTI benchmark [33,34]. The metrics are explained as below.

MOTA: The Multiple Object Tracking Accuracy $MOTA = 1 - \frac{\Sigma_t m_t - f_{p_t} + mm_t}{\Sigma_t g_t}$, where m_t, f_{p_t}, and mm_t are respectively the number of misses, of false positives, and of mismatches for time t.

MOTP: MOTP is the total position error for matched object hypothesis pairs over all frames, averaged by the total number of matches made. It shows the ability of the tracker to estimate precise object positions, independent of its skills at recognizing object configurations, keeping consistent trajectories, etc.

MT: Mostly tracked. Percentage of GT trajectories which are covered by tracker output for more than 80% in length.

ML: Mostly lost. Percentage of GT trajectories which are covered by tracker output for less than 20% in length. The smaller the value the better.

Fragments: The total number of times that a ground truth trajectory is interrupted in the tracking result. The smaller the value the better.

ID switches: The total number of times that a tracked trajectory changes its matched GT identity. The smaller the value the better.

4.3   Implementation Detail

We used two detectors in our experiments: the 3D detector PointPillar [3] and the 2D detector RRC [35]. Please see Table 1 for the performance of the two detectors. We trained the whole pipeline in an end-to-end manner. As stated in Sect. 3.2, we used PointNet [25] as the backbone of our 3D feature extractor and ResNet101 [28] with batch normalization as the backbone of the 2D feature extractor. The input image patch was resized to 112×112. The classification module was implemented as a three-layer MLP (i.e. Multi-layer Perceptron). We adapted the architecture of the data association module from [11]. We used Adam optimizer with the learning rate of 3e-4.

4.4   Ablation Study

Cross-Modal Attention Module. The first of the two ablation studies was on our cross-modal attention module. We stacked the sparse depth map with RGB image patch for attention mask generation. This treatment, as introduced in Sect. 3.3, was to overcome the inefficient feature extraction resulting from the depth sparsity. To establish the value of the stacked RGB-D input in the attention module, we designed an experiment to compare the tracking performance of three attention modules: one using the stacked RGB-D input, the second using pure RGB images, and the third using pure sparse depth maps. In addition, we had all three attention modules to compare performance with another architecture without any attention module. Table 2 demonstrated the evaluation results

Table 1. Statistics of detection results on KITTI validation subset. This table demonstrates the statics of detector performance for both the 2D [35] and 3D [3] detectors on our KITTI validation dataset. The third row lists statistics about the overlapped output proposals between the two detectors. The fourth row shows the statics of combined detection results from both detectors after the non-maximum suppression step.

Detector type	Proposal number	True positive	False positive
2D	12090	11528	562
3D	12642	10788	1854
Overlapped	10533	10308	225
Combination	14199	12008	2191
Ground truth	12363	–	–

Table 2. Ablation study on attention type.

	MOTA	MOTP	Recall	Precision	FP Rate
W/o attention	83.03%	85.75%	94.76%	92.11%	26.04%
W/Depth attention	82.70%	84.56%	94.75%	91.88%	31.25%
W/RGB attention	83.76%	84.53%	94.68%	92.91%	26.98%
Cross-modal attention	84.20%	85.43%	93.53%	93.74%	19.87%

in comparisons. It indicated that our cross-modal attention module (the last line on Table 2) had the best performance among all four settings.

Task-Specific Attention Module. As Sect. 3.3 mentioned, different tasks may have different requirements on the attended features. Therefore, we designed a second ablation study to compare three solutions: (1) a solution without any attention modules, (2) a solution with the association attention module only, and (3) a solution with both the association attention module and the classification attention module. A comparison between (1) and (2) revealed a performance boosting due to an attention module. A comparison between (2) and (3) further proved the value of using classification attention module in conjunction with an association attention module. Please see Table 3 for specific statistics of performance evaluation.

Figure 5 and Fig. 6 visualized the attention masks generated respectively for data association and classification.

4.5   Analysis on Multiple Detectors Performance

As Sect. 3.4 discussed, the classification module would be more important and more challenging in our multi-detector system than in prior single-detector tracking systems since we have more false positive proposals in our proposal pool. To prove our hypothesis and the strength of our framework in overcoming this challenge, we designed another set of experiments.

Table 3. The ablation study 2 on using or not using task specific attention module for classification and association.

Association Att	Cls Att	MOTA	MOTP	Recall	Precision	FP Rate
×	×	83.03%	85.75%	94.76%	92.11%	26.04%
✓	×	84.09%	85.33%	94.39%	93.04%	22.61%
✓	✓	84.20%	85.43%	93.53%	93.74%	19.87%

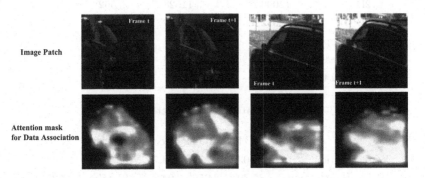

Fig. 5. Attention mask generated for data association module. The left four and the right four pictures respectively represent two different objects in different timestamps.

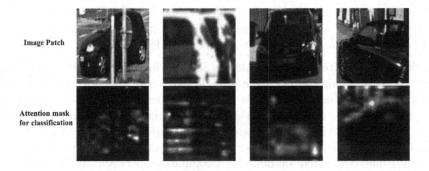

Fig. 6. Attention mask generated for the classification module.

First of all, we compared the performance of several detectors on the dataset described in Sect. 4.1. We argue that the recall of a detector is the most important metric to consider when we evaluate a detector used in a tracking task. A higher recall indicates more true positive proposals. Since a tracking-by-detection framework cannot produce additional positive proposals by itself - in addition to those provided by the detector, the number of true positive proposals that the detector provides may be regarded as the upper bound of what a tracking-by-detection system can achieve. The first three rows of Table 4 show that regarding the KITTI dataset, the 2D detector we used in the experiment performed better than the 3D detector judging their recalls, but the combined use of 2D and 3D detectors outperformed the 2D detector alone, yielding a recall about 4% higher than that of the 2D detector. We thus proved the superiority of a multiple-detector solution over single-detector solutions in incurring input of better quality for a tracking-by-detection system.

Secondly, the second three rows of Table 4 showed the results of the multi-modal tracking method [11], which is reproduced by using its official code and data. For comparison convenience, we replaced the original VGG-16 encoder by ResNet101 and adjusted the image patch to 112×112. The results demonstrated that when using a single detector, [11] was able to control the false positive rate while for a multiple detector setting, the false positive rate became much larger than the raw detection results. Namely, the classification module had problems in distinguishing true positives and false positives with too many distractions in a multiple detector setting.

A comparison between the second three rows and the last three rows of Table 4 demonstrated contribution of our framework. Our pipeline not only improved the performance of a multi-detector based tracking system but also single-detector based tracking systems with 2D or 3D detectors alone. This finding was supported by the higher MOTA statistics and lower false positive rates of our framework compared to [11]. Specially, in the multi-detector setting, our framework had a false positive rate that was 24% lower than that from [11]. This proved the ability of our proposed framework in successfully suppressing the false positive rate in tracking-by-detection systems even when the inputs come from multiple detectors.

Table 4. Results of experiments using different types of detectors.

Detector type	Model type	MOTA	MOTP	Recall	Precision	FP Rate	FP number
2D	–	–	–	93.24%	95.35%	4.64%	562
3D	–	–	–	87.26%	85.33%	14.66%	1854
Multi-detector	–	–	–	97.12%	84.56%	15.43%	2191
2D	[11]	89.49%	85.85%	92.84%	98.09%	6.94%	222
3D	[11]	75.90%	85.29%	85.06%	93.12%	19.67%	791
Multi-detector	[11]	83.03%	85.75%	94.76%	92.11%	26.04%	1007
2D	Ours	**89.66%**	85.83%	93.05%	98.07%	**5.59%**	**211**
3D	Ours	**76.31%**	85.20%	85.31%	93.63%	**18.25%**	**734**
Multi-detector	Ours	**84.20%**	85.43%	93.53%	93.74%	**19.87%**	**799**

4.6 Benchmark Evaluation

Lastly, we evaluated our framework on the KITTI tracking benchmark test split [36]. The authors of KITTI did not reveal their ground truth. We submitted to the benchmark our results on test split that were generated by the last model in our ablation study (see the last three columns of Table 3 for the model). The model used pure 2D detection results. We then compared our results to the other methods on the leader board. Without any fine-tuning, our model demonstrated promising results among the state-of-the-art methods in the benchmark. Table 5 listed our evaluation results in comparison with other methods on the KITTI tracking benchmark.

Table 5. KITTI benchmark evaluation

Method	MOTA↑	MOTP↑	MT↑	ML↓	IDS↓	FRAG↓	FP ↓
SASN-MCF_nano [37]	70.86 %	82.65 %	58.00 %	7.85 %	443	975	2344
CIWT [38]	75.39 %	79.25 %	49.85 %	10.31 %	165	660	954
SCEA [39]	75.58 %	79.39 %	53.08 %	11.54 %	104	448	1306
Complexer-YOLO [40]	75.70 %	78.46 %	58.00 %	5.08 %	1186	2092	1631
DSM[26]	76.15%	83.42%	60.00%	8.31%	296	868	578
FAMNet [41]	77.08 %	78.79 %	51.38 %	8.92 %	123	713	760
LP-SSVM [42]	77.63 %	77.80 %	56.31 %	8.46 %	62	539	1239
FANTrack [9]	77.72 %	82.33 %	62.62 %	8.77 %	150	812	1277
aUToTrack[43]	82.25%	80.52%	72.62 %	3.54 %	1025	1402	1040
Ours	79.93 %	84.77 %	66.00 %	10.00 %	278	716	671

5   Conclusion

In this paper, we propose a tracking-by-detection pipeline that uses multiple detectors and multiple sensors. Our pipeline successfully associates the proposals from different detectors and thereafter offers the tracking task a better starting point with more true positive proposals. To the best of our knowledge, our work is the first one that attempts to explore the potentials of a multi-detector setting in a tracking-by-detection system.

In the meantime, we propose a novel cross-modal attention module. It leverages the interaction between 3D features and 2D features to help extract 2D features with fewer distractions. The attended features, consequentially, help the classification module to suppress the high false positive rate brought by the multi-detector setting. With fewer distractions, the attended features are also more discriminative to better serve the data association module and to boost the performance of the framework.

The evaluation of our framework on the public benchmark proves the value and potential of our ideas as presented in the current study. Admittedly, though, there is still room for improvement regarding multi-detector settings (see Table 4 in the earlier passage). In future research, we will explore the possibilities of completing the sparse depth map generated by the LiDAR sensor to make the interaction between 2D and 3D features more natural.

References

1. Yoo, J.H., Kim, Y., Kim, J.S., Choi, J.W.: 3D-CVF: generating joint camera and lidar features using cross-view spatial feature fusion for 3D object detection (2020)
2. Liang, M., Yang, B., Chen, Y., Hu, R., Urtasun, R.: Multi-task multi-sensor fusion for 3D object detection. In: Proceedings of the IEEE Conference on Computer Vision and Pattern Recognition, pp. 7345–7353 (2019)
3. Lang, A.H., Vora, S., Caesar, H., Zhou, L., Yang, J., Beijbom, O.: Pointpillars: fast encoders for object detection from point clouds. In: Proceedings of the IEEE Conference on Computer Vision and Pattern Recognition, pp. 12697–12705 (2019)
4. Shi, S., et al.: PV-RCNN: point-voxel feature set abstraction for 3D object detection. In: Proceedings of the IEEE/CVF Conference on Computer Vision and Pattern Recognition, pp. 10529–10538 (2020)
5. Yilmaz, A., Javed, O., Shah, M.: Object tracking: a survey. ACM Comput. Surv. (CSUR) **38**, 13-es (2006)
6. Voigtlaender, P., et al.: MOTS: multi-object tracking and segmentation. In: The IEEE Conference on Computer Vision and Pattern Recognition (CVPR) (2019)
7. Chu, Q., Ouyang, W., Liu, B., Zhu, F., Yu, N.: DASOT: a unified framework integrating data association and single object tracking for online multi-object tracking. In: AAAI, pp. 10672–10679 (2020)
8. Xu, J., Cao, Y., Zhang, Z., Hu, H.: Spatial-temporal relation networks for multi-object tracking. In: Proceedings of the IEEE International Conference on Computer Vision, pp. 3988–3998 (2019)
9. Baser, E., Balasubramanian, V., Bhattacharyya, P., Czarnecki, K.: FANTrack: 3D multi-object tracking with feature association network. arxiv abs/1905.02843 (2019)
10. Weng, X., Kitani, K.: A baseline for 3D multi-object tracking (2019)
11. Zhang, W., Zhou, H., Sun, S., Wang, Z., Shi, J., Loy, C.C.: Robust multi-modality multi-object tracking. In: Proceedings of the IEEE International Conference on Computer Vision, pp. 2365–2374 (2019)
12. Weng, X., Wang, Y., Man, Y., Kitani, K.: GNN3DMOT: graph neural network for 3D multi-object tracking with multi-feature learning (2020)
13. Kuhn, H.W.: The hungarian method for the assignment problem. Naval Res. Logist. Q. **2**, 83–97 (1955)
14. Ristic, B., Arulampalam, S., Gordon, N.: Beyond the Kalman Filter: Particle Filters for Tracking Applications, vol. 685. Artech House, Boston (2004)
15. Zhang, L., Li, Y., Nevatia, R.: Global data association for multi-object tracking using network flows. In: 2008 IEEE Conference on Computer Vision and Pattern Recognition, pp. 1–8. IEEE (2008)
16. Frossard, D., Urtasun, R.: End-to-end learning of multi-sensor 3D tracking by detection. In: 2018 IEEE International Conference on Robotics and Automation (ICRA), pp. 635–642. IEEE (2018)
17. Bergmann, P., Meinhardt, T., Leal-Taixe, L.: Tracking without bells and whistles. In: Proceedings of the IEEE International Conference on Computer Vision, pp. 941–951 (2019)
18. Li, G., Gan, Y., Wu, H., Xiao, N., Lin, L.: Cross-modal attentional context learning for RGB-D object detection. IEEE Trans. Image Process. **28**, 1591–1601 (2018)
19. Chen, H., Li, Y.F., Su, D.: Attention-aware cross-modal cross-level fusion network for RGB-D salient object detection. In: 2018 IEEE/RSJ International Conference on Intelligent Robots and Systems (IROS), pp. 6821–6826. IEEE (2018)

20. Lee, K.-H., Chen, X., Hua, G., Hu, H., He, X.: Stacked cross attention for image-text matching. In: Ferrari, V., Hebert, M., Sminchisescu, C., Weiss, Y. (eds.) ECCV 2018. LNCS, vol. 11208, pp. 212–228. Springer, Cham (2018). https://doi.org/10.1007/978-3-030-01225-0_13

21. Huang, Y., Wang, W., Wang, L.: Instance-aware image and sentence matching with selective multimodal LSTM. In: 2017 IEEE Conference on Computer Vision and Pattern Recognition (CVPR) (2017)

22. Nam, H., Ha, J.W., Kim, J.: Dual attention networks for multimodal reasoning and matching. In: Proceedings of the IEEE Conference on Computer Vision and Pattern Recognition, pp. 299–307 (2017)

23. Ye, L., Rochan, M., Liu, Z., Wang, Y.: Cross-modal self-attention network for referring image segmentation. In: Proceedings of the IEEE Conference on Computer Vision and Pattern Recognition, pp. 10502–10511 (2019)

24. Wang, X., Wang, Y.F., Wang, W.Y.: Watch, listen, and describe: globally and locally aligned cross-modal attentions for video captioning. arXiv preprint arXiv:1804.05448 (2018)

25. Qi, C.R., Su, H., Mo, K., Guibas, L.J.: PointNet: deep learning on point sets for 3D classification and segmentation. In: Proceedings of the IEEE Conference on Computer Vision and Pattern Recognition, pp. 652–660 (2017)

26. Frossard, D., Urtasun, R.: End-to-end learning of multi-sensor 3D tracking by detection. In: ICRA. IEEE (2018)

27. Schulter, S., Vernaza, P., Choi, W., Chandraker, M.: Deep network flow for multi-object tracking. In: Proceedings of the IEEE Conference on Computer Vision and Pattern Recognition, pp. 6951–6960 (2017)

28. He, K., Zhang, X., Ren, S., Sun, J.: Deep residual learning for image recognition. In: Proceedings of the IEEE Conference on Computer Vision and Pattern Recognition, pp. 770–778 (2016)

29. Qi, C.R., Liu, W., Wu, C., Su, H., Guibas, L.J.: Frustum pointnets for 3D object detection from RGB-D data. In: Proceedings of the IEEE Conference on Computer Vision and Pattern Recognition, pp. 918–927 (2018)

30. Vaswani, A., et al.: Attention is all you need (2017)

31. Guan, Q., Huang, Y., Zhong, Z., Zheng, Z., Zheng, L., Yang, Y.: Diagnose like a radiologist: attention guided convolutional neural network for thorax disease classification (2018)

32. Geiger, A., Lenz, P., Urtasun, R.: Are we ready for autonomous driving? The KITTI vision benchmark suite. In: 2012 IEEE Conference on Computer Vision and Pattern Recognition, pp. 3354–3361. IEEE (2012)

33. Li, Y., Huang, C., Nevatia, R.: Learning to associate: hybridboosted multi-target tracker for crowded scene. In: 2009 IEEE Conference on Computer Vision and Pattern Recognition, pp. 2953–2960. IEEE (2009)

34. Bernardin, K., Stiefelhagen, R.: Evaluating multiple object tracking performance: the CLEAR MOT metrics. EURASIP J. Image Video Process. **2008**, 1–10 (2008)

35. Ren, J., et al.: Accurate single stage detector using recurrent rolling convolution. In: 2017 IEEE Conference on Computer Vision and Pattern Recognition (CVPR) (2017)

36. Geiger, A., Lenz, P., Urtasun, R.: Are we ready for autonomous driving? The KITTI vision benchmark suite. In: Conference on Computer Vision and Pattern Recognition (CVPR) (2012)

37. Gunduz, G., Acarman, T.: Efficient multi-object tracking by strong associations on temporal window. IEEE Trans. Intell. Veh. **4**(3), 447–455 (2019)

38. Osep, A., Mehner, W., Mathias, M., Leibe, B.: Combined image- and world-space tracking in traffic scenes. In: ICRA (2017)
39. Yoon, J.H., Lee, C.R., Yang, M.H., Yoon, K.J.: Online multi-object tracking via structural constraint event aggregation. In: IEEE International Conference on Computer Vision and Pattern Recognition (CVPR) (2016)
40. Simon, M., et al.: Complexer-YOLO: real-time 3D object detection and tracking on semantic point clouds. In: The IEEE Conference on Computer Vision and Pattern Recognition (CVPR) Workshops (2019)
41. Chu, P., Ling, H.: FAMNet: joint learning of feature, affinity and multi-dimensional assignment for online multiple object tracking. In: ICCV (2019)
42. Wang, S., Fowlkes, C.: Learning optimal parameters for multi-target tracking with contextual interactions. Int. J. Comput. Vis. **122**(3), 484–501 (2016)
43. Burnett, K., Samavi, S., Waslander, S., Barfoot, T., Schoellig, A.: aUToTrack: a lightweight object detection and tracking system for the SAE autodrive challenge. In: 2019 16th Conference on Computer and Robot Vision (CRV) (2019)

Dense Pixel-Wise Micro-motion Estimation of Object Surface by Using Low Dimensional Embedding of Laser Speckle Pattern

Ryusuke Sagawa[1]($\boxtimes$) (iD), Yusuke Higuchi[2], Hiroshi Kawasaki[2](iD),
Ryo Furukawa[3](iD), and Takahiro Ito[1](iD)

[1] National Institute of Advanced Industrial Science and Technology, Tokyo, Japan
`ryusuke.sagawa@aist.go.jp`
[2] Kyushu University, Fukuoka, Japan
[3] Hiroshima City University, Hiroshima, Japan

Abstract. This paper proposes a method of estimating micro-motion of an object at each pixel that is too small to detect under a common setup of camera and illumination. The method introduces an active-lighting approach to make the motion visually detectable. The approach is based on speckle pattern, which is produced by the mutual interference of laser light on object's surface and continuously changes its appearance according to the out-of-plane motion of the surface. In addition, speckle pattern becomes uncorrelated with large motion. To compensate such micro- and large motion, the method estimates the motion parameters up to scale at each pixel by nonlinear embedding of the speckle pattern into low-dimensional space. The out-of-plane motion is calculated by making the motion parameters spatially consistent across the image. In the experiments, the proposed method is compared with other measuring devices to prove the effectiveness of the method.

1 Introduction

The analysis of physical minute movements of objects is important to understand the behavior of various systems including mechanical systems, fluids analysis and biological studies. For example, mechanical systems vibrate at various frequency distributed over a wide range from several hertz to several kilohertz only with the extremely small amplitude, such as less than one millimeter. There are many approaches to measure such a minute movements, and typical methods are to use vibration sensors based on various measurement principles including accelerometers and displacement gauges. Although these methods can measure such a minute movements precisely, there is a severe limitation, such as only a

---

Electronic supplementary material The online version of this chapter (https://doi.org/10.1007/978-3-030-69532-3_42) contains supplementary material, which is available to authorized users.

H. Ishikawa et al. (Eds.): ACCV 2020, LNCS 12623, pp. 700–715, 2021.
https://doi.org/10.1007/978-3-030-69532-3_42

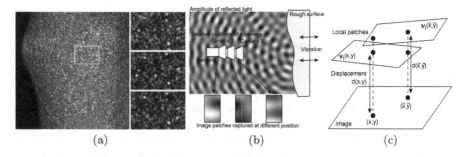

(a)   (b)   (c)

Fig. 1. An example of speckle pattern and modeling motion of piecewise planes. (a) An example of speckle pattern on an object's surface is shown. While the power of the incident light is uniform, the dotted pattern is observed by a camera. (b) The amplitude of light changes drastically according to the position due to the mutual interference. (c) The plane parameters $\psi_i(x, y)$ and $\psi_i(\tilde{x}, \tilde{y})$ are to be estimated.

single point can be measured by each sensor, because of necessity of physical contact, resulting in a measurement of only limited and small areas. In order to conduct accurate and robust analysis on spatio and temporal effect of vibration, measurement of micro movement of dense and wide region is required, which cannot be achieved by existing sensors and methods.

Acquiring such wide area's micro-motion like vibration of almost rigid but deformable object surfaces requires dense observation in time and space. One promising solution is to use a camera, since it can capture wide area information at a short period of time. Optical triangulation is a common method to measure displacement from captured image, however, since the movement by vibration is much smaller than the size of the object, *i.e.*, less than one pixel, it is impossible to measure such minute motion by the method. Another approach is to use optical interferometry. Since the method uses the difference of the length of multiple light paths, the accuracy mainly depends on the wavelength of the light, which indicates that the resolution of a camera is less dependent. The disadvantage of this approach is that it requires a complicated and precise setup with many optical components to generate the high quality reference light and path.

Speckle pattern, which is a phenomenon of light interference on object surface, has also been frequently used for detecting micro-motion. Since one of important characteristics of speckle pattern is high sensitivity of its appearance, it is utilized for observing minute phenomenon, such as micro-motion of object surface. Another unique characteristic of speckle pattern is that no reference light is necessary to observe the pattern, because it is mutual interference of the lights reflected from the multiple points on object's surface. Those characteristics enables a simple setup of devices to detect micro-motion in a wide field of view. A typical usage of speckle pattern for observing the minute movement is the frequency analysis, since the minute movement of object surface caused by vibration usually has a cyclic period, which can be effectively calculated by temporal analysis of the intensity at each pixel. One limitation of such speckle analyses is that since speckle is essentially an independent phenomenon at each pixel, it cannot extract temporal relationship, such as phase, between neighboring pixels, *i.e.*, wave propagation on object surface caused by vibration cannot be acquired. To the best of our knowledge, such wave propagation phenomenon has not been measured yet. In this paper, we propose a method to extract such spatio-temporal information of micro-motion on the surface by analyzing speckle pattern captured by a camera. In our method, series of speckle patterns of each patch are embedded into low-dimensional space and surface parameters at each pixel are estimated by joint optimization. The contribution of the paper is summarized as follows.

- The minute movement at each point of object's surface can be extracted as the low-dimensional embedding of laser speckle pattern.
- The spatial consistency of the embedded information is globally supported by smoothness constraint of the surface, which achieves the spatio-temporal analysis of speckle patterns.
- Various kind of wave propagation phenomena caused by vibration are first densely measured and visualized by our algorithm in real scene experiments.

2   Related Work

As methods to observe minute movement of an object, four methods can be considered. First, a contact sensor such as accelerometers is typically used to measure the vibration, but this approach is not suitable for spatial analysis that needs dense observation. Non-contact methods that observe vibration by using cameras have advantage in dense observation.

Both passive and active approaches have been studied to observe minute movements of objects by using a camera. As passive approaches, the methods based on optical flows and pattern matching by correlation have been proposed to observe vibrating objects [1,2]. Wu et al. [3] proposed a method to visualize subtle movements by magnifying the displacements based on spatio-temporal filtering. They have extended the method to recognize the sound by observing the vibration in the video [4] or the method to estimate material properties [5]. If the displacement is small, these methods need to zoom up the targets to detect the change of intensity due to their passive approach. Since passive approaches cannot be applied in the case that the vibration is smaller than the camera resolution, they have disadvantage in sensitivity.

As active approaches, laser-based methods have been proposed. When the wide field of view is illuminated by coherent laser light, Fig. 1(a) is an example of speckle pattern on an object's surface. While the power of the incident light is uniform, the dotted pattern is observed by a camera. When the surface vibrates, the pattern randomly changes as shown in the right three images, which are the zoom-up of the image patch in the red rectangle. The size of speckle depends on the aperture of the imaging system. If the aperture is large, the speckle of neighboring pixels is unrelated, and hard to distinguish from the noise of the

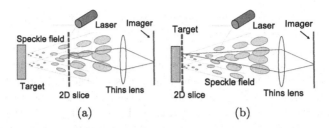

Fig. 2. The speckle field and observed 2D slices. (a) thin lens observation of fused speckle and (b) thin lens observation of independent speckle pattern.

imaging system in some cases. The irradiance of speckle pattern obeys negative exponential statistics, which indicates that some bright points exist while speckle patterns generally have many dark areas. The basic characteristics of speckle pattern have been studied in literature [6,7].

There are two approaches to extract the information from the images of speckle. First one that calculate the phase of vibration by using speckle pattern is based on interferometry, which is called electronic speckle pattern interferometry (ESPI) [8–10]. This approach uses a reference light and compare the length of the paths between the reference light and the light from an object. If the length changes by the deformation of the object, the intensity captured by a camera changes due to the interference of two lights. In this case, the object movement is called out-of-plane motion that is along the viewing direction of the camera. The absolute displacement by the movement can be calculated by using the wavelength of the light. But since this approach requires a highly calibrated setting, it have disadvantage in simplicity of the data acquisition. García et al. [11] measured distance between object and camera by out-of-plane motions, which are not based on interferometry but needs precise calibration to obtain the speckle beforehand that corresponds to each distance.

Second approach with speckle pattern, which is called speckle photography, do not require the setup for interference. If an object slightly moves in the direction parallel to the image plane, which is called in-plane motion, the movement of speckle pattern is simple translation [12]. The motion of the object therefore can be calculated by the techniques of pattern matching. This approaches are used for estimating blood flow [13], motion sensing [14], detecting small deformation [15]. For the analysis of out-of-plane motion, Zalevsky et al. [16] proposed a method to extract the vibration caused by sound and heart beat by using speckle patterns produced by projecting a point laser. Although the periodic signal is detected by calculating the correlation of the pattern, it is single-point observation and cannot applied to spatial analysis of the vibration. Synnergren [17] proposed to combine stereo vision and speckle photography, where measuring in-plane motions using speckle photography is used for estimate disparity between stereo images. Thus, out-of-plane displacements can be estimated. The speckle motion of a front-parallel object along out-of-plane axis becomes rotationally symmetric as analyzed in [18], which can be used to estimate out-of-plane motion. The methods [19–22] to estimate combined motion including in-plane and out-of-plane motions are also proposed. Although these methods are based on tracking speckle patterns, one of the problem is that a speckle pattern drastically change along out-of-plane motion if it is observed at the focal plane. They therefore used defocused or lens-less setups to observe moderate change of speckle. As the trade-off, the spatial resolution of the image is degraded and only a couple of motions are estimated at a time. In contrast, the method proposed in this paper observes speckles on the target surface using lens. It can obtain pixel-wise displacement information as a result, which is realized by multivariate analysis by using speckle pattern for spatial analysis of out-of-plane vibration instead of tracking pattern.

3   Overview of the Method

3.1   Principle

Generally, previous speckle photography methods observe 2D slices of 3D speckle field that is far from the target surface, which is generated by interference of reflected laser, as shown in Fig. 2(a). Since the speckle fields are magnified and fused, changes of the speckle pattern is analyzed as a whole. However, this makes the spatial resolution inevitably low, or large rigid motions of objects are assumed. One solution is to observe 2D slices near the object surface, where each speckle pattern is small and independent, by focusing on the target surface (Fig. 2(b)).

However, there are two problems in this approach: (1) the speckle pattern near object surface drastically changes its appearance w.r.t. out-of-plane motion, and (2) if focus plane is near the target, speckle image w.r.t. out-of-plane motion becomes totally different [18], because the speckle fields from local points are not fused. Thus, analysis of this type of speckle images needs a completely different approach. To overcome the problem, the intensities in a local image patch around a pixel is considered as a feature vector of the pixel and the distance between feature vectors can be used as a metric of the similarity/difference between the slices.

3.2   System Configuration and Algorithm

Figure 1(b) shows a configuration of the system. A coherent laser light is reflected on multiple points on the rough surface of an object and since the reflected lights have different phases, the mutual interference occurs between them, generating speckle field. When the relative position between the surface and camera changes along the out-of-plane axis, the observed image patches change drastically according to the position of the camera relative to the object surface. Although the amplitude of speckle pattern is almost random if the number of reflected points is very large, the image patches are reproducible if the relative position is the same. The proposed method consists of the following steps.

1. Capture sequence of speckle pattern near object surface using wide aperture lens.
2. Embed the feature vector of the local patch around each pixel into nonlinear low-dimensional space.
3. Make the low-dimensional space consistent between neighboring pixels.
4. Optimize the parameters of local surface to fit the low-dimensional space.

4   Implementation

4.1   Representation of Object Surface

The purpose of our method is to estimate subtle motion of object surface with pixel-wise density. The surface is assumed locally planer and the proposed method estimates 3D plane parameters around each pixel (x, y) at frame i defined as follows:

$$z = [\tilde{x} - x, \tilde{y} - y, 1]\boldsymbol{\psi}_i(x, y) \tag{1}$$

where $\boldsymbol{\psi}_i(x, y) = (\psi_1, \psi_2, \psi_3)^T$ is three dimensional vector as the plane parameters, and $(\tilde{x}, \tilde{y})$ are neighbor pixels around (x, y). The offset at the the origin of the local plane indicates surface displacement $d(x, y)$ as the movement at the pixel (x, y), which is calculated by $d(x, y) = [0, 0, 1]\boldsymbol{\psi}_i(x, y) = \psi_3$. The local plane is calculated for each pixel, and Fig. 1(c) shows a situation that the local patch of the plane for (x, y) and $(\tilde{x}, \tilde{y})$. Since the displacement is estimated from image patches, it is determined up to scale.

4.2   Embedding Speckle Pattern for Each Pixel

To observe the movement of surface, a video is captured during the movement with projecting the coherent light generated by a laser light source. Let $I_i(x, y)$ the intensity of a pixel (x, y) at frame i of the video. The pixels (x_k, y_k) in the local image patch $P(x, y)$ forms a feature vector $\boldsymbol{F}_i(x, y) = (I_i(x_1, y_1), \ldots, I_i(x_k, y_k))$ that describes the state of the local patch of surface. To analyze the movement between two frames i and j, the difference of two image patches is calculated by the Euclidean distance of the feature vectors.

$$D_{i,j}(x, y)^2 = \| \boldsymbol{F}_i(x, y) - \boldsymbol{F}_j(x, y) \|^2 \tag{2}$$

$$= \sum_{(x_k, y_k) \in P(x,y)} (I_i(x_k, y_k) - I_j(x_k, y_k))^2 \tag{3}$$

If the size of local patch is sufficiently large, the degree of freedom of the minute movement of the surface is much smaller than the dimension of $\boldsymbol{F}_i(x, y)$. It indicates that the distance is approximated by the distance of the low-dimensional vectors. Let $\boldsymbol{\Psi}_i(x, y) = (\psi_{i,1}(x, y), \ldots, \psi_{i,l}(x, y))$ a low-dimensional vector of which the dimension is $l(<< k)$. Namely, the distance becomes

$$D_{i,j}(x, y)^2 = \| \boldsymbol{\Psi}_i(x, y) - \boldsymbol{\Psi}_j(x, y) \|^2 \tag{4}$$

The low-dimensional vector can be obtained by the techniques of dimension-ality reduction, which embed the input vectors in the low-dimensional space so that the distance between two vectors are preserved after embedding. Since the movement is large, the speckle patterns between two frames becomes almost uncorrelated. Therefore, the relationship between the movement and the distance of speckle patterns is expected to be nonlinear. Various methods of dimension-ality reduction for nonlinear distances have been proposed such as Isomap [23], locally linear embedding [24], Laplacian eigenmaps [25], diffusion maps [26] and t-SNE [27]. Diffusion maps is used in this paper.

The input for the dimensionality reduction is a set of feature vectors $F_i(x, y)(i = 1, \ldots, N)$, which are created from the local image patches around a pixel (x, y) of frames $i = 1, \ldots, N$. In the experiments, the size of a patch is 11×11 pixels and the dimension of the feature vector is 11^2. The speckle pattern of a image patch is embedded into $\Psi_i(x, y)$ by the dimensionality reduction. The embedding is applied for each pixel independently and N vectors of dimension l are obtained as the outputs. The dimension l is 5 in the experiments.

4.3 Making the Embedded Vectors Spatially Consistent

The embedded vector $\Psi_i(x, y)$ has ambiguity in its sign because the speckle has no information about the direction of the movement. Since the embedded vectors are calculated independently for each pixel by the method described in Sect. 4.2, the parameters of adjacent pixels can be inconsistent each other. The second step of the proposed method is to make them spatially consistent.

A linear transformation is introduced to modify the embedded vectors as follows:

$$\psi_i(x, y) = M(x, y)\Psi_i(x, y) \tag{5}$$

where $M(x, y)$ is a $3 \times l$ matrix and $\Psi_i(x, y)$ is a $l \times 1$ column vector for the pixel (x, y). Since the local plane parameters of neighbor pixels should be similar, the following constraint is satisfied to make $\psi_i(x, y)$ spatially consistent

$$\min_{M} \sum_i \sum_{(x_1, y_1)} \sum_{(x_2, y_2)} E_s(i, x_1, y_1, x_2, y_2) \tag{6}$$

$$E_s(i, x_1, y_1, x_2, y_2) = \| [x_2 - x_1, y_2 - y_1, 1] M(x_1, y_1)\Psi_i(x_1, y_1) - \\ [0, 0, 1] M(x_2, y_2)\Psi_i(x_2, y_2) \|^2 \tag{7}$$

where (x_1, y_1) is a point in the whole image and (x_2, y_2) is a point in the neigh-borhood window of (x_1, y_1). This constraint means that the 3D local patches in Fig. 1(c) have the same height at the overlapping pixels in the image. The constraint for a pair of (x_1, y_1) and (x_2, y_2) becomes

$$(\Psi_i(x_1, y_1)[x_2 - x_1, y_2 - y_1, 1]) \circ M(x_1, y_1) \\ -(\Psi_i(x_2, y_2)[0, 0, 1]) \circ M(x_2, y_2) = \mathbf{0} \tag{8}$$

where $\circ$ is element-wise product. Let $\boldsymbol{m}$ the column vector by stacking $\boldsymbol{M}(x,y)$ for all pixels after vectorization. Since the constraints are expressed by $\boldsymbol{Am} = \boldsymbol{0}$, where $\boldsymbol{A}$ is the coefficient matrix calculated from Eq. (8), $\boldsymbol{m}$ is given as the eigenvector associated with the smallest eigenvalue of $\boldsymbol{A}^T \boldsymbol{A}$. Once $\boldsymbol{M}(x,y)$ is calculated, the modified embedded vectors $\boldsymbol{\psi}_i(x,y)$ calculated by Eq. (5) become spatially consistent. Note that the ambiguity of the movement direction in total remains due to the ambiguity of the eigenvector even after making it spatially consistent.

One of the problem in calculating the eigenvector is that the temporal distribution of $\boldsymbol{\Psi}_i(x,y)$ between pixels is different. If $\boldsymbol{\Psi}_i(x,y)$ of a pixel (x,y) is almost zero, the magnitude of $\boldsymbol{M}(x,y)$ is nearly equal to one and the parameters for other pixels become almost zero, because $\boldsymbol{\psi}_i(x,y)$ does not affect the error even if the magnitude of $\boldsymbol{M}(x,y)$ is dominant in the eigenvector. Therefore, the standard deviation of $\boldsymbol{\Psi}_i(x,y)$ is normalized before calculating the coefficient matrix $\boldsymbol{A}$ along the time axis as follows:

$$\Psi'_{ik} = \Psi_{ik}/(\sigma_k + \epsilon), \quad \sigma_k^2 = \frac{1}{N}\sum_i (\Psi_{ik} - \overline{\Psi_k})^2 \qquad (9)$$

where Ψ_{ik} is the k-th component of $\boldsymbol{\Psi}_i$, $\overline{\Psi_k}$ is the mean value of Ψ_{ik} and ϵ is a small number to avoid division by zero.

Since the cost of calculating the eigenvector in high resolution is large, $\boldsymbol{M}(x,y)$ is calculated after subsampling pixels. In the experiments, the original image is 512×512 pixels and subsampled to 64×64 pixels.

4.4   Optimizing Surface Parameters

The calculation of $\boldsymbol{M}(x,y)$ in Sect. 4.3 does not consider the distance between the features calculated by Eq. (2). In the third step, $\boldsymbol{M}(x,y)$ is optimized so that the embedded vector preserves the distance of the features.

By assuming the movement between adjacent two frames is sufficiently small, the constraint so that the distance of the embedded vectors preserves the distance of the features is added to the error function to be minimized as follows:

$$\min_{M} \sum_i \left[\sum_{(x,y)} E_t(i,x,y) + \lambda \sum_{(x_1,y_1)} \sum_{(x_2,y_2)} E_s(i,x_1,y_1,x_2,y_2) \right] \qquad (10)$$

$$E_t(i,x,y) = (\| \boldsymbol{\psi}_i(x,y) - \boldsymbol{\psi}_{i+1}(x,y) \| - \| \boldsymbol{F}_i(x,y) - \boldsymbol{F}_{i+1}(x,y) \|)^2 \qquad (11)$$

where E_s is the spatial constraint defined by Eq. (7) and λ is its weight. Once the transformation matrix $\boldsymbol{M}(x,y)$ is optimized, the plane parameter $\boldsymbol{\psi}_i(x,y)$ is obtained, and The displacement for each pixel is given as the third component of $\boldsymbol{\psi}_i(x,y)$.

The initial guess $\boldsymbol{\psi}'_i(x,y)$ for nonlinear minimization of Eq. (10) is given by $\boldsymbol{\psi}_i(x,y)$ calculated in Sect. 4.3 after normalizing the magnitude for each pixel as follows:

$$\psi_i'(x, y) = \frac{m_F}{m_\psi + \epsilon} \psi_i(x, y) \tag{12}$$

$$m_\psi = \frac{1}{N} \sum_i \| \psi_i(x, y) - \psi_{i+1}(x, y) \|^2 \tag{13}$$

$$m_F = \frac{1}{N} \sum_i \| F_i(x, y) - F_{i+1}(x, y) \|^2 \tag{14}$$

Since $M(x, y)$ calculated in Sect. 4.3 is subsampled, $M(x, y)$ is interpolated before optimizing parameters to obtain the displacement for the image of the original resolution. It is done by interpolating the displacement of the subsampled images calculated by using the initial guess $\psi_i'(x, y)$. Let $d(x, y)$ the linearly interpolated displacement at the pixel (x, y) of the original resolution. $M(x, y)$ at the interpolated pixels should satisfy the following equation for the neighboring pixels $(\tilde{x}, \tilde{y})$:

$$[\tilde{x} - x, \tilde{y} - y, 1] M(x, y) \Psi_i(x, y) = d(\tilde{x}, \tilde{y}) \tag{15}$$

Since this linear equation of $M(x, y)$ is obtained for all pixels in the local patch, $M(x, y)$ is calculated as the least-square solution. Once $M(x, y)$ is obtained for all pixels, the optimization is applied with the images of the original resolution.

5 Experiments

In the experiments, we used a high-speed monochrome camera that captures images at more than 1000 frames/second and a laser light source as the incident light to produce the speckle pattern. The resolution of the camera is 512×512 pixels. The light source and camera have about 40 degrees field of view.

5.1 Evaluating the Calculated Displacement with Respect to the Real Offset

The first experiment is to evaluate the displacement calculated by the proposed method with the images by changing the position with known offsets. Figure 3(a) shows the experimental setup. A planar object is illuminated by a laser projector and is observed by a camera. The camera is mounted on a microstage and the position is moved along the camera axis. A set of 100 images are obtained in total by capturing five images at each offset during changing the offset from 0 to 18 μm every 1 μm. The proposed method described in Sects. 4.2 and 4.3 is applied to the set of 100 images since the order of images cannot be used for the optimization for this dataset. In this experiment, we evaluate if the displacement calculated by the proposed method has linear relationship compared to the offset given by the microstage. Since speckle can be observed if an object has rough surface, three types of materials (wood, cardboard and sponge) are tested in this experiment to evaluate the relationship between the calculated displacement and the real offset.

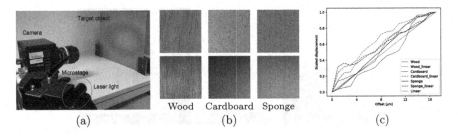

Wood   Cardboard   Sponge

(a)   (b)   (c)

Fig. 3. (a) A planar object is illuminated by a laser light source and observed by a camera mounted on a microstage, which moves the camera along the axis. (b) Three materials (wood, cardboard, sponge) are tested. The images in the upper row are illuminated by room light, and the ones in the lower row are illuminated by laser light. (c) The relationship between the calculated displacements and the real offsets are shown. The displacements are scaled from 0.0 to 1.0.

Figure 3(c) shows the results of the calculated displacements. Since the absolute values of displacements can not be obtained by the proposed method, the values are scaled from 0.0 to 1.0, which correspond from 0 to 18 μm of the real offset. The displacements are averaged at each offset. The results are compared with the linear approach calculating Euclidean distance between the patches of zero offset and the others. The root-mean-square errors of the displacements from the linear relationship are 0.080, 0.076 and 0.038 for the three materials, wood, cardboard and sponge, in the scaled displacement. The values correspond to 1.36 μm, 1.28 μm and 0.64 μm in the real scale. The root-mean-square errors of the linear approach are 0.171, 0.108 and 0.118 in the scaled displacement, and 2.91 μm, 1.83 μm and 2.01 μm in the real scale, respectively. These results show the proposed method is applicable for various materials to discriminate the minute displacements and the relationship with respect to the real movement is close to linear than by using linear distance.

5.2   Comparison with Accelerometers

Second, the proposed method is tested for a case of dynamic movement. The result is compared to the measurements by the accelerometers. Figure 4 shows the setup in the experiments. The distance from the camera to the target object (wood panel) is about 1m, and the field of view is 0.6 m square at the target's position. The object is in contact with a speaker as the vibration source, which generates 60 Hz sine wave. The direction of the vibration is nearly parallel to the viewing direction and the movement is out-of-plane. The image sequence of 256 frames is captured by a high speed camera at 1000 frames/second. Two accelerometers are placed on the object to measure the vibration and compare with the results by the proposed method.

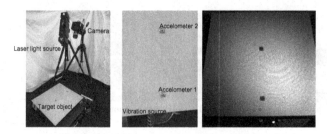

Fig. 4. The experimental setup consists of a camera and laser light source. A speaker is used as a source to vibrate the target object. Two accelerometers are placed on the object to measure the vibration. The right image is one of input images illuminated by the laser light.

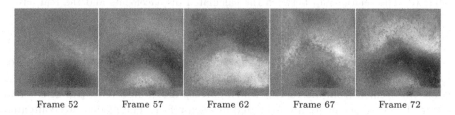

Frame 52   Frame 57   Frame 62   Frame 67   Frame 72

Fig. 5. The calculated displacements are shown for five frames in the sequence. The displacements are indicated by the brightness in these images.

Figure 5 shows the results of calculated displacement of five frames in the image sequence. The area of the same brightness indicates the same displacement. The vibration propagated from the bottom of the image at the beginning, and became a standing wave in the latter part. The measurements by the proposed method is compared to the values calculated by integrating the acceleration twice. Figure 6 shows the comparison with two measurements. Since the proposed method cannot calculate the absolute values of displacement, it is scaled to fit the mean magnitude of the measurements by the accelerometers. The two accelerometers are placed at the different distance from the vibration source. The accelerometer 2 is delayed about the half of the cycle from the accelerometer 1. The results by the proposed method is synchronized with the measurements by the both accelerometers. The normalized cross correlation of the signals between the proposed method and the accelerometers are 0.768 and 0.863. The high correlation indicates the proposed method can extract the phase of the minute vibration from the speckle pattern. Figure 7 shows the power spectrum of the vibration measured by the accelerometers and the proposed method. A strong peak at the same frequency is observed in all the results. Figure 8 shows the vertical slices of the displacements along the center line of the images of the two frames in Fig. 5. Since the spatial consistency of the displacements calculated for each pixel independently in Sect. 4.2 is obtained by the method

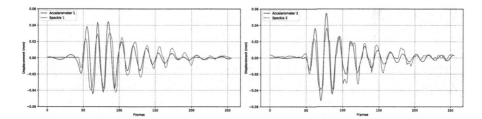

Fig. 6. The measurements by two accelerometers are compared to the results by the proposed method.

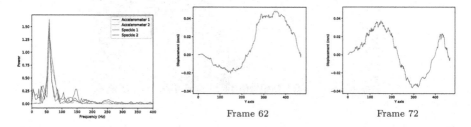

Frame 62   Frame 72

Fig. 7. The power spectrum   **Fig. 8.** The vertical slices of the displacements

described in Sect. 4.3, the wave propagated in the image can be observed by the displacements.

5.3 Visualizing Various Movements

Third, the proposed method is applied to various movements of different materials. In Fig. 9, a finger touches the canvas cloth and the movement occurs from the touching points. The movement propagates as a circular wave, which is reflected at the edge of the canvas. The left image in Fig. 9 shows one of the image sequences of the input images and the rest is the resulting displacement images. The images are captured at 1000 frames/second in this experiment. The canvas is pushed down by the finger at first and the position returns back after releasing the touch. The canvas cloth vibrates repeatedly during the touch.

Next, a hammering experiment of a wall made of metal panel is observed by the proposed method. The wall is painted and the speckle can be observed on the surface. Figure 10(a) shows the situation and one of the input images. In this experiment, the camera equips the band-pass filter to capture the infrared laser light and discard the illumination by room light. The image sequence is captured at 6400 frames/second in this experiment. Figure 11 shows the displacements for four frames in the sequence. The wave started from the hitting point and propagated the metal wall. Since the size of wall is known and the speed of the wave is about 17.5 pixel/frame, the speed of wave that propagates in the metal wall is about 250 m/s.

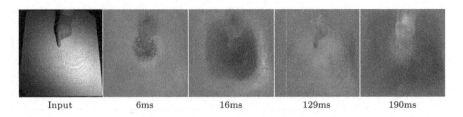

| Input | 6ms | 16ms | 129ms | 190ms |

Fig. 9. The movement is produced by touching the canvas by a finger in this sequence. The movement starts from the touching point, and propagates as a circular wave.

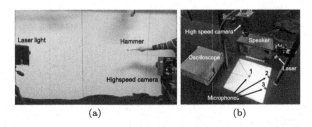

(a)   (b)

Fig. 10. Experimental setups: (a) The experiment of hitting a painted metal wall by a hammer. (b) The experiment of visualizing sound wave.

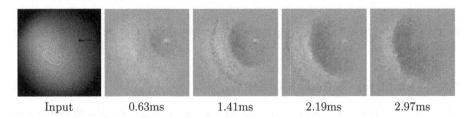

| Input | 0.63ms | 1.41ms | 2.19ms | 2.97ms |

Fig. 11. The displacements generated by hammering are calculated.

Finally, to visualize a sound wave, we set up a speaker and placed tissue papers that vibrates with the sound which propagates through the air. The tissue papers are fixed to the floor with tapes as shown in the setup image in Fig. 10(b) and captured by the high-speed camera with 10,000 fps. We also put three microphones to obtain ground truth data. The distances from the speaker to the microphones are 34 cm, 32 cm and 46 cm, respectively. Since the floor is hard enough, the tissue papers' motion is considered to be caused only by the air. The observed displacements are shown in Fig. 12. The wave-front propagates from the right to the left in wide images.

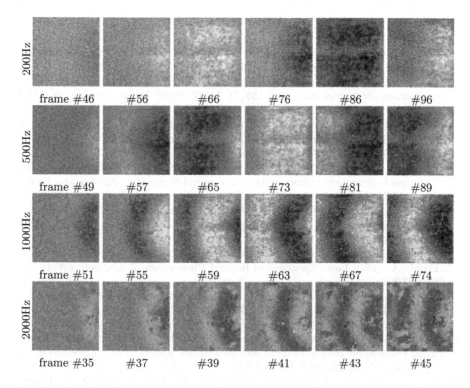

Fig. 12. Visualization of sound wave. Tissue papers are fixed to the floor with tapes, and a sound speaker is placed on the right of the images. The sound wave that propagates though the air moves the papers from the right to the left.

6 Conclusion

This paper proposed a method to observe the minute movement of objects by using the speckle that is generated by the illumination of laser light. Since the speckle varies sensitively to the out-of-plane movement, it enables to detect the minute movement of objects. Calculating the displacement without complex optical setup and calibration is realized based on the approach of embedding speckle pattern to low-dimensional space. The embedded vectors, which is calculated for each pixel independently, are made spatially consistent by estimating transformation matrices. The displacement is calculated by the consistent embedded vectors. In the experiments, the calculated displacement is compared to the movement measured by a micro-stage and accelerometers. Although the propose method cannot determine the scale of the movement, it can discriminate the displacement in micrometer accuracy. The proposed method is applied to various movement and materials, and succeeded to observe the minute movement of the objects. In future work, we plan to extend the proposed method to measure the real scale of the movement with simple and easy calibration.

References

1. D'Emilia, G., Razzè, L., Zappa, E.: Uncertainty analysis of high frequency image-based vibration measurements. Measurement **46**, 2630–2637 (2013)
2. Caetano, E., Silva, S., Bateira, J.: A vision system for vibration monitoring of civil engineering structures. Exp. Tech. **35**(4), 74–82 (2010). https://doi.org/10.1111/j.1747-1567.2010.00653.x
3. Wu, H.Y., Rubinstein, M., Shih, E., Guttag, J., Durand, F., Freeman, W.: Eulerian video magnification for revealing subtle changes in the world. ACM Trans. Graph. (Proc. SIGGRAPH 2012) **31**, 1–8 (2012)
4. Davis, A., Rubinstein, M., Wadhwa, N., Mysore, G., Durand, F., Freeman, W.: The visual microphone: passive recovery of sound from video. ACM Trans. Graph. (Proc. SIGGRAPH) **33**, 79:1–79:10 (2014)
5. Davis, A., Bouman, K., Chen, J., Rubinstein, M., Durand, F., Freeman, W.: Visual vibrometry: estimating material properties from small motions in video. IEEE TPAMI **39**, 732–745 (2017)
6. Goodman, J.: Some fundamental properties of speckle. JOSA **66**, 1145–1150 (1976)
7. Dainty, C. (ed.): Laser Speckle and Related Phenomena, 2 edn. Springer, Heidelberg (1984)
8. Løkberg, O., Høgmoen, K.: Vibration phase mapping using electronic speckle pattern interferometry. Appl. Opt. **15**, 2701–2704 (1976)
9. Creath, K.: Phase-shifting speckle interferometry. Appl. Opt. **24**, 3053–3058 (1985)
10. Bavigadda, V., Mihaylova, E., Jallapuram, R., Toal, V.: Vibration phase mapping using holographic optical element-based electronic speckle pattern interferometry. Opt. Lasers Eng. **50**, 1161–1167 (2012)
11. García, J., Zalevsky, Z., García-Martínez, P., Ferreira, C., Teicher, M., Beiderman, Y.: Three-dimensional mapping and range measurement by means of projected speckle patterns. Appl. Opt. **47**, 3032–3040 (2008)
12. Yamaguchi, I.: Real-time measurement of in-plane translation and tilt by electronic speckle correlation. Jpn. J. Appl. Phys. **19**, L133 (1980)
13. Fujii, H., Nohira, K., Yamamoto, Y., Ikawa, H., Ohura, T.: Evaluation of blood flow by laser speckle image sensing, part 1. Appl. Opt. **26**, 5321–5325 (1987)
14. Zizka, J., Olwal, A., Raskar, R.: Specklesense: fast, precise, low-cost and compact motion sensing using laser speckle. In: Proceedings the 24th Annual ACM Symposium on User Interface Software and Technology, pp. 489–498 (2011)
15. Chang Shih, Y., Davis, A., Hasinoff, S.W., Durand, F., Freeman, W.: Laser speckle photography for surface tampering detection. In: Proceedings/CVPR, IEEE Computer Society Conference on Computer Vision and Pattern Recognition, pp. 33–40 (2012)
16. Zalevsky, Z., et al.: Simultaneous remote extraction of multiple speech sources and heart beats from secondary speckles pattern. Opt. Expr. **17**, 21566–21580 (2009)
17. Synnergren, P.: Measurement of three-dimensional displacement fields and shape using electronic speckle photography. Opt. Eng. **36**, 2302–2310 (1997)
18. Jakobsen, M.L., Yura, H., Hanson, S.G.: Spatial filtering velocimetry of objective speckles for measuring out-of-plane motion. Appl. Opt. **51**, 1396–1406 (2012)
19. Jacquot, P., Rastogi, P.K.: Speckle motions induced by rigid-body movements in free-space geometry: an explicit investigation and extension to new cases. Appl. Opt. **18**, 2022–2032 (1979)
20. Jo, K., Gupta, M., Nayar, S.K.: SpeDo: 6 DOF ego-motion sensor using speckle defocus imaging. In: Proceedings of the IEEE International Conference on Computer Vision, pp. 4319–4327 (2015)

21. Smith, B.M., Desai, P., Agarwal, V., Gupta, M.: CoLux: multi-object 3D micro-motion analysis using speckle imaging. ACM Trans. Graph. (TOG) **36**, 1–12 (2017)
22. Smith, B.M., O'Toole, M., Gupta, M.: Tracking multiple objects outside the line of sight using speckle imaging. In: Proceedings of the IEEE Conference on Computer Vision and Pattern Recognition, pp. 6258–6266 (2018)
23. Tenenbaum, J.B., De Silva, V., Langford, J.C.: A global geometric framework for nonlinear dimensionality reduction. Science **290**, 2319–2323 (2000)
24. Roweis, S.T., Saul, L.K.: Nonlinear dimensionality reduction by locally linear embedding. Science **290**, 2323–2326 (2000)
25. Belkin, M., Niyogi, P.: Laplacian eigenmaps for dimensionality reduction and data representation. Neural Comput. **15**, 1373–1396 (2003)
26. Coifman, R.R., Lafon, S.: Diffusion maps. Appl. Comput. Harmonic Anal. **21**, 5–30 (2006)
27. Van der Maaten, L., Hinton, G.: Visualizing data using t-SNE. J. Mach. Learn. Res. **9**, 2579–2605 (2008)

Author Index

Printed in the United States
By Bookmasters